Cases

Part Ending Strategic Cases

MARKETING

MARKETING

SECOND CANADIAN EDITION

William M. Pride
Texas A & M University

O. C. Ferrell
University of New Mexico

Karen Blotnicky
Mount Saint Vincent University

Stephen Grant
University of New Brunswick

Houghton Mifflin Harcourt Publishing Company   Boston   New York

Karen Blotnicky:
I dedicate this book to my family whose energetic support was invaluable. In particular, I want to acknowledge my husband, Michael, for his patience, motivation, and guidance. I also want to thank my grown children, Pamela, Robert, and Christie, who provided both moral support and comic relief. I also want to thank my father, Walter, who continues to be my greatest fan, and my late mother, Ivy, whose commitment to lifelong learning continues to both motivate and inspire me.

Stephen Grant:
To my beautiful wife, Kimberly, fun daughter Rose, and supportive parents, Ernest and Treva. Thank you for your constant understanding and encouragement.

Project Manager: Timothy Cullen
Sponsoring Editor: Mike Schenk
Development Editor: Glen Herbert
Senior Project Editor: Fred Burns
Editorial Assistant: Jill Clark
Senior Marketing Manager: David Tonen
Art and Design Manager: Jill Haber
Cover Design Director: Tony Saizon
Senior Composition Buyer: Chuck Dutton
Manager of New Title Project Management: Patricia O'Neill

Cover image credit: (top image): Eisenhut & Mayer / FoodPix / Jupiter Images. Cover image description: Coffee beans in burlap (Image# 23044648). (bottom image): Ross Durant / FoodPix / Jupiter Images. Cover image description: Cup of coffee and coffee beans (Image# 23220489).

Printed in the U.S.A.

Library of Congress Control Number: 2008924240

ISBN 13: 978-0-618-88864-1

ISBN 10: 0-618-88864-0

1 2 3 4 5 6 7 8 9 — WEB — 12 11 10 09 08

Brief Contents

Contents

4 Social Responsibility and Ethics in Marketing   79

PART 3
Markets and Customer Behaviour   107

5 Consumer Buying Behaviour   108

6 Business Markets and Buying Behaviour   140

7 Reaching Global Markets   165

PART 4

Using Technology and Information to Reach Target Markets and Build Customer Relationships   199

8 Target Markets: Segmentation, Evaluation, and Positioning   200

9 E-Marketing and Customer Relationship Management   229

10 Marketing Research and Information Systems   255

PART 5
Product Decisions   283

11 Product Concepts   284

12 Developing and Managing Products   306

13 Services and Non-profit Marketing   338

PART 6

Pricing Decisions   363

14 Pricing Decisions   364

PART 7

Distribution Decisions   399

15 Marketing Channels, Supply Chain Management,   400
and Physical Distribution

16 Wholesaling, Retailing, and Direct Marketing   439

PART 8
Promotion Decisions · 473

17 Using Advertising, Public Relations, and Sales Promotion in Integrated Marketing Communications · 474

18 Personal Selling and Sales Management · 503

APPENDIX A Financial Analysis in Marketing · A-1

APPENDIX B Sample Marketing Plan

The Challenges of Teaching and Learning Marketing

Marketing continues to be one of the most dynamic dimensions of business. The global competitive environment has created new pressures to develop marketing strategies that reach beyond national boundaries.

Throughout, we maintain a hands-on approach to the course. The result is an integrated teaching package that is accurate, sound, and successful in reaching students, and one that fosters trust and confidence in the teaching package and in student learning outcomes.

Keeping Pace with the Challenges and the Changing World

The Internet and e-marketing strategies continue to create new opportunities for marketing success. Direct marketing, supply chain management, and growth of large retailers such as Wal-Mart, Canadian Tire, and IKEA—just some of the companies we feature in this edition—are changing the competitive forces. Starbucks' success reveals that consumers are trading up to services and experiences that provide enjoyment in a busy world. At the same time many of the companies we examine such as WestJet, Tim Horton's, and Nestlé are contributing more to society by providing environmentally responsible products and promoting fair trade activities to enhance the welfare of all marketing channel members. Ethics and social responsibility in marketing continue to be requirements—not options—in relating to customers and other stakeholders. All of these changes are emphasized in the content, examples, and boxes of this edition.

We also examine the challenges that marketers face in developing global marketing strategies. Consider that China, which has developed the second largest world economy in output behind the United States, has become the largest broadband DSL market, and companies such as Motorola and Intel have invested billions of dollars in China. Likewise, India's growing middle class, with more than 300 million consumers, is buying consumer products from companies such as Procter & Gamble and Coca-Cola. Conversely, Wal-Mart is now purchasing 20 percent of its merchandise from Chinese producers. These shifts in international markets mean that students need to understand how global marketing strategies are developed and implemented in a dynamic and complex world. We provide a revised chapter on this issue as well as exercises, boxed features, cases, examples, and content throughout the text.

Features of the Book

This text provides a comprehensive and practical introduction to marketing that is both easy to teach and to learn. The entire text is structured to excite students about the subject and to help them learn completely and efficiently.

- An *organizational model* at the beginning of each part provides a "roadmap" of the text and a visual tool for understanding the connection among various components.

- *Learning objectives* at the start of each chapter present concrete expectations about what students are to learn as they read the chapter.

- An *opening vignette* about a particular organization or current market trend introduces the topic for each chapter. Through these vignettes, students are exposed to contemporary marketing realities and are better prepared to understand and apply the concepts they will explore in the text.

- *Key term definitions* appear in the margins to help students build their marketing vocabulary.

- *Boxed features* reinforce students' awareness of the particular issues affecting marketing and the types of choices and decisions marketers must make. Topics range from ethics and global marketing to building customer relationships and ways to target ever-changing markets. Featured are trends such as yoga moms, aging baby boomers, and buzz marketing at teens, and companies such as Nickelodeon and Iams.

- *Snapshot features* engage students by highlighting interesting, up-to-date statistics that link marketing theory to the real world.

- *Recent research* that supports the frameworks and best practices for marketing is included throughout the text.

- *Advertisements* from well-known firms are employed to illustrate chapter topics. Experiences of real-world companies are used to exemplify marketing concepts and strategies throughout the text.

- A complete *chapter summary* reviews the major topics discussed, and the list of *important terms* provides another end-of-chapter study aid to expand students' marketing vocabulary.

- *Discussion and review questions* at the end of each chapter encourage further study and exploration of chapter content, and *application questions* enhance students' comprehension of important topics.

- *Internet exercises* at the end of each chapter ask students to examine a website and assess one or more strategic issues associated with the site. This section also points students to the various learning tools that are available on the text's website.

- *End of chapter cases* help students understand the application of chapter concepts.

- The *Marketing Entrepreneurs* feature highlights everyday individuals who have used innovative marketing to launch a new business.

- A *strategic case* at the end of each part helps students integrate the diverse concepts that have been discussed within the related chapters.

Text Organization

We have organized the eight parts of *Marketing* to give students a theoretical and practical understanding of marketing decision making.

Part 1 **Marketing Strategy and Customer Relationships**
Provides an overview of marketing, strategic marketing planning, and implementation

Part 2 **Environmental Forces, Social Responsibility, and Ethics**
Provides an overview of the marketing environment, social responsibility, and ethics

Part 3 **Markets and Customer Behaviour**
Focuses on consumer and business buying behaviour, and global and international marketing

Part 4 **Using Technology and Information to Reach Target Markets and Build Customer Relationships**
Covers e-marketing, customer relationship management, marketing research, information systems, target market segmentation, and positioning

Part 5 **Product Decisions**
Discusses product concepts, developing and managing products, branding, packaging, and services marketing

Part 6 **Pricing Decisions**
Covers pricing concepts and the setting of prices in a dynamic marketing environment

Part 7 **Distribution Decisions**
Provides coverage of marketing channels, supply chain management, wholesaling, physical distribution, retailing, and direct marketing

Part 8 **Promotion Decisions**
Focuses on integrated communications, advertising, public relations, personal selling, and sales promotion

A Comprehensive Instructional Resource Package

For instructors, this edition of *Marketing* includes an exceptionally comprehensive package of teaching materials.

■ *Canadian Instructor's Website.* This continually updated, password-protected site includes valuable tools to help design and teach the course. The website is designed so that you can spend your time preparing for class rather than clicking links. Website content includes sample syllabi, downloadable text files from the Canadian *Instructor's Resource Manual,* role-play exercises, Canadian PowerPoint® slides, *CRS (Classroom Response System) Clicker Content,* the new Integrated Lecture Outline, and more.

In addition, you can preview our unique custom content modules featuring extended content on the latest marketing topics. From here, you can determine which modules would enhance your instruction and your students' learning. To customize your text with modules, contact your Houghton Mifflin Harcourt sales representative.

■ Canadian *PowerPoint® slide presentations.* You can now enhance your lecture with our Premium PowerPoint slides that have been created to provide instructors with up-to-date unique content to increase student application and interest. The Premium PowerPoint slides offer such multimedia content as advertisements, video clips, weblinks, surveys and graphs, and important terms.

■ *Classroom Management Systems.* With *Eduspace* powered by Blackboard and *Blackboard/WebCT* course management tools, instructors can create and customize online course materials to use in distance learning, distributed learning, or as a supplement to traditional classes. Each system includes a variety of study aids for instructors, including a gradebook, the Instructor's Resource Manual, Integrated Lecture Outlines, test pools, PowerPoint slides, Classroom Response System (CRS) clicker content, ACE practice tests and auto-graded quizzes, links to web content, all end-of-chapter questions from the textbook with suggested answers, Video Activities, and more.

■ Canadian *Test Bank. HMTesting,* the computerized test bank, provides more than 4000 test items including true/false, multiple-choice, and essay questions. Each objective test item is accompanied by the correct answer, a main text page reference, and a key that shows whether the question tests knowledge, comprehension, or application. *HMTesting* also provides difficulty and discrimination ratings derived from actual class testing for many of the multiple-choice questions. When preparing a test, instructors are able to select, edit, and add questions, or generate randomly selected questions to produce a test master for easy duplication. An Online Testing System and gradebook function allows instructors to administer tests via a network system, modem, or personal computer, and sets up a new class, records grades from tests or assignments, analyzes grades, and produces class and individual statistics. This program can be used on both PCs and Macintosh computers.

■ Canadian *Instructor's Resource Manual.* The *Instructor's Resource Manual* includes a complete set of teaching tools. For each text chapter, there is (1) a teaching resources quick reference guide, (2) a purpose and perspective statement, (3) special class exercises, (4) a debate issue, (5) a chapter quiz, (6) answers to discussion and review questions, (7) comments on the end-of-chapter cases, and (8) video information.

■ *Integrated Lecture Outlines.* All multimedia instructor support is now integrated into a chapter outline prepared by the U.S. edition authors. This useful tool will provide cues for incorporating the video, PowerPoint slides—including appropriate video clips and ads—overhead transparencies, and additional text features. Encapsulate your students on everything our program has to offer!

■ *CRS (Classroom Response System) Clicker Content.* Using state-of-the-art wireless technology and text-specific content, a Classroom Response System (CRS) provides a convenient and inexpensive way to gauge student comprehension, deliver quizzes or exams, and provide "on-the-spot" assessment. Ideal for any classroom, a CRS is a customizable handheld response system that will complement any teaching style. Various answering modes, question types, and display options mean that a CRS is as functional as you want it to be. As a testing platform, as an assessment tool, or simply as a way to increase interactivity in the classroom, a CRS provides the technology you need to transform a lecture into a dynamic learning environment. Content is available on the Instructor Website.

■ *Marketing Video Series.* The *Instructor's Resource Manual* and *Integrated Lecture Outline* provide specific information about each video segment.

■ *Online colour transparencies.* A set of colour transparencies, available on the Online Teaching Centre, offers the instructor visual teaching assistance. About half of these are illustrations from the text. The rest are figures, tables, and diagrams that can be used as additional instructional aids.

■ *Role-play exercises.* Three role-play exercises that allow students to assume various roles within an organization are available in the *Instructor's Resource*

Manual and on the instructor's website. The exercises are designed to help students understand the real-world challenges of decision making in marketing. Decisions require a strategic response from groups or teams. These exercises simulate a real-world experience, and give students an opportunity to apply the marketing concepts covered in the text. Accompanying the exercises is in-depth information concerning their implementation and evaluation.

Supplements to Meet Student Needs

Supporting Supplements

The complete package available with *Marketing* includes support materials that facilitate student learning.

Our student website at **www.hmco.ca/marketing** contains the following:

■ *Your Guide to an 'A'* provides students with access to premium online study tools, designed to help students get a better grade. These assets include:
  - ACE+
  - MP3
  - Study Content in Flash
  - Interactive Marketing Plan
  - Flashcards and Crosswords
  - Marketing mini-cases and exercises

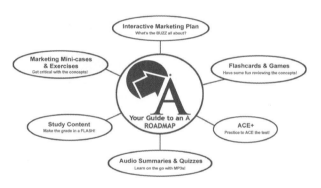

■ Please use the code in the *Your Guide to an A* passkey that came with new copies of your textbook. If you purchased a used textbook, the passkey is available for purchase through your bookstore.

■ *Interactive Marketing Plan.* The *Marketing Plan Worksheets* have been reproduced within an interactive and multimedia environment. A video program has been developed around the worksheets, allowing students to follow a company through the trials and tribulations of launching a new product. This video will help place the conceptual marketing plan into an applicable light and will be supported by a summary of the specific stages of the marketing plan as well as a sample plan based on the events of the video. These elements act as the 1-2-3 punch supporting the student while completing his or her own plan, the last step of the *Interactive Marketing Plan. The Plan* is broken up into three functional sections that can either be completed in one simple project or carried over throughout the semester. *Available with the "Guide to an 'A'" passkey in the* **Online Study Centre.**

■ *Audio Chapter Review MP3* downloadable files. The MP3 files provide unique audio chapter summaries and test-preppers for the on-the-go student. *Available with the "Guide to an 'A'" passkey in the* **Online Study Centre.**

■ *ACE & ACE+ online self-tests.* Written by the text authors, these questions allow students to practice taking tests and get immediate scoring results. ACE + questions *available with the "Guide to an 'A'" passkey in the* **Online Study Centre.**

■ *Online Study Content in Flash.* Written by the text's authors, this supplement helps students review and integrate key marketing concepts. The *Study Content* questions are different from those in the online study aids and include chapter outlines as well as matching, true/false, multiple-choice, and mini-case sample tests with answers. *Available with the "Guide to an 'A'" passkey in the* **Online Study Centre.**

■ *Flashcards.* These study tools will help students review concepts and prepare for tests. *Available with the "Guide to an 'A'" Media Passkey.*

■ *Company links.* Hot links to companies featured in the text are provided so that students can further their research and understanding of the marketing practices of these companies.

■ *Online glossary & chapter summary.* These sections help students review key concepts and definitions.

■ *Career Centre.* Downloadable "Personal Career Plan Worksheets" and links to various marketing careers websites will help students explore their options and plan their job search.

Acknowledgments

Like most textbooks, this one reflects the ideas of many academicians and practitioners who have contributed to the development of the marketing discipline. We'd especially like to thank the reviewers who were consulted throughout the development process:

Elaine MacNeil
Cape Breton University

Donna Sears
University of New Brunswick

Mehdi Zahaf
Lakehead University

Melanie Lang
University of Guelph

Rita Cossa
McMaster University

Shirley Lichti
Wilfrid Laurier University

Lisa Giguere
Wilfrid Laurier University

Perry Broome
Fanshawe College

Terry Champion
Niagara College

Beth Pett
Niagara College

Brian Harvey
Conestoga College

Gerry Taft
Mount Royal College

Webb Dussome
University of Alberta

Pat Browne
Kwantlen University College

Keith Wallace
Kwantlen University College

Rosemary Polegato
Mount Allison University

Marianne Marando
Seneca College

Jennifer Monk
Algonquin College

Brian Broadway
Kwantlen University College

Allen Richert
Confederation College

Derek Hassay
University of Calgary

Brent McKenzie
University of Western Ontario

A number of talented professionals at Houghton Mifflin have contributed to the development of this book. We are especially grateful to Glen Herbert, our developmental editor for his constant support and positive approach to text development. Thanks to David Tonen for his text development expertise and creative ideas that have made a real difference on this text. Thanks to Debbie Underhill for her successful efforts to launch this project and for her continued support. Also, thank you to Timothy Cullen for assisting with what seemed an infinite number of legal and administrative details. We also wish to thank the many members of the production team who have remained nameless but not unappreciated by the authors.

Karen Blotnicky
Stephen Grant

About the Authors

Karen Blotnicky is an Associate Professor of marketing in the Department of Business and Tourism and Hospitality Management at Mount Saint Vincent University in Halifax. Professor Blotnicky also holds a BA (honours sociology) and an MBA from Saint Mary's University in Halifax. She is completing a doctorate in international business at Northcentral University in Arizona.

Professor Blotnicky has been teaching marketing courses in both academic and professional venues since 1985. She is regarded as an energetic and student-centred professor who is passionate about marketing and greatly enjoys interacting with students.

Professor Blotnicky is also very involved in the marketing research community across Canada, having conducted marketing research and advised public, private, and nonprofit clients since 1993. She is a partner in The Marketing Clinic, a research and consulting firm based in Nova Scotia.

Professor Blotnicky is a member of the Entrepreneurs' Forum, and past member of the management board of the Centre for Women in Business in Halifax. She is a small business columnist for Halifax's *Chronicle-Herald* newspaper and was the small business columnist for Eastern Canada for CBC Radio One from 2005 through 2007.

E. Stephen Grant (BBA, MBA, PhD) is a Professor of Marketing and Entrepreneurship at the University of New Brunswick (UNB). He received his doctorate in Business Administration from The University of Memphis, Fogelman College of Business and Economics. His research has been published in a variety of journals and in national and international scholarly conference proceedings. Dr. Grant has co-authored leading textbooks with both Irwin/McGraw-Hill Ryerson and Pearson Education Canada.

Dr. Grant's research activities have been recognized through an assortment of awards, contracts, grants, and fellowships. Recently he received the UNB Merit Award for his performance in research, service, and teaching. Dr. Grant has a record of extensive service to his Faculty and to the University. In addition to other administrative positions, he served as Associate Dean–Research and Outreach from 2001 to 2004. More recently he served as Associate Dean–Programs. In addition to scholarly research, Dr. Grant is involved in applied contract research and consulting.

Dr. Grant's non-professional life interests involve spending quality time with family, which includes wife Kim, young daughter Rose, and two Scottish Terriers (Daisy and Kaylee). He is passionate about the car hobby and involves himself in the dissemination of knowledge on automotive repair and improvement via online forum discussions and technical non-peer reviewed articles.

William M. Pride is Professor of Marketing, Mays Business School at Texas A&M University. He received his Ph.D. from Louisiana State University. He is the author of Houghton Mifflin Company's *Business* text, a market leader.

Dr. Pride's research interests are in advertising, promotion, and distribution channels. Dr. Pride's research articles have appeared in major journals in the fields of advertising and marketing such as *Journal of Marketing, Journal of Marketing Research, Journal of the Academy of Marketing Science,* and the *Journal of Advertising.*

Dr. Pride is a member of the American Marketing Association, Academy of Marketing Science, Association of Collegiate Marketing Educators, Society for Marketing Advances and the Marketing Management Association.

Dr. Pride has taught principles of marketing and other marketing courses for more than 30 years at both the undergraduate and graduate levels.

O. C. Ferrell is Professor of Marketing and Creative Enterprise Scholar, Anderson Schools of Management, University of New Mexico. He recently served as the Bill Daniels Distinguished Professor of Business Ethics at the University of Wyoming and previously as Chair of the Colorado State University Marketing Department. He has also been on the faculties of the University of Memphis, Texas A&M University, and Illinois State University. He received his Ph.D. in Marketing from Louisiana State University.

He is past president of the Academic Council of the American Marketing Association and chaired the American Marketing Association Ethics Committee. Under his leadership, the committee developed the AMA Code of Ethics and the AMA Code of Ethics for Marketing on the Internet. He is currently a member of the advisory committee for the AMA marketing certification program. In addition, he is a former member of the Academy of Marketing Science Board of Governors and is a Society of Marketing Advances and Southwestern Marketing Association Fellow. He currently serves as Marketing Ethics and Social Issues Section Editor of the *Journal of Macromarketing.*

Ferrell is the co-author of 18 books and approximately 75 articles. His articles have been published in the *Journal of Marketing Research, Journal of Marketing, Journal of Business Ethics, Journal of Business Research, Journal of the Academy of Marketing Science, Journal of Public Policy Marketing,* as well as other journals.

Expert Panel

In today's world of increased complexity and continuous change we all need the assistance of experts to help us better understand facts, situations, and events. To help with your understanding of marketing principles and to inject realism into the development of this text, we assembled a panel of experts. All expert panel members contributed to the development of this text. Contributions were in the form of content reviews, fact checking, and/or the provision of material such as cases and content for the various features of the book. The biographies provided below illustrate the level of expertise of panel members and the diverse nature of expertise needed to gain an understanding of the real-world practice of marketing.

Michael G. Beairsto, Partner, Fraser Milner Casgrain LLP. Michael Beairsto is a partner with the firm of Fraser Milner Casgrain, practising corporate-commercial law with a specialization in technology and e-commerce matters. Mike is the head of the Technology Law Group practice in FMC's Toronto office. He has a Bachelor of Business Administration (1985) and an LL.B. (1987) from the University of New Brunswick.

Mr. Beairsto is recognized by *The Best Lawyers in Canada* as a leading lawyer in Information Technology, and is one of Canada's Leading Information Technology Lawyers in the Guide to the World's Leading Technology, Media & Telecommunications Lawyers, published by Euromoney Legal Media Group.

Rebecca Goldfarb, Principal, Goldfarb Intelligence Marketing. Dr. Rebecca Goldfarb is a Principal at Goldfarb Intelligence Marketing. Rebecca has more than ten years experience in market research, including qualitative and quantitative data analysis. She is a specialist in marketing strategy, branding, qualitative research techniques, and training. Rebecca is also an experienced quantitative researcher and has conducted satisfaction and public opinion studies. She has conducted numerous assignments in a variety of industries in North America, South America, and Europe.

Rebecca holds a Ph.D. in international relations from the Fletcher School of Law and Diplomacy at Tufts University in Boston (1997). She was a Fulbright Scholar in 1995/1996. Rebecca holds a Masters of Arts in Law Diplomacy (M.A.L.D.) from the Fletcher School of Law and Diplomacy (1993). Rebecca graduated with first class honours from Queen's University with a B.A.H. in Political Studies (1991).

Rebecca is a director of Soulpepper Theatre.

Ian Graham, Sales Director, Royal Canadian Mint. As Sales Director, Ian is responsible for the Royal Canadian Mint's sales of all collector coin products to domestic and international distributors in North America, Europe, Asia, and the Pacific. He has been involved with unique product development, custom issues, regional marketing, promotional opportunities, forecasting, customer relations, and establishment of new retail accounts. As a respected coin collector for over thirty years, he is often seen and heard on various media discussing the hobby of coin collecting and identifying those elusive coins found in many collections and accumulations. He also offers this expertise and passion when meeting with other collectors and those interested in the historical aspect of the hobby of numismatics, and is often called upon to act in official capacities such as exhibiting and speaking at collector forums.

Bruce MacLellan, APR, Fellow CPRS, President and CEO, Environics Communications Inc. Bruce MacLellan has been a public relations counsellor since 1980. In 1993, he won numerous industry awards including the Canadian Public Relations Society's Award of Excellence for External Communications. In 1994, he became the founding president and partner of Environics Communications Inc., a position he still holds. In 1995, Environics Communications became the first Canadian-owned PR agency to open an office in the United States. In 2007, the firm was chosen as number four on the list of Canada's 50 best workplaces by *Canadian Business* magazine. In 1996, Bruce was one of only four PR agency executives selected to *Marketing* magazine's Top 100 Communicators list. Bruce has a BA and an MA from the University of Toronto and is an active volunteer at his children's school as a communications advisor for The Nature Conservancy of Canada. He is the author of the local history book *Post Cards from Lake of Bays*, published in 2007.

Terry Malley, CEO, Malley Industries, Inc. Terry Malley founded Malley Industries with his father in 1979 while completing his degree at the University of New Brunswick. Terry has worked in all areas of the business from the manufacturing process through to sales and management. In January 2000 he became President and CEO of Malley Industries.

Terry is on the Advisory Board of the UNB Faculty of Business Administration and advisory board chair of the International Business and Entrepreneurship Center and is first vice-chair of the Greater Moncton Chamber of Commerce and National Director of the Excellence in Manufacturing Consortium. Terry received the K. C. Irving Award for Quality in Manufacturing in 1999 and the Greater Moncton Excellence Awards for Innovation in 2000, for Business Excellence in 2002 and 2006, and for Community Service in 2005. He was chosen as one of Atlantic Canada's Top 50 CEOs by Atlantic Business Magazine in 2002 and 2007 and was a finalist for the Ernst & Young Entrepreneur of the Year Award in 2004 and 2006.

In his spare time Terry is involved in the old car and collector car hobby both through involvement with organizing the Atlantic Nationals Automotive Extravaganza, Canada's largest car show festival, as well as enjoying his own old car, a 1940 Ford. Terry and his wife Kathy have two children, Myles 19 and Kayla 16.

Bill Moir, Executive Vice President, Marketing, The TDL Group Corp. Bill Moir joined The TDL Group Corp. in 1990 as Vice President, Marketing, and was promoted to Executive Vice President, Marketing in 1997. He is responsible for the strategic planning and execution of the chain's national advertising and marketing programs, as well as overseeing national brand advertising, regional marketing, and corporate communications.

Prior to joining Tim Hortons, Bill gained extensive marketing management experience in a variety of industries, with key positions at K-Tel, Shell Oil, and Labatt Breweries. He currently sits on the board for the Tim Horton Children's Foundation.

Bill has an Honours Business degree from the University of Manitoba.

Michael Schell, President, Thought Leader Publications & Training. After twenty years in corporate sales, Michael Schell decided to start his first company, Marketshare Communications, in 2001. With the tables turned and sales reps now pitching their products to him, Schell discovered just how rarely reps asked him insightful questions. Echoing the feelings of many organizational buyers, Schell notes that "life is too short, and business too important, to allow others [sales reps] to waste my time." In this revelation, Schell saw the need for a book written from the perspective of buyers who had years of experience meeting and interacting with sales reps. Thus came the formation of another company, Thought Leader Publications and Training, Inc., which began operations in 2006 (see www.thoughtleaderinc.com). There has been no looking back. Not only has the book sold more copies than Schell anticipated, praise has come from both corporate and academic reviewers.

Schell's success as an author has translated into success as a sales trainer. His first sales training workshop, which is based on his first book, is proving successful. Canon USA recently licensed the Buyer-Approved Selling Excellence workshop to train its national dealer sales force. Schell is in the process of replicating the success of his first book and training workshops with a growing list of new books, research services, and training products. All have a common theme - providing clients with practical, proven business advice from the decision-maker's side of the desk.

Brooke Yeates, Public Affairs Specialist, CVRD Inco Limited. Brooke Yeates was appointed Public Affairs Specialist with CVRD Inco's Ontario Operations in 2005. Brooke joined the company in 2002, holding the position of IT Communications Specialist at the Corporate Headquarters in Toronto. Her previous experience includes roles with EDS Canada, Ontario's Ministry of Tourism, and the Canadian Association of Insurance and Financial Advisors, all based in Toronto.

Brooke has an Honours degree in Arts from the University of New Brunswick and a Bachelor of Public Relations degree from Mount St. Vincent University.

A former board member of the Toronto chapter of the International Association of Business Communicators (IABC), Brooke maintains strong links to the public relations and communications community, often serving as a mentor to students entering the profession. Board member of the Art Gallery of Sudbury and member of the local Heart & Stroke Foundation Council, she also volunteers her time with a number of local organizations.

MARKETING

part 1

Marketing Strategy and Customer Relationships

Part One introduces the field of marketing and offers a broad perspective from which to explore and analyze various components of the marketing discipline. **Chapter 1** defines *marketing* and explores several key concepts, including customers and target markets, the marketing mix, the marketing concept, customer relationships, value-driven marketing, and the importance of marketing in the global economy. **Chapter 2** provides an overview of strategic marketing issues, such as the role of the mission statement, corporate, business-unit, and marketing strategies, as well as the creation of the marketing plan.

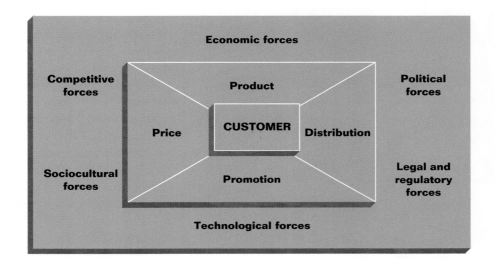

An Overview of Strategic Marketing

OBJECTIVES

1. **To be able to define marketing as focused on customers**

2. **To identify some important marketing terms, including target market, marketing mix, marketing exchanges, and marketing environment**

3. **To become aware of the marketing concept and marketing orientation**

4. **To understand the importance of building customer relationships**

5. **To learn about the process of marketing management**

6. **To recognize the role of marketing in our society**

Red Bull Has Wings

Sleek in its blue and silver can, Red Bull is a huge marketing success. While established cola giants struggle with flat sales, upstart Red Bull has brought new "energy" to the marketplace.

Red Bull, which originated in Austria, commands 60 percent of its market share against competitors like Hype, Rockstar, Monster, Pimp Juice, and Bong Water. In fact, without this berry-flavoured beverage featuring mysterious additives taurine and glucuronolactone, there would not even be a market for all the other energy drinks currently crowding the shelves. While still a relatively small market, the energy drink category grew 75 percent in 2005 to $3.3 billion in sales. Even giants Pepsi and Coke have introduced their own versions. Pepsi has Mountain Dew AMP and Mountain Dew MDX, while Coke offers Full Throttle and Tab Energy—a twist on the 1970s soft drink Tab, which is targeted at women.

Energy drinks have about three times the caffeine of a regular soft drink and are loaded with sugar—it's clear why they provide an instant rush. And people are willing to pay up to $3.00 for an 8-ounce can of Red Bull, more than double the price of a can of Coke. Red Bull's marketing group is broken into decentralized units throughout Canada. Each marketing and sales person is expected to take responsibility for the brand and act like an entrepreneur, working with distributors to find retail accounts at popular venues frequented by the local "in crowd." They select only five accounts in an area to give the product an aura of exclusivity and encourage retailers to aggressively merchandise the brand to keep the product franchise.

Red Bull's marketing teams use a variety of techniques to create brand awareness. Beyond traditional commercials, they have used dance clubs, deejays, and even cab drivers to spread the word. While others spend millions for superstars like Christina Aguilera, Red Bull relies on buzz from hip youngsters as well as the sponsorship of approximately 500 "extreme" athletes who surf in Nova Scotia in January or jump out of planes to swim the English Channel. One of the brand's favourite

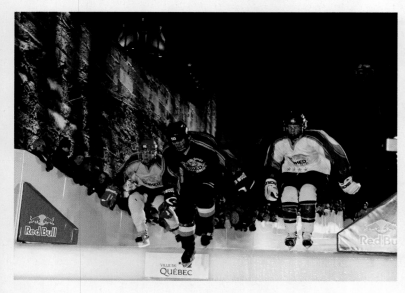

targets is alternative sports venues. It's involved in national and regional events, including the Red Bull Huckfest ski and snowboard competition in Utah. Its fleet of show planes, the Flying Bulls, appears at air shows around the world. These events are naturals for reaching potential customers.

Red Bull also uses consumer education teams, hiring hip locals in target areas to drive Red Bull cars (small sporty blue and silver vehicles with a large Red Bull can mounted on the back) and hand out samples. However, what consumers see in one city may be entirely different from what they see in another city. Red Bull's marketing philosophy is to adapt its approach to the local market. It's all part of the mystique![1] ■

Like all organizations, the maker of Red Bull attempts to develop products that customers want, communicate useful information about them to excite interest, price them appropriately, and make them available when and where customers want to buy them. Even if an organization does all these things well, however, competition from marketers of similar products, economic conditions, and other factors may affect the company's success. Such factors influence the decisions that all organizations must make in strategic marketing.

This chapter introduces the strategic marketing concepts and decisions covered throughout the text. First, we develop a definition of *marketing* and explore each element of the definition in detail. Next, we introduce the marketing concept and consider several issues associated with implementing it. We also take a brief look at the management of customer relationships and then at the concept of value, which customers are demanding today more than ever before. We next explore the process of marketing management, which includes planning, organizing, implementing, and controlling marketing activities to encourage marketing exchanges. Finally, we examine the importance of marketing in our global society.

Defining *Marketing*

marketing The process of creating, distributing, promoting, and pricing goods, services, and ideas to facilitate satisfying exchanges relationships with customers and develop and maintain favourable relationships with stakeholders in a dynamic environment

customers The purchasers of organizations' products; the focal point of all marketing activities

If you ask several people what *marketing* is you are likely to hear a variety of descriptions. Although many people think marketing is advertising or selling, marketing actually encompasses many more activities than most people realize. In this book, we define **marketing** as the process of creating, distributing, promoting, and pricing goods, services, and ideas to facilitate satisfying exchange relationships with customers and to develop and maintain favourable relationships with stakeholders in a dynamic environment. Our definition is consistent with that of the American Marketing Association (AMA), which defines marketing as "an organizational function and a set of processes for creating, communicating, and delivering value to customers and for managing customer relationships in ways that benefit the organization and its stakeholders."[2] Let's take a closer look at selected parts of our definition.

Marketing Focuses on Customers

As the purchasers of the products that organizations develop, promote, distribute, and price, **customers** are the focal point of all marketing activities (see Figure 1.1). Organizations must define their products not as what they produce but as what they do to satisfy customers. The Walt Disney Company, for example, is not in the business of establishing theme parks; it is in the business of making people happy. At Disney World, customers are guests, the crowd is an audience, and employees are cast members. Customer satisfaction and enjoyment can come from anything received when buying and using a product, and the product can be much more than just a physical item purchased for consumption.

The essence of marketing is to develop satisfying exchange relationships from which both customers and marketers benefit. The customer expects to gain a reward or benefit in excess of the costs incurred in a marketing transaction. The marketer

figure 1.1

COMPONENTS OF STRATEGIC MARKETING

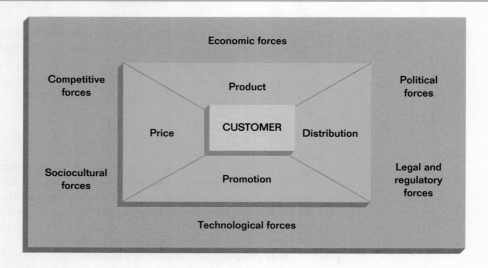

expects to gain something of value in return, generally the price charged for the product. Through buyer-seller interactions, a customer develops expectations about the seller's future behaviour. To fulfill these expectations, the marketer must deliver on promises made. Over time, this interaction results in interdependencies between the two parties. Fast-food restaurants such as Tim Horton's and Subway depend on repeat purchases from satisfied customers—many often live or work a few miles from these restaurants—while customer expectations revolve around quality food, good value, and dependable service.

Organizations generally focus their marketing efforts on a specific group of customers called a **target market.** Marketing managers may define a target market as a vast number of people or a relatively small group. Rolls-Royce, for example, targets its automobiles at a small, very exclusive market: wealthy people who want the ultimate in prestige in an automobile. Other companies target multiple markets, with different products, promotion, prices, and distribution systems for each one. Nike uses this strategy, marketing different types of shoes and apparel to meet specific needs of cross-trainers, rock climbers, basketball players, aerobics enthusiasts, and other athletic-shoe buyers. We explore the concept of target markets in more detail in Chapter 10.

Marketing Deals with Products, Place, Promotion, and Price

Marketing is more than simply advertising or selling a product; it involves developing and managing a product that will satisfy customer needs. It focuses on making the product available in the right place and at a price acceptable to buyers. It also requires communicating information that helps customers determine if the product will satisfy their needs. These activities are planned, organized, implemented, and controlled to meet the needs of customers within the target market. Marketers refer to these activities—the 4Ps: product, distribution (place), promotion, and pricing—as the **marketing mix** because they decide what type of each element to use and in what amounts. A primary goal of a marketing manager is to create and maintain the right mix of these elements to satisfy customers' needs for a general product type. Note in Figure 1.1 that the marketing mix is built around the customer.

Marketing managers strive to develop a marketing mix that matches the needs of customers in the target market. The marketing mix for DeWalt power tools, for example, combines rugged, high-quality products with coordinated distribution, promotion, and price appropriate for the target market of primarily professional con-

target market A specific group of customers on whom an organization focuses its marketing efforts

marketing mix Four marketing activities—product, distribution, promotion, and pricing—that a firm can control to meet the needs of customers within its target markets

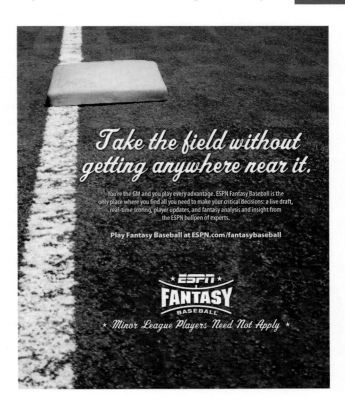

Appealing to Target Markets

This Neutrogena skin care advertisement targets young women. ESPN promotes its Fantasy Baseball primarily to men.

tractors. The marketing mix for Black & Decker power tools differs from that of DeWalt—even though the two brands are owned by the same firm—with lower prices and broader distribution.[3]

Before marketers can develop a marketing mix, they must collect in-depth, up-to-date information about customer needs. Such information might include data about the age, income, ethnicity, gender, and educational level of people in the target market, their preferences for product features, their attitudes toward competitors' products, and the frequency with which they use the product. In Chapter 9, we explore how organizations gather marketing research data. Armed with such data, marketing managers are better able to develop a marketing mix that satisfies a specific target market.

Let's look more closely at the decisions and activities related to each marketing mix variable.

product A good, a service, or an idea

The Product. Successful marketing efforts result in **products** that become a part of everyday life. Consider the satisfaction customers have had over the years from Coca-Cola, Levi's jeans, Visa credit cards, Tylenol pain relievers, and 3M Post-it Notes. The product variable of the marketing mix deals with researching customers' needs and wants and designing a product that satisfies them. The product marketed can be a good, a service, or a concept, such as an idea, a place or even a person. A good is a physical entity you can touch. A Honda Civic, an iPod, a Duracell battery, and a puppy available for adoption at an animal shelter are examples of goods. A service is the application of human and mechanical efforts to people or objects to provide intangible benefits to customers. Air travel, dry cleaning, hair cutting, banking, insurance, medical care, and day care are examples of services. Concepts include ideas (such as religious services, or your class lecture), places (travel destinations), or people (elected officials, movie celebrities, or even marketing yourself through a job interview).

The product variable also involves creating or modifying brand names and packaging, and may include decisions regarding warranty and repair services. Even one of the world's best hockey players is fast becoming a global brand. Sidney Crosby,

Nova Scotia's hockey ace, has signed on with the Pittsburgh Penguins, but he still takes time to be a spokesperson for a growing number of brands. He endorses Pepsi and Frito Lay in Canada, along with Reebok and Gatorade. He is also a fashion consultant for a Reebok clothing line, approving every design before it's launched.

Product variable decisions and related activities are important because they are directly involved in creating products that address customers' needs and wants. To maintain an assortment of products that help an organization achieve its goals, marketers must develop new products, modify existing ones, and eliminate those that no longer satisfy enough buyers or that yield unacceptable profits. In the funeral home industry, for example, some companies have developed new products such as DVD memoirs, grave markers that display photos along with a soundtrack, and caskets with drawers to hold mementos from the bereaved. Baby boomers, more than any other age group, prefer cremation to burial.[4] To appeal to this group firms are offering more cremation and memorial services. We consider such product issues and many more in Chapters 11 through 14.

The Place. To satisfy customers, products must be available at the right time and in convenient locations. For example, retail chains, including Wal-Mart, Superstore and Sobeys have opened in-store health clinics to make routine medical services such as sports physicals, flu shots, and strep-throat tests available to their customers without an appointment during pharmacy hours, including evenings and weekends. In dealing with the distribution (place) variable, a marketing manager makes products available in the quantities desired to as many target market customers as possible, keeping total inventory, transportation, and storage costs as low as possible. A marketing manager may also select and motivate intermediaries (wholesalers and retailers), establish and maintain inventory control procedures, and develop and manage transportation and storage systems. The Internet and other technologies have also dramatically influenced the distribution variable. Companies can now make their products available throughout the world without maintaining facilities in each country. We examine distribution issues in Chapters 15 through 17.

The Promotion. The promotion variable relates to activities used to inform individuals or groups about the organization and its products. Promotion can aim to increase public awareness of the organization and of new or existing products. Procter & Gamble, for example, is using NASCAR driver Tony Stewart to convey the masculinity and endurance of its Old Spice Red Zone antiperspirant.[5] Promotional activities can also educate customers about product features or urge people to take a particular stance on a political or social issue, such as smoking or drug abuse. The Ontario Ministry of Energy teamed up with six of the provinces' electrical distributors to launch a provocative public education and promotion program aimed at getting consumers to reduce their consumption of electricity. The *powerWISE*® campaign involved ads on television and in newspapers, as well as educational materials for use in schools and communities.[6] Promotion can also help sustain interest in established products that have been available for decades, such as Arm & Hammer baking soda or Ivory soap. Many companies are using the Internet and the Web to communicate information about themselves and their products. Ragu's website, for example, offers Italian phrases, recipes, and a sweepstakes, while Air Canada and Westjet websites enable customers to make flight reservations. In Chapters 18 through 20, we take a detailed look at promotion activities.

The Price. The price variable relates to decisions and actions associated with establishing pricing objectives and policies and determining product prices.

Number of cell phone users in Canada

1987   0.1
2001   9.5
2002   11.6
2006   16.6
2010   21.7

Users (in millions)

Source: Pay Phones: A dying breed? *CBC News Online*, June 28, 2006. Retrieved October 17, 2006 from http://www.cbc.ca/news/background/cellphones/payphones.html.

Price is a critical component of the marketing mix because customers are concerned about the value obtained in an exchange. Price is often used as a competitive tool, and intense price competition sometimes leads to price wars. Airlines, for example, develop complex systems for determining the right price for each seat on a specific flight. High prices can be used competitively to establish a product's image. The Gap is known as a higher-end retailer of clothing than discounters such as Wal-Mart or Zellers. Price makes a statement about clothing that effectively positions it in the minds of consumers, who may then use price to make a quality association about the product. We explore pricing decisions in more detail in Chapters 21 and 22.

The marketing mix variables are often viewed as controllable because they can be modified. However, there are limits to how much marketing managers can alter them. Economic conditions, competitive structure, or government regulations may prevent a manager from adjusting prices frequently or significantly. Making changes in the size, shape, and design of most tangible goods is expensive; therefore, such product features cannot be altered very often. In addition, promotional campaigns and methods used to distribute products ordinarily cannot be rewritten or revamped overnight.

Marketing Builds Relationships with Customers and Other Stakeholders

exchange The provision or transfer of goods, services, or ideas in return for something of value

Individuals and organizations engage in marketing to facilitate **exchanges,** the provision or transfer of goods, services, or ideas in return for something of value. Any product (good, service, or concept) may be involved in a marketing exchange. We assume only that individuals and organizations expect to gain a reward in excess of the costs incurred.

For an exchange to take place, four conditions must exist. First, two or more individuals, groups, or organizations must participate, and each must possess something of value that the other party desires. Second, the exchange should provide a benefit or satisfaction to both parties in the transaction. Third, each party must have confidence in the promise of the "something of value" held by the other. If you go to a Nickelback concert, for example, you go with the expectation of a great performance. Finally, to build trust, the parties to the exchange must meet expectations.

Figure 1.2 depicts the exchange process. The arrows indicate that the parties communicate that each has something of value available to exchange. An exchange will not necessarily take place just because these conditions exist; marketing activities can occur even without an actual transaction or sale. You may see an ad for a plasma TV, for instance, but you may never buy the product. When an exchange occurs, products are traded for other products or for financial resources.

Marketing activities should attempt to create and maintain satisfying exchange relationships. To maintain an exchange relationship, buyers must be satisfied with the obtained good, service, or concept, and sellers must be satisfied with the financial reward or something else of value received. A dissatisfied customer who lacks trust in the relationship often searches for alternative organizations or products.

figure 1.2

EXCHANGE BETWEEN BUYER AND SELLER

stakeholders Constituents who have a "stake" or claim in some aspect of a company's products, operations, markets, industry, and outcomes

marketing environment The competitive, economic, political, legal and regulatory, technological, and sociocultural forces that surround the customer and affect the marketing mix

Marketers are concerned with building relationships not only with customers but also with relevant stakeholders. **Stakeholders** include those constituents who have a "stake," or claim, in some aspect of a company's products, operations, markets, industry, and outcomes; these include customers, employees, investors and shareholders, suppliers, governments, communities, and many others. Besides customers, relevant stakeholders might include suppliers, employees, shareholders, governments, communities, and other entities. Developing and maintaining favourable relations with stakeholders is crucial to the long-term growth of an organization and its products.

Marketing Occurs in a Dynamic Environment

Marketing activities do not take place in a vacuum. The **marketing environment,** which includes competitive, economic, political, legal, regulatory, technological, and sociocultural forces, surrounds the customer and affects the marketing mix (see Figure 1.1). The effects of these forces on buyers and sellers can be dramatic and difficult to predict. They can create threats to marketers, but they can also generate opportunities for new products and new methods of reaching customers.

The forces of the marketing environment affect a marketer's ability to facilitate exchanges in three general ways. First, they influence customers by affecting their lifestyles, standards of living, and preferences and needs for products. Because a marketing manager tries to develop and adjust the marketing mix to satisfy customers, effects of environmental forces on customers also have an indirect impact on marketing mix components. The merging of telecommunications and computer technologies, for example, allows FedEx Corporation to interact with customers via the Web. FedEx customers can track packages from their home or office computers and send e-mail feedback to FedEx about its services. This technology thus enables FedEx to gather marketing research information directly from customers. Second, marketing environment forces help determine whether and how a marketing manager can perform certain marketing activities. For example, in a highly competitive marketplace, individual firms may have very little control over how they price their products. McDonald's was able to gain control in the highly competitive fast food market by selling burgers less expensively than A&W, while also focusing on product quality. Third, environmental forces may affect a marketing manager's decisions and actions by influencing buyers' reactions to the firm's marketing mix. For example, communities that are suffering from job losses in the automobile manufacturing industry will be more likely to support discount retailers than high-end retail offerings. Similarly, regions with a strong focus on protecting the environment are more likely to consist of buyers who seek the products and services of companies that also embrace a green philosophy. Marketing managers must design marketing strategies that appeal to such buyers.

Marketing environment forces can fluctuate quickly and dramatically, which is one reason why marketing is so interesting and challenging. Because these forces are closely interrelated, changes in one may cause changes in others. For example, evidence linking children's consumption of soft drinks and fast foods to health issues such as obesity, diabetes, and osteoporosis has exposed marketers of such products to negative publicity and generated calls for legislation regulating the sale of soft drinks in public schools. Some companies have responded to these concerns by reformulating products to make them healthier or even introducing new products. PepsiCo, for example, introduced Tropicana FruitWise bars and Life cereal with yogurt, and began a marketing campaign to help consumers identify healthier eating choices. The company placed a green "Smart Spot" on more than 200 products that met nutrition criteria of limits on fat, cholesterol, sodium, and added sugar, such as Baked Lay's potato chips and Tropicana orange juice.[7]

Changes in the marketing environment produce uncertainty for marketers and at times hurt marketing efforts, but they also create opportunities. Marketers who are alert to changes in environmental forces cannot only adjust to and influence these changes but also capitalize on the opportunities such changes provide. Linda Lundström Inc., the Toronto-based fashion design firm that became famous for creating the LAPARKA coat, suffered critical losses in the early 2000s. After establishing a design house that produced six fashion lines each year, with sales of more than $12 million, Linda Lundström realized that her firm might crumble. It took hard work to stabilize the firm, and tough decisions had to be made to deal with changes in the market. Five years later, the firm is back on solid ground, with three stores across Ontario and new product lines that reflect Canada's First Nations heritage.

Marketing mix elements—product, distribution, promotion, and price—are factors over which an organization has control; the forces of the environment, however, are far less controllable. But even though marketers know they cannot predict changes in the marketing environment with certainty, they must nevertheless plan for them. Because these environmental forces have such a profound effect on marketing activities, we explore each of them in considerable depth in Chapter 3.

Understanding the Marketing Concept

Some firms have sought success by buying land, building a factory, equipping it with people and machines, and then making a product they believe buyers need. However, these firms frequently fail to attract customers with what they have to offer because they defined their business as "making a product" rather than as "helping potential customers satisfy their needs and wants." For example, when compact discs became more popular than vinyl records, turntable manufacturers had an opportunity to develop new products to satisfy customers' needs for home entertainment. Companies that did not pursue this opportunity are no longer in business. Such organizations failed to implement the marketing concept. The growing popularity of MP3 technology has enabled firms such as Apple Computer to develop products like the iPod to satisfy consumers' desire to store customized music libraries. Instead of buying CDs, a consumer can download a song for 99 cents from Apple's iTunes.

marketing concept A philosophy that an organization should try to provide products that satisfy customers' needs through a coordinated set of activities that also allows the organization to achieve its goals

According to the **marketing concept,** an organization should try to provide products that satisfy customers' needs through a coordinated set of activities that also allow the organization to achieve its goals. Customer satisfaction is the major focus of the marketing concept. To implement the marketing concept, an organization strives to determine what buyers want and uses this information to develop satisfying products. It focuses on customer analysis, competitor analysis, and integration of the firm's resources to provide customer value and satisfaction as well as generate long-term profits.[8] The firm must also continue to alter, adapt, and develop products to keep pace with customers' changing desires and preferences. Ben & Jerry's, for example, continuously assesses customer demand for ice cream and sorbet. On its website, it maintains a "flavor graveyard" that lists combinations that were tried and ultimately failed. It also notes its top ten flavours each month. Pharmaceutical companies such as Merck and Pfizer continually strive to develop new products to fight infectious diseases, viruses, cancer, and other medical problems. Drugs that lower cholesterol, control diabetes, alleviate depression, or improve the quality of life in other ways also provide huge profits for the drug companies. When a new product is approved—such as a grape-flavoured chewable form of the allergy medication Zyrtec for young allergy sufferers—the company must undertake marketing activities to reach customers and communicate the product's benefits and

The Marketing Concept

State Farm's slogan, "Like a good neighbor, State Farm is there," indicates that this company is attempting to satisfy customers' needs.

any potential side effects. Thus, the marketing concept emphasizes that marketing begins and ends with customers. Research has found a positive association between customer satisfaction and shareholder value.[9]

The marketing concept is not a second definition of *marketing*. It is a management philosophy guiding an organization's overall activities. This philosophy affects all organizational activities, not just marketing. Production, finance, accounting, human resources, and marketing departments must work together.

The marketing concept is also not a philanthropic philosophy aimed at helping customers at the expense of the organization. A firm that adopts the marketing concept must satisfy not only its customers' objectives but also its own, or it will not stay in business long. The overall objectives of a business might relate to increasing profits, market share, sales, or a combination of the three. The marketing concept stresses that an organization can best achieve these objectives by being customer oriented. Thus, implementing the marketing concept should benefit the organization as well as its customers.

It is important for marketers to consider not only their current buyers' needs but also the long-term needs of society. Striving to satisfy customers' desires by sacrificing society's long-term welfare is unacceptable. For example, while many parents want disposable diapers that are comfortable, absorbent, and safe for their babies, society in general does not want non-biodegradable disposable diapers that create tremendous landfill problems now and for the future. Marketers are expected to act in a socially responsible manner, an idea we discuss in more detail in Chapter 4.

Evolution of the Marketing Concept

The marketing concept may seem to be an obvious approach to running a business. However, businesspeople have not always believed that the best way to make sales and profits is to satisfy customers (see Figure 1.3).

The Production Orientation. During the second half of the nineteenth century, the Industrial Revolution was in full swing. Electricity, rail transportation, division of labour, assembly lines, and mass production made it possible to produce goods more efficiently. With new technology and new ways of using labour, products poured into the marketplace, where demand for manufactured goods was strong. Management focus was on producing products

marketing ENTREPRENEURS

Sandra Wilson

THE BUSINESS: Robeez Shoes

FOUNDED: 1994

SUCCESS: Sold to Stride Rite Corporation in 2006 for $30.5 million

When she was downsized out of her job, Sandra Wilson decided to spend some quality time with her 18-month-old son, Robert. She also considered starting a home-based business. In 1994, she created a pair of shoes for young Robert, and the rest is history.

Robert loved his new, brightly coloured footwear. Thinking she may have tapped into a golden market opportunity, Sandra bought a booth at the Vancouver Gift Show and was overwhelmed by the response to the 20 pairs of tiny shoes that she had lovingly crafted. Before long, she had sold all 20 pairs and signed up retailers who were eager to sell Robeez Shoes.

Her first manufacturing operation was located in the basement of her home. She had to hire a sales representative a year after launching her firm. She quickly learned what she needed to know about being an entrepreneur: sales, marketing, accounting, management. She also decided to learn about the Internet, which prompted her to sell her products online beginning in 1997.

Five years after starting the firm, Sandra's business had outgrown her basement. By 2001, she was grossing more than a million dollars in sales. Ten years later, Robeez Shoes has exceeded $15 million in annual sales, with more than 4,500 stores around the world and 400 employees. Her firm was just ranked as the 11th fastest growing firm in Canada by *PROFIT* magazine. Robeez Shoes was ranked as 27th in profit by *PROFIT* magazine in 2005, and made the list of the best companies to work for in British Columbia in 2004. Wilson was ranked the top woman entrepreneur of the year, and top entrepreneur of the year, in 2004.

Today, Robeez Shoes is the world's leading supplier of soft-soled shoes for children with sales of $30 million. The firm also donates children's shoes to charities across the globe. On September 6, 2006, Sandra sold Robeez Shoes to Stride Rite Corporation of New York for $30.5 million.

for the masses, rather than producing products for which there were needs in the target market.

Production-oriented firms focus on the product first, and the customer second. The **production orientation** is based on the "field of dreams" approach of "build it and they will come." However, in today's modern consumer-driven society, many markets exist that have very distinctive needs. As a result, many production-oriented firms miss the market with their technology, leaving them with a lot of product but not a lot of sales. While most organizations understand that the production orientation is outdated by today's standards, some firms still pursue a production-oriented approach to marketing.

The Sales Orientation. In the 1920s, strong demand for products subsided, and businesses realized they would have to "sell" products to buyers. From the mid-1920s to the early 1950s, businesses viewed sales as the major means of increasing profits and came to adopt a **sales/selling orientation**. Businesspeople believed the most important marketing activities were personal selling, advertising, and distribution.

This era gave way to many unethical marketing practices as sales people resorted to high-pressure tactics and trickery to sell their products. Today's marketers understand that products that need to be shoved on consumers probably do not meet their needs, and may not have a market.

Today some people incorrectly equate marketing with a sales orientation. However, the marketing orientation puts the customer in the centre of the marketing strategy (see Figure 1.1), while the sales orientation focuses first on promotion, then on the customer.

The Marketing Orientation. By the early 1950s, some businesspeople began to recognize that efficient production and extensive promotion did not guarantee that customers would buy products. These businesses, and many others since, found they must first determine what customers want and then produce these products rather than making the products first and then trying to persuade customers that they need them. As more organizations realized the importance of satisfying customers' needs, businesses entered the marketing era, one of marketing orientation.

A **marketing orientation** requires the "organization-wide generation of market intelligence pertaining to current and future customer needs, dissemination of the intelligence across departments, and organization wide responsiveness to it."[10] Marketing orientation is linked to new product innovation by developing a strategic focus to explore and develop new products to serve target markets.[11] Top management, marketing managers, non-marketing managers (those in production, finance, human resources, and so on), and customers are all important in developing and carrying out a marketing orientation. Unless marketing managers provide continuous customer-focused leadership with minimal interdepartmental conflict, achieving a marketing orientation will be difficult. Non-marketing managers must communicate with marketing managers to share information important to understanding the customer. Finally, a marketing orientation involves being responsive to ever-changing customer needs and wants. For example, to accomplish this, Amazon.ca follows buyers' online purchases and recommends related purchases. Trying to assess what customers want, a difficult task to begin with, is further complicated by the speed with which fashions

Production orientation
A philosophy that an organization focuses first on the product and its production, believing that the product will draw customers

Sales/selling orientation
A philosophy that an organization focuses hiring aggressive sales people, or on promoting the good and service, over and above product quality, production efficiency or market needs

marketing orientation
An organization-wide commitment to researching and responding to customer needs

figure 1.3

THE EVOLUTION OF THE MARKETING CONCEPT

Production orientation   Sales orientation   Marketing orientation

1850   1900   1950   2000

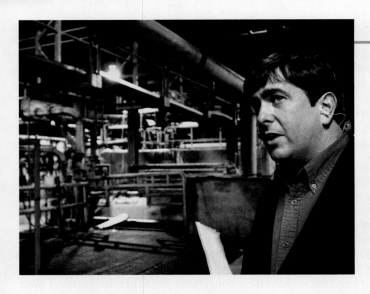

Through the use of socially responsible marketing, Minas Basin has distinguished itself as a company that is at the leading edge of environmentally responsible practices.

and tastes can change. Today businesses want to satisfy customers and build meaningful, long-term, buyer-seller relationships. Doing so helps a firm boost its own financial value.[12]

The Societal Marketing Orientation. Many of today's leading firms go beyond the marketing orientation to embrace a more global philosophy, which has a goal of meeting the needs of customers, as well as other stakeholders in the firm. The **societal marketing orientation** focuses on meeting the needs of customers, but when crafting the marketing mix (4 P's) care is taken to respect the concerns, rights and freedoms of other stakeholders who could be impacted by the firm's marketing activities.

societal marketing orientation
A philosophy that an organization focuses on meeting the needs of its customers, while respecting the needs of its other stakeholders

A societal marketing orientation requires looking beyond simply meeting the needs of the target market, towards being ethical in the interaction between the firm and its many publics. Minas Basin Pulp and Power is such a firm. Located in the small town of Hantsport, Nova Scotia, Minas Basin produces paper products from recycled paper products. Because they repulp existing paper, the firm has not cut down a tree in over a decade. This also eliminates the need to pulp wood. As a result, their air emissions are much cleaner and there is no odour. They have also reduced their landfill requirements by approximately 10.8 million cubic feet annually.

The mill produces its own hydroelectric power, and it has received the Canadian government's environmental logo, indicating that they are seen as being environmentally conscious and that they use renewable resources. The plant's waste water exceeds drinking water standards for purity.

In July 2006, Minas Basin Pulp and Power installed a state of the art heat recovery system; the first such installation of its kind for the North American pulp and paper industry. The new heat recovery system will further reduce sulfur dioxide and carbon dioxide emissions while also increasing the mill's heating efficiency, ultimately reducing heating costs by up to 25 percent.[13]

Minas Basin Pulp and Power has risen beyond simply trying to find markets for their paper products to finding ways to produce those products that respect the quality of life of those in their community. They are pursuing a societal marketing orientation.

Implementing the Marketing Concept

A philosophy may sound reasonable and look good on paper, but that does not mean it can be put into practice easily. To implement the marketing concept, a marketing-oriented organization must accept some general conditions and recognize and deal with several problems. Consequently, the marketing concept has yet to be fully accepted by all businesses. Management must first establish an information system to discover customers' real needs and then use the information to create satisfying products. Nissan, for example, conducted intensive marketing research before launching its first full-size pickup truck, the Titan. The company interviewed truck buyers about their needs and wants; sent researchers to hunting expos, gun shows, and other events frequented by pickup truck owners; and had researchers drive competing trucks for a month to learn firsthand about how the large vehicles handle in a variety of situations.[14] This example illustrates one technique marketers can use to obtain information about customers' desires and to respond in a way that forges a positive marketing relationship. An information system is usually expensive; management must commit money and time for its development and maintenance. But without an adequate information system, an organization cannot be marketing oriented.

To satisfy customers' objectives as well as its own, a company must also coordinate all its activities. This may require restructuring the internal operations and overall objectives of one or more departments. Nanotechnology, for example, represents opportunities for advances in pumps, gears, and switches to perform physical tasks.

Rutter Inc. Sets the Example in Societal Marketing Orientation

The following is from a website for Rutter Inc., which was ranked first in the *PROFIT* 100 Fastest Growing Canadian firms. What follows is the firm's values statement that demonstrates the views of a societal marketing-oriented firm.

Rutter Inc. is a marine technology and engineering firm located in St. John's, NL. Rutter was ranked first in *PROFIT* magazine's list of the 100 top growth firms in Canada. With revenues of $70.9 million in 2005, up from $223 800 only five years earlier, Rutter has grown into a world-class manufacturer and marketer. Rutter's value statement shows how the marketing orientation can be transformed into a societal marketing orientation through which a firm can satisfy its customers while also respecting the needs of other stakeholders.

Our Values

At Rutter we believe that listening and taking a long-term view of all the relationships in our world is important. We believe in conducting our business in an ethical socially responsible manner that respects the law of the land and benefits our shareholders, our employees and the communities in which we work. Our core values are based on this foundation and they include: partnership; trust; integrity; responsibility; entrepreneurship and teamwork; quality; growth; corporate strength; and corporate citizenship.

Partnership and Trust—We believe that partnerships and trust at many levels have contributed to

our success and will do so in the future. We are committed to being a good partner focused on collaborative trusting and beneficial relationships with all our stakeholders.

Integrity—We will be honest with ourselves and with others. We make decisions that are best for our customers and deliver on what we say we will do. We adhere to the highest ethical standards in all our business dealings.

Responsibility—We willingly take responsibility for our actions as individuals and as a company. We view accountability as synonymous with trust and we welcome scrutiny.

Entrepreneurship and Teamwork—We value it and look for it in those we hire. We encourage and reward teams and individuals that help us find new opportunities and better ways to operate our business and serve our customers.

Quality—At Rutter Technologies quality is a constant in the equation of who we are. We set standards that exceed regulatory requirements and strive to follow best management practices. We believe quality is at the heart of client satisfaction—the key to successful partnerships.

Growth—We foster a climate of innovation and embrace change. We will seek out new challenging opportunities that drive us to new levels of achievement both personally and corporately. We will be smart and choose the right tools for the job.

Corporate Strength—Rutter is focused on results and committed to top quartile performance. We will be profitable and deliver superior returns to our shareholders. We will take sustainable actions and maintain a strong balance sheet that gives us the ability to exceed customer service expectations and positions us for new growth opportunities.

Corporate Citizenship—We acknowledge the world around us and value what we receive from it economically, culturally and socially. We will give back in these same areas. As individuals and as a company, we strive to make a difference to the economic, social and cultural well being of the communities where we live and work. We respect our environment, will contribute to its preservation and conduct our business with appropriate sensitivity to it.

However, application and commercialization of this technology requires marketing knowledge related to customers' needs and product uses. If the head of the marketing unit is not a member of the organization's top-level management, a new technology may fail to sufficiently address actual customer needs and desires. Implementing the marketing concept demands the support not only of top management but also of managers and staff across all functions and levels of the organization.

There are also some inherent problems with the nature of the marketing concept itself, which can constrain its adoption. Firms whose products are very high technology-based may encounter problems when defining customer needs because customers cannot visualize the need nor can they understand the technology. For example, when microwave ovens were first being introduced many consumers feared them. They related microwave energy to nuclear energy and high profile nuclear accidents, such as Three Mile Island and Chernobyl. They feared that they could be zapped with radiation by walking through their kitchen when the microwave oven was turned on. A great deal of education is required to quell such fears.

There has also been some criticism that the marketing orientation focuses too much on the bottom line, on profitable sales, which has led many firms to modify existing products rather than pursue new innovations. After all, modifying existing products may cost less money and take less time to get to market, both of which are important considerations when one is being rated on their performance from fiscal quarter to fiscal quarter.

While firms may use these concerns as excuses to avoid embracing the marketing concept, there are ways to minimize such concerns, and firms will perform much better in the long run by becoming marketing oriented. Such approaches require the use of marketing research to develop better marketing strategies related to customers; needs. If a firm does not become market oriented, it may never make the transition to becoming societal marketing oriented, which builds on the marketing orientation.

Managing Customer Relationships

Achieving the full profit potential of each customer relationship should be the fundamental goal of every marketing strategy. Marketing relationships with customers are the lifeblood of all businesses. At the most basic level, profits can be obtained through relationships by (1) acquiring new customers, (2) enhancing the profitability of existing customers, and (3) extending the duration of customer relationships. Implementing the marketing concept means optimizing the exchange relationship—the relationship between a company's investment in customer relationships and the return generated by customers' loyalty and retention.[15]

relationship marketing
Establishing long-term, mutually satisfying buyer-seller relationships

Maintaining positive relationships with customers is an important goal for marketers. The term **relationship marketing** refers to "long-term, mutually beneficial arrangements in which both the buyer and seller focus on value enhancement through the creation of more satisfying exchanges."[16] Relationship marketing continually deepens the buyer's trust in the company, which, as the customer's confidence grows, in turn increases the firm's understanding of the customer's needs. Successful marketers respond to customer needs and strive to increase value to buyers over time. Eventually this interaction becomes a solid relationship that allows for cooperation and mutual dependency.

customer relationship management (CRM) Using information about customers to create marketing strategies that develop and sustain desirable customer relationships

To build long-term customer relationships, marketers are increasingly turning to marketing research and information technology. **Customer relationship management (CRM)** focuses on using information about customers to create marketing strategies that develop and sustain desirable customer relationships. By increasing customer value over time, organizations try to retain and increase long-term profitability through customer loyalty.[17]

Managing customer relationships requires identifying patterns of buying behaviour and using that information to focus on the most promising and profitable customers. Companies must be sensitive to customers' requirements and desires, and

customer lifetime value
The total value of purchases for a single customer received from a lifetime of loyal purchase behaviour

establish communication to build customers' trust and loyalty. A **customer's lifetime value** results from his or her frequency of purchases, average value of purchases, and brand-switching patterns.[18] For example, if a customer spends $25.00 on fast food each week, they will spend $1 300 each year, and $45 500 over 35 years. Discriminating firms will focus on customers with higher lifetime values. This can result in higher profits in future periods than when they focus on customers selected for other reasons.[19] Because the loss of a loyal potential lifetime customer can result in lower profits, managing customer relationships has become a major focus of strategic marketing today.

To some extent, developing relationships with customers is easier in the Canadian marketplace than in larger markets, such as those in the United States, where industries may be more competitive and the marketplace more divided. For example, Canada's five big banks can build customer relationships more effectively than banks can in the United States where numerous banks compete for the same consumer dollar.

Through the use of Internet-based marketing strategies (e-marketing), companies can personalize customer relationships on a nearly one-on-one basis. A wide range of products, such as computers, jeans, golf clubs, cosmetics, and greeting cards, can be tailored for specific customers. Dell has built a highly successful computer business by customizing its product offerings down to the individual customer level.

CRM provides a strategic bridge between information technology and marketing strategies aimed at long-term relationships with high-revenue customers.[20] Thus, information technology helps Amazon.ca manage customer relationships to build value and increase sales and satisfaction. We take a closer look at some of these e-marketing strategies in Chapter 8.

Is Canadian Tire Bank Coming to a Town Near You?

You may be banking at a Canadian Tire store near you. That opportunity may come soon if you reside in Calgary or Kitchener-Waterloo, two regions where Canadian Tire will pilot test its new approach to cementing customer relationships.

Taking a page from President's Choice Financial, Canadian Tire plans to offer financial products through its network of stores. They will invest $10.2 million to market financial services to their four million retail customers. But don't expect to see counter staff and wickets at the store level. Rather than creating physical banking facilities, Canadian Tire has decided to keep everything virtual, providing services online and via telephone.

Promotional literature will be provided in their stores, making each store into what management calls an "information channel." ING Direct is the banking facility behind Canadian Tire Financial, just like CIBC provides services for President's Choice.

Canadian Tire knows that the closer a company is to its market, the more products and services the customers will buy. One way to get closer to the market is to sell more services. Cross-selling allows firms to make money by increasing their share of the customer, not just their share of the market.

Canadian Tire also knows that it costs less to sell to an existing customer than to find a new customer. While they must do both, they hope that by offering more services, more customers will find them useful and affordable. By offering banking services, Canadian Tire will move closer to being a one-stop-shopping experience, adding more value for their customers, building customer relationships and increasing loyalty in a competitive marketplace.

Value-Driven Marketing

value A customer's subjective assessment of benefits relative to costs in determining the worth of a product

Value is an important element of managing long-term customer relationships and implementing the marketing concept. We view **value** as a customer's subjective assessment of benefits relative to costs in determining the worth of a product (customer value = customer benefits − customer costs). From a company's perspective, there is a tradeoff between increasing the value offered to a customer and maximizing the profits from a transaction.[21]

Customer benefits include anything a buyer receives in an exchange. Hotels and motels, for example, basically provide a room with a bed and bathroom, but each firm provides a different level of service, amenities, and atmosphere to satisfy its guests. Super Eight Motel offers the minimum services necessary to maintain a quality, efficient, low-price overnight accommodation. In contrast, the Holiday Inn Select provides many guest services and strives to ensure that all service is of the highest quality. Customers judge which type of accommodation offers the best value according to the benefits they desire and their willingness and ability to pay for the costs associated with those benefits.

Customer costs include anything a buyer must give up to obtain the benefits the product provides. The most obvious cost is the monetary price of the product, but non-monetary costs can be equally important in a customer's determination of value. Two non-monetary costs are the time and effort customers expend to find and purchase desired products. To reduce time and effort, a company can increase product availability, thereby making it more convenient for buyers to purchase the firm's products. Another non-monetary cost is risk, which can be reduced by offering good basic warranties or extended warranties for an additional charge.[22] Another risk reduction strategy is the offer of a 100 percent satisfaction guarantee. This strategy is increasingly popular in today's catalog/telephone/Internet shopping environment. Sears uses such a guarantee to reduce the risk involved in ordering merchandise from its catalogs and online store.

The process people use to determine the value of a product is not highly scientific. We all tend to get a feel for the worth of products based on our own expectations and previous experiences. We can, for example, compare the value of tires, batteries, and computers directly with the value of competing products. We evaluate movies, sporting events, and performances by entertainers on the more subjective basis of personal preferences and emotions. For most purchases, we do not consciously try to calculate the

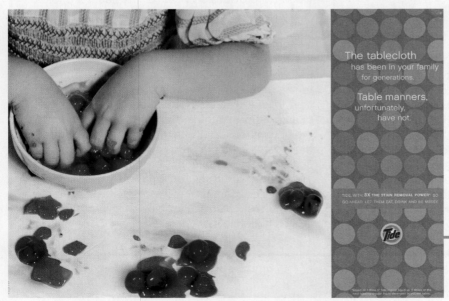

Value-Driven Marketing
Rapala uses value to promote its products. Tide promotes the value of its stain-fighting ability to those with family heirlooms.

associated benefits and costs. It becomes an instinctive feeling that Kellogg's Corn Flakes are a good value or that McDonald's is a good place to take children for a quick lunch. The purchase of an automobile or a mountain bike may have emotional components, but more conscious decision making may also figure in the process of determining value.

In developing marketing activities, it is important to recognize that customers receive benefits based on their experiences. For example, many computer buyers consider services such as fast delivery, ease of installation, technical advice, and training assistance to be important elements of the product. Customers also derive benefits from the act of shopping and selecting products. These benefits can be affected by the atmosphere or environment of a store, such as Red Lobster's nautical/seafood theme. Even the ease of navigating a website can have a tremendous impact on perceived value. For this reason, General Motors has developed a user-friendly way to navigate its website for researching and pricing vehicles. Using the Internet to compare a Saturn with a Mercedes could result in different customers viewing each automobile as an excellent value. Owners have highly rated the Saturn as providing low-cost, reliable transportation and having dealers who provide outstanding service. A Mercedes may cost twice as much but has been rated as a better-engineered automobile that also has a higher social status than the Saturn. Different customers may view each car as being an exceptional value for their own personal satisfaction.

The marketing mix can be used to enhance perceptions of value. A product that demonstrates value usually has a feature or an enhancement that provides benefits. Promotional activities can also help create an image and prestige characteristics that customers consider in their assessment of a product's value. In some cases, value may simply be perceived as the lowest price. Many customers may not care about the quality of the paper towels they buy; they simply want the cheapest ones for use in cleaning up spills because they plan to throw them in the trash anyway. On the other hand, more people are looking for the fastest, most convenient way to achieve a certain goal and therefore become insensitive to pricing. For example, many busy customers are buying more prepared meals in supermarkets to take home and serve quickly, even though these meals cost considerably more than meals prepared from scratch. In such cases, the products with the greatest convenience may be perceived as having the greatest value. The availability or distribution of products can also enhance their value. For example, many shoppers enjoy the convenience of ordering online. Others prefer to shop in a physical location, and preferably in one that is close to their home or workplace. The development of an effective marketing strategy requires understanding the needs and desires of customers and designing a marketing mix to satisfy them and provide the value they want.

Marketing Management

marketing management
The process of planning, organizing, implementing, and controlling marketing activities to facilitate exchanges effectively and efficiently

Marketing management is the process of planning, organizing, implementing, and controlling marketing activities to facilitate exchanges effectively and efficiently. Effectiveness and efficiency are important dimensions of this definition. *Effectiveness* is the degree to which an exchange helps achieve an organization's objectives. *Efficiency* refers to minimizing the resources an organization must spend to achieve a specific level of desired exchanges. Thus, the overall goal of marketing management is to facilitate highly desirable exchanges and to minimize the costs of doing so.

Planning is a systematic process of assessing opportunities and resources, determining marketing objectives, and developing a marketing strategy and plans for implementation and control. Planning determines when and how marketing activities are performed and who performs them. It forces marketing managers to think ahead, establish objectives, and consider future marketing activities and their impact on society. Effective planning also reduces or eliminates daily crises.

Organizing marketing activities involves developing the internal structure of the marketing unit. The structure is the key to directing marketing activities. The marketing unit can be organized by functions, products, regions, types of customers, or a combination of all four.

Proper implementation of marketing plans hinges on coordination of marketing activities, motivation of marketing personnel, and effective communication within the unit. Marketing managers must motivate marketing personnel, coordinate their activities, and integrate their activities both with those in other areas of the company and with the marketing efforts of personnel in external organizations, such as advertising agencies and research firms. If McDonald's runs a promotion advertising Big Macs for 99 cents, proper implementation of this plan requires that each of the company's restaurants has enough staff and product on hand to handle the increased demand. An organization's communication system must allow the marketing manager to stay in contact with high-level management, with managers of other functional areas within the firm, and with personnel involved in marketing activities both inside and outside the organization.

The marketing control process consists of establishing performance standards, comparing actual performance with established standards, and reducing the difference between desired and actual performance. We examine the development, organization, implementation, and controlling of marketing strategies in greater detail in the next chapter.

The Importance of Marketing in our Global Economy

Our definition of *marketing* and discussion of marketing activities reveal some of the obvious reasons the study of marketing is relevant in today's world. In this section, we look at how marketing affects us as individuals and at its role in our increasingly global society.

Marketing Costs Consume a Sizable Portion of Buyers' Dollars

Studying marketing will make you aware that many marketing activities are necessary to provide satisfying goods and services. Obviously these activities cost money. About one-half of a buyer's dollar goes toward marketing costs. If you spend $16 on a new compact disc, 50 to 60 percent goes toward marketing expenses, including promotion and distribution, as well as profit margin. The production (pressing) of the CD represents about $1, or 6.25 percent of its price. A family with a monthly income of $3 000 that allocates $600 to taxes and savings spends about $2 400 for goods and services. Of this amount, $1 200 goes for marketing activities. If marketing expenses consume that much of your dollar, you should know how this money is used.

Marketing Is Used in Non-Profit Organizations

Although the term *marketing* may bring to mind advertising for Estée Lauder, Toyota, and Microsoft, marketing is also important in organizations working to achieve goals other than ordinary business objectives such as profit. Government

Non-Profit Organizations Use Marketing

Non-profit organizations, such as CIBC in its promotion of Run For the Cure to benefit breast cancer research, use advertising to promote the cause and the event.

agencies at the federal, state, and local levels engage in marketing activities to fulfill their mission and goals. The Canadian Armed Forces uses promotion, including television advertisements and event sponsorships, to communicate the benefits of enlisting to potential recruits. Universities and colleges also engage in marketing activities to recruit new students as well as donations from alumni and businesses. The Canadian federal and provincial governments have used aggressive and emotionally charged marketing campaigns to educate people about workplace safety.

In the private sector, non-profit organizations employ marketing activities to create, distribute, promote, and even price programs that benefit particular segments of society. Habitat for Humanity, for example, must promote its philosophy of low-income housing to the public to raise funds and donations of supplies to build or renovate housing for low-income families who contribute "sweat equity" to the construction of their own homes. Much of the most compelling social marketing is linked to Mothers Against Drunk Driving, an organization that uses highly provocative and often disturbing imagery to educate the public about the hazards of drinking and driving.

Marketing Is Important to Business and the Economy

Businesses must sell products to survive and grow, and marketing activities help sell their products. Financial resources generated from sales can be used to develop innovative products. New products allow a firm to better satisfy customers' changing needs, which in turn enables the firm to generate more profits. Even non-profit businesses need to "sell" to survive.

All of the functions in a business that produce revenue are marketing functions. Marketing activities help produce the profits that are essential not only to the survival of individual businesses but also to the health and ultimate survival of the global economy. Profits drive economic growth because without them businesses find it difficult, if not impossible, to buy more raw materials, hire more employees, attract more capital, and create additional products that in turn make more profits. Without profits, marketers cannot continue to provide jobs and contribute to social causes.

Marketing Fuels Our Global Economy

Profits from marketing products contribute to the development of new products and technologies. Advances in technology, along with falling political and economic barriers combined with the universal desire for a higher standard of living, have made marketing across national borders commonplace while stimulating global economic growth. As a result of worldwide communications and increased international travel, many brands have achieved widespread acceptance around the world. At the same time, Canadians have greater choices among the products they buy as foreign brands such as Toyota (Japan), Bayer (Germany), and BP (Great Britain). People around the world watch CNN and MTV on Toshiba and Sony televisions they purchased at Wal-Mart. Some well-known brands have been sold to foreign companies: Lenovo, a Chinese firm, purchased IBM's personal computer unit.[23] Electronic commerce via the Internet now enables businesses of all sizes to reach buyers worldwide. We explore the international markets and opportunities for global marketing in Chapter 7.

Marketing Enhances Our Quality of Life

In Canada we benefit from a well-established marketing distribution system. We can go to shops and supermarkets and buy small amounts of products that are highly specialized, or that have been imported from exotic regions of the world. We can obtain various grades, products, sizes and packages to meet our own unique needs. We can explore unique tastes and products that cannot be produced in our Canadian climate. We have come to expect this level of service and we express dissatisfaction when such goods are in limited supply. We enjoy a quality of life that is among the most privileged in the world as a result of the well-integrated marketing system that has been developed in Canada.

Marketing Knowledge Enhances Consumer Awareness

Besides contributing to the well-being of our economy, marketing activities help improve the quality of our lives. Studying marketing allows us to assess a product's value and flaws more effectively. We can determine which marketing efforts need improvement and how to attain that goal. For example, an unsatisfactory experience with a warranty may make you wish for stricter law enforcement so that sellers would fulfill their promises. You may also wish you had more accurate information about a product before you purchased it. Understanding marketing enables us to evaluate corrective measures (such as laws, regulations, and industry guidelines) that could stop unfair, damaging, or unethical marketing practices. Thus, understanding how marketing activities work can help you be a better consumer.

Marketing Connects People Through Technology

Technology, especially computers and telecommunications, helps marketers understand and satisfy more customers than ever before. Over the phone and online, customers can provide feedback about their experiences with a company's products. Even products such as Dasani bottled water provide a customer service number and a website for questions or comments. This feedback helps marketers refine and improve their products to better satisfy customer needs. In addition to feedback, the Internet also allows companies to provide tremendous amounts of information about their products to consumers and to interact with them through e-mail. A consumer shopping for a personal digital assistant, for example, can visit the Blackberry website to compare its features to those of a smartphone such as the Palm Treo or visit a price comparison website to find the best price.

One Planet, One IKEA

As markets fragment, it is no surprise that companies with the biggest increases in brand value operate as a single brand globally. IKEA, the Swedish home furnishings company and the world's largest furniture retailer, has shown that a well-positioned brand with a strong marketing mix travels well. It has clearly learned that a single worldwide identity is easier to manage and more cost efficient than creating new brands for each country.

While other global brands make extensive changes to fit local environments, IKEA provides a nearly identical experience in its more than 200 blue and yellow stores. IKEA stores—each the size of five football fields—feature over 7 000 items ranging from self-assemble beds and kitchen cabinets to candlesticks and potted plants, all showcased in fully accessorized life-like settings. The shopping experience is as much a part of the product as the products themselves.

The 1.1 million customers who visit IKEA every day enter an environment that is emblematic of hip Scandinavian design and simplicity. The product displays and furniture showrooms appeal to the growing global middle class that aspires to success and a comfortable living. More than just a seller of furniture, the company conveys to people all over the world that IKEA is synonymous with good taste and smart value.

While IKEA refuses to change its basic concept—offering a broad variety of well-designed and functional home furnishing products at prices low enough that as many people as possible can afford them—it does adjust to ensure a pleasurable shopping experience for local cultures. When it was suggested that Americans wouldn't assemble furniture themselves, IKEA provided better instructions and offered an assembly service. To fit Japan's small urban apartments, IKEA offered smaller versions of its products. Stores in China carry chopsticks, woks, and cleavers—essential cooking tools in that country—and a department dedicated to balcony furniture to accommodate the many Chinese who live in apartments with balconies. But the basic model, complete with Swedish-named products such as Leksvik and Poang and restaurants featuring IKEA's popular cinnamon rolls, remains the same. IKEA clearly recognizes that the middle class it targets has similar needs and lifestyle aspirations across the globe.

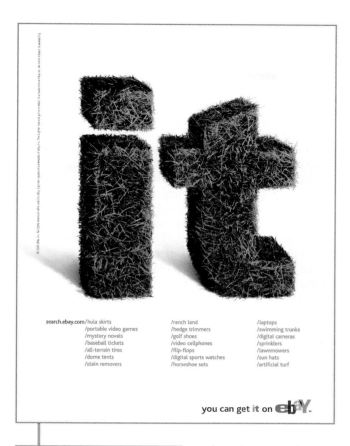

search.ebay.com/hula skirts
/portable video games
/mystery novels
/baseball tickets
/all-terrain tires
/dome tents
/stain removers

/ranch land
/hedge trimmers
/golf shoes
/video cellphones
/flip-flops
/digital sports watches
/horseshoe sets

/laptops
/swimming trunks
/digital cameras
/sprinklers
/lawnmowers
/sun hats
/artificial turf

you can get it on ebaY

Marketing and the Growth of Technology

eBay uses technology to facilitate the marketing of a multitude of products.

The Internet has also become a vital tool for marketing to other businesses. In fact, online sales now exceed $100 billion, accounting for more than 2 percent of all retail sales.[24] Successful companies are using technology in their marketing strategies to develop profitable relationships with these customers. We look more closely at marketing on the Internet in Chapter 8.

Socially Responsible Marketing: Promoting the Welfare of Customers and Society

The success of our economic system depends on marketers whose values promote trust and cooperative relationships in which customers are treated with respect. The public is increasingly insisting that social responsibility and ethical concerns be considered in planning and implementing marketing activities. Although some marketers' irresponsible or unethical activities end up in the media, more firms are working to develop a responsible approach to developing long-term relationships with customers and society. For example, Staples, the office-supply superstore chain, has provided financial support and donated more than $400 000 worth of school supplies to the School, Home & Office Products Association (SHOPA) Kids in Need Foundation, which provides school supplies to needy children and teachers in low-income schools, through its Staples Foundation for Learning.[25] By addressing concerns about the impact of marketing on society, a firm can protect the interests of the general public and the natural environment. We examine these issues and many others as we develop a framework for understanding more about marketing in the remainder of this book.

Marketing Offers Many Exciting Career Prospects

The marketing field offers a variety of interesting and challenging career opportunities throughout the world, such as personal selling, advertising, packaging, transportation, storage, marketing research, product development, wholesaling, and retailing. In addition, many individuals working for non-business organizations engage in marketing activities to promote political, educational, cultural, church, civic, and charitable activities. Whether a person earns a living through marketing activities or performs them voluntarily for a non-profit group, marketing knowledge and skills are valuable personal and professional assets. For more information about marketing jobs, go to the following websites: www.salaryexperts.com and www.WetFeet.com.

SUMMARY

Marketing is the process of creating, distributing, promoting, and pricing goods, services, and ideas to facilitate satisfying exchange relationships with customers and develop and maintain favourable relationships with stakeholders in a dynamic environment. As the purchasers of the products that organizations develop, promote, distribute, and price, customers are the focal point of all marketing activities. The essence of marketing is to develop satisfying exchanges from which both customers and marketers benefit. Organizations generally focus their marketing efforts on a specific group of customers called a target market.

Marketing involves developing and managing a product that will satisfy customer needs, making the product available in the right place and at a price acceptable to customers, and communicating information that helps customers determine if the product will satisfy their needs. These activities—product, distribution, promotion, and pricing—are known as the marketing mix because marketing managers decide what type of each element to use and in what amounts. Marketing managers strive to develop a marketing mix that matches the needs of customers in the target market. Before marketers can develop a marketing mix, they must collect in-depth, up-to-date information about customer needs. The product variable of the marketing mix deals with researching customers' needs and wants and designing a product that satisfies them. A product can be a good, a service, or an idea. In dealing with the distribution variable, a marketing manager tries to make products available in the quantities desired to as many customers as possible. The promotion variable relates to activities used to inform individuals or groups about the organization and its products. The price variable involves decisions and actions associated with establishing pricing policies and determining product prices. These marketing mix variables are often viewed as controllable because they can be changed, but there are limits to how much they can be altered.

Individuals and organizations engage in marketing to facilitate exchanges—the provision or transfer of goods, services, and ideas in return for something of value. Four conditions must exist for an exchange to occur. First, two or more individuals, groups, or organizations must participate, and each must possess something of value that the other party desires. Second, the exchange should provide a benefit or satisfaction to both parties involved in the transaction. Third, each party must have confidence in the promise of the "something of value" held by the other. Finally, to build trust, the parties to the exchange must meet expectations. Marketing activities should attempt to create and maintain satisfying exchange relationships.

The marketing environment, which includes competitive, economic, political, legal and regulatory, technological, and sociocultural forces, surrounds the customer and the marketing mix. These forces can create threats to marketers, but they also generate opportunities for new products and new methods of reaching customers. These forces can fluctuate quickly and dramatically.

According to the marketing concept, an organization should try to provide products that satisfy customers' needs through a coordinated set of activities that also allow the organization to achieve its goals. Customer satisfaction is the marketing concept's major objective. The philosophy of the marketing concept emerged during the 1950s after the production and sales eras. Organizations that develop activities consistent with the marketing concept become marketing-oriented organizations. To implement the marketing concept, a marketing-oriented organization must establish an information system to discover customers' needs and use the information to create satisfying products. It must also coordinate all its activities and develop marketing mixes that create value for customers in order to satisfy their needs.

Relationship marketing involves establishing long-term, mutually satisfying, buyer-seller relationships. Customer relationship management (CRM) focuses on using information about customers to create marketing strategies that develop and sustain desirable customer relationships. Managing customer relationships requires identifying patterns of buying behaviour and using that information to focus on the most promising and profitable customers.

Value is a customer's subjective assessment of benefits relative to costs in determining the worth of a product. Benefits include anything a buyer receives in an exchange; costs include anything a buyer must give up to obtain the benefits the product provides. The marketing mix can be used to enhance perceptions of value.

Marketing management is the process of planning, organizing, implementing, and controlling marketing activities to facilitate effective and efficient exchanges. Planning is a systematic process of assessing opportunities and resources, determining marketing objectives, developing a marketing strategy, and preparing for implementation and control. Organizing marketing activities involves developing the marketing unit's internal structure. Proper implementation of marketing plans depends on coordinating marketing activities, motivating marketing personnel, and communicating effectively within the unit. The marketing control process consists of establishing performance standards, comparing actual performance with established standards, and reducing the difference between desired and actual performance.

Marketing is important in our society in many ways. Marketing costs absorb about half of each buyer's dollar. Marketing activities are performed in both business and non-profit organizations. Marketing activities help business organizations generate profits and help fuel the increasingly global economy. Knowledge of marketing enhances consumer awareness and quality of life. New technology improves marketers' ability to connect with customers. Socially responsible marketing can promote the welfare of customers and society. Finally, marketing offers many exciting career opportunities.

Please visit the student website at **www.hmco.ca/marketing** for ACE Self-Test questions that will help you prepare for exams.

IMPORTANT TERMS

Marketing	Exchange	Marketing orientation	Customer relationship
Customers	Stakeholders	Societal marketing	management (CRM)
Target market	Marketing concept	orientation	Customer lifetime value
Marketing mix	Production orientation	Relationship	Value
Product	Sales/selling orientation	marketing	Marketing management

DISCUSSION & REVIEW QUESTIONS

1. What is marketing? How did you define the term before you read this chapter?

2. What is the focus of all marketing activities? Why?

3. What are the four variables of the marketing mix? Why are these elements known as variables?

4. What conditions must exist before a marketing exchange can occur? Describe a recent exchange in which you participated.

5. What are the forces in the marketing environment? How much control does a marketing manager have over these forces?

6. Discuss the basic elements of the marketing concept. Which businesses in your area use this philosophy? Explain why.

7. How can an organization implement the marketing concept?

8. What is customer relationship management? Why is it so important to "manage" this relationship?

9. What is value? How can marketers use the marketing mix to enhance customers' perception of value?

10. What types of activities are involved in the marketing management process?

11. Why is marketing important in our society? Why should you study marketing?

APPLICATION QUESTIONS

1. Identify several businesses in your area that have not adopted the marketing concept. What characteristics of these organizations indicate non-acceptance of the marketing concept?

2. Identify possible target markets for the following products:
   a. Kellogg's Corn Flakes
   b. Wilson tennis rackets
   c. Disney World
   d. Diet Pepsi

3. Discuss the variables of the marketing mix (product, price, promotion, and distribution) as they might relate to each of the following:
   a. a trucking company
   b. a men's clothing store
   c. a skating rink
   d. a campus bookstore

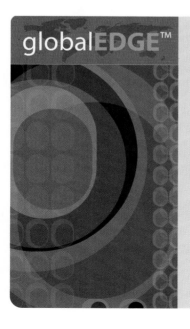

1. Forbes magazine publishes a composite ranking as a part of its Forbes Global 2000 based on four common business measures: sales, profit, assets, and market value. This information can be particularly useful if your firm intends to enter a new global market sector. Use the search term "composite ranking" at http://globaledge.msu.edu/ibrd or http://globaledge.msu.edu/ibrd/ibrd.asp to find the most recent Forbes 2000 ranking and then sort based on category. What are the top three semiconductor firms based on sales? In which country is each firm based?

2. Your firm is planning to develop a customer relationship management (CRM) initiative after it internationalizes. One way to understand the similarity or dissimilarity of markets and cultures is to use Hofstede's cultural dimensions, based on scores for 56 countries. Hofstede's cultural dimensions can be found using the search term "56 countries" at http://globaledge.msu.edu/ibrd or http://globaledge.msu.edu/ibrd/ibrd.asp to access the Geert Hofstede Resource Center and then the link called Hofstede Scores. The Power Distance Index (PDI) can be valuable in developing a CRM strategy. What are the five countries scoring lowest on Hofstede's PDI? Are these countries on the same continent? Are they geographically close?

The Canadian Marketing Association

The Canadian Marketing Association (CMA) is the marketing discipline's primary professional organization in Canada. In addition to sponsoring academic research, publishing marketing literature, and organizing meetings of local businesspeople with student members, it helps individual members find employment in member firms. To see what the CMA has to offer you, visit their website at http://www.the-cma.org.

1. What type of information is available for consumers at the CMA website?
2. What student programs are available at the Education link?
3. What regulations are noted on the site?

Case 1.1   Want Your Bagel Finagled?

Finagle A Bagel, a fast-growing Boston-based small business co-owned by Alan Litchman and Laura Trust, is at the forefront of one of the freshest concepts in the food service business: fresh food. The 20 stores bake a new batch of bagels every hour and receive deliveries of cheeses, vegetables, and other sandwich, soup, and salad ingredients every day. Store employees make everything to order to satisfy each "guest"—Finagle A Bagel's term for a customer. Patrons like this arrangement because they get fresh food prepared to their exact preferences—whether it's extra cheese on a bagel pizza or no onions in a salad—along with prompt, friendly service.

"Every sandwich, every salad is built to order, so there's a lot of communication between the customers and the cashiers, the customers and the sandwich makers, the customers and the managers," explains Trust. As a result, Finagle A Bagel's employees have ample opportunity to build customer relationships and encourage repeat business. Mirna Hernandez of the Tremont Street store in downtown Boston, for example, is so familiar with what many of the "regulars" order that she springs into action as soon as they enter the store. "We know what they want, and we just ring it in and take care of them," she says. Some employees even know their customers by name and make conversation as they create a sandwich or fill a coffee container.

Over time, the owners have introduced a wide range of bagels, sandwiches, soups, and salads linked to the core bagel product. Some of the most popular offerings include a breakfast bagel pizza, salads with bagel-chip croutons, and BLT (bacon-lettuce-tomato) bagel sandwiches. In any case, bagels—round, flat, seeded, plain, crowned with cheese, or cut into croutons—form the basis of every menu item at Finagle A Bagel. "So many

other shops will just grab onto whatever is hot, whatever is trendy, in a 'me-too' strategy," observes Heather Robertson, director of marketing, human resources, and research and development. In contrast, she says, "We do bagels—that's what we do best. And any menu item in our stores really needs to reaffirm that as our core concept." That's the first of Finagle A Bagel's marketing rules.

To identify a new product idea, Robertson and her colleagues conduct informal research by talking with both customers and employees. They also browse food magazines and cookbooks for ideas about out-of-the-ordinary flavours, taste combinations, and preparation methods. When developing a new bagel variety, Robertson looks for ideas that are innovative yet appealing: "If someone else has a sun-dried tomato bagel, that's all the more reason for me not to do it. People look at Finagle A Bagel as kind of the trendsetter." Once the marketing staff comes up with a promising idea, the next step is to write up a formula or recipe, walk downstairs to the dough factory, and mix up a test batch. Through trial and error, they refine the idea until they like the way the bagel or sandwich looks and tastes. One such idea is the scooped-out bagel, which has three-fourths of the calories and carbohydrates as a regular bagel, for those customers following a low-carb diet. To further reinforce the brand and reward customer loyalty, Finagle A Bagel introduced the Frequent Finagler card. Cardholders receive one point for every dollar spent in a Finagle A Bagel store and can redeem accumulated points for coffee, juice, sandwiches, or a dozen bagels (actually a *baker's dozen*, meaning 13 instead of 12). To join, customers register at the company's website (www.finagleabagel.com). From then on, says Litchman, "It's a Web-based program where customers can log on, check their points, and receive free gifts by mail. The Frequent Finagler is our big push right now to use technology as a means of generating store traffic."

Pricing is an important consideration in the competitive world of quick-serve food. This is where another of Finagle A Bagel's marketing rules comes in. Regardless of cost, the company will not compromise quality. Therefore, the first step in pricing a new product is to find the best possible ingredients and then examine the costs and calculate an approximate retail price. After thinking about what a customer might expect to pay for such a menu item, shopping the competition, and talking with some customers, the company settles on a price that represents "a great product for a fair value," says Robertson. Although Finagle A Bagel's rental costs vary, the owners' price menu items are the same in both higher-rent and lower-rent stores. "We have considered adjusting prices based upon the location of the store, but we haven't done it because it can backfire in a very significant way," Trust explains. "People expect to be treated fairly, regardless of where they live."

Although Finagle A Bagel competes with other bagel chains in and around Boston, its competition goes well beyond restaurants in that category. "You compete with a person selling a cup of coffee, you compete with a grocery store selling a salad," Litchman notes. "People only have so many 'dining dollars' and you need to convince them to spend those dining dollars in your store." Finagle A Bagel's competitive advantages are high-quality, fresh products; courteous and competent employees; and clean, attractive, and inviting restaurants.

Social responsibility is an integral part of Finagle A Bagel's operations. Rather than simply throwing away unsold bagels at the end of the day, the owners donate the bagels to schools, shelters, and other non-profit organizations. When local non-profit groups hold fund-raising events, the owners contribute bagels to feed the volunteers. Over the years, Finagle A Bagel has provided bagels to bicyclists raising money for St. Jude Children's Research Hospital, to swimmers raising money for breast cancer research, and to people building community playgrounds. Also, the owners are strongly committed to being fair to their customers by offering good value and a good experience. "Something that we need to remember and instill in our people all the time," Trust emphasizes, "is that customers are coming in and your responsibility is to give them the best that you can give them."

Even with 400-plus employees, the owners find that owning a business is a non-stop proposition. "Our typical day never ends," says Trust. They are continually visiting stores, dealing with suppliers, reviewing financial results, and planning for the future. Despite all these responsibilities, this husband-and-wife entrepreneurial team enjoys applying their educational background and business experience to build a business that satisfies thousands of customers every day.[26]

Questions for Discussion

1. Describe Finagle A Bagel's marketing mix.
2. What forces from the marketing environment provide opportunities for Finagle A Bagel?
3. What forces might threaten the firm's marketing strategy?
4. Does Finagle A Bagel appear to be implementing the marketing concept? Explain your answer.

Case 1.2   Indy: The Great Race

Championship Auto Racing Teams (CART) was created in 1978 when 18 out of 21 automobile racing team owners left the United States Auto Club (USAC) to form a new league for open-wheel racing. Originally sanctioned in the mid-1950s by the USAC, open-wheel racing refers to cars that have an open cockpit with the engine housed at the rear of the vehicle, typical of cars used in the Indianapolis 500 race each year. However, dissatisfaction with USAC's administration and promotion of open-wheel racing prompted Roger Penske, Dan Gurney, Pat Patrick, and 15 other highly respected figures in U.S. motor sports to found CART (whose name was changed to Champ Car in 2003).

During its first 17 years, Champ Car dominated auto racing in the United States, and open-wheel racing enjoyed greater attention than other forms of racing, including stock-car racing associated with NASCAR. In the 1980s, Champ Car attracted legendary driver Mario Andretti and gained further foreign media coverage when Formula 1 champion Nigel Mansell teamed up with Andretti and with Brazil's Emerson Fittipaldi for great finishes at Champ Car races.

Although Champ Car enjoyed increasing popularity in the early 1990s, Anton H. "Tony" George, whose family founded the Indianapolis 500 and developed it into the world-renowned auto race, was concerned that Champ Car was beginning to lose sight of the interests of open-wheel racing. Despite Champ Car's attempt to reorganize its board of directors to include Tony George, in 1994 he announced he was creating a new open-wheel league to compete with Champ Car beginning in 1996. His proposed Indy Racing League (IRL) was divisive to open-wheel racing as team owners were forced to choose whether to remain with Champ Car or move to the new league. George further deepened the rift when he proposed a "25/8" rule for the 1996 Indianapolis 500: the first 25 positions in the 33-car field would go to IRL members.

Despite the apparent duplication of open-wheel racing by Champ Car and IRL, there are significant differences between the two organizations. First, the leagues differ with respect to the types of racecourses employed. IRL races are held exclusively on oval tracks, whereas the majority of Champ Car races are run on road courses—either permanent racetrack facilities or temporary courses that run through the streets of an urban area. Because it is more difficult for racers to pass on road courses, they place a premium on drivers' skills to successfully navigate a track. On the other hand, oval track racing is influenced more by the horsepower and aerodynamics of the race cars, placing an emphasis on engineering and technical expertise to gain an edge over competitors.

Second, Champ Car and IRL differ in terms of the geographic scope of their leagues and drivers. The IRL is strictly a U.S. circuit. In contrast, Champ Car's drivers represent North America, South America, and Europe, and its 2006 schedule included races in Canada, the United States, Mexico, Australia, and South Korea. Champ Car also places greater emphasis on geographic allegiances with the Nations Cup, an award that recognizes the country whose drivers scored the best overall finish during the Champ Car season. As a result of Champ Car's international focus, it enjoys great television exposure as annually televised Champ Car races reach more than 980 million fans in 195 countries.

Champ Car has continued to be a dominant force in open-wheel racing after the initial split with the IRL. In fact, in 1998, Champ Car was incorporated and became a publicly traded company on the New York Stock Exchange. In 2000, two Champ Car teams resumed racing in the Indianapolis 500, and one won. Then Champ Car slowly began to lose ground against the IRL. Champ Car races in Brazil and Texas were cancelled during the 2001 season, resulting in public relations embarrassments for the organization. Top management turmoil was evident, too, as Champ Car went through four chief executive officers during 2000 and 2001.

When Champ Car and IRL split before the 1996 season, the breakup did more than split the racing teams. Fans tended to follow the league in which their favourite drivers raced rather than following both leagues. More important, sponsorship support was split between the two open-wheel leagues. Television broadcasts of Champ Car races could be instrumental in expanding the league's following, but Champ Car has been mired in an unfavourable television rights deal. Champ Car must pay to have its races broadcast, whereas IRL is paid by ABC for the rights to broadcast its races on ABC and ESPN. The limited reach of Champ Car's television broadcasts may have contributed to additional problems with sponsor relationships. Three major partners left Champ Car in recent seasons. Honda and Toyota, which provided engines and technical support to Champ Car and its teams, left for deals with IRL. FedEx, which shipped a great deal of cargo to Champ Car racing sites in foreign markets, discontinued its title-sponsor relationship with Champ Car after the 2002 season. Champ Car ART successfully enlisted two new major series sponsors for the 2003 season and renamed the Champ Car series "Bridgestone Presents Champ Car World Series Powered by Ford."

Champ Car's viability as a major racing league was also harmed by the defection of key racing teams to IRL, including Roger Penske, Michael Andretti, and Chip Ganassi. Their absence meant that Champ Car might not be able to field the 18 cars needed to hold races. Champ Car responded by offering financial incentives to team owners to ensure enough cars would participate in its races. Also, Champ Car was forced to become the promoter of its own races after losing promoters in some markets. The combined result of an unfavourable television deal, sponsor and team owner defections, and increased costs of holding races forced Champ Car into a perilous financial position.

Champ Car's financial position continued to deteriorate during 2003, and company reports of increased operating costs and sluggish advertising and sponsorship revenue ultimately sent the organization into bankruptcy proceedings. Shortly after that, a group of investors, including some Champ Car team owners, purchased the embattled company for 56 cents per share. The group formed Open Wheel Racing Series LLC and planned to continue operating under the name Bridgestone Presents The Champ Car World Series Powered by Ford.

The new owners have many decisions to consider, including ways to define their product, how to promote races, where to race, and how to price their product for their race fans (customers). They moved quickly to secure new sponsorships and race-car teams. By 2005, the organization had gained several new sponsors, including Bridgestone, Ford, and Sherwin-Williams, and new teams, like the Newman/Wachs team run by famed driver Eddie Wachs and actor Paul Newman, himself a race-car driver. Moreover, race attendance reached record levels in 2005. The organization is also exploring the possibility of new races in China and Japan.

Nonetheless, auto racing fans seem to prefer oval track racing, as evidenced by NASCAR's strong race attendance and television ratings. However, IRL races on many of the same oval tracks as NASCAR but draws a fraction of the fans, with the Indianapolis 500 being a notable exception. Moreover, proponents of street and road course racing point to the fact that such venues lend themselves to creating a festival atmosphere around a race, including concerts, volleyball games, and beer gardens. Some racing fans insist that IRL and Champ Car must reunite for the betterment of auto racing, but the notion remains controversial. In any case, to compete against the growing popularity of NASCAR and to continue to grow, Champ Car must carefully analyze its target market and create a marketing mix to develop a successful long-term marketing strategy.[27]

Questions for Discussion

1. Identify the product that the Champ Car World Series offers its race-car fans (customers).
2. What can the Champ Car World Series do to better promote its products? How should gaining sponsorships fit into its promotional plans?
3. How can the Champ Car World Series use the strengths of its international driver and race events to its advantage? Relate its selection of race courses and events to the concept of distribution presented in the chapter.

2

Planning, Implementing, and Controlling Marketing Strategies

It's Always Yesterday at A&W

For Vancouver-based A&W, the goal is to be a best friend to Canada's baby boomer generation. According to Don Maunders, A&W's vice-president of marketing, the strategy in the last few years has involved a focus on this demographic segment, one which is nine million strong.

In the late 1950s and early 1960s, A&W was big in Canada. McDonald's, Wendy's, and Burger King did not have the market presence as they do today. As a result, many Canadians have strong and positive memories of their "coming-of-age" while A&W was in the backdrop.

To help implement a strategy with a focus on the baby boomer generation, A&W used a 60-second television spot entitled "Drive," created by Vancouver agency Rethink, which shows a married couple cruising into A&W for some "grub." To help bring this scenario to life, A&W instituted the Cruisin' the Dub club. The groups regularly gather at the local A&W in their vintage '60s wheels. Strategy implementation did not end there, since 1999 A&W has made significant strides to bring its brand full circle by reintroducing The Burger Family, the Chubby Chicken line, and the Root Beer float. Also, A&W has established new freestanding stores in Ontario and Quebec (opposed to only focusing on mall locations, as it has in the past), and altered the design of its restaurants and packaging. Inside the stores, there are more nostalgia triggers like "memory posters" that reference the old drive-in days, even tray liners play a part, sharing feel-good stories from customers.

This strategy implementation is working. According to Don Maunder, "we've seen our same-store sales grow and consistently outpace the industry average, our market share has climbed continuously over the last five years, and there has also been growth in the number of boomers in our restaurants." A&W has demonstrated that a well planned and executed strategy can be used to sell a product as simple and traditional as the hamburger in the face of strong competition.[1] ∎

With competition increasing, A&W and many other companies are spending more time and resources on strategic planning, that is, on determining how to use their resources and abilities to achieve their objectives and satisfy their customers. Although most of this book deals with specific marketing decisions and strategies, this chapter focuses on "the big picture:" all the functional areas and activities—finance, production, human resources, and research and development, as well as marketing—that must be coordinated to reach organizational goals. To effectively implement the marketing concept of satisfying customers and achieving organizational goals, all organizations must engage in strategic planning.

We begin this chapter with an overview of the strategic planning process. Next, we examine how organizational resources and opportunities affect strategic planning and the role played by the organization's mission statement. After discussing the development of both corporate and business-unit strategy, we explore the nature of marketing strategy and the creation of the marketing plan. These elements provide a framework for the development and implementation of marketing strategies, as we will see throughout the remainder of this book.

Understanding the Strategic Planning Process

strategic planning The process of establishing an organizational mission and formulating goals, corporate strategy, marketing objectives, marketing strategy, and a marketing plan

Through the process of **strategic planning,** a firm establishes an organizational mission and formulates goals, corporate strategy, marketing objectives, marketing strategy, and, finally, a marketing plan.[2] A marketing orientation should guide the process of strategic planning to ensure that a concern for customer satisfaction is an integral part of the process. A marketing orientation is also important for the successful implementation of marketing strategies.[3] Figure 2.1 shows the components of strategic planning.

figure 2.1

COMPONENTS OF STRATEGIC PLANNING

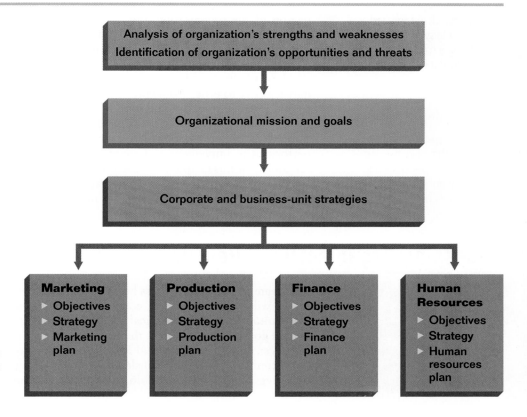

Source: From *Marketing Strategy,* 2nd edition, by O. C. Ferrell and Michael Hartline, 2002. Reprinted with permission of South-Western, a division of Thomson Learning: **www.thomson rights.com.** Fax 800-730-2215.

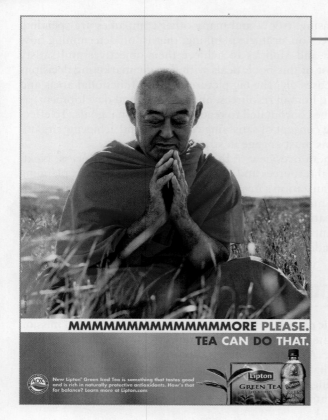

MMMMMMMMMMMMMMMORE PLEASE.
TEA CAN DO THAT.

New Lipton® Green Iced Tea is something that tastes good and is rich in naturally protective antioxidants. How's that for balance? Learn more at Lipton.com

Target Market Selection
Lipton targets health-conscience consumers with its green tea.

The process begins with a detailed analysis of the organization's strengths and weaknesses and with identification of opportunities and threats within the marketing environment. Based on this analysis, the firm can establish or revise its mission and goals, and then develop corporate strategies to achieve those goals. Next, each functional area of the organization (marketing, production, finance, human resources, etc.) establishes its own objectives and develops strategies to achieve them.[4] The objectives and strategies of each functional area must support the organization's overall goals and mission. The strategies of each functional area should also be coordinated with a focus on marketing orientation.

Because our focus is marketing, we are, of course, most interested in the development of marketing objectives and strategies. Marketing objectives should be designed so that their achievement will contribute to the corporate strategy and so they can be accomplished through efficient use of the firm's resources. To achieve its marketing objectives, an organization must develop a **marketing strategy,** which includes identifying and analyzing a target market and developing a marketing mix to meet the needs of individuals in that market. Thus, a marketing strategy includes a plan of action for developing, distributing, promoting, and pricing products that meet the needs of the target market. Marketing strategy is best formulated when it reflects the overall direction of the organization and is coordinated with all the firm's functional areas. When properly implemented and controlled, a marketing strategy will contribute to the achievement not only of marketing objectives but also of the organization's overall goals. Consider that Apple's successful marketing strategy for its iPod line of music players helped revitalize the computer firm's reputation for excellent design, which may transfer to other Apple products. The firm even designed its iMac G5 computer to mimic the look of an iPod with rounded corners and a translucent shell.[5]

The strategic planning process ultimately yields a marketing strategy that is the framework for a **marketing plan,** a written document that specifies the activities to be performed to implement and control the organization's marketing activities. In the remainder of this chapter, we discuss the major components of the strategic planning process: organizational opportunities and resources, organizational mission and goals, corporate and business-unit strategy, marketing strategy, and the role of the marketing plan.

marketing strategy A plan of action for identifying and analyzing a target market and developing a marketing mix to meet the needs of that market

marketing plan A written document that specifies the activities to be performed to implement and control the organization's marketing activities

Assessing Organizational Resources and Opportunities

The strategic planning process begins with an analysis of the marketing environment. As we will see in Chapter 3, economic, competitive, political, legal and regulatory, sociocultural, and technological forces can threaten an organization and influence its overall goals; they also affect the amount and type of resources the firm can acquire. However, these environmental forces can create favourable opportunities as well—opportunities that can be translated into overall organizational goals and marketing objectives. Organizational culture and information use affect the extent to which

core competencies Things a firm does extremely well, which sometimes give it an advantage over its competition

market opportunity A combination of circumstances and timing that permits an organization to take action to reach a particular target market

strategic windows Temporary periods of optimal fit between the key requirements of a market and the particular capabilities of a firm competing in that market

competitive advantage The result of a company's matching a core competency to opportunities it has discovered in the marketplace

SWOT analysis Assessment of an organization's strengths, weaknesses, opportunities, and threats

managers perceive such opportunities as situations on which they can successfully capitalize.[6]

Any strategic planning effort must assess the organization's available financial and human resources and capabilities, as well as how the level of these factors is likely to change in the future, as additional resources may be needed to achieve the organization's goals and mission.[7] Resources indirectly affect marketing and financial performance by helping to create customer satisfaction and loyalty.[8] Resources can also include goodwill, reputation, and brand names. The reputation and well-known brand names of Rolex watches and IBM computers, for example, are resources that give these firms an advantage over their competitors. Such strengths also include **core competencies,** things a firm does extremely well—sometimes so well that they give the company an advantage over its competition.

Analysis of the marketing environment involves not only an assessment of resources but also identification of opportunities in the marketplace. When the right combination of circumstances and timing permits an organization to take action to reach a particular target market, a **market opportunity** exists. For example, advances in computer technology and the growth of the Internet have enabled real estate firms to provide prospective homebuyers with databases of homes for sale all over the country. Realtor's Website allows buyers access to a wealth of information about homes for sale, including photos, floor plans, and virtual tours, as well as details about neighbourhoods, schools, and shopping. The Internet represents a powerful market opportunity for real estate firms because its visual nature is perfectly suited to the task of shopping for a home. Such opportunities are often called **strategic windows,** temporary periods of optimal fit between the key requirements of a market and the particular capabilities of a firm competing in that market.[9]

When a company matches a core competency to opportunities it has discovered in the marketplace, it is said to have a **competitive advantage.** In some cases, a company may possess manufacturing, technical, or marketing skills that it can match to market opportunities to create a competitive advantage. For example, eBay pioneered the online auction and built the premier site where 75 million users around the world buy and sell products. By analyzing its customer base, eBay found an opportunity to improve growth by targeting the nearly 23 million small businesses, many of which already use the auction site to buy and sell construction, restaurant, and other business equipment. To appeal to this important market, eBay sought ways to improve customers' online shopping experience.[10]

SWOT Analysis

One tool marketers use to assess an organization's strengths, weaknesses, opportunities, and threats is the **SWOT analysis.** Strengths and weaknesses are internal factors that can influence an organization's ability to satisfy its target markets. Strengths refer to competitive advantages or core competencies

You're the kid and we're the candy store.

LA-Z-BOY
The new look of comfort

Assessing Organizational Resources and Opportunities

Although La-Z-Boy's core competency is recliners, it is now expanding to other products.

Because so many people are pet owners, companies such as Petcetera have many market opportunities.

that give the firm an advantage in meeting the needs of its target markets. John Deere, for example, promotes its service, experience, and reputation in the farm equipment business to emphasize the craftsmanship used in its lawn tractors and mowers for city dwellers. Weaknesses refer to any limitations a company faces in developing or implementing a marketing strategy. Consider that America Online, the leading Internet service provider, brings in half the online advertising revenue of other online services such as Google, MSN, and Yahoo! at a time when online advertising has accelerated dramatically.[11] Both strengths and weaknesses should be examined from a customer perspective because they are meaningful only when they help or hinder the firm in meeting customer needs. Only those strengths that relate to satisfying customers should be considered true competitive advantages. Likewise, weaknesses that directly affect customer satisfaction should be considered competitive disadvantages. To boost online ad revenue, AOL has redesigned its website and added more content, such as a news ticker and more sports and music, to boost usage by members and thereby make it more attractive to online advertisers.[12]

Opportunities and threats exist independently of the firm and therefore represent issues to be considered by all organizations, even those that do not compete with the firm. *Opportunities* refer to favourable conditions in the environment that could produce rewards for the organization if acted on properly. That is, opportunities are situations that exist but must be exploited for the firm to benefit from them. *Threats*, on the other hand, refer to conditions or barriers that may prevent the firm from reaching its objectives. For example, consumers today are buying fewer music CDs, in part because many believe CD prices are too high. CD sales declined by 31 percent over a three-year period as consumers downloaded more music from online sharing networks, such as Kazaa, or shifted their entertainment dollars to video games and DVDs.[13] An organization must act on threats to prevent them from limiting its capabilities. For example, to counter the threat of declining music sales, Universal Music Group slashed the

Competitive Advantage in Doing It Yourself

Canadian Tire has been serving the "do-it-your selfer" market since 1922.

figure 2.2

THE FOUR-CELL SWOT MATRIX

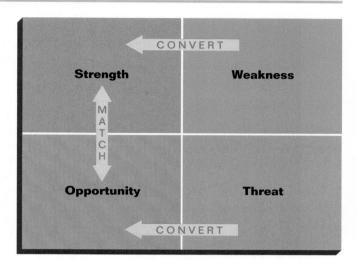

Source: Adapted from Nigel F. Piercy, *Market-Led Strategic Change.* Copyright © 1992 Butterworth-Heinemann Ltd., p. 371. Reprinted with permission.

wholesale price of CDs by artists such as Jay-Z and Shania Twain by as much as 31 percent.[14] Opportunities and threats can stem from many sources within the environment. When a competitor's introduction of a new product threatens a firm, a defensive strategy may be required. If the firm can develop and launch a new product that meets or exceeds the competition's offering, it can transform the threat into an opportunity.[15]

Figure 2.2 depicts a four-cell SWOT matrix that can help managers in the planning process. When an organization matches internal strengths to external opportunities, it creates competitive advantages in meeting the needs of its customers. In addition, an organization should act to convert internal weaknesses into strengths and external threats into opportunities. Ford Motor Company, for instance, converted the threats posed by rising gasoline prices and the growing acceptance of hybrid gas-electric cars from Japanese automakers into opportunities when it introduced a hybrid version of its Escape sport-utility vehicle. A firm that lacks adequate marketing skills can hire outside consultants to help convert a weakness into a strength.

Establishing an Organizational Mission and Goals

mission statement A long-term view, or vision, of what the organization wants to become

Once an organization has assessed its resources and opportunities, it can begin to establish goals and strategies to take advantage of those opportunities. The goals of any organization should derive from its **mission statement,** a long-term view, or vision, of what the organization wants to become. Herbal tea marketer Celestial Seasonings, for example, says that its mission is "To create and sell healthful, naturally oriented products that nurture people's bodies and uplift their souls."[16]

When an organization decides on its mission, it really answers two questions: Who are our customers? What is our core competency? Although these questions appear very simple, they are two of the most important questions any firm must answer. Defining customers' needs and wants gives direction to what the company must do to satisfy them.

Companies try to develop and manage their *corporate identity*—their unique symbols, personalities, and philosophies—to support all corporate activities including marketing. Managing identity requires broadcasting mission goals and values, sending a consistent image, and implementing visual identity with stakeholders. Mission statements, goals, and objectives must be properly implemented to achieve the desired corporate identity.[17] New Leaf Paper Company, for example, has developed a mission and identity based on principles of sustainability and ecology that are unique in the paper industry. Half the fibre New Leaf uses in its paper comes from post-consumer waste instead of virgin tree pulp. The small firm's sales have increased more than four times in the last six years, spurring larger paper companies to introduce their own "green" paper products.[18]

An organization's goals and objectives, derived from its mission statement, guide the remainder of its planning efforts. Goals focus on the end results the organization seeks. Starbucks' mission statement, for example, incorporates the company's goals of striving for a high-quality product, a sound financial position and community responsibility.

marketing objective
A statement of what is to be accomplished through marketing activities

A **marketing objective** states what is to be accomplished through marketing activities. A marketing objective of Ritz-Carlton hotels, for example, is to have more than 90 percent of its customers indicate they had a memorable experience at the hotel. Marketing objectives should be based on a careful study of the SWOT analysis and should relate to matching strengths to opportunities and/or converting weaknesses or threats. These objectives can be stated in terms of product introduction, product improvement or innovation, sales volume, profitability, market share, pricing, distribution, advertising, or employee training activities.

Marketing objectives should possess certain characteristics. First, a marketing objective should be expressed in clear, simple terms so that all marketing personnel understand exactly what they are trying to achieve. Second, an objective should be written so that it can be measured accurately. This allows the organization to determine if and when the objective has been achieved. If an objective is to increase market share by 10 percent, the firm should be able to measure market share changes accurately. Third, a marketing objective should specify a time frame for its accomplishment. A firm that sets an objective of introducing a new product should state the time period in which to do this. Finally, a marketing objective should be consistent with both business-unit and corporate strategy. This ensures that the firm's mission is carried out at all levels of the organization.

marketing ENTREPRENEURS

Chris Neville

THE BUSINESS: Lifeofsports.com

FOUNDED: 2004

SUCCESS: Rapid growth and profit margins of 65 percent

Having just completed his MBA at the University of New Brunswick with a focus on the study of start-ups, and having sold his distribution company to Nestlé, Canada, Chris Neville was looking for a start-up venture. Chris was an avid fantasy sports game player, which led to his vision of growing a massive database and daily online traffic, which would in turn result in advertising revenues. This vision became reality in December 2004 when he launched Lifeofsports.com.

Identifying opportunity has proven to be the key to Chris' success. Chris conceived the idea to partner with the number one poker player in Canada, and a national television channel to launch the first annual Canadian College Poker Championships. Two weeks later, Chris secured a deal with a leading national communications firm and Daniel Negreanu, the World Poker Champion and all time money leader on the World Poker Tour, to launch the first annual Canadian College Poker Championship. In 2006, The Daniel Negreanu Canadian College Poker Championship was produced for television. Meanwhile, Chris moved to increase his Web presence by adding www.maritimepokerclub.com, www.lifeofsports.com/ccpc, www.collegpokerlife.com, and www.collegepokerlife.com/nacpc (site of the North American College Poker Championship.) Also, www.allinpokernews.com has been launched as the largest and most extensive poker news site on the web. A second television show is being developed for the US market with American One Cable network for the North American College Poker Championships. The recent banning of online poker in the US threatens growth and the loss of television contracts but always up for a challenge, Chris remains excited and optimistic about the future of Lifeofsports.com.

Developing Corporate, Business-Unit, and Marketing Strategies

In any organization, strategic planning begins at the corporate level and proceeds downward to the business-unit and marketing levels. Corporate strategy is the broadest of these three levels and should be developed with the organization's overall mission in mind. Business-unit strategy should be consistent with the corporate strategy, and marketing strategy should be consistent with both the business-unit and corporate strategies. Figure 2.3 shows the relationships among these planning levels.

LEVELS OF STRATEGIC PLANNING

Corporate Strategy

corporate strategy A strategy that determines the means for utilizing resources in the various functional areas to reach the organization's goals

Corporate strategy determines the means for utilizing resources in the functional areas of marketing, production, finance, research and development, and human resources to reach the organization's goals. A corporate strategy determines not only the scope of the business but also its resource deployment, competitive advantages, and overall coordination of functional areas. In particular, top management's marketing expertise and deployment of resources for addressing markets contribute to sales growth and profitability.[19] Corporate strategy addresses the two questions posed in the organization's mission statement: Who are our customers? What is our core competency? The term *corporate* in this context does not apply solely to corporations; corporate strategy is used by all organizations, from the smallest sole proprietorship to the largest multinational corporation.

Corporate strategy planners are concerned with broad issues such as corporate culture, competition, differentiation, diversification, interrelationships among business units, and environmental and social issues. They attempt to match the resources of the organization with the opportunities and threats in the environment. Sara Lee, for example, sold its retail coffee unit including its well-known brand Chock Full o'Nuts for $82.5 million in order to make greater investments in its core businesses of food, beverages, and household and body care, as well as to increase its shareholder value through dividends.[20] Corporate strategy planners are also concerned with defining the scope and role of the firm's business units so that the units are coordinated to reach the ends desired. A firm's corporate strategy may affect its technological competence and ability to innovate.[21]

Business-Unit Strategy

After analyzing corporate operations and performance, the next step in strategic planning is to determine future business directions and develop strategies for individual

strategic business unit (SBU)
A division, product line, brand, or other profit centre within the parent company

market A group of individuals and/or organizations that have needs for products in a product class and have the ability, willingness, and authority to purchase those products

market share The percentage of a market that actually buys a specific product from a particular company

market growth/market share matrix A strategic planning tool based on the philosophy that a product's market growth rate and market share are important considerations in its determining marketing strategy

business units. A **strategic business unit (SBU)** is a division, product line, brand, or other profit centre within the parent company. Each of these units sells a distinct set of products to an identifiable group of customers, and each competes with a well-defined set of competitors. The revenues, costs, investments, and strategic plans of each SBU can be separated from those of the parent company and evaluated. SBUs operate in a variety of markets, all with differing growth rates, opportunities, degrees of competition, and profit-making potential.

Strategic planners should recognize the strategic performance capabilities of each SBU and carefully allocate scarce resources among those divisions. This requires market-focused flexibility in considering changes in the environment.[22] Several tools allow a firm's portfolio of strategic business units, or even individual products, to be classified and visually displayed according to the attractiveness of various markets and the business's relative market share within those markets. A **market** is a group of individuals and/or organizations that have needs for products in a product class and have the ability, willingness, and authority to purchase those products. The percentage of a market that actually buys a specific product from a particular company is referred to as that product's (or business unit's) **market share.** Nike, for example, is the leader in the athletic shoe market in Canada. Nike's share for the first six months of 2005 was 19.5 percent compared with 9.3 percent for Adidas and Reebok combined.[23] Product quality, order of entry into the market, and market share have been associated with SBU success.[24]

One of the most helpful tools is the **market growth/market share matrix,** the Boston Consulting Group (BCG) approach, which is based on the philosophy that a product's market growth rate and its market share are important considerations in determining its marketing strategy. All the firm's SBUs and products should be integrated into a single, overall matrix and evaluated to determine appropriate strategies for individual products and overall portfolio strategies. Managers can use this model to determine and classify each product's expected future cash contributions and future cash requirements. The BCG analytical approach is more of a diagnostic tool than a guide for making strategy prescriptions.

Figure 2.4, which is based on work by the BCG, enables the strategic planner to classify a firm's products into four basic types: stars, cash cows, dogs, and question marks.[25] *Stars* are products with a dominant share of the market and good prospects for growth. However, they use more cash than they generate to finance growth, add capacity, and increase market share. An example of a star might be Apple's iPod MP3 player. *Cash cows* have a dominant share of the market but low prospects for growth; typically they generate more cash than is required to maintain market share. Molson Canadian, one of the most recognized brands of beer in Canada, is a cash cow for Molson. *Dogs* have a subordinate share of the market and low prospects for growth; these products are often found in established

Corporate Strategy
Tim Horton's "always fresh" product is available for consumers who demand convenience and consistent quality.

markets. The Oldsmobile brand may have been considered a dog at General Motors; its declining profits and market share contributed to GM's decision to eliminate the brand. *Question marks,* sometimes called "problem children," have a small share of a growing market and generally require a large amount of cash to build market share. Mercedes mountain bikes, for example, are a question mark relative to Mercedes' automobile products.

The long-term health of an organization depends on having some products that generate cash (and provide acceptable profits) and others that use cash to support growth. Among the indicators of overall health are the size and vulnerability of the cash cows; the prospects for the stars, if any; and the number of question marks and dogs. Particular attention should be paid to those products with large cash appetites. Unless the company has an abundant cash flow, it cannot afford to sponsor many such products at one time. If resources, including debt capacity, are spread too thin, the company will end up with too many marginal products and will be unable to finance promising new-product entries or acquisitions in the future.

Marketing Strategy

The next phase in strategic planning is the development of sound strategies for each functional area of the organization, including marketing. Corporate strategy and marketing strategy must balance and synchronize the organization's mission and goals with stakeholder relationships. This means that marketing must deliver value and be responsible in facilitating effective relationships with all relevant stakeholders.[26] Consider that customers depend on the Coca-Cola Company to provide a standardized, reliable, satisfying soft drink or beverage anyplace in the world. Due to its efforts to expand distribution to every possible location, Coca-Cola sells 33 percent of its volume in Europe and the Middle East, 31 percent in North America, 22 percent in the Asian/Pacific region, 10 percent in Latin America, and 5 percent in Africa.[27] The company continues to introduce new products, expand distribution, and maintain a high-quality product. Coca-Cola is also a good "corporate citizen," donating millions

Sears Holdings: Merging to Success

Just 18 months after emerging from bankruptcy, Kmart announced that it would pay $11 billion to purchase Sears & Roebuck. The merged firm, Sears Holdings, has 3500 stores, making it the number three retailer after Wal-Mart and Home Depot. Many believe that the new company will be able to achieve tremendous cost savings that will result in lower prices for consumers—and give retail giant Wal-Mart more competition.

Although most individual Sears and Kmart stores retained their current names, some Kmart stores turned into Sears stores, and both stores began to promote each other's brands. The challenge will be to blend the two organizations into one customer-focused culture. One way to accomplish this is through the leveraging of current brands and reputations. Sears is well known for its Kenmore appliances and Craftsman tools, while Kmart is known for Martha Stewart Everyday products, which are offered exclusively in the U.S. by Kmart and in Canada by Sears Canada.

Allowing Sears and Kmart to sell each other's exclusive products is only one part of the strategy. Sears' long-time business model had relied on mall locations, but in recent years the retailing landscape has shifted to stand-alone "big box" retail stores. Many Kmart stores are located in prime locations outside malls and can now be converted to Sears stores.

For Sears Holdings to be successful, it will need to engage in the strategic planning process, establishing an organizational mission, goals, corporate strategy, marketing objectives, and a marketing strategy. Only by successfully assessing opportunities and appropriately implementing strategies can the new company be successful.

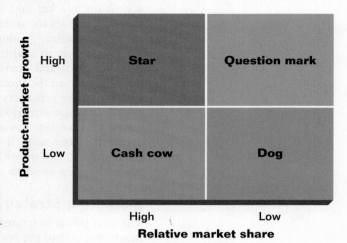

figure 2.4   GROWTH SHARE MATRIX DEVELOPED BY THE BOSTON CONSULTING GROUP

Source: *Perspectives,* No. 66, "The Product Portfolio." Reprinted by permission from The Boston Consulting Group, Inc., Boston, MA. Copyright © 1970.

of dollars to education, health and human services, and disaster-plagued regions each year. An effective marketing strategy must gain the support of key stakeholders including employees, investors, and communities, as well as channel members, such as franchisees. Consider what happened when Burger King launched a $340 million advertising campaign featuring a heavy metal band named Coq Roq. Franchisees, vital to the distribution of Burger King products, felt the marketing strategy targeted too narrow of a market—teenage males—and worried that it might alienate other desirable markets. Their dissatisfaction with the campaign and overall marketing strategy

Procter & Gamble Cleans Up Around the World

Consumers around the world trust Procter & Gamble (P&G). They count on Crest, Gillette, and Tide among many other brand names and hundreds of other products, to improve the quality of their lives. P&G markets nearly 300 brands in 140 countries, and employs almost 98 000 people in nearly 80 countries. P&G's core product categories—baby care, fabric care, feminine care, and hair care—are number one in terms of both global sales and

global market share and generate more than half of the company's total profits. One percentage point increase in market share across these four core businesses is worth about $1 billion in annual sales and more then $150 million in annual earnings.

P&G's foundation is household products, but it is moving toward balancing this group of products with those geared toward health and beauty, since healthcare and baby-care business now represent nearly half of the company's sales and profits. Personal healthcare sales have more than doubled in the past three years, significantly outpacing market growth. In China, P&G's laundry and oral-care market shares have more than doubled in the past three years. And in Russia, laundry, hair care, and oral care are all category leaders that have grown rapidly over the last three years.

P&G's ability to market superior products that improve the lives of its worldwide customers ensures that the company's future is indeed bright.

resulted in a complete communication breakdown in the Burger King national franchise organization.[28] The complexity of marketing strategy decisions requires the identification of key stakeholders and their support or reaction to marketing activities.[29] There is a need in marketing to develop more of a stakeholder orientation to go beyond markets, competitors, and channel members to understand and address all stakeholder concerns.[30]

Within the marketing area, a strategy is typically designed around two components: (1) the selection of a target market and (2) the creation of a marketing mix that will satisfy the needs of the chosen target market. A marketing strategy articulates the best use of the firm's resources and tactics to achieve its marketing objectives. It should also match customers' desire for value with the organization's distinctive capabilities. Internal capabilities should be used to maximize external opportunities. The planning process should be guided by a marketing-oriented organizational culture and processes.[31] A comprehensive strategy involves a thorough search for information, the analysis of many potential courses of action, and the use of specific criteria for making decisions regarding strategy development and implementation.[32] When properly implemented, a sound marketing strategy enables a company to achieve its business-unit and corporate objectives. Although corporate, business-unit, and marketing strategies all overlap to some extent, the marketing strategy is the most detailed and specific of the three.

Target Market Selection   Selecting an appropriate target market may be the most important decision a company has to make in the planning process because the target market must be chosen before the organization can adapt its marketing mix to meet this market's needs and preferences. Defining the target market and developing an appropriate marketing mix are the keys to strategic success. If a company selects the wrong target market, all other marketing decisions will be made in vain. Ford Motor, for example, experienced poor sales of its reintroduced Thunderbird, in part because its price tag was too steep for the retro-styled convertible's target market of younger baby boomers and older Generation Xers. However, the Thunderbird could not compete with similarly priced luxury, high-performance vehicles like the BMW Z4 and the Audi TT, which offer greater horsepower and more features.[33]

Accurate target market selection is crucial to productive marketing efforts. Products and even companies sometimes fail because marketers do not identify appropriate customer groups at whom to aim their efforts. Organizations that try to be all things to all people rarely satisfy the needs of any customer group very well. An organization's management therefore should designate which customer groups the firm is trying to serve and gather adequate information about those customers. Identification and analysis of a target market provide a foundation on which the firm can develop a marketing mix.

When exploring possible target markets, marketing managers try to evaluate how entering them would affect the company's sales, costs, and profits. Marketing information should be organized to facilitate a focus on the chosen target customers. Accounting and information systems, for example, can be used to track revenues and costs by customer (or group of customers.) In addition, managers and employees need to be rewarded for focusing on profitable customers. Teamwork skills can be developed with organizational structures that promote a customer orientation that allows quick responses to changes in the marketing environment.[34]

Marketers should also assess whether the company has the resources to develop the right mix of product, price, promotion, and distribution to meet the needs of a particular target market. In addition, they should determine if satisfying those needs is consistent with the firm's overall objectives and mission. When Amazon.com, the number one Internet bookseller, began selling electronics on its website, it made the decision with the belief that efforts to target this market would increase profits and be consistent with its objective to be the largest online retailer. The size and number of competitors already marketing products in potential target markets are concerns as well.

Creating the Marketing Mix The selection of a target market serves as the basis for creating a marketing mix to satisfy the needs of that market. (Recall that we defined the marketing mix as the four marketing activities—product, distribution, promotion, and pricing—that the firm can control to meet the needs of customers within its target market.) The decisions made in creating a marketing mix are only as good as the organization's understanding of its target market. This understanding typically comes from careful, in-depth research into the characteristics of the target market. Thus, while demographic information is important, the organization should also analyze customer needs, preferences, and behaviour with respect to product design, pricing, distribution, and promotion. For example, Toyota's marketing research about Generation Y drivers found that they practically live in their cars, and many even keep a change of clothes handy in their vehicles. As a result of this research, Toyota designed its Scion as a "home on wheels," with a 15-volt outlet for plugging in a computer, reclining front seats for napping, and a powerful audio system for listening to MP3 music files, all for a $12 500 price tag.[35]

Marketing mix decisions should have two additional characteristics: consistency and flexibility. All marketing mix decisions should be consistent with the business-unit and corporate strategies. Such consistency allows the organization to achieve its objectives on all three levels of planning. Flexibility, on the other hand, permits the organization to alter the marketing mix in response to changes in market conditions, competition, and customer needs. Marketing strategy flexibility has a positive influence on organizational performance. Marketing orientation and strategic flexibility complement each other to help the organization manage varying environmental conditions.[36]

The concept of the four marketing mix variables has stood the test of time, providing marketers with a rich set of questions for the four most important decisions in strategic marketing. Consider the efforts of Harley-Davidson to improve its competitive position. The company worked to improve its product by eliminating oil leaks and other problems, and prices that customers consider fair. The firm used promotional tools to build a community of Harley riders renowned for their camaraderie. Harley-Davidson also fostered strong relationships with the dealers that distribute the company's motorcycles and related products and that reinforce the firm's promotional messages. Even the Internet has not diminished the importance of finding the right marketing mix, although it has affected specific marketing mix elements. Amazon.com, for example, has exploited information technology to facilitate sales promotion by offering product feedback from other customers to help shoppers make purchase decisions.[37]

At the marketing mix level, a firm can detail how it will achieve a competitive advantage. To gain an advantage, the firm must do something better than its competition. In other words, its products must be of higher quality, its prices must be consistent with the level of quality (value), its distribution methods must be efficient and cost as little as possible, and its promotion must be more effective than the competition's. It is also important that the firm attempt to make these advantages sustainable. A **sustainable competitive advantage** is one that the competition cannot copy. Wal-Mart, for example, maintains a sustainable competitive advantage over Zellers because of its volume buying and highly efficient, low-cost distribution system. This advantage allows Wal-Mart to continuously offer consumers price roll-backs. Maintaining a sustainable competitive advantage requires flexibility in the marketing mix when facing uncertain competitive environments.[38]

sustainable competitive advantage An advantage that the competition cannot copy

Creating the Marketing Plan

A major concern in the strategic planning process is **marketing planning,** the systematic process of assessing marketing opportunities and resources, determining marketing objectives, defining marketing strategies, and establishing guidelines for implementation and control of the marketing program. The outcome of marketing planning is the

marketing planning The process of assessing marketing opportunities and resources, determining marketing objectives, defining marketing strategies, and establishing guidelines for implementation and control of the marketing program

development of a marketing plan. As noted earlier, a marketing plan is a written document that outlines and explains all the activities necessary to implement marketing strategies. It describes the firm's current position or situation, establishes marketing objectives for the product or product group, and specifies how the organization will attempt to achieve those objectives.

Developing a clear, well-written marketing plan, though time consuming, is important. The plan is the basis for internal communication among employees. It covers the assignment of responsibilities and tasks, as well as schedules for implementation. It presents objectives and specifies how resources are to be allocated to achieve those objectives. Finally, it helps marketing managers monitor and evaluate the performance of a marketing strategy.

Marketing planning and implementation are inextricably linked in successful companies. The marketing plan provides a framework to stimulate thinking and provide strategic direction, while implementation occurs as an adaptive response to day-to-day issues, opportunities, and unanticipated situations—for example, increasing interest rates or an economic slowdown—that cannot be incorporated into marketing plans. Implementation-related adaptations directly affect an organization's marketing orientation, rate of growth, and strategic effectiveness.[39]

Organizations use many different formats when devising marketing plans. Plans may be written for strategic business units, product lines, individual products or brands, or specific markets. Most plans share some common ground, however, by including many of the same components. Table 2.1 describes the major parts of a typical marketing plan.

table 2.1   COMPONENTS OF THE MARKETING PLAN

Plan Component	Component Summary	Highlights
Executive Summary	One- to two-page synopsis of the entire marketing plan	
Environmental Analysis	Information about the company's current situation with respect to the marketing environment	1. Assessment of marketing environment factors 2. Assessment of target market(s) 3. Assessment of current marketing objectives and performance
SWOT Analysis	Assessment of the organization's strengths, weaknesses, opportunities, and threats	1. Strengths 2. Weaknesses 3. Opportunities 4. Threats
Marketing Objectives	Specification of the firm's marketing objectives	Qualitative measures of what is to be accomplished
Marketing Strategies	Outline of how the firm will achieve its objectives	1. Target market(s) 2. Marketing mix
Marketing Implementation	Outline of how the firm will implement its marketing strategies	1. Marketing organization 2. Activities and responsibilities 3. Implementation timetable
Evaluation and Control	Explanation of how the firm will measure and evaluate the results of the implemented plan	1. Performance standards 2. Financial controls 3. Monitoring procedures (audits)

Implementing Marketing Strategies

marketing implementation
The process of putting marketing strategies into action

intended strategy The strategy the company decided on during the planning phase and wants to use

realized strategy The strategy that actually takes place

Marketing implementation is the process of putting marketing strategies into action. Although implementation is often neglected in favour of strategic planning, the implementation process itself can determine whether a marketing strategy succeeds. It is also important to recognize that marketing strategies almost always turn out differently than expected. In essence, all organizations have two types of strategy: intended strategy and realized strategy.[40] The **intended strategy** is the strategy the organization decided on during the planning phase and wants to use, whereas the **realized strategy** is the strategy that actually takes place. The difference between the two is often the result of how the intended strategy is implemented. For example, Chrysler's PT Cruiser was originally marketed to young drivers, but the retro-styled vehicle ultimately proved more popular with their nostalgic baby boomer parents. Just 4 percent of the PT Cruiser's buyers were from the car's intended target market of drivers under 25.[41] The realized strategy, though not necessarily any better or worse than the intended strategy, often does not live up to planners' expectations.

Approaches to Marketing Implementation

Just as organizations can achieve their goals by using different marketing strategies, they can implement their marketing strategies by using different approaches. In this section, we discuss two general approaches to marketing implementation: internal marketing and total quality management. Both approaches represent mindsets that marketing managers may adopt when organizing and planning marketing activities. These approaches are not mutually exclusive; indeed, many companies adopt both when designing marketing activities.

external customers Individuals who patronize a business

internal customers
A company's employees

Internal Marketing. **External customers** are the individuals who patronize a business—the familiar definition of customers—whereas **internal customers** are the company's employees. For implementation to succeed, the needs of both groups of customers must be met. If internal customers are not satisfied, it is likely external customers will not be satisfied either. Thus, in addition to targeting marketing activities at external customers, a firm uses internal marketing to attract, motivate, and retain qualified internal customers by designing internal products (jobs) that satisfy their wants and needs. **Internal marketing** is a management philosophy that coordinates internal exchanges between the organization and its employees to achieve successful external exchanges between the organization and its customers.[42]

internal marketing A management philosophy that coordinates internal exchanges between the organization and its employees to achieve successful external exchanges between the organization and its customers

Generally speaking, internal marketing refers to the managerial actions necessary to make all members of the marketing organization understand and accept their respective roles in implementing the marketing strategy. Thus, marketing managers need to focus internally on employees as well as externally on customers.[43] This means that all internal customers, from the president of the company down to the hourly workers on the shop floor, must understand the roles they play in carrying out their jobs and implementing the marketing strategy. In short, anyone invested in the firm, both marketers and those who perform other functions, must recognize the tenet of customer orientation and service that underlies the marketing concept.

Like external marketing activities, internal marketing may involve market segmentation, product development, research, distribution, and even public relations and sales promotion.[44] For example, an organization may sponsor sales contests to inspire sales personnel to boost their selling efforts. This helps employees (and ultimately the company) to understand customers' needs and problems, teaches them valuable new skills, and heightens their enthusiasm for their regular jobs. In addition, many companies use planning sessions, websites, workshops, letters, formal reports, and personal conversations to ensure that employees comprehend the corporate mission, the organization's goals, and the marketing strategy. The ultimate results are more satisfied employees and improved customer relations.

Total Quality Management. Quality has become a major concern in many organizations, particularly in light of intense foreign competition, more demanding custom-

total quality management (TQM) A philosophy that uniform commitment to quality in all areas of the organization will promote a culture that meets customers' perceptions of quality

ers, and poorer profit performance owing to reduced market share and higher costs. To regain a competitive edge, a number of firms have adopted a total quality management approach. **Total quality management (TQM)** is a philosophy that uniform commitment to quality in all areas of the organization will promote a culture that meets customers' perceptions of quality. Indeed, research has shown that quality orientation and marketing orientation are complementary and together are sources of superior performance.[45] TQM involves coordinating efforts to improve customer satisfaction, increasing employee participation and empowerment, forming and strengthening supplier partnerships, and facilitating an organizational culture of continuous quality improvement. It requires continuous quality improvement and employee empowerment.

benchmarking Comparing the quality of the firm's goods, services, or processes with that of its best-performing competitors

Continuous improvement of an organization's goods and services is built around the notion that quality is free; in contrast, *not* having high-quality goods and services can be very expensive, especially in terms of dissatisfied customers.[46] A primary tool of the continuous improvement process is **benchmarking,** comparing the quality of the organization's goods, services, or processes with that of the best-performing companies in the industry.[47] Benchmarking fosters organizational "learning" by helping firms identify and enhance valuable marketing capabilities.[48] Benchmarking lets the organization assess where it stands competitively in its industry, thus giving it a goal to aim for over time.

empowerment Giving customer-contact employees authority and responsibility to make marketing decisions without seeking approval of their supervisors

Ultimately TQM succeeds or fails because of the efforts of the organization's employees. Thus, employee recruitment, selection, and training are critical to the success of marketing implementation. **Empowerment** gives customer-contact employees the authority and responsibility to make marketing decisions without seeking the approval of their supervisors.[49] Although employees at any level in an organization can be empowered to make decisions, empowerment is used most often at the frontline, where employees interact daily with customers.

One characteristic of empowerment is that employees can perform their jobs the way they see fit, as long as their methods and outcomes are consistent with the organization's mission. However, empowering employees is successful only if the organization is guided by an overall corporate vision, shared goals, and a culture that supports the TQM effort.[50] For example, Ritz-Carlton hotels give each customer-contact employee permission to take care of customer needs as he or she observes issues. A great deal of time, effort, and patience is needed to develop and sustain a quality-oriented culture in an organization.

Organizing Marketing Activities

The structure and relationships of a marketing unit, including lines of authority and responsibility that connect and coordinate individuals, strongly affect marketing activities. Firms that truly adopt the marketing concept develop a distinct organizational culture: a culture based on a shared set of beliefs that makes the customer's needs the pivotal point of the firm's decisions about strategy and operations.[51] Instead of developing products in a vacuum and then trying to persuade customers to purchase them, companies using the marketing concept begin with an orientation toward their customers' needs and desires.

If the marketing concept serves as a guiding philosophy, the marketing unit will be closely coordinated with other functional areas such as production, finance, and human resources. Marketing must interact with other departments in a number of key areas. It needs to work with manufacturing in determining the volume and variety of the company's products. Those in charge of production rely on marketers for accurate sales forecasts. Research and development departments depend heavily on information gathered by marketers about product features and benefits consumers' desire. Decisions made by the physical distribution department hinge on information about the urgency of delivery schedules and cost/service tradeoffs. Information technology is often a crucial ingredient in effectively managing customer relationships, but successful customer relationship management programs must include every department involved in customer relations.[52]

How effectively a firm's marketing management can plan and implement marketing strategies also depends on how the marketing unit is organized. Organizing marketing activities in ways that mesh with a firm's strategic marketing approach enhances performance.[53] Effective organizational planning can give the firm a competitive advantage. The organizational structure of a marketing department establishes the authority relationships among marketing personnel and specifies who is responsible for making certain decisions and performing particular activities. This internal structure helps direct marketing activities.

One crucial decision regarding structural authority is centralization versus decentralization. In a **centralized organization,** top-level managers delegate little authority to lower levels. In a **decentralized organization,** decision making authority is delegated as far down the chain of command as possible. The decision to centralize or decentralize the organization directly affects marketing. Most traditional organizations are highly centralized. In these organizations, most, if not all, marketing decisions are made at the top levels. However, as organizations become more marketing oriented, centralized decision making proves somewhat ineffective. In these organizations, decentralized authority allows the company to respond to customer needs more quickly.

No single approach to organizing a marketing unit works equally well in all businesses. The best approach or approaches depends on the number and diversity of the firm's products, the characteristics and needs of the people in the target market, and many other factors. A marketing unit can be organized according to (1) functions, (2) products, (3) regions, or (4) types of customers. Firms often use some combination of these organizational approaches. Product features may dictate that the marketing unit be structured by products, whereas customer characteristics may require that it be organized by geographic region or by types of customers. By using more than one type of structure, a flexible marketing unit can develop and implement marketing plans to match customers' needs precisely.

Organizing by Functions Some marketing departments are organized by general marketing functions, such as marketing research, product development, distribution, sales, advertising, and customer relations. The personnel who direct these functions report directly to the top-level marketing executive. This structure is fairly common because it works well for some businesses with centralized marketing operations, such as Ford and General Motors. In more decentralized firms, such as grocery store chains, functional organization can cause serious coordination problems. However, the functional approach may suit a large, centralized company whose products and customers are neither numerous nor diverse.

Organizing by Products An organization that produces and markets diverse products may find the functional approach inadequate. The decisions and problems related to a single marketing function for one product may be quite different from those related to the same marketing function for another product. As a result, businesses that produce diverse products sometimes organize their marketing units according to product groups. Organizing by product groups gives a firm the flexibility to develop special marketing mixes for different products. Procter & Gamble, like many firms in the consumer packaged goods industry, is organized by product group. Although organizing by products allows a company to remain flexible, this approach can be rather expensive unless efficient categories of products are grouped together to reduce duplication and improve coordination of product management.

Organizing by Regions A large company that markets products nationally (or internationally) may organize its marketing activities by geographic regions. Managers of marketing functions for each region report to their regional marketing manager; all the regional marketing managers report directly to the executive marketing manager. Dahlgren & Company, Inc. (www.sunflowerseed.com), a world supplier of sunflower products for the snack, baking, and food-ingredient industries, organized its U.S. and Canadian market into three regional divisions enabling the company to be closer to its customers and respond more quickly to competitors. This form of organization is especially effective for a firm whose customers' characteristics and needs vary greatly from one region to another. Firms that try to penetrate the national market intensively may divide regions into subregions. A company could have multiple subregions in a large province like Ontario.

Organizing by Types of Customers   Sometimes a company's marketing unit is organized according to types of customers. This form of internal organization works well for a firm that has several groups of customers whose needs and problems differ significantly. For example, Bic may sell pens to large retail stores, wholesalers, and institutions. Retailers may want more rapid delivery of small shipments and more personal selling by the producer than do either wholesalers or institutional buyers. Because the marketing decisions and activities required for these two groups of customers differ considerably, the company may find it efficient to organize its marketing unit by types of customers.

Controlling Marketing Activities

marketing control process
Establishing performance standards, evaluating actual performance by comparing it with established standards, and reducing the differences between desired and actual performance

To achieve both marketing and general organizational objectives, marketing managers must effectively control marketing efforts. The **marketing control process** consists of establishing performance standards, evaluating actual performance by comparing it with established standards, and reducing the differences between desired and actual performance.

Organizations have both formal and informal control systems. The formal marketing control process, as mentioned earlier, involves performance standards, evaluation of actual performance, and corrective action to remedy shortfalls (see Figure 2.5). The informal control process involves self-control, social or group control, and cultural control through acceptance of the firm's value system. Which type of control system dominates depends on the environmental context of the firm.[54] We now discuss these steps in the formal control process and consider the major problems they involve.

performance standard
An expected level of performance against which actual performance can be compared

Establishing Performance Standards   Planning and controlling are closely linked because plans include statements about what is to be accomplished. For purposes of control, these statements function as performance standards. A **performance standard** is an expected level of performance against which actual performance can be compared. A performance standard might be a 20 percent reduction in customer complaints, a monthly sales quota of $150 000, or a 10 percent increase per month in new-

figure 2.5

THE MARKETING CONTROL PROCESS

customer accounts. General Motors, for example, had a goal of selling 31 000 Corvette C6s in 2005.[55] As stated earlier, performance standards should be tied to organizational goals.

Evaluating Actual Performance   To compare actual performance with performance standards, marketing managers must know what employees within the company are doing and have information about the activities of external organizations that provide the firm with marketing assistance. For example, Saturn, like many automakers, uses many measures to evaluate its product and service levels, including how well it ranks on the J. D. Power & Associates Customer Service Index. In 2005, Saturn ranked number three among all automakers, up from number six in 2004, behind only Lincoln and Cadillac.[56] Records of actual performance are compared with performance standards to determine whether and how much of a discrepancy exists. For example, if General Motors had determined that only 25 000 Corvettes were sold in 2005, a discrepancy would have existed because its goal was 31 000 vehicles.

Taking Corrective Action   Marketing managers have several options for reducing a discrepancy between established performance standards and actual performance. They can take steps to improve actual performance, reduce or totally change the performance standard, or do both. At Wal-Mart, for example, managers implemented a strategy not to employ its usual steep discounts during the holiday shopping season, but when that strategy resulted in sluggish sales, they quickly slashed prices on key products and ran full-page newspaper ads to promote the lower prices.[57] To improve actual performance, the marketing manager may have to use better methods of motivating marketing personnel or find more effective techniques for coordinating marketing efforts.

Problems in Controlling Marketing Activities   In their efforts to control marketing activities, marketing managers frequently run into several problems. Often the information required to control marketing activities is unavailable or is available only at a high cost. Although marketing controls should be flexible enough to allow for environmental changes, the frequency, intensity, and unpredictability of such changes may hamper control. In addition, the time lag between marketing activities and their results limits a marketing manager's ability to measure the effectiveness of specific marketing activities. This is especially true for all advertising activities.

Because marketing and other business activities overlap, marketing managers often cannot determine the precise costs of marketing activities. Without an accurate measure of marketing costs, it is difficult to know if the outcome of marketing activities is worth the expense. Finally, marketing control may be difficult because it is very hard to develop exact performance standards for marketing personnel.

SUMMARY

Through the process of strategic planning, a firm identifies or establishes an organizational mission and goals, corporate strategy, marketing goals and objectives, marketing strategy, and a marketing plan. To achieve its marketing objectives, an organization must develop a marketing strategy, which includes identifying a target market and developing a plan of action for developing, distributing, promoting, and pricing products that meet the needs of customers in that target market. The strategic planning process ultimately yields the framework for a marketing plan, a written document that specifies the activities to be performed for implementing and controlling an organization's marketing activities.

The marketing environment, including economic, competitive, political, legal and regulatory, sociocultural, and technological forces, can affect the resources a firm can acquire and create favourable opportunities. Resources may include core competencies, which are things that a firm does extremely well, sometimes so well that it gives the company an advantage over its competition. When the right combination of circumstances and timing permit an organization to take action toward reaching a particular target market, a market opportunity exists. Strategic windows are temporary periods of optimal fit between the key requirements of a market and the particular capabilities of a firm competing in that market. When a company matches a core competency to opportunities it has discovered in the marketplace, it is said to have a competitive advantage.

An organization's goals should be derived from its mission statement, a long-term view, or vision, of what the organization wants to become. A well-formulated mission statement helps give an organization a clear purpose and direction, distinguish it from competitors, provide direction for strategic planning, and foster a focus on customers. An organization's goals and objectives, which focus on the end results sought, guide the remainder of its planning efforts.

Corporate strategy determines the means for utilizing resources in the areas of production, finance, research and development, human resources, and marketing to reach the organization's goals. Business-unit strategy focuses on strategic business units (SBUs)—divisions, product lines, brands or other profit centres within the parent company used to define areas for consideration in a specific strategic market plan. Marketing strategies, the most detailed and specific of the three levels of strategy, are composed of two elements: the selection of a target market and the creation of a marketing mix that will satisfy the needs of the chosen target market. The selection of a target market serves as the basis for the creation of the marketing mix to satisfy the needs of that market. Marketing mix decisions should also be consistent with business-unit and corporate strategies and be flexible enough to respond to changes in market conditions, competition, and customer needs. Different elements of the marketing mix can be changed to accommodate different marketing strategies.

The outcome of marketing planning is the development of a marketing plan, which outlines all the activities necessary to implement marketing strategies. The plan fosters communication among employees, assigns responsibilities and schedules, specifies how resources are to be allocated to achieve objectives, and helps marketing managers monitor and evaluate the performance of a marketing strategy.

Marketing implementation is the process of executing marketing strategies. Marketing strategies do not always turn out as expected. Realized marketing strategies often differ from the intended strategies because of issues related to implementation. Proper implementation requires efficient organizational structures and effective control and evaluation.

One major approach to marketing implementation is internal marketing, a management philosophy that coordinates internal exchanges between the organization and its employees to achieve successful external exchanges between the organization and its customers. For strategy implementation to be successful, the needs of both internal and external customers must be met. Another approach is total quality management (TQM), which relies heavily on the talents of employees to continually improve the quality of the organization's goods and services.

Please visit the student website at **www.hmco.ca/marketing** for ACE Self-Test questions that will help you prepare for exams.

IMPORTANT TERMS

Strategic planning
Marketing strategy
Marketing plan
Core competencies
Market opportunity
Strategic window
Competitive advantage
SWOT analysis
Mission statement

Marketing objective
Corporate strategy
Strategic business unit (SBU)
Market
Market share
Market growth/market
   share matrix
Sustainable competitive
   advantage

Marketing planning
Marketing implementation
Intended strategy
Realized strategy
External customers
Internal customers
Internal marketing
Total quality management
   (TQM)

Benchmarking
Empowerment
Centralized organization
Decentralized organization
Marketing control process
Performance standard

DISCUSSION & REVIEW QUESTIONS

1. Identify the major components of strategic planning, and explain how they are interrelated.

2. What are the two major parts of a marketing strategy?

3. What are some issues to consider in analyzing a firm's resources and opportunities? How do these

issues affect marketing objectives and marketing strategy?

4. How important is the SWOT analysis to the marketing planning process?

5. How should organizations set marketing objectives?

6. Explain how an organization can create a competitive advantage at the corporate, business-unit, and marketing strategy levels.

7. Refer to question 6. How can an organization make its competitive advantages sustainable over time? How difficult is it to create sustainable competitive advantages?

8. What benefits do marketing managers gain from planning? Is planning necessary for long-run survival? Why or why not?

9. Why does an organization's intended strategy often differ from its realized strategy?

10. Why might an organization use multiple bases for organizing its marketing unit?

11. What are the major steps of the marketing control process?

APPLICATION QUESTIONS

1. Contact three organizations that appear to be successful. Ask one of the company's managers or executives if he or she would share with you the company's mission statement or organizational goals. Obtain as much information as possible about the statement and organizational goals. Discuss how the statement matches the criteria outlined in the text.

2. Assume you own a new, family-style restaurant that will open for business in the coming year. Formulate a long-term goal for the company, and then develop short-term goals to help you achieve the long-term goal.

3. Amazon.com identified an opportunity to capitalize on a desire of many consumers to shop at home. This strategic window gave Amazon.com a very competitive position in a new market. Consider the

opportunities that may be present in your city, your region, or in Canada as a whole. Identify a strategic window, and discuss how a company could take advantage of this opportunity. What kind of core competencies are necessary?

4. Marketing units may be organized according to functions, products, regions, or types of customers. Describe how you would organize the marketing units for the following:

a. A toothpaste with whitener; a toothpaste with extra-strong nicotine cleaners; a toothpaste with bubble-gum flavour

b. A national line offering all types of winter and summer sports clothing for men and women

c. A life insurance company that provides life, health, and disability insurance

globalEDGE™

1. Rankings of the world's largest manufacturing companies provide a variety of data. Rankings by industry can be found using the search term "largest manufacturing companies" at **http://globaledge.msu.edu/ibrd** or **http://globaledge.msu.edu/ibrd/ibrd.asp** to access *IndustryWeek*'s IW 1000 ranking. Perform a SWOT (i.e., Strengths, Weaknesses, Opportunities, and Threats) analysis of the top five firms in the apparel industry. From the information included, which firm has the strongest market position? Analyzing all firms in the apparel industry, which five firms have the weakest positions?

2. Your firm is currently developing a marketing strategy based on the expected age of both the Canadian and U.S. populations for the foreseeable future. By analyzing the population pyramids provided in the International Data Base (IDB) by the U.S. Census Bureau, you can better understand the estimated demographic shifts from 2000 to 2025 and 2050 for both countries. The population pyramids can be found using the search term "international data base" at **http://globaledge.msu.edu/ibrd** or **http://globaledge.msu.edu/ibrd/ibrd.asp** to reach the U.S. Census Bureau's IDB, and then choosing the Population Pyramid link. Provide a summary of your findings.

INTERNET Exercise

Sony

Internet analysts have praised Sony's website as one of the best organized and most informative on the Internet. See why by accessing **www.sony.com**.

1. Based on the information provided on the website, describe Sony's SBUs.
2. Based on your existing knowledge of Sony as an innovative leader in the consumer electronics industry, describe the company's primary competitive advantage. How does Sony's website support this competitive advantage?
3. Assess the quality and effectiveness of Sony's website. Specifically, perform a preliminary SWOT analysis comparing Sony's website with other high-quality websites you have visited.

Case 2.1 A Turnaround King Helps Burger King Recover

Burger King, founded in Miami in 1954 by James McLamore and David Edgerton, serves almost 12 million customers a day at more than 11 000 restaurants in 60 countries. In Canada there are over 345 Burger King restaurants from coast to coast, of which 221 are franchised. However, since the early 1990s the profits and success of Burger King restaurants have steadily declined, while rivals McDonald's and Wendy's grabbed its market share. While 10 CEOs passed through Burger King in 14 years, CEO number 11, Greg Brenneman, is finally turning things around. This charismatic, driven CEO has implemented new strategies that have boosted sales 6.8 percent in restaurants open more than a year—the largest increase in more than 10 years. The company's market share is also expected to show improvement this year after falling since 1999.

Brenneman certainly has experience with corporate turnarounds. Before taking the lead at Burger King, he helped turn around PwC Consulting and helped facilitate that company's merger with IBM Global Services. This merger earned the title of "deal of the year" from *Institutional Investor* magazine. Prior to that, Brenneman spent six years at the helm of Continental Airlines, helping to return the company to profitability after 16 years of losses. Although Brenne-

man has an MBA from Harvard Business School, he attributes much of his success to growing up on a farm, where days began at 6 a.m. and ended late in the evening, and where he developed a strong work ethic. His early jobs included manicuring golf courses and working at a furniture warehouse. Those who work with him view him as intelligent, aggressive, and quick. Even Edgerton feels Brenneman is the first CEO in a long time who listens to everyone.

To approach the issues facing Burger King, Brenneman took a simple path and initiated the "Go Forward Plan," which required a single sheet of paper to articulate. He set straightforward goals for the company: to earn money, bring in more customers/build enthusiasm in existing customers, and motivate BK employees. To reach those goals, he first slashed the costs of building new Burger King restaurants from $1.3 million to $970 000 by recommending that new stores be smaller. His idea was supported by research that suggested that most customers currently order food to go, so the new Burger King prototype has about half the previous number of seats. The kitchens of these new stores are also smaller to make preparation more efficient. In addition, Brenneman wants the new stores built with materials readily available at Home Depot. Doing all of this may enable franchisees to achieve profits more quickly. In addition to reducing the size of the new restaurants, the company has introduced a new "industrial chic" decoration scheme, which executives believe will be a major draw for customers. When Brenneman took the reins at Burger King, the company had just one project idea on the table. To take the company forward, he is determined that now there will always be at least 30 project ideas in the works. His first project was the Enormous Omelet Sandwich, which raised breakfast profits 20 percent.

One of Brenneman's biggest challenges is soothing franchisees, who are vital to the firm's continuing success. In particular, one group of franchisees is unhappy that a recent $340 million ad campaign targets teenage males at the expense of other market segments, especially women. While some franchisees worry that the advertising focus is too narrow, a spokeswoman for Burger King says that sales—the only way to measure success—have been up since the campaign began. Other issues of concern to franchisees relate to new menu items, pricing, and hours of operation. Given that 90 percent of Burger King restaurants are franchised, Brenneman clearly has work to do to settle these issues.

Despite these issues, Brenneman is optimistic about Burger King's future. There are signs to support his optimism. For example, customer satisfaction is at an all-time high according to the University of Michigan's American Customer Satisfaction Index, at a time when McDonald's has seen customer satisfaction decline. In 2005 Burger King opened more restaurants than it closed—a first since the 1990s. The company is also opening new restaurants overseas, with new locations in Brazil and China. All told, the company opened 300 to 350 international locations in 2005.

Even given the challenges to be faced, employees and franchisees alike are rooting for Brenneman and the success of Burger King. The company still has a way to go to return to the successful levels of the early 1990s, but Brenneman is certainly laying solid groundwork for success.

While it is simply a matter of watching to see how Burger King's future sales fare, Brenneman—who now rises at 4 a.m. and is at work by 4:30 and has successful company turnarounds under his belt—may be just the man to keep sales on the rise.[58]

Questions for Discussion

1. Briefly describe the target market and marketing mix used by Burger King.
2. Do you believe that targeting teenage males at the expense of other markets, especially women, is an appropriate strategy?
3. Have Burger King's strategic marketing planning efforts been successful? Why or why not?

Strategic Case 1 FedEx Packages Marketing for Overnight Success

In 1973, Frederick W. Smith founded Federal Express Corporation with part of an $8 million inheritance. At the time, ground mail was really the only means of delivering packages, and they often took several days or more to get packages to their destinations. While a student at Yale in 1965, Smith studied topology, a mathematical discipline dedicated to geometric configurations. He applied these principles to a business plan and envisioned a hub system from which packages could be delivered across the globe. Smith wrote a paper proposing an independent overnight delivery service. Although he received a C on the paper, Smith never lost sight of his vision. He believed many businesses would be willing to pay more to get letters, documents, and packages delivered overnight. He was right.

Federal Express began shipping packages overnight from Memphis, Tennessee, on April 17, 1973. On that first night of operations, the company handled six packages, one of which was a birthday present sent by Smith himself. Today FedEx Corporation handles more than three million overnight packages and documents a day and more than six million shipments a day around the world. FedEx controls more than 50 percent of the overnight delivery market, with an astounding $31 billion in total revenue. FedEx does not view itself as being in the package and document transport business; rather, it describes its business as delivering "certainty." FedEx delivers this certainty by connecting the global economy with a wide range of transportation, information, and supply chain services.

FedEx Express and FedEx Ground provide the bulk of the company's business, offering valuable services to anyone who needs to deliver letters, documents, and packages. Whether it is dropped off at one of nearly

42 000 drop boxes or 715 world service centres or picked up by FedEx courier, each package is taken to a local FedEx office, where it is trucked to the nearest airport. The package is flown to one of the company's distribution "hubs" for sorting and then flown to the airport nearest its destination. The package is then trucked to another FedEx office where a courier picks it up and hand delivers it to the correct recipient. All of this takes place overnight, with many packages delivered before 8:00 a.m. the following day. FedEx confirms that roughly 99 percent of its deliveries are made on time.

To achieve this highly successful delivery rate, FedEx maintains an impressive infrastructure of equipment and processes. The company owns more than 70 000 vehicles, and its 677 aircraft fly more than 500 000 miles every day. FedEx operates its own weather forecasting service, ensuring that most of its flights arrive within 15 minutes of schedule. The hub envisioned by Smith in university is located in Memphis, Tennessee. FedEx takes over control of Memphis International Airport at roughly 11:00 each night. For an hour every night, FedEx planes begin to arrive in Memphis and land side by side on parallel runways every minute. After the packages are sorted, all FedEx planes take off in time to reach their destinations. Beginning at 2:48 a.m. every Monday through Friday, FedEx dispatches eight to 12 aircraft every six minutes. By 4:12 a.m., FedEx has launched about 150 aircraft to over 136 domestic and international destinations. Not all packages are shipped via air; whenever possible, FedEx uses ground transportation to save on expenses. For international deliveries, FedEx uses a combination of direct services and independent contractors. To handle the logistics of its large number of planes, FedEx relies on high-tech software originally developed by NASA. The program displays real-time maps of the airport layout, runways, aircraft, and gates. With a single click of the mouse, the operator can receive detailed information about an individual airplane's arrival and departure times.

Growth and Expansion

FedEx has been expanding its reach by merging with Kinko's, partnering with its former competitor. FedEx purchased Kinko's in 2004 to provide new business services and expand FedEx shipping options at Kinko's nationwide stores. The purchase followed rival UPS' acquisition of 3 000 Mail Boxes Etc. stores. Renaming Mail Boxes Etc. to UPS put UPS closer to small- and medium-size customers and high-profit, infrequent shippers. FedEx's purchase of Kinko's, which operates in 11 countries, is expected to help the company reach new customers and expand in Asia and Europe.

One of the most important keys to success for FedEx is its flexibility. FedEx always has to be ready to deal with the unexpected or the uncontrollable. "That's the nature of the business," says Dave Bronczek, the head of FedEx's Express division. Natural disasters are a natural obstacle in the shipping business. In 2004 and 2005, FedEx had to rely on contingency plans to successfully navigate the 57 tropical storms that threatened to interrupt its business. "We're used to dealing with crisis," says Bronczek. When television reporters covered the inability of FEMA workers and Army personnel to communicate during post-Hurricane Katrina rescue operations, FedEx came to the rescue. The company contacted FEMA and offered use of its intact radio network to aid rescue workers. Every day, some part of the globe visited by FedEx is experiencing some type of political or natural unrest. This is the reason FedEx has implemented disaster drills covering everything from bioterrorism to typhoons. Each night eight planes sit in Memphis with fuel, supplies, and communications gear ready to deploy to a FedEx facility in need. Also, five cargoless planes roam the skies, ready to help out in cases of unexpected volume, air emergencies, or broken down planes.

FedEx Relies Heavily on Information Technology

Despite its tremendous successes, FedEx has faced some difficult times in its efforts to grow and compete against strong rivals. The overnight delivery market matured very rapidly in response to competitors as well as electronic document delivery (i.e., fax machines and e-mail), forcing FedEx to search for viable means of expansion.

Many analysts still argue that the overnight delivery market could eventually lose as much as 30 percent of its letter business to electronic document delivery, especially e-mail. This trend may be balanced by the enormous growth of online businesses that rely on shipping services to deliver merchandise.

FedEx constantly strives to improve its services by enhancing its distribution networks, transportation infrastructure, information technology, and employee performance. FedEx also continues to invest heavily in information technology by installing computer terminals at customers' offices and giving away its proprietary tracking software. Today the vast majority of FedEx customers—more than 70 percent—electronically generate their own pickup and delivery requests. FedEx has also moved more aggressively into e-commerce with respect to order fulfillment for business-to-business and business-to-consumer merchants.

FedEx offers several electronic tools, applications, and online interfaces for customers to integrate into their processes to shorten response time, reduce inventory costs, and generate better returns and to simplify their shipping. FedEx InSight was the first online application to offer proactive, real-time status information on inbound, outbound, and third-party shipments. It enables customers to identify issues instantly and address them before they become problems. In addition, FedEx

InSight allows customers to see the progress of their shipments without requiring a tracking number, giving them convenient and unprecedented data visibility critical to effective management of their supply chain systems. FedEx technology enables customers, couriers, and contract delivery personnel to access the company's information systems networks by wireless technology anytime, anywhere. In fact, FedEx was the first transportation company to embrace wireless technology—more than two decades ago—and continues to be a leader in the use of innovative wireless solutions.

Why Is FedEx Successful?

As FedEx moves ahead, the company has a lot going for it. No other carrier can match FedEx's global capabilities or one-stop shopping—at least not yet. To increase its competitiveness, FedEx is focusing on increasing revenue and reducing costs through tighter integration and consolidation, improved productivity, and reduced capital expenditures.

FedEx has been successful for many reasons. First, FedEx tries to stay focused on its mission statement, which is:

FedEx will produce superior financial returns for shareowners by providing high value-added supply chain, transportation, business and related information services through focused operating companies. Customer requirements will be met in the highest quality manner appropriate to each market segment served. FedEx will strive to develop mutually rewarding relationships with its employees, partners and suppliers. Safety will be the first consideration in all operations. Corporate activities will be conducted to the highest ethical and professional standards.

A second reason is the company's enviable corporate culture and workforce. Because employees are critical to the company's success, FedEx strives to hire the best people and offers them the best training and compensation in the industry. FedEx employees are loyal, highly efficient, and extremely effective in delivering good service. In fact, FedEx employees claim to have "purple blood" to match the company's official color. It is not surprising that FedEx has been named one of the "100 Best Companies to Work For" for eight consecutive years.

A third reason for FedEx's success is its technology and customer relationship management. The company's focus on "delivering certainty" has allowed it to home in on opportunities that give FedEx additional capabilities in innovative information technology solutions.

A final reason for FedEx's success is its highly effective marketing. FedEx is a master at recognizing untapped customer needs and building relationships. FedEx is also never content to sit on its laurels as it constantly strives to improve service and offer more options to its customers. After 30 years of success, there is little doubt that Fred Smith's C paper has become an indispensable part of the business world.[59]

Questions for Discussion

1. Which three environmental forces are likely to have the greatest effects on FedEx? Explain your answer.
2. What are the major strengths, weaknesses, opportunities, and threats (SWOT) associated with FedEx?
3. Is there evidence that FedEx has attempted to adopt and use the marketing concept? Explain.
4. Evaluate FedEx's mission statement. Explain the major strengths and weaknesses of this mission statement.

Environmental Forces, Social Responsibility, and Ethics

Part Two deals with the marketing environment and examines concepts, influences, and trends both in Canada and abroad. **Chapter 3** examines competitive, economic, political, legal, regulatory, technological, and sociocultural forces in the marketing environment, which can have profound effects on marketing strategies. **Chapter 4** explores the role of ethical and social responsibility issues in marketing decisions.

3

The Marketing Environment

OBJECTIVES

1. To recognize the importance of environmental scanning and analysis

2. To understand how competitive and economic factors affect organizations' ability to compete and customers' ability and willingness to buy products

3. To identify the types of political forces in the marketing environment

4. To understand how laws, government regulations, and self-regulatory agencies affect marketing activities

5. To explore the effects of new technology on society and on marketing activities

6. To analyze sociocultural issues marketers must deal with as they make decisions

The Canadian Airline Industry: What's Up?

Most Canadian air travellers have a story or two to share about lost baggage, cancelled flights, and expensive seats. Some even tell the story of being stranded by their financially troubled carrier, Jetsgo Corp., when it grounded its entire fleet. For most travellers, there are few alternatives when it comes time to book a flight. Moreover, most have come to expect better service from service providers than what they experience from airlines.

Over the last few years, Canada's remaining large commercial carriers—Air Canada and WestJet—have been engaged in a battle of the brands. In the beginning, this battle was a David and Goliath story. According to Ricardo Pilon, professor of airline management and marketing at the John Molson School of Business at Concordia University, "everyone felt sorry for WestJet, and Air Canada was always perceived as the big bad boy." Perceptions have since changed. A branding survey by Canadian Business magazine revealed some significant changes in public perception regarding the two carriers. Air Canada spent the last few years attempting to slim down and become more consumer-friendly by revamping prices, so that fares would be on par with WestJet and other low-cost carriers.

In addition to cost cutting, Air Canada has gone about adopting new uniforms and a new light blue colour scheme, introduced to the public with the help of

Céline Dion. While Air Canada was busy making changes, Calgary-based WestJet was scaling up, attempting to transform into a truly national airline. WestJet's success proves that Canadians want choice, and they like ambitious newcomers.

As long as these two carriers remain competitive, you can expect to see a battle of the brands play out in the marketing and advertising arenas, as the two carriers duke it out for the hearts and dollars of Canadian travellers. Neither airline wants to start a fare war that would only serve to destroy profit margins. Capital investments are huge, and the margins are very thin. One analyst noted, "an airline that is getting a 1 to 2 percent margin is doing great," . . . so when "your margins are that thin and the competition to get that is so intense, it's like legalized warfare."

Warfare indeed, the battle has even involved a case of alleged corporate espionage. Air Canada had WestJet and a WestJet employee served with a lawsuit. It alleged the WestJet employee had infiltrated an Air Canada employee website and collected sensitive competitive data, an act Air Canada branded "corporate espionage."

Not all businesses operate in a warfare environment as depicted here but all businesses need to understand that recognizing and addressing changes in the marketing environment are crucial to marketing success.[1] ■

Companies like Air Canada and WestJet are modifying marketing strategies in response to changes in the marketing environment. Because recognizing and addressing such changes in the marketing environment are crucial to marketing success, we will focus in detail on the forces that contribute to these changes.

This chapter explores the competitive, economic, political, legal and regulatory, technological, and sociocultural forces that constitute the marketing environment. First, we define the marketing environment and consider why it is critical to scan and analyze it. Next, we discuss the effects of competitive forces and explore the influence of general economic conditions: prosperity, recession, depression and recovery. We also examine buying power and look at the forces that influence consumers' willingness to spend. We then discuss the political forces that generate government actions affecting marketing activities and examine the effects of laws and regulatory agencies on these activities. After analyzing the major dimensions of the technological forces in the environment, we consider the impact of sociocultural forces on marketing efforts.

Examining and Responding to the Marketing Environment

The marketing environment consists of external forces that directly or indirectly influence an organization's acquisition of inputs (human, financial, natural resources and raw materials, and information) and creation of outputs (goods, services, or ideas). As we saw in Chapter 1, the marketing environment includes six such forces: competitive, economic, political, legal and regulatory, technological, and sociocultural.

Whether fluctuating rapidly or slowly, environmental forces are always dynamic. Changes in the marketing environment create uncertainty, threats, and opportunities for marketers. Consider that after uncertainty in the Middle East and the effects of hurricanes in the southern U.S. led to escalating fuel costs, many automakers saw sales of their gas-guzzling sport-utility vehicles plummet. For some firms, though, the situation proved fortuitous, as Honda, Nissan, and Toyota gained sales when many consumers switched to more fuel-efficient vehicles, like the Toyota Prius.[2] Although the future is not very predictable, marketers try to forecast what may happen. We can say with certainty that marketers continue to modify their marketing strategies and plans in response to dynamic environmental forces. Consider how technological changes have affected the products offered by computer companies and how the public's growing concern with health and fitness has influenced the products of clothing, food, exercise equipment, and health-care companies. Marketing managers who fail to recognize changes in environmental forces leave their firms unprepared to capitalize on marketing opportunities or to cope with threats created by those changes. Monitoring the environment is crucial to an organization's survival and to the long-term achievement of its goals.

Environmental Scanning and Analysis

environmental scanning
The process of collecting information about forces in the marketing environment

To monitor changes in the marketing environment effectively, marketers engage in environmental scanning and analysis. **Environmental scanning** is the process of collecting information about forces in the marketing environment. Scanning involves observation; secondary sources such as business, trade, government, and general-interest publications; and marketing research. The Internet has become a popular scanning tool since it makes data more accessible and allows companies to gather needed information quickly. Environmental scanning gives companies an edge over competitors in allowing them to take advantage of current trends. However, simply gathering information about competitors and customers is not enough; companies must know *how* to use that information in the strategic planning process. Managers must be careful not to gather so much information that sheer volume makes analysis impossible.

environmental analysis
The process of assessing and interpreting the information gathered through environmental scanning

Environmental analysis is the process of assessing and interpreting the information gathered through environmental scanning. A manager evaluates the information for accuracy, tries to resolve inconsistencies in the data, and, if warranted, assigns significance to the findings. Evaluating this information should enable the manager to identify potential threats and opportunities linked to environmental changes. Understanding the current state of the marketing environment and recognizing threats and opportunities arising from changes within it help companies in their strategic planning. In particular, it can help marketing managers assess the performance of current marketing efforts and develop future marketing strategies.

Responding to Environmental Forces

Marketing managers take two general approaches to environmental forces: accepting them as uncontrollable or attempting to influence and shape them. An organization that views environmental forces as uncontrollable remains passive and reactive toward the environment. Instead of trying to influence forces in the environment, its marketing managers adjust current marketing strategies to environmental changes. They approach with caution market opportunities discovered through environmental scanning and analysis. On the other hand, marketing managers who believe environmental forces can be shaped adopt a more proactive approach. For example, if a market is blocked by traditional environmental constraints, proactive marketing managers may apply economic, psychological, political, and promotional skills to gain access to and operate within it. Once they identify what is constraining a market opportunity, they assess the power of the various parties involved and develop strategies to overcome the obstructing environmental forces. Microsoft and Intel, for example, have responded to political, legal, and regulatory concerns about their power in the computer industry by communicating the value of their competitive approaches to various publics. The computer giants contend that their competitive success results in superior products for their customers.

A proactive approach can be constructive and bring desired results. To influence environmental forces, marketing managers seek to identify market opportunities or to extract greater benefits relative to costs from existing market opportunities. For example, a firm losing sales to competitors with lower-priced products develops a technology that makes its production processes more efficient, thus allowing it to lower prices of its own products. Political action is another way to affect environmental forces. However, managers must recognize that there are limits to the degree that environmental forces

snapshot

Got credit cards?

Nearly 40% of adults carry one or two credit cards.

38%
One or two

26%
None

20%
Three or four

15%
Five or more

First One To Save The Planet Wins.

We're all working for a better world. Cleaner air, a better environment and more natural resources. A worthy goal. At Toyota, we've been working on Hybrid Synergy Drive® for the past 40 years. The result? A technology that not only dramatically increases fuel economy but also creates far fewer smog-forming emissions. You'll find Hybrid Synergy Drive® on the Prius, Highlander Hybrid and, soon, the Camry Hybrid. In fact, we're working toward the day when you'll find it on all Toyota vehicles. Because we think you'll agree, better mileage and less pollution is a winning combination.

To learn more, visit toyota.com

HYBRID SYNERGY DRIVE

TOYOTA | moving forward ▶

Responding to Environmental Forces
By producing hybrid vehicles, car makers are responding to both customer demand and their own desires to exceed regulatory agency emissions standards.

can be shaped. Although an organization may be able to influence legislation through lobbying, it is unlikely that a single organization can significantly increase the national birthrate or move the economy from recession to prosperity.

We cannot say whether a reactive or a proactive approach to environmental forces is better. For some organizations the passive, reactive approach is more appropriate, but for others the aggressive approach leads to better performance. Selection of a particular approach depends on an organization's managerial philosophies, objectives, financial resources, customers, and human skills, as well as on the environment within which the organization operates. Both organizational factors and managers' personal characteristics affect the variety of responses to changing environmental conditions. Microsoft, for example, can take a proactive approach because of its financial resources and the highly visible image of its founder, Bill Gates.

In the remainder of this chapter, we explore in greater detail the six environmental forces—competitive, economic, political, legal and regulatory, technological, and sociocultural—that interact to create opportunities and threats that must be considered in strategic planning.

Competitive Forces

competition Other organizations that market products that are similar to or can be substituted for a marketer's products in the same geographic area

brand competitors Firms that market products with similar features and benefits to the same customers at similar prices

product competitors Firms that compete in the same product class but market products with different features, benefits, and prices

Few Canadian firms, if any, operate free of competition. In fact, for most goods and services, customers have many alternatives from which to choose. For example, the Big Three automakers—GM Canada, Ford Motor Co. of Canada, and DaimlerChrysler Canada—have lost market share to other manufacturers, year after year since the late 1990s.[3] Thus, when marketing managers define the target market(s) their firm will serve, they simultaneously establish a set of competitors.[4] In addition, marketing managers must consider the type of competitive structure in which the firm operates. In this section, we examine types of competition and competitive structures, as well as the importance of monitoring competitors' actions.

Types of Competitors
Broadly speaking, all firms compete with one another for customers' dollars. More practically, however, a marketer generally defines **competition** as other firms that market products that are similar to or can be substituted for its products in the same geographic area. These competitors can be classified into one of four types. **Brand competitors** market products with similar features and benefits to the same customers at similar prices. For example, a thirsty, calorie-conscious customer may choose a diet pop such as Diet Coke or Diet Pepsi from the soda machine. However, these sodas face competition from other types of beverages. **Product competitors** compete in the same product class but market products with different features, benefits, and

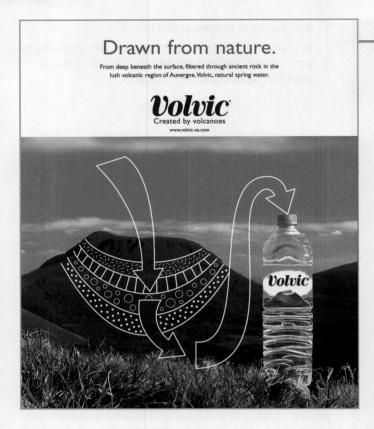

Drawn from nature.

From deep beneath the surface, filtered through ancient rock in the lush volcanic region of Auvergne, Volvic, natural spring water.

Volvic
Created by volcanoes
www.volvic-na.com

Brand Competition
Volvic bottled water has many competitors, including Evian and Dasani, as well as local brands.

prices. The thirsty dieter, for instance, might purchase iced tea, juice, mineral water, or bottled water instead of a pop. **Generic competitors** provide very different products that solve the same problem or satisfy the same basic customer need. Our dieter, for example, might simply have a glass of water from the kitchen tap to satisfy her thirst. **Total budget competitors** compete for the limited financial resources of the same customers.[5] Total budget competitors for Diet Coke, for example, might include gum, a newspaper, and bananas. Although all four types of competition can affect a firm's marketing performance, brand competitors are the most significant because buyers typically see the different products of these firms as direct substitutes for one another. Consequently marketers tend to concentrate environmental analyses on brand competitors.

Types of Competitive Structures

The number of firms that supply a product may affect the strength of competitors. When just one or a few firms control supply, competitive factors exert a different form of influence on marketing activities than when many competitors exist. Table 3.1 presents four general types of competitive structures: monopoly, oligopoly, monopolistic competition, and pure competition.

A **monopoly** exists when an organization offers a product that has no close substitutes, making that organization the sole source of supply. Because the organization has no competitors, it controls supply of the product completely and, as a single seller, can erect barriers to potential competitors. In reality, most monopolies surviving today are local utilities, which are heavily regulated by local, provincial or federal agencies. These monopolies are tolerated because of the tremendous financial resources needed to develop and operate them. For example, few organizations can obtain the financial or political resources to mount any competition against a local water supplier. On the other hand, competition is increasing in the electric and cable television industries.

An **oligopoly** exists when a few sellers control the supply of a large proportion of a product. In this case, each seller considers the reactions of other sellers to changes in marketing activities. Products facing oligopolistic competition may be homogeneous, such as aluminum, or differentiated, such as automobiles. Usually barriers of some sort make it difficult to enter the market and compete with oligopolies. For example, because of the enormous financial outlay required, few companies or individuals could afford to enter the oil-refining or steel-producing industry. Moreover, some industries demand special technical or marketing skills, a qualification that deters entry of many potential competitors.

Monopolistic competition exists when a firm with many potential competitors attempts to develop a marketing strategy to differentiate its product. For example, Levi Strauss has established an advantage for its blue jeans through a well-known trademark, design, advertising, and a reputation for quality. Although many competing brands of blue jeans are available, this firm has carved out a market niche by emphasizing differences in its products.

generic competitors Firms that provide very different products that solve the same problem or satisfy the same basic customer need

total budget competitors Firms that compete for the limited financial resources of the same customers

monopoly A competitive structure in which an organization offers a product that has no close substitutes, making that organization the sole source of supply

oligopoly A competitive structure in which a few sellers control the supply of a large proportion of a product

monopolistic competition A competitive structure in which a firm has many potential competitors and tries to develop a marketing strategy to differentiate its product

table 3.1	FOUR GENERAL TYPES OF COMPETITIVE STRUCTURES			
Type of Structure	Number of Competitors	Ease of Entry into Market	Product	Example
Monopoly	One	Many barriers	Almost no substitutes	Utilities Department, District of West Vancouver (municipal water supply)
Oligopoly	Few	Some barriers	Homogeneous or differentiated (with real or perceived differences)	General Motors (autos)
Monopolistic competition	Many	Few barriers	Product differentiation, with many substitutes	Levi Strauss (jeans)
Pure competition	Unlimited	No barriers	Homogeneous products	Vegetable farm (sweet corn)

pure competition A market structure characterized by an extremely large number of sellers, none strong enough to significantly influence price or supply

Pure competition, if it existed at all, would entail a large number of sellers, none of which could significantly influence price or supply. Products would be homogeneous, and entry into the market would be easy. The closest thing to an example of pure competition is an unregulated farmers' market, where local growers gather to sell their produce.

Pure competition is an ideal at one end of the continuum; monopoly is at the other end. Most marketers function in a competitive environment somewhere between these two extremes.

Monitoring Competition

Marketers need to monitor the actions of major competitors to determine what specific strategies competitors are using and how those strategies affect their own. Price is one marketing strategy variable that most competitors monitor. For example, as discussed in the chapter opener, Air Canada restructured to lower costs in order to be more price competitive with WestJet. Monitoring guides marketers in developing competitive advantages and in adjusting current marketing strategies and planning new ones.

In monitoring competition, it is not enough to analyze available information; the firm must develop a system for gathering ongoing information about competitors. Understanding the market and what customers want, as well as what the competition is providing, will help the firm maintain a marketing orientation.[6] Information about competitors allows marketing managers to assess the performance of their own marketing efforts and to recognize the strengths and weaknesses in their own marketing strategies. In addition, organizations are rewarded for taking risks and dealing with the uncertainty created by inadequate information.[7] Data about market shares, product movement, sales volume, and expenditure levels can be useful. However, accurate information on these matters is often difficult to obtain.

Economic Forces

Economic forces in the marketing environment influence both marketers' and customers' decisions and activities. In this section, we examine the effects of general economic conditions as well as buying power and the factors that affect people's willingness to spend.

Economic Conditions

The overall state of the economy fluctuates in all countries. Changes in general economic conditions affect (and are affected by) supply and demand, buying power, willingness to spend, consumer expenditure levels, and intensity of competitive behaviour. Therefore, current economic conditions and changes in the economy have a broad impact on the success of organizations' marketing strategies.

Fluctuations in the economy follow a general pattern, often referred to as the **business cycle.** In the traditional view, the business cycle consists of four stages: prosperity, recession, depression, and recovery. From a global perspective, different regions of the world may be in different stages of the business cycle during the same period. Throughout much of the last decade, for example, Canada experienced growth (prosperity). Japan, however, endured a recession during most of the last decade and into the early 2000s. Economic variation in the global marketplace creates a planning challenge for firms that sell products in multiple markets around the world.

During **prosperity,** unemployment is low and total income is relatively high. Assuming a low inflation rate, this combination ensures high buying power. If the economic outlook remains prosperous, consumers generally are willing to buy. In the prosperity stage, marketers often expand their product offerings to take advantage of increased buying power. They can sometimes capture a larger market share by intensifying distribution and promotion efforts.

Because unemployment rises during a **recession,** total buying power declines. These factors, usually accompanied by consumer pessimism, often stifle both consumer and business spending. As buying power decreases, many customers may become more price and value conscious, and look for basic, functional products. During a recession, some firms make the mistake of drastically reducing their marketing efforts, thus damaging their ability to survive. Obviously, however, marketers should consider some revision of their marketing activities during a recessionary period. Because consumers are more concerned about the functional value of products, a company should focus its marketing research on determining precisely what functions buyers want and make sure those functions become part of its products. Promotional efforts should emphasize value and utility. For example, KeepMedia, an online periodical content archive, discovered consumers wanted to pay for quality periodical content on the Internet but were unwilling to pay a separate fee for each title across the Web as they do for magazines offline. The company CEO put together recent editorial materials from recognizable publications at one flat fee.[8]

A prolonged recession may become a **depression,** a period in which unemployment is extremely high, wages are very low, total disposable income is at a minimum, and consumers lack confidence in the economy. A depression usually lasts for an extended period, often years, and has been experienced by Russia, Mexico, and Brazil in the last decade. Although evidence supports maintaining or even increasing spending during economic slowdowns, marketing budgets are more likely to be cut in the face of an economic downturn.

During **recovery,** the economy moves from recession or depression toward prosperity. During this period, high unemployment begins to decline, total disposable income increases, and the economic gloom that reduced consumers' willingness to buy subsides. Both the ability and the willingness to buy rise. Marketers face some problems during recovery; for example, it is difficult to ascertain how quickly and to what level prosperity will return. In this stage, marketers should maintain as much flexibility in their marketing strategies as possible so they can make the needed adjustments.

Buying Power

The strength of a person's **buying power** depends on economic conditions and the size of the resources—money, goods, and services that can be traded in an exchange— that enable the individual to make purchases. The major financial sources of buying

---

business cycle A pattern of economic fluctuations that has four stages: prosperity, recession, depression, and recovery

prosperity A stage of the business cycle characterized by low unemployment and relatively high total income, which together ensure high buying power (provided the inflation rate stays low)

recession A stage of the business cycle during which unemployment rises and total buying power declines, stifling both consumer and business spending

depression A stage of the business cycle when unemployment is extremely high, wages are very low, total disposable income is at a minimum, and consumers lack confidence in the economy

recovery A stage of the business cycle in which the economy moves from recession or depression toward prosperity

buying power Resources, such as money, goods, and services that can be traded in an exchange

income For an individual, the amount of money received through wages, rents, investments, pensions, and subsidy payments for a given period

power are income, credit, and wealth. For an individual, **income** is the amount of money received through wages, rents, investments, pensions, and subsidy payments for a given period, such as a month or a year. Normally this money is allocated among taxes, spending for goods and services, debt, and savings. The median household income in Canada is approximately $47 000, while the median total income for individuals is approximately $24 500.[9] However, because of regional disparities and differences in people's educational levels, abilities, occupations, and wealth, income is not equally distributed in this country.

disposable income After-tax income

Marketers are most interested in the amount of money left after payment of taxes because this **disposable income** is used for spending or saving. Because disposable income is a ready source of buying power, the total amount available in a nation is important to marketers. Several factors determine the size of total disposable income. One is the total amount of income, which is affected by wage levels, the rate of unemployment, interest rates, and dividend rates. Because disposable income is income left after taxes are paid, the number and amount of taxes directly affect the size of total disposable income. When taxes rise, disposable income declines; when taxes fall, disposable income increases.

discretionary income Disposable income available for spending and saving after an individual has purchased the basic necessities of food, clothing and shelter

Disposable income that is available for spending and saving after an individual has purchased the basic necessities of food, clothing, and shelter is called **discretionary income.** People use discretionary income to purchase entertainment, vacations, automobiles, education, pets, furniture, appliances, and so on. Changes in total discretionary income affect sales of these products, especially automobiles, furniture, large appliances, and other costly durable goods.

Credit enables people to spend future income now or in the near future. However, credit increases current buying power at the expense of future buying power. Several factors determine whether people use or forgo credit. First, credit must be available. Interest rates too affect buyers' decisions to use credit, especially for expensive purchases such as homes, appliances, and automobiles. When interest rates are low, the total cost of automobiles and houses becomes more affordable. In Canada, low interest rates over the past 10 years induced many buyers to take on the high level of debt necessary to own a home, fueling a boom in the construction of new homes and the sale of older homes. In contrast, when interest rates are high, consumers are more likely to delay buying such expensive items. Use of credit is also affected by credit terms, such as size of the down payment and amount and number of monthly payments.

wealth The accumulation of past income, natural resources, and financial resources

Wealth is the accumulation of past income, natural resources, and financial resources. It exists in many forms, including cash, securities, savings accounts, art, jewelry, and real estate. Like income, wealth is unevenly distributed. A person can have a high income and very little wealth. It is also possible, but not likely, for a person to have great wealth but little income. The significance of wealth to marketers is that as people become wealthier, they gain buying power in three ways: they can use their wealth to make current purchases, to generate income, and to acquire large amounts of credit.

Income, credit, and wealth equip consumers with buying power to purchase goods and services. Marketing managers need to be aware of current levels and expected changes in buying power in their own markets because buying power directly affects the types and quantities of goods and services customers purchase. Information about buying power is available from government sources, trade associations, and research agencies. One of the most current and comprehensive sources of buying power data is *Canadian Markets,* published annually by the Financial Post DataGroup. For U.S. buying power data, one of the most comprehensive sources is the *Sales & Marketing Management Survey of Buying Power,* published annually by *Sales & Marketing Management* magazine. Having buying power, however, does not mean consumers will buy. They must also be willing to use their buying power.

Willingness to Spend

willingness to spend An inclination to buy because of expected satisfaction from a product, influenced by the ability to buy and numerous psychological and social forces

People's **willingness to spend**—their inclination to buy because of expected satisfaction from a product—is, to some degree, related to their ability to buy. That is, people are sometimes more willing to buy if they have the buying power. However, a number of other elements also influence willingness to spend. Some elements affect specific products; others influence spending in general. A product's price and value influence almost all of us. Cross pens, for example, appeal to customers who are willing to spend more for fine writing instruments even when lower-priced pens are readily available. Increasingly, middle-class consumers seem more willing to spend on high-price luxury products, such as Juicy Couture handbags, BMW automobiles, and spa vacations, although they may shop for discounted groceries and other basic products at Wal-Mart and Zellers in order to afford the upscale products.[10] The amount of satisfaction received from a product already owned may also influence customers' desire to buy other products. Satisfaction depends not only on the quality of the currently owned product but also on numerous psychological and social forces.

Factors that affect consumers' general willingness to spend are expectations about future employment, income levels, prices, family size, and general economic conditions. Willingness to spend ordinarily declines if people are unsure whether or how long they will be employed, and usually increases if people are reasonably certain of higher incomes in the future. Expectations of rising prices in the near future may also increase willingness to spend in the present. For a given level of buying power, the larger the family, the greater the willingness to spend. One reason for this relationship is that as the size of a family increases, more dollars must be spent to provide the basic necessities to sustain family members.

Political Forces

Political, legal, and regulatory forces of the marketing environment are closely interrelated. Legislation is enacted, legal decisions are interpreted by courts, and regulatory agencies are created and operated, for the most part, by elected or appointed officials. Legislation and regulations (or their lack) reflect the current political outlook. Consequently the political forces of the marketing environment have the potential to influence marketing decisions and strategies.

Marketing organizations strive to maintain good relations with elected and appointed political officials for several reasons. Political officials well disposed toward particular firms or industries are less likely to create or enforce laws and regulations unfavourable to those companies. For example, political officials who believe oil companies are making honest efforts to control pollution are unlikely to create and enforce highly restrictive pollution control laws. In addition, governments are big buyers, and political officials can influence how much a government agency purchases and from whom. Finally, political officials can play key roles in helping organizations secure foreign markets.

Many marketers view political forces as beyond their control and simply adjust to conditions arising from those forces. Some firms, however, seek to influence the political process. In some cases, organizations publicly protest the actions of legislative bodies. More often, organizations help elect to political offices individuals who regard them positively. Much of this help is in the form of campaign contributions. As the result of a major overhaul of the Canada Elections Act in 2004, a number of restrictions and limits were introduced to regulate contributions for political activities. Individuals (Canadian citizens and permanent residents) may make financial contributions to registered parties, candidates, constituency associations, and leadership and nomination contestants, however, individuals are limited to a number of restrictions that cap calendar year contribution at $5000. Unions and corporations are no longer permitted to make political contributions to registered political parties and leadership contestants. They may, however, make maximum $1000 contributions to candidates, constituency associations and nomination contestants.[11]

Companies can also participate in the political process through lobbying to persuade public and/or government officials to favour a particular position in decision making. Many organizations concerned about the threat of legislation or regulation that may negatively affect their operations employ lobbyists to communicate their concerns to elected officials. For example, a World Health Organization (WHO) study suggested a relationship between food advertising and childhood obesity. These findings prompted the U.S. advertising industry to mount lobbying and public relations efforts to influence the regulation of food advertising.[12]

Legal and Regulatory Forces

A number of federal laws influence marketing decisions and activities. In addition to discussing these laws, which deal with competition and consumer protection, this section examines the effects of regulatory agencies and self-regulatory forces on marketing efforts.

Pro-competitive Legislation

Pro-competitive laws are designed to preserve competition. The Competition Act addresses pro-competitive business practices in two areas: restraint of trade and controlling mergers. The Competition Act prohibits such restraint of trade practices as group boycotting of suppliers or customers, price fixing, and bid rigging. However, it does allow businesses in the same industry to exchange information relating to statistics or credit information, and to cooperate in research and development.

The Competition Tribunal was established in 1986 with a mandate to maintain and encourage fair competition in Canada. The Competition Tribunal operates independently of the government and does not have investigative powers. Comprising experts in economics, business, and law, this court-like body has heard cases relating to mergers, abuse of dominant position, and unfair trade practices.

Consumer Protection Legislation

A second category of laws covered in the Competition Act relates to consumer protection. These laws address such practices as misleading advertising, bait and switch selling, and double ticketing. Under double-ticketing laws, when a product bears two price stickers, the customer is entitled to pay the lower price.

Promotion laws cover such practices as false or misleading advertising and misrepresentation of the original price. It is illegal to advertise a product that is not available in order to entice customers into the store. It is also illegal to state an original price for a product that is not accurate (bait and switch.) One Toronto-based modelling and talent agency pled guilty to charges under the Competition Act relating to misleading advertising and deceptive marketing practices. An earlier investigation had determined that the company was in the business not of securing modelling and acting jobs (as ads in the local print media suggested), but rather of selling courses or photographs. In this case, fines were imposed as a penalty.

Laws relating to product representation make it illegal to misrepresent a product or service in order to attract customers. All claims relating to the performance of the product or service must be substantiated.

Selling techniques covered under the Competition Act include pyramid sales schemes, referral selling, bait-and-switch practices, and promotional contest rules.

Encouraging Compliance with Laws and Regulations

Marketing activities are sometimes at the forefront of organizational misconduct. Legal violations usually begin when marketers develop programs that unwittingly overstep legal bounds. Many marketers lack experience in dealing with complex legal actions and decisions. Some test the limits by "pushing the envelope" of the law by operating in a questionable way to see how far they can get with certain practices before being prosecuted. Other marketers interpret regulations and statutes very strictly to avoid violating a vague law. When marketers interpret laws in relation to specific marketing practices, they often analyze recent court decisions both to better understand what the law is intended to do and to predict future court interpretations.

The enforcement of competition and consumer laws varies across the country. The Consumer Measures Committee of the Agreement on Internal Trade, a joint federal and provincial committee, works to develop cooperative enforcement of strategies and to promote harmonization between the federal and provincial governments and across provinces. Working groups under the umbrella of the committee focus their attention on specific problems such as identity theft and cost of credit disclosure.

Regulatory Agencies

Federal and provincial regulatory agencies influence many marketing activities, including product development, pricing, packaging, advertising, personal selling, and distribution. Federal agencies fall into two categories: those that have the power to regulate industries and those that provide advice and guidance to Canadian business. Because of this discretion and overlapping areas of responsibility, confusion or conflict regarding which agencies have jurisdiction over which marketing activities is common.

Regulatory agencies that have the power to govern industries usually have well-defined mandates. For example, the National Energy Board regulates the importing and exporting of natural gas, oil, and electricity, in addition to providing advice to the Minister of Natural Resources of Canada. Of particular interest to marketers is the Canadian Radio-television and Telecommunications Commission (CRTC), which supervises and regulates Canada's broadcasting and telecommunications systems. The CRTC works closely with this industry to set standards in a wide range of areas, including television violence, gender portrayal, ethnic and minority representation, and advertising aimed at children. The CRTC is also responsible for regulating the organizations that supply industry-related technology, including cable, satellite, and direct-to-home TV systems.[13]

Federal agencies that provide advice and guidance may facilitate the movement of businesses into new international markets or provide interpretations of industry specific laws. For example, the Canadian Environmental Assessment Agency provides

table 3.2 EXAMPLES OF FEDERAL AGENCIES

Agency	Major Areas of Responsibility
Canadian Radio-television and Telecommunications Commission (CRTC)	Supervises and regulates Canada's broadcasting and telecommunications systems
Canadian Environmental Assessment Agency	Administers and promotes environmental assessment policies and practices
Canadian Intellectual Property Office	Provides information on possible changes to intellectual property policies and legislation, and develops specific proposals relating to these areas
Canadian Tourism Commission	Expands marketing in domestic and major international markets in partnership with tourism industry
Communications Research Centre	Undertakes research on the interoperability and interconnectivity of radio, satcom, and fibre-optic systems
Measurement Canada	Ensures trade conformity with the Weights and Measures Act and the Electricity and Gas Inspection Act
Technology Partnerships Canada	Invests in research, development, demonstration, market development of environmental technologies, strategic enabling technologies, and the aerospace and defence industries
Office of Consumer Affairs	Protects consumer interests in the event of a market failure

information on environmental procedures and assessment of projects, while the Canadian Space Agency assists Canadian organizations with the objective of developing an internationally competitive space industry in Canada. Table 3.2 outlines areas of responsibility of eight federal agencies, all of which are part of Industry Canada.

In addition, all provinces, as well as many cities and towns, have regulatory bodies that enforce laws and regulations regarding marketing practices within their jurisdiction. Provinces and local regulatory agencies try not to establish regulations that conflict with those of federal regulatory agencies. They generally enforce laws dealing with the production and sale of particular goods and services. Education, health, electrical, credit unions, and liquor sales are commonly regulated by provincial regulatory agencies.

Self-Regulatory Forces

In an attempt to be good corporate citizens and prevent government intervention, some businesses try to regulate themselves. Kraft Foods, for example, stopped advertising sugary snacks and cereals to children under 12 in response to growing concerns about childhood obesity and its effects on children's long-term health. While some competitors were astonished by the decision, Kraft executives recognized that if food product marketers did not begin to police themselves, the government could impose restrictions on advertising to children and the businesses in the industry could face potential lawsuits.[14] Similarly, a number of trade associations have developed self-regulatory programs. Though these programs are not a direct outgrowth of laws, many were established to stop or stall the development of laws and governmental regulatory groups that would regulate the associations' members' marketing practices. Sometimes trade associations establish ethics codes by which their members must abide or risk censure or exclusion from the association. An example of such a code is the Canadian Marketing Association's Code of Ethics and Standards of Practice that will be discussed in Chapter 4. A particularly effective non-governmental standards association is the Canadian Standards Association, a standards development and certification organization that operates internationally.

Better Business Bureau (BBB)
A system of non-governmental, independent, local regulatory agencies supported by local businesses that helps settle problems between customers and specific business firms

Perhaps the best-known self-regulatory group is the **Better Business Bureau (BBB),** which is a system of non-governmental, independent, local regulatory agencies that are supported by local businesses. The Canadian Council of Better Business Bureaus is the governing body of the 14 Better Business Bureaus across Canada (www.ccbbb.ca). Each bureau acts to preserve good business practices in a locality, although it usually lacks strong enforcement tools for dealing with firms that employ questionable practices. When a firm continues to violate what the Better Business Bureau believes to be good business practices, the bureau warns consumers through local newspapers or broadcast media. If the offending organization is a BBB member, it may be expelled from the local bureau.

Another self-regulatory body, Advertising Standards Canada (ASC), administers the Canadian Code of Advertising Standards, handles complaints relating to advertising, provides clearance services for advertising of regulated products, and offers consultative services to the marketing communications industry. The Code sets the standards for acceptable advertising and helps ensure that the ads you see and hear are truthful, fair and accurate. Complaints received by the ASC that raise a potential Code issue are reviewed by independent, volunteer bodies—national and regional Consumer Response Councils comprising representatives from the advertising industry and the public. The Code and details of consumers' complaints regarding advertisements that were found by Council to contravene the Code can be reviewed at www.adstandards.com.

Self-regulatory programs have several advantages over governmental laws and regulatory agencies. Establishment and implementation are usually less expensive, and guidelines are generally more realistic and operational. In addition, effective self-regulatory programs reduce the need to expand government bureaucracy. However, these programs have several limitations. When a trade association creates a set of industry guidelines for its members, nonmember firms do not have to abide by them. Furthermore, many self-regulatory programs lack the tools or authority to enforce guidelines. Finally, guidelines in self-regulatory programs are often less strict than those established by government agencies.

Technological Forces

technology The application of knowledge and tools to solve problems and perform tasks more efficiently

The word *technology* brings to mind scientific advances such as information technology and biotechnology, which have resulted in the Internet, cell phones, cloning, stem-cell research, pharmaceutical products, lasers, and more. Technology has revolutionized the products created and offered by marketers, and the channels by which they communicate about those products. However, even though these innovations are outgrowths of technology, none of them *is* technology. **Technology** is the application of knowledge and tools to solve problems and perform tasks more efficiently. Technology grows out of research performed by businesses, universities, government agencies, and non-profit organizations. More than half of this research is paid for by the federal government, which supports research in such diverse areas as health, defence, agriculture, energy, and pollution.

The rapid technological growth of the last several decades is expected to accelerate. It has transformed Canada by changing how and where we work, the skills we require, and the functions of government and regulatory bodies.[15] Technology and technological advancements clearly influence buyers' and marketers' decisions, so let's take a closer look at the impact of technology and its use in the marketplace.

Impact of Technology

Technology determines how we, as members of society, satisfy our physiological needs. In various ways and to varying degrees, eating and drinking habits, sleeping patterns, sexual activities, health care, and work performance are all influenced by both existing technology and changes in technology. Because of the technological revolution in communications, for example, marketers can now reach vast numbers of people more efficiently through a variety of media. E-mail, voice mail, cell phones, pagers, and PDAs help marketers stay in touch with clients, make appointments, and handle last-minute orders or cancellations. Some companies, including Ford Motor, are even abandoning the use of traditional wired telephones in favour of exclusive use of cell phones in the workplace.[16] A growing number of households have given up their "land lines" in favour of using cell phones as their primary phones, and growth in wireless subscriptions is expected to continue for the foreseeable future.

Although we enjoy the benefits of communicating through the Internet, we are increasingly concerned about protecting our privacy and intellectual property. Likewise, although health and medical research have created new drugs that save lives, cloning and genetically modified foods have become controversial issues in many segments of society. In various ways and to varying degrees, home environments, health care, leisure, shopping, and work performance are all influenced by both current technology and advances in technology.[17] The impact of e-commerce on shopping behaviour is just one example. Canadians now order over $7.9 billion worth of goods and services over the Internet and place approximately 50 million orders online each year.[18]

The effects of technology relate to such characteristics as dynamics, reach, and the

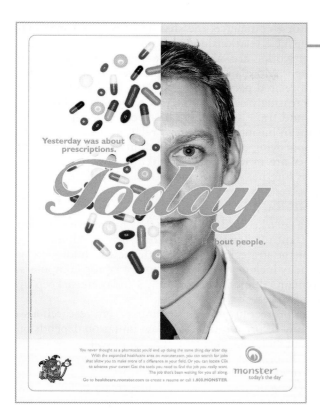

Yesterday was about prescriptions.

Today

...bout people.

You never thought as a pharmacist you'd end up doing the same thing day after day. With the expanded healthcare area on monster.com, you can search for jobs that allow you to make more of a difference in your field. Or you can locate CEs to advance your career. Get the tools you need to find the job you really want. The job that's been waiting for you all along.

Go to healthcare.monster.com to create a resume or call 1.800.MONSTER.

monster
today's the day™

The Impact of Technology

Monster.ca has changed the way people search for jobs by allowing them to post resumes online.

self-sustaining nature of technological progress. The *dynamics* of technology involve the constant change that often challenges the structures of social institutions, including social relationships, the legal system, religion, education, business, and leisure. *Reach* refers to the broad nature of technology as it moves through society. Consider the impact of cell phones. The ability to call from almost any location has many benefits but also negative side effects, including increases in traffic accidents, increased noise pollution, and fears about potential health risks.[19]

The *self-sustaining* nature of technology relates to the fact that technology acts as a catalyst to spur even faster development. As new innovations are introduced, they stimulate the need for more advancements to facilitate further development. For example, the Internet has created the need for ever-faster transmission of signals through broadband connections such as high-speed phone lines (DSL), satellites, and cable. Technology initiates a change process that creates new opportunities for new technologies in every industry segment or personal life experience that it touches. At some point, there is a multiplier effect that causes still greater demand for more change to improve performance.[20]

Technology Goes to the Dogs

We love our pets. A recent survey reveals that four out of five pet owners consider their pets to be their children, and market trends confirm this. The pet industry has more than doubled in size in the past 10 years. Fueling this trend are empty nesters and young adults who are having children later and spending their time and energy with their animals. As well, the pet industry has grown increasingly sophisticated at consumer marketing and has introduced a steady stream of new, high-tech pet products, all of which are vying for pet owners' dollars.

For example, the ThirstAlert! from JoBananas Club flashes red lights when the water level in your pet's bowl gets low. A deluxe version is scheduled for release next year that will send an e-mail or text message to let you know when your pet's bowl is empty. The Careful Clipper by Dogmatic marks the first renovation to the pet nail clipper in 20 years. It features an ergonomic handle and flexible snake light that allows you to see through almost any nail to avoid cutting the quick. The K&H Cool Bed absorbs heat from your pet and radiates the heat back into the air. And the Petmate Electronic Portion Control LeBistro is a programmable, electronic dispenser that holds more than five pounds (2.3 kg) of food and dispenses portions of up to three cups at selected times in the day.

With more of us falling in love with our pets, this industry is quickly growing and is proving to be as responsive to technology as any other market.

The expanding opportunities for e-commerce, the sharing of business information, and the ability to maintain business relationships and conduct business transactions via telecommunications networks are already changing the relationship between businesses and consumers.[21] More and more people are turning to the Internet to purchase computers and related peripherals, software, books, music, and even furniture. Consumers are increasingly using the Internet to book travel reservations, transact banking business, and trade securities. The forces unleashed by the Internet are particularly important in business-to-business relationships, where uncertainties are being reduced by improving the quantity, reliability, and timeliness of information. Numerous companies are moving toward making most of their purchases online. Business-to-business Internet sales are more than $5 trillion.[22]

Adoption and Use of Technology

Many companies lose their status as market leaders because they fail to keep up with technological changes. It is important for firms to determine when a technology is changing the industry and to define the strategic influence of the new technology. For example, wireless devices in use today include radios, cell phones, laptop computers, TVs, pagers, and car keys. To remain competitive, companies today must keep up with and adapt to technological advances.

The extent to which a firm can protect inventions stemming from research also influences its use of technology. How secure a product is from imitation depends on how easily others can copy it without violating its patent. If groundbreaking products and processes cannot be protected through patents, a company is less likely to market them and make the benefits of its research available to competitors.

Through a procedure known as *technology assessment*, managers try to foresee the effects of new products and processes on their firm's operations, on other business organizations, and on society in general. With information obtained through a technology assessment, management tries to estimate whether benefits of adopting a specific technology outweigh costs to the firm and to society at large. The degree to which a business is technologically based also influences its managers' response to technology.

Sociocultural Forces

sociocultural forces
The influences in a society and its culture(s) that change people's attitudes, beliefs, norms, customs, and lifestyles

Sociocultural forces are the influences in a society and its culture(s) that bring about changes in people's attitudes, beliefs, norms, customs, and lifestyles. Profoundly affecting how people live, these forces help determine what, where, how, and when people buy products. Like the other environmental forces, sociocultural forces present marketers with both challenges and opportunities. For a closer look at sociocultural forces, we examine three major issues: demographic and diversity characteristics, cultural values, and consumerism.

Demographic and Diversity Characteristics

Changes in a population's demographic characteristics—age, gender, race, ethnicity, marital and parental status, income, and education—have a significant bearing on relationships and individual behaviour. These shifts lead to changes in how people live and ultimately in their consumption of such products as food, clothing, housing, transportation, communication, recreation, education, and health services. We look at a few of the changes in demographics and diversity that are affecting marketing activities.

One major demographic change affecting the marketplace is the increasing proportion of older consumers. A Standing Senate Committee on Banking, Trade, and Commerce tabled a report on this issue in 2006, entitled, *The Demographic Time Bomb: Mitigating the Effects of Demographic Change in Canada*. Demographic change facts identified in the report include:

- Canada's birthrate is about 40 percent below the level needed to avoid long-term population loss;

- By 2031, about 25 percent of Canadians will be aged 65 years or older, up from 13 percent currently;

- Per capita public spending on health care for those age 65 and over is estimated to be almost five times greater than spending on the rest of the population;

- Since 2000, immigration has represented more than 60 percent of the population growth in Canada; and

- By 2030, it is predicted that there will be 40 retirees for every 100 working-age persons, up from 21 for every 100 in 2003.[23]

Consequently, we expect public policy to be amended to encourage strategically planned immigration, increased accountability measures for health-care services, and productivity growth as a means to improve Canadians' living standards. For marketers, we expect significant increases in the demand for health-care services, recreation, tourism, retirement housing, and selected skin-care products. Many organizations have already begun adapting their marketing strategies to accommodate and better serve the aging population. Real estate developers across Canada have begun providing housing options specifically designed for older residents. Also, many travel and tourism service providers, such as VIA Rail, Air Canada, and most hotel chains, offer seniors' discounts ranging from 10 to 25 percent. To reach older customers effectively, of course, marketers must understand the diversity within the mature market with respect to geographic location, income, marital status, and limitations in mobility and self-care.

The number of singles is also on the rise. This is the result of a combination of factors such as divorce, aging and living longer (thus outliving a spouse), and deliberate choice not to marry. Interestingly, cultural factors impact marriage expectations. For example, a Statistics Canada study found that the odds of not expecting marriage were

Demographic Changes

In Canada, we are building more old people than new people. Some marketers are changing their product offerings to provide a greater number of products that meet the needs of older people.

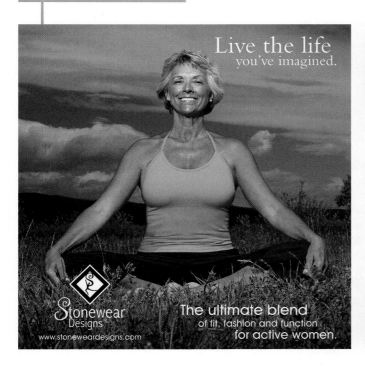

Live the life you've imagined.

Stonewear Designs®
www.stoneweardesigns.com

The ultimate blend of fit, fashion and function for active women.

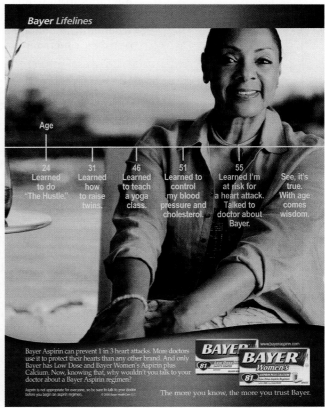

Bayer Lifelines

Age

24 Learned to do "The Hustle."

31 Learned how to raise twins.

46 Learned to teach a yoga class.

51 Learned to control my blood pressure and cholesterol.

55 Learned I'm at risk for a heart attack. Talked to doctor about Bayer.

See, it's true. With age comes wisdom.

Bayer Aspirin can prevent 1 in 3 heart attacks. More doctors use it to protect their hearts than any other brand. And only Bayer has Low Dose and Bayer Women's Aspirin plus Calcium. Now, knowing that, why wouldn't you talk to your doctor about a Bayer Aspirin regimen?

Aspirin is not appropriate for everyone, so be sure to talk to your doctor before you begin an aspirin regimen.

BAYER   BAYER Women's

The more you know, the more you trust Bayer.

Demographics and Diversity

Organizations understand the importance of responding to the needs of their ethnic customers.

five times higher for a male francophone than a male anglophone. Also, women living in Quebec have much higher odds of not expecting marriage compared with women living elsewhere in Canada.[24] Single people have quite different spending patterns than couples and families with children. They are less likely to own homes and thus buy less furniture and fewer appliances. They spend more heavily on convenience foods, restaurants, travel, entertainment, and recreation. In addition, they tend to prefer smaller packages, whereas families often buy bulk goods and products packaged in multiple servings. Services such as dating services have become increasingly popular in recent years. For example, Lavalife (www.lavalife.com) claims to be the number one dating site in Canada and reports having more than 600 000 active members exchanging over 1.3 million messages every day.[25]

Another noteworthy population trend is the increasingly multicultural nature of Canadian society. The last 40 years have seen dramatic changes in the country of origin of immigrants to Canada. Before 1960, the vast majority of those immigrants came from Europe. However, as a result of changes in Canada's immigration patterns, immigrants from China, Southeast Asia, the Middle East, the Americas (including the Caribbean), Africa, and India have come to outnumber those from Europe. Nowhere in Canada are these changes in immigration patterns more noticeable than in our major metropolitan cities.

Boomers: Not Babies Anymore

Few factors have influenced the North American marketing environment more than the emergence of the baby boom generation. Approximately one-third of Canadians fall into the category of baby boomers, or those born between the years 1947 and 1966. During this period, World War II veterans and their families reaped the benefits of an expanding economy. The Canadian boom was further encouraged by the arrival of immigrants displaced by the war. The birthrate started to decline in 1966, in part the result of increasing numbers of women in the workforce.

The baby boomers redefined every stage of the life cycle as they passed through it. They created the youth culture that brought us muscle cars, jeans, rock music, and sexual permissiveness. Many social—and therefore marketing—trends can be explained by the boomer phenomenon. Both the 1980s trend toward environmentally friendly products and the decline of this trend in the 1990s can be attributed to the boomer segment of the market. Boomers are also the driving force behind retirement related products, the popularity of golf, and the sales of products such as pharmaceuticals, motor homes, boats, and vacation properties.

As the boomers get older, their needs and tastes will change, and successful marketers will change with them. To identify necessary product changes, Ford has begun using a specially designed suit to simulate the challenges faced by elderly drivers. Whirlpool has unveiled elevated washers and dryers that make it easier to load and unload laundry. Home Depot has expanded the company's services to help older customers make home improvements.

Marketers need to recognize that these profound changes in the Canadian population bring unique problems and opportunities. A diverse population means a more diverse customer base, and marketing practices that must be modified—and diversified—to meet changing needs. Research indicates that ethnic Canadian minorities are more likely to purchase products if they are represented in advertisements for the products.[26] To respond to the needs of the increasing multicultural diversity in Canada, marketers have developed multicultural marketing programs designed to respond to the communication needs, lifestyles, and country-of-origin product preferences of ethnic markets.

According to Ashwin W. Joshi, professor of marketing at the Schulich School of Business at York University, there is a cultural disconnect between marketers and their customers. "Marketers are unhappy that their advertising campaigns toward Canadians are not working, and new Canadians complain that their needs are not being met." Accordingly, Joshi recommends that marketers gain an intimate knowledge of customers, "multicultural marketing involves becoming part of the cultural community." Joshi recommends that marketers need to learn the language, watch the movies, participate in community events, hire employees from the community—in short, marketers need to develop deep and enduring bonds if they want their multicultural marketing programs to work.[27]

Cultural Values

Changes in cultural values have dramatically influenced people's needs and desires for products. Although cultural values do not shift overnight, they do change at varying speeds. Marketers try to monitor these changes, knowing this information can equip them to predict changes in consumers' needs for products at least in the near future.

Starting in the late 1980s, issues of health, nutrition, and exercise grew in importance. People today are more concerned about the foods they eat and thus are choosing healthier products. Compared with those in the previous two decades, Canadians today are more likely to favour smoke-free environments and to consume less alcohol. They have also altered their sexual behaviour to reduce the risk of contracting sexually transmitted diseases. Marketers have responded with a proliferation of foods, beverages, and exercise products that fit this new lifestyle, as well as with programs to help people quit smoking and contraceptives that are safer and more effective. Canadians are also becoming increasingly open to alternative medicines and nutritionally improved foods. As a result, sales of organic foods, herbs and herbal remedies, vitamins, and dietary supplements have escalated. More marketers are investing in research into traditional herbal medicines and fortified foods to take advantage of this market opportunity. Celestial Seasonings, for example, has developed herbal teas like Mama Bear's Cold Care, with Echinacea and mint, and Sleepytime, with chamomile.

The major source of cultural values is the family. For years, when asked about the most important aspects of their lives, adults specified family issues and a happy marriage. Today, however, less than half of all

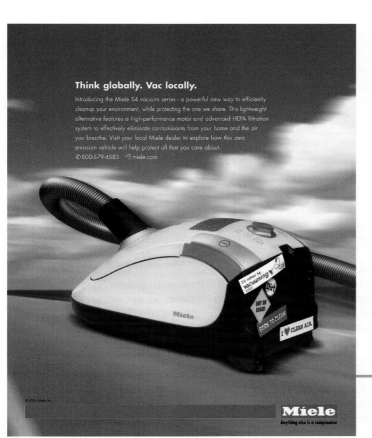

Think globally. Vac locally.

Introducing the Miele S4 vacuum series - a powerful new way to efficiently cleanup your environment, while protecting the one we share. This lightweight alternative features a high-performance motor and advanced HEPA filtration system to effectively eliminate contaminants from your home and the air you breathe. Visit your local Miele dealer to explore how this zero emission vehicle will help protect all that you care about.
800-579-4583   miele.com

Miele
Anything else is a compromise

Cultural Values

Changes in cultural values have resulted in a greater emphasis on preserving the environment. Vacuum cleaner maker Miele is responding to concerns about the environment.

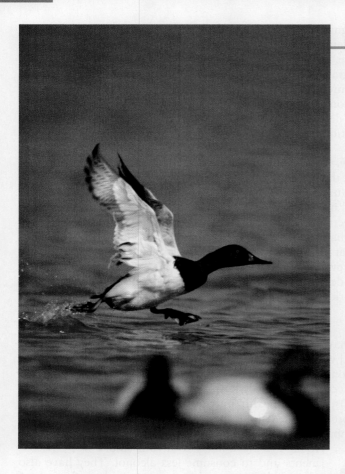

Cultural Values
Organizations respond to our cultural concern for environmental safety and conservation by supporting organizations such as Ducks Unlimited Canada.

marriages are predicted to last. Values regarding the permanence of marriage are changing. Because a happy marriage is prized so highly, more people are willing to give up an unhappy one and seek a different marriage partner or opt to stay single. Children remain important, however. Marketers have responded with safer, upscale baby gear and supplies, children's electronics, and family entertainment products. Marketers are also aiming more marketing efforts directly at children because children often play pivotal roles in purchasing decisions.

Children and family values are also factors in the trend toward more eat-out and take-out meals. Busy families in which both parents work are usually eager to spend less time in the kitchen and more time together enjoying themselves. Beneficiaries of this trend have primarily been fast-food and casual restaurants like McDonald's, Dairy Queen, and Boston Pizza. Also, most grocery stores have added more ready-to-cook or ready-to-serve meal components to meet the needs of busy customers. Some also offer dine-in cafés.

Today's consumers are more and more concerned about the natural environment. One of society's environmental hurdles is proper disposal of waste, especially of non-degradable materials such as disposable diapers and polystyrene packaging. Companies have responded by developing more environmentally-sensitive products and packaging. Procter & Gamble, for example, uses recycled materials in some of its packaging and sells environment-friendly refills. Raytheon has developed a new Amana refrigerator that does not use chlorofluorocarbons (CFCs), which harm the earth's ozone layer. A number of marketers sponsor recycling programs and encourage their customers to take part in them. Corporations can show their environmental responsibility by supporting organizations like Ducks Unlimited Canada (www.ducks.ca), which raises millions a year through cash donations (corporate and private), asset donations, and credit-card affinity programs to help conserve, restore and manage wetlands.

Consumerism

consumerism Organized efforts by individuals, groups, and organizations to protect consumers' rights

Consumerism involves organized efforts by individuals, groups, and organizations to protect consumers' rights. The movement's major forces are individual consumer advocates, consumer organizations and other interest groups, consumer education, and consumer laws.

To achieve their objectives, consumers and their advocates write letters or send e-mails to companies, lobby government agencies, broadcast public service announcements, and boycott companies whose activities they deem irresponsible. Consider that most consumers would like to eliminate telemarketing and e-mail spam, and many have joined organizations and groups attempting to stop these activities. Companies that consistently and willfully ignore society's wishes on these issues fuel public desire for a regulatory response.[28] For example, several organizations evaluate children's products for safety, often announcing dangerous products before Christmas so parents can avoid them. Other actions by the consumer movement have resulted in seat belts and air bags in automobiles, dolphin-safe tuna, the banning of unsafe three-wheel motorized vehicles, and numerous laws regulating product safety and information. We take a closer look at consumerism in the next chapter.

SUMMARY

The marketing environment consists of external forces that directly or indirectly influence an organization's acquisition of inputs (personnel, financial resources, raw materials, and information) and generation of outputs (goods, services, and ideas). The marketing environment includes competitive, economic, political, legal and regulatory, technological, and sociocultural forces.

Environmental scanning is the process of collecting information about forces in the marketing environment; environmental analysis is the process of assessing and interpreting information obtained in scanning. This information helps marketing managers predict opportunities and threats associated with environmental fluctuation. Marketing managers may assume either a passive, reactive approach or a proactive, aggressive approach in responding to these environmental fluctuations. The choice depends on the organization's structures and needs and on the composition of environmental forces that affect it.

All businesses compete for customers' dollars. A marketer, however, generally defines *competition* as other firms that market products that are similar to or can be substituted for its products in the same geographic area. These competitors can be classified into one of four types: brand competitors, product competitors, generic competitors, and total budget competitors. The number of firms controlling the supply of a product may affect the strength of competitors. The four general types of competitive structures are monopoly, oligopoly, monopolistic competition, and pure competition. Marketers monitor what competitors are currently doing and assess changes occurring in the competitive environment.

General economic conditions, buying power, and willingness to spend can strongly influence marketing decisions and activities. The overall state of the economy fluctuates in a general pattern known as the business cycle, which consists of four stages: prosperity, recession, depression, and recovery. Consumers' goods, services, and financial holdings make up their buying power, or ability to purchase. Financial sources of buying power are income, credit, and wealth. After-tax income used for spending or saving is disposable income. Disposable income left after an individual has purchased the basic necessities of food, clothes, and shelter is discretionary income. Factors affecting buyers' willingness to spend include product price; level of satisfaction obtained from currently used products; family size; and expectations about future employment, income, prices, and general economic conditions.

The political, legal, and regulatory forces of the marketing environment are closely interrelated. The political environment may determine what laws and regulations affecting specific marketers are enacted and how much the government purchases and from which suppliers. It can also be important in helping organizations secure foreign markets.

Federal legislation affecting marketing activities can be divided into pro-competitive legislation—laws designed to preserve and encourage competition—and consumer protection laws, which generally relate to issues such as pricing, misleading advertising, product misrepresentation, and selling techniques. Actual effects of legislation are determined by how marketers and courts interpret the laws.

Federal, provincial, and local regulatory agencies usually have power to enforce specific laws and some discretion in establishing operating rules and drawing up regulations to guide certain types of industry practices. Industry self-regulation represents another regulatory force; marketers view this type of regulation more favourably than government action because they have more opportunity to take part in creating guidelines. Self-regulation may be less expensive than government regulation, and its guidelines are generally more realistic. However, such regulation generally cannot ensure compliance as effectively as government agencies.

Technology is the application of knowledge and tools to solve problems and perform tasks more efficiently. Consumer demand, product development, packaging, promotion, prices, and distribution systems are all influenced directly by technology.

Sociocultural forces are the influences in a society and its culture that result in changes in attitudes, beliefs, norms, customs, and lifestyles. Major sociocultural issues directly affecting marketers include demographic and diversity characteristics, cultural values, and consumerism. Changes in a population's demographic characteristics, such as age, income, and ethnicity, can lead to changes in that population's consumption of products. Changes in cultural values, such as those relating to health, nutrition, family, and the natural environment, have had striking effects on people's needs for products and therefore are closely monitored by marketers. Consumerism involves the efforts of individuals, groups, and organizations to protect consumers' rights. Consumer rights organizations inform and organize other consumers, raise issues, help businesses develop consumer-oriented programs, and pressure lawmakers to enact consumer protection laws.

Please visit the student website at **www.hmco.ca/marketing** for ACE Self-Test questions that will help you prepare for exams.

IMPORTANT TERMS

Environmental scanning	Monopoly	Depression	Willingness to spend
Environmental analysis	Oligopoly	Recovery	Better Business Bureau
Competition	Monopolistic competition	Buying power	(BBB)
Brand competitors	Pure competition	Income	Technology
Product competitors	Business cycle	Disposable income	Sociocultural forces
Generic competitors	Prosperity	Discretionary income	Consumerism
Total budget competitors	Recession	Wealth	

DISCUSSION & REVIEW QUESTIONS

1. Why are environmental scanning and analysis important to marketers?

2. What are the four types of competition? Which is most important to marketers?

3. In what ways can each of the business cycle stages affect consumers' reactions to marketing strategies?

4. What business cycle stage are we experiencing currently? How is this stage affecting business firms in your area?

5. Define *income, disposable income,* and *discretionary income.* How does each type of income affect consumer buying power?

6. How do wealth and consumer credit affect consumer buying power?

7. What factors influence a buyer's willingness to spend?

8. Describe marketers' attempts to influence political forces.

9. What types of problems do marketers experience as they interpret legislation?

10. What is the role of the CRTC? List the ways in which the CRTC affects marketing activities. Do you think a single regulatory agency should have such a jurisdiction over marketing practices? Why or why not?

11. Name several non-governmental regulatory forces. Do you believe self-regulation is more or less effective than governmental regulatory agencies? Why?

12. What does the term *technology* mean to you? Do the benefits of technology outweigh its costs and potential dangers? Defend your answer.

13. Discuss the impact of technology on marketing activities.

14. What factors determine whether a business organization adopts and uses technology?

15. In what ways are cultural values changing? How are marketers responding to these changes?

16. Describe consumerism. Analyze some active consumer forces in your area.

APPLICATION QUESTIONS

1. Assume you are opening one of the following retail stores. Identify publications at the library or online that provide information about the environmental forces likely to affect the store. Briefly summarize the information each source provides.
   a. Convenience store
   b. Women's clothing store
   c. Grocery store
   d. Fast-food restaurant
   e. Furniture store

2. For both of the following products, identify brand competitors, product competitors, generic competitors, and total budget competitors.
   a. Dodge Caravan minivan
   b. Levi's jeans

3. Technological advances and sociocultural forces have a great impact on marketers. Identify at least one technological advance and one sociocultural change that has affected you as a consumer. Explain the impact of each change on your needs as a customer.

globalEDGE™

1. Free trade influences the global marketing environment in many ways. Though contingent on the bylaws of a specific free-trade agreement, such contracts between countries typically increase the number of competitors from abroad contending with current players in the market. The Free Trade Area of the Americas (FTAA) is one such example. More information about this trade agreement can be found using the search term "FTAA" at **http://globaledge.msu.edu/ibrd** or **http://globaledge.msu.edu/ibrd/ibrd.asp** to access the FTAA. How many FTAA members are there? Besides Canada, which are the most prominent members? Are there any countries that are conspicuously absent?

2. Globalization is a phenomenon that is affecting many countries. As a result, your firm is attempting to define its own role in a globalizing environment with a particular focus on western Europe. Public opinion regarding the globalization trend is likely to influence many competitive and market forces worldwide for a prolonged period of time. To gain valuable information about attitudes toward globalization in western European countries, use the search term "public opinion analysis" at **http://globaledge.msu.edu/ibrd** or **http://globaledge.msu.edu/ibrd/ibrd.asp** to access the Eurobarometer website and follow the Globalization link. To help your firm develop its European marketing strategy, identify the top two markets that support globalization and the top four markets that oppose globalization. From these results, what conclusions do you draw in your effort to enter these markets?

INTERNET Exercise

Visit **www.hmco.ca/marketing** for resources to help you master the material in this chapter, plus materials that will help you expand your marketing knowledge, including Internet exercise updates, ACE self-tests, hotlinks to companies featured in this chapter, and much more.

Industry Canada

To learn more about the Industry Canada and its mandate, look at IC's website at www.ic.gc.ca

1. Based on information on the website, describe Industry Canada's mandate.
2. Examine the section entitled Acts. Describe the degree to which legislation attempts to regulate Canadian business activities.
3. How could Industry Canada's website assist a company in avoiding misconduct?

Case 3.1   At Life is good.®, Life Is Great

Brothers John and Bert Jacobs believe in doing what you love and loving what you do. Not interested in the 9-to-5, they came up with the challenging—some might say crazy—idea of selling T-shirts with original designs door-to-door on New England college campuses. The pair travelled around and lived in a van, living off peanut butter and jelly and using their T-shirt inventory as pillows and blankets. "There were nights when it would be zero degrees and we'd be freezing in the van, burying ourselves in T-shirts," recalls John. "But we also had a lot of laughs. Life was good, even when we were sleeping in the van." It was this positive attitude, along with odd jobs delivering pizza and teaching skiing lessons, that kept the Jacobs brothers going.

John was an art major in college and designed a cartoon character the brothers named Jake, a shorter version of their last name that was their mutual high school nickname. Jake is a cartoon stick figure with a gigantic smile, an artist's beret, and very cool sunglasses. Armed with $78 dollars, John and Bert printed a run of T-shirts featuring the laid-back Jake and their own personal motto: "Life is good." At that point, a normal day of sales was around 20 shirts, so when the entire 48-shirt production of Jake sold out before noon, John and Bert knew they were onto something. Startled by the popularity of Jake and his "Life is good." attitude, the brothers scrapped all of their other designs and began printing only Jake. They sold $80 000 dollars of T-shirts the first year.

Today, life is indeed very good for the Jacobs brothers. Their company, aptly named Life is good., sells over $55 million dollars' worth of T-shirts and other merchandise annually. Jake is still the primary image of the brand. "Jake is our leader," claims Bert. An outdoorsy type who takes it easy and enjoys the simple things in life, "[Jake] could be any demographic; that's the beauty of him. He's just a free-thinking guy who doesn't take things too seriously." These days Jake appears hiking, rollerblading, golfing, practicing yoga, or relaxing in a hammock or beach chair. He has adopted a dog named Rocket and briefly had a female counterpart named Jackie. The character was dropped because the Jacobs felt that she detracted from Jake's ability to represent everyone. "Sure, Jake's a guy, but really, he's a stick figure. He's supposed to represent a feeling," explains Bert. And the feeling must be contagious because Jake has become a phenomenon.

But Jake and Rocket aren't limited to T-shirts anymore. Since the company officially started in 1994, the product catalog has grown from a single page to over 70 pages. There are successful lines of Life is good. hats, yoga apparel, baby clothes, Frisbees, stickers, beach towels, and coffee mugs. The company has also added metal and stone jewelry engraved with Jake's smiling face. Life is good. flip flops and sandals were a natural choice for this laid-back company because the Jacobs brothers wear them every day to work. The focus on sporting goods has increased, as the brothers have added performance items like river shorts for hiking and boating. Bert says that furniture is in the works as well. In fact, although the brothers insist that T-shirts are still the heart of the brand, they now make up only a small portion of the company's sales. Life is good. has adapted

its catalog to continue growth, but the broad appeal of its products increases the number of competitors to sporting goods, surf and skate, resort, running, spa and wellness, and golf apparel.

With outlets in the US, Canada, Mexico, Japan, Greece, and Germany—as well as many stores that carry the line—one of the most amazing parts of the Life is good. story is that the company has never used paid advertising. It has relied solely on word of mouth to spread its good cheer. Because of their focus on creating positive change, Bert and John have rejected several multi-million-dollar buyout offers. Instead, they are focusing on keeping Life is good. on the right track financially and socially. Although Life is good. is constantly adapting to change, the Jacobs brothers haven't changed a bit. They believe that the same positive outlook that got them through those cold nights in the back of their van is the key to their continued success. "The foundation of our brand is optimism, and optimism is timeless," explains Bert. "It always has a place in every demographic and in every economy, and it's always something that's in need."[29]

Questions for Discussion

1. Which marketing environment forces are likely to have the greatest impact on Life is good.?
2. What types of organizations are most likely to exert the greatest competitive forces on Life is good.?
3. Are there environmental forces that have contributed to the success of Life is good.? Explain.

Case 3.2 Chipping Away the Fat at Frito-Lay

Frito-Lay knows that yesterday's recipe for success is not necessarily today's. Owned by PepsiCo, Frito-Lay sells 15 billion bags of salty snacks every year under such well-known brands as Lay's, Doritos, Cheetos, Tostitos, and Ruffles. However, sales of potato chips and other similar snacks have flattened in recent years in part due to growing public concerns about widespread obesity and the health consequences of certain fats. The resulting changes in customer attitudes and regulatory guidelines have prompted Frito-Lay to reformulate both its recipes and its marketing efforts.

Food manufacturers turned to partially hydrogenated oils to enhance snack taste, texture, and stability after health experts linked the saturated fats in butter and palm oil to higher cholesterol levels and coronary heart disease. Years later, however, experts determined that these partially hydrogenated vegetable oils, also known as trans fats, were themselves linked to the risk of heart disease and diabetes. In Europe, Unilever took the early initiative in responding to these concerns by voluntarily reducing or eliminating trans fats. In fact, the success of Unilever's trans-fat-free margarine encouraged competing food manufacturers to introduce margarines made without trans fats.

In North America, governments have been slow to enact trans fats labelling requirements. In the United States, the Food and Drug Administration (FDA) deliberated for 10 years before requiring manufacturers to specify the amount of trans fats on food labels. In Canada, Health Canada in conjunction with the Heart and Stroke Foundation of Canada formed a multi-stakeholder task force on trans fat that made a number of recommendations to Health Canada in 2006.[30] As long as they did not have to change their labels, most major food manufacturers had resisted reducing or eliminating trans fats because of the expense of developing new products and changing processing systems. Meanwhile, however, customers were learning more about the dangers of trans fats, and some were switching to healthier snack alternatives. This benefited companies marketing organic and "all-natural" snacks without trans fats, but put more pressure on companies marketing snacks containing trans fats.

Frito-Lay was already offering some low-fat, reduced-fat, and no-fat snacks. For example, it made Lay's potato chips with corn oil rather than trans fats. Parent PepsiCo's senior management also recognized that customers' attitudes toward health and diet were changing. PepsiCo had invited prominent doctors to a health and wellness conference attended by representatives of Frito-Lay and other divisions. Frito-Lay's CEO vividly remembers that after the doctors told the group, "The single biggest thing you could do is to eliminate trans fats," he decided to do just that. Although this re-

quired investing in new production technologies and locating substitute ingredients, the CEO was convinced that the reformulated snacks would be more appealing to customers. Moreover, he believed the decision would demonstrate Frito-Lay's leadership within the industry, an important competitive consideration.

Based on this decision, Frito-Lay product developers came up with trans-fat-free recipes, and the company announced the changeover with a $2 million ad campaign. In addition, the company worked with a doctor to create a special Smart Snack label for products that meet certain nutritional guidelines for calorie, fat, trans fat, and sodium content. The company later changed that label to a green Smart Spot label to help customers find healthier snacks quickly. Frito-Lay's parent company also boosted promotional efforts of Smart Spot labelled products targeted at minority communities.

Eyeing the growing demand for natural products, Frito-Lay also created a line of natural, reduced-fat potato chips and introduced salty-snack alternatives such as snack bars and breakfast bars. "Today's consumers are more aware of what they eat, and we know they want better snack choices," explained Frito-Lay's vice president of North American marketing.

The company was the first in the industry to list trans-fat information on snack food labels, two years ahead of the January 2006 deadline for the new labelling rules set in the U.S. by the FDA and six months prior to Health Canada's receipt of the report from the multi-stakeholder task force on trans fat. Kraft and other Frito-Lay competitors also prepared for the change by revamping their products to reduce or replace trans fats and adding label information to comply with the new regulations. Nutrition experts agree that eliminating trans fats is a step in the right direction, but some express reservations about promoting chips and similar snacks on the basis of diet and health. "A no-trans-fat potato chip has just as many calories as a trans-fat chip," stresses a spokesperson at the Center for Science in the Public Interest.

Because Frito-Lay had addressed the trans-fat challenge in advance of new food labelling rules, it could seize the opportunity to introduce new flavours and new snacks based on feedback from marketing research. The vice president of potato chip marketing commented, "We're going back to basics with an emphasis on flavour. Consumers told us that flavour is the number one driver for eating chips." Other studies indicated that customers were choosing Procter & Gamble's Pringles crisps over Lay's chips because they wanted a "clean-eating snack." Therefore, after five years of research, development, and testing, the company introduced Lay's Stax—uniform, scoop-shaped potato crisps in a resealable plastic container—to compete head-on with Pringles.

Thanks to the new labelling requirement and increased public awareness of the health risks of trans fats, the $90 billion snack category will never be the same. Some customers will go out of their way to find snacks without trans fats, and some will use label information to compare the amount of trans fats when choosing among competing brands. Either way, Frito-Lay is in a position to benefit. Sales of Smart Spot labeled products have already climbed 13 percent and now account for 41 percent of PepsiCo's North American sales.[31]

Questions for Discussion

1. How did competition affect Frito-Lay's responses to the changes in the marketing environment? How did cultural values affect the decisions made by food manufacturers in the snack food industry?

2. Why would Frito-Lay make a point of being the first food manufacturer to eliminate trans fats from its best-selling snack products years before the new labelling requirement took effect?

CHAPTER 4

Social Responsibility and Ethics in Marketing

Cartoon Characters Lighten Up

Companies have been using cartoon characters in advertising since Mickey Mouse appeared on the Post Toasties cereal box in 1935. But today, children's advocates are growing increasingly concerned about the amount of advertising targeted at children, and particularly about the use of popular cartoon characters to promote unhealthy foods to children. Studies by the Kaiser Family Foundation (California) found that the average child sees about 40 000 advertisements a year on television, most of which endorse candy, cereal, fast food, and soft drinks. A report by the Institute of Medicine (Washington, D.C.) provided "strong evidence" that advertising is linked with obesity in young children.

The Kaiser studies suggest that food ads may not only influence the food choices children make but may confuse them regarding what is good for them and what is not. They also found that companies can have a positive impact on children by using their favourite characters to advertise healthier foods. The Institute of Medicine has also recommended that food companies use licensed characters to promote only healthful food choices.

Although some companies have been silent on the issue thus far, others are making positive changes. Kraft Foods, for example, decided to curtail advertising sugary snacks and cereals to children and has begun limiting its use of cartoon characters in an effort to support better nutrition for children younger than 12 years. PepsiCo has begun labelling some of its products to help children identify more healthful choices. Although Kellogg is using Chicken Little to advertise its cereal Fruit Loops, the cereal boxes show Chicken Little teaching children how to choose healthy breakfast foods, and Viacom recently agreed to place Sponge-Bob SquarePants on spinach packages. Although some companies are making efforts to encourage healthier food choices for children, the food industry as a whole needs to agree on the definition of a healthy food—no easy task and something many would rather not do.[1] ■

Most marketers operate responsibly and within the limits of the law. However, some companies engage in activities that customers, other marketers, and society in general deem unacceptable. Such activities include questionable selling practices, bribery, price discrimination, deceptive advertising, misleading packaging, and marketing defective products. Practices of this kind raise questions about marketers' obligations to society. Inherent in these questions are the issues of social responsibility and marketing ethics.

Because social responsibility and ethics often have profound impacts on the success of marketing strategies, we devote this chapter to their role in marketing decision making. We begin by defining social responsibility and exploring its dimensions. We then discuss social responsibility issues, such as the natural environment and the marketer's role as a member of the community. Next, we define and examine the role of ethics in marketing decisions. We consider ethical issues in marketing, the ethical decision-making process, and ways to improve ethical conduct in marketing. Finally, we incorporate social responsibility and ethics into strategic market planning.

The Nature of Social Responsibility

social responsibility An organization's obligation to maximize its positive impact and minimize its negative impact on society

In marketing, **social responsibility** refers to an organization's obligation to maximize its positive impact and minimize its negative impact on society. Social responsibility thus deals with the total effect of all marketing decisions on society. In marketing, social responsibility includes the managerial processes needed to monitor, satisfy, and even exceed stakeholder expectations and needs.[2] Remember from Chapter 1 that stakeholders are groups that have a "stake," or claim, in some aspect of a company's products, operations, markets, industry, and outcomes.

Ample evidence demonstrates that ignoring stakeholders' demands for responsible marketing can destroy customers' trust and even prompt government regulations. Irresponsible actions that anger customers, employees, or competitors may not only jeopardize a marketer's financial standing but have legal repercussions as well. For instance, after news reports that pharmaceutical giant Merck was aware that its arthritis-fighting drug Vioxx may cause heart problems, the firm's stock plummeted and hundreds of lawsuits were filed against the company. The company had already pulled the drug from the market.[3] In contrast, socially responsible activities can generate positive publicity, goodwill, and boost sales. Shoppers Drug Mart's annual Tree for Life campaign, for example, has enabled Shoppers' customers and employees to give back

The Nature of Social Responsibility

Recognizing their environmental responsibility, companies such as Canadian Tire and Shoppers Drug Mart have been recognized as good corporate and environmental citizens.

The Canadian Mint partners with Canadian organizations to allow exclusive distribution of special edition coins, such as this quarter commemorating Remembrance Day, first distributed in partnership with Tim Horton's restaurants.

marketing citizenship
The adoption of a strategic focus for fulfilling the economic, legal, ethical, and philanthropic social responsibilities expected by stakeholders

more than $5.3 million to communities in Canada. Shoppers Drug Mart is also founding sponsor of the Canadian Breast Cancer Foundation, and was exclusive distributor of the 25-cent coin featuring the iconic pink ribbon, the universal symbol of hope and awareness in the effort to create a future without breast cancer.[4]

Socially responsible efforts like Shoppers Drug Mart's have a positive impact on local communities; at the same time, they indirectly help the sponsoring organization by attracting goodwill, publicity, and potential customers and employees. Thus, while social responsibility is certainly a positive concept in itself, most organizations embrace it in the expectation of indirect long-term benefits. Our own research suggests that an organizational culture that is conducive to social responsibility engenders greater employee commitment and improved business performance.[5] Table 4.1 provides the Top 10 Corporate Citizens for 2006 as ranked in the fifth annual review ranking of Canada's Best 50 Corporate Citizens. These organizations make social responsibility a strategic long-term objective.

The Dimensions of Social Responsibility

Socially responsible organizations strive for **marketing citizenship** by adopting a strategic focus for fulfilling the economic, legal, ethical, and philanthropic social responsibilities that their stakeholders expect of them. Companies that consider the diverse perspectives of stakeholders in their daily operations and strategic planning are said to have a *stakeholder orientation*, an important element of social responsibility.[6] A stakeholder orientation in marketing goes beyond customers, competitors, and regulators to include understanding and addressing the needs of all stakeholders, including communities and special interest groups. As a result, organizations are now under pressure to undertake initiatives that demonstrate a balanced perspective on stakeholder interests.[7] Ford Motor, for example, has secured stakeholder input on a number of issues including human rights and climate change.[8] As Figure 4.1 shows, the economic, legal, ethical, and philanthropic dimensions of social responsibility can be viewed as a pyramid.[9] The economic and legal aspects have long been acknowledged, whereas ethical and philanthropic issues have gained recognition more recently.

table 4.1	CANADA'S TOP TEN CORPORATE CITIZENS FOR 2006
1	Shoppers Drug Mart
2	Rothmans Inc.
3	Reitman's (Canada) Ltd.
4	Maple Leaf Foods Inc.
5	Toyota Canada
6	Home Capital Group Inc.
7	TSX Group Inc.
8	DaimlerChrysler Canada Inc.
9	Bank of Montreal
10	Transat A.T. Inc.

Source: Press Release: "Shoppers Drug Mart Top Corporate Citizen in Canada," Corporate Knights, http://www.corporateknights.ca/info/pr/page.asp?name=best50_2006 (accessed November 11, 2006). Note: The 2006 Best 50 Corporate Citizens in Canada was sponsored by the Ethical Funds Company. Full results are available at: http://www.corporateknights.ca/downloads/best50_2006.pdf.

figure 4.1

THE PYRAMID OF CORPORATE SOCIAL RESPONSIBILITY

RESPONSIBILITIES

Philanthropic
Be a good corporate citizen
▶ Contribute resources to the community; improve quality of life

Ethical
Be ethical
▶ Obligation to do what is right, just, and fair
▶ Avoid harm

Legal
Obey the law
▶ Law is society's codification of right and wrong
▶ Play by the rules of the game

Economic
Be profitable
▶ The foundation upon which all others rest

Source: From Archie B. Carroll, "The Pyramid of Corporate Social Responsibility: Toward the Moral Management of Organizational Stakeholders," adaptation of Figure 3, p. 42. Reprinted from *Business Horizons*, July/Aug. 1991. Copyright © 1991 by the Foundation for the School of Business at Indiana University. Reprinted with permission.

At the most basic level, all companies have an economic responsibility to be profitable so they can provide a return on investment to their owners and investors, create jobs for the community, and contribute goods and services to the economy. How organizations relate to stockholders, employees, competitors, customers, the community, and the natural environment affects the economy. When economic downturns or poor decisions lead companies to lay off employees, communities often suffer as they attempt to absorb the displaced employees. Customers may experience diminished levels of service as a result of fewer experienced employees. Stock prices often decline when layoffs are announced, affecting the value of shareholders' investment portfolios. Moreover, stressed-out employees facing demands to reduce expenses may make poor decisions that affect the natural environment, product quality, employee rights, and customer service. An organization's sense of economic responsibility is especially significant for employees, raising such issues as equal job opportunities, workplace diversity, job safety, health, and employee privacy. Economic responsibilities require finding a balance between society's demand for social responsibility and investors' desire for profits.

The Dimensions of Social Responsibility

The Share Pink M&M's campaign engages in cause-related marketing by contributing $0.25 with each purchase of pink M&M's to the Canadian Breast Cancer Foundation.

Marketers also have an economic responsibility to compete fairly. Size frequently gives companies an advantage over rivals. Large firms can often generate economies of scale that allow them to put smaller firms out of business. Consequently small companies and even whole communities may resist the efforts of firms like Wal-Mart and Home Depot to open stores in their vicinity. These firms are able to operate at such low costs that small, local firms cannot compete. Though consumers appreciate lower prices, the failure of small businesses creates unemployment for some members of the community. Such issues create concerns about social responsibility for organizations, communities, and consumers.

Marketers are also expected, of course, to obey laws and regulations. The efforts of elected officials and special-interest groups to promote responsible corporate behaviour have resulted in laws and regulations designed to keep Canadian companies' actions within the range of acceptable conduct. When marketers engage in deceptive practices to advance their own interests over those of others, charges of fraud may result. In general, fraud is any purposeful communication that deceives, manipulates, or conceals facts in order to create a false impression. It is considered a crime, and convictions may result in fines, imprisonment, or both. According to a recent study released by the Canadian Coalition Against Insurance Fraud, at least 26 percent of all personal injury claims in Canada contain elements of fraud. Opportunistic fraud—exaggerating the extent of a legitimate injury for financial gain—represents the most frequent type of personal injury fraud committed. Ultimately all consumers bear the cost of this form of consumer fraud.[10]

When customers, interest groups, or businesses become outraged over what they perceive as irresponsibility on the part of a marketing organization, they may urge their

Nestlé in Africa: Doing the Right Thing

Since Nestlé, opened the first of 27 African factories in South Africa in 1927, African consumers have come to view Nestlé products as a familiar part of their lives. The company employs about 11 500 people in Africa, and only 120 of them are non-Africans. In addition, Nestlé's suppliers provide about 50 000 additional jobs there. In 2004, the dean of the University of Ibadan's Faculty of Social Sciences reported that in Nigeria "Nestlé employees earn more than the average in manufacturing. . . . More than 75 percent said that if given the choice to change jobs, they would decline."

Nestlé is the largest direct buyer of coffee in the world. Although it does not own farmland in Africa, it does work to help local farmers improve the quality of their crops and often their incomes. Improving the quality helps the farmers become more competitive in the global market.

The company is committed to improving farming labour standards, promoting local African products, preserving water, creating less waste, offering nutrition education, and fostering free trade. Nestlé also contributes to the United Nation's Millennium Development Goals in Africa, which are to eliminate extreme poverty and hunger, achieve universal primary education, promote gender equality and empower women, lessen child mortality, improve maternal health, combat HIV/AIDS and other diseases, foster environmental sustainability, and develop a global partnership for development. Peter Brabeck-Letmathe, Nestlé's chief executive, says, "We can really do good—not only for the communities and countries we're working with, but also for us."

legislators to draft new legislation to regulate the behaviour or engage in litigation to force the organization to "play by the rules."

Economic and legal responsibilities are the most basic levels of social responsibility for a good reason: failure to consider them may mean that a marketer is not around long enough to engage in ethical or philanthropic activities. Beyond these dimensions is **marketing ethics,** principles and standards that define acceptable conduct in marketing as determined by various stakeholders, including the public, government regulators, private-interest groups, consumers, industry, and the organization itself. The most basic of these principles have been codified as laws and regulations to encourage marketers to conform to society's expectations for conduct. However, marketing ethics goes beyond legal issues. Ethical marketing decisions foster trust, which helps build long-term marketing relationships. We take a more detailed look at the ethical dimension of social responsibility later in this chapter.

At the top of the pyramid of corporate responsibility (see Figure 4.1) are philanthropic responsibilities. These responsibilities, which go beyond marketing ethics, are not required of a company, but they promote human welfare or goodwill, as do the economic, legal, and ethical dimensions of social responsibility. That many companies have demonstrated philanthropic responsibility is evidenced by large donations to Canadian university fundraising campaigns, support for community-based events, and corporate initiatives such as Tim Horton's Children's Foundation. Some firms matched employee donations or provided mechanisms through which customers could donate

marketing ethics Principles and standards that define acceptable marketing conduct as determined by various stakeholders

Wal-Mart Struggles to Satisfy Stakeholders

Wal-Mart is the world's largest company with 5000 stores and 1.7 million employees around the globe; its revenues are in excess of $300 billion. It is often called a "retail giant," but some argue that this is an understatement given the enormous influence the company wields. This power has enormous ethical and social implications.

Suppliers report that Wal-Mart can dictate almost every aspect of their operations—from product design to prices—in an effort to deliver maximum savings to the consumer. To meet Wal-Mart's demands for lower prices, some suppliers have been forced to lay off employees or to move operations to countries where production costs are lower. Companies that balk risk finding their products replaced by a competitor's on Wal-Mart's lucrative shelves.

Wal-Mart stores can also wreak havoc on businesses and workers in communities. The demise of local businesses means the loss of jobs, and although Wal-Mart may rehire some workers, Wal-Mart employees generally receive lower pay and fewer benefits than workers at other retail stores. Other ethical and legal issues relate to allegations that Wal-Mart workers have been forced to work "off the clock" and that the company has discriminated against women and minorities in promotions to management positions.

Unquestionably there are benefits to Wal-Mart's philosophy: it has compelled suppliers to concentrate on efficiency and to innovate with new products, revived more than one floundering company, and directly and indirectly saved consumers an estimated $100 billion a year. But the real costs of Wal-Mart's philosophy have yet to be tallied. As the world's largest retailer, it must accept the public scrutiny and social responsibilities that come with the territory.

funds and supplies to help with relief efforts.[11] Even small companies participate in philanthropy through donations and volunteer support of local causes and international charities, such as the Red Cross and the United Way.

cause-related marketing
The practice of linking products to a particular social cause on an ongoing or short-term basis

More companies than ever are adopting a strategic approach to corporate philanthropy. Many firms link their products to a particular social cause on an ongoing or short-term basis, a practice known as **cause-related marketing.** Mothers Against Drunk Driving Canada (MADD Canada), for example, has partnered with MBNA Canada to create the first MADD Canada MasterCard. For every purchase on this card, a percentage of the value is donated directly to MADD Canada. Such cause-related programs tend to appeal to consumers because they provide an additional reason to "feel good" about their consumer spending. Marketers like the programs because well-designed ones increase sales and create feelings of respect and admiration for the companies involved. Indeed, research suggests that attitudes toward both the cause and the product may be enhanced when consumers view the association as plausible and favourable.[12] Research further indicates that such corporate support of causes generates trust in a company for 80 percent of those surveyed.[13]

strategic philanthropy
The synergistic use of organizational core competencies and resources to address key stakeholders' interests and achieve both organizational and social benefits

Some companies are beginning to extend the concept of corporate philanthropy beyond financial contributions by adopting a **strategic philanthropy** approach, the synergistic use of organizational core competencies and resources to address key stakeholders' interests and achieve both organizational and social benefits. Strategic philanthropy involves employees, organizational resources and expertise, and the ability to link those assets to the concerns of key stakeholders, including employees, customers, suppliers, and social needs. Strategic philanthropy involves both financial and non-financial contributions to stakeholders (employee time, goods and services, and company technology and equipment, as well as facilities), but it also benefits the company.[14]

marketing ENTREPRENEURS

Tom Szaky

THE BUSINESS: Terracycle, Inc.

FOUNDED: 2002

SUCCESS: Extensive product distribution in the U.S. and Canada; Exponential growth in 2006

TerraCycle Plant Food is the flagship product of Terra-Cycle, Inc. (www.terracycle .net). This product is a liquefied plant food made from worm-processed organic waste and packaged in reused soft drink bottles, many of which are collected in fund-raising efforts by school children and non-profit groups throughout the U.S. and Canada. TerraCycle, Inc. is a young, angel-funded company that was co-founded in 2002 by a Canadian entrepreneur named Tom Szaky. At the time, Tom was a 20-year-old Princeton University dropout.

TerraCycle, Inc. has received several noteworthy honours. TerraCycle Plant Food was introduced at Home Depot in Canada in 2005 and was honoured that year with Home Depot Canada's Environmental Stewardship Award. TerraCycle Plant Food is the first consumer product to earn the right to carry the Zerofootprint seal. This seal signifies that the materials and manufacturing process have virtually no negative impact on the environment (www.zerofootprint.net). Also, the Summerhill Group (www .summerhillgroup.ca) identified TerraCycle's products as "the most eco-friendly product" they have evaluated.

Zellers, with nearly 300 stores across Canada, stocks TerraCycle Plant Food throughout its locations. With its largest Canadian order coming from Zellers, TerraCycle broke the $1 000 000 mark for 2006 in Canada. Terra-Cycle's sales success here in Canada and in the U.S. has not gone unnoticed. The July 2006, *Inc.* magazine cover story touted TerraCycle Inc. the Coolest Little Startup in America.

Social Responsibility Issues

Although social responsibility may seem to be an abstract idea, managers make decisions related to social responsibility every day. To be successful, a business must determine what customers, government regulators, and competitors, as well as society in general, want or expect in terms of social responsibility. Table 4.2 summarizes three major categories of social responsibility issues: the natural environment, consumerism, and community relations.

Environmental Responsibility

The Natural Environment. One of the more common ways marketers demonstrate social responsibility is through programs designed to protect and preserve the natural environment. Many companies are making contributions to environmental protection organizations, sponsoring and participating in clean-up events, promoting recycling, retooling manufacturing processes to minimize waste and pollution, and generally reevaluating the effects of their products on the natural environment. Procter & Gamble, for example, uses recycled materials in some of its packaging and sells refills for some products, which reduces packaging waste. Canadian Tire provides on-site recycling for customers

table 4.2   SOCIAL RESPONSIBILITY ISSUES

Issue	Description	Major Social Concerns
Natural environment	Consumers insist not only on a good quality of life but on a healthful environment so they can maintain a high standard of living during their lifetimes	Conservation Water pollution Air pollution Land pollution
Consumerism	Activities undertaken by independent individuals, groups, and organizations to protect their rights as consumers	The right to safety The right to be informed The right to choose The right to be heard
Community relations	Society eager to have marketers contribute to its well-being, wishing to know what marketers do to help solve social problems	Equality issues Disadvantaged members of society Safety and health Education and general welfare

and encourages its suppliers to reduce wasteful packaging.[15] Such efforts generate positive publicity and often increase sales for the companies involved.

green marketing The specific development, pricing, promotion, and distribution of products that do not harm the natural environment

Green marketing refers to the specific development, pricing, promotion, and distribution of products that do not harm the natural environment. Toyota and Honda, for example, have succeeded in marketing "hybrid" cars that use electric motors to augment their internal-combustion engines, improving the vehicles' fuel economy without reducing their power. Ford Motor introduced the first hybrid SUV, the Escape, in 2005.[16] New Leaf Paper has taken a leadership role in the paper-production industry, producing paper made from 50–100 percent post-consumer waste instead of virgin tree pulp. The small firm's success has forced many larger competitors to introduce their own sustainable paper products. The growing trend of recycled papers is saving trees and reducing the amount of solid waste going into landfills.[17] On the other hand, some stakeholders, including customers, try to dictate companies' use of responsible suppliers and sources of products.[18] Aveda, for example, maker of earth-friendly personal-care products, only places magazine ads in magazines printed on recycled paper. The requirement has already prompted *Natural Health* to switch to recycled paper.[19]

Many products have been certified as "green" by environmental organizations such as Green Seal and carry a special logo identifying their organization as green marketers. Lumber products at Home Depot, for example, may carry a seal from

"I guess it is easy being green."

www.fordvehicles.com

Presenting the **36** mpg Ford Escape Hybrid, the most fuel-efficient SUV on Earth.* How green is that?   ESCAPE HYBRID   *Ford*

*Based on Automobil Revue, Transport Canada and US EPA. EPA estimated 36 city/31 hwy mpg, FWD. Actual mileage will vary. ©The Muppets Holding Company, LLC. All Rights Reserved.

Green Marketing

Ford recognizes the importance of producing hybrid vehicles to help protect the natural environment.

figure 4.2

EUROPE'S ECO-LABEL

the Forest Stewardship Council (FSC) to indicate they were harvested from sustainable forests using environmentally friendly methods.[20] The FSC is an international stakeholder owned network that promotes responsible management of the world's forests. Entitlement to use an FSC seal amounts to an international recognized "green" stamp of approval. A similar "green" stamp is awarded for most Chiquita bananas certified through the Rainforest Alliance's Better Banana Project as having been grown with more environmentally and labour-friendly practices.[21] In Europe, companies can voluntarily apply for an Eco-label to indicate that their products are less harmful to the environment than competing products, based on scientifically determined criteria (see Figure 4.2).

Although demand for economic, legal, and ethical solutions to environmental problems is widespread, the environmental movement in marketing includes many different groups whose values and goals often conflict. Some environmentalists and marketers believe companies should work to protect and preserve the natural environment by implementing the following goals:

1. *Eliminate the concept of waste.* Recognizing that pollution and waste usually stem from inefficiency, the question is not what to do with waste but how to make things without waste.

2. *Reinvent the concept of a product.* Products should be reduced to only three types and eventually just two. The first type is consumables, which are eaten or, when placed in the ground, turn into soil with few harmful side effects. The second type is durable goods—such as cars, televisions, computers, and refrigerators—which should be made, used, and returned to the manufacturer within a closed-loop system. Such products should be designed for disassembly and recycling. The third category is unsalables and includes such products as radioactive materials, heavy metals, and toxins. These products should always belong to the original makers who should be responsible for the products and their full life cycle effects. Reclassifying products in this way encourages manufacturers to design products more efficiently.

snapshot

Source: Data from TIAA-CREF Trust. Margin of error ±3 percentage points.

3. *Make prices reflect the cost.* Every product should reflect or at least approximate its actual cost—not only the direct cost of production but also the cost of air, water, and soil. For example, the cost of a gallon of gasoline, according to the World Resources Institute, is approximately $4.50 when pollution, waste disposal, health effects, and defense expenditures like those of the Persian Gulf and Iraq Wars are factored in.

4. *Make environmentalism profitable.* Consumers are beginning to recognize that competition in the marketplace should not occur between companies harming the environment and those trying to save it.[22]

Consumerism Another significant issue in socially responsible marketing is consumerism, which we defined in Chapter 3 as the efforts of independent individuals, groups, and organizations to protect the rights of consumers. A number of interest groups and individuals have taken action against companies they consider irresponsible by lobbying government officials and agencies, engaging in letter-writing campaigns and boycotts, and making public service announcements. Some consumers choose to boycott firms and products out of a desire to support a cause and make a difference.[23] How a firm handles customer complaints affects consumer evaluations and in turn customer satisfaction and loyalty.[24] Indeed, research suggests that angry consumers not only fail to make repeat purchases but may retaliate against the source of their dissatisfaction.[25] The consumer movement has been helped by news-format television programs, such as *CTV's W-FIVE, Dateline, 60 Minutes,* and *Prime Time Live,* as well as by 24-hour news coverage from CBC Newsworld, CNN, and MSNBC. The Internet too has changed the way consumers obtain information about companies' goods, services, and activities.

Ralph Nader, one of the best-known consumer activists, continues to crusade for consumer rights. Consumer activism by Nader and others has resulted in legislation requiring many features that make cars safer: seat belts, air bags, padded dashboards, stronger door latches, head restraints, shatterproof windshields, and collapsible steering columns. Activists' efforts have also facilitated the passage of several consumer protection laws, including the Personal Information Protection and Electronic Documents Act, also known as Canada's Privacy Act.

Also of great importance to the consumer movement are four basic rights collectively known as the consumer "bill of rights." These rights include the right to safety, the right to be informed, the right to choose, and the right to be heard.

Ensuring consumers' *right to safety* means marketers are obligated not to market a product that they know could harm consumers. This right can be extended to imply that all products must be safe for their intended use, include thorough and explicit instructions for proper and safe use, and have been tested to ensure reliability and quality.

Consumers' *right to be informed* means consumers should have access to and the opportunity to review all relevant information about a product before buying it. Many laws require specific labelling on product packaging to satisfy this right. In addition, labels on alcoholic and tobacco products must inform consumers that these products may cause illness and other problems.

The *right to choose* means consumers should have access to a variety of products and services at competitive prices. They should also be assured of satisfactory quality and service at a fair price. Activities that reduce competition among businesses in an industry might jeopardize this right.

The *right to be heard* ensures that consumers' interests will receive full and sympathetic consideration in the formulation of government policy. The right to be heard also promises consumers fair treatment when they complain to marketers about products. This right benefits marketers too because when consumers complain about a product, the manufacturer can use this information to modify the product and make it more satisfying.

Community Relations. Social responsibility also extends to marketers' roles as community members. Individual communities expect marketers to make philanthropic contributions to community projects and institutions and to be "good corporate citizens."

While most charitable donations come from individuals, corporate philanthropy is on the rise. Small- and medium-size firms can also make positive contributions to their communities. For example, Danny Murphy, owner of D.P. Murphy Inc., a corporation that operates Tim Horton's restaurants, Wendy's quick-service restaurants, and a Holiday Inn, most of which are located in Prince Edward Island, won Canada's Top Employer of Youth award, in large part to his firms lead by example philosophy. After many years of giving back to the community, people have come to anticipate Murphy's ski trips for underprivileged kids; food drives; highway cleanups; children's camps, one of which he personally runs and four others, to which he sends children; and the Easter Seals poster-child campaign. Other programs Murphy supports include a soup campaign each February (for the Heart & Stroke Foundation) and Alzheimer's Day (proceeds from every large coffee sold at select Tim Horton's locations benefit the Alzheimer's Society).[26] Danny Murphy's actions demonstrate that a marketer can significantly improve their community's quality of life through employment opportunities, a helping hand, and financial contributions to educational, health, cultural, and recreational causes.

The Nature of Ethics

As noted earlier, marketing ethics is a dimension of social responsibility involving principles and standards that define acceptable conduct in marketing. Acceptable standards of conduct in making individual and group decisions in marketing are determined by various stakeholders and by an organization's ethical climate.

Marketers should be aware of ethical standards for acceptable conduct from several viewpoints: company, industry, government, customers, special-interest groups, and society at large. When marketing activities deviate from accepted standards, the exchange process can break down, resulting in customer dissatisfaction, lack of trust, and lawsuits. In recent years, a number of ethical scandals have resulted in a massive loss of confidence in the integrity of North American businesses.[27] In fact, 73 percent of consumers say they would boycott the products of a socially irresponsible company, and 90 percent would consider switching to a competitor's products.[28] Sony BMG Music Entertainment, for example, was sharply criticized for including copy-protection software on millions of CDs. Although most marketers of music have sought innovative ways to stifle rampant CD piracy, many consumers felt that Sony's copy-protection software went too far because it could potentially disable computers or enable a hacker to unleash a virus if the CD was played on a Windows-based computer. At least one prosecutor launched an investigation into charges that the company used the software to secretly collect information on consumers' computers and send it back to the company. Sony ultimately recalled an estimated 4.7 million CDs, at a projected cost of $2 to $4 million, but not before generating considerable consumer anger and confusion over the technology as well as at least one class-action lawsuit.[29] When marketers engage in activities that deviate from accepted principles, continued marketing exchanges become difficult, if not impossible. The best time to deal with such problems is during the strategic planning process, not after major problems materialize.

As we already noted, marketing ethics goes beyond legal issues. Marketing decisions based on ethical considerations foster mutual trust in marketing relationships. Although we often try to draw a boundary between legal and ethical issues, the distinction between the two is frequently blurred in decision making. Marketers operate in an environment in which overlapping legal and ethical issues colour many decisions. To separate legal and ethical decisions, one must assume that marketing managers can instinctively differentiate legal and ethical issues. However, while the legal ramifications of some issues and problems may be obvious, others are not. Questionable decisions and actions often result in disputes that must be resolved through litigation. The legal system, therefore, provides a formal venue for marketers to resolve ethical disputes as well as legal ones. Most ethical disputes reported in the media involve the legal system at some level. In many cases, however, settlements are reached without requiring the decision of a judge or jury.

Before we proceed with our discussion of ethics in marketing, it is important to state that it is not our purpose to question anyone's ethical beliefs or personal convictions. Nor is it our purpose to examine the conduct of consumers, although some do behave unethically (engaging in, for instance, coupon fraud, shoplifting, returning clothing after wearing it, and other abuses). Instead, our goal here is to underscore the importance of resolving ethical issues in marketing and to help you learn about marketing ethics.

Ethical Issues in Marketing

An **ethical issue** is an identifiable problem, situation, or opportunity requiring an individual or organization to choose from among several actions that must be evaluated as

ethical issue An identifiable problem, situation, or opportunity requiring a choice among several actions that must be evaluated as right or wrong, ethical or unethical right or wrong, ethical or unethical. Any time an activity causes marketing managers or customers in their target market to feel manipulated or cheated, a marketing ethical issue exists, regardless of the legality of that activity. For example, organizational objectives that call for increased profits or market share may pressure marketers to knowingly bring an unsafe product to market. Such pressures represent ethical issues. Regardless of the reasons behind specific ethical issues, marketers must be able to identify those issues and decide how to resolve them. To do so requires familiarity with the many kinds of ethical issues that may arise in marketing. Research suggests that the greater the consequences associated with an issue, the more likely it will be recognized as an ethics issue and the more important it will be to making an ethical decision.[30] Some examples of ethical issues related to product, promotion, price, and distribution (the marketing mix) appear in Table 4.3.

Product-related ethical issues generally arise when marketers fail to disclose risks associated with a product or information regarding the function, value, or use of a product. Most automobile companies have experienced negative publicity associated with design or safety issues that resulted in a government-required recall of specific models. Pressures can build to substitute inferior materials or product components to reduce costs. Ethical issues also arise when marketers fail to inform customers about existing conditions or changes in product quality; such failure is a form of dishonesty about the nature of the product. Consider the introduction of a new size of candy bar, labelled with a banner touting its "new larger size." However, when placed in vending machines alongside older candy bars of the same brand, it was apparent that the product was actually slightly *smaller* than the candy bar it replaced. Although this could have been a mistake, the firm still has to defend and deal with the consequences of its actions.

Promotion can create ethical issues in a variety of ways, among them false or misleading advertising and manipulative or deceptive sales promotions, tactics, and publicity. One controversial issue in the area of promotion is the promotion of pharmaceuticals that require a doctor's prescription directly to consumers. Proponents of the practice argue that it arms consumers with more information about products that may be beneficial for their conditions. Critics worry about the potential for over treatment and have called for tighter guidelines on the promotion of drugs. With new studies suggesting that U.S. style direct-to-consumer advertising of pharmaceuticals is strongly influencing both doctors and consumers and consumers growing wary of the ads, the Pharmaceutical Research and Manufacturers of America announced plans to release voluntary guidelines to better self-regulate the industry.[31] In Canada, the Health Protection Branch of Health Canada restricts brand-specific promotion of prescription drugs. However, the Canadian drug lobby wants restrictions loosened that limit prescription drug advertising. The lobby claims the public would be well served by direct-to-consumer drug education. Many other ethical issues are linked to promotion,

table 4.3	SAMPLE ETHICAL ISSUES RELATED TO THE MARKETING MIX
Product Issue *Product information*	Covering up defects that could cause harm to a consumer; withholding critical performance information that could affect a purchase decision.
Distribution Issue *Counterfeiting*	Counterfeit products are widespread, especially in the areas of computer software, clothing, and audio and video products. The Internet has facilitated the distribution of counterfeit products.
Promotion Issue *Advertising*	Deceptive advertising or withholding important product information in a personal-selling situation.
Pricing Issue *Pricing*	Indicating that an advertised sale price is a reduction below the regular price when in fact that is not the case.

including the marketing of video games that allegedly promote violence and weapons to children, and the use of bribery in personal selling situations. In pricing, common ethical issues are price fixing, predatory pricing, and failure to disclose the full price of a purchase. The emotional and subjective nature of price creates many situations in which misunderstandings between the seller and buyer cause ethical problems. Marketers have the right to price their products to earn a reasonable profit, but ethical issues may crop up when a company seeks to earn high profits at the expense of its customers. Some pharmaceutical companies, for example, have been accused of pricing products at exorbitant levels and taking advantage of customers who must purchase the medicine to survive or to maintain their quality of life. Another issue relates to quantity surcharges that occur when consumers are effectively overcharged for buying a larger package size of the same grocery product.[32]

Ethical issues in distribution involve relationships among producers and marketing middlemen. Marketing middlemen, or intermediaries (wholesalers and retailers), facilitate the flow of products from the producer to the ultimate customer. Each intermediary performs a different role and agrees to certain rights, responsibilities, and rewards associated with that role. For example, producers expect wholesalers and retailers to honour agreements and keep them informed of inventory needs. Other serious ethical issues with regard to distribution include manipulating a product's availability for purposes of exploitation and using coercion to force intermediaries to behave in a specific manner. Several companies have been accused of channel stuffing, which involves shipping surplus inventory to wholesalers and retailers at an excessive rate, typically before the end of a quarter. The practice may conceal declining demand for a product or inflate financial statement earnings, misleading investors.[33]

The Nature of Marketing Ethics

To grasp the significance of ethics in marketing decision making, it is helpful to examine the factors that influence the ethical decision-making process. As Figure 4.3 shows, individual factors, opportunity, and organizational relationships interact to determine ethical decisions in marketing.

Individual Factors. When people need to resolve ethical conflicts in their daily lives, they often base their decisions on their own values and principles of right or wrong. For example, a study by the Josephson Institute of Ethics reported that 62 percent of students admitted to cheating on a test at least once in the past year, and 82 percent admitted to lying to their parents in the past year. One out of three students confessed to plagiarizing documents from the Internet in the same period.[34] People learn values and principles through socialization by family members, social groups, religion, and formal education. In the workplace, however, research has established that

figure 4.3

FACTORS THAT INFLUENCE THE ETHICAL DECISION-MAKING PROCESS IN MARKETING

Communication with your teens can be a form of prevention. In fact, teens whose parents lay out rules and expectations for them are far less likely to try pot and other drugs. Be clear. Be firm. Be a parent. For information, call 1-800-788-2800 or visit www.theantidrug.com.

if you're not telling them NO you're telling them YES

PARENTS.
THE ANTI-DRUG.

Office of National Drug Control Policy | Partnership for a Drug-Free America®

Individual Factors
Organizations such as "Parents—The Anti-Drug," focus on character development among teenagers.

an organization's values often have more influence on marketing decisions than do a person's own values.[35]

Organizational Relationships. Although people can and do make ethical choices pertaining to marketing decisions, no one operates in a vacuum.[36] Ethical choices in marketing are most often made jointly, in work groups and committees or in conversations and discussions with coworkers. Marketing employees resolve ethical issues based not only on what they learned from their own backgrounds but also on what they learn from others in the organization. The outcome of this learning process depends on the strength of each individual's personal values, opportunity for unethical behaviour, and exposure to others who behave ethically or unethically. Superiors, peers, and subordinates in the organization influence the ethical decision-making process. Although people outside the organization, such as family members and friends, also influence decision makers, organizational culture and structure operate through organizational relationships to influence ethical decisions.

Organizational (or corporate) culture is a set of values, beliefs, goals, norms, and rituals that members of

organizational (corporate) culture A set of values, beliefs, goals, norms, and rituals that members of an organization share

an organization share. These values also help shape employees' satisfaction with their employer, which may affect the quality of the service they provide to customers. A firm's culture may be expressed formally through codes of conduct, memos, manuals, dress codes, and ceremonies, but it is also conveyed informally through work habits, extracurricular activities, and anecdotes. An organization's culture gives its members meaning and suggests rules for how to behave and deal with problems within the organization.

With regard to organizational structure, most experts agree that the chief executive officer or vice president of marketing sets the ethical tone for the entire marketing organization. Lower-level managers obtain their cues from top managers, but they too impose some of their personal values on the company. This interaction between corporate culture and executive leadership helps determine the firm's ethical value system.

Coworkers' influence on an individual's ethical choices depends on the person's exposure to unethical behaviour. Especially in gray areas, the more a person is exposed to unethical activity by others in the organizational environment, the more likely he or she is to behave unethically. Most marketing employees take their cues from coworkers in learning how to solve problems, including ethical problems.[37] For example, the 2005 National Business Ethics Survey (NBES) found that 52 percent of employees had observed at least one type of misconduct in the past year; just over one-half of them (55 percent) had reported the misconduct to management.[38] Table 4.4 lists some commonly observed types of observed misconduct. Moreover, research suggests that marketing employees who perceive their work environment as ethical experience less role conflict and ambiguity, are more satisfied with their jobs, and are more committed to their employer.[39]

Organizational pressure plays a key role in creating ethical issues. For example, because of pressure to meet a schedule, a superior may ask a salesperson to lie to a customer over the phone about a late product shipment. Similarly, pressure to meet a

table 4.4   TYPES AND INCIDENCES OF OBSERVED MISCONDUCT

Type of Conduct Observed	Employees Observing It (%)
Abusive or intimidating behaviour toward employees	21
Lying to employees, customers, vendors, or the public	19
A situation that places employee interests over organizational interests	18
Safety regulation violations	16
Misreporting of actual time worked	16
Discrimination on the basis of race, colour, gender, age, or similar categories	12
Stealing or theft	11
Sexual harassment	9

Source: "Survey Documents State of Ethics in the Workplace," Ethics Resource Center, press release, Oct. 12, 2005, **www.ethics.org/nbes/nbes2005/release.html** (accessed Apr. 13, 2006). Reprinted by permission of Ethics Resource Center.

sales quota may result in overly aggressive sales tactics. Research in this area indicates that superiors and coworkers can generate organizational pressure, which plays a key role in creating ethical issues. Nearly all marketers face difficult issues whose solutions are not obvious or that present conflicts between organizational objectives and personal ethics.

Opportunity. Another factor that may shape ethical decisions in marketing is opportunity, that is, conditions that limit barriers or provide rewards. A marketing employee who takes advantage of an opportunity to act unethically and is rewarded or suffers no penalty may repeat such acts as other opportunities arise. For example, a salesperson who receives a raise after using a deceptive sales presentation to increase sales is being rewarded and thus will probably continue the behaviour. Indeed, opportunity to engage in unethical conduct is often a better predictor of unethical activities than are personal values.[40] Beyond rewards and the absence of punishment, other elements in the business environment may create opportunities. Professional codes of conduct and ethics-related corporate policy also influence opportunity by prescribing what behaviours are acceptable, as we will see later. The larger the rewards and the milder the punishment for unethical conduct, the greater is the likelihood that unethical behaviour will occur.

   However, just as the majority of people who go into retail stores do not try to shoplift at each opportunity, most marketing managers do not try to take advantage of every opportunity for unethical behaviour in their organizations. Although marketing managers often perceive many opportunities to engage in unethical conduct in their companies and industries, research suggests that most refrain from taking advantage of such opportunities. Moreover, most marketing managers do not believe unethical conduct in general results in success.[41] Individual factors as well as organizational culture may influence whether an individual becomes opportunistic and tries to take advantage of situations unethically.

Improving Ethical Conduct in Marketing

It is possible to improve ethical conduct in an organization by hiring ethical employees and eliminating unethical ones, and by improving the organization's ethical standards. One way to approach improvement of an organization's ethical standards is to use a "bad apple–bad barrel" analogy. Some people always do things in their own self-interest, regardless of organizational goals or accepted moral standards; they are

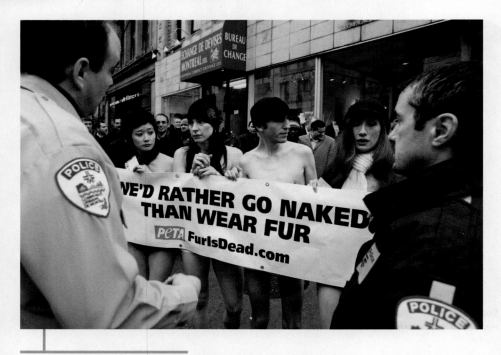

Improving Ethical Conduct in Marketing

Non-profit organizations, such as the Humane Society of Canada, are responsible for implementing ethics and compliance programs.

sometimes called "bad apples." To eliminate unethical conduct, an organization must rid itself of bad apples through screening techniques and enforcement of the firm's ethical standards. However, organizations sometimes become "bad barrels" themselves, not because the individuals within them are unethical but because the pressures to survive and succeed create conditions (opportunities) that reward unethical behaviour. One way to resolve the problem of the bad barrel is to redesign the organization's image and culture so that it conforms to industry and societal norms of ethical conduct.[42]

If top management develops and enforces ethical and legal compliance programs to encourage ethical decision making, it becomes a force to help individuals make better decisions. The 2005 National Business Ethics Survey found that formal ethics programs are an essential element of strong corporate cultures.[43] Ethics programs that include written standards of conduct, ethics training, ethics advice lines or offices, and systems for anonymous reporting increase the likelihood that employees will report misconduct observed in the workplace. When top managers talk about the importance of ethics, inform employees, keep promises, and model ethical behaviour, employees observe significantly fewer instances of unethical conduct. According to the 2005 NBES, employees who reported observations of misconduct to management did so because they thought it was the right thing to do. They also indicated that they felt they had the support of top management and that corrective action would result from their report. Figure 4.4 lists some of the reasons employees cited for not reporting observed misconduct.[44] When marketers understand the policies and requirements for ethical conduct, they can more easily resolve ethical conflicts. However, marketers can never fully abdicate their personal ethical responsibility in making decisions. Claiming to be an agent of the business ("the company

figure 4.4

REASONS EMPLOYEES DO NOT REPORT ETHICAL MISCONDUCT

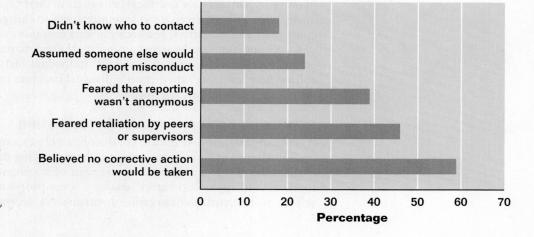

Source: From National Business Ethics Survey, "How Employees View Ethics in Their Organization 1994–2005," Ethics Resource Center 2005, p. 29. © Ethics Resource Center, Washington, D.C. Reprinted with permission.

told me to do it") is unacceptable as a legal excuse and is even less defensible from an ethical perspective.[45]

Codes of Conduct. Without compliance programs and uniform standards and policies regarding conduct, it is hard for employees to determine what conduct is acceptable within the company. In the absence of such programs and standards, employees will generally make decisions based on their observations of how coworkers and superiors behave. To improve ethics, many organizations have developed **codes of conduct** (also called *codes of ethics*) consisting of formalized rules and standards that describe what the company expects of its employees. Most large corporations have formal codes of conduct. Codes of conduct promote ethical behaviour by reducing opportunities for unethical behaviour; employees know both what is expected of them and what kind of punishment they face if they violate the rules. Codes help marketers deal with ethical issues or dilemmas that develop in daily operations by prescribing or limiting specific activities. Codes of conduct have also made companies that subcontract manufacturing operations abroad more aware of the ethical issues associated with supporting facilities that underpay and even abuse their workforce.

Codes of conduct do not have to be so detailed that they take every situation into account, but they should provide guidelines that enable employees to achieve organizational objectives in an ethical, acceptable manner. The Canadian Marketing Association's (CMA) Code of Ethics and Standards of Practice does not cover every possible ethical issue, but it provides a useful overview of what marketers believe are sound principles for guiding marketing activities. This document serves as a helpful model for structuring an organization's code of conduct. Topics covered in the document include disclosure, misrepresentation, privacy, product safety, special considerations in marketing to children and teenagers, and environmental responsibility. A full copy of the CMA's Code of Ethics and Standards of Practice is available at www.the-cma.org.

Ethics Officers. Organizational compliance programs must also have oversight by high-ranking persons in the organization known to respect legal and ethical standards. Ethics officers are typically responsible for creating and distributing a code of conduct, enforcing the code, and meeting with organizational members to discuss or provide advice about ethical issues. Many firms have created ethics officer positions, including the NovaGold Resources Inc, Nortel Networks, and Computer Associates International.[46] To assist with the ethical conduct of government, the Government of Canada created the Office of the Ethics Commissioner. The mandate of the Ethics Commissioner, carried on behalf of Parliament, is to administer conflict of interest codes, to provide confidential opinions to Members of the House of Commons, and to Public Office Holders, and to conduct inquiries on behalf of Parliament.[47]

Many ethics officers also employ toll-free telephone "hotlines" to provide advice, anonymously when desired, to employees who believe they face an ethical issue. Although the majority of incidents reported to these hotlines are minor infractions, callers have been known to identify kickbacks from suppliers, and to report on a multimillion-dollar falsified contract.[48]

Implementing Ethical and Legal Compliance Programs. To nurture ethical conduct in marketing, open communication and coaching on ethical issues are essential. This requires providing employees with ethics training, clear channels of communication, and follow-up support throughout the organization.

It is important that companies consistently enforce standards and impose penalties or punishment on those who violate codes of conduct and ethics policies. Clear Channel Communications, for example, fired two executives and disciplined other employees for violating the firm's policies on "payola," the illegal practice of accepting payment for playing songs on the air without divulging such deals. The firm, which owns approximately 1200 radio stations, also required station managers and programming personnel to undergo additional training on its policies.[49] In addition, companies must take reasonable steps in response to violations of standards and, as appropriate, revise their compliance programs to diminish the likelihood of future misconduct. To succeed, a compliance program must be viewed as a part of the overall marketing

codes of conduct Formalized rules and standards that describe what the company expects of its employees strategy implementation. If ethics officers and other executives are not committed to the principles and initiatives of marketing ethics and social responsibility, the program's effectiveness will be in question.

Although the virtues of honesty, fairness, and openness are often assumed to be self-evident and universally accepted, marketing strategy decisions involve complex and detailed matters in which correctness may not be so clear-cut. A high level of personal morality may not be sufficient to prevent an individual from violating the law in an organizational context in which even experienced lawyers debate the exact meaning of the law. Because it is impossible to train all members of an organization as lawyers, the identification of ethical issues and implementation of compliance programs and codes of conduct that incorporate both legal and ethical concerns constitute the best approach to preventing violations and avoiding litigation. Codifying ethical standards into meaningful policies that spell out what is and is not acceptable gives marketers an opportunity to reduce the probability of behaviour that could create legal problems. Without proper ethical training and guidance, it is impossible for the average marketing manager to understand the exact boundaries of illegality in the areas of price fixing, copyright violations, fraud, export/import violations, and so on. A corporate focus on ethics helps create a buffer zone around issues that could trigger serious legal complications for the company.

Incorporating Social Responsibility and Ethics into Strategic Planning

Although the concepts of marketing ethics and social responsibility are often used interchangeably, it is important to distinguish between them. *Ethics* relates to individual and group decisions—judgments about what is right or wrong in a particular decision-making situation—whereas *social responsibility* deals with the total effect of marketing decisions on society. The two concepts are interrelated because a company that supports socially responsible decisions and adheres to a code of conduct is likely to have a positive effect on society. Because ethics and social responsibility programs can be profitable as well, an increasing number of companies are incorporating them into their overall strategic market planning.

As we have emphasized throughout this chapter, ethics is one dimension of social responsibility. Being socially responsible relates to doing what is economically sound, legal, ethical, and socially conscious. One way to evaluate whether a specific activity is ethical and socially responsible is to ask other members of the organization if they approve of it. Contact with concerned consumer groups and industry or government regulatory groups may be helpful. A check to see whether there is a specific company policy about an activity may help resolve ethical questions. If other organization members approve of the activity and it is legal and customary within the industry, chances are the activity is acceptable from both an ethical and a social responsibility perspec-

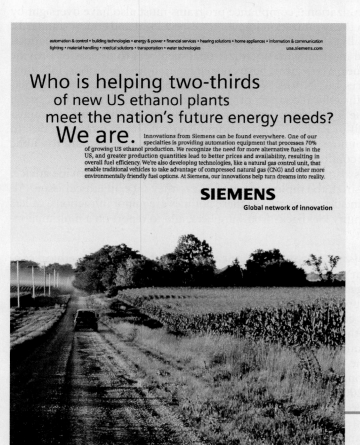

Incorporating Social Responsibility and Ethics
Siemens prides itself on global innovation, providing equipment that processes 70 percent of North American ethanol production.

table 4.5   ORGANIZATIONAL AUDIT OF SOCIAL RESPONSIBILITY AND ETHICS CONTROL MECHANISMS

Answer True or False for each statement.

T	F	
T	F	1. No mechanism exists for top management to detect social responsibility and ethical issues relating to employees, customers, the community, and society.
T	F	2. There is no formal or informal communication within the organization about procedures and activities that are considered acceptable behaviour.
T	F	3. The organization fails to communicate its ethical standards to suppliers, customers, and groups that have a relationship with the organization.
T	F	4. There is an environment of deception, repression, and cover-ups concerning events that could be embarrassing to the company.
T	F	5. Compensation systems are totally dependent on economic performance.
T	F	6. The only concerns about environmental impact are those that are legally required.
T	F	7. Concern for the ethical value systems of the community with regard to the firm's activities is absent.
T	F	8. Products are described in a misleading manner, with no information on negative impact or limitations communicated to customers.

True answers indicate a lack of control mechanisms, which, if implemented, could improve ethics and social responsibility.

tive. Table 4.5 provides an audit of mechanisms to help control ethics and social responsibility in marketing.

A rule of thumb for resolving ethical and social responsibility issues is that if an issue can withstand open discussion that results in agreement or limited debate, an acceptable solution may exist. Nevertheless, even after a final decision is reached, different viewpoints on the issue may remain. Openness is not the end-all solution to the ethics problem. However, it creates trust and facilitates learning relationships.[50]

The Challenge of Ethical and Socially Responsible Behaviour

To promote socially responsible and ethical behaviour while achieving organizational goals, marketers must monitor changes and trends in society's values. Consider that as aging baby boomers see increased rates of obesity, diabetes, heart conditions, and other chronic illnesses, many companies in the food industry are responding by introducing or adapting products to address their needs. Their approaches range from special brands and labels to introducing low-fat, low-sugar, whole-grain, and other specialty-food requirements to maintaining separate shelf space for products that target these conditions. Developing a more user-friendly grocery store for these consumers is both socially responsible and lucrative.[51] Likewise, when consumers began to demand greater transparency, or openness, from companies in the wake of a number of ethics scandals, transparency became a factor in most marketing and management decisions.[52] An organization's top management must assume some responsibility for employees' conduct by establishing and enforcing policies that address society's desires.

After determining what society wants, marketers must attempt to predict the long-term effects of decisions pertaining to those wants. Specialists outside the company, such as doctors, lawyers, and scientists, are often consulted, but sometimes there is a lack of agreement within a discipline as to what is an acceptable marketing decision. Forty years ago, for example, tobacco marketers promoted cigarettes as being good for one's health. Today, years after the discovery that cigarette smoking is linked to cancer and other medical problems, society's attitude toward smoking has changed, and marketers face new social responsibilities, such as providing a smoke-free atmosphere for customers.

Many of society's demands impose costs. For example, society wants a cleaner environment and the preservation of wildlife and their habitats, but it also wants low-priced products. Consider the plight of the gas station owner who asked his customers if they would be willing to spend an additional one cent per litre if he instituted an air filtration system to eliminate harmful fumes. The majority indicated they supported his plan. However, when the system was installed and the price increased, many customers switched to a lower-cost competitor across the street. Thus, companies must carefully balance the costs of providing low-priced products against the costs of manufacturing, packaging, and distributing their products in an environmentally responsible manner. Balancing society's demands to satisfy all members of society is difficult, if not impossible. Marketers must evaluate the extent to which members of society are willing to pay for what they want. For instance, customers may want more information about a product but be unwilling to pay the costs the firm incurs in providing the data. Marketers who want to make socially responsible decisions may find the task a challenge because, ultimately, they must ensure their economic survival.

Social Responsibility and Ethics Improve Marketing Performance

Do not think, however, that the challenge is not worth the effort. On the contrary, increasing evidence indicates that being socially responsible and ethical pays off. Research suggests that a relationship exists between a marketing orientation and an organizational climate that supports marketing ethics and social responsibility. This relationship implies that being ethically and socially concerned is consistent with meeting the demands of customers and other stakeholders. By encouraging employees to understand their markets, companies can help them respond to stakeholders' demands.[53]

There is a direct association between corporate social responsibility and profits.[54] In a survey of consumers, nearly 86 percent indicated that when quality and price are similar among competitors, they would be more likely to buy from the company associated with a particular cause. In addition, young adults aged 18–25 are especially likely to take a company's citizenship efforts into account when making not only purchasing but also employment and investment decisions.[55]

Thus, recognition is growing that the long-term value of conducting business in a socially responsible manner far outweighs short-term costs.[56] Companies that fail to develop strategies and programs to incorporate ethics and social responsibility into their organizational culture may pay the price with poor marketing performance and the potential costs of legal violations, civil litigation, and damaging publicity when questionable activities are made public. Because marketing ethics and social responsibility are not always viewed as organizational performance issues, many managers do not believe they need to consider them in the strategic planning process. Individuals also have different ideas as to what is ethical or unethical, leading them to confuse the need for workplace ethics and the right to maintain their own personal values and ethics. While the concepts are undoubtedly controversial, it is possible—and desirable—to incorporate ethics and social responsibility into the planning process.

SUMMARY

Social responsibility refers to an organization's obligation to maximize its positive impact and minimize its negative impact on society. It deals with the total effect of all marketing decisions on society. Although social responsibility is a positive concept, most organizations embrace it in the expectation of indirect long-term benefits.

Marketing citizenship involves adopting a strategic focus for fulfilling the economic, legal, ethical, and phil-

anthropic social responsibilities expected of organizations by their stakeholders, those constituents who have a stake, or claim, in some aspect of the company's products, operations, markets, industry, and outcomes. At the most basic level, companies have an economic responsibility to be profitable so they can provide a return on investment to their stockholders, create jobs for the community, and contribute goods and services to the economy. Marketers are also expected to obey laws and regulations. Marketing ethics refers to principles and standards that define acceptable conduct in marketing as determined by various stakeholders, including the public, government regulators, private-interest groups, industry, and the organization itself. Philanthropic responsibilities go beyond marketing ethics; they are not required of a company, but they promote human welfare or goodwill. Many firms use cause-related marketing, the practice of linking products to a social cause on an ongoing or short-term basis. Strategic philanthropy is the synergistic use of organizational core competencies and resources to address key stakeholders' interests and achieve both organizational and social benefits.

Three major categories of social responsibility issues are the natural environment, consumerism, and community relations. One of the more common ways marketers demonstrate social responsibility is through programs designed to protect and preserve the natural environment. Green marketing refers to the specific development, pricing, promotion, and distribution of products that do not harm the environment. Consumerism consists of the efforts of independent individuals, groups, and organizations to protect the rights of consumers. Consumers expect to have the right to safety, the right to be informed, the right to choose, and the right to be heard. Many marketers view social responsibility as including contributions of resources (money, products, and time) to community causes such as the natural environment, arts and recreation, disadvantaged members of the community, and education.

Whereas social responsibility is achieved by balancing the interests of all stakeholders in the organization, ethics relates to acceptable standards of conduct in making individual and group decisions. Marketing ethics goes beyond legal issues. Ethical marketing decisions foster mutual trust in marketing relationships.

An ethical issue is an identifiable problem, situation, or opportunity requiring an individual or organization to choose from among several actions that must be evaluated as right or wrong, ethical or unethical. A number of ethical issues relate to the marketing mix (product, promotion, price, and distribution).

Individual factors, organizational relationships, and opportunity interact to determine ethical decisions in marketing. Individuals often base their decisions on their own values and principles of right or wrong. However, ethical choices in marketing are most often made jointly, in work groups and committees or in conversations and discussions with coworkers. Organizational culture and structure operate through organizational relationships (with superiors, peers, and subordinates) to influence ethical decisions. Organizational, or corporate, culture is a set of values, beliefs, goals, norms, and rituals that members of an organization share. The more a person is exposed to unethical activity by others in the organizational environment, the more likely he or she is to behave unethically. Organizational pressure plays a key role in creating ethical issues, as does opportunity, conditions that limit barriers or provide rewards.

It is possible to improve ethical behaviour in an organization by hiring ethical employees and eliminating unethical ones, and by improving the organization's ethical standards. If top management develops and enforces ethics and legal compliance programs to encourage ethical decision making, it becomes a force to help individuals make better decisions. To improve company ethics, many organizations have developed codes of conduct, formalized rules and standards that describe what the company expects of its employees. A marketing compliance program must have oversight by a high-ranking organization member known to abide by legal and common ethical standards; this person is usually called an ethics officer. To nurture ethical conduct in marketing, open communication and coaching on ethical issues are essential. This requires providing employees with ethics training, clear channels of communication, and follow-up support throughout the organization. Companies must consistently enforce standards and impose penalties or punishment on those who violate codes of conduct.

An increasing number of companies are incorporating ethics and social responsibility programs into their overall strategic market planning. To promote socially responsible and ethical behaviour while achieving organizational goals, marketers must monitor changes and trends in society's values. They must determine what society wants and attempt to predict the long-term effects of their decisions. Costs are associated with many of society's demands, and balancing those demands to satisfy all of society is difficult. However, increasing evidence indicates that being socially responsible and ethical results in valuable benefits: an enhanced public reputation (which can increase market share), costs savings, and profits.

Please visit the student website at www.hmco.ca/marketing for ACE Self-Test questions that will help you prepare for exams.

IMPORTANT TERMS

Social responsibility	Cause-related marketing	Ethical issue	Codes of conduct
Marketing citizenship	Strategic philanthropy	Organizational (corporate)	
Marketing ethics	Green marketing	culture	

DISCUSSION & REVIEW QUESTIONS

1. What is social responsibility? Why is it important?

2. What are stakeholders? What role do they play in strategic marketing decisions?

3. What are four dimensions of social responsibility? What impact do they have on marketing decisions?

4. What is strategic philanthropy? How does it differ from more traditional philanthropic efforts?

5. What are some major social responsibility issues? Give an example of each.

6. What is the difference between ethics and social responsibility?

7. Why is ethics an important consideration in marketing decisions?

8. How do the factors that influence ethical or unethical decisions interact?

9. What ethical conflicts may exist if business employees fly on certain airlines just to receive benefits for their personal "frequent flier" programs?

10. Give an example of how ethical issues can affect each component of the marketing mix.

11. How can the ethical decisions involved in marketing be improved?

12. How can people with different personal values work together to make ethical decisions in organizations?

13. What tradeoffs might a company have to make to be socially responsible and responsive to society's demands?

14. What evidence exists that being socially responsible and ethical is worthwhile?

APPLICATION QUESTIONS

1. Some organizations promote their social responsibility. These companies often claim that being ethical is good business and that it pays to be a "good corporate citizen." Identify an organization in your community that has a reputation for being ethical and socially responsible. What activities account for this image? Is the company successful? Why or why not?

2. If you had to conduct a social audit of your organization's ethics and social responsibility, what information would most interest you? What key stakeholders would you want to communicate with? How could such an audit assist the company in improving its ethics and social responsibility?

3. Suppose that in your job you face situations that require you to make decisions about what is right or wrong and then act on these decisions. Describe such a situation. Without disclosing your actual decision, explain what you based it on. What and whom did you think of when you were considering what to do? Why did you consider them?

4. Consumers interact with many businesses daily and weekly. Not only do companies in an industry acquire a reputation for being ethical or unethical; entire industries also become known as ethical or unethical. Identify two types of businesses with which you or others you know have had the most conflict involving ethical issues. Describe those ethical issues.

1. Corporate social responsibility is an emerging area of interest for firms. As such, many companies have conducted research and developed reports on corporate social responsibility. One such report is the KPMG International Survey of Corporate Responsibility Reporting. This report can be accessed using the search term "international survey" at **http://globaledge.msu.edu/ibrd** or **http://globaledge.msu.edu/ibrd/ibrd.asp.** In the most recent report, which category of corporate social responsibility was most widely reported, and what does it say?

2. The use of bribery in the business setting is an important ethical dilemma many companies face both domestically and globally. While bribery is illegal for Canadian companies to use as a business strategy, there are still industries and countries in which it is perceived as acceptable. Transparency International's Bribe Payers Index, which assesses the perceived level of bribery in each country, can be found using the search term "bribe payers" at **http://globaledge.msu.edu/ibrd** or **http://globaledge.msu.edu/ibrd/ibrd.asp.** Using the most recent index, find the three industries in which bribery is perceived to be least prevalent. How does this compare with the three industries thought to have the largest problems with bribery?

INTERNET Exercise

Visit **www.prideferrell.com** for resources to help you master the material in this chapter, plus materials that will help you expand your marketing knowledge, including internet exercise updates, ACE self-tests, hotlinks to companies featured in this chapter, and much more.

Business for Social Responsibility

Business for Social Responsibility (BSR) is a non-profit organization for companies desiring to operate responsibly and demonstrate respect for ethical values, people, communities, and the natural environment. Founded in 1992, BSR offers members practical information, research, educational programs, and technical assistance as well as the opportunity to network with peers on current social responsibility issues. To learn more about this organization and access its many resources, visit www.bsr.org.

1. What types of businesses join BSR, and why?
2. Describe the services available to member companies. How can these services help companies improve their performances?
3. Peruse the "CRS Issue Areas and Information Links" and find the reports on ethics codes and training. Using these reports, list some examples of corporate codes of ethics and training.

Case 4.1   On Doing Good at Ford Motors

Ford Motor Company was founded in 1903 and grew into one of the world's largest corporations, selling nearly seven million vehicles worldwide. When founder Henry Ford ran the company in the early twentieth century, he often recycled materials—turning wooden crates into running boards, for example—to keep costs down. In more recent decades, however, Ford has not been known for its environmental record, as evidenced most recently by environmentalists' ridicule of the gas-guzzling Ford Expedition SUV and the firm's failure to achieve a much-publicized goal of improving fuel efficiency on SUVs by 25 percent. Now Henry Ford's grandson, chairman and CEO William Clay Ford, Jr., wants to change that record.

When Bill Ford stepped into the CEO's office in 2001, he brought his own values to the company and established far-reaching environmental, quality, and competitive goals for the company. Under his tenure, the company has improved quality, innovation, and cost efficiency. Ford also became the first carmaker to achieve ISO 14001 certification, a series of international environmental standards. Ford Motors also makes significant donations and grants to causes associated with education, environment, public policy, health and social programs, civic affairs and community development, and arts and humanities, typically through its Ford Motor Company Fund foundation.

One example of Bill Ford's environmental focus is a new assembly plant in the Ford Rouge Center that features efficient and flexible manufacturing processes as well as "breakthrough" environmental methods for storm-water management, energy use, air quality, and soil restoration. The roof of the Dearborn, Michigan, factory is a four-layer, mat-like system topped with drought-resistant plants, which acts like a giant sponge, absorbing rainfall and reducing polluted storm-water run-off, as well as an insulating blanket that helps sharply reduce energy consumption in all weather. Although the environmentally friendly roof added $3.6 million to the factory's cost, the firm will reap millions in savings by reducing energy expenses and eliminating the need for expensive storm sewers and storm-water treatment systems. The company has likewise invested in green facilities using solar, wind, and other technologies designed to reduce energy consumption and emissions.

At the Lima Engine Plant, for example, cold water from quarries on the plant site is used to help cool the facility, saving $300 000 a year in operating costs. These initiatives have helped Ford reap significant water and energy savings. Its facilities now use 18 percent less energy overall and five billion fewer gallons of water than they did in 2000.

Another example of the company's environmental focus is its new focus on technologies that promise to improve the fuel efficiency of and reduce emissions from vehicles wearing Ford-owned marques. The company is aggressively pursuing fuel-cell technology, which may allow cars of the future to have great fuel efficiency and zero emissions, and working to develop cleaner burning conventional and diesel engines. Ford's E-450 hydrogen engine shuttle buses are the first commercially available hydrogen vehicles in North America. In particular, Ford has taken a leadership position in the area of hybrid vehicles, which employ an electric engine to augment the traditional gasoline engine to improve fuel efficiency. The first of these hybrid vehicles is the Escape SUV. With demand for hybrids escalating along with gasoline prices, the company ultimately intends to offer hybrid engines on half its models.

Although Bill Ford has been criticized by some analysts and investors for applying his personal values to Ford operations, he strongly believes his approach is the right strategy for taking the firm into its second century of operations. He points out that reducing Ford's use of non-renewable materials will help it cut costs, and he believes that a stronger focus on social and environmental priorities will help better position Ford to respond to increasingly stringent government regulations around the world. He also recognizes that society's growing interest in environmental issues will foster a strong market for "green" products and technologies that can generate new revenue streams for the company. And perhaps most importantly, he acknowledges that consumers seem to assign greater value to brands that are associated with a strong commitment to social and environmental responsibility, and that more socially responsible companies can better attract and retain employees.

Will Ford's performance changes get environmentalists and other critics off of his back? He says, "Tackling environmental and social issues is not something a company does *after* it is profitable; it must be something we do to *be* more profitable." He believes that being more environmentally responsible will ultimately result in a better reputation with stakeholders, particularly customers and employees; a stronger bottom line; and a safer environment.[57]

Questions for Discussion

1. Describe the social responsibility issues that Ford Motor seems to be targeting. How do these issues relate to the firm's target markets? To other stakeholders?
2. What level of corporate social responsibility does Bill Ford have to his company and its stakeholders?
3. Debate Bill Ford's justifications for making Ford more environmentally and socially responsible.

Strategic Case 2   Texas Instruments

Introduction

Texas Instruments (TI) strives to develop the most effective organizational ethics and compliance program possible. The company knows it is vital to identify potential risks and uncover the existence of activities or events that relate to misconduct. It also understands that it must have the infrastructure and a plan in place to deal with unethical issues or events, which must include a rapid response system. Through explicit codes of conduct and statements of values and ethics documented in organizational communication, TI must maintain the values, the culture, and the expectations for conduct that employees hold about daily life within the firm. This same goal is also accomplished implicitly through stories about ethical decisions, by treatment of customer and employee complaints, and by the way that meetings are conducted. Another way employees learn a company's code of conduct is by noticing which behaviours and accomplishments get rewarded and recognized and which behaviours are criticized, ignored, or punished.

Texas Instruments Incorporated is headquartered in Dallas, Texas, and has manufacturing, design or sales operations in more than 25 countries. It has three separate business segments: 1) Semiconductor, which accounts for about 85 percent of its revenue; 2) Sensors & Controls, which accounts for about 10 percent of its revenue; and 3) Educational & Productivity Solutions, which accounts for about five percent of its revenue. Its largest geographic sources of revenue, in order, are Asia (excluding Japan), Europe, North America, and Japan. The company's vision is world leadership in digital solutions for the networked society. It wants to accomplish this with excellence in everything it does; by producing products and technologies that make them and its customers substantially different from the competition, by competing in high-growth markets and by providing consistently good financial performance.

Background and History

The company was founded in 1930 as Geophysical Service Inc. (GSI), a pioneering provider of seismic exploration services. In December 1941, four GSI managers purchased the company. During the war the company began manufacturing submarine detection equipment for the U.S. Navy, and following the war, became a supplier of defence systems and launched a strategy that would completely change the company. In 1951, the company changed its name to Texas Instruments (TI) to reflect the change in its business strategy, and entered the semiconductor business in 1952.

TI designed the first transistor radio in 1954, the hand-held calculator in 1967, and the single-chip microcomputer in 1971. It was assigned the first patent on a single-chip microprocessor in 1973. TI is usually given credit with Intel for the almost simultaneous invention of the microprocessor.

TI also created the first commercial silicon transistor and invented the integrated circuit. It continued to manufacture equipment for use in the seismic industry, as well as providing seismic services. TI sold its GSI subsidiary to Halliburton in 1988, and in the early 1990s began a strategic process of focusing on its semiconductor business, primarily digital signal processors and analog semiconductors. Few companies can match the 75-year record of innovations from TI. Today TI continues to work in processing and interpreting signals and its products are used in many things that are an integral part of our daily lives—from the single-chip mobile phone solution to cable modems, home theatres, wireless Internet, digital cameras, and advanced automotive systems. TI is also working on new signal processing innovations that will help create cars that drive themselves and allow the blind to see as well as much more.

The Business of TI

Semiconductors are the electronic building blocks used to create modern electronic systems and equipment.

Semiconductors come in two basic forms: individual transistors, and integrated circuits (generally known as "chips") that combine different transistors on a single piece of material to form a complete electronic circuit. TI's Semiconductor segment designs, manufactures, and sells integrated circuits.

The global semiconductor market is characterized by constant, though generally incremental advances in product designs and manufacturing methods. Typically, new chips are produced in limited quantities at first and then ramp to high-volume production over time. Chip prices and manufacturing costs tend to decline over time as manufacturing methods and product life cycles mature.

The "semiconductor cycle" is an important concept that refers to the ebb and flow of supply and demand. The semiconductor market is characterized by periods of tight supply caused by strong demand and/or insufficient manufacturing capacity, followed by periods of surplus products caused by declining demand and/or excess manufacturing capacity. This cycle is affected by the significant time and capital required to build and maintain semiconductor manufacturing facilities.

TI was the world's third-largest semiconductor company in 2004 in terms of revenue. Historically, its Semiconductor segment averages a significantly higher growth rate than its other two business segments. About 75 percent of Semiconductor revenue comes from its core products, which are analog semiconductors and digital signal processors, or DSPs. These products enhance, and often make possible, a variety of applications that serve the communications, computer, consumer, automotive and industrial markets. The company believes that virtually all of today's digital electronic equipment requires some form of analog or digital signal processing.

TI also designs and manufactures other types of semiconductors, such as Digital Light Processing™ devices that enable exceptionally clear video, and microprocessors that serve as the brains of high-end computer servers. Knowledge about the systems its products go into is becoming increasingly important, because it enables them to differentiate its product offerings for its customers. Where a customer may have previously required multiple chips for a system to operate, TI now uses its system-level knowledge to integrate the functionality of those multiple chips onto fewer chips. A recent example is its single-chip cell phone, which combines the functionality of many separate chips onto a single chip. The digitization of electronics also requires more high-performance analog functionality. With expertise in both digital signal processing and analog at the system level, TI believes it is one of a very few semiconductor companies capable of integrating both technologies onto a single chip.

In addition, TI enables its customers, particularly original design manufacturers (ODMs), to take advantage of its system-level knowledge. This speeds its customers' time to market by making available to them standard chipsets and reference designs. Reference designs are technical blueprints that contain all the essential elements in a system. Customers using its reference designs, such as cell phone ODMs, may enhance or modify the design as required. TI's ability to deliver integrated solutions and system-level knowledge allows its customers to create more advanced systems and products.

In each of its product categories, TI faces significant competition. TI believes that competitive performance in the semiconductor market depends upon several factors, including the breadth of a company's product line as well as technological innovation, quality, reliability, price, customer service, technical support, and scale.

Employee Stakeholders

TI employs approximately 35 200 people worldwide. During the last year TI's job growth was a negative six percent or a reduction of 1076 people, while its voluntary turnover was five percent. TI's workforce is made up of 34 percent minorities and 25 percent women. The company supports diversity through 30 employee-networking groups. Among them are the "Lesbian and Gay Employee Network," "Christian Values Initiative," and "Muslim Initiative." TI has also been mentioned as one of nine companies that have a "Best 401 (K) Match"—it offers a 100 percent match up to four percent of total compensation. In addition to financial incentives, Texas Instruments offers employees ancillary benefits such as flexible work options, an employee trip reduction program, an onsite concierge, a day-spa, elder care, a summer camp for kids, and even special interest clubs such as a flying club.

TI's flexible work arrangements include flex-time, part-time, compressed work-week schedules, and telecommuting. It has New Mothers Rooms for nursing mothers in all major facilities and an online parent's network for employees to share information on issues related to children and parenting. Onsite seminars on topics such as parenting, childcare, elder care, and other work-life balance issues are yet another benefit. TI also has corporate Wellness programs, services, and recreation associations, some which include child care. Its wellness programs include tobacco cessation programs, travel well programs for worldwide employees, and offers immunizations and preventive screenings for TI employees. TI also provides onsite walking and weight management programs as well as nutrition resources to ensure that its employees are as healthy as possible. Its benefits include discount programs at daycare centres, education assistance, adoption benefits, life insurance options, pretax reimbursement accounts for dependent care and health care, and an employee assistance program—which offers confidential counseling for TI employees and their family members. TI also offers a time bank program that allows accrued time off to be used for any reason.

TI is ranked 83rd on the *Fortune* list of 100 Best Companies to work for in 2006. It is the sixth year that TI has been on the list. This list is based on two criteria: an evaluation of the policies and culture of each company and the opinions of the company's employees. The opinions of employees are given a weight of two-thirds of the total score, and are based on responses to a 57-question survey, of 350 randomly selected employees. The remaining one-third of the score is based on an evaluation of each company's demographic makeup, pay, and benefits programs and culture. Companies are scored in four areas: credibility (communication to employees), respect (opportunities and benefits), fairness (compensation, diversity), and pride/camaraderie (philanthropy, celebrations).

TI also ranked 50th on the *Business Ethics Magazine*'s 100 Best Corporate Citizens in 2005. The aim of the list is to identify firms that excel at serving a variety of stakeholders with excellence and integrity. For each company the list rates eight categories—shareholders, community, minorities and women, employees, environment, human rights, customers, and governance. For each area, strengths and concerns are matched against each other to arrive at the final score. TI is also a member of the Domini 400 Social Index and has won numerous awards for corporate citizenship and ethics as well as for being a good employer and for its diversity.

TI Ethics Program

TI has always been concerned about ethics in its company. The company believes that maintaining the highest ethical standards requires a partnership between employees and employers. It proactively supports employees by communicating values and giving individual guidance, while empowered employees participate actively in problem-solving. In 1987, TI decided to actively support employees by establishing a TI Ethics Office and appointing a TI Ethics Director. The TI Ethics Office has three primary functions:

- to ensure that business policies and practices continue to be aligned with ethical principles;
- to clearly communicate ethical expectations; and
- to provide multiple channels for feedback through which people can ask questions, voice concerns and seek resolution to ethical issues.

TI has strong documented requirements for ethical business practices. These include the TI Standard Policies and Procedures, The TI Commitment, and "The Values and Ethics of TI" booklet. The TI Values and Principles are:

Integrity—respect and value people, be honest

Innovation—learn and create, act boldly

Commitment—take responsibility, commit to win.

The Ethics quick test is also an integral part of everything TI does. It is included in the Code of Ethics booklet as a punch out card to put in your wallet or purse as well as printed on the TI mouse pads given to employees.

The TI Ethics Quick Test:

Is the action legal?

Does it comply with our values?

If you do it, will you feel bad?

How will it look in the newspaper?

If you know it's wrong, don't do it!

If you're not sure, ask.

Keep asking until you get an answer.

There are many resources and alternative communication channels available to help ensure compliance—whether as an individual or as a company. The compliance procedures are:

Take Direct Action. The best and most effective approach is to fix problems on the spot. If employees are considering an action or see a proposed action that raises ethical concerns, they should raise the ethical concerns right away. Frequently—perhaps usually—merely highlighting and discussing the issue will result in actions that achieve the desired goal in full compliance with TI's Values and Ethics Statement and the Code of Business Conduct. Employees should use available resources, including the Code of Ethics, the Values and Ethics Statement, the Code of Business Conduct, the Ethics Quick Test, Policies, Business Rules, Chart of Accounts, and other guidance.

Consult Your Supervisor. TI supervisors know their employees' assignments and circumstances better than anyone else. TI supervisors can often help employees find answers and solutions if the one that is being tried just doesn't seem to fit.

Talk with Human Resources. If for any reason employees cannot communicate with their supervisor or local managers, they should contact Human Resources. The TI HR staff is there to help employees resolve many issues. Employees may counsel with them at any time.

Call the TI Law Department. For questions regarding contracts, pricing practices, or anything with a legal orientation, the TI Law Department can help employees find the answers. There are attorneys assigned to assist each business group, as well as attorneys who specialize in the areas of law that TI most frequently encounters.

Get Online. TI is an information-rich company. There are many sites on the Intranet where TI-specific information can be found.

Contact the TI Ethics Office. At any time, for any reason, employees can contact the TI Ethics Office for answers to its questions, including any concerns about accounting, internal accounting controls, or auditing matters. They may even remain anonymous.

Questions for Discussion

1. How effectively has TI managed the ethical and legal environment?
2. What are the ethical and legal risks associated with competing in TI's industries?
3. How you would describe TI's organizational culture?
4. Is there room for improvement in TI's ethics program?

Markets and Customer Behaviour

Part 3 focuses on consumer, business, and global markets and on buyer behaviour. The development of marketing strategy begins with customers. Understanding elements that affect buying decisions enables marketers to better analyze customers' needs and evaluate how specific marketing strategies can satisfy those needs. **Chapter 5** examines customer buying decision processes and factors that influence buying decisions. **Chapter 6** explores business markets, business customers, the buying centre, and the business buying decision process. **Chapter 7** focuses on the nature, involvement, and strategy of marketing in a global economy.

5

Consumer Buying Behaviour

1. To understand consumers' level of involvement with a product and describe the types of consumer problem-solving processes

2. To recognize the stages of the consumer buying decision process

3. To explore how situational influences may affect the consumer buying decision process

4. To understand the psychological influences that may affect the consumer buying decision process

5. To examine the social influences that may affect the consumer buying decision process

Why Leave the House? Use the Mouse!

Online shopping is big—BIG—business! Canadian households spent $7.9 billion on goods and services purchased over the Internet in 2005, with 41 percent of all adults who went online, having purchased online.[1] What accounts for such impressive growth? Well, since the dawn of e-commerce, there has been a steady stream of new online shoppers. Each year, more and more people have become Internet-savvy and have felt more and more confident about shopping securely online—for everything from iTunes at Apple to collectibles at eBay. Consumers are changing their attitudes toward buying products online. As consumer psychology changes, online retailing, or e-tailing, becomes a more profitable option. Consumers are learning to trust online retailers, and to forego some of their need to touch and feel products before making purchase decisions. People far and wide are learning about the benefits of shopping online; benefits such as the ease of comparing products and prices, and the ability to shop any time of the day or night. Plus, a recent study by MIT found that it is the ability to *find* products easily that prompts many consumers to shop the Internet. For example, while a brick and mortar bookstore may not be able to afford or have the space to keep titles on its shelves that sell only one or two copies a year, Amazon.com can fill an order without keeping millions of books in inventory. (When the company gets an order for an item not in inventory, it goes right to the publisher, gets the book, and processes the order.)

So what does all of this growth mean to marketers? Plenty. As online shopping matures, more people become online shoppers and eventually new customers are harder to come by. In response, online retailers and marketers will have to focus on growing their sales by attracting their competitor's customers and by keeping their current customers loyal. Coupons, free delivery, and "rewards" for frequent shoppers or users of the online store's credit card represent opportunities to attract new customers and keep existing customers devoted. Other routes for growth include improved processes:

one study suggests that online shoppers are likely to shop at sites that offer delivery services that are both reliable and flexible and that offer guaranteed online security.

Clearly, online shopping is big business—that's getting even bigger. What an opportunity![2] ■

Both online and traditional marketers go to great lengths to understand their customers' needs and gain a better grasp of customers' buying behaviour. Marketers attempt to understand buying behaviour for several reasons. First, customers' reactions to a firm's marketing strategy have a great impact on the firm's success. Second, as we saw in Chapter 1, the marketing concept stresses that a firm should create a marketing mix that satisfies customers. To find out what satisfies buyers, marketers must examine the main influences on what, where, when, and how consumers buy. Third, by gaining a deeper understanding of the factors that affect buying behaviour, marketers are in a better position to predict how consumers will respond to marketing strategies.

We begin this chapter by examining how a customer's level of involvement with a product affects the type of problem solving employed and by discussing the types of consumer problem-solving processes. Then we analyze the major stages of the consumer buying decision process, beginning with problem recognition, information search, and evaluation of alternatives and proceeding through purchase and postpurchase evaluation. Next, we examine situational influences—surroundings, time, purchase reason, and buyer's mood and condition—that affect purchasing decisions. We go on to consider psychological influences on purchasing decisions: perception, motives, learning, attitudes, personality and self-concept, and lifestyles. We conclude with a discussion of social influences that affect buying behaviour, including roles, family, reference groups and opinion leaders, social classes, and culture and subcultures.

Consumer Markets and Consumer Buying Behaviour

consumer market Purchasers and household members who intend to consume or benefit from the purchased products and do not buy products to make profits

buying behaviour
The decision processes and acts of people involved in buying and using products

consumer buying behaviour
The decision processes and purchasing activities of people who purchase products for personal or household use and not for business purposes

In Chapter 2, we defined a market as a group of individuals and/or organizations that have needs for products in a product class and have the ability, willingness, and authority to purchase those products. Markets can be divided into two categories: consumer markets and business markets. (Business markets are discussed in Chapter 6.) The division is based on the characteristics of the individuals and groups that comprise specific markets and the purposes for which they buy products. A **consumer market** consists of purchasers and household members who intend to consume or benefit from the purchased products and do not buy products for the primary purpose of making a profit. Each of us belongs to numerous consumer markets for products such as housing, food, clothing, vehicles, personal services, appliances, furniture, and recreational equipment. A firm's ability to develop and sustain satisfying customer relationships requires an understanding of **buying behaviour,** the decision processes and acts of people involved in buying and using products. **Consumer buying behaviour** refers to the buying behaviour of ultimate consumers, those who purchase products for personal or household use and not for business purposes.

Level of Involvement and Consumer Problem-Solving Processes

level of involvement
An individual's intensity of interest in a product and the importance of the product for that person

In order to acquire and maintain products that satisfy their current and future needs, consumers engage in problem solving. People engage in different types of problem-solving processes depending on the nature of the products involved. The amount of effort, both mental and physical, that buyers expend in solving problems also varies considerably. A major determinant of the type of problem-solving process employed depends on the customer's **level of involvement,** the degree of interest in a product and the importance the individual places on that product. High-involvement products tend to be those that are visible to others (such as clothing, furniture, or automobiles) and are expensive. High-importance issues, such as health care, are also associated with high levels of involvement. Low-involvement products tend to be less expensive and have less associated social risk, such as many grocery items. A person's interest in a product or product category that is ongoing and long term is referred to as *enduring involvement*. For example, a consumer interested in technology might always have the most advanced electronic devices, read electronics magazines, and work in a related field. However, most consumers have an enduring involvement with only a very few activities or items. In contrast, *situational involvement* is temporary and dynamic, and results from a particular set of circumstances, such as the need to buy a new car after being involved in an accident. For a short time period, the consumer will visit car dealerships, visit a car company's website, or even purchase automotive related magazines or books. However, once the car purchase is made, the consumer's interest and involvement tapers off. Consumer involvement may be attached to product categories (such as sports), loyalty to a specific brand, interest in a specific advertisement (e.g., a funny commercial) or a medium (such as a particular television show), or to certain decisions and behaviours (e.g., a love of shopping.) On the other hand, a consumer may find a particular advertisement entertaining, yet have little involvement with the brand advertised because of loyalty to another brand.[3] Involvement level, as well as other factors, affects a person's selection of one of three types of consumer problem solving: routinized response behaviour, limited problem solving, or extended problem solving (Table 5.1.)

A consumer uses **routinized response behaviour** when buying frequently purchased, low-cost items needing very little search-and-decision effort. When buying such items, a consumer may prefer a particular brand but is familiar with several brands in the product class and views more than one as acceptable. Typically, low-involvement products are bought through routinized response behaviour, that is, almost automatically. For example, most buyers spend little time or effort selecting soft drinks or cereals.

Buyers engage in **limited problem solving** when buying products occasionally or when they need to obtain information about an unfamiliar brand in a familiar product category. This type of problem solving requires a moderate amount of time for information gathering and deliberation. For example, if Procter & Gamble introduces an improved Tide laundry detergent, buyers will seek additional information about the new product, perhaps by asking a friend who has used it or watching a commercial about it, before making a trial purchase.

The most complex type of problem solving, **extended problem solving,** occurs when purchasing unfamiliar, expensive, or infrequently bought products—for instance, a car, home, or college education. The buyer uses many criteria to evaluate alternative brands or choices and spends much time seeking information and deciding on the purchase. Extended problem solving is frequently used for purchasing high-involvement products.

Purchase of a particular product does not always elicit the same type of problem-solving process. In some instances, we engage in extended problem solving the first time we buy a certain product but find that limited problem solving suffices when we

routinized response behaviour
A consumer problem-solving process used when buying frequently purchased, low-cost items that require very little search-and-decision effort

limited problem solving
A consumer problem-solving process used when purchasing products occasionally or needing information about an unfamiliar brand in a familiar product category

extended problem solving
A consumer problem-solving process employed when purchasing unfamiliar, expensive, or infrequently bought products

table 5.1   CONSUMER PROBLEM SOLVING

	Routinized Response	Limited	Extended
Product cost	Low	Low to moderate	High
Search effort	Little	Little to moderate	Extensive
Time spent	Short	Short to medium	Lengthy
Brand preference	More than one is acceptable, although one may be preferred	Several	Varies; usually many

impulse buying An unplanned buying behaviour resulting from a powerful urge to buy something immediately

buy it again. If a routinely purchased, formerly satisfying brand no longer satisfies us, we may use limited or extended problem solving to switch to a new brand. Thus, if we notice that the brand of pain reliever we normally buy is no longer effective, we may seek out a different brand through limited problem solving. Most consumers occasionally make purchases solely on impulse and not on the basis of any of these three problem-solving processes. **Impulse buying** involves no conscious planning but results from a powerful urge to buy something immediately.

Consumer Buying Decision Process

consumer buying decision process A five-stage purchase decision process that includes problem recognition, information search, evaluation of alternatives, purchase, and post-purchase evaluation

The **consumer buying decision process,** shown in Figure 5.1, includes five stages: problem recognition, information search, evaluation of alternatives, purchase, and post-purchase evaluation. Before we examine each stage, consider these important points. First, the actual act of purchasing is just one stage in the process, and usually not the first stage. Second, even though we indicate that a purchase occurs, not all decision processes lead to a purchase; individuals may end the process at any stage. Finally, not all consumer decisions include all five stages. People engaged in extended problem solving usually go through all stages of this decision process, whereas those engaged in limited problem solving and routinized response behaviour may omit some stages.

Problem Recognition

Problem recognition occurs when a buyer becomes aware of a difference between a desired state and an actual condition. Consider a student who owns a non-programmable calculator and learns she needs a programmable one for her math course. She recognizes that a difference exists between the desired state—having a programmable calculator—and her actual condition. She therefore decides to buy a new calculator.

The speed of consumer problem recognition can be quite rapid or rather slow. Sometimes a person has a problem or need but is unaware of it. Marketers use sales personnel, advertising, and packaging to help trigger recognition of such needs or problems. For example, a university bookstore may advertise programmable calculators

figure 5.1

CONSUMER BUYING DECISION PROCESS AND POSSIBLE INFLUENCES ON THE PROCESS

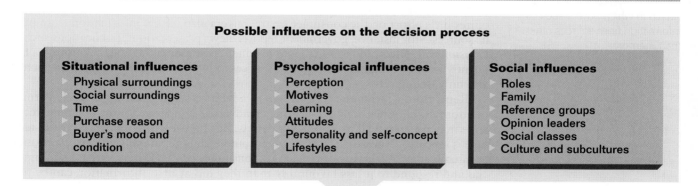

Possible influences on the decision process

Situational influences
- Physical surroundings
- Social surroundings
- Time
- Purchase reason
- Buyer's mood and condition

Psychological influences
- Perception
- Motives
- Learning
- Attitudes
- Personality and self-concept
- Lifestyles

Social influences
- Roles
- Family
- Reference groups
- Opinion leaders
- Social classes
- Culture and subcultures

Consumer buying decision process

Problem recognition → Information search → Evaluation of alternatives → Purchase → Postpurchase evaluation

Protect his habitat. And yours.

When you recycle your rechargeable batteries, you preserve his environment – and ours. Check the batteries in your cordless power tools, cordless and cellular phones, camcorders, laptop computers, digital cameras, and two-way radios. If they no longer hold a charge, recycle them by visiting one of many collection sites nationwide, including those retailers listed below. For a complete list of rechargeable battery drop-off locations, visit www.call2recycle.org or call toll free 877-2-RECYCLE.

Recycle your rechargeable batteries.

call2recycle
A Rechargeable Battery Recycling Corporation program

Recycle at one of these national retailers: BLACK & DECKER   HOME DEPOT   Lowe's   RadioShack   Sears   TARGET

Problem Recognition
In this advertisement, Call2Recycle stimulates problem recognition—in this case, what to do with used batteries. Problem recognition is the first stage in the consumer buying process.

internal search An information search in which buyers search their memories for information about products that might solve their problem

external search An information search in which buyers seek information from sources other than memory

consideration set A group of brands within a product category that a buyer views as alternatives for possible purchase

in the school newspaper at the beginning of the term. Students who see the advertisement may recognize that they need these calculators for their course work.

Information Search

After recognizing the problem or need, a buyer (if continuing the decision process) searches for product information that will help resolve the problem or satisfy the need. For example, after recognizing her need for a programmable calculator, the above-mentioned student may search for information about different types and brands of calculators. She acquires information over time from her surroundings. However, the information's impact depends on how she interprets it.

An information search has two aspects. In an **internal search,** buyers search their memories for information about products that might solve their problem. If they cannot retrieve enough information from memory to make a decision, they seek additional information from outside sources in an **external search.** The external search may focus on communication with friends or relatives, comparison of available brands and prices, marketer-dominated sources, and/or public sources. For example, one survey found that the Internet is the preferred information source among car shoppers in online households, especially for pricing information.[4] An individual's personal contacts—friends, relatives, and associates—often are influential sources of information because the person trusts and respects them. Utilizing marketer-dominated sources of information, such as salespeople, advertising, websites, package labelling, and in-store demonstrations and displays, typically requires little effort on the consumer's part. Buyers also obtain information from public sources—for instance, government reports, news presentations, publications such as *Consumer Reports,* and reports from product-testing organizations. Consumers frequently view information from public sources as highly credible because of its factual and unbiased nature.

Repetition, a technique well known to advertisers, increases consumers' learning of information. When seeing or hearing an advertising message for the first time, recipients may not grasp all its important details, but they learn more details as the message is repeated. Nevertheless, even when commercials are initially effective, repetition eventually may cause wear-out, meaning consumers pay less attention to the commercial and respond to it less favourably than they did at first. Information can be presented verbally, numerically, or visually. Marketers pay great attention to the visual components of their advertising materials.

Evaluation of Alternatives

A successful information search within a product category yields a group of brands that a buyer views as possible alternatives. This group of brands is sometimes called a **consideration set** (also called an *evoked set*.) For example, a consideration set of programmable calculators might include those made by Texas Instruments, Hewlett-Packard, Sharp, and Canon.

Framing Product Attributes

Gillette frames product attributes of its Fusion razor by advertising features such as "comfortable" and "stylish."

To assess the products in a consideration set, the buyer uses **evaluative criteria,** objective characteristics (such as fuel economy rating), and subjective characteristics (such as style) that are important to the buyer when purchasing a car. When buying a calculator, one buyer may want a rechargeable unit with a large display and large buttons, whereas another may have no size preferences but dislikes rechargeable calculators. The buyer also assigns a certain level of importance to each criterion: some features and characteristics carry more weight than others. Using the criteria, the buyer rates and eventually ranks brands in the consideration set. The evaluation stage may yield no brand the buyer is willing to purchase. In that case, a further information search may be necessary.

Marketers may influence consumers' evaluations by *framing* the alternatives, that is, describing the alternatives and their attributes in a certain manner. Framing can make a characteristic seem more important to a consumer and facilitate its recall from memory. For example, by stressing a car's superior comfort and safety features over those of a competitor's, a carmaker can direct consumers' attention toward these points of superiority. Framing probably influences the decision processes of inexperienced buyers more than those of experienced ones. If the evaluation of alternatives yields one or more brands the consumer is willing to buy, he or she is ready to move on to the next stage of the decision process: the purchase.

Marketers can also influence value perceptions of consumers by framing them in different ways, using information, product design, point of contact (customer interaction), physical store environments, and the process of transferring ownership. Smith and Colgate provided a practical framework for using strategic marketing to create four different kinds of consumer value-orientations. Since consumers often define value differently, the four value types provide guidance for marketers when they are making strategic decisions in the marketing plan.[5]

Smith and Colgate identified four different consumer value types. **Functional/ instrumental value** is focused on whether the product or service has the desired features, reliability, and benefits. For example, a buyer may want specific features in a car or an appliance. Perhaps fuel economy is important in the purchase of a car, or maybe having four-wheel drive for harsh winters is important. A busy household may seek a kitchen range with a self-cleaning oven in order to save time.

Experiential/hedonic value focuses on whether the good or service creates the desired feelings, experiences, or emotions for the consumer. For example, casinos try to create exciting and fast-paced environments that make it easier for patrons to spend a lot of time and spend a lot of money. The décor, the noise, and the excitement of other patrons are all part of the casino experience.

Symbolic/expressive value focuses on the level of meaning that consumers ascribe to the good or service. This meaning may involve how the product makes a customer feel about him or herself, or the extent to which it evokes good memories or feelings. If a restaurant serves blueberry pie as good as grandma's, chances are patrons will want to come back. Tourism operators are in the business of creating exciting experiences and relaxing vacations.

evaluative criteria Objective and subjective characteristics that are important to a buyer

functional/instrumental value Customer value orientation that focuses on product features, reliability and benefits

experiential/hedonic value Customer value orientation that focuses on whether or not the product creates desired feelings, experiences, or emotions

symbolic/expressive value Customer value orientation that focuses on how the product makes a customer feel about him/herself, or the extent to which it evokes memories

cost/sacrifice value Customer value orientation that focuses on how buyers attempt to minimize product cost or sacrifice to obtain the product

The last type of consumer value is **cost (or sacrifice) value.** This type of value is concerned with how buyers try to minimize the cost or sacrifice associated with acquiring the product. Risk related to loss, or failure to deliver a product, as well as purchase price, are all aspects that may impact the buyer's cost or sacrifice value.

Smith and Colgate maintain that marketers must use promotion (information), product design, customer service (interactions), selling environment (store features, locations, online selling), and ease of purchase (ownership, warranties, guarantees, and price) as ways to deliver the type of value that motivates customers in the firm's target market.

Purchase

In the purchase stage, the consumer chooses the product or brand to be bought. Selection is based on the outcome of the evaluation stage and on other dimensions. Product availability may influence which brand is purchased. For example, if the brand ranked highest in evaluation is unavailable, the buyer may purchase the brand ranked second. If a consumer wants a pair of black Nikes and cannot find them in his size, he may buy a pair of black Reeboks.

During this stage, buyers also pick the seller from which they will buy the product. The choice of seller may affect final product selection and therefore the terms of sale, which, if negotiable, are determined at this stage. Other issues, such as price, delivery, warranties, maintenance agreements, installation, and credit arrangements, are also settled. Finally, the actual purchase takes place during this stage, unless the consumer decides to terminate the buying decision process.

Post-Purchase Evaluation

cognitive dissonance A buyer's doubts shortly after a purchase about whether the decision was the right one

After the purchase, the buyer begins evaluating the product to ascertain if its actual performance meets expected levels. Many criteria used in evaluating alternatives are applied again during post-purchase evaluation. The outcome of this stage is either satisfaction or dissatisfaction, which influences whether the consumer complains, communicates with other possible buyers, and repurchases the brand or product.

Shortly after the purchase of an expensive product, evaluation may result in **cognitive dissonance,** doubts in the buyer's mind about whether purchasing the product was the right decision. For example, after buying a $200 iPod, the consumer may feel guilty about the purchase or wonder whether she purchased the right brand and quality. Cognitive dissonance is most likely to arise when a person has recently bought an expensive, high-involvement product that lacks some of the desirable features of competing brands. A buyer experiencing cognitive dissonance may attempt to return the product or seek positive information about it to justify choosing it. Marketers sometimes attempt to reduce cognitive dissonance by having salespeople telephone recent purchasers to make sure they are satisfied with their new purchases. At times, recent buyers are sent results of studies showing that other consumers are very satisfied with the brand.

As Figure 5.1 shows, three major categories of influences are believed to affect the consumer buying decision process: situational, psychological, and social. In the remainder of this chapter, we focus on these influences. Although we discuss each major influence separately, their effects on the consumer decision process are interrelated.

Marketers employ a number of marketing research techniques, some of which will be discussed in Chapter 9, to better understand their customers' buying decision processes and factors that influence those buying decision processes. Both conventional and unconventional marketing research methods are used.

Situational Influences on the Buying Decision Process

situational influences Influences resulting from circumstances, time, and location that affect the consumer buying decision process

Situational influences result from circumstances, time, and location that affect the consumer buying decision process. For example, buying an automobile tire after noticing while washing your car that the tire is badly worn is a different experience from buying a tire right after a blowout on the highway derails your vacation. Situational factors can influence the buyer during any stage of the consumer buying decision process and may cause the individual to shorten, lengthen, or terminate the process.

Situational factors can be classified into five categories: physical surroundings, social surroundings, time perspective, reason for purchase, and the buyer's momentary mood and condition.[6] Physical surroundings include location, store atmosphere, aromas, sounds, lighting, weather, and other factors in the physical environment in which the decision process occurs. Marketers at some banks, department stores, and specialty stores go to considerable effort and expense to create physical settings conducive to making purchase decisions. Numerous restaurant chains, such as Hard Rock Café and Montana's, invest heavily in facilities, often building from the ground up, to provide special surroundings that enhance customers' dining experiences.

In some settings, dimensions such as weather, traffic sounds, and odours are clearly beyond marketers' control; instead marketers must try to make customers more comfortable. General climatic conditions, for example, may influence a customer's decision to buy a specific type of vehicle (such as an SUV) and certain accessories (such as four-wheel drive). Current weather conditions, depending on whether they are favourable or unfavourable, may either encourage or discourage consumers to go shopping to seek out specific products. Social surroundings include characteristics and interactions of others who are present during a purchase decision, such as friends, relatives, salespeople, and other customers. Buyers may feel pressured to behave in a certain way because they are in a public place such as a restaurant, store, or sports arena. Thoughts about who will be around when the product is used or consumed is also a dimension of the social setting. An overcrowded store or an argument between a customer and a salesperson may cause consumers to stop shopping or even leave the store.

The time dimension also influences the buying decision process in several ways, such as the amount of time required to become knowledgeable about a product, to search for it, and to buy and use it. For instance, more men are buying diamond engagement rings online partly to make an informed decision at their own convenience. A high-end Internet jeweler like Blue Nile features interactive tools on its website to help men educate themselves about diamonds and then select a unique combination from its large inventory of diamonds and settings.[7] Time plays a major role in that the buyer considers the possible frequency of product use, the length of time required to use the product, and the length of the overall product life. Other time dimensions that influence purchases include time of day, day of the week or month, seasons, and holidays. The amount of time pressure a consumer is under affects how much time is devoted to purchase decisions. A customer under severe time constraints is likely either to make a quick purchase decision or to delay a decision.

The purchase reason raises the questions of what exactly the product purchase should accomplish and for whom. Generally, consumers purchase an item for their own use, for household use, or as a gift. For example, people who are buying a gift may buy a different product from one they would buy for themselves. If you own a Cross pen, for example, it is unlikely that you bought it for yourself.

The buyer's momentary moods (such as anger, anxiety, contentment) or momentary conditions (fatigue, illness, being flush with cash) may have a bearing on the consumer buying decision process. These moods or conditions immediately precede the current situation and are not chronic. Any of these moods or conditions can affect a person's ability and desire to search for information, receive information, or seek and evaluate alternatives. They can also significantly influence a consumer's post-purchase evaluation.

Psychological Influences on the Buying Decision Process

psychological influences
Factors that in part determine people's general behaviour, thus influencing their behaviour as consumers

Psychological influences partly determine people's general behaviour and thus influence their behaviour as consumers. Primary psychological influences on consumer behaviour are perception, motives, learning, attitudes, personality and self-concept, and lifestyles. Even though these psychological factors operate internally, they are very much affected by social forces outside the individual.

perception The process of selecting, organizing, and interpreting information inputs to produce meaning

information inputs Sensations received through sight, taste, hearing, smell, and touch

selective exposure The process by which some inputs are selected to reach awareness and others are not

selective distortion An individual's changing or twisting of information that is inconsistent with personal feelings or beliefs

selective retention Remembering information inputs that support personal feelings and beliefs and forgetting inputs that do not

Perception

Different people perceive the same thing at the same time in different ways. When you first look at the illustration below, do you see the fish changing into birds or the birds changing into fish? Similarly, an individual may perceive the same item in a number of ways at different times. **Perception** is the process of selecting, organizing, and interpreting information inputs to produce meaning. **Information inputs** are sensations received through sight, taste, hearing, smell, and touch. When we hear an advertisement, see a friend, smell polluted air or water, or touch a product, we receive information inputs.

As the definition indicates, perception is a three-step process. Although we receive numerous pieces of information at once, only a few reach our awareness. We select some inputs and ignore others because we cannot be conscious of all inputs at one time. This process is called **selective exposure** because an individual selects which inputs will reach awareness. If you are concentrating on this paragraph, you probably are not aware that cars outside are making noise, that the room light is on, or that you are touching this page. Even though you receive these inputs, they do not reach your awareness until they are pointed out.

An individual's current set of needs affects selective exposure. Information inputs that relate to one's strongest needs at a given time are more likely to be selected to reach awareness. It is not by random chance that many fast-food commercials are aired near mealtimes. Customers are more likely to tune in to these advertisements at these times.

The selective nature of perception may result not only in selective exposure but also in two other conditions: selective distortion and selective retention. **Selective distortion** is changing or twisting currently received information; it occurs when a person receives information inconsistent with personal feelings or beliefs. For example, on seeing an advertisement promoting a disliked brand, a viewer may distort the information to make it more consistent with prior views. This distortion substantially lessens the effect of the advertisement on the individual. In **selective retention,** a person remembers information inputs that support personal feelings and beliefs and forgets inputs that do not. After hearing a sales presentation and leaving a store, for example, a customer may forget many selling points if they contradict personal beliefs.

The second step in the process of perception is perceptual organization. Information inputs that reach awareness are not received in an organized form. To produce meaning, an individual must mentally organize and integrate new information with what is already stored in memory. People use several methods to organize. One method, called *closure,* occurs when a person mentally fills in missing elements in a pattern or statement. In an attempt to draw attention to its brand, an advertiser will capitalize on closure by using incomplete images, sounds, or statements in its advertisements.

Interpretation, the third step in the perceptual process, is the assignment of meaning to what has been organized. A person bases interpretation on what he or she expects or what is familiar. For this reason, a manufacturer that changes a product or its package faces a major problem: when people are looking for the old, familiar product or package, they may not recognize the new one. For instance, when Smucker's redesigned its packaging, marketers told designers that although they wanted a more contemporary package design, they also wanted a classic look so that customers would perceive the products to be the familiar ones they had been buying for years. Unless a product or package change is accompanied by a promotional

Fish or Fowl?

Do you see fish changing into birds or birds changing into fish?

program that makes people aware of the change, an organization may suffer a sales decline.

Although marketers cannot control buyers' perceptions, they often try to influence them through information. However, several problems may arise from such attempts. First, a consumer's perceptual process may operate such that a seller's information never reaches that person. For example, a buyer may block out a salesperson's presentation. Second, a buyer may receive a seller's information but perceive it differently than was intended. For example, when a toothpaste producer advertises that "35 percent of the people who use this toothpaste have fewer cavities," a customer might infer that 65 percent of users have more cavities. Third, a buyer who perceives information inputs to be inconsistent with prior beliefs is likely to forget the information quickly.

Motives

motive An internal energizing force that directs a person's behaviour toward satisfying needs or achieving goals

A **motive** is an internal energizing force that directs a person's activities toward satisfying needs or achieving goals. Buyers' actions are affected by a set of motives rather than by just one motive. At a single point in time, some of a person's motives are stronger than others. For example, a person's motives for having a cup of coffee are much stronger right after waking up than just before going to bed. Motives also affect the direction and intensity of behaviour. Some motives may help an individual achieve his or her goals, whereas others create barriers to goal achievement.

Maslow's hierarchy of needs The five levels of needs that humans seek to satisfy, from most to least important

Abraham Maslow, an American psychologist, conceived a theory of motivation based on a hierarchy of needs. According to Maslow, humans seek to satisfy five levels of needs, from most important to least important, as shown in Figure 5.2. This sequence is known as **Maslow's hierarchy of needs.** Once needs at one level are met, humans seek to fulfill needs at the next level up in the hierarchy.

At the most basic level are *physiological needs,* requirements for survival such as food, water, sex, clothing, and shelter, which people try to satisfy first. Food and beverage marketers often appeal to physiological needs. Marketers of whitening toothpastes such as Ultrabrite sometimes promote their brands based on sex appeal.

At the next level are *safety needs,* which include security and freedom from physical and emotional pain and suffering. Life insurance, automobile air bags, carbon monoxide detectors, vitamins, and decay-fighting toothpastes are products that consumers purchase to meet safety needs.

Next are *social needs,* the human requirements for love and affection and a sense of belonging. Advertisements frequently appeal to social needs. Ads for cosmetics and other beauty products, jewelry, and even cars often suggest that purchasing these products will bring love. Certain types of trendy clothing, such as Abercrombie jeans, Nike athletic shoes, or T-shirts imprinted with logos or slogans, appeal to the customer's need to belong.

figure 5.2

MASLOW'S HIERARCHY OF NEEDS

Maslow believed that people seek to fulfill five categories of needs.

At the level of *esteem needs,* people require respect and recognition from others as well as self-esteem, a sense of one's own worth. Owning a Lexus automobile, having a beauty makeover, or flying first class can satisfy esteem needs. At the top of the hierarchy are *self-actualization needs.* These refer to people's need to grow and develop and to become all they are capable of becoming. Some products that satisfy these needs include fitness centre memberships, education, self-improvement workshops, and skiing lessons. Motives that influence where a person purchases products on a regular basis are called **patronage motives.** A buyer may shop at a specific store because of such patronage motives as price, service, location, product variety, or friendliness of salespeople. To capitalize on patronage motives, marketers try to determine why regular customers patronize a particular store and to emphasize these characteristics in the store's marketing mix.

patronage motives Motives that influence where a person purchases products on a regular basis

Learning

learning Changes in an individual's thought processes and behaviour caused by information and experience

Learning refers to changes in a person's thought processes and behaviour caused by information and experience. Consequences of behaviour strongly influence the learning process. Behaviours that result in satisfying consequences tend to be repeated.

Stimulus-response theory dictates that living beings (animals and humans) can learn to associate a particular stimuli with a response. If the response to the stimuli is favourable, the stimuli will evoke a positive response through learned behaviour. Consumers learn to respond to the stimuli that give them the greatest satisfaction. For example, someone who enjoys a Tim Horton's cup of coffee will come to desire the coffee when they see the Tim Horton's sign. Loyal Big Mac buyers may actually salivate when they see the McDonald's sign. The sign becomes the stimulus that they have learned to associate with a Big Mac. McDonald's spent millions to draw this relationship with their "Big Mac Attack" advertising campaigns. In the same way, a consumer who buys a Snickers candy bar and enjoys the taste is more likely to buy a Snickers again. In fact, the individual will probably continue to purchase that brand until it no longer provides satisfaction. When effects of the behaviour are no longer satisfying, the person may switch brands or stop eating candy bars altogether.

Learning

Marketers attempt to change thought processes and behaviours with their advertisements.

When making purchasing decisions, buyers process information. Individuals' abilities in this regard differ. The type of information inexperienced buyers use may differ from the type used by experienced shoppers familiar with the product and purchase situation. Thus, two potential purchasers of an antique desk may use different types of information in making their purchase decisions. The inexperienced buyer may judge the desk's value by price, whereas the more experienced buyer may seek information about the manufacturer, period, and place of origin to judge the desk's quality and value. Consumers lacking experience may seek information from others when making a purchase and even take along an informed "purchase pal." More experienced buyers have greater self-confidence and more knowledge about the product and can recognize which product features are reliable cues to product quality.

Marketers help customers learn about their products by helping them gain experience with them. Free samples, sometimes coupled with coupons, can successfully encourage trial and reduce purchase risk. For example, because some consumers may be wary of exotic menu items, restaurants sometimes offer free samples. In-store demonstrations foster knowledge of product uses. A software producer may use point-of-sale product demonstrations to introduce a new product. Test drives give potential new-car purchasers some experience with the automobile's features.

Is it possible to reach new heights without any lows?

Kashi® GOLEAN Roll!® is designed for an optimized glycemic response – sustained energy from slow-release carbs. And it has high fiber and protein to help you stay satisfied. All natural, and all rolled up in nuts, crunchy whole grains and chocolate around a chewy center. The path to health now has fewer ups and downs. Follow it to kashi.com/golean.

See how far it takes you.

Consumers also learn by experiencing products indirectly through information from salespeople, advertisements, websites, friends, and relatives. Through sales personnel and advertisements, marketers offer information before (and sometimes after) purchases to influence what consumers learn and to create more favourable attitudes toward the product. However, their efforts are seldom fully successful. Marketers encounter problems in attracting and holding consumers' attention, providing consumers with important information for making purchase decisions, and convincing them to try the product.

Attitudes

attitude An individual's enduring evaluation of feelings about and behavioural tendencies toward an object or idea

attitude scale A means of measuring consumer attitudes by gauging the intensity of individuals' reactions to adjectives, phrases, or sentences about an object

An **attitude** is an individual's enduring evaluation of feelings about and behavioural tendencies toward an object or idea. The objects toward which we have attitudes may be tangible or intangible, living or non-living. For example, we have attitudes toward sex, religion, politics, and music, just as we do toward cars, football, and breakfast cereals. Although attitudes can change, they tend to generally remain stable and do not vary from moment to moment. However, all of a person's attitudes do not have equal impact at any one time; some are stronger than others. Individuals acquire attitudes through experience and interaction with other people.

An attitude consists of three major components: cognitive, affective, and behavioural. The cognitive component is the person's knowledge and information about the object or idea. The affective component comprises the individual's feelings and emotions toward the object or idea. The behavioural component manifests itself in the person's actions regarding the object or idea. Changes in one of these components may or may not alter the other components. Thus, a consumer may become more knowledgeable about a specific brand without changing the affective or behavioural components of his or her attitude toward that brand.

Consumer attitudes toward a company and its products greatly influence success or failure of the firm's marketing strategy. When consumers have strong negative attitudes toward one or more aspects of a firm's marketing practices, they may not only stop using its products but also urge relatives and friends to do likewise.

Because attitudes play such an important part in determining consumer behaviour, marketers should measure consumer attitudes toward prices, package designs, brand names, advertisements, salespeople, repair services, store locations, features of existing or proposed products, and social responsibility efforts. When marketers determine that a significant number of consumers have negative attitudes toward an aspect of a marketing mix, they may try to change those attitudes to make them more favourable. This task is generally lengthy, expensive, and difficult, and may require extensive promotional efforts. To alter consumers' responses so that more of them buy a given brand, a firm might launch an information-focused

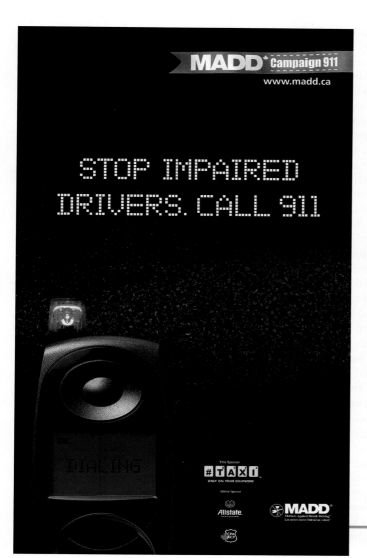

Attempting to Change Attitudes
Mothers Against Drunk Driving works to educate people about the dangers of drunk driving.

campaign to change the cognitive component of a consumer's attitude or a persuasive (emotional) campaign to influence the affective component. Distributing free samples might help change the behavioural component. Both business and non-business organizations try to change people's attitudes about many things, from health and safety to prices and product features.

Personality and Self-Concept

personality A set of internal traits and distinct behavioural tendencies that result in consistent patterns of behaviour in certain situations

Personality is a set of internal traits and distinct behavioural tendencies that result in consistent patterns of behaviour in certain situations. An individual's personality arises from hereditary characteristics and personal experiences that make the person unique. Personalities typically are described as having one or more characteristics, such as compulsiveness, ambition, gregariousness, dogmatism, authoritarianism, introversion, extroversion, and competitiveness. Marketing researchers look for relationships between such characteristics and buying behaviour. Even though a few links between several personality traits and buyer behaviour have been determined, results of many studies have been inconclusive. The weak association between personality and buying behaviour may be the result of unreliable measures rather than a lack of a relationship. A number of marketers are convinced that consumers' personalities do influence types and brands of products purchased. For example, the type of clothing, jewelry, or automobile a person buys may reflect one or more personality characteristics.

Some marketers believe that brands have their own personalities, and that individuals are drawn to brands with personalities that are a lot like their own. Brand personality is described as the set of human characteristics that a brand appears to have.[8] Traits that brands may have that mimic human characteristics include sincerity/honesty/wholesomeness, excitement/daring, competence/intelligence/reliability, charm and sophistication, and toughness or ruggedness.

At times marketers aim advertising at certain types of personalities. Marketers focus on positively valued personality characteristics, such as security consciousness, sociability, independence, or competitiveness, rather than on negatively valued ones, such as insensitivity or timidity. For example, ads for certain cigarette brands are directed toward specific personality types.

One of the best examples for advertising personalities was the Marlboro Man, the rugged cowboy that graced the ads for Phillip Morris' Marlboro cigarettes starting in 1955. Authors Karlan, Lazar, and Salter ranked The Marlboro Man number one out of 101 most influential people who never lived, a list of influential advertising personalities and fictional characters, in their book by the same name. The Marlboro Man and his fictional Marlboro Country became international symbols for masculinity. The impact of the Marlboro campaign continued intensely even after television advertising was banned in the United States in 1971. However, the death knell for the Marlboro Man came when both cowboy models for the icon, Wayne McLaran and David McLean, died of lung cancer. McLean was able to testify in favour of anti-smoking legislation before his death. Ironically, the death of the mythical Marlboro Man from illness caused by tobacco smoking became a compelling international anti-smoking campaign for people of all ages.[9]

self-concept A perception or view of oneself

A person's self-concept is closely linked to personality. **Self-concept** (sometimes called *self-image*) is a perception or view of oneself. Individuals develop and alter their self-concepts based on an interaction between psychological and social dimensions. Research shows that buyers purchase products that reflect and enhance their self-concepts and that purchase decisions are important to the development and maintenance of a stable self-concept. Consumers' self-concepts may influence whether they buy a product in a specific product category and may affect brand selection as well as where they buy.

There is some debate over whether individuals seek their real selves when buying goods and services, or whether they seek their ideal selves. Tweens, those between the ages of nine and 14, want to think of themselves as teens. The Canadian tween market consists of 2.4 million youths with $1.5 billion to spend: an average of over $130 each week. Advertisers know that due to the "age aspirations of tweens" they never address them as what they really are, but as they want to be, a teen.[10]

But youth aren't the only ones who are motivated more by their ideal selves, than their real selves. In the 1980s Johnson & Johnson introduced a special shampoo for women over the age of 40. The shampoo, named Affinity, was supposed to make older hair more manageable, but the product flopped when it became obvious that women over 40 didn't want to think of themselves as being over the age of forty, or of having "old" hair that required special care![11]

Vanity sizing in clothing is one innovation designed to appeal to a woman's self-concept, particularly as they grow older and naturally gain weight. Women's clothing sizes are getting smaller: at least on the label. This makes little sense in the face of an aging population, and a population that carries more body weight than previous generations.[12]

Vanity sizing is the approach taken by many clothing manufacturers to relabel fashion sizes downward in an attempt to cater to a woman's need to be seen as thin: the fashion ideal. Today's size zero was a size four thirty years ago, and a size eight fifty years ago.

More women's clothing retailers are also carrying sizes that are extremely small, often labeled XXS or XS, in order to attract girls to their clothing lines. If retailers can build relationships with girls and hold onto their consumer loyalty as they grow into women, the lifetime value for each shopper becomes much more attractive. Marketing to the self-concept, often based on the ideal self rather than the real self, is often the ticket to retail success.

Lifestyles

lifestyle An individual's pattern of living expressed through activities, interests, and opinions

A **lifestyle** is an individual's pattern of living expressed through activities, interests, and opinions. Lifestyle patterns include the ways people spend time, the extent of their interaction with others, and their general outlook on life and living. People partially determine their own lifestyles, but the pattern is also affected by personality and by demographic factors such as age, education, income, and social class. Lifestyles are measured through a lengthy series of questions.

Lifestyles have a strong impact on many aspects of the consumer buying decision process, from problem recognition to postpurchase evaluation. Lifestyles influence consumers' product needs, brand preferences, types of media used, and how and where they shop.

- VALS®, or Values-Attitudes-Lifestyles segments, provide an analytical tool to begin to understand the target market. Values provide an important element in consumer behaviour, helping to describe why one person would drive a Mercedes, while another equally affluent person would drive a family-oriented minivan. The VALS segments appear in Figure 5.3 on page 122. Try the VALS survey at the following website to see what VALS category you fit into http://www.sric-bi.com/VALS/presurvey.shtml.

Lifestyles

A variety of purchasing decisions are partially influenced by lifestyles.

figure 5.3

VALS SEGMENTS

VALS® Segments

Innovators

Innovators have the most resources, are very idealistic, and have a lot of self-esteem. They are natural leaders who are able to take control of many situations. They are very open to change and are very innovative. They are sophisticated, and tend to consume upscale, niche-oriented goods, and services.

Thinkers & Believers

These individuals are both motivated by idealism, but thinkers have much greater resources to bring their ideas to light than do believers. Thinkers are satisfied, comfortable, and reflective, while believers are very traditional and more driven by rules and authority. Thinkers are well-educated information seekers, who seek value by focusing on durability and functionality in what they buy. Believers are more likely to buy products that they already know, as well as name brand products.

Achievers & Strivers

Achievers and strivers are both achievement-oriented, but achievers have more resources at their disposal than strivers do. Achievers are very family-oriented, while strivers are more trendy and fun-loving. Achievers engage in conspicuous consumption, meaning that they buy things that reflect their social status and success. They are also adverse to risk and change. Strivers have too little income to follow in the footsteps of achievers, but they will try to buy things that make them look wealthier than they are.

Experiences & Makers

Experiencers and makers are both motivated primarily by self-expression. However, experiencers have more resources than do makers, which allows them to consume products that vent their self-expression. They spend a lot of money on fashion, socializing, and entertainment, and they seek out the new and offbeat in goods and services. Makers lack the financial ability to do so and rely primarily on more basic and practical goods and services. They spend leisure time with friends and family.

Survivors

Survivors have the least resources of any group and often feel powerless because of it. They tend to be brand loyal and buy discounted merchandise, focusing primarily on safety and security. They have very narrowly focused lives.

Social Influences on the Buying Decision Process

social influences The forces other people exert on one's buying behaviour

Forces that other people exert on buying behaviour are called **social influences.** As Figure 5.1 shows, they are grouped into five major areas: roles, family, reference groups and opinion leaders, social classes, and culture and subcultures.

Roles

role Actions and activities that a person in a particular position is supposed to perform based on expectations of the individual and surrounding persons

All of us occupy positions within groups, organizations, and institutions. Associated with each position is a **role,** a set of actions and activities a person in a particular position is supposed to perform based on expectations of both the individual and surrounding persons. Because people occupy numerous positions, they have many roles. For example, a man may perform the roles of son, husband, father, employee or employer, church member, civic organization member, and student in an evening college class. Thus, multiple sets of expectations are placed on each person's behaviour.

An individual's roles influence both general behaviour and buying behaviour. The demands of a person's many roles may be diverse and even inconsistent. Consider the various types of clothes that you buy and wear depending on whether you are going to class, to work, to a party, or to an aerobics class. You and others involved in these settings have expectations about what is acceptable clothing for these events. Thus, the expectations of those around us affect our purchases of clothing and many other products.

Family Influences and Consumer Buying Decisions

Family influences have a very direct impact on the consumer buying decision process. Parents teach children how to cope with a variety of problems, including those dealing with purchase decisions. **Consumer socialization** is the process through which a person acquires the knowledge and skills to function as a consumer. Often children gain this knowledge and set of skills by observing parents and older siblings in purchase situations, as well as through their own purchase experiences. Children observe brand preferences and buying practices in their families and, as adults, retain some of these brand preferences and buying practices as they establish and raise their own families. Buying decisions made by a family are a combination of group and individual decision making.

Although female roles continue to change, women still make buying decisions related to many household items, including health-care products, laundry supplies, paper products, and foods. Spouses participate jointly in the purchase of a variety of products, especially durable goods. Due to changes in men's roles, a significant proportion of men are major grocery shoppers. Children make many purchase decisions and influence numerous household purchase decisions. Knowing that children wield considerable influence over food brand preferences, H. J. Heinz is targeting them with EZ Squirt green, blue, or purple ketchup in a squeeze bottle. Kids like squeezing squiggly coloured patterns on their hamburgers, and parents like the ketchup's extra vitamin C.[13]

The family life cycle stage affects individual and joint needs of family members. (Family life cycle stages are discussed in Chapter 8.) For example, consider how the car needs of recently married "twenty-somethings" differ from those of the same couple when they are "forty-somethings" with a 13-year-old daughter and a 17-year-old son. Family life cycle changes can affect which family members are involved in purchase decisions and the types of products purchased.

The extent to which either one or both of the two adult family members take part in family decision making varies among families and product categories. As shown in Table 5.2, there are four types of family decisions: autonomic, husband-dominant, wife-dominant, and syncratic. In autonomic decision making, each adult household member makes an equal number of decisions. In husband-dominant or wife-dominant decision making, The husband or the wife makes most of the family decisions. Syncratic decision making means both partners jointly make most decisions concerning purchases. The type of family decision making employed depends on the values and

consumer socialization
The process through which a person acquires the knowledge and skills to function as a consumer

Enter the Gold Collar Aspirationalists

There is a unique group of young people in Canada—young people with high-end tastes, but limited income. These 18- to 25-year olds still live with their parents and they have a taste for the good life. As high school graduates not seeking post-secondary education, one might expect that they would share their parents' blue collar attitudes toward marketing and money, but nothing could be further from the truth.

A study has shown that these young people spend a tremendous amount of money on things that they really can't afford: facial cream valued at over $200 a jar, $300 sun glasses, designer duds, and more. Why? Because they like to stand out in a crowd.

These "gold collar aspirationalists" achieve through their consumption of high-priced goods and services. They do not have living expenses or student debt. They spend a lot of money to look like they come from a more well-heeled background. They buy their way into respectability, a process known as trading-up.

Marketers often overlook young adults without post-secondary education, assuming that they aren't profitable markets. The gold collar aspirationalists, worth an estimated $4 billion a year, may prove them wrong.

table 5.2   TYPES OF FAMILY DECISION MAKING

Decision-Making Type	Decision Maker	Types of Products
Husband-dominant	Male head-of-household	Lawn mowers, hardware and tools, stereos, refrigerators, washer and dryer
Wife-dominant	Female head-of-household	Children's clothing, women's clothing, groceries, pots and pans, toiletries, home decoration
Autonomic	Equally likely to be made by the husband or wife, but not by both	Men's clothing, luggage, toys and games, sporting equipment, cameras
Syncratic	Made jointly by husband and wife	Vacations, TVs, living room furniture, carpets, financial planning services, family cars

attitudes of family members. However, research indicates that women are the primary decision makers for 80–85 percent of all consumer buying decisions.[14]

There are some interesting trends in Table 5.2. Note that most of the husband's dominant shopping behaviour addresses household maintenance and appliances. Most of the wife's dominant shopping behaviour addresses household products, meal preparation, and home décor. She is also responsible for buying clothing for everyone including herself. Autonomic decisions for men's clothing indicate that it is equally likely to be purchased by her, or her husband, but not by both. A large proportion of men's underwear is actually purchased by women, who buy the items when buying

Linda Shops at Wal-Mart

Wal-Mart has a new planning guide and her name is Linda. Linda is Wal-Mart's typical target customer and she is helping to lead Wal-Mart into the next generation of Canadian retailing.

Linda is a hypothetical shopper who has been designed to reflect Wal-Mart's key consumer: the soccer mom, career woman, and wife who juggles many activities successfully and multi-tasks every day. Her retail solution? A one-stop shopping environment that delivers quality, service, selection, and overall value.

Linda is not an abstract concept to the Wal-Mart planning team. She has taken visual form through photographs of a woman between the ages of 35 and 45: an image that has also graced life-sized cardboard cutouts. Linda was the brainchild of the Mississauga Wal-Mart team, and she provides real direction for day-to-day marketing decisions.

Mario Pilozzi, CEO of Wal-Mart Canada, insists that it is very important to have a realistic core customer to guide decision making for the retail giant. By giving their core customer a real identity, the Wal-Mart team is better able to understand her needs and to work to make their store a success in a competitive market.

similar goods for the rest of the household. This is an important thing to know if you are Jockey®, Stanfields®, or Fruit of the Loom®. In a similar twist, a large percentage of women's cologne and jewelry (both popular gifts for women) are actually bought by men.

When two or more family members participate in a purchase, their roles may dictate that each is responsible for performing certain purchase-related tasks, such as initiating the idea, gathering information, determining if the product is affordable, deciding whether to buy the product, or selecting the specific brand. The specific purchase tasks performed depend on the types of products being considered, the kind of family purchase decision process typically employed, and the amount of influence children have in the decision process. Thus, different family members may play different roles in the family buying process.

Within a household, an individual may perform one or more roles related to making buying decisions. The gatekeeper is the household member who collects and controls information. This may include price and quality comparisons, locations of sellers, and assessment of which brand best suits the family's needs. For example, if a family is planning a summer vacation, the gatekeeper might compare prices for hotels and airfare. The influencer is a family member who expresses his or her opinions and tries to influence buying decisions. In the vacation example, an influencer might be a child who wants to go to Disney World or a teenager who wants only to go snowboarding. The decider is a member who makes the buying choice. This role switches based on the type and expense of the product being purchased. In the case of a vacation, the decider will more likely be the adults who use a combination of information, influences, and their own preferences. The buyer is a member who actually makes the purchase. After the family has decided to go to Disney World, the buyer will make all of the actual travel purchases. The user is a household member who consumes or uses the product. In this Disney World example, all members of the family would be users.

Reference Groups

A **reference group** is a group that a person identifies with so strongly that he or she adopts the values, attitudes, and behaviour of group members. Reference groups can be large or small. Most people have several reference groups, such as families, work-related groups, fraternities or sororities, civic clubs, professional organizations, or church-related groups.

In general, there are three major types of reference groups: membership, aspirational, and disassociative. A membership reference group is one to which an individual actually belongs; the individual identifies with group members strongly enough to take on the values, attitudes, and behaviours of people in that group. An aspirational reference group is a group to which a person aspires to belong; the individual desires to be like those group members. A group that a person does not wish to be associated with is a disassociative or negative reference group; the individual does not want to take on the values, attitudes, and behaviour of group members.

A reference group may serve as an individual's point of comparison and source of information. A customer's behaviour may change to be more in line with actions and beliefs of group members. For example, a person may stop buying one brand of shirts and switch to another based on reference group members' advice. An individual may also seek information from the reference group about other factors regarding a prospective purchase, such as where to buy a certain product.

The extent to which a reference group affects a purchase decision depends on the product's conspicuousness and on the individual's susceptibility to reference group influence. Generally, the more conspicuous a product, the more likely that the purchase decision will be influenced by reference groups. A product's conspicuousness is determined by whether others can see it and whether it can attract attention. Reference groups can affect whether a person does or does not buy a product at all, buys a type of product within a product category, or buys a specific brand.

A marketer sometimes tries to use reference group influence in advertisements by suggesting that people in a specific group buy a product and are highly satisfied with

reference group A group that a person identifies with so strongly that he or she adopts the values, attitudes, and behaviour of group members it. In this type of appeal, the advertiser hopes that many people will accept the suggested group as a reference group and buy (or react more favourably to) the product. Whether this kind of advertising succeeds depends on three factors: how effectively the advertisement communicates the message, the type of product, and the individual's susceptibility to reference group influence.

Opinion Leaders

opinion leader A member of an informal group who provides information about a specific topic to other group members

An **opinion leader** is a member of an informal group who provides information about a specific topic, like software, to other group members who seek that information. He or she is in a position or has knowledge or expertise that makes him or her a credible resource of information about a few topics. Opinion leaders are easily accessible and they are viewed by other group members as being well informed about a particular topic. While opinion leaders are not the foremost authority on all topics, because such individuals know they are opinion leaders, they feel a responsibility to remain informed about a topic and thus seek out advertisements, manufacturers' brochures, salespeople, and other sources of information.

An opinion leader is likely to be most influential when consumers have high product involvement but low product knowledge, when they share the opinion leader's values and attitudes, and when the product details are numerous or complicated. Possible opinion leaders and topics are shown in Table 5.3.

Big Spending on the Teen Scene

In 2006, 4.2 million teens represented a strong force in the marketplace. Canadian teens spend over $14 billion each year. They get their money from a variety of sources, including part-time jobs, parents, step-parents, and grandparents. The average teen has up to $500 a month to spend as they wish.

Favourite products of this age group include CDs, fast food, clothes, makeup, movie tickets, accessories, school supplies, books, magazines, shoes, and hair-care products. Teenage girls as well as boys like electronic gear, notably cell phones, which they use to stay in touch with each other almost constantly. Teenagers are also important sales drivers of video games and portable entertainment devices such as iPods and DVD players.

Teenagers shape their parents' consumer habits through what is becoming known as "pester power" or "kidfluence": the ability to encourage their parents to buy a variety of goods and services. Those in this age group are also strong influencers of family computer and consumer electronics purchases. Most parents wouldn't dare buy a computer or digital video recorder without consulting their techno-savvy teen.

Teenagers also influence what other teens buy. Research also shows that teens are much more concerned about having the right clothes to fit into a group. Peer influence, youth culture, and disposable income are key factors that shape Canada's youth market. According to one economist, "Consumption is a thoroughly social activity, and what one person buys, wears, drives or eats affects the desires and behaviours of those around them." This is especially true for teenagers, who are greatly influenced by the desires and behaviours of their peer groups.

Teenagers are a diverse, growing, and crucial market group in the United States today. Their beliefs, attitudes, and behaviours do and will affect buying trends for several years.

Today's teens are informed, savvy shoppers, and they are also the most culturally diverse group of young people to grace Canada's shopping scene. Shopping is also an activity that meets with parental approval in many immigrant families who work hard to see that their children get to socialize as much as possible with young people who were born in Canada. Given that immigrant families have larger families than most Canadian-born couples, the ethnic mix in the youth market continues to grow.

table 5.3   EXAMPLES OF OPINION LEADERS AND TOPICS

Opinion Leader	Possible Topics
Local religious leader	Charities to support, political ideas, lifestyle choices
Sorority president	Clothing and shoe purchases, hair styles, nail and hair salons
"Movie buff" friend	Movies to see in theatre or rent, DVDs to buy, television programs to watch
Family doctor	Prescription drugs, vitamins, health products
"Techie" acquaintance	Computer and other electronics purchases, software purchases, Internet service choices, video game purchases

Social Classes

social class An open group of individuals with similar social rank

In all societies, people rank others into higher or lower positions of respect. This ranking process, called social stratification, results in social classes. A **social class** is an open aggregate of people with similar social rank. A class is referred to as *open* because

table 5.4   SOCIAL CLASS BEHAVIOURAL TRAITS AND PURCHASING CHARACTERISTICS

Class (% of Population)	Behavioural Traits and Spending Patterns
Upper-upper (less than 1)	Upper-uppers have inherited wealth: they are the "old money" with very well-established cultural attributes and roles. These individuals also tend to be conservative in their dress and their spending patterns.
Lower-upper (2–4)	Lower-uppers include self-made millionaires or the "nouveau riche." Those with new money tend to carry on with many of their old cultural mannerisms, which may not sit well with the "old money" crowd. These individuals are more likely to spend in a very conspicuous way to show that they fit into high class society. They also tend to be very active in charitable activities.
Upper-Middle (12.5)	Professionals, managers, and independent business owners. These individuals are not wealthy but they are upwardly mobile and want the best for themselves and their families. They value education.
Lower-Middle (32)	Average-paid, white collar workers and blue collar friends. They live in the best possible neighbourhoods and try to do the right thing. They buy the popular items to keep up with fashionable things, and may seek brand name goods and services.
Working Class (38)	Average-paid, blue collar workers with working class lifestyle. They tend to rely on family members for help and support from time to time. They also seek advice on purchases.
Upper-Lower (9)	Working poor, but not welfare poor. These individuals have incomes just above the poverty line. Their behaviour may be considered to be "trashy" or "crude" by others outside of their peer groups. Individuals try to consume products to place themselves in a higher social stratum, but they are limited by their economic means.
Lower-Lower (7)	Welfare poor, chronically unemployed, and those who earn an income from unlawful means. Individuals in this group live a day-to-day existence and are seriously economically deprived.

Source: Adapted with permission from Richard P. Coleman, "The Continuing Significance of Social Class in Marketing," *Journal of Consumer Research*, Dec. 1983, pp. 265–280, with data from J. Paul Peter and Jerry C. Olson, *Consumer Behavior: Marketing Strategy Perspective.* (Homewood, Ill.: Irwin, 1987), p. 433.

people can move into and out of it. Criteria for grouping people into classes vary from one society to another. Canada and the United States share the same social class structure. Analyses of social class divides people into three to seven categories. Social scientist Richard P. Coleman suggests that for purposes of consumer analysis the population is divided into the four major status groups shown in Table 5.4. However, he cautions marketers that considerable diversity exists in people's life situations within each status group.

To some degree, individuals within social classes develop and assume common behavioural patterns. They may have similar attitudes, values, language patterns, and possessions. Social class influences many aspects of people's lives. Because people have the most frequent interaction with people from within their own social class, most people are more likely to be influenced by others within their own class than by those in other classes. For example, it affects their chances of having children and their children's chances of surviving infancy. It influences their childhood training, choice of religion, financial planning decisions, access to higher education, selection of occupation, and leisure time activities. Because social class has a bearing on so many aspects of a person's life, it also affects buying decisions.

Social class influences people's spending, saving, and credit practices. It determines to some extent the type, quality, and quantity of products a person buys and uses. For example, it affects purchases of clothing, foods, financial and health-care services, travel, recreation, entertainment, and home furnishings. The behaviours of people in one class can influence consumers in others. Most common is the "trickle-down" effect in which members of lower classes attempt to emulate members of higher social classes, such as purchasing expensive automobiles, homes, appliances, and other status symbols. For example, couture fashions designed for the upper class influence the clothing sold in department stores frequented by the middle class, who eventually influences the working class who shop at discount clothing stores. Less often, status float will occur, when a product that is traditionally associated with a lower class gains status and usage among upper classes. Blue jeans, for example, were originally worn exclusively by the working class. Youth of the 1950s began wearing them as a symbol of rebellion against their parents. By the 1970s and 1980s, jeans had also been adopted by upper-class youth when they began to acquire designer labels. Today, blue jeans are acceptable attire for all social classes and cost anywhere from $9.99 to the $2 million fetched by Jennifer Lopez's Sweetface diamond-covered denims that feature a 17-carat diamond on the top buckle.[15]

Social class also affects an individual's shopping patterns and types of stores patronized. In some instances, marketers attempt to focus on certain social classes through store location and interior design, product design and features, pricing strategies, personal sales efforts, and advertising. Many companies focus on the middle and working classes because they account for such a large portion of the population. Outside Canada, the middle class is growing in India, China, and other countries, making these consumers increasingly desirable to marketers as well. Some firms target different classes with different products. BMW, for example, introduced several models priced

Wealth and Life-style in Canada

Approximately 325 000 Canadians are worth at least $1 million. Seventy-seven percent of those millionaires are worth between $1 million and $5 million. Two thousand Canadians are worth $25 million, but the number drops to only 60 who have $500 million, and a mere 30 are actually billionaires.

The fastest growing number of wealthy Canadians is emerging from the ranks of entrepreneurs, most of whom are based in Toronto or Calgary. The largest percentage of wealthy Canadians (over 42 percent) live in Ontario.

The wealthiest Canadians tend to resist showing off their riches, choosing instead to live very conservative, if not frugal, lifestyles.

in the mid $20 000 range to target middle-class consumers, although it usually targets upper class customers with more expensive vehicles.

Culture and Subcultures

culture The accumulation of values, knowledge, beliefs, customs, objects, and concepts of a society

Culture is the accumulation of values, knowledge, beliefs, customs, objects, and concepts that a society uses to cope with its environment and passes on to future generations. Examples of objects are foods, furniture, buildings, clothing, and tools. Concepts include education, welfare, and laws. Culture also includes core values and the degree of acceptability of a wide range of behaviours in a specific society. Culture influences buying behaviour because it permeates our daily lives. Our culture determines what we wear and eat and where we reside and travel. Society's interest in the healthfulness of food affects food companies' approaches to developing and promoting their products. Culture also influences how we buy and use products and our satisfaction from them. Because culture determines product purchases and uses to some degree, cultural changes affect product development, promotion, distribution, and pricing. Food marketers, for example, have made a multitude of changes in their marketing efforts. Thirty years ago, most families ate at least two meals a day together, and the mother spent four to six hours a day preparing those meals. Today more than 75 percent of women between ages 25 and 54 work outside the home, and average family incomes have risen considerably. These shifts, along with scarcity of time, have resulted in dramatic changes in the national per capita consumption of certain food products, such as take-out foods, frozen dinners, and shelf-stable foods.

Global marketers find that people in other regions of the world have different attitudes, values, and needs, which call for different methods of doing business as well as different types of marketing mixes. Some international marketers fail because they do not or cannot adjust to cultural differences.

subcultures A group of individuals whose characteristic values and behaviour patterns are similar and different from those of the surrounding culture

A culture consists of various subcultures. **Subcultures** are groups of individuals whose characteristic values and behaviour patterns are similar and different from those of the surrounding culture. Subcultural boundaries are usually based on geographic designations and demographic characteristics, such as age, religion, race, and ethnicity.

Multicultural Canada Canadian culture is marked by a number of different subcultures, among them Quebec French, Acadian French, First Nations groups, African Canadian, White, and Anglo Canadian. In addition to the indigenous Canadian cultural groups, there is also the multicultural milieu that arises from immigration. Canada is a mosaic of various ethnicities, the most prevalent of which include Asians,

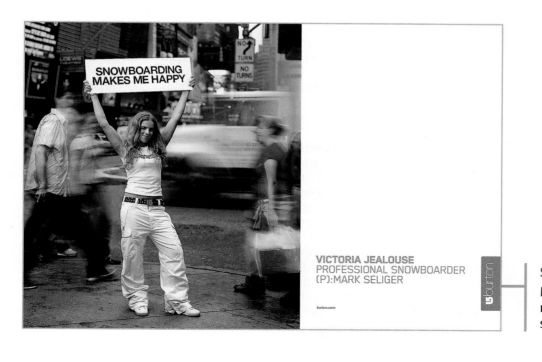

VICTORIA JEALOUSE
PROFESSIONAL SNOWBOARDER
(P):MARK SELIGER

burton.com

Subculture Based on Age

Marketers sometimes aim marketing mixes at age-based subcultures.

Europeans, and Arabic. There are also cultural differences among social class groups, teens, young adults, older adults, and seniors.

Multiculturalism has had a stabilizing effect on Canadian society, creating a tolerant nation that is a marvel in today's world, ultimately enhancing the lives of all Canadians. Some believe that multiculturalism has kept Canada intact despite Quebec's bid for nationhood, while also limiting American cultural influence within the Canadian marketplace. Clearly, multiculturalism provides new Canadians with a feeling of belonging and acceptance, enhancing their self-esteem, and making it easier for them to become contributing members of Canadian society.

Canada admitted 235 000 immigrants in 2004, compared with only 84 000 twenty years earlier. Nearly one-half of those arriving in Canada in 2004 were from Asian and South Asian nations. Eighteen percent of Canada's population was not born in Canada and less than two-thirds of all Canadians have a single ethnic origin. Nearly seven million Canadians speak languages other than English or French, and 23 percent of Canadians are first-generation immigrants.[16]

By 2011, four million people in the city of Toronto will have a distinctly different ancestry than that of the typical Canadian, and they will not identify with English, French, or aboriginal people. In addition, 2.5 million of those in the Toronto market will speak languages other than English, French, or aboriginal. This will open huge opportunities for marketers to communicate with new markets using ethnic media.

Within subcultures, greater similarities exist in people's attitudes, values, and actions than within the broader culture. Relative to other subcultures, individuals in one subculture may have stronger preferences for specific types of clothing, furniture, or foods. It is important to understand that a person can be a member of more than one subculture and that the behavioural patterns and values attributed to specific subcultures do not necessarily apply to all group members.

Immigrants also go through various stages of cultural adaptation when they come to Canada, all of which impact the marketing process. Initially, they focus on discovery and they are very excited about their new home. They have a touristic view of their new city and they want to see everything. Following the first year, some of the novelty wears off, and adjustment to life in Canada takes over. They may find differences in lifestyle, pace, and finances. The next stage requires balancing of both cultures: old and new. Advertising has more of an impact in the later stages of adaptation, while word of mouth from their cultural community within Canada provides more guidance when making purchase decisions in the earlier stages.

Ethnic media provides an excellent advertising vehicle throughout all phases of adaptation. There is also evidence that using traditional cultural values in such media will make newer immigrants feel more at ease, helping to sell product more quickly.

As time passes and immigrants become more mainstream in their views and preferences, they may respond more favourably to less culture-driven marketing appeals. When this happens it is critical that marketers avoid using stereotypes to communicate their message. Such stereotypes include casting blacks as athletes, or Asians as computer experts, using traditional ethnic garb (like Sikh turbans or Asian kimonos), or putting ethnic individuals in roles that are subservient or lacking in authority (Aunt Jemima or Oriental dolls.)[17]

Canadians and Americans: Culturally Similar, but Still Different While many marketers may treat Canada as a pocket of American culture, research continues to show that while Canadians and Americans are culturally similar, there are still important cultural differences between the two.

Canadians and Americans share the belief that individuals determine their own success through their actions, that they control their own destinies, and that governments have a role to play in taking care of the most vulnerable in society. However, Americans are more likely to feel that freedom to pursue individual goals is more important than taking care of those that are vulnerable. Canadians are more environmentally conscious than Americans, and they are more likely to put environmental issues above job growth than are their American counterparts.

There is considerable evidence that Canadians embrace change in values more easily than Americans do. Americans are also more likely to adopt traditional family values than are Canadians, with a belief in God and conservative moral values (including lack of acceptance of a homosexual lifestyle.) Thirty-seven percent of Americans believe that men should provide for the family and women should take care of the home and family, compared with 26 percent of Canadians. Compared with Americans, more Canadians believe in abortion on demand, legalization of marijuana, gay marriage, and the rights of gays to adopt children. Canadians also are more in favour of immigration than their American neighbours.

While Americans have been shown to be better personal communicators than Canadians, and in some ways, more self-confident, Canadians tend to be more subtle and quiet in their self-confidence. There is also a buffer where Canadian and American values blend. This buffer, sometimes referred to as borderland, is located along the Canada-U.S. border.

There are mixed views with regard to whether Canadians are more or less individualistic, with the belief that Canadians have grown more individualistic over the last two decades. However, the terrorist attacks of September 11, 2001, may have changed that to some extent, refocusing Canadians on the collective good, rather than individual rights and freedoms. These events seem to have gelled Canadian culture in a fundamental way that is quietly optimistic, uniquely Canadian and decidedly not American. Canadians are taking their place as both North Americans and Canadians, not one or the other. They are also defining themselves as unique unto themselves, rather than as different from Americans. They are also taking the issue of national security in stride, while continuing to focus most of their energies on matters like health care and the economy.

There are some documented differences in consumption between the two nations as well. Canadians consume three times as many doughnuts as their US counterparts, a trend that has contributed greatly to the success of the Tim Horton's coffee and doughnut chain in Canada. There are 10 times as many Tim Horton's outlets in Canada as there are Krispy Kreme outlets in the United States.[18]

There are also striking differences in how Canadians and Americans purchase automobiles. Canadians love their minivans, while Americans are much more inclined to purchase sport utility vehicles. Canadians are also more likely than Americans to buy compacts and foreign cars.

Canadians are more likely to engage in do-it-yourself mechanics, or to take their cars to the dealers for maintenance than Americans are, and Canadian Tire has been able to reach the do-it-yourself auto mechanic, rising to number one in the automotive aftermarket industry.

African Canadians   There were 662 210 African Canadians in Canada in the 2001 census. They accounted for 2.2 percent of the total Canadian population. Most were also young, with nearly half of all African Canadians under the age of 25. Over 60 percent of all Canadian blacks live in Ontario, but Ontario and Quebec account for over 85 percent of the African Canadian population. However, the highest proportion of Canadian-born blacks live in Halifax, Nova Scotia. Also, 52 percent of visible minorities in the city of Halifax are African Canadian.[19]

Having arrived as early as 1787, some arrived as freed slaves, while others came as slaves prior to the abolishment of slavery in British North America in 1834. The genuine culture for Canadian blacks is heavily rooted in deep love for family, community, and church, all of which provided strength during difficult times. These institutions continue to provide stability and belonging in many black communities.

The African community in Canada is culturally diverse in and of itself. Not only are there many black immigrants with distinct cultural identities, they are also Canadian-born blacks, and the overwhelming African American stereotype that flows into Canadian media through television and the music industry. This creates an environment where Canadian-born blacks may feel left out of the milieu and fighting to maintain their own cultural identity. These forces have led to a general belief among Canadian-born blacks that representations from, and to, their culture in Canada, are not authentic.

The search for authentic cultural representations in the African Canadian community is exacerbated by a lack of historical and cultural documentation about the roots and growth of the black Canadian people. Many black cultural historians have moved to American universities and no longer document the Canadian experience. Others are moving to fill this void by studying black Canadian history and culture, which has resulted in the launch of a new journal, *New Dawn: Journal of Black Canadian Studies,* at the University of Toronto.

The search for authentic reflections of African Canadian culture has extended to the media and marketers, with less than stellar results. Often, such media representation has simply communicated existing stereotypes that are not appropriate, or that are not realistic. For example, a fixation with the phrase "Whazzup" grew out of American Budweiser ads, reflecting what many black Canadians believed to be a white American interpretation of black culture, rather than genuine black culture. Finding examples of genuine African Canadian culture are even more rare. In many cases, blacks are portrayed in stereotypical roles, such as musicians or athletes.

The creation of Black Entertainment Television (BET) in the United States was originally heralded as a tremendous opportunity to capture and communicate the uniqueness of substance of African Canadian and American culture. Unfortunately, many in Canada's black communities are disillusioned with the images portrayed through music videos. By displaying negative images of black men and sexually explicit and degrading images of black women, many feel the network has little to offer in terms of offering a genuine glimpse into black culture. Many fear that such images will do more harm than good in regions where racism exists, and where non-blacks will not be exposed to real black culture.

Much of black culture, both north and south of the border, has been grouped into a single descriptor: urban. Urban culture is identified by various styles of dress, music, sports, language, and dance, including hip hop and R&B. These symbols of urban culture have extended beyond blacks to whites and Asians. The urban culture has given marketers a clear path to many of these consumers by using rap music to sell everything from cars to breakfast cereal. However, for most African Canadians this is simply another example of a failure to understand their unique culture, and to present authentic culture effectively in the mass media.

French Canada   Quebec French are culturally and linguistically distinct from the Acadian French, although both peoples have worked tirelessly to prevent cultural assimilation by the larger Anglo populace.

Quebec French are statistically more socially tolerant than their counterparts in English-speaking Canada. An acceptance of gay and lesbian lifestyles is greater than that shown by their fellow Canadians, and they continue to show respect and tolerance for many different cultures and lifestyles.

Research has shown that while Quebec French are very protective of their personal liberties, they are more influenced by their own culture, and less individualistic than English Canadians. They also tend to be more brand loyal, family-focused, and fashion-oriented. Researchers attribute these differences to cultural attributes.

There are nearly two million Acadian French in Canada. Nearly 300 000 live in Atlantic Canada. More than one million Acadians are spread out across Canada, with over one million residing in Quebec, and 200 000 in Ontario and Western Canada.

The Acadian nation continues to struggle to maintain its distinct culture, a struggle that began 250 years ago when all Acadians who refused to swear allegiance to the British crown were driven out of Canada. About 800 000 continue to reside in Louisiana, USA, where they are known as Cajuns. Approximately 400 000 live elsewhere in the Northeastern United States.

It appears that Canadians are now more supportive of bilingualism than they have been in years past. The 2006 Maclean's Poll revealed that Quebecers are strongly supportive (89 percent), as are Canadians overall, at 64 percent. Even previously staunch Anglo regions in Western Canada appear to support the policy, with nearly half of all British Columbia and prairies residents in agreement. This renewal of bilingual support has lessened the perceived threat of Quebec separation across Canada. Only 12 percent of all Canadians believe that the English-French issue is a serious problem, and only one-third expect that Quebec will separate from Canada. Among Quebecers, less than half believe that Quebec nationhood could happen, and only a quarter expects that it will.

Research has shown that there are some fundamental differences in how French and English Canadians spend their money on consumer goods. Compared with English-language households, French-language households are more likely to spend money on food products to do scratch-based cooking, and they are also more likely to purchase fresh vegetables over frozen, and to avoid buying canned or instant food products. They spend less on home furnishings, and they are likely to consume more wine and beer and less hard liquor than their English counterparts.[20]

First Nations Peoples, Inuit, and Métis Canada's First Nations peoples consist of the First Nations of North America, Métis, and Inuit. There is a great deal of diversity within the North American Indian people, who consist of numerous bands, some of which are the Cree, Maliseet, Dene, Ojibway, Mi'kmaq, and Mohawk.

In the 2001 census, peoples numbered 976 305, with the largest group consisting of First Nations, making up 62 percent of the total. The remaining aboriginal people consisted of 30 percent Métis and 5 percent Inuit.

Marketers have not approached aboriginal people seriously as a viable consumer group. This lack of interest was based on a variety of beliefs that no longer apply. As a result of this lack of attention, the aboriginal market is the least understood of all markets in Canada.

The majority of Canada's First Nations, Métis, and Inuit people are younger than the Canadian population as a whole. While the median age in Canada was 37.3 in the 2001 census, median ages were only 23.5 for First Nations, 27 for Métis, and 20.6 for Inuit. As well, the aboriginal population is also growing four times faster than that of other Canadian markets.

Many aboriginal businesses continue to develop. Aboriginal incomes are growing at twice the national average.

There are over 20 000 aboriginal-owned enterprises across Canada. A major success story is the Membertou Nation, located on Cape Breton Island in Nova Scotia. The Membertou Mi'kmaq community suffered the same fate as many small Cape Breton towns. In a region that was largely dependent on natural resources, loss of the coal and steel industries hit hard, devastating the local economy. Unemployment in Membertou peaked at 95 percent.

The last decade has seen a tremendous change of fortune for Membertou. Developing a local business base and partnering with other firms has enabled the community to turn around its dwindling economy. In 10 years, 95 percent unemployment has fallen to only 10 percent, a million dollar deficit has been transformed into a $44.5 million operating budget (10 times bigger than the operating budget 10 years ago), with a surplus. In addition, a workforce of 20 full-time staff has blossomed into 250 full-time workers. The goal for Membertou is to become fully self-sufficient, and to eliminate government subsidies.

Canada's Métis people number more than 100 000, with 65 percent living in urban areas.

The NWT Metis Development Corporation (MDC) Ltd. is an organization that purchases and resells properties. The firm has grown from $4 million in assets to $15 million in only five years. One of MDC's holdings is a $1.3 million dollar stake in Great Northern Lumber Co. Plans are to reinvest revenues to develop proper housing, schooling, and services in Métis communities, while also creating employment job training to improve the livelihood of Métis.

Nasittuq Corporation operates the North Warning System, a series of radar stations across Canada's far north that provide defence surveillance. The majority of the firm's northern employees are Inuit. Some revenues from the company are donated to training and development programs for the Inuit, as well as to Inuit businesses.

Tourism is fast becoming a key industry for First Nations communities, with thousands of tourists coming north to take part in cultural and historical tourist activities. Cultural tourists are usually well educated baby boomers with high incomes. Such activities help to finance the growth of the aboriginal market, while also educating non-aboriginals about aboriginal culture. As the market continues to grow, new opportunities to service the market will also emerge.[21]

Asian Canadians   The 2001 Census showed that there were 1.1 million Chinese immigrants living in Canada, with the largest concentration of Chinese living in Toronto (47 percent) and Vancouver (31 percent). English is no longer the most prevalent language in the city of Vancouver, where 56 percent of residents have another first language.

The Chinese make an attractive market segment. They are well educated with high incomes, and they make extensive use of Chinese-language media. This gives marketers a communication link to a very upscale and growing ethnic market.

The Chinese market is culturally distinct, with family-oriented values, respect for social customs, a desire for communal activities, placing great value on education and success. Trust is vital in the sales relationship, and Chinese shoppers may seek a lot of family input before making major purchases. Some of the need for consultation comes from a lack of understanding of the Canadian marketplace, while others desire more family input. There is clearly room to better serve the Asian market in Canada. Given the growth in the Asian market, it is time for marketers to seriously address this shortcoming.[22]

SUMMARY

A consumer market is comprised of purchasers and household members who intend to consume or benefit from the purchased products and do not buy products to make profits. Buying behaviour consists of the decision processes and acts of people involved in buying and using products. Consumer buying behaviour is the buying behaviour of ultimate consumers.

An individual's level of involvement—the importance and intensity of interest in a product in a particular situation—affects the type of problem-solving process used. Enduring involvement is an ongoing interest in a product class because of personal relevance, whereas situational involvement is a temporary interest stemming from the particular circumstance or environment in which buyers find themselves. There are three kinds of consumer problem solving: routinized response behaviour, limited problem solving, and extended problem solving. Consumers rely on routinized response behaviour when buying frequently purchased, low-cost items requiring little search-and-decision effort. Limited problem solving is used for products purchased occasionally or when buyers need to acquire information about an unfamiliar brand in a familiar product category. Consumers engage in extended problem solving when purchasing an unfamiliar, expensive, or infrequently bought product. Purchase of a certain product does not always elicit the same type of decision making. Impulse buying is not a consciously planned buying behaviour but involves a powerful urge to buy something immediately.

The consumer buying decision process includes five stages: problem recognition, information search, evaluation of alternatives, purchase, and post-purchase evaluation. Not all decision processes culminate in a purchase, nor do all consumer decisions include all five stages. Problem recognition occurs when buyers become aware of a difference between a desired state and an actual condition. After recognizing the problem or need, buyers search for information about products to help resolve the problem or satisfy the need. In the internal search, buyers search their memories for information about products that might solve the problem. If they cannot retrieve from memory enough information for a decision, they seek additional information through an external search. A successful search yields a group of brands, called a consideration set, that a buyer views as possible alternatives. To evaluate the products in the consideration set, the buyer establishes certain criteria by which to compare, rate, and rank different products. Marketers can influence consumers' evaluations by framing alternatives.

In the purchase stage, consumers select products or brands on the basis of results from the evaluation stage and on other dimensions. Buyers also choose the seller from whom they will buy the product. After the purchase, buyers evaluate the product to determine if its actual performance meets expected levels. Shortly after the purchase of an expensive product, for example, the post-purchase evaluation may result in cognitive dissonance, dissatisfaction brought on by the consumer's doubts as to whether he or she should have bought the product in the first place or would have been better off buying another desirable brand.

Three major categories of influences affect the consumer buying decision process: situational, psychological, and social. Situational influences are external circumstances or conditions existing when a consumer makes a purchase decision. Situational influences include surroundings, time, reason for purchase, and the buyer's mood and condition.

Psychological influences partly determine people's general behaviour, thus influencing their behaviour as consumers. The primary psychological influences on consumer behaviour are perception, motives, learning, attitudes, personality and self-concept, and lifestyles. Perception is the process of selecting, organizing, and interpreting information inputs (sensations received through sight, taste, hearing, smell, and touch) to produce meaning. The three steps in the perceptual process are selection, organization, and interpretation. Individuals have numerous perceptions of packages, products, brands, and organizations that affect their buying decision processes. A motive is an internal energizing force that orients a person's activities toward satisfying needs or achieving goals. Learning refers to changes in a person's thought processes and behaviour caused by information and experience. Marketers try to shape what consumers learn to influence what they buy. An attitude is an individual's enduring evaluation, feelings, and behavioural tendencies toward an object or idea and consists of three major components: cognitive, affective, and behavioural. Personality is the set of traits and behaviours that make a person unique. Self-concept, closely linked to personality, is one's perception or view of oneself. Research indicates that buyers purchase products that reflect and enhance their self-concepts. Lifestyle is an individual's pattern of living expressed through activities, interests, and opinions. Lifestyles influence consumers' needs, brand preferences, and how and where they shop.

Social influences are forces that other people exert on buying behaviour. They include roles, family, reference groups and opinion leaders, social class, and culture and subcultures. Everyone occupies positions within groups, organizations, and institutions, and each position has a role, a set of actions and activities that a person in a particular position is supposed to perform based on expectations of both the individual and surrounding persons. In a family, children learn from parents and older siblings how to make decisions, such as purchase decisions.

Consumer socialization is the process through which a person acquires the knowledge and skills to function as a consumer. The consumer socialization process is partially accomplished through family influences. A reference group is a group that a person identifies with so strongly that he or she adopts the values, attitudes, and behaviour of group members. The three major types of reference groups are membership, aspirational, and disassociative. An opinion leader is a member of an informal group who provides information about a specific topic to other group members.

A social class is an open group of individuals with similar social rank. Social class influences people's spending, saving, and credit practices. Social classes may also differ in terms of culture. Culture is the accumulation of values, knowledge, beliefs, customs, objects, and concepts that a society uses to cope with its environment and passes on to future generations. A culture is made up of subcultures, groups of individuals whose characteristic values and behaviour patterns are similar and different from those of the surrounding culture. Canadian marketers must learn to appreciate the subtle differences in culture in order to fully serve a unique, multicultural marketplace.

 Please visit the student website at www.hmco.ca/marketing for ACE Self-Test questions that will help you prepare for exams.

IMPORTANT TERMS

Consumer market
Buying behaviour
Consumer buying behaviour
Level of involvement
Routinized response behaviour
Limited problem solving
Extended problem solving
Impulse buying
Consumer buying decision process

Internal search
External search
Consideration set
Evaluative criteria
Functional/instrumental value
Experiential/hedonic value
Symbolic/expressive value
Cost/sacrifice value
Cognitive dissonance
Situational influences
Psychological influences

Perception
Information inputs
Selective exposure
Selective distortion
Selective retention
Motive
Maslow's hierarchy of needs
Patronage motives
Learning
Attitude
Attitude scale

Personality
Self-concept
Lifestyle
Social influences
Role
Consumer socialization
Reference group
Opinion leader
Social class
Culture
Subcultures

DISCUSSION & REVIEW QUESTIONS

1. How does a consumer's level of involvement affect his or her choice of problem-solving process?

2. Name the types of consumer problem-solving processes. List some products you have bought using each type. Have you ever bought a product on impulse? If so, describe the circumstances.

3. What are the major stages in the consumer buying decision process? Are all these stages used in all consumer purchase decisions? Why or why not?

4. What are the categories of situational factors that influence consumer buying behaviour? Explain how each of these factors influences buyers' decisions.

5. What is selective exposure? Why do people engage in it?

6. How do marketers attempt to shape consumers' learning?

7. Why are marketers concerned about consumer attitudes?

8. In what ways do lifestyles affect the consumer buying decision process?

9. How do roles affect a person's buying behaviour? Provide examples.

10. What are family influences, and how do they affect buying behaviour?

11. What are reference groups? How do they influence buying behaviour? Name some of your own reference groups.

12. How does an opinion leader influence the buying decision process of reference group members?

13. In what ways does social class affect a person's purchase decisions?

14. What is culture? How does it affect a person's buying behaviour?

15. Describe the subcultures to which you belong. Identify buying behaviour that is unique to one of your subcultures.

APPLICATION QUESTIONS

1. Consumers use one of three problem-solving processes when purchasing goods or services: routinized response behaviour, limited problem solving, or extended problem solving. Describe three buying experiences you have had (one for each type of problem solving), and identify which problem-solving type you used. Discuss why that particular process was appropriate.

2. The consumer buying process consists of five stages: problem recognition, information search, evaluation of alternatives, purchase, and post-purchase evaluation. Not every buying decision goes through all five stages, and the process does not necessarily conclude in a purchase. Interview a classmate about the last purchase he or she made. Report the stages used and those skipped, if any.

3. Attitudes toward products or companies often affect consumer behaviour. The three components of an attitude are cognitive, affective, and behavioural. Briefly describe how a beer company might alter the cognitive and affective components of consumer attitudes toward beer products and toward the company.

4. An individual's roles influence that person's buying behaviour. Identify two of your roles and give an example of how they have influenced your buying decisions.

5. Select three brands of toothpaste and explain how the appeals used in advertising these brands relate to Maslow's hierarchy of needs.

globalEDGE™

1. Marketers may define subcultures by a variety of demographic characteristics including ethnicity, income, or social class. Another attribute that can define a subculture is religion. To find information about religion in Canada and other countries, use the search term "global statistics" at **http://globaledge .msu.edu/ibrd** or **http://globaledge .msu.edu/ibrd/ibrd.asp**. Follow the link to Global Data and then to Religion by Country. Using this information, how might you segment the Canadian population according to religion? Are there any defining characteristics that marketers may use for the Canadian religions listed? Choose four other countries and report any commonalities or differences. Are there any differences in your sample of five countries that might be important to marketers?

2. Your firm is currently designing the next generation of mountain climbing accessories and footwear. To understand the needs and behaviours of this distinctive global market segment, you must perform market research in a variety of countries. From your own knowledge on the subject, you know that the number of Mt. Everest ascents per capita, developed by NationMaster.com, is an excellent measure of mountain climbing's popularity. To access this information, use the search term "compare various statistics" at **http://globaledge .msu.edu/ibrd** or **http://globaledge .msu.edu/ibrd/ibrd.asp**. Determine the top five countries in mountain climbing popularity. In which three countries would you conduct focus groups to develop your new product line?

INTERNET Exercise

Visit **www.prideferrell.com** for resources to help you master the material in this chapter, plus materials that will help you expand your marketing knowledge, including internet exercise updates, ACE self-tests, hotlinks to companies featured in this chapter, and much more.

Amazon.ca

Some mass market e-commerce sites, such as Amazon.ca, have extended the concept of customization to their customer base. Amazon.ca has created an affinity group by drawing on certain users' likes and dislikes to make product recommendations to other users. Check out this pioneering online retailer at www.amazon.ca.

1. What might motivate some consumers to read a "Top Selling" list?
2. Is the consumer's level of involvement with an online book purchase likely to be high or low?
3. Discuss the consumer buying decision process as it relates to a decision to purchase from Amazon.ca.

Case 5.1	Want the Low Down? Consumer Reports Has It

For more than 70 years, Consumer Reports has been helping people to buy right. A subsidiary of Consumer Union, Consumer Reports first began operations in 1936. The company is an independent, non-profit organization whose stated mission is to strive for a fair, just, and safe marketplace for all consumers. Also, Consumer Reports attempts to empower consumers to protect themselves by teaching them about products to make better buying decisions.

Credibility has been its key to success, and Consumer Reports works hard at maintaining its independence and impartiality by accepting no outside advertising or free samples and maintaining no other agenda than the interests of consumers. The company supports itself through the sale of information about products and services, individual contributions, and a few non-commercial grants. *Consumer Reports* magazine has about four million subscribers. ConsumerReports.org is the largest publication-based subscription website in the world with more than two million online subscribers.

Before a product enters one of Consumer Reports' dozens of labs, it has been carefully researched as to manufacturers' claims and consumer demand in the marketplace. Products are tested not only against government and industry standards but also on how consumers use them in everyday situations. Laboratory testing is supplemented through an annual questionnaire that is sent to subscribers that generates over 900 000 returns.

Consumer Reports also faces the risk of lawsuits. Obviously, companies are not happy when Consumer Reports disputes their claims or publishes test results that disparage their products. The company has been sued 15 times in its 70-year existence and has prevailed in every case. Clearly, the nature of Consumer Reports' type of business makes Consumer Union vulnerable to lawsuits. However, its track record speaks volumes about its accuracy and integrity.

Consumer Reports has continued to keep abreast of technology and consumer buying habits. Just prior to the Christmas buying season, Consumer Reports announced ShopSmart, a new service designed specifically for the way people shop. ShopSmart delivers independent expert ratings, reviews, and prices on thousands of popular consumer products to subscribers over their cell phones, wherever and whenever they shop. The service is available on major cell phone carriers for a monthly fee billed to the subscriber's cell phone account.

ShopSmart will change the way people shop by supplying them with detailed product and pricing information at the point of purchase. For example, a mom out shopping for a plasma screen TV for her family sees a sale on one of the latest models, and a salesperson assures her that it is flat-out the best TV at an unbeatable price. With a price tag of $2000, she wants to make sure she buys the best product at the best value. By dialing Shop-Smart on her cell phone, she can get a product rating, see the suggested price for the TV, and even determine if the same model is available in another store at a lower price.

"Consumer Reports ShopSmart was created with all types of shoppers in mind including the impulse buyer at the counter facing an aggressive salesperson and the researcher in the parking lot contemplating an important purchase," said the senior director and general manager of information products for Consumer Reports. "The service works for every lifestyle—from the teenager out shopping for a new MP3 player to expecting parents buying a new space heater."

Seventy years later, Consumer Reports is still helping customers to buy right.[22]

Questions for Discussion

1. What elements of the consumer buying decision process does Consumer Reports' information most impact? In what ways?
2. In what ways could information in Consumer Reports contribute to or help reduce cognitive dissonance? Explain.
3. How can Consumer Reports help a buyer to make a better purchase decision?

Case 5.2   AutoTrader.com Fuels Online Auto Buying

AutoTrader.com operates the largest virtual used-car lot in the world. Founded in 1997, this fast-growing company has accelerated beyond competitors eBay and cars.com to capture a dominant share of the online used-car market. At any one time, the AutoTrader website features classified ads for more than two million cars, both new and used. Buyers and sellers make contact through the site to negotiate the final terms for purchases.

When AutoTrader first opened its online business, few people had ever bought or sold a vehicle on the Internet. Therefore, the company's initial challenge was to change the habits of consumers and dealers who were accustomed to using newspaper classified advertising for used-car transactions. Instead of charging dealers for every listing, as newspapers did, AutoTrader decided to set a flat monthly fee for posting any number of descriptions and photos. Because dealers did not have to pay separately for every car listed, they could afford to post information about every vehicle in their inventories.

As more dealers signed up and listed cars for sale, the website became more attractive to consumers who wanted to choose from a large selection of vehicles. However, the company still had to educate its primary target market, 25- to 49-year-old men, about an unfamiliar buying process. AutoTrader's solution was to run informative television commercials showing step by step how to use its site. Its policy of charging buyers no fee to browse or buy was a plus. Soon the site was drawing more than 5.5 million visitors every month.

Next, AutoTrader targeted a slightly younger segment of 18- to 24-year-olds because research showed that these first-time buyers account for a significant percentage of used-car purchasers. The company hired a video game specialist to adapt the look of its fast-paced television commercials to an online promotion titled "Slide into Your Ride." Players earned prizes for correctly lining up three cars by matching their colours and were entered in a sweepstakes to win a $25 000 AutoTrader shopping spree and other prizes.

Knowing that students typically search for used cars before heading off for college in the fall, AutoTrader scheduled this promotional game for August and September. The company placed banner ads on popular websites and sent e-mail announcements to its online newsletter subscribers, as well as to people on a *Sports Illustrated* list. Although this promotion cost $1 million, it was a good investment because it raised brand awareness and drew an additional 500 000 visitors to the site during the first month alone.

More than half the visitors who played the game were women, and about one-third of the players were in the 18- to 24-year-old age group. More than 60 percent of the players signed up to receive AutoTrader's monthly online newsletter, enabling the company to continue building relationships with these potential buyers. Equally important, several hundred thousand players searched for used cars on the AutoTrader site during the promotional period.

Meanwhile AutoTrader noticed that online auctions were becoming more popular. At one time it cooperated with eBay, the world's best-known auction site, to link the two sites so consumers could search for cars on either one. After monitoring buyer behaviour for two years, AutoTrader ended the agreement and created its own vehicle auction operation, going into direct competition with eBay. "We did a lot of research and stud-ied very closely the behaviour of auction style users on our site," says Chip Perry, AutoTrader's CEO. He acknowledges that eBay is the "current major player in an extremely small niche segment of the car business." At the same time, he sees plenty of room for Auto-Trader to profitably serve customers in this $2 billion market segment.

As its annual vehicle sales accelerate past $100 million, AutoTrader is not putting on the brakes. The company continues to reinforce brand recognition through television advertising, especially during the weeks leading up to the busy fall buying season. And it constantly introduces new features to draw new visitors and serve the nearly 10 million qualified buyers who use the site every month to check the listings, compare prices, and buy or bid on vehicles. The firm's success can be measured in part by its number one rank in J. D. Powers & Associates satisfaction survey of used-vehicle dealers.[23]

Questions for Discussion

1. In what ways has AutoTrader helped potential car buyers learn how to buy cars online?
2. In which stage of the consumer buying decision process would AutoTrader's television commercials be most likely to influence potential car buyers to use AutoTrader's website? Why?
3. Why is it important for AutoTrader to influence first-time buyers' perceptions of its site through online promotions such as "Slide into Your Ride"?

6

Business Markets and Buying Behaviour

Blackberry for Business

While many Canadians scramble to update their Blackberries, businesses are looking just as seriously at RIM to enhance everything from manufacturing efficiency to customer service. Research in Motion, or RIM, as it is known, is a great Canadian success story. Launched in 1984 from Waterloo, Ontario, RIM has offices in North America, Europe, and Asia. They also offer a wealth of products for all kinds of businesses. If an organization can use wireless connectivity, there is a product for that organization within the Blackberry product line. Blackberry has also launched business solutions for small businesses, the backbone of the Canadian economy.

RIM specializes in Internet-based wireless communications. By utilizing wireless services managers can be in contact with their employees and customers anytime, anyplace. Organizations can also purchase servers to turn the workplace into a wireless environment to maximize flexibility for employees, whether they are mobile, or office-based.

RIM has focused very carefully on the organizational market, and it has made inroads into the business market in the United States. The infamous Blackberry is the choice of the American government workers, and there are more Blackberries in Washington, D.C. than in many Canadian cities. The Blackberry has also become the standard for most of the search and rescue services in the United States. RIM has also made considerable inroads into the courier and delivery service market with its wireless communications mobile devices. About 3 000 employees at United Parcel Service rely on Blackberries to get their jobs done quickly and efficiently.

In order to market their business solutions effectively across various business sectors, RIM's website offers a drop-down menu where potential business users can choose a sector for a more detailed description of suitable services. The list is shown in the screen capture of RIM's website below. Sectors serviced by RIM's state of the art technology include: financial services, government, healthcare, insurance, legal, manufacturing, pharmaceutical, public safety, real estate, wholesale, and retail.[1] ■

In this chapter, we look at organizational markets and buying decision processes. We first discuss various kinds of organizational markets and the types of buyers making up those markets. Next, we explore several dimensions of organizational buying, such as characteristics of transactions, attributes and concerns of buyers, methods of buying, and distinctive features of demand for products sold to business purchasers. We then examine how such buying decisions are made and who makes the purchases. Finally, we consider how organizational markets are analyzed.

Business Markets

business or organizational market Individuals or groups that purchase a specific kind of product for resale, direct use in producing other products, or use in general daily operations

A **business, or organizational, market** (also called a *business-to-business market* or *B2B market*) consists of individuals or groups that purchase a specific kind of product for one of three purposes: resale, direct use in producing other products, or use in general daily operations. Marketing to organizations employs the same concepts as marketing to ultimate consumers, such as defining target markets, understanding buying behaviour, and developing effective marketing mixes, but we devote a complete chapter to organizational marketing because there are structural and behavioural differences in business markets. A company marketing to another organization must understand how its product will affect other firms in the marketing channel, such as resellers and other manufacturers. Business products can also be technically complex and the market often consists of sophisticated buyers.

Because the organizational market consists of relatively smaller customer populations, a segment of the market could be as small as a few customers.[2] For example, the market for passenger jets in Canada is limited to a few major carriers. On the other hand, a business product can be a commodity, such as corn or a bolt or a screw, but the quantity purchased and the buying methods differ significantly from the consumer market. Cost and reliability are critical issues in the business to business market. In most cases, reliability of quality and supply will be more important to buyers than price. Organizational marketing is often based on long-term, mutually profitable relationships across members of the marketing channel. Networks of suppliers and customers recognize the importance of building strong alliances based on cooperation, trust, and collaboration.[3] Manufacturers may even codevelop new products with organizational customers sharing marketing research, production, scheduling, inventory management, and information systems. For example, when the largest distributor for independent book publishers, Consortium Book & Sales Distribution Inc., discovered its information technology system was obsolete, the firm partnered with Integrated Knowledge Systems, Inc., to develop a new database to track book sales in real time to let publishers know which titles sell well and which should be eliminated. In this case, the marketer custom designed IT solutions with the customer to resolve its operational services and efficiency concerns.[4] Although business marketing can be based on collaborative, long-term, buyer-seller relationships, there are also transactions based on timely exchanges of basic products at highly competitive market prices. For most business marketers, the goal is to understand customer needs and provide a value-added exchange that shifts from attracting customers to keeping customers and developing relationships.[5]

The four categories of organizational markets are producer, reseller, government, and institutional. In the remainder of this section, we discuss each of these types of markets.

Producer Markets

producer markets Individuals and business organizations that purchase products to make profits by using them to produce other products or using them in their operations

Individuals and business organizations that purchase products for the purpose of making a profit by using them to produce other products or using them in their operations are classified as **producer markets.** Producer markets include buyers of raw materials, as well as purchasers of semifinished and finished items, used to produce other products. For example, manufacturers buy raw materials and component parts for direct use in product production. Grocery stores and supermarkets are part of producer markets for numerous support products such as paper and plastic bags, counters, and scanners. Farmers are part of producer markets for farm machinery, fertilizer, seed, and livestock. Producer markets include a broad array of industries ranging from agriculture, forestry, fisheries, and mining to construction, transportation, communications, and utilities. As Table 6.1 indicates, the number of business establishments in national producer markets is enormous.

Reseller Markets

reseller markets Intermediaries that buy finished goods and resell them for profit

Reseller markets consist of intermediaries, such as wholesalers and retailers, which buy finished goods and resell them for profit. Aside from making minor alterations, resellers do not change the physical characteristics of the products they handle. Except for items producers sell directly to consumers, all products sold to consumer markets are first sold to reseller markets.

Wholesalers purchase products for resale to retailers, to other wholesalers, and to producers, governments, and institutions. Of the 63 206 wholesalers in Canada, 60 percent are located in Ontario and Quebec.[6] Although some products are sold directly to end users, many manufacturers sell their products to wholesalers, which in turn sell the products to other firms in the distribution system. Thus, wholesalers are very important in helping producers get products to customers. Professional buyers and buying committees make wholesalers' initial purchase decisions. Reordering is often automated.

table 6.1   NUMBER OF ESTABLISHMENTS IN INDUSTRY GROUPS

	Number of Establishments
Agriculture, forestry, fishing, hunting	193 935
Mining, Oil & Gas Extraction	8794
Construction	115 367
Manufacturing	60 585
Utilities	4234
Wholesalers	63 206
Transportation, warehousing	804 613
Finance, insurance, real estate	74 939
Services (not included in above classifications)	729 674

Source: Industry Canada. Canadian Industry Statistics. Strategis website. http://www.strategis.gc.ca/sc_ecnmy/sio/homepage.html.

Armand Wanted to Build a Snowmobile: The Bombardier Story

Joseph-Armand Bombardier had a dream: he wanted to build a snowmobile. Living in Eastern Townships, Quebec in the 1930s, Bombardier felt that a mechanical alternative to the dogsled would be a great idea. In 1937 he invented the first snowmobile that was a large affair, designed to haul many passengers. But he still hadn't realized his true dream, which was to build something much smaller: a one- or two-person, tracked snow vehicle. Joseph was successful in his quest for the snowmobile, launching the scaled down Ski-Doo in 1959.

Armand's dream was just the beginning of what would become a global empire in less than 50 years. At the time of his death in 1964, the firm, then known as L'Autoneige Bombardier Limitée, was a huge concern, with $20 million in revenues, equivalent to $160 million in 2004 Canadian dollars. His sons took over the reigns of the firm, renaming the company Bombardier Limited. The company went public in 1967, and today is listed on stock exchanges in Toronto, Montreal, and Frankfurt.

Bombardier grew rapidly due to astute marketing, acquisition of firms in international growth markets, an ability to carve out niche sectors in highly competitive international trade, and selling to private industry and government. Over the past 20 years, the firm has acquired major international and domestic manufacturers in railway, aerospace, missile systems, and recreational products. Bombardier has two main divisions: aerospace and transportation.

Bombardier Aerospace is responsible for over half of Bombardier's revenues, and is the world's third largest manufacturer of aircraft for the airline industry, behind competitors Boeing and Airbus. The aerospace division also competes in the regional jet market having acquired Canadair and de Havilland. Bombardier leads the regional jet market ahead of Brazilian-based Embraer. Bombardier has also distinguished itself in the business jet sector after acquiring Lear-

jet in 1990. Bombardier manufactures Challenger and Learjets, and is second to market to leader, Gulfstream.

Bombardier's transportation division is the world's largest manufacturer of railway equipment. The firm has signed contracts for high-speed rail, and subway trains for New York City, U.S.-based Amtrak, and The Underground in London, England. Bombardier was also a supplier for the monorail that unites casinos along the famous Las Vegas strip in Las Vegas, Nevada.

However, the firm ran into trouble shortly after signing these major contracts. Competition from Embraer was toughening in the regional jet market. The aerospace division was encountering stiff competition. In addition, there were complaints regarding rail products and services. Mechanical problems forced costly delays in the opening of the Las Vegas monorail. There had also been technical problems with high-speed Amtrak trains.

Bombardier was also being criticized for receiving government handouts. Subsidization of such major manufacturers is not unusual, with Embraer, Boeing, and Airbus rumoured to have received government subsidies. Governments fear job losses if major deals are not successful. Manufacturing in the transportation and aerospace sectors is very expensive, but also very lucrative. Heavy financing is required. Bombardier did

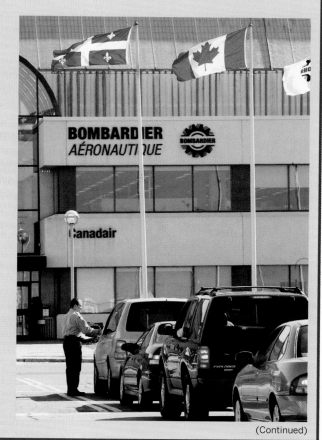

(Continued)

receive an interest rate subsidy on financing for the New York Subway deal.

Bombardier decided it was necessary to spin off several of its subsidiaries in order to remain financially viable and competitive. Bombardier sold its recreational business division in 2003, and divested itself of its defence contracting arm. An ambitious restructuring plan saw the firm spin off a number of subsidiaries and assets, generating more than $2.5 billion.

Bombardier is also working hard to become environmentally friendly. Over 85 percent of its global business sites are certified to the ISO 14001 environmental standard. The firm has also pledged to reduce its annual consumption of energy, CO_2 emissions, water consumption, and generation of hazardous waste by three percent by 2008.

Today Bombardier competes on five continents and has achieved impressive market presence in both North America and Europe. Bombardier is truly an international firm, with more than 90 percent of its sales originating from outside of Canada. Bombardier employs more than 55 000 people worldwide; however, losses of over 1700 jobs are expected in Quebec and Northern Ireland as the company works to restore its financial stregnth. Revenues for Bombardier Inc. for fiscal year ending January 31, 2006, were $14.6 billion. Sales for Bombardier Aerospace were $15.8 billion in 2006, up from a loss of $85 million in 2005.

And Bombardier continues to grow. In November, 2006, Bombardier signed a $43 million deal for 10 Bombardier CX-100 vehicles and upgrades to existing electrical and mechanical equipment for the Airport People Mover System at Las Vegas' McCarran International Airport. The vehicles will be delivered between 2008 and 2009. Bombardier proves that even a little dream, like wanting to build a snowmobile, can result in big business.

Retailers purchase products and resell them to final consumers. There are 217 924 retailers in Canada, but only 61 percent have employees apart from the owner.[7] Those retailers provide employment for 1.7 million people. Retailers reported total sales revenue of $371 billion in 2004.[8] Some retailers—Home Depot, Wal-Mart, and Staples, for example—carry a large number of items. Supermarkets may handle as many as 30 000 different products. In small, individually-owned retail stores, owners or managers make purchasing decisions. In chain stores, a central office buyer or buying committee frequently decides whether a product will be made available for selection by store managers. For most products, however, local managers make the actual buying decisions for a particular store.

When making purchase decisions, resellers consider several factors. They evaluate the level of demand for a product to determine in what quantity and at what prices the product can be resold. Retailers assess the amount of space required to handle a product relative to its potential profit, sometimes on the basis of sales per square foot of selling area. Because customers often depend on resellers to have products available when needed, resellers typically appraise a supplier's ability to provide adequate quantities when and where wanted. Resellers also take into account the ease of placing orders and the availability of technical assistance and training programs from producers. When resellers consider buying a product not previously carried, they try to determine whether the product competes with, or complements products they currently handle. These types of concerns distinguish reseller markets from other markets.

Government Markets

government markets Federal, provincial, territorial, or municipal governments that buy goods and services to support their internal operations and provide products to their constituencies

Federal, provincial, territorial, and municipal governments make up **government markets.** These markets spend billions of dollars annually for a variety of goods and services to support their internal operations and provide citizens with such products as highways, education, water, energy, and national defence. The revenue and spending for government in Canada is shown in Table 6.2. The amount spent by federal, municipal, provincial, and territorial governments has increased during the last 30 years because the level of services they provide has increased. Costs of providing these services have also risen. For example, governments spent $35.2 billion on hospital expenditures in 2005–2006, up 35 percent from 2001–2002.[9]

Canadian governments spend more than $532 billion on goods, services, and programs in 2005–2006. The largest percentage of spending was in the area of health care

(20 percent) and social services (25 percent). The types and quantities of products bought by government markets reflect social demands on various government agencies. As citizens' needs for government services change, so does demand for products by government markets.

Although it is common to hear of large corporations being awarded government contracts, in fact businesses of all sizes market to government agencies. Because government agencies spend public funds to buy the products needed to provide services, they are accountable to the public. This accountability explains their relatively complex set of buying procedures. Some firms do not even try to sell to government buyers because they want to avoid the tangle of red tape. However, many marketers have learned to deal efficiently with government procedures and do not find them a stumbling block. For certain products, such as defence-related items, the government may be the only customer.

Governments make purchases through bids or negotiated contracts. Although companies may be reluctant to approach government markets because of the complicated bidding process, once they understand the rules of this process, some firms routinely

table 6.2 THE GOVERNMENT AS PURCHASER	
Revenue and Expenditures for Canadian Federal, Provincial, Territorial, and Local Governments 2005–2006	
Revenue	**($ millions)**
Own source revenue	532 183
Income taxes	224 189
Consumption taxes	107 510
Property and related taxes	48 784
Health and drug insurance premiums	3253
Contributions to social security plans	32 458
Investment income	44 954
Other revenue from own sources	28 443
Total revenue	**532 183**
Expenditure	
General government services	19 797
Protection of persons and property	42 805
Transportation and communication	22 972
Health	102 286
Social services	131 146
Education	82 762
Resource conservation and industrial development	18 824
Environment	13 578
Recreation and culture	13 858
Labour, employment, and immigration	2465
Housing	3750
Foreign affairs and international assistance	6048
Regional planning and development	2355
Research establishments	2273
Debt charges	48 068
Other expenditures	2035
Total expenditures	**515 019**
Surplus (+) / deficit (−)	*17 163*

Source: Adapted from Statistics Canada, Table 3-1: Revenue and Expenditures—Consolidated Federal, Provincial, Territorial and Local Government Revenue and Expenditures. Statistics Canada Catalogue #63-213.

ISI Streamlines Procurement and Contracting Services for Atlantic Canadian Colleges and Universities

In an effort to make better use of scarce education dollars, ISI, a non-profit organization, was created to contract, coordinate, and manage many procurement services on behalf of its member institutions. ISI works on behalf of 18 member colleges and universities from across Atlantic Canada. Its members include Acadia University, Atlantic School of Theology, Cape Breton University, Dalhousie University, Holland College, Memorial University, Mount Allison University, Mount Saint Vincent University, Nova Scotia Community College, Nova Scotia College of Art and Design, Saint Mary's University, St. Francis Xavier University, St. Thomas University, Université de Moncton, Université Sainte Anne, University of King's College, University of New Brunswick, and the University of Prince Edward Island. In addition to providing services to its educational members, ISI also provides repair and service to scientific equipment in hospitals in the Atlantic region.

If you are selling office equipment, paper supplies, microscopes, courier services, stationery, or even employee benefits to universities and colleges in Atlantic Canada, your firm must deal with ISI. By pulling together the combined purchasing power of its members, ISI is a formidable buying agent, while also being a portal to extremely lucrative market opportunities. By buying in bulk, ISI is able to greatly reduce the prices that its members pay for goods and services. By selling in bulk, wholesalers and manufacturers are able to streamline their operations, reduce selling and logistics costs, and enjoy profitable sales.

penetrate government markets. To make a sale under the bid system, firms must apply and be approved for placement on a list of qualified bidders. When a government unit wants to buy, it sends out a detailed description of the products to qualified bidders. Businesses wishing to sell such products submit bids. The government unit is usually expected to accept the lowest bid, however, most tenders allow buyers to choose the vendor that offers the best overall value, but not necessarily the lowest price.

When buying non-standard or highly complex products, a government unit often uses a negotiated contract. Under this procedure, the government unit selects only a few firms and then negotiates specifications and terms; it eventually awards the contract to one of the negotiating firms. Although government markets can impose intimidating requirements, they can also be very lucrative.

Institutional Markets

institutional markets
Organizations with charitable, educational, community, or other non-business goals

Organizations with charitable, educational, community, or other non-business goals constitute **institutional markets.** Members of institutional markets include churches, hospitals, fraternities and sororities, charitable organizations, and community colleges and universities. Institutions purchase millions of dollars' worth of products annually to provide goods, services, and ideas to congregations, students, patients, and others. Because institutions often have different goals and fewer resources than other types of organizations, marketers may use special marketing efforts to serve them. To ease some of the administrative burden of coordinating procurement, some buying groups have emerged to assist such organizations. One such buying group, Interuniversity Services Inc. (ISI) provides procurement assistance to 18 educational institutions in Atlantic Canada (see box on page 146).

Dimensions of Marketing to Business Customers

Now that we have considered different types of business customers, we look at several dimensions of marketing to business customers. We examine characteristics of transactions with business customers and then discuss attributes of business customers and some of their primary concerns when making purchase decisions. Next, we consider buying methods and major types of purchases. Finally, we discuss the characteristics of demand for business products.

Characteristics of Transactions with Business Customers

Transactions between businesses differ from consumer sales in several ways. Orders by business customers tend to be much larger than individual consumer sales. An airline, for example, may order multiple jet airplanes costing several million dollars each. Suppliers often must sell products in large quantities to make profits; consequently they prefer not to sell to customers who place small orders. For example, Airborne Express competes successfully against FedEx and UPS by providing low-cost overnight delivery services primarily to businesses that buy such services in high volume.

Some business purchases involve expensive items, such as computer systems. Other products, such as raw materials and component items, are used continuously in production, and their supply may need frequent replenishing. The contract regarding terms of sale of these items is likely to be a long-term agreement.

Discussions and negotiations associated with business purchases can require considerable marketing time and selling effort. Purchasing decisions are often made by committee, orders are frequently large and expensive, and products may be custom built. Several people or departments in the purchasing organization are often involved. For example, one department expresses a need for a product, a second department develops the specifications, a third stipulates maximum expenditures, and a fourth places the order.

reciprocity An arrangement unique to business marketing in which two organizations agree to buy from each other

One practice unique to organizational markets is **reciprocity,** an arrangement in which two organizations agree to buy from each other. Reciprocal agreements that threaten competition are illegal. The Competition Bureau of Canada takes action to stop anticompetitive reciprocal practices. Nonetheless, a certain amount of reciprocal activity occurs among small businesses and, to a lesser extent, among larger companies. Because reciprocity influences purchasing agents to deal only with certain suppliers, it can lower morale among agents and lead to less than optimal purchases. The Competition Act focuses on any behaviour that lessens competition. This can include reciprocity if a firm:

> is a party or privy to, or assists in, any sale that discriminates to his knowledge, directly or indirectly, against competitors of a purchaser of articles from him in that any discount, rebate, allowance, price concession or other advantage is granted to the purchaser over and above any discount, rebate, allowance, price concession or other advantage that, at the time the articles are sold to the purchaser, is available to the competitors in respect of a sale of articles of like quality and quantity.[10]

If found guilty of lessening competition through illegal trade practices business decision makers may face up to two years in prison.

Attributes of Business Customers

Business customers typically demand detailed information about a product's functional features and technical specifications to ensure that it meets their needs. Personal goals, however, may also influence business buying behaviour. Most purchasing agents seek the psychological satisfaction that comes with organizational advancement and financial rewards. Agents who consistently exhibit rational business buying behaviour are likely to attain these personal goals because they help their firms achieve organizational objectives. Today many suppliers and their customers build and maintain mutually beneficial relationships, sometimes called *partnerships*. Researchers find that even in a partnership between a small vendor and a large corporate buyer, a strong partnership exists because high levels of interpersonal trust can lead to higher levels of commitment to the partnership by both organizations.[11]

Primary Concerns of Business Customers

When making purchasing decisions, business customers take into account a variety of factors. Among their chief considerations are price, product quality, service, and supplier relationships. Price matters greatly to business customers because it influences operating costs and costs of goods sold, which in turn affect selling price, profit margin, and ultimately the ability to compete. When purchasing major equipment, a business customer views price as the amount of investment necessary to obtain a certain level of return or savings. A business customer is likely to compare the price of a product with the benefits the product will yield to the organization.

Most business customers try to achieve and maintain a specific level of quality in the products they buy. To achieve this goal, most firms establish standards (usually stated as a percentage of defects allowed) for these products and buy them on the basis of a set of expressed characteristics, commonly called *specifications*. A customer evaluates the quality of the products being considered to determine whether they meet specifications. If a product fails to meet specifications or malfunctions for the ultimate consumer, the customer may drop that product's supplier and switch to a different one. On the other hand, customers are ordinarily cautious about buying products that exceed specifications because such products often cost more, thus increasing the organization's overall costs. Specifications are designed to meet a customer's wants, and anything that does not contribute to meeting those wants may be considered wasteful.

Business buyers value service. Services offered by suppliers directly and indirectly influence customers' costs, sales, and profits. In some instances, the mix of customer services is the major means by which marketers gain a competitive advantage. Typical services customers desire are market information, inventory maintenance, on-time delivery, and repair services. Business buyers are likely to need technical product

Aboriginal Business Launches Unique Partnership Opportunity

Aboriginal businesses have embraced partnerships with non-Aboriginal firms as a way of building a stronger Aboriginal business base, while also generating a greater understanding of Aboriginal communities in the Canadian business community. In 2001, the Canadian Council for Aboriginal Business (CCAB) launched the PAR program, an acronym for Progressive Aboriginal Relations. PAR allows non-Aboriginal entrepreneurs to partner with Aboriginal firms to market goods and services. In return for doing good business with such firms, non-Aboriginal firms will be able to display the PAR symbol, which provides the equivalent of a seal of approval. The PAR award is as a rating scheme that shows Aboriginal consumers that one's business is committed to working in a mutually advantageous way with Aboriginal communities.

PAR is focused on achieving goals in four key areas: employment, business development, individual professional development, and community relations. Firms do a self-assessment based in each of these four areas following standards created for PAR. The CCAB has partnered with the National Quality Institute to do an independent verification of each firm's self-assessment. The PAR certification is awarded based on assessment from an independent jury consisting of both Aboriginal and non-Aboriginal business leaders.

Non-Aboriginal businesses that work toward achieving a PAR certification can achieve three certification levels: gold, silver, and bronze. Today, 18 firms have achieved one of these levels. Firms which have achieved a gold PAR level include: Alberta-Pacific Forest Industries (Boyle, AB), BMO Bank of Montreal (Toronto, ON), Cameco Corporation (Saskatoon, SK), Diavik Diamond Mines Inc. (Lac De Gras, NWT), ESS Support Services (Burnaby, BC), Place Louis Riel All-Suite Hotel (Winnipeg, MB), Remote Sites Division, Sodexho (Montreal, PQ), Syncrude Canada (Fort McMurray, AB), and Xerox Canada (Toronto, ON). Five firms are currently at the silver level, four are at the bronze level, and seven are at the commitment level, having just embarked on their PAR certification.

information, data regarding demand, information about general economic conditions, or supply and delivery information. Maintaining adequate inventory is critical because it helps make products accessible when a customer needs them and reduces the customer's inventory requirements and costs. Because business customers are usually responsible for ensuring that products are on hand and ready for use when needed, on-time delivery is crucial. Furthermore, reliable, on-time delivery saves business customers money because it enables them to carry less inventory. For

The Focus Is on Service at IBM

IBM provides technology and support services to help companies operate. Based on earnings, IBM is number one in information technology (IT) services, hardware, and financing; it is number two in software. Over the years, IBM has transferred its focus from computer hardware to computer services.

In 2003, IBM made some big changes and refined its business model. The company sold its personal computer division to Lenovo, a Chinese firm, and phased out its presence in creating and selling hard disk drives, memory chips, and networking hardware. Instead, the company decided to focus on forming and maintaining collaborative relationships and providing services to solve the information management needs of its business customers. Some of the major shifts IBM has made are the restructuring of its busi-

ness skills, assets, and delivery capabilities to meet the needs of customers wanting to blend IT with business operations. IBM is always moving forward and reinventing its focus through effective customer relationship strategies.

Today, IBM continues to make its business more tangible, flexible, and innovative. The company vows to create a global reach and utilize the talent available worldwide by giving authority and resources to those working in close contact with its clients. IBM's target customers include companies such as General Motors, which is outsourcing $15 billion worth of IT contracts. To satisfy the auto giant, IBM will have to adjust to GM's demands for smaller contracts and standardized ways of doing things. In addition, it will need to develop a close partnership and craft the right value proposition to a company that is attempting to restructure in the highly competitive automotive market. IBM must also compete with EDS, Hewlett-Packard, and CapGemini, as well as other IT firms to get its share of GM's business. With IBM's new focus, every new customer represents a challenge to craft precisely the right service.

example, Dell opened an enterprise command centre similar to those it operates in the United States and in Limerick, Ireland, to provide around-the-clock support for its business customers in Europe, the Middle East, and Africa.[12] Purchasers of machinery are especially concerned about obtaining repair services and replacement parts quickly because inoperable equipment is costly. Caterpillar Inc., manufacturer of earth moving, construction, and materials-handling machinery, has built an international reputation, as well as a competitive advantage, by providing prompt service and replacement parts for its products around the world. Business customers are likely to resist a suppliers' effort to implement a new technology if there are questions about the technology's compatibility, reliability, or other factors that could cause the supplier to fail to deliver on promises.[13]

Quality of service is a critical issue because customer expectations about service have broadened. Using traditional service quality standards based only on traditional manufacturing and accounting systems is not enough. Communication channels that allow customers to ask questions, voice complaints, submit orders, and trace shipments are indispensable components of service. Marketers should strive for uniformity of service, simplicity, truthfulness, and accuracy. They should also develop customer service objectives and monitor customer service programs. Firms can monitor service by formally surveying customers or informally calling on customers and asking questions about the service they receive. Expending the time and effort to ensure that customers are happy can greatly benefit marketers by increasing customer retention. One study found that boosting customer retention by five percent could double a small firm's profitability.[14]

Finally, business customers are concerned about the costs of developing and maintaining relationships with their suppliers. By developing relationships and building trust with a particular supplier, buyers can reduce their search efforts and uncertainty about monetary prices.[15] Business customers have to keep in mind the overall fit of a purchase including its potential to reduce inventory and carrying costs as well as to increase inventory turnover and ability to move the right products to the right place at the right time. The entire business can be damaged by a single supplier's failure to be a good partner.[16]

Methods of Business Buying

Although no two business buyers do their jobs the same way, most use one or more of the following purchase methods: *description, inspection, sampling,* and *negotiation.* When products are standardized according to certain characteristics (such as size, shape, weight, and colour) and graded using such standards, a business buyer may be able to purchase simply by describing or specifying quantity, grade, and other attributes. Agricultural products often fall into this category. Sometimes buyers specify a particular brand or its equivalent when describing the desired product. Purchases on the basis of description are especially common between a buyer and seller with an ongoing relationship built on trust.

Certain products, such as industrial equipment, used vehicles, and buildings, have unique characteristics and may vary with regard to condition. For example, a particular used truck may have a bad transmission.

Methods of Buying
Titleist makes a standardized product that can be customized.

Consequently, business buyers of such products must base purchase decisions on inspection.

Sampling entails taking a specimen of the product from the lot and evaluating it on the assumption that its characteristics represent the entire lot. This method is appropriate when the product is homogeneous—for instance, grain—and examining the entire lot is not physically or economically feasible.

Some purchases by businesses are based on negotiated contracts. In certain instances, buyers describe exactly what they need and ask sellers to submit bids. They then negotiate with the suppliers that submit the most attractive bids. This approach may be used when acquiring commercial vehicles, for example. In other cases, the buyer may be unable to identify specifically what is to be purchased and can provide only a general description, as might be the case for a piece of custom-made equipment. A buyer and seller might negotiate a contract that specifies a base price and provides for the payment of additional costs and fees. These contracts are most commonly used for one-time projects such as buildings, capital equipment, and special projects.

Types of Business Purchases

new-task purchase An initial purchase by an organization of an item to be used to perform a new job or solve a new problem

straight rebuy purchase A routine purchase of the same products by a business buyer

modified rebuy purchase A new-task purchase that is changed on subsequent orders or when the requirements of a straight rebuy purchase are modified

Most business purchases are one of three types: new-task, straight rebuy, or modified rebuy purchase. Each type is subject to different influences and thus requires business marketers to modify their selling approaches appropriately.[17] In a **new-task purchase,** an organization makes an initial purchase of an item to be used to perform a new job or solve a new problem. A new-task purchase may require development of product specifications, vendor specifications, and procedures for future purchases of that product. To make the initial purchase, the business buyer usually needs much information. New-task purchases are important to suppliers because if business buyers are satisfied with the products, suppliers may be able to sell buyers large quantities of them for many years.

A **straight rebuy purchase** occurs when buyers purchase the same products routinely under approximately the same terms of sale. Buyers require little information for these routine purchase decisions and tend to use familiar suppliers that have provided satisfactory service and products in the past. These marketers try to set up automatic reordering systems to make reordering easy and convenient for business buyers. A supplier may even monitor the business buyer's inventories and indicate to the buyer what should be ordered and when. For example, when Aramark buys food products to use in servicing a campus café, straight rebuys make it possible to maintain a cost-effective and consistent food service operation.

In a **modified rebuy purchase,** a new-task purchase is changed the second or third time it is ordered or requirements associated with a straight rebuy purchase are modified. A business buyer might seek faster delivery, lower prices, or a different quality level of product specifications. A modified rebuy situation may cause regular suppliers to become more competitive to keep the account since other suppliers could obtain the business. When a

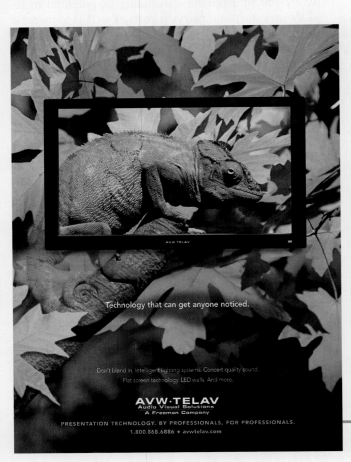

Technology that can get anyone noticed.

Don't blend in. Intelligent lighting systems. Concert quality sound.
Flat screen technology. LED walls. And more.

AVW·TELAV
Audio Visual Solutions
A Freeman Company

PRESENTATION TECHNOLOGY. BY PROFESSIONALS, FOR PROFESSIONALS.
1.800.868.6886 ◆ avwtelav.com

Types of Business Purchases
Audio visual solutions are often purchased for new-task applications linked to desired specifications.

firm changes the terms of a service contract, such as for telecommunication services, it has made a modified purchase. Gateway Computer Systems is expanding its commercial business by focusing on small businesses by offering on-site help and online educational resources. This effort may give Gateway a competitive advantage in serving small firms making modified rebuy purchases.[18]

Demand for Business Products

Unlike consumer demand, demand for business products (also called *industrial demand*) can be characterized as (1) derived, (2) inelastic, (3) joint, or (4) fluctuating.

derived demand Demand for industrial products that stems from demand for consumer products

Derived Demand. Because business customers, especially producers, buy products for direct or indirect use in the production of goods and services to satisfy consumers' needs, the demand for business products derives from the demand for consumer products; it is therefore called **derived demand.** In the long run, no demand for business products is totally unrelated to the demand for consumer products. The derived nature of demand is usually multilevel. Business marketers at different levels are affected by a change in consumer demand for a particular product. For instance, consumers have become concerned with health and good nutrition and, as a result, are purchasing more products with less fat, cholesterol, and sodium. When consumers reduced their purchases of high-fat foods, a change occurred in the demand for products marketed by food processors, equipment manufacturers, and suppliers of raw materials associated with these products. Change in consumer demand for a product affects demand for all firms involved in the production of that product.

inelastic demand Demand that is not significantly altered by a price increase or decrease

Inelastic Demand. With **inelastic demand,** a price increase or decrease will not significantly alter demand for a business product. Because some business products contain a number of parts, price increases affecting only one or two parts may yield only a slightly higher per-unit production cost. When a sizable price increase for a component represents a large proportion of the product's cost, demand may become more elastic because the price increase in the component causes the price at the consumer level to rise sharply. For example, if aircraft engine manufacturers substantially increase the price of engines, forcing Boeing to raise the prices of the aircraft it manufactures, the demand for airliners may become more elastic as airlines reconsider whether they can afford to buy new aircraft. An increase in the price of windshields, however, is unlikely to greatly affect either the price of or the demand for airliners.

Inelasticity applies only to industry demand for business products, not to the demand an individual firm faces. Suppose a spark plug producer increases the price of spark plugs sold to small-engine manufacturers, but its competitors continue to maintain lower prices. The spark plug company will probably experience reduced unit sales because most small-engine producers will switch to lower-priced brands. A specific firm is vulnerable to elastic demand, even if industry demand for a specific business product is inelastic. We will take another look at price elasticity in Chapter 14.

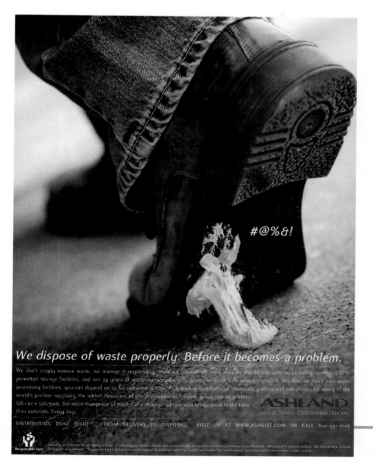

We dispose of waste properly. Before it becomes a problem.

#@%&!

ASHLAND
ASHLAND DISTRIBUTION

DISTRIBUTION DONE RIGHT™ FROM DELIVERY TO DISPOSAL. VISIT US AT WWW.ASHDIST.COM OR CALL 800-531-7106

Derived Demand
Ashland helps identify and resolve waste management issues.

joint demand Demand involving the use of two or more items in combination to produce a product

Joint Demand. Demand for certain business products, especially raw materials and components, is subject to joint demand. **Joint demand** occurs when two or more items are used in combination to produce a product. For example, a firm that manufactures axes needs the same number of axe handles as it does axe blades. These two products thus are demanded jointly. If a shortage of axe handles exists, the producer buys fewer axe blades. Understanding the effects of joint demand is particularly important for a marketer selling multiple jointly demanded items. Such a marketer realizes that when a customer begins purchasing one of the jointly demanded items, a good opportunity exists to sell related products.

Fluctuating Demand. Because the demand for business products is derived from consumer demand, it may fluctuate enormously. In general, when particular consumer products are in high demand, their producers buy large quantities of raw materials and components to ensure meeting long-run production requirements. In addition,

CHC Helicopters: a Canadian Success Story

October 7, 2006, was a sad day for one of Canada's foremost transportation service companies. Craig Dobbin, controlling shareholder and Executive Chairman, passed away. He was laid to rest in his home of Beachy Cove, NL. His passing noted the ending of a chapter in one of Canada's most successful transportation companies: CHC Helicopters.

CHC Helicopter Corporation is the world's largest provider of helicopter transportation services, providing services in more than 30 countries. CHC is a mainstay in the oil and gas industry, but it also provides emergency medical services, and service to the forestry, mining, and construction industries.

CHC is truly a Canadian company. In 1987, Craig Dobbin purchased Okanagan Helicopters Limited, the nation's first commercial helicopter service. Okanagan was the brainchild of three former military pilots, who started the firm in 1947 in British Columbia to spray crops. By 1954, Okanagan Helicopters Limited had grown to become the largest helicopter service firm in the world. Dobbin had established his own helicopter firm in Newfoundland and Labrador: Sealand Helicopters. The merger of Okanagan and Sealand would result in the formation of CHC Helicopter Corporation. Over the next 12 years, Dobbin would also acquire British International Helicopters, Helicopter Services Group of Norway, Lloyd Helicopters of Australia and Court Helicopters of South Africa. In 2004, CHC moved its head office from his native Newfoundland and Labrador, to Richmond, BC.

Today, CHC operates a fleet of 250 helicopters in 35 countries, employing nearly 3100 people. Bases of operation include: United Kingdom, Scandinavia, Australia, Brazil, Thailand, the Philippines, the Middle East, South Africa, South America, and North America. CHC is the leading provider of helicopter services in the North Sea.

Revenues for 2006 were $905.9 million, with sales growth of more than 26 percent over 2005. Major clients include BP, TotalFinaElf, Statoil, MobilExxon, Unocal, Chevron, and Norsk Hydro. CHC's shares are traded on the Toronto and New York stock exchanges, and the Dobbins family still controls 62 percent of the voting stock.

these producers may expand production capacity, which entails acquiring new equipment and machinery, more workers, and more raw materials and component parts. Conversely, a decline in demand for certain consumer goods significantly reduces demand for business products used to produce those goods.

Marketers of business products may notice changes in demand when customers alter inventory policies, perhaps because of expectations about future demand. For example, if several dishwasher manufacturers that buy timers from one producer increase their inventory of timers from a two-week to a one-month supply, the timer producer will have a significant, immediate increase in demand.

Sometimes price changes lead to surprising temporary changes in demand. A price increase for a business product may initially cause business customers to buy more of the item because they expect the price to rise further. Similarly, demand for a business product may decrease significantly following a price cut because buyers are waiting for further price reductions. Fluctuations in demand can be substantial in industries in which prices change frequently.

Business Buying Decisions

business (organizational) buying behaviour The purchase behaviour of producers, government units, institutions, and resellers

Business (organizational) buying behaviour refers to the purchase behaviour of producers, government units, institutions, and resellers. Although several factors affecting consumer buying behaviour (discussed in the previous chapter) also influence business buying behaviour, a number of factors are unique to the latter. In this section, we first analyze the buying centre to learn who participates in business purchase decisions. Then we focus on the stages of the buying decision process and the factors that affect it.

The Buying Centre

buying centre The people within an organization who make business purchase decisions

Relatively few business purchase decisions are made by just one person; often they are made through a buying centre. The **buying centre** is the group of people within the organization who make business purchase decisions. They include users, influencers, buyers, deciders, and gatekeepers.[19] One person may perform several roles. These participants share some goals and risks associated with their decisions.

Users are the organization members who actually use the product being acquired. They frequently initiate the purchase process and/or generate purchase specifications. After the purchase, they evaluate product performance relative to the specifications.

Influencers are often technical personnel, such as engineers, who help develop the specifications and evaluate alternative products. Technical personnel are especially important influencers when products being considered involve new, advanced technology.

Buyers select suppliers and negotiate terms of purchase. They may also become involved in developing specifications. Buyers are sometimes called purchasing agents or purchasing managers. Their choices of vendors and products, especially for new-task purchases, are heavily influenced by people occupying other roles in the buying centre. For straight rebuy purchases, the buyer plays a major role in vendor selection and negotiations.

Deciders actually choose the products. Although buyers may be deciders, it is not unusual for different people to occupy these roles. For routinely purchased items, buyers are commonly deciders. However, a buyer may not be authorized to make purchases exceeding a certain dollar limit, in which case higher-level management personnel are deciders.

Finally, gatekeepers, such as secretaries and technical personnel, control the flow of information to and among

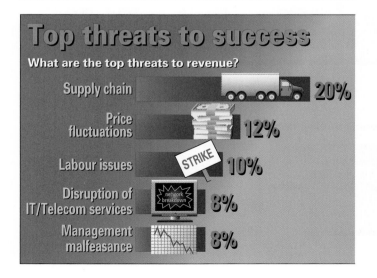

Top threats to success

What are the top threats to revenue?

Supply chain	20%
Price fluctuations	12%
Labour issues	10%
Disruption of IT/Telecom services	8%
Management malfeasance	8%

people occupying other roles in the buying centre. Buyers who deal directly with vendors also may be gatekeepers because they can control information flows. The flow of information from a supplier's sales representatives to users and influencers is often controlled by personnel in the purchasing department.

The number and structure of an organization's buying centres are affected by the organization's size and market position, the volume and types of products being purchased, and the firm's overall managerial philosophy regarding exactly who should be involved in purchase decisions. The size of a buying centre is influenced by the stage of the buying decision process and by the type of purchase. The size of the buying centre likely would be larger for a new-task purchase than for a straight rebuy. Varying goals among members of a buying centre can have both positive and negative effects on the purchasing process.

A marketer attempting to sell to a business customer should determine who is in the buying centre, the types of decisions each individual makes, and which individuals are most influential in the decision process. Because in some instances many people make up the buying centre, marketers cannot feasibly contact all participants. Instead, they must be certain to contact a few of the most influential.

Stages of the Business Buying Decision Process

Like consumers, businesses follow a buying decision process. This process is summarized in the lower portion of Figure 6.1. In the first stage, one or more individuals recognize that a problem or need exists. Problem recognition may arise under a variety of circumstances, for instance, when machines malfunction or a firm modifies an existing product or introduces a new one. Individuals in the buying centre, such as users, influencers, or buyers, may be involved in problem recognition, but it may be stimulated by external sources, such as sales representatives or advertisements.

The second stage of the process, development of product specifications, requires that buying centre participants assess the problem or need and determine what is nec-

---

figure 6.1 BUSINESS (ORGANIZATIONAL) BUYING DECISION PROCESS AND FACTORS THAT MAY INFLUENCE IT

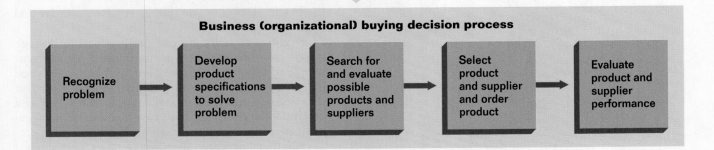

essary to resolve or satisfy it. During this stage, users and influencers, such as engineers, often provide information and advice for developing product specifications. By assessing and describing needs, the organization should be able to establish product specifications.

Searching for and evaluating potential products and suppliers is the third stage in the decision process. Search activities may involve looking in company files and trade directories; contacting suppliers for information; soliciting proposals from known vendors; and examining websites, catalogues, and trade publications. To facilitate a vendor search, some organizations, such as Wal-Mart, advertise their desire to build partnerships with specific types of vendors, such as those owned by women or by minorities. During this stage, some organizations engage in **value analysis,** an evaluation of each component of a potential purchase. Value analysis examines quality, design, materials, and possibly item reduction or deletion to acquire the product in the most cost-effective way. Some vendors may be deemed unacceptable because they are not large enough to supply needed quantities; others may be excluded because of poor delivery and service records. Sometimes the product is not available from any existing vendor and the buyer must find a company known for its innovation, such as 3M, to design and make it. Products are evaluated to make sure they meet or exceed product specifications developed in the second stage. Usually suppliers are judged according to multiple criteria. A number of firms employ **vendor analysis,** a formal, systematic evaluation of current and potential vendors focusing on such characteristics as price, product quality, delivery service, product availability, and overall reliability.

Results of deliberations and assessments in the third stage are used during the fourth stage to select the product to be purchased and the supplier from which to buy it. In some cases, the buyer selects and uses several suppliers, a process known as **multiple sourcing.** In others, only one supplier is selected, a situation called **sole sourcing.** For example, Best Buy and UPS recently agreed to an exclusive shipping relationship that resulted in greater savings, efficiencies, and customer loyalty for both companies.[20] Firms with federal government contracts are required to have several sources for an item. Sole sourcing has traditionally been discouraged except when a product is available from only one company. Sole sourcing is much more common today, however, partly because such an arrangement means better communications between buyer and supplier, stability and higher profits for suppliers, and often lower prices for buyers. However, many organizations still prefer multiple sourcing because this approach lessens the possibility of disruption caused by strikes, shortages, or bankruptcies. The actual product is ordered in this fourth stage, and specific details regarding terms, credit arrangements, delivery dates and methods, and technical assistance are finalized.

During the fifth stage, the product's performance is evaluated by comparing it with specifications. Sometimes the product meets the specifications, but its performance fails to adequately solve the problem or satisfy the need recognized in the first stage. In that case, product specifications must be adjusted. The supplier's performance is also evaluated during this stage. If supplier performance is inadequate, the business purchaser seeks corrective action from the supplier or searches for a new one. Results of the evaluation become feedback for the other stages in future business purchase decisions.

This business buying decision process is used in its entirety primarily for new-task purchases. Several stages, but not necessarily all, are used for modified rebuy and straight rebuy situations.

Influences on the Business Buying Decision Process

Figure 6.1 also lists four major categories of factors that influence business buying decisions: environmental, organizational, interpersonal, and individual.

Environmental factors include competitive and economic factors, political forces, legal and regulatory forces, technological changes, and sociocultural issues. These factors generate considerable uncertainty for an organization, which can make individuals in the buying centre apprehensive about certain types of purchases. Changes

---

value analysis An evaluation of each component of a potential purchase

vendor analysis A formal, systematic evaluation of current and potential vendors

multiple sourcing An organization's decision to use several suppliers

sole sourcing An organization's decision to use only one supplier in one or more environmental forces can create new purchasing opportunities and threats. For example, changes in competition and technology can make buying decisions difficult for products such as software, computers, and telecommunications equipment. On the other hand, many business marketers believe the Internet can reduce their customer service costs and allow firms to improve relationships with business customers.[21]

Organizational factors influencing the buying decision process include the company's objectives, purchasing policies, and resources, as well as the size and composition of its buying centre. An organization may have certain buying policies to which buying centre participants must conform. For instance, a firm's policies may mandate unusually long- or short-term contracts, perhaps longer or shorter than most sellers desire. General Motors, for example, limits technology contracts to five years, even though the industry standard is seven- or 10-year contracts. The company has also imposed strict standardized sets of operating rules governing its awarding of contracts. These rules give GM greater flexibility and control but create additional challenges for firms marketing to the auto giant.[22] An organization's financial resources may require special credit arrangements. Any of these conditions could affect purchase decisions.

Interpersonal factors are the relationships among people in the buying centre. Trust among all members of collaborative partnerships is crucial, particularly in purchases involving customized products.[23] Use of power and level of conflict among buying centre participants influences business buying decisions. Certain individuals in the buying centre may be better communicators and more persuasive than others. Often these interpersonal dynamics are hidden, making them difficult for marketers to assess.

Individual factors are personal characteristics of participants in the buying centre, such as age, education level, personality, and tenure and position in the organization. For example, a 55-year-old manager who has been in the organization for 25 years may affect decisions made by the buying centre differently than a 30-year-old person employed only two years. How influential these factors are depends on the buying situation, the type of product being purchased, and whether the purchase is new-task, modified rebuy, or straight rebuy. Negotiating styles of people vary within an organization and from one organization to another. To be effective, marketers must know customers well enough to be aware of these individual factors and their potential effects on purchase decisions.

Using Industrial Classification Systems

Marketers have access to a considerable amount of information about potential business customers since much of this information is available through government and industry publications and websites. Marketers use this information to identify potential business customers and to estimate their purchase potential.

Identifying Potential Business Customers

North American Industry Classification System (NAICS)
An industry classification system that generates comparable statistics among Canada, the United States, and Mexico

Much information about business customers is based on industrial classification systems. In the United States, marketers traditionally have relied on the *Standard Industrial Classification (SIC) system,* which the federal government developed to classify selected economic characteristics of industrial, commercial, financial, and service organizations. However, the SIC system has been replaced by a new industry classification system called the **North American Industry Classification System (NAICS.)** NAICS is a single industry classification system used by Canada, the United States, and Mexico to generate comparable statistics among the three partners of the North American Free Trade Agreement (NAFTA.) The NAICS classification is based on the types of production activities performed. NAICS is similar to the International Standard Industrial Classification (ISIC) system used in Europe and many other parts of the world. Whereas the SIC system divided industrial activity into 10 divisions, NAICS divides it into 20 sectors. NAICS contains 1172 industry classifications, compared with 1004 in the SIC system. NAICS is more comprehensive and up-to-date, and it

table 6.3   BREAKOUT OF NAICS CATEGORIES FOR MANUFACTURING

31–33 Manufacturing
    311   Food Manufacturing
    312   Beverage and Tobacco Product Manufacturing
    313   Textile Mills
    314   Textile Product Mills
    315   Clothing Manufacturing
    316   Leather and Allied Products Manufacturing
    321   Wood Product Manufacturing
    322   Paper Manufacturing
    323   Printing and Related Support Activities
    324   Petroleum and Coal Products Manufacturing
    325   Chemical Manufacturing
    326   Plastics and Rubber Products Manufacturing
    327   Non-Metallic Mineral Product Manufacturing
    331   Primary Metal Manufacturing
    332   Fabricated Metal Product Manufacturing
    333   Machinery Manufacturing
    334   Computer and Electronic Product Manufacturing
        3341   Computer and Peripheral Equipment Manufacturing
        3342   Communications Equipment Manufacturing
        3343   Audio and Video Equipment Manufacturing
        3344   Semiconductor and Other Electronic Component Manufacturing
        3345   Navigational, Measuring, Medical and Control Instruments Manufacturing
        3346 Manufacturing and Reproducing Magnetic and Optical Media
    335   Electrical Equipment, Appliance and Component Manufacturing
    336   Transportation Equipment Manufacturing
    337   Furniture and Related Product Manufacturing
    339   Miscellaneous Manufacturing

Value of Production
Principal Establishments**
Manufacturing Shipments
and
Manufacturing Value-Added
1994–2003
Computer and Electronic Product Manufacturing Subsector
(NAICS 334)

Measure of Production	Value in $billions		CAGR* 1994–2003	% Change 2002–2003
	1994	2003		
Manufacturing Shipments	18.1	21.2	1.8%	−5.5%
Manufacturing Value-Added	7.1	8.7	2.2%	3.1%

Notes:
* Compound annual growth rate
** Incorporated establishments with employees, primarily engaged in manufacturing and with sales of manufactured goods equal or greater than $30 000

Detailed statistical breakout by NAICS code retrievable for Canadian IPs from industry Canada's Canadian Industry Statistics from the Strategis Website:
http://strategis.ic.gc.ca/canadian_industry_statistics/cis.nsf/IDE/cis31-33prde.html

provides considerably more information about service industries and high-tech products.[24] A sample breakout of the classifications in the NAICS is shown in the Table 6.3 above. Also shown is a link to an information database through Industry Canada's Strategis website that will provide detailed statistical breakouts for each code level. Strategis can only be accessed by users of Canadian internet addresses (IPs).

Industrial classification systems are ready-made tools that enable marketers to categorize organizations into groups based mainly on the types of goods and services provided. Although an industrial classification system is a vehicle for segmentation, it is most appropriately used in conjunction with other types of data to determine exactly how many and which customers a marketer can reach.

Input-output analysis works well in conjunction with an industrial classification system. This type of analysis is based on the assumption that the output, or sales, of one industry are the input, or purchases, of other industries. **Input-output data** identify what types of industries purchase the products of a particular industry.

A marketer can take several approaches to determine the identities and locations of organizations in specific groups. One approach is to use regional directories or commercial industrial directories, such as *Standard & Poor's Register* and Dun & Bradstreet's *Million Dollar Directory*. These sources contain such information about a firm as its name, industrial classification, address, phone number, and annual sales. By referring to one or more of these sources, marketers isolate business customers with industrial classification numbers, determine their locations, and develop lists of potential customers by desired geographic area. A more expedient, although more expensive, approach is to use a commercial data service. Dun & Bradstreet, for example, can provide a list of organizations that fall into a particular industrial classification group. For each company on the list, Dun & Bradstreet gives the name, location, sales volume, number of employees, type of products handled, names of chief executives, and other pertinent information. Either method can effectively identify and locate a group of potential customers. However, a marketer probably cannot pursue all organizations on the list. Because some companies have greater purchasing potential than others, marketers must determine which customer or customer group to pursue.

input-output data Information that identifies what types of industries purchase the products of a particular industry

Estimating Purchase Potential

To estimate the purchase potential of business customers or groups of customers, a marketer must find a relationship between the size of potential customers' purchases and a variable available in industrial classification data, such as the number of employees. For example, a paint manufacturer might attempt to determine the average number of gallons purchased by a specific type of potential customer relative to the number of employees. A marketer with no previous experience in this market segment will probably have to survey a random sample of potential customers to establish a relationship between purchase sizes and numbers of employees. Once this relationship is established, it can be applied to customer groups to estimate their potential purchases. After deriving these estimates, the marketer is in a position to select the customer groups with the most sales and profit potential.

Despite their usefulness, industrial classification data pose several problems. First, a few industries do not have specific designations. Second, because a transfer of products from one establishment to another is counted as a part of total shipments, double counting may occur when products are shipped between two establishments within the same firm. Third, because Statistics Canada is prohibited from providing data that identify specific business organizations, some data, such as value of total shipments, may be understated. Finally, because government agencies provide industrial classification data, a significant lag usually exists between data collection time and the time the information is released.

SUMMARY

Business or organizational (B2B) markets consist of individuals and groups that purchase a specific kind of product for resale, direct use in producing other products, or use in day-to-day operations. Producer markets include those individuals and business organizations that purchase products for the purpose of making a profit by using them to produce other products or as part of their operations. Intermediaries that buy finished products and resell them to make a profit are classified as reseller markets. Government markets consist of federal, provincial, territorial or municipal governments, which spend billions of dollars annually for goods and services to support internal operations and to provide citizens with needed services. Organizations with charitable, educational, community, or other non-profit goals constitute institutional markets.

Transactions involving business customers differ from consumer transactions in several ways. Such transactions tend to be larger, and negotiations occur less frequently, though they are often lengthy. They frequently involve more than one person or department in the purchasing organization. They may also involve reciprocity, an arrangement in which two organizations agree to buy from each other. Business customers are usually better informed than ultimate consumers and more likely to seek information about a product's features and technical specifications.

When purchasing products, business customers are particularly concerned about quality, service, price, and supplier relationships. Quality is important because it directly affects the quality of products the buyer's firm produces. To achieve an exact level of quality, organizations often buy products on the basis of a set of expressed characteristics, called specifications. Because services have such a direct influence on a firm's costs, sales, and profits, factors such as market information, on-time delivery, and availability of parts are crucial to a business buyer. Although business customers do not depend solely on price to decide which products to buy, price is of primary concern because it directly influences profitability.

Business buyers use several purchasing methods, including description, inspection, sampling, and negotiation. Most organizational purchases are new-task, straight rebuy, or modified rebuy. In a new-task purchase, an organization makes an initial purchase of items to be used to perform new jobs or solve new problems. In a modified rebuy purchase, a new-task purchase is changed the second or third time it is ordered or requirements associated with a straight rebuy purchase are modified. A straight rebuy purchase occurs when a buyer purchases the same products routinely under approximately the same terms of sale.

Industrial demand differs from consumer demand along several dimensions. Industrial demand derives from demand for consumer products. At the industry level, industrial demand is inelastic. If an industrial item's price changes, product demand will not change as much proportionally. Some industrial products are subject to joint demand, which occurs when two or more items are used in combination to make a product. Finally, because organizational demand derives from consumer demand, the demand for business products can fluctuate widely.

Business (or organizational) buying behaviour refers to the purchase behaviour of producers, resellers, government units, and institutions. Business purchase decisions are made through a buying centre, the group of people involved in making such purchase decisions. Users are those in the organization who actually use the product. Influencers help develop specifications and evaluate alternative products for possible use. Buyers select suppliers and negotiate purchase terms. Deciders choose the products. Gatekeepers control the flow of information to and among individuals occupying other roles in the buying centre.

The stages of the business buying decision process are problem recognition, development of product specifications to solve problems, search for and evaluation of products and suppliers, selection and ordering of the most appropriate product, and evaluation of the product's and supplier's performance.

Four categories of factors influence business buying decisions: environmental, organizational, interpersonal, and individual. Environmental factors include competitive forces, economic conditions, political forces, laws and regulations, technological changes, and sociocultural factors. Business factors include the company's objectives, purchasing policies, and resources, as well as the size and composition of its buying centre. Interpersonal factors are the relationships among people in the buying centre. Individual factors are personal characteristics of members

of the buying centre, such as age, education level, personality, and tenure and position in the organization.

Business marketers have a considerable amount of information available for use in planning marketing strategies. Much of this information is based on an industrial classification system, which categorizes businesses into major industry groups, industry subgroups, and detailed industry categories. An industrial classification system—like the North American Industry Classification System (NAICS) used by Canada, the United States, and Mexico—provides marketers with information needed to identify business customer groups. It can best be used for this purpose in conjunction with other information, such as input-output data. After identifying target industries, a marketer can obtain the names and locations of potential customers by using government and commercial data sources. Marketers then must estimate potential purchases of business customers by finding a relationship between a potential customer's purchases and a variable available in industrial classification data.

 Please visit the student website at www.hmco.ca/marketing for ACE Self-Test questions that will help you prepare for exams.

IMPORTANT TERMS

Business or organizational market	Reciprocity	Joint demand	Multiple sourcing
Producer markets	New-task purchase	Business (organizational) buying behaviour	Sole sourcing
Reseller markets	Straight rebuy purchase	Buying centre	North American Industry Classification System (NAICS)
Government markets	Modified rebuy purchase	Value analysis	
Institutional markets	Derived demand	Vendor analysis	Input-output data
	Inelastic demand		

DISCUSSION & REVIEW QUESTIONS

1. Identify, describe, and give examples of the four major types of business markets.

2. Why might business customers generally be considered more rational in their purchasing behaviour than ultimate consumers?

3. What are the primary concerns of business customers?

4. List several characteristics that differentiate transactions involving business customers from consumer transactions.

5. What are the commonly used methods of business buying?

6. Why do buyers involved in straight rebuy purchases require less information than those making new-task purchases?

7. How does demand for business products differ from consumer demand?

8. What are the major components of a firm's buying centre?

9. Identify the stages of the business buying decision process. How is this decision process used when making straight rebuys?

10. How do environmental, business, interpersonal, and individual factors affect business purchases?

11. What function does an industrial classification system help marketers perform?

12. List some sources that a business marketer can use to determine the names and addresses of potential customers.

APPLICATION QUESTIONS

1. Identify organizations in your area that fit each business market category: producer, reseller, government, and institutional. Explain your classifications.

2. Indicate the method of buying (description, inspection, sampling, or negotiation) an organization would be most likely to use when purchasing each of the following items. Defend your selections.

   a. A building for the home office of a light bulb manufacturer

   b. Wool for a clothing manufacturer

   c. An Alaskan cruise for a company retreat, assuming a regular travel agency is used

   d. One-inch nails for a building contractor

3. Purchases by businesses may be described as new-task, modified rebuy, or straight rebuy. Categorize the following purchase decisions and explain your choices.

   a. Bob has purchased toothpicks from Smith Restaurant Supply for 25 years and recently placed an order for yellow toothpicks rather than the usual white ones.

   b. Jill's investment company has been purchasing envelopes from AAA Office Supply for a year and now needs to purchase boxes to mail year-end portfolio summaries to clients. Jill calls AAA to purchase these boxes.

   c. Reliance Insurance has been supplying its salespeople with small personal computers to assist in their sales efforts. The company recently agreed to begin supplying them with faster, more sophisticated computers.

4. Identifying qualified customers is important to the survival of any organization. NAICS provides helpful information about many different businesses. Go to the Strategis website at www.strategis.gc.ca and find the NAICS classification for manufacturing the following items.

   a. Chocolate candy bars

   b. Automobile tires

   c. Men's running shoes

globalEDGE™

1. The world market for steel plays a vital role on projects involving the construction of bridges, buildings, automobiles, and aircraft. After attending a conference sponsored by the International Iron and Steel Institute (IISI), you learn that the "World Steel in Figures" report can help your firm reassess its strategy for sourcing steel on the global market to be a better arbiter for clients. To access this report, use the search term "IISI" at **http://globaledge.msu.edu/ibrd** or **http://globaledge.msu.edu/ibrd/ ibrd.asp.** Currently, your sourcing strategy is similar to typical North American companies. As such, from which regions does your company source steel? Which countries might your firm aim to find new sources for steel?

2. Part of your firm's evaluation of a supplier's performance is based on the degree to which it seamlessly delivers goods and materials. A recent complication for global suppliers is an initiative to enhance shipping container security for international trade and transport. A report concerning container security for international trade and transportation can be found using the search term "international trade and transport" at **http://globaledge.msu.edu/ibrd** or **http://globaledge.msu.edu/ibrd/ ibrd.asp.** At the United Nations Conference on Trade and Development (UNCTAD) website, click on the Transport & Trade Logistics link, go to the Documents section, and look for a report on Container Security. What are the four parts of this program? Based on this, do you think your firm should change its evaluation of supplier performance?

General Electric Company

General Electric Company is a highly diversified, global corporation with many divisions. GEPolymerland.com is the online site for GE's resins business. Visit the site at **www.GEPolymerland.com.**

1. At what types of business markets are GE's resin products targeted?
2. How does GEPolymerland address some of the concerns of business customers?
3. What environmental factors do you think affect demand for GE resin products?

Case 6.1   ## Lextant Corporation: Design Research at Its Best

These days, competition is fierce. It's no longer possible just to make a product and hope that it sells; products must be designed with end users in mind. Lextant Corporation provides design research for its business customers, including PepsiCo, Procter & Gamble, Motorola, Goodyear, Whirlpool, Microsoft, and Hard Rock Café. Its name comes from the word *lexicon* meaning a vocabulary or language—in this case, a language of consumers. The privately held Columbus, Ohio-based company strives to translate this language into actionable insights, equipping its clients to design for the motivations, behaviours, and desires of their own customers.

Lextant was founded with one fundamental goal—to help companies achieve a sustainable competitive advantage by understanding their end users and designing products to satisfy them. To achieve this goal, Lextant examines what motivates and drives people and presents this information to its clients so that they can make informed decisions about the products they are designing. Lextant brings together teams of experts in psychology, sociology, anthropology, human factors, industrial design, and interaction design, and it combines ethnographic, participatory, marketing, behavioural, and usability research techniques to provide tools to make products better. Then researchers learn from consumers by following them in everything they do in their environment. Finally, researchers design systems that will yield the desired results for the firm's clients.

Lextant researchers discover what end users want by getting a broad view of people and trying to know and understand them, often by observing them in their own environment. They understand the importance of observing people actually using the products being studied in their place of usage. It is important in this

process to really listen to end users when they explain what matters to them. Lextant has two approaches for collecting data. The first is qualitative—through the context and environment of the user. The second is quantitative—based on what the client wants. The quantitative approach involves presenting prototypes of a product to a sample of end users. These clients then use the sample product and give feedback on what they like and don't like about the product, as well as suggestions on how the product could be improved.

In some cases, Lextant uses focus groups to discover information for its clients. Researchers bring people together at a central facility to use and test the product and provide feedback about its design, colour, and ease of use. This method is especially useful when budget or time is limited because it permits researchers to gather information at a central location in a short time and results in instant feedback.

Once researchers have collected the data from various sources, they are often confronted with an overwhelming amount of data. They must analyze the data to find the patterns and recognize anomalies that occur in only a few cases. Researchers use affinity diagrams and Post-it Notes stuck to the wall to help the process flow. By having Post-it Notes labelled with each important characteristic, it is easy to move the parts around until the relevant story becomes clear. By having many pictures of the users and the environments in which a product is used, it is possible for any person in the organization to come into the room and understand the consumers: their personas, attitudes, and motivations.

Employees at Lextant immerse themselves in the information that they gather to evaluate which information is relevant while at the same time discarding useless information. It is then possible to see where people say similar things and to focus on those and find out what is wrong with certain products.

Clients of Lextant are often surprised by the findings of the Lextant team, especially when it comes to identifying ways that they can modify their existing products to better satisfy end users. For example, Lextant helped Hard Rock Café, to answer the question, "Is our website experience helping or hurting our brand?" Indeed, its website was challenging to navigate and was sapping online sales. Lextant helped the restaurant chain develop an easy-to-use, compelling website to help rejuvenate the legendary brand. Lextant researchers examined the Hard Rock website from the customers' perspective, documented the user goals and ideal experiences, and then developed an architecture that facilitated desired activity flows. The research firm created a complete prototype featuring an intuitive Café locator, personalization features, and a stream-lined shopping process. This enabled Hard Rock to corroborate and refine site concepts before making significant investments in implementation.

Lextant provides a business product that has a derived demand from producing products that delight consumers. Design research is not about the what, but rather the why. If you understand why people do not like an existing design, then it is possible to design a new solution.[25]

Questions for Discussion

1. Why is the Lextant product a derived demand business product?
2. What types of business markets does Lextant serve?
3. When purchasing Lextant services, what type of buying method would be used: description, sampling, inspection, or negotiation?

CHAPTER 7

Reaching Global Markets

iPod: Surely One of Apple's Greatest Hits

Today, just about everyone has an iPod. Well, perhaps not everyone. But the Queen of England has one. So does the Pope. Fashion designer Karl Lagerfeld has more than 70 of them storing his collection of more than 60 000 CDs.

From its start in 1976 with the introduction of Apple I to the more recent phenomenon of the iPod, Apple Computer Inc. has achieved legendary status worldwide with its innovations. Whether it's the latest incarnation of the original iPod that was first introduced in October 2001 or the later additions such as the iPod shuffle or iPod nano, one of the most remarkable things about the iPod family is its almost universal appeal. It's been embraced not just by teenagers, but by people worldwide, young and old. Sit in a Tim Horton's in Calgary or venture out to a sidewalk cafe in Beijing, Melbourne, Rio de Janeiro, Stockholm, or Tokyo and the parade of iPods works like a universal ad for Apple. The company currently dominates the MP3 player market with its Microsoft-like 75 percent share worldwide.

The iPod is simply an entirely new way to listen to music, and the global marketplace is taking notice. Numerous companies are hopping on the bandwagon by developing products that go along with iPods. For example, Levi Strauss is launching its Levi's RedWire DLX jeans that have a docking station in the pocket and a control panel sewn into the coin pocket. "This brings blue jeans into the 21st century. . . . The idea is to merge fashion and technology," says Levi spokeswoman Amy Jasmer.

The automobile industry is also paying close attention to the iPod. "Customers have been asking for iPod connectivity," said Randy Ewers, director, Mopar Accessories Portfolio Team. Most carmakers now offer iPod integration. In cars made by the Chrysler Group—such as Chrysler, Jeep, and Dodge—seamless iPod integration means that drivers can listen to their iPods through their cars' audio systems. They have the traditional features of their iPods at their fingertips via the radio or steering wheel controls, and they can view selections on the radio display.

OBJECTIVES

1. To understand the nature of global marketing strategy

2. To analyze the environmental forces affecting international marketing efforts

3. To understand several important international trade agreements

4. To identify methods of international market entry

5. To examine various forms of global organizational structures

6. To examine the use of the marketing mix internationally

Accessories made specifically for iPod range from fashionable cases to Bose speaker systems. No doubt the iPod will continue to inspire new products and new marketing strategies the world over. It's time to Listen Up![1] ■

Before picking up an Egg McMuffin at McDonald's this morning, a young woman in Hong Kong may have brightened her smile with Colgate toothpaste and highlighted her eyes with Avon eye shadow. Her brother, on business that same day in Frankfurt, may cash a check in a local Citicorp branch bank. Elsewhere that day, a Polish office worker may lunch on a pizza from Pizza Hut, fried chicken from KFC, or a taco from Taco Bell. An Australian mother shopping for a birthday present in Melbourne may drop in at Daimaru, a Japanese department store, while a shopper in Hong Kong may shop for clothing at Roots, a Toronto-based retailer. The earth is now populated by about 6.5 billion people whose lives are intertwined in one tremendous global marketplace. In fact, global trade in goods and services reached $11 trillion in 2004, an increase of 18 percent compared with 2003.[2]

In deference to the increasingly global nature of marketing, we devote this chapter to the unique features of global markets and international marketing. We begin by exploring the environmental forces that create opportunities and threats for international marketers. Next, we consider several regional trade alliances, markets, and agreements. Finally, we examine the levels of commitment by firms to international marketing and their degree of involvement in it. These factors must be considered in any marketing plan that includes an international component.

The Nature of Global Marketing Strategy

international marketing
Developing and performing marketing activities across national boundaries

Technological advances and rapidly changing political and economic conditions are making it easier than ever for companies to market their products internationally as well as at home. **International marketing** involves developing and performing marketing activities across national boundaries. For example, Wal-Mart has more than 1.5 million employees and operates more than 5300 stores in 10 countries, including the United States, Brazil, Canada, and China, while Starbucks serves 20 million customers a week at more than 10 000 shops in 30 countries.[3]

Firms are finding that international markets provide tremendous opportunities for growth. At the same time, governments and industry leaders often argue that too few firms take full advantage of international opportunities. The result is a wide variance in trade balances for countries. For example, Canada enjoyed a trade surplus— more exports than imports— with the world in 2005, driven by large bilateral surplus with

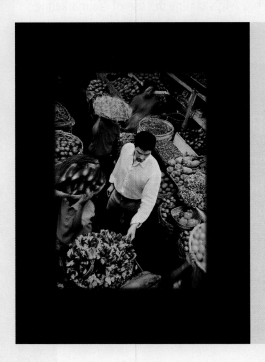

BE AN
EXPERT IN
OVERSEAS
MARKETS.

Do you live an InterContinental life?

INTERCONTINENTAL.
HOTELS & RESORTS

Global Strategy Thinking
InterContinental touts its global strategy capabilities.

the United States. In contrast, the trade balance of the United States has been significantly negative—more imports than exports—for decades.[4] To assist firms in their internationalization efforts, many countries offer significant practical assistance and valuable benchmarking research that will help their domestic firms become more competitive globally.

Canadian enterprise is served by Team Canada Inc., a network of federal departments and agencies working with the provinces, territories, and other partners to help Canadian businesses prepare for the global marketplace. Team Canada Inc. is a "one-stop shop" for information, skills, and assistance with an export venture. Team Canada Inc. offers a wide range of tools designed to help businesses become export-ready, develop export potential, and expand into new markets. Being **export-ready,** involves having the knowledge, skills, and resources necessary for export success. Most small- and medium-sized enterprises in Canada are not export-ready so could benefit greatly from the tools made available by Team Canada Inc. Examples of these tools include *Export Diagnostic* (an online diagnostic tool to test export readiness), and documents such as *Roadmap to Exporting, Step-by-Step Guide to Exporting,* and *Interactive Export Plan.* Team Canada Inc. also offers a half-day *Going Global* workshop at various locations across Canada. For access to and more information on these tools, check out ExportSource.ca.[5]

One noteworthy member of Team Canada Inc. is Export Development Canada (EDC). EDC is a Crown Corporation that provides Canadian exporters with financing, insurance, and bonding services as well as foreign market advise. In 2005, EDC's services and deal structuring capabilities helped to facilitate $57.5 billion in transactions for nearly 7000 Canadian organizations. Approximately 90 percent of EDC's customers are small- and medium-sized businesses. EDC's services can be utilized in virtually every world market; however, those services can be particularly effective in facilitating trade and investment in emerging markets that are opportunity rich but can also pose increased levels of risk.[6]

Before the so-called "born global" firm became a widespread viable organizational form around the early 1990s, most firms entered the international marketplace incrementally as they gained knowledge about various markets and opportunities. Becoming more internationally oriented was typically a slow and deliberate process. However, some firms had the knowledge and resources to speed up their commitment and investment in the international marketplace. Born globals—typically small technology-based firms operating in international markets within two years of their establishment and realizing as much as 70 percent of their sales outside the domestic home market—challenged the traditional internationalization process and especially its incremental nature and slow developmental speed.[7]

These born global firms export their products almost immediately after being established in market niches in which they compete with larger, more established firms. Whether the traditional approach, the born global approach, or an approach that merges attributes of both approaches is adopted to market the firm's products and services, international marketing strategy is a critical element of a firm's global operations. Today, global competition in most industries is intense and becoming increasingly fierce with the addition of newly emerging markets and firms.

For example, to combat new competition, online retailer Amazon.com has nine distribution centres from Nevada to Germany that fill their current flow of about 30 orders per second and ship them to customers in more than 200 countries.[8] In fact, most of the world's population and two-thirds of its total purchasing power are outside of the Canadian and U.S. markets. Accessing these markets can promote innovation, while intensifying global competition spurs companies to market better, less expensive products. Most automobile marketers, for instance, are now attempting to develop products for use by customers worldwide. In the future, only a few automobile brands may be recognized globally. Some of these are likely to be from General Motors, whose many globally recognized brands include Saab, Opel, Chevrolet, and Cadillac. Others may come from Japan's Toyota Motors, which aggressively markets automobiles and trucks around the world and looks to overtake GM as the top automaker in the next few years.[9]

Export-ready Having the knowledge, skills, and resources necessary for export success

Environmental Forces in Global Markets

Firms that enter international markets often find they must make significant adjustments in their marketing strategies. The environmental forces that affect foreign markets may differ dramatically from those affecting domestic markets. Thus, a successful international marketing strategy requires a careful environmental analysis. Conducting research to understand the needs and desires of international customers is crucial to global marketing success. Many firms have demonstrated that such efforts can generate tremendous financial rewards, increase market share, and heighten customer awareness of their products around the world. In this section, we explore how differences in the competitive, economic, political, legal and regulatory, technological, and sociocultural environmental forces in other countries can profoundly affect marketing activities.

Competitive Forces

Competition is often viewed as a staple of the global marketplace. Customers thrive on the choices offered by competition, and firms constantly seek opportunities to outmaneuver their competition to gain customers' loyalty. Firms typically identify their competition when they establish target markets worldwide. Customers seek alternative solutions to their product needs by identifying firms that can compete to solve their needs. However, the increasingly interconnected international marketplace and advances in technology have resulted in competitive forces that are unique to the international marketplace.

As in domestic markets, the products offered by the competition and the ways they are marketed are key competitive forces internationally. However, beyond the types of competition (i.e., brand, product, generic, and total budget competition) and types of competitive structures (i.e., monopoly, oligopoly, monopolistic competition, and pure competition) that are discussed in Chapter 3, firms operating internationally also need to

- attend to the competitive forces in the countries they target,

- identify the interdependence of countries and the global competitors in those markets, and

- be mindful of a new breed of customers—the global customer.

Each country has unique competitive aspects—often founded in the other environmental forces (i.e., sociocultural, technological, political, legal, regulatory, and economic forces)—that are often independent of the competitors in that country market. The most globally competitive countries are listed in Table 7.1. While competitors drive competition, country markets establish the infrastructure for the type of competition that can take place. For example, Microsoft's almost monopolistic dominance in the North American marketplace (and most countries' markets) has led the U.S. government and U.S. firms to a long-standing legal battle over the firm's business practices vis-à-vis its competition.[10] Other countries allow monopoly structures to exist. For example, similar to the situation in many Canadian provinces, most alcohol sales in Sweden are made through the governmental store Systembolaget, which is legally supported by the Swedish Alcohol Retail Monopoly.[11] According to Systembolaget, the Swedish

Staying Ahead of the Competition

DataPipe focuses on delivering services that make services competitive world-wide.

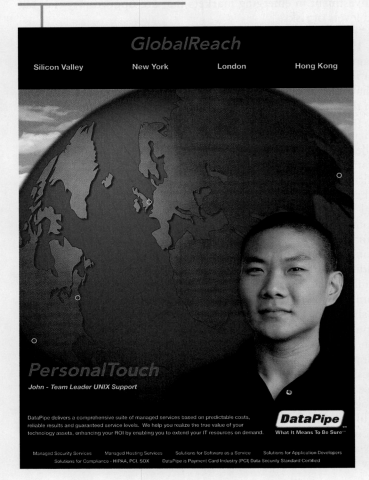

table 7.1	A RANKING OF THE MOST COMPETITIVE COUNTRIES IN THE WORLD		
1.	Finland	11.	Netherlands
2.	United States	12.	Japan
3.	Sweden	13.	United Kingdom
4.	Denmark	14.	Canada
5.	Taiwan	15.	Germany
6.	Singapore	16.	New Zealand
7.	Iceland	17.	South Korea
8.	Switzerland	18.	United Arab Emirates
9.	Norway	19.	Qatar
10.	Australia	20.	Estonia

Source: From Lopezcarlos/Porter/Schwab, *The Global Competitiveness Report 2005–2006,* World Economic Forum. Reproduced by permission of Palgrave Macmillan.

Alcohol Retail Monopoly exists for one reason, "To minimize alcohol-related problems by selling alcohol in a responsible way, without profit motive."

The interdependence between countries and their strategic relevance for multinational firms has long been a critical component of international competition.[12] These interdependencies are a function of governmental activity, trade agreements like the European Union (EU) and the North American Free Trade Agreement (NAFTA), and cultural differences. The result has been the formation of the "triad blocks" of North America, the EU, and Japan. Firms can clearly operate in more than the triad blocks, but the successful international firms typically need to have a solid position in each of the triad blocks to be successful in the long term. Success internationally is a function of the strategic interdependence firms can create across the triad blocks as well as across the other country and region markets targeted. In fact, in only a few industries—such as consumer electronics—should a firm strive to develop a global strategy. For most manufacturing firms and for almost all service firms, adopting a regional approach makes more sense (and in many cases, a country-specific approach is still needed).

The new breed of customer—the global customer—has changed the landscape of international competition drastically.[13] Firms used to simply produce products or services and provide local markets with information about the features and uses of their products or services. Customers seldom had opportunities to compare products from competitors, know details about the competing products' features, and compare other options beyond the local (country or region) markets. However, not only do customers who travel the globe expect to be able to buy the same product in most of the world's more than 200 countries, they also expect that the product they buy in their local store in Vancouver will have the same features as similar products sold in London or even in Beijing. If the quality of the product or its features are more advanced in an international market, customers will soon demand that their local markets offer the same product at the same or lower prices.

Economic Forces

Global marketers need to understand the international trade system, particularly the economic stability of individual nations, as well as trade barriers that may stifle marketing efforts. Economic differences among nations—differences in standards of living, credit, buying power, income distribution, national resources, exchange rates, and the like—dictate many of the adjustments firms must make in marketing internationally.

Canada, the United States, and Western Europe are more stable economically than many other regions of the world. However, even these economies have downturns in regular cycles. In recent years, a number of countries, including Korea, Russia,

Singapore, and Thailand, have experienced economic problems such as depressions, high unemployment, corporate bankruptcies, instability in currency markets, trade imbalances, and financial systems that need major reforms. Even more stable developing countries, such as Mexico and Brazil, tend to have greater fluctuations in their business cycles than Canada does. Economic instability can disrupt the markets for Canadian exports in places that otherwise might be excellent marketing opportunities.

Beyond assessing the stability of a nation's economy, marketers should consider whether that nation imposes trade restrictions, such as tariffs. An **import tariff** is any duty levied by a nation on goods bought outside its borders and brought in. Because they raise the prices of foreign goods, tariffs impede free trade between nations. Tariffs are usually designed either to raise revenue for a country or to protect domestic products.

Non-tariff trade barriers include quotas and embargoes. A **quota** is a limit on the amount of goods an importing country will accept for certain product categories in a specific period of time. An **embargo** is a government's suspension of trade in a particular product or with a given country. Embargoes are generally directed at specific goods or countries and are established for political, health, or religious reasons. For example, the United States forbids the importation of cigars from Cuba for political reasons. However, demand for Cuban cigars is so strong that many enter the U.S. market illegally.

Exchange controls, government restrictions on the amount of a particular currency that can be bought or sold, may also limit international trade. They can force business-people to buy and sell foreign products through a central agency, such as a central bank. On the other hand, to promote international trade, some countries have joined to form free trade zones, multinational economic communities that eliminate tariffs and other trade barriers. Such regional trade alliances are discussed later in the chapter. Foreign currency exchange rates also affect the prices marketers can charge in foreign markets. Fluctuations in the international monetary market can change the prices charged across national boundaries on a daily basis. Thus these fluctuations must be considered in any international marketing strategy.

Countries may limit imports to maintain a favourable balance of trade. The **balance of trade** is the difference in value between a nation's exports and its imports. When a nation exports more products than it imports, a favourable balance of trade exists because money is flowing into the country. Canada maintains a positive trade balance with the world. In June of 2005, Canada's positive balance of trade goods and services increased to just short of $5 billion as exports to countries other than the United States hit an all-time high. Canada's largest trading partner is the United States, which accounts for more than 80 percent of exports and more than 60 percent of imports. Other important trading partners include Japan, the United Kingdom, other European Economic Community countries, and Mexico.[14] The United States had a negative balance of trade for goods and services of $725 billion in 2005, the largest deficit ever.[15] Such a negative balance of trade is considered harmful because for the U.S. it means their dollars are supporting foreign economies at the expense of U.S. companies and workers. At the same time, individuals living in the United States benefit from the assortment of imported products and their typically lower prices.

In terms of the value of all products produced by a nation, Canada had a gross domestic product of nearly $1.08 trillion in 2005.[16] This is small relative to the United States, which has the largest gross domestic product in the world at nearly $12.5 trillion in 2005.[17] **Gross domestic product (GDP)** is an overall measure of a nation's economic standing; it is the market value of a nation's total output of goods and services for a given period. However, it does not take into account the concept of GDP in relation to population (GDP per capita.) Canada has a GDP per capita of approximately $23 074.

Although Switzerland's GDP is about one-fortieth the size of the United States' GDP, its GDP per capita is about the same. Even Canada, which is comparable in size with the United States, has a lower GDP and GDP per capita.[18] Table 7.2 provides a comparative economic analysis of Switzerland, Canada, and the United States.

import tariff A duty levied by a nation on goods bought outside its borders and brought in

quota A limit on the amount of goods an importing country will accept for certain product categories in a specific period of time

embargo A government's suspension of trade in a particular product or with a given country

exchange controls Government restrictions on the amount of a particular currency that can be bought or sold

balance of trade The difference in value between a nation's exports and its imports

gross domestic product (GDP) The market value of a nation's total output of goods and services for a given period; an overall measure of economic standing

table 7.2 **A COMPARATIVE ECONOMIC ANALYSIS OF CANADA, SWITZERLAND, AND THE UNITED STATES**

	Canada	Switzerland	United States
Land area (sq. mi.)	3 560 219	15 355	3 539 227
Population (millions)	32.21	7.41	290.34
Population density (persons per sq. mi.)	9	482	82
GDP, 2002 ($ billions)	$725	$268	$10 383
GDP per capita	$23 074	$36 722	$36 121

Source: U.S. Bureau of the Census, *Statistical Abstract of the United States, 2004* (Washington DC: Government Printing Office, 2005), pp. 841–843, 853.

Strategis and globalEDGE: The Net's Business Resources

Strategis is a comprehensive internet-based resource produced by Industry Canada. Strategis was launched in 1996 in order to harness the power of the Internet to provide business and consumer information to all Canadians without the constraint of geography. Since 1996, Strategis has grown and continues to evolve as the Internet develops.

Strategis' 30 000 subscribers enjoy new technologies that enable interactive applications such as customized benchmarking tools, cost calculators, and online business planning. Strategis contains more than 50 000 links to related business sites. Also, Industry Canada and Team Canada Inc. products and services can be accessed online through Strategis. For example, the site offers the following:

- Online application filing for patent
- **In the News:** latest business news highlights such as financial statistics
- Access to **Trade Data Online,** a service that provides customized reports on Canadian and U.S. trade in goods with over 200 countries

- Access to **exportsource.ca,** Canada's most comprehensive source of information and practical tools for new or experienced exporters[17]

Another valuable Internet based resource is globalEDGE. With over 5000 online resources and up-to-date statistics and business news for nearly 200 countries, globalEDGE is the world's leading online source of international business as ranked by Google, Yahoo!, MSN, and America Online. Created by the Center for International Business Education and Research at Michigan State University (MSU-CIBER), globalEDGE is a knowledge Web portal that connects international business professionals worldwide to a wealth of information, insights, and learning resources on global business activities.

The knowledge is free, providing you unlimited access to the information and tools needed to improve a firm's global competitiveness. The site offers the following:

- Global Resources, with more than 5000 online resources Country Insights, with a wealth of information on all countries
- **News & Views:** latest issues in international business and marketing
- **Academy:** extensive research and teaching resources
- **Diagnostic Tools:** decision-support tools for managers

If you are planning on exporting from Canada, starting a small business, providing business advice, or working on a class project, business and global answers can be found at Strategis and globalEDGE.

Knowledge about per capita income, credit, and the distribution of income provides general insights into market potential.

Opportunities for international trade are not limited to countries with the highest incomes. Some nations are progressing at a much faster rate than they were a few years ago, and these countries—especially in Latin America, Africa, eastern Europe, and the Middle East—have great market potential. An annual study by the Center for International Business Education and Research at Michigan State University provides updated rankings on emerging markets on the globalEDGE website (**http://globaledge .msu.edu/ibrd/marketpot.asp**). The 2006 update of the EMPI features Hong Kong and Singapore at the top of the most attractive emerging markets. China has been steadily climbing up in the index and now ranks third. Ranking as the fourth most attractive export market is South Korea. At the other extreme are South Africa, Venezuela, and Columbia, all suffering from extended economic recessions. However, marketers must understand the political and legal environments before they can convert buying power of customers in these countries into actual demand for specific products.

Political Forces

The political, legal, and regulatory forces of the environment are closely intertwined in Canada. To a large degree, the same is true in many countries internationally. Typically, legislation is enacted, legal decisions are interpreted, and regulatory agencies are operated by elected or appointed officials. A country's legal and regulatory infrastructure is a direct reflection of the political climate in the country. In some countries, this political climate is determined by the people via elections, while in other countries leaders are appointed or have assumed leadership based on certain powers. While laws and regulations have direct effects on a firm's operations in a country, political forces are indirect and often not clearly known in all country markets. For example, the need to work with the government of China to enter and establish operations in the country has been a highly political process since the Communist rule started.

To offset the potential political negatives that may exist in a country or region, firms (and often their home-country governments) strive to maintain good relations with political officials in the targeted countries. Some countries also establish specific mechanisms to better understand the political and business climates around the world, for the benefit of the country's firms and its economy. For example, Export Development Canada (EDC) provides risk assessment and risk management services such as accounts receivable insurance for Canadian exporters and investors. Also, Foreign Affairs and International Trade Canada offers the Canadian Trade Commissioners Service with professional staff located in offices in more than 140 cities worldwide. Trade Commissioners can assist the assessment of political, legal, and regulatory forces in a market, and help obtain advice and market intelligence.[19]

The political climate in a country or region, political officials in a country, and political officials in charge of trade agreements directly affect the legislation and regulations (or lack thereof.) Within industries, elected or appointed officials of influential industry associations also set the tone for the regulatory environment guiding operations in a particular industry. For example, the Canadian Marketing Association (CMA; **www.the-cma.org**) has established its Code of Ethics and Standards of Practice, with a revised edition that took effect in 2007, to guide the marketing profession in Canada.[20]

Legal and Regulatory Forces

A nation's political system, laws, regulatory bodies, special-interest groups, and courts all have great impact on international marketing. A government's policies toward public and private enterprise, consumers, and foreign firms influence marketing across national boundaries. Some countries have established import barriers. Many non-tariff barriers, such as quotas and minimum price levels set on imports, port-of-entry taxes, and stringent health and safety requirements, still make it difficult for Canadian companies to export their products. For example, the collectivistic nature of Japanese culture and the high-context nature of Japanese communication make some types of

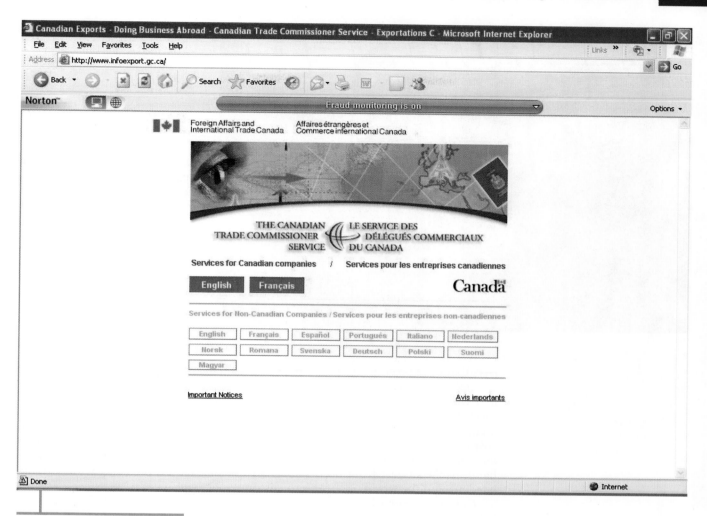

Legal and Regulatory Forces

The Canadian Trade Commissioner Service has officers located in more than 140 cities worldwide to provide relevant advice and intelligence.

direct marketing messages less effective and may predispose many Japanese to support greater regulation of direct marketing practices.[21] A government's attitude toward importers has a direct impact on the economic feasibility of exporting to that country.

Differences in national standards of ethics are illustrated by what the Mexicans call *la mordida*, "the bite." The use of payoffs and bribes is deeply entrenched in many governments. U.S. trade and corporate policy, as well as U.S. law, prohibits direct involvement in payoffs and bribes. While Canada has no law prohibiting the use of payoffs to secure foreign business, some organizations have imposed their own ban on the practice. The ultimate decision about whether to give small tips or gifts where they are customary must be based on a company's code of ethics.

Sociocultural Forces

Cultural, social, and ethical differences among countries (and their subcultures) can have significant effects on marketing activities. Because marketing activities are primarily social in purpose, they are influenced by beliefs and values regarding family, religion, education, health, and recreation. For example, in Greece, where sunbathing is a common form of recreation, products such as Johnson & Johnson Baby Sunblock have a large target market. By identifying major sociocultural variations among countries, marketers lay the groundwork for an effective adaptation of marketing strategy. For instance, when Little Caesars opened new franchise pizza outlets abroad, it made some menu changes to accommodate local tastes and social norms. In Japan, Little Caesars' pizzas are garnished with asparagus, potatoes, squid, or seaweed. Turkish menus include a local pastry for dessert, while Middle Eastern menus exclude

Cultural Differences
GM markets the Hummer in Canada, Mexico, and the U.S.

pork.[22] Although football is a popular sport in Canada and the United States, and a major opportunity for many television advertisers, soccer is the most popular televised sport in Europe (and the largest sport in the world). Most importantly, marketing communications often must be translated into other languages.

It can be difficult to transfer marketing symbols, trademarks, logos, and even products to international markets, especially if they are associated with objects that have profound religious or cultural significance in a particular culture. For example, when Big Boy opened a new restaurant in Bangkok, it quickly became popular with European and North American tourists, but the local Thais refused to eat there. Instead they placed gifts of rice and incense at the feet of the Big Boy statue—a chubby boy holding a hamburger—which reminded them of Buddha. In Japan, customers were forced to tiptoe around a logo painted on the floor at the entrance to an Athlete's Foot store because in Japan it is taboo to step on a crest. On the other hand, A&W's Great Root Beer is a Canadian icon that has been successfully translated around the world: it appeals to customers everywhere.[23]

Cultural differences may also affect marketing negotiations and decision-making behaviour. For example, consumers in Russia found the North American-style energetic happiness of McDonald's employees insincere and offensive when the company opened its first stores in the country.[24] Although North American and Taiwanese sales agents are equally sensitive to customer interests, research suggests that the Taiwanese are more sensitive to the interests of their companies and competitors and less attuned to the interests of colleagues. Identifying such differences in work-related values of employees across different nationalities helps companies design more effective sales management practices.[25] However, the use of North American sales management techniques among Polish retail salespeople has been successful despite many cultural, economic, and political differences in the environments.[26] Table 7.3 offers a sampling of behaviours that may be viewed as rude, insensitive, or offensive in global business negotiations. Cultural differences in the emphasis placed on personal relationships, status, and decision-making styles have been known to complicate dealings between North Americans and businesspeople from other countries. In the Far East, a gift may be considered a necessary introduction before negotiation, whereas in the United States or Canada, a gift may be misconstrued as an illegal bribe.

Buyers' perceptions of other countries can influence product adoption and use. For example, research indicates that Japanese consumers evaluate products from Japan more favourably than those from other countries regardless of product superiority. When people are unfamiliar with products from another country, their perceptions of the country itself may affect their attitude toward the product and help determine whether they will buy it. If a country has a reputation for producing quality products and therefore has a positive image in consumers' minds, marketers of products from that country will want to make the country of origin well known. For example, a generally favourable image of Western computer technology has fueled sales of U.S. personal computers and Microsoft software in Japan. On the other hand, marketers may

table 7.3	A SAMPLING OF CROSS-CULTURAL BEHAVIOURAL DIFFERENCES

Country Behaviours Viewed as Rude or Otherwise Unacceptable

Country	Behaviour
Belgium	Talking with your hands in your pockets
Egypt	Showing the sole of your shoe (as when legs are crossed)
England	Pushing your way in front of others standing in a line
Finland	Standing with your arms folded across your chest
France	Chewing gum, yawning, or conversing loudly in public
Hong Kong	Blinking conspicuously during conversation
India	Expressing anger
Japan	Talking about price during negotiations
New Zealand	Using toothpicks or chewing gum in public
Sri Lanka	Touching, leaning on, or sitting on an image of Buddha
Thailand	Stepping on a doorsill when entering a building
Zambia	Pointing directly at someone or something

Source: "Gestures Around the World," Web of Culture, www.webofculture.com/worldsmart/gestures.html (accessed July 5, 2001).

want to dissociate themselves from a particular country in some cases. For example, because the world has not always viewed Mexico as producing quality products, Volkswagen may not want to advertise that some of the models, including the New Beetle, are made in Mexico.

When products are introduced from one nation into another, acceptance is far more likely if similarities exist between the two cultures. It used to be that firms identified cultural differences and tried to modify their products and services to fit the customers' needs. Nowadays, firms identify similarities and stress those in their product offerings. For example, due to the global sensitivity regarding food, middle-class Canadian families are eating more like their counterparts in Japan, France, and the United States. Europeans are eating more like Canadians. For international marketers, cultural differences have implications for product development, advertising, packaging, and pricing.

Differences in ethical standards can also affect marketing efforts. For example, in China and Vietnam, standards regarding intellectual property differ dramatically from those in Canada, creating potential conflicts for marketers of computer software, music, and books. Because of differences in cultural and ethical standards, many companies are working both individually and collectively to establish ethics programs and standards for international business conduct.[27] Levi Strauss's code of ethics, for example, bars the firm from manufacturing in countries where workers are known to be abused. Starbucks' global code of ethics strives to protect agricultural workers who harvest coffee beans.

Technological Forces

Advances in technology have made international marketing much easier. Interactive web systems, instant messaging, and iPod downloads (along with the traditional vehicles of voice mail, e-mail, fax, and cell phones) make international marketing activities more affordable and convenient. Internet use has accelerated dramatically within Canada and abroad. In Europe, more than 50 percent of households have Internet access at home or work, pushing e-commerce revenues to $16.4 billion.[28] In Japan,

56 million are logging on to the Internet, and 18 million Russians have Internet access.[29] The majority of young adults (age 16 to 24) in Europe prefer advertisement on the Web over any other media vehicle; these ads are more directly targeting their needs.[30]

In many developing countries that lack the level of technological infrastructure found in Canada, marketers are beginning to capitalize on opportunities to "leap-frog" existing technology. For example, cellular and wireless phone technology is reaching many countries at a more affordable rate than traditional hard-wired telephone systems. Consequently opportunities for growth in the cell phone market remain strong in Southeast Asia, Africa, and the Middle East. In war-torn Iraq, many firms are fiercely competing for opportunities to rebuild the nation's telecommunications infrastructure, and MCI and Motorola have already won contracts to develop cell phone networks there.[31] Hewlett-Packard also hopes to bring new technologies to less developed countries. The company has launched World e-Inclusion, an economic development initiative that seeks to apply technology-based solutions to empower people in developing countries. Pilot programs for the initiative have already yielded high-speed Internet connections for remote villages in Central America and specialized software for coffee growers in Sumatra.[32]

Global Ethical and Social Responsibility Issues

dumping The practice of charging high prices for products sold in domestic markets while selling the same products in foreign markets at low prices, often below the costs of exporting them

When businesspeople travel, they sometimes perceive that other business cultures have different modes of operation. This uneasiness is especially pronounced for businesspeople who have not travelled extensively or interacted much with foreigners in business or social settings. For example, a perception exists among many in Canada that Canadian firms are often different from those in other countries. This implied perspective of "us" versus "them" is also common in other countries. Table 7.4 indicates the countries that businesspeople, risk analysts, and the general public perceived as the most and least corrupt. In business, the idea that "we" differ from "them" is called the self-reference criterion (SRC).

The SRC is the unconscious reference to one's own cultural values, experiences, and knowledge. When confronted with a situation, we react on the basis of knowledge we have accumulated over a lifetime, which is usually grounded in our culture of origin (and often rooted in our religious beliefs). Our reactions are based on meanings, values, and symbols that relate to our culture but may not have the same relevance to people of other cultures. In Canada, for example, **dumping**— the practice of charging high prices for products sold in domestic markets while selling the same products in foreign markets at low prices, often below the costs of exporting them—is viewed negatively, and Canada has anti-dumping legislation.

However, many businesspeople adopt the principle of "When in Rome, do as the Romans do." These businesspeople adapt to the cultural practices of the country they are in and use the host country's cultural practices as the rationalization for sometimes straying from their own ethical values when doing business

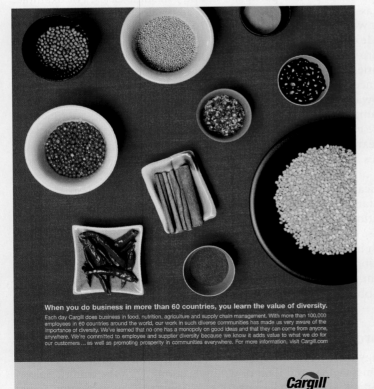

Global Diversity

Diversity is a value that can lead to increased competitiveness around the world.

table 7.4	PERCEPTIONS OF THE LEAST AND MOST CORRUPT COUNTRIES

Least Corrupt	Most Corrupt
1. Iceland (9.7)	1. Bangladesh (1.7), Chad
2. Finland (9.6), New Zealand	2. Haiti (1.8), Myanmar, Turkmenistan
3. Denmark (9.5)	3. Cote d'Ivoire (1.9), Equatorial Guinea, Nigeria
4. Singapore (9.4)	4. Angola (2.0)
5. Sweden (9.2)	5. Congo, Democratic Republic (2.1), Kenya, Pakistan, Paraguay, Somalia, Sudan, Tajikistan
6. Switzerland (9.1)	6. Azerbaijan (2.2), Cameroon, Ethiopia, Indonesia, Iraq, Liberia, Uzbekistan
7. Norway (8.9)	7. Burundi (2.3), Cambodia, Congo, Republic of, Georgia, Kyrgyzstan, Papua New Guinea, Venezuela
8. Australia (8.8)	8. Albania (2.4), Niger, Russia, Sierra Leon
9. Austria (8.7)	9. Afghanistan (2.5), Bolivia, Ecuador, Guatemala, Guyana, Libya, Nepal, Philippines, Uganda
10. United Kingdom (8.6), Netherlands	10. Belarus (2.6), Eritrea, Honduras, Kazakhstan, Nicaragua, Palestine, Ukraine, Vietnam, Zambia, Zimbabwe
11. Luxembourg (8.5)	11. Gambia (2.7), Macedonia, Swaziland, Yemen
12. Canada (8.4)	12. Algeria (2.8), Argentina, Madagascar, Malawi, Mozambique, Serbia & Montenegro
13. Hong Kong (8.3)	13. Armenia (2.9) Benin, Bosnia and Herzegovina, Gabon, India, Mali, Moldova, Tanzania
14. Germany (8.2)	14. Dominican Republic (3.0), Mongolia, Romania
15. United States (7.6)	15. Lebanon (3.1), Rwanda

Corruption Scale: 10 = Least Corrupt, 1 = Most Corrupt.

Source: "Transparency International Corruption Perceptions Index 2005," Transparency International, http://www.transparency.org/cpi/2005/dnld/media_pack_en.pdf (accessed Apr. 13, 2006). The results presented in this paper rely on data from the TI Corruption Perceptions Index 2005 provided by Transparency International. Reprinted by permission of Transparency International.

cultural relativism
The concept that morality varies from one culture to another and that business practices are therefore differentially defined as right or wrong by particular cultures

internationally. For example, by defending the payment of bribes or "greasing the wheels of business" and other questionable practices in this fashion, some business-people are resorting to **cultural relativism**—the concept that morality varies from one culture to another and that business practices are therefore differentially defined as right or wrong by particular cultures.

For example, Exxon Mobil Corporation and Royal Dutch/Shell Group have invested heavily in developing the oil reserves of Sakhalin Island, a Russian territory north of Japan. The companies have invested $22 billion in oil and gas drilling equipment not only because there may as much as 13 billion barrels of oil in its waters but also because Russia's environmental rules are almost non-existent and seldom enforced. However, the seismic blasting and toxic mud associated with developing the area's oil fields are hazardous to the endangered Western Pacific grey whale. If a spill or other accident were to occur, the nearest cleanup equipment is 50 miles away, making it impractical to save salmon and other animal species from harm.[33] Although the Russian government and people who live in the area are happy about the jobs created, in this case the multinational investment group seems to be applying Russian cultural values toward the natural environment rather than the more stringent ones of their own countries.

This example illustrates why multinational corporations (MNCs) have been the subject of much ethical criticism, and their impact on the countries in which they do business has been hotly debated. Their size and financial clout enable MNCs to control money supplies, employment, and even the economic well-being of less-developed countries.

At the same time, a large number of MNCs also strive to be good global citizens with strong ethical values. Texas Instruments (TI), for example, has adopted a three-level global approach to ethical integrity that asks: (1) "Are we complying with all legal requirements on a local level?" (2) "Are there business practices or requirements at the local level which impact how we interact with co-workers in other parts of the world?" and (3) "Do some of our practices need to be adapted based on the local laws and customers of a specific locale? On what basis do we define our universal standards that apply to TI employees everywhere?" TI generally follows conservative rules regarding the giving and receiving of gifts. TI specifies that gift-giving should not be used in a way that exerts undue pressure to win business or implies a quid pro quo.[34]

TI and many other firms, including Coca-Cola, Du Pont, Hewlett-Packard, Levi Strauss & Company, Texaco, and Wal-Mart, endorse following responsible business practices internationally. These companies support a globally based resource system called Business for Social Responsibility (BSR.) BSR tracks emerging issues and trends, provides information on corporate leadership and best practices, conducts educational workshops and training, and assists organizations in developing practical business ethics tools. It addresses such issues as community investment, corporate social responsibility, the environment, governance, and accountability. BSR has also established formal partnerships with other organizations that focus on corporate responsibility in Brazil, Israel, the United Kingdom, Chile, and Panama.[35]

Regional Trade Alliances, Markets, and Agreements

Although many more firms are beginning to view the world as one huge marketplace, various regional trade alliances and specific markets affect companies engaging in international marketing; some create opportunities, and others impose constraints. In fact, while trade agreements in various forms have been around for centuries, the last century can be classified as the trade agreement period in the world's international development. Today, there are about 180 trade agreements around the world compared with only a select handful in the early 1960s. In this section, we examine several of the more critical regional trade alliances, markets, and changing conditions affecting markets. These include the North American Free Trade Agreement, the European Union, the Common Market of the Southern Cone, Asia-Pacific Economic Cooperation, and the World Trade Organization.

The North American Free Trade Agreement (NAFTA)

North American Free Trade Agreement (NAFTA)
An alliance that merges Canada, Mexico, and the United States into a single market

The **North American Free Trade Agreement (NAFTA),** implemented in 1994, effectively merged Canada, Mexico, and the United States into one market of more than 430 million consumers.[36] NAFTA will eliminate virtually all tariffs on goods produced and traded among Canada, Mexico, and the United States to create a free trade area by 2009. The estimated annual output for this trade alliance is more than $11 trillion.[37]

NAFTA makes it easier for Canadian businesses to invest in Mexico and the United States; provides protection for intellectual property (of special interest to high-technology and entertainment industries); expands trade by requiring equal treatment of Canadian firms in both countries; and simplifies country-of-origin rules, hindering Japan's use of Mexico as a staging ground for further penetration

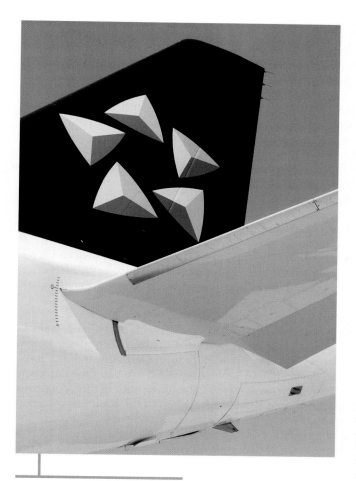

Worldwide Alliances

Star Alliance, the airline network for Earth™, with its member airlines, provides flexibility, services, and an array of reward benefits for frequent international travellers.

into North American markets. Although most tariffs on products coming to Canada will be lifted, duties on more sensitive products, such as household glassware, footwear, and some fruits and vegetables, will be phased out over a 15-year period.

Canada's 32.5 million consumers are relatively affluent, with a per capita GDP of $29 800.[38] Trade between the United States and Canada totals approximately $411 billion.[39] Currently exports to Canada support approximately 1.5 million U.S. jobs. Canadian investments in U.S. companies are also increasing, and various markets, including air travel, are opening as regulatory barriers dissolve.[40]

With a per capita GDP of $9000, Mexico's 105 million consumers are less affluent than Canadian consumers. However, Mexico has become the United States' second-largest trading market, after Canada.[41] Many U.S. companies, including Hewlett-Packard, IBM, and General Motors, have taken advantage of Mexico's low labour costs and close proximity to the United States to set up production facilities, sometimes called *maquiladoras*. Production at the *maquiladoras*, especially in the automotive, electronics, and apparel industries, has increased significantly as companies as diverse as Ford, John Deere, Motorola, Sara Lee, Kimberly-Clark, and VF Corporation set up facilities in north-central Mexican states. With the *maquiladoras* accounting for roughly half of Mexico's exports, Mexico has risen to become the world's twelfth-largest economy.[42] Although Mexico experienced financial instability throughout the 1990s, privatization of some government-owned firms and other measures instituted by the Mexican government and businesses have helped Mexico's economy.

Moreover, increasing trade between Canada and the United States constitutes a strong base of support for the ultimate success of NAFTA.

Mexico's membership in NAFTA links the United States and Canada with other Latin American countries, providing additional opportunities to integrate trade among all the nations in the Western Hemisphere. Indeed, efforts to create a free trade agreement among the 34 nations of North and South America are in process among the countries in the region (www.ftaa-alca.org). Like NAFTA, the Free Trade Area of the Americas (FTAA) will progressively eliminate trade barriers and create the world's largest free trade zone, with 800 million people.[43]

Despite its benefits, NAFTA has been controversial, and disputes continue to arise over its implementation. Archer Daniels Midland, for example, filed a claim against the Mexican government for losses resulting from a tax on soft drinks containing high-fructose corn syrup, which the company believes violates the provisions of NAFTA.[44] While many Americans feared the agreement would erase jobs in the United States, Mexicans have been disappointed that it failed to create more jobs. Moreover, Mexico's rising standard of living has increased the cost of doing business there; some 850 *maquiladoras* have closed their doors and transferred work to China and other nations where labour costs are lower.

Although NAFTA has been controversial, it has become a positive factor for Canadian firms wishing to engage in international marketing. Because licensing requirements have been relaxed under the pact, smaller businesses that previously could not afford to invest in Mexico and the United States will be able to do business in those markets without having to locate there. NAFTA's long phase-in period provides ample time for adjustment for those firms affected by reduced tariffs on imports. Furthermore, increased competition should lead to a more efficient market, and the long-term prospects of including most Western Hemisphere countries in the alliance promise additional opportunities for Canadian marketers.

The European Union (EU)

European Union (EU)
An alliance that promotes trade among its member countries in Europe

The **European Union (EU)**, sometimes also referred to as the *European Community* or *Common Market,* was established in 1958 to promote trade among its members, which initially included Belgium, France, Italy, West Germany, Luxembourg, and the Netherlands. In 1991 East and West Germany united, and by 1995 the United Kingdom, Spain, Denmark, Greece, Portugal, Ireland, Austria, Finland, and Sweden had joined as well. (Cyprus, Poland, Hungary, the Czech Republic, Slovenia, Estonia, Latvia, Lithuania, Slovakia, and Malta joined in 2004; Romania, Bulgaria, and Turkey have requested membership as well.[45])

Until 1993 each nation functioned as a separate market, but at that time the members officially unified into one of the largest single world markets, which today includes more than 450 million consumers in 25 countries. The EU is a relatively diverse set of democratic European countries. It is not a state that is intended to replace existing country states, nor is it an organization for international cooperation. Instead, its member states have common institutions to which they delegate some of their sovereignty to allow specific matters of joint interest to be decided at the European level. The primary goals of the EU are to establish European citizenship; ensure freedom, security, and justice; promote economic and social progress; and assert Europe's role in world trade.[46]

To facilitate free trade among members, the EU is working toward standardizing business regulations and requirements, import duties, and value-added taxes; eliminating customs checks; and creating a standardized currency for use by all members. Many European nations (Austria, Belgium, Finland, France, Germany, Ireland, Italy, Luxembourg, the Netherlands, Portugal, and Spain) are linked to a common currency, the *euro;* however, several EU members have rejected use of the euro in their countries (e.g., Denmark, Sweden, and the United Kingdom). Although the common currency requires many marketers to modify their pricing strategies and subjects them to increased competition, the use of a single currency frees companies that sell goods among European countries from the nuisance of dealing with complex exchange rates.[47] The long-term goals are to eliminate all trade barriers within the EU, improve the economic efficiency of the EU nations, and stimulate economic growth, thus making the union's economy more competitive in global markets, particularly against Japan and other Pacific Rim nations, and North America.

As the EU nations attempt to function as one large market, consumers in the EU may become more homogeneous in their needs and wants. Marketers should be aware, however, that cultural differences among the nations may require modifications in the marketing mix for customers in each nation. Differences in tastes and preferences in these diverse markets are significant for international marketers. But there is evidence that such differences may be diminishing, especially within the younger population that includes teenagers and young professionals. Gathering information about these distinct tastes and preferences is likely to remain a very important factor in developing marketing mixes that satisfy the needs of European customers.

The Common Market of the Southern Cone (MERCOSUR)

Common Market of the Southern Cone (MERCOSUR)
An alliance that promotes the free circulation of goods, services, and production factors, and has a common external tariff and commercial policy among member nations in South America

The **Common Market of the Southern Cone (MERCOSUR)** was established in 1991 under the Treaty of Asunción to unite Argentina, Brazil, Paraguay, and Uruguay as a free trade alliance. Venezuela became a new member in December 2005, and Bolivia is in the process of being invited to become a full member. Currently, Bolivia, Chile, Colombia, Ecuador, and Peru have associate member status. The alliance represents two-thirds of South America's population and has a combined GDP of more than $800 billion, making it the third-largest trading bloc behind NAFTA and the EU. Like NAFTA, MERCOSUR promotes "the free circulation of goods, services and production factors among the countries" and establishes a common external tariff and commercial policy.[48]

Asia-Pacific Economic Cooperation (APEC)

Asia-Pacific Economic Cooperation (APEC)
An alliance that promotes open trade and economic and technical cooperation among member nations throughout the world

The **Asia-Pacific Economic Cooperation (APEC)**, established in 1989, promotes open trade and economic and technical cooperation among member nations, which initially included Australia, Brunei Darussalam, Canada, Indonesia, Japan, Korea, Malaysia, New Zealand, the Philippines, Singapore, Thailand, and the United States. Since then the alliance has grown to include China, Hong Kong, Chinese Taipei, Mexico, Papua New Guinea, Chile, Peru, Russia, and Vietnam. The 21-member alliance represents 2.5 billion consumers, has a combined GDP of $19 trillion, and accounts for nearly 47 percent of global trade. APEC differs from other international trade alliances in its commitment to facilitating business and its practice of allowing the business/private sector to participate in a wide range of APEC activities.[49]

Despite economic turmoil and a recession in Asia in recent years, companies of the APEC have become increasingly competitive and sophisticated in global business in the last two decades. Moreover, the markets of the APEC offer tremendous opportunities to marketers who understand them. In fact, the APEC region has consistently been the most economically dynamic part of the world. In its first decade, the APEC countries generated almost 70 percent of worldwide economic growth and the APEC region consistently outperformed the rest of the world.[50]

Japanese firms in particular have made tremendous inroads on world markets for automobiles, motorcycles, watches, cameras, and audio-video equipment. Products from Sony, Sanyo, Toyota, Mitsubishi, Canon, Suzuki, and Toshiba are sold all over the world and have set standards of quality by which other products are often judged. Sony is often viewed as the benchmark of the global company. Despite the high volume of trade between the United States and Japan, the two economies are less integrated than the Canadian economy is with the U.S. If Japan imported goods at the same rate as other major nations, Canada and the United States would sell billions of dollars more each year to Japan.

The People's Republic of China, a country of 1.3 billion people, has launched a program of economic reform to stimulate its economy by privatizing many industries, restructuring its banking system, and increasing public spending on infrastructure (including railways and telecommunications.)[51] As a result, China has become a manufacturing powerhouse, with an economy growing at a rate of seven percent a year.[52] Many foreign companies, including General Motors, Volkswagen, and Toyota, are opening factories in China to take advantage of its low labour costs.[53] Nike and Adidas have shifted most of their shoe production to China, and recently China has become a major producer of CD players, cell phones, portable stereos, and personal computers. The potential of China's consumer market is so vast that it is almost impossible to measure, but doing business in China also entails many risks. Political and economic instability, especially inflation, corruption, and erratic policy shifts, have undercut marketers' efforts to stake a claim in what could become the world's largest market. Moreover, piracy is a major issue, and protecting a brand name in China is difficult. Because copying is a tradition in China and laws protecting copyrights and intellectual property are weak and minimally enforced, the country is flooded with counterfeit videos, movies, CDs, computer software, furniture, and clothing.

General Agreement on Tariffs and Trade (GATT) An agreement among nations to reduce worldwide tariffs and increase international trade

World Trade Organization (WTO) An entity that promotes free trade among member nations by eliminating trade barriers and educating individuals, companies, and governments about trade rules around the world

World Trade Organization (WTO)

Like NAFTA and the EU, the **General Agreement on Tariffs and Trade (GATT)** was based on negotiations among member countries to reduce worldwide tariffs and increase international trade in the wake of World War II. Originally signed by 23 nations in 1947, GATT was the precursor to the **World Trade Organization (WTO)** trading system that provides a forum for tariff negotiations, reduces trade restrictions, promotes discussion and resolution

marketing ENTREPRENEURS

Frank Hickingbotham

THE BUSINESS: TCBY Enterprises, Inc.

FOUNDED: 1981

During a shopping trip, Georgia Hickingbotham encouraged her husband Frank to try the Peach-flavoured frozen yogurt she bought while taking a break from shopping. Frank, not a yogurt fan, reluctantly did. "This can't be yogurt," he said, and, thus, the TCBY brand was born out of the initials of that outburst (although later the initials came to stand for "The Country's Best Yogurt.") The unique taste that melted "Mr. H.'s" dislike of yogurt was developed by Daniel Brackeen, a dairy genius from Dallas. The Hickingbothams arranged to purchase and distribute his product. And with that Frank—founder, chairman of the board, and CEO of TCBY Enterprises, Inc.—started the company with a first-day sale on September 23, 1981, of $153.69. There are now about 3000 TCBY locations in operation worldwide, and the TCBY brand is franchised in over 60 countries. In 2000, TCBY was acquired by Capricorn Investors for about $140 million (the startup cost in 1981 was about $150 000.)

of international trade problems, and provides rules to prevent dumping (i.e., the selling of products at unfairly low prices). As one of the youngest international organizations, the WTO came into being in 1995 as a result of the Uruguay Round (1988–1994) of negotiations. Broadly, WTO is the main worldwide organization that deals with the rules of trade between nations; its main function is to ensure that trade flows as smoothly, predictably, and freely as possible between nations. In 2006, 149 nations were members of the WTO.[54]

Fulfilling the purpose of the WTO requires eliminating trade barriers; educating individuals, companies, and governments about trade rules around the world; and assuring global markets that no sudden changes of policy will occur. At the heart of the WTO are agreements that provide legal ground rules for international commerce and trade policy. Based in Geneva, Switzerland, the WTO also serves as a forum for dispute resolution.[55] For example, the WTO made rulings in the United States–Canada softwood lumber dispute, which is one of the most significant and enduring trade disputes to impact Canadian business.

International Entry Modes

Marketers enter international markets and continue to engage in marketing activities at several levels of international involvement. Traditionally, firms have adopted one of four different modes of entering an international market; each successive "stage" represents different degrees of international involvement (i.e., the "Uppsala Model"):[56]

Stage 1: No regular export activities

Stage 2: Export via independent representatives (agents)

Stage 3: Establishment of one or more sales subsidiaries internationally

Stage 4: Establishment of international production/manufacturing facilities

Business Across Borders

The Orchard Network guides firms in their cross-border activities to reduce risk and increase the firm's potential.

As Figure 7.1 shows, today a firm's international involvement covers a wide spectrum from purely domestic marketing to global marketing. Domestic marketing involves marketing strategies aimed at markets within the home country; at the other extreme, global marketing entails developing marketing strategies for the entire world (or at least more than one major region of the world). Many firms with an international presence start out as small companies serving local and regional domestic markets and expand to national markets before considering opportunities in foreign markets (the born global firm, described earlier, is one exception to this internationalization process). Limited exporting may occur even if a firm makes little or no effort to obtain foreign sales. Foreign buyers may seek out the company and/or its products, or a distributor may discover the firm's products and export them. The level of commitment to international marketing is a major variable in global marketing strategies. In this section, we examine importing and exporting, trading companies, licensing and franchising, contract manufacturing, joint

business across borders

Overseas markets present enormous opportunities for expanding businesses, but setting out on an unfamiliar road can be hazardous for a Company of any size.

The Orchard Network is focussed on reducing the risk and increasing your potential. We will guide your Company along the right path.

Orchard Network

Our independent network brings together the most experienced and knowledgeable specialists in each country, ready to help you through the maze.

Visit our website www.orchardnetwork.com or send us an email to info@orchardnetwork.com and we will get things moving.

figure 7.1

LEVELS OF INVOLVEMENT IN GLOBAL MARKETING

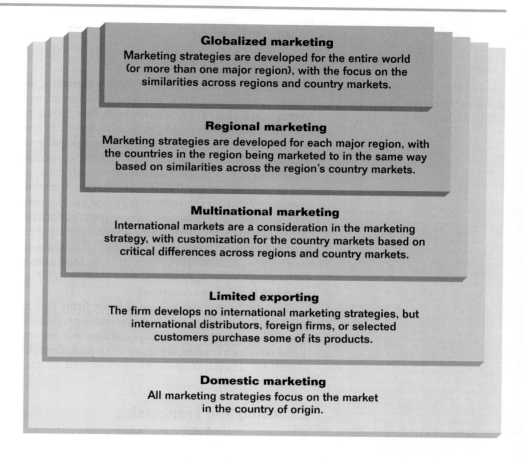

Globalized marketing
Marketing strategies are developed for the entire world (or more than one major region), with the focus on the similarities across regions and country markets.

Regional marketing
Marketing strategies are developed for each major region, with the countries in the region being marketed to in the same way based on similarities across the region's country markets.

Multinational marketing
International markets are a consideration in the marketing strategy, with customization for the country markets based on critical differences across regions and country markets.

Limited exporting
The firm develops no international marketing strategies, but international distributors, foreign firms, or selected customers purchase some of its products.

Domestic marketing
All marketing strategies focus on the market in the country of origin.

ventures, direct ownership, and some of the other approaches to international involvement.

Importing and Exporting

Importing and exporting require the least amount of effort and commitment of resources. **Importing** is the purchase of products from a foreign source. **Exporting,** the sale of products to foreign markets, enables firms of all sizes to participate in global business. A firm may find an exporting intermediary to take over most marketing functions associated with marketing to other countries. This approach entails minimal effort and cost. Modifications in packaging, labelling, style, or colour may be the major expenses in adapting a product for the foreign market.

Export agents bring together buyers and sellers from different countries and collect a commission for arranging sales. Export houses and export merchants purchase products from different companies and then sell them abroad. They are specialists at understanding customers' needs in global markets. Using exporting intermediaries involves limited risk because no foreign direct investment (FDI) is required.

Buyers from foreign companies and governments provide a direct method of exporting and eliminate the need for an intermediary. These buyers encourage international exchange by contacting overseas firms about their needs and the opportunities available in exporting to them. Indeed, research suggests that many small firms tend to rely heavily on such native contacts, especially in developed markets, and remain production oriented rather than marketing oriented in their approach to international marketing.[57] Domestic firms that want to export with minimal effort and investment

importing The purchase of products from a foreign source

exporting The sale of products to foreign markets

should seek out export intermediaries. Once a company becomes involved in exporting, it usually develops more knowledge of the country and becomes more confident in its competitiveness.[58] As discussed earlier in this chapter, the Canadian government offers a wealth of trade and exporting services at www.exportsource.ca, Team Canada Inc.'s website.

Trading Companies

trading company A company that links buyers and sellers in different countries

Marketers sometimes employ a **trading company,** which links buyers and sellers in different countries but is not involved in manufacturing and does not own assets related to manufacturing. Trading companies buy products in one country at the lowest price consistent with quality and sell them to buyers in another country. For instance, SCiNet (www.scinet-corp.com) offers a 24-hour-per-day online world trade system that connects 17 million companies in 245 countries, offering more than 50 million products and services. The SCiNet system offers online payments and handles customs, tariffs, and inspections of goods for their clients. A trading company acts like a wholesaler, taking on much of the responsibility of finding markets while facilitating all marketing aspects of a transaction. An important function of trading companies is taking title to products and performing all the activities necessary to move the products to the targeted foreign country. For example, large grain-trading companies control a major portion of the world's trade in basic food commodities. These trading companies sell homogeneous agricultural commodities that can be stored and moved rapidly in response to market conditions.

Trading companies reduce risk for firms seeking to get involved in international marketing. A trading company provides producers with information about products that meet quality and price expectations in domestic and international markets. Additional services a trading company may provide include consulting, marketing research, advertising, insurance, product research and design, legal assistance, warehousing, and foreign exchange.

Licensing and Franchising

licensing An alternative to direct investment requiring a licensee to pay commissions or royalties on sales or supplies used in manufacturing

When potential markets are found across national boundaries, and when production, technical assistance, or marketing know-how is required, **licensing** is an alternative to direct investment. The licensee (the owner of the foreign operation) pays commissions or royalties on sales or supplies used in manufacturing. The licensee may also pay an initial down payment or fee when the licensing agreement is signed. Exchanges of management techniques or technical assistance are primary reasons for licensing agreements. Yoplait, for example, is a French yogurt that is licensed for production in the Canada; the Yoplait brand tries to maintain a French image. Similarly, sports organizations such as the International Olympic Committee (IOC), which is responsible for the Olympic Games, typically concentrate on organizing their sporting events while licensing the merchandise and other products that are sold.

Licensing is an attractive alternative when resources are unavailable for direct investment or when the core competencies of the firm or organization are not related to the product being sold (such as in the case of Olympics merchandise). Licensing can also be a viable alternative when the political stability of a foreign country is in doubt. In addition, licensing is especially advantageous for small manufacturers wanting to launch a well-known brand internationally. For example, Questor Corporation owns the Spalding name but produces not a single golf club or tennis ball itself; all Spalding sporting products are licensed worldwide.

franchising A form of licensing in which a franchiser, in exchange for a financial commitment, grants a franchisee the right to market its product in accordance with the franchiser's standards

Franchising is a form of licensing in which a company (the franchiser) grants a franchisee the right to market its product, using its name, logo, methods of operation, advertising, products, and other elements associated with the franchiser's business, in return for a financial commitment and an agreement to conduct business in accordance with the franchiser's standard of operations. This arrangement allows franchisers to minimize the risks of international marketing in four ways: (1) the franchiser does not have to put up a large capital investment; (2) the franchiser's revenue stream is fairly consistent because franchisees pay a fixed fee and royalties; (3) the franchiser retains control of its name and increases global penetration of its product; and (4) franchise agreements ensure a certain standard of behaviour from franchisees, which protects the franchise name.[59] Subway, Pizza Hut, and KFC are "top ten" franchisers in the world; other well-known franchisers with international visibility include Holiday Inn, Marriott, McDonald's, and Wendy's. Tim Horton's is well known to Canadians as a Canadian franchising success story. Franchising is the mode of growth for the Tim Horton's brand as it attempts to duplicate its Canadian success in the U.S. market. There are now more than 295 Tim Horton's locations in the United States.[60]

Contract Manufacturing

contract manufacturing The practice of hiring a foreign firm to produce a designated volume of the domestic firm's product or a component of it to specification; the final product carries the domestic firm's name

Contract manufacturing occurs when a company hires a foreign firm to produce a designated volume of the firm's product (or a component of a product) to specification and the final product carries the domestic firm's name. The Gap, for example, relies on contract manufacturing for some of its apparel; Reebok uses Korean contract manufacturers to produce many of its athletic shoes. Marketing may be handled by the contract manufacturer or by the contracting company.

Three specific forms of contract manufacturing have become popular in the last decade: outsourcing, offshoring, and offshore outsourcing. **Outsourcing** is defined as the contracting of non-core operations or jobs from internal production within a business to an external entity that specializes in that operation. For example, outsourcing certain elements of a firm's operations to China and Mexico has become popular. The majority of all footwear is now produced in China regardless of the brand on the shoe you wear. **Offshoring** is defined as moving a business process that was done domestically at the local factory to a foreign country, regardless of whether the production accomplished in the foreign country is performed by the local company (e.g., in a wholly owned subsidiary) or a third party (e.g., subcontractor). Typically, the production is moved to reap the advantages of lower cost of operations in the foreign location. **Offshore outsourcing** is the practice of contracting with an organization to perform some or all business functions in a country other than the country in which the product or service will be sold.

outsourcing The practice of contracting non-core operations with an organization that specializes in those operation

offshoring The practice of moving a business process that was done domestically at the local factory to a foreign country, regardless of whether the production accomplished in the foreign country is performed by the local company (e.g. in a wholly owned subsidiary) or a third party (e.g. subcontractor)

offshore outsourcing The practice of contracting with an organization to perform some or all business functions in a country other than the country in which the product or service will be sold

Joint Ventures

joint venture A partnership between a domestic firm and a foreign firm or government

In international marketing, a **joint venture** is a partnership between a domestic firm and a foreign firm or government. Joint ventures are especially popular in industries that require large investments, such as natural resources extraction or automobile manufacturing. Control of the joint venture may be split equally, or one party may control decision making. Joint ventures are often a political necessity because of nationalism and government restrictions on foreign ownership. They may occur when acquisition or internal development is not feasible or when the risks and constraints leave no other alternative. They also provide legitimacy in the eyes of the host country's citizens. Local partners have firsthand knowledge of the economic and sociopolitical environment and the workings of available distribution networks, and they may have privileged access to local resources (raw materials, labour management, and so on). However, joint venture relationships require trust throughout the relationship to provide a foreign partner with a ready means of implementing its own marketing strategy.[61] Joint ventures are assuming greater global importance because of cost advantages and the number of inexperienced firms entering foreign markets. They may be the result of a tradeoff between a firm's desire for completely unambiguous control of an enterprise and its quest for additional resources.

strategic alliances A partnership formed to create a competitive advantage on a worldwide basis

Strategic alliances are partnerships formed to create competitive advantage on a worldwide basis. They are very similar to joint ventures, but while joint ventures are defined in scope, strategic alliances are typically represented by an agreement to work together (which can ultimately mean more involvement than a joint venture). In an international strategic alliance, the firms in the alliance may have been traditional rivals competing for the same market. They may also be competing in certain markets while working together in other markets where it is beneficial for both parties.

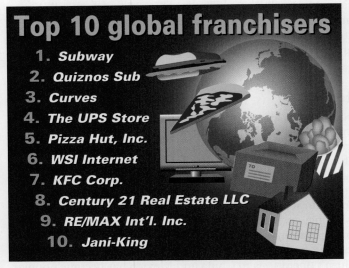

Source: "Top 10 Global Franchises for 2006," *Entrepreneur*, www.entrepreneur.com/franzone/rank/ 0,6584, 12-12-IN-2006-0,00 .html (accessed Apr. 13, 2006).

An example of such an alliance is New United Motor Manufacturing, Inc. (NUMMI), formed by Toyota and General Motors to make automobiles for both firms. This alliance united the quality engineering of Japanese cars with the marketing expertise and market access of General Motors. Today NUMMI manufactures the popular Toyota Tacoma compact pickup truck, as well as the Toyota Corolla, Pontiac Vibe, and a right-hand-drive Toyota Voltz for sale in Japan.[62] While joint ventures are formed to create a new identity, partners in international strategic alliances often retain their distinct identities, with each partner bringing a core competency to the union.

The success rate of international alliances could be higher if a better fit between the companies existed. A strategic alliance should focus on a joint market opportunity from which all partners can benefit.[63] In the automobile, computer, and airline industries, strategic alliances are becoming the predominant means of competing internationally. Competition in these industries is so fierce and the costs of competing on a global basis are so high that few firms have all the resources needed to do it alone. Firms that lack the internal resources essential for international success may seek to collaborate with other companies. A shared mode of leadership among partner corporations combines joint abilities and allows collaboration from a distance. Focusing on customer value and implementing innovative ways to compete create a winning strategy.[64] One such collaboration is the Sky Team Alliance—involving Northwest Airlines, KLM, Aero Mexico, Air France, Alitalia, Continental Airlines, TSA Czech Airlines, Delta, and Korean Air—which is designed to improve customer service among the nine firms.

Direct Ownership

Once a company makes a long-term commitment to marketing in a foreign country that has a promising market as well as a suitable political and economic environment, **direct ownership** of a foreign subsidiary or division is a possibility. Most foreign investment covers only manufacturing equipment or personnel because the expenses of developing a separate foreign distribution system can be tremendous. The opening of retail stores in Europe, Mexico, or the United States can require a staggering financial investment in facilities, research, and management.

The term **multinational enterprise,** sometimes called multinational corporation (MNC), refers to a firm that has operations or subsidiaries in many countries. Often the parent company is based in one country and carries on production, management, and marketing activities in other countries. The firm's subsidiaries may be autonomous so they can respond to the needs of individual international markets or they may be part of a global network that is led by the headquarters' operations.

At the same time, a wholly owned foreign subsidiary may be allowed to operate independently of the parent company to give its management more freedom to adjust to the local environment. Cooperative arrangements are developed to assist in marketing efforts, production, and management. A wholly owned foreign subsidiary may export products to the home country, its market may serve as a test market for the firm's global products, or it may be a component of the firm's globalization efforts. Some automobile manufacturers, for example, import cars built by their foreign subsidiaries. A foreign subsidiary offers important tax, tariff, and other operating advantages. Table 7.5 lists the ten largest global corporations.

One of the greatest advantages is the cross-cultural approach. A subsidiary usually operates under foreign management so that it can develop a local identity. In partic-

direct ownership A situation in which a company owns subsidiaries or other facilities overseas

multinational enterprise A firm that has operations or subsidiaries in many countries

table 7.5	THE 10 LARGEST GLOBAL CORPORATIONS			
Rank	Company	Country	Industry	Revenues (in millions)
1	Wal-Mart Stores	U.S.	General merchandiser	$287 989.0
2	BP	Britain	Petroleum refining	$285 059.0
3	Exxon Mobil	U.S.	Petroleum refining	$270 772.0
4	Royal Dutch/Shell Group	Netherlands/Britain	Petroleum refining	$268 690.0
5	General Motors	U.S.	Motor vehicles	$193 517.0
6	DaimlerChrysler	Germany	Motor vehicles	$176 687.5
7	Toyota Motor	Japan	Motor vehicles	$172 616.3
8	Ford Motor	U.S.	Motor vehicles	$172 233.0
9	General Electric	U.S.	Diversified financials	$152 866.0
10	Total	France	Petroleum refining	$152 609.5

Source: "Global 500: The World's Largest Corporations," *Fortune,* July 25, 2005. © 2005 Time Inc. Reprinted by permission. All rights reserved.

ular, the firm (i.e., seller) is often expected to adapt, if needed, to the buyer's culture. Interestingly, the cultural values of customers in the younger age group (30 years and younger) is becoming increasingly similar around the world. Today, a 20-year-old in Russia is increasingly similar in mindset to a 20-year-old in China and a 20-year-old in Canada. This makes marketing products and services to the younger population easier today than only 10 years ago. Nevertheless, there is still great danger involved in having a wholly owned subsidiary in some parts of the world due to political uncertainty, terrorism threats, and economic instability.

Global Organizational Structures

organizational structure
The way in which a firm divides its operations into separate functions and/or value-adding units and coordinates its activities

Firms develop their international marketing strategies and manage their marketing mix (i.e., product, distribution, promotion, and price) by developing and maintaining an organizational form that best leverages their resources and core competencies. This **organizational structure** is defined as the way in which a firm divides its operations into separate functions and/or value-adding units and coordinates its activities. The modes of entry, described in the previous section, can be adopted by any firm doing business internationally. However, most firms undergo a step-by-step development in their internationalization efforts of the firm's people, processes, functions, culture, and structure.[65]

The pyramid in Figure 7.2 symbolizes how deeply rooted the international operations and values are in the firm, with the base of the pyramid—structure—being the most difficult to change (especially in the short term.) Three basic structures of international organizations exist: export departments, international divisions, and internationally integrated structures (e.g., product division structures, geographic area structures, and matrix structures). The existing structure of the firm, or the structure that the firm chooses to adopt, has implications for international marketing strategy.

Export Departments

For most firms, the early stages of international development is often ad hoc and not fully planned. During this early internationalization effort, sales opportunities in the

figure 7.2

ORGANIZATIONAL ARCHITECTURE

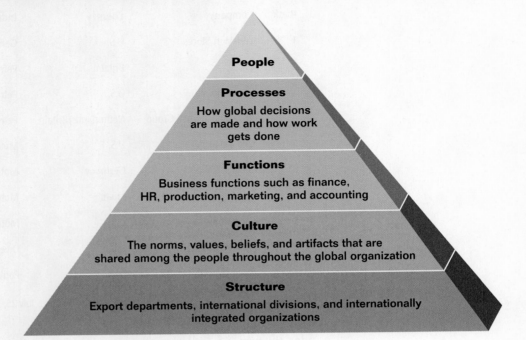

People

Processes
How global decisions are made and how work gets done

Functions
Business functions such as finance, HR, production, marketing, and accounting

Culture
The norms, values, beliefs, and artifacts that are shared among the people throughout the global organization

Structure
Export departments, international divisions, and internationally integrated organizations

global marketplace motivate the firm to engage internationally. For example, born global firms make exporting a primary objective from their inceptions. At the same time, for most firms engaging internationally for the first time, very minimal, if any, organizational adjustments take place to accommodate the international sales of the firm. Foreign sales—defined as sales outside the firm's home country—are typically so small that many firms cannot justify allocating structural or other resources to the internationalization effort in the infancy of internationalization.

Exporting, licensing, and using trading companies are preferred modes of international market entry for firms with an export department structure. Some firms develop the export department as a subunit of the marketing department while others organize it as a department that structurally coexists at an equal level with the other functional units. Clipsal, the Australian maker of more than 20 000 different lines of electrical accessories, has taken its number one position in Australia and achieved international success led by its high-quality products and operations of its export department. Clipsal's "Export Department offers global support in many areas and this has resulted in a level of teamwork that has significantly strengthened the Clipsal brand throughout the world."[66]

Another unique case of developing a successful export operation early after its inception is the born global firm of Logitech International. Logitech, founded in 1981, is a publicly traded Swiss company. Logitech designs personal peripherals that enable people to effectively work, play, and communicate in the digital world. Their products include webcams, mice, trackballs, keyboards, speakers, headsets, interactive gaming devices, digital pens, and advanced universal remote controls.

As demand for its products and services grows or commitments of the firm increase to internationalization efforts, the firm's structure develops. Many firms evolve from using their export department structure to forming an international division.

International Divisions

The international division of a firm centralizes all of the responsibility for international operations (and in many cases, all international activities also become centralized in the international division). The typical international division concentrates human resources (i.e., international expertise) into one unit and serves as the central point for all information flow related to international operations (e.g., international market opportunities, international research and development). At the same time, firms with an international division structure take advantage of economies of scale by keeping manufacturing and related functions within the domestic divisions. Firms with international divisions can be at a relatively early as well as a rather mature stage of their international development. As such, these firms use exporting, licensing and franchising, trading companies, contract manufacturing, and joint ventures as possible modes of international market entry.

This international division structure illustrates the critical importance of coordination and cooperation between domestic and international operations. Frequent interaction and strategic planning meetings are needed to make this structure work effectively. In particular, firms that use an international division structure are often organized domestically on the basis of functions or product divisions, while the international division operates based on geography. This means that coordination and strategic alignment across domestic divisions and the international division is critical to success. At the same time, lack of coordination between domestic and international operations is commonly the most significant flaw in the international division structure.

An example of a firm that has used the international division structure to achieve worldwide success is Abbott Laboratories, a $22 billion diversified health-care company that develops products and services that span prevention and diagnosis to treatment and cure. As international sales grew in the late 1960s, the firm added an international division to its structure. This international division structure has benefits and drawbacks for Abbott, as it does for other firms using it.

Some argue that to offset the natural "isolation" that may result between domestic and international operations in this structure, the international division structure should be used only when the firm (1) intends to market only a small assortment of products or services internationally and (2) when foreign sales account for only a small portion of total sales. When the product assortment increases or the percentage of foreign sales becomes significant, an internationally integrated structure should be adopted.

Internationally Integrated Structures

A number of different internationally integrated structures have been developed and implemented by firms in their quest to achieve success globally. The three most common structures are the product division structure, the geographic area structure, and the global matrix structure. Firms with these varied structures have multiple choices for international market entry similar to international divisions (e.g., exporting, licensing and franchising, trading companies, contract manufacturing, and joint ventures). However, firms with internationally integrated structures are the most likely to engage in direct ownership activities internationally.

The product division structure is the form used by the majority of multinational firms. This structure lends itself well to firms that are diversified, often driven by their current domestic operations. Each division is a self-contained entity with responsibility for its own operations, whether it is based on a country or regional basis. However, the worldwide headquarters maintains the overall responsibility for the strategic direction of the firm, while the product division is in charge of implementation. Procter & Gamble has a long-standing tradition of operating as a product division structure, with leading brands such as Pampers, Tide, Ariel, Always, Pantene, Bounty, Folgers, Pringles, Charmin, Downy, Crest, and Olay.

The geographic area structure lends itself well to firms with a low degree of diversification. Under this domestically influenced functional structure, the world is divided into logical geographical areas based on the firms' operations and the customers' characteristics. Accenture, a global management consulting firm, operates worldwide largely based on a geographic area structure. Each area tends to be relatively self-contained, and integration across areas is typically via the worldwide or the regional headquarters. This structure facilitates local responsiveness, but it is not ideal for reducing global costs and transferring core knowledge across the firm's geographic units. A key issue in geographic area structures, as in almost all multinational corporations, is the need to become more regionally and globally integrated.

The global matrix structure was designed to achieve both global integration and local responsiveness. Asea Brown Boveri (ABB), a Swedish-Swiss engineering multinational, is the best-known firm to implement a global matrix structure. ABB is an international leader in power and automation technologies that enable customers to improve their performance while lowering environmental impact. Global matrix structures theoretically facilitate a simultaneous focus on realizing local responsiveness, cost efficiencies, and knowledge transfers. However, few firms can operate a global matrix well since the structure is based on, for example, product and geographic divisions simultaneously (or a combination of any two traditional structures). This means that employees belong to two divisions and often report to two managers throughout the hierarchies of the firm. An effectively implemented global matrix structure has the benefit of being global in scope while also being nimble and responsive locally. However, a poorly implemented global matrix structure results in added bureaucracy and indecisiveness in leadership and implementation.

The International Marketing Mix: Customization versus Globalization

Like domestic marketers, international marketers develop marketing strategies to serve specific target markets. Traditionally international marketing strategies have customized marketing mixes according to cultural, regional, and national differences. Table 7.6 provides a sample of international issues related to product, distribution, promotion, and price. For example, many soap and detergent manufacturers adapt their products to local water conditions, equipment, and washing habits. Colgate-Palmolive even devised an inexpensive, plastic, hand-powered washing machine for use in households that have no electricity in less developed countries. Coca-Cola markets distinct versions of its soft drinks for the tastes of different regions of the world; it also contributes to local causes and customizes promotion to feature local people, humour, and sports teams in its advertising.[67] Realizing that both similarities and differences exist across countries is a critical first step to developing the appropriate marketing strategy effort targeted to particular international markets. Today, many firms strive to build their marketing strategies around similarities that exist instead of customizing around differences.

globalization The development of marketing strategies that treat the entire world (or its major regions) as a single entity

For many firms, **globalization** of marketing is the goal; it involves developing marketing strategies as though the entire world (or its major regions) were a single entity: a globalized firm markets standardized products in the same way everywhere.[68] Nike and Adidas shoes, for example, are standardized worldwide. Other examples of globalized products include electronic communications equipment, clothing brands, movies, soft drinks, rock and alternative music CDs, cosmetics, and toothpaste. Sony televisions, Levi jeans, and cigarette brands post year-to-year gains in the world market.

For many years, organizations have attempted to globalize their marketing mixes as much as possible by employing standardized products, promotion campaigns, prices, and distribution channels for all markets. The economic and competitive payoffs for globalized marketing strategies are certainly great. Brand name, product characteristics, packaging, and labelling are among the easiest marketing mix variables to standardize; media allocation, retail outlets, and price may be more difficult. In the end, the degree of similarity among the various environmental and market conditions determines the feasibility and degree of globalization. A successful globalization strategy often depends on the extent to which a firm is able to implement the idea of "think globally, act locally."[69] Even take-out food lends itself to globalization: McDonald's,

table 7.6	MARKETING MIX ISSUES INTERNATIONALLY

Sample International Issues

Product Element

Core Product	Is there a commonality of the customers' needs across countries? What will the product be used for and in what context?
Product Adoption	How is awareness created for the product in the various country markets? How and where is the product typically bought?
Managing Products	How are truly new products managed in the country markets vis-à-vis existing products or products that have been modified slightly?
Branding	Is the brand accepted widely around the world? Does the home country help or hurt the brand perception of the consumer?

Distribution Element

Marketing Channels	What is the role of the channel intermediaries internationally? Where is value created beyond the domestic borders of the firm?
Physical Distribution	Is the movement of products the most efficient from the home country to the foreign market or to a regional warehouse?
Retail Stores	What is the availability of different types of retail stores in the various country markets?
Retailing Strategy	Where do customers typically shop in the targeted countries—downtown, suburbs, or malls?

Promotion Element

Advertising	Some countries' customers prefer firm-specific advertising instead of product-specific advertising. How does this affect advertising?
Public Relations	How is public relations used to manage the stakeholders' interests internationally? Are the stakeholders' interests different worldwide?
Personal Selling	What product types require personal selling internationally? Does it differ from how those products are sold domestically?
Sales Promotion	Is coupon usage a widespread activity in the targeted international markets? What other forms of sales promotion should be used?

Pricing Element

Core Price	Is price a critical component of the value equation of the product in the targeted country markets?
Analysis of Demand	Is the demand curve similar internationally as it is domestically? Will a change in price drastically change demand?
Demand, Cost, and Profit Relationships	What are the fixed and variable costs when marketing the product internationally? Are they similar to the domestic setting?
Determination of Price	How does the pricing strategy, environmental forces, business practices, and cultural values affect price?

KFC, and Taco Bell restaurants satisfy hungry customers in every hemisphere, although menus may be altered slightly to satisfy local tastes.

International marketing demands some strategic planning if a firm is to incorporate foreign sales into its overall marketing strategy. International marketing activities often require customized marketing mixes to achieve the firm's goals. Globalization requires a total commitment to the world, regions, or multinational areas as an integral part of the firm's markets; world or regional markets become as important as domestic ones. Regardless of the extent to which a firm chooses to globalize its marketing strategy, extensive environmental analysis and marketing research are necessary to understand the needs and desires of the target market(s) and successfully implement the chosen marketing strategy. A global presence does not automatically result in a global competitive advantage. However, a global presence generates five opportunities for creating value: (1) to adapt to local market differences, (2) to exploit economies of global scale, (3) to exploit economies of global scope, (4) to mine optimal locations for activities and resources, and (5) to maximize the transfer of knowledge across locations.[70] To exploit these opportunities, marketers need to conduct marketing research and work within the constraints of the international environment and regional trade alliances, markets, and agreements.

Pacific Rim regions such as South Korea, Thailand, Singapore, Taiwan, and Hong Kong have become major manufacturing and financial centres. Even before Korean brand names such as Samsung, Daewoo, and Hyundai became household words, these

Indonesia: The New Economic Powerhouse?

With 25 percent of the world's total population, China's 1.3 billion people confer considerable market power, and its economy is growing at an astounding 9.5 percent a year. Likewise, India with its 1.1 billion people, information technology focus, and good GDP growth rate is getting the world's attention. Most firms today spend considerable resources on either sourcing from China and India or marketing their products in those countries. Is Indonesia the next country where substantial outsourcing and market gains can be found?

Indonesia, with its large population (more than 240 million people), a good GDP growth rate (4.9 percent in 2005), and a workforce that is more untapped by Western firms than those in China and India, presents itself as a strong possibility as the next country of note. Indonesia has a market-based economy, but the government plays a significant role. The Indonesian government owns close to 160 enterprises and is setting prices on several basic products such as fuel, rice, and electricity.

Inaugurated in 2004, Yudhoyono is Indonesia's first directly elected leader. Yudhoyono led a highly skilled response to the devastating tsunami in December 2004, and he then exhibited a leader's touch in signing an important peace pact to end the long-running rebellion in the province of Aceh. The ethnically and politically fractured Malay archipelago is increasingly becoming a stable market. In fact, Douglas Ramage, the Asia Foundation's Indonesia representative, calls Indonesia "the sleeper democratization success story" in Asia.

Indonesia has vast natural resources outside Java, including crude oil, natural gas, tin, copper, and gold. It is the world's second-largest exporter of natural gas (after Russia.) Major agricultural products include rice, tea, coffee, spices, and rubber. The country's major trading partners are Japan, the United States, and the surrounding nations of Singapore, Malaysia, and Australia.

products prospered under company labels, including GE, GTE, RCA, and JCPenney. Singapore boasts huge global markets for rubber goods and pharmaceuticals. Hong Kong is still a strong commercial centre after being transferred to Chinese control. Vietnam is becoming one of Asia's fastest-growing markets for North American businesses, but Taiwan may have the most promising future of all the Pacific Rim nations as a strong local economy and low import barriers draw increasing imports. Firms from Thailand and Malaysia are also thriving, carving out niches in the world markets for a variety of products from toys to automobile parts.

SUMMARY

International marketing involves developing and performing marketing activities across national boundaries. International markets can provide tremendous opportunities for growth and renewed opportunity for the firm.

A detailed analysis of the environment is essential before a company enters an international market. Environmental aspects of special importance include cultural, social, ethical, economic, political, legal, and technological forces. Because marketing activities are primarily social in purpose, they are influenced by beliefs and values regarding family, religion, education, health, and recreation. Cultural differences may affect marketing negotiations, decision-making behaviour, and product adoption and use. A nation's economic stability and trade barriers can affect marketing efforts. Significant trade barriers include import tariffs, quotas, embargoes, and exchange controls. Gross domestic product (GDP) and GDP per capita are common measures of a nation's economic standing. Political and legal forces include a nation's political system, laws, regulatory bodies, special-interest groups, and courts. Advances in technology have greatly facilitated international marketing.

Various regional trade alliances and specific markets create both opportunities and constraints for companies engaged in international marketing. These include the North American Free Trade Agreement, the European Union, the Common Market of the Southern Cone, Asia-Pacific Economic Cooperation, and the World Trade Organization.

There are several ways to get involved in international marketing. Importing (the purchase of products from a foreign source) and exporting (the sale of products to foreign markets) are the easiest and most flexible methods. Marketers may employ a trading company, which links buyers and sellers in different countries but is not involved in manufacturing and does not own assets related to manufacturing. Licensing and franchising are arrangements whereby one firm pays fees to another for the use of its name, expertise, and supplies. Contract manufacturing occurs when a company hires a foreign firm to produce a designated volume of the domestic firm's product to specification and the final product carries the domestic firm's name. Joint ventures are partnerships between a domestic firm and a foreign firm or government. Strategic alliances are partnerships formed to create competitive advantage on a worldwide basis. Finally, a firm can build its own marketing or production facilities overseas. When companies have direct ownership of facilities in many countries, they may be considered multinational enterprises.

Although most firms adjust their marketing mixes for differences in target markets, some firms standardize their marketing efforts worldwide. Traditional full-scale international marketing involvement is based on products customized according to cultural, regional, and national differences. Globalization, however, involves developing marketing strategies as if the entire world (or regions of it) were a single entity; a globalized firm markets standardized products in the same way everywhere. International marketing demands some strategic planning if a firm is to incorporate foreign sales into its overall marketing strategy.

Please visit the student website at www.hmco.ca/marketing for ACE Self-Test questions that will help you prepare for exams.

IMPORTANT TERMS

International marketing
Export-ready
Import tariff
Quota
Embargo

Exchange controls
Balance of trade
Gross domestic product (GDP)
Dumping

Cultural relativism
North American Free Trade Agreement (NAFTA)
European Union (EU)

Common Market of the Southern Cone (MERCOSUR)
Asia-Pacific Economic Cooperation (APEC)

General Agreement on
    Tariffs and Trade
    (GATT)
World Trade Organization
    (WTO)

Importing
Exporting
Trading company
Licensing
Franchising

Outsourcing
Offshoring
Offshore outsourcing
Joint venture
Strategic alliances

Direct ownership
Multinational enterprise
Organizational structure
Globalization

DISCUSSION & REVIEW QUESTIONS

1. How does international marketing differ from domestic marketing?

2. What factors must marketers consider as they decide whether to engage in international marketing?

3. Why are the largest industrial corporations in North America so committed to international marketing?

4. Why do you think this chapter focuses on an analysis of the international marketing environment?

5. If you were asked to provide a small tip (or bribe) to have a document approved in a foreign nation where this practice is customary, what would you do?

6. How will NAFTA affect marketing opportunities for Canadian products in North America (the United States, Mexico, and Canada)?

7. What should marketers consider as they decide whether to license or enter into a joint venture in a foreign nation?

8. Discuss the impact of strategic alliances on international marketing strategies.

9. Contrast globalization with customization of marketing strategies. Is one practice better than the other?

10. What are some of the product issues that you need to consider when marketing luxury automobiles in Australia, Brazil, Singapore, South Africa, and Sweden?

APPLICATION QUESTIONS

1. To successfully implement marketing strategies in the international marketplace, a marketer must understand the complexities of the global marketing environment. Which environmental forces (sociocultural, economic, political/legal, or technological) might a marketer need to consider when marketing the following products in the international marketplace, and why?

   a. Barbie dolls

   b. Beer

   c. Financial services

   d. Television sets

2. Many firms, including Procter & Gamble and FedEx, wish to do business in Eastern Europe and in the countries that were once part of the former Soviet Union. What events could occur that would make marketing in these countries more difficult? What events might make it easier?

3. This chapter discusses various organizational approaches to international marketing. Which would be the best arrangements for international marketing of the following products, and why?

   a. Construction equipment

   b. Cosmetics

   c. Automobiles

4. Procter & Gamble has made a substantial commitment to foreign markets, especially in Latin America. Its actions may be described as a "globalization of marketing." Describe how a shoe manufacturer (e.g., Wolverine World Wide) would go from domestic marketing, to limited exporting, to international marketing, and finally to a globalization of marketing. Give examples of some activities that might be involved in this process.

globalEDGE™

1. Tariffs play a significant role in global markets. Sometimes designed to protect industries from excessive foreign competition, tariffs may be imposed by countries for political, economic, or legal reasons. Find data pertaining to the Free Trade Area of America (FTAA) in the Trade and Tariff Database by using the search term "FTAA" at **http://globaledge.msu.edu/ibrd** or **http://globaledge.msu.edu/ibrd/ibrd.asp.** From the Trade and Tariff Database in the FTAA website, click on the Tariffs link, then the Tariffs button, and then choose Tariffs to Imports. Next, click on the Ranking button. Determine the top five industries in the United States benefiting from tariffs. Compare this list to the top five industries with tariffs in Mexico. Are there any differences or similarities that you notice?

2. An important element in designing your firm's internationalization strategy is to identify markets that are most similar and different culturally. Because your firm is based in Canada, one approach to determine this is to calculate the average difference in scores from Canada for each country based on Hofstede's five cultural dimensions for 56 countries. Hofstede's cultural dimensions can be found using the search term "56 countries" at **http://globaledge.msu.edu/ibrd** or **http://globaledge.msu.edu/ibrd/ibrd.asp.** At the Geert Hofstede Resource Center, there will be a link called Hofstede Scores. Which five countries are most similar to Canada? Which five countries are least similar?

INTERNET Exercise

Visit **www.prideferrell.com** for resources to help you master the material in this chapter, plus materials that will help you expand your marketing knowledge, including internet exercise updates, ACE self-tests, hotlinks to companies featured in this chapter, and much more.

FTD

Founded in 1910 as "Florists' Telegraph Delivery," FTD was the first company to offer a "flowers-by-wire" service. FTD does not itself deliver flowers but depends on local florists to provide this service. In 1994, FTD expanded its toll-free telephone-ordering service by establishing a website. Visit the site at **www.ftd.com.**

1. Click on International. Select a country to which you would like to send flowers. Summarize the delivery and pricing information that would apply to that country.
2. Determine the cost of sending fresh-cut seasonal flowers to Germany.
3. What are the benefits of this global distribution system for sending flowers worldwide? What other consumer products could be distributed globally through the Internet?

Case 7.1   One of P&G's Best Brands

For those of you who have ever used a wet razor, whether it was for shaving your face, legs, head, or other body parts, chances are you used a Gillette brand razor. After all, the Gillette Company, which also makes the popular Duracell battery, has a dominant share of the worldwide razor market. And the international marketplace is changing, at least for Gillette's competitors.

On October 1, 2005, the merger of the Gillette Company and the Procter & Gamble Company was completed.

This merger stands to profoundly affect the international marketplace. It represents a powerful merger of two giants spanning several global industries and centuries of experience and success (P&G was founded in 1837 and Gillette was founded in 1901).

Founded by King C. Gillette, the Gillette Company was one of the first great multinational organizations and, some would say, a marvel of marketing effectiveness—a trait that has also been synonymous with P&G. Just four years after founding Gillette in Boston, King

Gillette opened a branch office in London, and the company quickly gained sales and profits throughout western Europe. About 20 years later, Gillette said of his safety razor, "There is no other article for individual use so universally known or widely distributed. In my travels, I have found it in the most northern town in Norway and in the heart of the Sahara Desert." From the beginning, Gillette set out to offer consumers high-quality shaving products that would satisfy their basic grooming needs at a fair price. Having gained more than half of the entire razor and blades market, Gillette's manufacturing efficiency allowed it to implement marketing programs on a large scale, which helped the company gain both profits and market leadership.

Today the Gillette Company is the world leader in male grooming products, a category that includes blades, razors, and shaving preparations, and in selected female grooming products, such as wet-shaving products and hair removal devices. In addition, the company holds the number one position worldwide in alkaline batteries and in manual and power toothbrushes. Gillette's manufacturing operations are conducted at 32 facilities in 15 countries, and products are distributed through wholesalers, retailers, and agents in more than 200 countries and territories.

Gillette's Mach3 and Mach3 Turbo shaving systems, which reap $2 billion in sales annually, remain the best-selling men's shavers, and its line of Venus razors leads the women's shaver market. "Gillette's blade and razor business is the single most valuable franchise in the household products and cosmetics industries," said William H. Steele, an analyst at Bank of America Securities. The blade and razor segment accounts for roughly 40 percent of Gillette's sales and more than 70 percent of the company's profits. Sales in this segment have more than doubled in the last decade, and the outlook for this segment is promising as the shaving population increases, particularly in such locations as Asia, eastern Europe, and Latin America. The company's progress in its principal line of business reflects the success of its technologically advanced products, including the Mach3 system.

The worldwide success of the Mach3 was not a simple task, however. It took 10 years, 35 patents, $200 million in research and development, $550 million in capital investments, and $300 in marketing efforts to make Mach3 successful. And all of these resources were spent on an item that costs roughly $6.50 to consumers. The marketing campaign for Mach3 is a fascinating one. Specifically, Gillette's goal for Mach3 was a worldwide product launch, not just a domestic one. As such, the company needed to ensure that it had enough Mach3 products in the global supply chain to satisfy the likely strong global demand. Any stock-outs would be very costly to Gillette's market position and image and endanger its aggressive product launch. Mostly successful in its launch, the Mach3 razor set the tone for the marketplace and for how to launch such a product globally. Much of the launch success of the Venus razor for women is owed to the carefully delineated process of the Mach3 razor. Gillette used largely the same strategy for the Venus as it did for Mach3.

Gillette's current strategy in the personal care market is to focus resources on core grooming products such as deodorants/antiperspirants and shaving preparations while providing supporting products in key markets. The premier brand in this product mix is the Gillette Series, which includes shaving gels and foams, as well as Gillette Series antiperspirants and deodorants. The personal care segment also includes many of Gillette's best-known and most respected brands, including Foamy shaving cream and Right Guard, Soft & Dry, and Dry Idea deodorants/antiperspirants.

The Gillette Company also owns Braun, which turned in a record performance in 1997 but has since struggled to contribute profits. As a result, Braun is no longer considered one of the company's primary business segments. However, Gillette still values Braun's shaving products, oral care products, and hair removal (epilation) devices, which fit well with the company's emphasis on product innovation and with its other business segments. Other Braun products—namely kitchen appliances, personal-care products, and health-care instruments—do not fit as well with Gillette's focus. As a result, the company has contemplated selling most of the Braun line but keeping the key products in shaving, oral care, and hair removal.

Another brand in Gillette's stable is Oral-B, which develops and markets a broad range of superior oral care products worldwide in a strong and well-established partnership with dental professionals. Led by toothbrushes, the Oral-B line also includes interdental products, specialty toothpastes, mouth rinses, and professional dental products. Sales and profits continue to increase in this segment as a function of technological developments and product innovations. For example, the Oral-B Triumph toothbrush features innovative technology with a FlossAction brushhead for superior cleaning.

With the acquisition of Duracell International, Gillette instantly achieved worldwide leadership in the alkaline battery market. Duracell leads this market with approximately a 40 percent share. This segment is key to Gillette's portfolio and complements P&G's portfolio well. Duracell products generate sizable sales and profits. Also, Duracell and Gillette share many characteristics, including global brand franchises, common distribution channels, and geographic expansion potential. With the company's backing, Duracell enjoys significant economies of scale and greater market penetration through P&G's worldwide distribution network.

Each day around the world, more than one billion people interact with Gillette products while two billion times a day customers interact with P&G brands. Both Gillette and P&G have gained leadership positions through their strategies of managing their businesses with long-term, global perspectives. This ability to generate long-term, profitable growth in a changing global marketplace rests on several fundamental strengths, including a constantly increasing accumulation of scientific knowledge, innovative products that embody meaningful technological advances, and an immense manufacturing capability to produce billions of products every year reliably, efficiently, and cost effectively. Gillette's and P&G's strengths have created strong and enduring

consumer brand loyalty around the world. Now, what can these firms do together? One prediction is that the merger between Gillette and Procter & Gamble will make consumers' brand loyalty even stronger—could this be the case?[71]

QUESTIONS FOR DISCUSSION

1. What environmental factors have contributed to Gillette's success in global markets? What forces may have created challenges for the company?
2. What strategy does Gillette appear to have adopted for international marketing?
3. How can Gillette continue to compete effectively in the battery and grooming markets after the merger with Procter & Gamble?

Strategic Case 3 Mattel Takes on Global Challenges

Mattel, Inc., with about $5 billion in annual revenues, is the world leader in the design, manufacture, and marketing of children's toys. The company's major toy brands include Barbie (with more than 120 different Barbie dolls), Fisher-Price, Disney entertainment lines, Hot Wheels and Matchbox cars, Tyco Toys, and games such as UNO. In addition, Mattel promotes international sales by tailoring toys for specific global markets. Today, Mattel has offices in more than 40 countries and markets its products in more than 155 nations.

Mattel's marketing prowess and reach have paid off. In a poll conducted by the annual Power Brands study, Mattel had strong popularity among consumers. As many as 4 out of 10 people said that if they were shopping for toys, Mattel would be the brand they most prefer. Retailers also singled out Mattel as the number 1 performer, with more than 6 out of 10 mentions. This survey showed that both children and adults are enthused about Mattel and its line of products. Mattel and Fisher-Price names continually top surveys of consumers who are asked about their brand preferences when buying toys in discount stores or superstores. The same consumers mention Barbie and Hot Wheels repeatedly.

Customer Orientation at Mattel

Mattel's management philosophy focuses on satisfying customers' needs and wants. For example, Mattel redesigned Barbie to more naturally reflect a "normal" athletic woman in an attempt to meet the demand for a more realistic doll. Barbie has also taken on many different professions to reach a wider audience. These product modifications and extensions are designed to meet consumer and social demands while still accomplishing company objectives.

Mattel's pursuit of interactive multimedia is an attempt to adapt to the shorter span of time young girls spend playing with Barbie and other dolls and more traditional toys. Increasingly children are turning to more interactive toys, and Mattel acquired the Learning Company to meet and capitalize on this demand. This acquisition, however, did not prove profitable for Mattel, and the company eventually sold the division.

Mattel's Core Products—*Barbie*

The first Barbie doll sported open-toed shoes, a ponytail, sunglasses, earrings, and a zebra-striped bathing suit. Fashions and accessories were also available for the doll. Whereas buyers at the annual Toy Fair in New York City took no interest in Barbie, where the doll was introduced, little girls of the time certainly did. The intense demand seen at the retail stores was insufficiently met for several years; Mattel just could not produce the Barbie dolls fast enough. Today, Barbie is one of Mattel's major product lines, accounting for more than 50 percent of its total sales.

March 2005 marked the forty-fifth anniversary of Barbie. It also heralded a new Barbie campaign called "More than a Doll," which encourages girls to be anything from athletes to computer experts to dreamers. The campaign is an attempt to retain the interest of girls for a longer time, beyond the usual post-Barbie age of seven, by making Barbie more "real" to older girls.

"From fashion selection to vintage collection, she's everything." And in 2004 Barbie even split from Ken. After 43 years together, Barbie and Ken decided to break up—leaving Barbie as a more independent can-do (doll) woman.

Perhaps Barbie's slipping in popularity in the early part of the century had something to do with the breakup. Mattel reacted by introducing a line of My Scene dolls, which includes a multicultural Barbie, aimed at older girls referred to as "tweens."

Hot Wheels

With more than 15 million boys ages 5 to 15 collecting Hot Wheels cars, this line of small die-cast vehicles is now involved with almost every racing circuit in the world, including NASCAR (National Association for Stock Car Auto Racing), Formula One, NHRA (National Hot Rod Association), CART (Championship Auto Racing Teams), AMA (American Motorcycle Association), and many others. This immense popularity has created a group of young collectors: the average boy collector owns more than 41 Hot Wheels.

Hot Wheels celebrated its thirty-fifth anniversary in 2003 with a massive marketing campaign called the Hot Wheels Highway 35 World Race. Mattel created a story- and character-based package that included collectible cars, racetracks, comic books, home videos, a video game, a television network special, and an online race. The idea was to appeal to the many age groups of collectors Mattel has acquired in recent years.

Fisher-Price

Acquired in 1993 as a wholly owned subsidiary, Fisher-Price is the umbrella brand for all of Mattel's infant and preschool lines. The brand is trusted by parents all over the world and appears on everything from children's software to eyewear, books, and bicycles. Some of the classic products include the Rock-a-Stack and Little People play sets. Through licensing agreements, the brand also develops character-based toys such as *Sesame Street*'s Elmo and Big Bird and Disney's Winnie the Pooh and Mickey Mouse.

Fisher-Price has built trust with parents by creating products that are educational, safe, and useful. For example, during recent years, the brand has earned high regard for innovative car seats and nursery monitors. One project includes collaboration with Microsoft to develop an activity table that teaches infants through preschoolers with "smart technology." Fisher-Price keeps pace with the interests of today's families through innovative learning toys and award-winning baby gear.

Ethics and Responsibility at Mattel

Like most organizations, Mattel has recognized the different responsibilities it has to various stakeholders, including customers, employees, investors, suppliers, and the community, in its products, markets, and business outcomes. Mattel demonstrates a commitment to economic, legal, ethical, and philanthropic responsibilities.

Mattel's core products and business environment can present ethical issues. For example, because its products are designed primarily for children, the company must be sensitive to societal concerns about children's rights. In addition, the international environment often complicates business transactions, especially in the areas of employee rights and safety in manufacturing facilities. Different legal systems and cultural expectations about business can create ethical conflict. Finally, the use of technology may present ethical dilemmas, especially with regard to consumer privacy. Mattel has recognized these potential issues and has taken steps to strengthen its commitment to business ethics and social responsibility.

Advances in technology have created special issues for Mattel's marketing efforts. Mattel recognizes that because it markets to children, it has the responsibility to communicate with parents about corporate marketing strategy. The company has taken special steps to inform both children and adults about its philosophy regarding Internet-based marketing tools, such as the Hot Wheels website.

Today Mattel faces many market opportunities and threats, including the rate at which children are maturing and abandoning toys, the role of technology in consumer products, and purchasing power and consumer needs in global markets. Mattel's sales growth potential, especially in the international markets, continues to grow. For a company that began with two friends making picture frames, Mattel has demonstrated marketing dexterity. But the next few years will test the firm's resolve and strategy within the highly competitive but lucrative toy market.[72]

Questions for Discussion

1. Describe Mattel's target market for Barbie and Hot Wheels. How did the firm's marketing strategy appeal to this market internationally?
2. How has Mattel tried to be a socially responsible firm in its numerous world markets?
3. What environmental forces have created challenges for Mattel as it continues expansion into global markets? Which markets have created opportunities?

Using Technology and Information to Reach Target Markets and Build Customer Relationships

Part Four examines how marketers use technology to obtain and use information about customers to achieve organizational goals. **Chapter 8** explores how marketers use information technology to segment markets and create a viable marketing strategy. **Chapter 9** shows how organizations build long-term relationships with customers through e-marketing and customer relationship management. **Chapter 10** provides a foundation for analyzing buyers through a discussion of marketing information systems and the basic steps in the marketing research process.

Target Markets: Segmentation, Evaluation, and Positioning

Whole Foods and Baby Food

Whole Foods Markets is taking market segmentation to another level—it's targeting customers before they're born! Since 1980, the company has targeted customers with an interest in all-natural lifestyles. Today, it is the world's leading supermarket chain specializing in natural and organic foods. The company has sales in excess of $4 billion through more than 181 stores in the United States, Canada, and the United Kingdom.

Now Whole Foods, in partnership with *Mothering* magazine, has introduced a program called "Whole Baby" that targets expectant and new mothers. The Whole Baby program helps mothers prepare for their growing families by providing information on proper nutritional habits and on lifestyle topics ranging from prenatal care to baby's first foods.

In developing the program, Whole Foods commissioned a survey to evaluate the attitudes and interests of expectant and new mothers. When women were asked to identify their biggest concerns about having a baby, the issues most mentioned were money (56 percent), losing pregnancy weight (47 percent), and baby's health (44 percent). When asked about natural and organic foods, the survey found that 42 percent of the women thought that eating natural or organic foods was important, but that 38 percent didn't know the health advantages of these foods. Armed with this information, Whole Baby was developed to help new mothers learn about the benefits of healthier foods and lifestyles.

The program consists of free educational booklets available at Whole Foods Market stores. These guides contain money-saving coupons for the natural products that most appeal to mothers and information about parenting, as well as important nutritional information for pregnant women and new mothers. The program also includes free Whole Baby sample kits. These reusable tote bags contain product samples, information, and special offers from a variety of sponsors such as Burt's Bees, Earth's Best, Hylands, *Mothering* magazine, Seventh Generation, Stonyfield Farms, and Traditional Medicinals, which can be redeemed at Whole Foods Market stores.

Whole Foods Market is also partnering with *Mothering* magazine to offer a Whole Baby lecture series in selected regions. These free talks provide new mothers with everything they need to know about natural foods, nourishment, raising healthy children, and breastfeeding.

Whole Foods Markets knows that the birth of a baby often gets new parents thinking about adopting healthier lifestyles. The Whole Baby program seems to be a natural for introducing this target market to Whole Foods.[1] ■

To compete effectively, Whole Foods Markets has singled out specific customer groups toward which it will direct its marketing efforts. Any organization that wants to succeed must identify its customers and develop and maintain marketing mixes that satisfy the needs of those customers.

In this chapter, we explore markets and market segmentation. Initially we define the term *market* and discuss the major requirements of a market. Then we examine the steps in the target market selection process, including identifying the appropriate targeting strategy, determining which variables to use for segmenting consumer and business markets, developing market segment profiles, evaluating relevant market segments, and selecting target markets. Then we examine the concept of positioning products in customers' minds. Finally, we discuss various methods for developing sales forecasts.

What Are Markets?

The word *market* has a number of meanings. People sometimes use it to refer to a specific location where products are bought and sold—for example, a flea market. A large geographic area may also be called a market. Sometimes *market* refers to the relationship between supply and demand of a specific product, as in the question "How is the market for digital cameras?" *Market* may also be used as a verb, meaning to sell something.

We defined the term *market* in Chapter 2 as a group of people who, as individuals or as organizations, have needs for products in a product category and have the ability, willingness, and authority to purchase such products. In general use, the term *market* sometimes refers to the total population, or mass market, that buys products. However, our definition is more specific: it refers to groups of people seeking products in a specific product category. For example, students are part of the market for textbooks, as well as the markets for software, pens, paper, food, music, and other products. Obviously our complex economy has many different markets.

As stated in our definition, for a market to exist, the people in the aggregate must meet the following four requirements:

1. They must need or desire a particular product. If they do not, that aggregate is not a market.

2. They must have the ability to purchase the product. Ability to purchase is a function of buying power, which consists of resources such as money, goods, and services that can be traded in an exchange situation.

3. They must be willing to use their buying power.

4. They must have the authority to buy the specific products.

figure 8.1

TARGET MARKET SELECTION PROCESS

1 Identify the appropriate targeting strategy

2 Determine which segmentation variables to use

3 Develop market segment profiles

4 Evaluate relevant market segments

5 Select specific target markets

Individuals can have the desire, the buying power, and the willingness to purchase certain products but may not be authorized to do so. For example, teenagers may have the desire, the money, and the willingness to buy liquor, but a liquor producer does not consider them a market because teenagers are prohibited by law from buying alcoholic beverages. An aggregate of people that lacks any one of the four requirements thus does not constitute a market.

Target Market Selection Process

In Chapter 1, we pointed out that the first of two major components of developing a marketing strategy is to select a target market. Although marketers may employ several methods for target market selection, generally they use a five-step process. This process is shown in Figure 8.1, and we discuss it in the following sections.

Step 1: Identify the Appropriate Targeting Strategy

Recall from Chapter 1 that a target market is a group of people or organizations for which a business creates and maintains a marketing mix specifically designed to satisfy the needs of group members. The strategy used to select a target market is affected by target market characteristics, product attributes, and the organization's objectives and resources. Figure 8.2 illustrates the three basic targeting strategies: undifferentiated, concentrated, and differentiated.

Undifferentiated Targeting Strategy

An organization sometimes defines an entire market for a particular product as its target market. When a company designs a single marketing mix and directs it at the entire market for a particular product, it is using an **undifferentiated targeting strategy.** This strategy is sometimes also referred to as mass marketing. As Figure 8.2 shows, the strategy assumes that all customers in the target market for a specific kind of product have similar needs, and thus the organization can satisfy most customers with a single marketing mix. This mix consists of one type of product with little or no variation, one price, one promotional program aimed at everybody, and one distribution system to reach most customers in the total market. Products marketed successfully through the undifferentiated strategy include staple food items, such as sugar and salt, and certain kinds of farm produce.

The undifferentiated targeting strategy is effective under two conditions. First, a large proportion of customers in a total market must have similar needs for the product, a situation termed a **homogeneous market.** A marketer using a single marketing mix for a total market of customers with a variety of needs would find that the marketing mix satisfies very few people. A "universal car" meant to suit everyone would fulfill very few customers' needs for cars because it would not provide the specific attributes a particular person wants. Second, the organization must be able to develop and maintain a single marketing mix that satisfies customers' needs. The company must be able

undifferentiated targeting strategy A strategy in which an organization defines an entire market for a particular product as its target market, designs a single marketing mix, and directs it at that market

homogeneous market A market in which a large proportion of customers have similar needs for a product

figure 8.2

TARGETING STRATEGIES

The letters in each target market represent potential customers. Customers with the same letters have similar characteristics and similar product needs.

to identify a set of needs common to most customers in a total market and have the resources and managerial skills to reach a sizable portion of that market.

Although customers may have similar needs for a few products, for most products their needs decidedly differ. Most products today are very highly differentiated, making it very risky for some firms to follow an undifferentiated marketing strategy. In such instances, a company should use a concentrated or a differentiated strategy.

Concentrated Targeting Strategy Through Market Segmentation

Not everyone wants the same type of car, furniture, or clothes. A market made up of individuals or organizations with diverse product needs is called a **heterogeneous market.** For example, some individuals want an economical car, while others desire a status symbol, and still others seek a roomy and comfortable vehicle. The automobile market thus is heterogeneous.

For such heterogeneous markets, market segmentation is appropriate. **Market segmentation** is the process of dividing a total market into groups, or segments, consisting of people or organizations with relatively similar product needs. The purpose is to enable a marketer to design a marketing mix that more precisely matches the needs of customers in the selected market segment. A **market segment** consists of individuals, groups, or organizations sharing one or more similar characteristics that cause them to have relatively similar product needs. The automobile market is divided into many different market segments.

Hyundai, for example, aims its Sonata at the mid-size sedan market segment as opposed to aiming at all car buyers.[2] The main rationale for segmenting heterogeneous markets is that a company is better able to develop a satisfying marketing mix for a relatively small portion of a total market than to develop a mix that meets the needs of all people. Market segmentation is widely used. Fast-food chains, soft-drink companies, magazine publishers, hospitals, and banks are just a few types of organizations that employ market segmentation.

For market segmentation to succeed, five conditions must exist. First, customers' needs for the product must be heterogeneous; otherwise there is little reason to segment the market. Second, segments must be identifiable and divisible. The company must find a characteristic or variable for effectively separating individuals in a total market into groups containing people with relatively uniform needs for the product. Third, the total market should be divided so that segments can be compared with respect to estimated sales potential, costs, and profits. Fourth, at least one segment must have enough profit potential to justify developing and maintaining a special marketing mix for that segment. Finally, the company must be able to reach the chosen segment with a particular marketing mix. Some market segments may be difficult or impossible to reach because of legal, social, or distribution constraints. Therefore, market segments must be accessible, viable in terms of consumer demand, and profitable for the firm to target. A segment that is not profitable for one firm may be very profitable for another. When an organization directs its marketing efforts toward a single market segment using one marketing mix, it is employing a **concentrated targeting strategy,** or **single segmentation.** Porsche focuses on the luxury sports car segment and directs all its marketing efforts toward high-income individuals who want to own high-performance sports cars. Mont Blanc, a German company famous for its high-quality writing pens, targets its products to individuals within the writing instrument market who value high-end, collectable writing instruments.[3] Notice in Figure 8.2 that the organization using the concentrated strategy is aiming its marketing mix only at "B" customers.

The chief advantage of the concentrated strategy is that it allows a firm to specialize. The firm analyzes characteristics and needs of a distinct customer group and then focuses all its energies on satisfying that group's needs. A firm may generate a large sales volume by reaching a single segment. Also, concentrating on a single segment permits a firm with limited resources to compete with larger organizations that may have overlooked smaller segments. Many smaller firms become highly successful by meeting very unique needs of very small segments. With a high market penetration of a single segment, particularly one with high end products, such firms can be very profitable.

---

heterogeneous market
A market made up of individuals or organizations with diverse needs for products in a specific product class

market segmentation
The process of dividing a total market into groups with relatively similar product needs to design a marketing mix that matches those needs

market segment Individuals, groups, or organizations sharing one or more similar characteristics that cause them to have similar product needs

concentrated targeting strategy A market segmentation strategy in which an organization targets a single market segment using one marketing mix

Sometimes marketers will take different segments that have somewhat similar characteristics and combine them to make a larger marketing segment, then develop one marketing mix for it. While some marketers call this market combination, it is really another form of concentrated marketing strategy. It is not mass marketing because the strategy still involves selecting marketing segments out of the whole. Specialization, however, means that a company puts all its eggs in one basket, which can be hazardous. If a company's sales depend on a single segment and the segment's demand for the product declines, the company's financial strength also deteriorates. Moreover, when a firm penetrates one segment and becomes well entrenched, its popularity may keep it from moving into other segments. For example, it is very unlikely that Mont Blanc could or would want to compete with Bic in the low-end, disposable-pen market segment.

Differentiated Targeting Strategy Through Market Segmentation

differentiated targeting strategy A strategy in which an organization targets two or more segments by developing a separate marketing mix for each segment

With a **differentiated targeting strategy**, an organization directs its marketing efforts at two or more segments by developing a marketing mix for each segment (refer to Figure 8.2). This strategy is also called a multiple segmentation approach. After a firm uses a concentrated strategy successfully in one market segment, it sometimes expands its efforts to include additional segments. For example, Fruit of the Loom underwear has traditionally been aimed at one segment: men. However, the company now markets underwear for women and children as well. Marketing mixes for a differentiated strategy may vary as to product features, distribution methods, promotion methods, and prices.

A firm may increase sales in the aggregate market through a differentiated strategy because its marketing mixes are aimed at more people. For example, Gap, which established its retail apparel reputation by targeting people under 25, now targets several age groups, from infants to people over 60 with Gap, Banana Republic, and Old Navy stores. The company's newest stores, Forth & Towne, are aimed at women age

Differentiated Marketing

Many companies use differentiated strategy by targeting more than one market segment. In the ads shown here, VISA hopes to attract young parents and Mont Blanc targets those who give business gifts. Both organizations aim multiple marketing mixes at multiple target markets.

The Uploaded Photo at the End of the Bar

Many singles who are tired of the dating scene are going digital to search for a partner. And why not, when online dating boasts as high as a 94 percent success rate! Digital dating services use target marketing concepts to find singles the perfect mate. Today, online dating services are the biggest paid content on the Internet, with sales estimated at $1 billion.

Over one million Canadians have used online dating services and the market potential for online dating services is approximately three million men and women. All digital dating services require demographic information from their members, which allows these companies to be more precise in determining matches. Among the most sophisticated researchers is eHarmony.com, which asks its members to answer a 436-question assessment that will help match marriage-minded couples based on 29 dimensions of compatibility. These dimensions are grouped into core traits and vital attributes.

Canadians went online to find a date for specific reasons. Career obligations often result in little time to meet new people and the Internet provides a ready resource to meet interesting people who may also be interested in forming relationships. There is increased job mobility for young people, which creates barriers to being able to meet new people. There is also evidence that growing knowledge about sexual harassment, combined with various workplace policies about sexual conduct at work, are making it difficult for many to seek romance in the workplace.

But there are other reasons why Canadians went online to find romance. The Internet provides a place to meet new people that one would never get to meet on the street. It is private and confidential, and it is more convenient than social outings.

Internet users in general in Canada tend to be employed, well educated, with higher than average incomes. This demographic is certainly reflected in the online dating segment, but this segment also skews more toward divorced males, or single males, with paid employment, who dwell in urban areas. Most are single (80 percent) but up to 18 percent reported being married, or living common law.

Lifestyles of Canada's online daters indicate that most are social creatures who go out at least once a week with friends (53 percent), who spend time with family at least once a month (82 percent), who belong to clubs (41 percent), and who belong to religious organizations (24 percent).

With digital-assisted dating, your perfect mate may be just the press of a button away. Sixty percent of online daters had developed a long-term friendship, and 27 percent met someone they regarded as a partner. However, three percent ended up marrying the person they met online.

35 and up.[4] A company with excess production capacity may find a differentiated strategy advantageous because the sale of products to additional segments may absorb excess capacity. On the other hand, a differentiated strategy often demands more production processes, materials, and people. Thus, production costs may be higher than with a concentrated strategy. Many smaller firms may also find that it isn't financially viable for them to try to target more than one segment at a time.

When developing multiple marketing mixes to target multiple marketing segments it is only necessary to adjust the parts of the marketing mix that need tweaking to appeal to different consumer groups. For example, offering similar products with different features may allow a firm to target different groups without necessarily changing distribution or promotion. Firms may only adjust one or two aspects of the marketing mix to create a unique blend for each market segment.

Step 2: Determine Which Segmentation Variables to Use

segmentation variables
Characteristics of individuals, groups, or organizations used to divide a market into segments

Segmentation variables are the characteristics of individuals, groups, or organizations used to divide a market into segments. For example, location, age, gender, or rate of product usage can all be bases for segmenting markets.

To select a segmentation variable, several factors are considered. The segmentation variable should relate to customers' needs for, uses of, or behaviour toward the product. Stereo marketers might segment the stereo market based on income and age, but not on religion, because people's stereo needs do not differ due to religion. Furthermore, if individuals or organizations in a total market are to be classified accurately, the segmentation variable must be measurable. Age, location, and gender are measurable because such information can be obtained through observation or questioning. In contrast, segmenting a market on the basis of, say, intelligence is extremely difficult because this attribute is harder to measure accurately.

Gender-Based Segmentation

Razor manufacturers target both men and women.

A company's resources and capabilities affect the number and size of segment variables used. The type of product and degree of variation in customers' needs also dictate the number and size of segments targeted. In short, there is no best way to segment markets.

Choosing a segmentation variable or variables is a critical step in targeting a market. Selecting an inappropriate variable limits the chances of developing a successful marketing strategy. To help you better understand potential segmentation variables, we next examine the major types of variables used to segment consumer markets and the types used to segment business markets.

Variables for Segmenting Consumer Markets

A marketer using segmentation to reach a consumer market can choose one or several variables from an assortment of possibilities. As Figure 8.3 shows, segmentation variables can be grouped into four categories: demographic, geographic, psychographic, and behavioural.

Demographic Variables. Demographers study aggregate population characteristics such as the distribution of age and gender, fertility rates, migration patterns, and mortality rates. Demographic characteristics that marketers commonly use in segmenting markets include age, gender, race, ethnicity, income, education, occupation, family size, family life cycle, religion, and social class. Marketers rely on these demographic characteristics because they are often closely linked to customers' needs and purchasing behaviours and can be readily measured. Age is a commonly used variable for segmentation purposes. Everest Canada, LP, is using age as a key demographic variable to sell its unique funeral planning and concierge service. Everest works as an advisor to help families during times of grief, acting as an advocate in planning the funeral for a loved one. Everest has been endorsed by the Canadian Association for Retired Persons, and it has expanded its offerings to include life insurance designed to cover one's final expenses. It is currently attempting to sell its life insurance funeral package into the American market.

Marketers need to be aware of age distribution and how that distribution is changing. The fastest growing age group in Canada are those aged 80 years and over. This group grew by 41 percent between 1993 and 2003, and it is expected to grow an-

figure 8.3

SEGMENTATION VARIABLES FOR CONSUMER MARKETS

Demographic variables
- Age
- Gender
- Race
- Ethnicity
- Income
- Education
- Occupation
- Family size
- Family life cycle
- Religion
- Social class

Geographic variables
- Region
- Urban, suburban, rural
- City size
- County size
- State size
- Market density
- Climate
- Terrain

Psychographic variables
- Personality attributes
- Motives
- Lifestyles

Behaviouristic variables
- Volume usage
- End use
- Benefit expectations
- Brand loyalty
- Price sensitivity

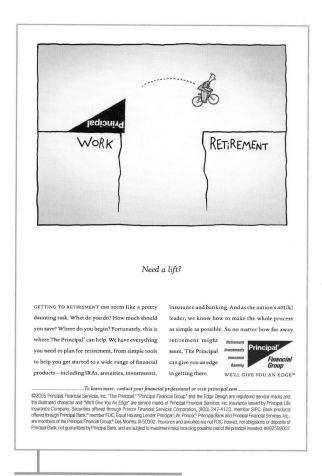

Need a lift?

Age-Based Segmentation

In this ad, Principle Financial Group touts its retirement plans and looks for potential customers among those people planning for retirement.

other 43 percent between 2001 and 2011. This population is characterized by more women than men, as men's life expectancy is less than that of women. This type of information is very important for firms like Everest who cater to the aging family.

Many marketers recognize the purchase influence of children and are targeting more marketing efforts at them. Numerous products are aimed specifically at children—toys, clothing, food and beverages, and entertainment such as movies and TV cable channels. In addition, children in this age group influence $500 billion of parental spending yearly.[5] In households with only one parent or those in which both parents work, children often take on additional responsibilities such as cooking, cleaning, and grocery shopping, and thus influence the types of products and brands these households purchase.

Gender is another demographic variable commonly used to segment markets, including the markets for clothing, soft drinks, non-prescription medications, toiletries, magazines, and even cigarettes. As of 2006, the Canadian population was almost evenly split by gender, with 50.5 percent women and 49.5 percent men.[6] Some deodorant marketers use gender segmentation: Secret and Soft and Dri are targeted specifically at women, whereas Degree and Mitchum are directed toward men. Food and beverage companies are paying close attention to women and have determined that all important food marketing trends are partially the result of women's influence in the home. Foods offering convenience, portability, and easy preparation have a good chance of success. For example, cereal maker Kellogg Company spun off its Rice Krispies Treats from its Rice Krispies line, and its convenience makes it one of the most popular snack bars in the country. Its easy portability and convenience, which appeals to women consumers, is a factor.[7]

Marketers also use race and ethnicity as variables for segmenting markets for such products as food, music, clothing, and cosmetics and for services such as banking and insurance. Even the marketing of cell phones has an ethnic niche. While most cell phones are marketed to users between the ages of 15 and 69, the core of users that is driving the market are those between the ages of 15 and 24 years. There is also a strong ethnic market consisting primarily of Chinese and East Indian cell phone users, many of whom buy phones with as many high-end features as possible because they see their cell phone as a status symbol.

Because income strongly influences people's product needs, it often provides a way to divide markets. Income affects people's ability to buy and their desires for certain lifestyles. Product markets segmented by income include sporting goods, housing, furniture, cosmetics, clothing, jewelry, home appliances, automobiles, and electronics.

Among the factors influencing household income and product needs are marital status and the presence and age of children. These characteristics, often combined and called the *family life cycle,* affect needs for housing, appliances, food and beverages, automobiles, and recreational equipment. Using the information in Table 8.1, consider how life cycle stages affect the purchase of beverages.

Marketers also use many other demographic variables. For instance, dictionary publishing companies segment markets by education level. Some insurance companies segment markets using occupation, targeting health insurance at college students and at younger workers with small employers that do not provide health coverage. Family life cycles can be broken down in various ways. Figure 8.5 shows a breakdown into nine categories based on the U.S. market. In Canada similar trends are

table 8.1   LIFE CYCLE STAGES INFLUENCE BEVERAGE PURCHASES

Percentage of all Dollars Spent Annually in Each Beverage Category, by Life Stage

	Carbonated Beverages	Coffee	Juices, Refrigerated	Soft Drinks, Non-carb.	Bottled Water	All Remaining Carb. Bev. (Diet)	All Remaining Carb. Bev. (Reg.)	Coffee, Liquid
Young singles (age 18–34)	2%	1%	2%	2%	2%	2%	1%	3%
Childless younger couples (two adults, 18–34)	4%	3%	4%	4%	6%	4%	4%	8%
New families (2 adults, 1 or more children <6)	5%	3%	5%	8%	6%	4%	5%	4%
Maturing families (2 adults, 1 or more children, not all <6 or +12)	26%	19%	22%	36%	22%	21%	30%	19%
Established families (1 or more children, all +12)	12%	9%	10%	10%	10%	9%	14%	12%
Middle-aged singles (35–54)	7%	5%	7%	4%	9%	9%	7%	7%
Middle-aged childless couples (2 adults, 35–54)	18%	17%	16%	14%	18%	19%	16%	18%
Empty-nesters (2 adults, +55, no children at home)	20%	32%	24%	17%	20%	24%	17%	21%
Older singles (55+)	7%	11%	10%	6%	7%	8%	6%	8%
Total	100%	100%	100%	100%	100%	100%	100%	100%

Source: *American Demographics,* "Drink Me" by Matthew Grimm. Feb. 2000, pp. 62–63. Copyright © 2000. Reprinted with permission from *American Demographics*.

Plus-Size Women Key Target Market

Despite the obsession with thinness in today's fashion and entertainment industries, more retailers are recognizing that a key target market for women's fashion has gone underserved for years: the plus-size woman. Women who wear size 14 and above are considered plus-size women in the fashion market. The reason for the growing popularity of this segment is that 30 percent of Canadian women are plus-size, and double as many American women fall into the same fashion category. Suddenly, the market is large enough to attract the attention of manufacturers and retailers. In fact, the plus-size woman, once considered to be outside of mainstream fashion, is today's average female shopper.

Targeting plus-size shoppers has resulted in a whirlwind of change for how the market segment is understood and served by the clothing industry. Fashion merchandisers are realizing that plus-size women desire, and are entitled to, the same selection and service that all customers should receive.

In 2002, Reitman's launched its MXM clothing line. It was followed by Wal-Mart in 2003 with the launch of Curvations, Wal-Mart's clothing line targeted to plus-size women. In 2004, The Bay introduced their Above Average line of fashionable clothing for women size 14 and up. These leading department stores joined other retail chains in offering attractive clothing options at various price points for plus-size women, such as Cotton Ginny Plus, Additionelle, and Pennington's.

Today, plus-size clothing lines lead the industry, with sales three times greater than sales of regular sized women's clothing, a trend that retailers and the fashion industry are happy to continue.

impacting families. There are more single parent households and people are marrying later and having children later in life. Sixteen percent of households in the 2001 census were headed by a single parent. Most of the single parents were women (81 percent).[8] Statistics Canada also revealed that a niche of mature adults do not expect to marry. About 50 percent of all mature singles in Canada do not expect to marry. Mature singles are defined as those over the typical marriage age but younger than 55 years.[9]

Marriage is still popular, although many individuals now choose common-law living arrangements either before, or instead, of traditional marriage.[10] However, 90 percent of married Canadians have been down the aisle only once, and have been married for an average of 23.5 years. The average age of first marriage in Canada is 25 years. Tracking these changes helps marketers satisfy the needs of particular target markets through new marketing mixes. There exists in Canada a unique generational shift, resulting from the combination of longer life spans, enhanced medical breakthroughs and the size of the baby boomer generation. This general shift has resulted in what has been called the Sandwich Generation: an environment where middle-aged adults may find themselves caring for elderly parents and dependent children at the same time. Statistics Canada reports that in 2002, nearly 30 percent of adults aged 45 to 64 were caught in the Sandwich Generation.[11]

Individuals caught in the Sandwich Generation make up a unique market for cell phones and medical supplies and equipment. They may also have to outfit their homes for people with special health needs. These individuals are also more likely to experience financial losses due to lost time at work or early retirement. They are also more likely to be experiencing stress from the additional demands of caregiving.

Geographic Variables. Geographic variables—climate, terrain, city size, population density, and urban/rural areas—also influence consumer product needs. Markets may be divided into regions because one or more geographic variables can cause customers to differ from one region to another. Many firms divide Canada into three distinct regions: Western (British Columbia through to Saskatchewan), Central (Manitoba, Ontario, Quebec), and Atlantic (the maritime provinces, and Newfoundland and Labrador). In some cases, Quebec is maintained as a separate market region. This kind of division simplifies logistics and may better capture regional cultural differences in the marketing plan.

City size can be an important segmentation variable. Some marketers focus efforts on cities of a certain size. For example, one franchised restaurant organization will not locate in cities of fewer than 200 000 people. It concluded that a smaller population

Movie Theatres and Drive-Ins: Geography Makes a Difference

Canada's movie theatres started to struggle in 2003–2004, with revenues down across the country. Revenues in 2003–2004 were $1.2 billion, down from one percent the previous year. This trend began to reverse in 2004–2005, with a two percent increase in revenues.

The drop in attendance in 2003–2004 can be attributed to a number of causes. In some cases, old theatres could not compete effectively with newly designed facilities. Other causes included the Severe Acute Respiratory illness (SARS) in the Toronto area and the amount of disposable income in the pockets of Canadians.

Despite the various causes for the drop in attendance to movie theatres and drive-ins there are still some clear geographic differences in attendance levels across the country. The most frequent moviegoers are still located in Alberta. Albertans spent $119 annually in the theatre, with up to 4.6 visits. Residents of Newfoundland and Labrador attended the movie theatre less often than any other region of Canada, averaging 2.4 visits per year.

base would result in inadequate profits. Other firms actively seek opportunities in smaller towns. A classic example is Wal-Mart, which initially only located in small towns.

Statistics Canada has developed a system to classify areas of various sizes. Larger cities, those with populations of 100 000 or more, are called Census Metropolitan Areas. In some cases, various municipalities may have been absorbed into CMAs. Census districts involve communities outside of CMAs. For example, the city of Ottawa is part of a Census Division, but the CMA is Ottawa-Hull. A breakout for Ottawa from Statistics Canada is shown in Figure 8.5.

market density The number of potential customers within a unit of land area

Market density refers to the number of potential customers within a unit of land area, such as a square kilometre. Although market density relates generally to population density, the correlation is not exact. For example, in two different geographic markets of approximately equal size and population, market density for office supplies would be much higher in one area if it contained a much greater proportion of business customers than the other area. Market density may be a useful segmentation variable because low-density markets often require different sales, advertising, and distribution activities than do high-density markets.

geodemographic segmentation A method of market segmentation that clusters people in zip code areas and smaller neighbourhood units based on lifestyle and demographic information

A number of marketers are using geodemographic segmentation. **Geodemographic segmentation** clusters people in postal code areas and even smaller neighbourhood units based on lifestyle information and especially demographic data such as income, education, occupation, type of housing, ethnicity, family life cycle, and level of urbanization. These small, precisely described population clusters help marketers isolate demographic units as small as neighbourhoods where the demand for specific products is strongest. Geodemographic segmentation allows marketers to engage in micromarketing. **Micromarketing** is the focusing of precise marketing efforts on very small geographic markets, such as community and even neighbourhood markets. Providers of financial and health-care services, retailers, and consumer products companies use micromarketing. Special advertising campaigns, promotions, retail site location analyses, special pricing, and unique retail product offerings are a few examples of micromarketing facilitated through geodemographic segmentation.

micromarketing An approach to market segmentation in which organizations focus precise marketing efforts on very small geographic markets

Climate is commonly used as a geographic segmentation variable because of its broad impact on people's behaviour and product needs. Product markets affected by

figure 8.5

STATISTICS CANADA CENSUS GEOGRAPHIC HIERARCHY BREAKOUTS FOR OTTAWA

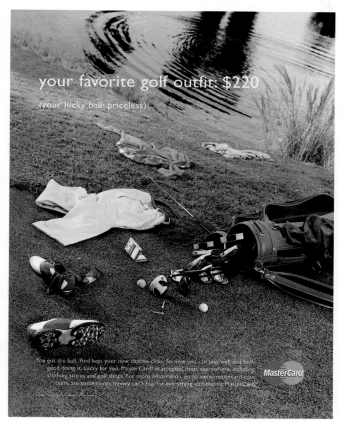

Lifestyle Segmentation

In these advertisements, the CESAR brand targets people who love their small dogs and MasterCard appeals to golfers.

climate include air-conditioning and heating equipment, clothing, gardening equipment, recreational products, and building materials.

Psychographic Variables. Marketers sometimes use psychographic variables, such as personality characteristics, motives, and lifestyles, to segment markets. A psychographic dimension can be used by itself to segment a market or combined with other types of segmentation variables.

Personality characteristics can be useful for segmentation when a product resembles many competing products and consumers' needs are not significantly related to other segmentation variables. However, segmenting a market according to personality traits can be risky. Although marketing practitioners have long believed consumer choice and product use vary with personality, until recently marketing research had indicated only weak relationships. It is hard to measure personality traits accurately, especially since most personality tests were developed for clinical use, not for segmentation purposes.

When appealing to a personality characteristic, a marketer almost always selects one that many people view positively. Individuals with this characteristic, as well as those who would like to have it, may be influenced to buy that marketer's brand. Marketers taking this approach do not worry about measuring how many people have the positively valued characteristic; they assume a sizable proportion of people in the target market either have it or want to have it.

When motives are used to segment a market, the market is divided according to consumers' reasons for making a purchase. Personal appearance, affiliation, status, safety, and health are examples of motives affecting the types of products purchased and the choice of stores in which they are bought. Marketing efforts based on health and fitness motives can be a point of competitive advantage. Lifestyle segmentation groups individuals according to how they spend their time, the importance of things in their surroundings (homes or jobs, for example), beliefs about themselves and broad issues, and some demographic characteristics, such as income and education.[12] Lifestyle analysis provides a broad view of buyers because it encompasses numerous characteristics related to people's activities (work, hobbies, entertainment, sports), interests (family, home, fashion, food, technology), and opinions (politics, social issues, education, the future). For example, homeownership is valued by most income and age segments. Recent studies show, however, that 49 percent of Generation Xers (born between 1964 and 1973) own homes and account for 16.5 percent of the home furnishing market and 19.9 percent of furniture purchases. Unlike baby boomers (born 1946–1963), Generation X homeowners often research products for their homes on the Web and later buy those products in-store. In addition, their decisions on major home improvements are often decided based on how those improvements will affect the home's resale value.[13]

One of the most popular consumer lifestyle frameworks is a survey from SRI Consulting Business Intelligence. The company's VALS Program uses a survey to help classify consumers into eight basic groups. The segmentation is based on psychological characteristics that are correlated with purchase behaviour and four key demographics.

figure 8.6

VALS TYPES AND SPORTS PREFERENCES

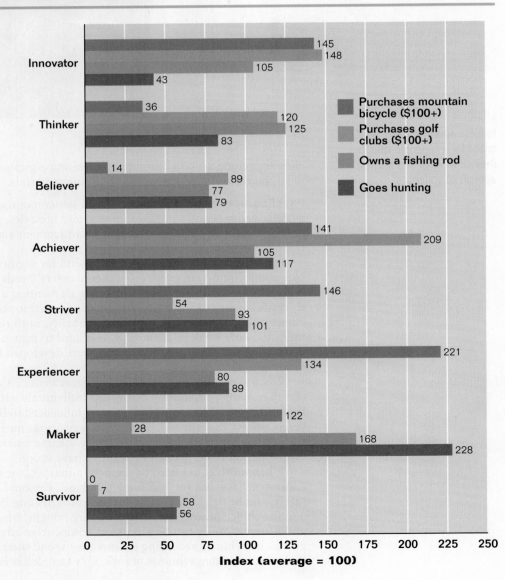

Source: VALS™ Program. SRI Consulting Business Intelligence. Reprinted with permission.

The eight groups are Innovators, Thinkers, Achievers, Experiencers, Believers, Strivers, Makers, and Survivors. This VALS questionnaire is then attached to larger surveys that focus on particular products, services, leisure activities, or media preferences to learn about the lifestyles of the eight groups. Figure 8.6 is an example of VALS data showing the proportion of each VALS group that purchased a mountain bike, purchased golf clubs, owns a fishing rod, and goes hunting. VALS research is also used to create new products as well as to segment existing markets. VALS systems have been developed for the United States, Japan, and the United Kingdom.[14]

Behavioural Variables. Firms can divide a market according to some feature of consumer behaviour toward a product, commonly involving some aspect of product use. For example, a market may be separated into users—classified as heavy, moderate, or light—and non-users. To satisfy a specific group, such as heavy users, marketers may create a distinctive product, set special prices, or initiate special promotion and distribution activities. Per capita consumption data help identify different levels of usage. How customers use or apply products may also determine the method of segmentation. To satisfy customers who use a product in a certain way, some feature—say, packaging, size, texture, or colour—may be designed precisely to make the product easier to use, safer, or more convenient.

benefit segmentation
The division of a market according to benefits that consumers want from the product

Benefit segmentation is the division of a market according to benefits that consumers want from the product. Although most types of market segmentation assume a relationship between the variable and customers' needs, benefit segmentation differs in that the benefits customers seek *are* their product needs. Consider that a customer who purchases over-the-counter cold relief medication may be specifically interested in two benefits: stopping a runny nose and relieving chest congestion. Thus, individuals are segmented directly according to their needs. By determining the desired benefits, marketers may be able to divide people into groups seeking certain sets of benefits. The effectiveness of such segmentation depends on three conditions:

Behavioural Factors in the Grocery Market

A study by researchers in Canada and New Zealand revealed that grocery shoppers belong to different behavioural segments, and that each behavioural segment is likely to shop at supermarkets with different price and service formats. Researchers Leszczyc, Sinha, and Sahgal determined that grocery shoppers belong to three different behavioural segments: time-constrained price-focused shopper, time-constrained service-seeking shoppers, and cherry-pickers.

The time-constrained price-focused shopper does not want to spend a lot of their day shopping, but still wants to find a deal. These shoppers respond better to the Every Day Low Price (EDLP) retail strategy that has been pursued by many supermarkets and discount department stores.

The time-constrained service-seeking shoppers are often looking for more than just food, which leads them to the nearest store that carries many different products. These shoppers may spend more time shopping than their counterpart, the time-constrained price-focused shopper, who is more likely to go to the store with the lowest prices.

The cherry pickers will go to a variety of stores looking for the best grocery purchases. Without a time constraint they can shop around to a variety of stores to be sure that they are getting the best deals. Cherry pickers will often travel out of their way to ensure that their grocery basket is the lowest possible price.

Cherry pickers are also the shoppers who respond readily to advertised and in-store specials, but retailers may find that cherry pickers don't make the best retail customers. Lack of store loyalty, and a tendency to buy only what is on sale, make cherry pickers less profitable and hard to serve.

(1) the benefits sought must be identifiable; (2) using these benefits, marketers must be able to divide people into recognizable segments; and (3) one or more of the resulting segments must be accessible to the firm's marketing efforts. Both Timberland and Avia, for example, segment the foot apparel market based on benefits sought.

As this discussion shows, consumer markets can be divided according to numerous characteristics. Business markets are segmented using different variables, as we will see in the following section.

Variables for Segmenting Business Markets

Like consumer markets, business markets are frequently segmented. Marketers segment business markets according to geographic location, type of organization, customer size, and product use.

Geographic Location. Earlier we noted that the demand for some consumer products can vary considerably among geographic areas because of differences in climate, terrain, customer preferences, and similar factors. Demand for business products also varies according to geographic location. For example, producers of certain types of lumber divide their markets geographically because their customers' needs vary from region to region. Geographic segmentation may be especially appropriate for reaching industries concentrated in certain locations. Furniture and textile producers, for example, are concentrated in the Southeast.

Type of Organization. A company sometimes segments a market by types of organizations within that market. Different types of organizations often require different product features, distribution systems, price structures, and selling strategies. Given these variations, a firm may either concentrate on a single segment with one marketing mix (a concentration targeting strategy) or focus on several groups with multiple mixes (a differentiated targeting strategy.) A carpet producer, for example, could segment potential customers into several groups, such as automobile makers, commercial carpet contractors (firms that carpet large commercial buildings), apartment complex developers, carpet wholesalers, and large retail carpet outlets.

Customer Size. An organization's size may affect its purchasing procedures and the types and quantities of products it wants. Size can thus be an effective variable for segmenting a business market. To reach a segment of a particular size, marketers may have to adjust one or more marketing mix components. For example, customers that buy in extremely large quantities are sometimes offered discounts. In addition, marketers often must expand personal selling efforts to serve large organizational buyers properly. Because the needs of large and small buyers tend to be quite distinct, marketers frequently use different marketing practices to reach various customer groups.

Product Use. Certain products, especially basic raw materials like steel, petroleum, plastics, and lumber, are used in numerous ways. How a company uses products affects the types and amounts of products purchased, as well as the purchasing method. For example, computers are used for engineering purposes, basic scientific research, and business operations such as word processing, accounting, and telecommunications. A computer maker therefore may segment the computer market by types of use because organizations' needs for computer hardware and software depend on the purpose for which products are purchased.

Order Size. Order size is an important segmentation variable in the business market. Some firms require very large lots of products for use in manufacturing operations. These buyers can only purchase from suppliers with the capacity to provide such large order sizes. Some smaller firms carve out a unique market niche by servicing smaller firms whose order sizes are not large. These smaller firms often find it hard to get a supplier because they do not purchase large enough order sizes, driving up suppliers' costs. Order size is not only an important segmentation variable for B2B marketing, it helps some firms carve out a market advantage.

Step 3: Develop Market Segment Profiles

A market segment profile describes the similarities among potential customers within a segment and explains the differences among people and organizations in different segments. A profile may cover such aspects as demographic characteristics, geographic factors, product benefits sought, lifestyles, brand preferences, and usage rates. Individuals and organizations within segments should be relatively similar with respect to several characteristics and product needs, and differ considerably from those within other market segments. Marketers use market segment profiles to assess the degree to which their possible products can match or fit potential customers' product needs. Market segment profiles help marketers understand how a business can use its capabilities to serve potential customer groups.

The use of market segment profiles benefits marketers in several ways. Such profiles help a marketer determine which segment or segments are most attractive to the organization relative to the firm's strengths, weaknesses, objectives, and resources. While marketers may initially believe certain segments are quite attractive, development of market segment profiles may yield information that indicates the opposite. For the market segment or segments chosen by the organization, the information included in market segment profiles can be highly useful in making marketing decisions.

Step 4: Evaluate Relevant Market Segments

After analyzing the market segment profiles, a marketer is likely to identify several relevant market segments that require further analysis and eliminate certain segments from consideration. To further assess relevant market segments, several important factors, including sales estimates, competition, and estimated costs associated with each segment, should be analyzed.

Sales Estimates

Potential sales for a market segment can be measured along several dimensions, including product level, geographic area, time, and level of competition.[15] With respect to product level, potential sales can be estimated for a specific product item (for example, Diet Coke) or an entire product line (Coca-Cola Classic, Caffeine-Free Coke, Diet Coke, Caffeine-Free Diet Coke, Vanilla Coke, Diet Vanilla Coke, Cherry Coca-Cola, and Diet Cherry Coca-Cola comprise one product line). A manager must also determine the geographic area to include in the estimate. In relation to time, sales estimates can be short range (one year or less), medium range (one to five years), or long range (longer than five years). The competitive level specifies whether sales are being estimated for a single firm or for an entire industry.

market potential The total amount of a product that customers will purchase within a specified period at a specific level of industry-wide marketing activity

Market potential is the total amount of a product that customers will purchase within a specified period at a specific level of industry-wide marketing activity. Market potential can be stated in terms of dollars or units. For example, with the aging of the large baby boomer generation, the market potential for medical instruments and medications to treat congestive heart failure, hypertension, and other cardiovascular conditions is estimated to reach over $20 billion by 2013.[16] A segment's market potential is affected by economic, sociocultural, and other environmental forces. Marketers must assume a certain general level of marketing effort in the industry when they estimate market potential. The specific level of marketing effort varies from one firm to another, but the sum of all firms' marketing activities equals industry-wide marketing efforts. A marketing manager must also consider whether and to what extent industry marketing efforts will change.

company sales potential The maximum percentage of market potential that an individual firm within an industry can expect to obtain for a specific product

Company sales potential is the maximum percentage of market potential that an individual firm within an industry can expect to obtain for a specific product. Several factors influence company sales potential for a market segment. First, the market potential places absolute limits on the size of the company's sales potential. Second, the

breakdown approach
Measuring company sales potential based on a general economic forecast for a specific period and the market potential derived from it

buildup approach Measuring company sales potential by estimating how much of a product a potential buyer in a specific geographic area will purchase in a given period, multiplying the estimate by the number of potential buyers, and adding the totals of all the geographic areas considered

magnitude of industry-wide marketing activities has an indirect but definite impact on the company's sales potential. Those activities have a direct bearing on the size of the market potential. When Domino's Pizza advertises home-delivered pizza, for example, it indirectly promotes pizza in general; its commercials may indirectly help sell Pizza Hut's and other competitors' home-delivered pizza. Third, the intensity and effectiveness of a company's marketing activities relative to competitors' affect the size of the company's sales potential. If a company spends twice as much as any of its competitors on marketing efforts and if each dollar spent is more effective in generating sales, the firm's sales potential will be quite high compared with competitors'.

There are two general approaches to measuring company sales potential: breakdown and buildup. In the **breakdown approach,** the marketing manager first develops a general economic forecast for a specific time period. Next, the manager estimates market potential based on this economic forecast. Then the manager derives the company's sales potential from the general economic forecast and estimate of market potential. In the **buildup approach,** the marketing manager begins by estimating how much of a product a potential buyer in a specific geographic area, such as a sales territory, will purchase in a given period. The manager then multiplies that amount by the total number of potential buyers in that area. The manager performs the same calculation for each geographic area in which the firm sells products and then adds the totals for each area to calculate market potential. To determine company sales potential, the manager must estimate, based on planned levels of company marketing activities, the proportion of the total market potential the company can obtain.

Competitive Assessment

Besides obtaining sales estimates, it is crucial to assess competitors already operating in the segments being considered. Without competitive information, sales estimates may be misleading. A market segment that seems attractive based on sales estimates may prove much less so following a competitive assessment. Such an assessment should ask several questions about competitors: How many exist? What are their strengths and weaknesses? Do several competitors have major market shares and together dominate the segment? Can our company create a marketing mix to compete effectively against competitors' marketing mixes? Is it likely that new competitors will enter this segment? If so, how will they affect our firm's ability to compete successfully? Answers to such questions are important for proper assessment of the competition in potential market segments.

The actions of a national food company that considered entering the dog food market illustrate the importance of competitive assessment. Through a segmentation study, the company determined that dog owners could be divided into three segments according to how they viewed their dogs and dog foods. One group treated their dogs as companions and family members. These individuals were willing to pay relatively high prices for dog foods and wanted a variety of types and flavours so their dogs would not get bored. The second group saw their dogs as performing a definite utilitarian function, such as protecting family members, playing with children, guarding the property, or herding farm animals. These people wanted a low-priced, nutritious dog food and were not interested in a wide variety of flavours. Dog owners in the third segment were found to actually hate their dogs. These people wanted the cheapest dog food they could buy and were not concerned with nutrition, flavour, or variety. The food company examined the extent to which competitive brands were serving all these dog owners and found that each segment contained at least three well-entrenched competing brands, which together dominated the segment. The company's management decided not to enter the dog food market because of the strength of the competing brands.

Cost Estimates

To fulfill the needs of a target segment, an organization must develop and maintain a marketing mix that precisely meets the wants and needs of individuals and organizations in that segment. Developing and maintaining such a mix can be expensive. Distinctive product features, attractive package design, generous product warranties, extensive advertising, attractive promotional offers, competitive prices, and high-quality personal service consume considerable organizational resources. Indeed, to reach certain segments, the costs may be so high that a marketer concludes the segment is inaccessible. Another cost consideration is whether the organization can effectively reach a segment at costs equal to or below competitors' costs. If the firm's costs are likely to be higher, it will be unable to compete in that segment in the long run.

Step 5: Select Specific Target Markets

An important initial consideration in selecting a target market is whether customers' needs differ enough to warrant the use of market segmentation. If segmentation analysis shows customer needs to be fairly homogeneous, the firm's management may decide to use the undifferentiated approach, discussed earlier. However, if customer needs are heterogeneous, which is much more likely, one or more target markets must be selected. On the other hand, marketers may decide not to enter and compete in any of the segments.

Assuming one or more segments offer significant opportunities to achieve organizational objectives, marketers must decide in which segments to participate. Ordinarily information gathered in the previous step—about sales estimates, competitors, and cost estimates—requires careful consideration in this final step to determine long-term profit opportunities. Also, the firm's management must investigate whether the organization has the financial resources, managerial skills, employee expertise, and facilities to enter and compete effectively in selected segments. Furthermore, the requirements of some market segments may be at odds with the firm's overall objectives, and the possibility of legal problems, conflicts with interest groups, and technological advancements could make certain segments unattractive. In addition, when prospects for long-term growth are taken into account, some segments may appear very attractive and others less desirable.

Selecting appropriate target markets is important to an organization's adoption and use of the marketing concept philosophy. Identifying the right target market is the key to implementing a successful marketing strategy, whereas failure to do so can lead to low sales, high costs, and severe financial losses. A careful target market analysis places an organization in a better position to both serve customers' needs and achieve its objectives.

Product Positioning and Repositioning

product positioning
Creating and maintaining a certain concept of a product in customers' minds

Once a target market is selected, a firm must consider how to position its product. **Product positioning** refers to the decisions and activities intended to create and maintain a certain concept of the firm's product (relative to competitive brands) in customers' minds. When marketers introduce a product, they try to position it so that it appears to have the characteristics that the target market most desires. This projected image is crucial. Crest is positioned as a fluoride toothpaste that fights cavities, and Close-Up is positioned as a whitening toothpaste that enhances the user's sex appeal, as shown in Figure 8.7.

Perceptual Mapping

A product's position is the result of customers' perceptions of the product's attributes relative to those of competitive brands. Buyers make numerous purchase decisions on a regular basis. To avoid a continuous reevaluation of numerous products, buyers tend to group, or "position," products in their minds to simplify buying decisions. Rather than allowing customers to position products independently, marketers often try to influence and shape consumers' concepts or perceptions of products through advertising. Marketers sometimes analyze product positions by developing perceptual figure 8.7

TOOTHPASTE PRODUCT POSITIONS

Brand	Product position
Colgate Total	Fights full range of oral health problems
Close-Up	Sexy, whitener, great breath for kissing
Crest	Powerful fluoride cavity fighter
Aim	Milder taste than other brands, kid-friendly
Arm & Hammer	Popular baking soda mixed with toothpaste
AquaFresh	Kills germs, for young adults
Biotene	Reduces bacteria and germs in mouth
Oral-B	High quality, dentist approved
Rembrandt	Higher quality whitening
Sensodyne	Especially for sensitive teeth
Mentadent	Baking soda and peroxide for fresh breath
Ultrabrite	Low priced whitener, removes stains

maps, as shown in Figure 8.8. Perceptual maps are created by questioning a sample of consumers about their perceptions of products, brands, and organizations with respect to two or more dimensions. To develop a perceptual map like the one in Figure 8.8, respondents would be asked how they perceive selected pain relievers in regard with price and type of pain for which the products are used. Also, respondents would be asked about their preferences for product features to establish "ideal points" or "ideal clusters," which represent a consensus about what a specific group of customers' desires in terms of product features. Then marketers can compare how their brand is perceived compared with the ideal points.

Bases for Positioning

Marketers can use several bases for product positioning. A common basis for positioning products is to use competitors. A firm can position a product to compete head-on with another brand, as PepsiCo has done against Coca-Cola, or to avoid competition, as 7Up has done relative to other soft-drink producers. Head-to-head competition may be a marketer's positioning objective if the product's performance characteristics are at least equal to those of competitive brands and if the product is priced lower. Head-to-head positioning may be appropriate even when the price is higher if the product's performance characteristics are superior. For example, the no-calorie sweetener Splenda is positioned as a healthier sugar substitute through its campaign slogan "Made from sugar so it tastes like sugar." Splenda also competes

figure 8.8

HYPOTHETICAL PERCEPTUAL MAP FOR PAIN RELIEVERS

Expensive

Excedrin ●

Bufferin ●
Aleve ●

● Nuprin

Orudis KT ●
● Advil

● Anacin

● Extra Strength
Tylenol

Tylenol ●

**For
headaches**

Motrin ●

**For
body aches**

● Bayer

St. Joseph's
●

● Norwich

Inexpensive

head-to-head through advertisements that indicate how it is unlike other no-calorie sweeteners because it is heat tolerant and can be used in baking as a cup-for-cup sugar substitute.[17] Conversely, positioning to avoid competition may be best when the product's performance characteristics do not differ significantly from competing brands. Moreover, positioning a brand to avoid competition may be appropriate when that brand has unique characteristics that are important to some buyers. Volvo, for example, has for years positioned itself away from competitors by focusing on the safety characteristics of its cars. Whereas some auto companies mention safety issues in their advertisements, many are more likely to focus on style, fuel efficiency, performance, or terms of sale. Avoiding competition is critical when a firm introduces a brand into a market in which the company already has one or more brands. Marketers usually want to avoid cannibalizing sales of their existing brands, unless the new brand generates substantially larger profits.

A product's position can be based on specific product attributes or features. For example, the Apple iPod is positioned based on product attributes such as its unique shape, its storage capacity (stores thousands of songs), and its access to iTunes music store. If a product has been planned properly, its features will give it the distinct appeal needed. Style, shape, construction, and colour help create the image and the appeal. If buyers can easily identify the benefits, they are, of course, more likely to

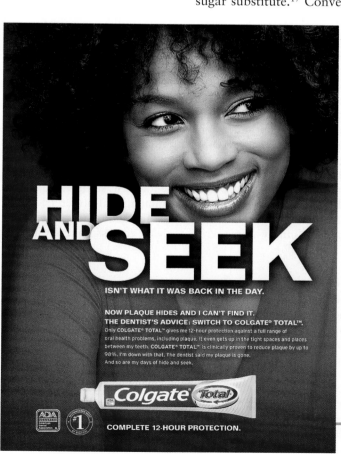

HIDE AND SEEK

ISN'T WHAT IT WAS BACK IN THE DAY.

NOW PLAQUE HIDES AND I CAN'T FIND IT.
THE DENTIST'S ADVICE: SWITCH TO COLGATE® TOTAL™.
Only COLGATE® TOTAL™ gives me 12-hour protection against a full range of oral health problems, including plaque. It even gets up in the tight spaces and places between my teeth. COLGATE® TOTAL™ is clinically proven to reduce plaque by up to 98%. I'm down with that. The dentist said my plaque is gone. And so are my days of hide and seek.

Colgate® Total

COMPLETE 12-HOUR PROTECTION.

Product Positioning

Colgate positions its Total toothpaste as the superior plaque fighter.

purchase the product. When the new product does not offer certain preferred attributes, there is room for another new product.

Other bases for product positioning include price, quality level, and benefits provided by the product. For example, Era detergent provides stain treatment and stain removal. Also, a positioning basis employed by some marketers is the target market. This type of positioning relies heavily on promoting the types of people who use the product.

Repositioning

Positioning decisions are not just for new products. Evaluating the positions of existing products is important because a brand's market share and profitability may be strengthened by product repositioning. For example, several years ago Kraft was on the verge of discontinuing Cheez Whiz because its sales had declined considerably. After Kraft marketers repositioned Cheez Whiz as a fast, convenient, microwavable cheese sauce, its sales rebounded and achieved new heights. When introducing a new product into a product line, one or more existing brands may have to be repositioned to minimize cannibalization of established brands and ensure a favourable position for the new brand.

Repositioning can be accomplished by physically changing the product, its price, or its distribution. Rather than making any of these changes, marketers sometimes reposition a product by changing its image through promotional efforts. Finally, a marketer may reposition a product by aiming it at a different target market.

Developing Sales Forecasts

sales forecast The amount of a product a company expects to sell during a specific period at a specified level of marketing activities

After a company targets its market and positioned its product, it needs a **sales forecast**—the amount of a product the company expects to sell during a specific period at a specified level of marketing activities. The sales forecast differs from the company sales potential. It concentrates on what actual sales will be at a certain level of company marketing effort, whereas the company sales potential assesses what sales are possible at various levels of marketing activities assuming certain environmental conditions will exist. Businesses use the sales forecast for planning, organizing, implementing, and controlling their activities. The success of numerous activities depends on this forecast's accuracy. Common problems in failing companies are improper planning and lack of realistic sales forecasts. Overly ambitious sales forecasts can lead to overbuying, overinvestment, and higher costs.

To forecast sales, a marketer can choose from a number of forecasting methods, some arbitrary and others more scientific, complex, and time consuming. A firm's choice of method or methods depends on the costs involved, type of product, market characteristics, time span of the forecast, purposes of the forecast, stability of the historical sales data, availability of required information, managerial preferences, and forecasters' expertise and experience.[18] Common forecasting techniques fall into five categories: executive judgment, surveys, time series analysis, regression analysis, and market tests.

Executive Judgment

jury of executive opinion A sales forecasting method based on the intuition of one or more executives

At times, a company forecasts sales chiefly on the basis of executive judgment. One forecasting approach, **the jury of executive opinion,** relies on the intuition of one or more executives. This approach is unscientific but expedient and inexpensive. Executive judgment may work reasonably well when product demand is relatively stable and the forecaster has years of market-related experience. However, because intuition is swayed most heavily by recent experience, the forecast may be overly optimistic or overly pessimistic. Another drawback to intuition is that the forecaster has only past experience as a guide for deciding where to go in the future. Also, those responsible for selling may feel that some executives are out of touch with what is happening on the ground in the marketplace. They may fear that this forecasting method may result in unrealistically high sales forecasts.

Surveys

Another way to forecast sales is to question customers, sales personnel, or experts regarding their expectations about future purchases. In a **customer survey,** marketers ask customers what types and quantities of products they intend to buy during a specific period. This approach may be useful to a business with relatively few customers. For example, Intel, which markets to a limited number of companies (primarily computer manufacturers), could conduct customer surveys effectively. PepsiCo, in contrast, has millions of customers and could not feasibly use a customer survey to forecast future sales.

customer survey A survey of customers regarding the quantities of products they intend to buy during a specific period

Customer surveys have several drawbacks. Customers must be able and willing to make accurate estimates of future product requirements. Although some organizational buyers can estimate their anticipated purchases accurately from historical buying data and their own sales forecasts, many cannot make such estimates. In addition, customers may not want to take part in a survey. Occasionally a few respondents give answers they know are incorrect, making survey results inaccurate. Moreover, customer surveys reflect buying intentions rather than actual purchases. Customers' intentions may not be well formulated, and even when potential purchasers have definite buying intentions, they do not necessarily follow through on them. Finally, customer surveys consume much time and money.

For the **sales force composite** the firm's salespeople estimate anticipated sales in their territories for a specified period. The forecaster combines these territorial estimates to arrive at a tentative forecast. A marketer may survey the sales staff for several reasons. The most important is that the sales staff is closer to customers on a daily basis than other company personnel and therefore should know more about customers' future product needs. Moreover, when sales representatives assist in developing the forecast, they are more likely to work toward its achievement. In addition, forecasts can be prepared for single territories, divisions consisting of several territories, regions made up of multiple divisions, and the total geographic market. Thus, the method provides sales forecasts from the smallest geographic sales unit to the largest.

sales force composite A survey of a firm's sales force regarding anticipated sales in their territories for a specified period

A sales force survey also has limitations. Salespeople may be too optimistic or pessimistic due to recent experiences. In addition, salespeople tend to underestimate sales potential in their territories when they believe their sales goals will be determined by their forecasts. They also dislike paperwork because it takes up time that could be spent selling. If preparation of a territorial sales forecast is time consuming, the sales staff may not do the job adequately.

Nonetheless, sales force surveys can be effective under certain conditions. The salespeople as a group must be accurate, or at least consistent, estimators. If the aggregate forecast is consistently over or under actual sales, the individual who develops the final forecast can make the necessary adjustments. Assuming the survey is well administered, the sales force can have the satisfaction of helping to establish reasonable sales goals and the assurance that its forecasts are not being used to set sales quotas.

When a company wants an **expert forecasting survey,** it hires professionals to help prepare the sales forecast. These experts are usually economists, management consultants, advertising executives, college professors, or other individuals outside the firm with solid experience in a specific market. Drawing on this experience and their analyses of available information about the company and the market, experts prepare and present forecasts or answer questions regarding a forecast. Using experts is expedient and relatively inexpensive. However, because they work outside the firm, these forecasters may be less motivated than company personnel to do an effective job.

expert forecasting survey Sales forecasts prepared by experts outside the firm, such as economists, management consultants, advertising executives, or college professors

A more complex form of the expert forecasting survey incorporates the Delphi technique. In the **Delphi technique,** experts create initial forecasts, submit them to the company for averaging, and have the results returned to them so they can make individual refined forecasts. The premise is that the experts will use the averaged results when making refined forecasts and these forecasts will be in a narrower range. The procedure may be repeated several times until the experts, each working separately, reach a consensus on the forecasts. The ultimate goal in using the Delphi technique is to develop a highly accurate sales forecast.

Delphi technique A procedure in which experts create initial forecasts, submit them to the company for averaging, and then refine the forecasts

Time Series Analysis

time series analysis An analysis of a firm's historical sales data to discover a pattern or patterns in the firm's sales over time

With **time series analysis,** the forecaster uses the firm's historical sales data to discover a pattern or patterns in the firm's sales over time. If a pattern is found, it can be used to forecast sales. This forecasting method assumes that past sales patterns will continue in the future. The accuracy, and thus usefulness, of time series analysis hinges on the validity of this assumption.

trend analysis An analysis of aggregate sales data, such as a company's annual sales figures, covering a period of many years to determine whether annual sales are generally rising, falling, or staying about the same

In a time series analysis, a forecaster usually performs four types of analysis: trend, cycle, seasonal, and random factor. **Trend analysis** focuses on aggregate sales data, such as the company's annual sales figures, covering a period of many years to determine whether annual sales are generally rising, falling, or staying about the same. Through **cycle analysis,** a forecaster analyzes sales figures (often monthly sales data) from a period of three to five years to ascertain whether sales fluctuate in a consistent, periodic manner. When performing a **seasonal analysis,** the analyst studies daily, weekly, or monthly sales figures to evaluate the degree to which seasonal factors, such as climate and holiday activities, influence sales. In a **random factor analysis,** the forecaster attempts to attribute erratic sales variations to random, non-recurrent events, such as a regional power failure, a natural disaster, or political unrest in a foreign market. After performing each of these analyses, the forecaster combines the results to develop the sales forecast. Time series analysis is an effective forecasting method for products with reasonably stable demand, but not for products with highly erratic demand.

cycle analysis An analysis of sales figures for a period of three to five years to ascertain whether sales fluctuate in a consistent, periodic manner

seasonal analysis An analysis of daily, weekly, or monthly sales figures to evaluate the degree to which seasonal factors influence sales

random factor analysis An analysis attempting to attribute erratic sales variations to random, non-recurrent events

Regression Analysis

Like time series analysis, regression analysis requires the use of historical sales data. In **regression analysis,** the forecaster seeks to find a relationship between past sales (the dependent variable) and one or more independent variables, such as population, per capita income, or gross domestic product. Simple regression analysis uses one independent variable, whereas multiple regression analysis includes two or more independent variables. The objective of regression analysis is to develop a mathematical formula that accurately describes a relationship between the firm's sales and one or more variables; however, the formula indicates only an association, not a causal relationship. Once an accurate formula is established, the analyst plugs the necessary information into the formula to derive the sales forecast.

regression analysis A method of predicting sales based on finding a relationship between past sales and one or more independent variables, such as population or income

Regression analysis is useful when a precise association can be established. However, a forecaster seldom finds a perfect correlation. Furthermore, this method can be used only when available historical sales data are extensive. Thus, regression analysis is futile for forecasting sales of new products.

Market Tests

market test Making a product available to buyers in one or more test areas and measuring purchases and consumer responses to marketing efforts

A **market test** involves making a product available to buyers in one or more test areas and measuring purchases and consumer responses to distribution, promotion, and price. Test areas are often cities with populations of 200 000 to 500 000, but can be larger metropolitan areas or towns with populations of 50 000 to 200 000. For example, ACNielsen Market Decisions, a marketing research firm, conducts market tests in numerous countries, including Canada.[19] A market test provides information about consumers' actual rather than intended purchases. In addition, purchase volume can be evaluated in relation to the intensity of other marketing activities such as advertising, in-store promotions, pricing, packaging, and distribution. Forecasters base their sales estimates for larger geographic units on customer response in test areas.

Because it does not require historical sales data, a market test is effective for forecasting sales of new products or sales of existing products in new geographic areas. A market test also gives a marketer an opportunity to test various elements of the marketing mix. However, these tests are often time consuming and expensive. In addition, a marketer cannot be certain that consumer response during a market test represents the total market response or that such a response will continue in the future.

Using Multiple Forecasting Methods

Although some businesses depend on a single sales forecasting method, most firms use several techniques. Sometimes a company is forced to use multiple methods when marketing diverse product lines, but even a single product line may require several forecasts, especially when the product is sold to different market segments. Thus, a producer of automobile tires may rely on one technique to forecast tire sales for new cars and on another to forecast sales of replacement tires. Variation in the length of needed forecasts may call for several forecasting methods. A firm that employs one method for a short-range forecast may find it inappropriate for long-range forecasting. Sometimes a marketer verifies results of one method by using one or more other methods and comparing outcomes.

SUMMARY

A market is an aggregate of people who, as individuals or as organizations, have needs for products in a product class and have the ability, willingness, and authority to purchase such products.

In general, marketers employ a five-step process when selecting a target market. Step 1 is to identify the appropriate targeting strategy. When a company designs a single marketing mix and directs it at the entire market for a particular product, it is using an undifferentiated targeting strategy. The undifferentiated strategy is effective in a homogeneous market, whereas a heterogeneous market needs to be segmented through a concentrated targeting strategy or a differentiated targeting strategy. Both these strategies divide markets into segments consisting of individuals, groups, or organizations that have one or more similar characteristics and thus can be linked to similar product needs. When using a concentrated strategy, an organization directs marketing efforts toward a single market segment through one marketing mix. With a differentiated targeting strategy, an organization directs customized marketing efforts at two or more segments.

Certain conditions must exist for effective market segmentation. First, customers' needs for the product should be heterogeneous. Second, the segments of the market should be identifiable and divisible. Third, the total market should be divided so that segments can be compared with respect to estimated sales, costs, and profits. Fourth, at least one segment must have enough profit potential to justify developing and maintaining a special marketing mix for that segment. Fifth, the firm must be able to reach the chosen segment with a particular marketing mix.

Step 2 is determining which segmentation variables to use. Segmentation variables are the characteristics of individuals, groups, or organizations used to divide a total market into segments. The segmentation variable should relate to customers' needs for, uses of, or behaviour toward the product. Segmentation variables for consumer markets can be grouped into four categories: demographic (e.g., age, gender, income, ethnicity, family life cycle), geographic (population, market density, climate), psychographic (personality traits, motives, lifestyles), and behavioural (volume usage, end use, expected benefits, brand loyalty, price sensitivity). Variables for segmenting business markets include geographic location, type of organization, customer size, and product use.

Step 3 in the target market selection process is to develop market segment profiles. Such profiles describe the similarities among potential customers within a segment and explain the differences among people and organizations in different market segments. Step 4 is evaluating relevant market segments, which requires that several important factors—including sales estimates, competition, and estimated costs associated with each segment—be determined and analyzed. Step 5 involves the actual selection of specific target markets. In this final step, the company considers whether customers' needs differ enough to warrant segmentation and which segments to target.

Product positioning relates to the decisions and activities that create and maintain a certain concept of the firm's product in customers' minds. It plays a role in market segmentation. Organizations can position a product to compete head to head with another brand or to avoid competition. Repositioning by making physical changes in the product, changing its price or distribution, or changing its image, can boost a brand's market share and profitability.

A sales forecast is the amount of a product the company actually expects to sell during a specific period at a specified level of marketing activities. To forecast sales, marketers can choose from a number of methods. The choice depends on various factors, including the costs involved, type of product, market characteristics, and time span and purposes of the forecast. There are five categories of forecasting techniques: executive judgment, surveys, time series analysis, regression analysis, and market tests. Executive judgment is based on the intuition of one or more executives. Surveys include customer, sales force, and expert forecasting surveys. Time series analysis uses the firm's historical sales data to discover patterns in the firm's sales over time and employs four major types of analyses: trend, cycle, seasonal, and random factor. With regression analysis, forecasters attempt to find a relationship between past sales and one or more independent variables. Market testing involves making a product available to buyers in one or more test areas and measuring purchases and consumer responses to distribution, promotion, and price. Many companies employ multiple forecasting methods.

Please visit the student website at www.hmco.ca/marketing for ACE Self-Test questions that will help you prepare for exams.

IMPORTANT TERMS

Undifferentiated targeting strategy
Homogeneous market
Heterogeneous market
Market segmentation
Market segment
Concentrated targeting strategy

Differentiated targeting strategy
Segmentation variables
Market density
Geodemographic segmentation
Micromarketing
Benefit segmentation
Market potential

Company sales potential
Breakdown approach
Buildup approach
Product positioning
Sales forecast
Jury of executive opinion
Customer survey
Sales force composite
Expert forecasting survey

Delphi technique
Time series analysis
Trend analysis
Cycle analysis
Seasonal analysis
Random factor analysis
Regression analysis
Market test

DISCUSSION & REVIEW QUESTIONS

1. What is a market? What are the requirements for a market?

2. In your local area, identify a group of people with unsatisfied product needs who represent a market. Could this market be reached by a business organization? Why or why not?

3. Outline the five major steps in the target market selection process.

4. What is an undifferentiated strategy? Under what conditions is it most useful? Describe a present market situation in which a company is using an undifferentiated strategy. Is the business successful? Why or why not?

5. What is market segmentation? Describe the basic conditions required for effective segmentation. Identify several firms that use market segmentation.

6. List the differences between concentrated and differentiated strategies, and describe the advantages and disadvantages of each.

7. Identify and describe four major categories of variables that can be used to segment consumer markets. Give examples of product markets that are segmented by variables in each category.

8. What dimensions are used to segment business markets?

9. Define *geodemographic segmentation*. Identify several types of firms that might employ this type of market segmentation, and explain why.

10. What is a market segment profile? Why is it an important step in the target market selection process?

11. Describe the important factors that marketers should analyze to evaluate market segments.

12. Why is a marketer concerned about sales potential when trying to select a target market?

13. Why is selecting appropriate target markets important for an organization that wants to adopt the marketing concept philosophy?

14. What is product positioning? Under what conditions would head-to-head product positioning be appropriate? When should head-to-head positioning be avoided?

15. What is a sales forecast? Why is it important?

16. What are the two primary types of surveys a company might use to forecast sales? Why would a company use an outside expert forecasting survey?

17. Under what conditions are market tests useful for sales forecasting? What are the advantages and disadvantages of market tests?

18. Under what conditions might a firm use multiple forecasting methods?

APPLICATION QUESTIONS

1. Generally marketers use one of three basic targeting strategies to focus on a target market: (1) undifferentiated, (2) concentrated, or (3) differentiated. Locate an article that describes the targeting strategy of a particular organization. Describe the target market, and explain the strategy being used to reach that market.

2. The stereo market may be segmented according to income and age. Discuss two ways the market for each of the following products might be segmented.
   a. Candy bars
   b. Travel agency services
   c. Bicycles
   d. Hair spray

3. Product positioning aims to create a certain concept of a product in consumers' minds relative to its competition. For example, Pepsi is positioned in direct competition with Coca-Cola, whereas Volvo has traditionally positioned itself away from competitors by emphasizing its cars' safety features. Following are several distinct positions in which an organization may place its product. Identify a product that would fit into each position.
   a. High price/high quality
   b. Low price
   c. Convenience
   d. Uniqueness

4. If you were using a time series analysis to forecast sales for your company for the next year, how would you use the following sets of sales figures?

   a.
1998	$145 000	2003	$149 000
1999	$144 000	2004	$148 000
2000	$147 000	2005	$180 000
2001	$145 000	2006	$191 000
2002	$148 000	2007	$227 000

   b.
	2005	2006	2007
Jan.	$12 000	$14 000	$16 000
Feb.	$13 000	$14 000	$15 500
Mar.	$12 000	$14 000	$17 000
Apr.	$13 000	$15 000	$17 000
May	$15 000	$17 000	$20 000
June	$18 000	$18 000	$21 000
July	$18 500	$18 000	$21 500
Aug.	$18 500	$19 000	$22 000
Sep.	$17 000	$18 000	$21 000
Oct.	$16 000	$15 000	$19 000
Nov.	$13 000	$14 000	$19 000
Dec.	$14 000	$15 000	$18 000

   c. 2005 sales increased 21.2 percent (opened an additional store in 2005); 2006 sales increased 18.8 percent (opened another store in 2006).

---

globalEDGE™

1. The level of a country's urbanization can have profound implications for marketers. While a variety of resources may provide insight on this topic, data from the Population Reference Bureau's website may be useful. This data can be found by using the search term "data query tool" at **http://www.prb.org/ datafind/datafinder7.htm.** Once you get to the Population Reference Bureau website, the level of urban population statistic can be found under the All Variables category. What is the level of urbanization of Canada? How does it compare with the level of urbanization in France, the United States, and the United Kingdom? What particular challenges might you need to consider in markets with higher or lower levels of urbanization?

INTERNET Exercise

Visit **www.hmco.ca/marketing** for resources to help you master the material in this chapter, plus materials that will help you expand your marketing knowledge, including Internet exercise updates, ACE self-tests, hotlinks to companies featured in this chapter, and much more.

iExplore

iExplore is an Internet company that offers a variety of travel and adventure products. Learn more about its goods, services, and travel advice through its website at **www.iexplore.com.**

1. Based on the information provided at the website, what are some of iExplore's basic products?
2. What market segments does iExplore appear to be targeting with its website? What segmentation variables is the company using to segment these markets?
3. How does iExplore appeal to comparison shoppers?

Case 8.1   IKEA's Leksvik and Klippan Sofas: Coming to a Living Room Near You

For more than 60 years, the Swedish firm IKEA has marketed simple but stylish home furnishings for cost-conscious customers who don't mind assembling their purchases to save money. In addition to welcoming shoppers in its stores, IKEA invites customers to shop online and through catalogues. Traditional furniture stores display beautiful home furnishings for high-end customers with deep pockets and little inclination to attach legs to a table or bolt together a bed frame. In contrast, IKEA's strategy is "to offer a wide range of home furnishings with good design and function at prices so low that as many people as possible will be able to afford them." Its products are of wide range—from frying pans and lamps to kitchen cabinets and living room suites—and come in styles that can be easily coordinated.

To keep prices low for its thrifty customers, IKEA is relentless in looking for ways to cut costs in manufacturing, marketing, warehousing, raw materials, and sales and then pass the savings along. For example, it buys raw materials in bulk and searches the world for efficient suppliers to keep per-unit costs low. It uses a special software package to collect price quotes from suppliers and streamline the purchasing process. For a company that buys from 1300 suppliers in 53 countries, even small efficiencies quickly add up to significant savings. More cost savings come from shipping furniture unassembled in flat boxes and having customers assemble their purchases at home. Low cost is not the only consideration, however. IKEA also requires its suppliers to abide by a code of conduct that forbids child labour, sets minimum standards for working conditions, and protects the environment.

Although IKEA's customers are frugal, they want to buy fashionable furniture that fits their personalities and lifestyles. In fact, the store's appeal cuts across demographic lines. Some customers who can well afford to shop at the poshest emporiums come to IKEA because they like the combination of chic design, down-to-earth functionality, and speedy assembly. Not every item must be assembled, but those that do are accompanied by simple, step-by-step instructions, which reassure even the most inexperienced do-it-yourselfer.

If customers get hungry as they walk through one of IKEA's cavernous stores, they can drop into the informal store restaurant for a quick snack or a light meal of delicacies from IKEA's home country. The most popular dish is Swedish meatballs: customers devour 150 million of these tiny meatballs every year.

Customers in many countries have responded enthusiastically to IKEA's formula of fashionable, affordable, and functional furniture. After expanding beyond Sweden to Norway and Denmark, the company opened stores in Europe, Australia, Canada, and the United States. More recently, IKEA has opened stores in Russia, Japan, and China.

Product names such as Leksvik bookcases and Klippan sofas are known throughout the world and reflect IKEA's Swedish origins. However, the company translates its catalogues into 36 languages and distributes 160 million copies every year. Here again, IKEA looks for ways to minimize expenses. It has all products photographed at one of Europe's largest studios and transmits the images electronically to printing facilities in the different regions where the catalogues will be distributed, saving on shipping and mailing costs. Every detail, from paper quality to type size, is scrutinized to identify new cost efficiencies.

IKEA's targeting strategy has helped it become a cult global brand. Every year, 410 million people go shopping in IKEA stores. The combined annual sales of home furnishings (and restaurant meals) in all of its 226 stores is nearly $18 billion. North America is one of IKEA's most important markets because it accounts for 16 percent of sales, and there are plans to have 50 stores open by 2010. No matter how large and fast IKEA grows, its focus will remain on keeping costs low to continue satisfying its target market's need for reasonably priced, well-designed assemble-it-yourself home furnishings.[20]

Questions for Discussion

1. Is IKEA's targeting strategy concentrated or undifferentiated? Explain your answer.
2. Which of the variables for segmenting consumer markets is IKEA using, and why are these variables appropriate?
3. What combination of techniques might IKEA apply when preparing sales forecasts for Canada?

E-Marketing and Customer Relationship Management

CHAPTER 9

"Hey, Hey . . . We're the Arctic Monkeys": E-Marketing Rocks

Thanks in great part to e-marketing, the Arctic Monkeys, a four-person indie rock band that was established in 2002 in Sheffield, England, skyrocketed to fame in three short years. About a year after the band's formation, demo CDs—handed out at small concert gigs—were downloaded to the Internet. Loyal fans shared the music via cyberspace, people began to take notice, and the band's fan base increased tremendously. In 2004, the band began to receive attention from BBC Radio 1 and the British press based on the offerings floating around the Net. In fact, some of their music is available only via download.

The Arctic Monkeys resisted the idea of signing with a record label for quite some time, even going as far as forbidding record company scouts from attending their concerts. Since the group had a large number of sold-out shows across the U.K., thanks primarily to electronic word of mouth, they weren't sure they needed representation. However, in 2005 they signed with Domino Records' owner Laurence Bell, a representative who signs only artists whose music he personally likes. The Arctic Monkeys' debut album, *Whatever People Say I Am, That's What I'm Not,* which includes the single "I Bet You Look Good on the Dance Floor," released in 2006. The album has become the fastest-selling debut album in U.K. chart history. In fact, the album is outselling all top 20 albums put together.

OBJECTIVES

1. To define electronic marketing and electronic commerce, and to recognize their increasing importance in strategic planning

2. To understand the characteristics of electronic marketing—addressability, interactivity, memory, control, accessibility, and digitalization—and how they differentiate electronic marketing from traditional marketing activities

3. To examine how the characteristics of electronic marketing affect marketing strategy

4. To understand how electronic marketing and information technology can facilitate customer relationship management

5. To identify legal and ethical considerations in electronic marketing

The band won "Best New Act" at the 2006 Brit Awards and made history yet again by being named both "Best New Band" and "Best British Band" in the same year at the 2006 NME Awards. The Arctic Monkeys' quick rise to fame has astounded those in the music business, some of whom say they haven't seen anything like it since the Beatles.[1] ■

The phenomenal growth of the Internet presents exciting opportunities for companies, including rock bands, to forge interactive relationships with consumers and business customers. The interactive nature of the Internet has made it possible to target markets more precisely and even reach markets that previously were inaccessible. It also facilitates customer relationship management, allowing companies to network with manufacturers, wholesalers, retailers, suppliers, and outsource firms to serve customers more efficiently. Because of its ability to enhance the exchange of information between customer and marketer, the Internet has become an important component of most firms' marketing strategies.

We devote this chapter to exploring this exciting frontier. We begin by defining *electronic marketing* and exploring its context within marketing strategies. Next, we examine the characteristics that differentiate electronic marketing activities from traditional ones and explore how marketers are using the Internet strategically to build competitive advantage. Then we take a closer look at the role of the Internet and electronic marketing in managing customer relationships. Finally, we consider some of the ethical and legal implications that affect Internet marketing.

Electronic Marketing

electronic commerce (e-commerce) Sharing business information, maintaining business relationships, and conducting business transactions by means of telecommunications networks

electronic marketing (e-marketing) The strategic process of creating, distributing, promoting, and pricing products for targeted customers in the virtual environment of the Internet

A number of terms have been coined to describe marketing activities and commercial transactions on the Internet. One of the most popular terms is **electronic commerce,** or **e-commerce,** defined as "the sharing of business information, maintaining business relationships, and conducting business transactions by means of telecommunications networks."[2] In this chapter, we focus on how the Internet, especially the World Wide Web, relates to all aspects of marketing, including strategic planning. Thus, we use the term **electronic marketing,** or **e-marketing,** to refer to the strategic process of creating, distributing, promoting, and pricing products for targeted customers in the virtual environment of the Internet.

There are three types of electronic marketing: B2C, B2B, and C2C. B2C marketing refers to business-to-consumer marketing, which is the activity that retailers are engaged in. One of the most important benefits of e-marketing is the ability of marketers and customers to share information. Through company websites, consumers can learn about a firm's products, including features, specifications, and even prices. Many websites also provide feedback mechanisms through which customers can ask questions, voice complaints, indicate preferences, and otherwise communicate about their needs and desires.

The Internet has changed the way marketers communicate and develop relationships not only with their customers but also with their employees and suppliers. B2B marketing refers to business-to-business marketing. Lockheed Martin, for example, created a global network linking 80 suppliers to help build a new stealth fighter jet. The company expects the project to save about $25 million a year during product development.[3] Many companies use e-mail, groupware (software that allows people in different locations to access and work on the same file or document over the Internet), instant messaging, blogs, videoconferencing, and other technologies to coordinate activities and communicate with employees. Because such technology facilitates and lowers the cost of communications, the Internet can contribute significantly to any industry or activity that depends on the flow of information, such as software, entertainment, health care, education, travel services, and government services.[4] Research has found that using the Internet for communication and administration activities has a greater effect on business performance than higher-profile activities such as order taking and procurement.[5]

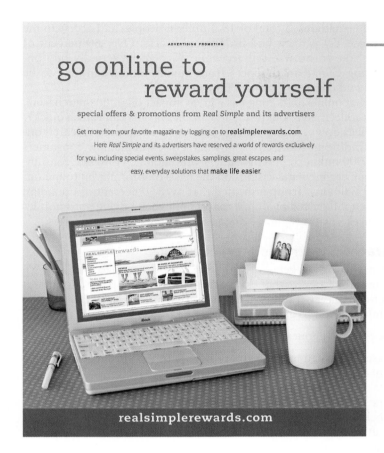

Electronic Marketing

Through the Internet, companies can offer customers unique services. RealSimpleRewards.com offers rewards and samples to subscribers of *Real Simple* magazine.

C2C marketing refers to consumer-to-consumer marketing, which has been greatly enhanced by the Internet. C2C includes E-Bay and other sites designed to help consumers find each other to sell goods and services.

Telecommunications technology offers many benefits to marketers, including rapid response, expanded customer service capability (e.g., 24 hours a day, 7 days a week, or 24/7), decreased operating costs, and reduced geographic barriers. Data networks have decreased cycle and decision times and permitted companies to treat customers more efficiently.[6] In today's fast-paced world, the ability to shop for books, clothes, and other merchandise at midnight, when traditional stores are usually closed, is a benefit for both buyers and sellers. The Internet allows even small firms to reduce the impact of geography on their operations.

Despite these benefits, many companies that chose to make the Internet the core of their marketing strategies—often called "dot-coms"—failed to earn profits or acquire sufficient resources to remain in business. Many dot-coms went bankrupt because they thought the only thing that mattered was brand awareness. In reality, however, Internet markets are more similar to traditional markets than they are different.[7] Thus, successful e-marketing strategies, like traditional marketing strategies, depend on creating, distributing, promoting, and pricing products that customers need or want, not merely developing a brand name or reducing the costs associated with online transactions.

Like the failed dot-coms, many Canadian retailers continue to go online only for promotional reasons, not considering the other attributes that the Internet offers to creative marketers. Costs of e-business are getting lower, and the ability to mine data from online sales to build lifetime relationships with customers is a key advantage to online marketing.

Not all online marketers do a good job of marketing in a virtual environment. A U.S. study revealed that seven percent of shoppers gave up trying to purchase online due to transaction problems. Key problems included a lack of information or incorrect information, getting stuck in endless processing loops, having poorly designed websites, or being kicked out of the website during the purchase process.[8]

Indeed, e-marketing has not changed all industries, although it has had more of an impact in some industries in which the costs of business and customer transactions are very high. Traditional retailers continue to do quite well in some areas that many people thought the Internet would dominate just a few years ago. It was anticipated that the Internet would take over a large percentage of retail sales. However, this hasn't happened. Online retail sales in 2004 totalled only $3 billion out of $26.5 billion, with 89 percent of online sales happening in the B2B market, not the B2C market. E-commerce accounted for less than one percent of all retail sales in Canada, to the relief of offline retailers.[9] But B2C online sales are growing rapidly. In 2005, B2C e-commerce totalled $5.2 billion, increasing 25 percent to $8.3 billion in 2006. Total online revenues for the B2C market are expected to grow to $10.5 billion in 2007, and to $16 billion by 2009.[10]

Fifty-eight percent of Canadians, a total of 19.3 million people, had access to the Internet in 2006. Of those, 59 percent had broadband access. Over 80 percent of Canadian Internet users like to browse online, while 56 percent actually buy online.[11] Key factors limiting Canadian shoppers from buying online continue to be fear of credit card fraud and control of private information.[12]

Research has shown that online marketing has a great impact on offline purchasing. Online shoppers are very concerned about price, and a firm's profits can vanish quickly as competition drives prices down. Many consumers choose to do their research online, while shopping in traditional store environments. For example, few consumers are willing to spend $30 000 online to purchase a new automobile. However, consumers are increasingly making car-buying decisions on the basis of information found online.[13] A study by the JC Williams Group indicated that over 60 percent of Canadian offline shoppers have been influenced by online marketing when buying automobiles and accessories, appliances, furniture, home and garden supplies, and groceries.

Consumer-Generated Electronic Marketing

While Internet-based marketing has generated exciting opportunities to interact with consumers, it is important to recognize that electronic marketing and related technologies are more consumer-driven than traditional markets. Two major factors have caused consumer-generated information to gain importance:

1. Consumers' desire to learn about other consumers' opinions and experiences

2. Consumers' increased ability to find information from other consumers' postings and to forward information about their own experiences[14]

Indeed, consumers often rely on the recommendations and suggestions from friends and family when making purchasing decisions. These informal exchanges of communication are often referred to as word of mouth, but online or electronic word-of-mouth practices are advancing rapidly.[15]

blogs Web-based journals in which people can editorialize and interact with other Internet users

wikis Software that creates an interface that enables users to add or edit the content of some types of websites (also called wikis or wikipages)

Today marketers must recognize the impact of not only websites but also instant messaging, blogs, online forums, mailing lists, and wikis, as well as text messaging via cell phones and podcasts via MP3 players (see Table 9.1). **Blogs** (short for "weblogs") are web-based journals in which writers can editorialize and interact with other Internet users, while **wikis** are software that create an interface that enables users to add or edit the content of some types of websites (also called wikis or wikipages). One of the best-known wikis is Wikipedia.com, an online encyclopedia. Marketers must also monitor websites with less than flattering names, such as

table 9.1	TECHNOLOGIES THAT PROVIDE CONSUMERS WITH MARKETING INFORMATION
Blogs	Online journals in which people can post entries about their personal experiences, interests, and hobbies
MP3 players	Allows users to listen to music or voice recordings in MP3 format
Handheld and wireless devices	Web-enabled devices including cell phones, personal digital assistants, and integrated devices such as Blackberries that permit users to access the Internet
Podcasts	Audio or video files, such as radio programs or videos, that can be downloaded from the Internet using either RSS or Atom syndication for listening on mobile devices and personal computers. The subscription feed of automatically delivered new content distinguishes a podcast from a simple download or real-time audio streaming

walmart-blows.com, ihatedell.net, or targetsucks.com in order to gain insight into public opinion about their firms. Social networks, such as MySpace.com, Youtube.com, CarSpace.com, livejournal.com, or Slashdot.com, allow subscribers to blog and share anecdotes and experiences, often with pictures, audio, or even videos. For example, after Jeff Jarvis had an unhappy experience with Dell's ineffective attempts to resolve problems with his new laptop, he wrote about it on his blog. Within days his blog became one of the most visited websites, and it triggered a surge of Dell horror stories across the Web. Soon after when people typed "Dell" into search engines, Jarvis's blog and websites with unflattering names would appear on the first listings page.[16]

Although one estimate indicates that Google handles an estimated two-thirds of the world's Internet search queries, people may use several different search engines, and new search engines are evolving for almost every subject. Each search engine may be tailored to a different specific task, such as searching blog postings, video clips, or Internet shopping sites like Become.com. They permit users to look for specific targeted information that traditional search engines cannot supply. Startups such as Jeteye and Kaboodle use the experiences of prior searchers to refine searches and offer more useful results. These "social searches" instill human preferences into computer search algorithms to unearth more relevant and useful information. Yahoo! recently acquired five startups focused on building online community content in the hopes that this will improve searching through people.[17]

Basic Characteristics of Electronic Marketing

Although e-marketing is similar to traditional marketing, it is helpful to understand the basic characteristics that distinguish this environment from the traditional marketing environment. These characteristics include addressability, interactivity, memory, control, accessibility, and digitalization.

Addressability. The technology of the Internet makes it possible for visitors to a website to identify themselves and provide information about their product needs and wants before making a purchase. The ability of a marketer to identify customers before they make a purchase is called **addressability.** Many websites encourage visitors to register to maximize their use of the site or to gain access to premium areas; some even require it. Registration forms typically ask for basic information, such as name,

addressability A marketer's ability to identify customers before they make a purchase

Canadian Youth Online

A landmark Canadian study conducted on behalf of the Media-Awareness Network has determined that youth spend a fair amount of time online, and they are not necessarily doing their homework! Ninety-four percent of young Canadians said they went online from home.

Almost six in 10 young said they use chat rooms. Seventy-one percent had their own e-mail account. Of those who did, eight in 10 had a free Web-based e-mail account. Almost six in 10 young people used Instant Messaging, including 27 percent who use it every day or almost every day. Almost 90 percent played games online. Online diaries or blogs have become popular as a form of self-expression, and most youth reported meeting new friends online, or socializing online with friends in their community.

As a homework tool, the Internet was ranked first among young people as their preferred information source (44 percent), followed by books from the public library (19 percent), and books from school (16 percent). Almost half used the Internet at least an hour every day, compared with 79 percent who say they watch television for an hour or more every day. Youth with their own Internet access spent twice as long online as those who shared Internet access on a family computer.

Most experts consider young people's abilities to integrate technology into their lives a positive thing. However, some reported having encountered online threats in chat rooms, as well as accidental exposure to pornographic images. Only 13 percent of youth were supervised by parents when they were online.

Addressability

Addressability is a company's ability to identify customers before they make a purchase.

cookie An identifying string of text stored on a website visitor's computer

e-mail address, age, and occupation, from which marketers can build user profiles to enhance their marketing efforts. CDNow (a partner of Amazon.com), for example, asks music lovers to supply information about their listening tastes so the company can recommend new releases. Some websites even offer contests and prizes to encourage users to register. Marketers can also conduct surveys to learn more about the people who access their websites, offering prizes as motivation to participate.

Addressability represents the ultimate expression of the marketing concept. With the knowledge about individual customers garnered through the Web, marketers can tailor marketing mixes more precisely to target customers with narrow interests, such as recorded blues music or golf. Addressability also facilitates tracking website visits and online buying activity, which makes it easier for marketers to accumulate data about individual customers to enhance future marketing efforts. Amazon.com, for example, stores data about customers' purchases and uses that information to make recommendations the next time they visit the site.

Some website software can store a **cookie,** an identifying string of text, on a visitor's computer. Marketers use cookies to track how often a particular user visits the website, what he or she may look at while there, and in what sequence. Cookies also permit website visitors to customize services, such as virtual shopping carts, as well as the particular content they see when they log onto a webpage. CNN, for example, allows visitors to its website to create a custom news page tailored to their particular interests. The use of cookies to store customer information can be an ethical issue, however, depending on how the data are used. If a website owner can use cookies to link a visitor's interests to a name and address, that information could be sold to advertisers and other parties without the visitor's consent or even knowledge. The potential for misuse of cookies has made many consumers wary of this technology. Because technology allows access to large quantities of data about customers' use of websites, companies must carefully consider how the use of such information affects individuals' privacy, as we discuss in more detail later in this chapter.

interactivity The ability to allow customers to express their needs and wants directly to the firm in response to the firm's marketing communications

Interactivity. Another distinguishing characteristic of e-marketing is **interactivity,** which allows customers to express their needs and wants directly to the firm in response to its marketing communications. This means marketers can interact with prospective customers in real time (or at least a close approximation of it). Of course, salespeople have always been able to do this, but at a much greater cost. The Web provides the advantages of a virtual sales representative, with broader market coverage and at lower cost.

Interactivity helps marketers maintain high-quality relationships with existing customers by shaping customer expectations and perceptions. Customers with a higher expectation of continuing a relationship with a marketer are more likely to maintain that relationship even after a less than satisfactory experience with that firm.[18] To help build such relationships, companies are using the Internet to share increasing levels of information with customers. Amazon.com, for example, launched Search Inside the Book, which enables customers to search for a word or phrase in 120 000 books. After the new feature was introduced, sales for searchable books rose by nine percent over books not included in the service.[19]

One implication of interactivity is that a firm's customers can also communicate with other customers (and non-customers) through mailing lists, blogs, and word of mouth. For this reason, differences in the amount and type of information possessed by marketers and their customers are less pronounced than in the past. One result is that the new- and used-car businesses have become considerably more competitive because buyers are coming into dealerships armed with more complete product and cost information obtained through comparison shopping on the Net. By providing information, ideas, and a context for interacting with other customers, e-marketers can enhance customers' interest in and involvement with their products.

community A sense of group membership or feeling of belonging by individual members

Interactivity also enables marketers to capitalize on the concept of community to help customers derive value from the firm's products and website. **Community** refers to a sense of group membership or feeling of belonging by individual members of a group.[20] One such community is Tripod, a website where Generation Xers can create their own webpages and chat or exchange messages on bulletin boards about topics ranging from cars and computers to health and careers. Another example is iVillage, a website targeted at women. Because such communities have well-defined demographics and share common interests, they represent a valuable audience for marketers, which typically fund the sites through advertising.

Another way to interact with customers is through blogs. There are an estimated five million blogs on a variety of topics, including companies, brands, and products, and they can be positive—raves about Manolo shoes, for example—or negative—such as rages against Wal-Mart, Kmart, and Best Buy. When Shayne McQuade invented a backpack with solar panels that let backpackers keep their gadgets charged, a friend mentioned the product on his blog, which soon led to references and discussions on other blogs, and ultimately, created a positive "buzz" and orders for the new product. Companies are increasingly establishing blogs to interact with customers. General Motors, for example, hosts the GM Smallblock Engine blog, where employees and customers marvel over Corvettes and other GM vehicles.[21]

memory The ability to access databases or data warehouses containing individual customer profiles and purchase histories and use these data in real time to customize a marketing offer

database A collection of information arranged for easy access and retrieval

Memory **Memory** refers to a firm's ability to access databases or data warehouses containing individual customer profiles and purchase histories and use these data in real time to customize its marketing offer to a specific customer. A **database** is a collection of information arranged for easy access and retrieval. Although companies have had database systems for many years, the information these systems contain did not become available on a real-time basis until fairly recently. Current software technology allows a marketer to identify a specific visitor to its website instantaneously, locate that customer's profile in its database, and then display the customer's past purchases or suggest new products based on past purchases while he or she is still at the site. For example, Bluefly, an online clothing retailer, asks visitors to provide their e-mail addresses, clothing preferences, brand preferences, and sizes so it can create a customized online catalogue of clothing that matches the customer's specified preferences. The firm uses customer purchase profiles to manage its merchandise buying. Whenever it adds new clothing items to its inventory, it checks them against its database of customer preferences and, if it finds a match, alerts the individual in an e-mail message. Applying memory to large numbers of customers represents a significant advantage when a firm uses it to learn more about individual customers each time they visit the firm's website.

control Customers' ability to regulate the information they view and the rate and sequence of their exposure to that information

Control. In the context of e-marketing, **control** refers to customers' ability to regulate the information they view and the rate and sequence of their exposure to that information. The Web is sometimes referred to as a *pull* medium because users determine what they view at websites; website operators' ability to control the content users look at and in what sequence is limited. In contrast, television can be characterized as a *push* medium because the broadcaster determines what the viewer sees once she or he has selected a particular channel. Both television and radio provide "limited exposure control" (you see or hear whatever is broadcast until you change the station).

Use of Internet for comparison shopping has shifted power from the retailer to the consumer. With the shift in power comes a more dramatic need for online retailers to facilitate customer service and provide reliable information to help consumers make decisions. In order to maximize the pull value of the medium, online marketers must be able to attract and hold a customer's interest. For e-marketers, the primary implication of control is that attracting—and retaining—customers' attention is more difficult. Marketers have to work harder and more creatively to communicate the value

The Smart Phone

Why settle for regular cellular communication when you can have much more? Why not have a cell phone that is also a computer and an e-mail machine? Why not play movies on your telephone as well as make videos and still photos? Do your day planning, answer your e-mail, check the news, weather and sports, all from the wireless comfort of your home, work, or car.

The wireless world is growing rapidly. There are nearly two billion wireless devices in use worldwide, and about 100 million are smart phones. The technology continues to grow with Research in Motion's (RIM) foray into the field with the famous Blackberry. As prices come down and features continue to be loaded into razor handheld devices, the devices will become more common and will have an even greater impact in the B2C, B2B, and C2C markets.

Canada's RIM introduced the Blackberry 880 in February 2007 at the 3GSM World Congress, a wireless-industry trade show in Barcelona, Spain. The Blackberry 880 contains a media player and an expandable memory slot for video and music. It also boasts GPS software and Bluetooth technology to accommodate wireless headsets. RIM will sell the new Blackberry worldwide going head-to-head with competing offerings.

of their websites clearly and quickly, or the viewer may lose interest and move on to another site. With literally hundreds of millions of unique pages of content available to any web surfer, simply putting a website on the Internet does not guarantee anyone will visit it or make a purchase. Publicizing the website may require innovative promotional activities. For this reason, many firms pay millions of dollars to advertise their products or websites on high-traffic sites such as AOL Canada. Because of AOL's growing status as a **portal** (a multi-service website that serves as a gateway to other websites), firms are eager to link to it and other such sites to help draw attention to their own sites. Indeed, consumers spend most of their time online on portal sites such as MSN and Yahoo!, checking e-mail, tracking stocks, and perusing news, sports, and weather.

portal A multiservice website that serves as a gateway to other websites

Accessibility. An extraordinary amount of information is available on the Internet. The ability to obtain information is referred to as **accessibility.** Because customers can access in-depth information about competing products, prices, reviews, and so forth, they are much better informed about a firm's products and their relative value than ever before. Someone looking to buy a new truck, for example, can go to the websites of Ford, Toyota, and Dodge to compare the features of the Ford F-150, the Toyota Tundra, and the Dodge Ram. The truck buyer can also access online magazines and pricing guides to get more specific information about product features, performance, and prices. Many new- and used-car buyers turn to independent websites such as Kelley Blue Book, Edmunds, and Autobytel for pricing information before they go to a dealership to negotiate for a new vehicle.

accessibility The ability to obtain information available on the Internet

Accessibility dramatically increases competition for Internet users' attention. Without substantial promotion, such as advertising on portals like AOL, MSN, Yahoo!, and other high-traffic sites, it is becoming increasingly difficult to attract a visitor's attention to a particular website. Consequently e-marketers have to be increasingly creative and innovative to attract visitors to their sites.

digitalization The ability to represent a product, or at least some of its benefits, as digital bits of information

Digitalization. **Digitalization** is the ability to represent a product, or at least some of its benefits, as digital bits of information. Digitalization allows marketers to use the Internet to distribute, promote, and sell those features apart from the physical item itself. FedEx, for example, has developed web-based software that allows consumers and business customers to track their own packages from starting point to destination. Distributed over the Web at very low cost, the online tracking system adds value to FedEx's delivery services. Digitalization can be enhanced for users who have broadband access to the Internet because broadband's faster connections allow streaming audio and video and other new technologies.

In addition to providing distribution efficiencies, digitizing part of a product's features allows new combinations of features and services to be created quickly and inexpensively. For example, a service station that keeps a customer's history of automotive oil changes in a database can e-mail that customer when the next oil change is due and at the same time suggest other types of preventive maintenance, such as tire rotation or a tune-up. Digital features are easy to mix and match to meet the demands of individual customers.

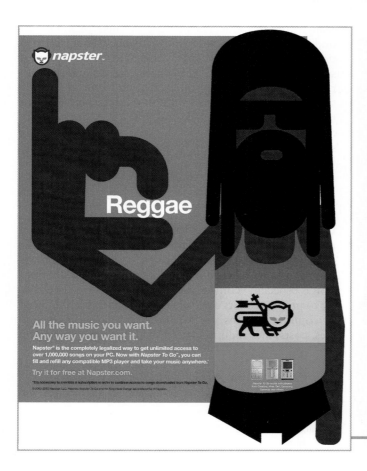

Digitalization
Napster offers music downloads of over one million songs.

E-Marketing Strategies

Now that we have examined some distinguishing characteristics of doing business on the Internet, let's consider how these characteristics affect marketing strategy. Marketing strategy involves creating a marketing mix to satisfy individuals in a target market, regardless of whether those individuals are accessible online or through more traditional avenues. However, there are significant differences in how the marketing mix components are developed and combined into a marketing strategy in the electronic environment of the Web. As we continue this discussion, keep in mind that the Internet is a very dynamic environment, and therefore e-marketing strategies may need to be modified frequently to keep pace.

Product Considerations. The growth of the Internet and the World Wide Web presents exciting opportunities for marketing products to both consumers and organizations. Computers and computer peripherals, industrial supplies, and packaged software are the leading business purchases online. Consumer products account for a small but growing percentage of Internet transactions, with food and beverage, sporting goods, and home goods among the fastest-growing online consumer purchases. Through e-marketing, companies can provide products, including goods, services, and ideas, that offer unique benefits and improve customer satisfaction.

The online marketing of goods such as computer hardware and software, books, videos, DVDs, CDs, toys, automobiles, and even groceries is accelerating rapidly. Services may have the greatest potential for online marketing success. Many websites offer or enhance services ranging from home- and car-buying assistance to travel reservations and stock trading. At Century 21's website, consumers can search for the home of their dreams, get information about mortgages and credit, read tips on buying real estate, and learn about the company's relocation services.

The Canadian tourism industry has been one of the most receptive to e-commerce. Up to 20 percent of all tourism revenues are booked online.[22] Tourism firms allocate approximately four percent of their revenues to advertising,[23] with about 1.8 percent of their promotional budgets allocated to online advertising.[24] The proliferation of information on the World Wide Web has itself spawned new services. Web search engines and directories such as Google, Yahoo!, Lycos, and Excite are among the most heavily accessed sites on the Internet. Without these services, which track and index the vast quantity of information available on the Web, the task of finding something of interest would be tantamount to searching for the proverbial needle in a haystack. Many of these services, most notably Yahoo!, have evolved into portals by offering additional services, including news, weather, chat rooms, free e-mail accounts, and shopping.

Distribution Considerations. The role of distribution is to make products available at the right time at the right place in the right quantities. The Internet can be viewed as a new distribution channel. Physical distribution is especially compatible with e-marketing. The ability to process orders electronically and increase the speed of communications via the Internet reduces inefficiencies, costs, and redundancies throughout the marketing

E-Marketing Strategies

The growth of the Internet has spawned immeasurable opportunity for online service companies such as Monster.com. Marketing messages are refined to appeal to both job hunters and head hunters.

channel. Most trucking firms now accept orders through the Internet, for example, but Yellow Transportation feeds order data from the Internet and the firm's call centres into a custom program to determine how many drivers it needs to schedule at its facilities around the world, saving $100 million a year.[25]

More firms are exploiting advances in information technology to synchronize the relationships between their manufacturing or product assembly and their customer contact operations. This increase in information sharing among the firm's various operations makes product customization easier to accomplish. Marketers can use their websites to query customers about their needs and then manufacture products that exactly fit those needs. Gateway and Dell, for example, help customers build their own computers by asking them to specify what components to include; the firms then assemble and ship the customized products directly to the customers in a few days. Imperial Sugar lets customers place orders, check stock, and track shipments via its website, which now accounts for 10 percent of the firm's sales.[26]

One of the most visible members of any marketing channel is the retailer, and the Internet is increasingly becoming a retail venue. The Internet provides an opportunity for marketers of everything from computers to travel reservations to encourage exchanges. Amazon.com, for example, sold more than $8 billion of books, CDs, DVDs, videos, toys, games, and electronics directly from its website in 2005.[27] Indeed, Amazon.com's success at marketing books online has been so phenomenal that many imitators have adopted its retailing model for everything from CDs to toys. Another retailing venture is online auctioneers, such as eBay, which auction everything from fine wines and golf clubs to computer goods and electronics.

ING Direct: Internet Banking—and Innovation—at Its Best

Nearly 20 million customers are served by ING Direct in Canada, the United States, Australia, Austria, France, Germany, Italy, Spain, and the United Kingdom.

What's the company's success secret? In a word: innovation. ING Direct has built a reputation as an easy-to-use, reliable bank, while it has rejected traditional banking conventions. Instead of providing high-service contact on every corner, it exploits a range of technological innovations that make it possible to move money around the world electronically. Instead of showering customers with free toasters, it offers them low-cost, simple banking products. Instead of interacting directly with its customers (such one-on-one service would be expensive and time-consuming), ING Direct relies on paperless transactions, which reduce costs and improve speed, efficiency, and service to its clients.

The company's marketing strategy is seamless. Its tagline states its aim succinctly: *Save your Money*. Its logo is no stately flag or imposing rock, but a simple bright orange, hard-to-miss circle. And you know those brick and mortar locations? They're *cafés*, where customers can attend seminars, surf the Net, ask questions of on-site sales associates, and yes, have a cup of coffee.

ING studied the lifestyles and habits of its most profitable customers and applied what it learned to attract prospects with similar characteristics. Its target customers are Internet-savvy, savings-minded parents aged 30 to 50. The bank's typical customer is comfortable but not wealthy, with average deposits of around $14 000.

ING Direct meets its goal of low-cost, simple transactions by letting savers open accounts with no fees and no minimums, and by consistently offering some of the best interest rates in Canada. Its mortgages have no application fee, a simple no-hassle application, and great rates that compared with the 30-year fixed mortgages offered by traditional banks can save customers thousands of dollars on their mortgages.

When ING Direct says it, they mean it: *Save your Money*.

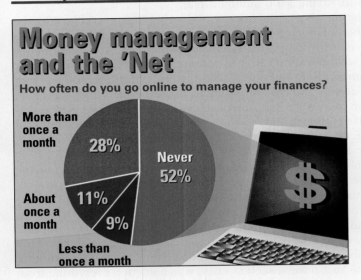

Money management and the 'Net

How often do you go online to manage your finances?

More than once a month — 28%

Never — 52%

About once a month — 11%

9% — Less than once a month

The Internet is quickly becoming part of a hybrid channel system for many retailers, who find that selling online is just one way to distribute their products. Hybrid channels are multi-channel systems that employ many different ways of getting the goods to the customer. Many retailers still rely on other direct marketing methods, including personal selling, in-home selling and catalogue sales.[28] Over 70 percent of online shoppers also received at least three catalogues over the last year.[29] The Direct Sellers Association of Canada reports that 62 percent of all direct sales happen in the home, with about 11 percent happening online.[30] The online channel makes an ideal complement to more traditional channels of distribution.

Promotion Considerations. The Internet is an interactive medium that can be used to inform, entertain, and persuade target markets to accept an organization's products. In fact, gathering information about goods and services is one of the main reasons people use the Internet. College students in particular say they are influenced by Internet ads when buying online or just researching product purchases.[31] The accessibility and interactivity of the Internet allow marketers to complement their traditional media usage for promotional efforts. The control characteristic of e-marketing means that customers who visit a firm's website are there because they choose to be, indicating they are interested in the firm's products and therefore can be at least somewhat involved in its website's message and dialogue. For these reasons, the Internet represents a highly cost-effective communication tool for small businesses.

Many companies augment their TV and print advertising campaigns with web-based promotions. Kraft, Ragu, and Splenda, for example, have created websites with recipes and entertaining tips to help consumers get the most out of their products. Many movie studios have set up websites at which visitors can view clips of their latest releases, and television commercials for new movies often encourage viewers to visit these sites. In addition, many companies choose to advertise their goods, services, and ideas on portals, search engines, and even other firms' websites. Table 9.2 describes the most common types of advertisements found on websites. More than 80 percent of companies now include the Internet as an advertising medium.[32]

Many marketers are also offering buying incentives and adding value to their products online through the use of sales promotions, especially coupons. Several websites,

table 9.2   TYPES OF ADVERTISING ON WEBSITES

Banner ads	Small rectangular, static, or animated ads that typically appear at the top of a webpage
Keyword ads	Ads that relate to text or subject matter specified in a web search
Button ads	Small square or rectangular ads bearing a corporate or brand name or logo and usually appearing at the bottom or side of a webpage
Pop-up ads	Large ads that open in a separate web browser window on top of the website being viewed
Pop-under ads	Large ads that open in a new browser window underneath the website being viewed
Sponsorship ads	Ads that integrate companies' brands and products with the editorial content of certain websites

including coolsavings.com, valupage.com, and valpak.com, offer online coupons for their members.

The characteristics of e-marketing make promotional efforts on the Internet significantly different from those using more traditional media. First, because Internet users can control what they see, customers who visit a firm's website are there because they choose to be, which implies, as pointed out previously, that they are interested in the firm's products and therefore may be more involved in the message and dialogue provided at the site. Second, the interactivity characteristic allows marketers to enter into dialogues with customers to learn more about their interests and needs. This information can then be used to tailor promotional messages to individual customers. In fact, customized communications can help reduce information overload and improve buying decisions, which can enhance customer relationships.[33] Finally, addressability can make marketing efforts directed at specific customers more effective. Indeed, direct marketing combined with effective analysis of customer databases may become one of e-marketing's most valuable promotional tools.

Pricing Considerations. Pricing relates to perceptions of value and is the most flexible element of the marketing mix. Electronic marketing facilitates both price and non-price competition because the accessibility characteristic of e-marketing gives consumers access to more information about the costs and prices of products than has ever been available to them before. A key benefit of online selling is that with the declining costs of having e-commerce, a firm's breakeven point is reduced and they can quickly reach the point where every new online customer provides incremental revenue. This can quickly add to the bottom line, particularly for firms that do not have a traditional retail outlet.

Shipping charges are an area of concern for many Internet buyers who claim that delivery costs make online purchasing too expensive. Over 70 percent of Canadian online shoppers indicated that they would buy from catalogues more often if shipping was free.[34] Many brick and mortar firms, like the Hudson Bay Company, utilize their store networks to facilitate easy pickup for online shoppers, helping to avoid high shipping charges. When ordering from HBC.com, customers can have products delivered to their door or to the nearest store. Sears has gone a step further by tying its online store with its existing network of catalogue delivery centres. This allows customers to choose whether to pay a fee to have their goods delivered to their door, or to travel to a nearby catalogue delivery centre to pick up their goods for free. It is important to remember that the total, delivered price, impacts the customer's overall perception of value.

Customer Relationship Management

One characteristic of companies engaged in e-marketing is a renewed focus on relationship marketing by building customer loyalty and retaining desired customers—in other words, on customer relationship management (CRM). As we noted in Chapter 1, CRM focuses on using information about customers to create marketing strategies that develop and sustain desirable long-term customer relationships. Procter & Gamble, for example, encourages Oil of Olay customers to join Club Olay, an online community with some four million members. In exchange for beauty tips, coupons, and special offers, the website collects some information about customers and their use of the skincare product.[35] CRM focuses on analyzing and using databases and leveraging technologies to identify strategies and methods that will maximize the lifetime value of each desirable customer to the firm.[36] Four dimensions of CRM include top management involvement and commitment; organizational alignment (people, systems, and processes); customer differentiation and management; and technology to develop analytical, collaborative, and operational management.[37]

A focus on customer relationship management is possible in e-marketing because of marketers' abilities to target individual customers. This effort is enhanced over time as customers invest time and effort into "teaching" the firm what they want. This investment in the firm also increases the costs a customer would incur by switching to another company. Once a customer has learned to trade stocks online through Charles Schwab, for example, there is a cost associated with leaving to find a new brokerage firm: another firm may offer less service, and it may take time to find a new firm and learn a new system. Any time a marketer can learn more about its customers to strengthen the match between its marketing mix and target customers' desires and preferences, it increases the perceived costs of switching to another firm. Strong customer identification with a company can also help build meaningful relationships and even turn customers into "champions" of those companies and their products.[38]

E-marketing permits companies to target customers more precisely and accurately than ever before. The addressability, interactivity, and memory characteristics of e-marketing allow marketers to identify specific customers, establish interactive dialogues with them to learn about their needs, and combine this information with their purchase histories to customize products to meet those needs. Like many online retailers, Amazon.com stores and analyzes purchase data to understand each customer's interests. This information helps the retailer improve its ability to satisfy individual customers and thereby increase sales of books, music, movies, and other products to each customer. The ability to identify individual customers allows marketers to shift their focus from targeting groups of similar customers to increasing their share of an individual customer's purchases. Thus, the emphasis shifts from *share of market* to *share of customer*. However, improving share of customer by maximizing customer loyalty can be difficult.[39]

Database Marketing

Database marketing uses an electronic information database.

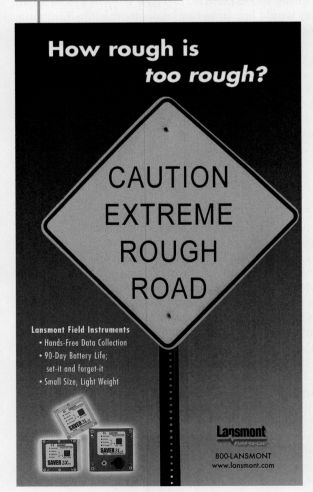

How rough is *too rough?*

CAUTION
EXTREME
ROUGH
ROAD

Lansmont Field Instruments
• Hands-Free Data Collection
• 90-Day Battery Life;
  set-it and forget-it
• Small Size, Light Weight

Lansmont
Field-to-Lab
800-LANSMONT
www.lansmont.com

Database Marketing

CRM employs database marketing techniques to identify different types of customers and develop specific strategies for interacting with each customer. It incorporates three elements:

1. Identifying and building a database of current and potential consumers, including a wide range of demographic, lifestyle, and purchase information

2. Delivering differential messages according to each consumer's preferences and characteristics through established and new media channels

3. Tracking customer relationships to monitor the costs of retaining individual customers and the lifetime value of their purchases[40]

It is important for marketers to distinguish *active* customers—those likely to continue buying from the firm—from *inactive* customers—those who are likely to defect and those who have already defected. This information should help to (a) identify profitable inactive customers who can be reactivated, (b) remove inactive unprofitable customers from the customer database, and (c) identify active customers who should be targeted with regular marketing activities.[41] Table 9.3 examines types of databases and how marketers can use them for customer relationship management.

Another aspect of CRM is supplier relationship marketing (SRM), which also uses databases to manage relationships and communications with vendors and other individuals and companies that supply goods, services, and ideas to a firm. SRM uses information technology to develop databases and measures for assessing and managing these relationships. It is necessary to monitor supplier relationships and track performance in order to assess quality and determine vendors' value to the overall operation. These systems and processes are important in creating value and effective relationships with a firm's own customers.[42]

table 9.3	TYPES OF DATABASES	
	What are they?	**What do they do?**
Customer databases	Contain information about a company's current customers and thereby form the core of any marketing database	Store basic data—name, address, zip code, and telephone number; demographic data—age, gender, marital status, education, income, and so on; psychographic data—values, activities, interests, preferences, and so on; transaction histories; inquiries and referrals
Prospect databases	Contain information about prospects—non-customers with profiles similar to those of existing customers; should include as much information about prospects as the customer database does about current customers	Supply information to be used to design marketing campaigns to target prospects and turn them into lifetime customers
Cluster databases	Contain information about relatively small clusters of people who can be defined based on geographic reference, affinity (e.g., clubs and associations), and lifestyle reference groups; people in the same cluster tend to have similar interests, attitudes, purchasing habits, and preferences	Help marketers identify clusters to which prospective customers belong and to customize marketing communications according to membership of prospective customers in specific clusters
Enhancement databases	Collect additional information about customers and prospects—demographic and psychographic data, transaction histories, address changes, income changes, privacy status, and new product categories recently purchased	Help marketers better target advertising and marketing campaigns, expand brand reach, improve acquisition and retention rates and thereby profitability

Source: Adapted from V. Kumar, "Customer Relationship Management," custom module for William M. Pride and O. C. Ferrell, *Marketing,* 14th ed. (Boston: Houghton Mifflin, 2006), www.prideferrell.com.

Customer Lifetime Value

Focusing on share of customer requires recognizing that all customers have different needs and that all customers do not have equal value to a firm. Thus, a firm should ensure that individual target customers have sufficient potential to justify such specialized efforts. Indeed, one benefit arising from the addressability characteristic of e-marketing is that firms can track and analyze individual customers' purchases and identify the most profitable and loyal customers. The most basic application of this idea is the 80/20 rule: 80 percent of business profits come from 20 percent of customers. Although this idea is not new, advances in technology and data collection techniques now permit firms to profile customers in real time. The goal is to assess the worth of individual customers and thus estimate their lifetime value to the firm. The concept of customer lifetime value (CLV) may include not only an individual's propensity to engage in purchases but also his or her strong word-of-mouth communication about the firm's products.[43] Some customers—those who require considerable hand holding or return products frequently—may simply be too expensive to retain given the low level of profits they generate. Companies can discourage these unprofitable customers by requiring them to pay higher fees for additional services. For example, many banks and brokerages charge hefty maintenance fees on small accounts. Such practices allow firms to focus their resources on developing and managing long-term relationships with more profitable customers.[44] Developing systematic CRM procedures is thus one of the most important steps in managing relationships.[45]

Thus, managing customer relationships requires allocating resources selectively to different customers based on the economic value of their relationship to the firm. CLV is a key measurement that forecasts a customer's lifetime economic contribution based on continued relationship marketing efforts. It can be calculated by taking the sum of the customer's present value contributions to profit margins over a specific timeframe. For example, the lifetime value of a Lexus customer could be predicted by how many new automobiles Lexus could sell the customer over a period of years and developing a summation of the contribution to margins across the time period. The sales value has been estimated at $600 000. Data from past customer and other information of the effectiveness of relationship efforts could assist in this projection. While this is not an exact science, knowing a customer's potential lifetime value can help marketers determine how best to allocate resources to marketing strategies to sustain that customer over a lifetime.

CLV is the only gauge that incorporates revenue, expense, and customer and adopts a customer-centric approach.[46] As such, the concept can help companies confront marketing issues with greater confidence by exploring these questions:

- Which customers should be provided with preferential and sometimes personal treatment?

- Which customers should the firm interact through inexpensive channels like the Internet or the telephone and which should be let go altogether?

- How do firms decide the timing of an offering to a customer?

- Which prospects will make good customers in the future, and therefore are worthwhile to attract now?

- How many and what resources should the firm allocate to secure future business with a current customer?

- How should firms monitor customer activity to determine whether adjustments to their marketing initiatives are required?[47]

If a company truly understands each customer's lifetime value, it can maximize its own value by boosting the number, scope, and duration of value-enhancing customer relationships. To do that, managers would have to determine how much revenue each customer would generate in the future and subtract the expected costs of acquiring, serving, and keeping that customer.[48] Thus the concept of CLV helps marketers adopt appropriate marketing activities today to increase future profitability.

Technology Drives CRM

CRM focuses on building satisfying exchange relationships between buyers and sellers by gathering useful data at all customer-contact points—telephone, fax, online, and personal—and analyzing those data to better understand customers' needs and desires. Companies are increasingly automating and managing customer relationships through technology. Indeed, one fast-growing area of CRM is customer support and call-centre software, which helps companies capture information about all interactions with customers and provides a profile of the most important aspects of the customer experience on the Web and on the phone. Using technology, marketers can analyze interactions with customers to identify performance issues and even build a library of "best practices" for customer interaction.[49] Customer support and call-centre software can focus on those aspects of customer interaction that are most relevant to performance, such as how long customers have to wait on the phone to ask a question of a service representative or how long they must wait to receive a response from an online request. This technology can also help marketers determine whether call-centre personnel are missing opportunities to promote additional products or provide better service. For example, after buying a new Saab automobile, the customer is supposed to meet a service mechanic who can answer any technical questions about the car during the first service visit. Saab follows up this visit with a telephone survey to determine whether the new-car buyer met the Saab mechanic and to learn about the buyer's experience with the first service call.

Sales automation software can link a firm's sales force to e-marketing applications that facilitate selling and providing service to customers. Often these applications enable customers to assist themselves instead of using traditional sales and service organizations. At Cisco, for example, 80 percent of all customer support questions can be answered online through the firm's website, eliminating 75 000 phone calls a month.[50] In addition, CRM systems can provide sales managers with information that helps them develop the best product solutions for customers and thus maximize service. Dell Computer, for example, employs CRM data to identify those customers with the greatest need for computer hardware and then provides these select customers with additional value in the form of free, secure, customized websites. These "premier pages" allow customers—typically large companies—to check their order status, arrange deliveries, and troubleshoot problems. Although Dell collects considerable data about its customers from its online sales transactions, the company avoids selling customer lists to outside vendors.[51] CRM applications such as that used by Dell include software for marketing automation, sales automation, and customer support and call centres.

It is important to distinguish between CRM systems and CRM processes. CRM systems, including computers and software, integrate relevant customer and product information. CRM processes involve the measures required to retain customers and provide effective marketing initiatives through continuous interaction with customers.[52] CRM systems provide the infrastructure needed to secure the data that generate information for marketing strategies.

Customer Satisfaction Is the End Result of CRM

Although technology drives CRM and can help companies build relationships with desirable customers, it is too often used as a cost reduction tactic or a tool for selling, with little thought toward developing and sustaining long-term relationships. Some

Mining Customer Opinions with Technology

Successful marketers take the time to study and understand consumer buying because it can influence the strategies a company uses to reach a particular target market. Increasingly, many companies such as Citigroup, Johnson & Johnson, Pfizer, and Procter & Gamble are turning to online software to create large-scale focus groups to help them understand their customers and their needs and wants. Companies that sell such software aim to help marketers listen to what their customers want rather than designing marketing campaigns based on generic strategies.

For years, companies have brought together small groups of people for traditional face-to-face focus groups to discuss products while marketers listen (often from another room) to their interactions. Edmund Sarraille, CEO of Informative, which markets the new focus-group software, says that the advantage of large-scale online focus groups is that they can reach a much larger audience and therefore capture a much wider range of ideas and opinions. This may yield more accurate information about what customers want.

Consider that for years, Lego has been producing the same Lego sets based on feedback from traditional focus groups. When Informative conducted an online focus group for the company involving 10 000 people—all Lego customers who were invited via e-mail to participate in an online contest regarding new products—the result was essentially brainstorming in cyberspace, which resulted in customers suggesting departures from Lego's traditional toys.

companies spend millions to develop CRM systems, yet fail to achieve the associated benefits. These companies often see themselves as sophisticated users of technology to manage customers, but they do not view customers as assets. CRM is effective only when it is developed as a relationship-building tool. CRM is a process of reaching out to customers and building trust, not a technology solution for customer sales.[53] In addition, service quality and satisfaction depend on customer contact employees' commitment to their company and its customers as well as technology.[54]

Perhaps because of the software and information technology associated with collecting information from consumers and responding to their desires, some critics view CRM as a form of manipulation. It is possible to use information about customers at their expense to obtain quick results—for example, charging higher prices whenever possible and using available data to maximize profits. However, using CRM to foster customer loyalty does not require collecting every conceivable piece of data from consumers or trying to sell customers products they don't want. Marketers should not try to control customers; they should try to develop relationships that derive from the trust gained over many transactions and are sustained by the customers' belief that the company genuinely desires their continued patronage.[55] Trust reduces the costs associated with worrying about whether expectations will be honoured and simplifies customers' buying efforts in the future.

What marketers can do with CRM technology is identify their most valuable customers so they can make an investment in building long-term relationships with those customers.[56] To be successful, marketers must measure the effectiveness of their CRM systems in terms of their progress toward developing satisfactory customer relationships. Fewer than 20 percent of companies track customer retention, but developing and assessing customer loyalty is important in managing long-term customer relationships. At **www.loyaltyeffect.com,** a survey asks customers whether a company is worthy of their loyalty. Companies that rank high in customer loyalty on the survey include Enterprise Rent-a-Car, Harley-Davidson, L. L. Bean, and Northwestern Mutual.[57]

The most important component of CRM is remembering that it is not about technology but about relationships with customers. It has proven useful for business-to-business, business-to-customer, and non-profit marketing. In all cases, high-contact relationships may require greater effort in developing organizational identity.[58] CRM systems should ensure that marketers listen to customers and then respond to their needs and concerns to build long-term relationships. The Internet can provide a valuable listening post and serve as a medium to manage customer relationships.[59]

Legal and Ethical Issues in E-Marketing

How marketers use technology to gather information—both online and offline—to foster long-term relationships with customers has raised numerous legal and ethical issues. The popularity and widespread use of the Internet grew so quickly that global legal systems have been unable to keep pace with advances in technology. Among the issues of concern are personal privacy, unsolicited e-mail, and misappropriation of copyrighted intellectual property.

One of the most significant privacy issues involves the personal information companies collect from website visitors. A survey by the Progress and Freedom Foundation found that 96 percent of popular commercial websites collect personally identifying information from visitors.[60] In response to privacy concerns, some companies are cutting back on the amount of information they collect. Public concerns about online privacy remain, however, and many professionals in the industry are urging self-policing on this issue to head off potential regulation. One effort toward self-policing is the online privacy program developed by the BBBOnLine subsidiary of the Council of Better Business Bureaus. The program awards a privacy seal to companies that clearly disclose to their website visitors what information they are collecting and how they are using it.[61] Another important development is the Personal Information Protection and Electronic Documents Act (PIPEDA) (see Figure 9.1) which was designed to protect the privacy of individuals in an electronic age.

PIPEDA incorporates 10 privacy principles which were originally developed as part of the Canadian Standards Association's Model Code for the Protection of Personal Information. These privacy principles are listed in Figure 9.1.

There are some exceptions to these privacy principles. These include:

- personal information collected, used or disclosed solely for journalistic, artistic, or literary purposes;

- if the action clearly benefits the individual or if obtaining permission could infringe on the information's accuracy;

- where such data can contribute to a legal investigation or aid in an emergency where people's lives and safety could be at stake; and

- if disclosure aids, in times of emergency, matters of legal investigation, or facilitates the conservation of historically important records.[62]

spam Unsolicited commercial e-mail

Spam, or unsolicited commercial e-mail (UCE), has become a major source of frustration with the Internet. Many Internet users believe spam violates their privacy and steals their resources. Over 60 percent of spam originates in the United States.

---

figure 9.1   **CANADIAN STANDARDS ASSOCIATION'S MODEL CODE FOR THE PROTECTION OF PERSONAL INFORMATION**

1. Accountability: An organization is responsible for personal information under its control and shall designate an individual or individuals who are accountable for the organization's compliance with the following principles.
2. Identifying Purposes: The purposes for which personal information is collected shall be identified by the organization at or before the time the information is collected.
3. Consent: The knowledge and consent of the individual are required for the collection, use or disclosure of personal information, except when inappropriate.
4. Limiting Collection: The collection of personal information shall be limited to that which is necessary for the purposes identified by the organization. Information shall be collected by fair and lawful means.
5. Limiting Use, Disclosure, and Retention: Personal information shall not be used or disclosed for purposes other than those for which it was collected, except with the consent of the individual or as required by the law. Personal information shall be retained only as long as necessary for fulfilment of those purposes.
6. Accuracy: Personal information shall be as accurate, complete, and up-to-date as is necessary for the purposes for which it is to be used.
7. Safeguards: Personal information shall be protected by security safeguards appropriate to the sensitivity of the information.
8. Openness: An organization shall make readily available to individuals specific information about its policies and practices relating to the management of personal information.
9. Individual Access: Upon request, an individual shall be informed of the existence, use and disclosure of his or her personal information and shall be given access to that information. An individual shall be able to challenge the accuracy and completeness of the information and have it amended as appropriate.
10. Challenging Compliance: An individual shall be able to address a challenge concerning compliance with the above principles to the designated individual or individuals for the organization's compliance.

Source: http://canada.justice.gc.ca/en/news/nr/1998/attback2.html

stop spam now

Shut it off with SurfControl E-mail Filter.

Only SurfControl E-mail Filter stops unwanted content using advanced Adaptive Reasoning Technology, artificial intelligence, and an Anti-Spam Agent™ that blocks virtually 100% of spam at the server. This simple-to-use enterprise solution also blocks inappropriate content, secures confidential data, optimizes network bandwidth and adds a layer of protection against viruses. And, it's easy to install on any SMTP or Exchange platform.

So get that spam out of your hair once and for all. Download SurfControl E-mail Filter now for a free 30-day evaluation.

Visit www.surfcontrol.com or call 1 800.368.3366

SurfControl®
The World's #1 Web & E-mail Filtering Company

Legal and Ethical Issues in E-Marketing
SurfControl stops unwanted e-mails, blocks inappropriate content, and secures confidential data.

Spam can be very lucrative for some businesses. The '419' spam was the most successful. Originating in Nigeria, the 419 spam requested that recipients send advance fees to cover costs of transferring money, with the promise of considerable monetary rewards in return. The 419 spam grossed $2 billion in 2003 and was actually Nigeria's second-largest business.

Many companies despise spam because it costs approximately $22 billion a year worldwide in lost productivity, new equipment, anti-spam filters, and labour. It is estimated that the average employee wastes 19 hours each year dealing with spam. Firms can visit www.cmsconnect.com and use an online calculator to determine how much spam is costing their firm each year.[63] Spam has been likened to receiving a direct-mail promotional piece with postage due. Some angry recipients of spam have organized boycotts against companies that advertise in this manner. Other recipients, however, appreciate the opportunity to learn about new products, as indicated in Figure 9.2.

Most commercial online services and Internet service providers offer their subscribers the option to filter out e-mail from certain Internet addresses that generate a large volume of spam. Businesses are installing software to filter out spam from outside their networks. Some firms have filed lawsuits against spammers; however, spammers appear to be ignoring the law and finding creative ways to get around spam filters.[64] The Internet has also created issues associated with intellectual property, the copyrighted or trade-

figure 9.2

TYPES OF GOODS AND SERVICES MARKETED THROUGH SPAM

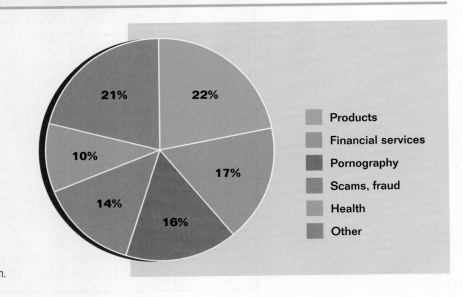

- Products
- Financial services
- Pornography
- Scams, fraud
- Health
- Other

Source: Ferris Research, in "Spam for Everyone," *The New York Times,* Jan. 31, 2005, www.nytimes.com.

marked ideas and creative materials developed to solve problems, carry out applications, and educate and entertain others. This issue has become a global concern because of disparities in enforcement of laws throughout the world. The software industry estimates that worldwide piracy costs its companies roughly $12 billion every year.[65]

Canada is one of the leading nations for illegal downloading of music. The Organization for Economic Development maintains that Canada has the largest file sharing population per capita of any country in the world. The Canadian Alliance Against Software Theft reported that Canadians were more likely to engage in illegal music downloading than their counterparts in other countries, including the U.S. The Canadian piracy rate is 36 percent, compared with 21 percent for the U.S., and 27 percent for Britain. A total of 1.6 billion Canadians downloaded music in 2005, resulting in 14 illegal downloads for each legal music download. Music revenues decreased by four percent in 2005, resulting in a loss of $23 million. The downward trend began in 1999, resulting in a loss of 41 percent of revenues to date, costing up to 14 000 jobs and $7 billion in spinoff revenue.[66]

Intellectual property rights issues have file-sharing services such as Napster, Kaaza, Grockster, and eDonkey scrambling to reinvent their business models to address a United States Supreme Court ruling supporting the Recording Industry Association of America's efforts to protect its members' copyrighted music. File-sharing via eDonkey, the most popular file-sharing service, accounts for more than one-third of the volume of data sent over the Web. Whether eDonkey can become a legal way to market and share music will determine whether the industry persists as a black market for illegal, pirated tunes or evolves to comprise legitimate businesses.[67] Even Google has run into problems related to copyrights in providing searches. In one case, Google was required to remove images that failed three of four tests of fair use. Because Google sells ads that run alongside search results, the image search service does not fall under the noncommercial freedom to transmit others' copyrighted images.[68]

Protecting trademarks can also be problematic. For example, some companies have discovered that another firm has registered a URL that duplicates or is very similar to their own trademarks. The "cyber-squatter" then attempts to sell the right to use the URL to the legal trademark owner. Companies such as Taco Bell, MTC, and KFC have paid thousands of dollars to gain control of domain names that match or parallel their company trademarks.[69] As the Internet continues to evolve, more legal and ethical issues will certainly arise. Recognizing this, the Canadian Marketing Association has developed a Code of Ethics that addresses Internet and Wireless marketing, as well as other marketing activities. Such self-regulatory policies may help head off government regulation of electronic marketing and commerce. Marketers and all other users of the Internet should make an effort to learn and abide by basic "netiquette" (Internet etiquette) to ensure they get the most out of the resources available on this growing medium. Fortunately, most marketers recognize the need for mutual respect and trust when communicating in any public medium. They know that doing so will allow them to maximize the tremendous opportunities the Internet offers to foster long-term relationships with customers.

SUMMARY

Electronic commerce (e-commerce) refers to sharing business information, maintaining business relationships, and conducting business transactions by means of telecommunications networks. Electronic marketing (e-marketing) is the strategic process of creating, distributing, promoting, and pricing products for targeted customers in the virtual environment of the Internet. The Internet has changed the way marketers communicate and develop relationships with their customers, employees, and suppliers. Telecommunications technology offers marketers potential advantages, including rapid response, expanded customer service capability, reduced costs of operation, and diminished geographic barriers. Despite these benefits, many Internet companies failed because they did not realize Internet markets are more similar to traditional markets than they are different and thus require the same marketing principles. Consumer-generated marketing information through instant messaging, blogs, online forums, mailing lists, and wikis, as well as text messaging and podcasts, has become more important.

Addressability is a marketer's ability to identify customers before they make a purchase. One way websites achieve addressability is through the use of cookies, strings of text placed on a visitor's computer. Interactivity allows customers to express their needs and wants directly to a firm in response to its marketing communications. It also enables marketers to capitalize on the concept of community and customers to derive value from the use of the firm's products and websites. Memory refers to a firm's ability to access collections of information in databases or data warehouses containing individual customer profiles and purchase histories. Firms can then use these data in real time to customize their marketing offers to specific customers. Control refers to customers' ability to regulate the information they view, as well as the rate and sequence of their exposure to that information. Accessibility refers to customers' ability to obtain the vast amount of information available on the Internet. Digitalization is the representation of a product, or at least the representation of some of its benefits, as digital bits of information.

The addressability, interactivity, and memory characteristics of e-marketing enable marketers to identify specific customers, establish interactive dialogues with them to learn their needs, and combine this information with their purchase histories to customize products to meet their needs. Thus, e-marketers can focus on building customer loyalty and retaining customers.

The growth of the Internet and the World Wide Web presents opportunities for marketing products (goods, services, and ideas) to both consumers and organizations. The Internet can also be viewed as a new distribution channel. The ability to process orders electronically and to increase the speed of communications via the Internet reduces inefficiencies, costs, and redundancies throughout the marketing channel. The Internet is an interactive medium that can be used to inform, entertain, and persuade target markets to accept an organization's products. The accessibility of the Internet presents marketers with an opportunity to expand and complement their traditional media promotional efforts. The Internet gives consumers access to more information about the costs and prices of products than has ever been available to them before.

One characteristic of companies engaged in e-marketing is a focus on customer relationship management (CRM), which employs information about customers to create marketing strategies that develop and sustain desirable long-term customer relationships. The addressability, interactivity, and memory characteristics of e-marketing allow marketers to identify specific customers, establish interactive dialogues with them to learn about their needs, and combine this information with customers' purchase histories to tailor products that meet those needs. It also permits marketers to shift their focus from share of market to share of customer. CRM employs database marketing techniques to identify different types of customers and develop specific strategies for interacting with each customer. The goal is to assess the worth of individual customers and thus estimate their customer lifetime value (CLV). Although technology drives CRM and can help companies build relationships with desirable customers, customer relationship management cannot be effective unless it is developed as a relationship-building tool.

One of the most controversial issues in e-marketing is personal privacy, especially the personal information companies collect from website visitors, often through the use of cookies. Additional issues relate to spam, or unsolicited commercial e-mail (UCE), and misappropriation of copyrighted or trademarked intellectual property. More issues are likely to emerge as the Internet and e-marketing continue to evolve.

Please visit the student website at **www.hmco.ca/marketing** for ACE Self-Test questions that will help you prepare for exams.

IMPORTANT TERMS

Electronic commerce (e-commerce)	Wikis	Memory	Digitalization
Electronic marketing (e-marketing)	Addressability	Database	Spam
Blogs	Cookie	Control	
	Interactivity	Portal	
	Community	Accessibility	

DISCUSSION & REVIEW QUESTIONS

1. How does addressability differentiate e-marketing from the traditional marketing environment? How do marketers use cookies to achieve addressability?

2. Define *interactivity* and explain its significance. How can marketers exploit this characteristic to improve relations with customers?

3. Memory gives marketers quick access to customers' purchase histories. How can a firm use this capability to customize its product offerings?

4. Explain the distinction between *push* and *pull* media. What is the significance of control in terms of using websites to market products?

5. What is the significance of digitalization?

6. How can marketers exploit the characteristics of the Internet to improve the product element of their marketing mixes?

7. How do the characteristics of e-marketing affect the promotion element of the marketing mix?

8. How does e-marketing facilitate customer relationship management?

9. How can technology help marketers improve their relationships with customers?

10. Electronic marketing has raised several ethical questions related to consumer privacy. How can cookies be misused? Should the government regulate the use of cookies by marketers?

APPLICATION QUESTIONS

1. Amazon.com is one of the Web's most recognizable marketers. Visit the company's website at **www.amazon.com,** and describe how the company adds value to its customers' buying experience.

2. Some products are better suited than others to electronic marketing activity. For example, Art.com specializes in selling art prints via its online store. The ability to display a variety of prints in many different categories gives customers a convenient and efficient way to search for art. On the other hand, General Electric has a website displaying its appliances, but customers must visit a retailer to purchase them.

Visit **www.art.com** and **www.geappliances.com,** and compare how each firm uses the electronic environment of the Internet to enhance its marketing efforts.

3. Visit the website **www.covisint.com** and evaluate the nature of the business customers attracted. Who is the target audience for this business marketing site? Describe the types of firms currently doing business through this exchange. What other types of organizations might be attracted? Is it appropriate to sell any banner advertising on a site such as this? What other industries might benefit from developing similar e-marketing exchange hubs?

globalEDGE™

1. If your firm wanted to market goods or services to potential customers via the Internet, your marketing efforts may be affected by the number of Internet service providers (ISPs) existing in a particular market. NationMaster.com's Internet Service Providers listing, which offers valuable assistance in comparing various statistics worldwide on the topic, can be found using the search term "compare various statistics" at **http://globaledge.msu.edu/ibrd** or **http://globaledge.msu.edu/ibrd/ibrd .asp.** Once you have reached NationMaster.com, select the Internet category and the subcategory of Internet Service Providers. What are the top 10 countries by number of ISPs? From this, divide these ten countries into two groups: highly decentralized and highly centralized per capita. What conclusions can be made from this?

2. Your firm wants to know which ten countries are most prepared for e-commerce. A ranking of the level of "e-readiness" of various markets worldwide can be accessed by using the search term "e-readiness" at **http:// globaledge.msu.edu/ibrd** or **http:// globaledge.msu.edu/ibrd/ibrd.asp.** If your firm was aiming to develop its international e-commerce competence, how can this information influence your firm's marketing strategy?

iVillage.com

One example of an online community is iVillage. Explore the content of this website at **www.ivillage.com.**

1. What target market can marketers access through iVillage?
2. How can marketers target this community to market their goods and services?
3. Based on your understanding of the characteristics of e-marketing, analyze the advertisements you observe on this website.

Case 9.1   The Gnome Helps Fuel a Turnaround at Travelocity

Travelocity was launched on March 12, 1996, by Sabre Interactive, a division of AMR Corporation, which at the time owned the Sabre Reservations System and American Airlines. Today Travelocity is the most popular travel service on the Web and the sixth-largest travel agency in the United States with sales of more than $500 million. Teams of employees working in seven U.S. offices work together to bring consumers the best in airline reservations, hotel rooms, cruises, vacation packages, car rentals, and last-minute deals. Travelocity operates or powers websites in five languages across four continents. It was named the "World's Leading Travel Internet Site" for the eighth consecutive year at the World Travel Awards in 2005, and it has led all travel sites—including airline and hotel sites—in customer respect, based on a study released by the Customer Respect Group. It holds the highest possible ranking from *Consumer Reports.*

When Travelocity began in 1996, it was one of the first Internet travel websites. By 2000 and 2001, however, it had stopped growing and was fading as the pioneer brand. Travelocity executives recognized that they needed to refocus the company on more profitable products. The reality is that selling airline tickets does not make money, but selling hotels and travel packages does. Consequently, Travelocity implemented a strategy of cross-selling and up-selling to help customers get a more complete travel experience. It focused on serving as a more complete advocate for travelers by providing a more affordable and more rewarding travel experience. The result: Travelocity's package segment grew by more than 100 percent a year between 2003 and 2005.

Despite the improving outlook, executives felt that the company needed to stand behind travelers in a way that no other online travel company did. They decided to spend a year developing a Customer Bill of Rights to guarantee that everything that customers book will be right and if it isn't, then the company will work with its partners to fix the problem. For example, if a customer books a hotel with a swimming pool, but finds the swimming pool closed upon arrival, Travelocity will, at its own expense, find a comparable or better quality hotel and move the customer there. Travelocity maintains a 24-hour hotline open seven days a week to ensure that customers get what they want. The Travelocity Guarantee allays the concerns of Travelocity customers who may be worried about booking online. The company stood by the guarantee even when it made a mistake and sold $0 tickets to Fiji for a short time.

The company paired the new guarantee with the "Roaming Gnome Enforcer of the Travelocity Guarantee" in television and other advertising. The Roaming Gnome advertising campaign represented an effort to humanize the Travelocity brand. The character embodied the joy of travel and symbolized getting out of the garden and seeing the world with new eyes. The advertising campaign created a tremendous buzz about Travelocity and boosted revenues by 37 percent. The gnome also won the American Marketing Association Gold EFIE award for Best Retail advertising campaign.

Travelocity partners with American Express Travel, AOL Travel, Yahoo! Travel, and many other firms. In this way, Travelocity has a much larger market share, and because it represents so many firms it has more power both with consumers and suppliers. The network partnering is especially important when it comes to marketing to customers. Travelocity can piggy-back off its partners to use their tried-and-tested marketing techniques with its own customers. In this way, Travelocity and its partners gain from the synergies of their partnerships.

Travelocity is also experimenting with creative ways of marketing to its customers. It was a sponsor of the

CBS series *Amazing Race,* and the competitors even had to find a gnome and carry him across the finish line. Although it was a huge investment for Travelocity, it paid off with increases in sales in only eight weeks. Executives believe that by going beyond 30-second commercials and banner ads, Travelocity is part of the complete entertainment mix of customers. Travelocity also uses search-engine marketing, spending much of its online advertising budget on paid keyword search ads. Although click-through advertising is vital, Travelocity has estimated that as many as a quarter of the people who came to Travelocity through search marketing would have come to the website anyway because Travelocity is such a well-known brand.

Travelocity also regularly tests its website for ease of use. It has seven testers in a room to find out where people are confused and where things can be improved. It has used this method to radically change its website.

One of the things it realized was that people forget passwords. To counteract this problem Travelocity changed the system so that customers re-entered their credit card information, address and e-mail address and used these things to pull up their profile, rather than relying on passwords. This change resulted in overnight increases in revenues of 10 percent. Executives realized that if you make using the website hard, then people will go elsewhere.[70]

Questions for Discussion

1. What is the role of consumer-generated information in helping Travelocity succeed?
2. Describe the marketing decisions that have helped Travelocity be so successful.
3. How did Travelocity use the Roaming Gnome as a symbol to communicate with its target market?

Case 9.2   eBay Auctions It All

One of the best-known Internet companies is eBay, whose stated mission is "to provide a global trading platform where practically anyone can trade practically anything." The leading online auction site has grown into a community of more than 100 million registered users around the world who can buy or sell literally anything from automobiles, boats, and furniture to jewelry, musical instruments, electronics, and collectibles. The auction site, described by CEO Meg Whitman as a "dynamic self-regulating economy," transacts nearly $15 billion in merchandise a year, more than the gross domestic product of many countries, giving it 80 percent of the online auction market. The firm sells more used vehicles than the nation's number one dealer, AutoNation. Unlike many high-tech dot-com companies, eBay has been profitable almost from the beginning. The company's revenues topped $4.5 billion in 2005, and its double-digit annual growth rate is expected to continue for the foreseeable future.

Why has eBay been so successful when so many other Internet startups have failed? Many people believe the company's success is due largely to the leadership of Whitman, who ranked first on a recent *Fortune* list of the most powerful women in business. Whitman, who gained experience at Hasbro, FTD, Stride Rite, Disney, and Procter & Gamble before taking the reins at eBay, keeps the company focused on the "big-picture" objectives and key priorities, such as keeping company expenses down and building a world-class executive team to keep the company on its fast-growing profitable pace. She expects to meet company objectives by making smart

acquisition decisions; reaching new customers, including more corporate ones; and opening a fixed-price bazaar. Whitman believes her most valuable contribution to eBay's success is the development of a work ethic and an organizational culture that focuses on a fun, open, and trusting environment.

Another reason for the company's success is its responsiveness to its users. For example, eBay's Voice of the Customer program brings in a dozen buyers and sellers every month to question about how they work and what else eBay could do to improve. In addition, the firm holds hour-long teleconferences at least twice a week to survey users on new features and policies.

Although eBay is known primarily for consumer-to-consumer actions, many small businesses have discovered they can sell older equipment and excess inventory through eBay. After a downturn in the aerospace industry, Reliable Tools Inc. sold a few items on eBay, including a $7000, 2300-pound milling machine. The California machine tool shop now sells about $1 million a month, accounting for 75 percent of its business. Increasingly, larger, multinational firms are setting up shop on eBay as well. Sun Microsystems and IBM, for example, have their own webpages within eBay's computer category from which they market products, primarily to small and midsize business customers.

For many small businesses, eBay serves as their retail outlet. An estimated 724000 individuals derive all or most of their income from selling products on the auction site; eBay has also spawned a number of "Trading Assistants," independent companies that act as intermediaries to help consumers and businesses sell goods on its site. AuctionDrop, for example, provides six sites in San Francisco where sellers can drop off goods for the small business to auction on eBay, after which it collects 40 percent of the sales price as a commission, on top of the transaction fee charged by eBay. The company, which handles up to 1000 items per day, plans to expand to four more locations around the United States.

To maintain customer confidence in auction transactions, eBay has taken numerous steps to avoid fraud. Although fraud occurs in only 0.01 percent of all eBay transactions, even a few fraudulent activities generate negative publicity and ill will, and could jeopardize the firm's reputation for quality transactions. To battle the potential for fraud, the company modified its user agreement to permit the barring of any user from the auction site and established feedback forms that allow buyers and sellers to rate each other based on their experiences. The company also offers escrow, payment processing, and credit card protection services through PayPal, Billpoint, and other providers, which further reduce the potential for fraud. The firm also established the Trust & Safety Department to look for suspicious activities and assist law enforcement agents in battling fraud.

By providing an easy-to-use site for consumers and businesses to buy and sell goods and remaining proactive, eBay has essentially become the poster child for a successful Internet venture. With strong leadership from Meg Whitman, Internet insiders believe the company will continue to serve as a model for electronic commerce.[71]

Questions for Discussion

1. Which of the basic characteristics of e-marketing is most important to eBay?
2. Describe eBay's marketing mix. How does this mix differ from that of a more traditional, "brick-and-mortar" discount store?
3. Online fraud has been a factor in some consumers' reluctance to use auction sites by eBay (and perhaps in the rise in intermediary companies). Has eBay done enough to prevent fraud on its site? What else could the company do to improve its services?

CHAPTER 10

Marketing Research and Information Systems

Mystery Shoppers on the Case

Since the 1940s, many companies have used "mystery shoppers" to visit their retail establishments and report on whether the stores were adhering to the companies' standards of service. Today, companies that would like a candid assessment of an average customer's experience at their places of business can hire a mystery shopping company—a firm that hires mystery shoppers to evaluate goods and services for corporate clients, analyzes the feedback, and provides that analysis to its corporate clients. Mystery shoppers enter establishments pretending to be regular customers. They evaluate the appearance of the store and assess how they are treated by employees. Some use digital cameras and computer equipment to document these observations. Many mystery shoppers work on a part-time basis and do so to earn free merchandise, meals, movies, and other goods. A few work full time.

These mystery shoppers provide valuable information that helps companies improve their organizations and refine their marketing strategies. Some companies take the input of mystery shoppers to heart and base company bonuses on employee performance during mystery inspections. Although a number of companies are now using online and phone customer surveys to judge performance—a practice that costs far less than employing mystery shoppers—many companies still rely on these mystery inspections and feel the results help them raise the bottom line—customer satisfaction.[1] ■

OBJECTIVES

1. To describe the basic steps in conducting marketing research

2. To explore the fundamental met of gathering data for marketing research

3. To describe the nature and role information systems in marketin decision making

4. To understand how such tools a databases, decision support syst and the Internet facilitate marke research

5. To identify key ethical and interna considerations in marketing rese

ystery shoppers enable marketers to implement the marketing concept by helping them acquire information about whether and how their goods and services satisfy the desires of target market customers. When used effectively, such information facilitates relationship marketing by helping marketers focus their efforts on meeting and even anticipating the needs of their customers. Marketing research and information systems that can provide practical and objective information to help firms develop and implement marketing strategies therefore are essential to effective marketing.

In this chapter, we focus on how marketers gather information needed to make marketing decisions. First, we define marketing research and examine the individual steps of the marketing research process, including various methods of collecting data. Next, we look at how technology aids in collecting, organizing, and interpreting marketing research data. Finally, we consider ethical and international issues in marketing research.

The Importance of Marketing Research

marketing research
The systematic design, collection, interpretation, and reporting of information to help marketers solve specific marketing problems or take advantage of marketing opportunities

Marketing research is the systematic design, collection, interpretation, and reporting of information to help marketers solve specific marketing problems or take advantage of marketing opportunities. As the word *research* implies, it is a process for gathering information not currently available to decision makers. The purpose of marketing research is to inform an organization about customers' needs and desires, marketing opportunities for particular goods and services, and changing attitudes and purchase patterns of customers. Market information increases marketers' ability to respond to customer needs, which leads to improved organizational performance.[2] Detecting shifts in buyers' behaviours and attitudes helps companies stay in touch with the ever-changing marketplace. Fast-food marketers, for example, would be very interested to know that young men ages 18 to 24 average 20 trips a month to fast-food establishments, compared with about 15 trips a month for all fast-food diners. The billions that consumers spend dining out represent a tremendous opportunity for those companies willing to invest the resources to understand this market.[3] Strategic planning requires marketing research to facilitate the process of assessing such opportunities or threats.

Marketing research can help a firm better understand market opportunities, ascertain the potential for success for new products, and determine the feasibility of a particular marketing strategy. A study by SPSS Inc. found that the most common reasons for conducting marketing research surveys included determining satisfaction (43 percent); product development (29 percent); branding (23 percent); segmentation (18 percent); awareness, trend tracking, and concept testing (18 percent); and business markets (11 percent).[4]

All sorts of organizations use marketing research to help them develop marketing mixes to match the needs of customers. Supermarkets, for example, have learned from marketing research that roughly half of all Americans prefer to have their dinners ready in 15 to 30 minutes. Such information highlights a tremendous opportunity for supermarkets to offer high-quality "heat and eat" meals to satisfy this growing segment of the food market. Political candidates also depend on marketing research to understand the scope of issues their constituents view as important. National political candidates may spend millions surveying voters to better understand issues and craft their images accordingly.

The real value of marketing research is measured by improvements in a marketer's ability to make decisions. Marketers should treat information in the same manner they use other resources, and they must weigh the costs of obtaining information against the benefits. Information should be judged worthwhile if it results in marketing activities that better satisfy the firm's target customers, lead to increased sales and profits, or help the firm achieve some other goal.

The Marketing Research Process

To maintain the control needed to obtain accurate information, marketers approach marketing research as a process with logical steps: (1) locating and defining problems or issues, (2) designing the research project, (3) collecting data, (4) interpreting research findings, and (5) reporting research findings (see Figure 10.1). These steps should be viewed as an overall approach to conducting research rather than as a rigid set of rules to be followed in each project. In planning research projects, marketers must consider each step carefully and determine how they can best adapt the steps to resolve the particular issues at hand.

Locating and Defining Problems or Research Issues

The first step in launching a research study is problem or issue definition, which focuses on uncovering the nature and boundaries of a situation or question related to marketing strategy or implementation. The first sign of a problem is typically a departure from some normal function, such as failure to attain objectives. If a corporation's objective is a 12 percent sales increase and the current marketing strategy resulted in a six percent increase, this discrepancy should be analyzed to help guide future marketing strategies. Declining sales, increasing expenses, and decreasing profits also signal problems. Customer relationship management (CRM) is frequently based on analysis of existing customers. However, research indicates that this information could be biased and therefore misleading when making decisions related to identifying and acquiring new customers.[5] Armed with this knowledge, a firm could define a problem as finding a way to adjust for biases stemming from existing customers when gathering data or to develop methods for gathering information to help find new customers. Conversely, when an organization experiences a dramatic rise in sales or some other positive event, it may conduct marketing research to discover the reasons and maximize the opportunities stemming from them.

Marketing research often focuses on identifying and defining market opportunities or changes in the environment. When a firm discovers a market opportunity, it may need to conduct research to understand the situation more precisely so it can craft an appropriate marketing strategy. For example, when General Motors saw that 42 percent of Hummer H3 buyers were women (compared to 26.3 percent of H2 buyers), it recognized an opportunity to position the smaller sport-utility vehicle to appeal to women buyers.[6]

To pin down the specific boundaries of a problem or an issue through research, marketers must define the nature and scope of the situation in a way that requires probing beneath the superficial symptoms. The interaction between the marketing manager and the marketing researcher should yield a clear definition of the research need. Researchers and decision makers should remain in the problem or issue definition stage until they have determined precisely what they want from marketing research and how they will use it. Deciding how to refine a broad, indefinite problem or issue into a precise, researchable statement is a prerequisite for the next step in the research process.

figure 10.1

THE FIVE STEPS OF THE MARKETING RESEARCH PROCESS

1 Locating and defining problems or issues

2 Designing the research project

3 Collecting data

4 Interpreting research findings

5 Reporting research findings

Designing the Research Project

research design An overall plan for obtaining the information needed to address a research problem or issue

Once the problem or issue has been defined, the next step is creating a **research design,** an overall plan for obtaining the information needed to address it. This step requires formulating a hypothesis and determining what type of research is most appropriate for testing the hypothesis to ensure the results are reliable and valid.

Developing a Hypothesis. The objective statement of a marketing research project should include hypotheses based on both previous research and expected research findings. A **hypothesis** is an informed guess or assumption about a certain problem or set of circumstances. It is based on all the insight and knowledge available about the problem or circumstances from previous research studies and other sources. As information is gathered, the researcher can test the hypothesis. For example, a food marketer such as H. J. Heinz might propose the hypothesis that children today have considerable influence on their families' buying decisions regarding ketchup and other grocery products. A marketing researcher would then gather data, perhaps through surveys of children and their parents, and draw conclusions as to whether the hypothesis is correct. Movie theatre, sports arena, and concert venue owners wondering why sales are down sharply have hypothesized that consumers are staying home more because of rising event prices, widespread availability of home theatres and broadband Internet access, as well as families' increasingly busy schedules.[7] Marketers could test these hypotheses by manipulating prices or offering strong incentives for consumers to return. Sometimes several hypotheses are developed during an actual research project; the hypotheses that are accepted or rejected become the study's chief conclusions.

hypothesis An informed guess or assumption about a certain problem or set of circumstances

Types of Research. The nature and type of research varies based on the research design and the hypotheses under investigation. Marketers may elect to conduct either exploratory research or conclusive research. While each has distinct purposes, the major differences between them are formalization and flexibility rather than the specific research methods used. Table 10.1 summarizes the differences.

Exploratory Research When marketers need more information about a problem or want to make a tentative hypothesis more specific, they may conduct **exploratory research.** The main purpose of exploratory research is to better understand a problem or situation and/or to help identify additional data needs or decision alternatives.[8] Consider that until recently, there was no research available to help marketers understand how consumers perceive the terms *clearance* versus *sale* in describing a discounted price event. An exploratory study asked one group of 80 consumers to write down their thoughts about a store window sign that said "sale" and another group of 80 consumers about a store window sign that read "clearance." The results revealed that consumers expected deeper discounts when the term *clearance* was used, and they expected the quality of the clearance products to be lower than that of products on sale.[9] This exploratory research helped marketers better understand how consumers view these terms and opened up the opportunity for additional research hypotheses about decision alternatives for retail pricing.

exploratory research Research conducted to gather more information about a problem or to make a tentative hypothesis more specific

conclusive research Research designed to verify insights through objective procedures and to help marketers in making decisions

Conclusive Research **Conclusive research** is designed to verify insights through an objective procedure to help marketers make decisions. It is used when the marketer has one or more alternatives in mind and needs assistance in the final stages of decision making.[10] For example, exploratory research revealed that clearance and sale terms send different signals to consumers, but in order to make a decision, a well-defined and structured research project could be used to help marketers decide which approach is best for a specific set of products and target consumers. The study would be specific to selecting a course of action and typically quantitative using methods that can be verified. Two types of conclusive research are descriptive and experimental research.

descriptive research Research conducted to clarify the characteristics of certain phenomena to solve a particular problem

If marketers need to understand the characteristics of certain phenomena to solve a particular problem, **descriptive research** can aid them. Descriptive studies may range from general surveys of customers' education, occupation, or age to specifics on how often teenagers consume sports drinks or how often customers buy new pairs of athletic shoes. For example, if Nike and Reebok want to target more young women, they

table 10.1	DIFFERENCES BETWEEN EXPLORATORY AND CONCLUSIVE RESEARCH	
Research Project Components	**Exploratory Research**	**Conclusive Research**
Research purpose	General: to generate insights about a situation	Specific: to verify insights and aid in selecting a course of action
Data needs	Vague	Clear
Data sources	Ill-defined	Well-defined
Data collection form	Open-ended, rough	Usually structured
Sample	Relatively small, often not randomly drawn; subjectively selected to maximize generalization of insights	Relatively large and randomly drawn; objectively selected to permit generalization of findings
Data collection	Often flexible; no set procedure	Generally rigid; well-laid-out procedure
Data analysis	Informal; typically non-quantitative	Formal; typically quantitative
Inferences/ recommendations	More tentative than final	More final than tentative

Adapted from: A. Parasuraman, Dhruv Grewal, and R. Krishnan, *Marketing Research* (Boston: Houghton Mifflin, 2004), p. 64. Copyright © 2004 by Houghton Mifflin Company. Used by permission.

might ask 15- to 35-year-old females how often they work out, how frequently they wear athletic shoes for casual use, and how many pairs of athletic shoes they buy in a year. Such descriptive research can be used to develop specific marketing strategies for the athletic-shoe market. Descriptive studies generally demand much prior knowledge and assume the problem or issue is clearly defined. For example, a survey of automobile buyers found that those who use the Internet to search for vehicles are more likely to be younger and more educated and to spend more time searching in general.[11] Some descriptive studies require statistical analysis and predictive tools. The marketer's major task is to choose adequate methods for collecting and measuring data.

experimental research
Research that allows marketers to make causal inferences about relationships

Descriptive research is limited in providing evidence necessary to make causal inferences (i.e., that variable X causes a variable Y). **Experimental research** allows marketers to make causal deductions about relationships.[12] Such experimentation requires that an independent variable (one not influenced by or dependent on other variables) be manipulated and the resulting changes in a dependent variable (one contingent on, or restricted to, one value or set of values assumed by the independent variable) be measured. For example, when Coca-Cola introduced Dasani flavoured waters, managers needed to estimate sales at various potential price points. In some markets, Dasani was introduced at $6.99/six pack. By holding variables such as advertising and shelf position constant, Coca-Cola could manipulate the price variable to study its effect on sales. If sales increased 40 percent when the price was reduced by $2, then managers could make an informed decision about the effect of price on sales. Coca-Cola could also use experimental research to manipulate other variables such as advertising or in-store shelf position to determine their effect on sales. Manipulation of the causal variable and control of other variables is what makes experimental research unique. As a result, it can provide much stronger evidence of cause and effect than data collected through descriptive research.

reliability A condition existing when a research technique produces almost identical results in repeated trials

validity A condition existing when a research method measures what it is supposed to measure

Research Reliability and Validity. In designing research, marketing researchers must ensure that research techniques are both reliable and valid. A research technique has **reliability** if it produces almost identical results in repeated trials. However, a reliable technique is not necessarily valid. To have **validity,** the research method must measure what it is supposed to measure, not something else. For example, although a group of customers may express the same level of satisfaction based on a rating scale, as individuals they may not exhibit the same repurchase behaviour because of different personal characteristics. This result may cause the researcher to question the validity of the satisfaction scale if the purpose of rating satisfaction was to estimate potential repurchase behaviour.[13] A study to measure the effect of advertising on sales would be valid if advertising could be isolated from other factors or variables that affect sales. The study would be reliable if replications of it produced the same results.

Collecting Data

The next step in the marketing research process is collecting data to help prove (or disprove) the research hypothesis. The research design must specify what types of data to collect and how they will be collected.

primary data Data observed and recorded or collected directly from respondents

secondary data Data compiled both inside and outside the organization for some purpose other than the current investigation

Types of Data. Marketing researchers have two types of data at their disposal. **Primary data** are observed and recorded or collected directly from respondents. This type of data must be gathered by observing phenomena or surveying people of interest. **Secondary data** are compiled both inside and outside the organization for some purpose other than the current investigation. Secondary data include general reports supplied to an enterprise by various data services and internal and online databases. Such reports might concern market share, retail inventory levels, and customers' buying behaviour. Commonly, secondary data are already available in private or public reports or have been collected and stored by the organization itself. Due to the opportunity to obtain data via the Internet, more than half of all marketing research now comes from secondary sources.

Sources of Secondary Data. Marketers often begin the data collection phase of the marketing research process by gathering secondary data. They may use available reports and other information from both internal and external sources to study a marketing problem.

Internal sources of secondary data can contribute tremendously to research. An organization's own database may contain information about past marketing activities, such as sales records and research reports, which can be used to test hypotheses and pinpoint problems. From sales reports, for example, a firm may be able to determine not only which product sold best at certain times of the year but also which colours and sizes customers preferred. Such information may have been gathered for management or financial purposes.[14]

Accounting records are also an excellent source of data but, surprisingly, are often overlooked. The large volume of data an accounting department collects does not automatically flow to other departments. As a result, detailed

Primary Data Collection
GMI works with physicians, nurses, and patients to help pharmaceutical companies collect primary data on over 100 ailments.

information about costs, sales, customer accounts, or profits by product category may not be easily accessible to the marketing area. This condition develops particularly in organizations that do not store marketing information on a systematic basis. A third source of internal secondary data is competitive information gathered by the sales force.

External sources of secondary data include trade associations, periodicals, government publications, unpublished sources, and online databases. Trade associations such as the Canadian and American Marketing Associations offer guides and directories rife with information. Periodicals such as *Business Week,* the *Wall Street Journal, Sales & Marketing Management, The Financial Post, Strategy Magazine, Advertising Age, Marketing Research,* and *Industrial Marketing* publish general information that can help marketers define problems and develop hypotheses. *Survey of Buying Power,* an annual supplement to *Sales & Marketing Management,* contains sales data for major industries on a county-by-county basis. Many marketers also consult federal government publications such as the *Census of Agriculture,* and the *Census of Population;* some of these government publications are available through online information services or the Internet. Although the government still conducts its primary census every five years, it now surveys households more often, providing marketers with a more up-to-date information about Canada's population every year. A very useful study includes the Survey on Household Spending. The report is available at the Statistics Canada website and may be downloaded for free. It provides detailed information on household spending for many different product categories for major cities, provinces and territories across Canada.

In addition, companies may subscribe to services, such as ACNielsen that track retail sales and other information. Small businesses may be unable to afford such services, but they can still find a wealth of information through industry publications and trade associations.[15]

Methods of Collecting Primary Data. Collection of primary data is a lengthier, more expensive, and more complex process than collection of secondary data. To gather primary data, researchers use sampling procedures, survey methods, and observation. These efforts can be handled in-house by the firm's own research department or contracted to a private research firm.

Sampling Because the time and resources available for research are limited, it is almost impossible to investigate all the members of a target market or other population. A **population,** or "universe," includes all the elements, units, or individuals of interest to researchers for a specific study. For example, for a Gallup poll designed to predict the results of a presidential election, all registered voters in the United States would constitute the population. By systematically choosing a limited number of units—a **sample**—to represent the characteristics of a total population, researchers can project the reactions of a total market or market segment. **Sampling** in marketing research, therefore, is the process of selecting representative units from a total population. Sampling techniques allow marketers to predict buying behaviour fairly accurately on the basis of the responses from a representative portion of the population of interest. Most types of marketing research employ sampling techniques.

Since a sample is a smaller group drawn from the entire population of interest, results drawn from the sample will not usually match the results that could have been obtained if the entire population was studied. The difference between these two sets of outcomes is called the **margin of error.** Professional researchers will ensure that samples are randomly drawn and sufficiently large to minimize the margin of error.

There are two basic types of sampling: probability sampling and non-probability sampling. With **probability sampling,** every element in the population being studied has a known chance of being selected for study. Random sampling is a form of probability sampling. When marketers employ **random sampling,** all the units in a population have an equal chance of appearing in the sample. The various events that can occur have an equal or known chance of taking place. For example, a specific card in a regulation deck of cards should have a 1/52 probability of being drawn at any one time. Sample units are ordinarily chosen by selecting from a table of random

population All the elements, units, or individuals of interest to researchers for a specific study

sample A limited number of units chosen to represent the characteristics of a total population

sampling The process of selecting representative units from a total population

margin of error The difference between study results drawn from a sample and the same results obtained from studying the entire population of interest

probability sampling A sampling technique in which every element in the population being studied has a known chance of being selected for study

random sampling A type of probability sampling in which all units in a population have an equal chance of appearing in the sample numbers statistically generated so that each digit, zero through 9, will have an equal probability of occurring in each position in the sequence. The sequentially numbered elements of a population are sampled randomly by selecting the units whose numbers appear in the table of random numbers.

Another type of probability sampling is **stratified sampling,** in which the population of interest is divided into groups according to a common attribute and a random sample is then chosen within each group. The stratified sample may reduce some of the error that could occur in a simple random sample. By ensuring that each major group or segment of the population receives its proportionate share of sample units, investigators avoid including too many or too few sample units from each group. Samples are usually stratified when researchers believe there may be variations among different types of respondents. For example, many political opinion surveys are stratified by gender, race, age, and/or geographic location.

The second type of sampling, **non-probability sampling,** is more subjective than probability sampling because there is no way to calculate the likelihood that a specific element of the population being studied will be chosen. Quota sampling, for example, is highly judgmental because the final choice of participants is left to the researchers. In **quota sampling,** researchers divide the population into groups and then arbitrarily choose participants from each group. A study of people who wear eyeglasses, for example, may be conducted by interviewing equal numbers of men and women who wear eyeglasses. In quota sampling, there are some controls—usually limited to two or three variables, such as age, gender, or race—over the selection of participants. The controls attempt to ensure that representative categories of respondents are interviewed. Because quota samples are not probability samples, not everyone has an equal chance of being selected, and sampling error therefore cannot be measured statistically. Quota samples are used most often in exploratory studies, when hypotheses are being developed. Often a small quota sample will not be projected to the total population, although the findings may provide valuable insights into a problem. Quota samples are useful when people with some common characteristic are found and questioned about the topic of interest. A probability sample used to study people allergic to cats, for example, would be highly inefficient.

Survey Methods Marketing researchers often employ sampling to collect primary data through mail, telephone, online, or personal interview surveys. The results of such surveys are used to describe and analyze buying behaviour. Selection of a survey method depends on the nature of the problem or issue; the data needed to test the hypothesis; and the resources, such as funding and personnel, available to the researcher. Marketers may employ more than one survey method depending on the goals of the research. Table 10.2 summarizes and compares the advantages of the various survey methods.

Gathering information through surveys is becoming increasingly difficult because fewer people are willing to participate. Many people believe responding to surveys takes up too much scarce personal time, especially as surveys become longer and more detailed.

stratified sampling A type of probability sampling in which the population of interest is divided into groups according to a common attribute and a random sample is then chosen within each group

non-probability sampling A sampling technique in which there is no way to calculate the likelihood that a specific element of the population being studied will be chosen

quota sampling A non-probability sampling technique in which researchers divide the population into groups and then arbitrarily choose participants from each group

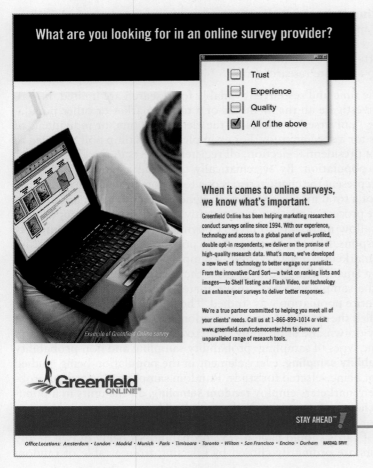

Collecting Data Through Survey
Greenfield Online creates and executes online surveys for clients who want to know more about their customers.

mail survey A research method in which respondents answer a questionnaire sent through the mail

Others have concerns about how much information marketers are gathering and whether their privacy is being invaded. These factors contribute to non-response rates for any type of survey.

In a **mail survey,** questionnaires are sent to respondents, who are encouraged to complete and return them. Mail surveys are used most often when the individuals in the sample are spread over a wide area and funds for the survey are limited. A mail survey is less expensive than a telephone or personal interview survey as long as the response rate is high enough to produce reliable results. The main disadvantages of this method are the possibility of a low response rate and of misleading results if respondents differ significantly from the population being sampled. One method of improving response rates involves attaching a brief note with a personal message on a Post-it note to the survey packet. Response rates to these surveys are not only higher, but the quality and the timeliness of the responses are also improved.[16]

Premiums or incentives that encourage respondents to return questionnaires have been effective in developing panels of respondents who are interviewed regularly by mail. Such mail panels, selected to represent a target market or market segment, are especially useful in evaluating new products and providing general information about customers, as well as records of their purchases (in the form of purchase diaries). Mail panels and purchase diaries are much more widely used than custom mail surveys, but both panels and purchase diaries have shortcomings. People who take the time to fill out a diary may differ from the general population based on income, education, or behaviour, such as the time available for shopping activities.

telephone survey A research method in which respondents' answers to a questionnaire are recorded by an interviewer on the phone

In a **telephone survey,** an interviewer records respondents' answers to a questionnaire over a phone line. A telephone survey has some advantages over a mail survey. The rate of response is higher because it takes less effort to answer the telephone and talk than to fill out and return a questionnaire. If there are enough interviewers, a telephone survey can be conducted very quickly. Thus, political candidates or

table 10.2   COMPARISON OF THE FOUR BASIC SURVEY METHODS

	Mail Surveys	Telephone Surveys	Online Surveys	Personal Interview Surveys
Economy	Potentially lower in cost per interview than telephone or personal surveys if there is an adequate response rate, but response rates are generally low.	Avoids interviewers' travel expenses; less expensive than in-home interviews.	The least expensive method if there is an adequate response rate, but it may be difficult to obtain a probability sample.	The most expensive survey method; shopping mall and focus-group interviews have lower costs than in-home interviews.
Flexibility	Inflexible; questionnaire must be short and easy for respondents to complete.	Flexible because interviewers can ask probing questions, but observations are impossible.	Less flexible; survey must be easy for online users to receive and return; short, dichotomous, or multiple-choice questions work best.	Most flexible method; respondents can react to visual materials; demographic data are more accurate; in-depth probes are possible.
Interviewer bias	Interviewer bias is eliminated; questionnaires can be returned anonymously.	Some anonymity; may be hard to develop trust in respondents.	Interviewer bias is eliminated, but e-mail address on the return eliminates anonymity.	Interviewers' personal characteristics or inability to maintain objectivity may result in bias.
Sampling and respondents' cooperation	Obtaining a complete mailing list is difficult; non-response is a major disadvantage.	Sample limited to respondents with telephones; devices that screen calls, busy signals, and refusals are a problem.	Sample limited to respondents with computer access; the available e-mail address list may not be a representative sample for some purposes.	Not-at-homes are a problem, which may be overcome by focus-group and shopping mall interviewing.

organizations seeking an immediate reaction to an event may choose this method. In addition, a telephone survey permits interviewers to gain rapport with respondents and ask probing questions.

However, only a small proportion of the population likes to participate in telephone surveys. Just one-third of respondents are willing to participate in telephone interviews, down from two-thirds 20 years ago.[17] This poor image can significantly limit participation and distort representation in a telephone survey. Moreover, telephone surveys are limited to oral communication; visual aids or observation cannot be included. Interpreters of results must make adjustments for individuals who are not at home or do not have telephones. Many households are excluded from telephone directories by choice (unlisted numbers) or because the residents moved after the directory was published. Potential respondents often use telephone answering machines, voice mail, or caller ID to screen or block calls. Moreover, an increasing number of younger Canadians are giving up their fixed telephone lines in favour of cellular or wireless phones.[18] These issues have serious implications for the use of telephone samples in conducting surveys. Some adjustment must be made for groups of respondents that may be undersampled because of a smaller-than-average incidence of telephone listings. Non-directory telephone samples can overcome such bias. Various methods are available, including random-digit dialing (adding random numbers to the telephone prefix) and plus-one telephone sampling (increasing the last digit of a directory number by one). These methods make it feasible to dial any working number, whether or not it is listed in a directory. Online surveys are evolving as an alternative to telephone surveys. In an **online survey,** questionnaires can be transmitted to respondents who have agreed to be contacted and have provided their e-mail addresses. Because e-mail is semi-interactive, recipients can ask for clarification of specific questions or pose questions of their own. The potential advantages of e-mail surveys are quick response and lower cost than traditional mail, telephone, and personal interview surveys if the response rate is adequate. In addition, more firms are using their websites to conduct surveys. Online surveys can also make use of online communities—such as chat rooms, web-based forums, blogs, and newsgroups—to identify trends in interests and consumption patterns. Movies, consumer electronics, food, and computers are popular topics in many online communities.[19] Indeed, by "listening in" on these ongoing conversations, marketers may be able to identify new product opportunities and consumer needs. Moreover, this type of online data can be gathered at little incremental cost compared to alternative data sources.[20] Evolving technology and the interactive nature of the Internet allow for considerable flexibility in designing online questionnaires. Sample Czar, an online research firm, conducts online research with consumer panels in Canada, the United States, Mexico, United Kingdom, France, Germany, Italy, Spain, China, Japan, South Korea, Australia, Brazil, Russia, and India.[21] Given the growing number of households that have computers with Internet access, marketing research is likely to rely heavily on online surveys in the future. Furthermore, as negative attitudes toward telephone surveys render that technique less representative and more expensive, the integration of e-mail, fax, and voicemail functions into one computer-based system provides a promising alternative for survey research. E-mail surveys have especially strong potential within organizations whose employees are networked and for associations that publish members' e-mail addresses. However, there are some ethical issues to consider when using e-mail for marketing research, such as spam (unsolicited e-mail) and privacy. Also, the increased use of spam blocking software makes it difficult to distribute invitations to complete surveys. It also makes it harder to obtain a random sample.

There are a number of organizations that invite web users to take a variety of surveys, although most of the organizations focus exclusively in American markets. There are also concerns that the web user who signs up to complete such surveys may actually differ demographically, or psychographically, from those who do not sign up. This disparity can result in sample bias. In a **personal interview survey,** participants respond to questions face to face. Various audiovisual aids—pictures, products, diagrams, or prerecorded advertising copy—can be incorporated into a personal interview. Rapport gained through direct interaction usually permits more in-depth interviewing,

online survey A research method in which respondents answer a questionnaire via e-mail or on a website

personal interview survey A research method in which participants respond to survey questions face to face including probes, follow-up questions, or psychological tests. In addition, because personal interviews can be longer, they may yield more information. Finally, respondents can be selected more carefully, and reasons for non-response can be explored.

One such research technique is the **in-home (door-to-door) interview.** The in-home interview offers a clear advantage when thoroughness of self-disclosure and elimination of group influence are important. In an in-depth interview of 45 to 90 minutes, respondents can be probed to reveal their real motivations, feelings, behaviours, and aspirations.

The object of a **focus-group interview** is to observe group interaction when members are exposed to an idea or a concept. General Motors, for example, used focus groups comprised of celebrity athletes, actors, and musicians, including XZibit, as part of its effort to redesign the Cadillac Escalade SUV and CTS sedan.[22] Focus-group interviews are often conducted informally, without a structured questionnaire, in small groups of eight to 12 people. They allow customer attitudes, behaviours, lifestyles, needs, and desires to be explored in a flexible and creative manner. Questions are open-ended and stimulate respondents to answer in their own words. Researchers can ask probing questions to clarify something they do not fully understand or something unexpected and interesting that may help explain buying behaviour. For example, Ford may use focus groups to determine whether to change its advertising to emphasize a vehicle's safety features rather than its style and performance. On the other hand, focus-group participants do not always tell the truth. Focus groups are also subject to group dynamics, and while focus group moderators try to limit such influence it can still bias the final results. Some participants may be less than honest in an effort to be sociable or to receive money and/or food in exchange for their participation. Research has found a poor correlation between stated intent and actual purchase behaviour.[23] It may be necessary to use separate focus groups for each major market segment studied—men, women, and age groups—and experts recommend the use of at least two focus groups per segment in case one group is unusually idiosyncratic.[24] Due to the unstructured and subjective nature of focus groups and the high costs of conducting them, it is impractical to attempt to collect data from a large number of respondents using the focus group interview method. As a result, focus groups are generally treated as exploratory research tools.

More organizations are starting **customer advisory boards,** which are small groups of actual customers who serve as sounding boards for new product ideas and offer insights into their feelings and attitudes toward a firm's products, promotion, pricing, and other elements of marketing strategy. While these advisory boards help companies maintain strong relationships with valuable customers, they can also provide great insight into marketing research questions.[25]

Still another option is the **telephone depth interview,** which combines the traditional focus group's ability to probe with the confidentiality provided by a telephone survey. This type of interview is most appropriate for qualitative research projects among a small targeted group that is difficult to bring together for a traditional focus group because of members' professions, locations, or lifestyles. Respondents can choose the time and day for the interview. Although this method is difficult to implement, it can yield revealing information from respondents who otherwise would be unwilling to participate in marketing research.[26]

The nature of personal interviews has changed. In the past, most personal interviews, which were based on random sampling or prearranged appointments, were conducted in the respondent's home. Today most personal interviews are conducted in shopping malls. **Shopping mall intercept interviews** involve interviewing a percentage of individuals passing by certain "intercept" points in a mall. Like any face-to-face interviewing method, mall intercept interviewing has many advantages. The interviewer is in a position to recognize and react to respondents' non-verbal indications of confusion. Respondents can be shown product prototypes, videotapes of commercials, and the like, and asked for their reactions. The mall environment lets the researcher deal with complex situations. For example, in taste tests, researchers know that all the respondents are reacting to the same product, which can be prepared and monitored from the mall test kitchen. In addition to the ability to conduct tests requiring bulky

in-home (door-to-door) interview A personal interview that takes place in the respondent's home

focus-group interview A research method involving observation of group interaction when members are exposed to an idea or a concept

customer advisory boards Small groups of actual customers who serve as sounding boards for new product ideas and offer insights into their feelings and attitudes toward a firm's products and other elements of marketing strategy

telephone depth interview An interview that combines the traditional focus group's ability to probe with the confidentiality provided by telephone surveys

shopping mall intercept interviews A research method that involves interviewing a percentage of individuals passing by "intercept" points in a mall equipment, lower cost and greater control make shopping mall intercept interviews popular.

on-site computer interview
A variation of the shopping mall intercept interview in which respondents complete a self-administered questionnaire displayed on a computer monitor

An **on-site computer interview** is a variation of the shopping mall intercept interview in which respondents complete a self-administered questionnaire displayed on a computer monitor. A computer software package can be used to conduct such interviews in shopping malls. After a brief lesson on how to operate the software, respondents can proceed through the survey at their own pace. Questionnaires can be adapted so that respondents see only those items (usually a subset of an entire scale) that may provide useful information about their attitudes.[27]

Questionnaire Construction A carefully constructed questionnaire is essential to the success of any survey. Questions must be clear, easy to understand, and directed toward a specific objective; that is, they must be designed to elicit information that meets the study's data requirements. Researchers need to define the objective before trying to develop a questionnaire because the objective determines the substance of the questions and the amount of detail. A common mistake in constructing questionnaires is to ask questions that interest the researchers but do not yield information useful in deciding whether to accept or reject a hypothesis. Finally, the most important rule in composing questions is to maintain impartiality.

The questions are usually of four kinds: open-ended, dichotomous, scaled, and multiple-choice.

Open-Ended Question
How do you feel about broadband Internet access for your computer?

_____

_____

_____

A Look-Look at Trendsetters

Look-Look.com is an online, real-time service that provides accurate and reliable information, research, and news about trendsetting youths ages 14 to 30. With this age group spending an estimated $140 billion a year, many companies are willing to shell out an annual subscription fee of about $20 000 for access to this valuable data.

Look-Look pays more than 35 000 handpicked, prescreened young people from all over the world to e-mail the company information about their styles, trends, opinions, and ideas. This group of selected youth represents the trendsetters—forward-thinking innovators who influence their peers. (Although trendsetters account for only about 20 percent of the youth population, they influence the other 80 percent.) Look-Look also has 20 photographers who travel the globe capturing youth trends in photos.

Through the Internet and the company's intranet, Look-Look clients have access to results of surveys and polls. These clients can uncover information on the latest fashion and technology trends, entertainment preferences, eating and drinking habits, and health and beauty issues of today's young people. They can also access the City Guide, which lists most preferred shops, hangouts, and restaurants in selected cities. Clients that may want to know the answer to a specific question can key that question into a search feature and reach a worldwide focus group 24 hours a day. Clients include an apparel company, video game manufacturers, a cosmetics company, beverage firms, and movie studios. Look-Look co-presidents DeeDee Gordon and Sharon Lee believe that full understanding of the youth culture requires a constant dialogue with young people—an understanding not achieved by a once- or twice-a-year focus group or by traditional market research. To find out more about how Look-Look taps into young opinion leaders around the world, view Look-Look's electronic media kit at http://look-look.com/looklook/multimedia/epk.mov.

Dichotomous Question
Do you presently have broadband access at home, work, or school?

Yes _____ No _____ Add Likert-scale question

Scaled Question
How would you rate the reliability of your current Internet Service Provider (ISP)? Would you say that it is

1___ Very unreliable 2___ Somewhat unreliable 3___ About average

4___ Somewhat reliable 5___ Very reliable

Multiple-Choice Question
What age group are you in?

Under 20 _____

20–29 _____

30–39 _____

40–49 _____

50–59 _____

60 and over _____

Problems may develop in the analysis of dichotomous or multiple-choice questions when responses for one outcome outnumber others. For example, a dichotomous question asking respondents to choose between "buy" or "not buy" might require additional sampling from the disproportionately smaller group if there were not enough responses to analyze.[28]

Researchers must also be very careful about questions that a respondent might consider too personal or that might require an admission of activities that other people are likely to condemn. Questions of this type should be worded to make them less offensive.

Observation Methods In using observation methods, researchers record individuals' overt behaviour, taking note of physical conditions and events. Direct contact with them is avoided; instead, their actions are examined and noted systematically. For instance, researchers might use observation methods to answer the question "How long does the average McDonald's restaurant customer have to wait in line before being served?" Observation may include the use of ethnographic techniques, such as watching customers interact with a product in a real-world environment.

Kimberly-Clark researchers employed ethnographic techniques when they asked a few consumers to wear a glasses-mounted camera so that they could observe how the consumers used Huggies baby wipes. The research revealed that parents were changing their babies on top of beds, floors, and even washing machines where they were struggling with wipe containers requiring two hands. Based on this research, the company redesigned the package so that the product can more easily be used with one hand.[29]

Observation may also be combined with interviews. For example, during a personal interview, the condition of a respondent's home or other possessions may be observed and recorded. The interviewer can also directly observe and confirm such demographic information as race, approximate age, and gender.

Data gathered through observation can sometimes be biased if the person is aware of the observation process. However, an observer can be placed in a natural market environment, such as a grocery store, without influencing shoppers' actions. If the presence of a human observer is likely to bias the outcome or if human sensory abilities are inadequate, mechanical means may be used to record behaviour. Mechanical observation devices include cameras, recorders, counting machines, scanners, and equipment that records physiological changes. A special camera can be used to record the eye movements of people as they look at an advertisement; the camera detects the sequence of reading and the parts of the advertisement that receive greatest attention.

The electronic scanners used in supermarkets are very useful in marketing research: they provide accurate data on sales and customers' purchase patterns, and marketing researchers may buy such data from the supermarkets.

Observation is straightforward and avoids a central problem of survey methods: motivating respondents to state their true feelings or opinions. However, observation tends to be descriptive. When it is the only method of data collection, it may not provide insights into causal relationships. Another drawback is that analyses based on observation are subject to the observer's biases or the limitations of the mechanical device.

Interpreting Research Findings

After collecting data to test their hypotheses, marketers need to interpret the research findings. Interpretation of the data is easier if marketers carefully plan their data analysis methods early in the research process. They should also allow for continual evaluation of the data during the entire collection period. They can then gain valuable insights into areas that should be probed during the formal interpretation.

The first step in drawing conclusions from most research is to display the data in table format. If marketers intend to apply the results to individual categories of the things or people being studied, cross-tabulation may be useful, especially in tabulating joint occurrences. For example, using the two variables of gender and purchase rates of automobile tires, a cross-tabulation could show how men and women differ in purchasing automobile tires.

statistical interpretation
Analysis of what is typical or what deviates from the average

After the data are tabulated, they must be analyzed. **Statistical interpretation** focuses on what is typical or what deviates from the average. It indicates how widely responses vary and how they are distributed in relation to the variable being measured. When marketers interpret statistics, they must take into account estimates of expected error or deviation from the true values of the population. The analysis of data may lead researchers to accept or reject the hypothesis being studied. Data require careful interpretation by the marketer. If the results of a study are valid, the decision maker should take action; if a question has been incorrectly or poorly worded, however, the results may produce poor decisions. Consider the research conducted for a food marketer that asked respondents to rate a product on criteria such as "hearty flavour," as well as how important each criterion was to the respondent. Although such results may have had utility for advertising purposes, they were less helpful in product development because it was not possible to discern respondents' meaning of "hearty flavour."[30] Managers must understand the research results and relate them to a context that permits effective decision making.

Reporting Research Findings

The final step in the marketing research process is to report the research findings. Before preparing the report, the marketer must take a clear, objective look at the findings to see how well the gathered facts answer the re-

Interpreting Research

Companies like Burke can help interpret data collected from market research and offer insights into the areas to be investigated.

search question or support or negate the initial hypotheses. In most cases, it is extremely doubtful that the study can provide everything needed to answer the research question. Thus, the researcher must point out the deficiencies and the reasons for them, in the report.

The report of research results is usually a formal, written document. Researchers must allow time for the writing task when they plan and schedule the project. Because the report is a means of communicating with the decision makers who will use the research findings, researchers need to determine beforehand how much detail and supporting data to include. They should keep in mind that corporate executives prefer reports that are short, clear, and simply expressed. Researchers often give their summary and recommendations first, especially if decision makers do not have time to study how the results were obtained. A technical report allows its users to analyze data and interpret recommendations because it describes the research methods and procedures and the most important data gathered. Thus, researchers must recognize the needs and expectations of the report user and adapt to them.

Bias and distortion can be a major problem if the researcher is intent on obtaining favourable results. For example, research analyzing consumers' reports of their frequency of using long-distance telephone calls, letters, cards, and visits for personal communication found that some groups under report their usage, whereas other groups over report it. In particular, researchers found that consumers underestimate the duration of lengthy telephone calls but overestimate the length of short ones; in general, people tend to overestimate both the frequency and duration of their telephone calls. Without this information, companies relying on survey results may get a distorted view of the market for long-distance telephone services by mistakenly judging it to be larger and more homogeneous than it really is.[31]

Marketing researchers want to know about behaviour and opinions, and they want accurate data to help them in making decisions. Careful wording of questions is very important because a biased or emotional word can dramatically change the results. Marketing research and marketing information systems can provide an organization with accurate and reliable customer feedback, which a marketer must have to understand the dynamics of the marketplace. As managers recognize the benefits of marketing research, they assign it a much larger role in decision making.

Using Technology to Improve Marketing Information Gathering and Analysis

Technology is making information for marketing decisions increasingly accessible. The ability of marketers to track customer buying behaviour and to better discern what buyers want is changing the nature of marketing. Customer relationship management is being enhanced by integrating data from all customer contacts and combining that information to improve customer retention. Information technology permits internal research and quick information gathering to help marketers better understand and satisfy customers. For example, company responses to e-mail complaints as well as to communications through mail, telephone, and personal contact can be used to improve customer satisfaction, retention, and value.[32] Armed with such information, marketers can fine-tune marketing mixes to satisfy their customers' needs.

The integration of telecommunications and computer technologies is allowing marketers to access a growing array of valuable information sources related to industry forecasts, business trends, and customer buying behaviour. Electronic communication tools can be effectively used to gain accurate information with minimal customer interaction. Most marketing researchers have e-mail, voicemail, teleconferencing, and fax machines at their disposal. In fact, many firms use marketing information systems to network all these technologies and organize all the marketing data available to them. In this section, we look at marketing information systems and specific technologies that are helping marketing researchers obtain and manage marketing research data.

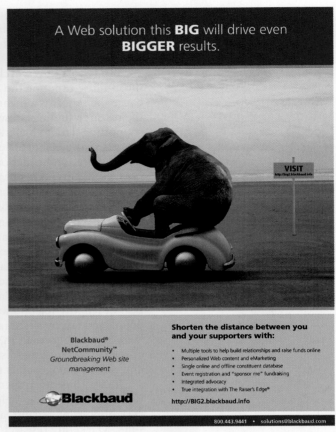
Using Technology

AVW Telav and Blackbaud provide high tech audience response systems to assist in data collection.

Marketing Information Systems

A **marketing information system (MIS)** is a framework for the day-to-day management and structuring of information gathered regularly from sources both inside and outside the organization. As such, an MIS provides a continuous flow of information about prices, advertising expenditures, sales, competition, and distribution expenses. The main focus of the MIS is on data storage and retrieval, as well as on computer capabilities and management's information requirements. The key components of a marketing information system are marketing research, marketing intelligence, and reporting. Marketing research consists of information retrieved from primary data collection, while marketing intelligence consists of information obtained through secondary data sources. Reporting provides managers with information upon which to make informed decisions.[33] Regular reports of sales by product or market categories, data on inventory levels, and records of salespeople's activities are examples of information that is useful in making decisions. In the MIS, the means of gathering data receive less attention than do the procedures for expediting the flow of information.

An effective MIS starts by determining the objective of the information, that is, by identifying decision needs that require certain information. The firm can then specify an information system for continuous monitoring to provide regular, pertinent information on both the external and internal environment. FedEx, for example, has developed interactive marketing systems to provide instantaneous communication between the company and its customers. Via either telephone or the Internet, customers can track their packages and receive immediate feedback concerning delivery. The company's website provides valuable information about customer usage and allows customers to express directly what they think about company services. The evolving telecommunications and computer technology is allowing marketing information systems to cultivate one-to-one relationships with customers.

marketing information system (MIS) A framework for managing and structuring information gathered regularly from sources inside and outside the organization

Interactive Marketing Research
Workplace Print Media helps its customers find customers.

Databases

Most marketing information systems include internal databases. As mentioned in Chapter 9, a database is a collection of information arranged for easy access and retrieval. Databases allow marketers to tap into an abundance of information useful in making marketing decisions: internal sales reports, newspaper articles, company news releases, government economic reports, bibliographies, and more, often accessed through a computer system. Information technology has made it possible to develop databases to guide strategic planning and help improve customer services. Many commercial websites require consumers to register and provide personal information to access the site or make a purchase. Frequent flier programs permit airlines to ask loyal customers to participate in surveys about their needs and desires, and to track their best customers' flight patterns by time of day, week, month, and year. Supermarkets gain a significant amount of data through checkout scanners tied to store discount cards. In fact, one of the best ways to predict market behaviour is the use of database information gathered through loyalty programs or other transaction-based processes.[34] ICOM Information and Communications has grown to be a leader in providing lists and market data to firms in the consumer packaged goods and pharmaceutical industries throughout North America. ICOM also manages North America's largest permission-based survey database. The Loyalty Group manages Airmiles.ca, one of the most successful loyalty programs in history. The Loyalty Group is a subsidiary of Alliance Data Systems Corporation, which employs over 7500 people throughout Canada and the United States. Alliance manages a database of 105 million consumer accounts and processes 2.7 billion transactions annually.[35]

Marketing researchers can also use commercial databases developed by information research firms, such as LexisNexis Canada, to obtain useful information for marketing decisions. Many of these commercial databases are accessible online for a fee. They can also be obtained in printed form or on computer compact discs (CD-ROMs). With most commercial databases, the user typically conducts a computer search by keyword, topic, or company, and the database service generates abstracts, articles, or reports that can then be printed out. Accessing multiple reports or a complete article may cost extra.

single-source data Information provided by a single marketing research firm

Information provided by a single firm on household demographics, purchases, television viewing behaviour, and responses to promotions such as coupons and free samples is called **single-source data.**[36] Ipsos-Reid is Canada's leading supplier of such market studies with expertise in many business sectors, including agriculture, automotive, consumer packaged goods, financial services, health care, retail, technology, travel, telecommunications and many others.

Pollara Inc. is the largest public opinion and marketing research firm in Canada, employing more than 600 people. Like Ipsos-Reid, Pollara boasts multi-sector research spanning financial travel, tourism, energy, pharmaceuticals, media and public affairs. In addition to traditional survey and focus group research, Pollara conducts online studies and uses a unique technology called the Perception Analyzer to track respondents' feelings about television commercials, speeches and other types of communications.

Marketing Decision Support Systems

marketing decision support system (MDSS) Customized computer software that aids marketing managers in decision making

A **marketing decision support system (MDSS)** is customized computer software that aids marketing managers in decision making by helping them anticipate the effects of certain decisions. Some decision support systems have a broader range and offer greater computational and modeling capabilities than spreadsheets; they let managers explore a greater number of alternatives. For example, an MDSS can determine how sales and profits might be affected by higher or lower interest rates or how sales forecasts, advertising expenditures, production levels, and the like might affect overall profits. For this reason, MDSS software is often a major component of a company's marketing information system. Customized decision support systems can support a customer orientation and customer satisfaction in business marketing.[37] Some decision support systems incorporate artificial intelligence and other advanced computer technologies.

The Internet and Online Information Services

The Internet has evolved as a most powerful communication medium, linking customers and companies around the world in computer networks via e-mail, forums, webpages, and more. Growth of the Internet, and especially the World Wide Web, has launched an entire industry that is working to make marketing information easily accessible to both marketing firms and customers. These technologies provide the backbone for modern direct marketing.

Table 10.3 lists a number of websites that can be valuable resources for marketing research. Among companies that exploit census data for marketing decisions, Blockbuster mines the data to help determine how many copies of a particular movie or video game to offer at each store.[38]

Data Mining at Wal-Mart

Wal-Mart is not only the world's largest retailer, it also operates the world's largest data warehouse, an organization wide data collection and storage system that gathers data from all of the firm's critical operation systems as well as from selected external data sources. Wal-Mart's data warehouse contains more than 460 terabytes of data stored on mainframe computers; experts believe the Internet comprises less than half that amount of data.

Wal-Mart collects reams of data about products and customers primarily from checkout scanners at its Wal-Mart discount and Sam's Club membership stores. Clerks and managers may also use wireless handheld units to gather additional inventory data. The company stores the detailed data and classifies it into categories such as product, individual store, or region. The system also serves as a basis for the Retail Link decision-support system between Wal-Mart and its suppliers.

Retail Link permits some vendors, like Kraft, to access data about how well their products are selling at Wal-Mart stores.

The mountain of data Wal-Mart collects helps boost efficiency dramatically by matching product supplies to demand. The data may also help the company track supplier performance, set ideal prices, and even determine how many cashiers to schedule at a certain store on a certain day. Most importantly, it helps the retailer avoid carrying too much inventory or not having enough to satisfy demand.

table 10.3   RESOURCES FOR MARKETING INFORMATION

	Government Sources
Statistics Canada	www.statscan.ca
2001 Census	www.12.statcan.ca/english/census01/home/index.cfm
Canadian Economy	www.canadianeconomy.gc.ca
Online Publications and Reports	www.canada.gc.ca/publications/publication_e.html
Society Statistics	http://www.canada.gc.ca/acanada/ViewCategory.htm?lang=eng&font=0&categoryId=74
Provincial and Territorial Links	http://www.canada.gc.ca/othergov/prov_e.html
Organization for Economic Co-operation and Development Statistical Portal	www.oecd.org/statsportal/0,2639,en_2825_293564_1_1_1_1_1,00.html
Strategis Economic Indicators	www.strategis.ic.gc.ca/engdoc/main.html
Statistics Canada Census of Agriculture	http://www.statcan.ca/english/agcensus2006/index.htm
National Industrial Profiles Human Resources and Social Development Canada	http://www.hrsdc.gc.ca/asp/gateway.asp?hr=/en/hip/hrp/sp/industry_profiles/IP_index.shtml&hs=hzp
	Commercial Sources
ACNielsen Canada	www.acnielsen.ca
Stats-Link Canada Market Research	www.stats-link-canada.com/Market.html
Cardmedia Online (retail sales)	www.cardmedia.com/tools/cma_retail.cfm
BBM Canada Audience Statistics	www.bbm.ca/en/home.html
GD Sourcing Canadian Marketing Resources	www.gdsourcing.com/works/conmarket3.asp
GD Sourcing Directory of Statistics Canada Data	www.gdsourcing.ca/works/StatCan.htm
Brewers' Association of Canada–Statistics	www.brewers.ca/EN/frames/enter_statistics.htm
	Periodicals and Books
Advertising Age	www.adage.com
Business Week	www.businessweek.com
Strategy Magazine	www.strategymag.com
Sales & Marketing Management	www.salesandmarketing.com

Companies can also mine their own websites for useful information. Amazon.com, for example, has built a relationship with its customers by tracking the types of books and music they purchase. Each time a customer logs on to the website, the company can offer recommendations based on the customer's previous purchases. Such a marketing system helps the company track the changing desires and buying habits of its most valued customers.

Marketing researchers can also subscribe to online services such as MSN, AOL Canada, and LexisNexis Canada. These services typically offer their subscribers such

Internet Research
Opinion Outpost provides its customers with research delivered by a readily available online panel.

specialized services as databases, news services, and forums, as well as access to the Internet itself. Marketers can subscribe to "mailing lists" that periodically deliver electronic newsletters to their computer screens, and they can participate in on-screen discussions with thousands of network users. This enhanced communication with a firm's customers, suppliers, and employees provides a high-speed link that boosts the capabilities of the firm's marketing information system. Many marketers turn to search engines like Google for free information.

While most webpages are open to anyone with Internet access, big companies like Cisco Systems also maintain internal webpages, called *intranets,* that allow employees to access such internal data as customer profiles and product inventory—information once hidden in databases only technicians could unlock. Such sensitive corporate information can be protected from outside users of the World Wide Web by special security software called *firewalls.* IBM uses its intranets to help its 300 000 employees around the world collaborate on projects. In addition to improving communications, the system has helped the company slash training and travel expenses by nearly $400 million.[39]

Issues in Marketing Research

The Importance of Ethical Marketing Research

Marketing managers and other professionals are relying more and more on marketing research, marketing information systems, and new technologies to make better decisions. It is therefore essential that professional standards be established by which to judge the reliability of marketing research. Such standards are necessary because of the ethical and legal issues that develop in gathering marketing research data. In addition, the relationships between research suppliers, such as marketing research agencies, and the marketing managers who make strategy decisions require ethical behaviour. Organizations such as the Marketing Research and Intelligence Association (MRIA) have developed codes of conduct and guidelines to promote ethical marketing research. To be effective, such guidelines must instruct marketing researchers on how to avoid misconduct. All members of MRIA must adopt the following Declaration of Principles when conducting customer research.

The activities of some firms may also be impacted by the federal Personal Information Protection and Electronics Documents Act (PIPEDA). The Act is designed to protect the personal information of employees and others who are impacted by a firm's activities. Personal information includes anything that can identify an individual, including personal contact information, gender, ethnicity, health data, medical history, religious affiliation, political beliefs, sexual preference, identification numbers, blood type, income, credit, and financial records. Firms that collect and/or store such information, or who sell lists of potential respondents or charitable donors, are impacted by the Act.[40] More information about the Privacy Principles in PIPEDA may be found in Figure 9.1 in Chapter 9 of this text. Additional information may be obtained from

Marketing Research and Intelligence Association Declaration of Principles

1. Interviews are to be conducted in an environment of trust and goodwill and in recognition of every Respondent's right to privacy.
2. Research will not be used to sell or develop leads for marketing purposes.
3. Any statement or assurance given to a Respondent in order to elicit cooperation will be factually correct and honoured.
4. Confidentiality of Respondent data will be maintained. Individual Respondents' personal data will not be provided to client or other third parties without the permission of the Respondent.
5. Respondents will not be badgered or harassed to answer questions and no comments will be made by interviewers about any response.
6. No audio recording of interviews will take place without having first informed the subject Respondent. No visual recording of interviews will take place without signed releases being obtained from the subject Respondent prior to the commencement of the interview.
7. Overly long questionnaires or confusing or misleading questions will not be employed in the conduct of Research.
8. Interviewers must carry time-dated company identification credentials. Immediately upon commencing a project, interviewers must identify themselves by their full names and the name of the Organization on whose behalf they are conducting the Research. Upon request, interviewers will provide the Respondent with the name, address and phone number of the head office of the Organization on whose behalf the interviewer is conducting the Research, as well as the MRIA research registration number and toll-free telephone number.
9. Members of the public should be advised of their right to complain to the CRTC where they have received unsolicited telecommunication for the purpose of sales or the purpose of developing leads for marketing.

Members of MRIA must also respect the following Charter of Respondent Rights:

Your participation in legitimate marketing, social or public opinion research is very important to us. We value your honest feedback and your time. Your opinions help companies develop new products, make existing ones better, and improve customer service. Your views also assist governments and non-profit organizations in advancing laws and policies that are in the public interest.

Our relationship with you is based on respect, trust and goodwill. When you participate in research conducted by our firm, or by any other corporate member of the Marketing Research and Intelligence Association (MRIA), you can be assured that:

Article 1: You will always be told the first name of the person contacting you, the research company's name and the nature of the study.

Article 2: You can verify that the research you have been invited to participate in is legitimate in one of two ways. You can either obtain a registration number and the MRIA's toll-free telephone number for any research registered with MRIA's Research Registration System or you can obtain the contact information of the research director who is conducting the study.

Article 3: You will not be sold anything or asked for money.

Article 4: Your privacy and the privacy of your answers will be respected and strictly preserved in accordance with the organization's privacy policy and applicable federal and provincial laws.

Article 5: You will be contacted at reasonable times, but if the time is inconvenient, you may ask to be re-contacted at a more convenient time.

Article 6: You are entitled to know the approximate duration of the interview.

Article 7: Your decision to participate in a study, answer specific questions, or discontinue your participation will be respected without question.

(Continued)

Article 8: You will be informed in advance if the interview will be recorded and the intended use of the recording. You may choose not to proceed with the interview if you do not want it to be recorded.

Article 9: You are assured that the highest standards of professional conduct will be upheld throughout all stages of the study.

the government's PIPEDA website at http://privacyforbusiness.ic.gc.ca/epic/site/pfb-cee .nsf/en/Home.

Legitimate marketing research firms differ from telemarketers in that they are not trying to sell items over the telephone, nor are they engaged in telephone-based fund-raising activities. These activities are not research-related, and they have been dubbed sugging (selling under the guise of research) and frugging (fundraising under the guise of research). Both practices would violate MRIA's Charter of Respondent Rights and should be avoided.

Canadian legislators have been working hard to create a "do not call list" similar to that in the United States that would allow Canadians to exempt themselves from telemarketing calls. Bill C37, the Canadian Telemarketing Do-Not-Call Registry, was originally introduced into law on November 25, 2005. The Canadian Radio-Television and Telecommunications Commission (CRTC) enforces the bill. The bill exempts non-telemarketers from the do not call list, including registered charities, political parties, existing business relationships going back 18 months, and survey research firms.[41]

International Issues in Marketing Research

As we saw in Chapter 7, sociocultural, economic, political, legal, and technological forces vary in different regions of the world. These variations create challenges for organizations attempting to understand foreign customers through marketing research. The marketing research process we describe in this chapter is used globally, but to ensure the research is valid and reliable, data-gathering methods may have to be modified to allow for regional differences. For example, experts have found that Latin Americans do not respond well to focus groups or in-depth interviews lasting more than 90 minutes. Researchers therefore need to adjust their tactics to generate information useful for marketing products in Latin America.[42] To ensure that global and regional differences are satisfactorily addressed, many companies retain a research firm with experience in the country of interest. Most of the largest marketing research firms derive a significant share of their revenues from research conducted in the United States and beyond.

Experts recommend a two-pronged approach to international marketing research. The first phase involves a detailed search for and analysis of secondary data to gain greater understanding of a particular marketing environment and to pinpoint issues that must be taken into account in gathering primary research data. Secondary data can be particularly helpful in building a general understanding of the market, including economic, legal, cultural, and demographic issues, as well as in assessing the risks of doing business in that market and in forecasting demand.[43] Marketing researchers often begin by studying country trade reports from www.strategis.gc.ca, the government website, as well as country-specific information from local sources, such as a country's website, and trade and general business publications such as *The Financial Post*. These sources can offer insights into the marketing environment in a particular country and can even indicate untapped market opportunities abroad.

The second phase involves field research using many of the methods described earlier, including focus groups and telephone surveys, to refine a firm's understanding of specific customer needs and preferences. Specific differences among countries can have a profound influence on data gathering. For example, in-home (door-to-door) interviews are illegal in some countries. In China, few people have regular telephone lines, making telephone surveys both impractical and non-representative of the total population. Primary data gathering may have a greater chance of success if the firm employs local researchers who better understand how to approach potential respondents and can do so in their own language.[44] Regardless of the specific methods used to gather primary data, whether in the United States or abroad, the goal is to better understand the needs of specific target markets to craft the best marketing strategy to satisfy the needs of customers in each market, as we will see in the next chapter.

SUMMARY

Marketing research is the systematic design, collection, interpretation, and reporting of information to help marketers solve specific marketing problems or take advantage of marketing opportunities. It is a process for gathering information not currently available to decision makers. Marketing research can help a firm better understand market opportunities, ascertain the potential for success for new products, and determine the feasibility of a particular marketing strategy. The value of marketing research is measured by improvements in a marketer's ability to make decisions.

To maintain the control needed to obtain accurate information, marketers approach marketing research as a process with logical steps: (1) locating and defining problems or issues, (2) designing the research project, (3) collecting data, (4) interpreting research findings, and (5) reporting research findings.

The first step in launching a research study, problem or issue definition, focuses on uncovering the nature and boundaries of a situation or question related to marketing strategy or implementation. When a firm discovers a market opportunity, it may need to conduct research to understand the situation more precisely so it can craft an appropriate marketing strategy.

In the second step, marketing researchers design a research project to obtain the information needed to address it. This step requires formulating a hypothesis and determining what type of research to employ to test the hypothesis so the results are reliable and valid. A hypothesis is an informed guess or assumption about a problem or set of circumstances. Marketers conduct exploratory research when they need more information about a problem or want to make a tentative hypothesis more specific; they use conclusive research to verify insights through an objective procedure. Research is considered reliable if it produces almost identical results in repeated trials; it is valid if it measures what it is supposed to measure.

For the third step of the research process, collecting data, two types of data are available. Primary data are observed and recorded or collected directly from respondents; secondary data are compiled inside or outside the organization for some purpose other than the current investigation. Sources of secondary data include an organization's own database and other internal sources, periodicals, government publications, unpublished sources, and online databases. Methods of collecting primary data include sampling, surveys, observation, and experimentation. Sampling involves selecting representative units from a total population. In probability sampling, every element in the population being studied has a known chance of being selected for study. Non-probability sampling is more subjective than probability sampling because there is no way to calculate the likelihood that a specific element of the population being studied will be chosen. Marketing researchers employ sampling to collect primary data through mail, telephone, online, or personal interview surveys. A carefully constructed questionnaire is essential to the success of any survey. In using observation methods, researchers record respondents' overt behaviour and take note of physical conditions and events. In an experiment, marketing researchers attempt to maintain certain variables while measuring the effects of experimental variables.

To apply research data to decision making, marketers must interpret and report their findings properly—the final two steps in the marketing research process. Statistical interpretation focuses on what is typical or what deviates from the average. After interpreting the research findings, the researchers must prepare a report on the findings that the decision makers can understand and use. Researchers must also take care to avoid bias and distortion.

Many firms use computer technology to create a marketing information system (MIS), a framework for managing and structuring information gathered regularly from sources both inside and outside the organization. A database is a collection of information arranged for easy access and retrieval. A marketing decision support system (MDSS) is customized computer software that aids marketing managers in decision making by helping them anticipate the effects of certain decisions. Online information services and the Internet also enable marketers to communicate with customers and obtain information.

Eliminating unethical marketing research practices and establishing generally acceptable procedures for conducting research are important goals of marketing research. Both domestic and international marketing use the same marketing research process, but international marketing may require modifying data-gathering methods to address regional differences.

Please visit the student website at **www.hmco.ca/marketing** for ACE Self-Test questions that will help you prepare for exams.

IMPORTANT TERMS

Marketing research
Research design
Hypothesis
Exploratory research
Conclusive research
Descriptive research
Experimental research
Reliability
Validity
Primary data

Secondary data
Population
Sample
Sampling
Margin of error
Probability sampling
Random sampling
Stratified sampling
Non-probability sampling
Quota sampling

Mail survey
Telephone survey
Online survey
Personal interview survey
In-home (door-to-door) interview
Focus-group interview
Customer advisory boards
Telephone depth interview

Shopping mall intercept interviews
On-site computer interview
Statistical interpretation
Marketing information system (MIS)
Single-source data
Marketing decision support system (MDSS)

DISCUSSION & REVIEW QUESTIONS

1. What is marketing research? Why is it important?

2. Describe the five steps in the marketing research process.

3. What is the difference between defining a research problem and developing a hypothesis?

4. Describe the different types of approaches to marketing research and indicate when each should be used.

5. Where are data for marketing research obtained? Give examples of internal and external data.

6. What is the difference between probability sampling and non-probability sampling? In what situation would random sampling be best? Stratified sampling? Quota sampling?

7. Suggest some ways to encourage respondents to cooperate in mail surveys.

8. If a survey of all homes with listed telephone numbers is to be conducted, what sampling design should be used?

9. Describe some marketing problems that could be solved through information gained from observation.

10. What is a marketing information system, and what should it provide?

11. Define a database. What is its purpose, and what does it include?

12. How can marketers use online services and the Internet to obtain information for decision making?

13. What role do ethics play in marketing research? Why is it important that marketing researchers be ethical?

14. How does marketing research in other countries differ from marketing research in Canada?

APPLICATION QUESTIONS

1. After observing customers' traffic patterns, Bashas' Markets repositioned the greeting card section in its stores, and card sales increased substantially. To increase sales for the following types of companies, what information might marketing researchers want to gather from customers?

   a. Furniture stores

   b. Gasoline outlets/service stations

   c. Investment companies

   d. Medical clinics

2. When a company wants to conduct research, it must first identify a problem or possible opportunity to market its goods or services. Choose a company in your city that you think might benefit from a research project. Develop a research question and outline a method to approach this question. Explain why you think the research question is relevant to the organi-

zation and why the particular methodology is suited to the question and the company.

3. Input for marketing information systems can come from internal or external sources. ACNielsen Canada is the largest provider of single-source marketing research in the world. Identify two firms in your city that might benefit from internal sources and two that might benefit from external sources. Explain why these sources would be useful to these companies. Suggest the type of information each company should gather.

4. Suppose you are opening a health insurance brokerage firm and want to market your services to small businesses with fewer than 50 employees. Determine which database for marketing information you will use in your marketing efforts, and explain why you will use it.

globalEDGE™

1. Your firm is considering entering the Japanese information technology market, and you have been asked to analyze the top 10 Japanese companies in this industry. One way to begin your research on this market segment is to access *BusinessWeek*'s Global 1000 firms by using the search term "top global companies" at **http://globaledge.msu.edu/ibrd** or **http://globaledge.msu.edu/ibrd/ibrd.asp.** Once there, click on the Country-by-Country scoreboard to find the best document for analysis. Considering the criteria given, prepare a summary that includes the largest and smallest firms. In addition, describe which firms are the most and least healthy.

2. For a marketing research company, an important element in gathering data for a market is the level of information technology (IT) infrastructure that exists. NationMaster.com's website offers a subcategory of Personal Computers (PCs) that can provide insight on the level of personal computer (PC) usage in a country. Use the search term "compare various statistics" at **http://globaledge.msu.edu/ibrd** or **http://globaledge.msu.edu/ibrd/ibrd.asp** to reach NationMaster.com. Once in the nationmaster.com site, select the Media category and then the subcategory of Personal Computers (PCs). Give a summary of the top 15 countries as ranked by the number of PCs used. From this specified list of markets, include an assessment of the three countries with the most and least access to PCs. What conclusions can you make?

INTERNET Exercise

Visit **www.hmco.ca/marketing** for resources to help you master the material in this chapter, plus materials that will help you expand your marketing knowledge, including Internet exercise updates, ACE self-tests, hotlinks to companies featured in this chapter, and much more.

World Association of Opinion and Marketing Research Professionals

The World Association of Opinion and Marketing Research Professionals (ESOMAR, founded as the European Society for Opinion and Marketing Research in 1948) is a non-profit association for marketing research professionals. ESOMAR promotes the use of opinion and marketing research to improve marketing decisions in companies worldwide and works to protect personal privacy in the research process. Visit the association's website at **www.esomar.nl.**

1. How can ESOMAR help marketing professionals conduct research to guide marketing strategy?
2. How can ESOMAR help marketers protect the privacy of research subjects when conducting marketing research in other countries?
3. ESOMAR introduced the first professional code of conduct for marketing research professionals in 1948. The association continues to update the document to address new technology and other changes in the marketing environment. According to ESOMAR's code, what are the specific professional responsibilities of marketing researchers?

Case 10.1   Best Buy Uncovers Angels in the Market

Best Buy Company, Inc. is a retailer of consumer electronics, home-office products, entertainment software, appliances, and related services. One of the company's goals is to make life easier and more fun for consumers. To meet that objective, the company's retail environment focuses on educating customers on the features and benefits of technology and entertainment products. The Minneapolis-based firm operates more than 930 retail stores across the United States and in Canada under the names Best Buy, Future Shop, GeekSquad,

and Magnolia Audio Video, as well as an outlet store on eBay.

Best Buy operates in the highly competitive consumer electronics retail industry and must compete against other electronics retailers, specialty home-office retailers, mass merchants, home improvement superstores, and a growing number of direct-to-consumer alternatives. It also competes against independent dealers, regional chain discount stores, wholesale clubs, video rental stores, and other specialty retail stores. There is also increasing pressure from online sites, which offer entertainment as downloads, as well as pay-per view cable television companies.

Best Buy collects data on nearly every transaction made, rain check issued, and call-centre problem resolved for 75 million customers. To discover what its customers want and need, the company developed a database that incorporated information from 19 customer touch points including point of sale, and enhanced it with Experians's INSOURCESM consumer marketing data to develop a complete picture of its customers. It gained further insight by using purchase histories to study its customers' current as well as their future needs through segmentation analysis. This allowed Best Buy to develop and identify new customer segments, to better understand existing customers, to more precisely target promotions and to identify key locations for expansion.

Best Buy collects data from its transactions and from mailing lists; it also has demographic information from local census numbers, surveys of customers, and targeted focus groups. In 2004 it launched a customer loyalty program called Reward Zone, which today has more than six million members from whom the company hopes to gain valuable insights. Best Buy retains Larry Selden, a professor at Columbia University's Graduate School of Business, as a consultant. Selden argued that losses produced by what he calls "devil" customers can wipe out profits generated by "angels." Through its consultation with Selden and its data analysis with Experian, Best Buy identified its angel and devil customers. The angels were customers who bought high definition TVs, portable electronics, and newly released DVDs without waiting for markdowns or rebates. The devils bought products, applied for their rebates, and then returned the products and bought them back again at returned-merchandise discounts. Best Buy then categorized its angel customers into five segments:

- The Small Business customer ("BBfB"): These customers use Best Buy's products and services to enhance the profitability of their businesses.
- The Young Entertainment Enthusiast ("Buzz"): These are active younger men who want the latest technology and entertainment. They are early adopters who are interested in buying and showing off the latest gadgets.
- The Affluent Professional ("Barry"): These customers want the best technology and entertainment experience, and they do not mind spending to get the best, regardless of the cost. They are enthusiasts of action movies and cameras.
- The Busy Suburban Mom ("Jill"): These customers want to enrich their children's lives with technology and entertainment. They are busy but willing to talk about helping their families. They are smart and affluent but usually avoid electronics stores because the products intimidate them. "Jills" are typically the main shopper for the family and will make purchases based on staff recommendations.
- The Tech-Savvy Family Man ("Ray"): These are family men who want technology to improve their lives. They are practical adopters of technology and entertainment.

Best Buy's new "customer-centric" operating model focuses on these five key segments. The company launched the initiative with 67 stores, each of which would analyze the demographics of its local market and then choose one or two of these groups to be their focus. Each store would then stock merchandise for and include elements designed to appeal to the targeted segments. Executives believe that this model offers customers a richer in-store experience, including better shopping assistance, and also provides more of the goods and service that they want. It also empowers employees to recognize unique sets of customers and to build offerings and experiences to meet their needs. In fact, employees receive training in how to differentiate the customer types and how to help each.

To encourage its angel customers, Best Buy sends out associates with pink umbrellas to escort the Jills to and from their cars on rainy days. Personal Shopping Assistants have been provided to help Jills from the moment they enter the stores till they leave via the express checkout. For Barrys, there are comfortable couches for watching large TVs hooked up to high-end sound systems; even popcorn is included to add to the atmosphere. Magnolia Home Theatre specialists provide personalized expert advice. For Buzzes, Best Buy has set up video game areas with leather chairs and game players hooked to mammoth plasma-screen TVs, and TVs and games just a short walk from the area.

To discourage the undesirable devil customers, Best Buy is cutting back on promotions and sales tactics that tend to attract them, and it is also removing many of them from mailing lists. The company is also enforcing a 15 percent restocking fee on returned merchandise to discourage customers who return items with the intention of repurchasing them at "open-box" discounts. Best Buy is experimenting with reselling returned merchandise over the Internet, so the products do not reappear in the store where they were originally purchased.

Best Buy has already converted 85 stores to the new customer centred-model and plans to convert all of its U.S. Best Buy stores within three years. The 67 stores that underwent conversion in 2005 have reported a sales increase of 8.2 percent for the portion of the year in which they operated under the customer centricity model. Compared to an average store sales gain of 1.9 percent at other U.S. Best Buy stores, this is a considerable gain.

However, due to one-time conversion costs and a higher expense structure, the selling, general, and administrative expenses for the converted stores were higher than for that of other U.S. Best Buy stores for the same period. Nonetheless, Best Buy believes that the profitability of stores operating under the customer-centred platform will improve over time, which is similar to its historical experience with new-store openings.[45]

Questions for Discussion

1. From what internal and secondary sources did Best Buy acquire the data that helped it develop its customer centricity initiative?
2. How did Best Buy employ database marketing to better satisfy its customers?
3. How are the data gathered by Best Buy useful in customer relationship management?

Strategic Case 4   Reebok Races into the Urban Market

Reebok wants to give front-runner Nike a run for its money in the race for market share in athletic footwear, apparel, and equipment. Reebok gained speed from the 1980s into the early 1990s by marketing special aerobics shoes for women. Then Nike pulled way ahead with new clothing and equipment endorsed by high-profile athletes such as Michael Jordan and Tiger Woods. Nike has remained the market leader, completely outdistancing all competitors to dominate the industry. Now Reebok is seeking to close the distance by changing its selection of target markets. In the process, it is aiming to change consumers' perceptions of and attitudes toward its brand and its products with the objective of boosting both sales and profits.

Breaking Tradition with Hip-Hop

Traditionally, sneaker manufacturers have captured market attention by signing successful or fast-rising sports stars to promote their shoes. Reebok still likes to link its brand to popular sports. Its multimillion-dollar contract with basketball's Yao Ming is one of the industry's most expensive deals, and it has many other sports figures under contract, including tennis star Venus Williams. The fierce rivalry with Nike continues on the playing field. Reebok has lucrative contracts to make branded hats for the National Basketball Association and to supply the National Football League with uniforms and equipment. Nike has an exclusive contract to provide performance apparel to all 30 major league baseball teams.

Looking beyond sports, Reebok's marketers investigated the urban market, where fashion rather than performance is the deciding factor in buying decisions. Urban teens tend to be extremely style conscious, buying as many as 10 pairs of athletic-style shoes a year so they can be seen in the very latest thing. Many are also fans of hip-hop music and buy clothing designed by hip-hop celebrities such as Jay-Z, Sean "Diddy" Combs, and Russell Simmons.

Reebok's marketing research confirmed this market's considerable buying power and the influence of hip-hop artists. To effectively reach this market, Reebok needed a new brand, new products, and new promotional efforts. First, the company took the focus off its mainstream Reebok brand by creating Rbk as a new brand specifically for the urban market. Next, it partnered with hip-hop artists such as Jay-Z and 50 Cent to develop special footwear collections, backed by targeted promotional efforts emphasizing style with attitude.

New Street Credibility

Reebok found it was tapping into a significant market opportunity. Right after Reebok introduced soft-leather, flat-soled S. Carter shoes (after Jay-Z's original name, Shawn Carter), the line sold out. Demand for the $100 shoes quickly spiked so high that eager buyers bid up to $250 for one pair on the eBay auction site. On the heels of this success, Reebok introduced G-Unit footwear, named after a hit song by the rapper 50 Cent, who says, "Reebok's Rbk Collection is the real thing when it comes to connecting with the street and hip-hop culture." Hip-hop's Eve was also asked to design a shoe. "She is one of the first artists in the campaign who has male and female appeal, urban and suburban," observes Reebok's director of global advertising. "She is as much a fashion icon as a music icon."

Moreover, the company found a way to bring sports and hip-hop together by launching the 13 Collection line of shoes by basketball star Allen Iverson. Iverson promoted the line by appearing in a series of fast-paced commercials filmed in rap-video style. Although he was shown playing basketball for a second or two, the commercials focused more on his off-court style than his on-court technique.

Despite the added credibility that such celebrities bring to the Reebok brand, the strategy entails some risks. Fads in street fashion and music can come and go at a dizzying pace, which means a shoe that is red-hot one day may be ice-cold the next. Moreover, Reebok might feel the repercussions if one of its celebrities gets into trouble. Still, the company's chief marketing officer is committed to the strategy. "With athletes, they wear the shoes for the length of a basketball season," he comments. "With hip-hop, the publicity is intense but short, just like movies." The advantage, he says, is that "You'll know very quickly whether you hit or miss."

Targeting Urban Markets in China

In pursuit of growth, Reebok is also targeting promising global markets. China is high on its list of priorities. Interest in sports is skyrocketing there, thanks in part to Chinese basketball star Yao Ming's move to the NBA. According to company research, 93 percent of Chinese males ages 13 to 25—a prime market for athletic shoes—watch NBA broadcasts on a regular basis. Reebok's Asia Pacific general manager cites one projection showing 50 percent annual growth in footwear sales. His prediction: "It's hard to say what the [actual sales] numbers are going to be, but they are going to be huge."

To make the most of this opportunity, Reebok has set up "Yao's House" basketball courts around central Shanghai. Each features the Reebok trademark and a giant *Sports Illustrated* cover showing the basketball star. By giving teens and young adults a place to hone their slam dunks, Reebok hopes to shape their attitudes toward its products. "The trends are made in the urban areas and on street basketball courts" says one Reebok executive.

Reebok is not the only athletic-shoe manufacturer entering this market. Nike sponsors a basketball court in Beijing, New Balance is building awareness of its shoes, and Pony is selling sneakers in Beijing, Shanghai, and Guandong. With the 2008 Summer Olympics in Beijing, sports fever is continuing to spread throughout the major cities.

Reebok's New Vector

Nike has its Swoosh, one of the most recognized trademarks in the world. Now Reebok has its Vector, a streamlined trademark designed to communicate the brand's attributes in a fast, fun way. The idea is to make the Vector synonymous with Reebok, just as the Swoosh is synonymous with Nike. "Our research suggests that consumers react better to logos than words, and it's a very effective marketing tool," stresses Reebok's head of marketing.[46]

Questions for Discussion

1. What segmentation variables is Reebok using for its products? Why are these variables appropriate?
2. Which of the three targeting strategies is Reebok applying? Explain.
3. What influences on the consumer buying decision process appear to have the most impact on Reebok's customers' purchase decisions?

5

Product Decisions

We are now prepared to analyze the decisions and activities associated with developing and maintaining effective marketing mixes. In Parts Five through Eight, we focus on the major components of the marketing mix: product, distribution, promotion, and price. **Part Five** explores the product component of the marketing mix. **Chapter 11** introduces basic concepts and relationships that must be understood to make effective product decisions. **Chapter 12** analyzes a variety of dimensions regarding product management, including line extensions and product modification, new-product development, product deletions branding, packaging, and labelling. **Chapter 13** explores the nature, importance, and characteristics of services.

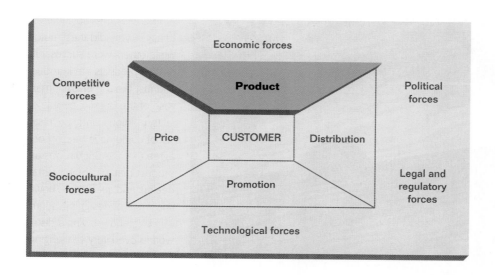

11

Product Concepts

Bricklin SV-1: The Cool Car That Never Made It

Like the Delorean DMC-12 of the early 1980s—which shared some of its exterior styling cues, including most notably the gull-wing doors—the Canadian built Bricklin SV-1 coupe was in many ways a "car of the future." When introduced in 1974 as a safety vehicle, *Playboy* magazine referred to the Bricklin as "safe, fast, sleek, sexy, and overprotective."

Designed to look sporty, the V8 powered coupe came with many saftey features that were innovative for the time: a bumper system 200 percent more efficient than regulation standards, a roll cage, enclosed engine and fuel tank, and doughnut-wide radial tires. Other features touted as safety features included the absence of an ashtray and cigarette lighter that were an industry standard at the time, steel framed gull-wing doors that only needed 12 inches to open, and a range of colour options, all referred to as safety colours (such as Safety Orange and Safety Green). The Bricklin's body panels were as unique as its design— a molded and colour impregnated acrylic outer shell bonded to fibreglass.

Unfortunately for its namesake and promoter Malcolm Bricklin, the SV-1 shares its place in automotive history with John Z. Delorean's DMC-12 and Preston Tucker's Tucker Torpedo of the 1940s. What do these automobiles have in common? All were launched as "cars of tomorrow," all three involved ventures that ended in financial ruin, and all are now valued by enthusiastic collectors.

Perhaps the most interesting question to ask is, why did these automobiles fail, while others were successful? Thousands of new products are introduced annually, and just like the Bricklin, many fail. In the case of the Bricklin, people cite many facts, opinions, and speculations about "what could have been, if only. . . ." Most agree that the Bricklin was an innovative product that was of interest to prospective dealers and car buyers; however, the challenge of designing, sourcing parts, building, and growing a distribution network proved very challenging and too expensive. In September 1975, Bricklin Canada Ltd. was placed into receivership after having built only 2854 cars. The true cost of this failure is unknown when you account for lost investment, jobs, and opportunity. What is certain, the province of New Brunswick had become the majority shareholder in Bricklin Canada Ltd. and guarantor of funds—an honourable mention in automotive history that cost the taxpayers of New Brunswick approximately $23 million.[1] ∎

The product is an important variable in the marketing mix. Products such as the Bricklin SV-1 can be a firm's and its investors' most important asset. If a company's products do not meet customers' desires and needs, the firm will fail unless it makes adjustments. Developing successful products requires knowledge of fundamental marketing and product concepts.

In this chapter, we first define *product* and discuss how buyers view products. Next, we examine the concepts of product line and product mix. We then explore the stages of the product life cycle and the effect of each life cycle stage on marketing strategies. Next, we outline the product adoption process. Finally, we discuss the factors that contribute to a product's failure or success.

What Is a Product?

good A tangible physical entity

service An intangible result of the application of human and mechanical efforts to people or objects

idea A concept, philosophy, image, or issue

As defined in Chapter 1, a *product* is a good, a service, or an idea received in an exchange. It can be either tangible or intangible and includes functional, social, and psychological utilities or benefits. It also includes supporting services, such as installation, guarantees, product information, and promises of repair or maintenance. Thus, the four-year/70 000-kilometre warranty that covers most new automobiles is part of the product itself. A **good** is a tangible physical entity, such as an iPod Nano music player or a Subway sandwich. A **service,** in contrast, is intangible; it is the result of the application of human and mechanical efforts to people or objects. Examples of services include a performance by Nelly Furtado, online travel agency bookings, medical examinations, child day care, real estate services, and martial arts lessons. (Chapter 13 provides a detailed discussion of services.) An **idea** is a concept, philosophy, image, or issue. Ideas provide the psychological stimulation that aids in solving problems or adjusting to the environment. For example, MADD (Mothers Against Drunk Driving) promotes safe consumption of alcohol and stricter enforcement of laws against drunk driving. It is helpful to think of a total product offering as having a combination of three interdependent elements: the core product itself, its supplemental features, and its symbolic or experiential value. See Figure 11.1 for an illustration. Consider that some people buy new tires for their basic utility (e.g., Canadian Tire's MotorMaster Tires), while some look for safety (e.g., Michelin), and others buy on the basis of brand name or exemplary performance (e.g., Pirelli).

The core product consists of a product's fundamental utility or main benefit. Broadband Internet services, for instance, offer speedy Internet access but some buyers want more additional features such as wireless connectivity anywhere they go. The core product usually addresses a fundamental need of the consumer. When you buy bottled water, you can buy a store brand, name brand such as Dasani and Aquafina brands, or more exclusive brands such as Voss of Norway. Regardless of price, each alternative will quench your thirst.

figure 11.1

THE TOTAL PRODUCT

Core product

Supplemental features

Symbolic and experimental benefits

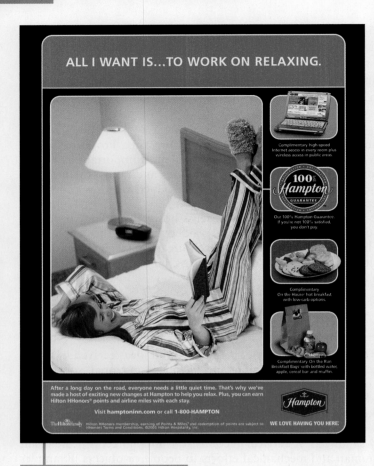

What Is a Product?

Hampton Inn provides a service based on consumers' expectations of a relaxing hotel environment.

Retailers such as Zellers and Wal-Mart specialize in offering core products of a generally acceptable quality level at competitive prices. Hotels such as Country Inns & Suites and the Holiday Inn specialize in providing quality services at affordable prices.

A product's supplemental features provide added value or attributes in addition to its core utility or benefit. Supplemental products can also provide installation, delivery, training, and financing. These supplemental attributes are not required to make the core product function effectively, but they help differentiate one product brand from another. The Hyatt, for example, offers a hotel concept that features larger rooms and work areas, free high-speed Internet, large flat screen TVs, CD and DVD players, and cordless phones.[2] These supplemental features add real value to the core product of overnight hotel stays.

Finally, customers also receive benefits based on their experiences with the product. In addition, many products have symbolic meaning for buyers. For some consumers, the simple act of shopping gives symbolic value and improves their attitudes. Some stores capitalize on this value by striving to create a special experience for customers. For example, you can buy stuffed toys at many retailers, but at Build-A-Bear, you can choose the type of animal, stuff it yourself, give it a heart, create a name complete with a birth certificate, as well as give the toy a bath, and clothe and accessorize it. The atmosphere and décor of a retail store, the variety and depth of product choices, the customer support, even the sounds and smells all contribute to the experiential element. These symbolic and experiential features are all part of the Build-A-Bear total product.

Thus, when buyers purchase a product, they are really buying the benefits and satisfaction they think the product will provide. A Rolex watch, for example, is purchased to make a statement of success, not just for telling time. Services in particular are purchased on the basis of expectations. Expectations, suggested by images, promises, and symbols, as well as processes and delivery, help consumers make judgments about tangible and intangible products. Products are formed by the activities and processes that help satisfy expectations. Starbucks, for example, did not invent the coffee shop, but it did make high-quality coffee beverages readily available around the world with standardized service and in stylish, comfortable stores. Often symbols and cues are used to make intangible products more tangible, or real, to the consumer. Allstate Insurance Company, for example, uses giant hands to symbolize security, strength, and friendliness.

Classifying Products

consumer products Products purchased to satisfy personal and family needs

business products Products bought to use in an organization's operations, to resell, or to make other products

Products fall into one of two general categories. Products purchased to satisfy personal and family needs are **consumer products.** Products bought to use in a firm's operations, to resell, or to make other products are **business products.** Consumers buy products to satisfy their personal wants, whereas business buyers seek to satisfy the goals of their organizations.

The same item can be both a consumer product and a business product. For example, when a consumer buys a 100-watt light bulb for lighting a closet, it is classified as a consumer product. However, when an organization purchases a 100-watt light bulb for lighting a reception area, it is considered a business product because it is used in daily operations. Thus, the buyer's intent—or the ultimate use of the product—determines whether an item is classified as a consumer or business product.

Product classifications are important because classes of products are aimed at particular target markets, which affect distribution, promotion, and pricing decisions. Furthermore, appropriate marketing strategies vary among the classes of consumer and business products. In short, how a product is classified can affect the entire marketing mix. In this section, we examine the characteristics of consumer and business products and explore the marketing activities associated with some of these products.

Consumer Products

The most widely accepted approach to classifying consumer products is based on characteristics of consumer buying behaviour. It divides products into four categories: convenience, shopping, specialty, and unsought products. However, not all buyers behave in the same way when purchasing a specific type of product. Thus, a single product can fit into several categories. To minimize this problem, marketers think in terms of how buyers *generally* behave when purchasing a specific item. In addition, they recognize that the "correct" classification can be determined only by considering a particular firm's intended target market. Examining the four traditional categories of consumer products can provide further insight.

convenience products
Relatively inexpensive, frequently purchased items for which buyers exert minimal purchasing effort

Convenience Products. **Convenience products** are relatively inexpensive, frequently purchased items for which buyers exert only minimal purchasing effort. They range from bread, soft drinks, and chewing gum to gasoline and newspapers. The buyer spends little time planning the purchase or comparing available brands or sellers. Today time has become one of our most precious assets, and many consumers therefore buy products at the closest location to preserve time for other activities. Even a buyer who prefers a specific brand will readily choose a substitute if the preferred brand is not conveniently available.

Classifying a product as a convenience product has several implications for a firm's marketing strategy. A convenience product is normally marketed through many retail outlets. Examples of typical outlets include Esso Gas Stations and Starbucks. Starbucks, for example, has opened locations inside airports, hotels, and grocery stores, and many of its company-owned stores now have drive-through lanes to ensure that customers can get coffee whenever or wherever the desire strikes.[3] Because sellers experience high inventory turnover, per-unit gross margins can be relatively low. Producers of convenience products, such as Altoid mints, expect little promotional effort at the retail level and thus must provide it themselves with advertising and sales promotion. Packaging is also an important

Kathy and Terry Malley

THE BUSINESS: Malley Industries

FOUNDED: 1979

SUCCESS: Exclusive build contracts and year-to-year growth

Malley Industries was founded in 1979 by the late A.J. Malley, his wife, Maudie and their son, Terry, who at the time was attending university. Twelve years earlier, the family had travelled to Expo '67 and found that accommodations were less than satisfactory. Upon their return home, A.J. and Terry built a camper in their basement. From that experience, a company was formed that began building truck campers, truck caps, and custom van conversions.

By the mid 1980s, Malley Industries had branched into manufacturing ambulances and modifying vehicles for persons with disabilities. Their impressive list of public and private sector contracts includes the manufacture of specialized law enforcement and prisoner transportation vehicles as well as custom fleet up-fitting for the transport of commodities, equipment, or people.

From the outset, the Malley family's philosophy was "if our name goes on a product, it has to be our best work." Where many companies strive for mass production, Malley Industries has positioned itself as a niche player, offering custom solutions for clients who have unique vehicle adaptation and transportation needs.

Since 1999, Malley Industries has been in an accelerated state of managed growth. This was due in part to acquiring a contract to replace a provincial fleet of ambulances, but also, to its aggressive approach to developing new markets. The company manufactures in excess of 500 vehicle conversions annually from facilities in both Moncton and Dieppe, N.B.

With growing market reach across Canada, the U.S., and abroad, the company sells civilian, public safety and military vehicles and components throughout Canada, the U.S., Mexico, the European Union, and the Caribbean. Future plans are to strengthen existing business relationships and continue to explore new market opportunities.

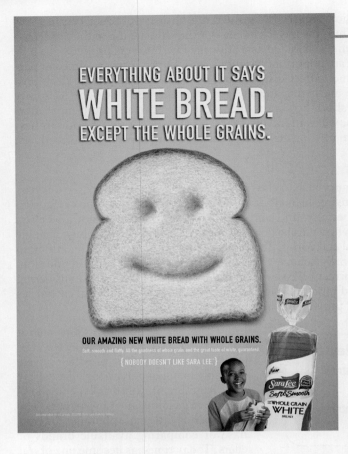

EVERYTHING ABOUT IT SAYS
WHITE BREAD.
EXCEPT THE WHOLE GRAINS.

OUR AMAZING NEW WHITE BREAD WITH WHOLE GRAINS.
Soft, smooth and fluffy. All the goodness of whole grain, and the great taste of white, guaranteed.
{ NOBODY DOESN'T LIKE SARA LEE. }

Convenience Products
White bread is a typical convenience product. Sara Lee adds whole grain to increase the health benefit.

shopping products Items for which buyers are willing to expend considerable effort in planning and making purchases

THE RECIPE FOR A GREAT DISH STARTS,
SURPRISINGLY, WITH A GREAT DISH.

Rediscover CorningWare bakeware. Great colors. Stylish lids.
Integrated handles. From baking to serving to cleanup,
creating your favorite masterpiece has never been easier.

CORNINGWARE.

Shopping Brands
Corning Ware produces reliable cookware, which are shopping products for most consumers.

---

element of the marketing mix for convenience products. The package may have to sell the product because many convenience items are available only on a self-service basis at the retail level.

Shopping Products. **Shopping products** are items for which buyers are willing to expend considerable effort in planning and making the purchase. Buyers spend much time comparing stores and brands with respect to prices, product features, qualities, services, and perhaps warranties. Shoppers may compare products at a number of outlets such as The Source, Sears, or Home Depot. Appliances, bicycles, furniture, stereos, cameras, and shoes exemplify shopping products. These products are expected to last a fairly long time and thus are purchased less frequently than convenience items. Although shopping products are more expensive than convenience products, few buyers of shopping products are particularly brand loyal. Most consumers, for example, are not brand loyal for computers and clothing. If they were, they would be unwilling to shop and compare among brands. Even when they are brand loyal, they may still spend considerable time comparing the features of different models of a brand. A consumer looking for a new Maytag washing machine, for example, may explore the company's website to compare the features of different washers before talking to a salesperson. Regardless of the number of brands of interest, buyers may also consult buying guides such as *Consumer Reports* or visit consumer information websites such as **www.epinions.com** to view others' opinions or ratings of brands and models before making an actual purchase.

To market a shopping product effectively, a marketer considers several key issues. Shopping products require fewer retail outlets than convenience products. Because shopping products are purchased less frequently, inventory turnover is lower, and marketing channel members expect to receive higher gross margins. Although large sums of money may be required to advertise shopping products, an even larger percentage of resources are likely to be used for personal selling. Usually the producer and the marketing channel members expect some cooperation from one another with respect to providing parts and repair services and performing promotional activities. In certain situations, both shopping products and convenience products may be marketed in the same location.

specialty products Items with unique characteristics that buyers are willing to expend considerable effort to obtain

Specialty Products. **Specialty products** possess one or more unique characteristics, and generally buyers are willing to expend considerable effort to obtain them. Buyers actually plan the purchase of a specialty product; they know exactly what they want and will not accept a substitute. Examples of specialty products include a Mont Blanc pen and a one-of-a-kind piece of hockey memorabilia, such as a hockey stick signed by Wayne Gretzky. When searching for specialty products, buyers do not compare alternatives; they are concerned primarily with finding an outlet that has the preselected product available.

The fact that an item is a specialty product can affect a firm's marketing efforts in several ways. Specialty products are often distributed through a limited number of retail outlets. Like shopping products, they are purchased infrequently, causing lower inventory turnover and thus requiring relatively high gross margins.

unsought products Products purchased to solve a sudden problem, products of which customers are unaware, and products that people do not necessarily think of buying

Unsought Products. **Unsought products** are products purchased when a sudden problem must be solved, products of which customers are unaware, and products that people do not necessarily think of purchasing. Emergency medical services and automobile repairs are examples of products needed quickly to solve a problem. A consumer who is sick or injured has little time to plan to go to a medical clinic or a hospital. Likewise, in the event of a broken fan belt on the highway, a consumer will likely seek out the nearest auto repair facility to get back on the road as quickly as possible. Computer users must purchase antivirus and spyware detection software to protect their computers even though they may not want to make such purchases. In such cases, speed and problem resolution are far more important than price and other features buyers might consider if they had more time for decision making. Companies such as ServiceMaster and Rainbow International Carpet Care & Restoration Specialists are making the purchases of these unsought products more bearable by building trust with consumers through recognizable brands and superior functional performance.[4]

Business Products

Business products are usually purchased on the basis of an organization's goals and objectives. Generally the functional aspects of the product are more important than the psychological rewards sometimes associated with consumer products. Business products can be classified into seven categories according to their characteristics and intended uses: installations, accessory equipment, raw materials, component parts, process materials, MRO supplies, and business services.

installations Facilities and non-portable major equipment

Installations. **Installations** include facilities, such as office buildings, factories, and warehouses, and major equipment that are non-portable, such as production lines and very large machines. Major equipment usually is used for production purposes. Some major equipment is custom made to perform specific functions for a particular organization; other items are standardized and perform similar tasks for many types of firms. Normally installations are expensive and intended to be used for a considerable

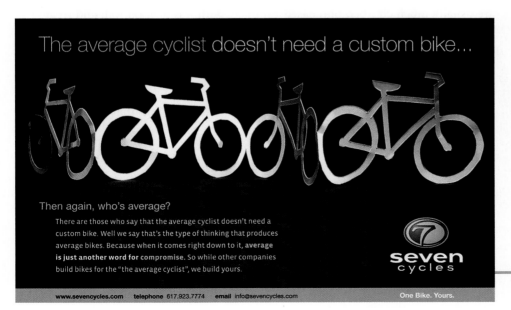

The average cyclist doesn't need a custom bike...

Then again, who's average?

There are those who say that the average cyclist doesn't need a custom bike. Well we say that's the type of thinking that produces average bikes. Because when it comes right down to it, **average is just another word for compromise.** So while other companies build bikes for the "the average cyclist", we build yours.

seven cycles

www.sevencycles.com   telephone 617.923.7774   email info@sevencycles.com   One Bike. Yours.

Specialty Products
Seven cycles makes custom bikes—a specialty product.

Business Products

Sato Barcode label printers are a business product, as are Caterpillar lift trucks.

accessory equipment
Equipment used in production or office activities that does not become a part of the final physical product but is used in production or office activities

raw materials Basic natural materials that become part of a physical product

component parts Items that become part of the physical product and are either finished items ready for assembly or items that need little processing before assembly

length of time. Because they are so expensive and typically involve a long-term investment of capital, purchase decisions are often made by high-level management. Marketers of installations frequently must provide a variety of services, including training, repairs, maintenance assistance, and even financial assistance.

Accessory Equipment. **Accessory equipment** does not become a part of the final physical product but is used in production or office activities. Examples include file cabinets, calculators, and tools. Compared with major equipment, accessory items are usually much cheaper, purchased routinely with less negotiation, and treated as expense items rather than capital items because they are not expected to last as long. Accessory products are standardized items that can be used in several aspects of a firm's operations. More outlets are required for distributing accessory equipment than for installations, but sellers do not have to provide the numerous services expected of installations marketers.

Raw Materials. **Raw materials** are the basic natural materials that actually become part of a physical product. They include minerals, chemicals, agricultural products, and materials from forests and oceans. They are usually bought and sold according to grades and specifications, and in relatively large quantities. Rose oil and jasmine are examples of raw materials in making perfume.

Component Parts. **Component parts** become a part of the physical product and are either finished items ready for assembly or products that need little processing before assembly. Although they become part of a larger product, component parts often can be easily identified and distinguished. Spark plugs, tires, clocks, brakes, and switches are all component parts of an automobile. German-based Robert Bosch GmbH, the world's largest auto parts maker, supplies 30 percent of the 46 million antilock brakes installed in vehicles worldwide.[5] Buyers purchase such items according to their own specifications or industry standards. They expect the parts to be of specified quality and delivered on time so that production is not slowed or stopped. Producers that are primarily assemblers, such as most lawn mower and computer manufacturers, depend heavily on suppliers of component parts.

process materials Materials that are used directly in the production of other products but are not readily identifiable

Process Materials. **Process materials** are used directly in the production of other products. Unlike component parts, however, process materials are not readily identifiable. For example, a salad dressing manufacturer includes vinegar in its salad dressing. The vinegar is a process material because it is included in the salad dressing but is not identifiable. As with component parts, process materials are purchased according to industry standards or the purchaser's specifications.

MRO supplies Maintenance, repair, and operating items that facilitate production and operations but do not become part of the finished product

MRO Supplies. **MRO supplies** are maintenance, repair, and operating items that facilitate production and operations but do not become part of the finished product. Paper, pencils, oils, cleaning agents, and paints are in this category. MRO supplies are commonly sold through numerous outlets and are purchased routinely. To ensure supplies are available when needed, buyers often deal with more than one seller.

business services Intangible products that many organizations use in their operations

Business Services. **Business services** are the intangible products that many organizations use in their operations. They include financial, legal, marketing research, information technology, and janitorial services. Firms must decide whether to provide their own services internally or obtain them from outside the organization. This decision depends on the costs associated with each alternative and how frequently the services are needed. For example, few firms have the resources to provide global overnight delivery services efficiently, so most companies rely on FedEx, UPS, and other service providers.

Product Line and Product Mix

Marketers must understand the relationships among all the products of their organization to coordinate the marketing of the total group of products. The following concepts help describe the relationships among an organization's products.

product item A specific version of a product

product line A group of closely related product items viewed as a unit because of marketing, technical, or end-use considerations

A **product item** is a specific version of a product that can be designated as a distinct offering among an organization's products. A Roots cotton pullover represents a product item. A **product line** is a group of closely related product items that are considered to be a unit because of marketing, technical, or end-use considerations. For example, Procter & Gamble, with the acquisition of Gillette, has hundreds of brands that fall into one of 22 product lines ranging from deodorants to paper products.[6] The exact boundaries of a product line (although sometimes blurred) are usually indicated by using descriptive terms such as "frozen dessert" product line or "shampoo" product line. To develop the optimal product line, marketers must understand buyers' goals. In the personal computer industry, for example, companies are likely to expand their product lines when industry barriers are low or perceived market opportunities exist. Firms with high market share are likely to expand their product lines aggressively, as are marketers with relatively high prices or limited product lines.[7] Specific product items in a product line usually reflect the desires of different target markets or the different needs of consumers.

product mix The composite, or total, group of products that an organization makes available to customers

width of product mix The number of product lines a company offers

depth of product mix The average number of different products offered in each product line

A **product mix** is the composite, or total, group of products that an organization makes available to customers. For example, all the health care, beauty care, laundry and cleaning, food and beverage, paper, cosmetic, and fragrance products that Procter & Gamble manufactures constitute its product mix. The **width of product mix** is measured by the number of product lines a company offers. Robert Bosch GmbH, for example, offers multiple product lines including automotive technology components such as brakes and stability control systems, consumer products such as household appliances, and business products such as packaging machines.[8] The **depth of product mix** is the average number of different products offered in each product line.

figure 11.2   THE CONCEPTS OF PRODUCT MIX WIDTH AND DEPTH APPLIED TO PROCTER & GAMBLE PRODUCTS

Laundry detergents	Toothpastes	Bar soaps	Deodorants	Shampoos	Tissue/Towel
Ivory Snow 1930	Gleem 1952	Ivory 1879	Old Spice 1948	Pantene 1947	Charmin 1928
Dreft 1933	Crest 1955	Camay 1926	Secret 1956	Head & Shoulders 1961	Puffs 1960
Tide 1946		Zest 1952	Sure 1972	Vidal Sassoon 1974	Bounty 1965
Cheer 1950		Safeguard 1963		Pert Plus 1979	
Bold 1965		Oil of Olay 1993		Ivory 1983	
Gain 1966				Infusium 23 1986	
Era 1972				Physique 2000	
Febreze Clean Wash 2000				Herbal Essence 2001	

Depth (vertical axis)   *Width* (horizontal axis)

Reprinted with permission of The Procter and Gamble Company.

Product Line and Product Mix

All natural salad dressings are among Newman's Own product lines. Horizon provides a complete line of dairy products.

Figure 11.2 shows the width and depth of a part of Procter & Gamble's product mix. Procter & Gamble is known for using distinctive branding, packaging, and consumer advertising to promote individual items in its detergent product line. Tide, Bold, Gain, Cheer, and Era—all Procter & Gamble detergents—share the same distribution channels and similar manufacturing facilities, but each is promoted as a distinctive product, adding depth to the product line.

Product Life Cycles and Marketing Strategies

product life cycle
The progression of a product through four stages: introduction, growth, maturity, and decline

Just as biological cycles progress from birth through growth and decline, so do product life cycles. As Figure 11.3 shows, a **product life cycle** has four major stages: introduction, growth, maturity, and decline. As a product moves through its life cycle, the strategies relating to competition, promotion, distribution, pricing, and market information must be periodically evaluated and possibly changed. Astute marketing managers use the life cycle concept to make sure the introduction, alteration, and termination of a product are timed and executed properly. By understanding the typical life cycle pattern, marketers are better able to maintain profitable products and drop unprofitable ones.

Introduction

introduction stage The initial stage of a product's life cycle; its first appearance in the marketplace when sales start at zero and profits are negative

The **introduction stage** of the product life cycle begins at a product's first appearance in the marketplace, when sales start at zero and profits are negative. Profits are below zero because initial revenues are low, and the company generally must cover large expenses for promotion and distribution. Notice in Figure 11.3 how sales should move upward from zero, and profits should also move upward from a position in which they are negative because of high expenses.

Kellogg Lures the Global Breakfast Bunch

Thanks to the vision of its founder, W. K. Kellogg, the Kellogg Company has been investing in international markets for almost 100 years. Many international consumers actually consider Kellogg brands to be "of local origin." And many of them are right: today, Kellogg products are produced in 17 countries and marketed in more than 180.

The United Kingdom is Kellogg's largest European area of business; popular products are Special K Lite Bites, Frosties Light, and yogurt-coated versions of Special K and All-Bran. The company uses a number of themed promotions and health challenges associated with various Kellogg products as successful marketing tools in Europe because of the region's focus on health and wellness.

Growth in Italy, Spain, and Latin America is strong, particularly in Mexico, where the company is building a manufacturing facility for producing cereals and snack foods. Anemia is a common problem in Latin America, so Kellogg initiated its Defensa K campaign to promote the nutritional value of its products, especially iron content. Popular brands in Latin America are Nutri-Grain and All-Bran cereals, Choco Krispies bars, and Pop-Tarts. Marketing campaigns with sports themes are popular.

The Asian Pacific is another growth front for Kellogg, where competition is strong. Kellogg offers new varieties of cereals and bars in Australia and a new version of Frosties with less sugar in South Korea. The initial response to these introductions is positive. Kellogg's campaigns in Australia, India, and Japan focus primarily on health.

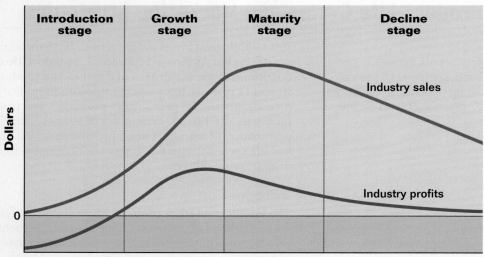

figure 11.3

THE FOUR STAGES OF THE PRODUCT LIFE CYCLE

Developing and introducing a new product can mean an outlay of $100 million or more. Cadbury Schweppes, for example, spent two years and millions of dollars to develop Trident Splash, a sugar-free gum with a candy shell and a liquid centre, which it markets to adults for 99 cents a package.[9] And while the importance of new products is significant, the risk of new-product failure is quite high, depending on the industry. Although LeapFrog introduced the LeapPad educational reading toy with tremendous success, the company has since struggled to find a successful follow-up. Parents today want their kids to learn while playing, but children just want to have fun. To thrive, LeapFrog must adapt to changing expectations from both children and their parents.[10] Because of high risks and costs, few product introductions represent revolutionary inventions. More typically, product introductions involve a new packaged convenience food, a new model of automobile, or a new fashion in clothing rather than a major product innovation. The more marketing oriented the firm, the more likely it will be to launch innovative, new-to-the-market products.[11]

Potential buyers must be made aware of the new product's features, uses, and advantages. Two difficulties may arise at this point. First, sellers may lack the resources, technological knowledge, and marketing know-how to launch the product successfully. Firms without large budgets can still attract attention by giving away free samples. Another small-budget tactic is to gain visibility through media appearances. Dave Dettman, a.k.a. Dr. Gadget, specializes in promoting new products on television news and talk programs. Companies such as Sony, Disney, Warner Brothers, and others have hired

New Products

Miracle-Gro LiquaFeed promotes new product adoption.

Dr. Gadget to help with the introduction of new products.[12] Second, the initial product price may have to be high to recoup expensive marketing research or development costs. Given these difficulties, it is not surprising that many products never get beyond the introduction stage.

Most new products start off slowly and seldom generate enough sales to bring immediate profits. As buyers learn about the new product, marketers should be alert for product weaknesses and make corrections quickly to prevent the product's early demise. Marketing strategy should be designed to attract the segment that is most interested in the product and has the fewest objections. As the sales curve moves upward and the break-even point is reached, the growth stage begins.

Growth

growth stage The product life cycle stage when sales rise rapidly and profits reach a peak, then start to decline

During the **growth stage,** sales rise rapidly and profits reach a peak, then start to decline (see Figure 11.3). The growth stage is critical to a product's survival because competitive reactions to the product's success during this period will affect the product's life expectancy. When Splenda, a sugar substitute, was introduced, sales rose quickly as consumers switched from other low-calorie sweeteners. Sales rose even more quickly when restaurants such as McDonald's and Starbucks began offering Splenda in single-serving packets.[13]

Profits begin to decline late in the growth stage as more competitors enter the market, driving prices down and creating the need for heavy promotional expenses. At this point, a typical marketing strategy encourages strong brand loyalty and competes with aggressive emulators of the product. During the growth stage, the organization tries to strengthen its market share and develop a competitive niche by emphasizing the product's benefits. Aggressive pricing, including price cuts, is also typical during this stage.

As sales increase, management must support the momentum by adjusting the marketing strategy. The goal is to establish and fortify the product's market position by encouraging brand loyalty. To achieve greater market penetration, segmentation may have to be used more intensely. That would require developing product variations to satisfy the needs of people in several different market segments. Apple, for example, introduced two variations on its wildly popular iPod MP3 player. The iPod Mini, a slimmer, more colourful device, and the iPod Shuffle, a more affordable iPod, have helped expand Apple's market penetration in the competitive MP3 player industry.[14] Marketers should also analyze competing brands' product positions relative to their own brands and take corrective actions.

Gaps in geographic market coverage should be filled during the growth period. As a product gains market acceptance, new distribution outlets usually become easier to obtain. Marketers sometimes move from an exclusive or a selective exposure to a more intensive network of dealers to achieve greater market penetration. Marketers must also make sure the physical distribution system is running efficiently so that customers' orders are processed accurately and delivered on time.

Promotion expenditures may be slightly lower than during the introductory stage, but are still quite substantial. As sales increase, promotion costs should drop as a percentage of total sales. A falling ratio between promotion expenditures and sales should contribute significantly to increased profits. The advertising messages should stress brand benefits. Coupons and samples may be used to increase market share.

After recovering development costs, a business may be able to lower prices. As sales volume increases, efficiencies in production can result in lower costs. These savings may be passed on to buyers. For example, when satellite navigation systems for cars were initially introduced, the price was $5000 or more. As demand soared, manufacturers were able to take advantage of economies

Crossover SUV sales soar

Crossover SUV sales grow as sales of traditional SUVs wane.

Traditional SUVs

Crossover SUVs

1.8 million

2.4 million

2.3 million

In millions

3

2

1

0

1995   2000   2006

of scale to reduce production costs and lower prices to less than $2000 within several years.[15] If demand remains strong and there are few competitive threats, prices tend to remain stable. If price cuts are feasible, they can help a brand gain market share and discourage new competitors from entering the market.

Maturity

maturity stage The stage of a product's life cycle when the sales curve peaks and starts to decline, and profits continue to fall

During the **maturity stage,** the sales curve peaks and starts to decline and profits continue to fall (see Figure 11.3). This stage is characterized by intense competition, as many brands are now in the market. Competitors emphasize improvements and differences in their versions of the product. As a result, during the maturity stage, weaker competitors are squeezed out or lose interest in the product.

During the maturity phase, the producers who remain in the market are likely to change their promotional and distribution efforts. Advertising and dealer-oriented promotions are typical during this stage of the product life cycle. Marketers must also take into account that as the product reaches maturity, buyers' knowledge of it attains a high level. Consumers of the product are no longer inexperienced generalists; instead they are experienced specialists. Marketers of mature products sometimes expand distribution into global markets. Often the products have to be adapted to more precisely fit differing needs of global customers.

Because many products are in the maturity stage of their life cycles, marketers must know how to deal with these products and be prepared to adjust their marketing strategies. As Table 11.1 shows, there are many approaches to altering marketing strategies during the maturity stage. As noted in the table, to increase the sales of mature products, marketers may suggest new uses for them. Arm & Hammer has boosted demand for its baking soda with this method. As customers become more experienced and knowledgeable about products during the maturity stage (particularly about bus-

Fifty Years of Pain Relief

In 2005, Tylenol celebrated 50 years of pain relief. Originally created to alleviate pain in children, McNeil Laboratories introduced Tylenol in 1955 as Children's Tylenol Elixir, available only with a prescription. After Johnson & Johnson bought McNeil Lab, it introduced Tylenol for adults in 1961. Since then, the acetaminophen-based pain reliever has become the most popular of its kind on the market for both children and adults.

Europeans began using acetaminophen in 1893, but it remained unfamiliar in North America until the Tylenol brand was launched. Today Tylenol is more popular than ever because it is less likely to interfere with other medications and has fewer complications than Vioxx, Bextra, ibuprofen, and naproxen. Although studies indicate that Aspirin is still the safest pain medication to use in most cases, many doctors and patients alike are confident in and prefer Tylenol for pain relief.

In 1982, seven people died from cyanide-laced Tylenol found in several bottles of Tylenol in Chicago. Johnson & Johnson worked swiftly to deal with the crisis, ultimately recalling 264 000 Tylenol bottles from Chicago stores and advising customers to exchange any bottles they had on hand for new, sealed ones. Although the recall cost the company about $100 million, it was a worthwhile investment. Given the company's straightforward response, consumer confidence in the brand rebounded after just a few months. As a result of the incident, the company introduced containers with multiple seals. Today consumers have tamperproof packaging on many items found at the pharmacy or grocery store due to Johnson & Johnson's response to the Tylenol-tampering crisis.

table 11.1   SELECTED APPROACHES FOR MANAGING PRODUCTS IN THE MATURITY STAGE

Approach	Examples
Develop new product uses	Arm & Hammer baking soda marketed as a refrigerator deodorant Cheez Whiz promoted as a microwavable cheese sauce
Increase product usage among current users	Multiple packaging used for products in which a larger supply at the point of consumption actually increases consumption (such as for soft drinks or beer)
Increase number of users	Global markets or small niches in domestic markets pursued
Add product features	Traditional SUVs slowly replaced by crossover vehicles Satellite radio systems in automobiles
Change package sizes	Single-serving sizes introduced Travel-size packages of personal-care products introduced
Increase product quality	Life of light bulbs increased Reliability and durability of U.S.-made automobiles increased
Change non-product marketing mix variables—promotion, price, distribution	A package of dishwasher detergent containing one-third more product offered for the same price Computer hardware marketed through mail-order outlets

iness products), the benefits they seek may change as well, necessitating product modifications. Consider that traditional truck-based sport-utility vehicles, such as the Ford Explorer and GMC Tahoe, have reached maturity and their sales are beginning to decline. Facing rising gasoline costs, consumers became interested in "crossovers," car-based utility vehicles like the Honda Pilot, BMW X3, Porsche Cayenne, and Saturn Vue. Automakers responded to this interest with more models and features. With their improved ride, handling, and fuel economy, crossovers are in a rapid sales growth stage at the expense of traditional SUVs.[16]

Three general objectives can be pursued during the maturity stage:

1. *Generate cash flow.* This is essential for recouping the initial investment and generating excess cash to support new products.

2. *Maintain share of market.* Companies with marginal market share must decide whether they have a reasonable chance to improve their position or whether they should drop out.

3. *Increase share of customer.* Whereas market share refers to the percentage of total customers a firm holds, *share of customer* relates to the percentage of each customer's needs that the firm is meeting. For example, many banks have added new services (life insurance, financial planning, etc.) to gain more of each customer's financial services business. Likewise, many supermarkets are seeking to increase share of customer by adding services such as restaurants, banks, movie rentals, and dry cleaning to provide one-stop shopping for their customers' household needs.[17]

During the maturity stage, marketers actively encourage dealers to support the product. Dealers may be offered promotional assistance in lowering their inventory costs. In general, marketers go to great lengths to serve dealers and provide incentives for selling their brands.

Maintaining market share during the maturity stage requires moderate, and sometimes large, promotion expenditures. Advertising messages focus on differentiating a brand from the field of competitors, and sales promotion efforts are aimed at both consumers and resellers.

A greater mixture of pricing strategies is used during the maturity stage. Strong price competition is likely and may ignite price wars. Firms also compete in ways other than price, such as through product quality or service. In addition, marketers develop price flexibility to differentiate offerings in product lines. Markdowns and price incentives are common. Prices may have to be increased, however, if distribution and production costs rise.

Decline

decline stage The stage of a product's life cycle when sales fall rapidly

During the **decline stage,** sales fall rapidly (refer to Figure 11.3). When this happens, the marketer considers pruning items from the product line to eliminate those not earning a profit. The marketer may also cut promotion efforts, eliminate marginal distributors, and, finally, plan to phase out the product.

An organization can justify maintaining a product only as long as the product contributes to profits or enhances the overall effectiveness of a product mix. Kodak, after spending $1 billion over eight years to develop its Advantix photography system, pulled the plug after sales declined by 75 percent.[18]

In this stage, marketers must determine whether to eliminate the product or try to reposition it to extend its life. Usually a declining product has lost its distinctiveness because similar competing products have been introduced. Competition engenders increased substitution and brand switching as buyers become insensitive to minor product differences. For these reasons, marketers do little to change a product's style, design, or other attributes during its decline. New technology or social trends, product substitutes, or environmental considerations may also indicate that the time has come to delete the product.

During a product's decline, outlets with strong sales volumes are maintained and unprofitable outlets are weeded out. An entire marketing channel may be eliminated if it does not contribute adequately to profits. An outlet not previously used, such as a factory outlet, is sometimes used to liquidate remaining inventory of an obsolete product. As sales decline, the product becomes more inaccessible, but loyal buyers seek out dealers who still carry it.

Spending on promotion efforts is usually reduced considerably. Advertising of special offers may slow the rate of decline. Sales promotions, such as coupons and premiums, may temporarily recapture buyers' attention. As the product continues to decline, the sales staff shifts its emphasis to more profitable products.

The marketing manager has two options during the decline stage: attempt to postpone the decline or accept its inevitability. Many firms lack the resources to renew a product's demand and are forced to consider harvesting or divesting the product or the strategic business unit (SBU). The *harvesting* approach employs a gradual reduction in marketing expenditures and a less resource-intensive marketing mix. A company adopting the *divesting* approach withdraws all marketing support from the declining product or SBU. It may continue to sell the product until losses are sustained or arrange for another firm to acquire the product.

Because most businesses have a product mix consisting of multiple products, a firm's destiny is rarely tied to one product. A composite of life cycle patterns forms when various products in the mix are at different cycle stages: as one product is declining, other products are in the introduction, growth, or maturity stage. Marketers must deal with the dual problem of prolonging the lives of existing products and introducing new products to meet organizational sales goals.

Product Adoption Process

Acceptance of new products—especially new-to-the-world products—usually doesn't happen overnight. In fact, it can take a very long time. People are sometimes cautious or even skeptical about adopting new products, as indicated by some of the remarks quoted in Table 11.2. Customers who eventually accept a new product do

table 11.2	MOST NEW IDEAS HAVE THEIR SKEPTICS

"I think there is a world market for maybe five computers."

—Thomas Watson, chairman of IBM, 1943

"This 'telephone' has too many shortcomings to be seriously considered as a means of communication. The device is inherently of no value to us."

—Western Union internal memo, 1876

"The wireless music box has no imaginable commercial value. Who would pay for a message sent to nobody in particular?"

—David Sarnoff's associates in response to his urgings for investment in the radio in the 1920s

"The concept is interesting and well-formed, but in order to earn better than a 'C,' the idea must be feasible."

—A Yale University management professor in response to Fred Smith's paper proposing reliable overnight delivery service (Smith went on to found Federal Express Corporation)

"Who the hell wants to hear actors talk?"

—H. M. Warner, Warner Brothers, 1927

"We don't like their sound, and guitar music is on the way out."

—Decca Recording Company rejecting the Beatles, 1962

product adoption process
The five-stage process of buyer acceptance of a product: awareness, interest, evaluation, trial, and adoption

so through an adoption process. The stages of the **product adoption process** are as follows:

1. *Awareness.* The buyer becomes aware of the product.

2. *Interest.* The buyer seeks information and is receptive to learning about the product.

3. *Evaluation.* The buyer considers the product's benefits and decides whether to try it.

4. *Trial.* The buyer examines, tests, or tries the product to determine if it meets his or her needs.

5. *Adoption.* The buyer purchases the product and can be expected to use it again whenever the need for this general type of product arises.[19]

In the first stage, when individuals become aware that the product exists, they have little information about it and are not concerned about obtaining more. Consumers enter the interest stage when they are motivated to get information about the product's features, uses, advantages, disadvantages, price, or location. During the evaluation stage, individuals consider whether the product will satisfy certain criteria that are crucial to meeting their specific needs. In the trial stage, they use or experience the product for the first time, possibly by purchasing a small quantity, taking advantage of free samples, or borrowing the product from someone. Supermarkets, for instance, frequently offer special promotions to encourage consumers to taste products. During this stage, potential adopters determine the usefulness of the product under the specific conditions for which they need it.

Individuals move into the adoption stage by choosing a specific product when they need a product of that general type. However, entering the adoption process does not mean the person will eventually adopt the new product. Rejection may occur at any stage, including the adoption stage. Both product adoption and product rejection can be temporary or permanent. This adoption model has several implications when launching a new product. First, the company must promote the product to create widespread awareness of its existence and its benefits. Samples or simulated trials should be arranged to help buyers make initial purchase decisions. At the same time, marketers should emphasize quality control and provide solid guarantees to reinforce buyer opinion during the evaluation stage. Finally, production and physical distribution must be linked to patterns of adoption and repeat purchases.

When an organization introduces a new product, people do not begin the adoption process at the same time, nor do they move through the process at the same speed. Of those who eventually adopt the product, some enter the adoption process rather quickly, whereas others start considerably later. For most products, there is also a group of non-adopters who never begin the process. For marketers, success in managing production innovation, diffusion, and adoption requires great adaptability and significant effort in understanding customers.[20]

Depending on the length of time it takes them to adopt a new product, consumers fall into one of five major adopter categories: innovators, early adopters, early majority, late majority, and laggards.[21] Figure 11.4 illustrates each adopter category and the percentage of total adopters it typically represents. **Innovators** are the first to adopt a new product; they enjoy trying new products and tend to be venturesome. **Early adopters** choose new products carefully and are viewed as "the people to check with" by those in the remaining adopter categories. People in the **early majority** adopt a new product just prior to the average person; they are deliberate and cautious in trying new products. Individuals in the **late majority** are quite skeptical of new products, but eventually adopt them because of economic necessity or social pressure. **Laggards,** the last to adopt a new product, are oriented toward the past. They are suspicious of new products, and when they finally adopt the innovation, it may already have been replaced by a new product.

Why Some Products Fail and Others Succeed

Thousands of new products are introduced annually, and many fail. Statistical bureaus, consulting firms, and trade publications estimate that one in three new products fails each year; others report an annual new-product failure rate as high as 80 to 90 percent. Failure and success rates vary from organization to organization, but in general consumer products fail more often than business products. Being one of the first brands launched in a product category is no guarantee of success. Table 11.3 shows examples of recent product successes and failures.

Products fail for many reasons. One of the most common reasons is the company's failure to match product offerings to customer needs. When products do not offer value and lack the features customers want, they fail in the marketplace. For example, Coca-Cola's C2 and PepsiCo's Pepsi Edge, both targeted at low-carbohydrate dieters with their mid-range calorie count, ultimately garnered just one percent share of the market together because low-carb dieters generally avoid products with any refined sugar.[22] Ineffective or inconsistent branding has also been blamed for product failures. Examples of products that failed due to failure to convey the right message

innovators First adopters of new products

early adopters Careful choosers of new products

early majority Individuals who adopt a new product just prior to the average person

late majority Skeptics who adopt new products when they feel it is necessary

laggards The last adopters, who distrust new products

---

figure 11.4

DISTRIBUTION OF PRODUCT ADOPTER CATEGORIES

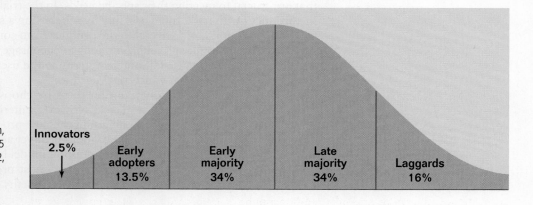

Innovators 2.5% | Early adopters 13.5% | Early majority 34% | Late majority 34% | Laggards 16%

table 11.3	PRODUCT SUCCESSES AND FAILURES	
Successes	**Failures**	
Smith Kline Beecham Nicoderm CQ	R. J. Reynolds Premier smokeless cigarettes	
Canon Elph digital camera	Cadillac Allante luxury cars	
Palm PDAs	Apple Lisa personal computer	
Coca-Cola Dasani water	Heinz Ketch Salsa	
Starbucks coffee shops	Nestle Panache coffee	
Procter & Gamble Pantene shampoos	Gillette For Oily Hair shampoo	
Tide High Efficiency laundry detergent	Drel Home Dry Cleaning Kits	
Procter & Gamble Swiffer mop and dusting cloths	S. C. Johnson Allercare aerosol spray, carpet powder, and dust mite powder	
Bacardi Breezers	Bricklin SV-1 safety vehicle	

or image include Gerber Singles (gourmet food for adults packaged in baby food jars), Microsoft's Bob (a "social interface" cartoon character that many users perceived as juvenile), and Gillette's For Oily Hair Only shampoo.[23] Other reasons cited for new-product failure include technical or design problems, poor timing, overestimation of market size, ineffective promotion, and insufficient distribution.

When examining the problem of product failure, it is important to distinguish the degree of failure. Absolute failure occurs when an organization loses money on a new product because it is unable to recover development, production, and marketing costs. This product usually is deleted from the product mix. Relative product failure occurs when a product returns a profit but does not meet a company's profit or market share objectives. If a company repositions or improves a relative product failure, that product may become a successful member of the product line. In contrast to this gloomy picture of new-product failure, some new products are very successful. Perhaps the most important ingredient for success is the product's ability to provide a significant and perceivable benefit (or relative advantage) to a sizable number of customers. New products with an observable advantage over similar available products, such as more features, ease of operation, or improved technology, have a greater chance to succeed. Critical to launching a product that will achieve market success is effective planning and management. Companies that follow a systematic, customer-focused plan for new-product development, such as Procter & Gamble, and 3M, are well positioned to launch successful products.

SUMMARY

A product is a good, a service, or an idea received in an exchange. It can be either tangible or intangible and includes functional, social, and psychological utilities or benefits. When consumers purchase a product, they are buying the benefits and satisfaction they think the product will provide.

Products can be classified on the basis of the buyer's intentions. Consumer products are those purchased to satisfy personal and family needs. Business products are purchased for use in a firm's operations, to resell, or to make other products. Consumer products can be subdivided into convenience, shopping, specialty, and unsought products.

Business products can be classified as installations, accessory equipment, raw materials, component parts, process materials, MRO supplies, or business services.

A product item is a specific version of a product that can be designated as a distinct offering among an organization's products. A product line is a group of closely related product items that are viewed as a unit because of marketing, technical, or end-use considerations. The product mix is the composite, or total, group of products that an organization makes available to customers. The width of the product mix is measured by the number of product lines the company offers. The depth of the product mix is the average number of different products offered in each product line.

The product life cycle describes how product items in an industry move through four stages: introduction, growth, maturity, and decline. The life cycle concept is used to ensure that the introduction, alteration, and termination of a product are timed and executed properly. The sales curve is at zero at introduction, rises at an increasing rate during growth, peaks at maturity, and then declines. Profits peak toward the end of the growth stage of the product life cycle. The life expectancy of a product is based on buyers' wants, the availability of competing products, and other environmental conditions. Most businesses have a composite of life cycle patterns for various products. It is important to manage existing products and develop new ones to keep the overall sales performance at a desired level.

When customers accept a new product, they usually do so through a five-stage adoption process. The first stage is awareness, when buyers become aware that a product exists. Interest, the second stage, occurs when buyers seek information about the product. In the third stage, evaluation, buyers consider the product's benefits and decide whether to try it. The fourth stage is trial, when buyers

examine, test, or try the product to determine if it meets their needs. The last stage is adoption, when buyers actually purchase the product and use it whenever a need for this general type of product arises.

Of the thousands of new products introduced every year, many fail. Absolute failure occurs when an organization loses money on a new product. Absolute failures are usually removed from the product mix. Relative failure occurs when a product returns a profit but fails to meet a company's objectives. Reasons for product failure include failure to match product offerings to customer needs, poor timing, and ineffective or inconsistent branding. New products that succeed provide significant and observable benefits to customers. Products that have perceivable advantages over similar products also have a better chance to succeed. Effective marketing planning and product management are important factors in a new product's chances of success.

Please visit the student website at **www.prideferrell.com** for ACE Self-Test questions that will help you prepare for exams.

IMPORTANT TERMS

Good	Unsought products	Product item	Maturity stage
Service	Installations	Product line	Decline stage
Idea	Accessory equipment	Product mix	Product adoption process
Consumer products	Raw materials	Width of product mix	Innovators
Business products	Component parts	Depth of product mix	Early adopters
Convenience products	Process materials	Product life cycle	Early majority
Shopping products	MRO supplies	Introduction stage	Late majority
Specialty products	Business services	Growth stage	Laggards

DISCUSSION & REVIEW QUESTIONS

1. List the tangible and intangible attributes of a pair of Nike athletic shoes. Compare its benefits with those of an intangible product such as a hairstyling in a salon.

2. A product has been referred to as a "psychological bundle of satisfaction." Is this a good definition of a product? Why or why not?

3. Is a personal computer sold at a retail store a consumer product or a business product? Defend your answer.

4. How do convenience products and shopping products differ? What are the distinguishing characteristics of each type of product?

5. In the category of business products, how do component parts differ from process materials?

6. How does an organization's product mix relate to its development of a product line? When should an

enterprise add depth to its product lines rather than width to its product mix?

7. How do industry profits change as a product moves through the four stages of its life cycle?

8. What is the relationship between the concepts of product mix and product life cycle?

9. What are the stages in the product adoption process, and how do they affect the commercialization phase?

10. What are the five major adopter categories describing the length of time required for a consumer to adopt a new product, and what are the characteristics of each?

11. In what ways does the marketing strategy for a mature product differ from the marketing strategy for a growth product?

12. What are the major reasons for new-product failure?

APPLICATION QUESTIONS

1. Choose a familiar clothing store. Describe its product mix, including its depth and width. Evaluate the mix and make suggestions to the owner.

2. Tabasco pepper sauce is a product that has entered the maturity stage of the product life cycle. Name products that would fit into each of the four stages: introduction, growth, maturity, and decline. Describe each product and explain why it fits in that stage.

3. Generally buyers go through a product adoption process before becoming loyal customers. Describe your experience in adopting a product you now use consistently. Did you go through all the stages of the process?

4. Identify and describe a friend or family member who fits into each of the following adopter categories. How would you use this information if you were product manager for a fashion-oriented, medium-priced clothing retailer such as?
   a. Innovator
   b. Early adopter
   c. Early majority
   d. Late majority
   e. Laggard

globalEDGE™

1. A firm's ability to innovate and develop new-product concepts is usually determined by the level of inventiveness and adeptness to adjust to market demands. As a result, successful firms generally benefit from an increase in revenue and publicity in magazines devoted to business innovation. *Business 2.0* annually ranks the fastest-growing companies, which often have the greatest rates of innovation. The ranking can be accessed by using the search term "business innovation" at **http://globaledge.msu.edu/ibrd** or **http://globaledge.msu.edu/ibrd/ibrd.asp.** Once you reach the *Business 2.0* website, click on Lists, and then choose the Fastest-Growing Companies option. Based on the *Business 2.0* List of Fastest-Growing Companies, what are the top ten fastest-growing companies? Which industry appears currently to have the most successful commercial innovativeness? Why do you think this industry is thriving?

2. The development of concepts for new products requires a firm to devote resources to research and development (R&D). While insight on different firms' R&D strategies and expenditures may be readily available in annual reports, *Technology Review,* a magazine of innovation, can consolidate this data in its Corporate R&D Scorecard to yield a more comprehensive analysis. The report can be accessed by using the search term "magazine of innovation" at **http://globaledge.msu.edu/ibrd** or **http://globaledge.msu.edu/ibrd/ibrd.asp.** Which three industries in a recent report devote the most resources to R&D? Which three industries allocate the least? What does this allow you to conclude about the characteristics of each industry?

INTERNET Exercise

Goodyear Tire & Rubber Company

In addition to providing information about the company's products, Goodyear's website helps consumers find the exact products they want and will even direct them to the nearest Goodyear retailer. Visit the Goodyear site at **www.goodyear.com.**

1. How does Goodyear use its website to communicate information about the quality of its tires?
2. How does Goodyear's website demonstrate product design and features?
3. Based on what you learned at the website, describe what Goodyear has done to position its tires.

Case 11.1   There's No Place like . . . Starbucks

Starbucks was founded in 1971 by three partners in Seattle's renowned open-air Pike Place Market. In 1982, after returning from a trip to coffee bar haven Milan, Italy (with its 1500 coffee bars), Howard Schultz recognized an opportunity to develop a similar retail coffee-bar culture in Seattle and joined the company as director of retail operations and marketing. Three years later, the company tested the first downtown Seattle coffeehouse, served the first Starbucks Café latte, and introduced its Christmas blend. Since then Starbucks expanded first across the United States and then around the globe. The company now operates 10 801 locations in 37 countries. It opens about three new stores a day and serves more than 30 million customers a week.

Starbucks purchases and roasts high-quality whole coffee beans and resells them, along with fresh brewed coffees, Italian-style espresso beverages, cold blended beverages, bottled water, complementary food items, coffee-related accessories and equipment, premium teas, and a line of CDs, primarily through company-operated retail stores. Starbucks also sells coffee and tea products and licenses its trademark through other channels, and, through some of its partners. Starbucks produces and sells bottled Frappuccino coffee drinks, DoubleShot espresso drinks, and a line of super-premium ice cream.

Starbucks locates its walk-in stores in high-traffic, high-visibility locations. While Starbucks can be found in a few shopping malls, the company generally focuses on locations that provide convenient access for pedestrians and drivers. The stores are designed to provide an inviting coffee bar environment that is an important part of the Starbucks experience. Because the company is flexible with regard to size and format, it can locate stores in or near a variety of settings, including downtown and suburban retail centres, office buildings, and university campuses. It can also situate retail stores in select rural and off-highway locations to serve a broader array of customers outside major metropolitan markets and further expand brand awareness. To provide a greater degree of access and convenience for non-pedestrian customers, the company has increased development of stores with drive-through lanes.

Starbucks constantly strives to update its products and introduces new drinks with each season. At Christmastime, drinks such as peppermint mochas and gingerbread lattes helped push earnings up 20 percent for the quarter. An eggnog latte introduced in 2004 proved so popular that the company introduced a new chai tea version of the drink the next year. Starbucks also tries hard to keep up with consumer desires and needs, for example, by introducing a low-calorie version of its popular frappuccino, which has about 30 to 40 percent fewer calories than the original. While the low-cal frappuccino has been very successful, not all new products are. In 2006 Starbucks pulled Chantico, its "drinkable dessert," from the menu. Chantico was marketed to resemble the thick, sweet hot chocolate drinks found in European cafés, but it was available without any variations in a six-ounce size. The limitations proved fatal: at Starbucks, customers are used to dictating not only the size of their coffee drinks but also the host of other specifics, such as whether they want them regular or decaf; with non-fat, whole or soy milk; with sugar-free or regular flavour shots; and with extras like whipped cream and caramel.

Starbucks has been ranked on *Fortune*'s "100 Best Companies to Work for" list for eight years and in 2005 ranked 29th. The company offers both full- and part-time employees a comprehensive benefits package that includes stock option grants through *Bean Stock,* as well as health, medical, dental, and vision benefits. It also embraces diversity as an essential component of doing business. The company has 91 056 employees; 11 444 are outside the United States. Of these, 28 percent are minorities and 64 percent are women. However, being a great employer does take its toll. In 2005, Starbucks spent more on health insurance for its employees than on raw materials required to brew its coffee. The company has faced double-digit increases in insurance costs each of the last four years. Nonetheless, the Starbucks' benefits policy is a key reason that it has notably low employee turnover and high productivity.

In the process of trying to establish Starbucks as the most recognized and respected brand of coffee in the world, the company has also built an excellent reputation for social responsibility and business ethics. Starbucks pays coffee farmers premium prices to help them make profits and support their families. It is also involved in social development programs that invest in programs to build schools, health clinics, and other projects that benefit coffee-growing communities. It collaborates with farmers through the Farmer Support Center, located in Costa Rica, to provide technical support and training that promotes high-quality coffee for the future. It strives to buy conservation and certified coffees including Fair Trade Certified, shade grown, and certified organic coffee, to promote responsible environmental and economic efforts. In 2005 Starbucks ranked 42nd on *Business Ethics'* "100 Best Corporate Citizens" list, up from its 2004 position of 45th. Starbucks' sense of social responsibility, fair trade, and support for the environment are a part of the total product it markets for consumers that are concerned about these social issues.[24]

Questions for Discussion

1. What is the total product that Starbucks markets?
2. What is the role of the development of new products in Starbucks' success?
3. Why do you think some new Starbucks products succeed and others, like Chantico, fail?

Case 11.2 Dell Mixes It Up

From MP3 music players and an online music store to flat-screen televisions to home theatre projectors, Dell is filling out its product mix with goods and services for the entire household. The company formerly known as Dell Computer wants to build on its dominance of the personal computer market by making inroads into the lucrative $100 billion world of consumer electronics. Based in Round Rock, Texas, Dell made its name selling computers directly to customers through its website. In the future, the company expects to derive an ever-larger portion of revenues and profits from a wider mix of products for use beyond the home office.

This drive for diversification started with the introduction of the Dell Axim handheld computer—in direct competition with Palm and other established rivals—followed one year later by a second Axim model. Because the Axims are priced lower than most comparable products, Dell's entry forced Hewlett-Packard and other competitors to lower prices to protect their market share. The company used the same approach when it began selling printers and ink cartridges on its website, again competing directly with Hewlett-Packard. Even some Dell insiders were surprised when printer sales in the first six months were two times higher than forecasted sales.

Now the stage was set for a more comprehensive move into electronics designed for the digital home. Founder Michael Dell and his team envisioned consumers using a personal computer (from Dell, of course) to control televisions, music players, and other products all around the house. They began the planning process by carefully examining electronics products made by nearly 90 manufacturers. They also analyzed consumers' needs, buying patterns, and complaints about incompatibility problems between new and older products. Based on all of this research, they developed an ultra-bright, flat-screen LCD television, a Dell Digital Jukebox (DJ) to store and play music files, and a home theatre projector for viewing DVDs and other entertainment. These new products were introduced in time for the holiday buying season, along with the Dell Music Store (selling downloadable music files) and software preloaded on Dell computers to help consumers manage digital entertainment files.

These new products, like the printers and handheld computers before them, put Dell squarely in the middle of a competitive battle with well-established rivals. The Dell DJ competes with Apple's iPod digital music player. The Dell Music Store sells downloadable music files in competition with Apple's iTunes store and other online retailers of digital music. The LCD television not only challenges Sony's television business but sets up a different kind of confrontation about which appliance will serve as the control centre of home entertainment. Dell is putting its brand and money behind the computer as the controlling appliance, whereas Sony is putting its resources behind the television as the controlling appliance. "Now is the time for TVs to be reborn," comments a Sony spokesperson.

Although Dell started with only a product or two in each new line, it is gradually adding depth and expanding the width of its product mix. The company is not looking to pioneer new lines; it specializes in applying new technology, adding new features, and making production more efficient. As Dell gains experience with consumer electronics products, it finds ways to lower costs while enhancing each new model. Meanwhile Hewlett-Packard is focusing more on consumer products with the introduction of more than 150 new products, including digital cameras designed for compatibility with its colour printers. Samsung and Sony are aggressively targeting segments of the home entertainment market with plasma televisions, home theatre projectors, and other products.

Can Dell triumph in such a dynamic and competitive environment? The company certainly knows how to keep prices low by wringing the most productivity out of its direct distribution method. It also knows how to stay close to customers and find out what they want. Finally, with a 20-year history of marketing technology-based products, Dell is among the best-known brands in the country. "We've come out of nowhere to be the number-three consumer brand in the U.S. in less than five years, while Coca-Cola has been doing it for 100 years," says Dell's general manager of consumer business for the United States. "We're not in this to be number three. Number one is the only target around here."[25]

Questions for Discussion

1. As a product, how can the Dell DJ music player be classified? Why?
2. While Dell has successfully marketed computers directly to customers, are customers likely to be willing to purchase consumer electronics such as home theatre systems direct from Dell?
3. How far can Dell widen its product mix without hurting the company's credibility? For example, what might be the impact of new products such as Dell motorcycles or Dell frozen pastries?

12

Developing and Managing Products

One Sweet Brand

By replacing three hydrogen-oxygen groups with three chlorine atoms in a sugar molecule, scientists at Tate & Lyle PLC and researchers at Queen Elizabeth College in London created sucralose—which we know as Splenda—in 1976. Six hundred times sweeter than sugar, Splenda is not absorbed by the body as a carbohydrate. To market the sweetener, Tate & Lyle partnered with McNeil Nutritional (part of Johnson & Johnson). It reached North America when it was approved for consumption in Canada in 1991; the U.S. Food and Drug Administration approved its use in food in 1998. Initially, Splenda was available in only limited quantities via the Internet, but it became available in grocery and other retail stores and restaurants in 2000. In just five short years, Splenda became a household word.

Analysts attribute the sweetener's success to an intelligent, gradual introduction strategy. McNeil Nutritional first targeted diabetics via the Internet to help build interest and demand. Only later did the company begin marketing to grocery stores and restaurants as well as to niche food and beverage companies such as Atkins Nutritional. Although you might think Splenda's marketers would take aim at its direct competition Sweet'N Low, Equal, and other artificial sweeteners, McNeil chose to go head to head against the sugar market. The company promoted Splenda as "made from sugar, so it tastes like sugar" with the implication that Splenda is more natural than other imitation sweeteners.

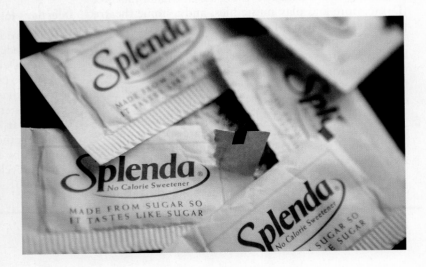

The strategy worked: by 2005 Splenda had revenues greater than sugar brands Domino and C&H; it surpassed sales of Equal and Sweet'N Low in 2004.

There are those that are critical of Splenda. In 2005 the Sugar Association and several other groups sued, not over the sweetener's safety, but over its "made from sugar, so it tastes like sugar" marketing claim. The association also launched a website (**www.truthaboutsplenda.com**) to inform consumers that Splenda is in fact a chemical. (A 2004 survey had revealed that 47 percent of Splenda users believed it was a "natural" product.)

Despite the lawsuits, Splenda continues to gain popularity. McDonald's is replacing Sweet'N Low packets with Splenda at 13 700 U.S. stores. Workers at Starbucks had to hide Splenda packets to keep customers from taking handfuls of them. Dunkin' Donuts and Peet's Coffee & Tea have also begun stocking it in response to high demand. Splenda is now used in more than 3000 foods and beverages, including Diet Coke, Diet Pepsi, and 7-Up, many displaying the Splenda logo on their own labels.

Building the Splenda brand is important not only for increasing revenue, but also in putting it at the forefront of the sucralose market. The patents on the process of making sucralose expired in 2006, opening the door for other companies to make products containing sucralose on their own. However, McNeil is not concerned. The company has plans to expand into Europe and to continue to innovate to keep the Splenda brand in the number one spot.[1] ■

Organizations like the marketer of Splenda must be able to adjust their product mixes in response to changes in customers' needs. To provide products that satisfy target markets and achieve the firm's objectives, a marketer must develop, alter, and maintain an effective product mix. An organization's product mix may require adjustment for a variety of reasons. Because customers' attitudes and product preferences change over time, their desire for certain products may wane. Coca-Cola, for example, has seen sales of carbonated drinks decline as consumers seek alternatives such as bottled water. The decline is particularly worrisome given that the cola giant gets 82 percent of its sales from soft drinks. Thus, the company introduced more than 1000 new products in 2005, including Diet Coke with Splenda, flavoured Dasani water, and low-calorie Powerade sports drink. Coke also plans to introduce new juice, water, coffee, and iced-tea products over the next few years.[2] In some cases, a company needs to alter its product mix for competitive reasons. A marketer may have to delete a product from the mix because a competitor dominates the market for that product. Similarly, a firm may have to introduce a new product or modify an existing one to compete more effectively or to take advantage of excess marketing and production capacity. Product mix decisions often involve adjustments to the brand, components of the brand, its package, or label. These are part of a product's tangible features, the verbal and physical cues that help customers identify the products they want and influence their choices when they are unsure. As such, branding and packaging play an important role in marketing strategy.

In this chapter, we examine several ways to improve an organization's product mix, including management of existing products, development of new products, product differentiation, and elimination of weak products from the product mix. We also discuss branding along with several relevant branding decisions and policies employed to aid product management. First, we discuss managing existing products through effective line extension and product modification. Then we examine the stages of new-product development, and look at the ways companies differentiate their products in the marketplace, discuss product positioning and repositioning, and examine the importance of deleting weak products. Next we discuss branding, its value to customers and marketers, brand loyalty, brand equity, and various types of brands. We consider how companies choose and protect brands, the various branding policies employed, co-branding, and brand licensing. We look at packaging's critical role as part of the product. Also, we explore the functions of packaging, issues to consider in packaging design, and packaging criticisms. Finally, we discuss the functions of labelling and relevant legal issues.

Managing Existing Products

An organization can benefit by capitalizing on its existing products. By assessing the composition of the current product mix, a marketer can identify weaknesses and gaps. This analysis can then lead to improvement of the product mix through line extension and product modification.

Line Extensions

line extension Development of a product that is closely related to existing products in the line but is designed specifically to meet different customer needs

A **line extension** is the development of a product closely related to one or more products in the existing product line but designed specifically to meet somewhat different customer needs. For example, Speedo, long known for its bathing suits, introduced high-performance winter-sport suits at the 2006 Winter Olympics.[3]

Many of the so-called new products introduced each year are in fact line extensions. Line extensions are more common than new products because they are a less expensive, lower-risk alternative for increasing sales. A line extension may focus on a different market segment or be an attempt to increase sales within the same market segment by more precisely satisfying the needs of people in that segment. Clorox, for example, introduced the Clorox Toilet Wand, which incorporates Clorox bleach.[4] Line extensions are also used to take market share from competitors. However, one side effect of employing a line extension is that it may result in a more negative evaluation of the core product.[5]

Product Modifications

product modification Changes in one or more characteristics of a product

quality modifications Changes relating to a product's dependability and durability

Product modification means changing one or more characteristics of a product. A product modification differs from a line extension in that the original product does not remain in the line. For example, North American automakers use product modifications annually when they create new models of the same brand. Once the new models are introduced, the manufacturers stop producing last year's model. Like line extensions, product modifications entail less risk than developing new products.

Product modification can indeed improve a firm's product mix, but only under certain conditions. First, the product must be modifiable. Second, customers must be able to perceive that a modification has been made. Third, the modification should make the product more consistent with customers' desires so it provides greater satisfaction. One drawback to modifying a successful product is that the consumer who had experience with the original version of the product may view a modified version as a riskier purchase.[6] There are three major ways to modify products: quality, functional, and aesthetic modifications.

Quality Modifications. Quality modifications are changes relating to a product's dependability and durability. The changes usually are executed by altering the materials or the production process. For example, Energizer increased its product's durability by using better materials—a larger cathode and anode interface—that make batteries last longer. For a service,

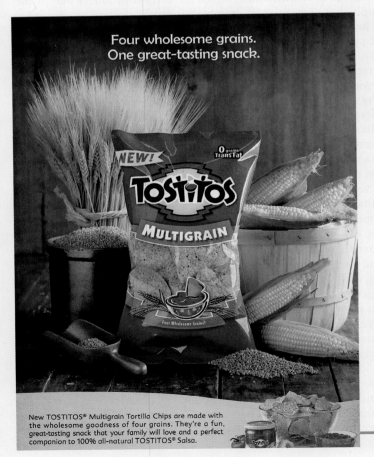

New TOSTITOS® Multigrain Tortilla Chips are made with the wholesome goodness of four grains. They're a fun, great-tasting snack that your family will love and a perfect companion to 100% all-natural TOSTITOS® Salsa.

Line Extensions

Tostitos grew through line extensions.

THE NEW ENVOY DENALI WITH AVAILABLE TOUCH-SCREEN NAVIGATION SYSTEM. OUR MOST LUXURIOUS APPOINTMENTS. OUR MOST ADVANCED IDEAS. AND OUR HIGHEST LEVEL OF ENGINEERING. ALL LIE BEHIND THIS GRILLE. VISIT GMC.COM/DENALI. WE ARE PROFESSIONAL GRADE. **ENVOY** DENALI

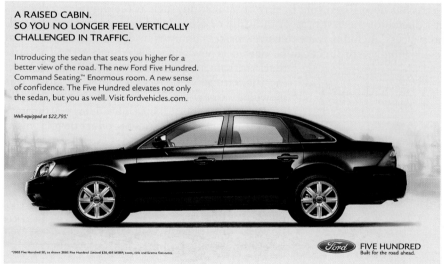

A RAISED CABIN.
SO YOU NO LONGER FEEL VERTICALLY
CHALLENGED IN TRAFFIC.

Introducing the sedan that seats you higher for a
better view of the road. The new Ford Five Hundred.
Command Seating.™ Enormous room. A new sense
of confidence. The Five Hundred elevates not only
the sedan, but you as well. Visit fordvehicles.com.

Well-equipped at $22,795.

*2005 Five Hundred SE; as shown 2005 Five Hundred Limited $28,495 MSRP; taxes, title and license fees extra.

Ford FIVE HUNDRED
Built for the road ahead.

Product Modification

Automakers often use product modification to grow. GM provides a touch screen navigation system in its Denali; the Ford Five Hundred offers a raised cabin for better road visibility.

such as a sporting event or air travel, quality modifications may involve enhancing the emotional experience that makes the consumer passionate and loyal to the brand.

Reducing a product's quality may allow an organization to lower its price and direct the item at a different target market. In contrast, increasing the quality of a product may give a firm an advantage over competing brands. Higher quality may enable a company to charge a higher price by creating customer loyalty and lowering customer sensitivity to price.

Functional Modifications. Changes that affect a product's versatility, effectiveness, convenience, or safety are called **functional modifications;** they usually require redesign of the product. Product categories that have undergone considerable functional modification include office and farm equipment, appliances, cleaning products, and telecommunications services. For example, Gillette, which has achieved great success with its three-blade Mach3 shaving system, introduced the five-blade Fusion in both manual and battery-powered versions

functional modifications
Changes affecting a product's versatility, effectiveness, convenience, or safety

and priced at a 30 percent premium. The new system's blades are 30 percent closer together than before.[7]

Functional modifications can make a product useful to more people and thus enlarge its market. They can place a product in a favourable competitive position by providing benefits that competing brands do not offer. They can also help an organization achieve and maintain a progressive image. Finally, functional modifications are sometimes made to reduce the possibility of product liability lawsuits.

aesthetic modifications
Changes relating to the sensory appeal of a product

Aesthetic Modifications.   **Aesthetic modifications** change the sensory appeal of a product by altering its taste, texture, sound, smell, or appearance. A buyer making a purchase decision is swayed by how a product looks, smells, tastes, feels, or sounds. Thus, an aesthetic modification may strongly affect purchases. For years, automobile makers have relied on quality and aesthetic modifications. For example, the Ford Mustang has been around in one form or another since 1964. The latest modification has a retro look that dates back to the Mustang's muscle car heritage but also includes new safety features.[8]

Aesthetic modifications can help a firm differentiate its product from competing brands and thus gain a sizable market share. The major drawback in using aesthetic modifications is that their value is determined subjectively. Although a firm may strive to improve the product's sensory appeal, customers may actually find the modified product less attractive.

Developing New Products

new-product development process A seven-phase process for introducing products: idea generation, screening, concept testing, business analysis, product development, test marketing, and commercialization

idea generation Seeking product ideas to achieve organizational objectives

A firm develops new products as a means of enhancing its product mix and adding depth to a product line. However, developing and introducing new products is frequently expensive and risky. As we discussed in the previous chapter, new-product failures occur frequently and can create major financial problems for organizations, sometimes even causing them to go out of business.

Failure to introduce new products is also risky. Both Ford Motor and General Motors have lost market share to Japanese and Korean automakers in recent years as sales of some of their most profitable models have declined. Chrysler, however, has maintained market share with successful new products.[9]

The term *new product* can have more than one meaning. A genuinely new product offers innovative benefits. However, products that are different and distinctly better are often viewed as new. The following items are product innovations of the last 30 years: Post-it Notes, cell phones, personal computers, PDAs, digital music players, satellite radio, and digital video recorders. Thus, a new product can be an innovative product that has never been sold by any organization, such as the digital camera was when introduced for the first time. A radically new product involves a complex developmental process, including an extensive business analysis to determine the potential for success.[10] Finally, a product can be viewed as new when it is brought to one or more markets from another market. For example, making the Saturn VUE SUV available in Japan was viewed as a new-product introduction in Japan.

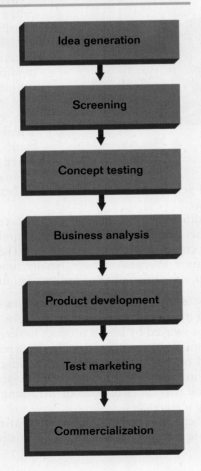

figure 12.1

PHASES OF NEW-PRODUCT DEVELOPMENT

Before a product is introduced, it goes through the seven phases of the **new-product development process** shown in Figure 12.1: (1) idea generation, (2) screening, (3) concept testing, (4) business analysis, (5) product development, (6) test marketing, and (7) commercialization. A product may be dropped (and many are) at any stage of development. In this section, we look at the process through which products are developed, from idea inception to fully commercialized product.

Idea Generation

Businesses and other organizations seek product ideas that will help them achieve their objectives. This activity is **idea generation.** The fact that only a few ideas are good enough to be commercially successful underscores the challenge of the task.

Although some organizations get their ideas almost by chance, firms that try to manage their product mixes effectively usually develop systematic approaches for generating new-product ideas. Indeed, in organizations there is a relationship between the amount of market information gathered and the number of ideas generated by work groups.[11] At the heart of innovation is a purposeful, focused effort to identify new ways to serve a market.

New-product ideas can come from several sources. They may stem from internal sources: marketing managers, researchers, sales personnel, engineers, or other organizational personnel. Brainstorming and incentives or rewards for good ideas are typical intrafirm devices for stimulating development of ideas. For example, the idea for 3M Post-it adhesive-backed notes came from an employee. As a church choir member, he used slips of paper to mark songs in his hymnal. Because the pieces of paper kept falling out, he suggested developing an adhesive-backed note. New-product ideas may also arise from sources outside the firm, such as customers, competitors, advertising agencies, management consultants, and private research organizations. Procter & Gamble gets 35 percent of its ideas from inventors and outside consultants.[12] Developing new-product alliances with other firms has also been found to enhance the acquisition and use of information useful for creating new-product ideas.[13] Asking customers what they want from products and organizations has helped many firms become successful and remain competitive.

screening Selecting the ideas with the greatest potential for further review

concept testing Seeking a sample of potential buyers' responses to a product idea

Screening

In the process of **screening,** the ideas with the greatest potential are selected for further review. During screening, product ideas are analyzed to determine whether they match the organization's objectives and resources. If a product idea results in a product similar to the firm's existing offerings, marketers must assess the degree to which the new product could cannibalize the sales of current products. The company's overall abilities to produce and market the product are also analyzed. Keeping the product idea in focus and on track by understanding consumer needs and wants is the key to success.[14] Other aspects of an idea to be weighed are the nature and wants of buyers and possible environmental changes. At times a checklist of new-product requirements is used when making screening decisions. This practice encourages evaluators to be systematic and thus reduces the chances of overlooking some pertinent fact. The largest number of new-product ideas is rejected during the screening phase.

marketing ENTREPRENEURS

A Seven-Person Committee Overseen by Event Chair, Bill Doherty

THEIR EVENT: Atlantic Nationals Automotive Extravaganza

EVENT'S FIRST YEAR: 2001

SUCCESS: Major sponsors, 1601 participating vehicles, 125 vendors, and 120 000 spectators with growth expected and significant economic spin-offs

Imagine an event with four fun-filled days of special interest cars and trucks, outdoor attractions, live entertainment, vendors, and cruising in a picturesque venue. Now, how do you plan such an event and implement it successfully year after year?

The Atlantic Nationals Automotive Extravaganza (**www.atlanticnationals.com**) was first conceived when an entrepreneurial group of committed volunteers (the Steering Committee) decided to address the growing demand experienced by the Greater Moncton Street Rods Club (who had hosted 18 previous Fun Run regional shows). According to Bill Doherty, then a Steering Committee member (in 1999), "with the demand for a larger show, the Steering Committee came up with the idea of a locally-grown major international event that would draw from Eastern Canada and the U.S. The event would have to retain a small-town, small-show feel with the full intention of growing the event into one of the countries' largest. The event would have to be a winning proposition for all stakeholders, participants, spectators, vendors, sponsors, and the general public."

With skilled planning and boundless effort and commitment, the vision of Bill's small Committee has grown Atlantic Nationals into a destination event for automotive enthusiasts. The event now draws participants and spectators from a growing list of distant states, provinces, and from as far away as Belgium. In addition to economic spin-offs that benefit the community, Atlantic Nationals is now recognized as a brand. Among its many accolades, this event has the largest prize pool in Canada—one of the largest in North America for a single event show.

Recognized by the CSRA (Canadian Street Rod Association) and by NSRA (National Street Rod Association), Atlantic Nationals Automotive Extravaganza has been featured on television on My Classic Car, as well as in numerous Canadian and U.S. magazines and newspapers. Simply put . . . a small group of entrepreneurial volunteers can make things happen!

Concept Testing

To evaluate ideas properly, it may be necessary to test product concepts. In **concept testing,** a small sample of potential buyers is presented with a product idea through a written or oral description (and perhaps a few drawings) to determine their attitudes and initial buying intentions regarding the product. Concept testing is a low-cost procedure that allows a company to determine customers' initial reactions to a product idea before it invests considerable resources in research and development. Input from online communities may also be beneficial in the product development process.[15] The results of concept testing can help product development personnel better understand which product attributes and benefits are most important to potential customers.

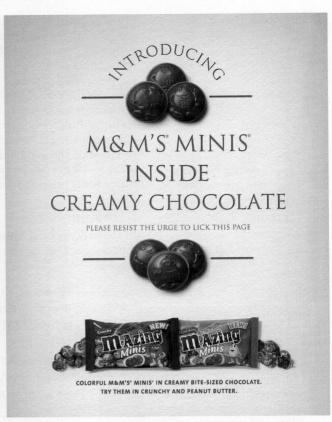

Example of a New Product
M&M introduced two new products—Mega M&M's and M&M's Minis—to satisfy consumer preferences.

Figure 12.2 shows a concept test for a proposed tick and flea control product. Notice that the concept is briefly described and then a series of questions is presented. The questions vary considerably depending on the type of product being tested. Typical questions are: In general, do you find this proposed product attractive? Which benefits are especially attractive to you? Which features are of little or no interest to you? Do you feel this proposed product would work better for you than the product you currently use? Compared with your current product, what are the primary advantages of the proposed product? If this product were available at an appropriate price, would you buy it? How often would you buy this product? How could this proposed product be improved?

Business Analysis

business analysis Evaluating the potential impact of a product idea on the firm's sales, costs, and profits

During the **business analysis** stage, the product idea is evaluated to determine its potential contribution to the firm's sales, costs, and profits. In the course of a business analysis, evaluators ask a variety of questions: Does the product fit in with the organization's existing product mix? Is demand strong enough to justify entering the market, and will the demand endure? What types of environmental and competitive changes can be expected, and how will these changes affect the product's future sales, costs, and profits? Are the organization's research, development, engineering, and production capabilities adequate to develop the product? If new facilities must be constructed, how quickly can they be built and how much will they cost? Is the necessary financing for development and commercialization on hand or obtainable at terms consistent with a favourable return on investment?

In the business analysis stage, firms seek market information. The results of customer surveys, along with secondary data, supply the specifics needed to estimate potential sales, costs, and profits.

For many products in this stage (when they are still just product ideas), forecasting sales accurately is difficult. This is especially true for innovative and completely

figure 12.2

CONCEPT TEST FOR A TICK AND FLEA CONTROL PRODUCT

Product description

An insecticide company is considering the development and introduction of a new tick and flea control product for pets. This product would consist of insecticide and a liquid dispensing brush for applying the insecticide to dogs and cats. The insecticide is in a cartridge that is installed in the handle of the brush. The insecticide is dispensed through the tips of the bristles when they touch the pet's skin (which is where most ticks and fleas are found). The actual dispensing works very much like a felt-tip pen. Only a small amount of insecticide actually is dispensed on the pet because of this unique dispensing feature. Thus, the amount of insecticide that is placed on your pet is minimal compared to conventional methods of applying a tick and flea control product. One application of insecticide will keep your pet free from ticks and fleas for fourteen days.

Please answer the following questions:

1. In general, how do you feel about using this type of product on your pet?

2. What are the major advantages of this product compared with the existing product that you are currently using to control ticks and fleas on your pet?

3. What characteristics of this product do you especially like?

4. What suggestions do you have for improving this product?

5. If it is available at an appropriate price, how likely are you to buy this product?

        Very likely   Semi-likely   Not likely

6. Assuming that a single purchase would provide 30 applications for an average-size dog or 48 applications for an average-size cat, approximately how much would you pay for this product?

new products. Organizations sometimes employ break-even analysis to determine how many units they would have to sell to begin making a profit. At times an organization also uses payback analysis, in which marketers compute the time period required to recover the funds that would be invested in developing the new product.

Product Development

product development
Determining if producing a product is feasible and cost effective

Product development is the phase in which the organization determines if it is technically feasible to produce the product and if it can be produced at costs low enough to make the final price reasonable. To test its acceptability, the idea or concept is converted into a prototype, or working model. The prototype should reveal tangible and intangible attributes associated with the product in consumers' minds. The product's design, mechanical features, and intangible aspects must be linked to wants in the marketplace. Through marketing research and concept testing, product attributes important to buyers are identified. These characteristics must be communicated to customers through the design of the product. Honda Motor, for example, developed a prototype minivan that targets Japan's growing population of pet owners with pet-friendly features such as panelled floors and seats that convert to a holding pen. Displayed at the Tokyo Auto Show, the prototype helped Honda assess interest in the concept.[16]

After a prototype is developed, its overall functioning must be tested. Its performance, safety, convenience, and other functional qualities are tested both in a laboratory

NOW CHEESE LOVERS REALLY HAVE SOMETHING TO SMILE ABOUT.

Baked!

Lay's

CHEDDAR & SOUR CREAM

NATURALLY BAKED FLAVORED POTATO CRISPS

The irresistible taste of real cheddar cheese on a baked potato crisp. They're delicious, yet sensible. This is snacking without the compromise.

Lay's get your smile on.

Product Development

In the product development stage, Lays tested consumer acceptance of its Cheddar & Sour Cream-flavoured potato chips.

and in the field. Functional testing should be rigorous and lengthy enough to test the product thoroughly. Manufacturing issues that come to light at this stage may require adjustments. When Cadbury Schweppes was developing its new Trident Splash gum, production problems necessitated changes in the ingredients. One combination resulted in a too-soft gum that jammed machines; another combination resulted in the gum's liquid centre leaking during trial deliveries. Finding just the right recipe required months.[17]

A crucial question that arises during product development is how much quality to build into the product. For example, a major dimension of quality is durability. Higher quality often calls for better materials and more expensive processing, which increase production costs and, ultimately, the product's price. In determining the specific level of quality, a marketer must ascertain approximately what price the target market views as acceptable. Obviously the quality of competing brands is also a consideration.

The development phase of a new product is frequently lengthy and expensive; thus, a relatively small number of product ideas are put into development. If the product appears sufficiently successful during this stage to merit test marketing, then, during the latter part of the development stage, marketers begin to make decisions regarding branding, packaging, labelling, pricing, and promotion for use in the test marketing stage.

Test Marketing

test marketing A limited introduction of a product in geographic areas chosen to represent the intended market

Test marketing is a limited introduction of a product in geographic areas chosen to represent the intended market. Its aim is to determine the extent to which potential customers will buy the product. Test marketing is not an extension of the development stage; it is a sample launching of the entire marketing mix. Test marketing should be conducted only after the product has gone through development and initial plans have been made regarding the other marketing mix variables. Companies use test marketing to lessen the risk of product mix failure. The dangers of introducing an untested product include undercutting already profitable products and, should the new product fail, loss of credibility with distributors and customers.

Test marketing provides several benefits. It lets marketers expose a product in a natural marketing environment to measure its sales performance. While the product is being marketed in a limited area, the company can strive to identify weaknesses in the product or in other parts of the marketing mix. A product weakness discovered after a nationwide introduction can be expensive to correct. Moreover, if consumers' early reactions are negative, marketers may be unable to persuade consumers to try the product again. Thus, making adjustments after test marketing can be crucial to the success of a new product. On the other hand, test marketing results may be positive enough to warrant accelerating the product's introduction. Test marketing also allows marketers to experiment with variations in advertising, pricing, and packaging in different test areas and to measure the extent of brand awareness, brand switching, and repeat purchases resulting from these alterations in the marketing mix.

Selection of appropriate test areas is very important because the validity of test marketing results depends heavily on selecting test sites that provide accurate representation of the intended target market. Table 12.1 lists some of the most popular

table 12.1	POPULAR TEST MARKETS IN CANADA		
London, Ont.	Kitchener, Ont.	Kingston, Ont.	Regina, Sask.
Saskatoon, Sask.	Halifax, N.S.	Fredericton, N.B.	Moncton, N.B.
Saint John, N.B.	Calgary, Alta.	Edmonton, Alta.	Winnipeg, Man.
Vancouver, B.C.	Victoria, B.C.	Toronto, Ont.	Guelph, Ont.

Source: AC Nielsen Canada.

test market cities in Canada. The criteria used for choosing test market locations depends on the product's attributes, the target market's characteristics, and the firm's objectives and resources.

Test marketing is not without risks. It is expensive, and competitors may try to interfere. A competitor may attempt to "jam" the test program by increasing its own advertising or promotions, lowering prices, and offering special incentives, all to combat recognition and purchase of the new brand. Any such tactics can invalidate test results. Sometimes, too, competitors copy the product in the testing stage and rush to introduce a similar product. It is therefore desirable to move to the commercialization phase as soon as possible after successful testing.

Because of these risks, many companies use alternative methods to measure customer preferences. One such method is simulated test marketing. Typically consumers at shopping centres are asked to view an advertisement for a new product and are given a free sample to take home. These consumers are subsequently interviewed over the phone and asked to rate the product. The major advantages of simulated test marketing are greater speed, lower costs, and tighter security, which reduce the flow of information to competitors and reduce jamming. Several marketing research firms, such as ACNielsen Canada, offer test marketing services to provide independent assessment of proposed products.

commercialization Refining and finalizing plans and budgets for full-scale manufacturing and marketing of a product

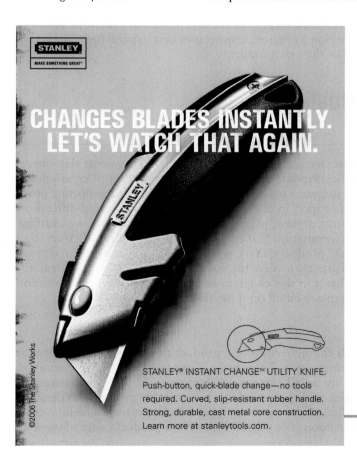

STANLEY® INSTANT CHANGE™ UTILITY KNIFE.
Push-button, quick-blade change—no tools required. Curved, slip-resistant rubber handle. Strong, durable, cast metal core construction. Learn more at stanleytools.com.

©2006 The Stanley Works

Commercialization

During the **commercialization** phase, plans for full-scale manufacturing and marketing must be refined and finalized and budgets for the project prepared. Early in the commercialization phase, marketing management analyzes the results of test marketing to find out what changes in the marketing mix are needed before introducing the product.

During the early part of this stage, marketers must not only gear up for larger-scale production but also make decisions about warranties, repairs, and replacement parts. The type of warranty a firm provides can be a critical issue for buyers, especially when expensive, technically complex goods such as appliances are involved. Maytag, for example, provides a money-back guarantee on its refrigerators. Establishing an effective system for providing repair services and replacement parts is necessary to maintain favourable customer relationships. The product enters the

Commercialization

Stanley develops innovative products and rolls them out nationally.

market during the commercialization phase. When introducing a product, a firm may spend enormous sums for advertising, personal selling, and other types of promotion, as well as for plant and equipment. Such expenditures may not be recovered for several years. Smaller firms may find this process difficult, but even so they may use press releases, blogs, podcasts, and other tools to capture quick feedback as well as promote the new product. Another low-cost promotional tool is product reviews in newspapers and magazines, which can be especially helpful when they are positive and target the same customers.

Usually products are not launched nationwide overnight but are introduced through a process called a *roll-out*. With a roll-out, a product is introduced in stages, starting in one set of geographic areas and gradually expanding into adjacent areas. It may take several years to market the product nationally.

Gradual product introduction is desirable for several reasons. First, it reduces the risks of introducing a new product. If the product fails, the firm will experience smaller losses if it introduced the item in only a few geographic areas than if it marketed the product nationally. Second, a company cannot introduce a product nationwide overnight because a system of wholesalers and retailers to distribute the product cannot be established so quickly; developing a distribution network may take considerable time. Third, if the product is successful, the number of units needed to satisfy nationwide demand for it may be too large for the firm to produce in a short time. Finally, it allows for fine tuning of the marketing mix to better satisfy target customers. Procter & Gamble, for example, originally conceived of Febreze deodourizer as a fabric-care product, but over time, the company's view of the highly successful brand evolved into an air freshening line because that's how consumers indicated they were using it.[18]

Despite the good reasons for introducing a product gradually, marketers realize this approach creates some competitive problems. A gradual introduction allows competitors to observe what the firm is doing and to monitor results just as the firm's own marketers are doing. If competitors see that the newly introduced product is successful, they may quickly enter the same target market with similar products. In addition, as a product is introduced region by region, competitors may expand their marketing efforts to offset promotion of the new product.

Product Differentiation Through Quality, Design, and Support Services

product differentiation
Creating and designing products so that customers perceive them as different from competing products

Some of the most important characteristics of products are the elements that distinguish them from one another. **Product differentiation** is the process of creating and designing products so that customers perceive them as different from competing products. Customer perception is critical in differentiating products. Perceived differences might include quality, features, styling, price, or image. In this section, we examine three aspects of product differentiation that companies must consider when creating and offering products for sale: product quality, product design and features, and product support services. These aspects involve the company's attempt to create real differences among products. Later in this chapter, we discuss how companies position their products in the marketplace based on these three aspects.

Product Quality

quality The overall characteristics of a product that allow it to perform as expected in satisfying customer needs

Quality refers to the overall characteristics of a product that allow it to perform as expected in satisfying customer needs. The words *as expected* are very important to this definition because quality usually means different things to different customers. For some, durability signifies quality. Among the most durable products on the market today is the Craftsman line of tools at Sears; indeed, Sears provides a lifetime guarantee on the durability of its tools. For other consumers, a product's ease of use may indicate quality.

The concept of quality also varies between consumer and business markets. Consumers consider high-quality products to be reliable, durable, and easy to maintain. For business markets, technical suitability, ease of repair, and company reputation are important characteristics. Unlike consumers, most organizations place far less emphasis on price than on product quality.

level of quality The amount of quality a product possesses

One important dimension of quality is **level of quality,** the amount of quality a product possesses. The concept is a relative one; that is, the quality level of one product is difficult to describe unless it is compared with that of other products. How high should the level of quality be? It depends on the product and the costs and consequences of a product failure.

consistency of quality The degree to which a product has the same level of quality over time

A second important dimension is consistency. **Consistency of quality** refers to the degree to which a product has the same level of quality over time. Consistency means giving consumers the quality they expect every time they purchase the product. Like level of quality, consistency is a relative concept; however, it implies a quality comparison within the same brand over time. The quality level of McDonald's french fries is generally consistent from one location to another.

The consistency of product quality can also be compared across competing products. It is at this stage that consistency becomes critical to a company's success. Companies that can provide quality on a consistent basis have a major competitive advantage over rivals. Many companies have taken major steps, such as implementing total quality management (TQM), to improve the quality of their products.

By and large, higher product quality means marketers will charge a higher price for the product. This fact forces marketers to consider quality carefully in their product-planning efforts. Not all customers want or can afford the highest-quality products available. Thus, some companies offer products with moderate quality.

Product Design and Features

product design How a product is conceived, planned, and produced

Product design refers to how a product is conceived, planned, and produced. Design is a very complex topic because it involves the total sum of all the product's physical characteristics. Many companies are known for the outstanding designs of their products: Sony for personal electronics, Hewlett-Packard for printers, and Apple for computers and music players. Good design is one of the best competitive advantages any brand can possess.

styling The physical appearance of a product

One component of design is **styling,** or the physical appearance of the product. The style of a product is one design feature that can allow certain products to sell very rapidly. Good design, however, means more than just appearance; it also involves a product's functioning and usefulness. Most consumers seek out products that both look good and function well.

product features Specific design characteristics that allow a product to perform certain tasks

Product features are specific design characteristics that allow a product to perform certain tasks. By adding or subtracting features, a company can differentiate its products from those of the competition. Chrysler promotes its line of minivans as having more features related to passenger safety—dual air bags, steel-reinforced doors, and integrated child safety seats—than any other auto company. Product features can also be used to differentiate products within the same company. For example, Nike offers both a walking shoe and a run-walk shoe for specific consumer needs.

For a brand to have a sustainable competitive advantage, marketers must determine the product designs and features that customers desire. Information from marketing research efforts and from databases can help in assessing customers' product design and feature preferences. Being able to meet customers' desires for product design and features at prices they can afford is crucial to a product's long-term success.

Product Support Services

customer services Human or mechanical efforts or activities that add value to a product

Many companies differentiate their product offerings by providing support services. Usually referred to as **customer services,** these services include any human or mechanical efforts or activities a company provides that add value to a product.[19] Examples of customer services include delivery and installation, financing arrangements, customer training, warranties and guarantees, repairs, layaway plans, convenient hours of operation, adequate parking, and information through toll-free numbers. For example, most hotel chains offer web-based reservation services for their customers' convenience. Their websites also provide information about the hotels' prices, amenities, and frequent-guest programs.

Whether as a major or minor part of the total product offering, all marketers of goods sell customer services. Providing good customer service may be the only way a company can differentiate its products when all products in a market have essentially the same quality, design, and features. This is especially true in the computer industry. When buying a laptop computer, for example, consumers shop more for fast delivery, technical support, warranties, and price than for product quality and design. Through research, a company can discover the types of services customers want and need. For example, some customers are more interested in financing, whereas others are more concerned with installation and training. The level of customer service a company provides can profoundly affect customer satisfaction.

Product Deletion

product deletion Eliminating a product from the product mix when it no longer satisfies a sufficient number of customers

Generally a product cannot satisfy target market customers and contribute to the achievement of the organization's overall goals indefinitely. **Product deletion** is the process of eliminating a product from the product mix, usually because it no longer satisfies a sufficient number of customers. Nikon, for example, discontinued seven film camera models, leaving the Japanese firm with just two film camera models on the market, in order to focus on digital cameras.[20] A declining product reduces an organization's profitability and drains resources that could be used to modify other products or develop new ones. A marginal product may require shorter production runs, which can increase per-unit production costs. Finally, when a dying product completely loses favour with customers, the negative feelings may transfer to some of the company's other products.

Most organizations find it difficult to delete a product. Basically there are three ways to delete a product: phase it out, run it out, or drop it immediately (see Figure 12.3). A *phase-out* allows the product to decline without a change in the marketing strategy; no attempt is made to give the product new life. Nikon, for example, simply allowed sales of its discontinued film cameras to continue until their supplies ran out.[21] A *run-out* exploits any strengths left in the product. Intensifying marketing efforts in core markets or eliminating some marketing expenditures, such as advertising, may cause a sudden jump in profits. This approach is commonly taken for technologically obsolete products, such as older models of computers and calculators. Often the price is reduced to generate a sales spurt. The third alternative, an *immediate drop* of an unprofitable product, is the best strategy when losses are too great to prolong the product's life.

figure 12.3
PRODUCT DELETION PROCESS

Source: Martin L. Bell, *Marketing: Concepts and Strategy,* 3rd ed., p. 267; Copyright © 1979, Houghton Mifflin Company. Reprinted by permission of Mrs. Martin L. Bell.

Branding

Brands, components of brands, packages, and labels are part of a product's tangible features, the verbal and physical cues that help customers identify the products they want and influence their choices when they are unsure. As such, branding and packaging play an important role in marketing strategy. A successful brand like Shoppers Drug Mart is distinct and memorable; without one, a firm could not differentiate its products and shoppers' choices would essentially be arbitrary. A good package design is cost effective, safe, environmentally responsible, and valuable as a promotional tool.

brand A name, term, design, symbol, or other feature that identifies a seller's products and differentiates them from competitors' products

brand name The part of a brand that can be spoken, including letters, words, and numbers

Marketers must make many decisions about products, including choices about brands, brand names, brand marks, trademarks, and trade names. A **brand** is a name, term, design, symbol, or any other feature that identifies one seller's good or service as distinct from those of other sellers. A brand may identify one item, a family of items, or all items of that seller.[22] A **brand name** is the part of a brand that can be spoken—including letters, words, and numbers—such as 7Up. A brand name is often a product's only distinguishing characteristic. Without the brand name, a firm could not differentiate its products. To consumers, a brand name is as fundamental as the product itself. Indeed, many brand names have become synonymous with the product, such as Scotch Tape and Xerox copiers. Through promotional activities, the owners of these brand names try to protect them from being used as generic names for tape and photocopiers.

brand mark The part of a brand not made up of words, such as a symbol or design

trademark A legal designation of exclusive use of a brand

trade name The full legal name of an organization

The element of a brand that is not made up of words—often a symbol or design—is a **brand mark** (also referred to as a visual brand icon). Examples of brand marks include McDonald's Golden Arches, Nike's "swoosh," and Scotiabank's stylized globe. A **trademark** is a legal designation indicating that the owner has exclusive use of a brand or a part of a brand and others are prohibited by law from using it. In Canada, an organization that registers a brand name or brand mark as a trademark under the federal Trademarks Act has an exclusive right to the use of the mark throughout Canada for a period of fifteen years, at which time the trademark protection can be renewed. Finally, a **trade name** is the full legal name of an organization, such as Ford Motor Company, rather than the name of a specific product.

Value of Branding

Both buyers and sellers benefit from branding. Brands help customers identify specific products that they do and do not like, which in turn facilitates the purchase of items that satisfy their needs and reduces the time required to purchase the product. Without brands, product selection would be quite random because buyers would have no assurance they were purchasing what they preferred. The purchase of certain brands can be a form of self-expression. For example, clothing brand names are important to many teenage boys; names such as Polo, Champion, Guess, and Nike give manufacturers an advantage in the marketplace. A brand also helps buyers evaluate the quality of products, especially when they are unable to judge a product's characteristics; that is, a brand may symbolize a certain quality level to a

Brand Mark

Scotiabank's stylized globe is an example of a brand mark.

customer, and in turn the person lets that perception of quality represent the quality of the item. A brand helps reduce a buyer's perceived risk of purchase. In addition, a psychological reward may come from owning a brand that symbolizes status. The Mercedes-Benz brand in North America is an example.

Sellers benefit from branding because each company's brands identify its products, which makes repeat purchasing easier for customers. Branding helps a firm introduce a new product that carries the name of one or more of its existing products because buyers are already familiar with those brands. Branding also facilitates promotional efforts because the promotion of each branded product indirectly promotes

Tim Hortons: The Double Double Travels South

In Canada, Tim Hortons enjoys far better market penetration than Starbucks. Census data for 2006 reveals that Starbucks has an average of one store per 37 000 people in the U.S., while Tim Hortons has an impressive one store per 12 000 in Canada. This degree of market penetration, in part the result of more than 3000 locations, leaves little room for competition. Little wonder Tim Hortons has become part of the country's retail and social fabric during its 40 plus years of operation.

So much a part of Canadian's social fabric, if you pull out a recent copy of the Canadian Oxford Dictionary you will find "double double" (the Tim Hortons' phrase for coffee with two creams and two sugars) has been added because the term has permeated the lexicon from coast-to-coast.

In Canada, Tim Hortons has helped establish an out-of-home coffee market, but this market category has not been so well developed in the U.S. Moreover, this market in the U.S. has many players, including chains such as Dunkin' Donuts and McDonald's, and thousands of gas station convenience stores. Coupled with a lack of awareness of the Tim Hortons' brand in the U.S., how can expansion of Tim Hortons into the U.S. be successful? According to Cathy Whelan Molloy, vice president of marketing and merchandising at the TDL Group Corp., "we know we have to enter the market in a big way . . . we need a strong enough store base to support it with marketing." She notes there are economies of scale in branding.

In order to make a real impact in the U.S., Whelan Molly says the company had to launch an introductory advertising campaign about the brand and what it stood for. "You have to be true to your brand. Who

Tim Hortons innately is and what it stands for is its 'always fresh' proposition. Everything else stems from there." Whelan Molloy says.

Thus far, the strategy is working. Today, 336 of its locations are in 10 U.S. states—CT, KY, MA, ME, MI, NY, OH, PA, RI, WV—and it's currently focusing on building its brand out along the Great Lakes states, an area encompassing about 90 million people, or almost three times the population of Canada. The plan is to have 500 Tim Hortons locations in the U.S. sometime in 2008.

"Tim Hortons is a strong brand that represents freshness, quality and friendly service and it's these attributes that customers are responding to on both sides of the border," said Bill Moir, Executive Vice President, Marketing, Tim Hortons.

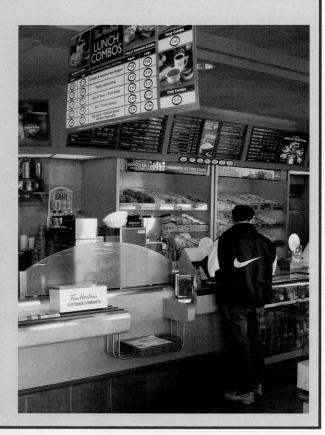

all other similarly branded products. Branding also fosters brand loyalty. To the extent that buyers become loyal to a specific brand, the company's market share for that product achieves a certain level of stability, allowing the firm to use its resources more efficiently. Once a firm develops some degree of customer loyalty for a brand, it can maintain a fairly consistent price rather than continually cutting the price to attract customers. A brand is as much of an asset as the company's building or machinery. When marketers increase their brand's value, they also raise the total asset value of the organization. (We discuss brand value in more detail later in this chapter.)

There is a cultural dimension to branding. Most brand experiences are individual, and each consumer confers his or her own social meaning onto brands. For some brands, such as Harley-Davidson and Apple, this can result in an almost cult-like following. These brands often develop a community of loyal customers that communicate through online forums, blogs, podcasts, and other means. These brands may even help consumers develop their identities and self-concepts and serve as forms of self expression. In fact, the term *cultural branding* has been used to explain how a brand conveys a powerful myth that consumers find useful in cementing their identities.[23]

It is important to recognize that because a brand exists independently in the consumer's mind, it is not directly controlled by the marketer. Every aspect of a brand is subject to a consumer's emotional involvement, interpretation, and memory. By understanding how branding influences purchases, marketers can foster customer loyalty.[24]

Brand Loyalty

brand loyalty A customer's favourable attitude toward a specific brand

brand recognition The degree of brand loyalty in which the customer is aware the brand exists and views the brand as an alternative purchase if their preferred brand is unavailable

brand preference The degree of brand loyalty in which a customer prefers one brand over competitive offerings

As we just noted, creating and maintaining customer loyalty toward a brand is a major benefit of branding. **Brand loyalty** is a customer's favourable attitude toward a specific brand. If brand loyalty is strong enough, customers may consistently purchase this brand when they need a product in that product category. Customer satisfaction with a brand is the most common reason for loyalty to that brand.[25] Development of brand loyalty in a customer reduces his or her risks and shortens the time spent buying the product. However, the degree of brand loyalty for products varies from one product category to another. For example, it is challenging to develop brand loyalty for most products because customers can usually judge a product's quality and do not need to refer to a brand as an indicator of quality.

Three degrees of brand loyalty exist: recognition, preference, and insistence. **Brand recognition** occurs when a customer is aware that the brand exists and views it as an alternative purchase if the preferred brand is unavailable or if the other available brands are unfamiliar. The term *loyalty* clearly is used very loosely here. One of the initial objectives when introducing a new brand is to create widespread awareness of the brand to generate brand recognition. Brand marks (also referred to as visual brand icons) are a tool used to assist in the generation of brand recognition. When used consistently, brand marks can trigger memories, opinions, rumors, and personal experiences with a brand.[26]

Brand preference is a stronger degree of brand loyalty: a customer definitely prefers one brand over competitive offerings and will purchase this brand if available. However, if the brand is not available, the customer will accept a substitute brand rather than expending additional effort finding and purchasing the preferred brand. A marketer is

Brand Marks as Recognition Tools

Brand marks (or visual brand icons) such as this caricature created by graphic artist Terry Malley for the Atlantic Nationals Automotive Extravaganza are an important brand recognition tool.

Always in season. *Enjoying the fresh taste of real fruit has never been easier. Now all the sweet goodness of DOLE comes in an unbreakable, resealable plastic jar. So the only thing that's going to get spoiled is you. Choose Mandarin Orange, Peach, Pineapple or Tropical Fruit. Each one is ripe and ready to be picked in the packaged fruit aisle.* **Life is Sweet.**

Brand Insistence
Many consumers insist on a particular brand of packaged fruit.

likely to be able to compete effectively in a market when a number of customers have developed brand preference for its specific brand.

When **brand insistence** occurs, a customer strongly prefers a specific brand, will accept no substitute, and is willing to spend a great deal of time and effort to acquire that brand. If a brand-insistent customer goes to a store and finds the brand unavailable, he or she will seek the brand elsewhere rather than purchase a substitute brand. Brand insistence is the strongest degree of brand loyalty; it is a brander's dream. However, it is the least common type of brand loyalty. Customers vary considerably regarding the product categories for which they may be brand insistent. Can you think of products for which you are brand insistent? Perhaps it's a brand of deodorant, soft drink, jeans, or even pet food (if your pet is brand insistent).

Brand loyalty in general seems to be declining, partly because of marketers' increased reliance on sales, coupons, and other short-term promotions and partly because of the sometimes overwhelming array of similar new products from which customers can choose. Several recent studies indicate that brand loyalty is declining for all age groups and especially among consumers age 50 and older.[27]

Building brand loyalty is a major challenge for many marketers. It is an extremely important issue. The creation of brand loyalty significantly contributes to an organization's ability to achieve a sustainable competitive advantage.

brand insistence The degree of brand loyalty in which a customer strongly prefers a specific brand and will accept no substitute

Brand Equity

A well-managed brand is an asset to an organization. The value of this asset is often referred to as brand equity. **Brand equity** is the marketing and financial value associated with a brand's strength in a market. Besides the actual proprietary brand assets, such as patents and trademarks, four major elements underlie brand equity: brand name awareness, brand loyalty, perceived brand quality, and brand associations (see Figure 12.4).[28]

brand equity The marketing and financial value associated with a brand's strength in a market

Awareness of a brand leads to brand familiarity, which in turn results in a level of comfort with the brand. A familiar brand is more likely to be selected than an unfamiliar brand because the familiar brand is often viewed as more reliable and of more acceptable quality. The familiar brand is likely to be in a customer's consideration set, whereas the unfamiliar brand is not.

Brand loyalty is an important component of brand equity because it reduces a brand's vulnerability to competitors' ac-

figure 12.4

MAJOR ELEMENTS OF BRAND EQUITY

Brand name awareness — Perceived brand equity — BRAND EQUITY — Brand associations — Brand loyalty

Source: Adapted with the permission of The Free Press, a division of Simon & Schuster Adult Publishing Group, from *Managing Brand Equity: Capitalizing on the Value of a Brand Name* by David A. Aaker. Copyright © 1991 by David A. Aaker. All rights reserved.

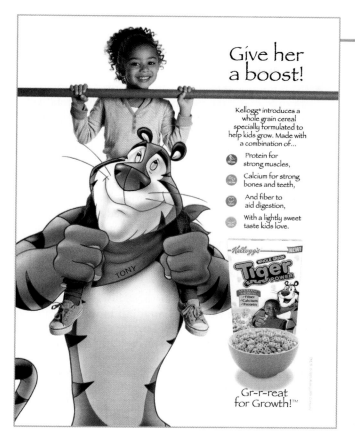

Give her
a boost!

Kellogg® introduces a
whole grain cereal
specially formulated to
help kids grow. Made with
a combination of...

Protein for
strong muscles,

Calcium for strong
bones and teeth,

And fiber to
aid digestion.

With a lightly sweet
taste kids love.

Gr-r-reat
for Growth!™

Stimulating Brand Associations
Kellogg's uses Tony the Tiger, a trademarked character, to stimulate favourable brand associations.

tions. Brand loyalty allows an organization to keep its existing customers and avoid spending an enormous amount of resources gaining new ones. Loyal customers provide brand visibility and reassurance to potential new customers. Because customers expect their brands to be available when and where they shop, retailers strive to carry the brands known for their strong customer following.

Customers associate a particular brand with a certain level of overall quality. A brand name may be used as a substitute for judgment of quality. In many cases, customers can't actually judge the quality of the product for themselves and instead must rely on the brand as a quality indicator. Perceived high brand quality helps support a premium price, allowing a marketer to avoid severe price competition. Also, favourable perceived brand quality can ease the introduction of brand extensions, since the high regard for the brand will likely translate into high regard for the related products.

The set of associations linked to a brand is another key component of brand equity. At times a marketer works to connect a particular lifestyle or, in some instances, a certain personality type with a specific brand. For example, customers associate Michelin tires with protecting family members and Coca-Cola with a unique taste. These types of brand associations contribute significantly to the brand's equity. Brand associations are sometimes facilitated by using trade characters, such as the Jolly Green Giant, and Tony the Tiger. Placing these trade characters in advertisements and on packages helps consumers link the ads and packages to the brands.

Although difficult to measure, brand equity represents the value of a brand to an organization. An organization may buy a brand from another company at a premium price because outright brand purchase may be less expensive and less risky than creating and developing a brand from scratch. Brand equity helps give a brand the power to capture and maintain a consistent market share, which provides stability to the organization's sales volume.

A brand's overall economic value rises and falls with the brand's profitability, brand awareness, brand loyalty, and perceived brand quality and with the strength of positive brand associations. Table 12.2 lists Interbrand's ranking of the 10 Canadian brands with the greatest economic value, as reported by *The Globe and Mail*'s Report on Business. In Interbrand's annual ranking of the world's most valuable brands, there has never been a Canadian brand. In the latest global ranking, just over half of the brands are from the U.S., the rest are from countries other than Canada. According to Interbrand's commentary on the state of branding in Canada, "it is an incredibly fast-paced and fluid set of factors that are rapidly making Canadian brands irrelevant [globally] due to size, penetration, perception and, arguably aggressiveness."[29] Interbrand has observed that well-performing Canadian brands share home-grown practices that have served them well, including:

■ A deep understanding of the consumer and an investment in segmentation. This ensures the brand experience is tailored to individual wants and needs.

■ Communication of the importance and commitment to community support. The Bay and Zellers missed an opportunity that Wal-Mart capitalized on through its telling of Canadian stories.

table 12.2	CANADA'S MOST VALUABLE BRANDS

Brand	Brand Value (In Million CAD $)
RBC Financial Group	3989.6
TD Canada Trust	3167.9
Petro-Canada	3064.0
Bell	2914.9
Shoppers Drug Mart	2830.6
Tim Hortons	1878.2
BMO Financial Group	1854.6
Canadian Tire	1634.2
Scotiabank	1378.7
Telus	1079.3

Source: Interbrand Candada, Inc. *Best Canadian Brands 2006: A Ranking by Brand Value.* July 2006, The Globe and Mail's *Report on Business* and *Interbrand*.

- A lack of pretentiousness that mirrors the Canadian personality. However, polite, almost deferential brands do well in Canada but do not translate well to other countries.

- Making due with less. The majority of Canadian brands that have the challenge of having relatively small marketing and communications budgets. Well performing brands coordinate marketing messages to deliver clear communications.

- Making honest efforts to communicate "Canada." Canadian Tire communicates Canada through nostalgia messaging highlighting its deep ties and contributions. Roots has mastered this in a visual sense through their casual clothing and personality. Tim Hortons has picked up on this as well, having featured Canadian Forces and students abroad in their national advertising.[30]

Interbrand cautions that these home-grown practices are less relevant for Canadian brands hoping to compete globally. Among concerns noted by Interbrand are a lack of investment in branding education and practice has meant that Canada suffers from a follower mentality, leaving brand leadership to organizations in other nations. An overall lack of investment in branding practice means that Canadian brands tend to be reactive rather than leaders in effective marketing communications.

Types of Brands

manufacturer brands A brand initiated by its producer

There are three categories of brands: manufacturer, private distributor, and generic. **Manufacturer brands** are initiated by producers and ensure that producers are identified with their products at the point of purchase—for example, McCain Cresendo Rising Crust Pizza, Chevrolet Corvette, and Levi's jeans. A manufacturer brand usually requires a producer to become involved in distribution, promotion, and, to some extent, pricing decisions. Brand loyalty is encouraged by promotion, quality control, and guarantees; it is a valuable asset to a manufacturer. The producer tries to stimulate demand for the product, which tends to encourage sellers and resellers to make the product available.

private distributor brands A brand initiated and owned by a reseller

Private distributor brands (also called *private brands, store brands,* or *dealer brands*) are initiated and owned by resellers, that is, wholesalers or retailers. The major characteristic of private brands is that the manufacturers are not identified on the products. Retailers and wholesalers use private distributor brands to develop more efficient promotion, generate higher gross margins, and change store image. There are private-label products at every price point and in every category from trash bags to ice cream.[31] Private distributor brands give retailers or wholesalers freedom to purchase products of a specified quality at the lowest cost without disclosing the identities of the manufacturers. Wholesaler brands include IGA (Independent Grocers' Alliance). Familiar retailer brand names include Sears' Kenmore and Loblaw's President's Choice. Many successful private brands are distributed nationally. Kenmore appliances are as well known as most manufacturer brands. Sometimes retailers with successful private distributor brands start manufacturing their own products to gain more control over product costs, quality, and design in the hope of increasing profits. Supermarket private brands are popular globally, too.

Competition between manufacturer brands and private distributor brands (sometimes called "the battle of the brands") is ongoing. To compete against manufacturer brands, retailers have tried to strengthen consumer confidence in private brands. For manufacturers, developing multiple manufacturer brands and distribution systems has been an effective means of combating the increased competition from private brands. By developing a new brand name, a producer can adjust various elements of its marketing mix to appeal to a different target market.

The growth of private brands has been steady. One reason is that retailers advertise the manufacturer brands that bring customers to their stores, but sell the private brands, especially to price-sensitive customers. Another reason is that retailers with private labels negotiate better prices from producers of manufacturer brands.[32] To compete against private brands, some manufacturer brand makers have stopped increasing prices or even have cut their prices, which has narrowed the price gap—the major advantage of buying a private brand. Traditionally private brands have appeared in packaging that directly imitates the packaging of competing manufacturers' brands without significant legal ramifications. However, the legal risks of using look-alike packaging are increasing for private branders.

Some private distributor brands are produced by companies that specialize in making only private distributor brands; others are made by producers of manufacturer brands. At times, producers of both types of brands find it difficult to ignore the opportunities that arise from producing private distributor brands. If a producer decides not to produce a private brand for a reseller, a competitor probably will. Moreover, the production of private distributor brands allows the producer to use excess production capacity. The ultimate decision of whether to produce a private or a manufacturer brand depends on a company's resources, production capabilities, and goals.

generic brands A brand indicating only the product category

Some marketers of traditionally branded products have embarked on a policy of not branding, often called *generic branding*. **Generic brands** indicate only the product category (such as aluminum foil) and do not include the company name or other identifying terms. Generic brands are usually sold at lower prices than comparable branded items. Although at one time generic brands may have represented as much as 10 percent of all retail grocery sales, today they account for less than half of one percent.

Selecting a Brand Name

Marketers consider a number of factors in selecting a brand name. First, the name should be easy for customers (including foreign buyers, if the firm intends to market its products in other countries) to say, spell, and recall. Short, one-syllable names, such as Cheer, often satisfy this requirement. Second, the brand name should indicate the product's major benefits and, if possible, suggest in a positive way the product's uses and special characteristics; negative or offensive references should be avoided. For example, the brand names of such household cleaning products as Ajax dishwashing liquid, Cascade dishwasher detergent, and Wisk laundry detergent connote strength and effectiveness. Research suggests that consumers are more likely to recall and to evaluate favourably names that convey positive attributes or benefits.[33] Third, to set it apart from competing brands, the brand should be distinctive. If a marketer intends to use a brand for a product line, that brand must be compatible with all products in the line. Finally, a brand should be designed so that it can be used and recognized in all types of media. Finding the right brand name has become a challenging task because many obvious product names have already been used.

How are brand names devised? Brand names can be created from single or multiple words—for example, Bic or Dodge Grand Caravan. Letters and numbers are used to create such brands as IBM PC or Z71. Words, numbers, and letters are combined to yield brand names such as Mazda MX-5 Miata or BMW Z4 Roadster. To avoid terms that have negative connotations, marketers sometimes use fabricated words that have absolutely no meaning when created—for example, Kodak and Exxon. Occasionally a brand is simply brought out of storage and used as is or modified. Firms often maintain banks of registered brands, some of which may have been used in the past. Cadillac, for example, has a bank of approximately 360 registered trademarks. The LaSalle brand, used in the 1920s and 1930s, could be called up for a new Cadillac model in the future. Possible brand names sometimes are tested in focus groups or other settings to assess customers' reactions.

Who actually creates brand names? Brand names can be created internally by the organization. Sometimes a name is suggested by individuals who are close to the product's development. Some organizations have committees that participate in brand name creation and approval. At times, outside consultants and companies that specialize in brand name development are used.

Although most of the important branding considerations apply to both goods and services, branding a service has some additional dimensions. The service brand is usually the same as the company name. Financial companies, such as CIBC Wood Gundy and BMO Nesbitt Burns, have established strong brand recognition. These companies have used their names to create an image of timely, responsible, accurate, and knowledgeable customer assistance. Service providers (such as Air Canada) are often perceived by customers as having one brand name, even though they offer multiple products (first class, business class, and coach.) Because the service brand name and company name are so closely interrelated, a service brand name must be flexible enough to encompass a variety of current services, as well as new ones the company may offer in the future. Geographical references such as *western* and descriptive terms such as *trucking* limit the scope of possible associations with the brand name. Because WestJet now flies to several destinations east of the western provinces, its name has become too limited in its scope of associations. Frequently a service marketer employs a symbol along with its brand name to make the brand distinctive and communicate a certain image.

Protecting a Brand

A marketer should also design a brand so that it can be protected easily through registration. A series of court decisions has created a broad hierarchy of protection based on brand type. From most protectable to least protectable, these brand types are fanciful (Esso), arbitrary (7Up), suggestive (Spray 'n Wash), descriptive (Minute Rice), and generic (aluminum foil). Generic brands are not protectable. Surnames and descriptive, geographic, or functional names are difficult to protect.[34] Therefore, "delicious" ice cream and "Atlantic" cod are marks that cannot be registered. Because of their designs, some brands can naturally be legally infringed on more easily than others. Although registration protects trademarks domestically for fifteen years and trademarks can be renewed indefinitely, a firm should develop a system for ensuring that its trademarks are renewed as needed.

To protect its exclusive rights to a brand, a company must ensure that the brand is not likely to be considered an infringement on any brand already registered with the Canadian Intellectual Property Office. This task may be complex because infringement is determined by the courts, which base their decisions on whether a brand causes consumers to be confused, mistaken, or deceived about the source of the product. McDonald's is one company that aggressively protects its trademarks against infringement; it has brought charges against a number of companies with *Mc* names because it fears the use of that prefix will give consumers the impression that these companies are associated with or owned by McDonald's.

Protecting a Brand

Xerox works hard to protect their brand name so that people do not use "Xerox" to mean generic photocopying.

Take your everyday business document, spice it up with Xerox color and it could attract 82% more attention. Now, that'll heat things up. Xerox Color. It makes business sense.

XEROX.

xerox.com/color 1-800-ASK-XEROX ext. COLOR

Technology | Document Management | Consulting Services

A marketer should guard against allowing a brand name to become a generic term used to refer to a general product category. Generic terms cannot be protected as exclusive brand names. For example, *Aspirin, escalator,* and *shredded wheat*—all brand names at one time—eventually were declared generic terms that refer to product classes. Thus, they could no longer be protected. To keep a brand name from becoming a generic term, the firm should spell the name with a capital letter and use it as an adjective to modify the name of the general product class, as in Kool-Aid Brand Soft Drink Mix.[35] Including the word *brand* just after the brand name is also helpful. An organization can deal with this problem directly by advertising that its brand is a trademark and should not be used generically. Canada's Trademarks Act does not require any marketing requirements; however, trademark owners often indicate their registration through symbols such as ® (registered), ™ (trademark), or ℠ (service mark).

A Canadian firm that tries to protect a brand in a foreign country frequently encounters problems. In many countries, brand registration is not possible; the first firm to use a brand in such a country automatically has the rights to it. In some instances, Canadian companies actually have had to buy their own brand rights from a firm in a foreign country because the foreign firm was the first user in that country.

Marketers trying to protect their brands must also contend with brand counterfeiting. For instance, one can purchase counterfeit General Motors parts, Rolex watches, Louis Vuitton handbags, Walt Disney character dolls, Mont Blanc pens, and a host of other products illegally marketed by manufacturers that do not own the brands. Annual losses caused by counterfeit products are estimated to be in the billions. Many counterfeit products are manufactured overseas—in Turkey, China, Thailand, Italy, and Colombia, for example—but some are counterfeited in North America. Counterfeit products are often hard to distinguish from the real brands. Products most likely to be counterfeited are well-known brands that appeal to a mass market and products whose physical materials are inexpensive relative to the products' prices. Microsoft estimates that its revenues would double if counterfeiting of its brand name products were eliminated. Some $40 billion a year are lost in the computer software business because of counterfeit and pirated products. Brand fraud results not only in lost revenue for the brand's owner; it also results in a low-quality product for customers, distorts competition, affects investment levels, reduces tax revenues and legitimate employment, creates safety risks, and affects international relations. It also likely affects customers' perceptions of the brand due to the counterfeit product's inferior quality.

Branding Policies

Before establishing branding policies, a firm must decide whether to brand its products at all. If a company's product is homogeneous and similar to competitors' products, it may be difficult to brand. Raw materials such as coal, sand, and farm produce are hard to brand because of the homogeneity and physical characteristics of such products.

individual branding A branding policy in which each product is given a different name

If a firm chooses to brand its products, it may opt for one or more of the following branding policies: individual, family, or brand extension branding. **Individual branding** is a policy of giving each product a different name. Sara Lee uses individual branding among its many divisions, which include Hanes underwear, L'eggs pantyhose, Champion sportswear, and other vastly diverse brands. A major advantage of individual branding is that if an organization introduces a poor product, the negative images associated with it do not contaminate the company's other products. An individual branding policy may also facilitate market segmentation when a firm wishes to enter many segments of the same market. Separate, unrelated names can be used and each brand aimed at a specific segment.

family branding Branding all of a firm's products with the same name or part of the name

In **family branding,** all of a firm's products are branded with the same name or part of the name, such as Kellogg's Frosted Flakes, Kellogg's Rice Krispies, and Kellogg's Corn Flakes. In some cases, a company's name is combined with other words to brand items. Arm & Hammer uses its name on all its products, along with a generic description of the item, such as Arm & Hammer Heavy Duty Detergent,

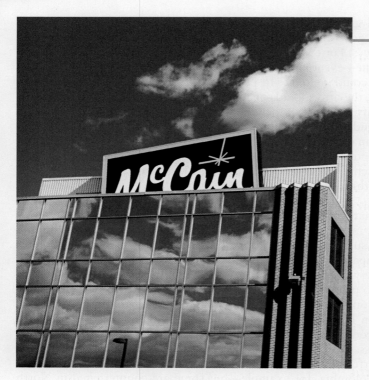

Family Branding
McCain brands its products with the same name.

Arm & Hammer Pure Baking Soda, and Arm & Hammer Carpet Deodorizer. Unlike individual branding, family branding means the promotion of one item with the family brand promotes the firm's other products. Other major companies that use family branding include McCain, Mitsubishi, Kodak, and Fisher-Price.

A **brand extension** occurs when a firm uses one of its existing brands to brand a new product in a different product category. For example, Procter & Gamble employed a brand extension when it named a new product Ivory Shampoo. Another example is when Bic, the maker of disposable pens, introduced Bic disposable razors and Bic lighters. A brand extension should not be confused with a line extension, which involves using an existing brand on a new product in the same product category, such as new flavours or sizes. For example, when the maker of Tylenol, McNeil Consumer Products, introduced Extra Strength Tylenol P.M., the new product was a line extension because it was in the same category. Researchers have found that there may be an opportunity

brand extension An organization uses one of its existing brands to brand a new product in a different product category

to charge a premium price relative to comparable products when extending a strong brand into a new product category because of consumers' perceptions of lower risk associated with a known brand name.[36]

Iams Aims at Pet Lovers

To many people today, pets are part of their families, and they want their pets to have the best. Iams, which markets the Iams and Eukanuba pet food brands, recognized this trend and shifted its focus. Today, it markets high-quality pet food, fancy pet treats, sauces, and other items that allow pet lovers to spoil their pets. For example, the company created Multi-Cat cat food for customers concerned about feeding cats in multi-cat households in which one cat might be overweight while another was not.

Now owned by Procter & Gamble, Iams has begun marketing pet products that mirror those intended for humans. For example, the company now applies a technology borrowed from P&G's Crest toothpaste to put a tartar-control coating on all adult pet food. The coating was added to pet treats in 2006. Iams also plans to produce a line of pet shampoo.

Iams continues to research new possibilities in pet supplies. For example, it is currently looking into creating pet products connected to P&G's Swiffer and Febreze brands. The company is also branching out by offering pet health insurance. As well, the company seeks to promote the brand in unique ways that will appeal to the customer base, such as sponsoring a dogsled race that is part of the annual Voyageur Festival in Winnipeg each year.

Marketers share a common concern that if a brand is extended too many times or extended too far outside its original product category, the brand can be significantly weakened. For example, in addition to an extensive list of family brand products (such as Labatt 50 and Labatt Lite) Labatt Breweries of Canada has extended its Labatt Blue brand to Labatt Blue Light and Labatt Blue Dry, but such extensions may confuse customers and encourage them to engage in considerable brand switching. Some evidence suggests that brands can be successfully extended to less closely related product categories through the use of advertisements that extend customers' perceptions of the original product category. For example, Waterford, an upscale Irish brand of crystal, extended its name to writing instruments when seeking sales growth beyond closely related product categories such as china, cutlery, and table linens.[37]

An organization is not limited to a single branding policy. A company that uses primarily individual branding for many of its products may also use brand extensions. Branding policy is influenced by the number of products and product lines the company produces, the characteristics of its target markets, the number and types of competing products available, and the size of the firm's resources.

Co-Branding

co-branding Using two or more brands on one product

Co-branding is the use of two or more brands on one product. Marketers employ co-branding to capitalize on the brand equity of multiple brands. It is popular in a number of processed food categories and in the credit card industry. The brands used for co-branding can be owned by the same company. For example, Kraft's Lunchables product teams the Kraft cheese brand with Oscar Mayer lunchmeats, another Kraft-owned brand. The brands may also be owned by different companies. Credit card companies such as Visa, and MasterCard, for instance, team up with other brands such as General Motors, Canadian Tire and many universities and airlines.

Effective co-branding capitalizes on the trust and confidence customers have in the brands involved. The brands should not lose their identities, and it should be clear to customers which brand is the main brand. For example, it is fairly obvious that Kellogg owns the brand and is the main brander of Kellogg's Healthy Choice Cereal. (The Choice brand is owned by ConAgra.) It is important for marketers to understand that when a co-branded product is unsuccessful, both brands are implicated in the product failure. To gain customer acceptance, the brands involved must represent a complementary fit in the minds of buyers. Trying to link a brand like Harley-Davidson with a brand like Healthy Choice will not achieve co-branding objectives because customers are not likely to perceive these brands as compatible.

Co-branding can help an organization differentiate its products from those of competitors. By using the product development skills of a co-branding partner, an organization can create a distinctive product. For example, fashion designer Giorgio Armani and carmaker Mercedes-Benz have teamed up to produce a Mercedes cabriolet with leather seats, dashboard, and leather steering wheel designed by Armani. The two are considering joint marketing events and advertising.[38] Co-branding can also allow the partners to take advantage of each other's distribution capabilities.

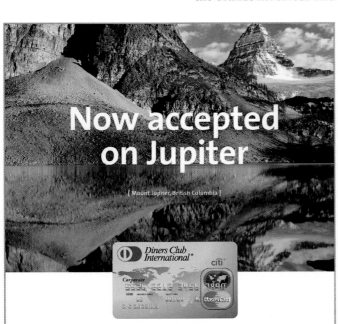

Now accepted on Jupiter

[Mount Jupiter, British Columbia]

And the millions of other places on Earth you do business.
The Diners Club® Card. Now accepted at nearly 24 million MasterCard® merchant locations worldwide.

The Diners Club Card with global MasterCard acceptance provides your business with a powerhouse end-to-end expense management tool that delivers the functionality and information needed to drive bottom-line savings. It's also a powerful tool in the hands of those who rely on your decisions. When you or your employees have a question, our best-in-class customer service connects you with a real person to speak with any time, day or night. Add our award-winning Club Rewards® Program†, and choosing the Diners Club Card is a smart business decision and an easy one to make.

For more information, go to dinersclubus.com/btn or call 1 800 999-9093

© 2006 Citicorp Diners Club Inc. All rights reserved.
† Diners Club has formed an alliance with MasterCard® in order to provide enhanced global merchant acceptance to Cardmembers with Cards issued in the U.S. and Canada. 'Award-winning Club Rewards (1997-2005) as voted by the readers of *Inside Flyer* magazine. Diners Club, Diners Club International with the Split Circle Logo and Club Rewards are trademarks of Diners Club International Ltd. Used under license. MasterCard is a registered trademark of MasterCard International Incorporated.

Co-Branding

MasterCard seeks co-branding alliances with established brands, such as in this partnership with Diners Club International. The Canadian Tire Options MasterCard is an example of a co-branding solution that encourages customer loyalty.

While co-branding has been used for a number of years, it began to grow in popularity in the 1980s when Monsanto aggressively promoted its NutraSweet product as an ingredient in such well-known brands as Diet Coke. Later a rival sweetener, Splenda, was co-branded with Diet Coke, Starbucks, and many other brands. Intel, too, has capitalized on ingredient co-branding through its "Intel Inside" program. The effectiveness of ingredient co-branding relies heavily on continued promotional efforts by the ingredient's producer.

Brand Licensing

brand licensing An agreement whereby a company permits another organization to use its brand on other products for a licensing fee

A popular branding strategy involves **brand licensing,** an agreement in which a company permits another organization to use its brand on other products for a licensing fee. Royalties may be as low as two percent of wholesale revenues or higher than 10 percent. Mattel, for example, licensed Warner Brothers' Harry Potter brand for use on board games and toys to tie in with the first movie based on the wildly popular book series. Warner was guaranteed royalties of $20 million from Mattel's licensing fee of 15 percent of gross revenues earned on these branded products.[39] The licensee is responsible for all manufacturing, selling, and advertising functions, and bears the costs if the licensed product fails. Not long ago only a few firms licensed their corporate trademarks, but today licensing is a multibillion-dollar business. The top North American licensing company is Walt Disney Company. The NFL, NASCAR, and Major League Baseball are all in the top ten in retail sales of licensed products.

The advantages of licensing range from extra revenues and low-cost or free publicity to new images and trademark protection. For example, Coca-Cola has licensed its trademark for use on glassware, radios, trucks, and clothing in the hope of protecting its trademark. However, brand licensing has drawbacks. The major disadvantages are a lack of manufacturing control, which could hurt the company's name, and bombarding consumers with too many unrelated products bearing the same name. Licensing arrangements can also fail because of poor timing, inappropriate distribution channels, or mismatching of product and name.

Packaging

Packaging involves the development of a container and a graphic design for a product. A package can be a vital part of a product, making it more versatile, safer, and easier to use. Like a brand name, a package can influence customers' attitudes toward a product and thus affect their purchase decisions. For example, several producers of jellies, sauces, and ketchups have packaged their products in squeezable containers to make use and storage more convenient. Package characteristics help shape buyers' impressions of a product at the time of purchase or during use. In this section, we examine the main functions of packaging and consider several major packaging decisions.

Packaging Functions

Effective packaging involves more than simply putting products in containers and covering them with wrappers. First, packaging materials serve the basic purpose of protecting the product and maintaining its functional form. Fluids such as milk, orange juice, and hair spray need packages that preserve and protect them. The packaging should prevent damage that could affect the product's usefulness and thus lead to higher costs. Because product tampering has become a problem, several packaging techniques have been developed to counter this danger. Some packages are also designed to deter shoplifting.

Another function of packaging is to offer convenience to consumers. For example, small aseptic packages—individual-size boxes or plastic bags that contain liquids and do not require refrigeration—strongly appeal to children and young adults with active lifestyles. The size or shape of a package may relate to the product's storage, convenience of use, or replacement rate. A third function of packaging is to promote a product by communicating its features, uses, benefits, and image. Sometimes a reusable package is developed to make the product more desirable. For example, the Cool Whip package doubles as a food storage container.

Finally, packaging can be used to communicate symbolically the quality or premium nature of a product. It can also evoke an emotional response. Packaging has been a major force in bath and body products, especially those associated with the spa industry. The goal is to communicate what the product stands for and trigger an expected experience.[40]

Major Packaging Considerations

In developing packages, marketers must take many factors into account. Obviously one major consideration is cost. Although a variety of packaging materials, processes, and designs are available, costs vary greatly. In recent years, buyers have shown a willingness to pay more for improved packaging, but there are limits. Marketers should conduct research to determine exactly how much customers are willing to pay for effective and efficient package designs.

As already mentioned, developing tamper-resistant packaging is very important for certain products. Although no package is tamperproof, marketers can develop packages that are difficult to contaminate. At a minimum, all packaging must comply with the Consumer Packaging and Labelling Act. However, packaging should also make any product tampering evident to resellers and consumers. Although effective tamper-resistant packaging may be expensive to develop, when balanced against the costs of lost sales, loss of consumer confidence and company reputation, and potentially expensive product liability lawsuits, the costs of ensuring consumer safety are minimal.

Marketers should also consider how much consistency is desirable among an organization's package designs. No consistency may be the best policy, especially if a firm's products are unrelated or aimed at vastly different target markets. To promote an overall company image, a firm may decide that all packages should be similar or include one major element of the design. This approach is called **family packaging.** Sometimes it is used only for lines of products, such as Campbell's soups, Weight Watchers' foods, and Planter's nuts.

family packaging Using similar packaging for all of a firm's products or packaging that has one common design element

A package's promotional role is an important consideration. Through verbal and non-verbal symbols, the package can inform potential buyers about the product's content, features, uses, advantages, and hazards. A firm can create desirable images and associations by its choice of colour, design, shape, and texture. Many cosmetics manufacturers, for example, design their packages to create impressions of richness, luxury, and exclusivity. A package performs a promotional function when it is designed to be safer or more convenient to use if such characteristics help stimulate demand.

Colours on packages are often chosen to attract attention, and colour can positively influence customers' emotions. People associate specific colours with certain feelings and experiences. For example:

- Blue is soothing; it is also associated with wealth, trust, and security.

- Gray is associated with strength, exclusivity, and success.

- Orange often signifies low cost.

- Red connotes excitement and stimulation.

- Purple is associated with dignity and stateliness.

- Yellow connotes cheerfulness and joy.

- Black is associated with being strong and masterful.[41]

When opting for colour on packaging, marketers must judge whether a particular colour will evoke positive or negative feelings when linked to a specific product. Rarely, for example, do processors package meat or bread in green materials because customers may associate green with mold. Marketers must also determine whether a specific target market will respond favourably or unfavourably to a particular colour. Cosmetics for women are more likely to be sold in pastel packaging than are personal care products for men. A relatively recent trend in packaging is colourless packages. Clear products and packaging connote a pure, natural product.

Packaging must also meet the needs of resellers. Wholesalers and retailers consider whether a package facilitates transportation, storage, and handling. Concentrated versions of laundry detergents and fabric softeners, for example, enable retailers to offer more product diversity within the existing shelf space. Resellers may refuse to carry certain products if their packages are cumbersome.

A final consideration is whether to develop packages that are environmentally responsible. Nearly one-half of all garbage consists of discarded plastic packaging, such as polystyrene containers, plastic soft drink bottles, and carryout bags. Plastic packaging material does not biodegrade, and paper requires the destruction of valuable forests. Consequently a number of companies have changed to environmentally sensitive packaging; they are also recycling more materials. Procter & Gamble markets several cleaning products in a concentrated form, which requires less packaging than the ready-to-use version. H. J. Heinz is looking for alternatives to its plastic ketchup squeeze bottles. Other companies are also searching for alternatives to environmentally harmful packaging. In some instances, however, customers have objected to such switches because the newer environmentally responsible packaging may be less effective or more inconvenient. Therefore, marketers must carefully balance society's desire to preserve the environment against customers' desire for convenience.

Criticisms of Packaging

The last several decades have brought a number of improvements in packaging. However, some packaging problems still need to be resolved. Some packages suffer from functional problems in that they simply do not work well. The packaging for flour and sugar is, at best, poor. Both grocers and consumers are very much aware that these packages leak and tear easily. Can anyone open and close a bag of flour without spilling at least a little bit? Certain packages, such as refrigerated biscuit cans, milk cartons with fold-out spouts, and potato chip bags, are frequently difficult to open. Research by Nestlé reveals that hard-to-open packages are among consumers' top complaints.[42] Although many steps have been taken to make packaging safer, critics still focus on the safety issues. Containers with sharp edges and breakable glass bottles are sometimes viewed as a threat to safety. Certain types of plastic packaging and aerosol containers represent possible health hazards.

At times, packaging is viewed as deceptive. Package shape, graphic design, and certain colours may be used to make a product appear larger than it actually is. The inconsistent use of certain size designations, such as giant, economy, family, king, and super, can lead to customer confusion.

Finally, although customers traditionally prefer attractive, effective, convenient packaging, the cost of such packaging is high.

Labelling

labelling Providing identifying, promotional, or other information on package labels

Labelling is very closely interrelated with packaging and is used for identification, promotional, and informational and legal purposes. Labels can be small or large relative to the size of the product and carry varying amounts of information. The sticker on a Chiquita banana, for example, is quite small and displays only the brand name of the fruit. A label can be part of the package itself or a separate feature attached to the package. Information presented on a label may include the brand name and mark, the registered trademark symbol, package size and content, product features, nutritional information, potential presence of allergens, type and style of the product, number of servings, care instructions, directions for use and safety precautions, the name and address of the manufacturer, expiration dates, seals of approval, and other facts.

universal product code (UPC) A series of electronically readable lines identifying a product and containing inventory and pricing information

For many products, the label includes a **universal product code (UPC),** a series of electronically readable lines identifying the product and providing inventory and pricing information for producers and resellers. The UPC is electronically read at the retail checkout counter.

Labels can facilitate the identification of a product by displaying the brand name in combination with a unique graphic design. For example, Heinz ketchup is easy to identify on a supermarket shelf because the brand name is easy to read and the label has a distinctive crown-like shape. By drawing attention to products and their benefits, labels can strengthen an organization's promotional efforts. Labels may contain such promotional messages as the offer of a discount or a larger package size at the same price, or information about a new or improved product feature.

Several federal laws (including the Consumer Packaging and Labelling Act, the Textile Labelling Act, and the Food and Drugs Act) deal directly or indirectly with packaging and labelling. For instance, federal laws require disclosure of such information as textile identification, potential hazards, and nutritional information. Although consumers have responded favourably to this type of information on labels, evidence as to whether they actually use it has been mixed. Despite legislation designed to make labels as accurate and informative as possible, questionable labelling practices persist. For example, consumers and consumer advocates continue to question the validity of label claims concerning such things as fat content and cholesterol, freshness, and the recyclability of the packaging.

SUMMARY

Organizations must be able to adjust their product mixes to compete effectively and achieve their goals. A product mix can be improved through line extension and product modification. A line extension is the development of a product closely related to one or more products in the existing line but designed specifically to meet different customer needs. Product modification is the changing of one or more characteristics of a product. This approach can be effective when the product is modifiable, when customers can perceive the change, and when customers want the modification. Quality modifications relate to a product's dependability and durability. Functional modifications affect a product's versatility, effectiveness, convenience, or safety. Aesthetic modifications change the sensory appeal of a product.

Developing new products can enhance a firm's product mix and add depth to the product line. A new product may be an innovation that has never been sold by any organization; a product that a given firm has not marketed previously, although similar products have been available from other organizations; or a product brought from one market to another.

Before a product is introduced, it goes through a seven-phase new-product development process. In the idea generation phase, new-product ideas may come from internal or external sources. In the process of screening, ideas are evaluated to determine whether they are consistent with the firm's overall objectives and resources. Concept testing, the third phase, involves having a small sample of potential customers review a brief description of the product idea to determine their initial perceptions of the proposed product and their early buying intentions. During the business analysis stage, the product idea is evaluated to determine its potential contribution to the firm's sales, costs, and profits. In the product development stage, the organization determines if it is technically feasible to produce the product and if it can be produced at a cost low enough to make the final price reasonable. Test marketing is a limited introduction of a product in areas chosen to represent the intended market. Finally, in the commercialization phase, full-scale production of the product begins and a complete marketing strategy is developed.

Product differentiation is the process of creating and designing products so that customers perceive them as different from competing products. Product quality, product design and features, and product support services are three aspects of product differentiation that companies consider when creating and marketing products. Product quality includes the overall characteristics of a product that allow it to perform as expected in satisfying customer needs. The level of quality is the amount of quality a product possesses. Consistency of quality is the degree to which a product has the same level of quality over time. Product design refers to how a product is conceived, planned, and produced. Components of product design include styling (the physical appearance of the product) and product features (the specific design characteristics that allow a product to perform certain tasks). Companies often differentiate their products by providing support services, usually called customer services. Customer services are human or mechanical efforts or activities that add value to a product.

Product deletion is the process of eliminating a product that no longer satisfies a sufficient number of customers. A product mix should be systematically reviewed to determine when to delete products. Products to be deleted can be phased out, run out, or dropped immediately.

A brand is a name, term, design, symbol, or any other feature that identifies one seller's good or service and distinguishes it from those of other sellers. A brand name is the part of a brand that can be spoken. A brand mark is the element not made up of words. A trademark is a legal designation indicating that the owner has exclusive use of the brand or part of the brand and others are prohibited by law from using it. A trade name is the legal name of an organization. Branding helps buyers identify and evaluate products, helps sellers facilitate product introduction and repeat purchasing, and fosters brand loyalty.

Brand loyalty is a customer's favourable attitude toward a specific brand. If brand loyalty is strong enough, customers may consistently purchase a particular brand when they need a product in this product category. The three degrees of brand loyalty are brand recognition, brand preference, and brand insistence. Brand recognition occurs when a customer is aware that the brand exists and views it as an alternative purchase if the preferred brand is unavailable. With brand preference, a customer prefers one brand over competing brands and will purchase it if available. Brand insistence occurs when a customer will accept no substitute.

Brand equity is the marketing and financial value associated with a brand's strength. It represents the value of a brand to an organization. The four major elements underlying brand equity include brand name awareness, brand loyalty, perceived brand quality, and brand associations.

A manufacturer brand, initiated by the producer, ensures that the firm is associated with its products at the point of purchase. A private distributor brand is initiated and owned by a reseller, sometimes taking on the name of the store or distributor. Manufacturers combat growing competition from private distributor brands by developing multiple brands. A generic brand indicates only the product category and does not include the company name or other identifying terms.

When selecting a brand name, a marketer should choose one that is easy to say, spell, and recall and that alludes to the product's uses, benefits, or special characteristics. Brand names can be devised from words, letters, numbers, nonsense words, or a combination of these. Brand names are created inside an organization by individuals, committees, or branding departments and by outside consultants. Services as well as products are branded, often with the company name and an accompanying symbol that makes the brand distinctive or conveys a desired image.

Producers protect ownership of their brands through registration with the Canadian Intellectual Property Office. A company must make certain the brand name it selects does not infringe on an already registered brand by confusing or deceiving consumers about the source of the product. In most foreign countries, brand registration is on a first-come, first-serve basis, making protection more difficult. Brand counterfeiting is becoming increasingly common and can undermine consumers' confidence in a brand.

Companies brand their products in several ways. Individual branding designates a unique name for each of a company's products, family branding identifies all of a firm's products with a single name, and brand extension branding applies an existing name to a new product in a different product category. Co-branding is the use of two or more brands on one product. Effective co-branding profits from the trust and confidence customers have in the brands involved. Finally, through a licensing agreement and for a licensing fee, a firm may permit another organization to use its brand on other products. Brand licensing enables producers to earn extra revenue, receive low-cost or free publicity, and protect their trademarks.

Packaging involves development of a container and a graphic design for a product. Effective packaging offers protection, economy, safety, and convenience. It can influence a customer's purchase decision by promoting features, uses, benefits, and image. When developing a package, marketers must consider the value to the customer of efficient and effective packaging, offset by the price the customer is willing to pay. Other considerations include making the package tamper resistant, whether to use multiple packaging and family packaging, how to design the package as an effective promotional tool, how best to accommodate resellers, and whether to develop environmentally responsible packaging. Firms choose particular colours, designs, shapes, and textures to create desirable images and associations. Consumers may criticize packaging that does not work well, poses health or safety problems, is deceptive in some way, or is not biodegradable or recyclable.

Labelling is closely interrelated with packaging and is used for identification, promotional, and informational and legal purposes. The labels of many products include a universal product code, a series of electronically readable lines identifying a product and containing inventory and pricing information. Various federal laws require that certain products be labelled or marked with warnings, instructions, nutritional information, manufacturer's identification, and the like. Despite legislation, questionable labelling practices persist, including misleading information about fat content and cholesterol, freshness, and recyclability of packaging.

 Please visit the student website at **www.hmco.ca/marketing** for ACE Self-Test questions that will help you prepare for exams.

IMPORTANT TERMS

Line extension	Functional	New-product development	Screening
Product modifications	modifications	process	Concept testing
Quality modifications	Aesthetic modifications	Idea generation	Business analysis

Product development
Test marketing
Commercialization
Product differentiation
Quality
Level of quality
Consistency of quality
Product design
Styling

Product features
Customer services
Product deletion
Brand
Brand name
Brand mark
Trademark
Trade name
Brand loyalty

Brand recognition
Brand preference
Brand insistence
Brand equity
Manufacturer brands
Private distributor
  brands
Generic brands
Individual branding

Family branding
Brand extension
Co-branding
Brand licensing
Family packaging
Labelling
Universal product code
  (UPC)

DISCUSSION & REVIEW QUESTIONS

1. What is a line extension, and how does it differ from a product modification?
2. Compare and contrast the three major approaches to modifying a product.
3. Identify and briefly explain the seven major phases of the new-product development process.
4. What is the major purpose of concept testing, and how is it accomplished?
5. What are the benefits and disadvantages of test marketing?
6. Why can the process of commercialization take a considerable amount of time?
7. What is product differentiation, and how can it be achieved?
8. Explain how the term *quality* has been used to differentiate products in the automobile industry in recent years. What are some makes and models of automobiles that come to mind when you hear the terms *high quality* and *poor quality?*
9. What is the difference between a brand and a brand name? Compare and contrast a brand mark and a trademark.
10. What are the three major degrees of brand loyalty?
11. What is brand equity? Identify and explain the major elements of brand equity.
12. Identify the factors a marketer should consider in selecting a brand name.
13. The brand name Xerox is sometimes used generically to refer to photocopiers, and Kleenex is used to refer to facial tissues. How can the manufacturers protect their brand names, and why would they want to do so?
14. What is co-branding? What major issues should be considered when using co-branding?
15. Describe the functions a package can perform. Which function is most important? Why?
16. What are the major criticisms of packaging?
17. What are the major functions of labelling?

APPLICATION QUESTIONS

1. When developing a new product, a company often test markets the proposed product in a specific area or location. Suppose you wish to test market your new, revolutionary SuperWax car wax, which requires only one application for a lifetime finish. Where and how would you test market your new product?
2. Phasing out a product from the product mix often is difficult for an organization. Visit a retail store in your area, and ask the manager what products he or she has had to discontinue in the recent past. Find out what factors influenced the decision to delete the product and who was involved in the decision. Ask the manager to identify any products that should be but have not been deleted, and try to ascertain the reason.
3. General Motors introduced the subcompact Geo with a name that appeals to a world market. Invent
a brand name for a line of luxury sports cars that also would appeal to an international market. Suggest a name that implies quality, luxury, and value.
4. For each of the following product categories, choose an existing brand. Then, for each selected brand, suggest a co-brand and explain why the co-brand would be effective.
   a. Cookies
   b. Pizza
   c. Long-distance telephone service
   d. A sports drink
5. Identify a package that you believe is inferior. Explain why you think the package is inferior, and discuss your recommendations for improving it.

globalEDGE™

1. Before your firm decides to develop a new product for a specific industry, you have been asked to survey the level and quality of innovation in the biotechnology, computer software, and semiconductor industries. *Technology Review,* a magazine of innovation, can help you identify the firms with the highest and lowest levels of innovation in each industry. Access this journal by using the search term "magazine of innovation" at **http://globaledge.msu.edu/ibrd** or **http://globaledge.msu.edu/ibrd/ibrd .asp** and then click on the pdf link in the first sentence of the welcome page to download the report. What are considered the top companies' core competencies? Given this information, what can you think may be important in the coming years in each industry?

2. Brands are no longer a domestic phenomenon. In fact, many consumers now associate global brands with higher degrees of quality or prestige than more localized or even regionalized brands. Find data on this topic at *Business Week*'s Global Brands section by using the search term "global brands" at **http://globaledge.msu.edu/ibrd** or **http://globaledge.msu.edu/ibrd/ibrd .asp.** Once there, click on the Top 100 Brands Scorecard to the right. What are the top 10 brands worldwide? Which countries are represented? Which brands from the overall study are from Germany? Summarize three German brands and compare each with a competing brand.

INTERNET Exercise

Visit **www.prideferrell.com** for resources to help you master the material in this chapter, plus materials that will help you expand your marketing knowledge, including internet exercise updates, ACE self-tests, hotlinks to companies featured in this chapter, and much more.

Merck & Company

Merck, a leading global pharmaceutical company, develops, manufactures, and markets a broad range of health-care products. The company has established a website to serve as an educational and informational resource for Internet users around the world. To learn more about the company and its research, visit its award-winning site at **www.merck.com**.

1. What products has Merck developed and introduced recently?
2. What role does research play in Merck's success? How does research facilitate new-product development at Merck?
3. Find Merck's mission statement. Is Merck's focus on research consistent with the firm's mission and values?
4. Does the Merck website promote brand loyalty? Explain.

Case 12.1 Using the 3Rs and 3M

3M, the $20 billion company formerly known as Minnesota Mining and Manufacturing, markets diverse products in nearly 200 countries. The century-old company has a long-held reputation for innovative, new products ranging from waterproof sandpaper and masking tape to Scotchguard fabric protector and Post-it Notes. It drives new-product development by carefully managing the 3Rs: risk, reward, and responsibility. 3M has more than a century of experience in successfully developing and managing a diverse mix of consumer and business products. Post-it Notes and Scotch-Brite scouring pads are just two of 3M's well-known brand names. The company also creates products for very specific uses, such as light-reflective coatings for street signs, and medicinal creams for fighting skin-based viruses.

Day in and day out, 6500 employees follow the 3R system as they search for new technologies and applications that could conceivably become 3M's next blockbuster product. The first R, risk, is a vital element in decisions about whether a product idea is promising enough to be developed into a prototype, test marketed, and ultimately brought to market through commercialization. Rather than take the safer path of incrementally improving existing products, 3M is taking calculated risks in its search for major breakthroughs. Its ambitious goals are to introduce twice the number of new products and triple the number of successful products that it has in the past.

Risks are evaluated relative to the second R, reward. Through the 3M Acceleration system, managers filter out ideas with lower profit potential and concentrate company resources on the few hundred ideas with higher profit potential. The point is to more productively support corporate growth by bringing high-potential products to market faster. Executives monitor all the ideas that make it into the Acceleration program to ensure speedy progress toward commercialization and measure the rewards in terms of revenue and profits.

With respect to the third R, responsibility, Lead User Teams—cross-functional groups of up to six employees—are responsible for new-product development. Along with technical and marketing staff, a team may have members from manufacturing, finance, procurement, or other departments, depending on its focus. Each team investigates product ideas to satisfy the unspoken or unrecognized needs of its customer segment. "They are taught to set their sights on exploring the areas where the possibilities for discovery are greatest because the pre-existing knowledge is most slim," says one 3M manager. This entails systematically examining trends that barely register today to consider products so advanced that "even the 'early adopters' have not yet arrived."

In addition to team responsibility, 3M has a long-standing tradition of nurturing independent research into potential new products. This encourages innovation from within and has led to new products and processes that benefited the company as well as its customers. Staff scientists are allowed to spend up to 15 percent of their time on self-directed projects that they think will blossom into commercially feasible products. They can request funding from their own business units or any other 3M unit to pursue the best ideas. If they are unable to obtain funding from a business unit, they can apply for a company-sponsored independent research grant of up to $100 000. Employees are also eligible for awards that honour outstanding achievement in new-product development, technology, and quality.

Along with the 3Rs, 3M is relying on DFSS—Design for Six Sigma—to boost product quality and development efficiency. The Six Sigma program takes quality far beyond simple error measurement and reduction: it teaches employees to incorporate the customer perspective early in the development process. More than 36 000 managers and scientists around the world have already received training in Six Sigma. These techniques "allow us to be more closely connected to the market and give us a much higher probability of success in our new-product designs," says 3M's vice president of research and development. The program has been so successful that the company is teaching its customers to apply Six Sigma techniques to improve their processes and products.

Finally, 3M is expediting new-product development by transferring 400 scientists from the corporate research and development department to specific business units. "By bringing more of our technical people into 3M businesses, we are strengthening our ability to commercialize new products now and well into the future," explains the CEO. "Now technical people can play more of a role in transforming pipeline projects into marketplace realities."[43]

Questions for Discussion

1. Why would 3M apply quality improvement techniques to the design of new products?
2. What effect is the 3M Acceleration program likely to have on each stage of the new-product development process?
3. Evaluate 3M's goals of launching twice the number of new products and triple the number of successful products compared with previous years. Are these goals practical and attainable? How might these goals affect the efforts of 3M's Lead User Teams?

13

Services and Non-profit Marketing

Are You Happy with Your Bank?

Often people can be heard complaining about their bank. Canadians frequently complain about their rising and ever-present service fees. These complaints seem to intensify when the banks announce record profits. Nevertheless, when surveyed about their primary bank, Canadians tend to provide favourable reports.

According to a nationwide study by Martiz Canada, almost four out of five (78 percent), an eight percent rise from the previous year, said their primary bank communicates effectively with them concerning their personal financial profile. Relatively good news; however, almost half (43 percent) of the survey's respondents said, "it wouldn't take a lot" for them to switch their primary bank if it meant they would receive better treatment at their new institution.

The same study investigated consumer expectations. It was found that Canadians rank convenience and customer service tops when it comes to what they want from their financial institions. Twenty-three percent of bank patrons want timely service, while another 22 percent want to deal with courteous and knowledgeable staff at their local branches. These two criteria outpaced votes for better interest rates (seven percent), a better fee structure (six percent), and a wider variety of financial services and products (one percent).

Another study by the technology company EDS Canada and Ipsos-Reid found that Canadians have a reasonably high level of trust in their banks: 40 percent indicate they are very confident in their bank's ability to protect their privacy and 54 percent are somewhat confident. Trust is an absolute requirement for bank clients. Failures to instill trust with bank clients could prove very costly to the banks. Twenty-one percent of consumers report they would close all accounts and move their business to another bank if their personal information were conpromised, and a further seven percent would close some accounts and use another bank.

Ultimately Canadians depend on banks to provide financial services, and to protect their information and investments.

Likewise, banks depend on their customers' continued patronage. A decline in service quality and any failure or mistake that would cause customers to question the trust they have in their bank could result in customers switching banks. ■

The products offered by Canadian banks—such as, investments, loans, and mortgages—are services rather than tangible goods. This chapter presents concepts that apply specifically to products that are services. The organizations that market service products include for-profit firms, such as those offering financial, personal, and professional services, and non-profit organizations, such as educational institutions, churches, charities, and governments.

We begin this chapter with a focus on the growing importance of service industries in our economy. We then address the unique characteristics of services. Next, we deal with the challenges these characteristics pose in developing and managing marketing mixes for services. We then discuss customers' judgment of service quality and the importance of delivering high-quality services. Finally, we define non-profit marketing and examine the development of non-profit marketing strategies.

The Nature and Importance of Services

All products, whether they are goods, services, or ideas, are intangible to some extent. We previously defined a service as an intangible product involving a deed, a performance, or an effort that cannot be physically possessed.[1] Services are usually provided through the application of human and/or mechanical efforts directed at people or objects. For example, a service such as education involves the efforts of service providers (teachers) directed at people (students), whereas janitorial and interior decorating services direct their efforts at objects. Services can also involve the use of mechanical efforts directed at people (air transportation) or objects (freight transportation). A wide variety of services, such as health care and landscaping, involve both human and mechanical efforts. Although many services entail the use of tangibles such as tools and machinery, the primary difference between a service and a good is that a service is dominated by the intangible portion of the total product.

Services as products should not be confused with the related topic of customer services. Customer service involves any human or mechanical activity that adds value to the product.[2] While the core product may be a good, complementary services help create the total product. While customer service is a part of the marketing of goods, service marketers also provide customer services. For example, many service companies offer guarantees to their customers in an effort to increase value. Hampton Inn, a U.S.-based chain of mid-price hotels, gives its guests a free night if they are not 100 percent satisfied with their stay (fewer than one-half of one percent of Hampton customers ask for a refund). In some cases, a 100 percent satisfaction guarantee or similar service commitment may motivate employees to provide high-quality service, not because failure to do so leads to personal penalties but because they are proud to be part of an organization that is so committed to good service.

The increasing importance of services in the Canadian economy has led many people to call the Canadian economy a service economy. In most developed countries, including Germany, Japan, Australia, and the United States, services account for about 70 percent of the gross domestic product (GDP). More than one-half of new businesses are service businesses, and service employment is expected to continue to grow. These industries have absorbed much of the influx of women and minorities into the work force.

One major catalyst in the growth of consumer services has been long-term economic growth (slowed only by a few economic turndowns) in Canada, which has led to increased interest in financial services, travel, entertainment, and personal care. Lifestyle changes have similarly encouraged expansion of the service sector. The need for child care, domestic services, and other time-saving services has increased, and many consumers want to avoid such tasks as meal preparation, house cleaning, yard

Service as Theatre

Service and sporting events, like theatre, have rules that standardize the performance.

maintenance, and tax preparation. Consequently, franchise service operations such as Subway, Merry Maids, Service Master, and H&R Block have experienced rapid growth. Also, because Canadians have become more health-, fitness-, and recreation-oriented, the demand for exercise and recreational facilities, such as golf courses, has escalated. In terms of demographics, the Canadian population is growing older, a fact that has promoted tremendous expansion of health-care and other services demanded by seniors. Finally, the increasing number and complexity of high-tech goods have spurred demand for support services. Indeed, the services sector has been enhanced by dramatic changes in information technology. Entrepreneurs have emerged taking advantage of inexpensive computer hardware, free software, and broadband Internet access to launch new service-oriented businesses or to transform existing businesses to focus on services.[3] Consider service companies such as Google, eBay, and Amazon.com, which use technology to provide services to challenge and change traditional ways of conducting business.

Business services have prospered as well. Business services include support and maintenance, consulting, installation, equipment leasing, marketing research, advertising, temporary office personnel, and janitorial services. Expenditures for business services have risen even faster than expenditures for consumer services. The growth in business services has been attributed to the increasingly complex, specialized, and competitive business environment. IBM, for example, has shifted from a focus on computer hardware to consulting services and software applications.

One way to view services is from a theatre framework with production elements such as actors, audience, a setting, and a performance. The actors (service workers) create a service (performance) for the audience (customers) in a setting (service environment) where the performance unfolds. Costumes (uniforms), props (devices, music, machines), and the setting (face-to-face or indirect through telephone or Internet) help complete the theatrical metaphor.[4] At Disney World, for example, all employees wear costumes; there is an entertainment setting; and most service contact with employees involves playing roles and engaging in planned skits. But the theatrical components are also visible in a Tim Hortons or on an Air Canada flight. In addition, a performance involves a "script," a chronologically ordered representation of the steps that comprise the service performance from the customer's perspective.[5] Even sporting events such as curling, football, and hockey have sequences of events and rules that standardize the performance, even if the outcome depends on the performance itself.

Characteristics of Services

The issues associated with marketing service products differ somewhat from those associated with marketing goods. To understand these differences, we need to look at the distinguishing characteristics of services. Services have six basic characteristics:

intangibility, inseparability of production and consumption, perishability, heterogeneity, client-based relationships, and customer contact.[6]

Intangibility

intangibility Cannot be perceived by the senses

As already noted, the major characteristic that distinguishes a service from a good is intangibility. **Intangibility** means a service is not physical and therefore cannot be perceived by the senses. For example, it is impossible to touch the education that students derive from attending classes; the intangible benefit is becoming more knowledgeable. In addition, services cannot be physically possessed. Students obviously cannot physically possess knowledge as they can an iPod or a car. There is a direct relationship between the level of intangibility and consumers' use of brands as a cue to the nature and quality of the service. This means that brand name is more important for financial services than for a cell phone.[7]

Figure 13.1 depicts a tangibility continuum from pure goods (tangible) to pure services (intangible). Pure goods, if they exist at all, are rare because practically all marketers of goods also provide customer services. Even a tangible product such as sugar must be delivered to the store, priced, and placed on a shelf before a customer can purchase it. Intangible, service-dominant products such as education or health care are clearly service products. But what about products near the centre of the continuum? Is a restaurant such as Boston Pizza a goods marketer or a service marketer? Services like airline flights have something tangible to offer, such as drinks and meals. An Internet search engine such as Google or news site such as CBC or CNN is service-dominant. Knowing where the product lies on the continuum is important in creating marketing strategies for service-dominant products.

Inseparability of Production and Consumption

inseparability The quality of being produced and consumed at the same time

Another important characteristic of services that creates challenges for marketers is **inseparability,** which refers to the fact that the production of a service cannot be separated from its consumption by customers. For example, air passenger service is produced and consumed simultaneously. In other words, services are often produced, sold, and consumed at the same time. In goods marketing, a customer can purchase a good, take it home, and store it until ready to use it. The manufacturer of the good may never

figure 13.1

THE TANGIBILITY CONTINUUM

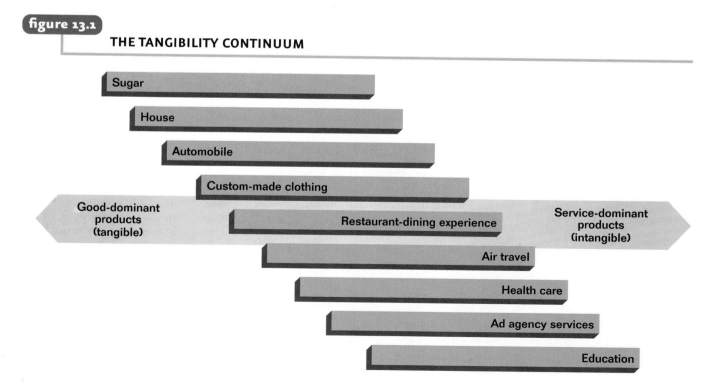

Good-dominant products (tangible)

Sugar
House
Automobile
Custom-made clothing
Restaurant-dining experience
Air travel
Health care
Ad agency services
Education

Service-dominant products (intangible)

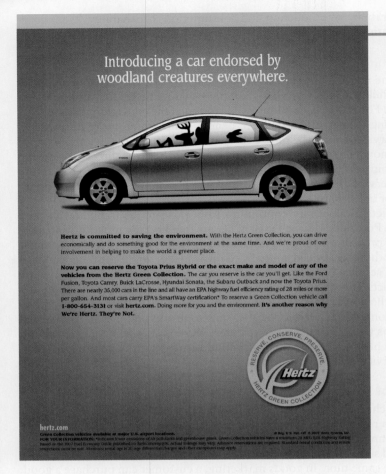

Introducing a car endorsed by
woodland creatures everywhere.

Hertz is committed to saving the environment. With the Hertz Green Collection, you can drive economically and do something good for the environment at the same time. And we're proud of our involvement in helping to make the world a greener place.

Now you can reserve the Toyota Prius Hybrid or the exact make and model of any of the vehicles from the Hertz Green Collection. The car you reserve is the car you'll get. Like the Ford Fusion, Toyota Camry, Buick LaCrosse, Hyundai Sonata, the Subaru Outback and now the Toyota Prius. There are nearly 35,000 cars in the line and all have an EPA highway fuel efficiency rating of 28 miles or more per gallon. And most cars carry EPA's SmartWay certification* To reserve a Green Collection vehicle call **1-800-654-3131** or visit **hertz.com**. Doing more for you and the environment. **It's another reason why We're Hertz. They're Not.**

hertz.com
Green Collection vehicles available at major U.S. airport locations.

Service Value
Hertz promotes both service and its ability to save the environment.

see an actual customer. Customers, however, often must be present at the production of a service (such as investment consulting or surgery) and cannot take the service home. Because of inseparability, customers not only want a specific type of service but expect it to be provided in a specific way by a specific individual. For example, the production and consumption of a medical exam occur simultaneously, and the patient knows in advance who the physician is and generally understands how the exam will be conducted. Inseparability implies a shared responsibility between the customer and service provider. As a result, training programs for employees should stress the customer's role in the service experience to elevate their perceptions of shared responsibility and positive feelings.[8]

Perishability

perishability The inability of unused service capacity to be stored for future use

Services are characterized by **perishability** in that the unused service capacity of one time period cannot be stored for future use. For example, empty seats on an airline flight today cannot be stored and sold to passengers at a later date. Other examples of service perishability include unsold basketball tickets, unscheduled dentists' appointment times, and empty hotel rooms. Although some goods, such as meat, milk, and produce, are perishable, goods generally are less perishable than services. If a pair of jeans has been sitting on a department store shelf for a week, someone can still buy them the next day. Goods marketers can handle the supply-demand problem through production scheduling and inventory techniques. Service marketers do not have the same advantage and face several hurdles in trying to balance supply and demand. They can, however, plan for demand that fluctuates according to day of the week, time of day, or season.

Heterogeneity

heterogeneity Variation in quality

Services delivered by people are susceptible to **heterogeneity,** or variation in quality. Quality of manufactured goods is easier to control with standardized procedures, and mistakes are easier to isolate and correct. Because of the nature of human behaviour, however, it is very difficult for service providers to maintain a consistent quality of service delivery. This variation in quality can occur from one organization to another, from one service person to another within the same service facility, and from one service facility to another within the same organization. For example, one bank may provide more convenient hours and charge fewer fees than the one next door, or the retail clerks in one bookstore may be more knowledgeable and therefore more helpful than those in another bookstore owned by the same chain. In addition, the service a single employee provides can vary from customer to customer, day to day, or even hour to hour. Although many service problems are onetime events that cannot be predicted or controlled ahead of time, training and establishment of standard procedures can help increase consistency and reliability. Because research suggests that service employees with greater sensitivity toward people of different countries and cultures are more attentive and have better interpersonal skills, job satisfaction, and social satisfaction, training that improves cultural sensitivity should improve consistency of service quality in cross-cultural environments.[9]

Heterogeneity usually increases as the degree of labour intensiveness increases. Many services, such as auto repair, education, and hairstyling, rely heavily on human labour. Other services, such as telecommunications, health clubs, and public transportation, are more equipment intensive. People-based services are often prone to fluctuations in quality from one time period to the next. For example, the fact that a hairstylist gives a customer a good haircut today does not guarantee that customer a haircut of equal quality from the same hairstylist at a later date or even a later hour. A morning customer may receive a better haircut than an end-of-the-day customer from the same stylist. Equipment-based services suffer from this problem to a lesser degree than people-based services. For instance, automated teller machines have reduced inconsistency in the quality of teller services at banks, and barcode scanning has improved the accuracy of service at checkout counters in grocery stores.

Client-Based Relationships

client-based relationships
Interactions that result in satisfied customers who use a service repeatedly over time

The success of many services depends on creating and maintaining **client-based relationships,** interactions that result in satisfied customers who use a service repeatedly over time.[10] In fact, some service providers, such as lawyers, accountants, and financial advisers, call their customers *clients* and often develop and maintain close, long-term relationships with them. For such service providers, it is not enough to attract customers. They are successful only to the degree to which they can maintain a group of clients who use their services on an ongoing basis. For example, an accountant may serve a family in his or her area for decades. If the members of this family like the quality of the accountant's services, they are likely to recommend the accountant to other families. If several families repeat this positive word-of-mouth communication, the accountant will likely acquire a long list of satisfied clients before long. This process

Heros in the Aftermath of Disaster

After Hurricane Katrina hit the Gulf Coast in 2005, Mississippi Power quickly and efficiently came to the rescue of its 195 000 customers—all of whom were left without power after the devastating storm. In only 12 days, the small utility managed to restore power to all customers for whom it was safe to do so, despite the loss of 65 percent of its transmission and distribution facilities.

Mississippi Power's values, as written on employees' ID badges, are "Unquestionable Trust, Superior Performance, Total Commitment." Facing the crisis, company executives had no choice but to take immediate action and trust that they could find solutions. Their resolve was strengthened by a "can-do" culture, years of hurricane experience, and a strong crisis-management plan. They appointed 20 storm directors and gave each complete authority to do whatever was necessary to get the job done. Each individual—from storm directors on down—was empowered to make decisions and solve problems on the spot. The results were phenomenal: people worked harder, found unconventional solutions, and restored power before the projected four-week deadline.

Those at Mississippi Power learned six valuable lessons in the wake of Katrina: (1) A good forecast pays off. (2) Back up your backup plans. (3) Know how to get help when you need it. (4) Seek breakthrough solutions. (5) Hard work and pride pay off. (6) Measure results. Although the Gulf Coast area is still recovering from Katrina, the people at Mississippi Power exceeded their own expectations by simply doing what needed to be done, and they saved money and restored service to their customers earlier than expected.

Characteristics of Services
Hairstylists develop close client-based relationships.

is the key to creating and maintaining client-based relationships. To ensure that it actually occurs, the service provider must take steps to build trust, demonstrate customer commitment, and satisfy customers so well that they become very loyal to the provider and unlikely to switch to competitors.

Customer Contact

customer contact The level of interaction between provider and customer needed to deliver the service

Not all services require a high degree of customer contact, but many do. **Customer contact** refers to the level of interaction between the service provider and the customer necessary to deliver the service. High-contact services include health care, real estate, and legal and spa services. Examples of low-contact services are tax preparation, auto repair, and dry cleaning. Note that high-contact services generally involve actions directed toward people, who must be present during production. A hairstylist's customer, for example, must be present during the styling process. Because the customer must be present, the process of production may be just as important as its final outcome. Although it is sometimes possible for the service provider to go to the customer, high-contact services typically require that the customer go to the production facility. Thus, the physical appearance of the facility may be a major component of the customer's overall evaluation of the service. For example, when the physical setting fosters customer-to-customer interactions, it can lead to greater loyalty to an establishment and positive word-of-mouth communications.[11] While low-contact services do not require the customer's physical presence during delivery, the customer will likely need to be present to initiate and terminate the service. For example, customers of auto-repair services must bring in the vehicle and describe its symptoms, but often do not remain during the preparation process.

Level of Customer Contact

Online universities, such as Lansbridge University, maintain the level of contact through technology.

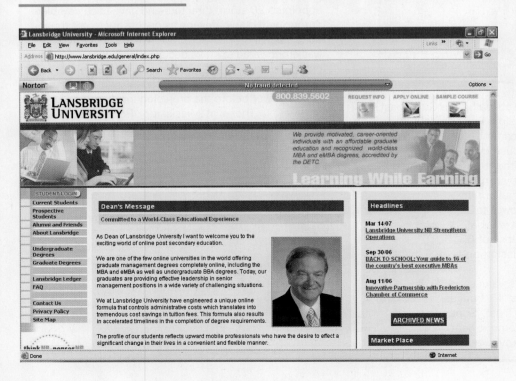

Employees of high-contact service providers are a very important ingredient in creating satisfied customers. A fundamental precept of customer contact is that satisfied employees lead to satisfied customers. In fact, employee satisfaction is the single most important factor in providing high-service quality. Thus, to minimize the problems customer contact can create, service organizations must take steps to understand and meet the needs of employees by adequately training them, empowering them to make more decisions, and rewarding them for customer-oriented behaviour.[12] To provide the quality of customer service that has made it the fastest-growing coffee retailer in the world, Starbucks provides extensive employee training. Employees receive about 25 hours of initial training, which includes memorizing recipes and learning the differences among a variety of coffees, proper coffee-making techniques, and many other skills that stress Starbucks' dedication to customer service. Starbucks has approximately 8500 coffee shops and about 96 700 employees worldwide.[13]

Developing and Managing Marketing Mixes for Services

The characteristics of services discussed in the previous section create a number of challenges for service marketers (see Table 13.1). These challenges are especially evident in the development and management of marketing mixes for services. Although such mixes contain the four major marketing mix variables—product, distribution, promotion, and price—the characteristics of services require that marketers consider additional issues.

Development of Services

A service offered by an organization generally is a package, or bundle, of services consisting of a core service and one or more supplementary services. A core service

table 13.1   SERVICE CHARACTERISTICS AND MARKETING CHALLENGES

Service Characteristics	Resulting Marketing Challenges
Intangibility	Difficult for customer to evaluate.
	Customer does not take physical possession.
	Difficult to advertise and display.
	Difficult to set and justify prices.
	Service process is usually not protectable by patents.
Inseparability of production and consumption	Service provider cannot mass produce services.
	Customer must participate in production.
	Other consumers affect service outcomes.
	Services are difficult to distribute.
Perishability	Services cannot be stored.
	Balancing supply and demand is very difficult.
	Unused capacity is lost forever.
	Demand may be very time sensitive.
Heterogeneity	Service quality is difficult to control.
	Service delivery is difficult to standardize.
Client-based relationships	Success depends on satisfying and keeping customers over the long term.
	Generating repeat business is challenging.
	Relationship marketing becomes critical.
Customer contact	Service providers are critical to delivery.
	Requires high levels of service employee training and motivation.
	Changing a high-contact service into a low-contact service to achieve lower costs is difficult to achieve without reducing customer satisfaction.

Sources: K. Douglas Hoffman and John E. G. Bateson, *Services Marketing: Concepts, Strategies, and Cases,* 3rd ed. (Cincinnati: Thomson/ South-Western, 2006); Valarie A. Zeithaml, A. Parasuraman, and Leonard L. Berry, *Delivering Quality Service: Balancing Customer Perceptions and Expectations* (New York: Free Press, 1990); Leonard L. Berry and A. Parasuraman, *Marketing Services: Competing Through Quality* (New York: Free Press, 1991), p. 5.

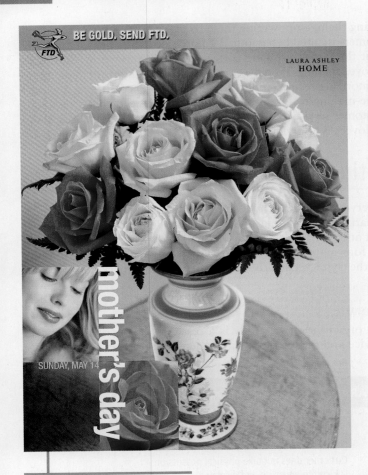

BE GOLD. SEND FTD.

LAURA ASHLEY
HOME

mother's day

SUNDAY, MAY 14

Development of Services

FTD provides many tangible cues to convey its delivery service.

is the basic service experience or commodity that a customer expects to receive. A supplementary service is a supportive one related to the core service and is used to differentiate the service bundle from competitors'. For example, Holiday Inn Express & Suites provides a room as a core service. Bundled with the room are such supplementary services as free local phone calls, cable television, and a complimentary continental breakfast.

As discussed earlier, heterogeneity results in variability in service quality and makes it difficult to standardize service delivery. However, heterogeneity provides one advantage to service marketers: it allows them to customize their services to match the specific needs of individual customers. Customization plays a key role in providing competitive advantage for the service provider. Being able to personalize the service to fit the exact needs of the customer accommodates individual needs, wants, or desires.[14] Subway, for example, tries to let each customer participate in developing his or her own customized sandwich. IBM determines a business's needs and then develops information technology services to provide a customized application. Health care is an example of an extremely customized service; the services provided differ from one patient to the next.

Such customized services can be expensive for both provider and customer, and some service marketers therefore face a dilemma: how to provide service at an acceptable level of quality in an efficient and economic manner and still satisfy individual customer needs. To cope with this problem, some service marketers offer standardized packages. For example, a spa may provide a number of treatments such as hair styling, facials, and massages for one price. When service bundles are standardized, the specific actions and activities of the service provider usually are highly specified. Automobile quick-lube providers frequently offer a service bundle for a single price; the specific work to be done on a customer's car is spelled out in detail. Various other equipment-based services are also often standardized into packages. For instance, cable television providers frequently offer several packages, such as "Basic," "Standard," and "Premier."

The characteristic of intangibility makes it difficult for customers to evaluate a service prior to purchase. A customer who is shopping for a pair of jeans can try them on before buying them, but how does she or he evaluate a legal advice before receiving the service? Intangibility requires service marketers such as attorneys to market promises to customers. The customer is forced to place some degree of trust in the service provider to perform the service in a manner that meets or exceeds those promises. Service marketers must guard against making promises that raise customer expectations beyond what they can provide.

To cope with the problem of intangibility, marketers employ tangible cues, such as well-groomed, professional-appearing contact personnel and clean, attractive physical facilities, to help assure customers about the quality of the service. Most service providers uniform at least some of their high-contact employees. Uniforms help make the service experience more tangible and serve as physical evidence to signal quality, create consistency, and send cues to suggest a desired image.[15] Consider the professionalism, experience, and competence conveyed by an airline pilot's uniform. Life insurance companies sometimes try to make the quality of their policies more tangible by printing them on premium-quality paper and enclosing them in leather sheaths. Because customers often rely on brand names as an indicator of product quality, service marketers at organizations whose names are the same as their service brand names should strive to build a strong national image for their companies. For example, Rogers,

McDonald's, eBay, London Life, and CIBC try to maintain strong, positive company images because these names are the brand names of the services they provide.

The inseparability of production and consumption and the level of customer contact also influence the development and management of services. The fact that customers take part in the production of a service means other customers can affect the outcome of the service. For instance, if a non-smoker were to dine in a restaurant, the overall quality of service experienced by the non-smoking customer declines. For this reason, even if not required by law to prohibit smoking, many service providers prohibit smoking anywhere on their premises. Service marketers can reduce these problems by encouraging customers to share the responsibility of maintaining an environment that allows all participants to receive the intended benefits of the service.

Distribution of Services

Marketers deliver services in a variety of ways. In some instances, customers go to a service provider's facility. For example, most health-care, dry-cleaning, and spa services are delivered at the provider's facilities. Some services are provided at the customer's home or business. Lawn care, air conditioning and heating repair, and carpet cleaning are examples. Other services are delivered primarily at "arm's length," meaning no face-to-face contact occurs between the customer and the service provider. A number of equipment-based services are delivered at arm's length, including electric, online, cable television, and telephone services. Providing high-quality customer service at arm's length can be costly but essential in keeping customers satisfied and maintaining market share. For example, many airlines, although trying to cut costs, are also increasing spending on refurbishing their websites to better serve customers. Companies such as WestJet are working on user-friendly websites as a way to draw customers to their online services as an alternative to going through an online travel agent like Orbitz or Travelocity.[16]

Marketing channels for services are usually short and direct, meaning the producer delivers the service directly to the end user. Some services, however, use intermediaries. For example, travel agents facilitate the delivery of airline services, independent insurance agents participate in the marketing of a variety of insurance policies, and financial planners market investment services.

Service marketers are less concerned with warehousing and transportation than are goods marketers. They are, however, very concerned about inventory management, especially balancing supply and demand for services. The service characteristics of inseparability and level of customer contact contribute to the challenges of demand management. In some instances, service marketers use appointments and reservations as approaches for scheduling delivery of services. Health-care providers, lawyers, accountants, auto mechanics, and restaurants often use appointments or reservations to plan and pace delivery of their services. To increase the supply of a service, marketers use multiple service sites and also increase the number of contact service providers at each site.

To make delivery more accessible to customers and increase the supply of a service, as well as reduce labor costs, some service providers have replaced some contact personnel with equipment. In other words, they have changed a high-contact service into a low-contact one. The banking industry is an example. By installing ATMs, banks have increased production capacity and reduced customer contact. In addition, a number of automated banking services are now available by telephone 24 hours a day. Such services have helped lower costs by reducing the need for customer service representatives. Changing the delivery of services from human to equipment has created some problems, however. Some customers complain that automated services are less personal. When designing service delivery, marketers must pay attention to the degree of personalization customers' desire.

Promotion of Services

The intangibility of services results in several promotion-related challenges to service marketers. Since it may not be possible to depict the actual performance of a service

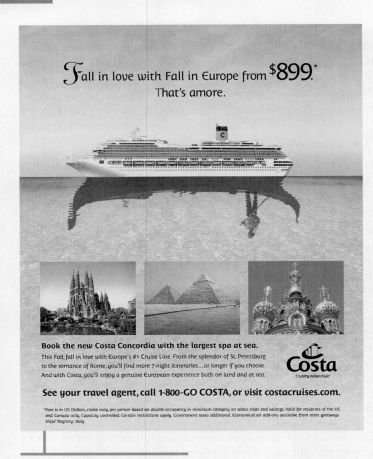

*F*all in love with Fall in Europe from $899*.
That's amore.

Book the new Costa Concordia with the largest spa at sea.
This Fall, fall in love with Europe's #1 Cruise Line. From the splendor of St. Petersburg
to the romance of Rome, you'll find more 7-night itineraries…or longer if you choose.
And with Costa, you'll enjoy a genuine European experience both on land and at sea.

Costa
Cruising Italian Style®

See your travel agent, call 1-800-GO COSTA, or visit costacruises.com.

*Fare is in US Dollars, cruise only, per person based on double occupancy in minimum category on select ships and sailings. Valid for residents of the US
and Canada only. Capacity controlled. Certain restrictions apply. Government taxes additional. Economical air add-ons available from most gateways.
Ships' Registry: Italy

Promotion of Services

Costa cruise lines promotes the
price of its European cruises.

in an advertisement or display it in a store, explaining
a service to customers can be a difficult task. Promotion of services typically includes tangible cues that
symbolize the service. For example, Mackenzie Investments uses the image of a castle's turret in its brand
mark to symbolize strength, security, and superior long-
term investment returns, important features associated with financial services. Similarly, the cupped hands
Allstate uses in its ads symbolize personalized service
and trustworthy, caring representatives. Although these
symbols have nothing to do with the actual services,
they make it much easier for customers to understand
the intangible attributes associated with insurance
services. To make a service more tangible, advertisements for services often show pictures of facilities,
equipment, and service personnel. Marketers may
also promote their services as a tangible expression of
consumers' lifestyles.

Compared with goods marketers, service providers
are more likely to promote price, guarantees, performance documentation, availability, and training and certification of contact personnel. The International Smart
Tan Network, a trade association for indoor tanning
salons, offers a certification course in professional standards for tanning facility operators. The association
encourages salons to promote their "Smart Tan Certification" in advertising and throughout the salon as a
measure of quality training.[17] When preparing advertisements, service marketers are careful to use concrete,
specific language to help make services more tangible
in customers' minds. They are also careful not to promise too much regarding their
services so that customer expectations do not rise to unattainable levels.

Through their actions, service contact personnel can be directly or indirectly involved in the personal selling of services. Personal selling is often important because
personal influence can help the customer visualize the benefits of a given service. Because service contact personnel may engage in personal selling, some companies invest heavily in training. Best Buy, for example, spends five percent of its payroll on
employee training. On a salesperson's first day on the job, he or she gets a four-hour
classroom session focused on how to fit into the company's sales force and the basics
for providing customer satisfaction.[18]

As noted earlier, intangibility makes experiencing a service prior to purchase difficult, if not impossible in some cases. A car can be test driven, a snack food can be
sampled in a supermarket, and a new brand of bar soap can be mailed to customers
as a free sample. Some services also can be offered on a trial basis at little or no risk
to the customer, but a number of services cannot be sampled before purchase. Promotional programs that encourage trial use of insurance, health care, or auto repair are
difficult to design because even after purchase of such services, assessing their quality may require a considerable length of time. For example, an individual may purchase
auto insurance from the same provider for 10 years before filing a claim, but the quality of the coverage is based primarily on how the customer is treated and protected
when a claim is made.

Because of the heterogeneity and intangibility of services, word-of-mouth communication is important in service promotion. What other people say about a service
provider can have a tremendous impact on whether an individual decides to use that
provider. Some service marketers attempt to stimulate positive word-of-mouth communication by asking satisfied customers to tell their friends and associates about the
service and may even provide incentives for doing so.

Pricing of Services

Prices for services can be established on several different bases. The prices of pest control services, dry cleaning, carpet cleaning, and health consultations are usually based on the performance of specific tasks. Other service prices are based on time. For example, lawyers, consultants, piano teachers, and plumbers often charge by the hour or day.

Some services use demand-based pricing. When demand for a service is high, the price also is high; when demand for a service is low, so is the price. The perishability of services means that when demand is low, the unused capacity cannot be stored and therefore is lost forever. Every empty seat on an airline flight or in a movie theatre represents lost revenue. Some services are very time sensitive in that a significant number of customers desire the service at a particular time. This point in time is called *peak demand*. A provider of time-sensitive services brings in most of its revenue during peak demand. For an airline, peak demand is usually early and late in the day; for cruise lines, peak demand occurs in the winter for Caribbean cruises and in the summer for Alaskan cruises. Providers of time-sensitive services often use demand-based pricing to manage the problem of balancing supply and demand. They charge top prices during peak demand and lower prices during off-peak demand to encourage more customers to use the service. This is why the price of a matinee movie is often half the price of the same movie shown at night. Major airlines maintain sophisticated databases to help them adjust ticket prices to fill as many seats as possible on every flight. On a single day, each airline makes thousands of fare changes to maximize the use of its seating capacity and thus maximize its revenues. To accomplish this objective, many airlines have to overbook flights and discount fares.

When services are offered to customers in a bundle, marketers must decide whether to offer the services at one price, price them separately, or use a combination of the two methods. For example, some hotels offer a package of services at one price, while others charge separately for the room, phone service, breakfast, and even in-room safes. Some service providers offer a one-price option for a specific bundle of services and make add-on bundles available at additional charges. For example, a number of cable television companies offer a standard package of channels for one price and offer add-on channel packages for additional charges. Telephone services, such as call waiting and caller ID, are frequently bundled and sold as a package for one price.

Because of the intangible nature of services, customers sometimes rely heavily on price as an indicator of quality. If customers perceive the available services in a service category as being similar in quality, and if the quality of such services is difficult to judge even after these services are purchased, customers may seek out the lowest-priced provider. For example, many customers seek auto insurance providers with the lowest rates. If the quality of different service providers is likely to vary, customers may rely heavily on the price-quality association. For certain types of services, market conditions may limit how much can be charged for a specific service, especially if the services in this category are perceived as generic in nature. For example, the prices charged by a self-serve laundromat are likely to be limited by the going price for laundromat services in a given community. Also, provincial and local government regulations may reduce price flexibility. Such regulations may substantially control the prices charged for auto insurance, utilities, and even housing rentals.

Service Quality

service quality Customers' perception of how well a service meets or exceeds their expectations

Delivery of high-quality services is one of the most important and most difficult tasks any service organization faces. Because of their characteristics, services are very difficult to evaluate. Hence customers must look closely at service quality when comparing services. **Service quality** is defined as customers' perceptions of how well a service meets or exceeds their expectations.[19] Research has found that 70 percent of consumers responding experienced "customer rage" indicating they were "extremely" or

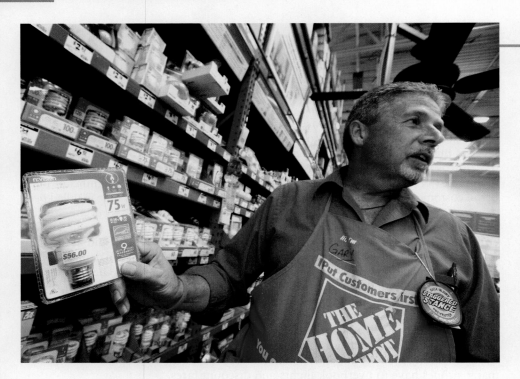

Quality of Service
Home Depot promotes its exceptional installation service.

"very" upset about a negative service experience. More than 33 percent indicated they had raised their voices, while 13 percent admitted to using profanity when interacting with customer service representatives. While 75 percent of respondents wanted an explanation of why the problem occurred, only 18 percent got an explanation, and only 25 percent heard "I'm sorry" from a customer service representative.[20] Note that customers, not the organization, evaluate service quality. This distinction is critical because it forces service marketers to examine quality from the customer's viewpoint. Thus, it is important for service organizations to determine what customers expect and then develop service products that meet or exceed those expectations.

Customer Evaluation of Service Quality

The biggest obstacle for customers in evaluating service quality is the intangible nature of the service. How can customers evaluate something they cannot see, feel, taste, smell, or hear? Evaluation of a good is much easier because all goods possess **search qualities,** tangible attributes such as colour, style, size, feel, or fit that can be evaluated prior to purchase. Trying on a new coat and taking a car for a test drive are examples of how customers evaluate search qualities. Services, on the other hand, have very few search qualities; instead, they abound in experience and credence qualities. **Experience qualities** are attributes, such as taste, satisfaction, or pleasure, which can be assessed only during the purchase and consumption of a service.[21] Restaurants and vacations are examples of services high in experience qualities. **Credence qualities** are attributes that customers may be unable to evaluate even after the purchase and consumption of the service. Examples of services high in credence qualities are surgical operations, automobile repairs, and legal representation. Most consumers lack the knowledge or skills to evaluate the quality of these types of services. Consequently they must place a great deal of faith in the integrity and competence of the service provider.

Despite the difficulties in evaluating quality, service quality may be the only way customers can choose one service over another. For this reason, service marketers live or die by understanding how consumers judge service quality. Table 13.2 defines five dimensions consumers use when evaluating service quality: tangibles, reliability, responsiveness, assurance, and empathy. Note that all of these dimensions have links to employee performance. Of the five, reliability is normally the most important in determining customer evaluations of service quality.[22]

Service marketers pay a great deal of attention to the tangibles of service quality. Tangible elements, such as the appearance of facilities and employees, are often the only aspects of a service that can be viewed before purchase and consumption. Indeed, research has found that a service provider's physical facilities have a very strong influence on customers' perceptions of quality.[23] Therefore, service marketers must ensure that these tangible elements are consistent with the overall image of the service.

search qualities Tangible attributes that can be judged before the purchase of a product

experience qualities Attributes that can be assessed only during purchase and consumption of a service

credence qualities Attributes that customers may be unable to evaluate even after purchasing and consuming a service

table 13.2   DIMENSIONS OF SERVICE QUALITY

Dimension	Evaluation Criteria	Examples
Tangibles: Physical evidence of the service	Appearance of physical facilities Appearance of service personnel Tools or equipment used to provide the service	A clean and professional-looking doctor's office A clean and neatly attired repairperson The freshness of food in a restaurant The equipment used in a medical exam
Reliability: Consistency and dependability in performing the service	Accuracy of billing or recordkeeping Performing services when promised	An accurate bank statement A confirmed hotel reservation An airline flight departing and arriving on time

Responsiveness:
Willingness or readiness of
  employees to provide the service
	Returning customer phone calls
	Providing prompt service
	Handling urgent requests
		A server refilling a customer's cup of tea
		  without being asked
		An ambulance arriving within 3 minutes

Assurance:
Knowledge/competence of
  employees and ability to
  convey trust and confidence
	Knowledge and skills of employees
	Company name and reputation
	Personal characteristics of employees
		A highly trained financial adviser
		A known and respected service provider
		A doctor's bedside manner

Empathy:
Caring and individual attention
  provided by employees
	Listening to customer needs
	Caring about customers' interests
	Providing personalized attention
		A store employee listening to and trying to
		  understand a customer's complaint
		A nurse counselling a heart patient

Sources: Adapted from Leonard L. Berry and A. Parasuraman, *Marketing Services: Competing Through Quality* (New York: Free Press, 1991); Valarie A. Zeithaml, A. Parasuraman, and Leonard L. Berry, *Delivering Quality Service: Balancing Customer Perceptions and Expectations* (New York: Free Press, 1990); A. Parasuraman, Leonard L. Berry, and Valarie A. Zeithaml, "An Empirical Examination of Relationships in an Extended Service Quality Model," *Marketing Science Institute Working Paper Series,* Report no. 90–112 (Cambridge, MA: Marketing Science Institute, 1990), p. 29.

Except for the tangibles dimension, the criteria customers use to judge service quality are intangible. For instance, how does a customer judge reliability? Since dimensions such as reliability cannot be examined with the senses, customers must rely on other ways of judging service. One of the most important factors in customer judgments of service quality is service expectations. Service expectations are influenced by past experiences with the service, word-of-mouth communication from other customers, and the service company's own advertising. For example, customers are usually eager to try a new restaurant, especially when friends recommend it. These same customers may have also seen advertisements placed by the restaurant. As a result, they have an idea of what to expect when they visit the restaurant for the first time. When they finally dine there, the quality they experience will change the expectations they have for their next visit. That is why providing consistently high service quality is important. If the quality of a restaurant, or of any service, begins to deteriorate, customers will alter their own expectations and change their word-of-mouth communication to others accordingly.

Delivering Exceptional Service Quality

Providing high-quality service on a consistent basis is very difficult. All consumers have experienced examples of poor service: late flight departures and arrivals, inattentive restaurant servers, rude bank employees, extended waits, long lines. Obviously it is impossible for a service organization to ensure exceptional service

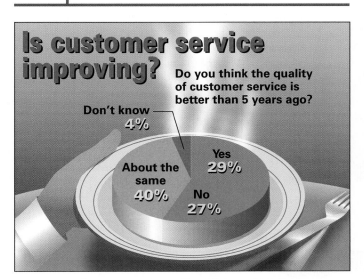

snapshot

Is customer service improving?

Do you think the quality of customer service is better than 5 years ago?

Don't know 4%

Yes 29%

About the same 40%

No 27%

Source: Data from DHL Roper Public Affairs and Media Survey. Margin of error ± 3 percentage points.

quality 100 percent of the time. However, an organization can take many steps to increase the likelihood of providing high-quality service. First, though, the service company must consider the four factors that affect service quality: (1) analysis of customer expectations, (2) service quality specifications, (3) employee performance, and (4) management of service expectations (see Figure 13.2).[24]

Analysis of Customer Expectations. Providers need to understand customer expectations when designing a service to meet or exceed those expectations. Only then can they deliver good service. Customers usually have two levels of expectations: desired and acceptable. The desired level of expectations is what the customer really wants. If this level of expectations is provided, the customer will be very satisfied. The acceptable level of expectations is what the customer views as adequate. The difference between these two levels of expectations is called the customer's *zone of tolerance*.[25]

Service companies sometimes use marketing research, such as surveys and focus groups, to discover customer needs and expectations. For instance, Ritz-Carlton Hotels conducted focus-group research to find out the level of service expected by high-tech executives and entrepreneurs, the target audience for one of its resort hotels. Based on this analysis, the resort began offering guests around-the-clock tech support as well as high-speed Web access, in-room video game consoles, safes to store laptop computers, and cell phone rentals.[26] Other service marketers, especially restaurants, use comment cards on which customers can complain or provide suggestions. Still another approach is to ask employees. Because customer contact employees interact daily with customers, they are in good positions to know what customers want from the company. Service managers should regularly interact with their employees by asking their opinions on the best way to serve customers.

Service Quality Specifications. Once an organization understands its customers' needs, it must establish goals to help ensure good service delivery. These goals, or

Stay Tuned: Nick Has the Right Mix

Cable television network Nickelodeon—Nick for short—has to satisfy a number of tough audiences. Toddlers want fun programs such as *Blue's Clues* and the bilingual *Dora the Explorer*. School-age viewers enjoy wacky cartoons such as *Jimmie Neutron*. Younger teens tune in for programs like *All That,* while older teens watch the celebrity specials. And parents want to be sure that Nick's programs entertain and educate without violence or sex. Nick delivers for all these audiences, with ratings that top the list of basic cable networks.

Nick is known for its in-depth marketing research and its careful control of animation and production. Of course, no one can predict which shows will resonate with viewers, and the network has had both successes and disappointments. One surprise was the popularity of *Sponge-Bob SquarePants,* which first aired as a weekend series but has now become a Nick staple.

Nick has been able to profit not only from selling advertising time but also from licensing its brand for an ever-widening mix of goods and services. One of Nick's newest licensing ventures is a theme resort in Florida, the Nickelodeon Family Suites by Holiday Inn. In addition to waterslides, pools, and game rooms, the hotel offers breakfast with Nick characters and stages live shows starring Nick characters. Nick believes that viewers who enjoy its characters will look forward to staying at a Nick-themed hotel and is working with Holiday Inn to open several more resorts soon. Can the resort deliver the kind of service that is consistent with the Nick brand? Stay tuned.

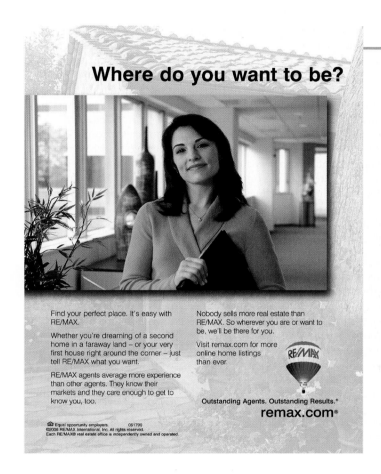

Where do you want to be?

Find your perfect place. It's easy with RE/MAX.

Whether you're dreaming of a second home in a faraway land – or your very first house right around the corner – just tell RE/MAX what you want.

RE/MAX agents average more experience than other agents. They know their markets and they care enough to get to know you, too.

Nobody sells more real estate than RE/MAX. So wherever you are or want to be, we'll be there for you.

Visit remax.com for more online home listings than ever.

RE/MAX

Outstanding Agents. Outstanding Results.®

remax.com®

Service Expectations

RE/MAX sets service expectations by asking customers to imagine the ideal living space.

service specifications, are typically set in terms of employee or machine performance. For example, a bank may require its employees to conform to a dress code. Likewise, the bank may require that all incoming phone calls be answered by the third ring. Specifications such as these can be very important in providing quality service as long as they are tied to the needs expressed by customers.

Perhaps the most critical aspect of service quality specifications is managers' commitment to service quality. Service managers who are committed to quality become role models for all employees in the organization. Such commitment motivates customer contact employees to comply with service specifications. It is crucial that all managers within the organization embrace this commitment, especially frontline managers, who are much closer to customers than higher-level managers.

Employee Performance. Once an organization sets service quality standards and managers are committed to them, the organization must find ways to ensure that customer contact employees perform their jobs well. Contact employees in most service industries (bank tellers, flight attendants, servers, sales clerks, etc.) are often the least trained and lowest-paid members of the organization. Service organizations must realize that contact employees are the most important link to the customer, and thus their performance is critical to customer perceptions of service quality. The way to ensure that employees perform well is to train them well so they understand how to do their jobs. Providing

figure 13.2

SERVICE QUALITY MODEL

Source: Adapted from A. Parasuraman, Leonard L. Berry, and Valarie A. Zeithaml, "An Empirical Examination of Relationships in an Extended Service Quality Model," *Marketing Science Institute Working Paper Series,* Report no. 90–112 (Cambridge, MA: Marketing Science Institute, 1990). Reprinted by permission of Marketing Science Institute and the authors.

Analysis of customer expectations
- Marketing research
- Open communication with employees

Service quality specifications
- Service goals
- Management commitment to service quality

Employee performance
- Employee training
- Evaluation and compensation systems

Management of service expectations
- Advertising
- Good internal communications

Service quality
- Tangibles
- Reliability
- Responsiveness
- Assurance
- Empathy

information about customers, service specifications, and the organization itself during the training promotes this understanding. The year-old company When Pigs Fly helps managers equip frontline workers at amusement parks, fairs, carnivals, and other amusement-related facilities with the training, tools, encouragement, and motivation they need to do their jobs well. Much of their training is targeted at the Generation Xers who staff these facilities. "Hospitality, customer service, safety—these things don't come naturally to kids," says company co-owner Patty Beazley.[27]

The evaluation and compensation system the organization uses also plays a part in employee performance. Many service employees are evaluated and rewarded on the basis of output measures, such as sales volume (automobile salespeople) or a low error rate (bank tellers). But systems using output measures overlook other major aspects of job performance, including friendliness, teamwork, effort, and customer satisfaction. These customer-oriented measures of performance may be a better basis for evaluation and reward. In fact, a number of service marketers use customer satisfaction ratings to determine a portion of service employee compensation.

Management of Service Expectations. Because expectations are so significant in customer evaluations of service quality, service companies recognize they must set realistic expectations about the service they can provide. They can set these expectations through advertising and good internal communication. In their advertisements, service companies make promises about the kind of service they will deliver. As already noted, a service company is forced to make promises because the intangibility of services prevents the organization from showing the benefits in the advertisement. However, the advertiser should not promise more than it can deliver. Doing so will likely mean disappointed customers.

To deliver on promises made, a company needs to have thorough internal communication among its departments, especially management, advertising, and store operations. Assume, for example, that a restaurant's radio advertisements guarantee service within five minutes or the meal is free. If top management or the advertising department fails to inform store operations about the five-minute guarantee, the restaurant will very likely fail to meet its customers' service expectations. Even though customers might appreciate a free meal, the restaurant will lose some credibility as well as revenue.

As mentioned earlier, word-of-mouth communication from other customers also shapes customer expectations. However, service companies cannot manage this "advertising" directly. The best way to ensure positive word-of-mouth communication is to provide exceptional service quality. It has been estimated that customers tell four times as many people about bad service as they do about good service.

Non-profit Marketing

non-profit marketing
Marketing activities conducted to achieve some goal other than ordinary business goals such as profit, market share, or return on investment

Non-profit marketing includes marketing activities conducted by individuals and organizations to achieve some goal other than ordinary business goals such as profit, market share, or return on investment. Non-profit marketing is divided into two categories: non-profit-organization marketing and social marketing. Non-profit-organization marketing is the use of marketing concepts and techniques by organizations whose goals do not include making profits. Social marketing promotes social causes, such as AIDS research and recycling.

Most of the previously discussed concepts and approaches to service products also apply to non-profit organizations. Indeed, many non-profit organizations provide mainly service products. In this section, we examine the concept of non-profit marketing to determine how it differs from marketing activities in for-profit business organizations. We also explore the marketing objectives of non-profit organizations and the development of their product strategies.

How Is Non-profit Marketing Different?

Many non-profit organizations strive for effective marketing activities. Charitable organizations and supporters of social causes are major non-profit marketers in this

SHARE WHAT YOU KNOW. BECOME A MENTOR.

It doesn't take special skills to mentor a young person—just a willingness
to listen, offer encouragement, and share what you've learned about life.
Mentoring programs in your community need more volunteers.

Visit **MENTORING.org**

 Harvard School of Public Health • MENTOR • MetLife Foundation

5TH ANNIVERSARY
NATIONAL
MENTORING MONTH
JANUARY 2006

Non-profit

Non-profit organizations promote volunteer programs such as mentoring.

country. Political parties, unions, religious sects, and fraternal organizations also perform marketing activities, but they are not considered businesses. Whereas the chief beneficiary of a business enterprise is whoever owns or holds stock in it, in theory the only beneficiaries of a non-profit organization are its clients, its members, or the public at large. The Canadian War Museum, for example, is a non-profit service organization (see www.warmuseum.ca).

Non-profit organizations have greater opportunities for creativity than most for-profit business organizations, but trustees or board members of non-profit organizations are likely to have difficulty judging the performance of the trained professionals they oversee. It is harder for administrators to evaluate the performance of professors or social workers than it is for sales managers to evaluate the performance of salespeople in a for-profit organization.

Another way non-profit marketing differs from for-profit marketing is that non-profit marketing is sometimes quite controversial. Non-profit organizations such as Greenpeace, the Right to Die Society of Canada, and the Canadian Hemophilia Society engage in lobbying efforts to persuade governments and even courts to support their interests, in part because acceptance of their aims by all of society is not always guaranteed. However, marketing as a field of study does not attempt to state what an organization's goals should be or to debate the issue of non-profit versus for-profit business goals. Marketing tries only to provide a body of knowledge and concepts to help further an organization's goals. Individuals must decide whether they approve or disapprove of a particular organization's goal orientation. Most marketers would agree that profit and consumer satisfaction are appropriate goals for business enterprises, but would probably disagree considerably about the goals of a controversial non-profit organization.

Non-profit Marketing Objectives

The basic aim of non-profit organizations is to obtain a desired response from a target market. The response could be a change in values, a financial contribution, the donation of services, or some other type of exchange. Non-profit marketing objectives are shaped by the nature of the exchange and the goals of the organization. These objectives should state the rationale for the organization's existence. An organization that defines its marketing objective as providing a product can be left without a purpose if the product becomes obsolete. However, servicing and adapting to the perceived needs and wants of a

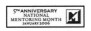

**marketing
ENTREPRENEURS**

Ercan Tutal

HIS BUSINESS: The Alternative Camp for Disabled Individuals

SUCCESS: Organization has served more than 200 000 people

Located in Turkey, the Alternative Camp is a non-profit organization that provides disabled persons with opportunities to participate in underwater sports such as diving. Tutal's organization has served more than 200 000 people and is funded entirely from the donations of generous businesses. So successful is his organization that the World Young Business Association granted him the Social Responsibility Award, and he recently was chosen to take part in the Olympic ceremonies as a torch bearer.

target public, or market, enhances an organization's chance to survive and achieve its goals.

Developing Non-profit Marketing Strategies

Non-profit organizations develop marketing strategies by defining and analyzing a target market and creating and maintaining a total marketing mix that appeals to that market.

Target Markets. We must revise the concept of target markets slightly to apply it to non-profit organizations. Whereas a business seeks out target groups that are potential purchasers of its product, a non-profit organization may attempt to serve many diverse groups. For our purposes, a **target public** is a collective of individuals who have an interest in or a concern about an organization, a product, or a social cause. The terms *target market* and *target public* are difficult to distinguish for many non-profit organizations. The target public of the Centre for Addiction and Mental Health, Canada's leading addiction and mental health teaching hospital, consists of parents, adults, and concerned teenagers. However, the target market for the organization's programs and services consists of potential and current drug users. When an organization is concerned about changing values or obtaining a response from the public, it views the public as a market.[28]

In non-profit marketing, direct consumers of the product are called **client publics** and indirect consumers are called **general publics**.[29] For example, the client public for a university is its student body, and its general public includes parents, alumni, and trustees. The client public usually receives most of the attention when an organization develops a marketing strategy.

Developing a Marketing Mix. A marketing mix strategy limits alternatives and directs marketing activities toward achieving organizational goals. The strategy should include a blueprint for making decisions about product, distribution, promotion, and price. These decision variables should be blended to serve the target market.

In developing the product, non-profit organizations usually deal with ideas and services. Problems may evolve when an organization fails to define what it is providing. What product, for example, does CUSO (formerly Canadian University Students Overseas) provide? Its services include placing skilled Canadians in under-developed nations to help change the world through volunteerism, linking people and organizations all over the world so they can better tackle social justice issues together, and working to increase public awareness of global issues. CUSO's product is more difficult to define than the average business product. As indicated in the first part of this chapter, services are intangible and therefore need special marketing efforts. The marketing of ideas and concepts is likewise more abstract than the marketing of tangibles, and much effort is required to present benefits.

Distribution decisions in non-profit organizations relate to how ideas and services will be made available to clients. If the product is an idea, selecting the right media to communicate the idea will facilitate distribution. By nature, services consist of assistance, convenience, and availability. Availability is thus part of the total service.

Developing a channel of distribution to coordinate and facilitate the flow of non-profit products to clients is a necessary task, but in a non-profit setting the traditional concept of the marketing channel may need to be revised. The independent wholesalers available to a business enterprise do not exist in most non-profit situations. Instead, a very short channel—non-profit organization to client—is the norm because production and consumption of ideas and services are often simultaneous.

Making promotional decisions may be the first sign that a non-profit organization is performing marketing activities. Non-profit organizations use advertising and publicity to communicate with clients and the public. Direct mail remains the primary means of fundraising for social services, such as those provided by the Salvation Army. Some non-profits use the immediacy of the Internet to reach fundraising and promotional goals. Non-profits use the Internet as a form of e-commerce to accept online gifts and conduct online auctions, and many use application service providers to maintain

---

target public A collective of individuals who have an interest in or concern about an organization, product, or social cause

client publics Direct consumers of a product of a non-business organization

general publics Indirect consumers of a product of a non-business organization software and save money.[30] Many non-profit organizations also use personal selling, although they may call it by another name. Churches and charities rely on personal selling when they send volunteers to recruit new members or request donations. Special events to obtain funds, communicate ideas, or provide services are also effective promotional activities. Amnesty International, for example, has held worldwide concert tours featuring well-known musical artists to raise funds and increase public awareness of political prisoners around the world.

Although product and promotional techniques may require only slight modification when applied to non-profit organizations, pricing is generally quite different and decision making is more complex. The different pricing concepts the non-profit organization faces include pricing in user and donor markets. Two types of monetary pricing exist: *fixed* and *variable*. There may be a fixed fee for users, or the price may vary depending on the user's ability to pay. When a donation-seeking organization will accept a contribution of any size, it is using variable pricing.

The broadest definition of price (valuation) must be used to develop non-profit marketing strategies. Financial price, an exact dollar value, may or may not be charged for a non-profit product. Economists recognize the giving up of alternatives as a cost. **Opportunity cost** is the value of the benefit given up by selecting one alternative over another. According to this traditional economic view of price, if a non-profit organization persuades someone to donate time to a cause or to change his or her behaviour, the alternatives given up are a cost to (or a price paid by) the individual. Volunteers who answer phones for a university counseling service or a suicide hotline, for example, give up the time they could spend studying or doing other things and the income they might earn from working at a for-profit business organization.

For other non-profit organizations, financial price is an important part of the marketing mix. Non-profit organizations today are raising money by increasing the prices of their services or are starting to charge for services if they have not done so before. They are using marketing research to determine what kinds of products people will pay for. Pricing strategies of non-profit organizations often stress public and client welfare over equalization of costs and revenues. If additional funds are needed to cover costs, the organization may solicit donations, contributions, or grants.

opportunity cost The value of the benefit given up by choosing one alternative over another

SUMMARY

Services are intangible products involving deeds, performances, or efforts that cannot be physically possessed. They are the result of applying human or mechanical efforts to people or objects. Services are a growing part of the Canadian economy. They have six fundamental characteristics: intangibility, inseparability of production and consumption, perishability, heterogeneity, client-based relationships, and customer contact. Intangibility means that a service cannot be seen, touched, tasted, or smelled. Inseparability refers to the fact that the production of a service cannot be separated from its consumption by customers. Perishability means unused service capacity of one time period cannot be stored for future use. Heterogeneity is variation in service quality. Client-based relationships are interactions with customers that lead to the repeated use of a service over time. Customer contact is the interaction between providers and customers needed to deliver a service.

Core services are the basic service experiences customers expect; supplementary services are those that relate to and support core services. Because of the characteristics of services, service marketers face several challenges in developing and managing marketing mixes. To address the problem of intangibility, marketers use cues that help assure customers about the quality of their services. The development and management of service products are also influenced by the service characteristics of inseparability and level of customer contact. Some services require that customers come to the service provider's facility; others are delivered with no face-to-face contact. Marketing channels for services are usually short and direct, but some services employ intermediaries. Service marketers are less concerned with warehousing and transportation than are goods marketers, but inventory management and balancing supply and demand for services are important issues. The intangibility of services poses several promotion-related challenges. Advertisements with tangible cues that symbolize the service and depict facilities, equipment, and personnel help address these challenges. Service providers are likely to promote price, guarantees, performance documentation, availability, and training and certification of contact personnel. Through their actions, service personnel can be involved directly or indirectly in the personal selling of services.

Intangibility makes it difficult to experience a service before purchasing it. Heterogeneity and intangibility make word-of-mouth communication an important means of promotion. The prices of services are based on task performance, time required, or demand. Perishability creates difficulties in balancing supply and demand because unused capacity cannot be stored. The point in time when a significant number of customers desire a service is called peak demand; demand-based pricing results in higher prices charged for services during peak demand. When services are offered in a bundle, marketers must decide whether to offer them at one price, price them separately, or use a combination of the two methods. Because services are intangible, customers may rely on price as a sign of quality. For some services, market conditions may dictate the price; for others, state and local government regulations may limit price flexibility.

Service quality is customers' perception of how well a service meets or exceeds their expectations. Although one of the most important aspects of service marketing, service quality is very difficult for customers to evaluate because the nature of services renders benefits impossible to assess before actual purchase and consumption. These benefits include experience qualities, such as taste, satisfaction, or pleasure, and credence qualities, which customers may be unable to evaluate even after consumption. When competing services are very similar, service quality may be the only way for customers to distinguish among them. Service marketers can increase the quality of their services by following the four-step process of understanding customer expectations, setting service specifications, ensuring good employee performance, and managing customers' service expectations.

Non-profit marketing is marketing aimed at non-business goals, including social causes. It uses most of the same concepts and approaches that apply to business situations. Whereas the chief beneficiary of a business enterprise is whoever owns or holds stock in it, the beneficiary of a non-profit enterprise should be its clients, its members, or its public at large. The goals of a non-profit organization reflect its unique philosophy or mission. Some non-profit organizations have very controversial goals, but many organizations exist to further generally accepted social causes.

The marketing objective of non-profit organizations is to obtain a desired response from a target market. Developing a non-profit marketing strategy consists of defining and analyzing a target market and creating and maintaining a marketing mix. In non-profit marketing, the product is usually an idea or a service. Distribution is aimed at the communication of ideas and the delivery of services. The result is a very short marketing channel. Promotion is very important to non-profit marketing. Non-profit organizations use advertising, publicity, and personal selling to communicate with clients and the public. Direct mail remains the primary means of fundraising for social services, but some non-profits use the Internet for fundraising and promotional activities. Price is more difficult to define in non-profit marketing because of opportunity costs and the difficulty of quantifying the values exchanged.

Please visit the student website at **www.hmco.ca/marketing** for ACE Self-Test questions that will help you prepare for exams.

IMPORTANT TERMS

Intangibility	Client-based relationships	Experience qualities	Client publics
Inseparability	Customer contact	Credence qualities	General publics
Perishability	Service quality	Non-profit marketing	Opportunity cost
Heterogeneity	Search qualities	Target public	

DISCUSSION & REVIEW QUESTIONS

1. How important are services in the Canadian economy?

2. Identify and discuss the major characteristics of services.

3. For each marketing mix element, which service characteristics are most likely to have an impact? Explain.

4. What is service quality? Why do customers find it difficult to judge service quality?

5. Identify and discuss the five components of service quality. How do customers evaluate these components?

6. What is the significance of tangibles in service marketing?

7. How do search, experience, and credence qualities affect the way customers view and evaluate services?

8. What steps should a service company take to provide exceptional service quality?

9. How does non-profit marketing differ from marketing in for-profit organizations?

10. What are the differences among clients, publics, and customers? What is the difference between a target public and a target market?

11. Discuss the development of a marketing strategy for a university. What marketing decisions must be made as the strategy is developed?

APPLICATION QUESTIONS

1. Imagine you are the owner of a new service business. What is your service? Be creative. What are some of the most important considerations in developing the service, training salespeople, and communicating about your service to potential customers?

2. As discussed in this chapter, the characteristics of services affect the development of marketing mixes for services. Choose a specific service and explain how each marketing mix element could be affected by these service characteristics.

3. In advertising services, a company must often use symbols to represent the offered product. Identify three service organizations you have seen in outdoor, television, or magazine advertising. What symbols do these organizations use to represent their services? What message do the symbols convey to potential customers?

4. Delivering consistently high-quality service is difficult for service marketers. Describe an instance when you received high-quality service and an instance when you experienced low-quality service. What contributed to your perception of high quality? Of low quality?

globalEDGE™

1. Service marketing is sometimes associated with franchise chains that deliver products to fulfill a global need in the marketplace. Though there are magazines that rank the leading franchisers, an examination of the top 50 gives the analyst information to understand the nature of franchising. Prepare a brief report based on information from the *Entrepreneur* Top Global Franchises. This ranking can be accessed by using the search term "top 200 franchisers" at **http://globaledge.msu.edu/ibrd** or **http://globaledge.msu.edu/ibrd/ibrd .asp**. In particular, which company has the highest startup costs? Given what you know, do you think the startup costs required for this company are justifiable?

2. To be a better "social enterprise" and deliver quality services, firms must better understand, communicate, and respond to customers. However, sometimes companies fail to interact with and help improve the communities they service. According to a report titled "The Three Ds of Customer Experience" by the Harvard Business School (HBS), as firms grow larger they sometimes fall into a dominance trap. This research can be accessed by using the search term "social enterprise" at **http:// globaledge.msu.edu/ibrd** or **http:// globaledge.msu.edu/ibrd/ibrd.asp**. Once you reach the HBS website, use the search term "dominance trap." The relevant research is entitled "The Three Ds of Customer Experience." Based on this paper, define the concept of a dominance trap. Also, define and present three imperatives that may prevent this from occurring in a firm.

INTERNET Exercise

Visit **www.prideferrell.com** for resources to help you master the material in this chapter, plus materials that will help you expand your marketing knowledge, including internet exercise updates, ACE self-tests, hotlinks to companies featured in this chapter, and much more.

Matchmaker.com

The Internet abounds with dating sites, but few offer as much information about their members as Matchmaker.com. Matchmaker profiles are gleaned from a survey of some 60 question and essay responses. Check out the site at **www.matchmaker.com.**

1. Classify Matchmaker.com's product in terms of its position on the service continuum.
2. How does Matchmaker.com enhance customer service and foster better client-based relationships through its Internet marketing efforts?
3. Discuss the degree to which experience and credence qualities exist in the services offered by Matchmaker.com and other dating websites.

Case 13.1   Meals on Wheels

Meals on Wheels of Fredericton Inc. is a non-profit organization dedicated to providing nutritious meals and social support for seniors, people with disabilities, and those recovering in their homes from illness, surgery or injury. The goal is to assist individuals in the enhancement of a healthy and independent lifestyle. The work of the organization is delivered through four paid staff members and a force of 350 community volunteers.

The organization meets its mission through the delivery of two community programs: Meals on Wheels and Wheels to Meals. The Meals on Wheels program is a home delivery service that was first made available in 1967. It operates every day of the year, providing close to 35 000 meals annually to clients in their homes. Clients range in age from 38 to 92. Hot meals are delivered by 300 volunteers who donate their time and the use of their own vehicles to transport the meals to those in need.

The Wheels to Meals program, for seniors only, aims to enhance the health and independence of seniors by helping them combat loneliness and isolation. Transportation is provided for seniors to "dine out" with other seniors at a local Church Hall, once a week. A freshly prepared and nutritionally balanced meal is served by volunteers and local performers entertain after the meal.

Although no formal referral is required for eligible individuals to access services, many individuals are referred to Meals on Wheels through health care professionals, government departments and community organizations. The organization also relies extensively on word-of-mouth to market its services.

Revenues for the organization are mostly generated from the meals delivered. Due to the fact that affordability is a major concern for many clients, pricing is a very sensitive issue for the Meals on Wheels organization. Unfortunately, in recent years, the criteria for government support has tightened, resulting in a decrease in the number of government subsidized clients. Currently, only 50 percent of clients are subsidized. Therefore, the organization must now heavily rely on financial support from the community in order to be able to offer an affordable, discounted rate to privately paying clients. The organization receives a yearly grant from United Way, receives donations from individuals, businesses and foundations, and conducts a number of annual fundraising events to cover the shortfall in its operating revenues.

Questions for Discussion

1. Describe the target public of Meals on Wheels of Fredericton, Inc.
2. Discuss the "marketing mix" of Meals on Wheels. How might their strategy be enhanced?
3. How might the extensive use of volunteers, by Meals on Wheels, pose challenges for ensuring quality services?

Source: Prepared by Professor, Lynn Haley, Faculty of Business Administration, University of New Brunswick. Used with permission. This case serves as a basis for discussion rather than an illustration of effective or ineffective handling of an administrative situation.

Strategic Case 5 · Radio Goes Sky-High at XM Satellite Radio

XM Satellite Radio is changing the world of radio. Until the company started on the road to static-free radio in 1997, when it paid more than $80 million for a federal license in the U.S. to broadcast digital radio, AM and FM radio stations had been free to all listeners, mainly because of commercial sponsorship. However, XM believed that commuters—and anyone else travelling by car for long periods—would be willing to pay for perfect 24-hour radio reception and dozens of channel choices. (After all, millions of viewers were paying for cable television service, even though they could watch broadcast television for free.) And it seems they were right. Today, XM has two satellites and offers 160 channels.

Getting Ready for the Launch

Turning the concept of digital radio into reality cost XM more than $1 billion. It sent two satellites into orbit, and built a reception and distribution infrastructure on the ground. In addition, XM created a vast library of digital recordings and built two performance studios to broadcast and record live musical performances.

Another big challenge was developing the radio equipment for customers' cars. XM planned to encode its satellite signals to prevent non-customers from listening to its channels. The radio had to be capable of receiving and decoding the satellite signals yet compact enough to fit in a car. After building and testing prototypes, XM began manufacturing a radio about the size of a suitcase, to be connected to an antenna on the car's roof for proper reception. Initially customers had to retrofit their cars with XM radios. In time, the company arranged for General Motors, Honda, Audi, Nissan, and several other big automakers to offer factory-installed XM radios as options in their new cars.

What to Broadcast, What to Charge?

At the same time the company was getting its technology in order, XM was conducting marketing research to determine the target market's listening tastes. Based on this research, the company decided to devote most of its radio stations to specific types of music, such as country, rap, jazz, blues, rock and roll, classic rock, international pop, instrumental classical music, and movie soundtracks. Some stations feature shows hosted by celebrities such as Bob Dylan, Snoop Dogg, and Wynton Marsalis. For more variety, it offers news-only, sports-only, talk-only, comedy-only, and children's stations, among other special-interest stations.

Pricing involved a delicate balancing act. On the one hand, XM wanted to build a sizable base of subscribers, so its pricing had to be within customers' reach. On the other hand, the company was planning for long-term profitability and wanted to recoup some of its high startup costs. In the end, XM set a monthly subscription fee of $9.95 (later raised to $12.95) and priced its first radios at $300 or less. Within a year, the company launched smaller, less expensive radios for the home and for listening on the go. "We are an entertainment company, but we also recognized that if we were going to be successful, we had to rapidly drive down the cost of the equipment people needed to get our service," recalls an XM marketing analyst.

Serious Competition from Sirius Satellite Radio

XM's new-product introduction has been successful. More than five million customers signed up in the first four years, and the company is preparing for even greater expansion, with profitability expected in the near future. In contrast, its only competitor, Sirius Satellite Radio, began operating a year after XM and has a smaller customer base, with three million customers. Like XM, Sirius paid millions for a digital radio broadcast license, launched sophisticated satellites, and created specialized programming for 120 stations. And like XM, Sirius is looking to sports and celebrities to draw in new subscribers.

Sirius charges a monthly subscription fee of $12.95 with discounts for multiyear contracts, but its channels are entirely commercial free. Sirius also sees drivers as the highest opportunity customer segment, so it has arranged for its radios to be preinstalled as options in cars manufactured by DaimlerChrysler, Ford, BMW, and several other automakers not covered by XM's deals. Sirius has also targeted the "aftermarket," retailers such as Best Buy, where consumers buy receivers for vehicles not already equipped with them.

Tuning into Satellite Radio's Future

Satellite radio is gaining popularity at a much faster rate than cable television, VCRs, and CDs did after their introductions. As early majority adopters start tuning in to satellite radio, the industry could be serving an estimated 25 million customers by 2010. Responding to critics who doubt that pay radio will become big business, Sirius's CEO observes, "People said no one would ever pay for satellite television, and now it has 21 million subscribers. The same thing is going to be true here."

One of XM's recent innovations is a $50 radio that can be connected to a personal computer, complete with software for switching between channels. It also began broadcasting local weather and traffic reports to draw listeners who otherwise would have tuned into local AM or FM stations for this information. Today radios capable of receiving either company's channels are available. Still, XM's CEO expects to maintain his company's market dominance by putting the emphasis on program content. "The technology is only the facilitator," he says.

"Music connects so personally to people. We're putting the passion back into radio."

Questions for Discussion

1. How is XM Satellite Radio differentiating its product from that of Sirius?
2. What role has quality played in XM's product development and management?
3. At what stage of the product life cycle is satellite radio? How is the rate of adoption affecting the product's progression through the life cycle?
4. Evaluate the brand names of XM Satellite Radio and Sirius Satellite Radio. What are the strengths and weaknesses of each brand name? Which is the better brand name? Why?

part 6

Pricing Decisions

To provide a satisfying marketing mix, an organization must set a price acceptable to target market members. Pricing decisions can have numerous effects on other parts of the marketing mix. For example, price can influence how customers perceive the product, what types of marketing institutions are used to distribute the product, and how the product is promoted. **Chapter 14** discusses the importance of price and looks at some characteristics of price and non-price competition. It explores fundamental concepts such as demand, elasticity, marginal analysis, and break-even analysis. Then the chapter examines the major factors that affect marketers' pricing decisions. The chapter concludes with a discussion of six major stages in a process marketers can use to establish prices.

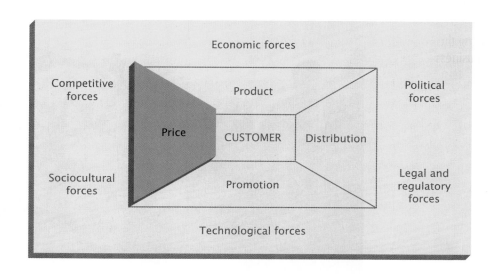

Pricing Decisions

The $1-Million Coin: Now That's Pricey

In early 2007, the Royal Canadian Mint launched the world's largest coin, a 100-kilogram coin that carries a face value of $1-million. This coin features a new Maple Leaf design and is one notch purer than any other bullion coin— 99.999 percent purity. A bullion coin is sold at a premium over the market spot commodity price and is usually considered as investment coins. With gold at $720.00/oz., this coin has a "gold" melt value of greater than $2.3 million.

It is over three times larger than the previous world champion, a 31-kilogram coin made by the Austrian Mint, which has been dubbed "Big Phil" after its namesake the Vienna Philharmonic Orchestra. Big Phil carries a face value of 100 000 euros (approximately $150 000 CDN).

When it comes to setting face value of bullion coins, mints typically keep the face value low relative to the issue price, to ensure that these coins are not actually used as legal tender. Mints don't want consumers showing up at banks or retailers and demanding cash for these coins, which has happened in the past and has caused some confusion.

Why introduce such a large and high value coin? The coin collector market has been very strong for a sustained period of years. The global coin trade is estimated to be at about $3 billion in total. More than half of the market is dominated by one-ounce gold coins. The Canadian Gold Maple Leaf coin had been the undisputed top seller in the 99.99 pure gold category since its introduction in 1979. In recent years competition has emerged with the introduction of new products such as the Panda series from China, Kangaroo Nuggets from Australia, and the American Buffalo that was recently launched by the United States Mint. The introduction of these coins has meant that the Royal Canadian Mint has lost some of its competitive edge in the industry. According to the regulatory filing necessary for the Mint to introduce a new coin, the coin "would create market visibility and excitement for the Royal Canadian Mint as it would be the world's largest, purest, and highest denomination gold coin." ∎

As illustrated in the opening vignette, the setting of price, whether it is the amount charged to consumers or the face value stamped on a coin, is an important decision. Unlike many other markets, the collector coin market does not have low-cost competitors who employ discount pricing as a major competitive tool. In other markets, successful organizations do not necessarily have the lowest or highest prices; rather, they use various other pricing strategies.

In this chapter, we focus first on the nature of price and its importance to marketers. We then consider some characteristics of price and non-price competition. Next, we discuss several pricing-related concepts such as demand, elasticity, and break-even analysis. Then we examine in some detail the numerous factors that can influence pricing decisions. Issues related to pricing products for business markets are also discussed. Finally, we examine six stages of a process marketers can use when setting prices. These stages are not rigid steps that all marketers must follow; rather, they are guidelines that provide a logical sequence for establishing prices.

The Nature of Price

price The value exchanged for products in a marketing exchange

The purpose of marketing is to facilitate satisfying exchange relationships between buyer and seller. **Price** is the value exchanged for products in a marketing exchange. Many factors may influence the assessment of value, including time constraints, price levels, perceived quality, and motivations to use available information about prices.[1] In most marketing situations, the price is apparent to both buyer and seller. However, price does not always take the form of money paid. In fact, trading of products, or barter, is the oldest form of exchange. Money may or may not be involved.

Buyers' interest in price stems from their expectations about the usefulness of a product or the satisfaction they may derive from it. Because buyers have limited resources, they must allocate those resources to obtain the products they most desire. Buyers must decide whether the utility gained in an exchange is worth the buying power sacrificed. Almost anything of value—ideas, services, rights, and goods—can be assessed by a price. In our society, financial price is the measurement of value commonly used in exchanges.

Terms Used to Describe Price

Value can be expressed in different terms for different marketing situations. For instance, students pay *tuition* for higher education. Automobile insurance companies charge a *premium* for protection from the cost of injuries or repairs stemming from an automobile accident. An officer who stops you for speeding writes a ticket that requires you to pay a *fine,* while a lawyer you hire to defend you in traffic court charges a *fee.* Airlines and taxi cabs charge a *fare.* A *toll* is charged for the use of bridges or toll roads. *Rent* is paid for the use of equipment or an apartment. A *commission* is remitted to a broker for the sale of real estate. *Dues* are paid for membership in a club or group. A *deposit* is made to hold or lay away merchandise. *Tips* help pay food servers for their services. *Interest* is charged for a loan, and *taxes* are paid for government services. Although price may be expressed in a variety of ways, its purpose is to quantify and express the value of the items in a marketing exchange.

The Importance of Price to Marketers

As pointed out in Chapter 11, developing a product may be a lengthy process. It takes time to plan promotion and to communicate benefits. Distribution usually requires a long-term commitment to dealers that will handle the product. Often price is the only thing a marketer can change quickly to respond to changes in demand or to actions of competitors. Under certain circumstances, however, the price variable may be relatively inflexible.

Price is a key element in the marketing mix because it relates directly to the generation of total revenue. The following equation is an important one for the entire organization:

$$\text{Profit} = \text{Total Revenue} - \text{Total Costs}$$

$$\text{Profits} = (\text{Price} \times \text{Quantity Sold}) - \text{Total Costs}$$

Prices affect an organization's profits in several ways because it is a key component of the profit equation and can be a major determinant of quantities sold. For example, price is a top priority for Hewlett-Packard in gaining market share and improving financial performance.[2] Furthermore, total costs are influenced by quantities sold.

Because price has a psychological impact on customers, marketers can use it symbolically. By pricing high, they can emphasize the quality of a product and try to increase the prestige associated with its ownership. By lowering a price, marketers can emphasize a bargain and attract customers who go out of their way to save a small amount of money. Thus, as this chapter details, price can have strong effects on a firm's sales and profitability.

Price and Non-price Competition

The competitive environment strongly influences the marketing mix decisions associated with a product. Pricing decisions are often made according to the price or non-price competitive situation in a particular market. Price competition exists when consumers have difficulty distinguishing competitive offerings and marketers emphasize low prices. Non-price competition involves a focus on marketing mix elements other than price.

Price Competition

price competition Emphasizing price as an issue and matching or beating competitors' prices

When engaging in **price competition,** a marketer emphasizes price as an issue and matches or beats competitors' prices. To compete effectively on a price basis, a firm should be the low-cost seller of the product. If all firms producing the same product charge the same price for it, the firm with the lowest costs is the most profitable. Firms that stress low price as a key marketing mix element tend to market standardized products. A seller competing on price may change prices frequently, or at least must be willing and able to do so. For example, Wal-Mart competes directly with Zellers by advertising price rollbacks on thousands of its items. Whenever competitors change their prices, Wal-Mart usually responds quickly.

Price competition gives marketers flexibility. They can alter prices to account for changes in their costs or respond to changes in demand for the product. If competitors try to gain market share by cutting prices, a company competing on a price basis can react quickly to such efforts. However, a major drawback of price competition is that competitors too have the flexibility to adjust prices. If they quickly match or beat a company's price cuts, a price war may ensue. Chronic price wars such as this one can substantially weaken organizations.

Non-price Competition

non-price competition Emphasizing factors other than price to distinguish a product from competing brands

Non-price competition occurs when a seller decides not to focus on price and instead emphasizes distinctive product features, service, product quality, promotion, packag-

Price Competition
Snapfish competes on price.

ing, or other factors to distinguish its product from competing brands. Thus, non-price competition allows a company to increase its brand's unit sales through means other than changing the brand's price. A major advantage of non-price competition is that a firm can build customer loyalty toward its brand. If customers prefer a brand because of non-price factors, they may not be easily lured away by competing firms and brands. In contrast, when price is the primary reason customers buy a particular brand, a competitor is often able to attract those customers through price cuts. However, some surveys show that the proportion of customers who base their purchase decisions solely on price is fairly small.[3]

Non-price competition is effective only under certain conditions. A company must be able to distinguish its brand through unique product features, higher product quality, effective promotion, distinctive packaging, or excellent customer service. Buyers not only must be able to perceive these distinguishing characteristics but must also view them as important. The distinguishing features that set a particular brand apart from competitors should be difficult, if not impossible, for competitors to imitate. Finally, the firm must extensively promote the brand's distinguishing characteristics to establish its superiority and set it apart from competitors in the minds of buyers. Examples of manufacturers that have used non-price competition effectively include Maytag (reliability and durability), Volvo (safety), and Caterpillar (quality and service).

Analysis of Demand

Determining the demand for a product is the responsibility of marketing managers, who are aided in this task by marketing researchers and forecasters. Marketing research and forecasting techniques yield estimates of sales potential, or the quantity of a product that could be sold during a specific period. These estimates are helpful in establishing the relationship between a product's price and the quantity demanded.

The Demand Curve

For most products, the quantity demanded goes up as the price goes down, and the quantity demanded goes down as the price goes up. Intel, for example, knows that lowering prices boosts demand for its Pentium PC processors. Thus, an inverse relationship exists between price and quantity demanded. As long as the marketing environment and buyers' needs, ability (purchasing power), willingness, and authority to buy remain stable, this fundamental inverse relationship holds.

Figure 14.1 illustrates the effect of one variable, price, on the quantity demanded. The classic **demand curve** (D_1) is a graph of the quantity of products expected to be sold at various prices if other factors remain constant.[4] It illustrates that as price falls, quantity demanded usually rises. Demand depends on other factors in the marketing mix, including product quality, promotion, and distribution. An improvement in any

demand curve A graph of the quantity of products expected to be sold at various prices if other factors remain constant

figure 14.1 **DEMAND CURVE ILLUSTRATING THE PRICE-QUANTITY RELATIONSHIP AND INCREASE IN DEMAND**

of these factors may cause a shift to, say, demand curve D_2. In such a case, an increased quantity (Q_2) will be sold at the same price (P).

Many types of demand exist, and not all conform to the classic demand curve shown in Figure 14.1. Prestige products, such as selected perfumes and jewelry, tend to sell better at high prices than at low ones. These products are desirable partly because their expense makes buyers feel elite. If the price fell drastically and many people owned these products, they would lose some of their appeal.

The demand curve in Figure 14.2 shows the relationship between price and quantity demanded for prestige products. Quantity demanded is greater, not less, at higher prices. For a certain price range—from P_1 to P_2—the quantity demanded (Q_1) goes up to Q_2. After a certain point, however, raising the price backfires: if the price goes too high, the quantity demanded goes down. The figure shows that if price is raised from P_2 to P_3, quantity demanded goes back down from Q_2 to Q_1.

Demand Fluctuations

Changes in buyers' needs, variations in the effectiveness of other marketing mix variables, the presence of substitutes, and dynamic environmental factors can influence demand. Restaurants and utility companies experience large fluctuations in demand daily. Toy manufacturers, fireworks suppliers, and air-conditioning and heating contractors also face demand fluctuations because of the seasonal nature of their products. The demand for online services, beef, and flat-screen TVs has changed over the last few years. In the case of flat-screen plasma and LCD TVs, demand accelerated as prices dropped by as much as 50 percent.[5] In some cases, demand fluctuations are predictable. It is no surprise to restaurants and utility company managers that demand fluctuates. However, changes in demand for other products may be less predictable, leading to problems for some companies.

price elasticity of demand
A measure of the sensitivity of demand to changes in price

Assessing Price Elasticity of Demand

figure 14.2 **DEMAND CURVE ILLUSTRATING THE RELATIONSHIP BETWEEN PRICE AND QUANTITY FOR PRESTIGE PRODUCTS**

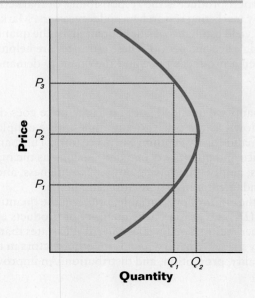

Up to this point, we have seen how marketers identify the target market's evaluation of price and its ability to purchase and how they examine demand to learn whether price is related inversely or directly to quantity. The next step is to assess price elasticity of demand. **Price elasticity of demand** provides a measure of the sensitivity of demand to changes in price. It is formally defined as the percentage change in quantity demanded relative to a given percentage change in price (see Figure 14.3). The percentage change in quantity demanded caused by a percentage change in price is much greater for elastic demand than for inelastic demand. For a product such as electricity, demand is relatively inelastic: when its price increases, say, from P_1 to P_2, quantity demanded goes down only a little, from Q_1 to Q_2. For products such as recreational vehicles, demand is relatively elastic: when price rises sharply, from P_1 to P_2, quantity demanded goes down a great deal, from Q_1 to Q_2.

If marketers can determine the price elasticity of demand, setting a price is much easier. By analyzing total revenues as prices change, marketers can determine whether a product is price elastic. Total revenue is price times quantity; thus, 10 000 rolls of wallpaper sold in one year at a price of $10 per roll equals $100 000 of total revenue. If demand

figure 14.3

ELASTICITY OF DEMAND

is *elastic,* a change in price causes an opposite change in total revenue: an increase in price will decrease total revenue, and a decrease in price will increase total revenue. *Inelastic* demand results in a change in the same direction as total revenue: an increase in price will increase total revenue, and a decrease in price will decrease total revenue. In the hotel industry, for example, research has found that demand for hotel rooms is inelastic regardless of whether they are in budget motels or luxury hotels.[6] The following formula determines the price elasticity of demand:

$$\text{Price Elasticity of Demand} = \frac{(\% \text{ Change in Quantity Demanded})}{(\% \text{ Change in Price})}$$

For example, if demand falls by eight percent when a seller raises the price by two percent, the price elasticity of demand is -4 (the negative sign indicating the inverse relationship between price and demand). If demand falls by two percent when price is increased by four percent, elasticity is $-\frac{1}{2}$. The less elastic the demand, the more beneficial it is for the seller to raise the price. Products without readily available substitutes and for which consumers have strong needs (for example, electricity or appendectomies) usually have inelastic demand.

Marketers cannot base prices solely on elasticity considerations. They must also examine the costs associated with different sales volumes and evaluate what happens to profits.

Demand, Cost, and Profit Relationships

The analysis of demand, cost, and profit is important because customers are becoming less tolerant of price increases, forcing manufacturers to find new ways to control costs. In the past, many customers desired premium brands and were willing to pay extra for those products. Today customers pass up certain brand names if they can pay less without sacrificing quality. To stay in business, a company must set prices that not only cover its costs but also meet customers' expectations. In this section, we explore two approaches to understanding demand, cost, and profit relationships: marginal analysis and break-even analysis.

Marginal Analysis

Marginal analysis examines what happens to a firm's costs and revenues when production (or sales volume) changes by one unit. Both production costs and revenues must be evaluated. To determine the costs of production, it is necessary to distinguish

fixed costs Costs that do not vary with changes in the number of units produced or sold

variable costs Costs that vary directly with changes in the number of units produced or sold

total cost The sum of average fixed and average variable costs times the quantity produced

marginal cost (MC) The extra cost incurred by producing one more unit of a product

marginal revenue (MR) The change in total revenue resulting from the sale of an additional unit of a product

among several types of costs. **Fixed costs** do not vary with changes in the number of units produced or sold. For example, a wallpaper manufacturer's cost of renting a factory does not change because production increases from one to two shifts a day or because twice as much wallpaper is sold. *Average fixed cost* is the fixed cost per unit produced and is calculated by dividing fixed costs by the number of units produced.

Variable costs vary directly with changes in the number of units produced or sold. The wages for a second shift and the cost of twice as much wallpaper are extra costs incurred when production is doubled. Variable costs are usually constant per unit; that is, twice as many workers and twice as much material produce twice as many rolls of wallpaper. *Average variable cost,* the variable cost per unit produced, is calculated by dividing the variable costs by the number of units produced.

Total cost is the sum of average fixed costs and average variable costs times the quantity produced. The *average total cost* is the sum of the average fixed cost and the average variable cost. **Marginal cost (MC)** is the extra cost a firm incurs when it produces one more unit of a product.

As Figure 14.4 shows, marginal cost equals average total cost at the latter's lowest level. Average total cost decreases as long as marginal cost is less than average total cost and increases when marginal cost rises above average total cost.

Marginal revenue (MR) is the change in total revenue that occurs when a firm sells an additional unit of a product. Figure 14.5 depicts marginal revenue and a demand curve. Most Canadian firms face downward-sloping demand curves for their products; in other words, they must lower their prices to sell additional units. This situation means that each additional unit of product sold provides the firm with less revenue than the previous unit sold. MR then becomes less than average revenue, as Figure 14.5 shows. Eventually MR reaches zero, and the sale of additional units actually hurts the firm.

However, before the firm can determine whether a unit makes a profit, it must know its cost, as well as its revenue, because profit equals revenue minus cost. If MR is a unit's addition to revenue and MC is a unit's addition to cost, MR minus MC tells us whether the unit is profitable.

Profit is the highest where MC = MR. Up to this point, the additional revenue generated from an extra unit sold exceeds the additional cost of producing it. Beyond this point, the additional cost of producing another unit exceeds the additional revenue generated, and profits decrease. If the price were based on minimum average total cost it would result in a lower profit.

Graphically combining Figures 14.4 and 14.5 into Figure 14.6 shows that any unit for which MR exceeds MC adds to a firm's profits, and any unit for which MC exceeds MR subtracts from profits. The firm should produce at the point where MR equals MC because this is the most profitable level of production.

This discussion of marginal analysis may give the false impression that pricing can be highly precise. If revenue (demand) and cost (supply) remained constant, prices could be set for maximum profits. In practice, however, cost and revenue change frequently.

figure 14.4

TYPICAL MARGINAL COST AND AVERAGE TOTAL COST RELATIONSHIP

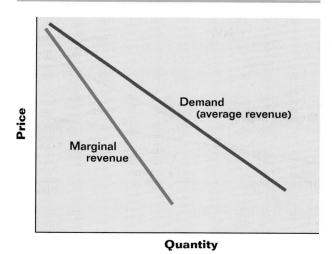

figure 14.5 **TYPICAL MARGINAL REVENUE AND AVERAGE REVENUE RELATIONSHIP**

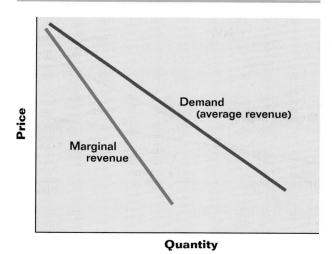

break-even point The point at which the costs of producing a product equal the revenue made from selling the product

The competitive tactics of other firms or government action can quickly undermine a company's expectations of revenue. Thus, marginal analysis is only a model from which to work. It offers little help in pricing new products before costs and revenues are established. On the other hand, in setting prices of existing products, especially in competitive situations, most marketers can benefit by understanding the relationship between marginal cost and marginal revenue.

Break-Even Analysis

The point at which the costs of producing a product equal the revenue made from selling the product is the **break-even point.** If the wallpaper manufacturer has total annual costs of $100 000 and sells $100 000 worth of wallpaper in the same year, the company has broken even.

Figure 14.7 illustrates the relationships among costs, revenue, profits, and losses involved in determining the break-even point. Knowing the number of units necessary to break even is important in setting the price. If a product priced at $100 per unit has an average variable cost of $60 per unit, the contribution to fixed costs is $40. If total fixed costs are $120 000, the break-even point in units is determined as follows:

$$\text{Break-Even Point} = \frac{\text{Fixed Costs}}{\text{Per-Unit Contribution to Fixed Costs}}$$

$$= \frac{\text{Fixed Costs}}{\text{Price} - \text{Variable Costs}}$$

$$= \frac{\$120\ 000}{\$40}$$

$$= 3000\ \text{Units}$$

To calculate the break-even point in terms of dollar sales volume, the seller multiplies the break-even point in units by the price per unit. In the preceding example,

figure 14.6

COMBINING THE MARGINAL COST AND MARGINAL REVENUE CONCEPTS FOR OPTIMAL PROFIT

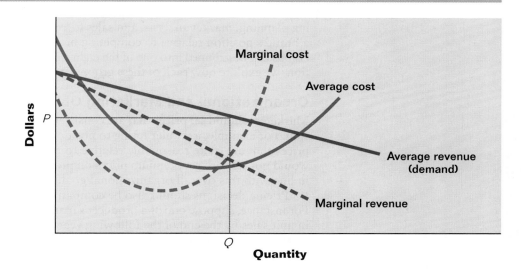

figure 14.7

DETERMINING THE BREAK-EVEN POINT

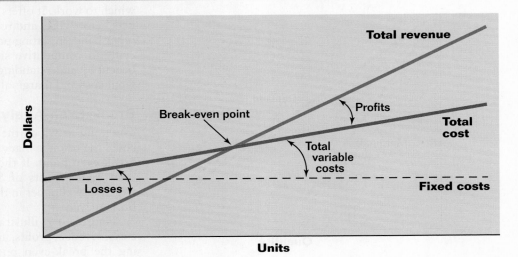

the break-even point in terms of dollar sales volume is 3000 (units) times $100, or $300 000.

To use break-even analysis effectively, a marketer should determine the break-even point for each of several alternative prices. This determination allows the marketer to compare the effects on total revenue, total costs, and the break-even point for each price under consideration.

Break-even analysis is simple and straightforward. It does assume, however, that the quantity demanded is basically fixed (inelastic) and that the major task in setting prices is to recover costs. It focuses more on how to break even than on how to achieve a pricing objective, such as percentage of market share or return on investment. Nonetheless, marketing managers can use this concept to determine whether a product will achieve at least a break-even volume.

Factors Affecting Pricing Decisions

Pricing decisions can be complex because of the number of factors to consider. Frequently there is considerable uncertainty about the reactions to price among buyers, channel members, and competitors. Price is also an important consideration in marketing planning, market analysis, and sales forecasting. It is a major issue when assessing a brand's position relative to competing brands. Most factors that affect pricing decisions can be grouped into one of the eight categories shown in Figure 14.8. In this section, we explore how each of these groups of factors enters into price decision making.

Organizational and Marketing Objectives

Marketers should set prices that are consistent with the organization's goals and mission. For example, a retailer trying to position itself as value oriented may wish to set prices that are quite reasonable relative to product quality. In this case, a marketer would not want to set premium prices on products but would strive to price products in line with this overall organizational goal.

Pricing decisions should also be compatible with the firm's marketing objectives. For instance, suppose one of a producer's marketing objectives is a 12 percent increase in unit sales by the end of the following year. Assuming buyers are price sensitive, increasing the price or setting a price above the average market price would not be in line with this objective.

figure 14.8

FACTORS THAT AFFECT PRICING DECISIONS

Types of Pricing Objectives

The types of pricing objectives a marketer uses obviously have considerable bearing on the determination of prices. For example, an organization that uses pricing to increase its market share would likely set the brand's price below those of competing brands of similar quality to attract competitors' customers. A marketer sometimes uses temporary price reductions in the hope of gaining market share. If a business needs to raise cash quickly, it will likely use temporary price reductions such as sales, rebates, and special discounts. We examine pricing objectives in more detail later in this chapter.

Costs

Clearly costs must be an issue when establishing price. A firm may temporarily sell products below cost to match competition, generate cash flow, or even increase market share, but in the long run it cannot survive by selling its products below cost. A marketer should be careful to analyze all costs so they can be included in the total cost associated with a product.

To maintain market share and revenue in an increasingly price-sensitive market, many marketers have concentrated on reducing costs. Labour-saving technologies, a focus on quality, and efficient manufacturing processes have brought productivity gains that translate into reduced costs and lower prices for customers. In the highly competitive computer industry, for example, IBM constantly looks for ways to lower the cost of developing, producing, and marketing computers and related products. As a cost-cutting move, the company recently relocated 4750 managerial and engineering jobs to India, where labour costs are significantly lower.[7]

Besides considering the costs associated with a particular product, marketers must take into account the costs the product shares with others in the product line. Products often share some costs, particularly the costs of research and development, production, and distribution. Most marketers view a product's cost as a minimum, or floor, below which the product cannot be priced.

Other Marketing Mix Variables

All marketing mix variables are highly interrelated. Pricing decisions can influence evaluations and activities associated with product, distribution, and promotion variables. A product's price frequently affects the demand for that item. A high price, for instance, may result in low unit sales, which in turn may lead to higher production costs per unit. Conversely, lower per-unit production costs may result from a low price. For many products, buyers associate better product quality with a high price and poorer product quality with a low price. This perceived price-quality relationship influences customers' overall image of products or brands.

The price of a product is linked to several dimensions of its distribution. Premium-priced products are often marketed through selective or exclusive distribution; lower-priced products in the same product category may be sold through intensive distribution. For example, Cross pens are distributed through selective distribution and Bic pens through intensive distribution. Moreover, an increase in physical distribution costs, such as shipping, may have to be passed on to customers.

Price may determine how a product is promoted. Bargain prices are often included in advertisements. Premium prices are less likely to be advertised, though they are sometimes included in advertisements for upscale items such as luxury cars or fine jewelry. Higher-priced products are more likely than lower-priced ones to require personal selling.

Channel Member Expectations

When making price decisions, a producer must consider what members of the distribution channel expect. A channel member certainly expects to receive a profit for the functions it performs. The amount of profit expected depends on what the intermediary could make if it were handling a competing product instead. Also, the amount of time and the resources required to carry the product influence intermediaries' expectations.

Channel members often expect producers to give discounts for large orders and prompt payment. At times, resellers expect producers to provide several support activities such as sales training, service training, repair advisory service, cooperative advertising, sales promotions, and perhaps a program for returning unsold merchandise to the producer. These support activities clearly have associated costs that a producer must consider when determining prices.

External Reference and Price

Duracell compares its quality with its direct competitors and justifies its price.

Why do you think they're so cheap?

You know the saying: You get what you pay for.
In this case, what you're getting are zinc batteries that rely on different, less powerful technology. That's why Duracell® will last up to 4 times longer than one of these so-called "Heavy Duty" batteries.

DURACELL
TRUS±ED EVERYWHERE

Customers' Interpretation and Response

When making pricing decisions, marketers should address a vital question: How will our customers interpret our prices and respond to them? *Interpretation* in this context refers to what the price means or what it communicates to customers. Does the price mean "high quality" or "low quality," or "great deal," "fair price," or "rip-off"? Customer *response* refers to whether the price will move customers closer to purchase of the product and the degree to which the price enhances their satisfaction with the purchase experience and with the product after purchase.

Customers' interpretation of and response to a price are to some degree determined by their assessment of value, or what they receive compared with what they give up to make the purchase. In evaluating what they receive, customers consider product attributes, benefits, advantages, disadvantages, the probability of using the product, and possibly the status associated with the product. In assessing the cost of the product, customers likely will consider its price, the amount of time and effort required to obtain it, and perhaps the resources required to maintain it after purchase.

At times, customers interpret a higher price as higher product quality. They are especially likely to make this price–quality association when they cannot judge the quality of the product themselves. This is not always the case, however; whether price is equated with quality depends on the types of customers and products involved. Obviously marketers that rely on customers making a price–quality association and that provide moderate-

or low-quality products at high prices will be unable to build long-term customer relationships.

When interpreting and responding to prices, how do customers determine if the price is too high, too low, or about right? In general, they compare prices with internal or external reference prices. An *internal reference price* is a price developed in the buyer's mind through experience with the product. It reflects a belief that a product should cost approximately a certain amount. To arrive at an internal reference price, consumers may consider one or more values including what they think the product "ought" to cost, the price usually charged for it, the last price they paid, the highest and lowest amounts they would be willing to pay, the price of the brand they usually buy, the average price of similar products, the expected future price, and the typical discounted price.[8] For the product categories with which we have less experience, we rely more heavily on external reference prices. An *external reference price* is a comparison price provided by others, such as retailers or manufacturers. For example, a retailer in an advertisement might state, "While this product is sold for $100 elsewhere, our price is only $39.95." When attempting to establish a reference price in customers' minds by advertising a higher price against which to compare the company's real price, a marketer must make sure the higher price is realistic, because if it is not, customers will not use this price when establishing or altering their reference prices.[9] Customers' perceptions of prices are also influenced by their expectations about future price increases, by what they paid for the product recently, and by what they would like to pay for the product. Other factors affecting customers' perceptions of whether the price is right include time or financial constraints, the costs associated with searching for lower-priced products, and expectations that products will go on sale.

Buyers' perceptions of a product relative to competing products may allow the firm to set a price that differs significantly from rivals' prices. If the product is deemed

Clearance? On Sale? Where's the Better Deal?

When you're out shopping, how do you respond to discounts labelled *sale* versus *clearance?* Although there have been legal actions against retailers for their use of the term *sale,* especially when used as a reference price ("Was $89.95. Now only $59.95"), there has been almost no research or regulatory guidance on the use of the term *clearance.* Researchers believe consumers associate *clearance* with the end of a season, excess inventories, or even products that may be discontinued. In reality, the term is used widely and in many different contexts that depend only on the seller's interpretation. Most retailers are aware that consumers want to buy at discount, but attitude toward and perception of price cues influence consumers' reaction to a discount. Almost 80 percent of automobiles, furniture, and kitchenware were purchased at a discount.

An experiment was conducted to provide greater insight into consumers' perception of the term *clearance.* One group of respondents was asked to write down their thoughts after driving past a store and seeing a large sign in the window saying *clearance.* Another was given the same task using the word *sale.* The experiment revealed that a *clearance* sign leads people to expect or maintain larger discounts, more favourable attitude toward promotion, a greater retailer obligation to reduce price, a greater sense that the retailer would be going out of business, and concerns about product quality. This research suggests that *clearance* is a more powerful term to use in influencing consumer perceptions about price discounts.

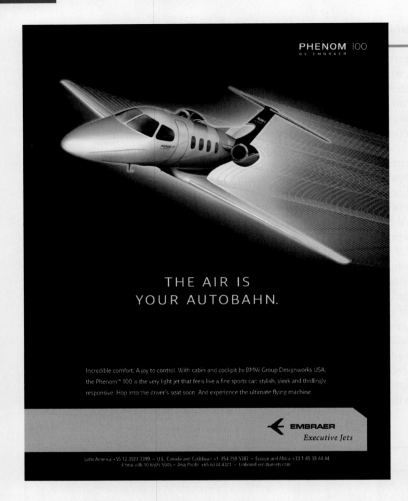

PHENOM 100
BY EMBRAER

THE AIR IS
YOUR AUTOBAHN.

Incredible comfort. A joy to control. With cabin and cockpit by BMW Group Designworks USA,
the Phenom™ 100 is the very light jet that feels like a fine sports car: stylish, sleek and thrillingly
responsive. Hop into the driver's seat soon. And experience the ultimate flying machine.

EMBRAER
Executive Jets

Latin America +55 12 3927 3399 ~ U.S. Canada and Caribbean +1 954 359 5387 ~ Europe and Africa +33 1 49 38 44 44
China +86 10 6505 5045 ~ Asia Pacific +65 6734 4121 ~ Embraerexecutivejets.com

Prestige Products
Embraer offers high-quality prestige products like the Phenom 100.

superior to most of the competition, a premium price may be feasible. However, even products with superior quality can be overpriced. Strong brand loyalty sometimes provides the opportunity to charge a premium price. On the other hand, if buyers view a product less than favourably (though not extremely negatively), a lower price may generate sales.

In the context of price, buyers can be characterized according to their degree of value consciousness, price consciousness, and prestige sensitivity. Marketers that understand these characteristics are better able to set pricing objectives and policies. **Value-conscious** consumers are concerned about both price and quality of a product.[10] These consumers may perceive value as quality per unit of price or as not only economic savings but also the additional gains expected from one product over a competitor's brand. The first view is appropriate for commodities such as bottled water, bananas, and gasoline. If a value-conscious consumer perceives that quality of gasoline to be the same for Ultramar and Shell, he or she will go to the station with the lower price. For consumers looking not just for economic value but additional gains they expect from one brand over another, a product differentiation value could be associated with benefits and features that are believed to be unique.[11]

value conscious Concerned about price and quality of a product

price conscious Striving to pay low prices

prestige sensitive Drawn to products that signify prominence and status

For example, a BMW may be considered to be better than a Cadillac. To appeal to the value-conscious consumer, Apple Computer recently introduced the Mac Mini and iPod Shuffle, more compact versions of their respective counterparts offered at discount prices.[12] **Price-conscious** individuals strive to pay low prices.[13] They want the lowest prices and would respond to Wal-Mart's claim that "we sell for less." **Prestige-sensitive** buyers focus on purchasing products that signify prominence and status.[14] For example, the Porsche Cayenne, one of the highest-priced sport-utility vehicles ever marketed, created record sales and profits for Porsche. Only 18 percent of Cayenne buyers had previously owned a Porsche; many of the rest were attracted to a vehicle with the prestige associated with the Porsche name.[15]

On the other hand, some consumers vary in their degree of value, price, and prestige consciousness. In some segments, consumers are increasingly "trading up" to higher-status products in categories such as automobiles, home appliances, restaurants, and even pet food, yet remain price conscious regarding cleaning and grocery products. This trend has benefited marketers such as Starbucks, and BMW, which can charge premium prices for high-quality, prestige products, as well as Wal-Mart and Costco, which offer basic household products at everyday low prices.[16] Indeed, it appears that a new "mass class" market is emerging in part due to technology and communication advances, the prevalence of designer goods, and the proliferation of counterfeit goods. As a result, more designers like Karl Lagerfeld are creating exclusive designer originals for upscale markets and less expensive mass market goods for a much broader target audience.[17]

Competition

A marketer needs to know competitors' prices so it can adjust its own prices accordingly. This does not mean a company will necessarily match competitors' prices; it

**Who knows.
You could be the next governor.**

Straight on Foothill. Left on Altadena.   goldsgym.com

**Competitive Industry
and Price**

Gold's Gym is part of a
competitive industry and
uses price to win customers.

may set its price above or below theirs. However, for some organizations (such as airlines), matching competitors' prices is an important strategy for survival.

When adjusting prices, a marketer must assess how competitors will respond. Will competitors change their prices and, if so, will they raise or lower them? In Chapter 3, we described several types of competitive market structures. The structure that characterizes the industry to which a firm belongs affects the flexibility of price setting. For example, because of reduced pricing regulation, firms in the telecommunications industry have moved from a monopolistic market structure to an oligopolistic one, which has resulted in significant price competition.

When an organization operates as a monopoly and is unregulated, it can set whatever prices the market will bear. However, the company may not price the product at the highest possible level to avoid government regulation or to penetrate a market by using a lower price. If the monopoly is regulated, it normally has less pricing flexibility; the regulatory body lets it set prices that generate a reasonable but not excessive return. A government-owned monopoly may price products below cost to make them accessible to people who otherwise could not afford them. Transit systems, for example, sometimes operate this way.

The automotive and aircraft industries exemplify oligopolies, in which only a few sellers operate and barriers to competitive entry are high. Companies in such industries can raise their prices in the hope competitors will do the same. When an organization cuts its price to gain a competitive edge, other companies are likely to follow suit. Thus, very little advantage is gained through price cuts in an oligopolistic market structure.

A market structure characterized by monopolistic competition has numerous sellers with product offerings that are differentiated by physical characteristics, features, quality, and brand images. The distinguishing characteristics of its product may allow a company to set a different price than its competitors. However, firms in a monopolistic competitive market structure are likely to practice non-price competition, discussed earlier in this chapter.

Under conditions of perfect competition, many sellers exist. Buyers view all sellers' products as the same. All firms sell their products at the going market price, and buyers will not pay more than that. This type of market structure, then, gives a marketer no flexibility in setting prices. Farming, as an industry, has some characteristics of perfect competition. Farmers sell their products at the going market price. At times, for example, corn, soybean, and wheat growers have had bumper crops and been forced to sell them at depressed market prices.

Legal and Regulatory Issues

As discussed in Chapter 3, legal and regulatory issues influence pricing decisions. To curb inflation, the federal government can invoke price controls, freeze prices at certain levels, or determine the rates at which firms may increase prices. Provincial governments may regulate prices on such products as gasoline, insurance, dairy goods, and electricity.

Many regulations and laws affect pricing decisions and activities. The Competition Act of 1986, amended in 1992, is the latest in a long history of competition legislation in Canada. The rationale for all such legislation is to foster a competitive environment among businesses, and to protect consumers from unfair business practices. The Competition Act has had a strong impact on pricing decisions, particularly in the areas of price fixing, price discrimination, resale price maintenance, and predatory pricing.

Price fixing occurs when competing sellers collude to set prices at a level generally higher than would otherwise exist in a free market. In Canada, fines for price fixing can be imposed on both organizations and individual executives. *Price discrimination,* the practice of employing price differentials that injure competition by giving one or more buyers a competitive advantage over other buyers, is also prohibited by law. However, not all price differentials are discriminatory. A marketer can use price differentials if they do not hinder competition, if they result from differences in the costs of selling or transportation to various customers, or if they arise because the firm has had to cut its price to a particular buyer to meet competitors' prices. There have been very few convictions for discriminatory pricing in Canada. In the U.S., it is legal to offer discounts to retailers and wholesalers based on the functions they perform. However, in Canada, as retailers and wholesalers are considered competitors, price differentials must be based on the quantity or quality of goods sold. *Deceptive pricing* occurs when price deals are used to mislead consumers. Unlike price discrimination, there have been many Canadian organizations found guilty and fined for deceptive pricing. To help organizations avoid unintentional deception of consumers, the Competition Bureau has published a guide called "Misleading Advertising Guidelines." *Resale price maintenance* occurs when a manufacturer exerts undue influence on the price at which a retailer resells a product. The desire to protect a brands premium or status image provides the temptation to exert such influence. The practice of establishing low prices with the intention of driving competition out of the market is known as *predatory pricing.*

Development of Pricing Objectives

pricing objectives Goals that describe what a firm wants to achieve through pricing

Pricing objectives are goals that describe what a firm wants to achieve through pricing. Developing pricing objectives is an important task because pricing objectives form the basis for decisions about other stages of pricing. Thus, pricing objectives must be stated explicitly, and the statement should include the time frame for accomplishing them. Figure 14.9 illustrates that the development of pricing objectives is the first of six stages of a process marketers can use when setting prices.

Marketers must ensure that pricing objectives are consistent with the organization's marketing objectives and with its overall objectives because pricing objectives influ-

figure 14.9

STAGES FOR ESTABLISHING PRICES

1 Development of pricing objectives
2 Assessment of target market's evaluation of price
3 Evaluation of competitors' prices
4 Selection of a basis for pricing
5 Selection of a pricing strategy
6 Determination of a specific price

table 14.1 PRICING OBJECTIVES AND TYPICAL ACTIONS TAKEN TO ACHIEVE THEM

Objective	Possible Action
Survival	Adjust price levels so the firm can increase sales volume to match organizational expenses
Profit	Identify price and cost levels that allow the firm to maximize profit
Return on investment	Identify price levels that enable the firm to yield targeted ROI
Market share	Adjust price levels so the firm can maintain or increase sales relative to competitors' sales
Cash flow	Set price levels to encourage rapid sales
Status quo	Identify price levels that help stabilize demand and sales
Product quality	Set prices to recover research and development expenditures and establish a high-quality image

ence decisions in many functional areas, including finance, accounting, and production. A marketer can use both short- and long-term pricing objectives and can employ one or multiple pricing objectives. For instance, a firm may wish to increase market share by 18 percent over the next three years, achieve a 15 percent return on investment, and promote an image of quality in the marketplace.

In this section, we examine some of the pricing objectives companies might set for themselves. Table 14.1 shows the major pricing objectives and typical actions associated with them.

Assessment of the Target Market's Evaluation of Price

Despite the general assumption that price is a major issue for buyers, the importance of price depends on the type of product, the type of target market, and the purchase situation. For example, buyers are probably more sensitive to gasoline prices than to luggage prices. With respect to the type of target market, adults may have to pay more than children for certain products. The purchase situation also affects the buyer's view of price. Most moviegoers would never pay in other situations the prices charged for soft drinks, popcorn, and candy at movie concession stands. By assessing the target market's evaluation of price, a marketer is in a better position to know how much emphasis to put on price. Information about the target market's price evaluation may also help a marketer determine how far above the competition the firm can set its prices.

Because some consumers today are seeking less expensive products and shopping more selectively, some manufacturers and retailers are focusing on the value of their products. Value combines a product's price and quality attributes, which customers use to differentiate among competing brands. Consumers are looking for good deals on products that provide better value for their money. They may also view products that have highly desirable attributes, such as organic content or time-saving features, as having great value. Consumers are increasingly willing to pay a higher price for food that is convenient and time saving. Even retail atmospherics can influence consumers' perceptions of price: the use of soft lights and colours has been found to have a positive influence on perception of price fairness.[18] Understanding the importance of a product to customers, as well as their expectations about quality and value, helps marketers correctly assess the target market's evaluation of price.

Evaluation of Competitors' Prices

In most cases, marketers are in a better position to establish prices when they know the prices charged for competing brands. Learning competitors' prices may be a regular function of marketing research. Some grocery and department stores, for example, have full-time comparative shoppers who systematically collect data on prices. Companies may also purchase price lists, sometimes weekly, from syndicated marketing research services.

Finding out what prices competitors are charging is not always easy, especially in producer and reseller markets. Competitors' price lists are often closely guarded. Even if a marketer has access to competitors' price lists, those lists may not reflect the actual prices at which competitive products are sold because those prices may be established through negotiation.

Knowing the prices of competing brands can be very important for a marketer. Competitors' prices and the marketing mix variables they emphasize partly determine how important price will be to customers. A marketer in an industry in which price competition prevails needs competitive price information to ensure its prices are the same as, or lower than, competitors' prices. In some instances, an organization's prices are designed to be slightly above competitors' prices to give its products an exclusive image. In contrast, another company may use price as a competitive tool and price its products below those of competitors. Category killers like Staples and Home Depot have acquired large market shares through highly competitive pricing.[19]

Selection of a Basis for Pricing

The three major dimensions on which prices can be based are cost, demand, and competition. The selection of the basis to use is affected by the type of product, the market structure of the industry, the brand's market share position relative to competing brands, and customer characteristics. In this section, we discuss each basis separately. However, when setting prices, an organization generally considers two or all three of these dimensions, even if one is the primary basis on which it determines prices. For example, if an organization is using cost as a basis for setting prices, marketers in that organization are also aware of and concerned about competitors' prices. If a company is using demand as a basis for pricing, those making pricing decisions still must consider costs and competitors' prices. Fairchild Semiconductor uses software to assess all three dimensions, as well as buying behaviour, manufacturing capacity, inventories, and product life cycles, in setting prices for its 44 000 products.[20]

Cost-Based Pricing

cost-based pricing Adding a dollar amount or percentage to the cost of the product

With **cost-based pricing**, a dollar amount or percentage is added to the cost of the product. This approach thus involves calculations of desired profit margins. Cost-based pricing does not necessarily take into account the economic aspects of supply and demand, nor must it relate to just one pricing strategy or pricing objective. Cost-based pricing is straightforward and easy to implement. Two common forms of cost-based pricing are cost-plus and markup pricing.

cost-plus pricing Adding a specified dollar amount or percentage to the seller's cost

Cost-Plus Pricing. With **cost-plus pricing,** the seller's costs are determined (usually during a project or after a project is completed), and then a specified dollar amount or percentage of the cost is added to the seller's cost to establish the price. Cost-plus pricing and competition-based pricing are in fact the most common bases for pricing services.[21] When production costs are difficult to predict, cost-plus pricing is appropriate. Projects involving custom-made equipment and commercial construction are often priced using this technique. One pitfall for the buyer is that the seller may increase costs to establish a larger profit base. Furthermore, some costs, such as overhead, may be difficult to determine. In periods of rapid inflation, cost-plus pricing is popular, especially when the producer must use raw materials that are fluctuating in price. In industries in which cost-plus pricing is common and sellers have similar costs, price competition may not be especially intense.

markup pricing Adding to the cost of the product a predetermined percentage of that cost

Markup Pricing. With **markup pricing,** commonly used by retailers, a product's price is derived by adding a predetermined percentage of the cost, called *markup,* to the cost of the product. Although the percentage markup in a retail store varies from one category of goods to another—35 percent of cost for hardware items and 100 percent of cost for greeting cards, for example—the same percentage is often used to determine the prices on items within a single product category, and the percentage markup may be largely standardized across an industry at the retail level. Using a rigid percentage markup for a specific product category reduces pricing to a routine task that can be performed quickly.

Markup can be stated as a percentage of the cost or as a percentage of the selling price. The following example illustrates how percentage markups are determined and points out the differences in the two methods. Assume a retailer purchases a can of tuna at 45 cents, adds 15 cents to the cost, and then prices the tuna at 60 cents. Here are the figures:

$$\text{Markup as a Percentage of Cost} = \frac{Markup}{Cost}$$

$$= \frac{15}{45}$$

$$= 33.3\%$$

$$\text{Markup as a Percentage of Selling Price} = \frac{Markup}{Selling\ Price}$$

$$= \frac{15}{60}$$

$$= 25.0\%$$

Obviously, when discussing a percentage markup, it is important to know whether the markup is based on cost or selling price.

Demand-Based Pricing

demand-based pricing Pricing based on the level of demand for the product

Marketers sometimes base prices on the level of demand for the product. When **demand-based pricing** is used, customers pay a higher price when demand for the product is strong and a lower price when demand is weak. For example, hotels that otherwise attract numerous travelers often offer reduced rates during lower-demand periods. Some long-distance telephone companies also use demand-based pricing by charging peak and off-peak rates. To use this pricing basis, a marketer must be able to estimate the amounts of a product consumers will demand at different prices. The marketer then chooses the price that generates the highest total revenue. Obviously the effectiveness of demand-based pricing depends on the marketer's ability to estimate demand accurately.

Competition-Based Pricing

competition-based pricing Pricing influenced primarily by competitors' prices

With **competition-based pricing,** an organization considers costs to be secondary to competitors' prices. The importance of this method increases when competing products are relatively homogeneous and the organization is serving markets in which price is a key purchase consideration. A firm that uses competition-based pricing may choose to price below competitors' prices, above competitors' prices, or at the same level. Airlines use competition-based pricing, often charging identical fares on the same routes. Online travel services such as Orbitz, Expedia, and Priceline.com have also employed competition-based pricing.

Although not all introductory marketing texts have exactly the same price, they do have similar prices. The price the bookstore paid to the publishing company for this textbook was determined on the basis of competitors' prices. Competition-based pricing can help a firm achieve the pricing objective of increasing sales or market share. Competition-based pricing may necessitate frequent price adjustments. For example, for many competitive airline routes, fares are adjusted often.

Selection of a Pricing Strategy

A pricing strategy is an approach or a course of action designed to achieve pricing and marketing objectives. Generally pricing strategies help marketers solve the practical problems of establishing prices. Table 14.2 lists the most common pricing strategies, which we discuss in this section.

Differential Pricing

An important issue in pricing decisions is whether to use a single price or different prices for the same product. Using a single price has several benefits. A primary advantage is simplicity. A single price is easily understood by both employees and customers, and since many salespeople and customers dislike having to negotiate a price, it reduces the chance of an adversarial relationship developing between marketer and customer. The use of a single price does create some challenges, however. If the single price is too high, a number of potential customers may be unable to afford the product. If it is too low, the organization loses revenue from those customers who would have paid more had the price been higher.

differential pricing Charging different prices to different buyers for the same quality and quantity of product

Differential pricing means charging different prices to different buyers for the same quality and quantity of product. For differential pricing to be effective, the market must consist of multiple segments with different price sensitivities, and the method should be used in a way that avoids confusing or antagonizing customers. Customers paying the lower prices should not be able to resell the product to the individuals and organizations paying higher prices, unless that is the seller's intention. Differential pricing can occur in several ways, including negotiated pricing, secondary-market discounting, periodic discounting, and random discounting.

negotiated pricing Establishing a final price through bargaining between seller and customer

Negotiated Pricing. **Negotiated pricing** occurs when the final price is established through bargaining between seller and customer. Negotiated pricing occurs in a number of industries and at all levels of distribution. Cutler-Hammer/Eaton streamlined its contract-negotiations process for more than 90 000 products by reducing quote

table 14.2	COMMON PRICING STRATEGIES	
Differential Pricing		**Psychological Pricing**
Negotiated pricing		Reference pricing
Secondary-market pricing		Bundle pricing
Periodic discounting		Multiple-unit pricing
Random discounting		Everyday low prices
New-Product Pricing		**Odd-Even Pricing**
Price skimming		Customary pricing
Penetration pricing		Prestige pricing
Product-Line Pricing		**Promotional Pricing**
Captive pricing		Price leaders
Premium pricing		Special-event pricing
Bait pricing		Comparison discounting
Price lining		
		Professional Pricing

response times and implementing automatic acceptance of offers.[22] Even when there is a predetermined stated price or a price list, manufacturers, wholesalers, and retailers may negotiate to establish the final sales price. Consumers commonly negotiate prices for houses, cars, and used equipment.

secondary-market pricing
Setting one price for the primary target market and a different price for another market

Secondary-Market Pricing. **Secondary-market pricing** means setting one price for the primary target market and a different price for another market. Often the price charged in the secondary market is lower. However, when the costs of serving a secondary market are higher than normal, secondary-market customers may have to pay a higher price. Examples of secondary markets include a geographically isolated domestic market, a market in a foreign country, and a segment willing to purchase a product during off-peak times. For example, some restaurants offer special "early-bird" prices during the late afternoon hours, movie theatres offer senior citizen and afternoon matinee discounts, and some textbooks and pharmaceutical products are sold for considerably less in certain foreign countries. Secondary markets give an organization an opportunity to use excess capacity and stabilize the allocation of resources.

periodic discounting
Temporary reduction of prices on a patterned or systematic basis

Periodic Discounting. **Periodic discounting** is the temporary reduction of prices on a patterned or systematic basis. Many retailers, for example, have annual holiday sales. Some women's apparel stores have two seasonal sales each year: a winter sale in the last two weeks of January and a summer sale in the first two weeks of July. Automobile dealers regularly discount prices on current models in the fall, when the next year's models are introduced. From the marketer's point of view, a major problem with periodic discounting is that because the discounts follow a pattern, customers can predict when the reductions will occur and may delay their purchases until they can take advantage of the lower prices.

random discounting
Temporary reduction of prices on an unsystematic basis

Random Discounting. To alleviate the problem of customers knowing when discounting will occur, some organizations employ **random discounting;** that is, they temporarily reduce their prices on an unsystematic basis. When price reductions of a product occur randomly, current users of that brand are likely unable to predict when the reductions will occur and thus will not delay their purchases. In the automobile industry, with the increasing reliance on sales, rebates, and incentives such as zero percent financing, random discounting has become nearly continuous discounting, and some analysts have expressed concern that automakers will find it difficult to "wean" consumers off the generous incentives as the economy improves.[23] Marketers also use random discounting to attract new customers.

Irrespective of whether they use periodic discounting or random discounting, retailers often employ tensile pricing when putting products on sale. *Tensile pricing* refers to a broad statement about price reductions as opposed to detailing specific price discounts. Examples of tensile pricing would be statements such as "20 to 50 percent off," "up to 75 percent off," and "save 10 percent or more." Generally, using and advertising the tensile price that mentions only the maximum reduction (such as "up to 50 percent off") generates the highest customer response.[24]

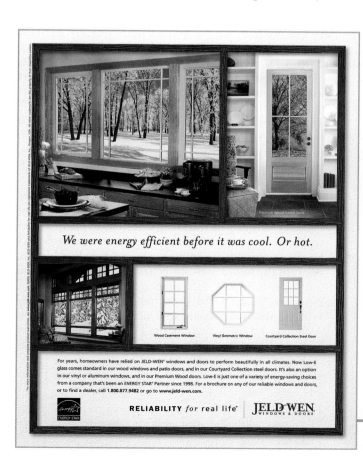

Secondary-Market Pricing
Because of the product type, purchasers of Jeld-Wen windows may be one-time customers.

New-Product Pricing

Setting the base price for a new product is a necessary part of formulating a marketing strategy. The base price is easily adjusted (in the absence of government price controls), and its establishment is one of the most fundamental decisions in the marketing mix. The base price can be set high to recover development costs quickly or provide a reference point for developing discount prices for different market segments. When a marketer sets base prices, it also considers how quickly competitors will enter the market, whether they will mount a strong campaign on entry, and what effect their entry will have on the development of primary demand. Two strategies used in new-product pricing are price skimming and penetration pricing.

price skimming Charging the highest possible price that buyers who most desire the product will pay

Price Skimming.   Price skimming means charging the highest possible price that buyers who most desire the product will pay. The Porsche Cayenne, for example, has a starting price of $58 900, considerably higher than those for other sport-utility vehicles.[25] This approach provides the most flexible introductory base price. Demand tends to be inelastic in the introductory stage of the product life cycle.

Price skimming can provide several benefits, especially when a product is in the introductory stage of its life cycle. A skimming policy can generate much-needed initial cash flows to help offset sizable development costs. Price skimming protects the marketer from problems that arise when the price is set too low to cover costs. When a firm introduces a product, its production capacity may be limited. A skimming price can help keep demand consistent with the firm's production capabilities. The use of a skimming price may attract competition into an industry because the high price makes that type of business appear quite lucrative. In reality, companies price new products for less than they could or should. In such cases, companies risk not only failing to maximize potential profits but also establishing a lower market value in buyers' minds.[26] New-product prices should be based on both the value to the customer and competitive products.

penetration pricing Setting prices below those of competing brands to penetrate a market and gain a significant market share quickly

Penetration Pricing.   With penetration pricing, prices are set below those of competing brands to penetrate a market and gain a large market share quickly. Perhaps the ultimate penetration pricing strategy was implemented by the Arctic Monkeys. The U.K. rock band handed out free CDs of its music at early performances, and fans e-mailed the music to friends. The resulting viral effort led to a recording contract for the band, which has the fastest-selling debut album in British music history.[27] This approach is less flexible for a marketer than price skimming because it is more difficult to raise a penetration price than to lower or discount a skimming price. It is not unusual for a firm to use a penetration price after having skimmed the market with a higher price.

Penetration pricing can be especially beneficial when a marketer suspects that competitors could enter the market easily. If penetration pricing allows the marketer to gain a large market share quickly, competitors may be discouraged from entering the market. In addition, because the lower per-unit penetration price results in lower per-unit profit, the market may not appear to be especially lucrative to potential new entrants. Apple prices its iPod digital music players at penetration prices. Although retailers such as the Future Shop earn very little profit on iPods, they benefit from selling iPod ac-

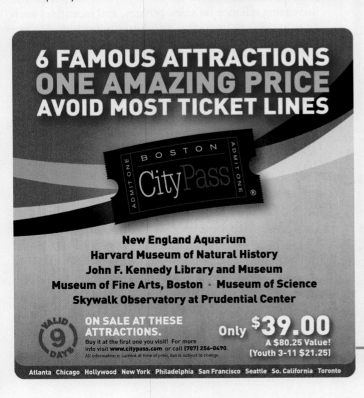

Penetration Pricing
CityPass uses penetration pricing to sell its discounts to city visitors.

cessories. Many iPod buyers purchase at least two accessories, and the market for accessories such as speakers and covers is expected to double. Moreover, 40 percent of vehicles sold in North America will offer some sort of iPod integration this year.[28]

Product-Line Pricing

product-line pricing
Establishing and adjusting prices of multiple products within a product line

Rather than considering products on an item-by-item basis when determining pricing strategies, some marketers employ product-line pricing. **Product-line pricing** means establishing and adjusting the prices of multiple products within a product line. When marketers use product-line pricing, their goal is to maximize profits for an entire product line rather than focusing on the profitability of an individual product. Product-line pricing can lend marketers flexibility in price setting. For example, marketers can set prices so that one product is quite profitable while another increases market share due to having a lower price than competing products.

Before setting prices for a product line, marketers evaluate the relationship among the products in the line. When products in a line are complementary, sales increases in one item raise demand for other items. For instance, desktop printers and toner cartridges are complementary products. When products in a line function as substitutes for one another, buyers of one product in the line are unlikely to purchase one of the other products in the same line. In this case, marketers must be sensitive to how a price change for one of the brands may affect the demand not only for that brand but also for the substitute brands. For example, if decision makers at Procter & Gamble were considering a price change for Tide detergent, they would be concerned about how the price change might influence sales of Cheer, Bold, and Gain.

Counting on the Games, Microsoft Prices Xbox Below Cost

Microsoft raised eyebrows when it used captive pricing for its Xbox 360 videogame system. According to an iSuppli survey, the parts used to make the 360 cost the company $470 prior to factoring in assembly; however, the system retails for $399—a $71 loss. Factoring in additional items such as power supply, cables, and controllers boosts the loss for each Xbox to $126. Microsoft has said that it may break even on the unit by 2007 with the help of sales on games for the Xbox, but in 2005, Microsoft's home entertainment division lost $391 million on sales of $3.3 billion. So why is the company producing a product on which it loses money?

For one thing, the cost of each game for the Xbox 360 has increased by $10 over the previous version. Also, multiplayer game functions cost $70 a year. Xbox users who network receive lots of online offers to buy more Microsoft products such as games and game add-ons. It appears that Microsoft expects to profit not only from game software and networking access but also from additional software buys made by those who want to make their Xboxes part of their home entertainment systems. The new Xbox system connects to a television and allows users to view photographs, play music, and more as well as playing games. Microsoft assumes that all the extra operating products will be purchased after the Xbox is purchased.

Bill Gates and the Microsoft team are confident that the Xbox will soon begin to turn a profit; time, of course, will tell. Let the games begin!

When marketers employ product-line pricing, they have several strategies from which to choose. These include captive pricing, premium pricing, bait pricing, and price lining.

captive pricing Pricing the basic product in a product line low while pricing related items higher

Captive Pricing. With **captive pricing,** the basic product in a product line is priced low while items required to operate or enhance it are priced higher. For example, a manufacturer of cameras and film may set the price of the cameras at a level low enough to attract customers but set the film price relatively high because to use the cameras, customers must continue to purchase film. Printer companies have used this pricing strategy providing relatively low-cost, low-margin printers and selling ink cartridges to generate significant profits. Gillette and other razor manufacturers know if you can sell a new razor handle to customers at little or no cost, you can generate revenues with blades. Likewise, Sirius and XM Satellite Radio cut the prices of receivers, which sell for as little as $30, to sell the annual radio service for about $150/year.[29]

premium pricing Pricing the highest-quality or most versatile products higher than other models in the product line

Premium Pricing. **Premium pricing** is often used when a product line contains several versions of the same product; the highest-quality products or those with the most versatility are given the highest prices. Other products in the line are priced to appeal to price-sensitive shoppers or to buyers who seek product-specific features.

Marketers that use a premium strategy often realize a significant portion of their profits from premium-priced products. Examples of product categories that commonly use premium pricing are small kitchen appliances, beer, ice cream, and cable television service.

bait pricing Pricing an item in a product line low with the intention of selling a higher-priced item in the line

price lining Setting a limited number of prices for selected groups or lines of merchandise

Bait Pricing. To attract customers, marketers may put a low price on one item in the product line with the intention of selling a higher-priced item in the line; this strategy is known as **bait pricing.** For example, a computer retailer might advertise its lowest-priced computer model, hoping that when customers come to the store they will purchase a higher-priced one. This strategy can facilitate sales of a line's higher-priced products. As long as a retailer has sufficient quantities of the advertised low-priced model available for sale, this strategy is considered acceptable. In contrast, *bait and switch* is an activity in which retailers have no intention of selling the bait product; they use the low price merely to entice customers into the store to sell them higher-priced products. Bait and switch is considered unethical, and is deemed a deceptive pricing practice by the Competition Act.

Price Lining. When an organization sets a limited number of prices for selected groups or lines of merchandise, it is using **price lining.** A retailer may have various styles and brands of similar-quality men's shirts that sell for $22 and another line of higher-quality shirts that sell for $39. Price lining simplifies customers' decision-making by holding constant one key variable in the final selection of style and brand within a line.

The basic assumption in price lining is that the demand for various groups or sets of products is inelastic. If the prices are attractive, customers will concentrate their purchases without responding to slight changes in price. Thus, a women's dress shop that carries dresses priced at $85, $55, and $35 may not attract many more sales with a drop to, say, $83,

Premium Pricing
Kohler uses unique ads to sell its high-end products.

figure 14.10

PRICE LINING

$85 price range

$55 price range

$35 price range

Price

Quantity

Demand

$53, and $33. The "space" between the price of $85 and $55, however, can stir changes in consumer response. With price lining, the demand curve looks like a series of steps, as shown in Figure 14.10.

Another type of price lining is subscription services. Cable or satellite TV subscribers choose different packages or groupings of channels with different prices. Likewise, subscribers to subscription DVD rental services such as Zip.ca or Netflix can choose a membership price based on the number of DVDs they want to receive at one time.

Psychological Pricing

Learning the price of a product is not always a pleasant experience for customers. It is sometimes surprising (as at a movie concession stand) and sometimes downright horrifying; most of us have been afflicted with "sticker shock." **Psychological pricing** attempts to influence a customer's perception of price to make a product's price more attractive. In this section, we consider several forms of psychological pricing: reference pricing, bundle pricing, multiple-unit pricing, everyday low prices (EDLP), odd-even pricing, customary pricing, and prestige pricing.

psychological pricing
Pricing that attempts to influence a customer's perception of price to make a product's price more attractive

reference pricing Pricing a product at a moderate level and positioning it next to a more expensive model or brand

bundle pricing Packaging together two or more complementary products and selling them at a single price

Reference Pricing. Reference pricing means pricing a product at a moderate level and positioning it next to a more expensive model or brand in the hope that the customer will use the higher price as an external reference price (i.e., a comparison price). Because of the comparison, the customer is expected to view the moderate price favourably. Reference pricing is based on the "isolation effect," meaning an alternative is less attractive when viewed by itself than when compared with other alternatives. When you go to the Future Shop to buy a DVD player, a moderately priced DVD player may appear especially attractive because it offers most of the important attributes of the more expensive alternatives on display and at a lower price. It is not unusual for an organization's moderately priced private brands to be positioned alongside more expensive, better-known manufacturer brands. On the other hand, many private store brands are raising their prices in an effort to boost these products' image.[30]

Bundle Pricing. Bundle pricing is packaging together two or more products, usually complementary ones, to be sold at a single price. Many fast-food restaurants, for example, offer combination meals at a price that is lower than the combined prices of each item priced separately. Most telephone and cable television providers bundle local telephone service, high-speed Internet access, and digital cable television for one monthly fee. To attract customers, the single bundled price is usually considerably less than the sum of the prices of the individual products. The opportunity to buy the bundled combination of products in a single transaction may be of value to the customer as well. Marketing research models suggest that marketers can develop heterogeneous bundles of products with optimal prices for different market segments.[31] Bundle pricing not only helps increase customer satisfaction; by bundling slow-moving products with products with higher turnover, an organization can also stimulate sales and increase revenues. It may also help build customer loyalty and reduce "churn," that is, losing dissatisfied customers to rivals.[32] Selling products as a package rather than individually may also result in cost savings. Bundle pricing is commonly used for banking and travel services, computers, and automobiles with option packages.

Some companies, however, are unbundling packages in favour of a more itemized approach sometimes called *a la carte pricing*. This approach gives customers the opportunity to pick and choose only the products they want without having to purchase additional products in the bundle that may not be right for their purposes.[33] For example, some television viewers have expressed a preference to subscribe only to their favourite channels rather than a predetermined package of channels.[34] At online music services such as iTunes and Rhapsody, customers can pick and choose individual songs to download instead of buying a complete CD.[35] Furthermore, with the help of the Internet, comparison shopping has become more convenient than ever, allowing customers to price items and create their own mixes. Nevertheless, bundle pricing continues to appeal to customers who prefer the convenience of a package.[36]

multiple-unit pricing
Packaging together two or more identical products and selling them at a single price

Multiple-Unit Pricing. Multiple-unit pricing occurs when two or more identical products are packaged together and sold at a single price. This normally results in a lower per-unit price than the price regularly charged. Multiple-unit pricing is commonly used for twin-packs of potato chips, four-packs of light bulbs, and six- and 12-packs of soft drinks. Customers benefit from the cost-saving and convenience this pricing strategy affords. A company may use multiple-unit pricing to attract new customers to its brands and, in some instances, to increase consumption of them. When customers buy in larger quantities, their consumption of the product may increase. For example, multiple-unit pricing may encourage a customer to buy larger quantities of snacks, which are likely to be consumed in higher volume at the point of consumption simply because they are available. However, this is not true for all products. For instance, greater availability at the point of consumption of light bulbs, bar soap, and table salt is not likely to increase usage.

Discount stores and especially warehouse clubs, such as Costco, are major users of multiple-unit pricing. For certain products in these stores, customers receive significant per-unit price reductions when they buy packages containing multiple units of the same product, such as an eight-pack of canned tuna fish.

everyday low prices (EDLP)
Pricing products low on a consistent basis

Everyday Low Prices (EDLP). To reduce or eliminate the use of frequent short-term price reductions, some organizations use an approach referred to as **everyday low prices (EDLP).** With EDLP, a marketer sets a low price for its products on a consistent basis rather than setting higher prices and frequently discounting them. Everyday low prices, though not deeply discounted, are set far enough below competitors' prices to make customers feel confident they are receiving a fair price. EDLP is employed by retailers such as Wal-Mart and manufacturers such as Procter & Gamble. A company that uses EDLP benefits from reduced losses from frequent markdowns, greater stability in sales, and decreased promotional costs.

A major problem with EDLP is that customers have mixed responses to it. Over the last several years, many marketers have inadvertently "trained" customers to expect and seek out deeply discounted prices. In some product categories, such as apparel, finding the deepest discount has become almost a national consumer sport. Thus, failure to provide deep discounts can be a problem for certain marketers.

odd-even pricing Ending the price with certain numbers to influence buyers' perceptions of the price or product

Odd-Even Pricing. Through **odd-even pricing**—ending the price with certain numbers—marketers try to influence buyers' perceptions of the price or the product. Odd pricing assumes more of a product will be sold at $99.95 than at $100. Theoretically, customers will think, or at least tell friends, that the product is a bargain—not $100, but $99 and change. Some claim, too, that certain types of customers are more attracted by odd prices than by even ones. Research has found a higher-than-expected demand associated with prices ending in 9 in print advertisements.[37] Odd prices are far more common today than even prices.

Even prices are often used to give a product an exclusive or upscale image. An even price supposedly will influence a customer to view the product as being a high-quality, premium brand. A shirt maker, for example, may print on a premium shirt package a suggested retail price of $42.00 instead of $41.95; the even price of the shirt is used to enhance its upscale image.

customary pricing Pricing on the basis of tradition

Customary Pricing. With **customary pricing,** certain goods are priced primarily on the basis of tradition. Recent economic uncertainties have made most prices fluctuate fairly widely, but the classic example of the customary, or traditional, price is the price of a candy bar. For years, a candy bar cost five cents. A new candy bar would have had to be something very special to sell for more than a nickel. This price was so sacred that rather than change it, manufacturers increased or decreased the size of the candy bar itself as chocolate prices fluctuated. Today, of course, the nickel candy bar has disappeared. However, most candy bars still sell at a consistent, but obviously higher, price. Thus, customary pricing remains the standard for this market.

prestige pricing Setting prices at an artificially high level to convey prestige or a quality image

Prestige Pricing. With **prestige pricing,** prices are set at an artificially high level to convey prestige or a quality image. Prestige pricing is used especially when buyers associate a higher price with higher quality. Typical product categories in which selected products are prestige priced include perfumes, liquor, jewelry, and cars. Although traditionally appliances have not been prestige priced, upscale appliances have appeared in recent years to capitalize on the willingness of some consumer segments to "trade up" for high-quality products. These consumers do not mind paying extra for a Sub-zero refrigerator, a Viking commercial range, or a Whirlpool Duet washer and dryer because these products offer high quality as well as a level of prestige. The Whirlpool Duet washer and dryer, for example, are priced about $1500–2000 more than conventional washers and dryers—but offer high performance, large loads, gentle cleaning, and energy efficiency.[38] If these producers lowered

professional pricing Fees set by people with great skill or experience in a particular field

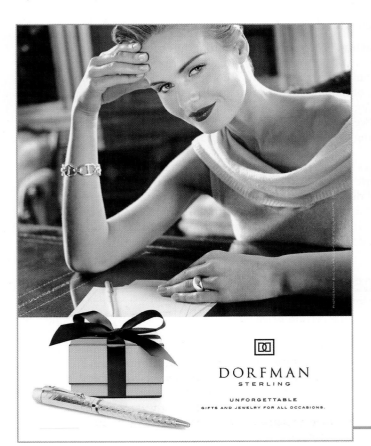

Prestige Pricing
Dorfman Jewelry uses prestige pricing.

their prices dramatically, the new prices would be inconsistent with the perceived high-quality images of their products. From gold clubs to handbags, prestige products are selling at record levels. For example, spending on pets has escalated, rivaling what some families spend on their children. Some consumers are willing to pay as much as $1000 for designer dogs like the "puggle," a beagle-pug mix, for their nice dispositions, intelligence, and smaller sizes.[39]

Professional Pricing

Professional pricing is used by people who have great skill or experience in a particular field. Professionals often believe their fees (prices) should not relate directly to the time and effort spent in specific cases; rather, a standard fee is charged regardless of the problems involved in performing the job. Some dentists' and lawyers' fees are prime examples, such as $75 for a checkup, $2000 for a root canal, and $995 for a divorce. Other professionals set prices in other ways. Like other marketers, professionals have costs associated with facilities, labour, insurance, equipment, and supplies. Certainly costs are considered when setting professional prices.

The concept of professional pricing carries the idea that professionals have an ethical responsibility not to overcharge customers. It also carries the responsibility to uphold the value of the profession by not undercutting the price of others. In some situations, a seller can charge customers a high price and continue to sell many units of the product. Medicine offers several examples. If a person with diabetes requires one insulin treatment per day to survive, she or he will probably buy that treatment whether its price is $1 or $10. In fact, the patient surely would purchase the treatment even if the price rose. In these situations, sellers could charge exorbitant fees. Drug companies claim that despite their positions of strength in this regard, they charge ethical prices rather than what the market will bear.

Promotional Pricing

As an ingredient in the marketing mix, price is often coordinated with promotion. The two variables are sometimes so closely interrelated that the pricing policy is promotion oriented. Types of promotional pricing include price leaders, special-event pricing, and comparison discounting.

Price Leaders. Sometimes a firm prices a few products below the usual markup, near cost, or below cost, which results in prices known as **price leaders** (also referred to as *loss-leaders*). This type of pricing is used most often in supermarkets and restaurants to attract customers by giving them especially low prices on a few items. Management hopes that sales of regularly priced products will more than offset the reduced revenues from the price leaders.

Special-Event Pricing. To increase sales volume, many organizations coordinate price with advertising or sales promotions for seasonal or special situations. **Special-event pricing** involves advertised sales or price cutting linked to a holiday, a season, or an event. If the pricing objective is survival, special sales events may be designed to generate the necessary operating capital. Special-event pricing entails coordination of production, scheduling, storage, and physical distribution. Whenever a sales lag occurs, special-event pricing is an alternative that marketers should consider.

Comparison Discounting. **Comparison discounting** sets the price of a product at a specific level and simultaneously compares it with a higher price. The higher price may be the product's previous price, the price of a competing brand, the product's price at another retail outlet, or a manufacturer's suggested retail price. Customers may find comparative discounting informative, and it can have a significant impact on their purchases. However, overuse of comparison pricing may reduce customers' internal reference prices, meaning they no longer believe the higher price is the regular or normal price.[40]

Some manufacturers' suggested retail prices are so high that very few products are actually sold at those prices. In such cases, comparison discounting would be deceptive. An example of deceptive comparison discounting occurred when a major retailer put 93 percent of its power tools on sale, with discounts ranging from 10 to 40 percent. The retailer's frequent price reductions meant the tools sold at sale prices most of the year. Thus, comparisons with regular prices were deemed to be deceptive.

price leader A product priced below the usual markup, near cost, or below cost

special-event pricing Advertised sales or price cutting linked to a holiday, a season, or an event

comparison discounting Setting a price at a specific level and comparing it with a higher price

Determination of a Specific Price

A pricing strategy will yield a certain price. However, this price may need refinement to make it consistent with pricing practices in a particular market or industry. When Blockbuster eliminated late fees for movie rentals, it probably did not anticipate that revenue would fall by nearly 10 percent. Given increasing competition from online movie rental and pay-per-view services, the company will need to evaluate its overall pricing strategy in light of decreased profitability.[41]

Pricing strategies should help in setting a final price. If they are to do so, marketers must establish pricing objectives; have considerable knowledge about target market customers; and determine demand, price elasticity, costs, and competitive factors. Also, the way pricing is used in the marketing mix will affect the final price.

In the absence of government price controls, pricing remains a flexible and convenient way to adjust the marketing mix. In many situations, prices can be adjusted quickly—over a few days or even in minutes. Such flexibility is unique to this component of the marketing mix.

Pricing for Business Markets

Business markets consist of individuals and organizations that purchase products for resale, for use in their own operations, or for producing other products. Establishing prices for this category of buyers sometimes differs from setting prices for consumers. Differences in the size of purchases, geographic factors, and transportation considerations require sellers to adjust prices. In this section, we discuss several issues unique to the pricing of business products, including discounts, geographic pricing, and transfer pricing.

Price Discounting

Producers commonly provide intermediaries with discounts, or reductions, from list prices. Although many types of discounts exist, they usually fall into one of five categories: trade, quantity, cash, seasonal, and allowance. Table 14.3 summarizes some reasons to use each type of discount and provides examples.

Geographic Pricing

geographic pricing Reductions for transportation costs or other costs associated with the physical distance between buyer and seller

Geographic pricing involves reductions for transportation costs or other costs associated with the physical distance between buyer and seller. Prices may be quoted as F.O.B. (free-on-board) factory or destination. An *F.O.B. factory* price indicates the price of the merchandise at the factory, before it is loaded onto the carrier, and thus

table 14.3	DISCOUNTS USED FOR BUSINESS MARKETS	
Type	**Reasons for Use**	**Examples**
Trade (functional)	To attract and keep effective resellers by compensating them for performing certain functions, such as transportation, warehousing, selling, and providing credit	A university bookstore pays about one-third less for a new textbook than the retail price a student pays
Quantity	To encourage customers to buy large quantities when making purchases and, in the case of cumulative discounts, to encourage customer loyalty	Large department store chains purchase some women's apparel at lower prices than do individually owned specialty stores
Cash	To reduce expenses associated with accounts receivable and collection by encouraging prompt payment of accounts	Numerous companies serving business markets allow a two percent discount if an account is paid within 10 days
Seasonal	To allow a marketer to use resources more efficiently by stimulating sales during off-peak periods	Florida hotels provide companies holding national and regional sales meetings with deeply discounted accommodations during the summer months
Allowance	In the case of a trade-in allowance, to assist the buyer in making the purchase and potentially earn a profit on the resale of used equipment; in the case of a promotional allowance, to ensure that dealers participate in advertising and sales support programs	A farm equipment dealer takes a farmer's used tractor as a trade-in on a new one\nNabisco pays a promotional allowance to a supermarket for setting up and maintaining a large, end-of-aisle display for a two-week period

excludes transportation costs. The buyer must pay for shipping. An *F.O.B. destination* price means the producer absorbs the costs of shipping the merchandise to the customer. This policy may be used to attract distant customers. Although F.O.B. pricing is an easy way to price products, it is sometimes difficult to administer, especially when a firm has a wide product mix or when customers are widely dispersed. Because customers will want to know about the most economical method of shipping, the seller must be informed about shipping rates.

To avoid the problems involved in charging different prices to each customer, *uniform geographic pricing,* sometimes called *postage-stamp pricing,* may be used. The same price is charged to all customers regardless of geographic location, and the price is based on average shipping costs for all customers. Gasoline, paper products, and office equipment are often priced on a uniform basis.

Zone pricing sets uniform prices for each of several major geographic zones; as the transportation costs across zones increase, so do the prices. For example, an Alberta manufacturer's prices may be higher for buyers in Atlantic Canada.

When the seller absorbs all or part of the actual freight costs, *freight absorption pricing* is being used. The seller might choose this method because it wishes to do business with a particular customer or to get more business; more business will cause the average cost to fall and counterbalance the extra freight cost. This strategy is used to improve market penetration and to retain a hold in an increasingly competitive market.

Transfer Pricing

transfer pricing Prices charged in sales between an organization's units

Transfer pricing occurs when one unit in an organization sells a product to another unit. Care must be taken by multinationals when setting transfer prices charged to subsidiaries because of the possible tax implications and product dumping regulations established to protect domestic markets. The price is determined by one of the following methods:

- *Actual full cost:* calculated by dividing all fixed and variable expenses for a period into the number of units produced

- *Standard full cost:* calculated based on what it would cost to produce the goods at full plant capacity

- *Cost plus investment:* calculated as full cost plus the cost of a portion of the selling unit's assets used for internal needs

- *Market-based cost:* calculated at the market price less a small discount to reflect the lack of sales effort and other expenses

The choice of transfer pricing method depends on the company's management strategy and the nature of the units' interaction. An organization must also ensure that transfer pricing is fair to all units involved in the transactions.

SUMMARY

Price is the value exchanged for products in marketing transactions. Price is not always money paid; barter, the trading of products, is the oldest form of exchange. Price is a key element in the marketing mix because it relates directly to generation of total revenue. The profit factor can be determined mathematically by multiplying price by quantity sold to get total revenue and then subtracting total costs. Price is the only variable in the marketing mix that can be adjusted quickly and easily to respond to changes in the external environment.

A product offering can compete on either a price or a non-price basis. Price competition emphasizes price as the product differential. Prices fluctuate frequently, and price competition among sellers is aggressive. Non-price competition emphasizes product differentiation through distinctive features, service, product quality, or other factors. Establishing brand loyalty by using non-price competition works best when the product can be physically differentiated and the customer can recognize these differences.

An organization must determine the demand for its product. The classic demand curve is a graph of the quantity of products expected to be sold at various prices if other factors hold constant. It illustrates that as price falls, the quantity demanded usually increases. However, for prestige products, there is a direct positive relationship between price and quantity demanded: demand increases as price increases. Next, price elasticity of demand, the percentage change in quantity demanded relative to a given percentage change in price, must be determined. If demand is elastic, a change in price causes an opposite change in total revenue. Inelastic demand results in a parallel change in total revenue when a product's price is changed.

Analysis of demand, cost, and profit relationships can be accomplished through marginal analysis or break-even analysis. Marginal analysis examines what happens to a firm's costs and revenues when production (or sales volume) is changed by one unit. Marginal analysis is only a model; it offers little help in pricing new products before costs and revenues are established.

Break-even analysis, determining the number of units that must be sold to break even, is important in setting price. The point at which the costs of production equal the revenue from selling the product is the break-even point. To use break-even analysis effectively, a marketer should determine the break-even point for each of several alternative prices. This makes it possible to compare the effects on total revenue, total costs, and the break-even point for each price under consideration. However, this approach assumes the quantity demanded is basically fixed and the major task is to set prices to recover costs.

Eight factors enter into price decision making: organizational and marketing objectives, pricing objectives, costs, other marketing mix variables, channel member expectations, customer interpretation and response, competition, and legal and regulatory issues. When setting prices, marketers should make decisions consistent with the organization's goals and mission. Pricing objectives heavily influence price-setting decisions. Most marketers view a product's cost as the floor below which a product cannot be priced. Because of the interrelationship among the marketing mix variables, price can affect product, promotion, and distribution decisions. The revenue channel members expect for their functions must also be considered when making price decisions.

Buyers' perceptions of price vary. Some consumer segments are sensitive to price, but others may not be. Thus, before determining price, a marketer needs to be aware of its importance to the target market. Knowledge of the prices charged for competing brands is essential to allow the firm to adjust its prices relative to competitors'. Government regulations and legislation also influence pricing decisions. Provincial governments may regulate prices on such products as gasoline, insurance, dairy goods, and electricity. The Competition Act is the federal legislation that has had a strong impact on pricing decisions, particularly in areas of price fixing, price discrimination, deceptive pricing, resale price maintenance, and predatory pricing.

The six stages in the process of setting prices are (1) developing pricing objectives, (2) assessing the target market's evaluation of price, (3) evaluating competitors' prices, (4) choosing a basis for pricing, (5) selecting a pricing strategy, and (6) determining a specific price.

The three major dimensions on which prices can be based are cost, demand, and competition. When using cost-based pricing, the firm determines price by adding a dollar amount or percentage to the cost of the product. Two common cost-based pricing methods are cost-plus and markup pricing. Demand-based pricing is based on the level of demand for the product. To use this method, a marketer must be able to estimate the amounts of a product buyers will demand at different prices. Demand-based pricing results in a high price when demand for a product is strong and a low price when demand is weak. In the case of competition-based pricing, costs and revenues are secondary to competitors' prices.

A pricing strategy is an approach or a course of action designed to achieve pricing and marketing objectives. Pricing strategies help marketers solve the practical problems of establishing prices. The most common pricing strategies are differential pricing (negotiated pricing, secondary-market pricing, periodic discounting, and random discounting), new-product pricing (price skimming and penetration pricing), product-line pricing (captive pricing, premium pricing, bait pricing, and price lining), psychological pricing (reference pricing, bundle pricing, multiple-unit pricing, everyday low prices, odd-even pricing, customary pricing, and prestige pricing), professional pricing, and promotional pricing (price leaders, special-event pricing, and comparison discounting).

Unlike consumers, business buyers purchase products for resale, for use in their own operations, or for producing other products. When adjusting prices, business sellers consider the size of the purchase, geographic factors, and transportation requirements. Producers commonly provide discounts off list prices to intermediaries. The categories of discounts include trade, quantity, cash, seasonal, and allowance.

Geographic pricing involves reductions for transportation costs or other costs associated with the physical distance between buyer and seller. With an F.O.B. factory price, the buyer pays for shipping from the factory. An F.O.B. destination price means the producer pays for shipping; this is the easiest way to price products, but it is difficult to administer. When the seller charges a fixed average cost for transportation, it is using uniform geographic pricing. Zone prices are uniform within major geographic zones; they increase by zone as transportation costs increase. Freight absorption pricing occurs when a seller absorbs all or part of the freight costs.

Please visit the student website at **www.hmco.ca/marketing** for ACE Self-Test questions that will help you prepare for exams.

IMPORTANT TERMS

Price
Price competition
Non-price competition
Demand curve
Price elasticity of demand
Fixed costs
Variable costs
Total cost
Marginal cost (MC)
Marginal revenue (MR)
Break-even point
Value conscious

Price conscious
Prestige sensitive
Pricing objectives
Cost-based pricing
Cost-plus pricing
Markup pricing
Demand-based pricing
Competition-based pricing
Differential pricing
Negotiated pricing
Secondary-market pricing
Periodic discounting

Random discounting
Price skimming
Penetration pricing
Product-line pricing
Captive pricing
Premium pricing
Bait pricing
Price lining
Psychological pricing
Reference pricing
Bundle pricing
Multiple-unit pricing

Everyday low prices
   (EDLP)
Odd-even pricing
Customary pricing
Prestige pricing
Professional pricing
Price leader
Special-event pricing
Comparison discounting
Geographic pricing
Transfer pricing

DISCUSSION & REVIEW QUESTIONS

1. Why are pricing decisions important to an organization?

2. Compare and contrast price and non-price competition. Describe the conditions under which each form works best.

3. List the characteristics of products that have inelastic demand, and give several examples of such products.

4. Chambers Company has just gathered estimates for conducting a break-even analysis for a new product. Variable costs are $7 a unit. The additional plant will cost $48 000. The new product will be charged $18 000 a year for its share of general overhead. Advertising expenditures will be $80 000, and $55 000 will be spent on distribution. If the product sells for $12, what is the break-even point in units? What is the break-even point in dollar sales volume?

5. In what ways do other marketing mix variables affect pricing decisions?

6. How do legal and regulatory forces influence pricing decisions?

7. Identify the six stages in the process of establishing prices.

8. Why must marketing objectives and pricing objectives be considered when making pricing decisions?

9. Under what conditions is cost-plus pricing most appropriate?

10. What is differential pricing? In what ways can it be achieved?

11. For what types of products would price skimming be most appropriate? For what types of products would penetration pricing be more effective?

12. Why do customers associate price with quality? When should prestige pricing be used?

13. Are price leaders a realistic approach to pricing? Explain your answer.

APPLICATION QUESTIONS

1. Customers' interpretations and responses regarding a product and its price are an important influence on marketers' pricing decisions. Perceptions of price are affected by the degree to which a customer is value conscious, price conscious, or prestige sensitive. Discuss how value consciousness, price consciousness, and prestige sensitivity influence the buying decision process for the following products:

   a. A new house
   b. Weekly groceries for a family of five
   c. An airline ticket
   d. A soft drink from a vending machine

2. Price skimming and penetration pricing are strategies commonly used to set the base price of a new product.

Which strategy is more appropriate for the following products? Explain.

   a. Short airline flights between cities in Ontario
   b. A DVD player
   c. A backpack or book bag with a lifetime warranty
   d. Season tickets for a newly franchised NHL hockey team

3. Price lining is used to set a limited number of prices for selected lines of merchandise. Visit a few local retail stores to find examples of price lining. For what types of products and stores is this practice most common? For what types of products and stores is price lining not typical or feasible?

globalEDGE™

1. A fundamental component of the price of newsprint in the world market is its supply and demand. At the national level, information can typically be gathered based on a country's imports and exports. Using the Food and Agriculture Organization of the United Nations (FAO) website as a resource devoted to food and agriculture, find Canadian, Mexican, and U.S. trade statistics concerning the newsprint industry. Use the search term "food and agriculture" at **http://globaledge.msu.edu/ibrd** or **http://globaledge.msu.edu/ibrd/ibrd.asp** to reach the FAO website. Then click on the Forestry link and then the "Pulp, Paper & Paperboard" link. Holding the CTRL key down for multiple choices in the same information boxes, choose Canada, Mexico, and the U.S. as countries, Newsprint as the category, Imports-Qty and Exports-Qty as the points of analysis, and the most recent year available as the year of analysis. From the three countries surveyed, which could be said to increase the price of newsprint in the world market? Which might decrease its price?

2. Business strategists and economists sometimes use a consumer price index (CPI) in their decision models. In fact, some organizations perform a comparison across countries to inform the public of consumer pricing trends. A report titled "Consumer Price Indices (CPI) for OECD Countries" should prove helpful in answering this question. Access this report by using the search term "comparison across countries" at **http://globaledge.msu.edu/ibrd** or **http://globaledge.msu.edu/ibrd/ibrd.asp**. Once you reach the OECD webpage, click on Consumer Price Indices (CPI) for OECD Countries. What is a CPI generally used to measure?

INTERNET Exercise

Visit **www.prideferrell.com** for resources to help you master the material in this chapter, plus materials that will help you expand your marketing knowledge, including internet exercise updates, ACE self-tests, hotlinks to companies featured in this chapter, and much more.

Rogers

Rogers has attempted to position itself as a low-cost, one-stop shop for all your phone, Internet, and television services. Rogers offers a comprehensive website to assist in pricing, scheduling, and bundling your choice of services. Visit this site at **www.shoprogers.com.**

1. How many different home phone plans and features are available in your city?
2. What type of pricing strategies is Rogers using for its services?
3. On a scale of one to 10, with 10 being excellent, how would you rate Rogers' website? Explain your rating.

Case 14.1   GM: Reducing Reliance on Rebates

Automakers have been using incentives to attract customers since 1912, when Henry Ford gave rebate checks to Model T buyers. The idea of incentives has remained popular throughout the years, although the offers themselves have varied, ranging from lease promotions and special financing offers to cash rebates. Incentives are a form of random discounting, temporary reductions of prices on an unsystematic basis; however, they have become almost ubiquitous in promoting sales of automobiles. Although incentives are credited with increasing sales and market share, automakers are now being criticized for abusing incentives, leading to decreased profits and poor brand image. The growing reliance on sales, rebates, and zero percent financing has made it difficult to wean consumers off incentives.

When General Motors introduced aggressive cash rebates and zero percent financing to boost sales after the attacks of September 11, 2001, the company never expected to keep riding on rebates for more than four years. GM executives credit the incentive program with providing many benefits for the company, including preserving market share and keeping GM's factories running. The latter is important because GM's labour costs are relatively fixed due to its contract with the United Auto Workers Union, which requires the firm to pay unemployment benefits equal to 95 percent of normal pay to any laid-off workers. Thus, even if the company cuts production, its labour cost would remain the same. GM has therefore chosen to use incentives to equalize sales and production rather than cutting production to meet demand. To understand General Motors' fear of reducing incentives, it is constructive to know that every percentage point of market share translates into millions of dollars in profit, according to Morgan Stanley.

Although GM has made several attempts to cut back on incentives (for example, launching the Chevrolet Cobalt with rebates no larger than $1500, compared with the $4000 rebate offered on the Chevrolet Cavalier that the Cobalt replaced), consumers have failed to cooperate. Between June and September 2005, GM extended its "employee discount" to every customer buying a new car or truck. However, the employee-discount promotion was quickly emulated by rivals Ford Motor and DaimlerChrysler (and soon after, even by marketers in other industries). But when the automakers ended the popular discount, vehicle sales hit the brakes. At GM, sales dove 26 percent in the month after the promotion ended. Thus, while the discounts gave all three automakers their third highest sales months in history, they did not help their bottom lines. The vice president of GM's North American marketing later admitted the promotion might have been a mistake.

The problem with incentives is that they erode profit. For example, in 2005 General Motors lost $5 billion on global auto sales, compared to 2002 when it netted $2.6 billion. Rebates may also give the impression of operating in a distressed atmosphere. There is little doubt that large rebates may suggest to consumers that a product's quality and reliability are not up to par. Because this concept is relative, a company that offers deep discounts may give consumers the impression of less quality. On the other hand, it would be desirable to use product design, styling, or other product features that would enhance and maintain a high-quality concept of the firm's product relative to competitive brands. Rebates and the cost of long-term loans can also undermine the resale value of an automaker's vehicles.

Alternatives to direct consumer incentives include discounting to dealers, who can then make decisions about how much of the discounts to pass along to consumers. Another approach is non-price competition, using promotions that encourage consumers to visit a dealership. Another approach is to build more niche cars that generate greater profits. Some "must-have" models include the Chevy SSR Pickup, Pontiac GTO, and Cadillac XLR. Volkswagen is also applying this approach.

An important question for all automobile companies is how to go about reducing incentives. Because incentive-driven sales persuaded many consumers to replace their cars during the economic downturn at the beginning of the century, little pent-up demand remains for new vehicles. Worse, consumers seem to have become addicted to incentives and unwilling to make a purchase without them. Volkswagen plans to "stick to its guns" and attempt to break consumers of the incentive habit. The company's new Touareg SUV is a good example of a unique, high-quality offering that can be sold at sticker price with few deals.

GM is now redesigning 90 percent of its passenger car lineup over the next three years in the hope of being able to compete on non-price attributes. It is also introducing value pricing for many models, eliminating the practice of haggling with dealers. However, in the face of sluggish sales during a period of rising fuel prices, GM and its rivals were forced to slash prices on sport-utility vehicles and to offer incentives such as free gas or zero percent financing to keep cars moving off showroom lots. The value of marketing in this industry is illustrated by the effectiveness of price incentives to manage demand. The challenge is to find other promotional methods that can effectively communicate the benefits and value of GM's products.[42]

Questions for Discussion

1. What pricing objectives does General Motors seem to be using? How do these objectives help dictate the firm's use of periodic discounting and incentives?
2. What type of pricing strategy is GM using?
3. What risks does an automaker such as Volkswagen, Toyota, or BMW face in going against the industry by avoiding price incentives?

Strategic Case 6   Direct Selling Mistine Cosmetics in Thailand

Better Way (Thailand) Company Limited was founded in 1988 by Thailand's "king of direct selling," Dr. Amornthep Deerojanawong, and Boonyakiat Chokwatana. Dr. Amornthep had worked as a medical doctor at Avon in Thailand, where he got the idea to start his own Thai-based cosmetics company. The company has become highly successful in Thailand using direct selling to launch its Mistine cosmetic brand. Although Thai people were not very familiar with the direct selling of cosmetics, within six years Mistine had become the leader in the consumer cosmetics market in Thailand, a market worth an estimated 25 billion baht (approximately $635 million) and growing at a rate of five to 10 percent annually.

Better Way began with fewer than 100 products. Today, the company markets more than 4000 makeup, skin-care, fragrance, and personal-care products. In addition, the company operates one retail store on the outskirts of Bangkok. Its warehouse is considered the largest cosmetics depot in Southeast Asia, with 1170 regular employees.

The company primarily targets women who have a high school, occupational certificate level, or high occupational certificate level of education and have a monthly income of about $125–200, as well as working women who have a monthly income of about $200–300. Mistine's core target market, which accounts for 70–80 percent of its total revenues, includes housewives with low-to-medium incomes. The company is expanding its customer base by targeting working people, men, and vocational school students, especially working people who have high purchasing power. There are now more than 420 000 customers nationwide.

Mistine positions itself as an Asian company marketing products developed and formulated specifically for the Asian woman. They are designed to blend well with the Asian skin tone and complexion. They are also made to better suit the warmer, more humid climate of the Asian region so that the product stays on longer and looks fresher.

Mistine's Marketing Activities

Mistine products are manufactured by the best quality cosmetics manufacturers all over the world. An experienced production team develops hundreds of new and unique products each year, with at least two to three new products launched each month.

Every Mistine product is thoroughly inspected and tested before being delivered to the warehouse. Customers can be assured that they will receive the highest quality products, and, indeed, Mistine will replace or offer a full refund for any product for which a customer is not completely happy. "Our customer's satisfaction is what we care about most" is one of Mistine's slogans, which helps it to maintain its leadership in a competitive market.

Direct selling companies normally depend on word of mouth to develop brand awareness, recruit salespersons, and encourage product purchases. Better Way decided to do things differently by being the first direct selling company in Thailand to use mass media advertising. The company's continuous and award-winning advertising campaigns have been used to build brand image and positioning in the customers' minds. Many products are promoted by popular celebrities.

Sales Force Characteristics

Mistine's direct-sales system is a simple, single-level marketing (SLM) approach. The company recruits district managers who in turn recruit as many salespersons as they can manage. This approach meshes well with Thai culture and lifestyle. The benefit of this approach is that each salesperson earns full commission without having to share his or her earnings with others. Thus the more sales a salesperson makes, the more income he or she receives.

The company welcomes anyone—male or female—who has some free time on their hands and would like to earn money, make new friends, and develop their self-confidence to become a salesperson. Salespersons can plan their own schedules and routes in order to reach sales objectives and obtain rewards. If a salesperson achieves no sales within three selling periods, then he or she is automatically terminated. The annual turnover rate for the sales force is about 200 percent because, for most salespersons, selling Mistine products is a second job. Moreover, most of the salespersons do not have any sales experience. Although they receive up to 25–30 percent commission, if they are not determined and committed, they leave. Generally, about 70 percent are terminated within six selling periods.

Sales goals are set according to the sales promotion plans and advertising budget spent for a particular distribution period. The company offers major incentives, such as trips to Europe and gold jewelry, to all district managers who achieve sales goals.

With the belief that the salespersons can live without Mistine but Mistine cannot live without the salespersons, several programs have been launched to create employee loyalty to the company. Internal relationship programs such as the "Mistine Thank-You Concert" were organized in nine provinces around Thailand, aimed at gathering Mistine salespersons together as a family, as well as at showing that the company cares about and is responsible for its employees. The company also provides life insurance with coverage of $50 000 for each salesperson, which is an unusual benefit in Thailand. Non-monetary rewards and recognition incentives for salespersons include crystal trophies and photos in the hall of fame.

Improving Sales Performance

In direct sales, the length of a selling period is crucial and shapes business operations. Normally, direct selling companies operate three-week selling periods, totaling 18 periods within a year. Mistine, however, found that most salespersons do not actually start selling products to customers until the last week of a selling period, meaning that the first two weeks are essentially wasted. Consequently, management decided to reduce the selling period to two weeks, resulting in 26 selling periods per year. This dramatic change was implemented despite objections. Ultimately, sales increased by 80 percent over the previous year, and salespersons became more active in selling the products.

These impressive sales increases occurred because of the reduced selling cycles and the positive attitude fostered throughout the company toward salespersons. One motto that employees of all levels still pledge to this day is "We will make Mistine No. 1."

Growth and Expansion

Despite Mistine's great success with direct cosmetic sales, the company continues to strategize to maintain its market share amidst intense competition. To achieve its goals, the firm intends to continue recruiting new salespersons in order to increase sales and expand its marketing coverage area. It has increased its local promotion budget by 50 percent and developed 400 new product items to maintain its leading position. After observing that the sales of men's personal care products have been increasing in department stores, Better Way launched nine men's products, including shampoo, deodorant, day and night cream, and sun protection lotion.

The company has formed a strategic alliance with DTAC, a leading telecommunications service provider, under the name "Mistine Corporate Solution," or MCS, which enables Mistine salespersons to call the 24-hour Mistine Call Center for free when using the DTAC cellphone network system. This innovative direct-selling tool will help the salespersons in ordering products, requesting product information, and asking about promotions. This strategic alliance will help the company cut costs of about $25 000 per month on phone charges.

To penetrate the teenage market segment, Mistine partnered with RS Promotions and employed D2B, an RS Promotions "boy band" popular among Thai teens, to present Mistine's Pink Magic lipstick. The campaign helped boost sales to teens by as much as 10 percent.

Recently Mistine has an aggressive strategy in its products and marketing communication in both domestic and international markets. The company opened manufacturing sites in the Philippines and Vietnam. Mistine has successfully offered products in Cambodia, Laos, Thailand and China. Moreover, its advertising campaigns that use popular actresses who are well known to people in those countries support its sales. Hungary and Russia are potential markets in the future.[43]

Questions for Discussion

1. Is it possible that having a retail outlet creates channel conflict? Explain.
2. From a customer's standpoint, what are the advantages or disadvantages of having a retail outlet? What about from the company's standpoint?
3. How would Mistine's use of mass media advertising influence the performance of its sales force?
4. Should Mistine's management expect to change marketing strategies when the company enters new international markets such as Hungary and Russia? Explain.
5. In what ways does the single-level direct-selling approach affect its turnover rates? Explain.

part 7

Distribution Decisions

Developing products that satisfy customers is important, but it is not enough to guarantee successful marketing strategies. Products must also be available in adequate quantities in accessible locations at the times when customers desire them. **Part Seven** deals with the distribution of products and the marketing channels and institutions that help make products available. **Chapter 15** discusses the structure and functions of marketing channels and presents an overview of institutions that make up these channels, as well as the decisions and activities associated with the physical distribution of products, such as order processing, materials handling, warehousing, inventory management, and transportation. **Chapter 16** analyzes the types of wholesalers and their functions, as well as focusing on retailing and direct marketing.

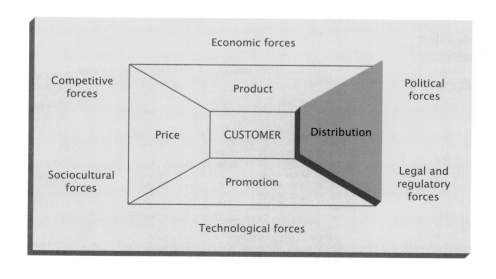

CHAPTER 15

Marketing Channels, Supply Chain Management, and Physical Distribution

Radio Shack's Channel Challenge

Radio Shack believes in channel integration and cooperation. The electronics specialty retailer operates 6000 company-owned stores, regional distribution centres, and a shopping website. Radio Shack also has 800 stores in Mexico, and it has recently closed its Canadian stores.

InterTAN, the firm that owned Radio Shack, was sold to Circuit City, the large U.S. electronics retailer, in 2004. Almost immediately, Radio Shack sued InterTAN for violating an agreement to use the Radio Shack name brand across Canada. Despite InterTAN's insistence that they had until 2010 to change the brand, courts ruled that InterTan would have to relinquish the Radio Shack brand name. The stores were then rebranded as The Source by Circuit City. However, that did not solve the dilemma for InterTAN.

Radio Shack had maintained a handful of stores in Canada under the Radio Shack banner. In January 2007, Radio Shack made the decision to close its Canadian stores in order to focus all of its resources on the highly competitive U.S. market.

Radio Shack's retail stores sell everything from high-end electronic products such as HDTVs, digital cameras, cell phones, and satellite navigational devices to low-end items like batteries, plugs, and connectors. The company faces competition from discounters such as Wal-Mart and Target as well as a growing range of stores owned by wireless service providers such as Verizon, AT&T, and T-Mobile.

To maintain its position in the U.S. wireless market, Radio Shack has agreements to operate wireless kiosks in Sam's Warehouse Club locations and a growing network of Sprint branded kiosks in shopping malls.

Under the agreements, the Radio Shack name cannot be used at these kiosk locations, and there is no brand tie-in with the retail stores. Nonetheless, Radio Shack sees benefits in the arrangements. For one, Radio Shack's marketers believe the company will make incremental sales and profits through these partnerships that it would not have otherwise made since these customers were not shopping at Radio Shack stores.

In general then, when you consider that the company's website is in competition with all of these retail outlets, it is easy to see why maintaining marketing channel harmony may be challenging to Radio Shack.

Unfortunately, even Circuit City has experienced problems in the competitive Canadian market. In February 2007 the company announced that it would be closing 62 of its 800 Canadian outlets with the loss of 300 full- and part-time jobs. Competitive pressures also impacted Circuit City south of the border, with the closure of seven superstores and one distribution centre. Losses were blamed on slow sales for flat panel television sets, a need to tighten the financial structure of the organization, as well as the need to refocus and build sales across the organization.[1] ■

distribution The activities that make products available to customers when and where they want to purchase them

Radio Shack expanded its operations to serve a greater number of customers through cost effective and efficient distribution practices. Decisions being made by Radio Shack marketers relate to the **distribution** component of the marketing mix, which focuses on the decisions and actions involved in making products available to customers when and where they want to purchase them. Choosing which channels of distribution to use is a major decision in the development of marketing strategies.

In this chapter, we focus on marketing channels. First, we discuss the nature of marketing channels and the need for intermediaries and then analyze the primary functions they perform. Next, we outline the types of marketing channels, discuss how they are selected, and explore how marketers determine the appropriate intensity of market coverage for a product. We then consider supply chain management, including behavioural patterns within marketing channels and forms of channel integration. Finally, we look at several legal issues affecting channel management.

The Nature of Marketing Channels

marketing channel A group of individuals and organizations that direct the flow of products from producers to customers

A **marketing channel** (also called a *channel of distribution* or *distribution channel*) is a group of individuals and organizations that direct the flow of products from producers to customers. The major role of marketing channels is to make products available at the right time at the right place in the right quantities. Providing customer satisfaction should be the driving force behind marketing channel decisions. Buyers' needs and behaviour are therefore important concerns of channel members.

Some marketing channels are direct, meaning that the product goes directly from the producer to customer. For example, when a customer orders a computer from Dell, this product is sent from the manufacturer to the customer. Most channels, however, have marketing intermediaries. A **marketing intermediary** (or *middleman*) links producers to other intermediaries or to ultimate consumers through contractual arrangements or through the purchase and reselling of products. Marketing intermediaries perform the activities described in Table 15.1. They also play key roles in customer relationship management, not only through their distribution activities but also by maintaining databases and information systems to help all members of the marketing channel maintain effective customer relationships. For example, eBay serves as a marketing intermediary between Internet sellers and buyers. eBay not only provides a forum for these exchanges, but it also keeps an extensive database of members' rankings to facilitate relationships among eBay channel members.[2]

marketing intermediary A middleman linking producers to other middlemen or ultimate consumers through contractual arrangements or through the purchase and resale of products

table 15.1	MARKETING CHANNEL ACTIVITIES PERFORMED BY INTERMEDIARIES
Category of Marketing Activities	**Possible Activities Required**
Marketing information	Analyze sales data and other information in databases and information systems Perform or commission marketing research
Marketing management	Establish strategic plans for developing customer relationships and organizational productivity
Facilitating exchanges	Choose product assortments that match the needs of customers Cooperate with channel members to develop partnerships
Promotion	Set promotional objectives Coordinate advertising, personal selling, sales promotion, publicity, and packaging
Price	Establish pricing policies and terms of sales
Physical distribution	Manage transportation, warehousing, materials handling, inventory control, and communication

Wholesalers and retailers are examples of intermediaries. Wholesalers buy and resell products to other wholesalers, to retailers, and to industrial customers. Retailers purchase products and resell them to ultimate consumers. For example, your local supermarket probably purchased the Tylenol or Advil on its shelves from a wholesaler, which purchased that product, along with other over-the-counter and prescription drugs, from manufacturers such as McNeil Consumer Labs and Whitehall-Robins. Chapters 16 and 17 discuss the functions of wholesalers and retailers in marketing channels in greater detail.

Marketing channel members share certain significant characteristics. Each member has different responsibilities within the overall structure of the channel. Mutual profit and success for channel members are attained most readily when channel members cooperate to deliver satisfying products to customers.

Although distribution decisions need not precede other marketing decisions, they are a powerful influence on the rest of the marketing mix. Channel decisions are critical because they determine a product's market presence and the product's accessibility to buyers. For example, because small businesses are more likely to purchase computers from office supply stores such as Staples or warehouse clubs such as Costco, computer companies may be at a disadvantage without distribution through these outlets. Channel decisions have additional strategic significance be-

Facilitating the Creation of Utility

Organizations like Capgemini, which delivers outsourcing services, help businesses create utility

COLLABORATIVE BUSINESS EXPERIENCE

BUSINESS

TOGETHER. When a single word makes all the difference.

Transforming your enterprise – whether you're making big or small changes – is never easy. Experience has shown us that if we define measurable objectives and set realistic schedules **together**, build joint teams, and above all, anticipate and mitigate risks **together**, then we improve our chances. Add to that motivation and commitment of over 60,000 people around the world and the knowledge and experience we share with you daily, and the result is faster, and more tangible success that lasts.

Together. One word that captures the difference between typical business practice and Capgemini's unique branded approach to delivering Consulting, Technology and Outsourcing Services - the Collaborative Business Experience.

Let's create a Collaborative Business Experience – together.

www.us.capgemini.com

Capgemini
CONSULTING.TECHNOLOGY.OUTSOURCING

cause they entail long-term commitments. Thus, it is usually easier to change prices or promotional strategies than to change marketing channels.

Marketing channels serve many functions, including creating utility and facilitating exchange efficiencies. Although some of these functions may be performed by a single channel member, most functions are accomplished through both independent and joint efforts of channel members. When managed effectively, the relationships among channel members can also form supply chains that benefit all members of the channel, including the ultimate consumer.

Marketing Channels Create Utility

Marketing channels create three types of utility: time, place, and possession. *Time utility* is having products available when customers want them. *Place utility* is created by making products available in locations where customers wish to purchase them. *Possession utility* means customers have access to the product to use or store for future use. Possession utility can occur through ownership or through arrangements that give the customer the right to use the product, such as a lease or rental agreement. Channel members sometimes create utility by assembling, preparing, or otherwise refining the product to suit individual customer needs.

Marketing Channels Facilitate Exchange Efficiencies

Marketing intermediaries can reduce the costs of exchanges by efficiently performing certain services or functions. Even if producers and buyers are located in the same city, exchanges have associated costs. As Figure 15.1 shows, when four buyers seek products from four producers, 16 transactions are possible. If one intermediary serves

figure 15.1

EFFICIENCY IN EXCHANGES PROVIDED BY AN INTERMEDIARY

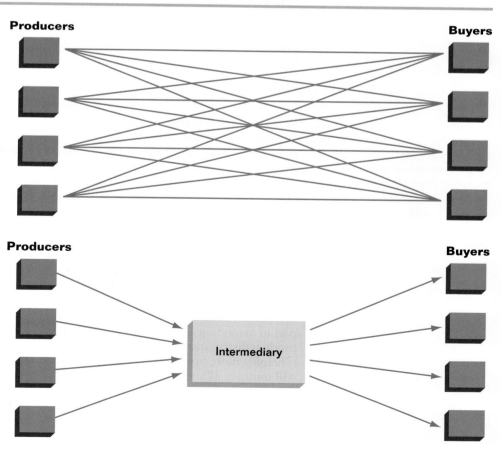

Producers   Buyers

Producers   Buyers

Intermediary

both producers and buyers, the number of transactions can be reduced to eight. Intermediaries are specialists in facilitating exchanges. They provide valuable assistance because of their access to and control over important resources used in the proper functioning of marketing channels.

Nevertheless, the media, consumers, public officials, and other marketers freely criticize intermediaries, especially wholesalers. Critics accuse wholesalers of being inefficient and parasitic. Buyers often wish to make the distribution channel as short as possible, assuming the fewer the intermediaries, the lower the price will be. Because suggestions to eliminate them come from both ends of the marketing channel, wholesalers must be careful to perform only those marketing activities that are truly desired. To survive, they must be more efficient and more customer-focused than other marketing institutions.

Critics who suggest that eliminating wholesalers would lower customer prices do not recognize that this would not eliminate the need for services wholesalers provide. Although wholesalers can be eliminated, the functions they perform cannot. Other channel members would have to perform those functions, and customers would still have to pay for them. In addition, all producers would have to deal directly with retailers or customers, meaning every producer would have to keep voluminous records and hire enough personnel to deal with a multitude of customers. Customers might end up paying a great deal more for products because prices would reflect the costs of less efficient channel members.

To illustrate the efficiency of wholesalers' services, assume all wholesalers have been eliminated. Because there are approximately 1.1 million retailers, a widely purchased consumer product—say, candy—would require an extraordinary number of sales contacts, possibly more than a million, to maintain the current level of product exposure. For example, Mars, Inc., would have to deliver candy, purchase and service thousands of vending machines, establish warehouses all over the country, and maintain fleets of trucks. Selling and distribution costs for candy would skyrocket. Instead of a few contacts with food brokers, large retail organizations, and merchant wholesalers, candy manufacturers would have to make thousands of expensive contacts with and shipments to smaller retailers. Such an operation would be highly inefficient, and costs would be passed on to consumers. Candy bars would cost more and be harder to find. Clearly wholesalers are often more efficient and less expensive.

Marketing Channels Form a Supply Chain

An important function of the marketing channel is the joint effort of all channel members to create a supply chain, a total distribution system that serves customers and creates a competitive advantage. **Supply chain management** refers to long-term partnerships among marketing channel members that reduce inefficiencies, costs, and redundancies in the marketing channel and develop innovative approaches to satisfy customers. Worldwide spending on supply chain management systems is over $19 billion.[3]

Supply chain management involves manufacturing, research, sales, advertising, shipping, and—most of all—cooperation and understanding of tradeoffs throughout the whole channel to achieve optimal levels of efficiency and service. Table 15.2 outlines the key tasks involved in supply chain management. Whereas traditional marketing channels tend to focus on producers, wholesalers, retailers, and customers, the supply chain is a broader concept that includes facilitating agencies such as shipping companies, communication companies, and other organizations that indirectly take part in marketing exchanges. Thus, the supply chain includes all entities that facilitate product distribution and benefit from cooperative efforts. Supply chain management is helping more firms realize that optimizing supply chain costs through partnerships will improve all members' profits. All parties should focus on cooperating to reduce the costs of all affected channel members. Supply chains start with the customer and require the cooperation of channel members to satisfy customer requirements. When the buyer, the seller, marketing intermediaries, and facilitating agencies work together, the cooperative relationship results in compromise and adjustments that meet customers' needs regarding delivery, scheduling, packaging, or other requirements.

supply chain management
Long-term partnerships among marketing channel members that reduce inefficiencies, costs, and redundancies and develop innovative approaches to satisfy customers

table 15.2	KEY TASKS IN SUPPLY CHAIN MANAGEMENT
Planning	Organizational and system wide coordination of marketing channel partnerships to meet customers' product needs
Sourcing	Purchasing of necessary resources, goods, and services from suppliers to support all supply chain members
Facilitating delivery	All activities designed to move the product through the marketing channel to the end user
Relationship building	All marketing activities related to selling, service, and the development of long-term customer relationships

Most companies do not set out to develop a supply chain. Typically they see a need to rework the way they serve their customers. Often they need to increase the quality of a good or service, which results in such goals as reducing the time from production to customer purchase, decreasing transportation costs, or lowering information management or administrative costs. Achieving these goals to attain a more competitive position often requires that channel members cooperate and share information as well as accommodate one another's needs.

Technology has dramatically improved the capability of supply chain management on a global basis. With integrated information sharing among channel members, costs can be reduced, service improved, and value provided to the customer enhanced. Tools such as electronic billing, purchase order verification, bar code technology, and image processing integrate needed data into the supply chain and improve

Technology Facilitates Supply Chain Management

Technology-based tools help supply chain managers improve efficiency and coordination.

overall performance. Intensely competitive industries operate the most sophisticated systems of supply chain management. Customer relationship management (CRM) systems exploit the information from supply chain partners' database and information systems to help all channel members make marketing strategy decisions that develop and sustain desirable customer relationships. Thus, managing relationships with supply chain partners is crucial to satisfying customers. CRM is gaining popularity with big companies like Hewlett-Packard and Amazon.ca, which spend large sums of money on implementation and support for data mining and CRM analytical applications. By 2008, companies that supply CRM technology, such as Siebel, SAS, and NetlQ, are expected to bring in over $11 billion in revenues.[4]

Supply chain management is not just a buzzword. Reducing inventory and transportation costs, speeding order cycle times, cutting administrative and handling costs, and improving customer service are all improvements that provide rewards for *all* channel members. The rewards will come as companies determine their positions in the supply chain, identify their partners and their roles, and establish partnerships that focus on customer relationships.

The Liquor Control Board of Ontario Wins Supply Chain Management Award

In 2005 the Liquor Control Board of Ontario (LCBO) was awarded the Innovation Award from the Council of Supply Chain Management Professionals (CSCMP). The Council is Canada's leading association for logistics and supply chain management professionals.

The LCBO was experiencing a number of challenges in 2000. Product offerings had expanded to include purchases from over 68 nations. The channel of distribution was long for many products, with a great deal of coordination needed in order to get the product where the customer wanted it, when they wanted it: the place part of the marketing mix.

LCBO storage facilities were filled, but product still wasn't making it onto store shelves quickly enough. In some cases, stores had too much of one product and too little of others. Despite sales of $100 million annually, the LCBO's distribution system was failing to fulfill organizational needs and customer demand.

To deal with growing demand and an inefficient logistics system, LCBO decided to launch a multi-year

Collaborative, Planning, Forecasting and Replenishment (CPFR) initiative. The first step of the plan was to determine and apply best practices standards for such things as sales, product delivery to stores and achieving profitable sales. In 2004, the organization introduced CPFR technology, which allowed real-time interaction for inventory control and movement of goods throughout the channel of distribution.

Achieving such coordination required total channel cooperation. Suppliers and resellers were required to work together to create seamless solutions throughout the channel network. This channel-wide perspective enhanced communication between members, enabling suppliers to understand LCBO's needs, and resulting in more efficient channel practices. In 2004, 18 suppliers (24 percent of the LCBO's supplier network) were included in the technologically-driven channel system.

Following the roll-out of technology in 2004 an evaluation was conducted of the channel system. Sales forecasts were much more accurate than before implementation of the supply chain management system. In addition, stock turnover in the LCBO's warehouses had doubled from 8.5 to 17 times. Correct order fulfillment for LCBO stores rose from 88 percent to 93 percent, and sales increased by $13 million. Gross margin return on inventory investment doubled and customer satisfaction rose from 74 percent to 80 percent.

By working on a long-term plan to determine logistics needs to meet customer demand, and developing strategies to achieve those goals, are the initial steps in creating a successful supply chain management system. Integrating technology throughout the channel and enhancing channel-wide communications gives firms the ability to use supply chain management strategically to increase efficiency, financial rewards and customer service.

Types of Marketing Channels

Because marketing channels appropriate for one product may be less suitable for others, many different distribution paths have been developed. The various marketing channels can be classified generally as channels for consumer products and channels for business products.

Channels for Consumer Products

Figure 15.2 illustrates several channels used in the distribution of consumer products. Channel A depicts the direct movement of goods from producer to consumers. Producers that sell goods directly from their factories to end users use direct marketing channels, as do companies that sell their own products via the Internet, such as Dell Computer. In fact, because Internet purchases have increased significantly, direct marketing via the Internet has become an important part of some companies' distribution strategies. Although direct marketing channels are the simplest, they are not necessarily the most effective distribution method. Faced with the strategic choice of going directly to the customer or using intermediaries, a firm must evaluate the benefits to customers of going direct versus the transaction costs involved in using intermediaries. Several companies provide supply chain management software to assist customers in managing sales orders, procurement, warehousing, transportation, and customer service.

Specialized supply chain management software can help firms achieve supply chain management goals. Radio identificiation tags, or RFID, is one form of such technology. The tags consist of silicon chips and antennas that send signals through a wireless receiver. Just as the use of the bar code revolutionized inventory management, the RFID is revolutionizing distribution management. Compared to the ubiquitous bar code, the RFID holds more information and can be read faster. The radio tags allow all members of the distribution channel, the supply chain, to electronically track goods from the manufacturer through to consumer.[5]

Channel B, which moves goods from the producer to a retailer and then to customers, is a frequent choice of large retailers since it allows them to buy in quantity from

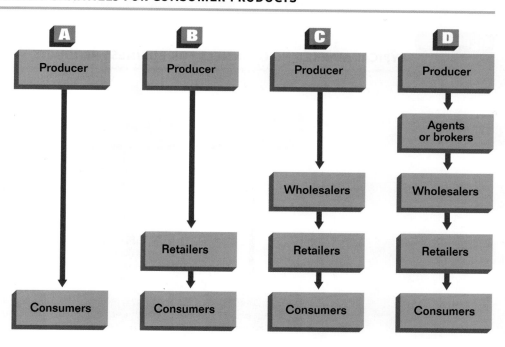

figure 15.2

TYPICAL MARKETING CHANNELS FOR CONSUMER PRODUCTS

manufacturers. Retailers such as Kmart and Wal-Mart sell clothing, stereos, and many other items purchased directly from producers. New automobiles and new college textbooks are also sold through this type of marketing channel. Primarily non-store retailers, such as L.L. Bean and J. Crew, also use this type of channel.

A long-standing distribution channel, especially for consumer products, channel C takes goods from the producer to a wholesaler, then to a retailer, and finally to consumers. It is a practical option for producers that sell to hundreds of thousands of customers through thousands of retailers. A single producer finds it hard to do business directly with thousands of retailers. Consider the number of retailers marketing Wrigley's chewing gum. It would be extremely difficult, if not impossible, for Wrigley to deal directly with each retailer that sells its brand of gum. Manufacturers of tobacco products, some home appliances, hardware, and many convenience goods sell their products to wholesalers, which then sell to retailers, which in turn do business with individual consumers.

Channel D, through which goods pass from producer to agents to wholesalers to retailers and then to consumers, is frequently used for products intended for mass distribution, such as processed foods. For example, to place its cracker line in specific retail outlets, a food processor may hire an agent (or a food broker) to sell the crackers to wholesalers. Wholesalers then sell the crackers to supermarkets, vending machine operators, and other retail outlets.

Contrary to popular opinion, a long channel may be the most efficient distribution channel for some consumer goods. When several channel intermediaries perform specialized functions, costs may be lower than when one channel member tries to perform them all.

Channels for Business Products

Figure 15.3 shows four of the most common channels for business products. As with consumer products, manufacturers of business products sometimes work with more than one level of wholesalers.

Channel E illustrates the direct channel for business products. In contrast to consumer goods, more than half of all business products, especially expensive equipment, are sold through direct channels. Business customers prefer to communicate directly with producers, especially when expensive or technically complex products are involved. For this reason, business buyers prefer to purchase expensive and highly complex mainframe computers directly from IBM and other mainframe producers. Intel has established direct marketing channels for selling its microprocessor chips to com-

figure 15.3

TYPICAL MARKETING CHANNELS FOR BUSINESS PRODUCTS

industrial distributor
An independent business organization that takes title to industrial products and carries inventories

puter manufacturers. In these circumstances, a customer wants the technical assistance and personal assurances that only a producer can provide.

In the second business products channel, channel F, an industrial distributor facilitates exchanges between producer and customer. An **industrial distributor** is an independent business that takes title to products and carries inventories. Industrial distributors usually sell standardized items such as maintenance supplies, production tools, and small operating equipment. Some industrial distributors carry a wide variety of product lines. Others specialize in one or a small number of lines. Industrial distributors are carrying an increasing percentage of business products. Industrial distributors can be most effectively used when a product has broad market appeal, is easily stocked and serviced, is sold in small quantities, and is needed on demand to avoid high losses.

Industrial distributors offer sellers several advantages. They can perform the needed selling activities in local markets at a relatively low cost to a manufacturer and reduce a producer's financial burden by providing customers with credit services. Also, because industrial distributors usually maintain close relationships with their customers, they are aware of local needs and can pass on market information to producers. By holding adequate inventories in their local markets, industrial distributors reduce producers' capital requirements.

Using industrial distributors has several disadvantages, however. Industrial distributors may be difficult to control since they are independent firms. Because they often stock competing brands, a producer cannot depend on them to sell its brand aggressively. Furthermore, since industrial distributors maintain inventories, they incur numerous expenses; consequently they are less likely to handle bulky or slow-selling items or items that need specialized facilities or extraordinary selling efforts. In some cases, industrial distributors lack the technical knowledge necessary to sell and service certain products.

The third channel for business products, channel G, employs a *manufacturers' agent,* an independent businessperson who sells complementary products of several producers in assigned territories and is compensated through commissions. Unlike an industrial distributor, a manufacturers' agent does not acquire title to the products and usually does not take possession. Acting as a salesperson on behalf of the producers, a manufacturers' agent has little or no latitude in negotiating prices or sales terms.

Using manufacturers' agents can benefit an organizational marketer. These agents usually possess considerable technical and market information and have an established set of customers. For an organizational seller with highly seasonal demand, a manufacturers' agent can be an asset because the seller does not have to support a year-round sales force. The fact that manufacturers' agents are paid on a commission basis may also be an economical alternative for a firm that has highly limited resources and cannot afford a full-time sales force.

Certainly the use of manufacturers' agents is not problem-free. Even though straight commissions may be cheaper, the seller may have little control over manufacturers' agents. Because of the compensation method, manufacturers' agents generally prefer to concentrate on their larger accounts. They are often reluctant to spend time following up sales, putting forth special selling efforts, or providing sellers with market information when such activities reduce the amount of productive selling time. Because they rarely maintain inventories, manufacturers' agents have a limited ability to provide customers with parts or repair services quickly.

Finally, channel H includes both a manufacturers' agent and an industrial distributor. This channel may be appropriate when the producer wishes to cover a large geographic area but maintains no sales force due to highly seasonal demand or because it cannot afford a sales force. This type of channel can also be useful for a business marketer that wants to enter a new geographic market without expanding its existing sales force.

Multiple Marketing Channels and Channel Alliances

To reach diverse target markets, manufacturers may use several marketing channels simultaneously, with each channel involving a different group of intermediaries. For

OVER 40 BLENDS
TO CHOOSE FROM.

PACE YOURSELF.

Find out what flavor you are at Millstone.com

© P&G 2006

dual distribution The use of
two or more marketing channels
to distribute the same product to
the same target market

strategic channel alliance
An agreement whereby the
products of one organization
are distributed through the
marketing channels of another

example, a manufacturer uses multiple channels when the same product is directed to both consumers and business customers. In some instances, a producer may prefer **dual distribution,** the use of two or more marketing channels to distribute the same products to the same target market. For example, Kellogg sells its cereals directly to large retail grocery chains (Channel B) and to food wholesalers that, in turn, sell them to retailers (Channel C). Another example of dual distribution is a firm that sells products through retail outlets and its own mail-order catalogue or website. Dual distribution, however, can cause dissatisfaction among wholesalers and smaller retailers when they must compete with large retail grocery chains that make direct purchases from manufacturers such as Kellogg. While the practice of dual distribution has been challenged as being anticompetitive, it is becoming far more common today with the development of direct marketing technologies that allow firms to bypass intermediaries altogether. Disintermediation is one term used to describe the fragmentation of traditional channel systems. Many channel options exist for firms today leading to disintermediation in the distribution channel. Another term used to describe this trend is hybrid channels, where firms combine various channel options to improve overall efficiency in getting the product to the consumer. A **strategic channel alliance** exists when the products of one organization are distributed through the marketing channels of another. The products of the two firms are often similar with respect to target markets or uses, but they are not direct competitors. For example, a brand of bottled water might be distributed through a marketing channel for soft drinks, or a domestic cereal producer might form a strategic channel alliance with a European food processor Alliances can provide benefits for both the organization that owns the marketing channel and the company whose brand is being distributed through the channel.

Selecting Marketing Channels

Selecting appropriate marketing channels is important. While the process varies across organizations, channel selection decisions usually are significantly affected by one or more of the following factors: customer characteristics, product attributes, type of organization, competition, marketing environmental forces, and characteristics of intermediaries (see Figure 15.4).

Customer Characteristics

Marketing managers must consider the characteristics of target market members in channel selection. As we have discussed, the channels appropriate for consumers are different than those for business customers. A different marketing channel will be required for business customers purchasing carpet for commercial buildings compared to consumers purchasing carpet for their homes. As already mentioned, business cus-

figure 15.4

SELECTING MARKETING CHANNELS

tomers often prefer to deal directly with producers (or very knowledgeable channel intermediaries such as industrial distributors), especially for highly technical or expensive products such as mainframe computers, jet airplanes, and large mining machines. Moreover, business customers are more likely to buy complex products requiring strict specifications and technical assistance and/or to buy in considerable quantities.

Consumers, on the other hand, generally buy limited quantities of a product, purchase from retailers, and often don't mind limited customer service. Additionally, when customers are concentrated in a small geographic area, a more direct channel may be ideal, but when many customers are spread across an entire provincial, territorial, or nation, distribution through multiple intermediaries is likely to be more efficient.

Product Attributes

The attributes of the product can have a strong influence on the choice of marketing channels. Marketers of complex and expensive products such as automobiles will likely employ short channels, as will marketers of perishable products such as dairy and produce. Less expensive, more standardized products, such as soft drinks and canned goods, can employ longer channels with many intermediaries. In addition, channel decisions may be affected by a product's sturdiness: fragile products that require special handling are more likely to be distributed through shorter channels to minimize the risk of damage. Firms that desire to convey an exclusive image for their products may wish to limit the number of outlets available.

Type of Organization

Clearly, the characteristics of the organization will have a great impact on the distribution channels chosen. Due to their sheer size, larger firms may be better able to negotiate better deals with vendors or other channel members. Compared to small firms, they may be in better positions to have more distribution centres, which may reduce delivery times to customers. A smaller regional company using regional or local channel members may be in a position to better serve customers in that region compared to a larger, less flexible organization. Compared with smaller organizations, large companies can use an extensive product mix as a competitive tool. Smaller firms may not have the resources to develop their own sales force, to ship their products long distances, to store or own products, or to extend credit. In such cases, they may have to include other channel members that have the resources to provide these services to customers efficiently and cost effectively.

Competition

Competition is also an important factor for supply chain managers to consider. The success or failure of a competitor's marketing channel may encourage or dissuade an organization from considering a similar approach. A firm may also be forced to adopt a similar strategy to remain competitive. In a highly competitive market, it is important for a company to keep its costs low so that it can underprice its competitors if necessary.

Marketing Environmental Forces

Environmental forces can also play a role in channel selection. Adverse economic conditions might force an organization to use a low-cost channel, even though customer satisfaction is reduced. In contrast, a booming economy might allow a company to choose a channel that previously had been too costly to consider. The introduction of new technology might cause an organization to add or modify its channel strategy. For instance, as the Internet became a powerful marketing communication tool, many companies were forced to go online to remain competitive. Government regulations can also affect channel selection. As new labour and environmental regulations are passed, an organization may be forced to modify its existing distribution channel structure. Firms may choose to make the changes before regulations are passed in order to appear compliant or to avoid legal issues. Governmental regulations can also include trade agreements with other countries that complicate the supply chain.

Characteristics of Intermediaries

When an organization believes that a current intermediary is not adequately promoting the organization's products, it may reconsider its channel choices. In these instances, the company may choose another channel member to handle its products or it may choose to eliminate intermediaries altogether and to perform the eliminated intermediaries' functions itself. Alternatively, an existing intermediary may not offer an appropriate mix of services, forcing an organization to change to another intermediary.

Intensity of Market Coverage

In addition to deciding which marketing channels to use to distribute a product, marketers must determine the intensity of coverage that a product should get, that is, the number and kinds of outlets in which it will be sold. This decision depends on the characteristics of the product and the target market. To achieve the desired intensity of market coverage, distribution must correspond to behaviour patterns of buyers. In Chapter 11, we divided consumer products into four categories—convenience products, shopping products, specialty products, and unsought products—according to how consumers make purchases. In considering products for purchase, consumers take into account replacement rate, product adjustment (services), duration of consumption, time required to find the product, and similar factors.[6] These variables directly affect the intensity of market coverage. As shown in Figure 15.5, the three major levels of market coverage are intensive, selective, and exclusive distribution.

intensive distribution
Using all available outlets to distribute a product

figure 15.5

INTENSITY OF MARKET COVERAGE

Intensive
Convenience products such as Coke, Pringles, and Duracell batteries

Available in many retail outlets

Selective
Shopping products such as iPods, televisions, DVD players, and shoes

Available in some outlets

Exclusive
Specialty products such as haute couture, Mont Blanc pens, BMWs, Fendi handbags

Available in very few outlets

Intensive Distribution

Intensive distribution uses all available outlets for distributing a product. Intensive distribution is appropriate for convenience products such as bread, chewing gum, soft drinks, and newspapers. Convenience products have a high replacement rate and require almost no service. To meet these demands, intensive distribution is necessary, and multiple channels may be used to sell through all possible outlets. For example, soft drinks, snacks, laundry detergent, and Aspirin are available at convenience stores, service stations, supermarkets, discount stores, and other types of retailers. To consumers, availability means a store is located nearby and minimum time is necessary to search for the product at the store. Sales may have a direct relationship to product availability. The successful sale of

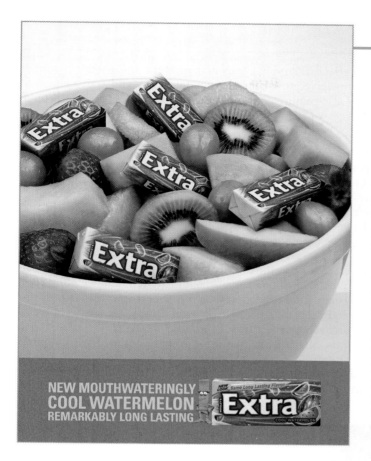

NEW MOUTHWATERINGLY
COOL WATERMELON
REMARKABLY LONG LASTING

Intensive Distribution

Chewing gum, like Extra, is distributed through intensive distribution.

such products as bread and milk at service stations or of gasoline at convenience grocery stores illustrates that the availability of these products is more important than the nature of the outlet. Companies such as Procter & Gamble that produce consumer packaged items rely on intensive distribution for many of their products (for example, soaps, detergents, food and juice products, and personal-care products) because consumers want ready availability.

Selective Distribution

Selective distribution uses only some available outlets in an area to distribute a product. Selective distribution is appropriate for shopping products; durable goods such as televisions, stereos, and home computers usually fall into this category. These products are more expensive than convenience goods, and consumers are willing to spend more time visiting several retail outlets to compare prices, designs, styles, and other features. Selective distribution is desirable when a special effort, such as customer service from a channel member, is important to customers. Shopping products require differentiation at the point of purchase. To motivate retailers to provide adequate presale service, selective distribution and company-owned stores are often used. Many business products are sold on a selective basis to maintain some control over the distribution process. For example, agricultural herbicides are distributed on a selective basis because dealers must offer services to buyers such as instructions about how to apply herbicides safely or the option to have the dealer apply the herbicide. Evinrude outboard motors are also sold by dealers on a selective basis.

selective distribution
Using only some available outlets to distribute a product

Exclusive Distribution

exclusive distribution
Using a single outlet in a fairly large geographic area to distribute a product

Exclusive distribution uses only one outlet in a relatively large geographic area. Exclusive distribution is suitable for products purchased infrequently, consumed over a long period of time, or requiring service or information to fit them to buyers' needs. It is also used for expensive, high-quality products, such as Porsche automobiles. It is not appropriate for convenience products and many shopping products.

Exclusive distribution is often used as an incentive to sellers when only a limited market is available for products. For example, automobiles such as the Bentley, made by Rolls-Royce, are sold on an exclusive basis, and Patek Philippe watches, which may sell for $10 000 or more, are available in only a few select locations. A producer using exclusive distribution generally expects dealers to carry a complete inventory, send personnel for sales and service training, participate in promotional programs, and provide excellent customer service. Some products are appropriate for exclusive distribution when first introduced, but as competitors enter the market and the product moves through its life cycle, other types of market coverage and distribution channels often become necessary. A problem that can arise with exclusive distribution (and selective distribution) is that unauthorized resellers acquire and sell products, violating the agreement between a manufacturer and its exclusive authorized dealers. This has been a problem for Rolex, another manufacturer of prestige watches.

Supply Chain Management

To fulfill the potential of effective supply chain management and ensure customer satisfaction, marketing channels require leadership, cooperation, and management of channel conflict. They may also require consolidation of marketing channels through channel integration.

Channel Leadership, Cooperation, and Conflict

Each channel member performs a different role in the distribution system and agrees (implicitly or explicitly) to accept certain rights, responsibilities, rewards, and sanctions for non-conformity. Moreover, each channel member holds certain expectations of other channel members. Retailers, for instance, expect wholesalers to maintain adequate inventories and deliver goods on time. Wholesalers expect retailers to honour payment agreements and keep them informed of inventory needs.

Channel partnerships facilitate effective supply chain management when partners agree on objectives, policies, and procedures for physical distribution efforts associated with the supplier's products. Such partnerships eliminate redundancies and reassign tasks for maximum system wide efficiency. One of the best-known partnerships is that between Wal-Mart and Procter & Gamble. Procter & Gamble locates some of its staff near Wal-Mart's purchasing department in Bentonville, Arkansas, to establish and maintain the supply chain. Sharing information through a cooperative computer system, Procter & Gamble monitors Wal-Mart's inventory and additional data to determine production and distribution plans for its products. The results are increased efficiency, decreased inventory costs, and greater satisfaction for the customers of both companies. At this time, some suppliers have been unwilling or unable to make this level of commitment. In this section we discuss channel member behaviour, including leadership, cooperation, and conflict, that marketers must understand to make effective channel decisions.

Channel Leadership

The manufacturer of Steve Madden shoes provides channel leadership in the distribution channels for its products.

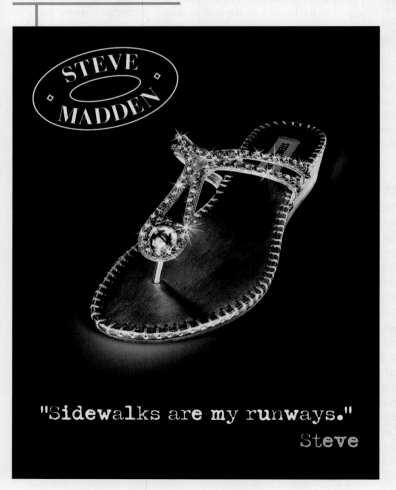

"Sidewalks are my runways."

Steve

Channel Cooperation. Channel cooperation is vital if each member is to gain something from other members. Cooperation enables retailers, wholesalers, and suppliers to speed up inventory replenishment, improve customer service, and cut the costs of bringing products to the consumer.[7] Without cooperation, neither overall channel goals nor member goals can be realized. All channel members must recognize that the success of one firm in the channel depends in part on other member firms. Thus, marketing channel members should make a coordinated effort to satisfy market requirements. Channel cooperation leads to greater trust among channel members and improves the overall functioning of the channel. It also leads to more satisfying relationships among channel members.

There are several ways to improve channel cooperation. If a marketing channel is viewed as a unified supply chain competing with other systems, individual members will be less likely to take actions that create disadvantages for other members. Similarly, channel members should agree to direct efforts toward common objectives so channel roles can be structured for maximum marketing effectiveness, which in turn can help members achieve individual objectives. A critical component in cooperation is a precise definition of each channel member's tasks. This provides a basis for reviewing the intermediaries' performance and helps reduce conflicts because each channel member knows exactly what is expected of it.

Channel Leadership and Conflict.   Many marketing channel decisions are determined by consensus. Producers and intermediaries coordinate efforts for mutual benefit. Some marketing channels, however, are organized and controlled by a single leader, or **channel captain** (also called *channel leader*). The channel captain may be a producer, wholesaler, or retailer. Channel captains may establish channel policies and coordinate development of the marketing mix. Wal-Mart, for example, dominates the supply chain for its retail stores by virtue of the magnitude of its resources (especially information management) and strong, nationwide customer base.

channel captain The dominant member of a marketing channel or supply chain

To become a captain, a channel member must want to influence overall channel performance. To attain desired objectives, the captain must possess **channel power,** the ability to influence another channel member's goal achievement. The member that becomes the channel captain will accept the responsibilities and exercise the power associated with this role.

channel power The ability of one channel member to influence another member's goal achievement

There are various kinds of channel power, each of which can render either negative control or positive control. For example, a firm may become a channel captain through positive approaches, such as by commanding respect or providing rewards for cooperation within the channel. Or a firm may take a negative or punitive approach using its size and the threat of leaving the channel to compel other channel members to do their bidding. Research has shown that positive sources of power are more effective than negative sources of power in creating strong and well coordinated channels of distribution.

When a manufacturer's large-scale production efficiency demands that it increase sales volume, the manufacturer may exercise power by giving channel members financing, business advice, ordering assistance, advertising services, sales and service training, and support materials. For example, domestic automakers provide these services to retail automobile dealerships. However, these manufacturers also place numerous requirements on their retail dealerships with respect to sales volume, sales and service training, and customer satisfaction.

As already noted, retailers may also function as channel captains. With the rise in power of national chain stores and private-brand merchandise, many large retailers such as Wal-Mart are doing so. Small retailers too may assume leadership roles when they gain strong customer loyalty in local or regional markets. These retailers control many brands and sometimes replace uncooperative producers. Increasingly, leading retailers are concentrating their buying power with fewer suppliers and, in the process, improving their marketing effectiveness and efficiency. Single-source supply relationships are often successful, whereas multiple-source supply relationships based on price competition are decreasing. Long-term commitments enable retailers to place smaller and more frequent orders as needed rather than waiting for large volume discounts or placing huge orders early in the season and assuming the risks associated with carrying a larger inventory.

Wholesalers assume channel leadership roles as well, although they were more powerful decades ago, when many manufacturers and retailers were smaller, under financed, and widely scattered. Today wholesaler leaders may form voluntary chains with several retailers, which they supply with bulk buying or management services; these chains may also market their own brands. In return, the retailers shift most of their purchasing to the wholesaler leader. The Independent Grocers' Alliance (IGA) is one of the best-known wholesaler leaders in the United States and formerly a major player in the Canadian grocery industry. IGA's power is based on its expertise in advertising, pricing, and purchasing knowledge that it makes available to independent business owners. Other wholesaler leaders help retailers with store layouts, accounting, and inventory control.

Although all channel members work toward the same general goal—distributing products profitably and efficiently—members may sometimes disagree about the best methods for attaining this objective. However, if self-interest creates misunderstanding about role expectations, the end result is frustration and conflict for the whole channel. For individual organizations to function together, each channel member must clearly communicate and understand role expectations. Communication difficulties are a potential form of channel conflict because ineffective communication leads to frustration, misunderstandings, and ill-coordinated strategies, jeopardizing further coordination.

The increased use of multiple channels of distribution, driven partly by new technology, has increased the potential for conflict between manufacturers and intermediaries. For example, Hewlett-Packard makes products available directly to consumers through its website (**www.hewlett-packard.com**), thereby competing directly with existing distributors and retailers.[8] Channel conflicts also arise when intermediaries overemphasize competing products or diversify into product lines traditionally handled by other intermediaries. Sometimes conflict develops because producers strive to increase efficiency by circumventing intermediaries. Such conflict is occurring in marketing channels for computer software. A number of software-only stores are establishing direct relationships with software producers, bypassing wholesale distributors altogether.

When a producer that has traditionally used franchised dealers broadens its retailer base to include other types of retail outlets, considerable conflict can arise. When Goodyear intensified its market coverage by allowing Sears and Discount Tire to market Goodyear tires, its action antagonized 2500 independent Goodyear dealers.

IBM: Outsupplying the Competition

Thirty years ago, it took 24 hours to rack up $10 billion in foreign exchange transactions. Today, the same amount of trade occurs in a single second. Globalization has raised the competitive stakes, forcing companies to compete on more than just product features and price. Companies can now achieve competitive differentiation based on how well they deliver the right product to the right place at the right time. For example, a Japanese manufacturer uses a logistics partner to configure its digital camera packaging to fit the requirements of individual retail chains. Free memory cards or carrying cases are packaged with the cameras, enabling retailers to differentiate themselves. By providing more value to its customers, this manufacturer has developed a competitive advantage over competing camera suppliers.

Bob Moffat, a senior vice president of IBM's integrated supply chain group, puts it this way, "When people work on a supply chain, they work on cost, but it's really how they take that cost and cash advantage and use it as a competitive advantage or weapon in the marketplace." Members of Moffat's organization have been working to reduce the number of days that sales revenue goes uncollected. That doesn't happen by changing terms and conditions, says Moffat. It comes from making sure the right data is in the billing system, that bills are accurate, and the necessary backup documentation is attached, all of which minimize the number of billing disputes initiated by customers.

For a corporation with more than $89 billion in annual sales, speeding collections by one day frees up almost $250 million in cash that can be used for new-product development, increased advertising, or other programs to give IBM an advantage over its competition. IBM's supply chain management has been so successful that it is now offering Business Transformation Outsourcing, a service that provides its own supply chain management solutions and technology to other companies.

The supply chain has clearly evolved to become more than a distribution system.

Although there is no single method for resolving conflict, partnerships can be reestablished if two conditions are met. First, the role of each channel member must be specified. To minimize misunderstanding, all members must be able to expect unambiguous, agreed-on performance levels from one another. Second, members of channel partnerships must institute certain measures of channel coordination, which requires leadership and benevolent exercise of control. To prevent channel conflict from arising, producers or other channel members may provide competing resellers with different brands, allocate markets among resellers, define policies for direct sales to avoid potential conflict over large accounts, negotiate territorial issues among regional distributors, and provide recognition to certain resellers for their importance in distributing to others.

Channel Integration

Channel members can either combine and control most activities or pass them on to another channel member. Channel functions may be transferred between intermediaries and to producers and even to customers. However, a channel member cannot eliminate functions; unless buyers themselves perform the functions, they must pay for the labour and resources needed to perform them.

Various channel stages may be combined under the management of a channel captain either horizontally or vertically. Such integration may stabilize supply, reduce costs, and increase coordination of channel members.

vertical channel integration
Combining two or more stages of the marketing channel under one management

Vertical Channel Integration.   **Vertical channel integration** combines two or more stages of the channel under one management. This may occur when one member of a marketing channel purchases the operations of another member or simply performs the functions of another member, eliminating the need for that intermediary.

Whereas members of conventional channel systems work independently, participants in vertical channel integration coordinate efforts to reach a desired target market. In this more progressive approach to distribution, channel members regard other members as extensions of their own operations. Vertically integrated channels are often more effective against competition because of increased bargaining power and sharing of information and responsibilities. At one end of a vertically integrated channel, a manufacturer might provide advertising and training assistance, and the retailer at the other end might buy the manufacturer's products in large quantities and actively promote them.

vertical marketing systems (VMSs) A marketing channel managed by a single channel member to achieve efficient, low-cost distribution aimed at satisfying target market customers

Integration has been successfully institutionalized in marketing channels called **vertical marketing systems (VMS),** in which a single channel member coordinates or manages channel activities to achieve efficient, low-cost distribution aimed at satisfying target market customers. VMSs essentially provide a method of resolving channel conflict by determining how disputes will be settled, and by identifying how individual channel members will contribute to the functioning of the channel.

Vertical integration brings most or all stages of the marketing channel under common control or ownership. The Limited, a retail clothing chain, uses a wholly owned subsidiary, Mast Industries, as its primary supply source. Radio Shack operates as a vertical marketing system, encompassing both wholesale and retail functions. Because efforts of individual channel members are combined in a VMS, marketing activities can be coordinated for maximum effectiveness and economy, without duplication of services. Vertical marketing systems are competitive, accounting for a significant share of retail sales in consumer goods.

Most vertical marketing systems take one of three forms: corporate, administered, or contractual. A *corporate VMS* combines all stages of the marketing channel, from producers to consumers, under a single owner. For example, the Limited established a corporate VMS that operates corporate-owned production facilities and retail stores. Supermarket chains that own food-processing plants and large retailers that purchase wholesaling and production facilities are other examples of corporate VMSs.

In an *administered VMS,* channel members are independent, but a high level of inter-organizational management is achieved through informal coordination. Essentially, channel conflict is reduced or controlled by information agreement between the parties. Members of an administered VMS, for example, may adopt uniform accounting and ordering procedures and cooperate in promotional activities for the benefit of all partners. Although individual channel members maintain autonomy, as in conventional marketing channels, one channel member (such as a producer or large retailer) dominates the administered VMS so that distribution decisions take the whole system into account. Because of its size and power, Intel exercises a strong influence over distributors and manufacturers in its marketing channels, as do Kellogg (cereal) and Magnavox (televisions and other electronic products).

Under a *contractual VMS,* the most popular type of vertical marketing system, channel members are linked by legal agreements spelling out each member's rights and obligations. Therefore, channel conflict is reduced or controlled by formal written agreement. Franchise organizations, such as McDonald's and KFC, are contractual VMSs. Other contractual VMSs include wholesaler-sponsored groups, such as IGA (Independent Grocers' Alliance) stores, in which independent retailers band

Family Owned Business Empire Ensures Channel Efficiency Through Corporate Vertical Marketing Systems

K.C. Irving founded Irving Oil in 1924. Since then, the company has grown into one of Canada's largest and more diversified industrial organizations. The company, still privately held, dominates the market in many key areas. Irving Oil Limited had integrated from refining through to retail, while J.D. Irving, Limited, has integrated from forest production through to retail for forestry-based products.

Irving Oil Limited employs over 7000 people in refineries, transportation, marine operations and 800 retail outlets. Irving's Saint John based refinery has a capacity of 300 000 barrels a day, and produces 75 percent of Canada's oil exports to the United States. The petroleum products refined at the Saint John location include award-winning ultra-low sulphur products that meet even the highest emission standards. Irving is planning to build a second refinery in Saint John, doubling its existing capacity, and creating 1000 jobs.

The firm also operates the Irving Canaport, the first deep water crude terminal in the Western Hemisphere, with a storage capacity of six million barrels. Irving Oil is also partnering with Repsol Ysf, S.A., to construct a liquefied-natural gas terminal (LNG) in Saint John. The Saint John location was ideal for the LNG terminal, allowing it to take advantage of the Bay of Fundy's high tides, with a water depth of 128 feet at low tide, in a port that is ice-free 365 days a year.

The location of the port is also important because of its proximity to key U.S. markets (it is only 105 kilometres from the U.S. border), and the fact that it is closer to key markets in South America and the North Sea than rival terminals on the Gulf Coast. At capacity, Canaport will hold one billion standard cubic feet of natural gas per day, and one billion barrels of oil. Canaport's LNG facility will be fully functional in 2008.

Irving Oil is able to refine petroleum products, sell them through existing channels, and retail them through their own chain of retail gasoline dealers. They are also able to sell other products through its chain of Bluecanoe convenience stores linked to its larger gasoline dealers.

J.D. Irving, Limited, is well known as the key player in the forestry industry in Atlantic Canada and the northeastern United States. The company owns 1.37 million hectares (3.4 million acres) of timberland in Nova Scotia, New Brunswick, and the state of Maine, contributing to a modern day belief that three out of every four trees in New Brunswick are owned by Irving. The firm also manages 1.13 million hectares (2.8 million acres) of crown land in New Brunswick.

The firm practices responsible forestry to bring top-quality lumber products to markets, having planted up to 750 million trees on crown land and its own landholdings since 1957. Being integrated vertically through corporate ownership, J.D. Irving Limited also owns mills, Kent Building Supplies and Kent Homes, and Irving Tissue product firms.

together under the contractual leadership of a wholesaler. Retailer-sponsored cooperatives, which own and operate their own wholesalers, are a third type of contractual VMS.

A third type of VMS is the corporate vertical marketing system, which exercises complete control through ownership of the entire channel. Firms that are vertically integrated from top to bottom, with sole ownership of all levels of the channel, constitute a corporate VMS. One example of a corporate VMS are the Irving family corporate holdings in New Brunswick. Irving Oil drills, refines and retails petroleum products, while J.D. Irving Limited manages forests, mills and sells lumber and construction-related services.

horizontal channel integration
Combining organizations at the same level of operation under one management

Horizontal Channel Integration.   Combining organizations at the same level of operation under one management constitutes **horizontal channel integration.** An organization may integrate horizontally by merging with other organizations at the same level in the marketing channel. The owner of a dry-cleaning firm, for example, might buy and combine several other dry-cleaning establishments. Horizontal integration may enable a firm to generate sufficient sales revenue to integrate vertically as well.

Although horizontal integration permits efficiencies and economies of scale in purchasing, marketing research, advertising, and specialized personnel, it is not always the most effective method of improving distribution. Problems of size often follow,

Partnering Helps Drive Toyota to the Top

To do a better job of reaching and satisfying customers through improved channel efficiencies, companies and channel members must choose their partners carefully, communicate clearly, and agree on the expectations and obligations of both sides.

Excelling at channel partnerships is one of the many reasons that Toyota is one of the world's leading automakers. Toyota has long been praised for its production system, which focuses on standardized processes and tooling. But the company believes in continual improvement, both for Toyota and its suppliers. Toyota's channel partnerships are based on the principle that product knowledge is intellectual property, but process knowledge is shared. Toyota offers process improvement lessons to its suppliers, disseminating information across Toyota's channel. The company even developed the Blue-

grass Automotive Manufacturers Association in the United States, which provides information on the best practices in the industry to all members.

Toyota also works with suppliers to help them develop more efficient practices, which brings the benefit of standardization beyond production and into supply chain management. Toyota believes that unless every partner is working together to lower costs and raise efficiency, the goal will never be met. Despite evidence of the importance of working with channel partners, however, only six percent of businesses that responded to a recent survey said that they standardize with supply channel partners.

Companies that do business globally face the challenge of partnering with hundreds or thousands of channel members, sometimes across vast distances. Toyota famously tackled this challenge by creating multiple short channels. Toyota has built 47 plants in 26 markets outside Japan to reduce costs by shortening the supply channel. Avoiding the high cost of importing has improved Toyota's profits. In fact, as U.S. car companies move overseas, Toyota is building more factories in the United States, including a strategically located truck factory in Texas.

Through partnering with suppliers, Toyota hopes to increase efficiencies to ensure its ability to remain highly competitive in the global automotive business.

resulting in decreased flexibility, difficulties in coordination, and the need for additional marketing research and large-scale planning. Unless distribution functions for the various units can be performed more efficiently under unified management than under the previously separate managements, horizontal integration will neither reduce costs nor improve the competitive position of the integrating firm.

Legal Issues in Channel Management

The numerous federal, provincial, and local laws governing channel management are based on the general principle that the public is best served by protecting competition and free trade. Under the authority of The Competition Act courts and regulatory agencies determine under what circumstances channel management practices violate this underlying principle and must be restricted. Although channel managers are not expected to be legal experts, they should be aware that attempts to control distribution functions may have legal repercussions. The following practices are among those frequently subject to legal restraint.

Dual Distribution

Earlier we noted that some companies may use dual distribution by using two or more marketing channels to distribute the same products to the same target market. Hewlett-Packard, for example, sells computers directly to consumers through a toll-free telephone line and a website, as well as through electronics retailers such as Best Buy. Courts do not consider this practice illegal when it promotes competition. A manufacturer can also legally open its own retail outlets. But the courts view as a threat to competition a manufacturer that uses company-owned outlets to dominate or drive out of business independent retailers or distributors that handle its products. In such cases, dual distribution violates the law. To avoid this interpretation, producers should use outlet prices that do not severely undercut independent retailers' prices.

Restricted Sales Territories

To tighten control over distribution of its products, a manufacturer may try to prohibit intermediaries from selling its products outside designated sales territories. Intermediaries themselves often favour this practice because it gives them exclusive territories, allowing them to avoid competition for the producer's brands within these territories. Although the courts have deemed restricted sales territories a restraint of trade among intermediaries handling the same brands, they have also held that exclusive territories can actually promote competition among dealers handling different brands. At present, the producer's intent in establishing restricted territories and the overall effect of doing so on the market must be evaluated for each individual case.

Tying Agreements

tying agreement An agreement in which a supplier furnishes a product to a channel member with the stipulation that the channel member must purchase other products as well

When a supplier (usually a manufacturer or franchiser) furnishes a product to a channel member with the stipulation that the channel member must purchase other products as well, a **tying agreement** exists. Suppliers may institute tying agreements to move weaker products along with more popular items, or a franchiser may tie purchase of equipment and supplies to the sale of franchises, justifying the policy as necessary for quality control and protection of the franchiser's reputation.

A related practice is *full-line forcing*, in which a supplier requires that channel members purchase the supplier's entire line to obtain any of the supplier's products. Manufacturers sometimes use full-line forcing to ensure that intermediaries accept new products and that a suitable range of products is available to customers.

The courts accept tying agreements when the supplier alone can provide products of a certain quality, when the intermediary is free to carry competing products as well, and when a company has just entered the market. Most other tying agreements are considered illegal.

Exclusive Dealing and Refusal to Deal

exclusive dealing A situation in which a manufacturer forbids an intermediary to carry products of competing manufacturers

When a manufacturer forbids an intermediary to carry products of competing manufacturers, the arrangement is called **exclusive dealing.** Manufacturers receive considerable market protection in an exclusive-dealing arrangement and may cut off shipments to intermediaries that violate the agreement.

The legality of an exclusive-dealing contract is generally determined by applying three tests. If the exclusive dealing blocks competitors from as much as 10 percent of the market, if the sales revenue involved is sizable, and if the manufacturer is much larger (and thus more intimidating) than the dealer, the arrangement is considered anticompetitive.[9] If dealers and customers in a given market have access to similar products or if the exclusive-dealing contract strengthens an otherwise weak competitor, the arrangement is allowed.

The Competition Act upholds the belief that producers have the right to choose channel members with which they will do business. However, within existing distribution channels, suppliers cannot legally refuse to deal with wholesalers or dealers merely because these wholesalers or dealers resist policies that are anticompetitive or in restraint of trade.[10]

The Nature of Physical Distribution

physical distribution Activities used to move products from producers to consumers and other end users

Physical distribution, also known as *logistics,* refers to the activities used to move products from producers to consumers and other end users. These activities include order processing, inventory management, materials handling, warehousing, and transportation. Planning an efficient physical distribution system is crucial to developing an effective marketing strategy because it can decrease costs and increase customer satisfaction. Speed of delivery, service, and dependability are often as important to customers as costs. Companies that have the right goods in the right place, at the right time, in the right quantity, and with the right support services are able to sell more than competitors that do not. For example, a construction equipment dealer with a low inventory of replacement parts requires fast, dependable service from component suppliers when it needs parts not in stock. Even when the demand for products is unpredictable, suppliers must be able to respond quickly to inventory needs. In such cases, physical distribution costs may be a minor consideration when compared with service, dependability, and timeliness.

Physical distribution deals with the physical movement and storage of products and supplies both within and among marketing channel members. Physical distribution systems must meet the needs of both the supply chain and customers. Distribution activities are thus an important part of supply chain planning and require the cooperation of all partners. Often one channel member manages physical distribution for all channel members.

outsourcing Contracting physical distribution tasks to third parties that do not have managerial authority within the marketing channel

Within the marketing channel, physical distribution activities may be performed by a producer, a wholesaler, or a retailer, or they may be outsourced. In the context of distribution, **outsourcing** is the contracting of physical distribution tasks to third parties that do not have managerial authority within the marketing channel. Most physical distribution activities can be outsourced to third-party firms that have special expertise in such areas as warehousing, transportation, inventory management, and information technology. Cooperative relationships with third-party organizations, such as trucking companies, warehouses, and data-service providers, can help reduce marketing channel costs and boost service and customer satisfaction for all supply chain partners. For example, a number of e-businesses, as well as some traditional brick-and-mortar ones, have outsourced physical distribution activities, including shipping and warehousing, to build a supply chain of strategic partners to maximize customer service. Such relationships are increasingly being integrated in the supply chain to achieve physical distribution objectives. When choosing companies through which to outsource, marketers take care to use efficient firms that will help the outsourcing company provide excellent customer service.

Physical Distribution Objectives

For most companies, the main objectives of physical distribution are to decrease costs and transit time while increasing customer service. However, few distribution systems achieve these goals in equal measure. The large inventories and rapid transportation necessary for good customer service drive up costs. Supply chain managers therefore strive for a reasonable balance among service, costs, and resources. They determine what level of customer service is acceptable and realistic, and then develop a "system" outlook to minimize total distribution costs and cycle time.

Meeting Customer Service Standards. In physical distribution, availability, timeliness, and accuracy are important dimensions of customer service. Companies set customer service standards based on one or a combination of these three dimensions. *Availability* refers to the percentage of orders that can be filled directly from a company's existing inventory. *Timeliness* refers to how quickly the product is shipped out to the customer. For example, some organizations set a service standard of shipping the product within 24 hours. *Accuracy* refers to whether the product the customer ordered is the product that is shipped to the customer. Some organizations have achieved better than a 99 percent order accuracy rate.

Customers seeking a high level of customer service may also want sizable inventories, efficient order processing, availability of emergency shipments, progress reports, post-sale services, prompt replacement of defective items, and warranties. Customers' inventory requirements influence the expected level of physical distribution service. Business customers seeking to reduce their inventory storage and shipping costs may expect wholesalers or third-party firms to take responsibility for maintaining inventory in the marketing channel or to assume the cost of premium transportation. Because service needs vary from customer to customer, companies must analyze, and adapt to, customer preferences. Attention to customer needs and preferences is crucial to increasing sales and obtaining repeat orders. Failure to provide the desired level of service may mean loss of customers.

Companies must also examine the service levels competitors offer and match or exceed those standards when the costs of providing the services are justified by the sales generated. Many companies guarantee service performance to win customers. Services are provided most effectively when service standards are developed and stated in measurable terms, for example, "98 percent of all orders filled within 48 hours." Standards should be communicated clearly to both customers and employees, and diligently enforced. Many service standards outline delivery times and specify provisions for back-ordering, returning goods, and obtaining emergency shipments.

Reducing Total Distribution Costs. Although physical distribution managers try to minimize the costs associated with order processing, inventory management, materials handling, warehousing, and transportation, decreasing costs in one area often raises costs in another. Figure 15.6 shows the percentage of total costs that physical distribution functions represent. A total-cost approach to physical distribution enables managers to view physical distribution as a system rather than a collection of unrelated activities. This approach shifts the emphasis from lowering the separate costs of individual activities to minimizing overall distribution costs.

The total-cost approach involves analyzing the costs of all distribution alternatives, even those considered too impractical or expensive. Total-cost analyses weigh inventory levels against warehousing expenses, materials costs against various modes of transportation, and all distribution costs against customer service standards. Costs of potential sales losses from lower performance levels must also be considered. In many cases, accounting procedures and statistical methods are used to figure total costs. When hundreds of combinations of distribution variables are possible, computer simulations are helpful. A distribution system's lowest total cost is never the result of using a combination of the cheapest functions. Instead, it is the lowest overall cost compatible with the company's stated service objectives. This means that the lowest cost option is not always the best choice, because lower cost usually means lower customer service.

For example, the Amerex Group buys materials and finished products from all over the world; consolidates them at various factories, where they are turned into men's,

figure 15.6   PROPORTIONAL COST OF EACH PHYSICAL DISTRIBUTION FUNCTION AS A PERCENTAGE OF TOTAL DISTRIBUTION COSTS

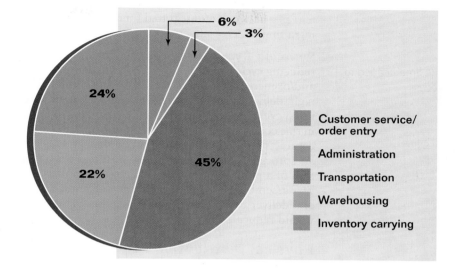

Source: Herbert W. Davis and Company/Establish, Inc., Fort Lee, NJ. *Davis Database,* June 2005, www.establishinc.com. Reprinted by permission of Herbert W. Davis and Company/Establish, Inc. *Davis Database,* Copyright © 2005 by Herbert W. Davis and Company/Establish, Inc.

Pie chart legend:
- Customer service/order entry
- Administration
- Transportation
- Warehousing
- Inventory carrying

Reducing Distribution Costs

Distribution-related organizations help companies improve efficiencies and reduce costs.

women's, and children's outwear; and then packs and ships either to customers or to warehouses. The firm's supply chain management system was inflexible, expensive to maintain, and not particularly helpful in tracking so many elements. The fast-growing company asked Computer Generated Solutions to craft and implement an automated system called Blue Cherry. The system ultimately helped Amerex save $650 000 a year and eliminate 22 positions.[11]

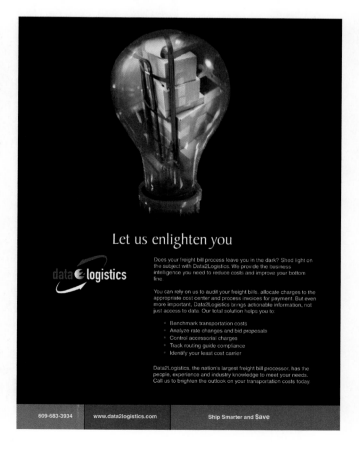

Physical distribution managers must be sensitive to the issue of cost tradeoffs. Higher costs in one functional area of a distribution system may be necessary to achieve lower costs in another. Tradeoffs are strategic decisions to combine (and recombine) resources for greatest cost effectiveness. When distribution managers regard the system as a network of integrated functions, tradeoffs become useful tools in implementing a unified, cost-effective distribution strategy.

Reducing Cycle Time.   Another important goal of physical distribution involves reducing **cycle time,** the time needed to complete a process. Doing so can reduce costs and/or increase customer service. Many companies, particularly manufacturers, overnight delivery firms, major news media, and publishers of books of current interest, are using cycle time reduction to gain a competitive advantage. FedEx believes so strongly in this concept that, in the interest of being the fastest provider of overnight delivery, it conducts research on reducing cycle time and identifying new management techniques and procedures for its employees. Seattle's Boeing Company is considering the construction of a plant to be run by two major suppliers and built next to Boeing's proposed 7E7 assembly plant. The plant would assemble about 75 percent of the 7E7's fuselage and deliver it to Boeing's final assembly plant next door. This arrangement not only would reduce cycle time but would save transportation costs on large pieces.[12]

cycle time The time needed to complete a process

Physical Distribution Functions

As we saw earlier, physical distribution includes the activities necessary to get products from producers to customers. In this section we take a closer look at these activities, which include order processing, inventory management, materials handling, warehousing, and transportation.

order processing The receipt and transmission of sales order information

Order Processing.   **Order processing** is the receipt and transmission of sales order information. Although management sometimes overlooks the importance of these activities, efficient order processing facilitates product flow. Computerized order processing provides a database for all supply chain members to increase their productivity. When carried out quickly and accurately, order processing contributes to customer satisfaction, decreased costs and cycle time, and increased profits.

Order processing entails three main tasks: order entry, order handling, and order delivery. Order entry begins when customers or salespeople place purchase orders via telephone, mail, e-mail, or website. Electronic ordering is less time consuming than a manual, paper-based ordering system and reduces costs. In some companies, sales representatives receive and enter orders personally, handle complaints, prepare progress reports, and forward sales order information.

Order handling involves several tasks. Once an order is entered, it is transmitted to a warehouse, where product availability is verified, and to the credit department, where prices, terms, and the customer's credit rating are checked. If the credit department approves the purchase, warehouse personnel (sometimes assisted by automated equipment) pick and assemble the order. If the requested product is not in stock, a production order is sent to the factory or the customer is offered a substitute.

Improving Order Processing
Many companies provide both hardware and software to improve order processing by making it more accurate and efficient.

When the order has been assembled and packed for shipment, the warehouse schedules delivery with an appropriate carrier. If the customer pays for rush service, overnight delivery by FedEx, UPS, or another overnight carrier is used. The customer is sent an invoice, inventory records are adjusted, and the order is delivered.

Whether to use a manual or an electronic order-processing system depends on which method provides the greater speed and accuracy within cost limits. Manual processing suffices for small-volume orders and is more flexible in certain situations. Most companies, however, use **electronic data interchange (EDI),** which uses computer technology to integrate order processing with production, inventory, accounting, and transportation. Within the supply chain, EDI functions as an information system that links marketing channel members and outsourcing firms together. It reduces paperwork for all members of the supply chain and allows them to share information on invoices, orders, payments, inquiries, and scheduling. Consequently many companies have pushed their suppliers toward EDI to reduce distribution costs and cycle times. For example, Dobbs, an airline food-service company, requires all of its vendors to be EDI-equipped.

electronic data interchange (EDI) A computerized means of integrating order processing with production, inventory, accounting, and transportation

Inventory Management. **Inventory management** involves developing and maintaining adequate assortments of products to meet customers' needs. Because a firm's investment in inventory usually represents a significant portion of its total assets, inventory decisions have a major impact on physical distribution costs and the level of customer

inventory management Developing and maintaining adequate assortments of products to meet customers' needs

Skechers Sprints Ahead with Wireless Inventory Management

How can a fashion footwear firm manage the flow of 60 000 individual products to thousands of retail stores around the world? In its early years, Skechers, a California company known for making stylish men's, women's, and children's shoes, relied on a network of wholesalers to service retail accounts outside the United States. Then it opened a huge distribution centre in Belgium to supplement its distribution centre in California. Now Skechers sells footwear worldwide through its online distribution site, skechers.com.

Because the popularity of specific fashion footwear can be unpredictable, the company must have inventory ready to ship at a moment's notice. Skechers holds extra inventory in outside warehouses and shifts products between facilities as needed to fill orders in each distribution centre. Searching the 1.5 million square feet of warehouse space to find a pair of shoes in a particular style, colour, and size would be a major

headache if not for the company's state-of-the art inventory management system.

When a case of shoes arrives from a Skechers factory, the wireless system picks up information about the contents and records where all items are transported and stored. As stores submit orders, the wireless system identifies each item's location, notes which products are being shipped to which store, deducts the products from current inventory levels, prepares shipping documents, and arranges for invoicing.

Thanks to this wireless system, Skechers can count all of its inventory in less than two days instead of the five days required before the company went wireless. The system automatically issues a warning if it detects any errors or discrepancies. This puts Skechers in a better position to fill store orders completely and correctly. Moreover, employees no longer have the tedious task of manually entering every shipment that enters or leaves the warehouse.

service provided. When too few products are carried in inventory, the result is *stock-outs,* or shortages of products, which in turn result in brand switching, lower sales, and loss of customers. When too many products (or too many slow-moving products) are carried, costs increase, as do risks of product obsolescence, pilferage, and damage. The objective of inventory management is to minimize inventory costs while maintaining an adequate supply of goods to satisfy customers. To achieve this objective, marketers focus on two major issues: when to order and how much to order.

To determine when to order, a marketer calculates the *reorder point,* the inventory level that signals the need to place a new order. Efficient inventory management with accurate reorder points is crucial for firms that use a **just-in-time (JIT)** approach, in which supplies arrive just as they are needed for use in production or for resale. When using JIT, companies maintain low inventory levels and purchase products and materials in small quantities whenever they need them. Usually there is no safety stock, and suppliers are expected to provide consistently high-quality products. Just-in-time inventory management requires a high level of coordination between producers and suppliers, but it eliminates waste and reduces inventory costs significantly. This approach has been used successfully by many well-known firms, including DaimlerChrysler, Harley-Davidson, and Dell Computer, to reduce costs and boost customer satisfaction. When a JIT approach is used in a supply chain, suppliers often move close to their customers.

just-in-time (JIT) An inventory management approach in which supplies arrive just when needed for production or resale

Materials Handling. **Materials handling,** the physical handling of tangible goods, supplies, and resources, is an important factor in warehouse operations, as well as in transportation from points of production to points of consumption. Efficient procedures and techniques for materials handling minimize inventory management costs, reduce the number of times a good is handled, improve customer service, and increase customer satisfaction. Systems for packaging, labelling, loading, and movement must be coordinated to maximize cost reduction and customer satisfaction. A growing number of firms are turning to radio waves to track materials tagged with radio frequency ID (RFID) through every phase of handling.

materials handling Physical handling of tangible goods, supplies, and resources

Product characteristics often determine handling. For example, the characteristics of bulk liquids and gases determine how they can be moved and stored. Internal packaging is also an important consideration in materials handling; goods must be packaged correctly to prevent damage or breakage during handling and transportation. Most companies employ packaging consultants to help them decide which packaging materials and methods will result in the most efficient handling.

Unit loading and containerization are two common methods used in materials handling. With *unit loading,* one or more boxes are placed on a pallet or skid; these units can then be efficiently loaded by mechanical means such as forklifts, trucks, or conveyor systems. *Containerization* is the consolidation of many items into a single large container, which is sealed at its point of origin and opened at its destination. Containers are usually 2.5 metres wide, 2.5 metres high, and three to 12 metres long. They can be conveniently stacked and shipped via train, barge, or ship. Once containers reach their destinations, wheel assemblies can be added to make them suitable for ground transportation. Because individual items are not handled in transit, containerization greatly increases efficiency and security in shipping.

Warehousing. **Warehousing,** the design and operation of facilities for storing and moving goods, is another important physical distribution function. Warehousing provides time utility by enabling firms to compensate for dissimilar production and consumption rates. When mass production creates a greater stock of goods than can be sold immediately, companies may warehouse the surplus until customers are ready to buy. Warehousing also helps stabilize prices and availability of seasonal items.

warehousing The design and operation of facilities for storing and moving goods

Warehousing is not simply the storage of products. The basic distribution functions warehouses perform include receiving, identifying, sorting, and dispatching goods to storage; holding goods in storage until needed; recalling and assembling stored goods for shipment; and dispatching shipments. When warehouses receive goods by carloads or truckloads, they break down the shipments into smaller quantities for individual customers.

Warehousing
Specialized information technology is helping managers to operate warehouses more efficiently.

The choice of warehouse facilities is an important strategic consideration. The right type of warehouse allows a company to reduce transportation and inventory costs or improve service to customers. The wrong type of warehouse may drain company resources. Beyond deciding how many facilities to operate and where to locate them, a company must determine which type of warehouse is most appropriate. Warehouses fall into two general categories: private and public. In many cases, a combination of private and public facilities provides the most flexible warehousing approach.

private warehouse
A company-operated facility for storing and shipping products

Companies operate **private warehouses** for storing and shipping their own products. A firm usually leases or purchases a private warehouse when its warehousing needs in a given geographic market are substantial and stable enough to warrant a long-term commitment to a fixed facility. Private warehouses are also appropriate for firms that require special handling and storage and that want control of warehouse design and operation. Retailers such as Sears and Radio Shack find it economical to integrate private warehousing with purchasing and distribution for their retail outlets. When sales volumes are fairly stable, ownership and control of a private warehouse may provide benefits such as property appreciation. Private warehouses, however, face fixed costs such as insurance, taxes, maintenance, and debt expense. They also limit flexibility when firms wish to move inventories to more strategic locations. Before tying up capital in a private warehouse or entering into a long-term lease, a company should consider its resources, level of expertise in warehouse management, and the role of the warehouse in its overall marketing strategy. Many private warehouses are being eliminated by direct links between producers and customers, reduced cycle times, and outsourcing to public warehouses.

public warehouse A business that leases storage space and related physical distribution facilities to other firms

Public warehouses lease storage space and related physical distribution facilities to other firms. They sometimes provide such distribution services as receiving, unloading, inspecting, and reshipping products; filling orders; providing financing; displaying products; and coordinating shipments. Public warehouses are especially useful to firms that have seasonal production or low-volume storage needs, have inventories that must be maintained in many locations, are testing or entering new markets, or own private warehouses but occasionally require additional storage space. Public warehouses also serve as collection points during product recall programs. Whereas private warehouses have fixed costs, public warehouses offer variable (and often lower) costs because users rent space and purchase warehousing services only as needed.

Many public warehouses furnish security for products being used as collateral for loans, a service provided at either the warehouse or the site of the owner's inventory. *Field public warehouses* are established by public warehouses at the owner's inventory location. The warehouser becomes custodian of the products and issues a receipt that can be used as collateral for a loan. Public warehouses also provide *bonded storage*, a warehousing arrangement in which imported or taxable products are not released until the products' owners pay U.S. customs duties, taxes, or other fees. Bonded warehouses enable firms to defer tax payments on such items until they are delivered to customers.

distribution centre A large, centralized warehouse that focuses on moving rather than storing goods

Distribution centres are large, centralized warehouses that receive goods from factories and suppliers, regroup them into orders, and ship them to customers quickly; their focus is on movement of goods rather than storage.[13] Distribution centres are specially designed for rapid flow of products. They are usually one-story buildings (to eliminate elevators) with access to transportation networks such as major highways or railway lines. Many distribution centres are highly automated, with computer-directed robots, forklifts, and hoists that collect and move products to loading docks. Although some public warehouses offer such specialized services, most distribution centres are privately owned. They serve customers in regional markets and, in some cases, function as consolidation points for a company's branch warehouses. Distribution centres typically are located within 500 miles of half of a company's market.

Distribution centres offer several benefits, the most important being improved customer service. Distribution centres ensure product availability by maintaining full product lines, and the speed of their operations cuts delivery time to a minimum. Distribution centres also reduce costs. Instead of making many smaller shipments to scattered warehouses and customers, factories ship large quantities of goods directly to distribution centres at bulk rates, thus lowering transportation costs. Furthermore, rapid inventory turnover lessens the need for warehouses and cuts storage costs. Overstock.com, for example, operates a 350 000 square foot distribution centre in Salt Lake City to process all the name-brand housewares, electronics, toys, sporting goods, and gifts it markets through a website. Efficiency in distribution operations helps the firm offer deep discounts and stay on top of busy holiday seasons.[14] Some distribution centres facilitate production by receiving and consolidating raw materials and providing final assembly for certain products.

transportation The movement of products from where they are made to where they are used

Transportation. **Transportation,** the movement of products from where they are made to where they are used, is the most expensive physical distribution function. Because product availability and timely deliveries depend on transportation functions, transportation decisions directly affect customer service. A firm may even build its distribution and marketing strategy around a unique transportation system if that system can ensure on-time deliveries and thereby give the firm a competitive edge. Companies may build their own transportation fleets (private carriers) or outsource the transportation function to a common or contract carrier.

Transportation Modes. There are five basic transportation modes for moving physical goods: railroads, trucks, waterways, airways, and pipelines. Each mode offers distinct advantages. Many companies adopt physical handling procedures that facilitate the use of two or more modes in combination. Table 15.3 shows typical transportation modes for various products. Table 15.3 indicates the relative ratings of various modes of transportation, ranked on key criteria.

table 15.3   TYPICAL TRANSPORTATION MODES FOR VARIOUS PRODUCTS

Railroads	Trucks	Waterways	Airways	Pipelines
Coal	Clothing	Petroleum	Flowers	Oil
Grain	Paper goods	Chemicals	Perishable food	Processed coal
Chemicals	Computers	Iron ore	Instruments	Natural gas
Lumber	Books	Bauxite	Emergency parts	Water
Automobiles	Livestock	Grain	Overnight mail	Chemicals
Steel				

Trucking

A number of transportation services are provided through trucks.

Railroads such as Canadian National carry heavy, bulky freight that must be shipped long distances over land. Railroads commonly haul minerals, sand, lumber, chemicals, and farm products, as well as low-value manufactured goods and an increasing number of automobiles. They are especially efficient for transporting full carloads, which can be shipped at lower rates than smaller quantities because they require less handling. Many companies locate factories or warehouses near major rail lines or on spur lines for convenient loading and unloading.

Trucks provide the most flexible schedules and routes of all major transportation modes because they can go almost anywhere. Because trucks have a unique ability to move goods directly from factory or warehouse to customer, they are often used in conjunction with other forms of transport that cannot provide door-to-door deliveries. Although trucks usually travel much faster than trains, they are more expensive and somewhat more vulnerable to bad weather. They are also subject to size and weight restrictions on the products they carry. Trucks are sometimes criticized for high levels of loss and damage to freight and for delays caused by rehandling small shipments. In response, the trucking industry has turned to computerized tracking of shipments and the development of new equipment to speed loading and unloading. Using a satellite-tracking system, a company can track when a driver arrives at a site and how long it takes to load and unload freight.

Waterways are the cheapest method of shipping heavy, low-value, non-perishable goods such as ore, coal, grain, and petroleum products. Water carriers offer considerable capacity. Powered by tugboats and towboats, barges that travel along intercoastal canals, inland rivers, and navigation systems can haul at least 10 times the weight of one rail car, and oceangoing vessels can haul thousands of containers. However, many markets are inaccessible by water transportation unless supplemented by rail or truck. Furthermore, water transport is extremely slow and sometimes comes to a standstill during freezing weather. Companies depending on waterways may ship their entire inventory during the summer and then store it for winter use. Droughts and floods also create difficulties for users of inland waterway transportation. Nevertheless, the extreme fuel efficiency of water transportation and the continuing globalization of marketing will likely increase its use in the future.

Air transportation is the fastest but most expensive form of shipping. It is used most often for perishable goods; for high-value, low-bulk items; and for products requiring quick delivery over long distances, such as emergency shipments. Some air carriers transport combinations of passengers, freight, and mail. Despite its expense, air transit can reduce warehousing and packaging costs and losses from theft and damage, thus helping to lower total costs (but truck transportation needed for pickup and final delivery adds to cost and transit time). Although air transport accounts for less than one percent of total tonne-miles carried, its importance as a mode of transportation is growing. In fact, the success of many businesses is now based on the availability of overnight air delivery service provided by such organizations as UPS, DHL, FedEx, RPS Air, and the U.S. Postal Service. Amazon.ca, for example, ships via UPS many products ordered online within a day of order. Pipelines, the most highly automated transportation mode, usually belong to the shipper and carry the shipper's products. Most pipelines carry petroleum products or chemicals. The Trans-Alaska Pipeline, owned and operated by a consortium of oil companies that includes Exxon, Mobil, and BP-Amoco, transports crude oil from remote oil-drilling sites in central Alaska to shipping terminals on the coast. Slurry pipelines carry pulverized coal, grain, or wood chips suspended in water. Pipelines move products slowly but continuously and at relatively low cost. They are dependable and minimize the problems of product damage and theft. However, contents are subject to as much as one percent shrinkage, usually from evaporation. Pipelines have also been a concern to environmentalists, who fear installation and leaks could harm plants and animals.

Choosing Transportation Modes. Distribution managers select a transportation mode based on the combination of cost, speed, dependability, load flexibility, accessibility, and frequency that is most appropriate for their products and generates the desired level of customer service. Table 15.4 shows relative ratings of each transportation mode by these selection criteria.

Marketers compare alternative transportation modes to determine whether benefits from a more expensive mode are worth higher costs. Air freight carriers such as FedEx promise many benefits, such as speed and dependability, but at much higher costs than other transportation modes. When such benefits are less important, marketers prefer lower costs. Bicycles, for instance, are often shipped by rail because an unassembled bicycle can be shipped more than 1000 miles on a train for as little as $3.60. Bicycle wholesalers plan purchases far enough in advance to capitalize on this cost advantage.

Speed is measured by the total time a carrier has possession of goods, including the time required for pickup and delivery, handling, and movement between points of

table 15.4	RELATIVE RATINGS OF TRANSPORTATION MODES BY SELECTION CRITERIA					
Mode	Cost	Speed	Dependability	Load Flexibility	Accessibility	Frequency
Railroads	Moderate	Average	Average	High	High	Low
Trucks	High	Fast	High	Average	Very high	High
Waterways	Very low	Very slow	Average	Very high	Limited	Very low
Airways	Very high	Very fast	High	Low	Average	Average
Pipelines	Low	Slow	High	Very low	Very limited	Very high

origin and destination. Speed obviously affects a marketer's ability to provide service, but other, less obvious implications are important as well. Marketers take advantage of transit time to process orders for goods en route, a capability especially important to agricultural and raw materials shippers. Some railroads also let carloads in transit be redirected for maximum flexibility in selecting markets. A carload of peaches, for instance, may be shipped to a closer destination if the fruit is in danger of ripening too quickly.

Dependability of a transportation mode is determined by the consistency of service provided. Marketers must be able to count on carriers to deliver goods on time and in an acceptable condition. Along with speed, dependability affects a marketer's inventory costs, including sales lost when merchandise is not available. Undependable transportation necessitates higher inventory levels to avoid stockouts, whereas reliable delivery service enables customers to carry smaller inventories at lower cost. Security problems vary considerably among transportation modes and are a major consideration in carrier selection. A firm does not incur costs directly when goods are lost or damaged because the carrier is usually held liable. Nevertheless, poor service and lack of security indirectly lead to increased costs and lower profits because damaged or lost goods are unavailable for immediate sale or use.

Load flexibility is the degree to which a transportation mode can provide appropriate equipment and conditions for moving specific kinds of goods and can be adapted for moving other products. Many products must be shipped under controlled temperature and humidity. Other products, such as liquids or gases, require special equipment or facilities for shipment. As Table 15.4 shows, waterways and railroads have the highest load flexibility, whereas pipelines have the lowest. *Accessibility* refers to a carrier's ability to move goods over a specific route or network. Some carriers differentiate themselves by serving areas their competitors do not. *Frequency* refers to how often a company can send shipments by a specific transportation mode. When using pipelines, shipments can be continuous. A marketer shipping by railroad or waterway is limited by the carriers' schedules.

Coordinating Transportation. To take advantage of the benefits offered by various transportation modes and compensate for deficiencies, marketers often combine and coordinate two or more modes. In recent years, **intermodal transportation**, as this integrated approach is sometimes called, has been facilitated by new developments within the transportation industry.

Several kinds of intermodal shipping are available. All combine the flexibility of trucking with the low cost or speed of other forms of transport. Containerization facilitates intermodal transportation by consolidating shipments into sealed containers for transport by *piggyback* (shipping that uses both truck trailers and railway flatcars), *fishyback* (truck trailers and water carriers), and *birdyback* (truck trailers and air carriers). As transportation costs have increased, intermodal shipping has gained popularity.

Specialized outsource agencies provide other forms of transport coordination. Known as **freight forwarders,** these firms combine shipments from several organizations into efficient lot sizes. Small loads (less than 500 pounds) are much more expensive to ship than full carloads or truckloads, which frequently requires consolidation. Freight forwarders take small loads from various marketers, buy transport space from carriers, and arrange for goods to be delivered to buyers. Freight forwarders' profits come from the margin between the higher, less-than-carload rates they charge each marketer and the lower carload rates they themselves pay. Because large shipments require less handling, use of freight forwarders can speed delivery. Freight forwarders can also determine the most efficient carriers and routes. They are useful for shipping goods to foreign markets because freight forwarders know how to clear customs, pay duties, and handle the necessary paperwork. Some companies prefer to outsource their shipping to freight forwarders because the latter provide door-to-door services.

Another transportation innovation is the development of **megacarriers,** freight transportation firms that offer several shipment methods, including rail, truck, and air

intermodal transportation Two or more transportation modes used in combination

freight forwarder An organization that consolidates shipments from several firms into efficient lot sizes

megacarrier A freight transportation firm that provides several modes of shipment service. CSX, for example, has trains, barges, container ships, trucks, and pipelines, thus offering a multitude of transportation services. In addition, air carriers have increased their ground transportation services. As they expand the range of transportation alternatives, carriers too put greater stress on customer service.

Strategic Issues in Physical Distribution

The physical distribution functions discussed in this chapter—order processing, inventory management, materials handling, warehousing, and transportation—account for about half of all marketing costs. Whether performed by a producer, wholesaler, or retailer, or outsourced to some other firm, these functions have a significant impact on customer service and satisfaction, which are of primary importance to all members of the supply chain.

The strategic importance of physical distribution is evident in all elements of the marketing mix. Product design and packaging must allow for efficient stacking, storage, transport, and tracking. Differentiating products by size, colour, and style must take into account additional demands placed on warehousing and shipping facilities. Competitive pricing may depend on a firm's ability to provide reliable delivery or emergency shipments of replacement parts. Firms trying to lower inventory costs may offer quantity discounts to encourage large purchases. Promotional campaigns must be coordinated with distribution functions so that advertised products are available to buyers and order-processing departments can handle additional sales orders efficiently. Channel members must consider warehousing and transportation costs, which may influence a firm's policy on stockouts or its decision to centralize (or decentralize) inventory.

Strategic Physical Distribution

Most organizations incorporate physical distribution functions into their marketing strategies.

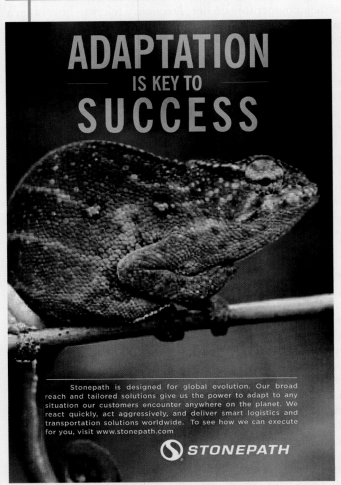

Improving physical distribution starts by closing the gap with customers. The entire supply chain must understand and meet customers' requirements. An effective way to improve physical distribution is to integrate processes across the boundaries of all members of the supply chain. The full scope of the physical distribution process includes suppliers, manufacturers, wholesalers, retailers, transportation firms, and warehouses. To work well, the process requires a formal, integrated plan to balance supply and demand within a defined time period. Physical distribution can also be improved by developing cooperative relationships with suppliers of component parts and services. These relationships should emphasize joint improvement. Cooperation can be enhanced through information technology that allows channel partners to work together to plan production and physical distribution activities; improve the efficiency and safety of product handling and movement; and reduce waste and costs for the benefit of all channel members, including the customer.

No single distribution system is ideal for all situations, and any system must be evaluated continually and adapted as necessary. Pressures to adjust service levels or to reduce costs may lead to a total restructuring of supply chain relationships. The ensuing changes in transportation, warehousing, materials handling, and inventory may affect speed of delivery, reliability, and economy of service. Recognizing that changes in any major distribution function may affect all other functions, marketing strategists consider customers' changing needs and preferences. Customer-oriented marketers analyze the characteristics of their target markets and plan distribution systems to provide products in the right place, at the right time, and at acceptable costs.

SUMMARY

A marketing channel, or channel of distribution, is a group of individuals and organizations that direct the flow of products from producers to customers. The major role of marketing channels is to make products available at the right time at the right place and in the right amounts. In most channels of distribution, producers and consumers are linked by marketing intermediaries, or middlemen. The two major types of intermediaries are retailers, which purchase products and resell them to ultimate consumers, and wholesalers, which buy and resell products to other wholesalers, retailers, and business customers.

Marketing channels serve many functions. They create time, place, and possession utility by making products available when and where customers want them and providing customers with access to product use through sale or rental. Marketing intermediaries facilitate exchange efficiencies, often reducing the costs of exchanges by performing certain services and functions. Although critics suggest eliminating wholesalers, someone must perform their functions in the marketing channel. Because intermediaries serve both producers and buyers, they reduce the total number of transactions that otherwise would be needed to move products from producer to ultimate users.

Marketing channels also form a supply chain, a total distribution system that serves customers and creates a competitive advantage. Supply chain management refers to long-term partnerships among channel members working together to reduce inefficiencies, costs, and redundancies and to develop innovative approaches to satisfy customers. The supply chain includes all entities—shippers and other firms that facilitate distribution, as well as producers, wholesalers, and retailers—that distribute products and benefit from cooperative efforts. Supply chains start with the customer and require the cooperation of channel members to satisfy customer requirements.

Channels of distribution are broadly classified as channels for consumer products and channels for business products. Within these two broad categories, different marketing channels are used for different products. Although consumer goods can move directly from producer to consumers, consumer product channels that include wholesalers and retailers are usually more economical and efficient. Distribution of business products differs from that of consumer products in the types of channels used. A direct distribution channel is common in business marketing. Also used are channels containing industrial distributors, manufacturers' agents, and a combination of agents and distributors. Most producers have multiple or dual channels so the distribution system can be adjusted for various target markets.

Selecting an appropriate marketing channel is a crucial decision for supply chain managers. To determine which channel is most appropriate, managers must think about customer characteristics, the type of organization, product attributes, competition, environmental forces, and the availability and characteristics of intermediaries. Careful consideration of these factors will assist a supply chain manager in selecting the correct channel.

A marketing channel is managed such that products receive appropriate market coverage. In choosing intensive distribution, producers strive to make a product available to all possible dealers. In selective distribution, only some outlets in an area are chosen to distribute a product. Exclusive distribution usually gives a single dealer rights to sell a product in a large geographic area.

Each channel member performs a different role in the system and agrees to accept certain rights, responsibilities, rewards, and sanctions for non-conformance. Although many marketing channels are determined by consensus, some are organized and controlled by a single leader, or channel captain. A channel captain may be a producer, wholesaler, or retailer. Channels function most effectively when members cooperate; when they deviate from their roles, channel conflict can arise.

Integration of marketing channels brings various activities under one channel member's management. Vertical integration combines two or more stages of the channel under one management. The vertical marketing system (VMS) is managed centrally for the mutual benefit of all channel members. Vertical marketing systems may be corporate, administered, or contractual. Horizontal integration combines institutions at the same level of channel operation under a single management.

Federal, provincial, territorial, and local laws regulate channel management to protect competition and free trade. Courts may prohibit or permit a practice depending on whether it violates this underlying principle. Various procompetitive legislation acts apply to distribution practices. Channel management practices frequently subject to legal restraint include dual distribution, restricted sales territories, tying agreements, exclusive dealing, and refusal to deal. When these practices strengthen weak competitors or increase competition among dealers, they may be permitted; in most other cases, when competition may be weakened considerably, they are deemed illegal.

Physical distribution, or logistics, refers to the activities used to move products from producers to customers and other end users. These activities include order processing, inventory management, materials handling, warehousing, and transportation. An efficient physical distribution system is an important component of an overall marketing strategy because it can decrease costs and increase customer satisfaction. Within the marketing channel, physical distribution activities are often performed by a wholesaler, but they may be performed by a producer or retailer, or outsourced to a third party.

The main objectives of physical distribution are to decrease costs and transit time while increasing customer service. Physical distribution managers strive to balance service, distribution costs, and resources. Because customers' service needs vary, companies must adapt to them. They must also offer service comparable to or better than competitors' and develop and communicate desirable customer service policies. Costs of providing service are minimized most effectively through the total-cost approach, which evaluates costs of the distribution system as a whole rather than as a collection of separate activities. Reducing cycle time, the time required to complete a process, is also important.

Order processing is the receipt and transmission of sales order information. It consists of three main tasks. Order entry begins when customers or salespeople place purchase orders by mail, e-mail, telephone, or computer. Order handling involves verifying product availability, checking customer credit, and preparing products for shipping. Order delivery is provided by the carrier most suitable for a desired level of customer service. Order processing can be done manually, but it is usually accomplished through electronic data interchange (EDI), a computerized system that integrates order processing with production, inventory, accounting, and transportation.

The objective of inventory management is to minimize inventory costs while maintaining a supply of goods adequate for customers' needs. To avoid stockouts without tying up too much capital in inventory, firms must have systematic methods for determining a reorder point, the inventory level that signals the need to place a new order. When firms use the just-in-time approach, products arrive just as they are needed for use in production or resale.

Materials handling, the physical handling of products, is an important factor in warehouse operations, as well as in transportation from points of production to points of consumption. Systems for packaging, labelling, loading, and movement must be coordinated to maximize cost reduction and customer satisfaction. Basic handling systems include unit loading, which entails placing boxes on pallets or skids and using mechanical devices to move them, and containerization.

Warehousing involves the design and operation of facilities for storing and moving goods. Private warehouses are operated by companies for the purpose of distributing their own products. Public warehouses are businesses that lease storage space and related physical distribution facilities to other firms. Distribution centres are large, centralized warehouses specially designed for rapid movement of goods to customers. In many cases, a combination of private and public facilities is the most flexible warehousing approach.

Transportation adds time and place utility to a product by moving it from where it is made to where it is purchased and used. The basic modes of transporting goods are railroads, trucks, waterways, airways, and pipelines. The criteria marketers use when selecting a transportation mode are cost, speed, dependability, load flexibility, accessibility, and frequency. Intermodal transportation allows marketers to combine advantages of two or more modes of transport. Freight forwarders coordinate transport by combining small shipments from several organizations into efficient lot sizes, while megacarriers offer several shipment methods.

Physical distribution functions account for about half of all marketing costs and have a significant impact on customer satisfaction. Effective marketers are therefore actively involved in the design and control of physical distribution systems. Physical distribution affects every element of the marketing mix: product, price, promotion, and distribution. To satisfy customers, marketers consider customers' changing needs and shifts within major distribution functions. They then adapt existing physical distribution systems for greater effectiveness.

Please visit the student website at **www.hmco.ca/marketing** for ACE Self-Test questions that will help you prepare for exams.

IMPORTANT TERMS

Distribution	Exclusive distribution	Exclusive dealing	Materials handling
Marketing channel	Channel captain	Physical distribution	Warehousing
Marketing intermediary	Channel power	Outsourcing	Private warehouse
Supply chain management	Vertical channel integration	Cycle time	Public warehouse
Industrial distributor	Vertical marketing systems (VMSs)	Order processing	Distribution centre
Dual distribution		Electronic data interchange (EDI)	Transportation
Strategic channel alliance	Horizontal channel integration	Inventory management	Intermodal transportation
Intensive distribution			Freight forwarder
Selective distribution	Tying agreement	Just-in-time (JIT)	Megacarrier

DISCUSSION & REVIEW QUESTIONS

1. Describe the major functions of marketing channels. Why are these functions better accomplished through combined efforts of channel members?

2. Can one channel member perform all the channel functions? Explain your answer.

3. "Shorter channels are usually a more direct means of distribution and therefore are more efficient." Comment on this statement.

4. List several reasons consumers often blame intermediaries for distribution inefficiencies.

5. Compare and contrast the four major types of marketing channels for consumer products. Through which type of channel is each of the following products most likely to be distributed?
   a. New automobiles
   b. Saltine crackers
   c. Cut-your-own Christmas trees
   d. New textbooks
   e. Sofas
   f. Soft drinks

6. Outline the four most common channels for business products. Describe the products or situations that lead marketers to choose each channel.

7. Describe an industrial distributor. What types of products are marketed through an industrial distributor?

8. Under what conditions is a producer most likely to use more than one marketing channel?

9. Identify and describe the factors that may influence marketing channel selection decisions.

10. Explain the differences among intensive, selective, and exclusive methods of distribution.

11. "Channel cooperation requires that members support the overall channel goals to achieve individual goals." Comment on this statement.

12. Name and describe firms that use (a) vertical integration and (b) horizontal integration in their marketing channels.

13. Explain the major characteristics of each of the three types of vertical marketing systems (VMSs): corporate, administered, and contractual.

14. Under what conditions are tying agreements, exclusive dealing, and dual distribution judged illegal?

APPLICATION QUESTIONS

1. *Supply chain management* refers to long-term partnerships among channel members working together to reduce inefficiencies, costs, and redundancies and to develop innovative approaches to satisfy customers. Select one of the following companies and explain how supply chain management could increase marketing productivity.
   a. Dell Computer
   b. FedEx
   c. Nike
   d. Liquor Control Board of Ontario (LCBO)

2. Organizations often form strategic channel alliances when they find it more profitable or convenient to distribute their products through the marketing channel of another organization. Find an article in a newspaper or on the Internet that describes such a strategic channel alliance. Briefly summarize the article and indicate the benefits each organization expects to gain.

3. Marketers can select from three major levels of market coverage when determining the number and kinds of outlets in which to sell a product: intensive, selective, or exclusive distribution. Characteristics of the product and its target market determine the intensity of coverage a product should receive. Indicate the intensity level best suited for the following products, and explain why it is appropriate.
   a. Personal computer
   b. Deodorant
   c. Canon digital cameras
   d. Nike athletic shoes

4. Describe the decision process you might go through if you were attempting to determine the most appropriate distribution channel for one of the following:
   a. Shotguns for hunters
   b. Women's lingerie
   c. Telephone systems for small businesses
   d. Toy trucks for two-year-olds

globalEDGE™

1. Go to **http://globaledge.msu.edu/ibrd** and click on Country Insights, and Tools and Games. Click on Country Comparator. Using the table compare Canada, China, France, United Kingdom and United States, for airports, railways, highways, for the most recent year of data. How do they compare? Now use the same tool to compare imports and exports. How do five countries rank?

2. Go to **http://globaledge.msu.edu/ibrd** and click on Resource Desk, and Logistics. Scroll down the page to click on PBB Incoterms. Within that website, click on Tools and Resources, then International Borders, then click on Status of Border Crossings, and Canada-US Land Crossings. If you were a Canadian exporter shipping products to the United States would there be any delays? Explain.

INTERNET Exercise

Visit **www.hmco.ca/marketing** for resources to help you master the material in this chapter, plus materials that will help you expand your marketing knowledge, including Internet exercise updates, ACE self-tests, hotlinks to companies featured in this chapter, and much more.

iSuppli

Distribution bottlenecks can be an expensive problem for any business. Trying to prevent such problems is iSuppli, an Internet supply chain management tool that links all members of a supply chain from the supplier's system to the retailer's storefront system. Learn more about this innovative tool at **www.isuppli.com.**

1. Does iSuppli represent a new type of marketing channel? Why or why not?
2. Why would firms be cautious when deciding whether to use iSuppli?
3. Do you think iSuppli represents the future of supply chain management? Why or why not?

Case 15.1   Stuffing It at Coca-Cola

The Coca-Cola Company, founded in the late 1800s, is the largest beverage company in the world with customers in more than 200 countries. The company's brands are many of the most recognized; they include Coca-Cola, Diet Coke, Fanta, Sprite, Powerade, Minute Maid, and Dasani bottled water. Although Coca-Cola focused primarily on customers in the United States in its early years, it has since recognized and relentlessly pursued international opportunities. By the late 1990s, Coca-Cola dominated its market with more than 50 percent of international soft-drink sales. The company has always maintained a strong focus on bringing in, satisfying, and keeping loyal customers. Strategic, recognizable designs on bottles and cans and well-liked global advertising have contributed to the strong reputation the company holds. Coca-Cola consistently is rated the most valuable brand in the world.

Coca-Cola has long focused on social responsibility issues. It makes donations to several foundations that focus on education and community improvement. Coca-Cola is also involved in issuing grants and scholarships both in the United States and internationally. It is also concerned with preserving the environment and helping stem the AIDS/HIV crisis in Africa. All of these contributions help Coca-Cola develop an emotional, trusting relationship with its customers. In 2005, Coca-Cola issued a 50-page report on corporate responsibility in Great Britain. Key accomplishments include supplier compliance and audits, recycling, open work environment, community investment, and an environmental advisory board. Coca-Cola has always prided itself on its strong reputation. The Harris Interactive and the Reputation Institute (creating reputation quotients for companies by measuring 20 perceived attributes) ranked Coca-Cola second in overall reputation in 1999. The company had long been featured on *Fortune* magazine's "America's Most Admired Companies" list. However, the company failed to make the 2000 *Fortune* list due to problems with performance and leadership in 1999. It was also eliminated from *Business Ethics* magazine's

"100 Best Corporate Citizens" list in 2001. The 2005 *Business Ethics* 100 Best Corporate Citizens also did not include Coca-Cola.

Coca-Cola's problems in 1999 began with a contamination scare that had a negative effect on its European reputation. That year also brought a racial discrimination lawsuit by about 2000 current and former African American employees against the company. The company settled the suit by paying $193 million. And then-CEO Doug Invester raised concentrate prices—a strategy that did not go over well with the company's bottlers. Overall, it was thought that the company did not handle these crises well. In addition to reflecting poorly on Coca-Cola's reputation, these crises had a negative impact on the firm's bottlers, distributors, suppliers, and other related third parties.

A major problem that Coca-Cola faced during this period was accusations of channel stuffing. Channel stuffing is the practice of shipping extra inventory to wholesalers and retailers at an excessive rate, typically before the end of a quarter. Essentially, a company counts the shipments as sales although the products often remain in warehouses or are later returned to the manufacturer. Channel stuffing tends to create the appearance of strong demand (or conceals declining demand) for a product, which may result in inflated financial statement earnings, misleading investors. Accusations of channel stuffing have been made recently against companies such as Krispy Kreme Donuts, Harley-Davidson, Clear One Communications, Symbol Technologies, Network Associates, Bristol-Myers, Taser International, and Intel.

In Coca-Cola's case, the company was accused of sending extra concentrate to Japanese bottlers from 1997 through 1999 in an effort to inflate its profit. The company was already under investigation after a former employee filed a lawsuit in 2000 accusing the company of fraud and improper business practices. In 2004, former finance officials for Coca-Cola reported finding statements of inflated earnings due to the company's shipping extra concentrate to Japan. Although the company settled the allegations, the Securities and Exchange Commission (SEC) did find that channel stuffing had occurred. However, what Coca-Cola had done was to pressure bottlers into buying additional concentrate in exchange for extended credit. Therefore, the sales were technically considered legitimate.

To settle with the SEC, Coke agreed to avoid engaging in channel stuffing in the future. The company also created an ethics and compliance office and is required to verify each financial quarter that it has not altered the terms of payment or extended special credit. The company further agreed to work to reduce the amount of concentrate held by international bottlers. Although the company settled with the SEC and the Justice Department, it still faces a shareholder lawsuit regarding channel stuffing in Japan, North America, Europe, and South Africa.

Despite a solid focus on building and maintaining a strong, positive reputation and a firm dedication to social responsibility, Coca-Cola has had its major problems in competing with its major rival PepsiCo. The use of channel stuffing and other questionable practices has not been the answer to making the numbers.[15]

Questions for Discussion

1. How could channel stuffing at Coca-Cola affect its relationships with channel members such as bottlers?
2. In what ways could channel stuffing impact its own customer service standards?
3. Why would Coca-Cola risk its reputation by engaging in channel stuffing?

Case 15.2   Distribution Technology: Wal-Mart's Power Tool

How does the world's largest retailer keep the shelves stocked at 6000 stores while keeping prices low enough to attract 138 million shoppers worldwide every week? Physical distribution is the key. Since the first Wal-Mart opened in Rogers, Arkansas, in 1962, management has carefully balanced its inventory levels, delivery schedules, and transportation costs to ensure products arrive at the right stores at the right time and at the right price. Today the company uses information technology to coordinate the movement of products from suppliers to the loading docks of its 62 distribution centres and on to the company's Wal-Mart discount stores, SuperCenter combination food/general merchandise outlets, Sam's Club warehouse stores, and Neighborhood Market grocery stores. Every day, Wal-Mart tracks 718 million items.

Through its Retail Link network, Wal-Mart collaborates with suppliers to forecast sales, plan future orders, and replenish stock automatically. Here is how the system works. The point-of-sale scanning equipment in each store captures item-by-item, brand-by-brand sales data. Using sophisticated database technology, Wal-Mart analyzes the sales patterns and historical results for the previous 65 weeks with all of its suppliers. Next, Wal-Mart and its suppliers agree on forecasts for future sales. Then they jointly decide on an order and delivery schedule to ensure inventory levels at each distribution centre are appropriate for the forecasted store sales. Wal-Mart makes the system available to suppliers free of charge. In exchange, suppliers share detailed analyses of results and forecasts with Wal-Mart officials.

Retail Link works. During a pilot test with the maker of Listerine, Wal-Mart was able to boost its in-stock position from 87 percent to 98 percent while cutting the order fulfillment cycle time from 21 to 11 days. The supplier also benefited because it sold Wal-Mart an additional $8.5 million of Listerine and was able to better manage its production and delivery activities. Customers benefited because they were able to pick up bottles of Listerine from store shelves when they wanted, and they saved money because low costs allow Wal-Mart to set everyday low prices.

Another technology that helps Wal-Mart streamline its physical distribution system is radio frequency identification (RFID). Wal-Mart requires its 100 largest suppliers to attach an RFID tag (bearing a computer chip, radio antenna, and identification number) to each case or pallet of merchandise. Using readers in its distribution centres, Wal-Mart picks up radio signals indicating which products are being received and in what quantities. Now the company can track inbound inventory on conveyer belts travelling 540 feet per minute without individually counting each container—and with complete accuracy. The technology has already yielded a 16 percent reduction of stockouts for certain products. Next-generation RFID technology will enable Wal-Mart to track shipments on much faster-moving conveyer belts.

Despite a global roster of 20 000 suppliers, Wal-Mart is always looking for ways to improve its supply chain management and gain flexibility, slash costs, and identify new supply sources around the world. For example, the company imports $12 billion worth of merchandise from China every year. It also maintains a private procurement website to request and receive supplier bids on contracts, centrally negotiate purchasing, and arrange shipping.

As the most powerful channel captain on the planet, Wal-Mart can command ever-higher efficiencies from its suppliers, squeeze additional costs from physical distribution due to economies of scale, and pass the savings on to consumers in the form of lower retail prices. Consider its private-brand George jeans, which were originally priced at $26.67. Wal-Mart reduced costs by purchasing in high volume directly from suppliers in Asia rather than working through wholesalers. It cut costs even further by refining materials handling and transportation. Now George jeans sell for $7.85—less than one-third of the old price.

As Wal-Mart spreads farther from its Arkansas base, management continues opening distribution centres and arranging transportation to ship merchandise to clusters of stores in the area. The company operates a huge truck fleet to transfer products from distribution centres to stores, but it also contracts with independent trucking firms to transport food and other specialized products. In the Northeast, for example, Wal-Mart receives and stores grocery products at an 868 000-square-foot food distribution centre in Johnstown, New York. From there, trucks operated by Clarksville Refrigerated Lines bring orders to Wal-Mart stores across New England, New York, and Pennsylvania. Similarly, a fleet of refrigerated trucks operated by M. S. Carriers transports perishable food products from Wal-Mart's food distribution centre in Monroe, Georgia, to Sam's Club warehouse stores in five surrounding states.

Rather than reinvent the wheel for every distribution centre and store in North America, Argentina, Brazil, Germany, the United Kingdom, Japan, China, and Korea, the company encourages each region to share its best distribution practices. As a result, Wal-Mart's German stores are benefiting from the U.S. stores' experience in reducing inventory levels and restocking more rapidly. Its Korean stores are replicating the Mexican operation's popular and profitable web-based grocery delivery program. The world's largest retailer is not finished expanding. As it opens hundreds of new stores in the coming years, it will keep honing its distribution skills to keep shelves stocked at the lowest possible cost.[16]

Questions for Discussion

1. Why is physical distribution so important to Wal-Mart's marketing strategy?
2. Why does Wal-Mart prefer to deal directly with suppliers rather than buying from wholesalers?
3. How does Retail Link help Wal-Mart better control order processing and inventory management?

Wholesaling, Retailing, and Direct Marketing

CHAPTER 16

Wholesalers in Canada: Leading the Pack

Wholesaling may not have the allure of manufacturing, or the glamour of retail, but it has become a powerhouse for revenue and employment across Canada. Canada's wholesalers grossed $470 billion in 2005, up 48 percent from 1997. This growth rate averaged six percent each year, outperforming Canada's economic growth and resulting in the highest growth rate of any industrial sector. Sales growth between 2004 and 2005 was the largest single year-to-year growth rate in the last six years at 7.8 percent, after adjusting for inflation.

Wholesalers employed approximately 739 000 people in 2005, up 30 percent from 2004, and up 60 percent from 1997. In 2004, wholesale trade accounted for three percent of the nation's workforce. Employment increased 30 percent between 1997 and 2004, outperforming that of retail and manufacturing sectors with growth rates of 13 percent.

Statistics Canada reported that employees in the wholesale sectors also bring home more money than their counterparts in retail or manufacturing. In 2004, the average wholesale worker's weekly earnings were over $800: 23 percent higher than wages of manufacturing workers, and nearly double the wages of retail workers.

The wholesale industry has been dramatically impacted by increases in technology, all of which have also impacted employee productivity. Once again, wholesalers outperformed retailers and manufacturers. Wholesale labour productivity rose 36 percent between 1997 and 2004, compared to increases of 20 percent in retail and 25 percent in manufacturing.

Wholesalers provide a vital service to the Canadian economy, providing access to import products that Canadians demand, while also helping producers and retailers to more efficiently respond to changing consumer tastes in everything from fashion, to automobiles, to food. In a time when many firms seek to save money but "cutting out the middleman" Canadian wholesalers have found ways to further integrate themselves into Canada's major supply chains by providing added value services that make each channel member more efficient, and ultimately, more profitable.[1] ■

Wholesalers help make products available to customers when and where they want them. Wholesalers often play a key role in supply chain management and physical distribution. Companies rely heavily on physical distribution, a crucial set of functions in supply chain management, because it includes those activities associated with handling and moving products through the marketing channel.

In this chapter, we explore the role of wholesaling and physical distribution in supply chain management. First, we examine the importance of wholesalers in marketing channels, including their functions and classifications. Next, we will examine the retailing function in the distribution channel. We conclude this chapter by examining some strategic implications of retailing.

The Nature of Wholesaling

wholesaling Transactions in which products are bought for resale, for making other products, or for general business operations

wholesaler An individual or organization that sells products that are bought for resale, for making other products, or for general business operations

Wholesaling refers to all transactions in which products are bought for resale, for making other products, or for general business operations. A **wholesaler** is an individual or organization that sells products that are bought for these purposes. In other words, wholesalers buy products and resell them to reseller, government, and institutional users. Wholesaling does not include exchanges with ultimate consumers. For example, SYSCO, a leading North American food-service distributor, supplies restaurants, hotels, schools, industrial caterers, and hospitals with everything from frozen and fresh food and paper products to medical and cleaning supplies. Table 16.1 lists the major activities wholesalers perform, but individual wholesalers may perform more or fewer functions than the table shows. Distribution of all goods requires wholesaling activities whether or not a wholesaling firm is involved. Wholesaling activities are not limited to goods; service companies, such as financial institutions, also use active wholesale networks. For example, some banks buy loans in bulk from other financial institutions as well as making loans to their own retail customers.

Wholesalers perform services for other organizations in the marketing channel. They bear primary responsibility for the physical distribution of products from manufacturers to retailers. In addition, they may establish information systems that help producers and retailers better manage the supply chain from producer to customer. Many wholesalers are using information technology and the Internet to allow their employees, customers, and suppliers to share information between intermediaries and facilitating agencies such as trucking companies and warehouse firms. For example, FedEx, which serves as a facilitating agency in providing overnight or even same-day delivery of packages, provides online tracking of packages for the benefit of its customers. Other firms are making their databases and marketing information systems available to their supply chain partners to facilitate order processing, shipping, and product development and to share information about changing market conditions and customer desires. As a result, some wholesalers play a key role in supply chain management decisions.

Services Provided by Wholesalers

Wholesalers provide essential services to both producers and retailers. By initiating sales contacts with a producer and selling diverse products to retailers, wholesalers

table 16.1 MAJOR WHOLESALING FUNCTIONS	
Supply chain management	Creating long-term partnerships among channel members
Promotion	Providing a sales force, advertising, sales promotion, and publicity
Warehousing, shipping, and product handling	Receiving, storing, and stock keeping Packaging Shipping outgoing orders Materials handling Arranging and making local and long-distance shipments
Inventory control and data processing	Processing orders Controlling physical inventory Recording transactions Tracking sales data for financial analysis
Risk taking	Assuming responsibility for theft, product obsolescence, and excess inventories
Financing and budgeting	Extending credit Borrowing Making capital investments Forecasting cash flow
Marketing research and information systems	Providing information about markets Conducting research studies Managing computer networks to facilitate exchanges and relationships

serve as an extension of the producer's sales force. Wholesalers also provide financial assistance. They often pay for transporting goods; they reduce a producer's warehousing expenses and inventory investment by holding goods in inventory; they extend credit and assume losses from buyers who turn out to be poor credit risks; and when they buy a producer's entire output and pay promptly or in cash, they are a source of working capital. Wholesalers also serve as conduits for information within the marketing channel, keeping producers up to date on market developments and passing along the manufacturers' promotional plans to other intermediaries. Using wholesalers therefore gives producers a distinct advantage because the specialized services wholesalers perform allow producers to concentrate on developing and manufacturing products that match customers' needs and wants.

Many producers would prefer more direct interaction with retailers. Wholesalers, however, are more likely to have closer contact with retailers because of their strategic position in the marketing channel. Although a producer's own sales force is probably more effective at selling, the costs of maintaining a sales force and performing functions normally done by wholesalers are sometimes higher than the benefits received from an independent sales staff. Wholesalers can spread sales costs over many more products than can most producers, resulting in lower costs per product unit. For these reasons, many producers shift informational, financing, and physical distribution activities, such as transportation and warehousing, to wholesalers. Thus, the wholesaler often becomes a major link in the supply chain, creating an optimal level of efficiency and customer service.

Wholesalers support retailers by assisting with marketing strategy, especially the distribution component. Wholesalers also help retailers select inventory. They are often specialists on market conditions and experts at negotiating final purchases. In industries in which obtaining supplies is important, skilled buying is indispensable. For example, Atlanta-based Genuine Parts Company (GPC), the nation's top automotive parts wholesaler, has more than 70 years of experience in the auto parts business, which helps the company serve its customers effectively. GPC supplies more than 300 000 replacement parts (from 150 different suppliers) to 6000 NAPA Auto Parts stores.[2] The firm also supplies 1800 service outlets throughout Canada, the United States, and Mexico.

Effective wholesalers make an effort to understand the businesses of their customers. They can reduce a retailer's burden of looking for and coordinating supply sources. If the wholesaler purchases for several buyers, all customers can share expenses. Furthermore, whereas a manufacturer's salesperson offers retailers only a few products at a time, independent wholesalers always have a wide range of products available. Thus, through partnerships, wholesalers and retailers can forge successful relationships for the benefit of customers.

Buying in large quantities and delivering to customers in smaller lots enable wholesalers to perform physical distribution activities efficiently. These activities (discussed later in this chapter) include order processing, inventory planning, materials handling, warehousing, and transportation. Wholesalers furnish greater service than might be feasible for a producer's or retailer's own physical distribution system. Furthermore, wholesalers offer quick and frequent delivery even when demand fluctuates and can do so at low cost, which lets the producer and the wholesalers' customers avoid risks associated with holding large inventories.

The distinction between services performed by wholesalers and those provided by other businesses has blurred in recent years. Changes in the competitive nature of business, especially the growth of strong retail chains such as Wal-Mart, Home Depot, and Best Buy, are changing supply chain relationships. In many product categories, such as electronics, furniture, and even food products, retailers have discovered they can deal directly with producers, performing wholesaling activities themselves at a lower cost. An increasing number of retailers are relying on computer technology to expedite ordering, delivery, and handling of goods. Technology is thus allowing retailers to take over many wholesaling functions. When a wholesaler is eliminated from a marketing channel, the functions, listed in Table 16.1, still have to be performed by a member of the marketing channel, whether a producer, retailer, or facilitating agency. These wholesaling activities are critical components of supply chain management.

Types of Wholesalers

Wholesalers are classified according to several criteria. Whether a wholesaler is independently owned or owned by a producer influences how it is classified. Wholesalers can also be grouped according to whether they take title to (own) the products they handle. The range of services provided is another criterion used for classification. Finally, wholesalers are classified according to the breadth and depth of their product lines. Using these criteria, we discuss three general types of wholesaling establishments: merchant wholesalers, agents and brokers, and manufacturers' sales branches and offices.

merchant wholesaler
An independently owned business that takes title to goods, assumes ownership risks, and buys and resells products to other wholesalers, business customers, or retailers

Merchant Wholesalers. **Merchant wholesalers** are independently owned businesses that take title to goods, assume risks associated with ownership, and generally buy and resell products to other wholesalers, business customers, or retailers. A producer is likely to rely on merchant wholesalers when selling directly to customers would be economically unfeasible. Merchant wholesalers are also useful for providing market coverage, making sales contacts, storing inventory, handling orders, collecting market information, and furnishing customer support. Some merchant wholesalers are even involved in packaging and developing private brands to help retail customers be competitive. Merchant wholesalers go by various names, including *wholesaler, jobber, distributor, assembler, exporter,* and *importer.* They fall into one of two broad categories: full-service and limited-service (see Figure 16.1).

full-service wholesaler
A merchant wholesaler that performs the widest range of wholesaling functions

Full-Service Wholesalers. **Full-service wholesalers** perform the widest possible range of wholesaling functions. Customers rely on them for product availability, suitable assortments, breaking large quantities into smaller lots, financial assistance, and technical advice and service. Full-service wholesalers handle either consumer or business products and provide numerous marketing services to their customers. Many large grocery wholesalers help retailers with store design, site selection, personnel training,

figure 16.1

TYPES OF MERCHANT WHOLESALERS

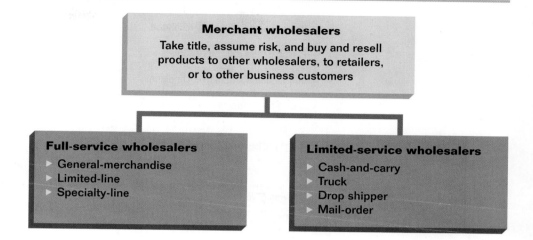

financing, merchandising, advertising, coupon redemption, and scanning. Although full-service wholesalers often earn higher gross margins than other wholesalers, their operating expenses are also higher because they perform a wider range of functions. Full-service wholesalers are categorized as general-merchandise, general-line, and specialty-line wholesalers.

General-merchandise wholesalers carry a wide product mix but offer limited depth within product lines. They deal in such products as drugs, non-perishable foods, cosmetics, detergents, and tobacco. **General-line wholesalers** carry only a few product lines, such as groceries, lighting fixtures, or oil-well drilling equipment, but offer an extensive assortment of products within those lines. Bergen Brunswig Corporation, for example, is a general-line wholesaler of pharmaceuticals and health and beauty aids. General-line wholesalers provide a range of services similar to those of general-merchandise wholesalers. Bergen Brunswig's products are sold through the 1750 Safeway supermarket outlets across North America.

Specialty-line wholesalers offer the narrowest range of products, usually a single product line or a few items within a product line. Wholesalers that specialize in shellfish, fruit, or other food delicacies are specialty-line wholesalers. **Rack jobbers** are a type of specialty-line wholesalers that own and maintain display racks in supermarkets, drugstores, and discount and variety stores. They set up displays, mark merchandise, stock shelves, and keep billing and inventory records; retailers need to furnish only space. Rack jobbers specialize in non-food items with high profit margins, such as health and beauty aids, books, magazines, hosiery, and greeting cards.

Limited-Service Wholesalers. **Limited-service wholesalers** provide fewer marketing services than full-service wholesalers and specialize in just a few functions. Producers perform the remaining functions or pass them on to customers or to other intermediaries. Limited-service wholesalers take title to merchandise but often do not deliver merchandise, grant credit, provide marketing information, store inventory, or plan ahead for customers' future needs. Because they offer restricted services, limited-service wholesalers are compensated with lower rates and have smaller profit margins than full-service wholesalers. The decision about whether to use a limited-service or a full-service wholesaler depends on the structure of the marketing channel and the need to manage the supply chain to provide competitive advantage. Although certain types of limited-service wholesalers are few in number, they are important in the distribution of such products as specialty foods, perishable items, construction materials, and coal. Table 16.2 summarizes the services provided by four typical limited-service wholesalers: cash-and-carry wholesalers, truck wholesalers, drop shippers, and mail-order wholesalers.

general-merchandise wholesaler A full-service wholesaler with a wide product mix but limited depth within product lines

general-line wholesaler A full-service wholesaler that carries only a few product lines but many products within those lines

specialty-line wholesaler A full-service wholesaler that carries only a single product line or a few items within a product line

rack jobber A type of specialty-line wholesaler that owns and maintains display racks in stores

limited-service wholesaler A merchant wholesaler that provides some services and specializes in a few functions

table 16.2	SERVICES THAT LIMITED-SERVICE WHOLESALERS PROVIDE			
	Cash-and-Carry	Truck	Drop Shipper	Mail-Order
Physical possession of merchandise	Yes	Yes	No	Yes
Personal sales calls on customers	No	Yes	No	No
Information about market conditions	No	Some	Yes	Yes
Advice to customers	No	Some	Yes	No
Stocking and maintenance of merchandise in customers' stores	No	No	No	No
Credit to customers	No	No	Yes	Some
Delivery of merchandise to customers	No	Yes	No	No

cash-and-carry wholesaler
A limited-service wholesaler whose customers pay cash and furnish transportation

truck wholesaler A limited-service wholesaler that transports products directly to customers for inspection and selection

drop shipper A limited-service wholesaler that takes title to goods and negotiates sales but never actually takes possession of products

mail-order wholesaler
A wholesaler who uses catalogues instead a sales force to sell products to retail and business buyers

agent An intermediary that represents either buyers or sellers on a permanent basis

broker An intermediary that brings buyers and sellers together temporarily

Cash-and-carry wholesalers are intermediaries whose customers—usually small businesses—pay cash and furnish transportation. Cash-and-carry wholesalers typically handle a limited line of products with a high turnover rate, such as groceries, building materials, and electrical or office supplies. Many small retailers whose accounts are refused by other wholesalers survive because of cash-and-carry wholesalers. **Truck wholesalers,** sometimes called *truck jobbers,* transport a limited line of products directly to customers for on-the-spot inspection and selection. They are often small operators who own and drive their own trucks. They usually have regular routes, calling on retailers and other institutions to determine their needs. **Drop shippers,** also known as *desk jobbers,* take title to goods and negotiate sales but never actually take possession of products. They forward orders from retailers, business buyers, or other wholesalers to manufacturers and arrange for carload shipments of items to be delivered directly from producers to these customers. They assume responsibility for products during the entire transaction, including the costs of any unsold goods. **Mail-order wholesalers** use catalogues instead of sales forces to sell products to retail and business buyers. Wholesale mail-order houses generally feature cosmetics, specialty foods, sporting goods, office supplies, and automotive parts. This is a convenient and effective method of selling small items to customers in remote areas that other wholesalers might find unprofitable to serve. The Internet has enabled mail-order wholesalers to sell products via their own websites and have the products shipped by the manufacturers.

Agents and Brokers. Agents and brokers negotiate purchases and expedite sales but do not take title to products (see Figure 16.2). Sometimes called *functional middlemen,* they perform a limited number of services in exchange for a commission, which is generally based on the product's selling price. **Agents** represent either buyers or sellers on a permanent basis, whereas **brokers** are intermediaries that buyers or sellers employ temporarily.

Although agents and brokers perform even fewer functions than limited-service wholesalers, they are usually specialists in particular products or types of customers and can provide valuable sales expertise. They know their markets well and often form long-lasting associations with customers. Agents and brokers enable manufacturers to expand sales when resources are limited, to benefit from the services of a trained sales force, and to hold down personal selling costs. Despite the advantages they offer, agents and brokers face increased competition from merchant wholesalers, manufacturers' sales branches and offices, and direct-sales efforts through manufacturer-owned websites. We look here at three types of agents—manufacturers' agents, selling agents, and commission merchants—and at the broker's role in bringing about exchanges between buyers and sellers. Table 16.3 summarizes the services agents and brokers provide.

figure 16.2

TYPES OF AGENTS AND BROKERS

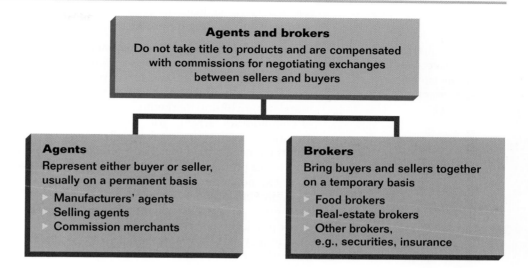

Agents and brokers
Do not take title to products and are compensated with commissions for negotiating exchanges between sellers and buyers

Agents
Represent either buyer or seller, usually on a permanent basis
- Manufacturers' agents
- Selling agents
- Commission merchants

Brokers
Bring buyers and sellers together on a temporary basis
- Food brokers
- Real-estate brokers
- Other brokers, e.g., securities, insurance

manufacturers' agent
An independent intermediary that represents two or more sellers and usually offers customers complete product lines

Manufacturers' Agents. **Manufacturers' agents,** which account for more than half of all agent wholesalers, are independent intermediaries that represent two or more sellers and usually offer customers complete product lines. They sell and take orders year-round, much as a manufacturer's sales force does. Restricted to a particular territory, a manufacturers' agent handles non-competing and complementary products. The relationship between the agent and the manufacturer is governed by written contracts that outline territories, selling price, order handling, and terms of sale related to delivery, service, and warranties. Manufacturers' agents have little or no control over producers' pricing and marketing policies. They do not extend credit and may be unable to provide technical advice. They do occasionally store and transport products, assist producers with planning and promotion, and help retailers advertise. Some maintain a service organization; the more services offered, the higher the agent's commission. Manufacturers' agents are commonly used in sales of apparel, machinery and equipment, steel, furniture, automotive products, electrical goods, and certain food items.

selling agent An intermediary that markets a whole product line or a manufacturer's entire output

Selling Agents. **Selling agents** market either all of a specified product line or a manufacturer's entire output. They perform every wholesaling activity except taking title to products. Selling agents usually assume the sales function for several producers simultaneously and are often used in place of marketing departments. In fact, selling agents are used most often by small producers or by manufacturers that have difficulty maintaining a marketing department because of seasonal production or other factors. In

table 16.3   SERVICES THAT AGENTS AND BROKERS PROVIDE

	Manufacturers' Agents	Selling Agents	Commission Merchants	Brokers
Physical possession of merchandise	Some	Some	Yes	No
Long-term relationship with buyers or sellers	Yes	Yes	Yes	No
Representation of competing product lines	No	No	Yes	Yes
Limited geographic territory	Yes	No	No	No
Credit to customers	No	Yes	Some	No

contrast to manufacturers' agents, selling agents generally have no territorial limits and have complete authority over prices, promotion, and distribution. To avoid conflicts of interest, selling agents represent non-competing product lines. They play a key role in advertising, marketing research, and credit policies of the sellers they represent, at times even advising on product development and packaging.

commission merchant
An agent that receives goods on consignment from local sellers and negotiates sales in large, central markets

Commission Merchants. **Commission merchants** receive goods on consignment from local sellers and negotiate sales in large, central markets. Sometimes called *factor merchants,* these agents have broad powers regarding prices and terms of sale. They specialize in obtaining the best price possible under market conditions. Most often found in agricultural marketing, commission merchants take possession of truckloads of commodities, arrange for necessary grading or storage, and transport the commodities to auctions or markets where they are sold. When sales are completed, the agents deduct commissions and sales expenses, and then turn over the remaining revenue to the producer. Commission merchants also offer planning assistance and sometimes extend credit, but usually do not provide promotional support.

A broker's primary purpose is to bring buyers and sellers together. Thus, brokers perform fewer functions than other intermediaries. They are not involved in financing or physical possession, have no authority to set prices, and assume almost no risks. Instead they offer customers specialized knowledge of a particular commodity and a network of established contacts. Brokers are especially useful to sellers of certain types of products, such as supermarket products and real estate. Food brokers, for example, sell food and general merchandise to retailer-owned and merchant wholesalers, grocery chains, food processors, and business buyers.

sales branches A manufacturer-owned intermediary that sells products and provides support services to the manufacturer's sales force

Manufacturers' Sales Branches and Offices. Sometimes called *manufacturers' wholesalers,* manufacturers' sales branches and offices resemble merchant wholesalers' operations. **Sales branches** are manufacturer-owned intermediaries that sell products and provide support services to the manufacturer's sales force. Situated away from the manufacturing plant, they are usually located where large customers are concentrated and demand is high. They offer credit, deliver goods, give promotional assistance, and furnish other services. In many cases, they carry inventory (although this practice often duplicates functions of other channel members and is now declining). Customers include retailers, business buyers, and other wholesalers. Manufacturers of electrical supplies, such as Westinghouse Electric, and of plumbing supplies, such as American Standard, often have branch operations. Sales branches are also common in the lumber and automotive parts industries.

sales office A manufacturer-owned operation that provides services normally associated with agents

Sales offices are manufacturer-owned operations that provide services normally associated with agents. Like sales branches, they are located away from manufacturing plants; unlike branches, they carry no inventory. A manufacturer's sales office (or branch) may sell products that enhance the manufacturer's own product line. Companies such as Campbell Soup provide diverse services to their wholesale and retail customers. Hiram Walker, a liquor producer, imports wine from Spain to increase the number of products its sales offices can offer wholesalers.

Manufacturers may set up these branches or offices to reach their customers more effectively by performing wholesaling functions themselves. A manufacturer may also set up such a facility when specialized wholesaling services are not available through existing intermediaries. A manufacturer's performance of wholesaling and physical distribution activities through its sales branch or office may strengthen supply chain efficiency. In some situations, though, a manufacturer may bypass its sales office or branches entirely—for example, if the producer decides to serve large retailer customers directly.

Retailers such as the Container Store, Home Depot, and Victoria's Secret are highly visible and accessible channel members to consumers. They are important links in the marketing channel because they are both marketers for and customers of producers and wholesalers. They perform many marketing functions, such as buying, selling, grading, risk taking, and developing and maintaining information databases about customers. Retailers are in strategic positions to develop relationships with consumers and partnerships with producers and intermediaries in the marketing channel.

In this chapter, we examine the nature of retailing and its importance in supplying consumers with goods and services. We discuss the major types of retail stores. Then we describe direct marketing and two other types of non-store retailing. Next we look at franchising, a retailing form that continues to grow in popularity. Finally, we explore several strategic issues in retailing, including location, retail positioning, store image, scrambled merchandising, and the wheel of retailing.

The Nature Of Retailing

retailing All transactions in which the buyer intends to consume the product through personal, family, or household use

retailer An organization that purchases products for the purpose of reselling them to ultimate consumers

Retailing includes all transactions in which the buyer intends to consume the product through personal, family, or household use. Buyers in retail transactions are therefore the ultimate consumers. A **retailer** is an organization that purchases products for the purpose of reselling them to ultimate consumers. Although most retailers' sales are made directly to the consumer, non-retail transactions occasionally occur when retailers sell products to other businesses. Retailing often takes place in stores or service establishments, but it also occurs through direct selling, direct marketing, and vending machines outside stores.

Retailing is important to the national economy. Most personal income is spent in retail stores, and nearly one out of eight people employed works in a retail operation (Figure 16.3).

Retailers add value, provide services, and assist in making product selections. They can enhance the value of the product by making the shopping experience more convenient, as in home shopping. Through its location, a retailer can facilitate comparison shopping; for example, car dealerships often cluster in the same general vicinity. Product value is also enhanced when retailers offer services, such as technical advice, delivery, credit, and repair services. Finally, retail sales personnel can demonstrate to customers how a product can help address their needs or solve a problem.

The value added by retailers is significant for both producers and ultimate consumers. Retailers are the critical link between producers and ultimate consumers because they provide the environment in which exchanges with ultimate consumers occur. Ultimate consumers benefit through retailers' performance of marketing functions that result in availability of broader arrays of products. Retailers play a major role in creating time, place, and possession utility and, in some cases, form utility.

Leading retailers such as Wal-Mart, Home Depot, and Toys 'R' Us offer consumers a place to browse and compare merchandise to find exactly what they need. However, such traditional retailing is being challenged by direct marketing channels that provide home shopping through catalogues, television, and the Internet. Traditional retailers are responding to this change in the retail environment in various ways. Wal-Mart, for example, is offering more upscale merchandise such as plasma TVs and more fashionable apparel as well as more extended warranties on merchandise.[3] It has also joined forces with fast-food giants McDonald's and KFC to attract consumers and offer them the added convenience of eating where they shop. In response to competition from Amazon.com, Barnes & Noble developed a website to sell books via the Internet.

New store formats and advances in information technology are making the retail environment highly dynamic and competitive. Instant-messaging technology is enabling online retailers to converse with customers so they don't click away to another site. For example, shoppers on the Lands' End website can chat, via keyboard, directly with a customer service representative about sizes, colours, or other product details. The key to success in

figure 16.3

THE IMPORTANCE OF RETAILING IN THE U.S. ECONOMY

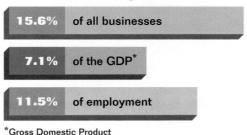

In the U.S., retailing accounts for:

15.6% of all businesses

7.1% of the GDP*

11.5% of employment

*Gross Domestic Product

Source: U.S. Bureau of the Census, *Statistical Abstract of the United States,* 2006 (Washington, DC: Government Printing Office, 2006), pp. 407, 444, 513, 671.

retailing is to have a strong customer focus with a retail strategy that provides the level of service, product quality, and innovation that consumers desire. Partnerships among non-competing retailers and other marketing channel members are providing new opportunities for retailers. For example, airports are leasing space to retailers such as Sharper Image, McDonald's, Sunglass Hut, and The Body Shop.

Retailers are also finding global opportunities. For example, both McDonald's and the Gap are now opening more international stores than domestic ones, a trend that is likely to continue for the foreseeable future. Wal-Mart and Home Depot are opening stores in Canada, Mexico, and South America. Increasingly, retailers from abroad, such as IKEA, Zara, and BP, are opening stores in the United States.

Major Types Of Retail Stores

Many types of retail stores exist. One way to classify them is by the breadth of products offered. Two general categories include general-merchandise retailers and specialty retailers.

General-Merchandise Retailers

general-merchandise retailer A retail establishment that offers a variety of product lines that are stocked in considerable depth

department store A large retail organization characterized by a wide product mix and organized into separate departments to facilitate marketing efforts and internal management

A retail establishment that offers a variety of product lines stocked in considerable depth is referred to as a **general-merchandise retailer.** The types of product offerings, mixes of customer services, and operating styles of retailers in this category vary considerably. The primary types of general-merchandise retailers are department stores, discount stores, supermarkets, superstores, hypermarkets, warehouse clubs, and warehouse and catalogue showrooms (see Table 16.4).

Department Stores. **Department stores** are large retail organizations characterized by wide product mixes and staffs of at least 25 people. To facilitate marketing efforts and internal management in these stores, related product lines are organized into

table 16.4 GENERAL-MERCHANDISE RETAILERS

Type of Retailer	Description	Examples
Department store	Large organization offering a wide product mix and organized into separate departments	Macy's, JCPenney, Sears
Discount store	Self-service, general-merchandise store offering brand name and private-brand products at low prices	Wal-Mart, Zellers
Convenience store	Small self-service store offering narrow product assortment in convenient locations	7-Eleven, Need, Green Gables
Supermarket	Self-service store offering a complete line of food products and some non-food products	Sobey's, A&P, Overwaitea, Dominion
Superstore	Giant outlet offering all food and non-food products found in supermarkets, as well as most routinely purchased products	Wal-Mart Supercentres, AtlanticSuperstore
Warehouse club	Large-scale, members-only establishment combining cash-and-carry wholesaling and discount retailing	Sam's Club, Costco
Warehouse showroom	Facility in a large, low-cost building with large on-premises inventories and minimal service	IKEA, Leon's
Catalogue showroom	Warehouse showroom in which consumers use catalogues to place orders for products, which are then filled directly in the warehouse area and picked up by buyers in the showroom	Service Merchandise, Consumer's Distributing

separate departments, such as cosmetics, housewares, apparel, home furnishings, and appliances. Often each department functions as a self-contained business, and buyers for individual departments are fairly autonomous.

Department stores are distinctly service oriented. Their total product may include credit, delivery, personal assistance, merchandise returns, and a pleasant atmosphere.

Although some so-called department stores are actually large, departmentalized specialty stores, most department stores are shopping stores: consumers can compare price, quality, and service at one store with those at competing stores. Along with large discount stores, department stores are often considered retailing leaders in a community and are found in most places with populations of more than 50 000.

Typical department stores, such as Sears, The Bay, and Neiman Marcus, obtain a large proportion of sales from apparel, accessories, and cosmetics. Other products these stores carry include gift items, luggage, electronics, home accessories, and sports equipment. Some department stores offer such services as automobile insurance, hair care, income tax preparation, and travel and optical services. In some cases, space for these specialized services is leased out, with proprietors managing their own operations and paying rent to the store.

discount store A self-service, general-merchandise store offering brand name and private-brand products at low prices

Discount Stores. **Discount stores** are self-service, general-merchandise outlets that regularly offer brand name and private-brand products at low prices. Discounters accept lower margins than conventional retailers in exchange for high sales volume. To keep inventory turnover high, they carry a wide but carefully selected assortment of products, from appliances to housewares and clothing. Major discount establishments also offer food products, toys, automotive services, garden supplies, and sports equipment. Most operate in large no-frills facilities ranging in size from more than 4000 to over 7000 square metres (50 000 to 80 000 square feet). Discount stores usually offer everyday low prices rather than relying on sales events.

Discount retailing developed on a large scale in the early 1950s, when post-war production began catching up with consumer demand for appliances, home furnishings, and other hard goods. Discount stores were often cash-only operations in warehouse districts, offering goods at savings of 20 to 30 percent over conventional retailers. Facing increased competition from department stores and other discount stores, some discounters have improved store services, atmosphere, and location, raising prices and sometimes blurring the distinction between discount store and department store. Other discounters continue to focus on price alone.

convenience store A small self-service store that is open long hours and carries a narrow assortment of products, usually convenience items

Convenience Stores. **Convenience stores** are small self-service stores that are open long hours and carry a narrow assortment of convenience items such as soft drinks and other beverages, snacks, newspapers, tobacco, and gasoline, and provide services such as automatic teller machines. The primary product offered by these stores is convenience. 7-Eleven's director of processed foods says, "When consumers visit a

7-Eleven, they seek something that will solve their immediate need. They are in the mood for a consumable product and want it right now, and expect the convenience store to deliver it."[4] According to Statistics Canada, convenience and specialty food stores accounted for 13.2 percent of all food sales in Canada in 2006, totalling more than $9.5 billion.[5] Convenience stores are typically less than 5000 square feet, are open 24 hours a day, seven days a week, and stock about 500 items. In addition to many national chains, there are many family-owned independent convenience stores in operation.[6]

supermarket A large, self-service store that carries a complete line of food products, along with some non-food products

Supermarkets. **Supermarkets** are large, self-service stores that carry a complete line of food products, as well as some non-food products such as cosmetics and non-prescription drugs. Supermarkets are arranged in departments for maximum efficiency in stocking and handling products, but have central checkout facilities. They offer lower prices than smaller neighbourhood grocery stores, usually provide free parking, and may also cash checks. Supermarkets must operate efficiently because net profits after taxes are usually less than one percent of sales. Supermarkets may be independently owned but are often part of a chain operation.

Loblaw Companies is Canada's largest supermarket chain, with more than 1000 stores across Canada. The stores vary in size by community and are known by the following banners: Real Atlantic Superstore, Loblaws, Extra Foods, Fortinos, No Frills, Provigo, Your Independent Grocer, Zehrs Markets, Atlantic Grocery and SaveEasy. Loblaws employs 139 000 from coast to coast making it one of the nation's largest employers. Loblaw had sales of $23.8 billion in 2005, with growth of more than 20 percent over the previous year. Loblaw is also known for its highly successful private label brands: President's Choice and No Name.[7]

Today consumers make more than three-quarters of all grocery purchases in supermarkets. Even so, supermarkets' total share of the food market is declining because consumers now have widely varying food preferences and buying habits. Furthermore, in many communities shoppers can choose from a number of convenience stores, discount stores, and specialty food stores, as well as a wide variety of restaurants. Wal-Mart has also created a more competitive marketplace by choosing to add grocery lines, and organics, to its retail selection.

superstore A giant retail outlet that carries food and non-food products found in supermarkets, as well as most routinely purchased consumer products

Superstores. **Superstores,** which originated in Europe, are giant retail outlets that carry not only food and non-food products ordinarily found in supermarkets but also routinely purchased consumer products. Besides a complete food line, superstores sell housewares, hardware, small appliances, clothing, personal-care products, garden products, and tires—about four times as many items as supermarkets. Services available at superstores include dry cleaning, automotive repair, check cashing, bill paying, and snack bars.

Superstores combine features of discount stores and supermarkets. There are several examples of superstores in the United States, including Wal-Mart Supercentres, and Super Kmart Centres. To cut handling and inventory costs, superstores use sophisticated operating techniques and often have tall shelving that displays entire assortments of products. Superstores can have an area of larger than 18 500 square metres, compared to only 1900 square metres in a traditional supermarket. Sales volume is two to three times that of supermarkets, partly because locations near good transportation networks help generate the in-store traffic needed for profitability. Wal-Mart is opening three Wal-Mart Superstores in Ontario. The stores will be about twice the size of a regular Wal-Mart store, with over 17 600 square metres of retail space. The Wal-Mart superstores will sell regular Wal-Mart merchandise as well as baked goods, meat, and produce.[8]

hypermarket A store that combines supermarket and discount store shopping in one location

Hypermarkets. **Hypermarkets** combine supermarket and discount store shopping in one location. Larger than superstores, they range from 4200 to 31 000 square metres and offer 45 000 to 60 000 different types of low-priced products. They commonly allocate 40 to 50 percent of their space to grocery products and the remainder to general merchandise, including athletic shoes, designer jeans, and other apparel; refrigerators, televisions, and other appliances; housewares; cameras; toys; jewelry;

hardware; and automotive supplies. Many lease space to non-competing businesses such as banks, optical shops, and fast-food restaurants. All hypermarkets focus on low prices and vast selections. Although Kmart, Wal-Mart, and Carrefour (a French retailer) have operated hypermarkets in the United States, most of these stores were unsuccessful and closed. Such stores are too big for time-constrained American shoppers. However, hypermarkets are successful in Europe, South America, and Mexico. For example, the hypermarket has become such a success in Mexico that the leading chains are currently waging a retail war. Wal-Mart de Mexico is leading the battle with annual sales of $11.7 billion, but competitors such as Soriana, with annual sales of $3.2 billion, are taking risks and fighting back.[9]

warehouse club A large-scale, members-only establishment that combines features of cash-and-carry wholesaling with discount retailing

Warehouse Clubs.   Warehouse clubs, a rapidly growing form of mass merchandising, are large-scale, members-only selling operations combining cash-and-carry wholesaling with discount retailing. For a nominal annual fee (usually about $35), small retailers purchase products at wholesale prices for business use or for resale. Warehouse clubs also sell to ultimate consumers affiliated with government agencies, credit unions, schools, hospitals, and banks, but instead of paying a membership fee, individual consumers may pay about five percent more on each item than do business customers.

Sometimes called *buying clubs,* warehouse clubs offer the same types of products as discount stores, but in a limited range of sizes and styles. Whereas most discount stores carry around 40 000 items, a warehouse club handles only 3500 to 5000 products, usually acknowledged brand leaders. Costco leads the warehouse club industry with sales of $52.9 billion. Costco has 371 outlets in the U.S. and Puerto Rico, 70 in Canada, 30 in Mexico, 18 in the United Kingdom, five in Korea, and four in Hong Kong.[10]

Warehouse clubs offer a broad product mix, including food, beverages, books, appliances, housewares, automotive parts, hardware, and furniture. Warehouse clubs appeal to many price-conscious consumers and small retailers unable to obtain wholesaling services from large distributors. The average warehouse club shopper has more education, a higher income, and a larger household than the average supermarket shopper.

To keep prices lower than those of supermarkets and discount stores, warehouse clubs provide few services. They generally do not advertise, except through direct mail. Their facilities, often located in industrial areas, have concrete floors and aisles wide enough for forklifts. Merchandise is stacked on pallets or displayed on pipe racks. Customers must transport purchases themselves.

warehouse showroom A retail facility in a large, low-cost building with large on-premise inventories and minimal services

Warehouse and Catalogue Showrooms.   Warehouse showrooms are retail facilities with five basic characteristics: large, low-cost buildings; warehouse materials handling technology; vertical merchandise displays; large on-premises inventories; and minimal services. IKEA, a Swedish company, sells furniture, household goods, and kitchen accessories in warehouse showrooms and through catalogues around the world. Consumer's Distributing, based in Mississauga, Ontario, was once solely a catalogue showroom retailer, but now relies heavily on web-based sales. These high-volume, low-overhead operations stress fewer personnel and services. Lower costs are possible because some marketing

Warehouse Showroom
IKEA, a Swedish company, is a warehouse showroom that markets furniture and accessories.

functions have been shifted to consumers, who must transport, finance, and perhaps store merchandise. Most consumers carry away purchases in the manufacturers' cartons, although stores will deliver for a fee.

catalogue showroom

A warehouse showroom in which consumers use catalogues to place orders for products, which are then filled directly in the warehouse area and picked up by buyers in the showroom

In **catalogue showrooms,** one item of each product is displayed, often in a locked case, with remaining inventory stored out of the buyer's reach. Using catalogues that have been mailed to their homes or are on store counters, customers order products by phone or in person. Clerks fill orders from the warehouse area, and products are presented in the manufacturers' cartons. In contrast to traditional catalogue retailers, which offer no discounts and require that customers wait for delivery, catalogue showrooms regularly sell below list price and often provide goods immediately.

Catalogue showrooms usually sell jewelry, luggage, photographic equipment, toys, small appliances and housewares, sporting goods, and power tools. They advertise extensively and carry established brands and models that are not likely to be discontinued. Because catalogue showrooms have higher product turnover, fewer losses through shoplifting, and lower labour costs than department stores, they are able to feature lower prices. However, they offer minimal services and customers often have to stand in line to examine items or place orders.

Specialty Retailers

In contrast to general-merchandise retailers with their broad product mixes, specialty retailers emphasize narrow and deep assortments. Despite their name, specialty retailers do not sell specialty items (except when specialty goods complement the overall product mix). Instead, they offer substantial assortments in a few product lines. We examine three types of specialty retailers: traditional specialty retailers, off-price retailers, and category killers.

traditional specialty retailers

A store that carries a narrow product mix with deep product lines

Traditional Specialty Retailers. Traditional specialty retailers are stores that carry a narrow product mix with deep product lines. Sometimes called *limited-line retailers,* they may be referred to as *single-line retailers* if they carry unusual depth in one main product category. Specialty retailers commonly sell such shopping products as apparel, jewelry, sporting goods, fabrics, computers, and pet supplies. The Limited, Radio Shack, Hickory Farms, Gap, and Foot Locker are examples of retailers offering limited product lines but great depth within those lines.

Although the number of chain specialty stores is increasing, many specialty stores are independently owned. Florists, bakery shops, and bookstores are among the small, independent specialty retailers that appeal to local target markets, although these stores can be owned and managed by large corporations. Even if this kind of retailer adds a few supporting product lines, the store may still be classified as a specialty store.

Because they are usually small, specialty stores may have high costs in proportion to sales, and satisfying customers may require carrying some products with low turnover rates. However, these stores sometimes obtain lower prices from suppliers by purchasing limited lines of merchandise in large quantities. Successful specialty stores understand their customer types and know what products to carry, thus reducing the risk of unsold merchandise. Specialty stores usually offer better selections and more sales expertise than department stores, their main competitors. By capitalizing on fashion, service, personnel, atmosphere, and location, specialty retailers position themselves strategically to attract customers in specific

The Container Store™
The Original Storage and Organization Store®

Chestnut Hill, MA 27 Boylston, Route 9 (just east of The Mall at Chestnut Hill) (617) 566-7480
Natick, MA Route 9 (just west of Natick Mall) (508) 655-8500
Store Hours: Monday - Saturday 9 am - 9 pm; Sunday 11 am - 6 pm
www.containerstore.com   1-800-733-3532

Traditional Specialty Retailers

The Container Store is a traditional specialty store that offers organizational products.

market segments. Specialty stores may even become exclusive dealers in their markets for certain products. Through specialty stores, small-business owners provide unique services to match consumers' varied desires. For consumers dissatisfied with the impersonal nature of large retailers, the close, personal contact offered by a small specialty store can be a welcome change.

off-price retailer A store that buys manufacturers' seconds, overruns, returns, and off-season merchandise for resale to consumers at deep discounts

Off-Price Retailers. **Off-price retailers** buy manufacturers' seconds, overruns, returns, and off-season production runs at below-wholesale prices for resale to consumers at deep discounts. Unlike true discount stores, which pay regular wholesale prices for goods and usually carry second-line brand names, off-price retailers offer limited lines of national-brand and designer merchandise, usually clothing, shoes, and/or housewares. The number of off-price retailers has grown since the mid-1980s.

Off-price stores charge 20 to 50 percent less than department stores for comparable merchandise but offer few customer services. They often feature community dressing rooms and central checkout counters. Some of these stores do not take returns or allow exchanges. Off-price stores may or may not sell goods with original labels intact. They turn over their inventory nine to 12 times a year, three times as often as traditional specialty stores. They compete with department stores for the same customers: price-conscious customers who are knowledgeable about brand names.

Another form of off-price retailer is the manufacturer's outlet mall, which makes available manufacturer overstocks and unsold merchandise from other retail outlets at discounted prices. Diverse manufacturers are represented in these malls.

To ensure a regular flow of merchandise into their stores, off-price retailers establish long-term relationships with suppliers that can provide large quantities of goods at reduced prices. Manufacturers may approach retailers with samples, discontinued products, or items that have not sold well. Also, retailers may seek out manufacturers, offering to pay cash for goods produced during the manufacturers' off season. Although manufacturers benefit from such arrangements, they also risk alienating their specialty and department store customers. Department stores tolerate off-price stores as long as they do not advertise brand names, limit merchandise to lower-quality items, and are located away from the department stores. When off-price retailers obtain large stocks of in-season, top-quality merchandise, tension builds between department stores and manufacturers.

category killer A very large specialty store that concentrates on a major product category and competes on the basis of low prices and enormous product availability

Category Killers. Over the last two decades, a new breed of specialty retailer, the category killer, has evolved. A **category killer** is a very large specialty store that concentrates on a major product category and competes on the basis of low prices and enormous product availability. The stores are referred to as category killers because they expand rapidly and gain sizable market shares, taking business away from smaller, high-cost retail outlets. Examples of category killers include Home Depot; Staples (office-supply chain); Chapters (booksellers); Toys 'R' Us (toys); PETCO and PetSmart (pet-supply chains); and Circuit City (consumer electronics).

Category Killers
Stores like Chapters-Indigo are referred to as category killers because of their product mixes and their low prices.

Direct Marketing

direct marketing The use of the telephone, Internet, and non-personal media to introduce products to customers, who can then purchase them via mail, telephone, or the Internet

non-store retailing The selling of products outside the confines of a retail facility

catalogue marketing A type of marketing in which an organization provides a catalogue from which customers make selections and place orders by mail, telephone, or the Internet

Direct marketing is the use of the telephone, Internet, and non-personal media to communicate product and organizational information to customers, who can then purchase products via mail, telephone, or the Internet. Direct marketing is one type of non-store retailing. **Non-store retailing** is the selling of products outside the confines of a retail facility. This form of retailing accounts for an increasing percentage of total sales. Direct marketing can occur through catalogue marketing, direct-response marketing, telemarketing, television home shopping, and online retailing.

Catalogue Marketing

In **catalogue marketing,** an organization provides a catalogue from which customers make selections and place orders by mail, telephone, or the Internet. Catalogue marketing began in 1872, when Montgomery Ward issued its first catalogue to rural families. Sears is Canada's most long-standing catalogue retailer, and while Sears has department stores in most Canadian cities, the catalogue is the only outlet for Sears customers who live in smaller towns or remote locations.

The advantages of catalogue retailing include efficiency and convenience for customers. The retailer benefits by being able to locate in remote, low-cost areas; save on expensive store fixtures; and reduce both personal selling and store operat-

Beyond the Maine Woods: L.L. Bean Branches Out

L.L. Bean, the well-known seller of outdoor clothing and equipment, is facing another hurdle in its successful history—how to change its way of doing business without changing its image.

Leon Leonwood Bean founded his company in Freeport, Maine, in 1912, the year after he made the first rubber-bottomed hunting boots. He sold his boots through a four-page mailer that he sent to hunters in Maine and to out-of-staters who held Maine hunting licenses. The business prospered as the company expanded its product line to outdoor clothing and hunting and fishing gear. Today the company is a global organization with annual sales in excess of $1.4 billion. About 40 percent of its merchandise is sold through catalogues,

40 percent over the Internet, and 20 percent through five retail stores and 14 factory stores in or near Maine.

L.L. Bean's success has been primarily due to its high-quality, dependable products and a carefully constructed image of a Maine-based company that embraces the region's old-fashioned values of integrity, frugality, and quality.

In recent years, the marketplace has changed due to the emergence of savvy and aggressive competitors, three of which are each approaching annual sales of $1 billion. Eddie Bauer has over 400 locations across the United States; Eastern Mountain Sports (EMS) has 100 stores; and Gander Mountain has 98. For the most part, these competitors have built their businesses through retail sales outlets.

L.L. Bean plans to open more retail stores across the country to compete more effectively and grow long term. The challenge is to expand to new areas while maintaining its rustic Maine image. According to the current CEO, the important goal for the future is to convince people that the company still stands for the same things it did 40 years ago: outdoors, service, and quality products.

ing expenses. On the other hand, catalogue retailing is inflexible, provides limited service, and is most effective only for a selected set of products.

Even though the cost of mailing catalogues continues to rise, catalogue sales are growing at double the rate of in-store retailing. Catalogue sales have been increasing due to the convenience of catalogue shopping. Product quality is often high, and because consumers can order by phone or Internet 24 hours a day, charge purchases to a credit card, and have the merchandise delivered to their door in one to two days, such shopping is much easier than going to a store.

Direct-Response Marketing

direct-response marketing A type of marketing in which a retailer advertises a product and makes it available through mail or telephone orders

Direct-response marketing occurs when a retailer advertises a product and makes it available through mail or telephone orders. Generally a purchaser may use a credit card, but other forms of payment are acceptable. Examples of direct-response marketing include a television commercial offering a recording artist's musical collection available through a toll-free number, a newspaper or magazine advertisement for a series of children's books available by filling out the form in the ad or calling a toll-free number, and even a billboard promoting floral services available by calling 1-800-Flowers. Direct-response marketing is also conducted by sending letters, samples, brochures, or booklets to prospects on a mailing list and asking that they order the advertised products by mail or telephone. In general, products must be priced above $20 to justify the advertising and distribution costs associated with direct-response marketing.

Telemarketing

telemarketing The performance of marketing-related activities by telephone

A number of organizations use the telephone to strengthen the effectiveness of traditional marketing methods. **Telemarketing** is the performance of marketing-related activities by telephone. Some organizations use a prescreened list of prospective clients. Telemarketing can help generate sales leads, improve customer service, speed up payments on past-due accounts, raise funds for non-profit organizations, and gather marketing data.

Television Home Shopping

television home shopping A form of selling in which products are presented to television viewers, who can buy them by calling a toll-free number and paying with a credit card

Television home shopping presents products to television viewers encouraging them to order through toll-free numbers and pay with credit cards. There are several home shopping cable channels. A few of these channels specialize in certain product categories. The most popular products sold through television home shopping are jewelry (40 percent of total sales), clothing, housewares, and electronics.

Home Shopping Network and QVC are two of the largest home shopping networks. Approximately 60 percent of home shopping sales revenues come from repeat purchasers.

The television home shopping format offers several benefits. Products can be easily demonstrated, and an adequate amount of time can be spent showing the product in order to make viewers well informed. The length of time a product is shown depends not only on the time required for doing demonstrations but also on whether the product is selling. Once the calls peak and begin to decline, a new product is shown. Another benefit is that customers can shop at their convenience from the comfort of their homes.

Online Retailing

online retailing Retailing that makes products available to buyers through computer connections

Online retailing makes products available to buyers through computer connections. The phenomenal growth

snapshot

Benefits of online marketing

Researchers report that the four major advantages of online marketing are increased revenue, greater visibility, cost savings, and reaching new customers.

Increased revenue 73%

Greater visibility 58%

Cost savings 56%

Reaching new customers 54%

Search [GO]

Clothing Footwear Accessories Home

Online Retailing

Expedia is an online retailer of travel-related services.

of Internet use has created new retailing opportunities. Many retailers have set up websites to disseminate information about their companies and products. Although most retailers with websites use them primarily to promote products, a number of companies, including Chapters, Sears, and HBC (Zeller's, The Bay, and Home Outfitters) sell goods online. Consumers can purchase hard-to-find items, such as Pez candy dispensers and Elvis memorabilia, on eBay. Banks and brokerage firms have established websites to give customers direct access to manage their accounts and enable them to trade online. With advances in computer technology continuing and consumers ever more pressed for time, online retailing will continue to escalate.

Although online retailing represents a major retailing venue, security remains an issue. In a recent survey conducted by the Business Software Alliance, about 75 percent of Internet users expressed concerns about shopping online. The major issues are identity theft and credit card theft.

Other Types Of Non-store Retailing

Besides direct marketing, there are two other major types of non-store retailing: direct selling and automatic vending.

Direct Selling

direct selling Marketing products to ultimate consumers through face-to-face sales presentations at home or in the workplace

Direct selling is the marketing of products to ultimate consumers through face-to-face sales presentations at home or in the workplace. Although direct sellers historically used a cold-canvass, door-to-door approach to finding prospects, many companies today, such as World Book, Amway, Mary Kay, and Avon, use other approaches. They initially identify customers through the mail, the telephone, the Internet, or shopping mall intercepts and set up appointments.

Direct selling sometimes uses the "party plan," which can occur in the customer's home or workplace. With a party plan, the customer acts as a host and invites a number of friends and associates to view merchandise in a group setting, where a salesperson demonstrates products. The congenial party atmosphere helps to overcome customers' reluctance and encourages them to buy. Direct selling through the party plan requires effective salespeople who can identify potential hosts and provide encouragement and incentives for them to organize a gathering of friends and associates. Tupperware and Mary Kay were the pioneers of this selling technique, paving the way for companies like the Pampered Chef to grow from a basement business into a corporation that brings in over $700 million in revenues annually.[11]

Direct selling has both benefits and limitations. It gives the marketer an opportunity to demonstrate the product in an environment—usually customers' homes—where it would most likely be used. The door-to-door seller can give the customer personal attention, and the product can be presented to the customer at a convenient time and location. Personal attention to the customer is the foundation on which some direct sellers, such as Mary Kay, have built their businesses. Because commissions for salespeople are so high, ranging from 30 to 50 percent of the sales price, and great effort is required to isolate promising prospects, overall costs of direct selling make it the most expensive form of retailing. Furthermore, some customers view direct selling negatively, owing to unscrupulous and fraudulent practices used by some direct sellers in the past. Some communities even have local ordinances that control or, in some cases, prohibit direct selling. Despite these negative views held by some individuals, direct selling is still alive and well, bringing in revenues of over $29 billion a year.[12]

Automatic Vending

automatic vending The use of machines to dispense products

Automatic vending is the use of machines to dispense products. It accounts for less than two percent of all retail sales. Video game machines provide an entertainment service, and many banks offer automatic teller machines (ATMs), which dispense cash and perform other services.

Automatic vending is one of the most impersonal forms of retailing. Small, standardized, routinely purchased products (e.g., chewing gum, candy, newspapers, cigarettes, soft drinks, coffee) can be sold in machines because consumers usually buy them at the nearest available location. Machines in areas of heavy traffic provide efficient and continuous service to consumers. Such high-volume areas may have more diverse product availability—for example, hot and cold sandwiches, and even hot pizza. Since vending machines need only a small amount of space and no sales personnel, this retailing method has some advantages over stores. The advantages are partly offset, however, by the high costs of equipment and frequent servicing and repairs.

Franchising

franchising An arrangement in which a supplier (franchiser) grants a dealer (franchisee) the right to sell products in exchange for some type of consideration

Franchising is an arrangement in which a supplier, or franchiser, grants a dealer, or franchisee, the right to sell products in exchange for some type of consideration. The franchiser may receive some percentage of total sales in exchange for furnishing equipment, buildings, management know-how, and marketing assistance to the franchisee. The franchisee supplies labour and capital, operates the franchised business, and agrees to abide by the provisions of the franchise agreement. Because of changes in the international marketplace, shifting employment options in Canada, the expanding service economy, and corporate interest in more joint venture activity, franchising is rapidly increasing.

Major Types of Retail Franchises

Retail franchise arrangements fall into three general categories. In one arrangement, a manufacturer authorizes a number of retail stores to sell a certain brand name item. This franchise arrangement, one of the oldest forms, is common in sales of cars and trucks, farm equipment, shoes, paint, earth-moving equipment, and petroleum. In the second type of retail franchise, a producer licenses distributors to sell a given product to retailers. This arrangement is common in the soft-drink industry. Most national manufacturers of soft-drink syrups, including Coca-Cola, Dr Pepper, and PepsiCo, grant franchises to bottlers, which in turn serve retailers. In the third type of retail franchise, a franchiser supplies brand names, techniques, or other services instead of complete products. The franchiser may provide certain production and distribution services, but its primary role in the arrangement is careful development and control of marketing strategies. This approach to franchising is very common today and is used by such organizations as Holiday Inn, Curves, McDonald's, Dairy Queen, KFC, and Century 21 Real Estate. Top franchises in Canada are shown in Table 16.5.

Advantages and Disadvantages of Franchising

Franchising offers several advantages to both the franchisee and the franchiser. It enables a franchisee to start a business with limited capital and benefit from the business experience of others. Moreover, nationally advertised franchises, such as ServiceMaster and Subway, are often assured of customers as soon as they open. If business problems arise, the franchisee can obtain guidance and advice from the franchiser at little or no cost. Franchised outlets are generally more successful than

table 16.5   POPULAR CANADIAN FRANCHISES AND THEIR STARTUP COSTS*

Franchise	Description	# Franchise Outlets Worldwide	Startup Costs
Subway	Sandwiches, salads	26 197	$73 000–$197 000
Curves	Women's fitness and weight loss	9900	$38 400–$53 500
UPS Store	Postal, business, communications services	5760	$138 700–$266 800
Jani-King	Commercial cleaning	12 140	$11 300–$34 100
RE/MAX Int'l	Real estate	6898	$20 000–$199 000
Pizza Hut	Pizza	9722	$1.1 million–$1.7 million
Century 21 Real Estate	Real estate	8096	$11 800–$522 800
Jan-Pro Franchising	Commercial cleaning	5371	$3300–$49 900
McDonald's	Hamburgers, chicken, salads	22 554	$506 000–$1.6 million
ServiceMaster Clean	Commercial/residential cleaning and disaster restoration	4540	$19 100–$109 200
Kumon Math & Reading Centers	Supplemental education	25 642	$30 000–$110 000
Coldwell Banker Real Estate	Real estate	2892	$23 500–$490 500
Jiffy Lube	Fast oil change	1946	$214 000–$273 000

*Ranking is based primarily on financial strength and stability, growth rate, size of the system, number of years in business, startup costs, litigation, percentage of terminations, and whether the company provides financing.
Source: Franchises & Opportunities. Entrepreneur.com. Retrieved May 2, 2006 from http://www.entrepreneur.com/franchiseopportunities/index.html.

independently owned businesses. Fewer than 10 percent of franchised retail businesses fail during the first two years of operation, compared with approximately 50 percent of independent retail businesses. Also, the franchisee receives materials to use in local advertising and can benefit from national promotional campaigns sponsored by the franchiser.

Through franchise arrangements, the franchiser gains fast and selective product distribution without incurring the high cost of constructing and operating its own outlets. The franchiser therefore has more capital for expanding production and advertising. It can also ensure, through the franchise agreement, that outlets are maintained and operated according to its own standards. The franchiser benefits from the fact that the franchisee, being a sole proprietor in most cases, is likely to be very highly motivated to succeed. Success of the franchise means more sales, which translate into higher income for the franchiser.

Franchise arrangements also have several drawbacks. The franchiser can dictate many aspects of the business: decor, design of employees' uniforms, types of signs, and numerous details of business operations. In addition, franchisees must pay to use the franchiser's name, products, and assistance. Usually there is a one-time franchise fee and continuing royalty and advertising fees, often collected as a percentage of sales. For example, Subway requires franchisees to come up with $70 000 to $220 000 in startup costs. Franchisees often must work very hard, putting in 10- to 12-hour days, six or seven days a week. In some cases, franchise agreements are not uniform; one franchisee may pay more than another for the same services. Finally, the franchiser gives up a certain amount of control when entering into a franchise agreement. Consequently individual establishments may not be operated exactly according to the franchiser's standards.

Strategic Issues in Retailing

Consumers often have vague reasons for making retail purchases. Whereas most business purchases are based on economic planning and necessity, consumer purchases may result from social and psychological influences. Because consumers shop for a variety of reasons—to search for specific items, escape boredom, or learn about something new—retailers must do more than simply fill space with merchandise. They must make desired products available, create stimulating shopping environments, and develop marketing strategies that increase store patronage. In this section, we discuss how store location, retail positioning, store image, scrambled merchandising, and the wheel of retailing affect retailing objectives.

Location of Retail Stores

Location, the least flexible of the strategic retailing issues, is one of the most important because location dictates the limited geographic trading area from which a store draws its customers. Retailers consider a variety of factors when evaluating potential locations, including location of the firm's target market within the trading area, kinds of products being sold, availability of public transportation, customer characteristics, and competitors' locations.

In choosing a location, a retailer evaluates the relative ease of movement to and from the site, including such factors as pedestrian and vehicular traffic, parking, and transportation. Some retailers prefer sites with high pedestrian traffic. Preliminary site investigations sometimes include a pedestrian count to determine how many passersby are prospective customers. The nature of the area's vehicular traffic is also analyzed. Because customers of certain retailers, such as service stations and many convenience stores, drive to these retail sites, overly congested locations should be avoided. Parking space must be adequate for projected demand, and transportation networks (major thoroughfares and public transit) must accommodate customers and delivery vehicles.

Retailers also evaluate the characteristics of the site itself: types of stores in the area; size, shape, and visibility of the lot or building under consideration; and rental, leasing, or ownership terms. Retailers look for compatibility with nearby retailers because stores that complement one another draw more customers for everyone. When making site location decisions, retailers select from among several general types of locations: freestanding structures, traditional business districts, traditional shopping centres, or non-traditional shopping centres.

Retail Location

The location of a retail store is crucial. There are a number of organizations that assist retailers to make retail site location decisions.

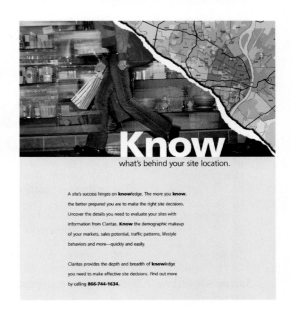

Freestanding Structures. Freestanding structures are buildings unconnected to other buildings. Organizations may build such structures or lease or buy them. A retailer, for example, may find that its most successful stores are in freestanding structures close to a shopping mall but not in the mall. Use of freestanding structures allows retailers to physically position themselves away from or close to competitors. Quick-service oil change dealers and fast-food restaurants frequently use freestanding structures and locate close to each other. Toys 'R' Us and Home Depot also tend to locate in freestanding structures.

Traditional Business Districts. A traditional business district—the "downtown shopping district"—usually consists of structures attached to one another and located in a central part of a town or city. Often these structures are aging, and, in some cities, traditional business districts are decaying and are viewed as non-viable locations for retailers. However, many towns and cities are preserving or revitalizing their traditional business districts, thus making them attractive locations for certain types of retailers. Some cities have enclosed walkways, shut off streets from traffic, and provided free parking and transportation systems to help traditional business districts compete more effectively with shopping malls.

neighbourhood shopping centre A shopping centre usually consisting of several small convenience and specialty stores

Shopping Centres. The major types of shopping centres are identified and described in Table 16.6. **Neighbourhood shopping centres** usually consist of several small convenience and specialty stores, such as small grocery stores, gas stations, and fast-food restaurants. Many of these retailers consider their target markets to be consumers who live within two to three miles of their stores, or ten minutes' driving time. Because most purchases are based on convenience or personal contact, there is usually little coordination of selling efforts within a neighbourhood shopping centre. Generally product mixes consist of essential products, and depth of product lines is limited. Convenience stores are most successful when they are closer to consumers than, for example, supermarkets. A good strategy for neighbourhood centres is to locate near hotels or interstate highways, or on the route to regional shopping centres.

community shopping centre A shopping centre with one or two department stores, some specialty stores, and convenience stores

Community shopping centres include one or two department stores and some specialty stores, as well as convenience stores. They draw consumers looking for shopping and specialty products not available in neighbourhood shopping centres. Because these centres serve larger geographic areas, consumers must drive longer distances to

table 16.6   TYPES AND CHARACTERISTICS OF SHOPPING CENTRES

Type	Concept	Open or Enclosed?	Acreage	Number of Anchors	Radius of primary trade area (kilometres)
Neighbourhood centre	Convenience	Open	3–15	1 or more	5
Community centre	General merchandise, convenience	Open	10–40	2 or more	5–10
Regional centre	General merchandise, fashion	Enclosed	40–100	2 or more	8–24
Superregional centre	More variety than regional centre	Enclosed	60–120	3 or more	8–40
Lifestyle centre	Upscale specialty, dining, and entertainment, usually national chains	Open	10–40	0–2	13–19
Power centre	Category-dominant anchors, a few small businesses	Open	25–80	3 or more	8–16
Outlet centre	Manufacturers' outlet stores	Open	10–50	N/A	25–75

Source: Adapted from "ICSC Shopping Centre Definitions," International Council of Shopping Centers, p. 4, www.icsc.org/srch/lib/SCDEefinitions.pdf (accessed Feb. 3, 2006).

community shopping centres than to neighbourhood centres. Community shopping centres are planned and coordinated to attract shoppers. Special events, such as art exhibits, automobile shows, and sidewalk sales stimulate traffic. Overall management of a community shopping centre looks for tenants that complement the centre's total assortment of products. Such centres have wide product mixes and deep product lines.

regional shopping centre
A type of shopping centre with large department stores, the wide product mix, and the deep-product lines of all shopping centres

Regional shopping centres usually have the largest department stores, the widest product mixes, and the deepest product lines of all shopping centres. Many shopping malls are regional shopping centres, although some are community shopping centres. Regional shopping centres carry most products found in a downtown shopping district. With 150 000 or more consumers in their target market, regional shopping centres must have well-coordinated management and marketing activities. Target markets may include consumers travelling from a distance to find products and prices not available in their hometowns.

Because of the expense of leasing space in regional shopping centres, tenants are more likely to be national chains than small, independent stores. Large centres usually advertise, have special events, furnish transportation to some consumer groups, maintain their own security forces, and carefully select the mix of stores. The largest of these centres, sometimes called **superregional shopping centres,** have the widest and deepest product mixes and attract customers from many miles away. These centres might host exclusive or high-end stores with fewer locations than most retail chains. Superregional centres often have special attractions such as skating rinks, amusement centres, or upscale restaurants.

superregional shopping centre A type of shopping centre with the largest department stores, the widest product mix, and the deepest product lines of all shopping centres

The biggest mall in the world is the West Edmonton Mall, located in a fashionable section of the Alberta city. The mall is the province's largest tourist attraction, featuring over 800 retail and service outlets, over 100 restaurants, a theme hotel and nine entertainment venues. The mall occupies the equivalent of 48 city blocks. Entertainment attractions include a water park, amusement park, an ice rink and various other types of attractions.[13]

Despite the success of many malls, some regional shopping centres are viewed as being out of touch with the needs of a changing population, struggling with massive debt accumulation, and in need of significant structural repair.[14] Indeed, fewer enclosed regional malls have been built in recent years; instead, developers have been opening shopping centres that often focus as much on entertainment as on shopping.[15]

lifestyle shopping centre
A type of shopping centre that is typically open-air and features upscale specialty, dining, and entertainment stores

A **lifestyle shopping centre** is typically an open-air shopping centre that features upscale specialty, dining, and entertainment stores, usually owned by national chains, as well as fountains, benches, and other amenities that encourage "casual browsing." They are often located near affluent neighbourhoods. Architectural design is an important aspect of these "mini-cities," which may include urban streets or parks, and is intended to encourage consumer loyalty by creating a sense of place. Some lifestyle centres are designed to resemble traditional "Main Street" shopping centres or have a central theme suggested by architecture.[16]

Some shopping centres may not include a traditional anchor department store. Most malls have one to three main anchor department stores to ensure a continuous stream of mall traffic. With traditional mall sales declining, this more recent type of shopping mall may be anchored by a store such as the Gap. Other likely stores for such malls include Toys 'R' Us, Circuit City, PetSmart, and Home Depot. Shopping centre developers are combining off-price stores and small stores with category killers in **power shopping centre** formats. The number of power shopping centres is growing, resulting in a variety of formats vying for the same retail dollar. To compete, existing region malls may have to adapt by changing their store mixes.

power shopping centre
A type of shopping centre that features off-price and small stores combined with category killers

outlet shopping centre
A type of shopping centre that features discount and factory outlet stores carrying manufacturer brands

Outlet shopping centres feature discount and factory outlet stores carrying traditional manufacturer brands. Some outlet centres feature upscale products. Manufacturers own these stores and make a special effort to avoid conflict with traditional retailers of their products. Manufacturers claim their stores are in non-competitive locations; indeed, most factory outlet centres are located outside metropolitan areas. Not all factory outlets stock closeouts and irregulars, but most avoid comparison with discount houses. Factory outlet centres attract value-conscious customers seeking quality and major brand names. They operate in much the same way as regional shopping centres, but usually draw customers from a larger shopping radius; a portion of these stores' customers are sometimes tourists. Promotional activity is at the heart of these shopping centres. Craft and antique shows, contests, and special events attract a great deal of traffic.

Retail Positioning

retail positioning Identifying an unserved or underserved market segment and serving it through a strategy that distinguishes the retailer from others in the minds of consumers in that segment

The large variety of shopping centres and expansion of product offerings by stores has intensified retailing competition. Retail positioning is therefore an important consideration. **Retail positioning** involves identifying an unserved or underserved market segment and serving it through a strategy that distinguishes the retailer from others in the minds of those customers.

A retailer may position itself as a seller of high-quality, premium-priced products and provide many services. Neiman Marcus, for example, specializes in expensive, high-fashion clothing and jewelry, sophisticated electronics, and exclusive home furnishings, and provides wrapping and delivery, valet parking, and personal shopping consultants. Another type of retail organization may be positioned as a marketer of reasonable-quality products at everyday low prices. Pizza Hut, for example, has positioned itself as the value alternative by offering a variety of large pizzas at low prices. Its rival, Papa John's, has established a product quality position with the slogan "Better ingredients. Better pizza."

Store Image

To attract customers, a retail store must project an image—a functional and psychological picture in the consumer's mind—that appeals to its target market. Store environment, category management, merchandise quality, and service quality are key determinants of store image.

PetSmart: Barking Up the Right Tree

PetSmart, Inc., the world's largest retailer of pet-related products, operates more than 800 pet stores and offers more than 12 000 products in the United States and Canada. In addition to operating its retail outlets, the company runs a growing number of in-store PetsHotels, has a large pet-supply catalogue business, and leads in online sales of pet products and information. PetSmart also offers pet training, grooming, day care, and adoption services.

PetSmart employs over 30 000 people in North America. In addition to its sales and store personnel, the retailer employs 1500 accredited trainers who train more than 300 000 dogs annually. With its SmartPet Promise, customers are guaranteed 100 percent satisfaction, or their pets can take the training class again for free. PetSmart also has 6600 certified pet stylists who groom and bathe more than five million dogs a year.

PetSmart is testing a Doggie Day Camp concept at its store in Pasadena, California, that provides daytime care and exercise for dogs. The Day Camp is an extension of its 26 PetsHotels that provide overnight and long-term boarding for pets. All PetsHotels feature caregivers who are hand-picked for their love of pets and are on the premises 24 hours a day.

The company is not resting on its laurels. PetSmart has opened close to 200 new stores the last two years and a new distribution centre in the Midwest. The company's CEO envisions the retailer eventually having 1400 stores in North America. In 2005, the company changed its name from PetsMart to PetSmart because management felt the organization's primary goal was offering superior solutions rather than simply serving as a retailer of pet products.

atmospherics The physical elements in a store's design that appeal to consumers' emotions and encourage buying

Atmospherics, the physical elements in a store's design that appeal to consumers' emotions and encourage buying, help to create an image and position a retailer. Barnes and Noble, for example, uses murals of authors and framed classic book covers to convey a literary image.

Exterior atmospheric elements include the appearance of the storefront, display windows, store entrances, and degree of traffic congestion. Exterior atmospherics are particularly important to new customers, who tend to judge an unfamiliar store by its outside appearance and may not enter if they feel intimidated by the building or inconvenienced by the parking lot. Interior atmospheric elements include aesthetic considerations such as lighting, wall and floor coverings, dressing facilities, and store fixtures. Interior sensory elements contribute significantly to atmosphere. Colour can attract shoppers to a retail display. Many fast-food restaurants use bright colours, such as red and yellow, because research suggests that these colours make customers feel hungrier and eat faster, which increases turnover. Sound is another important sensory component of atmosphere and may range from silence to subdued background sounds to music. One study indicated that retail customers shop for a longer period when exposed to unfamiliar music than they do when exposed to familiar music.[17] Many retailers believe shoppers who remain in their stores longer will, in fact, purchase more. A store's layout—arrangement of departments, width of aisles, grouping of products, and location of checkout areas—is another determinant of atmosphere. Department stores, restaurants, hotels, service stations, and specialty stores combine these elements in different ways to create specific atmospheres that may be perceived as warm, fresh, functional, or exciting. In one study, 90 percent of surveyed consumers ranked cleanliness—particularly in supermarkets—as the most important atmospheric element in choosing a shopping destination. Lighting, temperature, and aisle width were also ranked highly. Active elements such as in-store televisions were rated among the least influential.[18]

Retailers must assess the atmosphere the target market seeks and then adjust atmospheric variables to encourage desired consumer awareness and action. High-fashion boutiques generally strive for an atmosphere of luxury and novelty. Ralph Lauren's Polo Shops offer limited merchandise in large, open areas with props such as saddles or leather chairs adding to the exclusive look and image. On the other hand, discount department stores strive *not* to seem too exclusive and expensive. To appeal to multiple market segments, a retailer may create different atmospheres for different operations within the store; for example, the discount basement, the sports department, the housewares department, and the women's shoe department may each have a unique atmosphere.

Although heavily dependent on atmospherics, a store's image is also shaped by its reputation for integrity, number of services offered, location, merchandise assortments, pricing policies, promotional activities, and community involvement. Characteristics of the target market—social class, lifestyle, income level, and past buying behaviour—help form store image as well. How consumers perceive the store can be a major determinant of store patronage. Consumers from lower socioeconomic groups tend to patronize small, high-margin, high-service food stores and prefer small, friendly loan companies over large, impersonal banks, even though the former charge higher interest. Affluent consumers tend to look for exclusive establishments offering high-quality products and prestigious labels. Retailers should be aware of the multiple factors contributing to store image and recognize that perceptions of image vary.

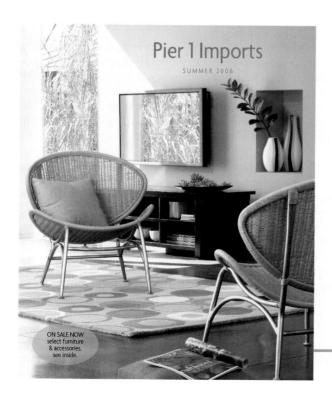

Store Image

Pier 1 Imports stores utilize atmospherics, such as soft lighting, to attract customers.

Category Management

Category management is a retail strategy of managing groups of similar, often substitutable products produced by different manufacturers. An assortment of merchandise is customer and strategically driven to improve performance. Performance can be profit-per-square-metre of category space or average dollars purchased by customers in each category. Category management developed in the food industry because supermarkets were concerned about highly competitive behaviour between manufacturers. Category management is a move toward a collaborative supply chain initiative to enhance consumer value. Wal-Mart, for example, has developed strong supplier relationships with firms such as Procter & Gamble. For category management to be successful, there should be the acquisition, analysis, and sharing of sales and consumer information between the retailer and manufacturer. The development of information about demand, consumer behaviour, and optimal allocations of products, should be available from one source. Firms such as SAS provide software to manage data associated with each step of the category management decision cycle. The key is cooperative interaction between the manufacturers of category products and the retailer to create maximum success for all parties in the supply chain. For example, supermarkets such as Safeway use category management to determine space for products such as cosmetics, cereals, and soups.

Scrambled Merchandising

When retailers add unrelated products and product lines—particularly fast-moving items that can be sold in volume—to an existing product mix, they are practicing **scrambled merchandising.** Retailers adopting this strategy hope to accomplish one or more of the following: (1) convert stores into one-stop shopping centres, (2) generate more traffic, (3) realize higher profit margins, and (4) increase impulse purchases. In scrambled merchandising, retailers must deal with diverse marketing channels. Scrambled merchandising can also blur a store's image in consumers' minds, making it more difficult for a retailer to succeed in today's highly competitive, saturated markets. Finally, scrambled merchandising intensifies competition among traditionally distinct types of stores and forces suppliers to adjust distribution systems to accommodate new channel members.

The Wheel of Retailing

As new types of retail businesses evolve, they strive to fill niches in a dynamic retailing environment. One hypothesis regarding the evolution and development of new types of retail stores is the **wheel of retailing.** According to this theory, new retailers enter the marketplace with low prices, margins, and status. Their low prices are usually the result of innovative cost-cutting procedures and soon attract imitators. Gradually, as these businesses attempt to broaden their customer base and increase sales, their operations and facilities become more elaborate and more expensive. They may move to more desirable locations, begin to carry higher-quality merchandise, or add services. Eventually they emerge at the high end of the price, cost, and service scales, competing with newer discount retailers following the same evolutionary process.[19]

Supermarkets, for example, have undergone many changes since their introduction in 1921. Initially they offered limited services and low food prices. Over time they developed a variety of new services, including free coffee, gourmet food sections, and children's play areas. Today supermarkets are being challenged by superstores, which offer more product choices and undercut supermarket prices.

Consider the evolution of department stores, discount stores, warehouse clubs, category killers, and online retailers. Department stores such as Sears started out as high-volume, low-cost merchants competing with general stores and other small retailers. Discount stores developed later in response to rising expenses of services in department stores. Many discount outlets now appear to be following the wheel of retailing by offering more services, better locations, quality inventories, and therefore higher prices. Some discount stores are almost indistinguishable from department stores. In response have emerged category killers, such as PetSmart and Toys 'R' Us, which concentrate on a major product category and offer enormous product depth, in many cases at lower prices than discount stores. Even these retailers, however, seem to be following the wheel. Lowe's, a home improvement retailer, has added big-ticket items and more upscale brands, such as Laura Ashley.

The wheel of retailing, along with other changes in the marketing environment and in buying behaviour itself, requires that retailers adjust to survive and compete. Consumers have less time than ever to shop. Shopping today centres on "needs fulfillment" and thus is more utilitarian and work oriented, a fact that many major retailing executives have noticed. As consumers have less time to shop and greater access to more sophisticated technology, retailing venues such as catalogue retailing, television home shopping, and online retailing will take on greater importance. New retailers will evolve to capitalize on these opportunities, while those that cannot adapt will not survive.

SUMMARY

Wholesaling consists of all transactions in which products are bought for resale, for making other products, or for general business operations. Wholesalers are individuals or organizations that facilitate and expedite exchanges that are primarily wholesale transactions. For producers, wholesalers are a source of financial assistance and information; by performing specialized accumulation and allocation functions, they allow producers to concentrate on manufacturing products. Wholesalers provide retailers with buying expertise, wide product lines, efficient distribution, and warehousing and storage.

Merchant wholesalers are independently owned businesses that take title to goods and assume ownership risks. They are either full-service wholesalers, offering the widest possible range of wholesaling functions, or limited-service wholesalers, providing only some marketing services and specializing in a few functions. Full-service merchant wholesalers include general-merchandise wholesalers, which offer a wide but relatively shallow product mix; general-line wholesalers, which offer extensive assortments within a few product lines; specialty-line wholesalers, which carry only a single product line or a few items within a line; and rack jobbers, which own and service display racks in supermarkets and other stores. Limited-service merchant wholesalers include cash-and-carry wholesalers, which sell to small businesses, require payment in cash, and do not deliver; truck wholesalers, which sell a limited line of products from their own trucks directly to customers; drop shippers, which own goods and negotiate sales but never take possession of products; and mail-order wholesalers, which sell to retail and business buyers through direct-mail catalogues.

Agents and brokers, sometimes called functional middlemen, negotiate purchases and expedite sales in exchange for a commission, but they do not take title to products. Usually specializing in certain products, they can provide valuable sales expertise. Whereas agents represent buyers or sellers on a permanent basis, brokers are intermediaries that buyers and sellers employ on a temporary basis to negotiate exchanges. Manufacturers' agents offer customers the complete product lines of two or more sellers.

Selling agents market a complete product line or a producer's entire output and perform every wholesaling function except taking title to products. Commission merchants are agents that receive goods on consignment from local sellers and negotiate sales in large, central markets.

Manufacturers' sales branches and offices are owned by manufacturers. Sales branches sell products and provide support services for the manufacturer's sales force in a given location. Sales offices carry no inventory and function much as agents do.

Retailing includes all transactions in which buyers intend to consume products through personal, family, or household use. Retailers, organizations that sell products primarily to ultimate consumers, are important links in the marketing channel because they are both marketers for and customers of wholesalers and producers. Retailers add value, provide services, and assist in making product selections.

Retail stores can be classified according to the breadth of products offered. Two broad categories are general-merchandise retailers and specialty retailers. The primary types of general-merchandise retailers include department stores, discount stores, supermarkets, superstores, hypermarkets, warehouse clubs, and warehouse and catalogue showrooms. Department stores are large retail organizations employing at least 25 people and characterized by wide product mixes of considerable depth for most product lines. Their products are organized into separate departments that function like self-contained businesses. Discount stores are self-service, low-price, general-merchandise outlets. A convenience store is a small self-service store that is open long hours and carries a narrow assortment of products, usually convenience items. Supermarkets are large, self-service food stores that also carry some non-food products. Superstores are giant retail outlets that carry all the products found in supermarkets and most consumer products purchased on a routine basis. Hypermarkets offer supermarket and discount store shopping at one location. Warehouse clubs are large-scale, members-only discount operations. Warehouse and catalogue showrooms are low-cost operations characterized by warehouse methods of materials handling and display, large inventories, and minimal services.

Specialty retailers offer substantial assortments in a few product lines. They include traditional specialty retailers, which carry narrow product mixes with deep product lines; off-price retailers, which sell brand name manufacturers' seconds and production overruns at deep discounts; and category killers, large specialty stores that concentrate on a major product category and compete on the basis of low prices and enormous product availability.

Direct marketing is the use of the telephone, Internet, and non-personal media to communicate product and organizational information to customers, who can then purchase products via mail, telephone, or the Internet. Direct marketing is a type of non-store retailing, the selling of goods or services outside the confines of a retail facility. Forms of direct marketing include catalogue marketing, direct-response marketing, telemarketing, television home shopping, and online retailing. Two other types of non-store retailing are direct selling and automatic vending. Direct selling is the marketing of products to ultimate consumers through face-to-face sales presentations at home or in the workplace. Automatic vending is the use of machines to dispense products.

Franchising is an arrangement in which a supplier grants a dealer the right to sell products in exchange for some type of consideration. Retail franchises are of three general types. A manufacturer may authorize a number of retail stores to sell a certain brand name item; a producer may license distributors to sell a given product to retailers; or a franchiser may supply brand names, techniques, or other services instead of a complete product. Franchise arrangements have a number of advantages and disadvantages over traditional business forms, and their use is increasing.

To increase sales and store patronage, retailers must consider strategic issues. Location determines the trading area from which a store draws its customers and should be evaluated carefully. When evaluating potential sites, retailers take into account a variety of factors, including the location of the firm's target market within the trading area, kinds of products sold, availability of public transportation, customer characteristics, and competitors' locations. Retailers can choose among several types of locations, including freestanding structures, traditional business districts, or shopping centres. The major types of shopping centres are neighbourhood shopping centres, community shopping centres, regional shopping centres, superregional shopping centres, lifestyle shopping centres, power shopping centres, and outlet shopping centres.

Retail positioning involves identifying an unserved or underserved market segment and serving it through a strategy that distinguishes the retailer from others in those customers' minds. Store image, which various customers perceive differently, derives not only from atmosphere but also from location, products offered, customer services, prices, promotion, and the store's overall reputation. Atmospherics refers to the physical elements of a store's design that can be adjusted to appeal to consumers' emotions and thus induce them to buy. Category management is a retail strategy of managing groups of similar, often substitutable products produced by different manufacturers. Scrambled merchandising adds unrelated product lines to an existing product mix and is being used by a growing number of stores to generate sales.

The wheel of retailing hypothesis holds that new retail institutions start out as low-status, low-margin, and low-price operations. As they develop, they increase services and prices, and eventually become vulnerable to newer organizations, which enter the market and repeat the cycle.

Please visit the student website at **www.hmco.ca/marketing** for ACE Self-Test questions that will help you prepare for exams.

IMPORTANT TERMS

Wholesaling
Wholesaler
Merchant wholesaler
Full-service wholesaler
General-merchandise wholesaler
General-line wholesaler
Specialty-line wholesaler
Rack jobber
Limited-service wholesaler
Cash-and-carry wholesaler
Truck wholesaler
Drop shipper
Mail-order wholesaler
Agent
Broker

Manufacturers' agent
Selling agent
Commission merchant
Sales branches
Sales office
Retailing
Retailer
General-merchandise retailer
Department store
Discount store
Convenience store
Supermarket
Superstore
Hypermarket
Warehouse club

Warehouse showroom
Catalogue showroom
Traditional specialty retailers
Off-price retailer
Category killer
Direct marketing
Non-store retailing
Catalogue marketing
Direct-response marketing
Telemarketing
Television home shopping
Online retailing
Direct selling
Automatic vending
Franchising

Neighbourhood shopping centre
Community shopping centre
Regional shopping centre
Superregional shopping centre
Lifestyle shopping centre
Power shopping centre
Outlet shopping centre
Retail positioning
Atmospherics
Category management
Scrambled merchandising
Wheel of retailing

DISCUSSION & REVIEW QUESTIONS

1. What is wholesaling?

2. What services do wholesalers provide to producers and retailers?

3. What is the difference between a full-service merchant wholesaler and a limited-service merchant wholesaler?

4. Drop shippers take title to products but do not accept physical possession of them, whereas commission merchants take physical possession of products but do not accept title. Defend the logic of classifying drop shippers as wholesale merchants and commission merchants as agents.

5. Why are manufacturers' sales offices and branches classified as wholesalers? Which independent wholesalers are replaced by manufacturers' sales branches? Which independent wholesalers are replaced by manufacturers' sales offices?

6. Discuss the cost and service tradeoffs involved in developing a physical distribution system.

7. What factors must physical distribution managers consider when developing a customer service mix?

8. What are the main tasks involved in order processing?

9. Discuss the advantages of using an electronic order-processing system. Which types of organizations are most likely to use electronic order processing?

10. Explain the tradeoffs inventory managers face when reordering products or supplies. How is the reorder point computed?

11. How does a product's package affect materials handling procedures and techniques?

12. What is containerization? Discuss its major benefits.

13. Explain the major differences between private and public warehouses. What is a field public warehouse?

14. Distribution centres focus on the movement of goods. Describe how distribution centres are designed for the rapid flow of products.

15. Compare and contrast the five major transportation modes in terms of cost, speed, dependability, load flexibility, accessibility, and frequency.

16. Discuss ways marketers can combine or coordinate two or more modes of transportation. What is the advantage of doing so?

17. What value do retailers add to a product? What value do retailers add for producers and ultimate consumers?

18. Differentiate between the two general categories of retail stores based on breadth of product offering.

19. What are the major differences between discount stores and department stores?

20. How does a superstore differ from a supermarket?

21. In what ways are traditional specialty stores and off-price retailers similar? How do they differ?

22. Describe direct marketing and the other two major types of non-store retailing. List some products you have purchased through these types of non-store retailing in the last six months. Why did you choose this method for making your purchases instead of going to a retail outlet?

23. How is door-to-door selling a form of retailing? Some consumers believe direct-response orders bypass the retailer. Is this true? Explain.

24. Evaluate the following statement: "Telemarketing, television home shopping, and online retailing will eventually eliminate the need for traditional forms of retailing."

25. If you were opening a retail business, would you prefer to open an independent store or own a store under a franchise arrangement? Explain your preference.

26. What major issues should be considered when determining a retail site location?

27. Describe the major types of shopping centres. Give an example of each type in your area.

28. Discuss the major factors that help determine a retail store's image.

29. How does atmosphere add value to products sold in a store? How important is atmospherics for convenience stores?

30. Is it possible for a single retail store to have an overall image that appeals to sophisticated shoppers, extravagant buyers, and bargain hunters? Why or why not?

31. In what ways does the use of scrambled merchandising affect a store's image?

APPLICATION QUESTIONS

1. Contact a local retailer with which you do business, and ask the manager to describe the store's relationship with one of its wholesalers. Using Table 16.1 as a guide, identify the activities the wholesaler performs. Are any of the functions shared by both the retailer and the wholesaler?

2. Assume you are responsible for the physical distribution of computers at a mail-order company.

What would you do to ensure product availability, timely delivery, and quality service for your customers?

3. The type of warehouse facilities used has important strategic implications for a firm. What type of warehouse would be most appropriate for the following situations, and why?

   a. A propane gas company recently entered the market in the state of Washington. The company's customers need varied quantities of propane on a timely basis and, at times, on short notice.

   b. A suntan lotion manufacturer has little expertise in managing warehouses and needs storage space in several locations in the Southeast.

   c. A book publisher must have short cycle time to get its products to customers quickly and needs to send the products to many different retailers.

4. Marketers select a transportation mode based on cost, speed, dependability, load flexibility, accessibility, and frequency (see Table 16.5). Identify a product and then select a mode of transportation based on these criteria. Explain your choice.

Juanita wants to open a small retail store that specializes in high-quality, high-priced children's clothing. With what types of competitors should she be concerned in this competitive retail environment? Why?

5. Location of retail outlets is a primary issue in strategic planning. Juanita wants to open a small business. What initial steps would you recommend to Juanita when she considers a location for her store?

6. Different types of stores offer varying breadth and depth of assortments. Godiva Chocolate stores, for example, offer a very narrow assortment of products but provide great depth. Visit a discount store, a specialty store, or a department store, and report on the number of different product lines offered and the depth within each line.

7. Atmospherics is an important tool used by retailers in their efforts to position stores. Visit a retail store you shop in regularly. Identify the store and describe its atmospherics. Be specific about both exterior and interior elements, and indicate how the store is being positioned through its use of atmospherics.

---

globalEDGE™

1. Go to **http://globaledge.msu.edu/** and click on Industry Profiles, and then Retail. Then click on Resources and Retail Food World. In the Retail Food World site choose any three of the following retailer profiles: A&P, Loblaws, Wal-Mart, Sobeys, Costco, Tesco, or Metro (Canada). For the profiles you have selected compare the retailers regarding number of stores and number of employees in Canada.

2. Click on the Leading Retailers link at the Retail World Food site. Where do the leading Canadian-based rate in terms of gross revenues, in terms of dollars and placement on the Leading Retailers list? Who are their greatest retail threats in the Canadian market?

INTERNET Exercise

Visit **www.hmco.ca/marketing** for resources to help you master the material in this chapter, plus materials that will help you expand your marketing knowledge, including Internet exercise updates, ACE self-tests, hotlinks to companies featured in this chapter, and much more.

FedEx

FedEx has become a critical link in the distribution network of both small and large firms. With its efficient and strategically located superhub in Memphis, FedEx has truly revolutionized the shipping industry. View the company's website at **www.fedex.com.**

1. Comment on how the website's overall design reflects the services the site promotes.
2. Why does FedEx so prominently display a "News" area on its website?
3. Does FedEx differentiate between small and large customers on its website? Why or why not?

Case 16.1   Low Prices and Lots of Suprises at Costco

More than 20 years after Costco opened its first warehouse club store in Seattle, the company's philosophy can still be summed up as "pile 'em high, price 'em low." Costco stores are anything but fancy; in fact, the first store was located inside a warehouse. Yet today millions of customers both in Canada, the U.S. and beyond pay $45 (fee may vary) annually so they can save on everything from mayonnaise to snow tires. In fact, customers never really know what products they will find each time they visit one of the 471 Costco warehouse stores around the world. Surprises are all part of the shopping experience at Costco.

"The art form of our business is intuition," says CEO James D. Sinegal. His buyers must choose carefully, because the typical Costco carries less than 10 percent of the number of products displayed in a Wal-Mart store. Moreover, Costco aims for a profit margin of no more than 14 percent, which means inventory must sell quickly. If products sell slowly, they will tie up precious cash that could be better spent on newer or more popular merchandise. Therefore, Costco's buyers watch for particularly hot products and product categories.

Costco's main competitor is Sam's Club, owned by Wal-Mart. Given Wal-Mart's buying power and channel leadership, Sam's Club can buy products at very low prices and get them to stores with unusual efficiency. Nonetheless, Costco tops Sam's Club in a number of ways. In recent years, Costco has expanded by offering new services at low prices. For example, members can log onto the retailer's website and sign up for long-distance telephone service, apply for a mortgage, buy life insurance, or price a vacation trip. The company has also started a new chain of stores, Costco Home, which specializes in home furnishings. In warehouse retailing, however, Sam's Club remains the competitor to beat. Before Sam's Club opened stores in Canada, Costco prepared for the increased competition by remodeling some of its stores. And price wars sometimes break out when the two competitors battle for customers. The parent company of Sam's Club is by far the largest company in the world, but Costco is so adept at warehouse retailing that it continues to hold its own.[20]

Questions for Discussion

1. How do Costco's atmospherics support its retail positioning?
2. How is Costco's retail positioning likely to be affected by its target profit margin of 14 percent?

Strategic Case 7   T-Mobile Promotes with Celebrity Sidekicks

With the purchase of U.S. wireless carrier Voice-Stream Wireless, Germany's Deutsche Telekom became the first European company to cross the Atlantic and join the highly competitive North American wireless phone market. Deutsche Telekom envisioned becoming the world's first single-branded international cell phone service. Operating as T-Mobil in Germany, it added an 'e' for a more English-friendly calling card. T-Mobile, in six different countries, was born.

Promoting a product in any market can be difficult, but T-Mobile was faced with the unique challenge of promoting its single brand in six different markets and across continents. Nikesh Arora, who heads up global marketing for T-Mobile, was up for the challenge: ". . . on the marketing side you need a one-brand approach, which means you have common products and common ways of representing the business. We have to make sure we have exciting offers for our customers in every market," says Arora. "I have to build a solid, sustainable, and differentiated brand." When developing the promotion strategy, Arora and his team decided to look at the positive: "We had to sit down and decide what is common across all of the markets and what the key strength of T-Mobile today is." To reach its goal of promoting a consistent brand image, T-Mobile uses a single advertising agency that handles all of its advertising in all six countries.

T-Mobile started out as a genuine underdog; pitting itself against strong competitors. The company has more than met the challenge. T-Mobile is the fastest growing wireless carrier on the continent.

T-Mobile's Star-Studded Promotion Efforts

As an unknown European brand, T-Mobile had to seek ways to create a definitive brand image. To create a recognizable brand, T-Mobile hired Academy Award-winning actress Catherine Zeta-Jones. The highly recognizable Welsh-born actress has been instrumental in building the brand image by appearing in television, print, and radio ads. Because Zeta-Jones is so well known, customers not only noticed the company's ads but also remembered them. Although Zeta-Jones is the official spokesperson, she isn't the only star behind T-Mobile's promotion. The company rolled out the red carpet when introducing its high-end multimedia device, the Sidekick. T-Mobile used a long lineup of celebrities in television ads and promotional events. The television commercials featured rapper Snoop Dogg using his T-Mobile Sidekick to message a long series of celebrities—such as Paris Hilton, Wee Man from MTV's *Jackass,* Wayne Newton, and Burt Reynolds—for help in doing his laundry. The goal of the advertisement wasn't just to sell a lot of Sidekicks but to establish T-Mobile as a hip, young, and cool brand.

The company reinforces this message by sponsoring events such as ESPN's X Games and parties featuring hot musical acts such as the Black Eyed Peas and the Pussycat Dolls. T-Mobile has made sure that its Sidekick is photographed in the hands of Hollywood's hottest trendsetting stars, such as Beyoncé, Lindsay Lohan, Jessica Simpson, and Nicky and Paris Hilton. T-Mobile also offers special editions of the Sidekick, partnered by hip L.A. clothing line Juicy Couture and urban artist Mister Cartoon. The Juicy Couture Sidekick is baby pink with the designer brand's signature Scottie dogs emblazoned on the back. Juicy Couture also offers jewelry charms, velour wristlets, and trendy carrying cases customized for the T-Mobile Sidekick. The Mister Cartoon Sidekick is decorated with the artist's drawings. T-Mobile also partners with NYC Peach, the company that decorated Paris Hilton's infamously hijacked Sidekick. NYC Peach will completely customize a Swarovski crystal design for T-Mobile Sidekicks.

T-Mobile doesn't rely on celebrities just for its Sidekick. It sponsors the T-Mobile All Access Concert Series featuring intimate venues with hot musical acts such as Gavin DeGraw, Simple Plan, and Good Charlotte. To cross-promote the tour, subscribers could download free ring tones of performances or wallpapers of the touring musicians.

T-Mobile also has a multiyear marketing partnership as Official Wireless Services Partner with the NBA and WNBA. This agreement allows T-Mobile to reach a wide market of basketball fans. T-Mobile is integrated into all NBA and WNBA broadcasts and events. It also offers special basketball-related content on its phones, such as participation in NBA All-Star balloting, MVP voting for the NBA All-Star Game and the championship finals, as well as the latest NBA-related news, statistics, and other fun features. T-Mobile is confident that this partnership will broaden its exposure and enhance its youth-targeted image.

Some of T-Mobile's ads poke fun at competitors. One commercial featured two grocery store employees locked in a walk-in freezer. Although suffering from hypothermia, they refuse to call for help because they are outside of their network and don't want to be charged roaming fees. Another ad features a series of parents angry at their children because of high cell phone overages. To promote its flat-rate text messaging plan, a T-Mobile ad shows a suspicious dad roaming the house hoping to catch his children sending text messages. These ads poke fun at common consumer complaints within the wireless phone industry and provide T-Mobile as the provider with a solution. These ads set T-Mobile apart as the company that understands the frustration of wireless bills and overage charges.

T-Mobile's Customers "Get More" Customer Service

T-Mobile lacks some of the multimedia services offered by competitors such as iTunes and live TV. T-Mobile attributes their growth without multimedia to exceptional customer service. It ranked number 1 on J. D. Power & Associates' industry survey in "Overall Customer Satisfaction," "Customer Care," and "Call Quality." Its mission is not only to remain at the top of its industry in customer service but also to eventually become the most highly respected service company across industries. To maintain this goal, T-Mobile's CEO Robert Dotson and Chief Marketing Officer Mike Butler visit a large number of T-Mobile stores every quarter. Butler says that the purpose of the visits is not to lecture employees but to learn from them: "We come away with a list of items we're going to address to help deliver better customer service in the future." Many of the ideas expressed by T-Mobile store employees have been incorporated by the company. One suggested change was to provide more detailed information to potential customers about service coverage. T-Mobile developed colour-coded maps that allow potential customers to view the coverage in their area as specifically as at street level. "[W]e would rather they went down the street to someone else than sign up with us and be unhappy," says Butler. T-Mobile even christened its headquarters as "T-Mobile Field Service," because it feels that the purpose of its headquarters is to assist field employees with the necessary tools to deliver outstanding customer service. Many of T-Mobile's ads focus on this dedication to customer service. It believes that "Get More" is not just a tagline but a promise that every customer will get more service, more savings, and more features.

What's Ahead for T-Mobile?

Some industry analysts speculate that T-Mobile might be the next target of a buyout or that it will be unable to compete against the multimedia features being offered by other service providers. But T-Mobile remains optimistic and fully expects to continue growing by focusing on excellent customer service and more traditional cell phone features. T-Mobile is betting on the idea that cell phone users find chatting with friends and family more important than other features. Only time will tell if this strategy will pay off; but T-Mobile's track record indicates they might be right.[21]

Questions for Discussion

1. What kind of brand image does T-Mobile want to build through its celebrity-packed promotion efforts?
2. What celebrities should T-Mobile use in its advertisements? Why?
3. How would T-Mobile's choice of promotional partners, such as Juicy Couture and the NBA, attract or discourage customers from selecting T-Mobile's phone services?
4. In what ways is T-Mobile supporting its personal selling activities at the retail level?
5. T-Mobile promotes its highly rated customer service as a selling point. Do you think it is effective against competitors that promote high-tech multimedia features? Explain.

8

Promotion Decisions

Part Eight focuses on communication with target market members and, at times, other groups. A specific marketing mix cannot satisfy people in a particular target market unless they are aware of the product and know where to find it. Some promotion decisions relate to a specific marketing mix; others are geared toward promoting the entire organization. **Chapter 17** discusses integrated marketing communications. It describes the communication process and the major promotional methods that can be included in promotion mixes. It also discusses the major steps in developing an advertising campaign, what public relations is and how it can be used. This chapter also explores the general characteristics of sales promotion and describes sales promotion techniques. **Chapter 18** deals with personal selling and professional sales management and the critical role it plays in a firm's promotional efforts.

Using Advertising, Public Relations, and Sales Promotion in Integrated Marketing Communications

WestJet Celebrates Brand Success

WestJet celebrated its eleventh year in 2007, while also reveling in a year of record sales. WestJet, Air Canada's nemesis in Canada's airline industry, reached record profit levels of $76.1 million in the third quarter.

WestJet has been able to develop a loyal following, tying up nearly a third of the flying public. Its success is based on textbook branding: focus on the entire flying experience, from booking to landing, then working hard to further personalize the service experience.

Its creative advertising set them apart. Their promotion featuring employee-owners stuck a chord with Canadians, raising return on investment from 35 per cent to an impressive 175 percent. These numbers boosted brand familiarity from 51 percent to 69 percent, with an equally bullish increase in top-of-mind awareness for airlines from 23 percent to 33 percent.

What is it that makes WestJet's promotion so effective? Experts at *Strategy Magazine* attribute the airline's promotional success to building a solid brand foundation, and then leveraging that image to further develop brand loyalty. Advertising that focuses on employees who are also owners captures the imagination of the marketplace while also focusing on high levels of personalized customer service. Canadians really seem to love the message.

WestJet has worked hard to develop a unique brand. Today, WestJet has an image of being a fun and entertaining airline to fly. Add to that crews of employee-owners who will stop at nothing to ensure their passengers are well served and comfortable, and a successful airline brand becomes even more golden.

WestJet is following up its successful branding by focusing closely on growth markets of baby boomers across Canada, expanding routes to sun-filled destinations, and continuing to pour on the WestJet charm.[1] ■

Organizations such as WestJet employ a variety of promotional methods to communicate with their target markets. Providing information to customers and other stakeholders is vital to initiating and developing long-term relationships with them.

This chapter looks at the general dimensions of promotion. First, we discuss the nature of integrated marketing communications. Next, we analyze the meaning and process of communication. We then define and examine the role of promotion and explore some of the reasons promotion is used. Then we consider major promotional methods and the factors that influence marketers' decisions to use particular methods. Next, we explain the positive and negative effects of personal and electronic word-of-mouth communication. Finally, we examine criticisms and defenses of promotion.

The Nature of Integrated Marketing Communications

integrated marketing communications
Coordination of promotion and other marketing efforts for maximum informational and persuasive impact

Integrated marketing communications refer to the coordination of promotion and other marketing efforts to ensure maximum informational and persuasive impact on customers. Coordinating multiple marketing tools to produce this synergistic effect requires a marketer to employ a broad perspective. A major goal of integrated marketing communications is to send a consistent message to customers. For example, Mars has attempted to integrate its well-known M&Ms brand with iconic consumer events such as the Academy Awards to help reinforce the fact that M&Ms are the number one snack food at the movies. In addition to humorous appearances by its "Red" and "Yellow" spokescharacters at pre-Oscar events, print ads for M&Ms featured a bingo game that consumers could play along with the awards ceremony, while television commercials offered tips for using M&Ms to host an Oscar party.[2] Indeed, research suggests that the use of such spokespersons results in more favourable brand images in integrated marketing communications.[3]

Because various units both inside and outside most companies have traditionally planned and implemented promotional efforts, customers have not always received consistent messages. Integrated marketing communications allow an organization to coordinate and manage its promotional efforts to transmit consistent messages. Integrated marketing communications also enable synchronization of promotion elements and can reduce overspending on elements that may produce a smaller return on investment.[4] Thus, this approach fosters not only long-term customer relationships but also the efficient use of promotional resources.

Communication Channels
Numerous communications channels such as Yahoo! are available for use in integrated marketing communication programs.

The concept of integrated marketing communications has been increasingly accepted for several reasons. Mass media advertising, a very popular promotional method in the past, is used less frequently today because of its high cost and lower effectiveness in reaching some target markets.[5] Marketers can now take advantage of more precisely targeted promotional tools, such as cable TV, direct mail, the Internet, special-interest magazines, CDs and DVDs, cell phones, and iPods. Database marketing is also allowing marketers to more precisely target individual customers. Until recently, suppliers of marketing communications were specialists. Today a number of promotion-related companies provide one-stop shopping for the client seeking advertising, sales promotion, and public relations, thus reducing coordination problems for the sponsoring company.

The specific communication vehicles employed and the precision with which they are used are changing as both information technology and customer interests become increasingly dynamic. For example, an increasing number of companies are running short advertisements during podcasts of TV shows and other videos that users download to their video iPods.[6] Earthlink sponsored podcasts from Washingtonpost.com for a month and ran 15-second ads in front of video clips.[7] Today marketers and customers have almost unlimited access to data about each other. Integrating and customizing marketing communications while protecting customer privacy has become a major challenge. However, research indicates that 75 percent of adult consumers want products customized to their personal needs, and 70 percent say they would be more loyal to companies that make an effort to discover their needs and tastes.[8] Through the Internet, companies can provide product information and services that are coordinated with traditional promotional activities. Communication relationships with customers can actually determine the nature of the product. For example, Reflect.com, an online cosmetics firm, mixes makeup for different skin types based on information exchanges with customers. Thus, consumers may be willing to exchange personal information for customized products.[9] The sharing of information and use of technology to facilitate communication between buyers and sellers are essential for successful customer relationship management.

Promotion and the Communication Process

Communication is essentially the transmission of information. For communication to take place, both the sender and receiver of information must share some common ground. They must have a common understanding of the symbols, words, and pictures used to transmit information. An individual transmitting the following message may believe he or she is communicating with you:

在工廠吾人製造化粧品,在商店吾人銷售希望。

However, communication has not taken place if you don't understand the language in which the message is written.[10] Thus, we define **communication** as a sharing of meaning.[11] Implicit in this definition is the notion of transmission of information because sharing necessitates transmission.

As Figure 17.1 shows, communication begins with a source. A **source** is a person, group, or organization with a meaning it attempts to share with an audience. A source could be a salesperson wishing to communicate a sales message or an organization wanting to send a message to thousands of customers through an advertisement. Developing a strategy can enhance the effectiveness of the source's communication. For example, a strategy in which a salesperson attempts to influence a customer's decision by eliminating competitive products from consideration has been found to be effective.[12] A **receiver** is the individual, group, or organization that decodes a coded message, and an *audience* is two or more receivers.

To transmit meaning, a source must convert the meaning into a series of signs or symbols representing ideas or concepts. This is called the **coding process,** or *encoding.*

communication A sharing of meaning through the transmission of information

source A person, group, or organization with a meaning it tries to share with a receiver or an audience

receiver The individual, group, or organization that decodes a coded message

coding process Converting meaning into a series of signs or symbols

figure 17.1

THE COMMUNICATION PROCESS

When coding meaning into a message, the source must consider certain characteristics of the receiver or audience. To share meaning, the source should use signs or symbols familiar to the receiver or audience. Research has shown that persuasive messages from a source are more effective when the appeal matches an individual's personality.[13] Marketers that understand this realize the importance of knowing their target market and ensuring that an advertisement, for example, uses language the target market understands. Thus, when General Mills advertises Cheerios, it does not mention all the ingredients used to make the cereal because some ingredients would have little meaning to consumers. Some notable problems have occurred in translating English advertisements into other languages to communicate with customers in global markets. For example, Coors' "Turn it loose" campaign was translated into Spanish as "Drink Coors and get diarrhea," while KFC's long-running slogan, "Finger lickin' good," was translated into Chinese as "Eat your fingers off." And Parker Pen was dismayed to learn that "Avoid embarrassment" (from a leaking pen) had been translated into "Avoid pregnancy" in Spanish.[14] Clearly it is important that people understand the language used in promotion.

When coding a meaning, a source needs to use signs or symbols that the receiver or audience uses to refer to the concepts the source intends to convey. Instead of technical jargon, explanatory language that helps consumers understand is more likely to result in positive attitudes and purchase intentions.[15] Marketers try to avoid signs or symbols that may have several meanings for an audience. For example, *soda* as a general term for soft drinks may not work well in national advertisements. Although in some parts of the United States the word means "soft drink," in other regions it may connote bicarbonate of soda, an ice cream drink, or something one mixes with Scotch whiskey.

To share a coded meaning with the receiver or audience, a source selects and uses a **communications channel,** the medium of transmission that carries the coded message from the source to the receiver or audience. Transmission media include ink on paper, airwave vibrations produced by vocal cords, chalk marks on a chalkboard, and electronically produced vibrations of air waves (in radio and television signals, for example).

When a source chooses an inappropriate communication channel, several problems may arise. The coded message may reach some receivers, but the wrong ones. For example, dieters embracing the Atkins low-carbohydrate diet are more likely to focus on communications relating to their food concerns, such as "Eat Meat Not Wheat" T-shirts, QVC's Low-Carb Hour, and fast-food chain advertisements that communicate information about the carbohydrate content of menu items.[16] An advertiser attempting to reach this group would need to take this information into account when choosing an appropriate communications channel. Coded messages may also

communications channel
The medium of transmission that carries the coded message from the source to the receiver

reach intended receivers in incomplete form because the intensity of the transmission is weak. For example, radio and broadcast television signals are received effectively only over a limited range, which varies according to climatic conditions. Members of the target audience living on the fringe of the broadcast area may receive a weak signal; others well within the broadcast area may also receive an incomplete message if, for example, they listen to the radio while driving or studying.

decoding process Converting signs or symbols into concepts and ideas

In the **decoding process,** signs or symbols are converted into concepts and ideas. Seldom does a receiver decode exactly the same meaning the source coded. When the result of decoding differs from what was coded, noise exists. **Noise** is anything that reduces the clarity and accuracy of the communication; it has many sources and may affect any or all parts of the communication process. Noise sometimes arises within the communications channel itself. Radio static, poor or slow Internet connections, and laryngitis are sources of noise. Noise also occurs when a source uses signs or symbols that are unfamiliar to the receiver or have a meaning different from the one intended. Noise may also originate in the receiver; a receiver may be unaware of a coded message when perceptual processes block it out.

noise Anything that reduces a communication's clarity and accuracy

The receiver's response to a decoded message is **feedback** to the source. The source usually expects and normally receives feedback, although perhaps not immediately. During feedback, the receiver or audience is the source of a message directed toward the original source, which then becomes a receiver. Feedback is coded, sent through a communications channel, and decoded by the receiver, the source of the original communication. Thus, communication is a circular process, as indicated in Figure 17.1.

feedback The receiver's response to a decoded message

During face-to-face communication, such as occurs in personal selling and product sampling, verbal and non-verbal feedback can be immediate. Instant feedback lets communicators adjust messages quickly to improve the effectiveness of their communications. For example, when a salesperson realizes through feedback that a customer does not understand a sales presentation, the salesperson adapts the presentation to make it more meaningful to the customer. This may be why face-to-face sales presentations create higher behavioural intentions to purchase services than do telemarketing sales contacts.[17] In interpersonal communication, feedback occurs through talking, touching, smiling, nodding, eye movements, and other body movements and postures.

channel capacity The limit on the volume of information a communication channel can handle effectively

When mass communication such as advertising is used, feedback is often slow and difficult to recognize. Also, it may be several years before the effects of this promotion will be known. Feedback does exist for mass communication in the form of measures of changes in sales volume or in consumers' attitudes and awareness levels.

Each communication channel has a limit on the volume of information it can handle effectively. This limit, called **channel capacity,** is determined by the least efficient component of the communication process. Consider communications that depend on speech. An individual source can speak only so fast, and there is a limit to how much an individual receiver can take in aurally.

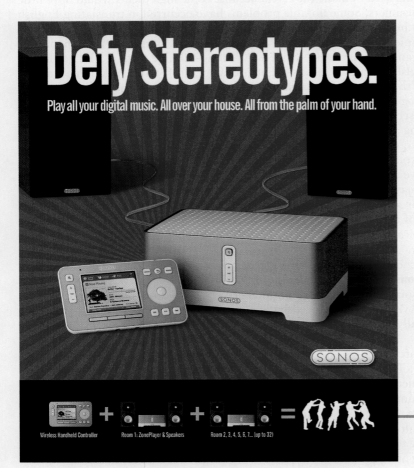

The Role and Objectives of Promotion

Marketers use promotional efforts to achieve a broad spectrum of objectives. What is the objective of this advertisement?

Beyond that point, additional messages cannot be decoded; thus, meaning cannot be shared. Although a radio announcer can read several hundred words a minute, a one-minute advertising message should not exceed 150 words because most announcers cannot articulate words into understandable messages at a rate beyond 150 words per minute.

The Role and Objectives of Promotion

promotion Communication to build and maintain relationships by informing and persuading one or more audiences

Promotion is communication that builds and maintains favourable relationships by informing and persuading one or more audiences to view an organization positively and to accept its products. Toward this end, many organizations spend considerable resources on promotion to build and enhance relationships with current and potential customers. For example, the lumber, pork, and milk industries promote the use of these products to stimulate demand with such catch phrases as "Be Constructive," "Pork: The Other White Meat," and "Got Milk?"[18] Marketers also indirectly facilitate favourable relationships by focusing information about company activities and products on interest groups (such as environmental and consumer groups), current and potential investors, regulatory agencies, and society in general. For example, some organizations promote responsible use of products criticized by society such as tobacco, alcohol, and violent movies. Companies sometimes promote programs that help selected groups. Yoplait, for instance, supports the Susan G. Komen Breast Cancer Research Foundation with its "Save Lids to Save Lives" campaign, which contributes 10 cents to the charity for every pink yogurt lid sent in by consumers.[19] Such cause-related marketing, as we discussed in Chapter 4, links the purchase of products to philanthropic efforts for one or more causes. By contributing to causes that its target markets support, cause-related marketing can help marketers boost sales and generate goodwill.

For maximum benefit from promotional efforts, marketers strive for proper planning, implementation, coordination, and control of communications. Effective management of integrated marketing communications is based on information about and feedback from customers and the marketing environment, often obtained from an organization's marketing information system (see Figure 17.2). How successfully marketers use promotion to maintain positive relationships depends to some extent on the quantity and quality of information the organization receives. Because customers derive information and opinions from many different sources, integrated marketing communications planning also takes into account informal methods of communication such as word of mouth and independent information sources on the Internet. Because promotion is communication that can be managed, we now analyze what communication is and how the communication process works.

Promotional objectives vary considerably from one organization to another and within organizations over time. Large firms with multiple promotional programs operating simultaneously may have quite varied promotional objectives. For the purpose of analysis, we focus on the eight promotional objectives shown in Table 17.1. Although the list is not exhaustive, one or more of these objectives underlie many promotional programs.

figure 17.2

INFORMATION FLOWS ARE IMPORTANT IN INTEGRATED MARKETING COMMUNICATIONS

table 17.1	POSSIBLE OBJECTIVES OF PROMOTION
Create awareness	Retain loyal customers
Stimulate demand	Facilitate reseller support
Encourage product trial	Combat competitive promotional efforts
Identify prospects	Reduce sales fluctuations

Create Awareness

A considerable amount of promotion efforts focus on creating awareness. For an organization introducing a new product or a line extension, making customers aware of the product is crucial to initiating the product adoption process. A marketer that has invested heavily in product development strives to create product awareness quickly to generate revenues to offset the high costs of product development and introduction. To create awareness of its new Spicy Premium Chicken sandwich, for example, McDonald's passed out samples of the sandwich, coupons, T-shirts, and iPod covers in 14 cities.[20]

Creating awareness is important for existing products, too. Promotional efforts may aim to increase awareness of brands, product features, image-related issues (such as organizational size or socially responsive behaviour), or operational characteristics (such as store hours, locations, and credit availability). Some promotional programs are unsuccessful because marketers fail to generate awareness of critical issues among a significant portion of target market members. For example, Chrysler Group effectively dropped an expensive campaign to launch its new Pacifica when sales failed to meet expectations. Chrysler wanted to target the new vehicle at younger, more affluent consumers. However, the company chose Celine Dion, the popular Canadian singer, to appear in television commercials for the campaign and only later discovered that she appeals to a much older audience, with an average age of 52.[21]

Stimulate Demand

When an organization is the first to introduce an innovative product, it tries to stimulate **primary demand**—demand for a product category rather than for a specific brand of product—through pioneer promotion. **Pioneer promotion** informs potential customers about the product: what it is, what it does, how it can be used, and where it can be purchased. Because pioneer promotion is used in the introductory stage of the product life cycle, meaning there are no competing brands, it neither emphasizes brand names nor compares brands. When Apple introduced the iPod, for instance, it initially attempted to stimulate primary demand by emphasizing the benefits of music players in general rather than the benefits of its specific brand. Primary-demand stimulation is not just for new products. At times an industry trade association rather than a single firm uses promotional efforts to stimulate primary demand.

primary demand Demand for a product category rather than for a specific brand

pioneer promotion Promotion that informs consumers about a new product

4000-YEAR-OLD MAN FOUND FROZEN IN ICE, FEET STILL WARM AND DRY.

THE BUGASTORM™ LIGHT WEIGHT SKI SOCK: With 73% non-itch Merino wool for warmth, moisture wicking and breathability • Comfy over-calf length, arch support and selective cushioning • 800-MA BOYLE or columbia.com

TESTED TOUGH

◆ Columbia
Sportswear Company.

Selective Demand

In its advertisement for ski socks, Columbia attempts to stimulate selective demand.

selective demand Demand for a specific brand

To build **selective demand,** demand for a specific brand, a marketer employs promotional efforts that point out the strengths and benefits of a specific brand. Building selective demand also requires singling out attributes important to potential buyers. Selective demand can be stimulated by differentiating the product from competing brands in the minds of potential buyers. Increasing the number of product uses and promoting them through advertising campaigns, as well as through price discounts, free samples, coupons, consumer contests and games, and sweepstakes can also stimulate selective demand. Bennigan's, for example, launched an advertising campaign and held a 30th anniversary party to coincide with St. Patrick's Day to remind customers that the Irish-themed restaurant chain provides a fun environment where people can share good food.[22] Promotions for large package sizes or multiple-product packages are directed at increasing consumption, which in turn can stimulate demand. In addition, selective demand can be stimulated by encouraging existing customers to use more of the product.

Encourage Product Trial

When attempting to move customers through the product adoption process, a marketer may successfully create awareness and interest, but customers may stall during the evaluation stage. In this case, certain types of promotion—such as free samples; coupons; test drives; or limited free-use offers, contests, and games—are employed to encourage product trial. Silk, for example, distributed coupons and samples to promote its new Silk Live! Smoothie product.[23] Whether a marketer's product is the first in a new product category, a new brand in an existing category, or simply an existing brand seeking customers, trial-inducing promotional efforts aim to make product trial convenient and low risk for potential customers.

Identify Prospects

Certain types of promotional efforts aim to identify customers who are interested in the firm's product and are most likely to buy it. A marketer may use a magazine advertisement with a direct-response information form, requesting the reader to complete and mail the form to receive additional information. Some advertisements have toll-free numbers to facilitate direct customer response. Customers who fill out information blanks or call the organization usually have higher interest in the product, which makes them likely sales prospects. The organization can respond with phone calls, follow-up letters, or personal contact by salespeople. Dun & Bradstreet, for example, offered a free article on customer relationship management to businesses that mailed in a card or called a toll-free number. This helped the consulting firm identify prospects to sell data used to develop and maintain customer relationships.

Encouraging Product Trial

Sun Microsystems encourages product trial by offering free use for a selected time period.

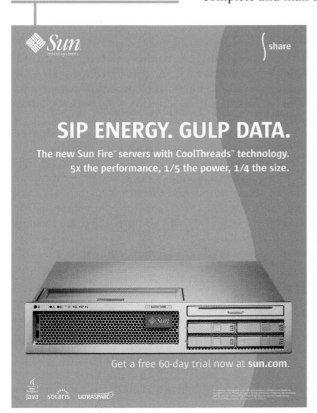

Retain Loyal Customers

Clearly, maintaining long-term customer relationships is a major goal of most marketers. Such relationships are quite valuable. Promotional efforts directed at customer retention can help an organization control its costs because the costs of retaining customers are usually considerably lower than those of acquiring new ones. Frequent-user programs, such as those sponsored by airlines, car rental agencies, and hotels, aim to reward loyal customers and encourage them to remain loyal. Moët Hennessy, for example, introduced the Sparkling Circle, a membership club for 15 000 loyal customers.[24] Some organizations employ special offers that only their existing customers can use. To retain loyal customers, marketers not only advertise loyalty programs but also use reinforcement advertising, which assures current users they have made the right brand choice and tells them how to get the most satisfaction from the product.

Facilitate Reseller Support

Reseller support is a two-way street: producers generally want to provide support to resellers to maintain sound working relationships, and in turn they expect resellers to support their products. When a manufacturer advertises a product to consumers, resellers should view this promotion as a form of strong manufacturer support. In some instances, a producer agrees to pay a certain proportion of retailers' advertising expenses for promoting its products. When a manufacturer is introducing a new consumer brand in a highly competitive product category, it may be difficult to persuade supermarket managers to carry this brand. However, if the manufacturer promotes the new brand with free sample and coupon distribution in the retailer's area, a supermarket manager views these actions as strong support and is much more likely to handle the product. To encourage wholesalers and retailers to increase their inventories of its products, a manufacturer may provide them with special offers and buying allowances. In certain industries, a producer's salesperson may provide support to a wholesaler by working with the wholesaler's customers (retailers) in the presentation and promotion of the products. Strong relationships with resellers are important to a firm's ability to maintain a sustainable competitive advantage. The use of various promotional methods can help an organization achieve this goal.

Combat Competitive Promotional Efforts

At times a marketer's objective in using promotion is to offset or lessen the effect of a competitor's promotional program. This type of promotional activity does not necessarily increase the organization's sales or market share, but it may prevent a sales or market share loss. A combative promotional objective is used most often by firms in extremely competitive consumer markets, such as the fast-food and automobile industries. When some automakers began advertising their automobiles' ability to withstand collisions, as determined by crash tests conducted by various federal and private agencies, Volkswagen, BMW, Saturn, Mercedes-Benz, Toyota, and other firms quickly followed suit to combat their competitors' advertising. Although these ads were trying to promote safety records, the companies were also trying to prevent market share loss in a very competitive market.[25]

Reduce Sales Fluctuations

Demand for many products varies from one month to another because of such factors as climate, holidays, and seasons. A business, however, cannot operate at peak efficiency when sales fluctuate rapidly. Changes in sales volume translate into changes in production, inventory levels, personnel needs, and financial resources. When promotional techniques reduce fluctuations by generating sales during slow periods, a firm can use its resources more efficiently.

Promotional techniques are often designed to stimulate sales during sales slumps. For example, advertisements promoting price reduction of lawn care equipment can increase sales during fall and winter months. During peak periods, a marketer may refrain from advertising to prevent stimulating sales to the point where the firm cannot handle all the demand. On occasion, an organization advertises that customers can be better served by coming in on certain days. A pizza outlet, for example, might distribute coupons that are valid only Monday through Thursday because on Friday through Sunday the restaurant is extremely busy.

To achieve the major objectives of promotion discussed here, companies must develop appropriate promotional programs. In the next section, we consider the basic components of such programs: the promotion mix elements.

The Promotion Mix

Several promotional methods can be used to communicate with individuals, groups, and organizations. When an organization combines specific methods to manage the integrated marketing communications for a particular product, that combination

figure 17.3   **THE FOUR POSSIBLE ELEMENTS OF A PROMOTION MIX**

promotion mix A combination of promotional methods used to promote a specific product

constitutes the promotion mix for that product. The four possible elements of a **promotion mix** are advertising, personal selling, public relations, and sales promotion (see Figure 17.3). For some products, firms use all four elements; for others, they use only two or three. In this section, we provide an overview of each promotion mix element; they are covered in greater detail in the next chapter.

Advertising

Advertising is a paid non-personal communication about an organization and its products transmitted to a target audience through mass media, including television, radio, the Internet, newspapers, magazines, direct mail, outdoor displays, and signs on mass transit vehicles. One company even placed advertisements—in the form of temporary tattoos of company logos—on the foreheads of college students.[26] Individuals and organizations use advertising to promote goods, services, ideas, issues, and people. Being highly flexible, advertising can reach an extremely large target audience or focus on a small, precisely defined segment. For instance, Burger King's advertising focuses on a large audience of potential fast-food customers, ranging from children to adults, whereas advertising for Gulfstream jets aims at a much smaller and more specialized target market.

Advertising offers several benefits. It is extremely cost efficient when it reaches a vast number of people at a low cost per person. For example, the cost of a four-colour, full-page advertisement in *Time* magazine is $246 000. Because the magazine reaches more than four million subscribers, the cost of reaching 1000 subscribers is about $62.[27] Advertising also lets the source repeat the message several times. Levi Strauss, for example, advertises on television, in magazines, and in outdoor displays. Advertising repetition has been found to be especially effective for brand name extensions beyond the original product category.[28] Furthermore, advertising a product a certain way can add to the product's value, and the visibility an organization gains from advertising can enhance its image. At times a firm tries to enhance its own or its product's image by including celebrity endorsers in advertisements. For example, the "milk moustache" campaign."[29] Advertising has disadvantages as well. Even though the cost per person reached may be low, the absolute dollar outlay can be extremely high, especially for commercials during popular television shows. High costs can limit, and sometimes preclude, use of advertising in a promotion mix. Moreover, advertising rarely provides rapid feedback. Measuring its effect on sales is difficult, and it is ordinarily less persuasive than personal selling. In most instances, the time available to communicate a message to customers is limited to seconds, since people look at a print advertisement for only a few seconds and most broadcast commercials are 30 seconds or less. Of course, the use of infomercials can increase exposure time for viewers.

Advertising Aimed at Prevention
Merck uses the "Tell someone" campaign to heighten awareness of the risks of cervical cancer.

institutional advertising
Advertising that promotes organizational images, ideas, and political issues

advocacy advertising
Advertising that promotes a company's position on a public issue

product advertising Advertising that promotes the uses, features, and benefits of products

pioneer advertising
Advertising that tries to stimulate demand for a product category rather than a specific brand by informing potential buyers about the product

competitive advertising
Advertising that points out a brand's special features, uses, and advantages relative to competing brands

comparative advertising
Advertising that compares two or more brands on the basis of one or more product characteristics

reminder advertising
Advertising used to remind consumers about an established brand's uses, characteristics, and benefits

reinforcement advertising
Advertising that assures users they chose the right brand and tells them how to get the most satisfaction from it

objective-and-task approach
Budgeting for an advertising campaign by first determining its objectives and then calculating the cost of all the tasks needed to attain them

percent-of-sales approach
Budgeting for an advertising campaign by multiplying the firm's past and expected sales by a standard percentage

Classifying Advertising. Advertising is used to promote goods, services, ideas, images, issues, people, and anything else advertisers want to publicize or foster. Depending on what is being promoted, advertising can be classified as institutional or product advertising. **Institutional advertising** promotes organizational images, ideas, and political issues. It can be used to create or maintain an organizational image. Institutional advertisements may deal with broad image issues, such as organizational strength or the friendliness of employees. They may also aim to create a more favourable view of the organization in the eyes of non-customer groups such as shareholders, consumer advocacy groups, potential stockholders, or the general public. When a company promotes its position on a public issue—for instance, a tax increase, abortion, gun control, or international trade coalitions—institutional advertising is referred to as **advocacy advertising.** Institutional advertising may be used to promote socially approved behaviour such as recycling and moderation in consuming alcoholic beverages. Research has identified a number of themes that advertisers can use to increase the effectiveness of antismoking messages for adolescents.[30] This type of advertising not only has societal benefits but also helps build an organization's image.

Product advertising promotes the uses, features, and benefits of products. There are two types of product advertising: pioneer and competitive. **Pioneer advertising** focuses on stimulating demand for a product category (rather than a specific brand) by informing potential customers about the product's features, uses, and benefits. This type of advertising is employed when the product is in the introductory stage of the product life cycle. **Competitive advertising** attempts to stimulate demand for a specific brand by promoting the brand's features, uses, and advantages, sometimes through indirect or direct comparisons with competing brands. Advertising effects on sales must reflect competitors' advertising activities. The type of competitive environment will determine the most effective industry approach.

To make direct product comparisons, marketers use a form of competitive advertising called **comparative advertising,** which compares the sponsored brand with one or more identified competing brands on the basis of one or more product characteristics. Often the brands promoted through comparative advertisements have low market shares and are compared with competitors that have the highest market shares in the product category. Product categories that commonly use comparative advertising include soft drinks, toothpaste, pain relievers, foods, tires, automobiles, and detergents. Under the provisions of the 1988 Trademark Law Revision Act, marketers using comparative advertisements in the United States must not misrepresent the qualities or characteristics of competing products. Other countries may have laws that are stricter or less strict with regard to comparative advertising.

Other forms of competitive advertising include reminder and reinforcement advertising. **Reminder advertising** tells customers that an established brand is still around and still offers certain characteristics, uses, and advantages. **Reinforcement advertising** assures current users they have made the right brand choice and tells them how to get the most satisfaction from the choice that they have made.

Determining Advertising Budgets. Of the many techniques used to determine the advertising budget, one of the most logical is the **objective-and-task approach.** Using this approach, marketers determine the objectives a campaign is to achieve and then attempt to list the tasks required to accomplish them. The costs of the tasks are calculated and added to arrive at the total appropriation. While this is usually the best way to determine what is really needed to accomplish a firm's advertising goals, this approach has one main problem: marketers sometimes have trouble accurately estimating the level of effort needed to attain certain objectives. A coffee marketer, for example, may find it extremely difficult to determine how much of an increase in national television advertising is needed to raise a brand's market share from eight to 10 percent.

In the more widely used **percent-of-sales approach,** marketers simply multiply the firm's past sales, plus a factor for planned sales growth or decline, by a standard percentage based on both what the firm traditionally spends on advertising and the industry average. This approach, too, has a major flaw: it is based on the incorrect assumption that sales create advertising rather than the reverse. A marketer using this approach during declining sales will reduce the amount spent on advertising, but such a reduction may further diminish sales. Though illogical, this technique has been favoured because it is easy to use.

Another way to determine advertising appropriation is the **competition-matching, or parity, approach.** Marketers following this approach try to match their major competitors' appropriations in absolute dollars or to allocate the same percentage of sales for advertising that their competitors do. Although a marketer should be aware of what competitors spend on advertising, this technique should not be used alone because the firm's competitors probably have different advertising objectives and different resources available for advertising. Many companies and advertising agencies review competitive spending on a quarterly basis, comparing competitors' dollar expenditures on print, radio, and television with their own spending levels. Competitive tracking of this nature occurs at both the national and regional levels.

At times marketers use the **arbitrary approach,** which usually means a high-level executive in the firm states how much to spend on advertising for a certain period. The arbitrary approach often leads to underspending or overspending. Although hardly a scientific budgeting technique, it is expedient.

Deciding how large the advertising appropriation should be is critical. If the appropriation is set too low, the campaign cannot achieve its full potential. When too much money is appropriated, overspending results and financial resources are wasted.

Creating a Media Plan

Advertisers spend tremendous amounts on advertising media. These amounts have grown rapidly during the past two decades. To derive maximum results from media expenditures, marketers must develop effective media plans. A **media plan** sets forth the exact media vehicles to be used (specific magazines, television stations, newspapers, and so forth) and the dates and times the advertisements will appear. The plan determines how many people in the target audience will be exposed to the message. It also determines, to some degree, the effects of the message on those individuals. Media planning is a complex task requiring thorough analysis of the target audience. Sophisticated computer models have been developed to attempt to maximize the effectiveness of media plans.

To formulate a media plan, the planners select the media for the campaign and prepare a time schedule for each medium. The media planner's primary goal is to reach the largest number of people in the advertising target that the budget will allow. A secondary goal is to achieve the appropriate message reach and frequency for the target audience while staying within budget. *Reach* refers to the percentage of consumers in the target audience actually exposed to a particular advertisement in a stated period. *Frequency* is the number of times these targeted consumers are exposed to the advertisement.

Media planners begin with broad decisions but eventually make very specific ones. They first decide which kinds of media to use: radio, television, the Internet, newspapers, magazines, direct mail, outdoor displays, or signs on mass transit vehicles. Internet advertising in particular is growing, with companies spending $4 billion in 2004 to run ads alongside Internet searches in sites like Yahoo! and Google.[31] They assess different formats and approaches to determine which are most effective. Some media plans are highly focused and use just one medium. The media plans of manufacturers of consumer packaged goods can be quite complex and dynamic.

Media planners take many factors into account when devising a media plan. They analyze location and demographic characteristics of consumers in the target audience because people's tastes in media differ according to demographic groups and locations. There are radio stations especially for teenagers, magazines for men ages 18 to 34, and television cable channels aimed at women in various age groups. Media planners also consider the sizes and types of audiences that specific media reach. Anheuser-Busch, for example, cut back on network television advertising in favour of more cable television and Internet advertising in response to changing consumer media habits.

competition-matching, or parity, approach Determining an advertising budget by trying to match competitors' advertising outlays

arbitrary approach Budgeting for an advertising campaign as specified by a high-level executive in the firm

media plan A plan that specifies the media vehicles to be used and the schedule for running advertisements

Declining broadcast television ratings have led many companies to explore alternative media, including not only cable television and Internet advertising but also ads on cell phones and product placements in video games. Several data services collect and periodically provide information about circulations and audiences of various media.

The content of the message sometimes affects media choice. Print media can be used more effectively than broadcast media to present complex issues or numerous details in single advertisements. If an advertiser wants to promote beautiful colours, patterns, or textures, media offering high-quality colour reproduction, such as magazines or television, should be used instead of newspapers. For example, food can be effectively promoted in full-colour magazine advertisements but far less effectively in black and white.

The cost of media is an important but troublesome consideration. Planners try to obtain the best coverage possible for each dollar spent. The concept of integrated marketing communications stresses the benefits of coordinating and building synergy across various media to build brand equity. Overspending is less likely with an integrated approach to multimedia advertising.[32] However, there is no accurate way to compare the cost and impact of a television commercial with the cost and impact of a newspaper advertisement. A **cost comparison indicator** lets an advertiser compare the costs of several vehicles within a specific medium (such as two magazines) in relation to the number of people each vehicle reaches. The *cost per thousand (CPM)* is the cost comparison indicator for magazines; it shows the cost of exposing 1000 people to a one-page advertisement.

Figure 17.4 shows the extent to which each medium is used and how it has changed since 1985. For example, the proportion of total advertising dollars spent on television has risen since 1985 and surpassed that spent on newspapers. The major media classes are show in Table 17.2.

Like media selection decisions, media scheduling decisions are affected by numerous factors, such as target audience characteristics, product attributes, product seasonality, customer media behaviour, and size of the advertising budget. There are three general types of media schedules: continuous, flighting, and pulsing. When a *continuous* schedule is used, advertising runs at a constant level with little variation throughout the campaign period. With a *flighting* schedule, advertisements run for set periods of

cost comparison indicator
A means of comparing the costs of advertising vehicles in a specific medium in relation to the number of people reached

---

figure 17.4

PERCENTAGE OF SPENDING BY MEDIA CATEGORY: 1985 VS. 2005

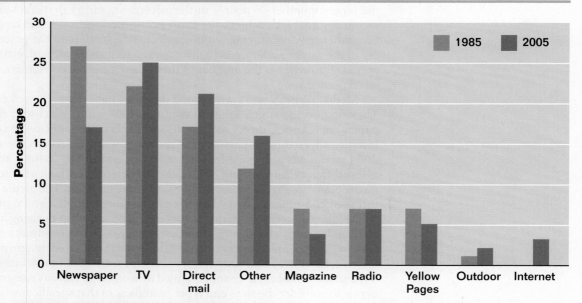

Sources: "Ad Spending Totals by Media," *Advertising Age*, June 27, 2005, p. S-21; Robert J. Coen, "Coen: Little Ad Growth," *Advertising Age*, May 6, 1991, pp. 1, 16.

| table 17.2 | ADVANTAGES AND DISADVANTAGES OF MAJOR MEDIA CLASSES |

Medium	Advantages	Disadvantages
Newspapers	Reaches large audience; purchased to be read; geographic flexibility; short lead time; frequent publication; favourable for cooperative advertising; merchandising services	Not selective for socioeconomic groups or target market; short life; limited reproduction capabilities; large advertising volume limits exposure to any one advertisement
Magazines	Demographic selectivity; good reproduction; long life; prestige; geographic selectivity when regional issues are available; read in leisurely manner	High costs; 30–90 day average lead time; high level of competition; limited reach; communicates less frequently
Direct mail	Little wasted circulation; highly selective; circulation controlled by advertiser; few distractions; personal; stimulates actions; use of novelty; relatively easy to measure performance; hidden from competitors	Very expensive; lacks editorial content to attract readers; often thrown away unread as junk mail; criticized as invasion of privacy; consumers must choose to read the ad
Radio	Reaches 95 percent of consumers; highly mobile and flexible; very low relative costs; ad can be changed quickly; high level of geographic and demographic selectivity; encourages use of imagination	Lacks visual imagery; short life of message; listeners' attention limited because of other activities; market fragmentation; difficult buying procedures; limited media and audience research
Television	Reaches large audiences; high frequency available; dual impact of audio and video; highly visible; high prestige; geographic and demographic selectivity; difficult to ignore	Very expensive; highly perishable message; size of audience not guaranteed; amount of prime time limited; lack of selectivity in target market
Internet	Immediate response; potential to reach a precisely targeted audience; ability to track customers and build databases; highly interactive medium	Costs of precise targeting are high; inappropriate ad placement; effects difficult to measure; concerns about security and privacy
Yellow Pages	Wide availability; action and product category oriented; low relative costs; ad frequency and longevity; non-intrusive	Market fragmentation; extremely localized; slow updating; lack of creativity; long lead times; requires large space to be noticed
Outdoor	Allows for frequent repetition; low cost; message can be placed close to point of sale; geographic selectivity; operable 24 hours a day; high creativity and effectiveness	Message must be short and simple; no demographic selectivity; seldom attracts readers' full attention; criticized as traffic hazard and blight on countryside; much wasted coverage; limited capabilities

Sources: William F. Arens, *Contemporary Advertising* (Burr Ridge, IL: Irwin/McGraw-Hill, 2004); George E. Belch and Michael Belch, *Advertising and Promotion* (Burr Ridge, IL: Irwin/McGraw-Hill, 2004).

time, alternating with periods in which no ads run. For example, an advertising campaign might have an ad run for two weeks, then suspend it for two weeks, and then run it again for two weeks. A *pulsing* schedule combines continuous and flighting schedules: during the entire campaign, a certain portion of advertising runs continuously, and during specific time periods of the campaign, additional advertising is used to intensify the level of communication with the target audience.

Creating the Message

The basic content and form of an advertising message are a function of several factors. A product's features, uses, and benefits affect the content of the message. Characteristics of the people in the target audience—gender, age, education, race, income, occupation, lifestyle, and other attributes—influence both content and form. When Procter & Gamble promotes Crest toothpaste to children, the company emphasizes daily brushing and cavity control. When marketing Crest to adults, Procter & Gamble stresses tartar and plaque control. To communicate effectively, advertisers use words, symbols, and illustrations that are meaningful, familiar, and appealing to people in the target audience.

An advertising campaign's objectives and platform also affect the content and form of its messages. If a firm's advertising objectives involve large sales increases, the message may include hard-hitting, high-impact language and symbols. When campaign objectives aim to increase brand awareness, the message may use much repetition of the brand name and words and illustrations associated with it. Thus, the advertising platform is the foundation on which campaign messages are built.

copy The verbal portion of advertisements

Copy is the verbal portion of an advertisement and may include headlines, subheadlines, body copy, and signature. Not all advertising contains all of these copy elements. Even handwritten notes on direct-mail advertising that say, "Try this. It works!" seem to increase requests for free samples.[33] The headline is critical because often it is the only part of the copy that people read. It should attract readers' attention and create enough interest to make them want to read the body copy. The subheadline, if there is one, links the headline to the body copy and sometimes serves to explain the headline.

Body copy for most advertisements consists of an introductory statement or paragraph, several explanatory paragraphs, and a closing paragraph. Some copywriters have adopted guidelines for developing body copy systematically: (1) identify a specific desire or problem, (2) recommend the product as the best way to satisfy that desire or solve that problem, (3) state product benefits and indicate why the product is best for the buyer's particular situation, (4) substantiate advertising claims, and (5) ask the buyer to take action. When substantiating claims, it is important to present the substantiation in a credible manner. The proof of claims should help strengthen both the image of the product and company integrity. Typeface selection can help advertisers create a desired impression using fonts that are engaging, reassuring, or very prominent.[34]

Personal Selling

Personal selling is a paid personal communication that seeks to inform customers and persuade them to purchase products in an exchange situation. The phrase *purchase products* is interpreted broadly to encompass acceptance of ideas and issues. Telemarketing, described in Chapter 16 as direct selling over the telephone, relies heavily on personal selling. However, negative consumer attitudes and legislation restricting telemarketing have lessened its effectiveness as a personal selling technique.

Personal selling has both advantages and limitations when compared with advertising. Advertising is general communication aimed at a relatively large target audience, whereas personal selling involves more specific communication directed at one or several individuals. Reaching one person through personal selling costs considerably more than through advertising, but personal selling efforts often have greater impact on customers. Personal selling also provides immediate feedback, allowing marketers to adjust their messages to improve communication. It helps them determine and respond to customers' information needs.

Public Relations

While many promotional activities focus on a firm's customers, other stakeholders—suppliers, employees, stockholders, the media, educators, potential investors, government officials, and society in general—are important to an organization as well. To communicate with customers and stakeholders, a company employs public relations. Public relations is a broad set of communication efforts used to create and maintain favourable relationships between an organization and its stakeholders. Maintaining a positive relationship with one or more stakeholders can affect a firm's current sales and profits, as well as its long-term survival.

Public relations uses a variety of tools, including annual reports, brochures, event sponsorship, and sponsor-

snapshot

Customer response rates to direct marketers

Media	Rate
Telephone	8.55%
Coupon	4.29%
Catalogue	3.67%
Banner/rich media ads	3.52%
Direct mail	2.77%
Email	2.48%
Radio	1.35%
Newspaper	0.5%
Magazine	0.17%

Direct marketers' average rate by media type across twenty-one industries.

ship of socially responsible programs aimed at protecting the environment or helping disadvantaged individuals. Nintendo, for example, is targeting older game players by hosting Super Bowl parties with men's magazines *Maxim* and *FHM,* as well as Spring Break parties and music tours, and it sponsored the Burton snowboarding championships.[35] Merrill Lynch sponsored a "Women of the World" art exhibit, which featured art by women artists from around the world, to help the financial services firm achieve its goal of targeting more affluent women.[36]

Other tools arise from the use of publicity, which is a component of public relations. Publicity is non-personal communication in news story form about an organization or its products, or both, transmitted through a mass medium at no charge. A few examples of publicity-based public relations tools are news releases, press conferences, and feature articles. When TiVo launched the personal video recorder, the company initially gave free devices to sports celebrities and select members of the entertainment industry to stimulate awareness and product trial. The company gained further publicity with news stories, product reviews, and strategic product placements in the mass media. TiVo may have chosen a public relations campaign over a more traditional advertising effort because its product enables consumers to bypass television commercials; use of personal video recorders is expected to reduce viewing of television advertisements by 19 percent by 2007.[37] Ordinarily public relations efforts are planned and implemented to be consistent with and support other elements of the promotion mix. Public relations efforts may be the responsibility of an individual or of a department within the organization, or the organization may hire an independent public relations agency.

Unpleasant situations and negative events such as product tampering or an environmental disaster may generate unfavourable public relations for an organization. For example, after Wal-Mart suffered negative publicity due to news stories and lawsuits related to its hiring practices, union management, and aggressive expansion policies, the company ran a full-page newspaper ad in more than 100 newspapers promoting its job creation, employee diversity, and employee-benefit packages.[38] To minimize the damaging effects of unfavourable coverage, effective marketers have policies and procedures in place to help manage any public relations problems.

Public relations should not be viewed as a set of tools to be used only during crises. To get the most from public relations, an organization should have someone responsible for public relations either internally or externally, and should have an ongoing public relations program.

Companies use a variety of public relations tools to convey messages and create images. Public relations professionals prepare written materials, such as brochures, newsletters, company magazines, news releases, and annual reports that reach and influence their various stakeholders.

Public relations personnel also create corporate identity materials, such as logos, business cards, stationery, and signs that make firms immediately recognizable. Speeches are another public relations tool. Because what a company executive says publicly at meetings or to the media can affect the organization's image, the speech must convey the desired message clearly.

Event sponsorship, in which a company pays for part or all of a special event, such as a benefit concert or a tennis tournament, is another public relations tool. Examples are Home Depot's sponsorship of NASCAR and the U.S. Olympic team. Sponsoring special events can be an effective means of increasing company or brand recognition with relatively minimal investment. Event sponsorship can gain companies considerable amounts of free media coverage. An organization tries to ensure that its product and the sponsored event target a

Sales Promotion as a Promotion Mix Element

Simdesk uses sales promotion (a free trial) and other elements in its promotion mix.

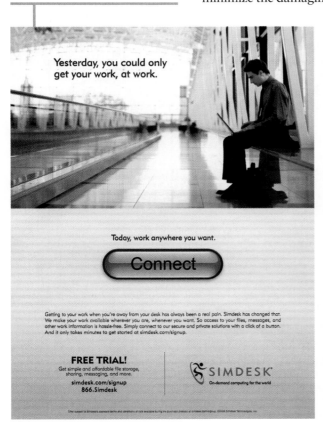

Yesterday, you could only get your work, at work.

Today, work anywhere you want.

Connect

Getting to your work when you're away from your desk has always been a real pain. Simdesk has changed that. We make your work available wherever you are, whenever you want. So access to your files, messages, and other work information is hassle-free. Simply connect to our secure and private solutions with a click of a button. And it only takes minutes to get started at simdesk.com/signup.

FREE TRIAL!
Get simple and affordable file storage, sharing, messaging, and more.
simdesk.com/signup
866.Simdesk

SIMDESK
On-demand computing for the world

consumer sales promotion methods Sales promotion techniques that encourage consumers to patronize specific stores or try particular products

Consumer sales promotion methods encourage or stimulate consumers to patronize specific retail stores or try particular products. Consumer sales promotion methods initiated by retailers often aim to attract customers to specific locations, whereas those used by manufacturers generally introduce new products or promote established brands. Consumer sales promotion methods include coupons, cents-off offers, money refunds and rebates, frequent shopping incentives (like point clubs or Airmiles), point-of-purchase displays, product demonstration booths, free samples, gift with purchase, consumer contests and games, and consumer sweepstakes.

trade sales promotion methods Methods intended to persuade wholesalers and retailers to carry a producer's products and market them aggressively

Trade sales promotion methods attempt to persuade wholesalers and retailers to carry a producer's products and market them more aggressively. These methods include temporary price reductions for buying special items (known as buying allowances), cooperative advertising, free merchandise, and sales contests. When deciding which sales promotion methods to use, marketers must consider several factors, particularly product characteristics (size, weight, costs, durability, uses, features, and hazards) and target market characteristics (age, gender, income, location, density, usage rate, and shopping patterns). How products are distributed and the number and types of resellers may determine the type of method used. The competitive and legal environment may also influence the choice.

The use of sales promotion has increased dramatically over the last 20 years, primarily at the expense of advertising. This shift in how promotional dollars are used has occurred for several reasons. Heightened concerns about value have made customers more responsive to promotional offers, especially price discounts and point-of-purchase displays. Thanks to their size and access to checkout scanner data, retailers have gained considerable power in the supply chain and are demanding greater promotional efforts from manufacturers to boost retail profits. Declines in brand loyalty have produced an environment in which sales promotions aimed at persuading customers to switch brands are more effective. Finally, the stronger emphasis placed on improving short-term performance results calls for greater use of sales promotion methods that yield quick (although perhaps short-lived) sales increases.

Selecting Promotion Mix Elements

Marketers vary the composition of promotion mixes for many reasons. Although a promotion mix can include all four elements, frequently a marketer selects fewer than four. Many firms that market multiple product lines use several promotion mixes simultaneously.

Promotional Resources, Objectives, and Policies

The size of an organization's promotional budget affects the number and relative intensity of promotional methods included in a promotion mix. If a company's promotional budget is extremely limited, the firm is likely to rely on personal selling because it is easier to measure a salesperson's contribution to sales than to measure the sales effectiveness of advertising. Businesses must have sizable promotional budgets to use regional or national advertising. Procter & Gamble, for example, spends nearly $4 million a year on advertising its personal care and cleaning products in the United States.[42] Organizations with extensive promotional resources generally include more elements in their promotion mixes, but having more promotional dollars to spend does not necessarily mean using more promotional methods.

An organization's promotional objectives and policies also influence the types of promotion selected. If a company's objective is to create mass awareness of a new convenience good, such as a breakfast cereal, its promotion mix probably leans heavily toward advertising, sales promotion, and possibly public relations. If a company hopes to educate consumers about the features of a durable good, such as a home appliance, its promotion mix may combine a moderate amount of advertising, possibly some sales promotion designed to attract customers to retail stores, and a great deal of personal selling because this method is an efficient way to inform customers about such products. If a firm's objective is to produce immediate sales of non-durable services, the promotion mix will probably stress advertising and sales promotion. For example, dry cleaners and carpet-cleaning firms are more likely to use advertising with a coupon or discount rather than personal selling.

Characteristics of the Target Market

Size, geographic distribution, and demographic characteristics of an organization's target market help dictate the methods to include in a product's promotion mix. To some degree, market size determines composition of the mix. If the size is limited, the promotion mix will probably emphasize personal selling, which can be very effective for reaching small numbers of people. Organizations selling to industrial markets and firms marketing products through only a few wholesalers frequently make personal selling the major component of their promotion mixes. When a product's market consists of millions of customers, organizations rely on advertising and sales promotion because these methods reach masses of people at a low cost per person.

Geographic distribution of a firm's customers also affects the choice of promotional methods. Personal selling is more feasible if a company's customers are concentrated in a small area than if they are dispersed across a vast region. When the company's customers are numerous and dispersed, advertising may be more practical.

Distribution of a target market's demographic characteristics, such as age, income, or education, may affect the types of promotional techniques a marketer selects, as well as the messages and images employed. The 2000 U.S. census found that so-called traditional families—those composed of married couples with children—account for fewer than one-quarter of all U.S. households, down from 30 percent in 1980 and 45 percent in 1960. To reach the three-quarters of households consisting of single parents, unmarried couples, singles, and "empty nesters" (whose children have left home), more companies are modifying the images used in their promotions. Charles Schwab, for example, featured celebrity single mother Sarah Ferguson, the Duchess of York, in commercials for its financial services.

Characteristics of the Product

Generally promotion mixes for business products concentrate on personal selling, whereas advertising plays a major role in promoting consumer goods. This generalization should be treated cautiously, however. Marketers of business products use some advertising to promote products. Advertisements for computers, road-building equipment, and aircraft are fairly common, and some sales promotion is also used occasionally to promote business products. Personal selling is used extensively for consumer durables, such as home appliances, automobiles, and houses, whereas consumer convenience items are promoted mainly through advertising and sales promotion. Public relations appears in promotion mixes for both business and consumer products.

Marketers of highly seasonal products often emphasize advertising and sales promotion, because off-season sales generally will not support an extensive year-round sales force. Although most toy producers have sales forces to sell to resellers, many of these companies depend chiefly on advertising to promote their products.

A product's price also influences the composition of the promotion mix. High-priced products call for personal selling because consumers associate greater risk with the purchase of such products and usually want information from a salesperson. Few people, for example, are willing to purchase a refrigerator from a self-service establishment. For low-priced convenience items, marketers use advertising rather than personal selling. Research suggests that consumers visiting a store specifically to purchase a product on sale are more likely to have read flyers and to have purchased other sale-priced products than consumers visiting the same store for other reasons.[43]

Another consideration in creating an effective promotion mix is the stage of the product life cycle. During the introduction stage, much advertising may be necessary for both business and consumer products to make potential users aware of them. For many products, personal selling and sales promotion are also helpful in this stage. In the growth and maturity stages, consumer services require heavy emphasis on adver-

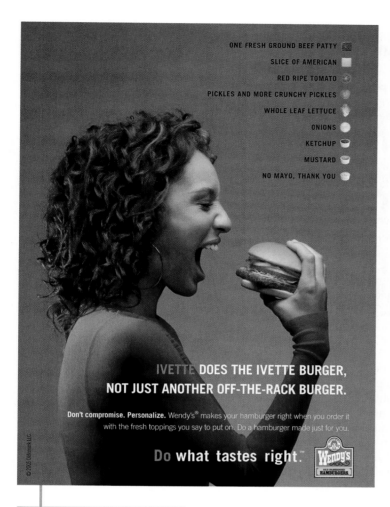

ONE FRESH GROUND BEEF PATTY

SLICE OF AMERICAN

RED RIPE TOMATO

PICKLES AND MORE CRUNCHY PICKLES

WHOLE LEAF LETTUCE

ONIONS

KETCHUP

MUSTARD

NO MAYO, THANK YOU

IVETTE DOES THE IVETTE BURGER,
NOT JUST ANOTHER OFF-THE-RACK BURGER.

Don't compromise. Personalize. Wendy's® makes your hamburger right when you order it
with the fresh toppings you say to put on. Do a hamburger made just for you.

Do what tastes right.™   Wendy's

Product Characteristics

Inexpensive, frequently purchased convenience products, like those advertised here, require significant levels of advertising.

tising, whereas business products often call for a concentration of personal selling and some sales promotion. In the decline stage, marketers usually decrease all promotional activities, especially advertising.

Intensity of market coverage is still another factor affecting composition of the promotion mix. When products are marketed through intensive distribution, firms depend strongly on advertising and sales promotion. Many convenience products, such as lotions, cereals, and coffee, are promoted through samples, coupons, and money refunds. When marketers choose selective distribution, promotion mixes vary considerably. Items handled through exclusive distribution, such as expensive watches, furs, and high-quality furniture, typically require a significant amount of personal selling.

A product's use also affects the combination of promotional methods. Manufacturers of highly personal products, such as laxatives, non-prescription contraceptives, and feminine hygiene products, depend on advertising because many customers do not want to talk with salespeople about these products.

Costs and Availability of Promotional Methods

Costs of promotional methods are major factors to analyze when developing a promotion mix. National advertising and sales promotion require large expenditures. However, if these efforts succeed in reaching extremely large audiences, the cost per individual reached may be quite small, possibly a few pennies. Some forms of advertising are relatively inexpensive. Many small, local businesses advertise products through local newspapers, magazines, radio and television stations, outdoor displays, and signs on mass transit vehicles.

Another consideration that marketers explore when formulating a promotion mix is availability of promotional techniques. Despite the tremendous number of media vehicles in the United States, a firm may find that no available advertising medium effectively reaches a certain target market. The problem of media availability becomes more pronounced when marketers advertise in foreign countries. Some media, such as television, simply may not be available, or advertising on television may be illegal. In China, the State Administration for Radio, Film, and Television banned a Nike commercial that featured basketball star LeBron James besting a kung fu master and a pair of dragons in a video game. In recent years, the agency has cracked down on U.S. and Japanese advertisements that fail to "uphold national dignity and interest, and respect the motherland's culture."[44] Available media may not be open to certain types of advertisements. In some countries, advertisers are forbidden to make brand comparisons on television. Other promotional methods also have limitations. For instance, a firm may wish to increase its sales force but be unable to find qualified personnel.

Push and Pull Channel Policies

push policy Promoting a product only to the next institution down the marketing channel

Another element marketers consider when planning a promotion mix is whether to use a push policy or a pull policy. With a **push policy,** the producer promotes the product only to the next institution down the marketing channel. In a marketing channel with wholesalers and retailers, the producer promotes to the wholesaler because in this case, the wholesaler is the channel member just below the producer (see Figure 17.5). Each channel member in turn promotes to the next channel member. A push policy

figure 17.5

COMPARISON OF PUSH AND PULL PROMOTIONAL STRATEGIES

Push policy

Producer → Wholesalers → Retailers → Consumers

Pull policy

Producer → Wholesalers → Retailers → Consumers

↓ Flow of products

↓ Flow of communications

normally stresses personal selling. Sometimes sales promotion and advertising are used in conjunction with personal selling to push the products down through the channel.

As Figure 17.5 shows, a firm using a **pull policy** promotes directly to consumers to develop strong consumer demand for its products. It does so primarily through advertising and sales promotion. Because consumers are persuaded to seek the products in retail stores, retailers in turn go to wholesalers or the producers to buy the products. This policy is intended to pull the goods down through the channel by creating demand at the consumer level. Consumers are told that if the stores don't have it, ask them to get it.

Push and pull policies are not mutually exclusive. At times an organization uses both simultaneously.

pull policy Promoting a product directly to consumers to develop strong consumer demand that pulls products through the marketing channel

Personal and Electronic Word-of-Mouth Communication

word-of-mouth communication Personal informal exchanges of communication that customers share with one another about products, brands, and companies

buzz marketing An attempt to gain acceptance of a product through word-of-mouth communications

When making decisions about the composition of promotion mixes, marketers should recognize that commercial messages, whether from advertising, personal selling, sales promotion, or public relations, are limited in the extent to which they can inform and persuade customers and move them closer to making purchases. Depending on the type of customers and the products involved, buyers to some extent rely on word-of-mouth communication from personal sources such as family members and friends. **Word-of-mouth communication** is personal informal exchanges of communication that customers share with one another about products, brands, and companies.[45] Most customers are likely to be influenced by friends and family members when making purchases. Word-of-mouth communication is very important when people are selecting restaurants and entertainment, and automotive, medical, legal, banking, and personal services such as hair care. Effective marketers who understand the importance of word-of-mouth communication attempt to identify opinion leaders and encourage them to try their products in the hope they will spread favourable word about them. Apple Computer, for example, relies on its devoted consumer following to spread by word of mouth their satisfaction with Apple products such as PowerBooks and iPods. Apple has built an "army of evangelists," ranging from teenagers to middle-aged adults, to make the product more visible and communicate the quality of the products to those around them.[46]

Buzz marketing is an attempt to create a trend or acceptance of a product through word-of-mouth communications. The idea is that an accepted member of a social group will always be more credible than any other form of paid communication.[47] For example, Vespa Scooters paid models to ride and park its trendy motorbikes around the "in" cafés and fashionable retail establishments in Los Angeles in the hope of generating favourable word-of-mouth communication about the reissued European bikes. And Toyota parked its new Scions outside of raves and hip cafes, coffee shops, and clothing stores, where shoppers could take informal test drives to get the "buzz" going about the new marque.[48] Buzz marketing works best as a part of an integrated marketing communication program that also uses advertising, personal selling, sales promotion, and publicity. Marketers should not underestimate the importance of both word-of-mouth communication and personal influence, nor should they have unrealistic expectations about the performance of commercial messages.

In addition, customers are increasingly going online for information and opinions about goods and services as well as about the companies. Electronic word of mouth is communicating about products through websites, blogs, e-mail, or online forums. Users can go to a number of consumer-oriented websites, such as epinions.com and ConsumerReview.com. At these sites, they can learn about other consumers' feelings toward and experiences with specific products. Users can also search within product categories and compare consumers' viewpoints on various brands and models. Buyers can peruse Internet-based newsgroups, forums, and blogs to find word-of-mouth information. A consumer looking for a new cell phone service, for example, might inquire in forums about other participants' experiences and level of satisfaction to gain more information before making a purchase decision. A study by Forrester and Intelliseek found that more than 90 percent of consumers trust such recommendations they get from other consumers.[49] Electronic word of mouth is particularly important to consumers staying abreast of trends. For example, Facebook.com serves as an online social

P&G Buzzes Minors, Alarming Consumer Activists

U sing a buzz marketing website called Tremor, Procter & Gamble (P&G) recruited 250 000 "connectors"—teens with lots of social connections—to talk up its products to other teenagers. P&G does not tell members of the "Tremor Crew" what to say and it does not pay them, but it does bestow coupons, samples, discounts, and free downloads. Members are not required to disclose their membership to anyone—not even their own parents.

Commercial Alert, a consumer-activist group, filed a complaint with the Federal Trade Commission, arguing that Tremor inappropriately targets minor children. The group also asked the federal agency to investigate whether such viral and buzz marketing efforts violate laws requiring the disclosure of commercial relationships. Commercial Alert argues that buzz marketing is deceptive and intrusive, takes advantage of the kindness of strangers, and involves turning people's friends and family against them for profit. P&G, however, contends that "we have been upfront with [our teens] to let them know that we are part of Procter & Gamble and a word-of-mouth marketing program."

Buzz marketing, now a $60 million business, has been controversial from the beginning. Consider the case of Sony Ericsson Mobile, which deployed fake tourists to ask bystanders in New York's Times Square to take their photos with a new camera phone and then chat with them about the phones. The "tourists" however, did not disclose their relationship to the company.

network. Originally designed for college and university students, and now open to all Internet users, Facebook allows users to share interests as well as favourite movies, books, and television shows. The Pulse on Facebook tracks trends relating to each school. Students, for instance, can see which band is the most popular on their campus and how it compares to all schools. Consumers can also read or text-message their own reviews of movies or restaurants via their cell phones.

Word of mouth, no matter how it's transmitted, is not effective in all product categories. It seems to be most effective for new-to-market and more expensive products. Despite the obvious benefits of positive word of mouth, marketers must also recognize the potential dangers of negative word of mouth. This is particularly important in dealing with online platforms that can reach more people and encourage consumers to "gang up" on a company or product. For example, music giant Sony BMG received negative press over a protest campaign that moved from online to the front of its office building. Sony had stopped production on the third album of its artist Fiona Apple after it decided the record was not radio-friendly. A copy of the album was mysteriously "leaked" on the Internet and soon became one of the most downloaded items online. Fans organized at websites and online forums to create petitions and mail apples to Sony's executives every day for several months. Sony agreed to release the album to stores after members of the online campaign picketed Sony's offices in New York and the story reached the mainstream media.[50]

viral marketing A strategy to get Internet users to share ads and promotions with their friends

Viral marketing is a strategy to get Internet users to share ads and promotions among friends. The concept is based on viral activities that are spread among users through e-mail and website links. Burger King, for example, created the "Subservient Chicken" website, where visitors seem to be able to control a person in a chicken suit by typing in commands. Viral communications resulted in nearly 14 million visitors to the website in less than a year.[51]

Criticisms and Defences of Promotion

Even though promotional activities can help customers make informed purchasing decisions, social scientists, consumer groups, government agencies, and members of society in general have long criticized promotion. There are two main reasons for such criticism: promotion does have flaws, and it is a highly visible business activity that pervades our daily lives. Although complaints about too much promotional activity are almost universal, a number of more specific criticisms have been lodged. In this section, we discuss some of the criticisms and defenses of promotion.

Is Promotion Deceptive?

One common criticism of promotion is that it is deceptive and unethical. During the nineteenth and early twentieth centuries, much promotion was blatantly deceptive. Although no longer widespread, some deceptive promotion still occurs. For example, T-Mobile paid $135 000 to the city of New York to settle a lawsuit accusing the company of misleading and confusing consumers with deceptive cell phone advertisements.[52] Questionable weight loss claims are made about various exercise devices and diet programs. Some promotions are unintentionally deceiving; for instance, when advertising to children, it is easy to mislead them because they are more naive than adults and less able to separate fantasy from reality. For this reason, the Federal Trade Commission monitors the ratings systems of the film, music, and electronic games industries as well as their advertising to children.[53] A promotion may also mislead some receivers because words can have diverse meanings for different people. However, not all promotion should be condemned because a small portion is flawed. Laws, government regulation, and industry self-regulation have helped decrease deceptive promotion.

Does Promotion Increase Prices?

Promotion is also criticized for raising prices, but in fact it often tends to lower them. The ultimate purpose of promotion is to stimulate demand. If it does, the business should be able to produce and market products in larger quantities and thus reduce per-unit production and marketing costs, which can result in lower prices. For example, as demand for flat-screen TVs and MP3 players has increased, their prices have dropped. When promotion fails to stimulate demand, the price of the promoted product increases because promotion costs must be added to other costs. Promotion also helps keep prices lower by facilitating price competition. When firms advertise prices, their prices tend to remain lower than when they are not promoting prices. Gasoline pricing illustrates how promotion fosters price competition. Service stations with the highest prices seldom have highly visible price signs.

Does Promotion Create Needs?

Some critics of promotion claim that it manipulates consumers by persuading them to buy products they do not need, hence creating "artificial" needs. In his theory of motivation, Abraham Maslow (discussed in Chapter 5) indicates that an individual tries to satisfy five levels of needs: physiological needs, such as hunger, thirst, and sex; safety needs; needs for love and affection; needs for self-esteem and respect from others; and self-actualization needs, that is, the need to realize one's potential. When needs are viewed in this context, it is difficult to demonstrate that promotion creates them. If there were no promotional activities, people would still have needs for food, water, sex, safety, love, affection, self-esteem, respect from others, and self-actualization.

Although promotion may not create needs, it does capitalize on them (which may be why some critics believe promotion creates needs). Many marketers base their appeals on these needs. For example, several mouthwash, toothpaste, and perfume advertisements associate these products with needs for love, affection, and respect. These advertisers rely on human needs in their messages, but they do not create the needs.

Does Promotion Encourage Materialism?

Another frequent criticism of promotion is that it leads to materialism. The purpose of promoting goods is to persuade people to buy them; thus, if promotion works, consumers will want to buy more and more things. Marketers assert that values are instilled in the home and that promotion does not change people into materialistic consumers. However, the behaviour of today's children and teenagers contradicts this view; many insist on high-priced, brand name apparel such as Gucci, Coach, Ralph Lauren, and Hummer.

Does Promotion Help Customers Without Costing Too Much?

Every year firms spend billions of dollars for promotion. The question is whether promotion helps customers enough to be worth the cost. Consumers do benefit because promotion informs them about product uses, features, advantages, prices, and locations where they can buy the products. Consumers thus gain more knowledge about available products and can make more intelligent buying decisions. Promotion also informs consumers about services—for instance, health care, educational programs, and day care—as well as about important social, political, and health-related issues. For example, several organizations, such as the California Department of Health Services, inform people about the health hazards associated with tobacco use.

Should Potentially Harmful Products Be Promoted?

Finally, some critics of promotion, including consumer groups and government officials, suggest that certain products should not be promoted at all. Primary targets are products associated with violence and other possibly unhealthy activities, such as handguns, alcohol, and tobacco. Cigarette advertisements, for example, promote smoking, a behaviour proven to be harmful and even deadly. Tobacco companies, which spend billions on promotion, have countered criticism of their advertising by pointing out that advertisements for red meat and coffee are not censured even though these products may also cause health problems. Those who defend such promotion assert that as long as it is legal to sell a product, promoting that product should be allowed.

SUMMARY

Integrated marketing communications is the coordination of promotion and other marketing efforts to ensure maximum informational and persuasive impact on customers.

Communication is a sharing of meaning. The communication process involves several steps. First, the source translates meaning into code, a process known as coding or encoding. The source should employ signs or symbols familiar to the receiver or audience. The coded message is sent through a communications channel to the receiver or audience. The receiver or audience then decodes the message and usually supplies feedback to the source. When the decoded message differs from the encoded one, a condition called noise exists.

Promotion is communication to build and maintain relationships by informing and persuading one or more audiences. Although promotional objectives vary from one organization to another and within organizations over time, eight primary objectives underlie many promotional programs. Promotion aims to create awareness of a new product, a new brand, or an existing product; to stimulate primary and selective demand; to encourage product trial through the use of free samples, coupons, limited free-use offers, contests, and games; to identify prospects; to retain loyal customers; to facilitate reseller support; to combat competitive promotional efforts; and to reduce sales fluctuations.

The promotion mix for a product may include four major promotional methods: advertising, personal selling, public relations, and sales promotion. Advertising is paid non-personal communication about an organization and its products transmitted to a target audience through a mass medium. Personal selling is paid personal communication that attempts to inform customers and persuade them to purchase products in an exchange situation. Public relations is a broad set of communication efforts used to create and maintain favourable relationships between an organization and its stakeholders. Sales promotion is an activity or material that acts as a direct inducement, offering added value or incentive for the product, to resellers, salespeople, or consumers.

The promotional methods used in a product's promotion mix are determined by the organization's promotional resources, objectives, and policies; characteristics of the target market; characteristics of the product; and cost and availability of promotional methods. Marketers also con-

sider whether to use a push policy or a pull policy. With a push policy, the producer promotes the product only to the next institution down the marketing channel. Normally, a push policy stresses personal selling. Firms that use a pull policy promote directly to consumers, with the intention of developing strong consumer demand for the products. Once consumers are persuaded to seek the products in retail stores, retailers go to wholesalers or the producer to buy the products.

Most customers are likely to be influenced by friends and family members when making purchases. Word-of-mouth communication is personal, informal exchanges of communication that customers share with one another about products, brands, and companies. Customers may also choose to go online to find electronic word of mouth about products or companies. Buzz marketing is an attempt to gain acceptance of a product through word-of-mouth communications. Viral marketing is a strategy to get Internet users to share ads and promotions with their friends.

Promotional activities can help consumers make informed purchasing decisions, but they have also evoked many criticisms. Promotion has been accused of deception. Although some deceiving or misleading promotions do exist, laws, government regulation, and industry self-regulation minimize deceptive promotion. Promotion has been blamed for increasing prices, but it usually tends to lower them. When demand is high, production and marketing costs decrease, which can result in lower prices. Moreover, promotion helps keep prices lower by facilitating price competition. Other criticisms of promotional activity are that it manipulates consumers into buying products they do not need, that it leads to a more materialistic society, and that consumers do not benefit sufficiently from promotional activity to justify its high cost. Finally, some critics of promotion suggest that potentially harmful products, especially those associated with violence, sex, and unhealthy activities, should not be promoted at all.

Please visit the student website at **www.hmco.ca/marketing** for ACE Self-Test questions that will help you prepare for exams.

IMPORTANT TERMS

Institutional advertising	Comparative advertising	Percent-of-sales approach	Cost comparison indicator
Advocacy advertising	Reminder advertising	Competition-matching, or	Copy
Product advertising	Reinforcement advertising	parity, approach	Publicity
Pioneer advertising	Objective-and-task	Arbitrary approach	Consumers sales
Competitive advertising	approach	Media plan	promotion methods

Trade sales promotion methods	Receiver	Channel capacity	Push policy
Intergrated marketing communications	Coding process	Promotion	Pull policy
	Communications channel	Primary demand	Word-of-mouth communication
Communication	Decoding process	Pioneer promotion	
Source	Noise	Selective demand	Buzz marketing
	Feedback	Promotion mix	Viral marketing

DISCUSSION & REVIEW QUESTIONS

1. What does the term *integrated marketing communications* mean?

2. Define *communication* and describe the communication process. Is it possible to communicate without using all the elements in the communication process? If so, which elements can be omitted?

3. Identify several causes of noise. How can a source reduce noise?

4. What is the major task of promotion? Do firms ever use promotion to accomplish this task and fail? If so, give several examples.

5. Describe the possible objectives of promotion and discuss the circumstances under which each objective might be used.

6. What factors affect the size of an advertising budget? What techniques are used to determine an advertising budget?

7. What is the difference between competitive advertising and comparative advertising?

8. How do target market characteristics determine which promotional methods to include in a promotion mix? Assume a company is planning to promote a cereal to both adults and children. Along what major dimensions would these two promotional efforts have to differ from each other?

9. How can a product's characteristics affect the composition of its promotion mix?

10. What types of sales promotion methods have you observed recently? Comment on their effectiveness.

11. Explain the difference between a pull policy and a push policy. Under what conditions should each policy be used?

12. What is sales promotion? Why is it used?

13. Which criticisms of promotion do you believe are the most valid? Why?

14. Should organizations be allowed to promote offensive, violent, sexual, or unhealthy products that can be legally sold and purchased? Support your answer.

APPLICATION QUESTIONS

1. Developing a promotion mix is contingent on many factors, including the type of product and the product's attributes. Which of the four promotional methods—advertising, personal selling, public relations, or sales promotion—would you emphasize if you were developing the promotion mix for the following products? Explain your answers.
   a. Washing machine
   b. Cereal
   c. Halloween candy
   d. CD

2. Marketers must consider whether to use a push or a pull policy when deciding on a promotion mix (see Figure 17.4). Identify a product for which marketers should use each policy and a third product that might best be promoted using a mix of the two policies. Explain your answers.

globalEDGE™

1. Go to **http://www.globaledge.msu.edu** and click on Resource Desk, then Rankings. Scroll down to Industry Specific links and choose AdAge Advertising and Marketing Data Centre. Scroll down the page to choose reports that compare advertising spending in the U.S. and globally. What are the top U.S. advertisers? The top global advertisers? Are any Canadian firms featured in the listings?

2. Go to **http://www.globaledge.msu.edu** and click on Resource Desk, then Rankings. Scroll down to Company Specific links and click on Interbrand: Global Brands Scoreboard. What brands are the highest ranked. What is it about their image that prompted Business Week to rank them so highly? Are these brands owned by the top advertisers (referred to in Question 1)?

MySpace Is the Music Place

MySpace isn't just for friends. It's also a unique promotional platform for musical artists, especially unsigned and independent artists. By creating a MySpace page, musicians can share their songs, post important dates, or even blog. MySpace music pages are different from record company websites because they feel more personal. Artists also take advantage of MySpace's viral nature by allowing other MySpace members to post their pictures, songs, and music videos on their own MySpace profile pages. Visit the website at **http://music.myspace.com** and look for your favourite artist or explore a new one.

1. Who is the target market for members?
2. What is being promoted to these individuals?
3. What are the promotional objectives of this website?
4. Is word-of-mouth communication occurring at this website? Explain.

Case 17.1

Recruiting Volunteer Business Executives for Corporate Fundraising: Using Sales Promotions and Direct Marketing Communications

How does an unknown performing arts centre, perceived to be an amateur, community theatre, attract corporate support in a cost-effective manner? Just ask Bill Murray.

Bill Murray was the Audience and Business Development Officer for a newly opened nonprofit performing arts centre located in a major suburb of Vancouver, British Columbia. Bill's primary objectives were to increase the Centre's corporate profile in the surrounding business community, and to recruit business executives who would volunteer their time for corporate fundraising.

The performing arts centre had been open two years and most of the events presented in the theatre were local amateur productions of theatre, dance, and music. Other events booked into the Centre were nonperformance related, such as seminars, workshops, and conferences.

Unfortunately, there were not enough local performing and non-performing events to generate the rental and ticket sale revenues required by the Centre to break even. As well, the Centre had an image of being a "community theatre" as opposed to a "professional-regional" performing arts centre.

To address the issues of revenue shortfalls and poor quality image, the Board of Directors decided to put on its own professional theatre and children's music series. The theatre series consisted of five professional theatrical productions per year. Each production ran for 14 days, whereby the Centre produced three of the productions in house and purchased two touring productions. The children's series consisted of five children's entertain-

ers who performed two shows per day running over a three-day period. Both the theatre and the children's music series were sold on annual season subscriptions or by single tickets.

Bill's Solution

An integrated direct marketing communications strategy was developed and employed over a 12-month period. The four-step strategy was as follows:

1) *Introduce the Centre and its key personnel to the local business community.* The Centre joined the suburb's 525-member Chamber of Commerce. Along with Bill, the Centre's General Manager and the Board's President made a presentation to the Chamber members at one of its business luncheons.

2) *Invite the business community to the Centre's professional theatre productions.* All 525 business executives who were members of the Chamber were invited to opening night performances of the Centre's first two theatrical productions. The invitations were designed so that invitees attending had to fill out information about themselves and their company, and then provide it to the box office officials upon their arrival. Box office staff then issued a pair of tickets for the best house seats, two free refreshment tickets, and a special reception name tag allowing them to attend a backstage cast reception. To assess the level of excitement and appreciation towards the Centre, Bill mingled with attendees prior to the performance, during intermissions, and at the post-show reception.

3) *Recruit business executive attendees to become involved in the volunteer corporate fundraising campaign.* Bill recruited a Campaign Chair from the invited attendees. Then on behalf of the Campaign Chair, Bill sent a letter to all attendees asking them to attend a corporate fundraising campaign meeting. At the campaign meeting, those who attended were officially recruited to be on the Centre's corporate fundraising team. Team members received a volunteer appreciation gift, a bronze key chain in the shape of the Centre' ticket stub.

4) *Implement the corporate fundraising campaign.* Fundraising team members were each asked to identify 10 companies as potential corporate supporters. The Centre, on the volunteer's behalf, mailed these 10 identified company executives information on the corporate campaign and the Centre's operations. The volunteers followed up with a personal phone call and/or visit to encourage their 10 identified companies to financially support the Centre.

The following results were associated with Bill's corporate fundraising campaign:

■ Of the 525 invitations sent out, 64 business executives accepted and attended the theatrical production (a response rate of 12%).

■ Of the 64 business executives, 20 were recruited to be volunteers for the corporate fundraising campaign (a response rate of 31%).

■ Of the 200 companies identified and approached by the 20 member fundraising team, 110 compa-

nies (a response rate of 55%) gave an average financial donation of $105, for a total of $11 500.

■ Of the 20 volunteers, 15 purchased corporate theatre subscriptions for the next theatre season, which amounted to $3600 in revenue (a response rate of 75%).

■ The campaign also identified six companies interested in sponsoring Centre events the following season. Five of these companies became sponsors and contributed a total of $30 000.

Bill was very pleased with the results of his fundraising strategy. He estimated the direct costs associated with this strategy (mailings, stationery, etc.) to be $1500. More important perhaps than the revenues associated with the strategy to date, Bill believed a number of marketing relationships had been formed that would serve to ensure the continued success of the Centre for many years to come.[54]

Questions for Discussion

1. What type(s) of sales promotion were used?
2. Critically assess the strengths and weaknesses of Bill's solution. Identify sales promotions not incorporated in Bill's solution that you believe could enhance the effectiveness of the campaign.
3. What feature of Bill's solution qualifies it as a form of direct marketing communications?
4. Review the response rates reported above for the first four results items. Why did the response rates increase?

Case 17.2   One Tough Mother at Columbia Sportswear

Eighty-one-year-old Gert Boyle is "one tough mother." Not only is she the chairman of the board for Columbia Sportswear, she's also their spokeswoman. Gert assumed control of Columbia Sportswear 35 years ago after her husband Neil passed away from a sudden heart attack. Gert reported for duty a mere four days after Neil's death to take the reins of the growing company—a company that has flourished under her tough leadership.

Founded by Neil Boyle in 1938, Columbia Sportswear Company is a global leader in the design, sourcing, marketing, and distribution of active outdoor apparel and footwear. The $1.1 billion company employs more than 1800 people and distributes and sells products in

more than 70 countries to more than 12 000 retailers internationally. As one of the largest outerwear brands in the world and the leading seller of skiwear in the United States, the company has developed an international reputation for quality, performance, functionality, and value.

Columbia Sportswear has worked hard over the years to develop its image of offering high-quality products. It promotes itself and its products through event sponsorships, print and television advertising, and a strong public relations program. It is actively involved in event marketing. For example, the company signed up to be the official apparel sponsor of Jeep's "King of the Mountain" series, proclaimed as the richest and most prestigious professional snow racing series in the world.

Columbia Sportswear will outfit the event staff and volunteers, as well as VIPs attending the event. Other sponsorships include events such as the Mt. Baker Banked Slalom snowboarding competition, which draws world-class snow boarders; the annual World Superpipe Championships; and the Ski Mountaineering Competition in Korea.

The company has used many approaches to promote the quality of its products. Their greatest success however, is a campaign featuring Gert and her son, Tim Boyle. This positioning is an outgrowth of the relationship that has existed between Gert and Tim since they began running the company together. According to people who know them, Tim and his mother have argued from the beginning about how to run Columbia Sportswear. A director of the company says, "Tim and Gert are a lot like the Jack Lemmon and Walter Matthau characters in *The Odd Couple*. They complain all the time, and yet they cherish each other."

Over 20 years ago, Borders, Perrin & Norrander, the company's advertising agency, came up with an idea to use the well-known relationship between Gert and her son to develop an identity for the company—an identity beyond technical claims about product quality. They developed an ad campaign that portrays Gert as "one tough mother" who uses her son to demonstrate that Columbia Sportswear clothes will protect whoever wears them under any weather conditions. In the many spots, Gert appears as a hard-driving mother who refuses to accept anything but the highest quality of products, both for her son and her company. The ads were so successful at positioning and promoting Columbia Sportswear's products, that Gert and Tim are now the company's ad staples.

Showing Gert put her son through a series of catastrophic tests to demonstrate the durability of the company's products doesn't just communicate product quality; it also establishes an identity in the customers'

minds. In one commercial, Gert drives an SUV with Tim strapped on top through a series of severe weather situations to show that his clothing is protecting him. The ending scene is a close-up of the jacket he is wearing with the tagline "Tested Tough." This theme is continued throughout a series of commercials that depict Tim in a number of cold weather survival situations, such as being dropped on the top of a snow covered mountain by a helicopter piloted by Gert, being under the ice in a hockey arena (staying alive with a breathing tube), and being covered by snow with Gert driving the snow plow. In all cases, Tim is unharmed and Gert is unconcerned—all because he is wearing Columbia outerwear.

Columbia Sportswear's signature spot shows Gert in a biker bar. The audio track says: "In a world of rugged individuals only one is the toughest mother of them all. Mother Gert Boyle—maker of tough mother jeans." There is a close-up of Gert with a tattoo on her bicep that reads: "Born to Nag" and the spot ends with a product shot of Columbia jeans. These irreverent and memorable ads appear to be working. Since their inception, Columbia Sportswear has carved out a 50 percent market share in its category. Now that's one tough mother![55]

Questions for Discussion

1. Identify the key objectives of Columbia Sportswear's promotion program. Are the objectives the same or different for its advertising and for its event sponsorships?

2. Does Columbia Sportswear use integrated marketing communications? What suggestions, if any, would you make to strengthen the coordination of Columbia's promotion activities?

3. Describe the characteristics of Columbia's target market. Are they the same for advertising and event sponsorships? Explain.

CHAPTER 18

Personal Selling and Sales Management

Goodbye to the Back-slapping Salesperson

Gone are the days of salespeople being the fast-talking, back-slapping, con-game players as depicted in the movie *Tin Men*. Today's successful organizations consider sales professionals the vital link between the organization and customer. Often it is the sales professional who is given the responsibility to cultivate customer relationships and implement marketing strategy. The importance of this responsibility cannot be underestimated in today's competitive marketplace. Thus organizations are expecting their salespeople to develop and manage customer relationships in a professional manner. Likewise, salespeople understand the need to continuously improve themselves to maintain a competitive edge in their abilities to deal with customers and other stakeholders.

Aware of these expectations and needs, the Canadian Professional Sales Association's (CPSA) Sales Institute is dedicated to maintaining progressive competency standards for sales professionals and to providing timely, relevant and quality services to support and enhance the role of the sales professional. It's the CPSA's mission "to enhance the value and credibility of the sales profession through the setting of professional standards and certification." To those who qualify, the CPSA Sales Institute offers the Certified Sales Professional (CSP) designation.

The CSP designation identifies the holder as a highly qualified sales professional in tune with today's global environment. In a recent survey of CSP designates, 86 percent said their professional designation gave them a competitive advantage in the marketplace. The path to accomplishing qualification for the CSP designation is thorough and challenging. Candidates need to demonstrate competence in consultative selling, must have a minimum of two years verified sales experience, and must complete a written and oral examination. Also, CSPs must agree to abide by the CPSA Code of Ethics, and must agree to adhere to the CPSA's Maintenance of Certification requirement.

Fast-talking, back-slapping, and con-game playing salespeople have no place in today's competitive environment. The professional approach endorsed by the CPSA via its Code of Ethics and CSP designation is a proven approach to sales success.[1] ■

Personal selling plays an important role in marketing strategies. As discussed in the opening of this chapter, personal selling has become more professional and sophisticated. Today's salespeople are expected to act ethically, and often they act as consultants and advisers, in addition to selling.

In this chapter, we focus on personal selling and sales management. We first consider the purposes of personal selling and then examine its basic steps. Next, we look at types of salespeople and how they are selected. After taking a look at several new types of personal selling, we discuss major sales force management decisions, including setting objectives for the sales force and determining its size; recruiting, selecting, training, compensating, and motivating salespeople; managing sales territories; and controlling and evaluating sales force performance.

The Nature of Personal Selling

personal selling Paid personal communication that attempts to inform customers and persuade them to buy products in an exchange situation

Personal selling is paid personal communication that attempts to inform customers and persuade them to purchase products in an exchange situation. For example, a Xerox Canada salesperson describing the benefits of the company's copiers to a small-business customer is engaging in personal selling. Personal selling gives marketers the greatest freedom to adjust a message to satisfy customers' information needs. It is the most precise of all promotion methods, enabling marketers to focus on the most promising sales prospects. Other promotion mix elements are aimed at groups of people, some of whom may not be prospective customers. However, personal selling is generally the most expensive element in the promotion mix. The average cost of a sales call is more than $400.[2]

More than a million members of the Canadian workforce are employed in sales positions, including an increasing number of women who are earning their living through selling services, such as advertising, real estate, and insurance. Sales careers can offer high income, a great deal of freedom, a high level of training, and a high degree of job satisfaction. Although the public may harbour negative perceptions of personal selling, unfavourable stereotypes of salespeople are changing thanks to the efforts of major corporations, professional sales associations, and academic institutions. Research indicates that personal selling will continue to gain respect as professional sales associations, such as the Canadian Professional Sales Association develop and enforce ethical codes of conduct.[3]

Personal selling goals vary from one firm to another. However, they usually involve finding prospects, persuading prospects to buy, and keeping customers satisfied. Identifying potential buyers interested in the organization's products is critical. Because most potential buyers seek information before making purchases, salespeople can ascertain prospects' informational needs and then provide relevant information. To do so, sales personnel must be well trained regarding both their products and the selling process in general.

Salespeople must be aware of their competitors. They must monitor the development of new products and keep abreast of competitors' sales efforts in their sales territories, how often and when the competition calls on their accounts, and what the competition is saying about their product in relation to its own. Salespeople must emphasize the benefits their products provide, especially when competitors' products do not offer those specific benefits.

Few businesses survive solely on profits from one-time customers. For long-run survival, most marketers depend on repeat sales and thus need to keep their customers satisfied. In addition, satisfied customers provide favourable word-of-mouth communications, thus attracting new customers. Although the whole organization is responsible for achieving customer satisfaction, much of the burden falls on salespeople because they are almost always closer to customers than anyone else in the company and often provide buyers with information and service after the sale. Indeed, research shows that a firm's marketing orientation has a positive influence on salespeople's attitudes, commitment, and influence on customer purchasing intentions.[4] Such contact gives salespeople an opportunity to generate additional sales and offers them a good vantage point for evaluating the strengths and weaknesses of the company's products and other marketing mix components. Their observations help develop and maintain a marketing mix that better satisfies both the firm and its customers.

Elements of the Personal Selling Process

prospecting Developing a list of potential customers

The specific activities involved in the selling process vary among salespeople and selling situations. No two salespeople use exactly the same selling methods. Nonetheless, many salespeople move through a general selling process as they sell products. This process consists of seven steps, outlined in Figure 18.1: prospecting, preapproach, approach, making the presentation, overcoming objections, closing the sale, and following up.

marketing ENTREPRENEURS

Michael Schell

THE BUSINESS: Thought Leader Publications and Training, Inc., Vancouver, B.C.

FOUNDED: 2006

SUCCESS: A growing list of successful publications, training products, and customer research contracts.

After 20 years in corporate sales, Michael Schell decided to start his first company, Marketshare Communications in 2001. With the tables turned and sales reps now pitching their products to him, Schell discovered just how rarely reps asked him insightful questions. Despite the fact that most of these reps were from leading organizations, Schell also noticed reps typically disregarded basics like setting agendas for meetings and doing research before a sales call. Echoing the feelings of many organizational buyers, Schell notes that "life is too short, and business too important, to allow others [sales reps] to waste my time."

For Schell, the shift in perspective from sales professional to business owner was like being "hit-in-the-head" with a hammer. His biggest revelation was the realization that the single biggest contributor to success in sales is a switch in focus from working *in* your job to working *on* your job. In this revelation, Schell saw the need for a book written from the perspective of buyers who had years of experience meeting and interacting with sales reps.

Recognizing the relevance of his idea, Schell developed a research design to gather insights from buyers, collected this information, then authored his book, entitled "Buyer Approved Selling: Sales Secrets from the Buyer's Side of the Desk." Thus the formation of another company, Thought Leader Publications and Training, Inc., began operations in 2006 (see www.thoughtleaderinc.com). There has been no looking back. Not only has the book sold more copies than Schell anticipated, praise has come from both corporate and academic reviewers.

Schell's success as an author has translated into success as a sales trainer. His first sales training workshop, which is based on his first book, is proving successful. Canon USA recently licensed the Buyer-Approved Selling Excellence workshop to train its national dealer sales force.

What's next? Schell is in the process of replicating the success of his first book and training workshops with a growing list of new books, research services, and training products. All have a common theme—providing clients with practical, proven business advice from the decision-maker's side of the desk.

Prospecting

Developing a list of potential customers is called **prospecting.** Salespeople seek names of prospects from company sales records, trade shows, commercial databases, newspaper announcements (of marriages, births, deaths, and so on), public records, telephone directories, trade association directories, and many other sources. Sales personnel also use responses to advertisements that encourage interested persons to send in information request forms. Seminars and meetings targeted at particular types of clients, such as attorneys or accountants, may also produce leads.

A number of salespeople prefer to use referrals—recommendations from current customers—to find prospects. Obtaining referrals requires that the salesperson have a good relationship with the current customer and therefore must have performed well before asking the customer for help. As might be expected, a customer's trust in and satisfaction with a salesperson influences his or her willingness to provide referrals.[5] Research shows that one referral is as valuable as 12 cold calls. Also, 80 percent of clients are willing to give referrals, but only 20 percent are ever asked. According to sales experts, the advantages of using referrals are that the resulting sales leads are highly qualified, sales rates are higher, initial transactions are larger, and the sales cycle is shorter.[6] Some companies even reward customers for referring their salespeople to new prospects by offering discounts off future purchases.[7]

Consistent activity is critical to successful prospecting. Salespeople must actively search the customer base for qualified prospects who fit the target market profile.

figure 18.1   GENERAL STEPS IN THE PERSONAL SELLING PROCESS

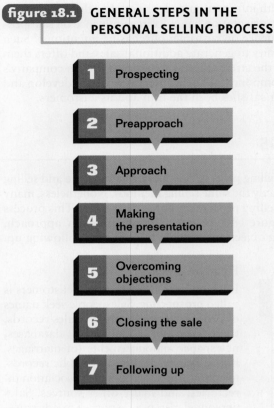

1   Prospecting

2   Preapproach

3   Approach

4   Making the presentation

5   Overcoming objections

6   Closing the sale

7   Following up

approach The manner in which a salesperson contacts a potential customer

After developing the prospect list, a salesperson evaluates whether each prospect is able, willing, and authorized to buy the product. Based on this evaluation, prospects are ranked according to desirability or potential.

Preapproach

Before contacting acceptable prospects, a salesperson finds and analyzes information about each prospect's specific product needs, current use of brands, feelings about available brands, and personal characteristics. In short, salespeople need to know what potential buyers and decision makers consider most important and why they need a specific product.[8] The most successful salespeople are thorough in their preapproach, which involves identifying key decision makers, reviewing account histories and problems, contacting other clients for information, assessing credit histories and problems, preparing sales presentations, identifying product needs, and obtaining relevant literature. Many companies employ information technology and customer relationship management systems to scour their databases and thus identify the most profitable products and customers. These systems can also help sales departments manage leads, track customers, develop sales forecasts, and measure performance.[9] A salesperson with a lot of information about a prospect is better equipped to develop a presentation that precisely communicates with that prospect.

Approach

The **approach,** the manner in which a salesperson contacts a potential customer, is a critical step in the sales process. In more than 80 percent of initial sales calls, the purpose is to gather information about the buyer's needs and objectives. Creating a favourable impression and building rapport with prospective clients are important tasks in the approach because the prospect's first impressions of the salesperson are usually lasting ones. During the initial visit, the salesperson strives to develop a relationship rather than just push a product. Indeed, coming across as a "salesperson" may not be the best approach because some people are put off by strong selling tactics. Experts recommend using a neutral tone and normal conversational speech to improve the odds of making a sale.[10] The salesperson may have to call on a prospect several times before the product is considered. The approach must be designed to deliver value to targeted customers. If the sales approach is inappropriate, the salesperson's efforts are likely to have poor results.

One type of approach is based on referrals: the salesperson approaches the prospect and explains that an acquaintance, an associate, or a relative suggested the call. The salesperson who uses the "cold canvass" approach calls on potential customers without prior consent. Repeat contact is another common approach: when making the contact, the salesperson mentions a previous meeting. The exact type of approach depends on the salesperson's preferences, the product being sold, the firm's resources, and the prospect's characteristics.

Making the Presentation

During the sales presentation, the salesperson must attract and hold the prospect's attention, stimulate interest, and spark a desire for the product. The salesperson should have the prospect touch, hold, or use the product. If possible, the salesperson should demonstrate the product or invite the prospect to use it. Automobile salespeople, for example, typically invite potential buyers to test drive the vehicle that interests them. Audiovisual equipment and software may also enhance the presentation.

During the presentation, the salesperson must not only talk but also listen. The sales presentation gives the salesperson the greatest opportunity to determine the prospect's specific needs by listening to questions and comments and observing responses.

Enhancing Sales Presentations
A variety of technology-based products, such as Webex and InFocus projectors, are used to enhance sales presentations.

Even though the salesperson plans the presentation in advance, she or he must be able to adjust the message to meet the prospect's informational needs. Research demonstrates that adapting the message in response to the customer's needs generally enhances performance, particularly in new-task or modified rebuy purchase situations.[11]

Overcoming Objections

An effective salesperson usually seeks out a prospect's objections in order to address them. If they are not apparent, the salesperson cannot deal with them, and the prospect may not buy. One of the best ways to overcome objections is to anticipate and counter them before the prospect raises them. However, this approach can be risky because the salesperson may mention objections that the prospect would not have raised. If possible, the salesperson should handle objections as they arise. They can also be addressed at the end of the presentation.

Closing the Sale

closing The stage in the personal selling process when the salesperson asks the prospect to buy the product

Closing is the stage in the personal selling process when the salesperson asks the prospect to buy the product. During the presentation, the salesperson may use a *trial close* by asking questions that assume the prospect will buy. The salesperson might ask the potential customer about financial terms, desired colours or sizes, or delivery arrangements. Reactions to such questions usually indicate how close the prospect is to buying. Properly asked questions may allow prospects to uncover their own problems and identify solutions themselves. One questioning approach uses broad questions (*what, how, why*) to probe or gather information and focused questions (*who, when, where*) to clarify and close the sale. A trial close allows prospects to indicate indirectly that they will buy the product without having to say those sometimes difficult words, "I'll take it."

A salesperson should try to close at several points during the presentation because the prospect may be ready to buy. An attempt to close the sale may result in objections. Thus,

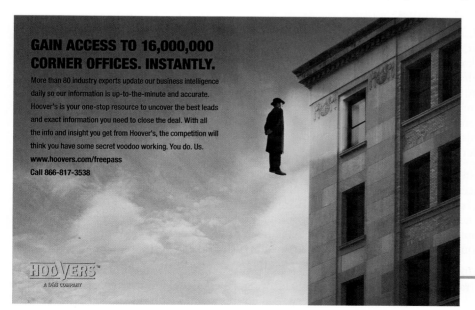

Closing the Sale
Hoover's Online provides detailed information that can help close sales.

closing can uncover hidden objections, which the salesperson can then address. One closing strategy involves asking the potential customer to place a low-risk tryout order.

Following Up

After a successful closing, the salesperson must follow up the sale. In the follow-up stage, the salesperson determines whether the order was delivered on time and installed properly, if installation was required. He or she should contact the customer to learn if any problems or questions regarding the product have arisen. The follow-up stage is also used to determine customers' future product needs.

Types of Salespeople

To develop a sales force, a marketing manager decides what kind of salesperson will sell the firm's products most effectively. Most business organizations use several different kinds of sales personnel. Based on the functions performed, salespeople can be classified into three groups: order getters, order takers, and support personnel. One salesperson can, and often does, perform all three functions.

Order Getters

order getter A salesperson who sells to new customers and increases sales to current customers

To obtain orders, a salesperson informs prospects and persuades them to buy the product. The **order getter's** job is to increase sales by selling to new customers and increasing sales to present customers. This task is sometimes called *creative selling*. It requires that salespeople recognize potential buyers' needs and give them necessary information. Order getting is frequently divided into two categories: current-customer sales and new-business sales.

Current-Customer Sales. Sales personnel who concentrate on current customers call on people and organizations that have purchased products from the firm before. These salespeople seek more sales from existing customers by following up previous sales. Current customers can also be sources of leads for new prospects.

New-Business Sales. Business organizations depend to some degree on sales to new customers. New-business sales personnel locate prospects and convert them into buyers. In many organizations, salespeople help generate new business, but organizations that sell real estate, insurance, appliances, heavy industrial machinery, and automobiles depend in large part on new-customer sales.

Order Takers

order takers A salesperson who primarily seeks repeat sales

Taking orders is a repetitive task salespeople perform to perpetuate long-lasting, satisfying customer relationships. **Order takers** primarily seek repeat sales, generating the bulk of many firms' total sales. One of their major objectives is to be certain customers have sufficient product quantities where and when needed. Most order takers handle orders for standardized products that are purchased routinely and do not require extensive sales efforts. The role of order takers is changing, however, as the position moves more toward one that identifies and solves problems to better meet the needs of customers. There are two groups of order takers: inside order takers and field order takers.

Inside Order Takers. In many businesses, inside order takers, who work in sales offices, receive orders by mail, telephone, and the Internet. Certain producers, wholesalers, and retailers have sales personnel who sell from within the firm rather than in the field. Some inside order takers communicate with customers face to face; retail salespeople, for example, are classified as inside order takers. As more orders are placed through the Internet, the role of the inside order taker continues to change.

Field Order Takers. Salespeople who travel to customers are outside, or field, order takers. Often customers and field order takers develop interdependent relationships. The buyer relies on the salesperson to take orders periodically (and sometimes to deliver them), and the salesperson counts on the buyer to purchase a certain quantity of products periodically. Use of small computers has improved the field order taker's inventory and order-tracking capabilities.

Support Personnel

support personnel Sales staff members who facilitate selling but usually are not involved solely with making sales

Support personnel facilitate selling but usually are not involved solely with making sales. They engage primarily in marketing industrial products, locating prospects, educating customers, building goodwill, and providing service after the sale. There are many kinds of sales support personnel; the three most common are missionary, trade, and technical salespeople.

missionary salespeople Support salespeople, usually employed by a manufacturer, who assist the producer's customers in selling to their own customers

Missionary Salespeople. **Missionary salespeople,** usually employed by manufacturers, assist the producer's customers in selling to their own customers. Missionary salespeople may call on retailers to inform and persuade them to buy the manufacturer's products. When they succeed, retailers purchase products from wholesalers, which are the producer's customers. Manufacturers of medical supplies and pharmaceuticals often use missionary salespeople, called *detail reps,* to promote their products to physicians, hospitals, and retail druggists.

trade salespeople Salespeople involved mainly in helping a producer's customers promote a product

Trade Salespeople. **Trade salespeople** are not strictly support personnel because they usually take orders as well. However, they direct much effort toward helping customers, especially retail stores, promote the product. They are likely to restock shelves, obtain more shelf space, set up displays, provide in-store demonstrations, and distribute samples to store customers. Food producers and processors commonly employ trade salespeople.

technical salespeople Support salespeople who give technical assistance to a firm's current customers

Technical Salespeople. **Technical salespeople** give technical assistance to the organization's current customers, advising them on product characteristics and applications, system designs, and installation procedures. Because this job is often highly technical, the salesperson usually has formal training in one of the physical sciences or in engineering. Technical sales personnel often sell technical industrial products such as computers, heavy equipment, and steel.

When hiring sales personnel, marketers seldom restrict themselves to a single category because most firms require different types of salespeople. Several factors dictate how many of each type a particular company should have. Product use, characteristics, complexity, and price influence the kind of sales personnel used, as do the number and characteristics of customers. The types of marketing channels and the intensity and type of advertising also affect the composition of a sales force.

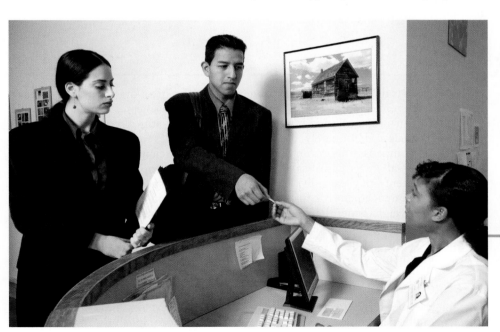

Missionary Salespeople
Pharmaceutical reps are missionary salespeople. They are employed by manufacturers to promote products to physicians, hospitals, and retail druggists.

Selected Types of Selling

Personal selling has become an increasingly complex process due in large part to rapid technological innovation. Most importantly, the focus of personal selling is shifting from selling a specific product to building long-term relationships with customers by finding solutions to their needs, problems, and challenges. As a result, the roles of salespeople are changing. Among the new philosophies for personal selling are team selling and relationship selling.

Team Selling

team selling The use of a team of experts from all functional areas of a firm, led by a salesperson, to conduct the personal selling process

Many products, particularly expensive high-tech business products, have become so complex that a single salesperson can no longer be expert in every aspect of the product and purchase process. **Team selling,** which involves the salesperson joining with people from the firm's financial, engineering, and other functional areas, is appropriate for such products. The salesperson takes the lead in the personal selling process, but other members of the team bring their unique skills, knowledge, and resources to the process to help customers find solutions to their own business challenges. Selling teams may be created to address a particular short-term situation or they may be formal, ongoing teams. Team selling is advantageous in situations calling for detailed knowledge of new, complex, and dynamic technologies such as jet aircraft and medical equipment. It can be difficult, however, for highly competitive salespersons to adapt to a team-selling environment.

Relationship Selling

relationship selling The building of mutually beneficial long-term associations with a customer through regular communications over prolonged periods of time

Relationship selling, also known as consultative selling, involves building mutually beneficial long-term associations with a customer through regular communications over prolonged periods of time. Like team selling, it is especially used in business-to-business marketing. Relationship selling involves finding solutions to customers' needs by listening to them, gaining a detailed understanding of their organizations, understanding and caring about their needs and challenges, and providing support after the sale. At Computer Discount Warehouse (CDW), relationship selling is based on helping customers succeed. Before hurricanes struck Florida, for example, some CDW account managers contacted clients in the paths of the storms and suggested computer back-up storage and battery solutions that could help their businesses weather the storms with greater confidence.[12]

Managing the Sales Force

The sales force is directly responsible for generating one of an organization's primary inputs: sales revenue. Without adequate sales revenue, businesses cannot survive. In addition, a firm's reputation is often determined by the ethical conduct of its sales force. The morale and ultimately the success of a firm's sales force depend in large part on adequate compensation, room for advancement, sufficient training, and management support—all key areas of sales management. Salespeople who are not satisfied with these elements may leave. Evaluating the input of salespeople is an important part of sales force management because of its strong bearing on a firm's success.

We explore eight general areas of sales management: establishing sales force objectives, determining sales force size, recruiting and selecting salespeople, training sales personnel, compensating salespeople, motivating salespeople, managing sales territories, and controlling and evaluating sales force performance.

Establishing Sales Force Objectives

To manage a sales force effectively, sales managers must develop sales objectives. Sales objectives tell salespeople what they are expected to accomplish during a specified time period. They give the sales force direction and purpose, and serve as standards for evaluating and controlling the performance of sales personnel. Sales objectives should be stated in precise, measurable terms and should specify the time period and geographic areas involved.

Sales objectives are usually developed for both the total sales force and individual salespeople. Objectives for the entire force are normally stated in terms of sales volume, market share, or profit. Volume objectives refer to dollar or unit sales. For example, the objective for an electric drill producer's sales force might be to sell $18 million worth of drills, or 600 000 drills annually. When sales goals are stated in terms of market share, they usually call for an increase in the proportion of the firm's sales relative to the total number of products sold by all businesses in that industry. When sales objectives are based on profit, they are generally stated in terms of dollar amounts or return on investment.

Sales objectives, or quotas, for individual salespeople are commonly stated in terms of dollar or unit sales volume. Other bases used for individual sales objectives include average order size, average number of calls per time period, and ratio of orders to calls.

Determining Sales Force Size

Sales force size is important because it influences the company's ability to generate sales and profits. Moreover, size of the sales force affects the compensation methods used, salespeople's morale, and overall sales force management. Sales force size must be adjusted periodically because a firm's marketing plans change along with markets and forces in the marketing environment. One danger in cutting back the size of the sales force to increase profits is that the sales organization may lose strength and resiliency, preventing it from rebounding when growth occurs or better market conditions prevail.

Several analytical methods can help determine optimal sales force size. One method involves determining how many sales calls per year are necessary for the organization to serve customers effectively and then dividing this total by the average number of sales calls a salesperson makes annually. A second method is based on marginal analysis, in which additional salespeople are added to the sales force until the cost of an additional salesperson equals the additional sales generated by that person. Although marketing managers may use one or several analytical methods, they normally temper decisions with subjective judgments.

Recruiting and Selecting Salespeople

recruiting Developing a list of qualified applicants for sales positions

To create and maintain an effective sales force, sales managers must recruit the right type of salespeople. In **recruiting,** the sales manager develops a list of qualified applicants for sales positions. Effective recruiting efforts are a vital part of implementing the strategic sales force plan and can help assure successful organizational performance.[13] Costs of hiring and training a salesperson are soaring, reaching more than $60 000 in some industries. Thus, recruiting errors are expensive.

To ensure the recruiting process results in a pool of qualified applicants, a sales manager establishes a set of qualifications before beginning to recruit. Although marketers have tried for years to identify a set of traits characterizing effective salespeople, no set of generally accepted characteristics yet exists. Experts agree that good salespeople exhibit optimism, flexibility, self-motivation, empathy, and the ability to network and maintain long-term customer relationships. One trait that may be useful in sensing customer reactions and generally being flexible is emotional intelligence: being in touch with one's own feelings and those of others.[14] Today companies are increasingly seeking applicants capable of employing relationship-building and consultative approaches.[15]

Sales managers must determine what set of traits best fits their companies' particular sales tasks. Two activities help establish this set of required attributes. First, the sales manager should prepare a job description listing specific tasks salespeople are to perform. Second, the manager should analyze characteristics of the firm's successful salespeople, as well as those of ineffective sales personnel. From the job description and analysis of traits, the sales manager should be able to develop a set of specific requirements and be aware of potential weaknesses that could lead to failure.

A sales manager generally recruits applicants from several sources: departments within the firm, other firms, employment agencies, educational institutions, respondents to advertisements, and individuals recommended by current employees. The specific sources depend on the type of salesperson required and the manager's experiences with particular sources.

The process of recruiting and selecting salespeople varies considerably from one company to another. Companies intent on reducing sales force turnover are likely to have strict recruiting and selection procedures. State Farm Life Insurance, for example, strives to retain customers by having low sales force turnover. Applicants for the job of State Farm insurance agent must go through a year-long series of interviews, tests, and visits with agents before finding out if they have been hired. Approximately 80 percent of State Farm agents are still employed four years after being hired, compared with an industry average of only 30 percent.

Sales management should design a selection procedure that satisfies the company's specific needs. Some organizations use the specialized services of other companies to hire sales personnel. The process should include steps that yield the information required to make accurate selection decisions. However, because each step incurs a certain amount of expense, there should be no more steps than necessary. Stages of the selection process should be sequenced so that the more expensive steps, such as a physical examination, occur near the end. Fewer people will then move through higher-cost stages.

Recruitment should not be sporadic; it should be a continuous activity aimed at reaching the best applicants. The selection process should systematically and effectively match applicants' characteristics and needs with the requirements of specific selling tasks. Finally, the selection process should ensure that new sales personnel are available where and when needed.

Sales Training

Companies like Thought Leader Publications offer specialized publications and training workshops to assist sales professionals.

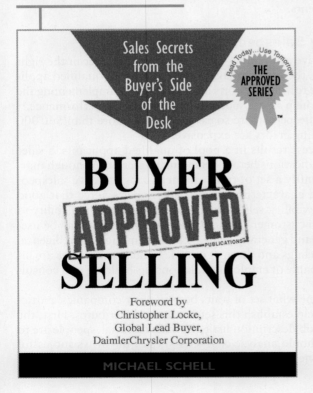

Training Sales Personnel Many organizations have formal training programs; others depend on informal, on-the-job training. Some systematic training programs are quite extensive, whereas others are rather short and rudimentary. Whether the training program is complex or simple, developers must consider what to teach, whom to train, and how to train them.

A sales training program can concentrate on the company, its products, or selling methods. Training programs often cover all three. Such programs can be aimed at newly hired salespeople, experienced salespeople, or both. Training for experienced company salespeople usually emphasizes product information, although salespeople must also be informed about new selling techniques and changes in company plans, policies, and procedures. Ordinarily, new sales personnel require comprehensive training, whereas experienced personnel need both refresher courses on established products and training regarding new-product information.

Sales training may be done in the field, at educational institutions, in company facilities, and/or online using web-based technology. For many companies, online training saves time and money, and helps salespeople learn about new products quickly. Some firms train new employees before assigning them to a specific sales position. Others put them into the field immediately, providing formal training only after they have gained some experience. Training programs for new personnel can be as short as several days or as long as three years; some are even longer. Sales training for experienced personnel is often scheduled when sales activities are not too demanding. Because experienced salespeople usually need periodic retraining, a firm's sales management must determine the frequency, sequencing, and duration of these efforts.

Sales managers, as well as other salespeople, often engage in sales training, whether daily on the job or periodically during sales meetings. Salespeople sometimes receive training from technical specialists within their own organizations. In addition, a number of outside companies and associations like the Canadian Professional Sales Association specialize in providing sales training programs. Materials for sales training programs range from videos, texts, online materials, manuals, and cases to programmed learning devices and audio- and videocassettes. Lectures, demonstrations, simulation exercises, and on-the-job training can all be effective teaching methods. The choice of methods and materials for a particular sales training program depends on type and number of trainees, program content and complexity, length and location, size of the training budget, number of teachers, and teacher preferences.

Compensating Salespeople

To develop and maintain a highly productive sales force, a business must formulate and administer a compensation plan that attracts, motivates, and retains the most effective individuals. The plan should give sales management the desired level of control and provide sales personnel with acceptable levels of income, freedom, and incentive. It should be flexible, equitable, easy to administer, and easy to understand. Good compensation programs facilitate and encourage proper treatment of customers. Obviously it is quite difficult to incorporate all of these requirements into a single program.

Developers of compensation programs must determine the general level of compensation required and the most desirable method of calculating it. In analyzing the required compensation level, sales management must ascertain a salesperson's value to the company on the basis of the tasks and responsibilities associated with the sales position. Sales managers may consider a number of factors, including salaries of other types of personnel in the firm, competitors' compensation plans, costs of sales force turnover, and non-salary selling expenses. An entry level salesperson can earn $50 000 annually (including commissions and bonuses), whereas a high-level, high-performing salesperson can make as much as $155 000 or more a year.

Pampered Chef

Doris Christopher's experience as a home economics teacher and homemaker helped her recognize a need for kitchen tools and techniques to minimize the time busy moms spend cooking. Inspired to help others preserve the tradition of family mealtimes, she founded the Pampered Chef out of the basement of her Chicago home in 1980.

Christopher modelled her business around home demonstration parties, which are sales presentations in which she showed people how to use the proper kitchen tools with real food. These parties offered the kind of show-and-tell that gave customers a "try-before-you-buy" experience. Christopher sold $175 worth of kitchenware at her first in-home show. She expanded her direct-selling organization by following the personal selling process with in-home presentation as the heart of the sales process.

At first, Christopher handled all of the demonstrations herself, but in 1981 she took on her first outside "kitchen consultant" salesperson. By the end of that year, she had a dozen sales consultants and had established a commission incentive for selling the products. She also began holding sales meetings in her home, training sales consultants in effective techniques for making presentations, demonstrating recipes, and introducing new products.

Today more than 70 000 Pampered Chef Kitchen consultants sell more than 200 products with annual sales of $700 million. In addition to a network of Pampered Chef Kitchen consultants in the U.S. and Canada, Pampered Chef has grown a network of consultants in both Deutschland and the United Kingdom. Doris Christopher's approach to personal selling, inspired by her dedication to family and home, helped to create a successful privately held company.

straight salary compensation plan Paying salespeople a specific amount per time period, regardless of selling effort

straight commission compensation plan Paying salespeople according to the amount of their sales in a given time period

combination compensation plan Paying salespeople a fixed salary plus a commission based on sales volume

Sales compensation programs usually reimburse salespeople for selling expenses, provide some fringe benefits, and deliver the required compensation level. To achieve this, a firm may use one or more of three basic compensation methods: straight salary, straight commission, or a combination of salary and commission. Table 18.1 lists the major characteristics, advantages, and disadvantages of each method. In a **straight salary compensation plan,** salespeople are paid a specified amount per time period, regardless of selling effort. This sum remains the same until they receive a pay increase or decrease. Although this method is easy to administer and affords salespeople financial security, it provides little incentive for them to boost selling efforts. In a **straight commission compensation plan,** salespeople's compensation is determined solely by sales for a given period. A commission may be based on a single percentage of sales or on a sliding scale involving several sales levels and percentage rates. While this method motivates sales personnel to escalate their selling efforts, it offers them little financial security, and it can be difficult for sales managers to maintain control over the sales force. For these reasons, many firms offer a **combination compensation plan** in which salespeople receive a fixed salary plus a commission based on sales volume. Some combination programs require that a salesperson exceed a certain sales level before earning a commission; others offer commissions for any level of sales. This method is the most popular, as indicated in Table 18.1.

When selecting a compensation method, sales management weighs the advantages and disadvantages listed in the table. Research suggests that sales managers may be moving away from individual performance-based commissions and toward salary- and team-based compensation methods.[16] For example, the Container Store, which markets do-it-yourself organizing and storage products, prefers to pay its sales staff salaries that are 50 to 100 percent higher than those offered by rivals instead of basing pay on commission plans.[17]

Motivating Salespeople

Although financial compensation is an important incentive, additional programs are necessary for motivating sales personnel. A sales manager should develop a systematic

---

table 18.1 CHARACTERISTICS OF SALES FORCE COMPENSATION METHODS

Compensation Method	Use (%)*	When Especially Useful	Advantages	Disadvantages
Straight salary	17.5	Compensating new salespersons; firm moves into new sales territories that require developmental work; sales requiring lengthy presale and postsale services	Gives salespeople security; gives sales managers control over salespeople; easy to administer; yields more predictable selling expenses	Provides no incentive; necessitates closer supervision of salespeople; during sales declines, selling expenses remain constant
Straight commission	14.0	Highly aggressive selling is required; non-selling tasks are minimized; company uses contractors and part-timers	Provides maximum amount of incentive; by increasing commission rate, sales managers can encourage salespeople to sell certain items; selling expenses relate directly to sales resources	Salespeople have little financial security; sales managers have minimum control over sales force; may cause salespeople to give inadequate service to smaller accounts; selling costs less predictable
Combination	68.5	Sales territories have relatively similar sales potential; firm wishes to provide incentive but still control sales force activities	Provides certain level of financial security; provides some incentive; can move sales force efforts in profitable direction	Selling expenses less predictable; may be difficult to administer

*Figures computed from *Dartnell's 30th Sales Force Compensation Survey,* Dartnell Corporation, Chicago, 1999.
Source: Charles Futrell, *Sales Management* (Ft. Worth: Dryden Press), 2001, pp. 307–316.

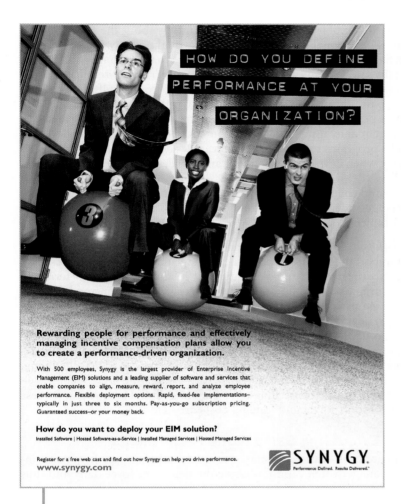

Rewarding people for performance and effectively managing incentive compensation plans allow you to create a performance-driven organization.

With 500 employees, Synygy is the largest provider of Enterprise Incentive Management (EIM) solutions and a leading supplier of software and services that enable companies to align, measure, reward, report, and analyze employee performance. Flexible deployment options. Rapid, fixed-fee implementations—typically in just three to six months. Pay-as-you-go subscription pricing. Guaranteed success—or your money back.

How do you want to deploy your EIM solution?
Installed Software | Hosted Software-as-a-Service | Installed Managed Services | Hosted Managed Services

Register for a free web cast and find out how Synygy can help you drive performance.
www.synygy.com

SYNYGY
Performance Defined. Results Delivered.

Motivating Salespeople

Synygy provides sales compensation management solutions. Properly managed incentive programs motivate appropriate sales force behaviour, and thus sales performance.

approach for motivating salespeople to be productive. Effective sales force motivation is achieved through an organized set of activities performed continuously by the company's sales management.

Sales personnel, like other people, join organizations to satisfy personal needs and achieve personal goals. Sales managers must identify those needs and goals and strive to create an organizational climate that allows each salesperson to fulfill them. Enjoyable working conditions, power and authority, job security, and opportunity to excel are effective motivators, as are company efforts to make sales jobs more productive and efficient. At the Container Store, for example, sales personnel receive hundreds of hours of training about the company's products every year so they can help customers solve organization and storage problems.[18] Sales contests and other incentive programs can also be effective motivators. Sales contests can motivate salespeople to increase sales or add new accounts, promote special items, achieve greater volume per sales call, and cover territories more thoroughly. However, companies need to understand salespersons' preferences when designing contests in order to make them effective in increasing sales.[19] Some companies find such contests powerful tools for motivating sales personnel to achieve company goals. In smaller firms lacking the resources for a formal incentive program, a simple but public "thank-you" from management at a sales meeting, along with a small-denomination gift card, can be rewarding.[20]

Properly designed incentive programs pay for themselves many times over, and sales managers are relying on incentives more than ever. Recognition programs that acknowledge outstanding performance with symbolic awards, such as plaques, can be very effective when carried out in a peer setting. The most common incentive offered by companies is cash, followed by gift cards and travel.[21] Travel reward programs can confer a high-profile honour, provide a unique experience that makes recipients feel special, and build camaraderie among award-winning salespeople. However, some recipients of travel awards may feel they already travel too much on the job. Cash rewards are easy to administer, are always appreciated by recipients, and appeal to all demographic groups. However, cash has no visible "trophy" value and provides few "bragging rights." The benefits of awarding merchandise are that the items have visible trophy value, recipients who are allowed to select the merchandise experience a sense of control, and merchandise awards can help build momentum for the sales force. The disadvantages of using merchandise are that employees may have lower perceived value of the merchandise and that the company may experience greater administrative problems. Some companies outsource their incentive programs to companies that specialize in the creation and management of such programs.

Managing Sales Territories

The effectiveness of a sales force that must travel to customers is somewhat influenced by management's decisions regarding sales territories. When deciding on territories, sales managers must consider size, shape, routing, and scheduling.

Creating Sales Territories. Several factors enter into the design of a sales territory's size and shape. First, sales managers must construct territories that allow sales potential to be measured. Sales territories often consist of several geographic units, such as cities or provinces, for which market data are obtainable. Sales managers usually try to create territories with similar sales potential or requiring about the same amount of work. If territories have equal sales potential, they will almost always be unequal in geographic size. Salespeople with larger territories have to work longer and harder to generate a certain sales volume. Conversely, if sales territories requiring equal amounts of work are created, sales potential for those territories will often vary. If sales personnel are partially or fully compensated through commissions, they will have unequal income potential. Many sales managers try to balance territorial workloads and earning potential by using differential commission rates. At times sales managers use commercial programs to help them balance sales territories. Although a sales manager seeks equity when developing and maintaining sales territories, some inequities always prevail.

A territory's size and shape should also help the sales force provide the best possible customer coverage and should minimize selling costs. Customer density and distribution are important factors.

Routing and Scheduling Salespeople. The geographic size and shape of a sales territory are the most important factors affecting the routing and scheduling of sales calls. Next in importance are the number and distribution of customers within the territory, followed by sales call frequency and duration. Those in charge of routing and scheduling must consider the sequence in which customers are called on, specific roads or transportation schedules to be used, number of calls to be made in a given period, and time of day the calls will occur. In some firms, salespeople plan their own routes and schedules with little or no assistance from the sales manager; in others, the sales manager draws up the routes and schedules. No matter who plans the routing and scheduling, the major goals should be to minimize salespeople's non-selling time (time spent travelling and waiting) and maximize their selling time. Planners should try to achieve these goals so that a salesperson's travel and lodging costs are held to a minimum.

Controlling and Evaluating Sales Force Performance

To control and evaluate sales force performance properly, sales management needs information. A sales manager often cannot observe the field sales force daily and thus relies on salespeople's call reports, customer feedback, and invoices. Call reports identify the customers called on and present detailed information about interactions with those clients. Sales personnel often must file work schedules indicating where they plan to be during specific time periods. Data about a salesperson's interactions with customers and prospects can be included in the company's customer relationship management system. This information provides insights about the salesperson's performance.

Dimensions used to measure a salesperson's performance are determined largely by sales objectives, normally set by the sales manager. If an individual's sales objective is stated in terms of sales volume, that person should be evaluated on the basis of sales volume generated. Even if a salesperson is assigned a major objective, he or she is ordinarily expected to achieve several related objectives as well. Thus, salespeople are often judged along several dimensions. Sales managers evaluate many performance indicators, including average number of calls per day, average sales per customer, actual sales relative to sales potential, number of new-customer orders, average cost per call, and average gross profit per customer.

To evaluate a salesperson, a sales manager may compare one or more of these dimensions with predetermined performance standards. However, sales managers commonly compare a salesperson's performance with that of other employees operating under similar selling conditions or the salesperson's current performance with past performance. Sometimes management judges factors that have less direct bearing on sales performance, such as personal appearance, product knowledge, and ethical standards. One concern is the tendency to reprimand top sellers less severely than poor performers for engaging in unethical selling practices.[22]

After evaluating salespeople, sales managers should take any needed corrective action to improve sales force performance. They may adjust performance standards, provide additional training, or try other motivational methods. Corrective action may demand comprehensive changes in the sales force.

SUMMARY

Personal selling is the process of informing customers and persuading them to purchase products through paid personal communication in an exchange situation. The three general purposes of personal selling are finding prospects, persuading them to buy, and keeping customers satisfied.

Many salespeople, either consciously or unconsciously, move through a general selling process as they sell products. In prospecting, the salesperson develops a list of potential customers. Before contacting prospects, the salesperson conducts a preapproach that involves finding and analyzing information about prospects and their needs. The approach is the manner in which the salesperson contacts potential customers. During the sales presentation, the salesperson must attract and hold the prospect's attention to stimulate interest in and desire for the product. If possible, the salesperson should handle objections as they arise. During the closing, the salesperson asks the prospect to buy the product or products. After a successful closing, the salesperson must follow up the sale.

In developing a sales force, marketing managers consider which types of salespeople will sell the firm's products most effectively. The three classifications of salespeople are order getters, order takers, and support personnel. Order getters inform both current customers and new prospects and persuade them to buy. Order takers seek repeat sales and fall into two categories: inside order takers and field order takers. Sales support personnel facilitate selling, but their duties usually extend beyond making sales. The three types of support personnel are missionary, trade, and technical salespeople. The roles of salespeople are changing. Team selling involves the salesperson joining with people from the firm's financial, engineering, and other functional areas. Relationship selling involves building mutually beneficial long-term associations with a customer through regular communications over prolonged periods of time.

Sales force management is an important determinant of a firm's success because the sales force is directly responsible for generating the organization's sales revenue. Major decision areas and activities are establishing sales force objectives; determining sales force size; recruiting, selecting, training, compensating, and motivating salespeople; managing sales territories; and controlling and evaluating sales force performance.

Sales objectives should be stated in precise, measurable terms and specify the time period and geographic areas involved. The size of the sales force must be adjusted occasionally because a firm's marketing plans change along with markets and forces in the marketing environment.

Recruiting and selecting salespeople involves attracting and choosing the right type of salesperson to maintain an effective sales force. When developing a training program, managers must consider a variety of dimensions, such as who should be trained, what should be taught, and how training should occur. Compensation of salespeople involves formulating and administering a compensation plan that attracts, motivates, and retains the right types of salespeople. Motivated salespeople should translate into high productivity. Managing sales territories focuses on such factors as size, shape, routing, and scheduling. To control and evaluate sales force performance, sales managers use information obtained through salespeople's call reports, customer feedback, and invoices.

Please visit the student website at **www.hmco.ca/marketing** for ACE Self-Test questions that will help you prepare for exams.

IMPORTANT TERMS

Personal selling
Prospecting
Approach
Closing
Order getter

Order takers
Support personnel
Missionary salespeople
Trade salespeople
Technical salespeople

Team selling
Relationship selling
Recruiting
Straight salary
  compensation plan

Straight commission
  compensation plan
Combination
  compensation plan

DISCUSSION & REVIEW QUESTIONS

1. What is personal selling? How does personal selling differ from other types of promotional activities?

2. What are the primary purposes of personal selling?

3. Identify the elements of the personal selling process. Must a salesperson include all these elements when selling a product to a customer? Why or why not?

4. How does a salesperson find and evaluate prospects? Do you consider any of these methods to be ethically questionable? Explain.

5. Are order getters more aggressive or creative than order takers? Why or why not?

6. Why are team selling and relationship selling becoming more prevalent?

7. Identify several characteristics of effective sales objectives.

8. How should a sales manager establish criteria for selecting sales personnel? What do you think are the general characteristics of a good salesperson?

9. What major issues or questions should management consider when developing a training program for the sales force?

10. Explain the major advantages and disadvantages of the three basic methods of compensating salespeople. In general, which method would you prefer? Why?

11. What major factors should be taken into account when designing the size and shape of a sales territory?

12. How does a sales manager, who cannot be with each salesperson in the field on a daily basis, control the performance of sales personnel?

APPLICATION QUESTIONS

1. Briefly describe an experience you have had with a salesperson at a clothing store or an automobile dealership. Describe the steps the salesperson used. Did the salesperson skip any steps? What did the salesperson do well? Not so well? Would you describe the salesperson as an order getter, an order taker, or a support salesperson? Why? Did the salesperson perform more than one of these functions?

2. Leap Athletic Shoe, Inc., a newly formed company, is in the process of developing a sales strategy. Market research indicates sales management should segment the market into five regional territories. The sales potential for the West Coast (B.C.) region is

$1.2 million, for the Western region $1 million, for the Ontario region $1.3 million, for the Quebec region $1.1 million, and for the Eastern region $.5 million. The firm wishes to maintain some control over the training and sales processes because of the unique features of its new product line, but Leap marketers realize the salespeople need to be fairly aggressive in their efforts to break into these markets. They would like to provide the incentive needed for the extra selling effort. What type of sales force compensation method would you recommend to Leap? Why?

globalEDGE™

1. Your firm has recently developed a revolutionary new chemical that is widely applicable, nearly costless, and does not harm the environment. However, before widespread production, you must identify the largest manufacturing companies worldwide that may be interested in your new product. The *IndustryWeek*'s IW 1000 ranking should prove useful for this task. This can be found using the search term "largest manufacturing companies" at **http://globaledge.msu.edu/ibrd** or **http://globaledge.msu.edu/ibrd/ibrd.asp.** From there, follow the link to the IW 1000 Database and then choose the Chemicals industry as a choice criterion. What are the ten largest chemical companies as ranked by sales? Because your firm plans to export to the United States and focused on growing that market, which companies are feasible to target for a comprehensive sales

strategy? If you were planning to enter a new market, which would it be?

2. Your Vancouver-based maritime business is currently enjoying profitable conditions. Because your firm and other competitors have been catching an overabundance of fresh shrimp in recent weeks, you have noticed that the North American market is currently saturated. You are unsure of the options that may exist internationally, so you decide to export through a local agent to assist in selling your products overseas. Find potential agents by using the search term "products overseas" at **http://globaledge.msu.edu/ibrd** or **http://globaledge.msu.edu/ibrd/ibrd.asp** to reach the FASonline website. Enter appropriate criteria. How many agents do you find that are near your offices when you search FASonline's website? Which will you choose?

INTERNET Exercise

Visit **www.prideferrell.com** for resources to help you master the material in this chapter, plus materials that will help you expand your marketing knowledge, including internet exercise updates, ACE self-tests, hotlinks to companies featured in this chapter, and much more.

TerrAlign

The TerrAlign Group offers consulting services and software products world-wide that are designed to help firms maximize control and deployment of field sales representatives. In addition to helping firms with control and deployment, TerrAlign, also assists clients with issues of sales force sizing, customer targeting, and sales call planning. Review its website at **www.terralign.com.**

1. Identify three features of TerrAlign software that are likely to benefit salespeople.
2. Identify three features of TerrAlign software that are likely to benefit sales managers.
3. Why might field sales professionals object to the use of software from TerrAlign?

Case 18.1   IBM Sales Force Sells Solutions

In recent years, IBM has worked hard to reposition itself from a supplier of information technology hardware and software to a company that provides business solution services. In their own words, "We measure ourselves today by how well we help clients solve their biggest and most pressing problems." Obviously, successful problem solving leads to an increase in customers and an increase in goods and services sold.

Although IBM is still the world's largest provider of IT hardware and software, it regards this as the means to an end. The company relies heavily on its global sales force to make the transition from a goods to a solution services provider. The enormous task of changing the company's focus cannot be overstated.

Personal selling has always been a fundamental aspect of IBM's business philosophy and is one of the foundations of the company's success: IBM has customers in 174 countries who speak 165 languages. The company's sales force makes 18 billion client contacts a year and addresses 350 000 sales opportunities per day.

As in all organizations, IBM's change comes from the top. Last year Samuel J. Palmisano, IBM's chairman, president, and chief executive officer, led a process of examining and redefining the company's core values. One of the first core values identified was "dedication to every client's success." From a sales perspective, this is achieved through consultative or solution selling, which brings all of IBM's resources and expertise together to solve customer problems. This requires that the sales force thoroughly understand their customers' business environments and deliver the correct answers to their questions. As Palmisano points out, the company's business model has changed. It used to be "invent, build, and sell." Today it is "craft, solve, and deliver the solution."

Not surprisingly, solution selling has brought new challenges to the sales force. IBM believes that salespeople are not born, but trained. The company puts its salespeople through an extensive five-month training program that encompasses three major areas of focus: IBM's commitment to its customers, techniques of collaborative selling, and techniques for gaining understanding of a company's resources and infrastructure. For large projects, salespeople often work in teams comprised of one sales leader and four to five sales specialists who have expertise relevant to the project.

For the most part, IBM salespeople use the Socratic method of selling. This involves asking open-ended questions to better understand their customers' problems, desires, and needs. As might be expected, solution (or pull) selling is more complex than product (or push) selling. The salesperson's role in solution selling is to gather information concerning the customer's business problem, provide a point of view, solve the problem (with the help of other team members), and determine the potential impact on the customer's business once the recommended solution is implemented.

The most accurate and important indicator of the success of the solutions service is customer reaction. An example of IBM achieving its sales objective of "insuring our clients are successful," is their Sales Connections Program. Actuate, an Independent Software Vendor (ISV) and IBM customer, used the Sales Connection website to express concerns about a customer dragging its feet on an applications deal. IBM discovered that the person Actuate was working with lacked the authority to close the deal. IBM provided Actuate with the correct contact person and the sale was quickly closed.

Another example is IBM's Software-as-a-Service program. Software-as-a-Service delivers software via the

Internet. This eliminates the need for companies to buy, build, manage, and maintain applications that address areas such as accounting, human resources, customer relationship management, and enterprise resource planning. Companies benefit from this concept because they can reduce their operational costs and maintenance expenses, therefore increasing profits. In an effort to sell this service more broadly, an IBM sales team designed a sales incentive that awards a 10 percent referral fee and additional marketing incentives to IBM customers that submit leads resulting in business for IBM. The marketing incentives include direct mail, telemarketing, advertising, and technical resources to help businesses generate leads. This program enabled one of IBM's customers to generate 800 sales leads in one year.

With this kind of dedication, there is little doubt that IBM's solutions service will continue its success.[23]

Questions for Discussion

1. What are the advantages for IBM in selling solutions rather than goods?
2. Why is solution selling more complex than hardware and software selling? Identify the sales skills needed for each approach.
3. What are some ways that IBM can measure the effectiveness of its solutions or consultative selling?

Case 18.2   Sales Ethics: the Pros and Cons of Leasing a Car

When Mike and Alda Kiani decided they needed a new vehicle, they went to a dealership looking for a good used car. Like so many others in their situation, what they walked out with was a brand new leased car. Why? The salesperson asked enough questions to find out that the monthly payment was a major factor in their buying decision. The salesperson told them that the monthly payments for leasing were lower than for buying.

What the salesperson didn't tell them was just how much more expensive the lease was going to be in the long run. It would have been almost impossible for the Kianis to figure this out themselves because the car dealership did not disclose all the financial details of the leasing agreement. (Such disclosure is now required in many provinces.) Hidden charges such as a so-called acquisition fee can add $1000 to $3000 to the lease cost over the life of the lease, according to Parkway Honda Sales Manager Alexander Degenis, in Toronto.

Automobile analyst Dennis Desrosiers says that car leases are so complex that it's just about impossible for consumers to decide if they are getting a good deal. Many people in his position are pushing to have all dealers use simpler, more understandable lease agreements and to disclose all the financial details upfront.

Had they known all the facts, the Kianis may still have decided to lease; but, like many other Canadian car shoppers who rely on the information that the salesperson provides, they just weren't given the chance to make a well-informed decision.

Questions for Discussion

1. What kinds of questions might the salesperson have asked the Kianis to ascertain their needs?
2. If you were a car salesperson, how would you feel about the practice of not disclosing all costs of a lease to a customer?
3. If you were a sales force manager for a car dealership, how would you react upon learning one of your salespeople intentionally failed to disclose all costs of a lease to a customer?

Strategic Case 8   Napster 2.0: The Cat Is Back

Napster was the brainchild of Shawn Fanning, a 17-year-old student at Northeastern University in Boston, Massachusetts, who left university to develop a technology to trade music over the Internet. The technology was commercialized through Napster, which allowed computer users to share high-quality digital recordings (MP3s) of music via the Internet using its proprietary MusicShare software. Napster didn't actually store the recordings on its own computers; rather, it provided an index of all the songs available on the computers of members who were logged on to the service. In other words, Napster functioned as a sort of clearinghouse through which members could search by artist or song title, identify MP3s of interest, and download their choices from other members' hard drives. Napster quickly became one of the most popular sites on the Internet, claiming some 15 million users in little more than a year. Indeed, so many students were downloading songs from Napster that many colleges and universities were forced to block the site from their systems to regain bandwidth.

From the beginning, Napster's service was as controversial as it was popular. Barely a year after its 1999 launch, Napster was sued by the Recording Industry Association of America (RIAA), which represents major recording companies such as Universal Music, BMG, Sony Music, Warner Music Group, and EMI. The RIAA claimed that Napster's service violated copyright laws by allowing users to swap music recordings for free. The RIAA also sought an injunction to stop the downloading of copyrighted songs and damages for lost revenue. The RIAA argued that song swapping via Napster and similar firms had cost the music industry more than $300 million in lost sales. Metallica, a heavy-metal band, and rap star Dr. Dre filed separate lawsuits accusing Napster of copyright infringement and racketeering. Lars Ulrich, Metallica's drummer, told a Senate committee that he believed Napster users were basically stealing from the band every time they downloaded one of its songs.

The Fall of Napster

Within months, Napster was found guilty of direct copyright infringement of RIAA members' musical recordings. Napster was ordered to stop allowing its millions of users to download and share copyrighted material without properly compensating the owners of that material. The company agreed to pay $26 million for past distribution of unauthorized music and made a proposal that would let songwriters and musicians distribute their music on Napster for a fee. This settlement would have covered as many as 700 000 songs, but Napster still needed an agreement before it could legally distribute the music. However, after several failed attempts

to reach a suitable compromise with the recording industry, and with litigation expenses mounting, the company filed for bankruptcy.

The final nail in the coffin for Napster came on September 3, 2002, when a bankruptcy judge blocked the sale of the company to Bertelsmann, ruling that negotiations with the German media company had not been made at arm's length and in good faith. Bertelsmann had agreed to pay creditors $8 million for Napster's assets. According to the bankruptcy petition, the company had assets of $7.9 million and debts of $101 million. Napster appeared to be doomed.

The Digital Music Revolution

North America is the largest music market in the world, accounting for 40 percent of all global sales and almost 33 percent of all unit sales. However, the future of traditional music sales—CDs and albums—appears bleak. CD sales declined by 31 percent over a three-year period; the sale of DVDs increased, but only by a slight four percent. One major reason for the decline in music sales is changing consumer preferences. Although consumers value CDs because they provide "long-term" entertainment, an RIAA survey found that many believe CDs cost too much.

With Napster out of the picture and the RIAA bringing lawsuits against individual downloaders of music online, other online music providers were rapidly getting their houses in order. One of the first was AOL, which launched MusicNet with 20 music streams and 20 downloads for $3.95 per month. Apple's iTunes was by far the heaviest hitter to join the foray into online music with 99-cent downloads.

Worldwide, there are now 335 legal downloading services, with more than two million songs available. The number of registered users of Napster and other music download services grew from 1.5 million to 2.8 million in 2005. Thus it has become clear to both sides of the music-downloading controversy that online music distribution is here to stay. It was only a matter of time until a compromise could be reached among the recording studios, the artists, and the various online music providers.

Some thorny issues remained to be resolved, however. First, because even pay-for-download services are not immune to piracy, the recording industry wanted to develop technology that would prevent downloaders from swapping files on their own even after making a legitimate purchase. To protect the artists, the industry also wanted to limit the number of times a song can be downloaded and copied. Suggestions included using the MD5 hash—a digital fingerprint—or using software that monitors sound patterns to detect illegal copies. A second issue was the development of a revenue model. Should MP3 files be available individually, as one file in a complete album, or both? Should pricing be based on a per-download basis or on an unlimited basis for a monthly subscription fee?

The Rise of Napster 2.0

In late 2002, Napster's name and assets were purchased by Roxio, a company well known for its "CD-burning" software. After much fanfare and excitement, Roxio revived Napster as Napster 2.0 on October 29, 2003. The new fee-based service offers one million songs for download—giving it one of the largest online catalogues currently available in the industry—at 99 cents per track or $9.95 per album. Users can also pay $9.95 per month for unlimited music streaming to their desktops. Perhaps most important, Napster's relaunch came with the blessing of five major record labels. Napster has also developed a number of partnerships with Microsoft, Gateway, Yahoo!, and Samsung that gave it an advantage during its relaunch. Napster's partnership with Samsung led to the creation of the Samsung YP-910GS, a 20-gigabyte digital audio player that is fully integrated with Napster 2.0. The device allows users to transfer songs from Napster directly to the unit via a USB connection. The player also boasts an integrated FM transmitter that allows users to broadcast MP3 playback through their home or car stereo systems. In addition, Napster subscribers receive the industry's leading CD creation software package, developed by parent company Roxio, as a bonus.

Although the reborn Napster currently offers a large catalogue of songs, it continues to face competition from a growing number of firms, particularly iTunes. iTunes currently offers more than two million songs and adds thousands more weekly. It also offers a wide selection of audio books, music videos, and television show episodes. Moreover, the popularity of Apple's iPod MP3 player confers on Apple a distinct advantage: the iPod provides customers with a perfect vehicle to get the music they desire. The iTunes software application works for both Macintosh and Windows operating systems. The service is easy to use and boasts fewer restrictions than MusicNet and other brand competitors. As a result, iTunes has developed a high customer satisfaction rating.

Other competitors include the thousands of offline and online music record stores that offer CDs and other merchandise, as well as satellite radio and, increasingly, music downloads via mobile phones. Moreover, there are still websites from which music can be downloaded free of charge, albeit illegally. Some potential customers would rather risk getting caught than pay for the music.

As with any technology-based service, new competition is often unseen and swift. With subscribers of peer-to-peer networks being targeted by the Recording Industry Association of America, any or all of these services may move toward a pay-for-play service to avoid being hassled by the RIAA. In addition, competition exists from major retailers such as Wal-Mart and Amazon.com and from traditional music retailers. Given the existing and future competition, it is imperative that Napster make its brand the market leader in a short period of time.[24]

Questions For Discussion

1. What factors seem to have the greatest influence on Napster 2.0's pricing decisions? Explain.
2. What appear to be Napster's primary pricing objectives?
3. Assess the level of price competition in the music industry as a whole and within the online music distribution business specifically.
4. Evaluate Napster's pricing strategy of charging 99 cents per song. Under what circumstances should the company consider changing that strategy?

Financial Analysis in Marketing*

Our discussion in this book focuses more on fundamental concepts and decisions in marketing than on financial details. However, marketers must understand the basic components of financial analyses to be able to explain and defend their decisions. In fact, they must be familiar with certain financial analyses to reach good decisions in the first place. To control and evaluate marketing activities, they must understand the income statement and what it says about their organization's operations. They also need to be familiar with performance ratios, which compare current operating results with past results and with results in the industry at large. We examine the income statement and some performance ratios in the first part of this appendix. In the second part, we discuss price calculations as the basis for price adjustments. Marketers are likely to use all these areas of financial analysis at various times to support their decisions and make necessary adjustments in their operations.

The Income Statement

The income, or operating, statement presents the financial results of an organization's operations over a certain period. The statement summarizes revenues earned and expenses incurred by a profit centre, whether a department, a brand, a product line, a division, or the entire firm. The income statement presents the firm's net profit or net loss for a month, quarter, or year.

Table A.1 is a simplified income statement for Stoneham Auto Supplies, a fictitious retail store. The owners, Rose Costa and Nick Schultz, see that net sales of $250 000 are decreased by the cost of goods sold and by other business expenses to yield a net income of $83 000. Of course, these figures are only highlights of the complete income statement, which appears in Table A.2.

The income statement can be used in several ways to improve the management of a business. First, it enables an owner or a manager to compare actual results with budgets for various parts of the statement. For example, Rose and Nick see that the total amount of merchandise sold (gross sales) is $260 000. Customers returned merchandise or received allowances (price reductions) totaling $10 000. Suppose the budgeted amount was only $9000. By checking the tickets for sales returns and allowances, the owners can determine why these events occurred and whether the $10 000 figure could be lowered by adjusting the marketing mix.

After subtracting returns and allowances from gross sales, Rose and Nick can determine net sales, the amount the firm has available to pay its expenses. They are pleased with this figure because it is higher than their sales target of $240 000.

A major expense for most companies that sell goods (as opposed to services) is the cost of goods sold. For Stoneham Auto Supplies, it amounts to 18 percent of net sales. Other expenses are treated in various ways by different companies. In our example, they are broken down into standard categories of selling expenses, administrative expenses, and general expenses.

*We gratefully acknowledge the assistance of Jim L. Grimm, in writing this appendix.

table A.1   SIMPLIFIED INCOME STATEMENT FOR A RETAILER

Stoneham Auto Supplies
Income Statement for the Year Ended
December 31, 2007

Net Sales	$250 000
Cost of Goods Sold	45 000
Gross Margin	$205 000
Expenses	122 000
Net Income	$ 83 000

The income statement shows that for Stoneham Auto Supplies, the cost of goods sold was $45 000. This figure was derived in the following way. First, the statement shows that merchandise in the amount of $51 000 was purchased during the year. In paying the invoices associated with these inventory additions, purchase (cash) discounts of $4000 were earned, resulting in net purchases of $47 000. Special requests for selected merchandise throughout the year resulted in $2000 in freight charges, which increased the net cost of delivered purchases to $49 000. When this amount is added to the beginning inventory of $48 000, the cost of goods available for sale during 2007 totals $97 000. However, the records indicate that the value of inventory at the end of the year was $52 000. Because this amount was not sold, the cost of goods that were sold during the year was $45 000.

Rose and Nick observe that the total value of their inventory increased by 8.3 percent during the year:

$$\frac{\$52\,000 - \$48\,000}{\$48\,000} = \frac{\$4000}{\$48\,000} = \frac{1}{12} = .0825, \text{ or } 8.3\%$$

Further analysis is needed to determine whether this increase is desirable or undesirable. (Note that the income statement provides no details concerning the composition of the inventory held on December 31; other records supply this information.) If Nick and Rose determine that inventory on December 31 is excessive, they can implement appropriate marketing action.

Gross margin is the difference between net sales and cost of goods sold. Gross margin reflects the markup on products and is the amount available to pay all other expenses and provide a return to the owners. Stoneham Auto Supplies had a gross margin of $205 000:

Net sales	$250 000
Cost of goods sold	45 000

Stoneham's expenses (other than cost of goods sold) during 2007 totaled $122 000. Observe that $53 000, or slightly more than 43 percent of the total, constituted direct selling expenses:

$$\frac{\$53\,000 \text{ selling expenses}}{\$122\,000 \text{ total expenses}} = .434, \text{ or } 43\%$$

The business employs three salespeople (one full time) and pays competitive wages. The selling expenses are similar to those in the previous year, but Nick and Rose wonder whether more advertising is necessary because the value of inventory increased by more than 8 percent during the year.

The administrative and general expenses are essential for operating the business. A comparison of these expenses with trade statistics for similar businesses indicates that the figures are in line with industry amounts.

Net income, or net profit, is the amount of gross margin remaining after deducting expenses. Stoneham Auto Supplies earned a net profit of $83 000 for the fiscal year ending December 31, 2007. Note that net income on this statement is figured before payment of income taxes.

Income statements for intermediaries and for businesses that provide services follow the same general format as that shown for Stoneham Auto Supplies in Table A.2.

table A.2   INCOME FOR A RETAILER

Stoneham Auto Supplies
Income Statement for the Year Ended December 31, 2007

Gross Sales			**$260 000**
Less: Sales returns and allowances			$ 10 000
Net Sales			**$250 000**
Cost of Goods Sold			
Inventory, January 1, 2007 (at cost)		$48 000	
Purchases	$51 000		**$260 000**
Less: Purchase discounts	4000		
Net purchases	$47 000		
Plus: Freight-in	2000		
Net cost of delivered purchases		$49 000	
Cost of goods available for sale		$97 000	
Cost of goods sold			$ 45 000
Gross Margin			**$205 000**
Expenses			
Selling expenses			
Sales salaries and commissions	$32 000		
Advertising	16 000		
Sales promotions	3000		
Delivery	2000		
Total selling expenses		$53 000	
Administrative expenses			
Administrative salaries	$20 000		
Office salaries	20 000		
Office supplies	2000		
Miscellaneous	1000		
Total administrative expenses		$43 000	
General expenses			
Rent	$14 000		
Utilities	7000		
Bad debts	1000		
Total general expenses		$26 000	
Total expenses			$122 000
Net Income			**$ 83 000**

table A.3   COST OF GOODS SOLD FOR A MANUFACTURER

ABC Manufacturing
Income Statement for the Year Ended December 31, 2007

Cost of Goods Sold			$ 50 000
Finished goods inventory January 1, 2007			
Cost of goods manufactured			
Work-in-process inventory, January 1, 2007		$ 20 000	
Raw materials inventory, January 1, 2007	$ 40 000		
Net cost of delivered purchases	$240 000		
Cost of goods available for use	$280 000		
Less: Raw materials inventory, December 31, 2007	$ 42 000		
Cost of goods placed in production		$238 000	
Direct labour		32 000	
Manufacturing overhead			
Indirect labour	$ 12 000		
Supervisory salaries	10 000		
Operating supplies	6000		
Depreciation	12 000		
Utilities	$ 10 000		
Total manufacturing overhead		$ 50 000	
Total manufacturing costs		$320 000	
Total work-in-process		$340 000	
Less: Work-in-process inventory, December 31, 2007		$ 22 000	
Cost of Goods Manufactured			$318 000
			$368 000
Cost of Goods Available for Sale			48 000
Less: Finished goods inventory, December 31, 2007			
Cost of Goods Sold			**$320 000**

The income statement for a manufacturer, however, differs somewhat in that "purchases" portion is replaced by "cost of goods manufactured." Table A.3 shows the entire Cost of Goods Sold section for a manufacturer, including cost of goods manufactured. In other respects, income statements for retailers and manufacturers are similar.

Performance Ratios

Rose and Nick's assessment of how well their business did during fiscal year 2007 can be improved through use of analytical ratios. Such ratios enable a manager to compare the results for the current year with data from previous years and industry statistics. However, comparisons of the current income statement with income statements and industry statistics from other years are not very meaningful because factors such as inflation are not accounted for when comparing dollar amounts. More useful comparisons can be made by converting these figures to a percentage of net sales, as this section shows.

The first analytical ratios we discuss, the operating ratios, are based on the net sales figure from the income statement.

Operating Ratios

Operating ratios express items on the income, or operating, statement as percentages of net sales. The first step is to convert the income statement into percentages of net sales, as illustrated in Table A.4. After making this conversion, the manager looks at several key operating ratios: two profitability ratios (the gross margin ratio and the net income ratio) and the operating expense ratio.

For Stoneham Auto Supplies, these ratios are determined as follows (see Tables A.2 and A.4 for supporting data):

$$\text{Gross Margin Ratio} = \frac{Gross\ Margin}{Net\ Sales} = \frac{\$205\,000}{\$250\,000} = 82\%$$

$$\text{Net Income Ratio} = 33.2\%$$

$$\text{Operating Expenses Ratio} = \frac{Total\ Expenses}{Net\ Sales} = \frac{\$122\,000}{\$250\,000} = 48.8\%$$

The gross margin ratio indicates the percentage of each sales dollar available to cover operating expenses and achieve profit objectives. The net income ratio indicates the percentage of each sales dollar that is classified as earnings (profit) before payment of income taxes. The operating expense ratio calculates the percentage of each dollar needed to cover operating expenses.

If Nick and Rose believe the operating expense ratio is higher than historical data and industry standards, they can analyze each operating expense ratio in Table A.4 to determine which expenses are too high and then take corrective action. After reviewing several key operating ratios, Nick and Rose, like many managers, will probably want to analyze all the items on the income statement. By doing so, they can determine whether the 8 percent increase in the value of their inventory was necessary.

Inventory Turnover Rate

The inventory turnover rate, or stock-turn rate, is an analytical ratio that can be used to answer the question "Is the inventory level appropriate for this business?" The inventory turnover rate indicates the number of times an inventory is sold (turns over) during one year. To be useful, this figure must be compared with historical turnover rates and industry rates.

The inventory turnover rate is computed (based on cost) as follows:

$$\text{Inventory Turnover} = \frac{Cost\ of\ Goods\ Sold}{Average\ Inventory\ at\ Cost}$$

Rose and Nick would calculate the turnover rate from Table A.2 as follows:

$$\frac{Cost\ of\ Goods\ Sold}{Average\ Inventory\ at\ Cost} = \frac{\$45\,000}{\$50\,000} = 0.9\%$$

Their inventory turnover is less than once per year (0.9 times). Industry averages for competitive firms are 2.8 times. This figure convinces Rose and Nick that their investment in inventory is too large and they need to reduce their inventory.

Return on Investment

Return on investment (ROI) is a ratio that indicates management's efficiency in generating sales and profits from the total amount invested in the firm. For Stoneham Auto Supplies, the ROI is 41.5 percent, which compares well with competing businesses.

We use figures from two different financial statements to arrive at ROI. The income statement, already discussed, gives us net income. The balance sheet, which states the firm's assets and liabilities at a given point in time, provides the figure for total assets (or investment) in the firm.

table A.4   INCOME STATE COMPONENTS AS PERCENTAGE OF NET SALES

Stoneham Auto Supplies
Income Statement as a Percentage of Net Sales for the Year Ended
December 31, 2007

			Percentage of Net Sales
Gross Sales			103.8%
Less: Sales returns and allowances			3.8
Net Sales			100.0%
Cost of Goods Sold			
Inventory, January 1, 2007 (at cost)		19.2%	
Purchases	20.4%		
Less: Purchase discounts	1.6		
Net purchases	18.8%		
Plus: Freight-in	0.8		
Net cost of delivered purchases		19.6	
Cost of goods available for sale		38.8%	
Less: Inventory, December 31, 2007 (at cost)		20.8	
Cost of goods sold			18.0
Expenses			
Selling expenses			
Sales salaries and commissions	12.8%		
Advertising	6.4		
Delivery	0.8		
Total selling expenses		21.2%	
Administrative expenses			
Administrative salaries	8.0%		
Office salaries	8.0		
Office supplies	0.8		
Miscellaneous	0.4		
Total administrative expenses		17.2%	
General expenses			
Rent	5.6%		
Utilities	2.8		
Bad debts	0.4		
Miscellaneous	1.6		
Total general expenses		10.4%	
Total expenses			48.8
Net Income			33.2%

The basic formula for ROI is

$$ROI = \frac{Net\ Income}{Total\ Investment}$$

For Stoneham Auto Supplies, net income is $83 000 (see Table A.2). If total investment (taken from the balance sheet for December 31, 2007) is $200 000, then

$$ROI = \frac{\$83\,000}{\$200\,000} = 0.415,\ or\ 41.5\%$$

The ROI formula can be expanded to isolate the impact of capital turnover and the operating income ratio separately. Capital turnover is a measure of net sales per dollar of investment; the ratio is figured by dividing net sales by total investment. For Stoneham Auto Supplies,

$$Capital\ Turnover = \frac{Net\ Sales}{Total\ Investment} = \frac{\$250\,000}{\$200\,000} = 1.25$$

ROI is equal to capital turnover times the net income ratio. The expanded formula for Stoneham Auto Supplies is

$$ROI = \frac{Net\ Income}{Net\ Sales}$$

$$= \frac{\$250\,000}{\$200\,000} \times \frac{\$83\,000}{\$250\,000}$$

$$= (1.25)\,(33.2\%) = 41.5\%$$

Price Calculations

An important step in setting prices is selecting a basis for pricing. The systematic use of markups, markdowns, and various conversion formulas helps in calculating the selling price and evaluating the effects of various prices.

Markups

As discussed in the text, markup is the difference between the selling price and the cost of the item; that is, selling price equals cost plus markup. The markup must cover cost and contribute to profit; thus, markup is similar to gross margin on the income statement.

Markup can be calculated on either cost or selling price as follows:

$$Markup\ as\ Percentage\ of\ Cost = \frac{Amount\ Added\ to\ Cost}{Cost} = \frac{Dollar\ Markup}{Cost}$$

$$Markup\ as\ Percentage\ of\ Selling\ Price = \frac{Amount\ Added\ to\ Cost}{Selling\ Price} = \frac{Dollar\ Markup}{Selling\ Price}$$

Retailers tend to calculate the markup percentage on selling price.

To review the use of these markup formulas, assume an item costs $10 and the markup is $5:

$$Selling\ Price = Cost + Markup$$

$$\$15 = \$10 + \$5$$

Thus,

$$\text{Markup Percentage on Selling Price} = \frac{\$5}{\$10} = 50\%$$

$$\text{Markup Percentage on Selling Price} = \frac{\$5}{\$15} = 33\tfrac{1}{3}\%$$

It is necessary to know the base (cost or selling price) to use markup pricing effectively. Markup percentage on cost will always exceed markup percentage on price, given the same dollar markup, as long as selling price exceeds cost.

On occasion, we may need to convert markup on cost to markup on selling price, or vice versa. The conversion formulas are as follows:

$$\text{Markup Percentage on Selling Price} = \frac{\textit{Markup Percentage on Cost}}{100\% + \textit{Markup Percentage on Cost}}$$

$$\text{Markup Percentage on Cost} = \frac{\textit{Markup Percentage on Selling Price}}{100\% - \textit{Markup Percentage on Selling Price}}$$

For example, if the markup percentage on cost is $33\tfrac{1}{3}$ percent, the markup percentage on selling price is

$$\frac{33\tfrac{1}{3}\%}{100\% + 33\tfrac{1}{3}\%} = \frac{33\tfrac{1}{3}\%}{1.33\tfrac{1}{3}\%} = 25\%$$

If the markup percentage on selling price is 40 percent, the corresponding percentage on cost is as follows:

$$66\tfrac{2}{3}\%$$

Finally, we can show how to determine selling price if we know the cost of the item and the markup percentage on selling price. Assume an item costs $36 and the usual markup percentage on selling price is 40 percent. Remember that selling price equals markup plus cost. Thus, if

$$100\% = 40\% \text{ of Selling Price} + \text{Cost}$$

then,

$$60\% \text{ of Selling Price} = \text{Cost}$$

In our example, cost equals $36. Therefore,

$$0.6X = \$36$$

$$X = \frac{\$36}{0.6}$$

$$\text{Selling Price} = \$60$$

Alternatively, the markup percentage could be converted to a cost basis as follows:

$$66\tfrac{2}{3}\%$$

The selling price would then be computed as follows:

$$\text{Selling Price} = 66\tfrac{2}{3}\%(\text{COST}) + \text{COST}$$

$$= 66\tfrac{2}{3}\%(\$36) + \$36$$

$$= \$24 + \$36 = \$60$$

If you keep in mind the basic formula—selling price equals cost plus markup—you will find these calculations straightforward.

Markdowns

Markdowns are price reductions a retailer makes on merchandise. Markdowns may be useful on items that are damaged, priced too high, or selected for a special sales event. The income statement does not express markdowns directly because the change in price is made before the sale takes place. Therefore, separate records of markdowns would be needed to evaluate the performance of various buyers and departments.

The markdown ratio (percentage) is calculated as follows:

$$\text{Markdown Percentage} = \frac{\text{Dollar Markdowns}}{\text{Net Sales in Dollars}}$$

In analyzing their inventory, Nick and Rose discover three special automobile jacks that have gone unsold for several months. They decide to reduce the price of each item from $25 to $20. Subsequently these items are sold. The markdown percentage for these three items is

$$\text{Markdown Percentage} = \frac{3(\$5)}{3(\$20)} = \frac{\$15}{\$60} = 25\%$$

Net sales, however, include all units of this product sold during the period, not just those marked down. If ten of these items were already sold at $25 each, in addition to the three items sold at $20, the overall markdown percentage would be

$$\text{Markdown Percentage} = \frac{3(\$5)}{\$10(\$25) + 3(\$20)}$$

$$= \frac{\$15}{\$250 + \$60} = \frac{\$15}{\$310} = 4.8\%$$

Sales allowances are also a reduction in price. Thus, the markdown percentage should include any sales allowances. It would be computed as follows:

$$\text{Markdown Percentage} = \frac{\text{Dollar Markdowns} + \text{Dollar Allowances}}{\text{Net Sales in Dollars}}$$

Discussion and Review Questions

1. How does a manufacturer's income statement differ from a retailer's income statement?

2. Use the following information to answer questions a through c:

TEA COMPANY

Fiscal year ended June 30, 2007

Net sales	$500 000
Cost of goods sold	300 000
Net income	50 000
Average inventory at cost	100 000
Total assets (total investment)	200 000

a. What is the inventory turnover rate for TEA Company? From what sources will the marketing manager determine the significance of the inventory turnover rate?

b. What is the capital turnover ratio? What is the net income ratio? What is the return on investment (ROI)?

c. How many dollars of sales did each dollar of investment produce for TEA Company?

3. Product A has a markup percentage on cost of 40 percent. What is the markup percentage on selling price?

4. Product B has a markup percentage on selling price of 30 percent. What is the markup percentage on cost?

5. Product C has a cost of $60 and a usual markup percentage of 25 percent on selling price. What price should be placed on this item?

6. Apex Appliance Company sells 20 units of product Q for $100 each and 10 units for $80 each. What is the markdown percentage for product Q?

Sample Marketing Plan

This sample marketing plan for a hypothetical company illustrates how the marketing planning process might be implemented. If you are asked to create a marketing plan, this model may be a helpful guide.

① The Executive Summary, one of the most frequently read components of a marketing plan, is a synopsis of the marketing plan. Although it does not provide detailed information, it does present an overview of the plan so readers can identify key issues pertaining to their roles in the planning and implementation processes. Although this is the first section in a marketing plan, it is usually written last.

② The Environmental Analysis presents information regarding the organization's current situation with respect to the marketing environment, the current target market(s), and the firm's current marketing objectives and performance.

③ This section of the environmental analysis considers relevant **external environmental forces** such as competitive, economic, political, legal and regulatory, technological, and sociocultural forces.

Star Software, Inc., Marketing Plan

① I. EXECUTIVE SUMMARY

Star Software, Inc., is a small, family-owned corporation in the first year of a transition from first-generation to second-generation leadership. Star Software sells custom-made calendar programs and related items to about 400 businesses, which use the software mainly for promotion. As Star's business is highly seasonal, its eighteen employees face scheduling challenges, with greatest demand during October, November, and December. In other months, the equipment and staff are sometimes idle. A major challenge facing Star Software is how to increase profits and make better use of its resources during the off-season.

An evaluation of the company's internal strengths and weaknesses and external opportunities and threats served as the foundation for this strategic analysis and marketing plan. The plan focuses on the company's growth strategy, suggesting ways it can build on existing customer relationships, and on the development of new products and/or services targeted to specific customer niches. Since Star Software markets a product used primarily as a promotional tool by its clients, it is currently considered a business-to-business marketer.

② II. ENVIRONMENTAL ANALYSIS

Founded as a commercial printing company, Star Software, Inc., has evolved into a marketer of high-quality, custom-made calendar software and related business-to-business specialty items. In the mid-1960s, Bob McLemore purchased the company and, through his full-time commitment, turned it into a very successful family-run operation. In the near future, McLemore's 37-year-old son, Jonathan, will take over as Star Software's president and allow the elder McLemore to scale back his involvement.

③ A. THE MARKETING ENVIRONMENT

1. *Competitive forces.* The competition in the specialty advertising industry is very strong on a local and regional basis, but somewhat weak nationally. Sales figures for the industry as a whole are difficult to obtain since very little business is conducted on a national scale.

   The competition within the calendar industry is strong in the paper segment and weak in the software-based segment. Currently paper calendars hold a dominant market share of approximately 65 percent; however, the software-based segment is growing rapidly. The 35 percent market share held by software-based calendars is divided among many different firms. Star Software, which holds 30 percent of the software-based calendar market, is the only company that markets a software-based calendar on a national basis. As software-based calendars become more popular, additional competition is expected to enter the market.

2. *Economic forces.* Nationwide, many companies have reduced their overall promotion budgets as they face the need to cut expenses. However, most of these reductions have occurred in the budgets for mass media advertising (television, magazines, and newspapers). While overall promotion budgets are shrinking, many companies are diverting a larger percentage of their budgets to sales promotion and specialty advertising. This trend is expected to continue as a slow-growth economy forces most companies to focus more on the "value" they receive from their promotion dollars. Specialty advertising, such as can be done with a software-based calendar, provides this value.

3. *Political forces.* There are no expected political influences or events that could affect the operations of Star Software.

4. *Legal and regulatory forces.* In recent years, more attention has been paid to "junk mail." A large percentage of specialty advertising products are distributed by mail, and some of these products are considered "junk." Although this label is attached to the type of products Star Software makes, the problem of junk mail falls on Star's clients and not on the company itself. While legislation may be introduced to curb the tide of advertising delivered through the mail, the fact that more companies are diverting their promotion dollars to specialty advertising indicates that most do not fear the potential for increased legislation.

5. *Technological forces.* A major emerging technological trend involves personal digital assistants (PDAs). A PDA is a handheld device, similar in size to a large calculator that can store a wide variety of information, including personal notes, addresses, and a calendar. Some PDAs, such as the BlackBerry, can be loaded with a cell phone and walkie-talkie. The user can e-mail and schedule on the electronic calendar. As this trend continues, current software-based calendar products may have to be adapted to match the new technology.

6. *Sociocultural forces.* In today's society, consumers have less time for work or leisure. The hallmarks of today's successful products are convenience and ease of use. In short, if the product does not save time and is not easy to use, consumers will simply ignore it. Software-based calendars fit this consumer need quite well. A software-based calendar also fits in with other societal trends: a move to a paperless society, the need to automate repetitive tasks, and the growing dependence on computers, for example.

4 The analysis of current target markets assesses demographic, geographic, psychographic, and product usage characteristics of the target markets. It also assesses the current needs of each of the firm's target markets, anticipated changes in those needs, and how well the organization's current products are meeting those needs.

4 B. Target Market(s)

By focusing on commitment to service and quality, Star Software has effectively implemented a niche differentiation strategy in a somewhat diverse marketplace. Its ability to differentiate its product has contributed to superior annual returns. Its target market consists of manufacturers or manufacturing divisions of large corporations that move their products through dealers, distributors, or brokers. Its most profitable product is a software program for a PC-based calendar, which can be tailored to meet client needs by means of artwork, logos, and text. Clients use this calendar software as a promotional tool, providing a disk to their customers as an advertising premium. The calendar software is not produced for resale.

The calendar software began as an ancillary product to Star's commercial printing business. However, due to the proliferation of PCs and the growth in technology, the computer calendar soon became more profitable for Star than its wall and desktop paper calendars. This led to the sale of the commercial printing plant and equipment to employees. Star Software has maintained a long-term relationship with these former employees, who have added capabilities to reproduce computer disks and whose company serves as Star's primary supplier of finished goods. Star's staff focuses on further development and marketing of the software.

C. Current Marketing Objectives and Performance

Star Software's sales representatives call on potential clients and, using a template demonstration disk, help them create a calendar concept. Once the sale has been finalized, Star completes the concept, including design, copywriting, and customization of the demonstration disk. Specifications are then sent to the supplier, located about 1000 miles away, where the disks are produced. Perhaps what most differentiates Star from its competitors is its high level of service. Disks can be shipped to any location the buyer specifies. Since product development and customization of this type can require significant amounts of time and effort, particularly during the product's first year, Star deliberately pursues a strategy of steady, managed growth. Star Software markets its products on a company-specific basis. It has an annual reorder rate of approximately 90 percent and an average customer-reorder relationship of about eight years. The first year in dealing with a new customer is the most stressful and time consuming for Star's salespeople and product developers. Subsequent years are faster and significantly more profitable.

A company must set marketing objectives, measure performance against those objectives, and then take corrective action if needed.

The company is currently debt free except for the mortgage on its facility. However, about 80 percent of its accounts receivable are billed during the last three months of the calendar year. Seasonal account billings, along with the added travel of Star's sales staff during the peak season, pose a special challenge to the company. The need for cash to fund operations in the meantime requires the company to borrow significant amounts of money to cover the period until customer billing occurs. Star Software's marketing objectives include increases in both revenues and profits of approximately 10 percent over the previous year. Revenues should exceed $4 million, and profits are expected to reach $1.3 million.

III. SWOT ANALYSIS

> **5** **Strengths** are competitive advantages or core competencies that give the organization an advantage in meeting the needs of its customers.

5 ## A. Strengths

1. Star Software's product differentiation strategy is the result of a strong marketing orientation, commitment to high quality, and customization of products and support services.

2. There is little turnover among employees, who are well compensated and liked by customers. The relatively small staff size promotes camaraderie with co-workers and clients, and fosters communication and quick response to clients' needs.

3. A long-term relationship with the primary supplier has resulted in shared knowledge of the product's requirements, adherence to quality standards, and a common vision throughout the development and production process.

4. The high percentage of reorder business suggests a satisfied customer base, as well as positive word-of-mouth communication, which generates some 30 percent of new business each year.

6 **Weaknesses** are limitations a firm has in developing or implementing a marketing strategy.

6 B. Weaknesses

1. The highly centralized management hierarchy and lack of managerial backup may impede creativity and growth. Too few people hold too much knowledge.

2. Despite the successful, long-term relationship with the supplier, single-sourcing could make Star Software vulnerable in the event of a natural disaster, strike, or dissolution of the current supplier. Contingency plans for suppliers should be considered.

3. The seasonal nature of the product line creates bottlenecks in productivity and cash flow, places excessive stress on personnel, and strains the facilities.

4. Both the product line and the client base lack diversification. Dependence on current reorder rates could breed complacency, invite competition, or create a false sense of customer satisfaction. The development of a product that would make the software calendar obsolete would probably put Star out of business.

5. While the small size of the staff fosters camaraderie, it also impedes growth and new-business development.

6. Star Software is reactive rather than assertive in its marketing efforts because of its heavy reliance on positive word-of-mouth communication for obtaining new business.

7. Star's current facilities are crowded. There is little room for additional employees or new equipment.

7 **Opportunities** are favourable conditions in the environment that could yield rewards for an organization if acted on properly.

7 C. Opportunities

1. Advertising expenditures in Canada exceed $10 billion annually. More than $2.5 billion of this is spent on direct-mail advertising and another $2 billion on specialty advertising. Star Software's potential for growth is significant in this market.

2. Technological advances have not only freed up time for Canadians and brought greater efficiency but have also increased the amount of stress in their fast-paced lives. Personal computers have become commonplace, and personal information managers have gained popularity.

3. As Canadian companies look for ways to develop customer relationships rather than just close sales, reminders of this relationship could come in the form of acceptable premiums or gifts that are useful to the customer.

4. Computer-based calendars are easily distributed nationally and globally. The globalization of business creates an opportunity to establish new client relationships in foreign markets.

8 **Threats** are conditions or barriers that may prevent the organization from reaching its objectives.

8 **D. Threats**

1. Reengineering, right-sizing, and outsourcing trends in management may alter traditional channel relationships with brokers, dealers, and distributors or eliminate them altogether.

2. Calendars are basically a generic product. The technology, knowledge, and equipment required to produce such an item, even a computer-based one, is minimal. The possible entry of new competitors is a significant threat.

3. Theft of trade secrets and software piracy through unauthorized copying is difficult to control.

4. Specialty advertising through promotional items relies on gadgetry and ideas that are new and different. As a result, product life cycles may be quite short.

5. Single-sourcing can be detrimental or even fatal to a company if the buyer-supplier relationship is damaged or if the supplying company has financial difficulty.

6. Competition from traditional paper calendars and other promotional items is strong.

9 During the development of a marketing plan, marketers attempt to match internal strengths to external opportunities. In addition, they try to convert internal weaknesses into strengths and external threats into opportunities.

9 **E. Matching Strengths to Opportunities/Converting Weaknesses and Threats**

1. The acceptance of technological advances and the desire to control time create a potential need for a computer-based calendar.

2. Star Software has more opportunity for business growth during its peak season than it can presently handle because of resource (human and capital) constraints.

3. Star Software must modify its management hierarchy, empowering its employees through a more decentralized marketing organization.

4. Star Software should discuss future growth strategies with its supplier and develop contingency plans to deal with unforeseen events. Possible satellite facilities in other geographic locations should be explored.

5. Star Software should consider diversifying its product line to satisfy new market niches and develop nonseasonal products.

6. Star Software should consider surveying its current customers and its customers' clients to gain a better understanding of their changing needs and desires.

10 The development of marketing objectives is based on environmental analysis, SWOT analysis, the firm's overall corporate objectives, and the organization's resources. For each objective, this section should answer the question "What is the specific and measurable outcome and time frame for completing this objective?"

11 The marketing plan clearly specifies and describes the target market(s) toward which the organization will aim its marketing efforts. The difference between this section and the earlier section covering target markets is that the earlier section deals with present target markets, whereas this section looks at future target markets.

10 ## IV. MARKETING OBJECTIVES

Star Software, Inc., is in the business of helping other companies market their products and/or services. Besides formulating a marketing-oriented and customer-focused mission statement, Star Software should establish an objective to achieve cumulative growth in net profit of at least 50 percent over the next five years. At least half of this 50 percent growth should come from new, non-manufacturing customers and from products that are nonseasonal or that are generally delivered in the off-peak period of the calendar cycle.

To accomplish its marketing objectives, Star Software should develop benchmarks to measure progress. Regular reviews of these objectives will provide feedback and possible corrective actions on a timely basis. The major marketing objective is to gain a better understanding of the needs and satisfaction of current customers. Since Star Software is benefiting from a 90 percent reorder rate, it must be satisfying its current customers. Star could use the knowledge of its successes with current clients to market to new customers. To capitalize on its success with current clients, the company should establish benchmarks to learn how it can improve the products it now offers through knowledge of clients' needs and specific opportunities for new product offerings. These benchmarks should be determined through marketing research and Star's marketing information system.

Another objective should be to analyse the billing cycle Star now uses to determine if there are ways to bill accounts receivable in a more evenly distributed manner throughout the year. Alternatively, repeat customers might be willing to place orders at off-peak cycles in return for discounts or added customer services.

Star Software should also create new products that can use its current equipment, technology, and knowledge base. It should conduct simple research and analyses of similar products or product lines with an eye toward developing specialty advertising products that are software based but not necessarily calendar related.

V. MARKETING STRATEGIES

11 ### A. Target Market(s)

Target market 1: Large manufacturers or stand-alone manufacturing divisions of large corporations with extensive broker, dealer, or distributor networks

Example: An agricultural chemical producer, such as Dow Chemical, distributes its products to numerous rural "feed and seed" dealers. Customizing calendars with relevant agricultural information and dates would be beneficial to these potential clients.

Target market 2: Nonmanufacturing, nonindustrial segments of the business-to-business market with extensive customer networks, such as banks, medical services, or financial planners

Example: Various sporting goods manufacturers distribute to specialty shop dealers. Calendars could be customized to the particular sport, such as golf (with PGA and other tour dates), or running (with various national marathon dates).

Target market 3: Direct consumer markets for brands with successful licensing arrangements for consumer products, such as Coca-Cola

Example: Products with major brand recognition and fan club membership, such as Harley-Davidson motorcycles or Corvette clubs, could provide additional markets for customized computer calendars. Environmental or political groups represent a nonprofit market. Brands with licensing agreements for consumer products could provide a market for consumer computer calendars in addition to the specialty advertising product, which would be marketed to manufacturers/dealers.

Target market 4: Industry associations that regularly hold or sponsor trade shows, meetings, conferences, or conventions

Example: National associations, such as the Dairy Farmers of Canada or the Canadian Marketing Association, host meetings or conventions. Customized calendars could be developed for any of these groups.

12

> **12** Though the marketing mix section in this plan is abbreviated, this component should provide considerable details regarding each element of the marketing mix: product, price, distribution, and promotion.

B. Marketing Mix

1. *Products.* Star Software markets not only calendar software but also the service of specialty advertising to its clients. Star's intangible attributes are its ability to meet or exceed customer expectations consistently, its speed in responding to customers' demands, and its anticipation of new customer needs. Intangible attributes are difficult for competitors to copy, thereby giving Star Software a competitive advantage.

2. *Price.* Star Software provides a high-quality specialty advertising product customized to its clients' needs. The value of this product and service is reflected in its premium price. Star should be sensitive to the price elasticity of its product and overall consumer demand.

3. *Distribution.* Star Software uses direct marketing. Since its product is compact, lightweight, and nonperishable, it can be shipped from a central location direct to the client via UPS, FedEx, or Canada Post. The fact that Star can ship to multiple locations for each customer is an asset in selling its products.

4. *Promotion.* Since 90 percent of Star's customers reorder each year, the bulk of promotional expenditures should focus on new product offerings through direct-mail advertising and trade journals or specialty publications. Any remaining promotional dollars could be directed to personal selling (in the form of sales performance bonuses) of current and new products.

VI. MARKETING IMPLEMENTATION

13

> **13** This section of the marketing plan details how the firm will be organized—by functions, products, regions, or types of customers—to implement its marketing strategies. It also indicates where decision-making authority will rest within the marketing unit.

A. Marketing Organization

Because Star's current and future products require extensive customization to match clients' needs, it is necessary to organize the marketing function by customer groups. This will allow Star to focus its marketing efforts exclusively on the needs and specifications of each target customer segment. Star's marketing efforts will be organized around the following customer groups: (1) manufacturing group; (2) nonmanufacturing, business-to-business group; (3) consumer product licensing group; and (4) industry associations group. Each group will be headed by a sales manager who will report to the marketing director (these positions must be created). Each group will be responsible for marketing Star's products within that customer segment. In addition, each group will have full decision-making authority. This represents a shift from the current, highly centralized management hierarchy. Frontline salespeople will be empowered to make decisions that will better satisfy Star's clients.

These changes in marketing organization will enable Star Software to be more creative and flexible in meeting customers' needs. Likewise, these changes will overcome the current lack of diversification in Star's product lines and client base. Finally, this new marketing organization will give Star a better opportunity to monitor the activities of competitors.

14 This component of the marketing plan outlines the specific activities required to implement the marketing plan, who is responsible for performing these activities, and when these activities should be accomplished based on a specified schedule.

B. Activities, Responsibility, and Timetables for Completion

All implementation activities are to begin at the start of the next fiscal year on April 1. Unless specified, all activities are the responsibility of Star Software's next president, Jonathan McLemore.

- On April 1, create four sales manager positions and the position of marketing director. The marketing director will serve as project leader of a new business analysis team, to be composed of nine employees from a variety of positions within the company.

- By April 15, assign three members of the analysis team to each of the following projects: (1) research potential new product offerings and clients, (2) analyse the current billing cycle and billing practices, and (3) design a customer survey project. The marketing director is responsible.

- By June 30, the three project groups will report the results of their analyses. The full business analysis team will review all recommendations.

- By July 31, develop a marketing information system to monitor client reorder patterns and customer satisfaction.

- By July 31, implement any changes in billing practices as recommended by the business analysis team.

- By July 31, make initial contact with new potential clients for the current product line. Each sales manager is responsible.

- By August 31, develop a plan for one new product offering, along with an analysis of its potential customers. The business analysis team is responsible.

- By August 31, finalize a customer satisfaction survey for current clients. In addition, the company will contact those customers who did not reorder for the 2007 product year to discuss their concerns. The marketing director is responsible.

- By January, implement the customer satisfaction survey with a random sample of 20 percent of current clients who reordered for the 2007 product year. The marketing director is responsible.

- By February, implement a new product offering, advertising to current customers and to a sample of potential clients. The business analysis team is responsible.

- By March, analyse and report the results of all customer satisfaction surveys and evaluate the new product offering. The marketing director is responsible.

- Reestablish the objectives of the business analysis team for the next fiscal year. The marketing director is responsible.

15 This section details how the results of the marketing plan will be measured and evaluated. The control portion of this section includes the types of actions the firm can take to reduce the differences between the planned and the actual performance.

15 VII. EVALUATION AND CONTROL

A. Performance Standards and Financial Controls

A comparison of the financial expenditures with the plan goals will be included in the project report. The following performance standards and financial controls are suggested:

- The total budget for the billing analysis, new-product research, and the customer survey will be equal to 60 percent of the annual promotional budget for the coming year.

- The breakdown of the budget within the project will be a 20 percent allocation to the billing cycle study, a 30 percent allocation to the customer survey and marketing information system development, and a 50 percent allocation to new-business development and new-product implementation.

- Each project team is responsible for reporting all financial expenditures, including personnel salaries and direct expenses, for its segment of the project. A standardized reporting form will be developed and provided by the marketing director.

- The marketing director is responsible for adherence to the project budget and will report overages to the company president on a weekly basis. The marketing director is also responsible for any redirection of budget dollars as required for each project of the business analysis team.

- Any new product offering will be evaluated on a quarterly basis to determine its profitability. Product development expenses will be distributed over a two-year period, by calendar quarters, and will be compared with gross income generated during the same period.

Monitoring Procedures

To analyse the effectiveness of Star Software's marketing plan, it is necessary to compare its actual performance with plan objectives. To facilitate this analysis, monitoring procedures should be developed for the various activities required to bring the marketing plan to fruition. These procedures include, but are not limited to, the following:

● A project management concept will be used to evaluate the implementation of the marketing plan by establishing time requirements, human resource needs, and financial or budgetary expenditures.

● A perpetual comparison of actual and planned activities will be conducted on a monthly basis for the first year and on a quarterly basis after the initial implementation phase. The business analysis team, including the marketing director, will report its comparison of actual and planned outcomes directly to the company president.

● Each project team is responsible for determining what changes must be made in procedures, product focus, or operations as a result of the studies conducted in its area.

Chapter 1

1. Burt Helm, "The Sport of Extreme Marketing," *Business Week,* Mar. 14, 2005; Kerry A. Dolan, "The Soda with Buzz," *Forbes,* Mar. 28, 2005; Kathryn Masterson, "Crank Juice—As Energy Drinks Gain on Sodas in THR Market Selection Grows Too," *Chicago Tribune,* Dec. 5, 2005.

2. *Marketing News,* Sept. 15, 2004, p. 1.

3. Julie Schlosser, "DeWalt," in "Breakaway Brands," *Fortune,* Oct. 31, 2005, pp. 156–158.

4. Source: Lanciaut, J.C. (2005). Bereavement Industry Adapting to Consumer Demands. New Media Journalism. University of Western Ontario. Retrieved October 17, 2006 from http://www.fims.uwo.ca/newmedia2005/default.asp?id=93.

5. James Tenser, "Endorser Qualities Count More Than Ever," *Advertising Age,* Nov. 8, 2004, pp. S-2, S-4.

6. Sources: Ontario Ministry of Energy. (January 31, 2006). "Ontario Government Joins Electricity Distribution Companies to Promote Energy Conservation: powerWISE® Education Campaign Targets Ontario Consumers." http://www.energy.gov.on.ca/index.cfm?fuseaction=english.news&body=yes&news_id=118; http://www.powerwise.ca/. Retrieved October 17, 2006.

7. Chad Terhune, "Pepsi Outlines Ad Campaign for Healthy Food," *The Wall Street Journal,* Oct. 15, 2005, p. A4, http://online.wsj.com/public/us.

8. Ajay K. Kohli and Bernard J. Jaworski, "Market Orientation: The Construct, Research Propositions, and Managerial Implications," *Journal of Marketing,* Apr. 1990, pp. 1–18; O. C. Ferrell, "Business Ethics and Customer Stakeholders," *Academy of Management Executive* 18 (May 2004): 126–129.

9. Eugene W. Anderson, Claes Fornell, and Sanal K. Mazvancheryl, "Customer Satisfaction and Shareholder Value," *Journal of Marketing* 68 (Oct. 2004): 172–185.

10. Kohli and Jaworski, "Market Orientation."

11. Kwaku Atuahene-Gima, "Resolving the Capability-Rigidity Paradox in New Product Innovation," *Journal of Marketing* 69 (Oct. 2005): 61–83.

12. Sunil Gupta, Donald R. Lehmann, and Jennifer Ames Stuart, "Valuing Customers," *Journal of Marketing Research* 41(Feb. 2004): 7–18

13. Source: Graham, Rodden. (June, 2006). Minas Basin is a Survivor. Pulp and Paper. http://findarticles.com/p/articles/mi_qa3636/is_200606/ai_n17178310/print. Retrieved August 29, 2007.

14. Jean Halliday, "Nissan Delves into Truck Owner Psyche," *Advertising Age,* Dec. 1, 2003, p. 11.

15. Alan Grant and Leonard Schlesinger, "Realize Your Customers' Full Profit Potential," *Harvard Business Review,* Sept./Oct. 1995, p. 59; Peter C. Verhoef, "Understanding the Effect of Customer Relationship Management Efforts on Customer Retention and Customer Share Development," *Journal of Marketing,* Oct. 2003, p. 30.

16. Jagdish N. Sheth and Rajendras Sisodia, "More Than Ever Before, Marketing Is Under Fire to Account for What It Spends," *Marketing Management,* Fall 1995, pp. 13–14.

17. Lynette Ryals and Adrian Payne, "Customer Relationship Management in Financial Services: Towards Information-Enabled Relationship Marketing," *Journal of Strategic Marketing,* Mar. 2001, p. 3.

18. Roland T. Rust, Katherine N. Lemon, and Valarie A. Zeithaml, "Return on Marketing: Using Customer Equity to Focus Marketing Strategy," *Journal of Marketing* 68 (Jan. 2004): 109–127

19. Rajkumar Venkatesan and V. Kumar, "A Customer Lifetime Value Framework for Customer Selection and Resource Allocation Strategy," *Journal of Marketing* 68 (Oct. 2004): 106–125.

20. Ibid.

21. Natalie Mizik and Robert Jacobson, "Trading Off Between Value Creation and Value Appropriation: The Financial Implications of Shifts in Strategic Emphasis," *Journal of Marketing,* Jan. 2003, pp. 63–76.

22. Ferrell and Hartline, *Marketing Strategy,* p. 104.

23. Steve Lohr, "Is IBM's Lenovo Proposal a Threat to National Security?" *The New York Times,* Jan. 31, 2005, www.nytimes.com.

24. Keith Regan, "Report: Online Sales Top $100 Billion," *E-Commerce Times,* June 1, 2004, www.ecommercetimes.com/story/34148.html.

25. "A Perfect Fit: Staples and Kids in Need," *Chain Store Age,* Oct. 2005, p. 78.

26. Sources: Thomas Caywood, "Bagel Company Finagles Hollow New Idea," *The Boston Herald,* Jan. 6, 2005, via LexisNexis; Donna Hood Crecca, "Higher Calling," Chain Leader, Dec. 2002, p. 14; Finagle a Bagel, www.finagleabagel.com (accessed Apr. 13, 2005); "Finagle Sees a Return to More Normal Business Mode," *Foodservice East,* Fall 2002, pp. 1, 17; "Sloan Grads Bet Their Money on Bagels," *Providence Business News,* Oct. 25, 1999, p. 14; "State Fare: Finagle A Bagel, Boston," *Restaurants and Institutions,* Oct. 1, 2002, www.rimag.com/1902/sr.htm; interview with Laura B. Trust and Alan Litchman, Feb. 25, 2003.

27. Sources: "A Brief History of CART and Champ Car Racing," *Fullspeed Database,* Feb. 17, 2003, www.fsdb.net/champcar/history/index.htm; "Champ Car Announces Management Changes," Motorsport.com, July 16, 2005, www.motorsport.com/news/article.asp?ID=197605&FS=BUSINESS; "Champ Car Team Owner and Legendary Actor Paul Newman Partners with Friend and Fellow Racer Eddie Wachs to Form Newman/Wachs Racing Atlantic Team," Champ Car World Series, Nov. 4, 2005, www.champcarworldseries.com/News/Article.asp?ID=9816; Mark Cipollini, "Branding CART and Their Race Cars," AutoRacing1.com, Nov. 9, 2000, www.autoracing1.com/MarkC/001109Branding.htm; Daniel Kaplan, "CART Tries Turnaround," *Sports Business Journal,* www.sportsbusiness journal.com/article.cms?articleId=26881&s=1; Robin Miller, "New Owners Could Focus on Streets," RPM//espn.go.com/ rpm/cart/2003/0810/159430.html; Robin Miller, "Pook Looking to Privatize Company," RPM//espn.go.com/rpm/cart/2003/ 0615/1568383.html; "Open Wheel Racing Series Pursues the Acquisition of Championship Auto Racing Teams," *Champ Car News,* Sept. 18, 2003, www.cart.com/News/Article.asp?ID= 7058&print=true; Chapman Rackaway, "Eccelstone to the Rescue?" *Racing News Online,* Oct. 23, 2002, www.racingnewsonline.com/story.do?id=55630; "Sherman-Williams Brings Colorful New Outlook to Partnership with Champ Car World Series and Champ Car Atlantic Series," Champ Car World Series, press release, Nov. 2, 2005,

www.champcarworldseries.com/News/Article.asp?ID=9814; "State of the Series: Steve Johnson," Champ Car World Series, Sept. 20, 2005, www.champcarworldseries.com/News/ Article.asp?ID=9665; Bob Zeller, "CART vs. IRL: Who Won the War?" *Car and Driver Online*, Feb. 2004, www.caranddriver .com/article.asp ?section_id=4&article_id=7719&page _numbers=1. Don Roy, Middle Tennessee State University, assisted in the preparation of this case.

Chapter 2

1. Adapted from: Lisa D'Innocenzo (2005), "Culture Club," *Strategy*, April, pp. 9–13.
2. O. C. Ferrell and Michael Hartline, *Marketing Strategy* (Mason, OH: South-Western, 2005), p. 10.
3. Christian Homburg, Karley Krohmer, and John P. Workman, Jr., "A Strategy Implementation Perspective of Market Orientation," *Journal of Business Research*, 57 (2004): 1331–1340.
4. Ferrell and Hartline, *Marketing Strategy*.
5. Abraham Lustgarten, "iPod," in "Breakaway Brands," *Fortune*, Oct. 31, 2005, pp. 154–156.
6. J. Chris White, P. Rajan Varadarajan, and Peter A. Dacin, "Market Situation Interpretation and Response: The Role of Cognitive Style, Organizational Culture, and Information Use," *Journal of Marketing*, July 2003, pp. 63–79.
7. Ferrell and Hartline, *Marketing Strategy*, p. 51.
8. Graham J. Hooley, Gordon E. Greenley, John W. Cadogan, and John Fahy, "The Performance Impact of Marketing Resources," *Journal of Business Research*, 58 (2005): 18–27.
9. Derek F. Abell, "Strategic Windows," *Journal of Marketing*, July 1978, p. 21.
10. Michael Krauss, "EBay 'Bids' on Small-Biz Firms to Sustain Growth," *Marketing News*, Dec. 8, 2003, p. 6.
11. Catherine Yang with Jay Green, "You've Got Mail—But Not Enough Ads," *Business Week*, Oct. 25, 2004, p. 48.
12. Ibid.
13. Michael McCarthy, "CD Prices Hit Sour Note with Retail Buyers," *USA Today*, Dec. 2003, pp. 1B, 2B.
14. Ibid.
15. Douglas Bowman and Hubert Gatignon, "Determinants of Competitor Response Time to a New Product Introduction," *Journal of Marketing Research*, Feb. 1995, pp. 42–53.
16. "Our Mission," *Celestial Seasonings*, www.celestialseasonings .com/whoweare/corporatehistory/mission.php (accessed Apr. 13, 2006).
17. Cláudia Simões, Sally Dibb, and Raymond P. Fisk, "Managing Corporate Identity," *Journal of the Academy of Marketing Science*, 33 (Apr. 2005):154–168.
18. Peter Asmus, "17th Annual Business Ethics Awards," *Business Ethics*, Fall 2005, pp. 18–20.
19. Laurence G. Weinzimmer, Edward U. Bond III, Mark B. Houston, and Paul C. Nystrom, "Relating Marketing Expertise on the Top Management Team and Strategic Market Aggressiveness to Financial Performance and Shareholder Value," *Journal of Strategic Marketing*, June 2003, pp. 133–159.
20. "Sara Lee Sells Coffee Business," *The Wall Street Journal*, Oct. 26, 2005, http://online.wsj.com/public/us.
21. Thomas Ritter and Hans Georg Gemünden, "The Impact of a Company's Business Strategy on Its Technological Competence, Network Competence and Innovation Success," *Journal of Business Research*, 57 (2004): 548–556.
22. Jean L. Johnson, Ruby Pui-Wan Lee, Amit Saini, and Bianca Grohmann, "Market-Focused Flexibility: Conceptual Advances and an Integrative Model," *Journal of the Academy of Marketing Science*, 31, no. 1 (2003):74–89.
23. Information Resouces, Inc., reported in Stephanie Thompson,

"Nestlé, Hershey Figure Sticks Will Be Big Sellers," *Advertising Age*, Oct. 3, 2005, p. 3.
24. Robert D. Buzzell, "The PIMS Program of Strategy Research: A Retrospective Appraisal," *Journal of Business Research*, 57 (2004): 478–483.
25. George S. Day, "Diagnosing the Product Portfolio," *Journal of Marketing*, Apr. 1977, pp. 30–31.
26. Isabelle Maignan, O. C. Ferrell, and Linda Ferrell, "A Stakeholder Model for Implementing Social Responsibility in Marketing," *European Journal of Marketing*, 39 (Sept./Oct. 2005): 956–977.
27. Coca-Cola 2004 Annual Report, www2.coca-cola.com/ investors/annualandotherreports/2004/pdf/Coca-Cola_10-K_ Item_01.pdf (accessed Apr. 13, 2006).
28. Kate MacCarthur, "Franchisees Turn on Crispin's King," *Advertising Age*, Oct. 24, 2005, pp. 1, 42
29. M. Fry and Michael J. Polonsky, "Examining the Unintended Consequences of Marketing," *Journal of Business Research*, 57 (2005):1303–1306.
30. Maignan, Ferrell, and Ferrell, "A Stakeholder Model for Implementing Social Responsibility in Marketing."
31. G. Tomas, M. Hult, David W. Cravens, and Jagdish Sheth, "Competitive Advantage in the Global Marketplace: A Focus on Marketing Strategy," *Journal of Business Research*, Jan. 2001, pp. 1–3.
32. Kwaku Atuahene-Gima and Janet Y. Murray, "Antecedents and Outcomes of Marketing Strategy Comprehensiveness," *Journal of Marketing*, 68 (Oct. 2004): 33–46.
33. Nancy Einhart, "How the New T-Bird Went Off Course," *Business 2.0*, Nov. 2003, pp. 74–76.
34. Christian Homburg, John P. Workman, and Ove Jensen, "Fundamental Changes in Marketing Organization: The Movement Toward a Customer-Focused Organizational Structure," *Journal of the Academy of Marketing Science*, Fall 2000, pp. 459–478.
35. Weiss, "To Be About to Be," pp. 28–36.
36. Rajdeep Grewal and Patriya Tansuhaj, "The Chain of Effects from Brand Trust and Brand Affect to Brand Performance: The Role of Brand Loyalty," *Journal of Marketing*, Apr. 2001, pp. 67–80.
37. Steve Watkins, "Marketing Basics: The Four P's Are as Relevant Today as Ever," *Investor's Business Daily*, Feb. 4, 2002, p. A1.
38. Bent Dreyer and Kjell Grønhaug, "Uncertainty, Flexibility, and Sustained Competitive Advantage," *Journal of Business Research* 57 (2004): 484–494.
39. Hemant C. Sashittat and Avan R. Jassawalla, "Marketing Implementation in Smaller Organizations: Definition, Framework, and Propositional Inventory," *Journal of the Academy of Marketing Science*, Winter 2001, pp. 50–69.
40. Ferrell and Hartline, *Marketing Strategy*, p. 257.
41. Weiss, "To Be About to Be," pp. 28–36.
42. Adapted from Nigel F. Piercy, *Market-Led Change* (Newton, MA: Butterworth, Heinemann, 1992), pp. 374–385.
43. Ian N. Lings, "Internal Market Orientation: Construct and Consequences," *Journal of Business Research*, 57 (2004): 405–413.
44. Sybil F. Stershic, "Internal Marketing Campaign Reinforces Service Goals," *Marketing News*, July 31, 1998, p. 11.
45. Kee-hung Lee and T. C. Edwin Cheng, "Effects of Quality Management and Marketing on Organizational Performance," *Journal of Business Research*, 58 (2005): 446–456; Wuthichai Sittimalakorn and Susan Hart, "Market Orientation Versus Quality Orientation: Sources of Superior Business Performance," *Journal of Strategic Marketing*, 12 (Dec. 2004): 243–253.
46. Philip B. Crosby, Quality Is Free: *The Art of Making Quality Certain* (New York: McGraw-Hill, 1979), pp. 9–10.

47. Piercy, *Market-Led Change.*
48. Douglas W. Vorhies and Neil A. Morgan, "Benchmarketing Marketing Capabilities for Sustainable Competitive Advantage," *Journal of Marketing,* 69 (Jan. 2005): 80–94.
49. Kenneth W. Thomas and Betty A. Velthouse, "Cognitive Elements of Empowerment: An 'Interpretive' Model of Intrinsic Task Motivation," *Academy of Management Review,* Oct. 1990, pp. 666–681.
50. Ferrell and Hartline, *Marketing Strategy.*
51. Rohit Deshpande and Frederick E. Webster, Jr., "Organizational Culture and Marketing: Defining the Research Agenda," *Journal of Marketing,* Jan. 1989, pp. 3–15.
52. Kathleen Cholewka, "CRM: Lose the Hype and Strategize," *Sales & Marketing Management,* June 2001, pp. 27–28.
53. Eric M. Olson, Stanley F. Slater, and G. Tomas Hult, "The Performance Implications of Fit Among Business Strategy, Marketing Organization Structure, and Strategic Behavior," *Journal of Marketing,* 69 (July 2005): 49–65.
54. Bernard J. Jaworski, "Toward a Theory of Marketing Control: Environmental Context, Control Types, and Consequences," *Journal of Marketing,* July 1988, pp. 23–39.
55. James R. Healey, "Hot, Fun, and Even Functional," *USA Today,* Nov. 26, 2004, p. 10D.
56. "Lincoln Continues to Break Records for Customer Satisfaction with Dealer Service," J. D. Powers & Associates, press release, July 20, 2005, www.jdpa.com/news/releases/pressrelease .asp?ID=2005092.
57. Brian Steinberg and Ann Zimmerman, "Lesson Learned, Wal-Mart Touts Lower Prices," *The Wall Street Journal,* Dec. 3, 2004, http://online.wsj.com/public/us.
58. Sources: "Greg Brenneman, Chairman and Chief Executive Officer, Burger King Corporation," Burger King Corporation, www.bk.com/CompanyInfo/bk_corporation/executive_team/ brenneman.aspx (accessed Jan. 31, 2006); "Global Fact Sheet," Burger King, www.bk.com/CompanyInfo/bk_corporation/ fact_sheets/global_facts.aspx (accessed Apr. 13, 2006); Bruce Horovitz, "CEO Turns the Flame Up," USA Today, May 23, 2005, p. 3B; Kate MacArthur, "Franchisees Turn on Crispin's King," *Advertising Age,* Oct. 24, 2005, pp. 1, 42; Elaine Walker, "Whopper of a Recovery?" *The Kansas City Star,* Sept. 24, 2005, pp. C-1, C-2.
59. Sources: Kate MacArthur, "Visa, FedEx Pony Up For Future Fund," *Advertising Age,* Nov. 14, 2005, pp. 1, 37; Ellen Florian Kratz, "For FedEx, It Was Time to Deliver," *Fortune,* Oct. 3, 2005, p. 65; "Pass the Parcel," *Economist,* Feb. 11, 2006, p. 61; Robert W. Mooman, "The IT Traffic Solution," *Air Transport World,* Sep. 2005, p. 58; Patricia Sellers, "Bigger and BIGGER," *Fortune,* Sep. 5, 2005, pp. 104–107; "BW50: Delivering the Goods at FedEx," *Business Week Online,* June 13, 2005, www.businessweek.com; "DHL/Airborne Deal Could Shake Up U.S. Express Market," Logistics Management, Apr. 1, 2003, www.manufacturing.net; FedEx Corporation, 2003 Annual Report; FedEx Corporation, www.fedex.com (accessed Jan. 24, 2006); "FedEx to Buy Kinko's for $2.4B," CNN/Money, Dec. 30, 2003, http://money.cnn.com; "FedEx to Create Shanghai Hub Office," *AirWise News,* Oct. 24, 2003, http://news.airwise.com; "FedEx Ground Opens 'Super Hub,'" *Transportation & Distribution,* Nov. 2000, pp. 12–13; Kristin S. Krause, "Handling the Holiday Crush," *Traffic World,* Dec. 4, 2000, p. 33; Betsy McKay and Rick Brooks, "FedEx Will Buy Kinko's for $2.4 Billion in Cash," *The Wall Street Journal,* Dec. 30, 2003, http://online.wsj.com; Theo Mullen, "Delivery Wars Go High-Tech—FedEx Ground Sends Message with $80M Investment to Improve Package Tracking," *Internetweek,* Oct. 23, 2000, p. 18; Jayne O'Donnell, "FedEx–Postal Service Alliance Delivers Goods," *USA Today Online,* Jan. 11, 2001, www.usatoday.com/; "Post Office, FedEx to Work Together," *USA Today Online,* Jan. 10, 2001, www.usatoday.com/; Monica Roman, "FedEx Hitches Up a New Trucker," *Business Week,* Nov. 27, 2000, p. 66; Marc L. Songini, "FedEx Expects CRM System to Deliver," *Computerworld,* Nov. 6, 2000, p. 10; "UPS Wants Fed Probe into DHL–Airborne Deal," *San Francisco Business Times,* Mar. 27, 2003, http://www.bizjournals.com.

Chapter 3

1. Laura Bogomolny (2005), "Battle of the Brands: Air Canada vs. WestJet," *Canadian Business* (June), http://www .canadianbusiness.com/companies/article.jsp?content=200 . . . , Extracted November 14, 2006; Matthew McCleam (2005), "Spy vs. Spy," Canadian Business, (January), http://www .canadianbusiness.com/companies/article.jsp?content+200 . . . , Extracted November, 14, 2006.
2. Gina Chon, "Sales of SUVs Fall Sharply," *The Wall Street Journal,* Oct. 4, 2005, p. D1, http://online.wsj.com/public/us
3. "U.S. Soft Drink Sales Flat in 2003, "Beverage Marketing Corporation Reports," Beverage Marketing Corporation, press release, Mar. 4, 2004, www.beveragemarketing.com/news2oo.htm
4. O. C. Ferrell and Michael Hartline, *Marketing Strategy* (Mason, OH: South-Western, 2005), p. 58.
5. Ibid.
6. Rodolfo Vazquez, Maria Leticia Santos, and Luis Ignacio Álvarez, "Market Orientation, Innovation and Competitive Strategies in Industrial Firms," *Journal of Strategic Marketing,* Mar. 2001, pp. 69–90.
7. Eberhard Stickel, "Uncertainty Reduction in a Competitive Environment," *Journal of Business Research,* 51, no. 3 (2001): 169–177.
8. EContent, Nov. 2003, p. 23.
9. Source: Anon. (2006), "Income of Individuals," The Daily. Tues, May 23, http://www.statcan.ca/Daily/English/060523/ d060523c.htm, Extracted November 16, 2006; 2000 Household Income, Statistics Canada, http://www12.statcan.ca/english/ census01/products/standard/theme., Extracted November 21, 2006.
10. Lorrie Grant, "Scrimping to Splurge," *USA Today,* Jan. 28, 2005, p. 1B.
11. Spano, Sebastian (2006) "Political Finnacing and Campaign Regulations," Library of Parliament, (February 23), http://www.parl .gc.ca/information/library/PRBpubs/prb0579-e.htm, Extracted: November, 17, 2006.
12. Hall Dickler Kent Goldstein & Wood LLC, "Controversy over Food Advertising to Children," *AdLaw,* Oct. 20, 2003.
13. "About the CRTC," http://www.crtc.gc.ca/eng/about.htm, Extracted November 17, 2006.
14. Sarah Ellison, "Why Kraft Decided to Ban Some Food Ads to Children," *The Wall Street Journal,* Oct. 31, 2005, p. A1, http://online.wsj.com/public/us.
15. Deirdre McMurdy, "Building the New Economy: The Push Is On to Position Business for Changing Times," Maclean's, June 27, 1994, p. 28.
16. Chris Woodward, "Some Offices Opt for Cellphones Only," *USA Today,* Jan. 25, 2005, p. B1.
17. Debbie McAlister, Linda Ferrell, and O. C. Ferrell, *Business and Society* (Boston: Houghton Mifflin, 2005), p. 85.
18. "E-commerce: Shopping on the Internet," The Daily, Statistics Canada, November 1, 2006.
19. McAlister, Ferrell, and Ferrell, *Business and Society* p. 85.
20. Ibid.
21. Vladimir Zwass, "Electronic Commerce: Structures and

Issues," *International Journal of Electronic Commerce,* Fall 2000, pp. 3–23.

22. "Peace Corp. Seeks to Launch First PEO Business-to-Business Online Marketplace," *Business Wire,* July 31, 2003, p. 2086.

23. Source: "The Demographic Time Bomb: Mitigating the Effects of Demographic Change in Canada," Report of the Senate Committee on Banking, Trade, and Commerce, June 2006, http://parl.gc.ca/39/1/parlbus.commbus/senate/com-e-bank-e/ rep . . . , Extracted November 18, 2006.

24. Source: "Study: Mature Singles Who Don't Expect to Marry," The Daily, Statistics Canada, June 2, 2005, http://statcan.ca/ Daily/English/050607/d050607a.htm, Extracted November 19, 2006.

25. Source: http://www.lavalife.com, Accessed November 19, 2006.

26. "Markets Seek Ways to Lure Ethnic Consumers: Canadian Advertising Foundation Study," *Canadian Press Newswire,* September 15, 1995.

27. Ashwin W. Joshi (2005), "The Visible Majority," Marketing Magazine, August 29, http://marketingmag.ca/magazine/current/ multicultural/article.js . . . , Accessed November 19, 2006.

28. William H. Redmond, "Intrusive Promotion as Market Failure: How Should Society Impact Marketing?" *Journal of Macromarketing* 25 (June 2005): 12–21.

29. Sources: Jennifer Soong, "The Sunshine Boys," *Worthwhile,* Premiere Issue 2004, p. 43; Thomas J. Ryan, "Lust for Life," SBG, Jan. 2006, p. 30; Jill Rose, "The Right Thing," *American Executive,* Aug. 2005; Rachel Bowie, "Good Feelings," *Boston Common,* Winter 2006, p. 62; Melonee McKinney Hurt, "Life Is good.," *American Profile,* Oct.–Nov. 2005; Life is good., www.lifeisgood.com (accessed Apr. 13, 2006); Susan Reimer, "Brothers Spread Positive T-shirt Vibes," *Mail Tribune,* Sept. 1, 2005, Local Section; Brooke Donald, "Life Is (Very) Good for Brothers Selling T-Shirts One at a Time," *USA Today,* July 9, 2005; Christopher O'Carroll, "It's Hip to Be Happy," *UMass Magazine,* Fall 2004, www.umassmag.com.

30. "Multi-stakeholder Task Force on Trans Fat," Health Canada, http://www.hc-sc.gc.ca/ahc-asc/public-consult/sonsultations/ col/trans-f . . . , Accessed November 19, 2006; and "Transforming the Food Supply," Final Report of the Trans Fat Task Force, http://www.hc.sc.gc.ca/fn-an/nutrition/gras-trans/tf -ge/tf-gt_ rep-r . . . , Accessed November 19, 2006.

31. Sources: "Frito-Lay Introduces New Lineup of Low-Carb Chips," *Long Island Business News,* Jan. 16, 2004; Theresa Howard, "Frito-Lay's New Stax to Take a Stand," *USA Today,* Aug. 15, 2003, p. 12B; Debbie Howell, "Good-for You Munchies Best News in Snacks," *DSN Retailing Today,* Jan. 24, 2005, p. F6; Sonia Reyes, "Strategy: R-R-R-Ruffles Hopes Its Past Gives Future a Blast," *Brandweek,* June 23, 2003; "Snacking Now Made Easier with Frito-Lay's New Smart Snack Ribbon Label," PR Newswire, Aug. 5, 2003, www.prnewswire.com; Chad Terhune, "Frito-Lay to Refocus Marketing," *The Wall Street Journal,* Feb. 25, 2005, p. B3; Chad Terhune, "Pepsi Outlines Ad Campaign for Healthy Food," *The Wall Street Journal,* Oct. 15, 2005, p. A4; Stephanie Thompson, "Frito-Lay Defends Its Snack Turf Against all Comers, Salty or Sweet," *Advertising Age,* May 16, 2005, p. 16; Suzanne Vranica, "PepsiCo Sets Health-Snack Effort," *The Wall Street Journal,* Sept. 23, 2003, p. B6; Andrea K. Walker, "Potato-Chip Maker Now Targets 'Bad Fat,'" *FSView and Florida Flambeau,* Oct. 2, 2003; Judith Weinraub, "Getting the Fat Out," *Washington Post,* Nov. 12, 2003, p. F1.

Chapter 4

1. Sources: Sarah Ellison, "Why Kraft Decided to Ban Some Food Ads to Children," *The Wall Street Journal,* Oct. 31, 2005, p. A1, http://online.wsj.com/public/us; Sarah Ellison and Janet Adamy, "Panel Faults Food Packaging for Kid Obesity," *The Wall Street*

Journal, Dec. 7, 2005, http://online.wsj.com/public/us; "Kaiser Family Foundation Releases New Report on Role of Media in Childhood Obesity," Kaiser Family Foundation, press release, Feb. 24, 2004, www.kff.org/entmedia/entmedia 022404nr.cfm; "Supersizing Europeans," in William M. Pride and O. C. Ferrell, *Foundations of Marketing,* 2nd ed. (Boston: Houghton Mifflin, 2006), p. 122; Melanie Warner, "Under Pressure, Food Producers Shift to Healthier Products," *The New York Times,* Dec. 16, 2005, www.nytimes.com.

2. Isabelle Maignan and O. C. Ferrell, "Corporate Social Responsibility and Marketing: An Integrative Framework," *Journal of the Academy of Marketing Science* 32 (Jan. 2004): 3–19.

3. Isabelle Maignan and O. C. Ferrell, "Corporate Social Responsibility and Marketing: An Integrative Framework," *Journal of the Academy of Marketing Science* 32 (Jan. 2004): 3-19.

4. As adapted from Shoppers Drug Mart website, http://www .shoppersdrugmart.ca/english/corporate_information/ab. Extracted Nov. 11, 2006.

5. Isabelle Maignan and O. C. Ferrell, "Antecedents and Benefits of Corporate Citizenship: An Investigation of French Businesses," *Journal of Business Research* 51, no. 1 (2001): 37–51.

6. Debbie McAlister, Linda Ferrell, and O. C. Ferrell, *Business and Society: A Strategic Approach to Social Responsibility* (Boston: Houghton Mifflin, 2005), pp. 38–40.

7. O. C. Ferrell, "Business Ethics and Customer Stakeholders," *Academy of Management Executive* 18 (May 2004): 126–129.

8. "Corporate Citizenship Report 2003–2004," Ford Motor Company, www.ford.com/en/company/about/corporateCitizenship/ report/ (accessed Apr. 13, 2006).

9. Archie Carroll, "The Pyramid of Corporate Social Responsibility: Toward the Moral Management of Organizational Stakeholders," *Business Horizons,* July/Aug. 1991, p. 42.

10. Adapted from "Fraud cost half a billion a year, new study says," Press Release, Insurance-Canada.ca, www.insurance-canada.ca/ claims/canada/CCAIF20010.php, Extracted November 9, 2006.

11. Jessica Stannard-Friel, "Corporate Giving Responds to Hurricane Katrina," on Philanthropy, Aug. 30, 2005, www .onphilanthropy.com/onthescene/os2005-08-30.html.

12. Barbara A. Lafferty, Ronald E. Goldsmith, and G. Tomas M. Hult, "The Impact of the Alliance on the Partners: A Look at Cause-Brand Alliances," *Psychology & Marketing* 21, no. 7 (July 2004): 509-531, via ABI/INFORM Global.

13. As reported by MADD Canada at www.madd.ca/english/ donationg/causerelated.html. Extracted November 11, 2006.

14. McAlister, Ferrell, and Ferrell, *Business and Society,* p. 335.

15. Steve Quinn, "Wal-Mart Green with Energy," *The* [Fort Collins] *Coloradoan,* July 24, 2005, p. E1.

16. Keith Naughton, with Patrick Crowley, "Green," *Newsweek,* Nov. 22, 2004, pp. 50–56.

17. Peter Asmus, "17th Annual Business Ethics Awards," *Business Ethics,* Fall 2005, pp. 18–20.

18. Isabelle Maignan and Debbie Thorne McAlister, "Socially Responsible Organizational Buying: How Can Stakeholders Dictate Purchasing Policies?" *Journal of Macromarketing* 23 (Dec. 2003): 78–89.

19. Stephanie Thompson, "Aveda Pressures Mags to Go Green," *Advertising Age,* Nov. 29, 2004, p. 19.

20. "Certification," Home Depot, www.homedepot.com/HDUS/ EN_US/corporate/corp_respon/certification.shtml (accessed Jan. 31, 2006).

21. "Better Banana Project," Chiquita, www.chiquita.com/chiquita/ discover/owbetter.asp (accessed Apr. 13, 2006).

22. Paul Hawken and William McDonough, "Seven Steps to Doing Good Business," *Inc.,* Nov. 1993, pp. 79–90.

23. Jill Gabrielle Klein, N. Craig Smith, and Andrew John, "Why We Boycott: Consumer Motivations for Boycott Participation," *Journal of Marketing* 68 (July 2004): 92–109.

24. Christian Homburg and Andreas Fürst, "How Organizational Complaint Handling Drives Customer Loyalty: An Analysis of the Mechanistic and the Organic Approach," *Journal of Marketing* 69 (July 2005): 95–114..

25. Roger Bougie, Rik Pieters, and Marcel Zeelenberg, "Angry Customers Don't Come Back, They Get Back: The Experience and Behavioral Implications of Anger and Dissatisfaction in Services," *Journal of the Academy of Marketing Science* 31, no. 4 (2003): 377–393.

26. Adapted from "For good CAUSE—1999 Socially Responsible Franchisee of the Year Awards," *Entrepreneur,* July, 1999, by Karen E. Spaeder.

27. Thomas L. Carson, "Self-Interest and Business Ethics: Some Lessons of the Recent Corporate Scandals," *Journal of Business Ethics,* April 2003, pp. 389–394.

28. "Multi-Year Study Finds 21% Increase in Americans Who Say Corporate Support of Social Issues Is Important in Building Trust," Cone, Inc., press release, Dec. 8, 2004, www.coneinc.com/Pages/pr_30.html.

29. Mark Lisheron, "Texas Sues Sony Over Hidden Software That Can Hurt PCs," *The Austin American-Statesman,* Nov. 22, 2005, www.statesman.com; Ethan Smith, "Sony BMG Pulls Millions of CDs Amid Antipiracy-Software Flap," *The Wall Street Journal,* Nov. 17, 2005, p. D5, http://online.wsj.com/public/us.

30. Tim Barnett and Sean Valentine, "Issue Contingencies and Marketers' Recognition of Ethical Issues, Ethical Judgments and Behavioral Intentions," *Journal of Business Research* 57 (2004): 338–346.

31. Betsy Querna, "The Big Pill Pitch," *U.S. News & World Report,* June 6, 2005, pp. 52–53.

32. David E. Sprott, Kenneth C. Mannign, and Anthony D. Miyazaki, "Grocery Price Setting and Quantity Surcharges," *Journal of Marketing,* July 2003, pp. 34–46.

33. Stephen Taub, "SEC Probing Harley Statements," CFO.com, July 14, 2005, www.cfo.com/article.cfm/4173321/c_4173841?f=archives&origin=archive.

34. Michael Josephson, "2004 Report Card: The Ethics of American Youth," Josephson Institute of Ethics, press release, www.josephsoninstitute.org/Survey2004/2004reportcard_press release.htm.

35. Peggy H. Cunningham and O. C. Ferrell, "The Influence of Role Stress on Unethical Behavior by Personnel Involved in the Marketing Research Process" (working paper, Queens University, Ontario, 2004), p. 35.

36. Joseph W. Weiss, *Business Ethics: A Managerial, Stakeholder Approach* (Belmont, CA: Wadsworth, 1994), p. 13.

37. O. C. Ferrell, Larry G. Gresham, and John Fraedrich, "A Synthesis of Ethical Decision Models for Marketing," *Journal of Macromarketing,* Fall 1989, pp. 58–59.

38. Ethics Resource Center, "The Ethics Resource Center's 2005 *National Business Ethics Survey: How Employees View Ethics in Their Organizations,* 1994–2005" (Washington, DC: Ethics Resource Center, 2005), p. 16.

39. Barry J. Babin, James S. Boles, and Donald P. Robin, "Representing the Perceived Ethical Work Climate Among Marketing Employees," *Journal of the Academy of Marketing Science* 28, no. 3 (2000): 345–358.

40. Ferrell, Gresham, and Fraedrich, "A Synthesis of Ethical Decision Models for Marketing."

41. Lawrence B. Chonko and Shelby D. Hunt, "Ethics and Marketing Management: A Retrospective and Prospective Commentary," *Journal of Business Research* 50, no. 3 (2000): 235–244.

42. Linda K. Trevino and Stuart Youngblood, "Bad Apples in Bad Barrels: A Causal Analysis of Ethical Decision Making Behavior," *Journal of Applied Psychology* 75, no. 4 (1990): 378–385.

43. "Survey Documents State of Ethics in the Workplace," Ethics Resource Center, press release, Oct. 12, 2005, www.ethics.org/nbes/nbes2005/release.html.

44. Ethics Resource Center, "The Ethics Resource Center's 2005 *National Business Ethics Survey,*" p. 29.

45. Gene R. Laczniak and Patrick E. Murphy, *Ethical Marketing Decisions: The Higher Road* (Boston: Allyn & Bacon, 1993), p. 14.

46. James C. Hyatt, "Birth of the Ethics Industry," *Business Ethics,* Summer 2005, pp. 20–26.

47. Adapted from Office of the Ethics Commissioner, Mandate, Role, and Responsibilities, http://www.parl.gc.ca/oec/en/office_ethics_commissioner/mandate, Extracted November 13, 2006.

48. Hyatt, "Birth of the Ethics Industry"; Del Jones, "Law Rings up Growth in Worker Hotline Industry," *USA Today,* May 26, 2003, www.usatoday.com.

49. Jeff Leeds, "2 Are Fired at Clear Channel After a Misconduct Inquiry," *The New York Times,* Oct. 12, 2005, www.nytimes.com.

50. Sir Adrian Cadbury, "Ethical Managers Make Their Own Rules," *Harvard Business Review,* Sept./Oct. 1987, p. 33.

51. Caren Epstein, "Food Companies Marketing Products to People Living with Chronic Disease," *The* [Fort Colllins] *Coloradoan,* Nov. 13, 2005, p. E4.

52. Don Tapscott and David Ticoll, "The Naked Corporation," *The Wall Street Journal,* Oct. 14, 2003, http://online.wsj.com/public/us.

53. Ferrell, Fraedrich, and Ferrell, *Business Ethics,* pp. 27–30.

54. Isabelle Maignan, O. C. Ferrell, and Linda Ferrell, "A Stakeholder Model for Implementing Social Responsibility in Marketing," *European Journal of Marketing* 39 (Sept./Oct. 2005): 956–977.

55. "Multi-Year Study Finds 21% Increase in Americans Who Say Corporate Support of Social Issues Is Important in Building Trust."

56. Maignan, Ferrell, and Ferrell, "A Stakeholder Model for Implementing Social Responsibility in Marketing."

57. Sources: Ford Motor Company, www.ford.com (accessed Apr. 13, 2006); John S. McClenahen, "Ford's Formidable Challenge," *Industry Week,* Feb. 1, 2003, www.industryweek.com/current Articles/asp/articles.asp?ArticleID=1379; Joann Muller, "Lean Green Machine," *Forbes,* Feb. 3, 2003, www.forbes.com/ global/2003/0203023_print.html; "Our Route to Sustainability: Ford Sustainability Report," 2004/2005, Ford Motor Company, www.ford.com (accessed Apr. 13, 2006); Chuck Salter, "Ford's Escape Route," *Fast Company,* Oct. 2004, pp. 106+; Jason Sapsford, Phred Dvorak, and Jeffrey McCracken, "Ford Plans to Speed Up Production of Hybrid Vehicles," *The Wall Street Journal,* Sept. 22, 2005, p. A1, http://online.wsj.com/public/us.

Chapter 5

1. Source: Statistics Canada. (Nov. 1, 2006). *E-Commerce: Shopping on the Internet.* The Daily. Retrieved Nov.8, 2006 from http://www.statcan.ca/Daily/English/061101/d061101a.htm.

2. PR Newswire, Packaged Facts, http://biz.yahoo.com/prnews (accessed Feb. 20, 2006); "Broadband Biggest Factor in Online Sales Growth," *The Retail Bulletin,* www.theretailbulletin.com (accessed Feb. 21, 2006); Juan Carlos Perez, "Online Sales in US to Grow Briskly through 2010, Study Says," ComputerWorld.com, www.computerworld.com (accessed Feb. 16, 2006); Kate Maddox, "Outsell Predicts Strong Growth in Online Marketing," BtoB, www.Btobonline.com (accessed Feb. 16, 2006).

3. Wayne D. Hoyer and Deborah J. MacInnis, *Consumer Behavior,* 3rd ed. (Boston: Houghton Mifflin, 2004), pp. 57–59.

4. "First Source for Car Shoppers in Online Households," *USA Today* Snapshot, Nov. 16, 2001, www.usatoday.com/snapshot.

5. Russell W. Belk, "Situational Variables and Consumer Behavior," *Journal of Consumer Research*, Dec. 1975, pp. 157–164.

6. "Sorry Cupid, Santa's the One Handing Out Engagement Rings This Year—and He's Buying Them Online," *PR Newswire*, Dec. 6, 2004.

7. Source: Aaker, Jennifer. (August, 1997). Dimensions of Brand Personality. Journal of Marketing Research, Vol.34. 347–356.

8. Sources for brand personalities: Karlan, D. (2007). 101 Most Influential People Who Never Lived. Retrieved August 31, 2007 from http://www.101influential.com/.; Barbara & David P. Mikkelson. (2007). Marlboro Manslaughter. Retrieved August 31, 2007 from http://www.snopes.com/radiotv/tv/marlboro.asp.; National Public Radio. (October 21, 2002). The Marlboro Man. Retrieved August 31, 2007 from http://www.npr.org/programs/morning/features/patc/marlboroman/.

9. Source: Clark, Andrew, Deziel, Shanda, McClelland, Susan and Oh, Susan. (March 22, 1999). Gen Y has the cash, the cool—and a burgeoning consumer culture. Macleans, 112(12).

10. Source: Schewem Charles D. (May-June 1991). Strategically positioning your way into the aging marketplace. Business Horizons, May-June 1991. Retrieved Nov. 8, 2006 from http://findarticles.com/p/articles/mi_m1038/is_n3_v34/ai_10816677/print.

11. Source for information about sizing of women's clothing and appealing to girls: Jackson, Kate M. (May 5, 2006). 0 is the new 8: As waistlines grow, women's clothing sizes shrink incredibly. *The Boston Globe*. Retrieved August 31, 2007 from http://www.boston.com/news/nation/articles/2006/05/05/0_is_the_new_8/.

12. "Heinz Unveils New Blue Ketchup," *USA Today*, Apr. 7, 2003, www.usatoday.com/money/industries/food/2003-04-07-blue-ketchup_x.htm; Casey Keller, "So Far, It's Easy Being Green," *The New York Times*, Oct. 22, 2000, sec. 3, p. 2.

13. Maria Mooshil, "More Retailers Take Steps to Capture Women's Consumer Allegiance," *Chicago Tribune*, Jun 15, 2005, http://web.lexis-nexis.com.

14. Eric Wilson, "Her Name Already in Lights, A Star Seeks Fashion Credibility," *New York Times*, Feb. 11, 2005, Fashion, p. 11.

15. Baxter, David. (June 3, 2002). From dim sum to doughnuts: People in today's global village are not defined by their ethnic origins any more than by their age or generation. *Marketing Magazine*, 107(22), p.16.; Salloum, Habeeb. (March, 1997). Contemporary Review, 270(1574).; Gregg, Alan. (April 1, 2006). Identity Crisis. *Walrus Magazine*. Retreived October 23, 2006 from http://allangregg.com/?p=43#more-43.; Minogue, Sarah. (September 22, 2006). Reaching new Canadians: Multicultural experts offer their best practice advice to niche marketers. *Strategy Magazine*. Retrieved November 4, 2006 from http://www.strategymag.com/articles/magazine/20030922/panel.html?print=yes; Siu, Bobby. (September 30, 1996). Ethnic marketing: Blanket approach won't work in ethnic marketing. *Strategy Magazine*. Retrieved November 8, 2006 from http://www.strategymag.com/articles/magazine/19960930/12628.html?print-yes.; Pitt. Andeen. (September 22, 2003). Multicultural is mainstream—but rare in ads. *Strategy Magazine*. Retrieved November 9, 2006 from http://www.strategymag.com/articles/magazine/20030922/pitt.html?print=yes.

16. See Sui, Bobby. (April 14, 1997). Ethnic marketing: make sure you're not thinking in stereotypes. *Strategy Magazine*. Retrieved November 8, 2006 from http://www.strategymag.com/articles/magazine/19970414/13372.html?print=yes.

17. Source: Faguy, Denise. (n.d.) Inside Canada's Aftermarket. Retrieved August 30, 2007 from http://www.doityourself.com/stry/subtledifferences.

18. Sources: *Statistics Canada*. (2001). Visible minority population, by age group. 2001 Census. Retrieved November 9, 2006 from http://www.40.statcan.ca/101/cst01/demo50a.html.; *Statistics Canada*. (2001). Visible minority population, by province and territory. 2001 Census. Retrieved November 9, 2006 from http://www40.statcan.ca/101/cst01/demo52c.html.; Runstedler, Theresa. (2005). Caught between the devil and the deep white sea: Black Canada's diasporic dys-funk-tion. *Canadian Issues*, p.41.; Watts, Eric King and Orbe, Mark P. (2002). The spectacular consumption of "true" African American culture: "Whassup" with the Budweiser guys? *Critical Studies in Mass Communication*, 19(1), p.1–20;Okalow, Samson,. (July 28, 2003). Holla! Exploiting the urban boom. *Strategy Magazine*. Retrieved November 8, 2006 from http://www.strategymag.com/articles/magazine/20030728/urban.html?print=yes; Siu, Bobby. (April 14, 1997). Ethic marketing: Make sure you're not thinking in stereotypes. *Strategy Magazine*. Retrieved November 8, 2006 from http://www.strategymag.com/articles/magazine/19970414/13372html?print=yes; Jones, Vernon Clement. (February, 2001). Not black like me. *The Globe and Mail*. http://www.globeandmail.com.; The Black Cultural Centre of Nova Scotia. (n.d.). The History of Slavery. Retrieved November 9, 2006 from http://www.bccns.com/history_slavery.html.; New Dawn: *The Journal of Black Canadian Studies*. http://aries.oise.utoronto.ca/dawn/journal; Barrington, Walker. (2006). Marginality, interdisciplinarity and Black Canadian history. New Dawn: *The Journal of Black Canadian Studies*. 1(1). Retrieved from http://aries.oise.utoronto.ca/dawn/journal; Mackay, Maria. (August 13, 2005). New documentary charts story of churches in Canada's black communities. *Christian Today*. Retrieved November 10, 2006 from http://www.christiantoday.com/articledir/print.html?id=3687; Anonymous. (February 24, 2003). The new Canada. *Strategy Magazine*. Retrieved November 4, 2006 from ; http://www.strategymag.com/articles/magazine/20030224/newcanada.html?print=yes.

19. Sources: Benoit, Auben. (December 31, 2001. Where the solitudes meet: It's hard to tell Quebec's responses from the national results. Maclean's Retrieved Oct. 23, 2006 from http://www.macleans.ca/topstores/article/jsp?content=88861928#; Mourali, Mehdi, Laroche, Mihceal and Pons, Frank. (2005). Individualistic orientation and consumer susceptibility to interpersonal influence. The Journal of Services Marketing, 19(3), p.164.; Laroche, Michel, Teng, Lefa, Michon, Richard, and Chebat, Jean-Charles. (2005). Incorporating service quality into consumer mall shopping decision-making: A comparison between English and French Canadian consumers. *The Journal of Services Marketing*, 19(3), p.157.; Fick, Stephen and Shilts, Elizabeth. (Mar/Apr.2004). Return of the dispossessed. Canadian Geographic. 124(2).; Demont, John and Harris, Becky. (March 24, 2003). Survival of the most spirited. Maclean's. 116(2). ; Gatehouse, John. (July 7, 206). Maclean's Poll 2006: Divided we stand. Maclean's. Retrieved October 23, 2006 from http://www.macleans.ca/topstories/polls/article.jsp?content=20060701_130286_130296.

20. Sources: Normand, Josee. (Winter, 1996). Canadian Social Trends, Statistics Canada Catalogue #11-008-XPE; *Statistics Canada*. (2002). Aboriginal Identity Population, Median Age, for Canada, Provinces and Territories—20% Sample Data. 2001 Census of the Population; http www12.statcan.ca/egnlish/census01/products/highlight/Aboriginal/PrintFriendly.cfm.; Southerst, John. (September, 1992). *Canadian Business*, 65(9), p.105.; Kolybabi, Deanie. (September, 2003). *Marketing Magazine*, 108(32) p.27.; Waytuik, Judy. (May, 2000). The new native niche: The west's aboriginal market is growing and growing more wealthy. *Marketing Magazine*, 105(20), p.13.; Halloway, Andy. (April 25, 2004). Band on a run. *Canadian Business*, 77(8), p.10.; Lasarus, Eve. (May, 1999). Native hospitality: Well-heeled tourists are so keen to experience Canada's traditional native culture that aboriginal groups are having trouble keeping up with the demand. *Marketing Magazine*,

104(18), p.12–15.; Holloway, Andy. (April 11, 2004). Aboriginal Voices. *Canadian Business,* 77(7), p.49.

21. Sources: Barrington, Stephen. (January 13, 1997). *Advertising Age,* 68(2).; Minogue, Sarah. (September 22, 2006). Reaching new Canadians: Multicultural experts offer their best practice advice to niche marketers. *Strategy Magazine.* Retrieved November 4, 2006 from http://www.strategymag.com/articles/magazine/20030922/panel.html?print=yes; Siu, Bobby. (July 6, 1998). *Ethnic marketing*: Demographic wave well worth riding. *Strategy Magazine.* Retrieved November 8, 2006 from http://www.strategymag.com/articles/magazine/19980706/22100.html?print=yes.

22. Sources: *Consumer Reports,* www.consumerreports.com (accessed Jan. 26, 2006); "Winner: Consumer Reports Staff," *The Quill,* June/July 2005; Roger Parloff, "The Ionic Breeze Is No Match for Consumer Reports," *Fortune,* Dec. 13, 2004; "Holiday Shopping Made Easy: Consumer Reports ShopSmart Mobile Subscription Service Helps On-the-Go Holiday Shoppers Buy the Best Gifts at the Best Prices," *AScribe Newswire,* Dec. 12, 2005, www.highbeam.com.

23. Sources: AutoTrader.com, www.autotrader.com (accessed Apr. 13, 2006); "AutoTrader.com Continues Summer Marketing Blitz with Television Buy," *PR Newswire,* June 30, 2003, www.prnewswire.com; "AutoTrader.com Gears Up for One-of-a-Kind Interactive Online Gaming Experience," Auto-Trader, news release, Aug. 2, 2001, www.autotrader.com; "AutoTrader.com Has Highest Overall Satisfaction Among Used Vehicle Independent Sites in J. D. Power and Associates Study," AutoTrader.com, press release, Sept. 21, 2005, www.autotrader.com/about/pressroom/media/pressrelease_detail.jsp?article_id=18299; "How to Translate a TV Ad into an Online Promotion," MarketingSherpa.com, Nov. 1, 2001, www.emarketingtoher.com; Steve Jarvis, "Pedal to the Cyber-Metal," *Marketing News,* Jan. 21, 2002, pp. 6–7; Gregory Jordan, "Online, Used Car Lots That Cover the Nation," *The New York Times,* Oct. 22, 2003, p. G13; Chaz Osburn, "AutoTrader Adds Online Auction Listings," *Automotive News,* Jan. 13, 2003, p. 28.

Chapter 6

1. Sources: Stoughton, Stephanie. (February 19, 2006). "End to BlackBerry patent feud may finally be at hand." *USA Today.* Retrieved February 19, 2006 from http://www.usatoday.com/tech/news/2006-02-19-blackberry-suit_x.htm?POE=TECISVA. RIM Website: URL = http://www.blackberry.com/solutions/index.shtml. Retrieved November 14, 2006.

2. "STP: Segmentation, Targeting, Positioning," American Marketing Association, www.marketingpower.com/content1488C381S3.php (accessed Dec. 17, 2005.

3. Ibid.

4. Matt Kelly, "Consortium Finds a Happy Ending," *eWeek,* Sept. 19, 2005, pp. C1, C4.

5. Michael D. Hutt and Thomas W. Speh, *Business Marketing Management* (Mason, OH: Thomson/South-Western, 2004), p. 93.

6. Source: Industry Canada. Canadian Industry Statistics. Strategis website. http://www.strategis.gc.ca/sc_ecnmy/sio/homepage.html. Accessed November 13, 2006.

7. Source: *Statistics Canada.* Table: Employment by Enterprise Size. Retrieved November 14, 2006 from http://www40.statcan.ca/l01/cst01/labr75a.htm.

8. *Statistics Canada.* (March 27, 2006). Annual retail trade. *The Daily.* Retrieved November 14, 2006 from http://www.statcan.ca/Daily/English/060327/d060327a.htm.

9. Source: *Statistics Canada,* Table 3-1: Revenue and Expenditures—Consolidated Federal, Provincial, Territorial and Local Government Revenue and Expenditures. *Statistics Canada Catalogue #63-213.* Retrieved November 14, 2006

from http://www.statcan.ca/english/freepub/68-213-XIE/2006000/t016_en.htm?.

10. Department of Justice. Part IV: Offences Related to Competition. Illegal Trade Practices. Retrieved November 14, 2006 from http://laws.justice.gc.ca/en/C-34/229088.html.

11. Das Narayandas and V. Kasturi Rangan, "Building and Sustaining Buyer-Seller Relationships in Mature Industrial Markets," *Journal of Marketing,* July 2004, p. 63.

12. "Dell Expands Global Services Capabilities with European Command Center," *Business Wire,* Dec. 1, 2004.

13. Alex R. Zablah, Wesley J. Johnston, and Danny N. Bellenger, "Transforming Partner Relationships Through Technological Innovation," *Journal of Business & Industrial Marketing* 20 (Aug. 2005): 355–363.

14. Moin Uddin, "Loyalty Programs: The Ultimate Gift," *DSN Retailing Today,* Mar. 5, 2001, p. 12.

15. Cindy Claycomb and Gary L. Frankwick, "Dynamics of Buyers' Perceived Costs During a Relationship Development Process: An Empirical Assessment," *Journal of Business Research* 58 (2005): 1662–1671.

16. Lisa Harrington, "Right Moves," *Inbound Logistics,* Nov. 2005, pp. 37–40.

17. Leonidas C. Leonidou, "Industrial Buyers' Influence Strategies: Buying Situation Differences," *Journal of Business & Industrial Marketing* 20 (Jan. 2005): 33–42.

18. Jeffrey Burt, "Gateway Eyes Small Businesses," *eWeek,* Sept. 5, 2005, www.eweek.com.

19. Frederick E. Webster, Jr., and Yoram Wind, "A General Model for Understanding Organizational Buyer Behavior," *Marketing Management,* Winter/Spring 1996, pp. 52–57.

20. Laura Heller, *DSN Retailing Today,* Jan. 10, 2005, pp.13–14.

21. George S. Day and Katrina J. Bens, "Capitalizing on the Internet Opportunity," *Journal of Business & Industrial Marketing* 20 (2005): 160–168.

22. Steve Hamm, "GM's Way or the Highway," *Business Week,* Dec. 19, 2005, pp. 48–49.

23. Niklas Myhr and Robert E. Spekman, "Collaborative Supply-Chain Partnerships Built upon Trust and Electronically Mediated Exchange," *Journal of Business & Industrial Marketing* 20 (2005): 179–186.

24. "Development of NAICS," U.S. Census Bureau, www.census.gov/epcd/www/naicsdev.htm (accessed Apr. 13, 2006).

25. Sources: Lextant, www.lextant.com (accessed Apr. 13, 2006); Jon Udell, "Art and Science of Usability Analysis," *InfoWorld,* June 4, 2004, www.infoworld.com/article/04/06/04/23FEuser-sb_1.html?INTEGRATED%20DEVELOPMENT%20ENVIRONMENT%20-%20IDE.

Chapter 7

1. Sources: Leander Kahney, "The Cult of iPod," *Playlist,* http://playlistmag.com (accessed Jan. 18, 2006); iPod, www.apple.com/ipod.html (accessed Apr. 13, 2006); Louise Lee, "Sewing Up the iPod Market," *BusinessWeek,* Jan. 12, 2006, http:\\www.businessweek.com/technology/content/jan2006/tc20060112_086932.htm (accessed June 2, 2006); Mary Bellis, "Inventors of the Modern Computer," *About,* http://inventors.about.com/library/weekly/aa121598.htm (accessed Apr. 13, 2006); Apple Computer Inc., www.apple.com (accessed Apr. 13, 2006); Carol Glatz, "Vatican Radio Employees Present Pope with Specially Loaded iPod Nano," *The Catholic News Service,* www.catholicnews.com/data/stories/cns/0601282.htm (accessed Apr. 13, 2006).

2. U.S. Bureau of the Census, World Population Clock, www.census.gov/cgi-bin/ipc/popclockw (accessed Jan. 19, 2006); "Trade Statistics 2005," World Trade Organization, http://www.wto.org/english/res_e/statis_e/its2005_e/its2005_e.pdf (accessed Apr. 13, 2006).

3. Export.gov, www.export.gov/comm_svc/about_us/about _home.html (accessed Apr. 13, 2006).

4. The Progressive Policy Institute, www.ppionline.org (accessed Apr. 13, 2006).

5. Adapted from "About Us," Team Canada Inc., http://www.exportsource.ca/gol/exportsource/site.nsf/en/ es02470.html, Extracted November 28, 2006.

6. Adapted from "Introduction to Who We Are," Export Development Canada, http://www.edc.ca/english/whoweare.htm, Extracted November 28, 2006.

7. Gary A. Knight and S. Tamer Cavusgil, "Innovation, Organizational Capabilities, and the Born-Global Firm," *Journal of International Business Studies,* Mar. 2004, pp. 124–141.

8. Investor Relations at Amazon.com, http://amazon.com (accessed Feb. 8, 2006); *People's Daily Online,* http://english.people.com .cn/200501/27/eng20050127_172143.html (accessed Feb. 9, 2006).

9. Brian Bremner and Chester Dawson, "Can Anything Stop Toyota?" *Business Week,* Nov. 17, 2003, pp. 114–122.

10. United States of America v. Microsoft Corporation, http:// usvms.gpo.gov (accessed Mar. 30, 2006); BBC News, Microsoft Corporation v. America Online (AOL), http://news.bbc .co.uk/1/hi/business/2949778.stm (accessed Mar. 30, 2006).

11. This Is Systembolaget, www.systembolaget.se/Applikationer/ Knappar/InEnglish/Swedish_alcohol_re.htm (accessed Apr. 13, 2006).

12. George S. Yip, *Total Global Strategy* II (Upper Saddle River, NJ: Prentice Hall, 2003), Alan M. Rugman, *The Regional Multinationals: MNEs and "Global" Strategic Management* (Cambridge: Cambridge University Press, 2005).

13. Global Customers, Kimberly-Clark, www.kimberly-clark.com/ investorinfo/AnnualReport2001/kc_customers.pdf (accessed Apr. 13, 2006); Oracle—Global Customer Program, www.oracle .com/customers/gcp/index.html (accessed Apr. 13, 2006); Sony—Customer Satisfaction, www.sony.net/SonyInfo/ Environment/people/customers/satisfaction/index.html (accessed Apr. 13, 2006).

14. "Canadian International Merchandise Trade," The Daily, Statistics Canada, Friday, August 12, 2005, http://www.statcan./ ca/Daily/English/050812/d050812a.htm, Extracted December 11, 2006; and "Imports, exports and trade balances of goods on a balance-of-payments basis, by country or country grouping," *Statistics Canada,* http://www40.statcan.ca/101/cst01/ gblec02a.htm, Extracted December 11, 2006.

15. "Background Note: Canada," U.S. Department of State, Bureau of Western Hemisphere Affairs, http://www.state.gov/pa/ei/ bgn/2089.htm., Extracted November 28, 2006.

16. "Strategis—About Us," Strategis.gc.ca: Canada's Business and Consumer Site, http://strategis.ic.gc.ca/epic/internet/inabout _us-contexte.nsf/en/h_au..., Extracted November 26, 2006.

17. Bureau of Economic Analysis, U.S. Department of Commerce, www.bea.gov/bea/dn/home/gdp.htm (accessed Apr. 13, 2006).

18. Ibid., pp. 824–826, 834.

19. "Introduction to Who We Are," Export Development Canada, http://www.edc.ca/english/whoweare.htm, Extracted November 28, 2006; "Highlights," Foreign Affairs and International Trade Canada, The Canadian Trade Commissioner Service, http:// www.infoexport.gc.ca/ie-en/ MarketReportsAndServices.jsp, Extracted November 28, 2006.

20. See Code of Ethics and Standards of Practice, http://www.the-cma.org/regulatory/codeofethics.cfm.

21. Charles R. Taylor, George R. Franke, and Michael L. Maynard, "Attitudes Toward Direct Marketing and Its Regulation: A Comparison of the United States and Japan," *Journal of Public Policy & Marketing,* Fall 2000, pp. 228–237.

22. "Product Pitfalls Proliferate in Global Cultural Maze," *The Wall Street Journal,* May 14, 2001, p. B11.

23. Ibid.

24. Greg Botelho, "2003 Global Influentials: Selling to the World," CNN, Dec. 9, 2003, www.cnn.com.

25. Jeffrey G. Blodgett, Long-Chuan Lu, Gregory M. Rose, and Scott J. Vitell, "Ethical Sensitivity to Stakeholder Interests: A Cross-Cultural Comparison," *Journal of the Academy of Marketing Science* 29, no. 2 (2001): 190–202.

26. Thomas G. Brashear, Elzbieta Lepkowska-White, and Cristian Chelariu, "An Empirical Test of Antecedents and Consequences of Salesperson Job Satisfaction Among Polish Retail Salespeople," *Journal of Business Research,* Dec. 2003, pp. 971–978.

27. Dave Izraeli and Mark S. Schwartz, "What We Can Learn from the Federal Sentencing Guidelines for Organizational Ethics," *Journal of Business Ethics,* July 1998, pp. 9–10.

28. "European Consumers Getting Comfortable with Online Channel," CyberAtlas, July 6, 2001, http://cyberatlas.internet .com/big_picture/geographics/article/0.5911_794321,00.html.

29. "Population Explosion!" CLickZ Stats, Nov. 3, 2005, www.clickz.com/stats/sectors/geographics/article.php/5911 _151151.

30. Click Z Network, "Euro Teens Respond to Online Advertising," www.clickz.com/stats/sectors/demographics/article.php/ 3586966 (accessed Apr. 13, 2006).

31. Elisa Batista, "Telcos Duke It Out over Iraq," Wired News, June 27, 2003, www.wired.com/news/politics/0,1283,59410,00.html; Ben Charny, "Study: Cell Phone Use to Double," cnet, Aug. 2003, http://news.com.com/2100–1039_3–5060745.html.

32. Louisa Kasdon Sidell, "The Economics of Inclusion," *Continental,* Apr. 2001, pp. 64–67.

33. Jim Carlton, "Stymied in Alaska, Oil Producers Flock to a New Frontier," *The Wall Street Journal,* Sept. 4, 2002, pp. A1, A15.

34. "Ethics in the Global Market," Texas Instruments, www.ti.com/ corp/docs/company/citizen/ethics/market.shtml (accessed Apr. 13, 2006).

35. Business for Social Responsibility, www.bsr.org (accessed Apr. 13, 2006).

36. Geri Smith and Cristina Lindblad, "Mexico: Was NAFTA Worth It?" *Business Week,* Dec. 22, 2003, pp. 66–72.

37. U.S. Bureau of the Census, *Statistical Abstract of the United States, 2002* (Washington, DC: Government Printing Office, 2003), pp. 824–826, 834; U.S. Department of Commerce, "NAFTA: A Decade of Strengthening a Dynamic Relationship," pamphlet, 2003, available at www.ustr.gov.

38. globalEDGE, Country Insights, http://globaledge.msu.edu (accessed Feb. 26, 2006).

39. U.S. Bureau of the Census, "Canada-U.S. Trade Statistics," www.census.gov/foreign-trade/balance/c1220.html#2006 (accessed Apr. 13, 2006).

40. William C. Symonds, "Meanwhile, to the North, NAFTA Is a Smash," *Business Week,* Feb. 27, 1995, p. 66.

41. U.S. Bureau of the Census, *Statistical Abstract of the United States, 2006* (Washington, DC: Government Printing Office, 2006), www.census.gov/statab/www (accessed Apr. 13, 2006).

42. globalEDGE, Country Insights, http://globaledge.msu.edu (accessed Feb. 26, 2006).

43. "Antecedents of the FTAA Process," FTAA, www.ftaa-alca.org/ View_e.asp (accessed Apr. 8, 2004); "FTAA Fact Sheet," Market Access and Compliance, U.S. Department of Commerce, www.mac.doc.gov/ftaa2005/ftaa_fact_sheet.html (accessed Apr. 8, 2004).

44. "Archer Daniels to File NAFTA Claim Against Mexico," Inbound Logistics, Oct. 2003, p. 30.

45. "The European Union at a Glance," Europa (European Union online), http://europa.eu.int/abc/index_en.htm (accessed Mar. 28, 2006).

46. Gateway to the European Union, http://europa.eu.int/ index_en.htm (accessed Mar. 28, 2006).

47. Stanley Reed, with Ariane Sains, David Fairlamb, and Carol Matlack, "The Euro: How Damaging a Hit?" *Business Week,* Sept. 29, 2003, p. 63; "The Single Currency," CNN, July 3, 2001, www.cnn.com/SPECIALS/2000/eurounion/story/currency/.

48. "Common Market of the South (MERCOSUR): Agri-Food Regional Profile Statistical Overview," Agriculture and Agri-food Canada, Oct. 2002, http://atn-riae.agr.ca/latin/e3431.htm.

49. "About APEC," Asia-Pacific Economic Cooperation, www.apecsec.org.sg/apec/about_apec.html (accessed Apr. 13, 2006).

50. Asian Pacific Economic Cooperation, www.apec.org/content/apec/about_apec/achievements_and_benefits.html (accessed Apr. 13, 2006).

51. Smith and Lindblad, "Mexico."

52. Clay Chandler, "How to Play the China Boom," *Fortune,* Dec. 22, 2003, pp. 141–142.

53. Dexter Roberts and Frederik Balfour, "Is This Boom in Danger?" *Business Week,* Nov. 3, 2003, pp. 48–50.

54. World Trade Organization, www.wto.org/index.htm (accessed Apr. 13, 2006).

55. "What Is the WTO?" World Trade Organization, www.wto.org/ english/thewto_e/whatis_e/whatis_e.htm (accessed Apr. 13, 2006).

56. Jan Johanson and Finn Wiedersheim-Paul, "The Internationalization of the Firm," *Journal of Management Studies,* Oct. 1975, pp. 305–322; Jan Johanson and Jan-Erik Vahlne, "The Internationalization Process of the Firm—A Model of Knowledge Development and Increasing Foreign Commitments," *Journal of International Business Studies,* Spring/Summer 1977, pp. 23–32; S. Tamer Cavusgil and John R. Nevin, "Internal Determinants of Export Marketing Behavior: An Empirical Investigation," *Journal of Marketing Research,* Feb. 1981, pp. 114–119.

57. Pradeep Tyagi, "Export Behavior of Small Business Firms in Developing Economies: Evidence from the Indian Market," *Marketing Management Journal,* Fall/Winter 2000, pp. 12–20.

58. Berrin Dosoglu-Guner, "How Do Exporters and Non-Exporters View Their 'Country of Origin' Image Abroad?" *Marketing Management Journal,* Fall/Winter 2000, pp. 21–27.

59. Farok J. Contractor and Sumit K. Kundu, "Franchising Versus Company-Run Operations: Model Choice in the Global Hotel Sector," *Journal of International Marketing,* Nov. 1997, pp. 28–53.

60. Franchising, Tim Hortons, http://www.timhortons.com/en/franchise/franchise_us.html, Extracted December, 10, 2006.

61. Margreet F. Boersma, Peter J. Buckley, and Pervez N. Ghauri, "Trust in International Joint Venture Relationships," *Journal of Business Research,* Dec. 2003, pp. 1031–1042.

62. "What We're About," NUMMI, http://www.nummi.com/co_info.html (accessed Apr. 13, 2006).

63. William Q. Judge and Joel A. Ryman, "The Shared Leadership Challenge in Strategic Alliances: Lessons from the U.S. Healthcare Industry," *Academy of Management Executive,* May 2001, pp. 71–79.

64. Ibid.

65. Jan Johanson and Finn Wiedersheim-Paul, "The Internationalization of the Firm," *Journal of Management Studies,* Oct. 1975, pp. 305–322; Jan Johanson and Jan-Erik Vahlne, "The Internationalization Process of the Firm—A Model of Knowledge Development and Increasing Foreign Commitments," *Journal of International Business Studies,* Spring/Summer 1977, pp. 23–32; D. Naidler, M. Gerstein, and R. Shaw, *Organization Architecture* (San Francisco: Jossey-Bass, 1992).

66. Clipsal Export Department, www.clipsal.com.au/trade/about_us/Export (accessed Apr. 13, 2006).

67. Botelho, "Selling to the World."

68. Theodore Levitt, "The Globalization of Markets," *Harvard Business Review,* May/June 1983, p. 92.

69. Deborah Owens, Timothy Wilkinson, and Bruce Keillor, "A Comparison of Product Attributes in a Cross-Cultural/Cross-National Context," *Marketing Management Journal,* Fall/Winter 2000, pp. 1–11.

70. Anil K. Gupta and Vijay Govindarajan, "Converting Global Presence into Global Competitive Advantage," *Academy of Management Executive,* May 2001, pp. 45–58.

71. Sources: Rekha Balu, "Hop Faster, Energizer Bunny: Rayovac Batteries Roll On," *The Wall Street Journal,* June 15, 1999, p. B4; "Battle of the Blades Draws Corporate Blood," "For Mighty Gillette, These Are the Faces of War," *The New York Times,* Oct. 12, 2003, sec. 3, p. 1; The Gillette Company, www.gillette.com (accessed Apr. 13, 2006); Gillette 1999–2005 Annual Reports, http://www.pg.com/investors/annualreports.jhtml (accessed June 2, 2006); "Gillette's Edge," *Business Week,* Jan. 19, 1998, pp. 70–77; "Gillette, Schick End Legal War, but Battle in Market Rages On," Boston.com, www.boston.com/business/healthcare/articles/2006/02/17/gillette_schick_end_legal_war_but_battle_in_market_rages_on (accessed Apr. 13, 2006); "Wal-Mart Selling Its Own Brand of Alkaline Batteries," *The Wall Street Journal,* Dec. 10, 1999, pp. C4–C5. Don Roy, Middle Tennessee State University; Michael D. Hartline, Florida State University; and G. Tomas M. Hult, Michigan State University, assisted in the development of these case materials.

72. Deborah Adamson, "Trouble in Toyland," CBS MarketWatch, Mar. 8, 2000, http://cbs.marketwatch.com/; American Girl, www.americangirl.com (accessed Apr. 3, 2006); Bandai, www.bandai.com (accessed May 27, 2003); "Barbie Is Banned from Russia, Without Love," *The Observer,* Nov. 24, 2002, www.observer.co.uk/; Lisa Bannon, "Mattel Sees Untapped Market for Blocks: Little Girls," *The Wall Street Journal,* June 6, 2002, p. B-1; Lisa Bannon, "New Playbook: Taking Cues from GE, Mattel's CEO Wants Toy Maker to Grow Up," *The Wall Street Journal,* Nov. 14, 2001, p. A-1; Barbie, www.barbie.com (accessed May 27, 2003); Sherri Day, "As It Remakes Itself, Mattel Does Same for Barbie," *New York Times,* Nov. 9, 2002, p. C-1; Hot Wheels, www.hotwheels.com/ (accessed Apr. 3, 2006); Debbie Howell, "Top Brands 2002: A Longing for Labels' Returns," *DSN Retailing Today,* Oct. 28, 2002, pp. 24–27; Interbrand, "The 100 Best Brands," *Business Week Online,* Aug. 5, 2002, www.businessweek.com; "Iran Enforces Barbie Ban," Associated Press, May 23, 2002; Kate MacArthur, "Plastic Surgery: Barbie Gets Real Makeover," *Advertising Age,* Nov. 4, 2002, pp. 4, 53; Mattel, www.mattel.com (accessed Apr. 3, 2006); "Mattel Combines Girls, Boys Divisions, Cuts Management," Associated Press, Feb. 28, 2003; "Mattel, Inc. Launches Global Code of Conduct Intended to Improve Workplace, Workers' Standard of Living," Canada NewsWire, Nov. 21, 1997 (for more information on Mattel's code, contact the company at 310-252-3524); "Mattel Lands WB Master Toy Licenses," *Home Textiles Today,* Sep. 2002, p. 14; "Mattel Swings to Better Than Expected Profit," Reuters News & Financial Intelligence, Apr. 13, 2003, http:// www.reuters.com/; My Scene Barbie, www.myscene.com (accessed May 27, 2003); Christopher Palmeri, "Mattel's New Toy Story," *Business Week,* Nov. 18, 2002, pp. 72–74; J. Alex Tarquino, "Barbie & Co. Reviving Mattel," *New York Times,* March 9, 2003, Section 3, p. 7. This case was prepared by Debbie Thorne McAlister and Laura Leigh Saenz, Texas State University–San Marcos, for classroom discussion rather than to illustrate either effective or ineffective handling of an administration situation. The authors acknowledge the work of Kevin Sample on previous versions of this case.

Chapter 8

1. Sources: "Whole Baby Program Introduces New Moms to Advantages of Natural and Organic Lifestyle for Their Growing Families, Whole Foods Market and *Mothering* Magazine Partner to Launch Informational Lecture Tour About Benefits of Natural Parenting," *PR Newswire,* Aug. 11, 2005; "Whole Foods Market Survey Reveals Expectant Moms Are Hungry for Natural and Organic Nutrition Guidance, Whole Baby Lecture Series Kicks-Off in New York City Sept. 22, National Experts Promote Health to Growing Families," *PR Newswire,* Sept. 19, 2005; Whole Foods Market, www.wholefoodsmarket.com (accessed Apr. 17, 2006); Whole Baby Lecture Series, www .wholebaby lecture.com (accessed Apr. 17, 2006).

2. Mark Rechtin, "Hyundai Targets Sedan Superstars," *Automotive News,* Jan. 17, 2005, pp. 14–15.

3. Dan Higgins, "Pens, A Fountain of Inspiration," *The Times Union,* Nov. 5, 2004, p. E1.

4. Andrew Blum, with Louise Lee, "It Sure Ain't Old Navy," *Business Week,* Oct. 17, 2005, pp. 62–64.

5. "Kids and Commercialism," Center for New American Dream, http://newdream.org/kids/facts.php (accessed Apr. 17, 2006).

6. Source: *Statistics Canada* (October 26, 2006). Population by Sex and Age Group. Retrieved January 14, 2007 from http://www40.statcan.ca/l01/cst01/demo10a.htm.

7. Marvin Maties, "The New Product Game: Why Targeting Women Is Key," *Prepared Foods,* June 2003, p. 35.

8. Source: *Statistics Canada.*(Dec. 12, 2004). Census families in private households by family structure and presence of children, by province and territory (2001 Census). Retrieved January 14, 2007 from http://www40.statcan.ca/l01/cst01/famil54a.htm.

9. Source: *Statistics Canada.* (June 7, 2005). Study: Mature singles who don't expect to marry. Retrieved January 14, 2007 from http://www.statcan.ca/Daily/English/050607/d050607a.htm.

10. Source: CBC News. (June 28, 2006) Wedding bells ring only once for most Canadians: study. Retrieved July 2006 from http://www.cbc.ca/canada/story/2006/06/28/marriage-survey .html#skip300x250.

11. *Statistics Canada.* (September 28, 2002). Study: The Sandwich Generation. The Daily. Retrieved November 2006 from http://www.statcan.ca/Daily/English/040928/d040928b.htm.

12. Joseph T. Plummer, "The Concept and Application of Life Style Segmentation," *Journal of Marketing,* Jan. 1974, p. 33.

13. "Catching Up with the Next Generation: They're Not Slackers Anymore," *PR Newswire,* Oct. 26, 2004.

14. SRI Consulting Business Intelligence, www.sric-bi.com/VALS (accessed Apr. 17, 2006).

15. "Analysis: Huge Cardiovascular Market Potential in Aging Baby Boomers," *Heart Disease Weekly* via NewsRX.com and NewsRX.net, Apr. 11, 2004, p. 92.

16. Sara Schaefer Munoz, "Food Group Joins Sugar Producers Critical of Splenda," *The Wall Street Journal,* Feb. 15, 2005, p. D4; Marian Burros, "Splenda's 'Sugar' Claim Unites Odd Couple of Nutrition Wars," *The New York Times,* Feb. 15, 2005, p. A12.

17. Charles W. Chase, Jr., "Selecting the Appropriate Forecasting Method," *Journal of Business Forecasting,* Fall 1997, pp. 2, 23, 28–29.

18. "ACNielsen Market Decisions: Controlled Market Testing," ACNielsen, http://us.acnielsen.com/products/rms_amd _controlledmktest.shtml (accessed Apr. 17, 2006).

19. Sources: Jordan's Furniture, www.jordans.com (accessed Apr. 17, 2006); "Three Customer-Centric Retailers," *Chain Store Age,* Oct. 2005, pp. 26–29.

20. Sources: Kerry Capell, "IKEA: How the Swedish Retailer Became a Global Brand," *Business Week,* Nov. 14, 2005, pp. 96–106; "Facts and Figures," IKEA, www.ikea.com/ms/en_US (accessed Apr. 17, 2006); "IKEA's Growth Limited by Style Issues, Says CEO," *Nordic Business Report,* Jan. 21, 2004, www .nordicbusinessreport.com; "IKEA Sets New Heights with Cat," *Printing World,* Aug. 21, 2003, p. 3; "Stylish, Swedish, 60-ish: IKEA's a Global Phenomenon," *Western Mail,* May 20, 2003, p. 1; "Verticalnet's Supply Chain Software Upgrade, Packaging Wins Customers," *InternetWeek,* Sept. 3, 2003, www.internet world.com.

Chapter 9

1. "More Monkeyshines? Or the Real Deal?," Jac Chebatoris, *Newsweek,* Feb. 6, 2006, p. 10; "Arctic Monkeys Earn Fastest-Selling U.K. Debut," Paul Sexton, *Billboard.com,* Jan. 30, 2006, www.billboard.com/bbcom/news/article_display.jsp?vnu _content_id=1001920504; "Arctic Monkeys Make Chart History," BBC News, Jan. 29, 2006, http://news.bbc.co.uk/go/pr/fr/-/1/hi/entertainment/4660394.stm; "Arctic Monkeys," Wikipedia.

2. Vladimir Zwass, "Electronic Commerce: Structures and Issues," *International Journal of Electronic Commerce,* Fall 1996, pp. 3–23.

3. Stan Crock, "Lockheed Martin," *Business Week,* Nov. 24, 2003, p. 85.

4. Michael J. Mandel and Robert D. Hof, "Rethinking the Internet," *Business Week,* Mar. 26, 2001, pp. 116–122.

5. Fang Wu, Vijay Mahajan, and Sridhar Balasubramanian, "An Analysis of E-Business Adoption and Its Impact on Business Performance," *Journal of the Academy of Marketing Science,* Fall 2003, pp. 425–447.

6. Michael Totty, "The Researcher," *The Wall Street Journal,* July 16, 2001, p. R20.

7. David W. Stewart and Qin Zhao, "Internet Marketing, Business Models, and Public Policy," *Journal of Public Policy & Marketing,* Fall 2000, pp. 287–296.

8. Campanelli, Melissa (Sept. 26, 2006). Online Transaction Issues Can Have Negative Effect. *DM News.* http://www.dmnews.com/cms/dm-.

9. Source: Uhrback, Mark. (November, 2005). *How Business-to-Business Sales Dominate e-Commerce.* Sciene, Innovation and Electronic Information Division, Industry Canada.

10. Canada B2C E-Commerce. (December, 2006). Retrieved February 13, 2007 from http://www.emarketer.com.

11. Canada Online. (May, 2006). Retrieved February 13, 2007 from http://www.emarketer.com.

12. J.C.Williams Group (2006). Multi-Channel Shopping: Canadian Style. Retrieved February 13, 2007 from http://www.jcwg.com

13. Totty, "The Researcher."

14. Christopher Hart and Pete Blackshaw, "Internet Inferno," *Marketing Management,* Jan./Feb. 2006, p. 19.

15. John Eaton, "e-Word-of-Mouth Marketing," custom module for William M. Pride and O. C. Ferrell, *Marketing,* 14th ed. (Boston: Houghton Mifflin, 2006), www.prideferrell.com.

16. Christopher Hart and Pete Blackshaw, "Internet Inferno," *Marketing Management,* Jan./Feb. 2006, p. 21.

17. Ben Elgin, "A Search Engine for Every Subject," *Business Week,* Feb. 20, 2006, pp. 66–67.

18. Ronald L. Hess, Shankar Ganesan, and Noreen M. Klein, "Service Failure and Recovery: The Impact of Relationship Factors on Customer Satisfaction," *Journal of the Academy of Marketing Science,* Spring 2003, pp. 127–145.

19. "Turning to Tech," *Business Week,* Dec. 22, 2003, p. 83.

20. Jon Mark Giese, "Place Without Space, Identity Without Body: The Role of Cooperative Narrative in Community and Identity Formation in a Text-Based Electronic Community" (unpublished dissertation, Pennsylvania State University, 1996).

21. David Kirkpatrick and Daniel Roth, "Why There's No Escaping the Blog," *Fortune,* Jan. 10, 2005, pp. 44–50.

22. Source: emarketer.com. Tourism Industry Association of Canada. Retrieved August 28, 2006 from www.tiac-aitc.com.

23. 2002 Small Business Profiles—Canada—NAICS 4541—Electronic Shopping and Mail-Order Houses. Retrieved September 29, 2005 from www.strategis.gc.ca.

24. Hairong, Li. Advertising Media. Retrieved October 7, 2005 from www.admedia.org.

25. Michael Arndt, "Yellow," *Business Week,* Nov. 24, 2003, pp. 100, 101.

26. Andrew Park, "Imperial Sugar," *Business Week,* Nov. 24, 2003, p. 98.

27. "Amazon.com Announces Free Cash Flow Surpasses $500 Million for the First Time; Customers Joined Amazon Prime at an Accelerated Rate," Amazon.com, press release, Feb. 2, 2006, http://phx.corporate-ir.net/phoenix.zhtml?c=176060&p=irolnewsArticle&ID=812301&highlight=.

28. *Direct Marketing: An Integrated Approach* by William J. McDonald, Irwin-McGraw Hill, 1998.

29. JC Williams Group. (2006).Multi-Channel Shopping: Canadian Style.

30. Direct Sellers Association. (2006). Location of Sales. Retrieved September, 2006 from http://www.dsa.ca/industryfacts-locationofsales.htm

31. Enid Burns, "Online Ads Influence Collegiate Set," ClickZ, Feb. 10, 2006, www.clickz.com/stats/sectors/demographics/article.php/3584441.

32. Enid Burns, "Online Seizes More of the Advertising Mix," ClickZ, Feb. 13, 2006, www.clickz.com/stats/sectors/advertising/article.php/3584801.

33. Asim Ansari and Carl F. Mela, "E-Customization," *Journal of Marketing Research,* May 2003, pp. 131–145.

34. JC Williams Group. (2006). Multi-Channel Shopping: Canadian Style.

35. Stephanie Stahl and John Soat, "Feeding the Pipeline: Procter & Gamble Uses IT to Nurture New Product Ideas," *Information Week,* Feb. 24, 2003, www.informationweek.com.

36. V. Kumar, "Customer Relationship Management," custom module for William M. Pride and O. C. Ferrell, *Marketing,* 14th ed. (Boston: Houghton Mifflin, 2006), www.prideferrell.com.

37. Ilaria Dalla Pozza and Guiliano Noci, "The Impact of Customer Relationship Management on Performance," in Jean L. Johnson and John Hulland, eds., 2006: AMA Winter Educators' Conference; *Marketing Theory and Applications* 17 (Winter 2006): 144–145.

38. C. B. Bhattacharya and Sankar Sen, "Consumer-Company Identification: A Framework for Understanding Consumers' Relationships with Companies," *Journal of Marketing,* Apr. 2003, pp. 76–88.

39. Peter C. Verhoef, "Understanding the Effect of Customer Relationship Management Efforts on Customer Retention and Customer Share Development," *Journal of Marketing,* Oct. 2003, pp. 30–45.

40. D. Aaker, V. Kumar, and G. Day, *Marketing Research,* 8th ed. (New York: Wiley & Sons, 2004).

41. Marlus Wübben and Florian von Wangenheim, "Predicting Customer Lifetime Duration and Future Purchase Levels: Simple Heuristics vs.Complex Models," in Jean L. Johnson and John Hulland, eds., 2006: AMA Winter Educators' Conference; *Marketing Theory and Applications* 17 (Winter 2006): 83–84.

42. Kumar, "Customer Relationship Management."

43. V. Kumar, J. Andrew Peterson, and Robert P. Leone, "The Power of Customer Advocacy," in Jean L. Johnson and John Hulland, eds., 2006: AMA Winter Educators' Conference; *Marketing Theory and Applications* 17 (Winter 2006): 81–82.

44. O. C. Ferrell and Michael D. Hartline, *Marketing Strategy,* 3rd ed. (Mason, OH: South-Western, 2005), p. 72.

45. Werner J. Reinartz and V. Kumar, "The Impact of Relationship Characteristics on Profitable Lifetime Duration," *Journal of Marketing,* Jan. 2003, pp. 77–99.

46. Kumar, "Customer Relationship Management."

47. V. Kumar, G. Ramani, and T. Bohling, "Customer Lifetime Value Approaches and Best Practices Applications," *Journal of Interactive Marketing* 18, no. 3 (2004): 60–72.

48. Kumar, "Customer Relationship Management."

49. J. Bonasia, "Eyeing Growth in Customer Relationship Management Software," *Investors Business Daily,* Jan. 8, 2002, p. 7.

50. "Better Relationships, Better Business," *Business Week,* Special Advertising Section, Apr. 29, 2002.

51. Edward Prewitt, "How to Build Customer Loyalty in an Internet World," CIO, Jan. 1, 2002, www.cio.com/archive/010102/loyalty_content.html.

52. G. S. Day, *Capabilities for Forging Customer Relationships* (Cambridge, MA: Marketing Science Institute, 2000).

53. Michael Krauss, "At Many Firms, Technology Obscures CRM," *Marketing News,* Mar. 18, 2002, p. 5.

54. Emin Babakus, Ugur Yavas, Osman M. Karatepe, and Turgay Avci, "The Effect of Management Commitment to Service Quality on Employees' Affective and Performance Outcomes," *Journal of the Academy of Marketing Science,* Summer 2003, pp. 272–286.

55. Prewitt, "How to Build Customer Loyalty in an Internet World."

56. Ibid.

57. Ibid.

58. Dennis B. Arnett, Steve D. German, and Shelby D. Hunt, "The Identity Salience Model of Relationship Marketing Success: The Case of Nonprofit Marketing," *Journal of Marketing,* Apr. 2003, pp. 89–105.

59. David Pottruck and Terry Peace, "Listening to Customers in the Electronic Age," *Fortune,* May 2000, www.business2.com/articles/mag/0,1640,7700,00.html.

60. Peter Loftus, "Yahoo Modifies Its Privacy Policy to Allow More Sharing of User Data," *The Wall Street Journal,* Mar. 28, 2002, http://online.wsj.com/public/us.

61. "BBBOnLine Privacy Seal," BBBOnLine, www.BBBOnLine.org/privacy/index.asp (accessed Apr. 13, 2006).

62. See http://canada.justice.gc.ca/en/news/nr/1998/attback2.html

63. Sources: Analyzing the Impact of Spam. (2006). ITSecurity. Retrieved December 2, 2006 from http://www.itsecurity.com/security.htm?s=802 ; Industry Canada. (2005). Stopping spam: Creating a stronger, safer Internet. Report of the Task Force on Spam. Retrieved December 2, 2006 from http://www.strategis.gc.ca/epic/internet/inecic-ceac.nsf/vwapj/stopping_spam_May 2005.pdf/ ; E-privacy Group. (2003). Spam by the Numbers. Retrieved December 2, 2006 from http://www/pettingers.org/media/SpamByTheNumbers.pdf.

64. Tim Hanrahan and Jason Fry, "Spammers, Human Mind Do Battle over Spelling," *The Wall Street Journal,* Feb. 9, 2004, http://online.wsj.com/public/us; Tom Zeller, "Law Barring Junk E-Mail Allows a Flood Instead," *The New York Times,* Feb. 1, 2005, www.nytimes.com.

65. Stephen H. Wildstrom, "Can Microsoft Stamp Out Piracy?" *Business Week Online,* Oct. 2, 2000, www.businessweek.com.

66. Sources: Anonymous. (March, 2006). Music sales in Canada fall 4 percent in 2005: downward trend resumes as international body calls on Canada to act on copyright reform and curb illegal file swapping. The Canadian Recording Industry Association. Retrieved September 6, 2006 from http://www.cria.ca/news/020306a_n.php. ; Anonymous. (September 29, 2005). Recording Industry Launches Campaign to Protect and Promote Products of the Mind, Citing the Results of Two New National Polls. The Canadian Recording Industry Association. Retrieved September 6, 2006 from http://www.cria.ca/news/290905a_n.php. ; Anonymous. (August 29, 2006). Universal plans free music

downloads. Canoe Network - Tech News. Retrieved September 6, 2006 from http://cnews.canoe.ca/CNEWS/TechNews/TechInvestor/2006/08/29/1784358-cp.html; Barefoot, Darren. (March 2006). Come to Canada, Steal Music. Retrieved September 6, 2006 from http://www.darrenbarefoot.com/archives/2006/03/come-to-canada-steal-music.html; Cash, Andrew. (May 18, 2006). Rocking in free world: How fans can download tunes and we musicians still get paid. *NOW Magazine*. Retrieved September 6, 2006 from http://www.nowtoronto.com/issues/2006-05-18/news_story2_p.html; Copyright Board of Canada. (December 12, 2003). Copyright Board's Private Copying 2003–2004 Decision. Retrieved September 6, 2006 from http://www.cb-cda.gc.ca/news/c20032004fs-e.html; Garcia, Michelle. (January 5, 2006). Canadians #1 Illegal Downloaders. Retrieved September 6, 2006 from http://www.soulshine.ca/news/newsarticle.php?nid=2995; Lametti, DAvid. (May, 2005). File-sharing & Music in Canada: Threats, Lies and Digital Tape. Retrieved September 6, 2006 from http://www.cipp.mcgill.ca/data/newsletters/00000056.pdf.; Maffin, Tod. (March 2006). Canada: A music pirate's haven? Retrieved September 6, 2006 from http://todmaffin.com/blogs/radio/2006/03/06/canada-a-music-pirates-haven/; McCoy, Heath. (January, 2006). Downloading complaints abound as music sales slide. The *Vancouver Sun*. Retrieved September 6, 2006 from http://www.canada.com/vancouversun/news/story.html?id=eb5451f1-0267-4f77-a8a4-ae38341c03cd&k=27805.

67. Burt Helm, "A Hard Ride for eDonkey," *Business Week*, Oct. 24, 2005, pp. 90–92.
68. Richard Waters, "Google's Image Search Breaches Publisher's Rights," *Financial Times*, Feb. 23, 2006, p. 15.
69. William T. Neese and Charles R. McManis, "Summary Brief: Law, Ethics and the Internet: How Recent Federal Trademark Law Prohibits a Remedy Against Cyber-squatters," Proceedings from the Society of Marketing Advances, Nov. 4–7, 1998.
70. Sources: Marty Gast, "Travelocity.com: A Glimpse Through History," *Travel News*, Dec. 23 2003, www.breakingtravelnews.com/article.php?story=20031222221110443&mode=print; Josh Roberts, "Travelocity, Expedia Aim to Prove Their Differences," *USA Today*, May 11, 2005, www.usatoday.com/travel/deals/inside/2005-05-11-column_x.htm; Travelocity, www.travelocity.com (accessed Apr. 13, 2006); "Travelocity.com LP," Hoovers, www.hoovers.com/travelocity/–ID_100249–/free-co-factsheet.xhtml (accessed Apr. 13, 2006).
71. Sources: Karen Bannan, "Sole Survivor," *Sales & Marketing Management*, July 2001, pp. 36–41; "eBay Announces Fourth Quarter and Full Year 2005 Results," eBay, press release, Jan. 18, 2006, http://investor.ebay.com/news/; "eBay: The World's Online Marketplace," eBay, http://pages.ebay.com/aboutebay/thecompany/companyoverview.html (accessed Apr. 13, 2006); Robert Goff, "Ebay's Cop," *Forbes*, June 25, 2001, p. 42; "Fiorina Tops Fortune List of Most Powerful Women," *Mercury News*, Oct. 1, 2003, www.mercurynews.com/mld/mercurynews/business/6904474.htm; Robert D. Hof, "The eBay Economy," *Business Week Online*, Aug. 25, 2003, www.businessweek.com/magazine/content/03_34/b3846650.htm; Robert D. Hof, "Online Extra: Q&A with eBay's Meg Whitman," *Business Week Online*, May 14, 2001, www.businessweek.com; Julia King, "Websites Crack Down on Fraud," *ComputerWorld*, Sept. 13, 1999, p. 1113; Chuck Lenatti, "Auction Mania," Upside, July 11, 1999, pp. 84–92; Ellen Messmer, "Ebay Acts to Curtail Internet Fraud," *Network World*, July 24, 2000, pp. 31, 34; "New Study Reveals 724,000 Americans Rely on eBay Sales for Income," eBay, press release, July 21, 2005, http://investor.ebay.com/ReleaseDetail.cfm?ReleaseID=170073&FYear=; Paul Sloan, "Retail Without the Risk," *Business 2.0*, Mar. 1, 2006, http://money.cnn.com/magazines/business2/business2_archive/2006/03/01/8370575/; Jon

Swartz, "'E' in eBay Might Stand for Expansion," *USA Today*, Mar. 28, 2001, www.usatoday.com; Lizette Wilson, "Businesses Build Profits Helping Others Use Ebay," *San Francisco Business Times*, May 26, 2003, http://sanfrancisco.bizjournals.com/sanfrancisco/stories/2003/05/26/story8.html; Eric Young, "Ebay Says Fixed-Price Bazaar Will Open Next Quarter," *The Standard*, May 25, 2001, www.thestandard.com.

Chapter 10

1. Sources: "Company History," Pacific Research Group, http://65.119.21.227/company/history.asp (accessed Apr. 14, 2006); Robert Frank, "How One Entrepreneur Lives Large—For Free," from *The Wall Street Journal Online*, June 11, 2003, www.startupjournal.com/ideas/services/20030611-frank.html; Matthew Heimer, "Mystery Shopper," *Smart Money*, Dec. 2005, pp. 96–101; "Our Programs: Digital On-Site Mystery Shopping," Pacific Research Group, http://65.119.21.227/programs/digital_onsite_shopping.asp (accessed Apr. 14, 2006).
2. Anne L. Souchon, John W. Cadogan, David B. Procter, and Belinda Dewsnap, "Marketing Information Use and Organisational Performance: The Mediating Role of Responsiveness," *Journal of Strategic Marketing*, 12 (Dec. 2004): 231–242.
3. Suzanne Vranica, "McDonald's Tries for 'Viral' Buzz," *The Wall Street Journal*, Feb. 8, 2005, http://online.wsj.com/public/us.
4. Catherine Arnold, "Self-Examination: Researchers Reveal State of MR in Survey," *Marketing News*, Feb. 1, 2005, pp. 55, 56.
5. Jacquelyn S. Thomas, "A Methodology for Linking Customer Acquisition to Customer Retention," *Journal of Marketing Research*, May 2001, pp. 262–268.
6. Jamie Lareau, "Hummer's H3 Thrives in Slow SUV Market Despite Higher Gas Prices," *AutoWeek*, Oct. 11, 2005, www.autoweek.com/news.cms?newsId=103335.
7. "Trading the Bleachers for the Couch," *Business Week Online*, Aug. 22, 2005, www.businessweek.com.
8. A. Parasuraman, Dhruv Grewal, and R. Krishnan, *Marketing Research* (Boston: Houghton Mifflin, 2004), p. 63.
9. Ken Manning, O. C. Ferrell, and Linda Ferrell, "Consumer Expectations of Clearance vs. Sale Prices," University of Wyoming, working paper, 2006.
10. Parasuraman, Grewal, and Krishnan, *Marketing Research*, p. 64.
11. Brian T. Ratchford, Myung-Soo Lee, and Debabrata Talukdar, "The Impact of the Internet on Information Search for Automobiles," *Journal of Marketing Research*, May 2003, pp. 193–209.
12. Parasuraman, Grewal, and Krishnan, *Marketing Research*, p. 73.
13. Vikas Mittal and Wagner A. Kamakura, "Satisfaction, Repurchase Intent, and Repurchase Behavior: Investigating the Moderating Effects of Customer Characteristics," *Journal of Marketing Research*, Feb. 2001, pp. 131–142.
14. "Internal Secondary Market Research," CCH Business Owner's Toolkit, www.toolkit.cch.com/text/P03_3020.asp (accessed Apr. 14, 2006).
15. "External Secondary Market Research," CCH Business Owner's Toolkit, www.toolkit.cch.com/text/P03_3011.asp (accessed Apr. 14, 2006).
16. Randy Garner, "Post-It Note Persuasion: A Sticky Influence," *Journal of Consumer Psychology* 15 (2005): 230–237.
17. John Harwood and Shirley Leung, "Hang-Ups: Why Some Pollsters Got It So Wrong This Election Day," *The Wall Street Journal*, Nov. 8, 2003, pp. A1, A6.
18. Ibid.
19. Robert V. Kozinets, "The Field Behind the Screen: Using Netnography for Marketing Research in Online Communities," *Journal of Marketing Research* 39 (Feb. 2002): 61–72.
20. Glen L. Urban and John R. Hauser, "'Listening In' to Find and Explore New Combinations of Customer Needs," *Journal of Marketing* 68 (Apr. 2004): 72–87.

21. Source: http://www.sampleczar.com/operational.html.
22. "Where the Stars Design the Cars," *Business 2.0,* July 2005, p. 32.
23. Daniel Gross, "Lies, Damn Lies, and Focus Groups," *Slate,* Oct. 10, 2003, http://slate.msn.com/id/2089677/.
24. Peter DePaulo, "Sample Size for Qualitative Research," *Quirk's Marketing Research Review,* Dec. 2000, www.quirks.com.
25. Sean Geehan and Stacy Sheldon, "Connecting to Customers," *Marketing Management,* Nov./Dec. 2005, pp. 37–42.
26. Barbara Allan, "The Benefits of Telephone Depth Sessions," *Quirk's Marketing Research Review,* Dec. 2000, www.quirks.com.
27. Jagdip Singh, Roy D. Howell, and Gary K. Rhoads, "Adaptive Designs for Likert-Type Data: An Approach for Implementing Marketing Surveys," *Journal of Marketing Research,* Aug. 1990, pp. 304–321.
28. Bas Donkers, Philip Hans Franses, and Peter C. Verhoef, "Selective Sampling for Binary Choice Models," *Journal of Marketing Research,* Nov. 2003, pp. 492–497.
29. David Kiley, "Shoot the Focus Group," *Business Week Online,* Nov. 14, 2005, www.businessweek.com.
30. Thomas T. Semon, "Determine Survey's Purpose for Best Results," *Marketing News,* Jan. 6, 2003, p. 7.
31. Eunkyu Lee, Michael Y. Hu, and Rex S. Toh, "Are Consumer Survey Results Distorted? Systematic Impact of Behavioral Frequency and Duration on Survey Response Errors," *Journal of Marketing Research,* Feb. 2000, pp. 125–133.
32. Judy Strauss and Donna J. Hill, "Consumer Complaints by E-mail: An Exploratory Investigation of Corporate Responses and Customer Reactions," *Journal of Interactive Marketing,* Winter 2001, pp. 63–73.
33. Source: Vencil, John (2003). Marketing Information System (MIS) Basics: Information flow is critical to a sustainable marketing effort. VPI Strategies. Retrieved February 19, 2007 from http://www.vpistrategies.com/articles_pdf/MIS_Bsic.pdf.
34. Noah Rubin Brier, John McManus, David Myron, and Christopher Reynolds, "'Zero-In' Heroes," *American Demographics,* Oct. 2004, pp. 36–45.
35. Source: http://www.loyalty.com/who/corporate_info/.
36. Laurence N. Goal, "High Technology Data Collection for Measurement and Testing," *Marketing Research,* Mar. 1992, pp. 29–38.
37. Behrooz Noori and Mohammad Hossein Salimi, "A Decision-Support System for Business-to-Business Marketing," *Journal of Business & Industrial Marketing* 20 (2005): 226–236.
38. Amy Merrick, "New Population Data Will Help Marketers Pitch Their Products," *The Wall Street Journal,* Feb. 14, 2001, http://online.wsj.com/public/us.
39. Spencer E. Ante, "IBM," *Business Week,* Nov. 24, 2003, p. 84.
40. PIPEDA Overview (http://privacyforbusiness.ic.gc.ca/epic/site/pfb-cee.nsf/en/hc00005e.html.
41. http://www.mria-arim.ca/NEWS/Telemarketing.asp.
42. Carlos Denton, "Time Differentiates Latino Focus Groups," *Marketing News,* Mar. 15, 2004, p. 52.
43. Lambeth Hochwald, "Are You Smart Enough to Sell Globally?" *Sales & Marketing Management,* July 1998, pp. 52–56.
44. Ibid.
45. Sources: Best Buy, www.bestbuy.com (accessed Apr. 14, 2006); "Best Buy Case Study," Experian, www.Experian.com (accessed Apr. 14, 2006); Ariana Eunjung Chu, "In Retail Profiling for Profit; Best Buy Stores Cater to Specific Customer Types," *The Washington Post,* Aug. 17, 2005, p. A1; Stacey Collett, "Turning Data into Dollars," *Computer World,* Sept. 23, 2004, www.computerworld.com; *Fiscal 2005 Annual Report,* Best Buy; Gary McWilliams, "Minding the Store: Analyzing Customers, Best Buy Decides Not All Are Welcome," *The Wall Street Journal,* Nov. 8, 2004, http://online.wsj.com/public/us.
46. Sources: Jennifer Carofano, "The Turnaround Gunning for the No. 1 Spot in Athletic Footwear, Reebok Cranked Up the Heat in 2003," *Footwear News,* Dec. 8, 2003, p. 22; Polly Devaney, "Reebok Shoots from the Hip-Hop in Sneaker Wars," *Marketing Week,* July 31, 2003, p. 21; Rosemary Feitelberg, "Eve to Rap Up Reebok Classic," *Women's Wear Daily,* Mar. 20, 2003, p. 8; www.hoovers.com; Morag Cuddeford Jones, "Reebok Has Spring in Its Step," *Brand Strategy,* Oct. 2003, p. 9; David Lipke, "Reebok Targets Men with New NYC Store," *Daily News Record,* Oct. 27, 2003, p. 14; Wayne Niemi, "Chasing China: With Several Major Athletic Players Betting Big on China, the Sneaker Wars Are Heating Up," *Footwear News,* Dec. 15, 2003, p. 12; Elizabeth Olson, "Being Chased by the Big Boys," *New York Times,* Nov. 27, 2003, p. C4; Joseph Pereira and Stephanie Kang, "Phat News: Rappers Choose Reebook Shoes," *The Wall Street Journal,* Nov. 14, 2003, p. B1; Reebok, www.rbk.com (accessed Jan. 24, 2006); Scott Van Voorhis, "Reebok Pitching Licensing Deal to MLB," *Boston Herald,* Jan. 15, 2004, p. 40.

Chapter 11

1. Adapted from Eric Peters (2004) , *Automotive Atrocities: The Cars We Love To Hate,* Motorbooks International, pp. 35-37; Anon, (1974) "SAFETY FAST sleek, sexy and overprotective, the Bricklin is trying to gull-wing its way into America's heart," *Playboy,* September, pp. 158-159; Anon, "A History of Bricklin," http://bricklin.org/BI_HistoryOfBricklin.htm, Extracted December 18, 2006; H.A. Fredericks and Allan Chambers (1977), *Bricklin,* Brunswick Press.
2. Jay Boehmer, "Three Hotel Chains Introduce Select Service Prototypes," *Business Travel News,* Oct. 17, 2005, pp. 10–34.
3. Greg Moss, "Starbucks Sees Growing Demand for Drive-Thrus," 9News.com, Dec. 27, 2005, www.9news.com.
4. Karen Richardson, "First Service's Odd Mix Works," *The Wall Street Journal,* Dec. 22, 2004, p. C4.
5. Joann Muller, "Parts for the Sensitive Car," *Forbes,* Nov. 28, 2005, pp. 204–208.
6. Traci Pardum, "Procter & Gamble: Adding More Goods to Its Bag," *IndustryWeek,* Oct. 13, 2005, www.industryweek.com/ReadArticle.aspx?ArticleID=10862&SectionID=5.
7. William P. Putsis, Jr., and Barry L. Bayus, "An Empirical Analysis of Firms' Product Line Decisions," *Journal of Marketing Research,* Feb. 2001, pp. 110–118.
8. Muller, "Parts for the Sensitive Car."
9. Deborah Ball, "Snack Attack: As Chocolate Sags, Cadbury Gambles on a Piece of Gum," *The Wall Street Journal,* Jan. 12, 2006, p. A1, http://online.wsj.com/public/us.
10. Susanna Hamner, "Why the Kids Are Dissing LeapFrog," *Business 2.0,* Nov. 2005, www.business2.com.
11. Brian A. Lukas and O. C. Ferrell, "The Effect of Market Orientation on Product Innovation," *Journal of the Academy of Marketing Science,* Feb. 2000, pp. 239–247.
12. "Who Is Dr. Gadget?" The Dettman Group, 2005, www.doctor gadget.com/Who_Is_Dr._Gadget.html.
13. Elizabeth Esfahani, "Finding the Sweet Spot," *Business 2.0,* Nov. 2005, www.business2.com.
14. Peter Lewis, "Play That Funky Music, White Toy," *Fortune,* Feb. 7, 2005, pp. 38–39.
15. Lee G. Cooper, "Structure Marketing Planning for Radically New Products," *Journal of Marketing,* Jan. 2000, pp. 1–16.
16. James R. Healey and Jayne O'Donnell, "Popularity of Crossovers Leaves SUVs in Dust," *USA Today,* Dec. 8, 2005, pp. 1B, 3B.
17. O. C. Ferrell and Michael Hartline, *Marketing Strategy* (Mason, OH: South-Western, 2005), pp. 172–173.
18. Adam Horowitz, Mark Athitakis, Mark Lasswell, and Owen Thomas, "101 Dumbest Moments in Business," *Business 2.0,* Jan/Feb. 2005, pp. 103–112.

19. Adapted from Everett M. Rogers, *Diffusion of Innovations* (New York: Macmillan, 1962), pp. 81–86.

20. Arch G. Woodside and Wim Biemans, "Managing Relationships, Networks, and Complexity in Innovation, Diffusion, and Adoption Processes," *Journal of Business & Industrial Marketing* 20 (July 2005): 335–338.

21. Ibid., pp. 247–250.

22. Horowitz, Athitakis, Lasswell, and Thomas, "101 Dumbest Moments in Business."

23. Susan Casey, "Object-Oriented: Everything I Ever Needed to Know About Business I Learned in the Frozen Food Aisle," *eCompany,* Oct. 2000, www.ecompany.com.

24. Sources: "100 Best Corporate Citizens 2005," *Business Ethics,* Spring 2005, pp. 22–23; "Brewing Up a Strong Starbucks Alternative," MSNBC, Feb. 5, 2006, www.msnbc.msn.com/id/4163701/; "Coca-Cola May Take on Starbucks," MSNBC, Jan. 30, 2006, www.msnbc.msn.com/id/11101825/; "Company Fact Sheet," Starbucks, Feb. 2006, www.starbucks.com/aboutus/Company_Fact_Sheet_Feb06.pdf; "'Fortune 100 Best Companies to Work for 2006," *Fortune,* Jan. 12, 2005, http://money.cnn.com/magazines/fortune/bestcompanies/snapshots/1267.html; "Health Care Takes Its Toll on Starbucks," MSNBC, Sep. 14, 2005, www.msnbc.msn.com/id/9344634/; Adam Horowitz, David Jacobson, Mark Lasswell, and Owen Thomas, "101 Dumbest Moments in Business," *Business 2.0,* Feb. 1, 2006, http://money.cnn.com/magazines/business2/101dumbest/full_list/page6.html; "In Rare Flop, Starbucks Scraps Chocolate Drink," MSNBC, Feb. 10, 2006, www.msnbc.msn.com/id/11274445/; Starbucks, www.starbucks.com (accessed Apr. 17, 2006); Starbucks Annual Report 10-K; Winter, "Starbucks Everywhere," www.starbuckseverywhere.net/ (accessed Apr. 17, 2006).

25. Sources: "Dell at a Glance," Dell, www1.us.dell.com/content/topics/global.aspx/corp/background/en/facts?c=us&l=en&s=corp&~section=000&~ck=mn (accessed Apr. 17, 2006); Heather Green, "Consumer Electronics: Free-Falling Prices and Rocketing Sales," *Business Week,* Jan. 12, 2004, pp. 99–101; Bolaji Ojo, "Equipped with Hard Drive," EBN, Oct. 27, 2003, p. 2; Cathy Booth Thomas, "Dell Wants Your Home," *Time,* Oct. 6, 2003, pp. 48–50; Cynthia L. Webb, "Battle of the Consumer Electronics Giants," Washingtonpost.com, Sept. 26, 2003, www.washingtonpost.com.

Chapter 12

1. Sources: Elizabeth Esfahani, "Finding the Sweet Spot," *Business 2.0,* Nov. 2005, www.business2.com; Judith Blake, "Splenda under Fire over Claims," *The Seattle Times,* Mar. 2, 2005, http://seattletimes.nwsource.com/html/foodwine/2002193747_splenda02.html; "Splenda Brand Timeline," Splenda, www.splenda.com/page.jhtml?id=splenda/newspromotions/press/timelines.inc (accessed Mar. 2, 2006).

2. Mary Jane Credeur, "Coke Poured Out 1,000 New Products in 2005," *USA Today,* Dec. 8, 2005, p. B5.

3. Bruce Horovitz, "Speedo Speeds Suits to Winter Athletes," *USA Today,* Dec. 1, 2005, p. 3B.

4. Brian Hindo, "Clorox: The Dirt on Innovation," *Business Week Online,* Nov. 3, 2005, www.businessweek.com.

5. Chung K. Kim, Anne M. Lavack, and Margo Smith, "Consumer Evaluation of Vertical Brand Extensions and Core Brands," *Journal of Business Research,* Mar. 2001, pp. 211–222.

6. Maria Sääksjärvi and Minttu Lampinen, "Consumer Perceived Risk in Successive Product Generations," *European Journal of Innovation Management* 8 (June 2005): 145–156.

7. William C. Symonds, "Gillette's Five-Blade Wonder," *Business Week,* Sept. 15, 2005, www.businessweek.com.

8. Warren Brown, "Add Sunshine, Be Stirred: 2005 Mustang Convertible," *The Washington Post,* Jan. 16, 2005, p. G1.

9. Scott Sprinzen and Robert Schulz, "Running on Empty in Detroit," *Business Week Online,* Dec. 9, 2005, www.business week.com.

10. Lee G. Cooper, "Strategic Marketing Planning for Radically New Products," *Journal of Marketing,* Jan. 2000, pp. 1–16.

11. Lisa C. Troy, David M. Szymanski, and P. Rajan Varadarajan, "Generating New Product Ideas: An Initial Investigation of the Role of Market Information and Organizational Characteristics," *Journal of the Academy of Marketing Science,* Jan. 2001, pp. 89–101.

12. "A. G. Lafley: Procter & Gamble," *Business Week,* Dec. 19, 2005, p. 62.

13. Aric Rindfleisch and Christine Moorman, "The Acquisition and Utilization of Information in New Product Alliances: A Strength-of-Ties Perspective," *Journal of Marketing,* Apr. 2001, pp. 1–18.

14. Jack Gordon and Bill Vernick, "What All Brands, CEOs Must Know About Developing Great New Products," *Cost Engineering* 47 (Nov. 2005): 8–9.

15. Dennis A. Pitta and Danielle Fowler, "Online Consumer Communities and Their Value to New Product Developers," *Journal of Product & Brand Management* 14 (2005): 283–291.

16. Jathon Sapsford, "Honda Caters to Japan's Pet Population Boom," *The Wall Street Journal,* Oct. 5, 2005, p. B1, http://online.wsj.com/public/us.

17. Deborah Ball, "As Chocolate Sags, Cadbury Gambles on a Piece of Gum," *The Wall Street Journal,* Jan. 12, 2006, p. A1, http://online.wsj.com/public/us.

18. Jack Neff, "Swiffer by Another Name," *Advertising Age,* Apr. 11, 2005, p. 11.

19. Adapted from Michael Levy and Barton A. Weitz, *Retailing Management* (Burr Ridge, IL: Irwin/McGraw-Hill, 2001), p. 585.

20. "Nikon Will Stop Making Most Film Cameras," CNN, Jan. 12, 2006, www.cnn.com.

21. "Nikon Will Stop Making Most Film Cameras."

22. "Dictionary of Marketing Terms," American Marketing Association, www.marketingpower.com/mg-dictionary.php (accessed Jan. 18, 2006).

23. Douglas B. Holt, *How Brands Become Icons: The Principles of Cultural Branding* (Boston: Harvard Business School Press, 2004).

24. Nigel Hollis, "Branding Unmasked," *Marketing Research,* Fall 2005, pp. 24–29.

25. Don E. Schultz, "The Loyalty Paradox," *Marketing Management,* Sept./Oct. 2005, pp. 10–11.

26. Mike Moser (2003), *United We Brand,* Harvard Business School Press, Boston, Mass. p. 95.

27. David J. Lipke, "Pledge of Allegiance," *American Demographics,* Nov. 2000, pp. 40–42.

28. David A. Aaker, *Managing Brand Equity: Capitalizing on the Value of a Brand Name* (New York: Free Press, 1991), pp. 16–17.

29. Interbrand Canada Inc., *Best Canadian Brands 2006: A Ranking by Brand Value.* The Globe and Mail's Report on Business and Interbrand. July 2006, p. 4.

30. Ibid, pp. 5–6.

31. Kelly Pate, "Private Brands Help Grocers Compete, Offer Higher Profit Margins," *The Denver Post,* July 30, 2003.

32. Marcel Corstjens and Rajiv Lal, "Building Store Loyalty Through Store Brands," *Journal of Marketing Research,* Aug. 2000, pp. 281–291.

33. Chiranjeev S. Kohli, Katrin R. Harich, and Lance Leuthesser, "Creating Brand Identity: A Study of Evaluation of New Brand Names," *Journal of Business Research* 58 (2005): 1506–1515.

34. Dorothy Cohen, "Trademark Strategy," *Journal of Marketing,* Jan. 1986, p. 63.

35. U.S. Trademark Association, "Trademark Stylesheet," no. 1A.
36. Devon Del Vecchio and Daniel C. Smith, "Brand-Extension Price Premiums: The Effects of Perceived Fit and Extension Product Category Risk," *Journal of Marketing Science* 33 (Apr. 2005): 184–196.
37. Vicki R. Lane, "The Impact of Ad Repetition and Ad Content on Consumer Perceptions of Incongruent Extensions," *Journal of Marketing,* Apr. 2000, pp. 80–91.
38. Alessandra Galloni, "Armani, Mercedes to Form Marketing, Design Venture," *Wall Street Journal Online,* Sept. 30, 2003, http://online.wsj.com/article/0,,SB106487258836292400,00 .html.
39. Christopher Palmeri, "Mattel: Up the Hill Minus Jill," *Business Week,* Apr. 9, 2001, pp. 53–54.
40. Jeff Falk, "Splish, Splash—Packaging Takes a Bath," *Global Cosmetic Industry,* Dec. 2005, pp. 44+.
41. Thomas J. Madden, Kelly Hewett, and Martin S. Roth, "Managing Images in Different Cultures: A Cross-National Study of Color Meanings and Preferences," *Journal of International Marketing,* Winter 2000, p. 90.
42. Ball, "The Perils of Packaging."
43. Sources: Jennifer Bjorhus, "3M Unveils Drastic Shakeup of Research and Development Division," *Saint Paul Pioneer Press,* Sept. 27, 2003, www.twincities.com/mld/pioneerpress; John S. McClenahen, "New World Leader: 3M Co.'s James McNerney, CEO of the Year," *Industry Week,* Jan. 2004, pp. 36+; Rita Shor, "Managed Innovation: 3M's Latest Model for New Products," *Manufacturing and Technology News* (n.d.), www.manufacturingnews.com/news/editorials/shor.html; Tim Studt, "3M—Where Innovation Rules," *R&D,* Apr. 2003, pp. 20+; Robert Westervelt, "3M Reorganizes R&D Effort," *Chemical Week,* Oct. 5, 2003, p. 11; "Who We Are," 3M, http://solutions.3m.com/wps/portal/!ut/p/kcxml/04 _Sj9SPykssy0xPLMnMz0vM0Q9KzYsPDdaP0I8yizeID3 LUL8hwVAQAOeGPLw!! (accessed Apr. 17, 2006).

Chapter 13

1. Leonard L. Berry and A. Parasuraman, *Marketing Services: Competing Through Quality* (New York: Free Press, 1991), p. 5.
2. Michael Levy and Barton A. Weitz, *Retailing Management* (Burr Ridge, IL: Irwin/McGraw-Hill, 2001), p. 585.
3. Matthew Maier, "Building the Next Google," *Business 2.0,* Nov. 1, 2005, p. 117.
4. Raymond P. Fisk, Stephen J. Grove, and Joby John, *Interactive Services Marketing* (Boston: Houghton Mifflin, 2003), p. 25.
5. Ibid., p. 59.
6. The information in this section is based on K. Douglas Hoffman and John E. G. Bateson, *Services Marketing: Concepts, Strategies, and Cases,* 3rd ed. (Cincinnati: Thomson/South-Western, 2006); Valarie A. Zeithaml, A. Parasuraman, and Leonard L. Berry, *Delivering Quality Service: Balancing Customer Perceptions and Expectations* (New York: Free Press, 1990).
7. Michael K. Brady, Brian L. Bourdeau, and Julia Heskel, "The Importance of Brand Cues in Intangible Service Industries: An Application to Investment Services," *Journal of Services Marketing* 19 (Oct. 2005): 401–410.
8. Jeremy J. Sierra and Shaun McQuitty, "Service Providers and Customers: Social Exchange Theory and Service Loyalty," *Journal of Services Marketing* 19 (Oct. 2005): 392–400.
9. Steve Sizoo, Richard Plank, Wilifried Iskat, and Hendrick Serrie, "The Effect of Intercultural Sensitivity on Employee Performance in Cross-Cultural Service Encounters," *Journal of Services Marketing* 29 (June 2005): 245–255.
10. J. Paul Peter and James H. Donnelly, *A Preface to Marketing Management* (Burr Ridge, IL: Irwin/McGraw-Hill, 2003), p. 212.

11. Robert Moore, Melissa L. Moore, and Michael Capella, "The Impact of Customer-to-Customer Interactions in a High Personal Contact Service Setting," *Journal of Services Marketing* 19 (July 2005): 482–491.
12. Michael D. Hartline and O. C. Ferrell, "Service Quality Implementation: The Effects of Organizational Socialization and Managerial Actions of Customer Contact Employee Behavior," *Marketing Science Institute Report,* no. 93–122 (Cambridge, MA: Marketing Science Institute, 1993).
13. Starbucks Corporation Fact Sheet, *Hoover's Online,* www.hoovers.com/starbucks/–ID_15745–/free-co-factsheet .xhtml (accessed May 1, 2006).
14. Fisk, Grove, and John, *Interactive Services Marketing,* p. 56
15. Ibid., p. 91.
16. Sam Schechner, "Testing Out Airline Web Sites," *The Wall Street Journal,* Feb. 15, 2005, p. D5.
17. International Smart Tan Network, www.smarttan.com/beta/ page.php?pid=4 (accessed May 1, 2006).
18. Lesley Kump, "Teaching the Teachers," *Forbes,* Dec. 12, 2005, p. 121.
19. Zeithaml, Parasuraman, and Berry, *Delivering Quality Service.*
20. Dayana Yochim, "'Customer Rage' Is on the Rise," *The Motley Fool,* Nov. 3, 2005, via AOL.
21. Valarie A. Zeithaml, "How Consumer Evaluation Processes Differ Between Goods and Services," in *Marketing of Services,* ed. James H. Donnelly and William R. George (Chicago: American Marketing Association, 1981), pp. 186–190.
22. A. Parasuraman, Leonard L. Berry, and Valarie A. Zeithaml, "An Empirical Examination of Relationships in an Extended Service Quality Model," *Marketing Science Institute Working Paper Series,* no. 90–112 (Cambridge, MA: Marketing Science Institute, 1990), p. 29.
23. Anja Reimer and Richard Kuehn, "The Impact of Servicescape on Quality Perception," *European Journal of Marketing* 39 (Jan. 2005): 785–808.
24. Valarie A. Zeithaml, Leonard L. Berry, and A. Parasuraman, "Communication and Control Processes in the Delivery of Service Quality," *Journal of Marketing,* Apr. 1988, pp. 35–48.
25. Valarie A. Zeithaml, Leonard L. Berry, and A. Parasuraman, "The Nature and Determinants of Customer Expectations of Service," *Journal of the Academy of Marketing Science,* Winter 1993, pp. 1–12.
26. Linda Himelstein, "'Room Service, Send Up a Techie,'" *Business Week,* Apr. 9, 2001, p. 10.
27. James Zoltak, "'When Pigs Fly' Teaches GenXers the Meaning of Customer Service," *Amusement Business,* Sept. 1, 2003.
28. Philip Kotler, *Marketing for Nonprofit Organizations,* 2nd ed. (Englewood Cliffs, NJ: Prentice-Hall, 1982), p. 37.
29. Ibid.
30. "Non-Profits Discover the Benefits of Using Software Through the Internet," *Fund Raising Management,* Apr. 2001, p. 36.
31. Sources: Dan Thanh Dang, "Satellite Radio Industry Continues to Grow, Enter Mainstream," *The Baltimore Sun,* Nov. 16, 2003, www.sunspot.net; Stephen Holden, "High-Tech Quirkiness Restores Radio's Magic," *The New York Times,* Dec. 26, 2003, pp. E1+; "In Brief, Radio: XM Radio Ends '03 with 1.36 Million Users," *The Los Angeles Times,* Jan. 8, 2004, p. C3; David Pogue, "Satellite Radio Extends Its Orbit," *The New York Times,* Dec. 18, 2003, p. G1; "Satellite Scramble," *The Wall Street Journal,* http://online.wsj.com/documents/ info-satellite04 .html?printVersion=true (accessed Jan. 24, 2006); "Sirius Satellite Radio Hits Three Million Subscribers," *The Wall Street Journal,* Dec. 27, 2005, http://online.wsj.com; Brad Stone, "Greetings, Earthlings: Satellite Radio for Cars Is Taking Off and Adding New Features—Now Broadcasters Are Starting to Fight Back," *Newsweek,* Jan. 26, 2003, p. 55; David Welch, "Satellite Radio: Two for the Road," *Business Week,* Nov. 24, 2003, p. 144+.

Chapter 14

1. Rajneesh Suri and Kent B. Monroe, "The Effects of Time Constraints on Consumers' Judgments of Prices and Products," *Journal of Consumer Research,* June 2003, p. 92.

2. "Hewlett-Packard," case study, Professional Pricing Society, www.pricingsociety.com/case_studies_details4.asp (accessed May 5, 2006).

3. David Aaker and Erich Joachimsthaler, "An Alternative to Price Competition," *American Demographics,* Sept. 2000, p. 11.

4. Dictionary of Marketing Terms, American Marketing Association, www.marketingpower.com/mg-dictionary.php (accessed May 5, 2006).

5. Gary McWilliams and Evan Ramstad, "Where the TV Bargains Are," *The Wall Street Journal,* Jan. 17, 2006, p. D1, http://online.wsj.com/public/us.

6. "Study: Hotel Demand Is Price Inelastic—So What Now?" *Hotels,* July 1, 2003, p. 14.

7. Carleen Hawn, "The Global Razor's Edge," *Fast Company,* Feb. 2004, pp. 27, 28.

8. Russell S. Winer, *Pricing* (Cambridge, MA: Marketing Science Institute, 2005), p. 20.

9. Bruce L. Alford and Brian T. Engelland, "Advertised Reference Price Effects on Consumer Price Estimates, Value Perception, and Search Intention," *Journal of Business Research,* May 2000, pp. 93–100.

10. Lichtenstein, Ridgway, and Netemeyer, "Price Perceptions and Consumer Shopping Behavior."

11. Gerald E. Smith and Thomas T. Nagle, "A Question of Value," *Marketing Management,* July/Aug. 2005, pp. 39–40.

12. Peter Burrows, "Apple's Down Market Gamble; By Launching a Much Cheaper Mac and iPod, Steve Jobs Is Appealing to Hordes of Price-Conscious Consumers," *Business Week Online,* Jan. 12, 2005.

13. Lichtenstein, Ridgway, and Netemeyer, "Price Perceptions and Consumer Shopping Behavior."

14. Ibid.

15. Gail Edmondson, "This SUV Can Tow an Entire Carmaker," *Business Week,* Jan. 19, 2004, pp. 40, 41.

16. Lorrie Grant, "Scrimping to Splurge," *USA Today,* Jan. 28, 2005, p. 1B; Linda Tischler, "The Price Is Right," *Fast Company,* Nov. 2003, p. 83.

17. Diane Brady, "Best Ideas," *Business Week,* Dec. 19, 2005, p. 80.

18. Barry J. Babin, David M. Hardesty, and Tracy A. Suter, "Color and Shopping Intentions: The Intervening Effect of Price Fairness and Perceived Affect," *Journal of Business Research,* July 2003, pp. 541–551.

19. David Moin, "Category Killers' Concerns: Overgrowth and Extinction," *WWD,* Jan. 6, 2005, p. 17.

20. "Fairchild Dynamic Pricing Team," Professional Pricing Society, case study, www.pricingsociety.com/case_studies_details3.asp (accessed May 6, 2006).

21. George J. Avlonitis and Kostis A. Indounas, "Pricing Objectives and Pricing Methods in the Services Sector," *Journal of Services Marketing* 19 (Jan. 2005): 47–57.

22. "Cutler-Hammer/Eaton Corporation," case study, Professional Pricing Society, www.pricingsociety.com/case_studies_details2.asp (accessed May 6, 2006).

23. "Can Detroit Break the Rebate Habit?" *Business Week,* Jan. 12, 2004, p. 110; Joann Muller, "Outpsyching the Car Buyer," *Forbes,* Feb. 17, 2003, p. 52.

24. Marla Royne Stafford and Thomas F. Stafford, "The Effectiveness of Tensile Pricing Tactics in the Advertising of Services," *Journal of Advertising,* Summer 2000, pp. 45–56.

25. Gail Edmondson, "This SUV Can Tow an Entire Carmaker," *Business Week,* Jan. 19, 2004, pp. 40, 41.

26. Michael Marn, Eric V. Roegner, and Craig C. Zawada, "Pricing New Products," *Inc.,* July 2003, http://pf.inc.com/articles/2003/07/pricing.html.

27. "Arctic Monkeys Play on Web Hype," CNN/Money, Feb. 2, 2006, www.cnnmoney.com.

28. Amanda Cantrell, "iPod Add-Ons: Boombox Purses, and More," CNN/Money, Jan. 12, 2006, www.cnnmoney.com.

29. John W. Schoen, "Stern's Move to Sirius a Hard Act to Follow," MSNBC, Jan. 9, 2006, www.msnbc.msn.com.

30. Daniel A. Sheinin and Janet Wagner, "Pricing Store Brands across Categories and Retailers," *Journal of Product & Brand Management* 12, no. 4 (2003): 201–220.

31. Jaihak Chung and Vithala R. Rao, "A General Choice Model for Bundles with Multiple-Category Products: Application to Market Segmentation and Optimal Pricing for Bundles," *Journal of Marketing Research,* May 2003, pp. 115–130.

32. Keith Damsell, "Telecom Bundling Seen Luring Customers," *The Globe and Mail,* Sept. 29, 2003, p. B8, via www.globetechnology.com.

33. George Mannes, "The Urge to Unbundle," *Fast Company,* Feb. 2005, pp. 23–25.

34. Doug Halonen, "Watchdog Sets Sights on a la Carte," *TelevisionWeek,* Jan. 10, 2005, p. 8.

35. Russell S. Winer, *Pricing* (Cambridge, MA: Marketing Science Institute, 2005), p. 31.

36. Mannes, "The Urge to Unbundle."

37. Keith S. Coulter, "The Influence of Print Advertisement Organization on Odd-Ending Price Image Effects," *Journal of Product & Brand Management* 11, no. 4 (2002): 319.

38. Lorrie Grant, "Scrimping to Splurge," *USA Today,* Jan. 28, 2005, p. 1B; Linda Tischler, "The Price Is Right," *Fast Company,* Nov. 2003, p. 83.

39. "Best Ideas," *Business Week,* Dec. 19, 2005, pp. 76–77.

40. Bruce L. Alford and Brian T. Engelland, "Advertised Reference Price Effects on Consumer Price Estimates, Value Perception, and Search Intention," *Journal of Business Research,* May 2000, pp. 93–100. "Blockbuster Plans to Eliminate 300 Jobs," *Business Week Online,* Feb. 8, 2006 (accessed May 6, 2006).

41. "Blockbuster Plans to Eliminate 300 Jobs," *Business Week Online,* Feb. 8, 2006 (accessed May 6, 2006).

42. Sources: Gina Chon, "Car Makers Forced to Pile on More Discounts," *The Wall Street Journal,* Oct. 25, 2005, p. D1, http://online.wsj.com/public/us; General Motors, www.gm.com (accessed May 6, 2006); "GM Exec Said to Regret Employee Discount," CNN, Jan. 5, 2006, www.cnn.com; David Guilford, "Apologize for Incentives? GM Loves 'Em," *Automotive News,* Aug. 18, 2003, p. 1, via Lexis-Nexis Academic Database; Lee Hawkins, "GM Cuts Prices on Most Vehicles," *The Wall Street Journal,* Jan. 11, 2006, p. D1, http://online.wsj.com/public/us; Chris Isidore, "GM Execs: No Let-Up on Incentives," CNN/Money, Jan. 5, 2004, via Lexis-Nexis Academic Database; Kathleen Kerwin and David Welch, "Can Detroit Break the Rebate Habit?" *Business Week,* Jan. 12, 2004, pp. 110–111; David Kiley, "GM Tries to Cut Cord on Costly Rebates," *USA Today,* Jan. 23, 2004, pp. 1B–2B; David Kiley, "The Incentive Trap: Owing More Than Trade-in's Worth," *USA Today,* Jan. 23, 2004, p. 2B; Alisa Priddle and David E. Zoia, "Are Incentives a Carrot or Noose?" *Ward's Dealer Business,* Aug. 1, 2003, p. 8, via Lexis-Nexis Academic Database; Jennifer Saranow, "Employee Discounts Now Everywhere," *The [Fort Collins] Coloradoan,* Aug. 28, 2005, pp. E1, E2.

43. Sources: "The Digital Music Report—2006," IFPI, www.ifpi.org/site-content/press/20060119d.html (accessed Feb. 23, 2006); "GartnerG2 Says 'Big 5' Record Labels Must Standardize Digital Music Delivery to Profit from the Market Opportunity," The Gartner Group, press release, Aug. 29, 2001, http://

gartner.com/5_about/press_releases/2001/pr20010829c.html; Stephen Hinkle, "RIAA, Surrender Now!" Dmusic.com, http://news.dmusic.com/print/5026 (accessed Nov. 20, 2003); Bob Keefe, "Music File-Sharers Hit by New Round of Lawsuits," *The Austin American-Statesman,* Jan. 22, 2004, www.statesman.com; Michael McCarthy, "CD Prices Hit Sour Note with Retailers, Buyers," *USA Today,* Dec. 8, 2003, pp. 2B, 2B; "Napster, But in Name Only," *Wired News,* July 28, 2003, www.wired.com/news/digiwood/0,1412,59798,00.html; Napster, www.napster.com (accessed Feb. 23, 2006); Michael Pastore, "The Online Music Debate Rambles On," Cyberatlas, July 24, 2000, http://cyberatlas.internet.com/markets/retailing article/0,,6061_420571,00.html; Plunkett Research, www.plunkettresearch.com/technology/infotech_trends.htm (accessed Nov. 20, 2003); "U.S. Electronic Media and Entertainment," theinfoshop.com, www.the-infoshop.com/study/fi13558_electronic_media.html (accessed Nov. 20, 2003); Andrew Wallmeyer, "Wal-Mart to Offer Songs at 88 Cents a Download," *Wall Street Journal,* Dec. 18, 2003, http://online.wsj.com. Michael D. Hartline and O. C. Ferrell prepared this case for classroom discussion rather than to illustrate effective or ineffective handling of an administrative, legal, or ethical situation.

Chapter 15

1. Sources: Jonathan Birchall, "Radio Shack Seeks the Right Retail Wavelength," *Financial Times (US Edition),* May 31, 2005, Business Life Section, p. 9; Laura Heller, "Radio Shack Inks Two Wireless Deals," *DSN Retailing Today,* Oct. 25, 2004, p. 5; Radio Shack, www.radioshackcorporation.com (accessed May 1, 2006); Sources: RadioShack Corporation. (n.d.). *Corporate Information.* Retrieved May 1, 2007 from http://www.radioshack.com/; *RadioShack Corporation* (n.d.). History. Retrieved May 1, 2007 from http://www.radioshackcorporation.com/history.html; Anonymous. (March 28, 2005). Court orders end to RadioShack branding in Canada. CBC News. Retrieved May 1, 2007 from http://www.cbc.ca/money/story/2005/03/24 /radioshack050324.html; Anonymous. (February 8, 2007). Circuit City closing 62 stores in Canada. *CBC News.* Retrieved May 1, 2007 from http://www.cbc.ca/money/story/2007/02/08/circuitcity.html.

2. "eBay: The World's Online Marketplace," ebay.com, http://pages.ebay.com/aboutebay/thecompany/companyoverview.html (accessed May 1, 2006).

3. "When Complexity Pays Off," CFO, *The Magazine for Financial Executives,* Winter 2003, p. 14.

4. "Trendspotting," *Intelligent Enterprises,* Mar. 2005, p. 17; Doug Henschen, "Content and CRM: Completing the Picture Intelligent Enterprise," *Intelligent Enterprises,* Mar. 2005, pp. 34+.

5. Source: Mayfield, Kendra. (May 20, 2002). Radio ID tags: Beyond bar codes. *Wired Magazine.* Retrieved May 2, 2007 from http://www.wired.com/science/discoveries/news/2002/05/52343.

6. Leo Aspinwall, "The Marketing Characteristics of Goods," in *Four Marketing Theories* (Boulder: University of Colorado Press, 1961), pp. 27–32.

7. Wroe Alderson, *Dynamic Marketing Behavior* (Homewood, IL: Irwin, 1965), p. 239.

8. Jonathan D. Hibbard, Nirmalya Kumar, and Louis W. Stern, "Examining the Impact of Destructive Acts in Marketing Channel Relationships," *Journal of Marketing Research,* Feb. 2001, pp. 45–61.

9. Anne T. Coughlan, Erin Anderson, Louis W. Stern, and Adel I. El-Ansary, *Marketing Channels* (Upper Saddle River, NJ: Prentice-Hall, 2001), pp. 368–369.

10. Sources: The Competition Bureau (2005). Conspiracies. Retrieved May 2, 2007 from http://www.competitionbureau.gc.ca/internet/index.cfm?itemID=112&lg=e; The Competition Bureau (2005). Refusal to Deal. Retrieved May 2, 2007 from http://www.competitionbureau.gc.ca/internet/index.cfm?itemID=665&lg=e; The Competition Bureau (2005). Vertical Restraints. Retrieved May 2, 2007 from http://www.competitionbureau.gc.ca/internet/index.cfm?itemID=111&lg=e.

11. Amy Roach Partridge, "Apparel Logistics & Technology: A Perfect Fit," *Inbound Logistics,* Nov. 2005, www.inboundlogistics.com/articles/features/1105_feature04.shtml.

12. Dominic Gates, "Boeing 7E7 Site Winner Will Get Second-Plant Bonus," *Seattle Times,* Nov. 19, 2003.

13. Anne T. Coughlan, Erin Anderson, Louis W. Stern, and Adel I. El-Ansary, *Marketing Channels* (Upper Saddle River, NJ: Prentice-Hall, 2001), p. 510.

14. Leslie Hansen Harps, "Best Practices in Today's Distribution Center," *Inbound Logistics,* May 2005, www.inboundlogistics.com/articles/features/0505_feature01.shtml.

15. Sources: Katrina Brooker, "The Pepsi Machine." *Fortune,* Feb. 6, 2006, pp. 68–72; "Coca-Cola Company: Crisis and Reputation Management," in Debbie Thorne McAlister, O. C. Ferrell, and Linda Ferrell, *Business and Society: A Strategic Approach to Social Responsibility,* 2nd ed. (Boston: Houghton Mifflin, 2005), pp. 394–401; T. C. Doyle, "Channel Stuffing Rears Its Ugly Head," *VARBusiness,* May 6, 2003, www.varbusiness.com/showArticle.jhtml;jsessionid=PCVHTC51ICHQ0QSNDBCSKHSCJUMEKJVN?articleID=18823602; "Grand Jury to Investigate Coke on Channel Stuffing Allegations," *Atlanta Business Chronicle,* May 3, 2004, http://atlanta.bizjournals.com/atlanta/stories/2004/05/03/daily2.html; Majorie Kelly, "100 Best Corporate Citizens," *Business Ethics,* Spring 2005, pp. 20–23; Betsy McKay and Chad Terhune, "Coca-Cola Settles Regulatory Probe; Deal Resolves Allegations by SEC That Firm Padded Profit by 'Channel Stuffing,'" *The Wall Street Journal,* via http://proquest.umi.com/pqdweb?did=823831501&sid=1&Fmt=3&clientld=2945&RQT=309&Vname=PQD (accessed Nov. 8, 2005); Stephen Taub, "SEC Probing Harley Statements," CFO.com, July 13, 2005, www.cfo.com/article.cfm/4173321/c_4172651?f=archives&origin=archive.

16. Sources: Larisa Brass, "Technology Keeps Wal-Mart Out Front," *Knight Ridder Tribune Business News,* Feb. 24, 2005, p. 1; Anthony Bianco and Wendy Zellner, "Is Wal-Mart Too Powerful?" *Business Week,* Oct. 6, 2003, pp. 100–110; Alorie Gilbert, "Retail's Super Supply Chains—Wal-Mart Inks Deal to Roll Out Private Trading Hub; Kmart Readies an Overhaul of Its Planning Systems," *InformationWeek,* Oct. 16, 2000, p. 22; Kris Hudson, "Wal-Mart Aims to Recharge Growth in Operating Profit," *The Wall Street Journal,* Nov. 9, 2005, http://online.wsj.com/public/us; Jean Kinsey, "A Faster, Leaner Supply Chain: New Uses of Information Technology," *American Journal of Agricultural Economics,* Nov. 15, 2000, p. 1123; Jack Neff, "Wal-Marketing: How to Benefit in Bentonville," *Advertising Age,* Oct. 6, 2003, p. 1; Liz Parks, "Wal-Mart Gets Onboard Early with Collaborative Planning," *Drug Store News,* Feb. 19, 2001, p. 14; "Ready for RFID?" *Information Week,* Jan. 5, 2004; "Trucking Company to Expand to Accommodate Wal-Mart," *Capital District Business Review,* May 7, 2001, p. 8; Wal-Mart, www.walmart.com (accessed May 1, 2006); "Wal-Mart Fuels Expansion at M.S. Carriers," *Memphis Business Journal,* July 28, 2000, p. 3; "World-Class Merchandising Model Leverages Global Synergies," *DSN Retailing Today,* June 2001, p. 15.

Chapter 16

1. Source: Hays, Alex. (2005). Wholesalers: A key link in Canada's economy—Analytical Paper. Distributive Trade Division:

Statistics Canada. Catalogue No. 11-621-MIE-No.026. Retrieved May 2, 2007 from http://www.statcan.ca/english/research/11-621-MIE/11-621-MIE2005026.pdf; Lebreaux, Jean. (2006). Between the producer and retailer: A review of wholesale trade for 2005—Analytical Paper. Distributive Trade Division: *Statistics Canada*. Catalogue No. 11-621-MIE-No.040. Retrieved May 2, 2007 from http://www.statcan.ca/english/research/11-621-MIE/11-621-MIE2006040.pdf.

2. Genuine Parts Company Fact Sheet, Hoover's Online, www.hoovers.com/free (accessed May 1, 2006).

3. Ann Zimmerman and Kris Hudson, "Looking Upscale, Wal-Mart Begins a Big Makeover," *The Wall Street Journal*, Sept. 17, 2005, p. A1, http://online.wsj.com/public/us; Robert Berner, "Watch Out, Best Buy and Circuit City," *Business Week*, Nov. 21, 2005, pp. 46–48.

4. "A Different Type of Sears Store," *The New York Times*, Feb. 9, 2005, p. C5.

5. Source: *Statistics Canada*. (2007). Retail trade by industry. Retrieved May 2, 2007 from http://www40.statcan.ca/l01/cst01/trad15a.htm.

6. "Testing Ground, Why the Convenience Channel Is the Ideal Environment to Spur Consumer Trial," *Stagnito's New Products Magazine*, May 2005, p. 38.

7. Source: Loblaw Company Limited (n.d.) Retrieved May 2, 2007 from http://www.answers.com/topic/loblaw-companies-limited ; About Us (n.d.) Loblaw Company Limited. Retrieved May 2, 2007 from http://www.loblaw.ca/en/abt_corprof.html.

8. Source: CBC News (December 14, 2005). Wal-Mart bringing superstores to Canada: Report. CBC News. Retrieved May 2, 2007 from http://www.cbc.ca/money/story/2005/12/14/walmart-051214.html.

9. Richard C. Morais, "One Hot Tamale," *Forbes*, Dec. 27, 2004, p. 137.

10. Source: Costco Wholesale. (November 30, 2006). Costco wholesale corporation reports November sales results. Press Release. Retrieved May 2, 2007 from http://www.marketwire.com/mw/release_html_b1?release_id=189694.

11. Lucinda Hahn, "Pampered Life," *Chicago Tribune*, Jan. 18, 2005, p. 1.

12. "Fact Sheet: U.S. Direct Selling 2004," *Direct Selling Association*, www.dsa.org/pubs/numbers/05gofactsheet.pdf (accessed May 1, 2006).

13. Source: About (n.d.) West Edmonton Mall website. Retrieved May 2, 2007 from http://www.westedmall.com/about/default.asp.

14. Nora Ganim Barnes, "As the Mall Falls: Is Mall Entertainment Too Little, Too Late?" *Marketing Advances in the New Millennium*, Proceedings of the Society for Marketing Advances, 2000, pp. 51–54.

15. David Bodamer, "The Mall Is Dead," *Retail Traffic*, Apr. 1, 2005, www.retailtrafficmag.com/mag/retail_mall_dead/index.html.

16. Kurt Blumenau, "Are Target, Best Buy Really Upscale? Owners of 'Lifestyle' Shopping Centers Still Signing Retail Tenants," *The [Allentown, Pennsylvania] Morning Call*, May 29, 2005, via LexisNexis; "ICSC Shopping Center Definitions," International Council of Shopping Centers, www.icsc.org/srch/l.ib/SCDefinitions.pdf (accessed Feb. 2, 2006); Debra Hazel, "Wide-Open Spaces," *Chain Store Age*, Nov. 2005, p. 120.

17. Richard F. Yalch and Eric R. Spangenberg, "The Effects of Music in a Retail Setting on Real and Perceived Shopping Times," *Journal of Business Research*, Aug. 2000, pp. 139–147.

18. "Store Atmospherics Provide Competitive Edge," *Chain Store Age*, Dec. 2005, p. 74.

19. Stephen Brown, "The Wheel of Retailing: Past and Future," *Journal of Retailing*, Summer 1990, pp. 143–149.

20. Sources: "The Costco Way," *Business Week*, Apr. 12, 2004, www.businessweek.com/magazine/content/04_15/b3878084 _mz021.htm; Doug Desjardins, "Costco Comps Up 7%, Despite 4Q Lag," *DSN Retailing Today*, Oct. 27, 2003, p. 8; Doug Desjardins, "Costco Home to Expand in '04," *DSN Retailing Today*, Dec. 15, 2003, p. 8; John Helyar, "The Only Company Wal-Mart Fears," *Fortune*, Nov. 24, 2003, p. 158; Kris Hudson, "Warehouses Go Luxe," *The Wall Street Journal*, Nov. 11, 2005, p. B1, http://online.wsj.com/public/us; "Investor Relations: Company Profile," Costco, http://phx.corporate-ir.net/phoenix.zhtml?c=83830&p=irol-homeprofile (accessed May 1, 2006).

21. Sources: Better Way (Thailand) Company, www.mistine.co.th; Grammy Entertainment Public Company, www.gmmgrammy.com; RS Promotion Public Company, www.rs-promotion.co.th; Total Access Communication Public Company, www.dtac.co.th; "Mistine," Superbrands International, Nov. 24, 2004, www.superbrandsinternational.com/thailand/vol1/images/member/pdf/Mistine_TH20041229.pdf; Jaturong Kobkaew, King of Direct Sales (Bangkok: Thai Public Relations and Publishing, 2002); Anuwat Dharamadhaj, "How Direct Selling Is Regulated and Managed in Different Markets in Thailand," 2002, www.hkdsa.org.hk/symposium/anuwat _ppt.pdf; "U*Star and GMM Grammy Artists," Krungthep Turakij, Oct. 2, 2004, www.bangkokbiznews.com; "Branding for Direct Selling," *Business Thai*, Dec. 12, 2003, http://bcm .arip.co.th; "Direct Selling," *Marketeer*, September 2003, p. 62; "U*Star to the Market," GoToManager, Sep. 13, 2003, www.gotomanager.com; "Direct Selling War," Krungthep Turakij, March 24, 2003, www.bangkokbiznews.com; "Big Five Direct Sellers," *Business Thai*, Oct. 12, 2001, http://bcm .arip.co.th; MK621 Competitive Strategies in Marketing; Reports on Thailand Direct Selling from MIM Class 16, Thammasat University, 2004; MIM Class 17, Thammasat University, 2005, prepared this case under the direction of Dr. O. C. Ferrell, Colorado State University, and Dr. Linda Ferrell, University of Wyoming, as the basis for classroom discussion.

Chapter 17

1. Sources: Poulton, Terry. (March 2006). An ideal marketer: Sean Durfy-Gold. Strategy Magazine. Retrieved November 13, 2007 from http://www.strategymag.com/articles/magazine/20060301/durfy.html; Jang, Brent. (Nov.8, 2007). WestJet soars to record profit. The Globe and Mail. Retrieved November 13, 2007 from http://www.theglobeandmail.com/servlet/ArticleNews/freeheadlines/LAC/20071108/RAIRLINES08/business/ROB.

2. Stephanie Thompson, "Masterfoods Ties M&M's to Movies with Oscar Effort," *Advertising Age*, Jan. 24, 2005, pp. 4, 54.

3. Judith A. Garretson and Scot Burton, "The Role of Spokespersons as Advertisement and Package Cues in Integrated Marketing Communications," *Journal of Marketing* 69 (Oct. 2005): 118–135.

4. Prasad A. Naik and Kalyon Raman, "Understanding the Impact of Synergy in Multimedia Communications," *Journal of Marketing Research*, Nov. 2003, pp. 375–388.

5. Ibid.

6. Suzanne Vranica, "Marketers Aim New Ads at Video iPod Users," *The Wall Street Journal*, Jan. 31, 2006, p. B1, http://online.wsj.com/public/us.

7. Pamela Parker, "Earthlink Runs Ads on Video Podcasts," ClickZ, Dec. 13, 2005, www.clickz.com/news/article.php/3570421.

8. Rebecca Gardyn, "Swap Meet: Customers Are Willing to Exchange Personal Information for Personalized Products," *American Demographics*, July 2001, pp. 51–55.

9. Ibid.

10. The message, prepared by Chih Kang Wang, says, "In the factory we make cosmetics, and in the store we sell hope."

11. Terence A. Shimp, *Advertising, Promotion, and Supplemental*

Aspects of Integrated Marketing Communications (Cincinnati: South-western, 2003), p. 81.

12. Judy A. Wagner, Noreen M. Klein, and Janet E. Keith, "Selling Strategies: The Effects of Suggesting a Decision Structure to Novice and Expert Buyers," *Journal of the Academy of Marketing Science* 29, no. 3 (2001): 289–306.

13. Salvador Ruiz and María Sicilia, "The Impact of Cognitive and/or Affective Processing Styles on Consumer Response to Advertising Appeals," *Journal of Business Research* 57 (2004): 657–664.

14. Anton Piësch, "Speaking in Tongues" *Inc.,* June 2003, p. 50.

15. Samuel D. Bradley III and Robert Meeds, "The Effects of Sentence-Level Context, Prior Word Knowledge, and Need for Cognition on Information Processing of Technical Language in Print Ads," *Journal of Consumer Psychology* 14, no. 3 (2004): 291–302.

16. Mathew Boyle, "Atkins World," *Fortune,* Jan. 12, 2004, pp. 94–96.

17. David M. Szymanski, "Modality and Offering Effects in Sales Presentations for a Good Versus a Service," *Journal of the Academy of Marketing Science* 29, no. 2 (2001): 179–189.

18. Chad Terhune, "Wood Folks Hope for 'Got Milk' Success," *The Wall Street Journal,* Feb. 9, 2001, p. B7.

19. "Yoplait Is Committed to Fighting Breast Cancer!" Yoplait, www.yoplait.com/breastcancer_commitment.aspx (accessed May 5, 2006).

20. Amy Johannes, "McDonald's Debuts Coupons, Sampling Effort for Chicken Sandwich," *Promo,* Feb. 8, 2006, http://promomagazine.com/othertactics/mcds_spicychicken_020806/.

21. "Inside Chrysler's Celine Dion Advertising Disaster," *Advertising Age,* Nov. 24, 2003, www.adage.com/news.cms/newsID39262; Thomas Mucha, "Why the Caveman Loves the Pitchman," *Business 2.0,* Apr. 2005, p. 39.

22. "Bennigan's Celebrates 30th Anniversary with Irish Bash," *Promo,* Jan. 12, 2006, http://promomagazine.com/eventmarket ing/bennigans_30anniversary_011206/.

23. Patricia Odell, "Silk Goes Guerilla to Sample New Smoothie," *Promo,* Aug. 18, 2004, http://promomagazine.com/sampling/silk_goes_guerrilla/.

24. Betsy Spethmann, "Moët Fine Tunes Loyalty Premiums," *Promo,* Feb. 8, 2006, http://promomagazine.com/interactivemarketing/moet_loyaltypremiums_020806/.

25. Karen Lundegaard, "Car Crash Ads May Lose Impact," *The Detroit News,* Apr. 15, 2001, p. C1.

26. "Ad Space," *Business Week,* Jan. 12, 2004, p. 14.

27. "2006 Rates and Editions," *Time,* www.time.com/time/mediakit/editions/national/index.html (accessed May 5, 2006).

28. Vicki R. Lane, "The Impact of Ad Repetition and Ad Content on Consumer Perceptions of Incongruent Extensions," *Journal of Marketing,* Apr. 2000, pp. 80–91.

29. "Got Milk," National Fluid Milk Processor Promotion Board, www.whymilk.com (accessed May 5, 2006).

30. Cornelia Pechmann, Guangzhi Zhao, Marvin E. Goldberg, and Elen Thomas Reibling, "What to Convey in Antismoking Advertisements for Adolescents: The Use of Protection Motivation Theory to Identify Effective Message Themes," *Journal of Marketing,* Apr. 2003, pp. 1–18.

31. Marcelo Prince, "Red Hot Online Ad Market Boosts Google, Yahoo," *The Wall Street Journal,* Feb. 2, 2005, http://online.wsj.com/public/us.

32. "Notion of Ad Overspending Lessens with Integrated Communications," *Marketing News,* Nov. 24, 2003, pp. 28, 30.

33. Daniel J. Howard and Roger A. Kerin, "The Effects of Personalized Product Recommendations on Advertisement Response Rates: The 'Try This. It Works!' Technique," *Journal of Consumer Psychology* 14, no. 3 (2004): 271–279.

34. Pamela W. Henderson, Joan L. Giese, and Joseph A. Cote, "Impression Management Using Typeface Design," *Journal of Marketing* 68 (Oct. 2004): 60–72.

35. Beth Snyder Bulik, "Nintendo 'Maximi'-izes to Lure Older Generation of Gamers," *Advertising Age,* Feb. 7, 2005, p. 8.

36. Colleen DeBaise, "To Draw Women Investors, Firms Appeal to Senses," *Marketing News,* Feb. 15, 2005, p. 14.

37. Michael Krauss, "Television Advertising in a Time of TiVo," *Marketing News,* Jan. 6, 2003, p. 4.

38. "Wal-Mart on PR Blitz," CNN, Jan. 13, 2005, www.cnn.com.

39. Deborah L. Vence, "Serves Them Right," *Marketing News,* Feb. 1, 2005, pp. 13, 16.

40. Jack Neff, "Clorox Gives in on Glad, Hikes Trade Promotion," *Advertising Age,* July 19, 2001, www.adage.com.

41. Harald J. Van Heerde, Sachin Gupta, and Dick R. Wittink, "Is 75% of the Sales Promotion Bump Due to Brand Switching? No, Only 33% Is," *Journal of Marketing Research,* Nov. 2003, pp. 481–491.

42. "National Advertisers Ranked 1 to 50," *Advertising Age,* June 27, 2005, pp. S2–S3.

43. Rockney G. Walters and Maqbul Jamil, "Exploring the Relationships Between Shopping Trip Type, Purchases of Products on Promotion, and Shopping Basket Profit," *Journal of Business Research* 56 (2003): 17–29.

44. Geoffrey A. Fowler, "China Bans Nike's LeBron Ad as Offensive to Nation's Dignity," *The Wall Street Journal,* Dec. 7, 2004, http://online.wsj.com/public/us.

45. John Eaton, "e-Word-of-Mouth Marketing," Teaching Module, Houghton Mifflin Company, 2006.

46. Alice Z. Cuneo, "Apple Transcends as Lifestyle Brand," *Advertising Age,* Dec. 15, 2003, pp. S-2, S-6.

47. Gerry Khermouch and Jeff Green, "Buzz Marketing," *Business Week,* July 30, 2001, pp. 50–51.

48. *Business 2.0,* Jan./Feb. 2005, pp. 67–68; Michael J. Weiss, "To Be About to Be," *American Demographics,* Sept. 2003, pp. 28–36.

49. "The New Realities of a Low-Trust World," *Advertising Age,* Feb. 13, 2006, www.adage.com.

50. Scott D. Lewis, "Fiona Apple vs. Sony," *The Oregonian,* Apr. 15, 2005, p. D1.

51. Nat Ives, "Interactive Viral Campaigns Ask Consumers to Spread the Word," *The New York Times,* Feb. 18, 2005, www.nytimes.com.

52. "T-Mobile Pays $135,000 to Settle City's Lawsuit for Deceptive Ads," New York City Department of Consumer Affairs, press release, Dec. 14, 2005, www.nyc.gov/html/dca/html/pr2005/pr_121405.shtml.

53. Deborah L. Vence, "Marketing to Minors Still Under Careful Watch," *Marketing News,* Mar. 31, 2003, p. 5.

54. Source: Prepared by Lloyd Salmone, President of Precisions Target Marketing Ltd., Fredericton, NB. Used with permission. Names and locations have been disguised. This case serves as a basis for discussion rather than as an illustration of either effective or ineffective handling of an administrative situation.

55. Sources: "Columbia Sportswear Named Official Apparel Sponsor of Jeep Ski/Snowboard Series," The Auto Channel, Dec. 1, 2005, www.theautochannel.com/news/2005/12/01/153912.html (accessed May 5, 2006); Erica Iacono, "Corporate Case Study—Columbia Spo rtswear Speaks to Many with One Voice," *PR Week,* Jan. 16, 2006; George Anders, "Drama's Profitable at Sportswear Maker—Columbia Run by Mother and Son," *The Seattle Times,* Oct. 12, 2005; Columbia Sportswear, www.columbia.com (accessed May 5, 2006).

Chapter 18

1. Source: Canadian Professional Sales Associate's Website: http://www.cpsa.com. Extracted February 15, 2007. John Burnett, Sandra Moriarty, E. Stephen Grant. *Introduction to Integrated Marketing Communications.* Prentice Hall, 2001 p. 357.

2. Research and Markets: The Cost of the Average Sales Call Today Is More Than 400 Dollars," *M2 Presswire,* Feb. 28, 2006.

3. Jon M. Hawes, Anne K. Rich, and Scott M. Widmier, "Assessing the Development of the Sales Profession," *Journal of Personal Selling & Sales Management* 24 (Winter 2004): 27–37.

4. Eli Jones, Paul Busch, and Peter Dacin, "Firm Market Orientation and Salesperson Customer Orientation: Interpersonal and Intrapersonal Influence on Customer Service and Retention in Business-to-Business Buyer–Seller Relationships," *Journal of Business Research* 56 (2003): 323–340.

5. Julie T. Johnson, Hiram C. Barksdale, Jr., and James S. Boles, "Factors Associated with Customer Willingness to Refer Leads to Salespeople," *Journal of Business Research* 56 (2003): 257–263.

6. Sarah Lorge, "The Best Way to Prospect," *Sales & Marketing Management,* Jan. 1998, p. 80.

7. Andy Cohen, "Success with Referrals," *Sales & Marketing Management,* Sept. 2003, p. 12.

8. Bob Donath, "Tap Sales 'Hot Buttons' to Stay Competitive," *Marketing News,* Mar. 1, 2005, p. 8.

9. J. Bonasia, "Keep Sales Up by Finding New Customers, Focusing on Strengths," *Investor's Business Daily,* Mar. 25, 2002, p. A4.

10. "Lose the Sales Act," *Sales & Marketing Management,* Jan. 2004, p. 22.

11. Stephen S. Porter, Joshua L. Wiener, and Gary L. Frankwick, "The Moderating Effect of Selling Situation on the Adaptive Selling Strategy—Selling Effectiveness Relationship," *Journal of Business Research* 56 (2003): 275–281.

12. Chuck Salter, "The Soft Sell," *Fast Company,* Jan. 2005, pp. 72+.

13. Michael A. Wiles and Rosann L. Spiro, "Research Notes: Attracting Graduates to Sales Positions and the Role of Recruiter Knowledge: A Reexamination," *Journal of Personal Selling & Sales Management* 24 (Winter 2004): 39–48.

14. Julia Chang, "Born to Sell?" *Sales & Marketing Management,* July 2003, p. 34.

15. Greg W. Marshall, Daniel J. Goebel, and William C. Moncrief, "Hiring for Success at the Buyer–Seller Interface," *Journal of Business Research* 56 (2003): 247–255.

16. Susan Mudambi, "Salesforce Compensation and the Web: Managing Change in the Information Age," *American Marketing Association,* Winter 2002, p. 489.

17. Kirk Shinkle, "All of Your People Are Salesmen: Do They Know? Are They Ready?" *Investor's Business Daily,* Feb. 6, 2002, p. A1.

18. Ibid.

19. William H. Murphy, Peter A. Dacin, and Neil M. Ford, "Sales Contest Effectiveness: An Examination of Sales Contest Design Preferences of Field Sales Forces," *Journal of the Academy of Marketing Science* 32, no. 2 (2004): 127–143.

20. Eilene Zimmerman, "Motivation on Any Budget," *Sales & Marketing Management,* Jan. 2004, pp. 37, 38.

21. Patricia Odell, "Motivating the Masses," *Promo,* Sept. 1, 2005, http://promomagazine.com.

22. Joseph A. Bellizzi and Ronald W. Hasty, "Supervising Unethical Sales Force Behavior: How Strong Is the Tendency to Treat Top Sales Performers Leniently?" *Journal of Business Ethics,* Apr. 2003, pp. 337–351.

23. Sources: "IBM Steps Up Efforts to Drive the Adoption of Software as a Service—Offers Broadest Range of Resources Enabling Business Partners to Transition to Rapid Delivery Model," Market Wire, Feb. 23, 2006, www.marketwire.com/mw/release_html_b1?release_id=110803; Dan Neel, IBM Connects the Partner Dots," *Computer Reseller News,* Nov. 7, 2005; IBM, www.ibm.com (accessed May 5, 2006); Video Interviews with IBM employees: Dan Pelino, Greg Pushalla, Karen Lowe, Monica Chambers (accessed Feb. 28, 2006).

24. Sources: Li Yuan, "Cellphone Accessories Enter Realm of Couture," *Wall Street Journal,* Mar. 1, 2006, p. D5; Brad Stone, "More Fun For Your Mobile; Forget Mere Ringtones. 'Mobile Media' Have Arrived," *Newsweek,* Nov. 14, 2005, p. 36; Bob Garfield, "T-Mobile Spots Succeed Because They Ring True," *Advertising Age,* Aug. 22, 2005, p. 57; Alice Z. Cuneo, "T-Mobile's Novel Sell: Great Cell Service," *Advertising Age,* Nov. 28, 2005, p. 12; Matt Richtel and Ken Belson, "Yes, T-Mobile Is Profitable, But What to Do with It?," *The New York Times,* July, 11, 2005, C5 p. 6; "T-Mobile Heats Up Hollywood's Elite with the Debut of the New Limited Edition Versions of the T-Mobile Sidekick II," *PR Newswire,* Oct. 19, 2005; "T-Mobile Inks Broad Marketing Partnership with NBA and WNBA," *Business Wire,* Oct. 3, 2005; "T-Mobile Brings Today's Hottest Artists Up Close and Personal," *PR Newswire US,* July 27, 2005, www.prnewswire.com; "The Ideas Behind the Big Pink T," *Global Telecom Business,* Jan.–Feb. 2004, p. 40; "Deutsche Telekom AG: T-Mobile USA Posts Gain of 1.4 Million New Subscribers," *Wall Street Journal,* Jan. 27, 2006, p. 1; Alice Z. Cuneo, "T-Mobile Sprinkles Stardust on Sidekick II," *Advertising Age,* Nov. 22, 2004, p. 6; Kelly Hill, "T-Mobile USA Tops J.D. Power Customer Care Survey," *RCR Wireless News,* Jan. 30, 2006, p. 3; Dan Meyer, "Can T-Mobile USA Make It Alone?," *RCR Wireless News,* Apr. 18, 2005, p. 1; T-Mobile USA, www.t-mobile.com (accessed Mar. 17, 2006).

Chapter 1

Page 10: www.robeez.ca/en-us/about/sandra.htm (Sandra's Story) accessed October 18, 2006; www.robeez.ca/en-us/about/awardspress.htm

Page 13: http:ruttertech.com/overview2.html.

Page 15: Paddon, David. (October 12, 2006). Canadian Tire Financial to offer savings accounts, mortgages and GICs. Canadian Business. Retrieved October 18, 2006 from http://www.canadianbusiness.com/markets/headline_news/article.jsp?content=b101257A.

Chapter 2

Page 34: Based on author interview with Chris Neville. Content used with permission.

Page 37: Cynthia Crossen and Kortney Stringer, "A Merchant's Evolution," *The Wall Street Journal,* Nov. 18, 2004, pp. B1–B2; David Lieberman, "Retailing Giants Team Up," *USA Today,* Nov. 18, 2004, p. 1A; Amy Merrick and Dennis Berman, "Kmart to Buy Sears for $11.5 Billion," *The Wall Street Journal,* Nov. 18, 2004, pp. A1, A8; David Runk, "The Mind Behind the Merger," *The [Fort Collins] Coloradoan,* Nov. 18, 2004, pp. D7, D8; Allan Sloan, "It's Not About Retailing," *Newsweek,* Nov. 29, 2004, p. 41.

Page 38: David Gaffen, "Gillette Sparkles on Merger," *The Wall Street Journal,* Jan. 28, 2005, http://online.wsj.com/public/us; Atifa Hargrave-Silk, "P&G Broadening China Sweet Spot," *Media Asia,* Jan. 16, 2004, p. 3, accessed via Business Source Premier; Cliff Peale, "P&G in Deal to Buy Gillette," *USA Today,* Jan. 28, 2005, p. 1B; Procter & Gamble Annual Report, 2004, Procter & Gamble, www.pg.com/company/who_we_are/index.jhtml (accessed Apr. 13, 2006).

Chapter 3

Page 66: "The Able Jo Waldron," WomenOf, www.womenof.com/Articles/cb_3_29_04.asp (accessed May 2, 2006); "Now Hear This," ColoradoBiz 30 (Aug. 2003): 14; Christine Turner, "Inventing Technology That Matters," *Colorado Company,* Jan./Feb. 2004, www.coloradocompany.biz/jan_feb/inventing_technology.shtml.

Page 67: "Hottest New Pet Products Unleashed at Global Pet Expo," *Business Wire,* Mar. 29, 2005, www.businesswire.com; Laura Koss-Feder, "Critter Comforts: The Boom in Pet Businesses Has Entrepreneurs Vying for Their Spots as Top Dog," *Entrepreneur,* Nov. 2005, p. 124; Kathleen M. Mangan, "Perks for Pets: Nutritional Supplements for Fluffy and Fido," E: *The Enforcement Magazine,* Nov.–Dec., 2004, www.emagazine.com.

Page 70: "New National Poll Shows Boomers Have Ambitious Expectations for Active Retirement Lifestyle," accessed November 19, 2006; David K. Foot and Daniel Stoffman, Boom, Bust & Echo, (Toronto: Macfarlane Walter and Ross, 1996); "The Green Devolution: Why Only a Handful of Environmentally Friendly Products Survived the Green Revolution of the Late 1980s," Marketing Magazine, April 15, 1996, p. 9.

Chapter 4

Page 83: "Nestlé Boss Starts an African Crusade," *The Sunday Times,* Mar. 13, 2005, www.timesonline.co.uk/article/0,,2095-1522290,00.html; "The Nestlé Coffee Report," Faces of Coffee, Mar. 2004, Nestlé S.A., Public Affairs, www.nestle.com/NR/rdonlyres/4F893E04-4129-4E4C-92F1-91AF4C8C4738/0/2003_Coffee_Report.pdf; "The Nestlé Commitment to Africa," Africa Report, Nestlé, www.nestle.com/Our_Responsibility/Africa+ Report/Overview/Africa+Report.htm (accessed Apr. 13, 2006). p. 90 Anthony Bianco and Wendy Zellner, "Is Wal-Mart Too Powerful?" *Business Week,* Oct. 6, 2003, pp. 102–110; Cora Daniels, "Women vs. Wal-Mart," *Fortune,* July 21, 2003, pp. 79–82; Charles Fishman, "The Wal-Mart You Don't Know: Why Low Prices Have a High Cost," *Fast Company,* Dec. 2003, pp. 70–80; Daren Fonda, "Will Wal-Mart Steal Christmas?" *Time,* Dec. 8, 2003, pp. 54–56; WalMart, www.walmart.com (accessed Apr. 13, 2006).

Page 84: Anthony Bianco and Wendy Zellner, "Is Wal-Mart Too Powerful?" *Business Week,* Oct. 6, 2003, pp. 102–110; Cora Daniels, "Women vs. Wal-Mart," *Fortune,* July 21, 2003, pp. 79–82; Charles Fishman, "The Wal-Mart You Don't Know: Why Low Prices Have a High Cost," *Fast Company,* Dec. 2003, pp. 70–80; Daren Fonda, "Will Wal-Mart Steal Christmas?" *Time,* Dec. 8, 2003, pp. 54–56; Wal-Mart, www.walmart.com (accessed Apr. 13, 2006).

Page 85: Adapted from TerraCycle Inc. press releases extracted Nov. 11, 2006 from www.terracycle.net/press_releases.htm.

Chapter 5

Page 123: Daniel, Chris. (May 9, 2005). The other working class. Marketing Magazine, 110(7), p.5.

Page 124: Strauss, Marina. (November 8, 2006). What would Linda buy? Wal-Mart needs to know. The Globe and Mail, p.B12.

Page 128: Source: Macklem, Katharine. (August 2, 2004). The myth of rich. Maclean's, 117(31), 24-30

Chapter 6

Pages 143-144: Sources: Anonymous. (October 25, 2006). Bombadier announces layoffs. Political Gateway. Retrieved November 23, 2006 from http://www.politicalgateway.com/news/read/43481. Bombardier Website. http://www.bombardier.com Retrieved November 22, 2006.; Bombardier Inc., Hoover's Directory. Retrieved November 22, 2006.; Bombardier Aerospace, Hoover's Directory. Retrieved November 22, 2006.; Bombardier Inc. Canadian Business Resource. Retrieved November 23, 2006 from http://www.cbr.ca/CompanyProfile.aspx?CompanyID=2559.

Page 149: Sources: Blotnicky, Karen. (Sunday, November 12, 2006). First Nations Making Their Mark. The Sunday Herald. Halifax, NS. Retrieved November 14, 2006 from http://www.herald.ns.ca/Search/540310.html.; Website: Progressive Aboriginal Relations from the Canadian Council for Aboriginal Business website: http://www.ccab.com/par/. Retrieved November 14, 2006.; Canadian Council for Aboriginal Business, Backgrounder-Oct. 6. Received November 13, 2006 in personal email communication from Ken Tufts, CCAB.

Page 150: "Press Room: Background," IBM, www03.ibm.com/press/us/en/background.wss (accessed Apr. 13, 2006); Steve Hamm, "GM's Way or the Highway," *Business Week,* Dec. 19, 2005, pp. 48–49; IBM Annual Report 2004, IBM, pp. 1–7; Understanding Our Company, An IBM Prospectus, IBM, Mar. 2005.

Chapter 7

Page 171: "Strategis- About Us," Strategis.gc.ca: Canada's Business and Consumer Site, http://strategis.ic.gc.ca/epic/internet/inabout_us-contexte.nsf/en/h_au..., Extracted November 26, 2006.

Page 181: TCBY, www.tcby.com (accessed Apr. 13, 2006); Merger Place, "TCBY to Be Acquired by Capricorn Investors," http://mergerplace.bison.com/press/pr2-10tcby.html (accessed Apr. 13, 2006); *Entrepreneur.com,* www.entrepreneur.com/franzone/rank/0,6584,12-12-F5-2003-30,00.html (accessed Jan. 19, 2006).

Page 192: George Wehrfritz and Joe Cochrane, "The Biggest Sleeper," *NewsWeek International,* Mar. 6, 2006, http://www.msnbc.msn.com/id/11569226/site/newsweek (accessed June 2, 2006); globalEDGE Country Insights: Indonesia, http://globaledge.msu.edu/ibrd (accessed Apr. 13, 2006).

Chapter 8

Page 211: Source: Statistics Canada. (June 28, 2005). Move theatres and drive-ins. Retrieved November 2006 from http://www.statcan.ca/Daily/English/050628/d050628b.htm

Page 215: Source: Lexczcyc, P., Sinha, A. and Sahgal, A. (2004). The effect of multi-purpose shopping on pricing and location strategy for grocery stores. *Journal of Retailing,* 80, p.85-99.

Chapter 9

Page 233: Source: http://www.media-awareness.ca/english/research/YCWW/phaseII/key_findings.cfm

Page 236: Sources: Rosenbush, Steve. (May 3, 2005). Smart Phones: Intelligence Spreads. BusinessWeek Online. Retrieved February 13, 2007 from http://www.businessweek.com/technology/content/may2005/tc2005053_1044.htm

Page 239: "About Us," ING Direct, http://home.ingdirect.com/about/about.asp (accessed Oct. 25, 2006); "ING Direct Bank Does One Thing Noticeably Well," ING Direct, news release, March 7, 2004, http://home.ingdirect.com/about/aboutus_news.html#03072004; Lisa Sanders, "ING Café: Coffee, Tea or Mortgage," *Advertising Age,* June 14, 2004, p. 8; Matthew Sibel, "Where Money Doesn't Talk," *Forbes,* May 24, 2004, p. 176.

Page 245: About Us," Informative, www.informative.com/aboutUs.html (accessed Oct. 25, 2006); Allison Fass, "Collective Opinion, Forget the Up-Close Focus Group. Newfangled Software Lets Lego, Procter & Gamble and Others Mine Ideas from Tens of Thousands of Opinionated Customers," *Forbes,* Nov. 28, 2005, pp. 76–79; "The Communispace Difference," Communispace, www.communispace.com/difference.htm (accessed Oct. 25, 2006); "Customer Communities," Communispace, www.communispace.com/customer_c.htm (accessed Oct. 25, 2006); "Solutions and Services," Informative, www.informative.com/solutionsServices.html (accessed Oct. 25, 2006); "Technology and Services," Communis-pace, www.communispace.com/technology.htm (accessed Oct. 25, 2006).

Chapter 10

Page 266: Stephanie Kang, "Trying to Connect with a Hip Crowd," *The Wall Street Journal,* Oct. 13, 2005, p. B3, http://online.wsj.com/public/us; Sarah Moore, "On Your Markets," *Working Woman,* Feb. 2001, p. 26; "Quest for Cool," *Time,* Sept. 2003, via www.looklook.com/looklook/html/Test_Drive_Press_Time.html; "What We Do," Look-Look.com, www.look-look.com/dynamic/looklook/jsp/What_We_Do.jsp (accessed Apr. 14, 2006); "Who We Are," Look-Look.com, www.look-look.com/looklook/html/Test_Drive_Who_We_Are.html (accessed Apr. 14, 2006).

Page 272: Constance L. Hays, "What Wal-Mart Knows About Customers' Habits," *The New York Times,* Nov. 14, 2004, www.nytimes.com; Skip Kaltenheuser, "Innovative Air Force Data Warehouse Integrates Millions of Parts into One-Stop Supply Chain Visibility," *World Trade Magazine,* Jan. 1, 2005, www.worldtrademag.com/CDA/ArticleInformation/features/BNP__Features__Item/0,3483,140201,00.html; "Wal-Mart Expands Its Teradata Warehouse to Optimize Decision Support Capabilities 10/13/04," *Teradata,* press release, Oct. 13, 2004, www.teradata.com/t/page/128640/index.html.

Page 275: Sources: http://www.mria-arim.ca/SURVEYREGISTRATION/SurveyRegprinciples.asp; http://www.mria-arim.ca/NEWS/PDF/RespondentCharter.pdf.

Chapter 11

Page 287: Prepared by Kathy Malley. Used with permission.

Page 293: Janet Adamy, "Kellogg Posts 11% Rise in Profits But Warns of Fuel-Cost Impact," *The Wall Street Journal,* Nov. 1, 2005, p. B5, http://online.wsj.com/public/us; "Kellogg Around the World," Kellogg, www.kelloggcompany.com/kelloggco/kellogg_around_the_world/index.html (accessed Apr. 17, 2006); "Our Company," Kellogg, www.kelloggcompany.com/kelloggco/our_company/index.html (accessed Apr. 17, 2006); Staying on Track, Annual Report 2004, Kellogg Company, pp. 14–17.

Page 296: "At 50, Tylenol Brand Still Gaining Steam," MSNBC.com, Oct. 31, 2005, http://msnbc.msn.com/id/9879888; Linda A. Johnson, "Tylenol Turns 50, Best-Known Acetaminophen Brand Gaining Steam on Its Safety Image," *The [Fort Collins] Coloradoan,* Nov. 6, 2005, pp. E1, E3.

Chapter 12

Page 320: Developed based on "Tim Hortons Power Play" by Renée Alexander, extracted February 4, 2007 from www.brandchannel.com/features_profile.asp?pr_id=253; with material from *Best Canadian Brands 2006,* a report produced by The Globe and Mail's Report on Business and Interbrand (July 2006); and based on E. Stephen Grant's correspondence on February 22, 2007 with Tim Hortons' Bill Moir, Executive Vice President, Marketing via Rachel M. Douglas, Director, Public Affairs, Tim Hortons.

Page 328: Good Boy!" 2005 Fast 50, *Fast Company,* www.fastcompany.com/fast50_05/winners/1.html (accessed May 1, 2006); Diane Brady, "Pets Are People, Too, You Know," *Business Week,* Nov. 28, 2005, p. 114; "The Iams Company," Iams, www.iamsco.com/en_US/jhtmls/iamsco/home/sw_ih_Home_page. jhtml?pti=IH&li=en_US&bc=C (accessed May 1, 2006); "The Iams Company Hires Dean of The Ohio State University's College of Veterinary Medicine," *Business Wire,* Jan. 9, 2004, www.findarticles.com/p/articles/mi_m0EIN/is_2004_Jan_9/ai_112007046/print

Chapter 13

Page 343: Dennis Cauchon, "The Little Company That Could," *USA Today,* Oct. 10, 2005, www.usatoday.com/money/companies/management/2005-10-09-mississippi-power-usat_x.htm; "News and Information," Mississippi Power, http://newsinfo.southernco.com/printArticle.asp?mnuType=sub&mnuItem=ni&id=1868& mnuOpco=mpc&category=000&layout=print (accessed May 1, 2006).

Page 352: Diane Brady and Gerry Khermouch, "How to Tickle a Child," *Business Week,* July 7, 2003, pp. 48–50; Joe Flint, "Testing Limits of Licensing," *The Wall Street Journal,* Oct. 9, 2003, p. B1; "He Lives in a Pineapple Under the Sea," *Hotel & Motel Management,* Nov. 3, 2003, p. 126; "Nickelodeon Sits Atop the Basic Cable Heap," MSNBC, Dec. 30, 2005, http://msnbc.msn.com/id/10562945; Karyn Strauss, "Move Over, Disney," *Hotels,* Jan. 2004, p. 13.

Page 355: Alternative Camp," www.alternativecamp.org (accessed May 1, 2006); "Ashoka Fellows-Turkey," Ashoka, www.ashoka.org/global/aw_ce_turkey.cfm (accessed May 1, 2006);

Ercan Baysal, "World Acclaim for Young Business Achiever," *Zaman Daily Online,* Dec. 3, 2004, www.zaman.com/?bl=national&alt=&trh=20041203&hn=14389.

Chapter 14

Page 375: Mercedes M. Cardona, "Affluent Shoppers Like Their Luxe Goods Cheap,"*Advertising Age,* Dec. 1, 2003; Donald R. Lichtenstein, Scot Burton, and Paul M. Herr, "An Examination of the Effects of Information Consistency and Distinctiveness in a Reference Price Advertisement Context," *Journal of Applied Social Psychology,* Dec. 1993; Donald R. Lichtenstein, Scot Burton, and Eric Karson, "The Effect of Semantic Cues on Consumer Perceptions of Reference Price Advertisements," *Journal of Consumer Research,* Dec. 1991; Ken Manning, O. C. Ferrell, and Linda Ferrell, "A Comparison of Clearance and Sale Prices: An Empirical Investigation," working paper, University of Wyoming, 2006.

Page 385: Arik Hesseldahl, "For Every Xbox, A Big Fat Loss," *UP-Front,* Dec. 5, 2005, p. 13; Thomas Jackson, "War of the New Machines," *Forbes,* Dec. 13, 2005, pp. 81–83, via EBSCO Host Research Database; Stephen Manes, "Generation X," *Forbes,* Dec. 12, 2005, pp. 70–72, via EBSCO Host Research Database; Frank Michael Russell, "Xbox 360 Pricing Strategy: Less than the Sum of Its Parts?" *Mercury News,* Nov. 23, 2005 (accessed January 18, 2006); Stephen H. Wildstrom, "Xbox: A Winner Only at Games," *Business Week,* Dec. 12, 2005 (accessed January 18, 2006), via EBSCO Host Research Database.

Page 387: Jacky Johnson, "Young and Inventive," *St. Petersburg Times,* Mar. 3, 2003, www.sptimes.com/2003/03/03/Xpress/Young_and_inventive.shtml; "Kid Inventors," *Wild Planet Kid Inventor Challenge,* www.kidinventorchallenge.com/kid_inventors/rich_stachowski.php (accessed May 6, 2006); "Teen Titans," *People,* Nov. 8, 2004, p. 129.

Chapter 15

Page 406: Source: LCBO. (July 14, 2005). Case Study: CPFR - Partnerships & Profits. Retrieved May 1, 2007 from http://www.cscmp.org/Downloads/public/Resources/LCBO.pdf.

Page 416: "IBM to Enhance Its Supply Chain BTO Offering," *Market Wire,* Feb. 8, 2006; Mike Eskew, "The Art of Delivery: Why More CEOs Are Becoming Supply Chain Experts," *Chief Executive,* Aug.–Sept. 2004, p. 16; David Drickhamer, "Supply-Chain Superstars," *Industry Week,* May 2004, p. 58; Mike McInerney, "Supply Chain Strategic Alliances Can Help Logistics Teams Provide Value," *Pulp & Paper,* Oct. 2003, p. 58.

Page 419: Philip Evans and Bob Wolf, "Collaboration Rules," *Harvard Business Review,* July–Aug. 2005, p. 96; Kate Vitasek, Karl B. Manrodt, and Jeff Abbott, "What Makes a Supply Chain Lean?" *Supply Chain Management,* Oct. 1, 2005, p. 39; Clay Chandler, "Full Speed Ahead," *Fortune,* Feb. 7, 2005, p. 78.

Page 425: Ann Bednarz, "Footwear Maker Treads Wirelessly," *Network World,* Nov. 17, 2003, p. 23; Rishawn Biddle,

"Skechers' Executives Dispute Wrongdoing in Distribution Deals," *Los Angeles Business Journal,* Apr. 21, 2003, p. 3; Karen M. Kroll, "Better Selling Through Kiosks," *MultiChannel Merchant,* Dec. 1, 2005; "Psion Teklogix's Wireless Inventory Management System Implemented at Skechers," *Canadian Corporate News,* Sept. 16, 2003.

Chapter 16

Page 454: Paul Grimaldi, "Out of the Woods—After 93 years in Freeport, Maine, L.L. Bean Says It Has to Open a String of Retail Stores to Fend Off Its Competitors," *The Providence Journal,* July 24, 2005; Tux Terkel, "L.L. Bean Considers Retail, Distribution Expansion in Freeport, Maine," *Portland Press Herald,* Sept. 22, 2005; Clarke Canfield, "L.L. Bean Reports 17 Percent Surge in Holiday Sales," *The Associated Press State & Local Wire,* Jan. 9, 2006; L.L. Bean, www.llbean.com (accessed May 1, 2006).

Page 462: Doug Desjardins, "PetSmart Rolls Out New Store Format: All Stores to Be Converted to Eagle II by End of 2006," *DSN Retailing Today,* Nov. 8, 2004; "PetSmart Selects Unicru to Find People Passionate About Pets—Top Specialty Retailer of Pet Food and Supplies Looks to Unicru to Hire the Best," *Business Wire,* Jan. 17, 2006; "Multimedia News Release—Mart or Smart?—Nations Largest Pet Retailer Grooms Smart New Brand," *PR Newswire,* Aug. 25, 2005.

Chapter 17

Page 495: Claire Atkinson, "Commercial Alert Seeks FTC Buzz Marketing Investigation," *Advertising Age,* Oct. 18, 2005, www.adage.com; "Buzz Marketing," Commercial Alert, www.commercialalert.org/issues-landing.php?subcategory_id=90&category=1 (accessed May 5, 2006); Matthew Creamer, "Is Buzz Marketing Illegal?" *Advertising Age,* Oct. 4, 2005, www.adage.com; Jeff Gelles, "New Buzz Tactic: Manipulating Teens," *Philadelphia Inquirer,* Oct. 31, 2005, via www.commercialalert.org/issues-article.php?article_id=816&subcategory_id=90&category=1; Andy Sernovitz, "'Is Buzz Marketing Illegal' Story Rebutted," letter to the editor, *Advertising Age,* Oct. 10, 2005, www.adage.com.

Chapter 18

Page 505: Source: E-Mail correspondence with Michael Schell conducted by E. Stephen Grant, February 8, 2007. Thought Leader Publications' Website:http://www.thoughtleaderinc.com. Extracted February 14, 2007. Michael Schell, *Buyer-Approved Selling: Sales Strategies from the Buyer's Side of theDesk.* Approved Publications, Inc. 2003, p. xvii.

Page 513: Gregory K. Ericksen, "A Woman Entrepreneur Tells Her Story: Doris Christopher," in *Women Entrepreneurs Only: 12 Women Entrepreneurs Tell Their Success* (New York: Wiley, 1999); The Pampered Chef, www.pamperedchef.com (accessed May 5, 2006); "The Pampered Chef, Ltd.," Hoover's, www.hoovers.com (accessed May 5, 2006).

Inc.; Page 292: (left) Reprinted with permission of Newman's Own, Inc.; (right) Reprinted with permission of Horizon Organic; Page 293: MedioImages/Jupiter Images; Page 294: Reprinted with permission of The Scotts Miracle-Gro Company; Page 296: James Keyser/Time Life Pictures.

Chapter 12   Page 306: Mario Tama/Getty Images News; Page 308: Reprinted with permission of Frito-Lay, Inc.; Page 309: (top) General Motors Corp. Used with permission, GM Media Archives; (bottom) Photographer: Ken Stidwill www.acmephoto .com; Page 312: M&M's® and MY M&M's® are registered trademarks owned by Mars, Inc. and its affiliates. These trademarks are used with permission. Mars, Inc. is not associated with Houghton Mifflin Company. Advertisements printed with permission of Mars, Inc. © Mars, Inc., 2008. Page 314: Reprinted with permission of Frito-Lay, Inc.; Page 315: Reprinted with permission of The Stanley Works; Page 319: CP Images/Adrian Brown; Page 320: CP Images/Rich Buchan; Page 322: Reprinted with permission of Dole Food Company, Inc.; Page 323: ©2007 Kellogg North America Company; Page 326: Reprinted with permission of Xerox Corporation; Page 328: (top) ©xela/Alamy; (bottom) CP Images/The Winnipeg Free Press/Joe Bryksa; Page 329: Reprinted with permission of Citicorp Diners Club Inc. Ad published in 2005.

Chapter 13   Page 338: CP Photo/Adrian Wyld; Page 340: CP Photo/Adrian Wyld; Page 342: ©2008 Hertz Systems, Inc. Hertz is a registered service mark and trademark of Hertz Systems, Inc.; Page 343: Photodisc Red/Getty Images; Page 344: (top) Reprinted with permission of Amy Schiappa, Fringe Salon NY; (bottom) Reprinted with permission of Lansbridge University; Page 346: Reprinted with permission of FTD; Page 348: Reprinted with permission of Costa Cruise Lines, N.V.; Page 350: AP Photo/ Joanne Carole; Page 352: AP Photo/Wilfredo Lee; Page 353: Reprinted with permission of RE/MAX International, Inc. Photo by Ed Dosien; Page 355: Reprinted with permission of Harvard School of Public Health.

Chapter 14   Page 364: CP Photo/Tom Hanson; Page 367: Reprinted with permission of Snapfish; Page 374: Reprinted with permission of The Gillette Company; Page 375: Arthur S. Aubry/ Getty Images; Page 376: Reprinted with permission of Leliam de Castro Raña, Embraer; Page 377: Reprinted with permission of Gold's Gym International; Page 383: Reprinted with permission of JELD-WEN © Windows & Doors, www.jeld-wen.com; Page 384: Reprinted with permission of CITYPASS, Inc.; Page 385: Joan Joannides/Alamy; Page 386: Reprinted with permission of Kohler.

Photo courtesy of Jean Claude Maillard; Page 389: Reprinted with permission of Dorfman Sterling.

Chapter 15   Page 400: Royalty Free Corbis; Page 402: Reprinted with permission of Capgemini; Page 405: (left) Reprinted with permission of Luther Brown, nVision Global Technology Solutions, Inc.; (right) Reprinted with permission of TechTarget Inc.; Page 410: Reprinted with permission of Procter & Gamble; Page 413: Reprinted with permission of Wm. Wrigley Jr. Company; Page 414: Reprinted with permission of Steve Madden Ltd.; Page 416: Age Fotostock/Fotosearch; Page 419: Cut and Deal/Gambling Stock Photography/Alamy; Page 423: (left) Reprinted with permission of New Breed Logistics, Inc.; (right) Reprinted with permission of Data2Logistics, LLC; Page 424: Reprinted with permission of Ryder System, Inc.; Page 425: Image Source/Getty Images; Page 427: Reprinted with permission of SeayCo Integrators, Inc.; Page 429: (left) Reprinted with permission of Con-Way Inc.; (right) Reprinted with permission of Horizon Lines Inc. & BSY Associates; Page 432: Reprinted with permission of Stonepath Group.

Chapter 16   Page 439: Jupiter Images; Page 449: AP Photo; Page 451: CP Photo/Steve White; Page 452: Reprinted with permission of The Container Store; Page 453: CP Photo/Steve White; Page 454: Image Ideas/Jupiter Images; Page 456: Reprinted with permission of Expedia, Inc.; Page 459: (left) Reprinted with permission of the Corporate Marketing Department of MapInfo Corporation; (right) Reprinted with permission of Claritas Inc.; Page 462: Digital Vision/Getty Images; Page 463: Reprinted with permission of Pier 1 Imports.

Chapter 17   Page 474: CP Photo/Adrian Wyld; Page 475: ©2007 Yahoo! Inc. Yahoo! And the Yahoo! Logo are trademarks of Yahoo! Inc.; Page 478: Reprinted with permission of Sonos; Page 480: Reprinted with permission of Columbia Sportswear Company; Page 481: Copyright 2006 Sun Microsystems Inc. All rights reserved. Reprinted with permission of Sun Microsystems; Page 483: Reprinted with permission of Merck & Co., Inc.; Page 489: Reprinted with permission of Simdesk Technologies; Page 493: Reprinted with permission of Wendy's International, Inc.; Page 495: Peter Lowe/ Stock Image Pixland/Alamy.

Chapter 18   Page 503: Image Source; Page 507: (top) CP Photo/ Aaron Harris; (bottom) Reprinted with permission of Hoover's, Inc., a D&B Company; Page 509: Custom Medical Stock Photo/ Alamy; Page 512: Thought Leader; Page 513: Steve Lupton/ Corbis; Page 515: Reprinted with permission of Synygy, Inc. Photo by Coneyl Jay/Getty Images.

The terms shown in bold are defined in the margin glossary on the page indicated.

Miracle-Gro, 294
Mississippi Power, 343
Mitchum, 209
Mitsubishi, 181, 328
M&M's, 82, 312, 475
MobilExxon, 154
Moët Hennessy, 481
Molson Canadian, 36
Monsanto, 330
Monster, 2, 67, 238
Montana's, 115
Mont Blanc, 204, 205, 289, 327
Montgomery Ward, 454
Mothering magazine, 201
Motorola, 163, 176, 179
MSN, 32, 171, 237, 273
MSNBC, 88
MTC, 249
MTV, 19
D. P. Murphy, 88
MusicNet, 521, 522
MySpace.com, 233, 500

NAPA Auto Parts stores, 442
Napster, 237, 249, 521–522
NASCAR (National Association for Stock
    Car Auto Racing), 198
Nasittuq, 134
National Business Ethics Survey, 94
National Hot Rod Association, 198
National Street Rod Association, 311
NBA, 282
Need, 448
Neiman Marcus, 449, 462
Nestlé, 83, 301, 332
Netflix, 387
Network Associates, 437
Neutrogena, 5
New Balance, 282
New Breed, 423
New Leaf Paper, 86
Newman's Own, 292
News & Views, 171
New United Motor Manufacturing, 186
Nickelodeon, 352
Nickelodeon Family Suites by Holiday
    Inn, 352
Nike, 36, 114, 117, 181, 190, 258–259,
    281, 282, 317, 319, 493
Nikon, 318
Nintendo, 489
Nissan, 12, 55, 361, 490
No Frills, 450
No Name, 450
Norsk Hydro, 154
Nortel Networks, 95
Northwest Airlines, 186
Northwestern Mutual, 246
NovaGold Resources, 95
nVision, 405

Oil of Olay, 241
Okanagan, 154
Old Navy, 205
Old Spice, 6
1-800-Flowers, 455
Ontario Ministry of Energy, 6

Opinion Outpost, 274
Oral-B, 196, 220
Orbitz, 347, 381
Orchard Network, 182
Oscar Mayer, 329
Ottawa-Hull, 212
Overstock.com, 428
Overwaitea, 448

Palm, 301
Pampered Chef, 456, 513
Papa John's, 462
Patek Philippe watches, 413
PayPal, 254
Peet's Coffee & Tea, 307
Pennington's, 210
PepsiCo., 8, 57, 77–78, 79, 163, 220, 223,
    300, 307, 457
Petcetera, 32
PETCO, 453
PetSmart, 453, 461, 462, 464–465
Pfizer, 9, 245
Pharmaceutical Research and Manufactur-
    ers of America, 90
Phillip Morris, 120
Pimp Juice, 2
Pirelli, 285
Pizza Hut, 166, 185, 218, 458, 462
Place Louis Riel All-Suite Hotel, 149
Planter's, 331
Pollara, 271
Porsche, 297, 376, 384
Postal Service, United States (USPS), 430,
    444
President's Choice, 450
Priceline.com, 381
Prime Time Live, 88
Principle Financial Group, 209
Procter & Gamble (P&G), 38, 44, 72, 77,
    85, 110, 163, 189, 195–197, 241,
    245, 253, 291, 292–293, 301, 311,
    316, 325, 328, 332, 385, 388, 413,
    414, 464, 487, 491, 495
Provigo, 450

Questor, 184
QVC, 455, 477

Radio Shack, 400–401, 417, 427, 452
Ragu, 6, 240
Rainbow International Carpet Care &
    Restoration Specialists, 289
Ralph Lauren's Polo Shops, 463
Rapala, 16
Raytheon, 72
RCA, 193
Real Atlantic Superstore, 450
realsimplerewards.com, 231
Realtor's Web, 31
Recording Industry Association of Amer-
    ica (RIAA), 249, 521
Red Bull, 2–3
Red Cross, 85
Red Lobster, 17
Reebok, 6, 36, 114, 185, 258–259,
    281–282
ReeferPlus, 429

Reflect.com, 476
Reitman's (Canada) Ltd., 81, 210
Reliable Tools, 253
RE/MAX, 353
RE/MAX Int'l, 458
Rembrandt, 220
Remote Sites Division, Sodexho, 149
Research in Motion (RIM), 140–141, 236
Retail Link, 272
R. J. Reynolds, 301
Rhapsody, 388
Right to Die Society of Canada, 355
Ritz-Carlton Hotels, 34, 43, 352
Robeez Shoes, 10
Robert Bosch GmbH, 290, 291
Rockstar, 2
Rogers, 346
Rolex, 31, 286, 327
Rolls-Royce, 4, 413
Roots, 166
Rothmans, 81
Roxio, 522
Royal Canadian Mint, 364–365
Royal Dutch/Shell Group, 177
RPS Air, 430
Rutter, 13
Ryder, 424

Saab, 245
Safeway, 443
salaryexperts.com, 21
Sales & Marketing Management (maga-
    zine), 61, 261
    Survey of Buyting Power, 61
Salvation Army, 356
Sam's Club, 272, 401, 437, 448, 469
Samsung, 305
Sanyo, 181
Sara Lee, 35, 179, 288, 327
SAS, 464
Sato Barcode, 290
Saturn, 46, 297, 310, 482
SaveEasy, 450
Schick, 207
School, Home & Office Products Associa-
    tion (SHOPA) Kids in Need Founda-
    tion, 21
Scotch Tape, 319
Scotiabank, 319
Sealand Helicopters, 154
Sears, 16, 288, 316, 324, 416, 427, 448,
    449, 454, 456
SeayCo Integrators, 427
Secret, 209
Sensodyne, 220
ServiceMaster Clean, 289, 340, 457, 458
Service Merchandise, 448
7-Eleven, 448, 450
7Up, 326
Seven Cycles, 289
Seventh Generation, 201
SGiNet, 184
Sharp, 112
Sharper Image, 448
Shell, 376
Sherwin-Williams, 26
Shoppers Drug Mart, 80–81, 319

The terms shown in bold are defined in the margin glossary on the page indicated.